Frederic William Farrar

The Early Days of Christianity

Frederic William Farrar

The Early Days of Christianity

ISBN/EAN: 9783742862716

Manufactured in Europe, USA, Canada, Australia, Japa

Cover: Foto ©ninafisch / pixelio.de

Manufactured and distributed by brebook publishing software (www.brebook.com)

Frederic William Farrar

The Early Days of Christianity

THE EARLY DAYS

OF

CHRISTIANITY.

BY

FREDERIC W. FARRAR, D.D., F.R.S.;

LATE FELLOW OF TRINITY COLLEGE, CAMBRIDGE;
ARCHDEACON AND CANON OF WESTMINSTER; AND CHAPLAIN IN ORDINARY
TO THE QUEEN.

POPULAR EDITION.

CASSELL & COMPANY, LIMITED:
LONDON, PARIS & NEW YORK.
1884.

[ALL RIGHTS RESERVED.]

Google

TO

ROBERT BROWNING, Esq.,

AUTHOR OF "A DEATH IN THE DESERT,"

AND OF MANY OTHER POEMS OF THE DEEPEST INTEREST TO ALL

STUDENTS OF SCRIPTURE,

I Dedicate

THIS VOLUME

WITH SINCERE ADMIRATION AND ESTEEM.

Google

PREFACE.

I COMPLETE in this volume the work which has absorbed such leisure as could be spared from many and onerous duties during the last twelve years. My object has been to furnish English readers with a companion, partly historic and partly expository, to the whole of the New Testament. By attention to the minutest details of the original, by availing myself to the best of my power of the results of modern criticism, by trying to concentrate upon the writings of the Apostles and Evangelists such light as may be derived from Jewish, Pagan, or Christian sources, I have endeavoured to fulfil my ordination vow and to show diligence in such studies as help to the knowledge of the Holy Scriptures. The "Life of Christ" was intended mainly as a commentary upon the Gospels. It was written in such a form as should reproduce whatever I had been able to learn from the close examination of every word which they contain, and should at the same time set forth the living reality of the scenes recorded. In the "Life of St. Paul" I wished to incorporate the details of the Acts of the Apostles with such biographical incidents as can be derived from the Epistles of St. Paul; and to take the reader through the Epistles themselves in a way which might enable him, with keener interest, to judge of their separate purpose and peculiarities by grasping the circumstances under which each of them was written. The present volumes are an attempt to set forth, in their distinctive characteristics, the work and the writings of St. Peter, St. James, St. Jude, St. John, and the author of the Epistle to the Hebrews. If my effort has been in any degree successful, the reader should carry away from these pages some conception of the varieties of religious thought which prevailed in the schools of Jerusalem and of Alexandria, and also of those phases of theology which are represented by the writings of the two greatest of the twelve Apostles.

In carrying out this design I have gone, almost verse by verse, through the seven Catholic Epistles, the Epistle to the Hebrews, and the Revelation of St. John—explaining their special difficulties, and developing their general characteristics. Among many Christians there is a singular ignorance of the Books of Scripture as a whole. With a wide knowledge of particular texts, there is a strange lack of familiarity with the bearings of each separate Gospel and Epistle. I have hoped that by considering each book in connexion with all that we can learn of its author, and of the circumstances under which it was written, I might perhaps contribute to the intelligent study of Holy Writ. There may be some truth in the old motto, *Bonus textuarius bonus theologus;* but he whose knowledge is *confined* to "texts," and who has never studied them, first with their context, then as forming fragments of entire books, and lastly in their relation to the whole of Scripture, incurs the risk of turning theology into an erroneous and artificial system. It is thus that the Bible has been misinterpreted by substituting words for things; by making the dead letter an instrument wherewith to murder the living spirit; and by reading into Scripture a multitude of meanings which it was never intended to express. Words, like the chameleon, change their colour with their surroundings. The very same word may in different ages involve almost opposite connotations. The vague and differing notions attached to the same term have been the most fruitful sources of theological bitterness, and of the internecine opposition of contending sects. The abuse of sacred phrases has been the cause, in age after age, of incredible misery and mischief. Texts have been perverted to sharpen the sword of the tyrant and to strengthen the rod of the oppressor—to kindle the fagot of the Inquisitor and to rivet the fetters of the slave. The terrible wrongs which have been inflicted upon mankind in their name have been due exclusively to their isolation and perversion. The remedy for these deadly evils would have been found in the due study and comprehension of Scripture as a whole. The Bible does not all lie at a dead level of homogeneity and uniformity. It is a progressive revelation. Its many-coloured wisdom was made known "fragmentarily and multifariously"—in many parts and in many manners.

In the endeavour to give a clearer conception of the books here considered I have followed such different methods as each particular passage seemed to require. I have sometimes furnished a very close and literal translation; sometimes a free paraphrase; sometimes a rapid abstract; sometimes a running commentary. Avoiding all parade of learned references, I have thought that the reader would generally prefer the brief expression of a definite opinion to the reiteration of many bewildering theories. Neither in this, nor in the previous volumes, have I wilfully or consciously avoided a single difficulty. A passing sentence often expresses a conclusion which has only been formed after the study of long and tedious monographs. In the foot-notes especially I have compressed into the smallest possible space what seemed to be most immediately valuable for the illustration of particular words or allusions. In the choice of readings I have exercised an independent judgment. If my choice coincides in most instances with that of the Revisers of the New Testament, this has only arisen from the fact that I have been guided by the same principles as they were. This volume, like the "Life of Christ" and the "Life of St. Paul," was written before the readings adopted by the Revisers were known, and without the assistance which I should otherwise have derived from their invaluable labours.*

The purpose which I have had in view has been, I trust, in itself a worthy one, however much I may have failed in its execution. A living writer of eminence has spoken of his works in terms which, in very humble measure, I would fain apply to my own. "I have made," said Cardinal Newman—in a speech delivered in 1879—"many mistakes. I have nothing of that high perfection which belongs to the writings of the saints, namely, that error cannot be found in them. But what I trust I may claim throughout all I have written is this—an honest intention; an absence of personal ends; a temper of obedience; a willingness to be corrected; a dread of error; a desire to serve the Holy Church; and" (though this is perhaps more than I have any right to say) "through the Divine mercy a fair measure of success."

F. W. FARRAR.

St. Margaret's Rectory, Westminster,
June 7th, 1882.

---

* I take this opportunity of thanking the Rev. John de Soyres and Mr. W. R. Brown for the assistance which they have rendered in preparing this book for the press.

TABLE OF CONTENTS.

Book I.
THE WORLD.
CHAPTER I.
MORAL CONDITION OF THE WORLD.

Degradations which accompanied the Decadence of Paganism—The Slaves—The Rich and Noble—The Emperor—Fatal Degeneracy—Greeklings—Literature, Art, and Drama—The Senate—Scepticism and Superstition—Stoic Virtue—The Holy Joy of Christians . . 1

CHAPTER II.
THE RISE OF THE ANTICHRIST.

The Nemesis of Absolutism—Reign of Nero—Christians and the Roman Government—St. Paul and the Empire—Horrors of Cæsarism—The Palace of the Antichrist—Agrippina the Younger—Infancy of Nero—Evil Auguries—Intrigues of Agrippina—Her Marriage with Claudius—Her Career as Empress—Her Plots to Advance her Son—Her Crimes—Her Peril—Murder of Claudius—Accession of Nero 10

CHAPTER III.
THE FEATURES OF THE ANTICHRIST.

Successful Guilt—Fresh Crimes—The "Golden Quinquennium"—Follies of Nero—Threats of Agrippina—Jealousy of Britannicus—Murder of Britannicus—Nero estranged from Agrippina—Influence of Poppæa—Plot to Murder Agrippina—Burrus and Seneca—Murder of Agrippina—A Tormented Conscience—The Depths of Satan 20

CHAPTER IV.
THE BURNING OF ROME AND THE FIRST PERSECUTION.

The Era of Martyrdom—The Fire of Rome—Was Nero Guilty?—Devastation of the City—Confusion and Agony—The Golden House—Nero Suspected—The Christians Accused—Strangeness of this Circumstance—Tacitus—Popular Feeling against the Christians—Secret Jewish Suggestions—Poppæa a Proselyte—Incendiarism attributed to Christians—Æsthetic Cruelty—A Huge Multitude—Dreadful Forms of Martyrdom—Martyrs on the Stage—The Antichrist—Retribution—Awful Omens—The Revolt of Vindex—Suicide of Nero—Expectation of his Return 29

Book II.
ST. PETER AND THE CHURCH CATHOLIC.
CHAPTER V.
WRITINGS OF THE APOSTLES AND EARLY CHRISTIANS.

Annals of the Church—End of the Acts—Obscurity of Details—Little known about the Apostles—St. Andrew—St. Bartholomew—St. Matthew—St. Thomas—St. James the Less—St. Simon Zelotes—Judas—Late and Scanty Records—Writings of the Great Apostles—Invaluable as illustrating different Phases of Christian Thought—They Explain the opposite Tendencies of Heretical Development—The Revelation—The

Epistle to the Hebrews—The Seven Catholic Epistles—The Epistle of St. Jude—The Epistle of St. James—The Epistles of St. Peter—Catholicity of St. Peter—The Three Epistles of St. John—Genuineness of these Writings—Contrasts between different Apostles—Difference between St. Paul and St. John—Superiority of the New Testament to the Writings of the Apostolic Fathers—The Epistle of St. Clemens—Its Theological and Intellectual Weakness—The Epistle of Barnabas—Its exaggerated Paulinism—Its Extravagant Exegesis—The Christian Church was not ideally Pure—Yet its Chief Glory was in the Holiness of its Standard 45

CHAPTER VI
ST. PETER.

Outline of his early Life—Events recorded in the Acts—Complete Uncertainty as to his Subsequent Career—Legends—Domine quo vadis?—The Legends embellished and Doubtful—Legend about Simon Magus—Was Peter Bishop of Rome?—Improbability of the Legend about his Crucifixion head downwards—His Martyrdom—His Visit to Rome 60

CHAPTER VII.
SPECIAL FEATURES OF THE FIRST EPISTLE OF ST. PETER.

Date of the Epistle—Its certain Genuineness—Style of the Epistle—A Christian Treatise—Natural Allusions to Events in the Gospels—Vivid Expressions—Resemblance to the Speeches in the Acts—Allusions to the Law—Resemblances to St. Paul and St. James—Plasticity of St. Peter's Nature—Struggle after Unity—Originality—His View of REDEMPTION—His View of FAITH—His Views upon REGENERATION and BAPTISM—Not Transcendental but Practical—Christ's Descent into Hades—Great Importance of the Doctrine—Attempts to Explain it away—Reference to the Epistle to the Galatians—Addressed to both Jews and Gentiles—Crisis at which it was Composed—A Time of Persecution—Keynote of the Letter—Analysis 67

CHAPTER VIII.
THE FIRST EPISTLE OF ST. PETER.

Title which he Adopts—Address—Provinces of Asia—Thanksgiving—Exhortation to Hope—Special Appeals—Duty of Blameless Living—Duty of Civil Obedience—Humble Submission—Address to Servants—To Christian Wives—Exhortation to Love and Unity—Christ Preaching to the Spirits in Prison—Obvious Import of the Passage—Ruthlessness of Commentators—The approaching End—Address to Elders—Conclusion . . 83

CHAPTER IX.
PECULIARITIES OF THE SECOND EPISTLE.

Overpositiveness in the Attack and Defence of its Genuineness—Its Canonicity—Exaggeration of the Arguments urged in its Favour—Extreme Weakness of external Evidence—Tardy Acceptance of the Epistle—Views of St. Jerome, &c.—Cessation of Criticism—The Unity of its Structure—Outline of the Letter—Internal Evidence—Resemblance to First Epistle—Difference of Style—Peculiarity of its Expressions—Difference in general Form of Thought—Irrelevant Arguments about the Style—Marked Variations—Dr. Abbott's Proof of the Resemblance to Josephus—Could Josephus have Read it?—Reference to the Second Advent—What may be Urged against these Difficulties—Priority of St. Jude—Extraordinary Relation to St. Jude—Method of Dealing with the stranger Phenomena of St. Jude's Epistle—Possible Counter-considerations—Allusion to the Transfiguration—Ancientness of the Epistle—Superiority of the Epistle to the Post-Apostolic Writings—The Thoughts may have been Sanctioned and Adopted by St. Peter 97

CHAPTER X.
THE SECOND EPISTLE OF ST. PETER.

Reasons for offering a Literal Translation of the Epistle—Translation and Notes—Abrupt Conclusion 116

CHAPTER XI.
THE EPISTLE OF ST. JUDE.

Its Authenticity—Who was the Author?—Jude, the Brother of James—Not an Apostle—One of the Brethren of the Lord—Why he does not use this Title—Why he Calls himself "Brother of James"—Story of his Grandchildren—Circumstances which may have called forth the Epistle—Corruption of Morals—Who were the Offenders thus Denounced?—Resemblances to Second Epistle of St. Peter—Translation and Notes—Style of Greek—Simplicity of Structure—Fondness for Apocryphal Allusions—Methods of Dealing with these Peculiarities—"Verbal Dictation"—Rabbinic Legends—Corrupt, Gnosticising Sects 122

Book III.

APOLLOS, ALEXANDRIAN CHRISTIANITY, AND THE EPISTLE TO THE HEBREWS.

CHAPTER XII.
JUDAISM, THE SEPTUAGINT, ETC.

Unity of Christian Faith—Diversity in Unity—Necessity and Blessing of the Diversity—Individuality of the Sacred Writers—Phases of Christian Truth—*Alexandrian Christianity*—The Jews and Greek Philosophy—Hebraism and Hellenism—Glories of Alexandria—Prosperity of the Jews in Alexandria—The Diaspleuston—Favour shown the Jews by the Ptolemies—The Septuagint—Delight of the Hellenists—Anger of the Hebraists—Effects of Judaism—Bias of the Translators—Harmless Variations from the Hebrew—Hagadoth—Avoidance of Anthropomorphism and Anthropopathy—Deliberate Manipulation of the Original—Aristobulus—The Wisdom of Solomon—Semi-Ethnic Jewish Literature—Philo not wholly Original 136

CHAPTER XIII.
PHILO AND THE DOCTRINE OF THE LOGOS.

Family of Alexander the Alabarch—Life of Philo—Classification of his Works—Those that bear on the Creation—On Abraham—Allegorising Fancies—The Life of Moses—Arbitrary Exegesis—Meanings of the word LOGOS—Personification of the Logos—The High Priest—A Cupbearer—Other Comparisons—Vague Outlines of the Conception—Contrast with St. John 146

CHAPTER XIV.
PHILONISM—ALLEGORY—THE CATECHETICAL SCHOOL.

Influence of Philo on the Sacred Writers—Sapiental Literature of Alexandria—Defects of Philonism—The School of St. Mark—Motto of the Alexandrian School—Allegory applied to the Old Testament—The *Pardes* of the Kabbalists—History of Allegory in the Alexandrian School—Allegory in the Western Church 153

CHAPTER XV.
AUTHORSHIP AND STYLE OF THE EPISTLE TO THE HEBREWS.

Continuity of Scripture—Manifoldness of Wisdom—Ethnic Inspiration—the Epistle Alexandrian—External Evidence—Summary—Superficial Custom—Misuse of Authorities—Later Doubts and Hesitations—Indolent Custom—Phrases common to the Author with St. Paul—Differences of Style not Explicable—The Epistle not a Translation—Fondness of the Writer for Sonorous Amplifications 157

CHAPTER XVI.
THEOLOGY OF THE EPISTLE TO THE HEBREWS.

Difference from the Theological Conceptions of St. Paul—Three Cardinal Topics—"The People"—Christianity and Judaism—Alexandrianism of the Writer—Prominence of the Jews—Method of treating Scripture—Indebtedness to Philo—Particular Expressions—"the Cutter-Word"—Stern Passages—Melchizedek-Priesthood of Christ—Superiority to Philo—Fundamental Alexandrianism—Judaism not regarded as a Law but as a System of Worship—"The Pattern shown thee in the Mount"—Effectiveness of the Argument—A Præ-existent Ideal—The World of Ideas—View of Hope—FAITH, in this Epistle and in St. Paul—RIGHTEOUSNESS—CHRISTOLOGY—REDEMPTION—Prominence given to PRIESTHOOD and SACRIFICE—Peculiar Sentences—The Author could not have been St. Paul 166

CHAPTER XVII.

WHO WROTE THE EPISTLE TO THE HEBREWS?

Absence of Greeting—Certainties about the Writer—by some known Friend of St. Paul—Yet not by AQUILA—Nor by TITUS—Nor by SILAS—Nor by ST. BARNABAS—Nor by ST. CLEMENS OF ROME—Nor by ST. MARK—Nor by ST. LUKE—Strong Probability that the Writer was APOLLOS—This would not necessarily be known to the Church of Alexandria—Suggested by Luther—Generally and increasingly Accepted—Date of the Epistle—Allusion to Timothy—Addressed to Jewish Christians—Not Addressed to the Church of Jerusalem—Nor to Corinth—Nor to Alexandria—May have been Addressed to Rome—or to Ephesus—"They of Italy"—Apollos 182

CHAPTER XVIII.

THE EPISTLE TO THE HEBREWS.

SECTION I.—*The Superiority of Christ.*—Comparison between Judaism and Christianity—Outline of the Epistle—Its Keynotes—Striking Opening—Christ Superior to Angels—Peculiar Method of Scriptural Argument—Use of Quotations—An Admitted Method—Partial Change of View—The Style of Argument less important to us . . . 191

SECTION II.—*A Solemn Exhortation.*—Translation and Notes—Christ Superior to Moses—Parallelism of Structure—Appeal 198

SECTION III.—*The High Priesthood of Christ.*—Transitional Exhortation—Qualifications of High Priesthood—Sketch of the great Argument of the Epistle—Translation and Notes—Explanation of Difficulties respecting the Nature of Christ—Digression—Post-Baptismal Sin—Indefectibility of Grace—Calvinistic View of the Passage—Arminian View—Neither View Tenable—Obvious Limitations of the Meaning of the Passage—"Near a Curse"—"For Burning"—A Better Hope 203

SECTION IV.—*The Order of Melchizedek.*—Translation and Notes—All that is known of Melchizedek—Salem—El Elion—Allusion in Psalm cx.—Hagadoth—Philo—Mystery attached to Melchizedek—Fantastic Hypotheses—Who Melchizedek was—Only Important as a Type—Semitic Phraseology and Modes of Arguing from the Silence of Scripture—Translation and Notes—Argument of the Passage—Superiority of the Melchizedek to the Levitic Priesthood in Seven Particulars—Summary and Notes . 216

SECTION V.—*The Day of Atonement.*—Grandeur of the Day—Translation and Notes—A New Covenant—Its Superior Ordinances of Ministration—Translation and Notes—Symbolism of Service—The Tabernacle, not the Temple—"*Vacua omnia*"—Contents of the Ark—The Thumiaterion—Censer (?)—Altar of Incense—Translation and Notes—Meanings of the word *Diatheke*—An obvious Play on its Second Meaning of "Testament"—Translation and Notes—Familiarity with the Hagadoth and the Halacha—Grandest Phase of Levitic Priesthood—Feelings Inspired by the Day—Careful Preparation of the High Priest—Legendary Additions to the Ritual—Peril of the Function—Chosen as the Highest Point of Comparison—Superiority of Christian Privileges in every respect 226

SECTION VI.—*A Recapitulation.*—Translation and Notes—Triumphant Close of the Argument—Summary 242

SECTION VII.—*A Third Solemn Warning.*—Exhortation—Its Solemnity—Translation and Notes 245

SECTION VIII.—*The Glories of Faith.*—FAITH—What is Faith?—Exhibited in its Issues—Beginning of the Illustration—Instances from each Period of Sacred History—Translation and Notes 248

SECTION IX.—*Final Exhortations.*—Exhortation to Endurance—God's Fatherhood—Translation and Notes—Faith and Patience—Superior Grandeur of Christianity—Moral Appeal of the last Chapter—Translation and Notes—Modern Controversies—"We have an Altar"—Explanation of the Passage—Exhortation to Obedience—Final Clauses—Their Bearing on the Authorship of the Epistle 254

Book IV.

JUDAIC CHRISTIANITY.

CHAPTER XIX.

THE LORD'S BROTHER.

A New Phase of Christianity—The Name "James"—The Author was not James the Son of Zebedee—Untenable Arguments—Nor James the Son of Alphæus—Untenable Arguments—Alphæus—He is James, Bishop of Jerusalem, and the Lord's Brother—Is he

Identical with the Son of Alphæus?—"Neither did His Brethren Believe on Him"— Paucity of Jewish Names—Helvidian Theory—The Simplest and Fairest explanation of the Language of the Evangelists—The Language not Absolutely Decisive—Dogma of the *Aeiparthenia*—The Evangelists give no Hint of it—What the Gospels Say—Utter Baselessness of the Theory of St. Jerome—Entirely Untrue that the Terms "Cousins" and "Brothers" are Identical—The Theory an Invention due to *à priori* Conceptions—Not a single Argument can be Adduced in its favour—Tendencies which Led to the Dogma of the *Aeiparthenia*—Unscriptural and Manichæan Disparagement of the Sanctity of Marriage—The Theory arises from Apollinarian Tendencies—Theory of Epiphanius—Derived from the Apocryphal Gospels—Their Absurdities and Discrepancies—Conclusion 265

CHAPTER XX.
LIFE AND CHARACTER OF ST. JAMES.

Inimitable Truthfulness of Scripture Narrative—Childhood and Training of St. James— A Boy's Education—"A Just Man"—Levitic Precision—The Home at Nazareth— Familiarity with Scripture—"Wisdom"—Knowledge of Apocryphal Books—Curious Phenomenon—A Nazarite—Scrupulous Holiness—A Lifelong Vow—Shadows over the Home at Nazareth—Alienation of Christ's "Brethren"—Their Interferences—His Calm and Gentle Rebukes—Their Last Interference—Their Complete Conversion—Due to the Resurrection—"He was Seen of James"—Legend in the Gospel of the Hebrews —St. James and St. Paul—Death of the Son of Zebedee—James, Bishop of Jerusalem —Deep Reverence for his Character—*Obliam*—St. James and St. Peter—Bearing of St. James in the Synod of Jerusalem—Wisdom which he Showed—Importance of the Question at Stake—His Decision—Its Results—"Certain from James"—A Favourite of the Ebionites—Judaic Type of his Character and of his Views—The Results of his Training—"The Just"—Title which he Adopts—Unfortunate Advice to St. Paul— Martyrdom of St. James—Josephus—Hegesippus—Narrative of Hegesippus—Talmudic Legends of St. James—Rapid Retribution 280

CHAPTER XXI.
CHARACTERISTICS OF THE EPISTLE OF ST. JAMES.

Canonicity of St. James—Judaic Tone of Thought—Absence of Distinctively Christian Dogmas—Luther's Rash Assertion—Ideal of St. James—Readers whom he had in View —Date of the Epistle—Where Written—Phenomena of the Epistle Explained by its Palestinian Origin—State of the Jewish Church at Jerusalem—Tyrannous Sadducean Priests—Maledictions against them in the Talmud—Their Greed and Luxury—St. James in Writing to Christians was Thinking partly of Jews—And his Words would be Respected by Jews as well as Christians—Asserted Essenism and Ebionism of St. James—Orphic Colouring—Style of St. James—Outline of the Epistle—Its one Predominant Thought—Controversial Aspect—Parties in the Christian Church—A Last Appeal to Jews—Uniqueness of the Epistle—Its Usefulness and Grandeur . . . 307

CHAPTER XXII.
THE EPISTLE OF ST. JAMES.

The Title which he Adopts—The Dispersion—The Greeting—Translation and Notes— Temptation and Trial—Need of Wisdom—Need of Prayer—Address to Rich and Poor —Meaning of the Words addressed to them—Transitoriness of Riches—Blessing of Endurance—God always in the Meridian—A Pregnant Clause—The True Ritual— Respect of Persons—Justification by Works—Translation and Notes—Oracular Egotism —Sins of the Tongue—Heavenly Wisdom—Translation and Notes—State of the Christian Communities—St. James is Thinking of Jerusalem—False Religionism— "The Spirit that Dwelleth in us Lusteth to Envy"—Various Exhortations—Overconfidence—Denunciation of Greed—Of Whom is he Thinking?—Sadducean Hierarchs— The Impending Doom—The Murder of the "Just One"—Despised Warnings—Last Exhortations—Efficacy of Prayer—Perversion of the Passage—A Last Exhortation . 324

CHAPTER XXIII.
ST. JAMES AND ST. PAUL ON FAITH AND WORKS.

St. Paul and St. James Contrasted—Is there a Real Contradiction?—Views of the Tübingen School—Is St. James thinking of St. Paul at all?—The Questions often Discussed— Jewish Reliance on the Benefit of Theoretic Monotheism—On Circumcision—On National Privileges—On Externalism Generally—St. James probably Intended to Correct Perversions of Pauline Teaching—St. Paul's Views Misrepresented even in his Lifetime, and still often Perverted—No Intention to *Refute* St. Paul—Is the Language of the Apostles Reconcilable?—They are using the same Words in Different

CONTENTS. xiii

PAGE

Senses—"Faith" in St. Paul and in St. James—"Works" in St. Paul and in St. James—"Justification" in St. Paul and in St. James—Illustrations drawn from *different* Periods in the Life of Abraham—St. Paul was Dealing with the Vanity of Legalism, St. James with the Vanity of Orthodoxy—Fundamental Agreement between the two Apostles shown by what they say of Faith and of Works in other Passages—No Bitter Controversy between them—They used Different Expressions, and looked on Christianity from Different Points of View—What Both would have Accepted—Blessing of Truth revealed under Many Lights 349

Book V.

THE EARLIER LIFE AND WORKS OF ST. JOHN.

CHAPTER XXIV.

ST. JOHN.

The Pillar-Apostles—Individuality of Each—St. Paul Meets them at Jerusalem—The Special Work of St. John—His Growth in Spiritual Enlightenment—Continuity of his Godliness—His Boyhood—A Disciple of the Baptist—His Natural Gifts—Independence of Galileans—Messianic Hopes—Becomes a Disciple of Jesus—Why St. John Lived at Jerusalem—Teaching of the Baptist—Was St. John Married?—"Follow Me"—Belonged to the Innermost Group of Apostles—Not Ideally Faultless—He had Much to Unlearn—His Exclusiveness—His Intolerance at En Gannim—Mixture of Humane Motives with His Zeal—"As Elias did"—"Ye Know not what Spirit ye are of"—Christ's Last Journey to Jerusalem—Ambition of the Sons of Zebedee—The Cup and the Baptism—Leaning on the Lord's Bosom—Flight at Gethsemane—The Earliest to Rejoin his Lord—In the High Priest's Palace—A Witness of the Trials—A Witness of the Crucifixion—"Behold thy Mother!"—"To his own Home"—Blood and Water—At the Tomb—A Witness of the Resurrection—On the Lake of Galilee—"If I Will that he Tarry till I Come"—Mistaken Interpretation of the Words 362

CHAPTER XXV.

LIFE OF ST. JOHN AFTER THE ASCENSION.

In the Upper Room—Healing of the Cripple—Threatened and Scourged—With Peter in Samaria—Years of Contemplation—Once Mentioned by St. Paul—At the Synod of Jerusalem—A Judaist—Recognised the Mission of St. Paul—Took no Part in the Debate—No further Records of him in Scripture—At Patmos—Date of this Banishment—Causes which led to his Departure from Jerusalem—Legends of his Banishment to Patmos—The Boiling Oil and the Poison—Was he ever at Rome?—Certainty that he Resided in Asia Minor—"The Nebulous Presbyter"—John the Presbyter was John the Apostle—The Quartodeciman Controversy—Greek of the Apocalypse—Revealing Effect of the Fall of Jerusalem—The Apocalypse Judaic in Tone—St. John at Ephesus —Patmos 381

CHAPTER XXVI.

LEGENDS OF ST. JOHN.

Legend of his Meeting Cerinthus at the Thermae—Reasons for believing the Story to be a mere Invention—Spirit of Religious Intolerance in which the Story Originated—Strange Legend about the Messianic Grapes—Credulity of Papias—Possible Explanation of the Story—Error of Irenaeus—Vehemence of Polycarp—Legend of St. John and the Robber —Legend of St. John and the Tame Partridge—Tenderness to Animals—St. John and the *Petalon*—Other Legends—St. John's Last Sermons—Legends of the Death of St. John—Legends of his Immortality 394

CHAPTER XXVII.

GENERAL FEATURES OF THE APOCALYPSE

The Earliest of St. John's Books—What we Lose by the Unchronological Arrangement of the Book—The Apocalypse Written before the Fall of Jerusalem—Impossibility that it should have been Written after the Gospel 404

SECTION I.—*Date of the Apocalypse.*—The Apocalypse could Not have been Written in the Time of Domitian—Possible Causes of the Error of Irenaeus—Key to the Apocalypse found in the Neronian Persecution—Why the Book has been so grievously Misunderstood

—Theological Romances of Commentary—The Neronian Persecution and the Jewish War—Lesson of the Apocalypse—Nero the Antichrist—Nero amid the Ashes of Rome—All Apocalypses deal with Events on the Contemporary Horizon—Outbreak of the Jewish War—The Temple still Standing—The Flight of the Christians to Pella—The Date of the Apocalypse Implied in Rev. xiii. 3, and xvii. 10, 11—Written in the Reign of Galba—Or possibly a little later—The Woes of the Messiah—The Doom of Rome . . 407

SECTION II.—*The Revolt of Judæa.*—Delinquencies of Pilate—Threatening Symptoms—Hatred of the Jews for the Romans—The Air full of Prodigies—Wickedness of Gessius Florus—Insolence of the Greeks at Cæsarea—Disgraceful Tyranny of Florus—The Jews Appeal to Cestius Gallus—Rise of the Zealots—Seizure of the Tower of Antonia—Epidemic of Massacre—March of Cestius Gallus—His Pusillanimity—His Defeat at Bethhoron—Vespasian Despatched to Judæa—Leading Citizens Involved in the Revolt—Josephus in Galilee—Siege of Jotapata—Massacres—Siege of Gamala—Mount Tabor—Giscala—Atrocities of the Zealots in Jerusalem—The Idumeans Admitted—Horrible Orgies—Advance of Vespasian Marked by fresh Massacres—A River of Blood—Increasing Horrors—Factions in Jerusalem—Dreadful Condition of the City—Aspect of the World—Physically—Morally—Socially—Politically—Incessant Civil Wars—General Terror—The Era of Martyrdoms—Style, Metaphors, and Meaning of the Apocalypse—Dislike felt for the Book—Accounted for by the Perversions to which it has been subjected—Strange Systems of Interpretation—The Præterists—The Futurists—The Historical Interpreters—Gleams of Tradition as to the True View of the Book—Increasing Conviction that it Dealt with Events mainly Contemporary—Multitudes of Fantastic Guesses—Their Extreme Diversity—Essential Sacredness of the Book—Apocalyptic Literature—Necessity for its Cryptographic Form 415

CHAPTER XXVIII.

THE APOCALYPSE.

St. John "The Theologian" 437

SECTION I.—*The Letters to the Seven Churches.*—Only a Rapid Outline of the Apocalypse offered—Sections of the Book—The Seven Churches—The Letters Normally Sevenfold—The Letter to Ephesus, &c.—The Heresies alluded to—Theory that they are Aimed at the Followers of St. Paul—Absurdity of the Theory—The Nicolaitans—"The Depths of Satan"—"The False Apostles"—Volkmar—The Tübingen School—Extravagant Opinions 438

SECTION II.—*The Seals.*—The Vision—The First Seal—The White Horse: The Messiah—The Second Seal—The Red Horse: Slaughter—The Third Seal—The Black Horse: Famine—"The Oil and the Wine"—The Fourth Seal—The Livid Horse: Pestilence—The Fifth Seal—The Cry for Vengeance—The Sixth Seal—Universal Catastrophe—Apocalyptic Style—The Pause—The Sealing of the 144,000—Symbols Iterative and Progressive 443

SECTION III.—*The Trumpets.*—The Censer Hurled to Earth—The First Trumpet—Storms, Earthquakes, Portents—The Second Trumpet—The Burning Mountain and the Sea Turned into Blood—The Third Trumpet—The Star Absinth—The Fourth Trumpet—The Smiting of Sun, Moon, and Stars—The Eagle screaming "Woe!"—The Fifth Trumpet—The Fallen Star—The Scorpion-Locusts—The Sixth Trumpet—Two Hundred Million Horsemen 450

SECTION IV.—*An Episode.*—The Sunlike Angel—The Seven Thunders—The Book—The Measuring—Character of the Symbols—The Two Witnesses—The Earthquake - Difficulties of Interpretation—Remarks on these Visions 456

SECTION V.—*The Wild Beast from the Sea.*—The Star-Crowned Woman; the Child; the Dragon—Meaning of the Symbols—Flight of the Church to Pella—Certainty that by the Wild Beast from the Sea is mainly meant the Emperor Nero—The Sixteen Distinctive Indications—Every one of them Points Directly to Nero and the Roman Empire—Especially in those Particulars which seem most Enigmatical—Widespread Belief among Christians that Nero would Return—The Number of the Beast—Sole Element of Difficulty—Ancient Guesses—Its Kabbalistic Character—Its Certain Solution—Commonness of these Isopsephic Enigmas—The Solution Confirmed by the Ancient Various Readings—The Belief about Nero Redivivus—*A priori* Dogmas—Domitian was a Nero Redivivus 461

SECTION VI.—*The Second Beast and the False Prophet.*—Absence of Definite Traditions—Ten Indications as to the Person Intended—Idle Guesses—Various Conjectures—The Roman Augurial System—Simon Magus—Probability that Vespasian was Intended—Remarkable Adaptation to him of every one of the Ten Indications, even in the most unexpected Particulars—Possibility that it is a *Composite* Symbol—Nero and Domitian—The Name "Nero" often given to Domitian 474

SECTION VII.—*The Vials.*—The Remainder of the Apocalypse—The Vials—The Seventh Vial—Judgment of the Harlot City—Pæan over the Fall of Babylon—General Conception of the Apocalypse 483

CHAPTER XXIX.
THE FALL OF JERUSALEM

Sources of the History—Advance of Titus—Rage and Despair of the Jews—Destruction of the Temple—Massacre and Devastation—A Second Advent—Close of the Æon—Tremendous Significance of the Event—Rightly Apprehended by Ancient Christian Historians—Effects of the Event on the Mind of St. John—How he came to Write the Apocalypse—Resemblance and Differences of the Apocalypse and the Fourth Gospel . 486

CHAPTER XXX.
THE GROWTH OF HERESY.

The Growth of Heresy Gradual—Original Meaning of the Word—Real and Imaginary Heretics—Sources of Heresy—Sects—Jewish Sects—Strange Vitality of Judaism—Rabbinism—A Nomocracy—Jewish Sects—Nazarenes—Ebionites—Gentile Sects—Simon Magus—Legends of him—An Antichrist—Cerinthus—His Errors—Gradual Rise of Docetism—Gnostic Systems—Gnostics before Gnosticism—Opposite Tendencies—How St. John met Heresy 494

CHAPTER XXXI.
LATER WRITINGS OF ST. JOHN.

The First Epistle of St. John—Christianity had Entered on a New Phase—Speculations and Errors—St. John's Method of Argument—The Incarnation of the Divine—Tradition about the Gospel—The Last of the Apostles—A New Era—Supreme Utterances—Righteousness, Sonship, Sanctification 504

CHAPTER XXXII.
THE STAMP OF FINALITY ON THE WRITINGS OF ST. JOHN

St. John sets the Seal to Former Revelations—Stamp of Finality upon his Writings—The Idea of Eternity—The Logos—"God is Righteous"—"God is Light"—"God is Love"—Importance of these Utterances—Simplification of Essential Elements—St. Paul and St. John—The Gospel—The Epistle—Where Written—Tradition—Tone of the Epistle—Dangers which St. John Contemplates—Calm of the Style 509

CHAPTER XXXIII.
CHARACTERISTICS OF THE MIND AND STYLE OF ST. JOHN.

His Contemplativeness—His Repose—His Style—His Sternness—How Accounted for—The Personal Question—Ideas of Righteousness and Love 519

CHAPTER XXXIV.
OBJECT AND OUTLINE OF THE FIRST EPISTLE.

Object of the Epistle—Not Aphoristic—First Attempts at Analysis—Full Analysis of the Epistle, showing its Remarkable Symmetry—Illustrates the Characteristics of his Methods—Prevalent Triplicity of Arrangement—Certain Genuineness of the Epistle—An Epistle not a Treatise 525

CHAPTER XXXV.
THE FIRST EPISTLE OF ST. JOHN.

SECTION I.—*Eternal Life.*—Translation and Notes—Introductory Theme—An Apparent Contradiction—"God is Light"—Meaning of the Phrase—"Walking in Light"—Translation, Notes, Comments—Propitiation—Prevalent Misunderstandings as to the Style and Manner of St. John—Symmetries of Statement—Parallels—"Knowing God"—Love—"Abiding in God"—The New and Old Commandment—In what sense "New" and "Old"—The Ideal and the Actual—A Test of Professions—"Little Children, Fathers, Young Men"—Meaning of the Passage—Warning against Love of the World—What is Meant by "Antichrist"—Prevalence of Antichrists—The Unction from the Holy Spirit is the Christian's Security—Abiding in the Truth—Eternal Life 531

SECTION II.—*The Confidence of Sonship.*—Confidence of Sonship a Sign that we Possess Eternal Life—The "Manifestation" of Christ—"Children of God"—How it will be Tested—Translation and Notes—Awful Conceptions of Sin—Severity of Language—

Doing Righteousness—Love to Man the Purpose of Revelation—Cain—Christ—Perfect Love—Difficult Recapitulation—Self-condemnation—God's Judgments—Confidence towards God—Last Discourses of Christ 546

SECTION III.—*The Source of Sonship.*—"Abide in Him"—Denial of Christ—"Testing the Spirits"—Confessing "Christ come in the Flesh"—Interesting Variation of Reading—What is meant by "Severing Jesus"—Argument for the Genuineness of the Reading—The Recognition of God—"God is Love"—Summary and Gathering up of the leading Conceptions 554

SECTION IV.—*Assurance.*—The Witnesses—Spurious Verse—The Water and the Blood—Sevenfold Witnesses in the Gospel—Witnesses in the Epistle—No Direct Allusion to the Sacraments—Distinct Reference to the Crucifixion—Meaning of the Passage—Confirmation of the Divine Testimony 561

SECTION V.—*Conclusion.*—Recapitulation—Aim of the Epistle—Prayer—"The Sin unto Death"—No One Definite Sin—Desperate Apostasy—The Prayer Not Forbidden—Parallels in the Old Testament—"Delivering to Satan"—The Limitation belongs to the Realm of the Ideal—Rabbi Meier—Prayer for all Men—Conclusion of the Epistle—"Little Children, keep yourselves from Idols" 567

CHAPTER XXXVI.

THE SECOND EPISTLE OF ST. JOHN.

Brief Christian Epistles—Probability of their Genuineness—External Evidence—Internal Evidence—John the Elder—To whom was the Second Epistle addressed—Electa?—Kyria?—A Lady or a Church?—Theory of Bishop Wordsworth—Founded on very Uncertain Hypothesis—Theories of German Critics—Fantastic and Untenable—Improbability of the Letter being Addressed to a Church—The Address better understood in its Simplest Sense—Where the Letter was Written—Analysis—Translation and Notes—Keynotes of the Letter—Wrong Use made of One Passage—Sin of Dogmatic Intolerance—Hatred can never be a Christian Virtue—What St. John really Meant . . . 575

CHAPTER XXXVII.

THE THIRD EPISTLE OF ST. JOHN.

Gaius—Commonness of the Name—Object of the Letter—Translation and Notes—*Filioli, diligite alterutrum* 589

APPENDIX.

EXCURSUS I.—Asserted Primacy of St. Peter 593
EXCURSUS II.—Patristic Evidence of St. Peter's Visit to Rome 594
EXCURSUS III.—Use of the name "Babylon" for Rome in 1 Peter. v. 13 . . . 595
EXCURSUS IV.—The Book of Enoch 597
EXCURSUS V.—Rabbinic Allusions in St. Jude 598
EXCURSUS VI.—Specimens of Philonian Allegory 600
EXCURSUS VII.—Additional Illustrations of Philo's Views about the Logos . . 602
EXCURSUS VIII.—Patristic Evidence as to the Authorship of the Epistle to the Hebrews . 603
EXCURSUS IX.—Minor Resemblances between the Epistle to the Hebrews and the Works of Philo 611
EXCURSUS X.—"Salem" and Jerusalem 612
EXCURSUS XI.—The Altar of Incense and the Holiest Place 613
EXCURSUS XII.—Ceremonies of the Day of Atonement 614
EXCURSUS XIII.—Impressions left on the Minds of the Jews by the Ceremonies of the Day of Atonement 615
EXCURSUS XIV.—The Identity of "John the Presbyter" with John the Apostle . . 618

THE EARLY DAYS OF CHRISTIANITY.

Book I.
THE WORLD.

CHAPTER I.
MORAL CONDITION OF THE WORLD.

> " Quem vocet divum populus ruentis
> Imperi rebus? prece qua fatigent
> Virgines sanctae minus audientem
>   Carmina Vestam?"
>   —Hor. *Od.* I. ii. 25.

> " Nona aetas agitur pejoraque saecula ferri
> Temporibus, quorum sceleri non invenit ipsa
> Nomen, et a nullo posuit natura metallo."
>   —Juv. *Sat.* xiii. 28—30.

" From Mummius to Augustus the Roman city stands as the living mistress of a dead world, and from Augustus to Theodosius the mistress becomes as lifeless as her subjects."—Freeman's *Essays*, ii. 330.

The epoch which witnessed the early growth of Christianity was an epoch of which the horror and the degradation have rarely been equalled, and perhaps never exceeded, in the annals of mankind. Were we to form our sole estimate of it from the lurid picture of its wickedness, which St. Paul in more than one passage has painted with a few powerful strokes, we might suppose that we were judging it from too lofty a standpoint. We might be accused of throwing too dark a shadow upon the crimes of Paganism, when we set it as a foil to the lustre of an ideal holiness. But even if St. Paul had never paused amid his sacred reasonings to affix his terrible brand upon the pride of Heathenism, there would still have been abundant proofs of the abnormal wickedness which accompanied the decadence of ancient civilisation. They are stamped upon its coinage, cut on its gems, painted upon its chamber-walls, sown broadcast over the pages of its poets, satirists, and historians. "Out of thine own mouth will I judge thee, thou wicked servant!" Is there any age which stands so instantly condemned by the bare mention of its rulers as that which recalls the successive names of Tiberius, Gaius, Claudius, Nero, Galba, Otho, and Vitellius, and which after a brief gleam of better examples under Vespasian and Titus, sank at last under the hideous tyranny of a Domitian? Is there any age of which the evil characteristics force themselves so instantaneously upon the mind as that of which we mainly learn the history and moral condition from the relics of Pompeii and Herculaneum, the satires of Persius and Juvenal, the epigrams of Martial, and the terrible records of Tacitus, Suetonius, and Dion Cassius? And yet even beneath this lowest deep, there is a lower deep; for not even on their dark pages are the depths of Satan so shamelessly laid bare to human gaze as they are in the sordid fictions of Petronius and of Apuleius. But to dwell upon the crimes and the retributive misery of that period is happily not my duty. I need but make a passing allusion to its enormous wealth; its unbounded self-indulgence; its coarse and tasteless luxury; its greedy avarice; its sense of insecurity and terror;[1] its apathy, debauchery, and cruelty;[2] its hopeless fatalism;[3] its unspeakable sadness and weariness;[4] its strange extravagances alike of infidelity and of superstition.[5]

At the lowest extreme of the social scale were millions of slaves, without family, without religion, without possessions, who had no recognised rights, and towards whom none had any recognised duties, passing normally from a childhood of degradation to a manhood of hardship, and an old age of unpitied neglect.[6] Only a little above the slaves stood the lower classes, who formed the vast majority of the freeborn inhabitants of the Roman Empire. They were, for the most

---

[1] 2 Cor. vii. 10; "Interciderat sortis humanae commercium vi metûs," Tac. *Ann.* vi. 19; "Pavor internus occupaverat animos," *id.* iv. 76. See the very remarkable passage of Pliny ("At Hercule homini plurima ex homine mala sunt," *H. N.* vii. 1).

[2] Mart. *Ep.* ii. 66; Juv. vi. 491.

[3] Lucan, *Phars.* i. 70, 81; Suet. *Tib.* 69; Tac. *Agric.* 42; *Ann.* iii. 18, iv. 26; "Sed mihi haec et talia audienti in incerto judicium est, fatone res mortalium et necessitate immutabili an forte volvantur," *Ann.* vi. 22; Plin. *H. N.* ii. 7; Sen. *De Benef.* iv. 7.

[4] Tacitus, with all his resources, finds it difficult to vary his language in describing so many suicides.

[5] See my *Witness of History to Christ*, p. 101; *Seekers after God*, p. 38. The "taurobolies" and "kriobolies" (baths in the blood of bulls and rams) mark the extreme sensuality of superstition. See Döllinger, *Gentile and Jew*, ii. 179; De Pressensé, *Trois Premiers Siècles*, ii. 1—60, etc.

[6] Some of the *loci classici* on Roman slavery are: Cic. *De Rep.* xiv. 23; Juv. vi. 219, x. 183, xiv. 16—24; Sen. *Ep.* 47; *De Irâ*, iii. 35, 40; *De Clem.* 18; *Controv.* v. 33; *De Vit. Beat.* 17; Plin. *H. N.* xxxiii. 11; Plut. *Cato*, 21. Vedius Pollio and the lampreys (Plin. *H. N.* ix. 23). In the debate on the murder of Pedanius Secundus (Tac. *Ann.* xiv. 42—45) many eminent senators openly advocated the brutal law that when a master was murdered, his slaves, often to the number of hundreds, should be put to death. These facts, and many others, will be found collected in Wallon, *De l'Esclavage dans l'Antiquité*; Friedländer, *Sittengesch. Roms*; Becker, *Gallus*, E. T. 199—225; Döllinger, *Judenth. u. Heidenth.* ix 1, § 2. It is reckoned that in the Empire there cannot have been fewer than 60,000,000 slaves (Le Maistre, *Du Pape*, i. 283). They were so numerous as to be divided according to their nationalities (Tac. *Ann.* iii. 53), and every slave was regarded as a potential enemy (Sen. *Ep.* xlvii.).

part, beggars and idlers, familiar with the grossest indignities of an unscrupulous dependence. Despising a life of honest industry, they asked only for bread and the games of the circus, and were ready to support any Government, even the most despotic, if it would supply these needs. They spent their mornings in lounging about the Forum, or in dancing attendance at the levées of patrons, for a share in whose largesses they daily struggled.[1] They spent their afternoons and evenings in gossiping at the Public Baths, in listlessly enjoying the polluted plays of the theatre, or looking with fierce thrills of delighted horror at the bloody sports of the arena. At night they crept up to their miserable garrets in the sixth and seventh storeys of the huge *insulae*— the lodging houses of Rome—into which, as into the low lodging-houses of the poorer quarters of London, there drifted all that was most wretched and most vile.[2] Their life, as it is described for us by their contemporaries, was largely made up of squalor, misery, and vice.

Immeasurably removed from these needy and greedy freemen, and living chiefly amid crowds of corrupted and obsequious slaves, stood the constantly diminishing throng of the wealthy and the noble.[3] Every age in its decline has exhibited the spectacle of selfish luxury side by side with abject poverty; of—

"Wealth, a monster gorged
Mid starving populations:"—

but nowhere, and at no period, were these contrasts so startling as they were in Imperial Rome. There a whole population might be trembling lest they should be starved by the delay of an Alexandrian corn-ship, while the upper classes were squandering a fortune at a single banquet,[4] drinking out of myrrhine and jewelled vases worth hundreds of pounds,[5] and feasting on the brains of peacocks and the tongues of nightingales.[6] As a consequence, disease was rife, men were short-lived, and even

---

[1] Suet. *Ner.* 16; Mart. iv. 8, viii. 50; Juv. i. 100, 128, iii. 269, etc.
[2] Juv. *Sat.* iii. 60—65; Athen. i. 17, § 36; Tac. *Ann.* xv. 44, "quo cuncta undique atrocia aut pudenda confluunt;" Vitruv. ii. 8; Suet. *Ner.* 38. There were 44,000 *insulae* in Rome to only 1,780 *domus* (Becker, *Gallus*, E. T., p. 232).
[3] Among the 1,200,000 inhabitants of ancient Rome, even in Cicero's time, there were scarcely 2,000 proprietors (Cic. *De Off.* ii. 21).
[4] See Tac. *Ann.* iii. 55. 400,000 sesterces (Juv. xi. 19). Taking the standard of 100,000 sesterces to be in the Augustan age £1,080 (which is a little below the calculation of Hultsch), this would be £4,320. 30,000,000 sesterces (Sen. *Ep.* xcv.; Sen. *ad. Helv.* 9). In the days of Tiberius three mullets had sold for 30,000 sesterces (Suet. *Tib.* 34). Even in the days of Pompey Romans had adopted the disgusting practice of preparing for a dinner by taking an emetic. Vitellius set on the table at one banquet 2,000 fishes and 7,000 birds, and in less than eight months spent in feasts a sum that would now amount to several millions.
[5] Plin. *H. N.* viii. 48, xxxvii. 18.
[6] "Portenta luxuriae," Sen. *Ep.* cx.; Plin. *H. N.* ix. 18, 32, x. 51, 72. Petron. 93; Juv. xi. 1—55, v. 92—100; Macrob. *Sat.* iii. 12, 13; Sen. *Ep.* lxxxix. 21; Mart. *Ep.* lix. 5; Lampridius, *Elagab.* 20; Suet. *Vitell.* 13. On the luxury of the age in general, see Sen. *De Brev. Vit.* 12; *Ep.* xcv.

women became liable to gout.¹ Over a large part of Italy most of the freeborn population had to content themselves, even in winter, with a tunic, and the luxury of the toga was reserved only, by way of honour, to the corpse.² Yet at this very time the dress of Roman ladies displayed an unheard-of splendour. The elder Pliny tells us that he himself saw Lollia Paulina dressed for a betrothal feast in a robe entirely covered with pearls and emeralds, which had cost forty million sesterces,³ and which was known to be less costly than some of her other dresses.⁴ Gluttony, caprice, extravagance, ostentation, impurity, rioted in the heart of a society which knew of no other means by which to break the monotony of its weariness, or alleviate the anguish of its despair.

> "On that hard Pagan world disgust
> And secret loathing fell;
> Deep weariness and sated lust
> Made human life a hell.
> In his cool hall, with haggard eyes,
> The Roman noble lay;
> He drove abroad in furious guise
> Along the Appian Way;
> He made a feast, drank fierce and fast,
> And crowned his hair with flowers—
> No easier nor no quicker past
> The impracticable hours."

At the summit of the whole decaying system—necessary, yet detested—elevated indefinitely above the very highest, yet living in dread of the very lowest, oppressing a population which he terrified, and terrified by the population which he oppressed⁵—was an Emperor, raised to the divinest pinnacle of autocracy, yet conscious that his life hung upon a thread;⁶—an Emperor who, in the terrible phrase of Gibbon, was at once a priest, an atheist, and a god.⁷

The general condition of society was such as might have been expected from the existence of these elements. The Romans had entered on a stage of fatal degeneracy from the first day of their close intercourse with Greece.⁸ Greece learnt from Rome her cold-blooded cruelty; Rome learnt from Greece her voluptuous corruption. Family

---

¹ Sen. *Ep.* xcv. 15—29. At Herculaneum many of the rolls discovered were cookery books.
² Juv. i. 171; Mart. ix. 58, 8.
³ £432,000.
⁴ Pliny, *H. N.* ix. 35, 56. He also saw Agrippina in a robe of gold tissue, *id.* xxxiii. 19.
⁵ Juv. iv. 153; Suet. *Domit.* 17.
⁶ Tac. *Ann.* vi. 6; Suet. *Claud.* 35.
⁷ "Coelum decretum," Tac. *Ann.* i. 73; "Dis aequa potestas Caesaris," Juv. iv. 71; Plin. *Paneg.* 74—5, "Civitas nihil felicitati suae putat adstrui, posse nisi ut *Di Caesarem imitentur.*" (Cf. Suet. *Jul.* 88; *Tib.* 13, 58; *Aug.* 59; *Calig* 33; *Vesp.* 23 *Domit.* 13). Lucan, vii. 456; Philo, *Leg. ad Gaium passim;* Dion Cass. lxiii. 5, 20; Martial, *passim;* Tert. *Apol.* 33, 34; Boissier, *La Rel. Romaine,* i. 122—208.
⁸ The degeneracy is specially traceable in their literature from the days of Plautus onwards.

life among the Romans had once been a sacred thing, and for 520 years divorce had been unknown among them.[1] Under the Empire marriage had come to be regarded with disfavour and disdain.[2] Women, as Seneca says, married in order to be divorced, and were divorced in order to marry; and noble Roman matrons counted the years not by the Consuls, but by their discarded or discarding husbands.[3]

To have a family was regarded as a misfortune, because the childless were courted with extraordinary assiduity by crowds of fortune-hunters.[4] When there were children in a family, their education was left to be begun under the tutelage of those slaves who were otherwise the most decrepit and useless,[5] and was carried on, with results too fatally obvious, by supple, accomplished, and abandoned Greeklings.[6] But, indeed, no system of education could have eradicated the influence of the domestic circle. No care[7] could have prevented the sons and daughters of a wealthy family from catching the contagion of the vices of which they saw in their parents a constant and unblushing example.[8]

Literature and art were infected with the prevalent degradation. Poetry sank in great measure into exaggerated satire, hollow declamation, or frivolous epigrams. Art was partly corrupted by the fondness for glare, expensiveness, and size,[9] and partly sank into miserable triviality, or immoral prettinesses,[10] such as those which decorated the walls of Pompeii in the first century, and the Parc aux Cerfs in the eighteenth. Greek statues of the days of Phidias were ruthlessly decapitated, that their heads might be replaced by the scowling or imbecile features of a Gaius or a Claudius. Nero, professing to be a connoisseur, thought that he improved the Alexander of Lysimachus by gilding it from head to foot. Eloquence, deprived of every legitimate aim, and used almost solely for purposes of insincere display, was tempted to supply the lack of genuine fire by sonorous euphony and

---

[1] The first Roman recorded to have divorced his wife was Sp. Carvilius Ruga, B.C. 234 (Dionys. ii. 25; Aul. Gell. xvii. 21).
[2] Hor. *Od.* iii. 6, 17. "Haraque in hoc aevo quae velit esse parens," Ov. *Nux.* 15. Hence the Lex Papia Poppaea, the Jus trium liberorum, etc. Suet. *Oct.* 34; Aul. Gell. i. 6. See Champagny, *Les Césars*, i. 258, *seq.*
[3] "Non consulum numero sed maritorum annos suos computant," Sen. *De Benef.* iii. 16; "Repudium jam votum erat, et quasi matrimonii fructus," Tert. *Apol.* 6; "Corrumpere et corrumpi saeculum vocatur," Tac. *Germ* .19. Comp. Suet. *Calig.* 34.
[4] Tac. *Germ.* 20; *Ann.* xiii. 52; Plin. *H. N.* xiv. proœm; Sen. *ad Marc. Consol.* 19; Plin. *Epp.* iv. 16; Juv. *Sat.* xii. 114, *seq.*
[5] Plut. *De Lib. Educ.*
[6] Juv. vii. 187, 219.
[7] Juv. *Sat.* xiv.
[8] Juv. *Sat.* xiv. *passim*; Tac. *De Orat.* 28, 29; Quinct. i. 2; Sen. *De Ira*, ii. 22; *Ep.* 95.
[9] It was the age of Colossi (Plin. *H. N.* xxxiv. 7; Mart. *Ep.* i. 71, viii. 44; Stat. *Sylv.* i. 1, etc.).
[10] Ῥωπογραφία. Cic. *Att.* xv. 16; Plin. xxxv. 37. See Champagny, *Les Césars*, iv. 138, who refers to Vitruv. vii. 5; Propert. ii. 5; Plin. *H. N.* xiv. 22, and xxxv. 10 (the painter Arellius, etc.).

theatrical affectation. A training in rhetoric was now understood to be a training in the art of emphasis and verbiage, which was rarely used for any loftier purpose than to make sycophancy plausible, or to embellish sophistry with speciousness.[1] The Drama, even in Horace's days, had degenerated into a vehicle for the exhibition of scenic splendour or ingenious machinery. Dignity, wit, pathos, were no longer expected on the stage, for the dramatist was eclipsed by the swordsman or the ropedancer.[2] The actors who absorbed the greatest part of popular favour were pantomimists, whose insolent prosperity was generally in direct proportion to the infamy of their character.[3] And while the shamelessness of the theatre corrupted the purity of all classes from the earliest age,[4] the hearts of the multitude were made hard as the nether millstone with brutal insensibility, by the fury of the circus, the atrocities of the amphitheatre, and the cruel orgies of the games.[5] Augustus, in the document annexed to his will, mentioned that he had exhibited 8,000 gladiators and 3,510 wild beasts. The old warlike spirit of the Romans was dead among the gilded youth of families in which distinction of any kind was certain to bring down upon its most prominent members the murderous suspicion of irresponsible despots. The spirit which had once led the Domitii and the Fabii "to drink delight of battle with their peers" on the plains of Gaul and in the forests of Germany, was now satiated by gazing on criminals fighting for dear life with bears and tigers, or upon bands of gladiators who hacked each other to pieces on the encrimsoned sand.[6] The languid enervation of the delicate and dissolute aristocrat could only be amused by magnificence and stimulated by grossness or by blood.[7] Thus the gracious illusions by which true Art has ever aimed at purging the passions of terror and pity, were extinguished by the realism of tragedies ignobly horrible, and comedies intolerably base. Two phrases sum up the characteristics of Roman

---

[1] Tac. *Dial.* 36—41; *Ann.* xv. 71; Sen. *Ep.* cvi. 12; Petron. *Satyr.* i.; Dion Cass. lix. 20.
[2] Juv. xiv. 250; Suet. *Nero*, 11; *Galb.* 6.
[3] Mnester (Tac. *Ann.* xi. 4, 36); Paris (Juv. vi. 87, vii. 88); Aliturus (Jos. *Vit.* 3); Pylades (Zosim. i. 6); Bathyllus (Dion Cass. liv. 17; Tac. *Ann.* i. 54).
[4] Isidor. xviii. 39.
[5] "Mera homicidia sunt," Sen. *Ep.* vii. 2; "Nihil est nobis... cum insaniâ circi, cum impudicitia theatri, cum atrocitate arenae, cum vanitate xysti," Tert. *Apol.* 38. Cicero inclined to the prohibition of games which imperilled life (*De Legg.* ii. 15), and Seneca (*l.c.*) expressed his compassionate disapproval, and exposed the falsehood and sophism of the plea that after all, the sufferers were only criminals. Yet in the days of Claudius the number of those thus butchered was so great that the statue of Augustus had to be moved that it might not constantly be covered with a veil (Dion Cass. lx. 13, who in the same chapter mentions a lion that had been trained to devour men). In Claudius's sham sea-fight we are told that the incredible number of 19,000 men fought each other (Tac. *Ann.* xii. 56). Titus, the "darling of the human race," in one day brought into the theatre 5,000 wild beasts (Suet. *Tit.* 7), and butchered thousands of Jews in the games at Berytus. In Trajan's games (Dion Cass. lxviii. 15) 11,000 animals and 10,000 men had to fight.
[6] Suet. *Claud.* 14, 21, 34; *Ner.* 12; *Calig.* 35; Tac. *Ann.* xiii. 49; Plin. *Paneg.* 33.
[7] Tac. *Ann.* xv. 32.

civilisation in the days of the Empire—heartless cruelty, and unfathomable corruption.[1]

If there had been a refuge anywhere for the sentiments of outraged virtue and outraged humanity, we might have hoped to find it in the Senate, the members of which were heirs of so many noble and austere traditions. But—even in the days of Tiberius—the Senate, as Tacitus tells us, had rushed headlong into the most servile flattery,[2] and this would not have been possible if its members had not been tainted by the prevalent deterioration. It was before the once grave and pure-minded Senators of Rome—the greatness of whose state was founded on the sanctity of family relationships—that the Censor Metellus had declared in A.U.C. 602, without one dissentient murmur, that marriage could only be regarded as an intolerable necessity.[3] Before that same Senate, at an earlier period, a leading Consular had not scrupled to assert that there was scarcely one among them all who had not ordered one or more of his own infant children to be exposed to death.[4] In the hearing of that same Senate in A.D. 59, not long before St. Paul wrote his letter to Philemon, C. Cassius Longinus had gravely argued that the only security for the life of masters was to put into execution the sanguinary Silanian law, which enacted that, if a master was murdered, every one of his slaves, however numerous, however notoriously innocent, should be indiscriminately massacred.[5] It was the Senators of Rome who thronged forth to meet with adoring congratulations the miserable youth who came to them with his hands reeking with the blood of matricide.[6] They offered thanksgivings to the gods for his worst cruelties,[7] and obediently voted Divine honours to the dead infant, four months old, of the wife whom he afterwards killed with a brutal kick.[8]

And what was the religion of a period which needed the sanctions and consolations of religion more deeply than any age since the world began? It is certain that the old Paganism was—except in country places—practically dead. The very fact that it was necessary to

---

[1] Eph. iv. 19; 2 Cor. vii. 10. Merivale, vi. 452; Champagny, *Les Césars*, iv. 161, sq. Seneca, describing the age in the tragedy of *Octavia*, says:—

"Saeculo premimur gravi
Quo scelera regnant, saevit impietas furens," etc.
—*Oct.* 379—437.

[2] Tac. *Ann.* iii. 65, vi. 2, xiv. 12, 13, etc.

[3] Comp. Tac. *Ann.* ii. 37, 38, iii. 34, 35, xv. 19; Aul. Gell. *N. A.* i. 6; Liv. *Epit.* 50.

[4] This abandonment of children was a *normal* practice (Ter. *Heaut.* iv. 1, 37; Ovid, *Amor.* ii. 14; Suet. *Calig.* 5; *Oct.* 65; Juv. *Sat.* vi. 592; Plin. *Ep.* iv. 15 [comp. ii. 20]; Sen. *ad Marciam*, 19; *Controv.* x. 6). Augustine (*De Civ. Dei*, iv. 11) tells us that there was a goddess *Levana*, so called "quia *lerat* infantes;" if the father did not take the new-born child in his arms, it was exposed (Tac. *Hist.* v. 5; *Germ.* 19; Tert. *Apol.* 9; *Ad Natt.* 15; Minuc. Fel. *Octav.* xxx. 31; Stobaen's *Floril.* lxxv. 15; Epictet. i. 23; Paulus, *Dig.* xxv. 3, etc. And see Denis, *Idées morales dans l'Antiquité*, ii. 203).

[5] Tac. *Ann.* xiv. 43, 44; *v. supra*, p. 2.

[6] Tac. *Ann.* xiv. 13, "festo cultu Senatum."

[7] "Quotiens fugas et caedes jussit princeps, toties grates Deis actas," Tac. *An* xiv. 64.

[8] Tac. *Ann.* xvi. 6; Suet. *Ner.* 25; Dion Cass. lxii. 27.

prop it up by the buttress of political interference shows how hollow and ruinous the structure of classic Polytheism had become.[1] The decrees and reforms of Claudius were not likely to reassure the faith of an age which had witnessed in contemptuous silence, or with frantic adulation, the assumption by Gaius of the attributes of deity after deity, had tolerated his insults against their sublimest objects of worship, and encouraged his claim to a living apotheosis.[2] The upper classes were "destitute of faith, yet terrified at scepticism." They had long learnt to treat the current mythology as a mass of worthless fables, scarcely amusing enough for even a schoolboy's laughter,[3] but they were the ready dupes of every wandering quack who chose to assume the character of a *mathematicus* or a *mage*.[4] Their official religion was a decrepit Theogony; their real religion was a vague and credulous fatalism, which disbelieved in the existence of the gods, or held with Epicurus that they were careless of mankind.[5] The mass of the populace either accorded to the old beliefs a nominal adherence which saved them the trouble of giving any thought to the matter,[6] and reduced their creed and their morals to a survival of national habits; or else they plunged with eager curiosity into the crowd of foreign cults[7]—among which a distorted Judaism took its place[8]—such as made the Romans familiar with strange names like Sabazius and Anchialus, Agdistis, Isis, and the Syrian goddess.[9] All men joined in the confession that "the oracles were dumb." It hardly needed the wail of mingled lamentations as of departing deities which swept over the astonished crew of the vessel off Palodes to assure the world that the reign of the gods of Hellas was over—that "Great Pan was dead."[10]

Such are the scenes which we must witness, such are the sentiments with which we must become familiar, the moment that we turn away

---

[1] Suet. *Tib.* 36.
[2] Suet. *Calig.* 51. See Mart. *Ep.* v. 8, where he talks of the "edict of our Lord and God," *i.e.*, of Domitian; and vii. 60, where he says that he shall pray to Domitian, and not to Jupiter.
[3] "Esse aliquos manes et subterranea regna...
Nec pueri credunt nisi qui nondum aere lavantur."
—Juv. *Sat.* ii. 149, 152.
[4] Tac. *H.* i. 22; *Ann.* vi. 20, 21, xii. 68; Juv. *Sat.* xiv. 248, iii. 42, vii. 200, etc.; Suet. *Aug.* 94; *Tib.* 14; *Ner.* 26; *Otho,* 4; *Domit.* 15, etc.
[5] Lucr. vi. 445—455; Juv. *Sat.* vii. 189—202, x. 129, xiii. 86—89; Plin. *H.N.* ii. 21; Quinct. *Instt.* v. 6, § 3; Tac. *H.* i. 10—18, ii. 69—82; *Agric.* 13; *Germ.* 33; *Ann.* vi. 22, etc.
[6] Juv. *Sat.* iii. 144, vi. 342, xiii. 75—83.
[7] "Nec turba deorum talis ut est hodie," Juv. *Sat.* xiii. 46; "Ignobilem Deorum turbam quam longo aevo longa superstitio congessit," Sen. *Ep.* 110. See Boissier, *Les Religions Etrangères* (*Rel. Rom.* i. 374—450); Liv. xxxix. 8; Tac. *Ann.* ii. 85; Val. Max. I. iii. 2.
[8] Juv. *Sat.* xiv. 96—106; Jos. *Antt.* xviii. 3; Pers. *Sat.* v. 180.
[9] Cic. *De Legg.* ii. 8; *De Div.* ii. 24; Tert. *ad Natt.* i. 10; Juv. *Sat.* xiv. 263, xv. 1—32.
[10] Plut. *De Def. Orac.*, p. 419. Some Christian writers connect this remarkable story with the date of the Crucifixion. See Niedner, *Lehrbuch d. Chr. K. G.*, p. 64.

our eyes from the spectacle of the little Christian churches, composed chiefly as yet of slaves and artisans, who had been taught to imitate a Divine example of humility and sincerity, of purity and love. There were, indeed, a few among the Heathen who lived nobler lives, and professed a purer ideal than the Pagans around them. Here and there in the ranks of the philosophers a Demetrius, a Musonius Rufus, an Epictetus; here and there among Senators an Helvidius Priscus, a Paetus Thrasea, a Barea Soranus; here and there among literary men a Seneca or a Persius—showed that virtue was not yet extinct. But the Stoicism on which they leaned for support amid the terrors and temptations of that awful epoch utterly failed to provide a remedy against the universal degradation. It aimed at cherishing an insensibility which gave no real comfort, and for which it offered no adequate motive. It aimed at repressing the passions by a violence so unnatural that with them it also crushed some of the gentlest and most elevating emotions. Its self-satisfaction and exclusiveness repelled the gentlest and sweetest natures from its communion. It made a vice of compassion, which Christianity inculcated as a virtue; it cherished a haughtiness which Christianity discouraged as a sin. It was unfit for the task of ameliorating mankind, because it looked on human nature in its normal aspects with contemptuous disgust. Its marked characteristic was a despairing sadness, which became specially prominent in its most sincere adherents. Its favourite theme was the glorification of suicide, which wiser moralists had severely reprobated,[1] but which many Stoics belauded as the one sure refuge against oppression and outrage.[2] It was a philosophy which was indeed able to lacerate the heart with a righteous indignation against the crimes and follies of mankind, but which vainly strove to resist, and which scarcely even hoped to stem, the ever-swelling tide of vice and misery. For wretchedness it had no pity; on vice it looked with impotent disdain. Thrasea was regarded as an antique hero for walking out of the Senate-house during the discussion of some decree which involved a servility more than usually revolting.[3] He gradually drove his few admirers to the

[1] Virg. Æn. vi. 450, seq.; Tusc. Disp. i. 74; Cic. De Senect. 73; De Rep. vi. 15; Somn. Scip. 3; Sen. Ep. 70. Comp. Epict. Enchir. 52.
[2] Both Zeno and Cleanthes died by suicide. For the frequency of suicide under the Empire see Tac. Ann. vi. 10, 26, xv. 60; Hist. v. 26; Suet. Tib. 49; Sen. De Benef. ii. 27; Ep. 70; Plin. Ep. i. 12, iii. 7, 16, vi. 24. For its glorification, Lucan, Phars. iv.:—

"Mors utinam pavidos vitae subducere nolles,
Sed virtus te sola daret."

"Mortes repentinae, hoc est summa vitae felicitas," Plin. H. N. vii. 53, cf. 51. The practice of suicide became in the days of Trajan almost a "national usage" (see Merivale, vii. 317, viii. 107). The variety of Latin phrases for suicide shows the frequency of the crime. On the pride of Stoicism see Tac. Ann. xiv. 57; Juv. xiii. 93.
[3] On the motion against the memory of Agrippina (Tac. Ann. xiv. 12). He had also opposed the execution of Antistius (id. xiv. 48). It was further remembered against him that he had not attended the obsequies of the deified Poppaea, or offered sacrifice for the preservation of Nero's "divine voice."

conviction that, even for those who had every advantage of rank and wealth, nothing was possible but a life of crushing sorrow ended by a death of complete despair.[1] St. Paul and St. Peter, on the other hand, were at the very same epoch teaching in the same city, to a few Jewish hucksters and a few Gentile slaves, a doctrine so full of hope and brightness that letters, written in a prison with torture and death in view, read like idylls of serene happiness and pæans of triumphant joy. The graves of these poor sufferers, hid from the public eye in the catacombs, were decorated with an art, rude indeed, yet so triumphant as to make their subterranean squalor radiant with emblems of all that is brightest and most poetic in the happiness of man.[2] While the glimmering taper of the Stoics was burning pale, as though amid the vapours of a charnel-house, the torch of Life upheld by the hands of the Tarsian tent-maker and the Galilæan fisherman had flashed from Damascus to Antioch, from Antioch to Athens, from Athens to Corinth, from Corinth to Ephesus, from Ephesus to Rome.

CHAPTER II.

THE RISE OF THE ANTICHRIST.

"Hic hostis Deum
Hominumque templis expulit superos suis,
Civesque patria; spiritum fratri abstulit
Hausit cruorem matris;—et lucem videt!"
—SEN. *Octav.* 239.

"Praestare Neronem
Securum valet haec aetas."
—JUV. *Sat.* viii. 173.

ALL the vice, all the splendour, all the degradation of Pagan Rome seemed to be gathered up in the person of that Emperor who first placed himself in a relation of direct antagonism against Christianity. Long before death ended the astute comedy in which Augustus had so gravely borne his part,[3] he had experienced the Nemesis of

---

[1] Suet. *Ner.* 37.

[2] "There the ever-green leaf protests in sculptured silence that the winter of the grave cannot touch the saintly soul; the blossoming branch speaks of vernal suns beyond the snows of this chill world; the good shepherd shows from his benign looks that the mortal way so terrible to nature had become to those Christians as the meadow-path between the grassy slopes and beside the still waters." (Martineau, *Hours of Thought,* p. 155).

[3] On his death-bed he asked his friends "whether he had fitly gone through the play of life," and, if so, begged for their applause like an actor on the point of leaving the stage (Suet. *Octav.* 99).

Absolutism, and foreseen the awful possibilities which it involved. But neither he, nor any one else, could have divined that four such rulers as Tiberius, Gaius, Claudius, and Nero—the first a sanguinary tyrant, the second a furious madman, the third an uxorious imbecile, the fourth a heartless buffoon—would in succession afflict and horrify the world. Yet these rulers sat upon the breast of Rome with the paralysing spell of a nightmare. The concentration of the old prerogatives of many offices in the person of one, who was at once Consul, Censor, Tribune, Pontifex Maximus, and perpetual Imperator, fortified their power with the semblance of legality, and that power was rendered terrible by the sword of the Prætorians, and the deadly whisper of the informers. No wonder that Christians saw the true type of the Antichrist in that omnipotence of evil, that apotheosis of self, that disdain for humanity, that hatred against all mankind besides, that gigantic aspiration after the impossible, that frantic blasphemy and unlimited indulgence, which marked the despotism of a Gaius or a Nero. The very fact that their power was precarious as well as gigantic—that the lord of the world might at any moment be cut off by the indignation of the *canaille* of Rome, nay, more, by the revenge of a single tribune, or the dagger-thrust of a single slave [1]— did but make more striking the resemblance which they displayed to the gilded monster of Nebuchadnezzar's dream. Their autocracy, like that visionary idol, was an image of gold on feet of clay. Of that colossus many a Christian would doubtless be reminded when he saw the huge statue of Nero, with the radiated head and the attributes of the sun-god, which once towered 120 feet high on the shattered pediment still visible beside the ruins of the Flavian Amphitheatre.[2]

The sketch which I am now presenting to the reader is the necessary introduction to the annals of that closing epoch of the first century, which witnessed the early struggle of Christianity with the Pagan power. In the thirteen years of Nero's reign all the worst elements of life which had long mingled with the sap of ancient civilisation seem to have rushed at once into their scarlet flower. To the Christians of that epoch the dominance of such an Emperor presented itself in the aspect of wickedness raised to superhuman exaltation, and engaged in an impious struggle against the Lord and against His saints.

Till the days of Nero the Christians had never been brought into collision with the Imperial Government. We may set aside as a worthless fiction the story that Tiberius had been so much interested in the account of the Crucifixion forwarded to him by Pontius Pilate, as to consult the Senate on the advisability of admitting Jesus among

[1] Out of 43 persons in Lipsius's *Stemma Caesarum*, 32 died violent deaths, *i.e.*, nearly 75 per cent.
[2] Suet. *Ner.* 31; Mart. *Spect. Ep.* 2.

the gods of the Pantheon.[1] It is very unlikely that Tiberius ever heard of the existence of the Christians. In its early days the Faith was too humble to excite any notice out of the limits of Palestine. Gaius, absorbed in his mad attempt to set up in the Holy of Holies "a desolating abomination," in the form of a huge image of himself, entertained a savage hatred of the Jews, but had not learned to discriminate between them and Christians. Claudius, disturbed by tumults in the Ghetto of Jewish freedmen across the Tiber, had been taught to look with alarm and suspicion on the name of Christus distorted into "Chrestus;" but his decree for the expulsion of the Jews from Rome, which had been a dead letter from the first, only affected Christianity by causing the providential migration of Priscilla and Aquila, to become at Corinth and Ephesus the hosts, the partners, and the protectors of St. Paul.[2] Nero was destined to enter into far deadlier and closer relations with the nascent Faith, and to fill so vast a space in the horrified imaginations of the early Christians as to become by his cruelties, his blasphemies, his enormous crimes, the nearest approach which the world has yet seen to the "Man of Sin." He was the ideal of depravity and wickedness, standing over against the ideal of all that is sinless and Divine. Against the Christ was now to be ranged the Antichrist,—the man-god of Pagan adulation, in whom was manifested the consummated outcome of Heathen crime and Heathen power.

Up to the tenth year of Nero's reign the Christians had many reasons to be grateful to the power of the Roman Empire. St. Paul, when he wrote from Corinth to the Thessalonians, had indeed seen in the fabric of Roman polity, and in Claudius, its reigning representative, the "check" and the "checker" which must be removed before the coming of the Lord.[3] Yet during his stormy life the Apostle had been shielded by the laws of Rome in more than one provincial tumult. The Roman politarchs of Thessalonica had treated him with humanity. He had been protected from the infuriated Jews in Corinth by the disdainful justice of Gallio. In Jerusalem the prompt interference of Lysias and of Festus had sheltered him from the plots of the Sanhedrin. At Cæsarea he had appealed to Cæsar as his best security from the persistent hatred of Ananias and the Sadducees. If we have taken a correct view of the latter part of his career, his appeal had not been in vain, and he owed the last two years of his missionary activity to the impartiality of Roman Law. Hence, apart from the general

---

[1] Ps. Clem. *Hom.* i. 6; Tert. *Apol.* 5; Euseb. *H. E.* ii. 2; Jer. *Chron. Pasch.* i. 430. Braun (*De Tiberii Christum in Deorum numerum referendi consilio*, Bonn, 1834) vainly tried to support this fable. Tiberius, more than any Emperor, was "circa Deos et religiones negligentior" (Suet. *Tib.* 69).

[2] See Tert. *Apol.* 3; *ad Natt.* i. 3; my *Life and Work of St. Paul*, i. 559. I cannot accept the view of Herzog (*Real-Encykl.*, s.v. Claudius), that *Chrestus* was some seditious Roman Jew.

[3] *Life and Work of St. Paul*, i. 584, fg.

principle of submission to recognised authority, he had special reason to urge the Roman Christians "to be subject to the higher powers," and to recognise in them the ordinance of God.[1] With the private wickednesses of rulers the Christians were not directly concerned. Rumours, indeed, they must have heard of the poisoning of Claudius and of Britannicus; of Nero's intrigues with Acte; of his friendship with the bad Otho; of the divorce and legal assassination of Octavia; of the murders of Agrippina and Poppæa, of Burrus and Seneca. Other rumours must have reached them of nameless orgies, of which it was a shame even to speak. But knowing how the whole air of the bad society around them reeked with lies, they may have shown the charity that hopeth all things, and imputeth no evil, and rejoiceth not in iniquity, by tacitly setting aside these stories as incredible or false. It was not till A.D. 64, when Nero had been nearly ten years on the throne, that the slow light of History fully revealed to the Church of Christ what this more than monster was.

A dark spirit was walking in the house of the Cæsars—a spirit of lust and blood which destroyed every family in succession with which they were allied. The Octavii, the Claudii, the Domitii, the Silani, were all hurled into ruin or disgrace in their attempt to scale, by intermarriage with the deified race of Julius, "the dread summits of Cæsarian power." It has been well said that no page even of Tacitus has so sombre and tragic an eloquence as the mere *Stemma Cæsarum*. The great Julius, robbed by death of his two daughters, was succeeded by his nephew Augustus,[2] who, in ordering the assassination of Cæsarion, the natural son of Julius by Cleopatra, extinguished the direct line of the greatest of the Cæsars. Augustus by his three marriages was the father of but one daughter, and that daughter disgraced his family and embittered his life. He saw his two elder grandsons die under circumstances of the deepest suspicion; and being induced to disinherit the third for the asserted stupidity and ferocity of his disposition, was succeeded by Tiberius, who was only his stepson, and had not one drop of the Julian blood in his veins. Tiberius had but one son, who was poisoned by his favourite, Sejanus, before his own death. This son, Drusus, left but one son, who was compelled to commit suicide by his cousin, Guius; and one daughter, whose son, Rubellius Plautus, was put to death by order of Nero. The marriage of Germanicus, the nephew of Tiberius, with the elder Agrippina, grand-daughter of Augustus, seemed to open new hopes to the Roman people and the imperial house. Germanicus was a prince of courage,

---

[1] Rom. xiii. 1—7.
[2] It is characteristic of the manners of the age that Julius Cæsar had married four times, Augustus thrice, Tiberius twice, Gaius thrice, Claudius six times, and Nero thrice. Yet Nero was the last of the Cæsars, even of the adoptive line. No descendants had survived of the offspring of so many unions, and, as Merivale says, "a large proportion, which it would be tedious to calculate, were the victims of domestic jealousy and politic assassination" (*Hist* vi. 366).

virtue, and ability, and the elder Agrippina was one of the purest and noblest women of her day. Of the nine children of this virtuous union six alone survived. On the parents, and the three sons in succession, the hopes of Rome were fixed. But Germanicus was poisoned by order of Tiberius, and Agrippina was murdered in banishment, after the endurance of the most terrible anguish. Their two elder sons, Nero and Drusus, lived only long enough to disgrace themselves, and to be forced to die of starvation.[1] The third was the monster Gaius. Of the three daughters, the youngest, Julia Livia, was put to death by the orders of Messalina, the wife of her uncle Claudius. Drusilla died in prosperous infamy, and Agrippina the younger, after a life of crime so abnormal and so detestable that it throws into the shade even the monstrous crimes of many of her contemporaries, murdered her husband, and was murdered by the orders of the son for whose sake she had waded through seas of blood.

That son was Nero! Truly the Palace of the Cæsars must have been haunted by many a restless ghost, and amid its vast and solitary chambers the guilty lords of its splendour must have feared lest they should come upon some spectre weeping tears of blood. In yonder corridor the floor was still stained with the life-blood of the murdered Gaius;[2] in that subterranean prison, the miserable Drusus, cursing the name of his great-uncle Tiberius, tried to assuage the pangs of hunger by chewing the stuffing of his mattress;[3] in that gilded saloon Nero had his private interviews with the poison-mixer, Locusta, whom he salaried among "the instruments of his government;"[4] in that splendid hall Britannicus fell into convulsions after tasting his brother's poisoned draught; that chamber, bright with the immoral frescoes of Arellius, witnessed the brutal kick which caused the death of the beautiful Poppæa. Fit palace for the Antichrist—fit temple for the wicked human god!—a temple which reeked with the memory of infamies—a palace which echoed with the ghostly footfall of murdered men!

Agrippina the Second, mother of Nero, was the Lady Macbeth of that scene of murder, but a Lady Macbeth with a life of worse stains and a heart of harder steel. Born at Cologne in the fourteenth year of the reign of Tiberius, she lost her father, Germanicus, by poison when she was three years old, and her mother, Agrippina, first by exile when she was twelve years old, and finally by murder when she was seventeen. She grew up with her wicked sisters and her wicked brother Gaius in the house of her grandmother Antonia, the widow of the elder Drusus. She was little more than fourteen years old when

---

[1] Tac. *Ann.* v. 3, vi. 24.
[2] "The Verres of a single province sank before the majesty of the law, and the righteous eloquence of his accuser; against the Verres of the world there was no defence except in the dagger of the assassin" (Freeman, *Essays*, ii. 330).
[3] Tac. *Ann.* vii. 23.   [4] Tac. *Ann.* xii. 66, xiii. 5.

Tiberius married her to Cnæus Domitius Ahenobarbus. The Domitii were one of the noblest and most ancient families of Rome, but from the time that they first emerged into the light of history they had been badly pre-eminent for the ferocity of their dispositions. They derived the surname of Ahenobarbus, or brazen-beard, from a legend of their race intended to account for their physical peculiarity.[1] Six generations earlier the orator Crassus had said of the Domitius Ahenobarbus of that day, "that it was no wonder his beard was of brass, since his mouth was of iron and his heart of lead." But though the traditions of cruelty and treachery had been carried on from generation to generation,[2] they seem to have culminated in the father of Nero, who added a tinge of meanness and vulgarity to the brutal manners of his race. His loose morals had been shocking even to a loose age, and men told each other in disgust how he had cheated in his prætorship; how he had killed one of his freedmen only because he had refused to drink as much as he was bidden; how he had purposely driven over a poor boy on the Appian Road; how in a squabble in the Forum he had struck out the eye of a Roman knight; how he had been finally banished for crimes still more shameful. It was a current anecdote of this man, who was "detestable through every period of his life," that when, nine years after his marriage, the birth of his son Nero was announced to him, he answered the congratulations of his friends with the remark, that from himself and Agrippina nothing could have been born but what was hateful, and for the public ruin.

Agrippina was twenty-one when her brother Gaius succeeded to the throne. Towards the close of his reign she was involved in the conspiracy of Lepidus, and was banished to the dreary island of Pontia. Gaius seized the entire property both of Domitius and of Agrippina. Nero, their little child, then three years old, was handed over as a penniless orphan to the charge of his aunt Domitia, the mother of Messalina. This lady entrusted the education of the child to two slaves, whose influence is perhaps traceable for many subsequent years. One of them was a barber, the other a dancer.

On the accession of Claudius, Agrippina was restored to her rank and fortune, and once more undertook the management of her child. He was, as we see from his early busts, a child of exquisite beauty. His beauty made him an object of special pride to his mother. From this time forward it seems to have been her one desire to elevate the boy to the rank of Emperor. In vain did the astrologers warn her that his elevation involved her murder. To such dark hints of the future

---

[1] Suet. *Ner.* 1; Plut. *Æmil.* 25.
[2] "The grandfather of Nero had been checked by Augustus from the bloodshed of his gladiatorial shows . . . his great-grandfather, 'the best of his race,' had changed sides three times, not without disgrace, in the civil wars . . . . his great-great-grandfather had rendered himself infamous by cruelty and treachery at Pharsalia, and was also charged with most un-Roman pusillanimity" (see Suet. *Ner.* 1—5; Merivale. vi. 62, *seq.*).

she had but one reply—*Occidat dum imperet!* "Let him slay me, so he do but reign!"

By her second marriage, with Crispus Passienus, she further increased her already enormous wealth. She bided her time. Claudius was under the control of his freedmen, Narcissus and Pallas, and of the Empress Messalina, who had borne him two children, Britannicus and Octavia. The fierce and watchful jealousy of Messalina was soon successful in securing the banishment and subsequent murder of Julia, the younger sister of Agrippina,[1] and in spite of the retirement in which the latter strove to withdraw herself from the furious suspicion of the Empress, she felt that her own life and that of her son were in perpetual danger. A story prevailed that when Britannicus, then about seven years old, and Nero, who was little more than three years older,[2] had ridden side by side in the Trojan equestrian game, the favour of the populace towards the latter had been so openly manifested that Messalina had despatched emissaries to strangle him in bed, and that they had been frightened from doing so by seeing a snake glide from under the pillow.[3] Meanwhile, Messalina was diverted from her purpose by the criminal pursuits which were notorious to every Roman with the single exception of her husband. She was falling deeper and deeper into that dementation preceding doom which at last enabled her enemy Narcissus to head a palace conspiracy and to strike her to the dust. Agrippina owed her escape from a fate similar to that of her younger sister solely to the infatuated passion of the rival whose name through all succeeding ages has been a byword of guilt and shame.

But now that Claudius was a widower, the fact that he was her uncle, and that unions between an uncle and a niece were regarded as incestuous, did not prevent Agrippina from plunging into the intrigues by which she hoped to secure the Emperor for her third husband. Aided by the freedman Pallas, brother of Felix, the Procurator of Judæa, and by the blandishments which her near relationship to Claudius enabled her to exercise, she succeeded in achieving the second great object of her ambition. The twice-widowed matron became the sixth wife of the imbecile Emperor within three months of the execution of her predecessor. She had now but one further design to accomplish, and that was to gain the purple for the son whom she loved with all the tigress affection of her evil nature. She had been the sister and the wife, she wished also to be the mother of an Emperor.

The story of her daring schemes, her reckless cruelty, her incessant intrigues, is recorded in the stern pages of Tacitus. During the five years of her married life,[4] it is probable that no day passed without her thoughts brooding upon the guilty end which she had kept steadily

---

[1] Suet. *Claud.* 29. [2] Tacitus says two years; but see Merivale, v. 517, vi. 88.
[3] Suetonius thinks that the story arose from a snake's skin which his mother gave him as an amulet, and which for some time he wore in a bracelet (*Ner.* 6).
[4] She was married in A.D. 49, and poisoned her husband in October, A.D. 54.

in view during so many vicissitudes. Her first plan was to secure for Nero the hand of Octavia, the only daughter of Claudius. Octavia had long been betrothed to the young and noble Lucius Junius Silanus, a great-great-grandson of Augustus, who might well be dreaded as a strong protector of the rights of his young brother-in-law, Britannicus. As a favourite of the Emperor, and the betrothed of the Emperor's daughter, Silanus had already received splendid honours at the hands of the Senate, but at one blow Agrippina hurled him into the depths of shame and misery. The infamous Vitellius—Vitellius who had once begged as a favour a slipper of Messalina, and carried it in his bosom and kissed it with profound reverence—Vitellius who had placed a gilded image of the freedman Pallas among his household gods—trumped up a false charge against Silanus, and, as Censor, struck his name off the list of the Senate. His betrothal annulled, his prætorship abrogated, the high-spirited young man, recognising whose hand it was that had aimed this poisoned arrow at his happiness, waited till Agrippina's wedding-day, and on that day committed suicide on the altar of his own Penates. The next step of the Empress was to have her rival Lollia Paulina charged with magic, to secure her banishment, to send a tribune to kill her, and to identify, by personal inspection, her decapitated head. Then Calpurnia was driven from Rome because Claudius, with perfect innocence, had praised her beauty. On the other hand, Seneca was recalled from his Corsican exile, in order to increase Agrippina's popularity by an act of ostensible mercy, which restored to Rome its favourite writer, while it secured a powerful adherent for her cause and an eminent tutor for her son. The next step was to effect the betrothal of Octavia to Nero, who was twelve years old. A still more difficult and important measure was to secure his adoption. Claudius was attached to his son Britannicus, and, in spite of his extraordinary fatuity, he could hardly fail to see that his son's rights would be injured by the adoption of an elder boy of most noble birth, who reckoned amongst his supporters all those who might have natural cause to dread the vengeance of a son of Messalina. Claudius was an antiquary, and he knew that for 800 years, from the days of Attus Clausus downwards, there had never been an adoption among the patrician Claudii. In vain did Agrippina and her adherents endeavour to poison his mind by whispered insinuations about the parentage of Britannicus. But he was at last overborne, rather than convinced, by the persistence with which Agrippina had taken care that the adoption should be pressed upon him in the Senate, by the multitude, and even in the privacy of his own garden. Pallas, too, helped to decide his wavering determination by quoting the precedents of the adoption of Tiberius by Augustus, and of Gaius by Tiberius. Had he but well weighed the fatal significance of those precedents, he would have hesitated still longer ere he sacrificed to an intriguing alien the birthright, the happiness, and ultimately the lives of the young son and daughter whom he so dearly loved.

And now Agrippina's prosperous wickedness was bearing her along full sail to the fatal haven of her ambition. She obtained the title of Augusta, which even the stately wife of Augustus had never borne during her husband's lifetime. Seated on a lofty throne by her husband's side, she received foreign embassies and senatorial deputations. She gained permission to antedate the majority of her son, and secured for him a promise of the Consulship, admission to various priesthoods, a proconsular *imperium*, and the title of "Prince of the Youth." She made these honours the pretext for obtaining a largess to the soldiery, and Circensian games for the populace, and at these games Nero appeared in the manly toga and triumphal insignia, while Britannicus, utterly eclipsed, stood humbly by his side in the boyish *praetexta*—the embroidered robe which marked his youth. And while step after step was taken to bring Nero into splendid prominence, Britannicus was kept in such deep seclusion, and watched with such jealous eyes, that the people hardly knew whether he was alive or dead. In vain did Agrippina lavish upon the unhappy lad her false caresses. Being a boy of exceptional intelligence, he saw through her hypocrisy, and did not try to conceal the contemptuous disgust which her arts inspired. Meanwhile he was a prisoner in all but name: every expedient was invented to keep him at the greatest distance from his father; every friend who loved him, every freedman who was faithful to him, every soldier who seemed likely to embrace his cause, was either secretly undermined, or removed under pretext of honourable promotion. Tutored as he was by adversity to conceal his feelings, he one day through accident or boyish passion returned the salutation of his adoptive brother by the name of Ahenobarbus, instead of calling him by the name Nero, which was the mark of his new rank as the adopted son of Claudius. Thereupon the rage of Agrippina and Nero knew no bounds; and such insolence —for in this light the momentary act of carelessness or venial outburst of temper was represented to Claudius—made the boy a still more defenceless victim to the machinations of his stepmother. Month after month she wove around him the web of her intrigues. The Prætorians were won over by flattery, gifts, and promises. The double præfecture of Lucius Geta and Rufius Crispinus was superseded by the appointment of Afranius Burrus, an honest soldier, but a partisan of the Empress, to whom he thus owed his promotion to the most coveted position in the Roman army. From the all-powerful freedmen of Claudius, Agrippina had little to fear. Callistus was dead, and she played off against each other the rival influences of Pallas and Narcissus. Pallas was her devoted adherent and paramour; Narcissus was afraid to move in opposition to her, because the accession of Britannicus would have been his own certain death-warrant, since he had been the chief agent in the overthrow of Messalina.

As for the phenomena on which the populace looked with terror—

the fact that the skies had seemed to blaze with fire on the day of
Nero's adoption, and violent shocks of earthquake had shaken Rome on
the day that he assumed the manly toga—Agrippina cared nothing
for them. She would recognise no omen which did not promise success
to her determination. Nothing could now divert her from her purpose.
When Domitia, the aunt under whose roof the young Nero had been
trained, began to win his smiles by the contrast between her flatteries
and presents and the domineering threats of his mother, Agrippina
at once brought against her a charge of magic, and in spite of the
opposition of Narcissus, Domitia was condemned to death. The
Empress hesitated at no crime which helped to pave the way of
her son to power, but at the same time her ambition was so far selfish
that she intended to keep that son under her own exclusive influence.

Many warnings now showed her that the time was ripe for her
supreme endeavour. Her quarrel with Narcissus had broken out into
threats and recriminations in the very presence of the Emperor. The
Senate showed signs of indignant recalcitrance against her attacks
on those whose power she feared, or whose wealth she envied. Her
designs were now so transparent, that Narcissus began openly to show
his compassion for the hapless and almost deserted Britannicus. But,
worst of all, it was clear that Claudius himself was becoming conscious
of his perilous mistake, and was growing weary both of her and of
her son. He had changed his former wife for a worse. If Messalina
had been unfaithful to him, so, he began to suspect, was Agrippina, and
he could not but feel that she had changed her old fawning caresses for
a threatening insolence. He was sick of her ambition, of her intrigues,
of the hatred she always displayed to his oldest and most faithful
servants, of her pushing eagerness for her Nero, of her treacherous
cruelty towards his own children. He was heard to drop ominous
expressions. He began to display towards Britannicus a yearning
affection, full of the passionate hope that when he was a little older
his wrongs would be avenged. All this Agrippina learnt from her
spies. Not a day was to be lost. Narcissus, whose presence was
the chief security for his master's life, had gone to the baths of Sinuessa
to find relief from a fit of the gout. There lay at this time in prison,
on a charge of poisoning, a woman named Locusta, whose career recalls
the Mrs. Turner of the reign of James I., and the Marchioness de
Brinvilliers of the court of Louis XIV. To this woman Agrippina
repaired with the promise of freedom and reward, if she would provide
a poison which would disturb the brain without too rapidly destroying
life. Halotus, the Emperor's *praegustator*, or taster, and Xenophon,
his physician, had been already won over to share in the deed. The
poison was infused into a fine and delicious mushroom of a kind of
which Claudius was known to be particularly fond, and Agrippina gave
this mushroom to her husband with her own hand. After tasting it he
became very quiet, and then called for wine. He was carried off to

bed senseless, but the quantity of wine which he had drunk weakened the effects of the poison, and at a sign from Agrippina the faithless physician finished the murder by tickling the throat of the sufferer with a poisoned feather. Before the morning of Oct. 13, A.D. 54, Claudius was dead.

His death was concealed from the public and from his children, whom Agrippina with hypocritical caresses and false tears kept by her side in her own chamber, until everything was ready for the proclamation of Nero. At noon, which the Chaldæans had declared would be the only lucky hour of an unlucky day, the gates of the palace were thrown open, and Nero walked forth with Afranius Burrus by his side. The Prætorian Præfect informed the guard that Claudius had appointed Nero his successor. A few faithful voices asked, "Where is Britannicus?" But as no one answered, and the young prince was not forthcoming, they accepted what seemed to be an accomplished fact. Nero went to the Prætorian camp, promised a donation of 15,000 sesterces (more than a £130) to each soldier, and was proclaimed Emperor. The Senate accepted the initiative of the Prætorians, and by sunset Nero was securely seated on the throne of the Roman world. The dream of Agrippina's life was accomplished. She was now the mother, as she had been the sister and the wife of an Emperor; and that young Emperor, when the tribune came to ask him the watchword for the night, answered in the words—*Optimae Matri!* "To the Best of Mothers!"

CHAPTER III.

THE FEATURES OF THE ANTICHRIST.

Ἔσχατος Αἰνεαδῶν μητροκτόνος ἡγεμονεύσει.—Orac. Sib. *ap.* Xiphilin. lxii. p. 709.

"Nero . . . ut erat exsecrabilis ac nocens tyrannus, prosilivit ad excidendum coeleste templum delendamque justitiam."—Lactant. *De Mort. Persec.* 2.

"Quid Nerone pejus?"—Mart. *Epig.* vii. 34.

FROM the very moment of her success, the awful Nemesis began to fall upon Agrippina, as it falls on all sinners—that worst Nemesis, which breaks crowned with fire out of the achievement of guilty purposes. Of Agrippina on the night of Claudius's murder it might doubtless have been said, as has been said of another queen on the tragic night on which her husband perished in the explosion at Kirk o' Fields, that she "retired to rest—to sleep, doubtless—sleep with the soft tranquillity of an innocent child. Remorse may disturb the slumbers of the man who is dabbling with his first experiences of wrong. When the pleasure has been tasted and is gone, and nothing is left of the crime but the ruin it has wrought, then, too, the Furies take their seats upon the midnight pillow. But the meridian of evil is for the most part left unvexed; and when human creatures have chosen their road, they are left alone to follow it to the end."[1]

From the day that she had won her own heart's desires, Agrippina found that her hopes had vanished, and that her life was to be plunged in retributive calamities. She found that crime ever needs the support of further crime; that the evil spirits who serve the government of an abandoned heart demand incessant sacrifices at their altar. She had brought about the ruin of the young Lucius Junius Silanus. His elder brother, Marcus, was a man of such a gentle and unassuming character that Gaius had nicknamed him "the Golden Sheep;" and though the blood of the imperial family flowed in his veins, he excited so little jealousy that he had been raised to the consulship, and even sent to Asia with proconsular command. Yet Agrippina dreaded that he might avenge the death of his brother, and, without the knowledge of Nero, sent the freedman Helius, with P. Celer, a Roman knight, who poisoned Silanus at a banquet, so openly that the whole world was aware of what had been done.

The aged Narcissus was her next victim; and more murders would have followed had not Burrus and Seneca taken measures to prevent them. Their influence was happily sufficient, since they were still regarded as tutors of the young Cæsar, who was only seventeen years old. They also endeavoured to veil, and as far as possible to cloak, the audacious intrusions into state affairs, which showed that Agrippina was not content with the exceptional honours showered upon her. Of those honours, strange to say, one of the chief was her appointment to be a priestess of the now deified Emperor whom she had so recently poisoned! It is clear that, though she had again and again proved herself to be the most ungrateful of women, she expected from her son a boundless gratitude. Indeed, she so galled the vanity and terrified the cowardice of his small and mean nature by her constant threats and upbraidings, that he feared her far more than he had ever loved. The consequence was that she had at once to struggle for her ascendency. It was threatened on the one hand by the influence of Burrus and Seneca, and on the other by the blandishments of bad companions and fawning slaves. Bent on pleasure, fond of petty accomplishments, flattered into the notion that he was a man of consummate artistic taste, Nero occupied himself with *dilettante* efforts in sculpture, painting, singing, verse-making, and chariot-driving, and was quite content to leave to his tutors the graver affairs of state. His tiger nature had not yet tasted blood. Seneca in his treatise on clemency, written at the close of Nero's first year, had informed the delighted world that the gentle youth, on being required to sign the order for

---

[1] Froude, *Hist.* vii. 511.

a criminal's execution, had expressed the fervent wish that he had never learnt to write. Seneca also composed for him the admired speeches which he was now and then called upon to deliver. The government of the world was practically in the hands of an upright soldier and an able philosopher; and however glaring were the inconsistencies of the latter, he had yet attained to a moral standard incomparably superior to that professed by the majority of his contemporaries. If the political machine worked with perfect smoothness, if Rome for five years was shocked by no public atrocities, if informers to some extent found their occupation gone, if no noble blood was wantonly shed, if the Senate was respected and the soldiers were orderly, the glory of that "golden quinquennium"—which, in the opinion of Trajan, eclipsed the merits of even the worthiest princes—was due, not to the small-minded and would-be æsthetic youth who figured as Emperor, but to the tutors who kept in check the wild passions of his mother, and directed the acts which ostensibly proceeded from himself.

But in order to keep him amused they thought it either inexpedient or impossible to maintain too strict a discipline over his moral character. Nero was nominally married to the daughter of Claudius, but from the first they were separated from each other by a mutual and instinctive repulsion. When he entered into an intrigue with Acte, a beautiful Greek freedwoman, his tutors held it desirable to connive at vices which the spirit of the age scarcely pretended to condemn. Agrippina, however, treated him as though he were still a child, and, when she observed his resentment, forfeited all his confidence by passing from the extreme of furious reproach to the extreme of fulsome complaisance. Hence, alike in affairs of state and in his domestic pleasures he was alienated from his mother, and in his daily life he fell unreservedly under the influence of corrupt associates like Marcus Otho and Claudius Senecio, two bad specimens of the *jeunesse dorée* of their day, the dandies of an age when dandyism was a far viler thing than it is in modern times.[1] At last the quarrel between Nero and Agrippina became so fierce that she did not hesitate to reveal to him all the crimes which she had committed for his sake, and if she could not retain her sway over his mind by gratitude, she terrified him with threats that she who had raised him to the throne could hurl him from it. Britannicus was the true heir; Nero, but for her, would have remained a mere Ahenobarbus. She was the daughter of Germanicus; she would go in person to the Prætorian camp, with Britannicus by her side, and then let the maimed Burrus and the pedagogic Seneca see whether they could prevent her from restoring to the throne of his fathers the injured boy who had been ousted by her intrigues on behalf of an adopted alien. "I made you Emperor, I can unmake you. Bri-

---

[1] Niebuhr.

tannicus is the true Emperor, not you." She dinned such taunts and threats into the ears of a son who was already vitiated in character, who already began to feel his power, until he too was driven to protect, by the murder of a brother, the despotism which his mother had won for him by the murder of a husband. Thus in every way she became the evil angel of his destiny. She drove him into the crimes of which she had already set the fatal example. It was her fault if he rapidly lost sight of the lesson which Seneca had so assiduously inculcated, that the one impregnable bulwark of a monarch is the affection of his people.[1]

Nero began to look on the young Britannicus as King John looked on the young Arthur. Even civilised, even Christian ages have shown how perilous is the position of a hated heir to a usurped throne. The threats of Agrippina had deepened dislike into detestation, and uneasiness into terror. Britannicus was a fine, strong, well-grown boy, who showed signs of a vigorous character and a keen intellect. A little incident which occurred in December, A.D. 54, had alarmed Nero still further. The Saturnalia were being celebrated with their usual effusive joy, and at one of the feasts Nero—who had become by lot the *Rex bibendi*, or Master of the Revel—had issued his mimic commands to the other guests in a spirit of harmless fun; but in order to put the shyness of Britannicus to the blush, he had ordered the lad to go out into the middle of the room and sing a song. Without the least trepidation or awkwardness Britannicus had stepped out and sung a magnificent fragment of a tragic chorus, in which he had indicated how he was expelled from his rights by violence and crime. The scene would have been an awkward one under any circumstances; it was rendered still more so by the fact that in the darkening hall a deep murmur had expressed the admiration and sympathy of the guests. Yet no steps could be taken against a young prince whom it was impossible to put to death openly, and against whom there was no pretence for a criminal accusation.

But the first century, like the fifteenth, was an age of poisoners. Locusta was still in prison, and Nero employed the Prætorian tribune Julius Pollio to procure from her a poison which might effect a slow death. There was no need to win over the *praegustator*, or the personal attendants of the young prince. Care had long been taken that the poor boy should only be surrounded by the creatures of his enemies. The poison was administered, but it failed. Nero grew wild with alarm. Stories, which probably gained their darkest touches from the horror of his subsequent career, told how he had threatened the tribune and struck Locusta for her cowardice in not doing her work well, "as though *he*, forsooth, need have any fear about the Julian law." Deadlier poison was then concocted outside his own bed-chamber, and tried upon

---

[1] "Unum est inexpugnabile munimentum amor civium" (Sen. *De Clement.* i. 19, 5).

animals, until its effects were found to be sufficiently rapid. Setting aside these stories as crude exaggerations, all authorities are agreed as to the circumstances of the death of Britannicus. It was a custom established by Augustus that the young princes of the imperial house should sit at dinner with nobles of their own age at a lower and less luxuriously served table than that at which the Emperor dined. While Britannicus was thus dining, a draught was handed to him which had been tasted by his *praegustator*, but was too hot to drink. He asked for water to cool it, and in that cold water the poison was administered. He drank, and instantly sank down from his seat silent and breathless. The guests, among whom was the young Titus, the future Emperor of Rome, started from the table in consternation. The countenance of Agrippina, working with astonishment, anguish, and terror, showed that she at least had not been admitted into the terrible secret. Octavia looked on with the self-possession which in such a palace had taught her on all occasions to hide her emotions under a simulated apathy. The banqueters were disturbed until Nero, with perfect coolness, bade them resume their mirth and conversation. "Britannicus," he said, "will soon be well. He has only been seized with one of the epileptic fits to which he is liable." It was no epileptic fit—the last of the Claudii was dead. That night, amid storms which seemed to mark the wrath of heaven, the corpse was carried with hurried privacy to a mean funeral pyre on the Field of Mars. We may disbelieve the ghastly story that the rain washed off the chalk which had been used to disguise the livid indications of poison; but it seems certain that the last rites were paid with haste and meanness little suited to the last male descendant of a family which had been famous for so many centuries—to the sole inheritor of the glorious traditions of so many of the noblest lines.

The Romans acquiesced too easily in this terrible crime, because it fell in with the Machiavellian policy which would gladly rid itself of a source of future disturbances. But they were punished for their facile tolerance by the change which every year developed in the character of their Emperor. Agrippina felt that even-handed justice was indeed beginning to commend the ingredients of the poisoned chalice to her own lips. Her enemies began to see that their opportunity was come. Her prosperity was instantly swallowed up in the "chaos of hatreds" which she had aroused by her unscrupulous ambition. The coward conscience of the Emperor was worked upon by a plot, contrived by Silana and Domitia Lepida, which charged Agrippina with the intention of raising Rubellius Plautus to the throne. This plot she overbore by the force of her own passionate indignation. Scornfully ignoring the false evidence trumped up against her, she claimed an interview with her son, and instead of entering on her own defence, demanded and secured the death or exile of her enemies. But she had by this time been deprived of her body-guard, of her sentinels, of all public honours, even of her home in the palace. Her son rarely visited her, and then only among a number of centurions, and he always left her after a brief and chilling salutation. She was living deserted by her friends, and exposed to deliberate insults, in alarmed isolation amid the hatred of the populace. Worse dangers thickened around her. Nero became deeply enamoured of Poppæa Sabina, the wife of his friend Otho, and one of the most cruel and cold-blooded intriguers amid the abandoned society of Roman matrons. Nero was deeply smitten with her infantile features, the soft complexion, which she preserved by daily bathing in warm asses'-milk, her assumed modesty, her genial conversation and sprightly wit. He was specially enchanted with the soft, abundant hair, the envy of Roman beauties, for which he invented the fantastic, and, to Roman writers, the supremely ludicrous epithet of "amber tresses." If Otho was one of the worst corrupters of Nero's character, he was punished by the loss of his wife, and Nero was punished by forming a connexion with a woman who instigated him to yet more frightful enormities. Up to this time his crimes had been mainly confined to the interior of the palace, and his follies had taken no worse form than safe and cowardly outrages on defenceless passengers in the streets at night, after the fashion of the Mohawks of the days of Queen Anne. But from the day that he first saw Poppæa a headlong deterioration is traceable in his character. She established a complete influence over him, and drove him by her taunts and allurements to that crime which, even among his many enormities, is the most damning blot upon his character—the murder of his mother.

That wretched princess was spending the last year of a life which had scarcely passed its full prime in detested infamy, such as in our own history attended the last stage in the career of the Countess of Somerset, the wife of James's unworthy favourite, Robert Carr. Worse than this, she lived in daily dread of assassination. Her watchfulness evaded all attempts at poisoning, and she was partly protected against them by the current fiction that she had fortified herself by the use of antidotes. Plots to murder her by the apparently accidental fall of the fretted roof in one of the chambers of her villa were frustrated by the warning which she received from her spies. At last, Anicetus, a freedman, admiral of the fleet at Misenum, promised Nero to secure her end in an unsuspicious manner by means of a ship which should suddenly fall to pieces in mid-sea. Nero invited her to a banquet at Baiæ, which was to be the sign of their public reconciliation. Declining, however, to sail in the pinnace which had been surreptitiously fitted up for her use, she was carried to her son's villa in her own litter. There she was received with such hilarity and blandishment, such long embraces and affectionate salutations, that her suspicions were dispelled. She consented to return by water, and went on board the treacherous vessel. It had not proceeded far when the heavily-weighted canopy under which she reclined was made to fall with a great crash. One of her ladies was killed on the spot. Immediately afterwards the bolts which held the vessel together were pulled out, and Agrippina, whose life had been saved by the projecting sides of her couch, found herself struggling in the waves. A lady who was with her, named Acerronia, thinking to save her own life, exclaimed that she was the empress, and was instantly beaten down with poles and oars. Agrippina kept silence, and, escaping with a single bruise on her shoulder, she swam or floated safely till she was picked up by a boat sent from the shore, which was glittering with lights and thronged with visitors who were enjoying the cool evening air. The wretched victim saw through the whole plot, but thought it best to treat the matter as an accident, and sent one of her freedmen, named Agerinus, to announce to Nero her fortunate escape. Nero had already received the news with unfeigned alarm. Would the haughty, vindictive woman fire the soldiery with the tale of her wrongs? would she throw herself on the compassion of the Senate and the people? would she arm her slaves to take vengeance on her murderer? Burrus and Seneca were hastily summoned. To them the Emperor appealed in the extreme agitation of unsuccessful guilt. In silence and anguish the soldier and the Stoic felt, as they listened to the tale, how fatal to their reputation was their prosperous complicity with the secrets of such a court. Seneca was the first to break the silence. He asked his colleague "whether the Prætorians should be ordered to put her to death." In that hour he must have tasted the very dregs of the bitter cup of moral degradation. Perhaps the two ministers excused themselves with the sophism that things had now gone too far to prevent the commission of a crime, and that either Agrippina or Nero must perish. But Burrus replied that "the Prætorians would never lift a hand against the daughter of their beloved Germanicus. Let Anicetus fulfil his promises." Miserable soldier! miserable philosopher! Stoicism has been often exalted at the expense of Christianity. Let the world remember the two scenes, in one of which the polished Stoic, in the other the Christian Apostle stood—the one a magnificent minister, the other a fettered prisoner—in the presence of the lord of the world!

Anicetus rose to the occasion, and, amid the ecstatic expressions of Nero's gratitude, claimed as his own the consummation of the deed. On the arrival of Agerinus with the message of Agrippina, Anicetus suddenly flung a dagger at the wretched man's feet, and then, declaring that Agrippina had sent him to murder her son, loaded him with chains. By this transparent device he hoped to persuade the world that Agrippina had been detected in a conspiracy, and had committed suicide from very shame. The news of her recent peril had caused the wildest excitement among the idlers on the shore. Anicetus, with his armed emissaries, had to assume a threatening attitude, as he made his way through the agitated throng. Surrounding the villa and bursting open the door, he seized the few slaves who yet lingered near the chamber of their mistress. Within that chamber, by the light of a single lamp, Agrippina, attended by only one handmaid, was awaiting in intense anxiety and with misgivings which became deeper and deeper at every moment, the suspicious delay in the return of her faithful messenger. The slave-girl rose and left the room. "Do you too desert me?" she exclaimed; and at that moment the door was darkened by the entrance of Anicetus, with the trierarch Herculeius and the naval centurion Obaritus. "If you have come to inquire about my health," said the undaunted woman, "say that I have recovered. If to commit a crime, I will not believe that you have my son's orders; he would not command a matricide." Returning no answer, the murderers surrounded her bed, and the trierarch struck her on the head with his stick. "Strike my womb," she exclaimed, as the centurion drew his sword, "it bore a Nero." These were her last words before she sank down slain with many wounds. There is no need to darken with further and unaccredited touches of horror the dreadful story of her end. The old presage which she had accepted was fulfilled. She had made her son an Emperor, and he had rewarded her by assassination. Such was the awful unpitied end of one on whose birthday and in whose honour in that very year altars had smoked with sacrifices offered at the feet of the god *Honour* and the goddess *Concordia*.[1]

When the crime was over, Nero first perceived its magnitude, and was seized with the agony of a too brief terror and remorse. There is in great crimes an awful power of illumination. They light up the conscience with a glare which shows all things in their true hideousness. He spent the night in oppressive silence. For the first time in his life his sleep was disturbed by dreams. He often started up in terror, and dreaded the return of dawn. The gross flattery and hypocritical congratulations of his friends soon dissipated all personal alarm. But scenes cannot change their aspect so easily as the countenances of men, and there was to him a deadly look in the sea and shore. From the lofty summit of Misenum ghostly wailings and the blast of a solitary trumpet seemed to reach him from his mother's grave. He despatched a letter to the Senate, full of the ingenious and artificial turns of expression which betrayed, alas! the style of Seneca; and in it he charged his mother's memory with the very crimes of which he had himself been guilty. But though he recalled her enemies from exile, and threw down her statues, and raked up every evil action of her life, and insinuated that she had been the cause of the enormities which had disgraced the reign of Claudius, men hardly affected to believe his exculpation, and the very mob charged him with matricide in their epigrams and scribblings on the statues and walls of Rome.[2] But yet when he returned to Rome, the whole populace, from the Senate downwards, poured forth to give him a reception so enthusiastic and

---

[1] As shown by inscriptions of the Fratres Arvales (De Rossi, *Bull. Archéol.* 1866). See Champagny, *Les Césars*, ii. 194.
[2] Suet. *Ner.* 3; Dion Cass. lxi. 16.

triumphant that every remnant of shame was dispelled from his mind. Feeling for the first time that no wickedness was too abnormal to shake his absolute power over a nation of slaves, he plunged without stint or remorse into that career of infamy which has made his name the synonym of everything which is degraded, cruel, and impure.[1]

Through the separate details of that career we need not follow him. The depths[2] into which he sank are too abysmal for utterance. Even Pagan historians could not without a blush hold up a torch in those crypts of shame.[3] How he established games in which he publicly appeared upon the stage, and compelled members of the noblest Roman families to imitate his degradation; on how vast a scale, and with how vile a stain, he deliberately corrupted the whole tone of Roman society; how he openly declared that the consummation of art was a false aestheticism, corrupt and naked, and not ashamed;[4] how he strove to revive the flagging pulse of exhausted pleasure by unheard-of enormities, and strove to make shame shameless by undisguised publicity; how he put to death the last descendant of Augustus,[5] the last descendant of Tiberius, and the last descendant of the Claudii; how he ended the brief but heartrending tragedy of the life of Octavia by defaming her innocence, driving her to the island of Pandataria, and there enforcing her assassination under circumstances so sad as might have moved the hardiest villain to tears; how he hastened by poison the death of Burrus, and entrusted the vast power of the Prætorian command to Tigellinus, one of the vilest of the human race; how, when he had exhausted the treasures amassed by the dignified economy of Claudius, he filled his coffers by confiscating the estates of innocent victims; how he caused the death of his second wife, Poppæa, by a kick inflicted on her when she was in a delicate condition; how, after the detection of the conspiracy of Piso, he seemed to revel in blood; how he ordered the death of Seneca; how, by the execution of Pætus Thrasea and Barea Soranus, he strove to extinguish the last embers of Roman magnanimity, and to slay "virtue itself;"[6] how wretches like Vatinius became the cherished favourites of his court; how his reign degenerated into one perpetual orgy, at once monstrous and vulgar;—into these details, fortunately, we need not follow his awful career. His infamous follies and cruelties in Greece; his dismal and disgraceful fall—a tragedy without pathos, and a ruin without dignity—all this must be read in the pages of contemporary historians. Probably no man who ever lived has crowded into fourteen years of life so black a catalogue of iniquities as this Collot d'Herbois upon an imperial throne. The seeds of innumerable vices were latent in the soil of his disposition, and the hot-bed

---

[1] Tac. *Ann.* xiv. 13.   [2] Rev. ii. 24.   [3] 2 Cor. iv. 2.
[4] Suet. *Ner.* lxxx. 29, 30. Dion Cass. lxi. 4, 5.
[5] A son of the M. Jun. Silanus whom Gaius called "the golden sheep" (Tac. *Ann.* xvi. 9).
[6] Tac. *Ann.* xvi. 21.

of absolutism forced them into rank growth. To speak thus much of him and of his reign has been necessary, because he was the epitome of tho age in which he lived—the consummate flower of Pagan degradation at the time when the pure bud of Christian life was being nurtured into beauty amid cold and storm. But here we must for the present leave the general story of his reign, to give our attention to the one event which brought him into collision with the Christian Church

CHAPTER IV.

THE BURNING OF ROME, AND THE FIRST PERSECUTION.

> "Mira Nero de Tarpeya
> A Roma como se ardia
> Gritos dan niños y viejos
> Y él de nada se dolia.
>   Que alegre vista!"—*Spanish Song.*

HAD it not been for one crime with which all ancient writers have mixed up his name, Christianity might have left Nero on one side, not speaking of him, but simply looking and passing by, while he, on his part, might scarcely so much as have heard of the existence of Christians amid the crowded thousands of his capital. That crime was the burning of Rome; and by precipitating the Era of Martyrdom, it brought him into immediate and terrible connexion with the Church of Christ.

Whether he was really guilty or not of having ordered that immense conflagration, it is certain that he was suspected of it by his contemporaries, and has been charged with it by many historians of his country.[1] It is certain, also, that his head had been full for years of the image of flaming cities; that he used to say that Priam was to be congratulated on having seen the ruin of Troy; that he was never able to resist the fixed idea of a crime;[2] that the year following he gave a public recitation of a poem called *Troica*, from the orchestra of the theatre, and that this was only the burning of Rome under a thin disguise;[3] and that just before his flight he meditated setting fire

---

[1] Tac. *Ann.* xv. 67 (cf. 38); Suet. *Ner.* 38; Dion Cass. lxii. 16; Pliny, *H.N.* xvii. 1, 1; followed by Orosius, Sulpicius, Severus, Eutropius, etc.
[2] Renan, *L'Antechrist*, p. 144.
[3] Dion Cass. lxii. 29; Juv. viii. 221. Eutropius says that he burnt Rome: "Ut spectaculi ejus imaginem cerneret quali olim Troja capta evaserat." Ampère says, "Pour moi j'incline à l'admettre" (*Hist. Rom.* ii. 56). Renan thinks that this poem may have originated the metaphor that he played his lyre over the ruins of his country—which was afterwards taken literally.

to Rome once more.[1] It was rumoured that when some one had told him how Gaius used to quote the phrase of Euripides—

"When I am dead, sink the whole earth in flames!"

he replied, "Nay, but while I live!" He was accused of the ambition of destroying Rome, that he might replace its tortuous and narrow lanes with broad, regular streets and uniform Hellenic edifices, and so have an excuse for changing its name from Rome to Neropolis. It was believed that in his morbid appetite for new sensations he was quite capable of devising a truly artistic spectacle which would thrill his jaded æstheticism, and supply him with vivid imagery for the vapid antitheses of his poems. It was both believed and recorded that during the terrors of the actual spectacle he had climbed the Tower of Mæcenas, had expressed his delight at what he called "the flower and loveliness of the flames," and in his scenic dress had sung on his own private stage the "Capture of Ilium."[2] It was said that all attempts to quench the fire had been forcibly resisted; that men had been seen hurling lighted brands upon various buildings, and shouting that they had orders for what they did; that men of even Consular rank had detected Nero's slaves on their own property with tow and torches, and had not ventured to touch them; that when the wind had changed, and there was a lull in the conflagration, it had burst out again from houses that abutted on the gardens of his creature Tigellinus. At any rate, the Romans could hardly have been mistaken in thinking that Nero might have done much more than he did to encourage the efforts made to extinguish the flames. It was remembered that, a few years earlier, Claudius, during a conflagration, had been seen, two nights running, seated in a little counting-office with two baskets full of silver at his side, to encourage the firemen, and secure the assistance of the people and the soldiers. Nero certainly, in this far more frightful crisis, did nothing of the kind. Even if some of the rumours which tended to implicate him in having caused the calamity had no better foundation than idle rumour, or the interested plots of robbers, who seized the opportunity for promiscuous plunder, they acquired plausibility from the whole colour of Nero's character and conversation, and they seemed to be justified by the way in which he used for his own advantage the disaster of his people. For immediately after the fire he seized a much larger extent of ground than he had previously possessed, and began to rear with incredible celerity his "Golden House"—a structure unexampled in the ancient world for gorgeous magnificence. It was in this amazing structure,

---

[1] Suet. *Ner.* 43.

[2] The one circumstance which tends to exculpate him from some of these motives is that he was at Antium when the fire broke out, and did not arrive in Rome till the third day, when the flames had rolled to the gardens of Mæcenas, and his own "Domus Transitoria" (Tac. *Ann.* xv.). The late Mr. G. H. Lewes attempted to "rehabilitate" the character of Nero; but the evidence against him is too unanimous to be set aside.

on which the splendour of the whole Empire was recklessly squandered, that Nero declared, with a smirk of self-satisfaction, that now at last he was lodged like a human being!

But whether Nero was guilty of this unparalleled outrage on the lives and fortunes of his subjects or not, certain it is that on July 19, A.D. 64, in the tenth year of his reign, a fire broke out in shops full of inflammable materials which lined the valley between the Palatine and Cælian Hills. For six days and seven nights it rolled in streams of resistless flame over the greater part of the city, licking up the palaces and temples of the gods which covered the low hills, and raging through whole streets of the wretched wooden tenements in which dwelt myriads of the poorer inhabitants who crowded the lower regions of Rome. When its course had been checked by the voluntary destruction of a vast mass of buildings which lay in its path, it broke out a second time, and raged for three days longer in the less crowded quarters of the city, where its spread was even more fatal to public buildings and the ancient shrines of the gods. Never since the Gauls burnt Rome had so deadly a calamity fallen on the afflicted city. Of its fourteen districts, four alone escaped untouched; three were completely laid in ashes; in the seven others were to be seen the wrecks of many buildings, scathed and gutted by the flames. The disaster to the city was historically irreparable. If Nero was indeed guilty, then the act of a wretched buffoon, mad with the diseased sensibility of a depraved nature, has robbed the world of works of art, and memorials, and records, priceless and irrecoverable. We can rather imagine than describe the anguish with which the Romans, bitterly conscious of their own degeneracy, contemplated the destruction of the relics of their national glory in the days when Rome was free. What could ever replace for them or their children such monuments as the Temple of Luna, built by Servius Tullius; and the *Ara Maxima*, which the Arcadian Evander had reared to Hercules; and the Temple of Jupiter Stator, built in accordance with the vow of Romulus; and the little humble palace of Numa; and the shrine of Vesta with the Penates of the Roman people and the spoils of conquered kings? What structural magnificence could atone for the loss of memorials which the song of Virgil and of Horace had rendered still more dear?[1] The city might rise more regular from its ashes, and with broader streets, but its artificial uniformity was a questionable boon. Old men declared that the new streets were far less healthy, in consequence of their more scorching glare, and they muttered among themselves that many an object of national interest had been wantonly sacrificed to gratify the womanish freak of a miserable actor.

But the sense of permanent loss was overwhelmed at first by the

---

[1] Virg. Æn. viii. 271; Hor. Od.

immediate confusion and agony of the scene. Amid the sheets of flame that roared on every side under their dense canopy of smoke, the shrieks of terrified women and the wail of infants and children were heard above the crash of falling houses. The incendiary fires seemed to be bursting forth in so many directions that men stood staring in dumb stupefaction at the destruction of their property, or rushed hither and thither in helpless amazement. The lanes and alleys were blocked up with the concourse of struggling fugitives. Many were suffocated by the smoke, or trampled down in the press. Many others were burnt to death in their own burning houses, some of whom purposely flung themselves into the flames in the depth of their despair. The density of the population that found shelter in the huge many-storeyed lodging-houses increased the difficulty of escape; and when they had escaped with bare life, a vast multitude of homeless, shivering, hungry human beings—many of them bereaved of their nearest and dearest relatives, many of them personally injured, and most of them deprived of all their possessions, and destitute of the means of subsistence—found themselves huddled together in vacant places in one vast brotherhood of hopeless wretchedness. Incidents like these are not often described by ancient authors. As a rule, the classic writers show themselves singularly callous to all details of individual misery; but this disaster was on a scale so magnificent that it had impressed the imaginations of men who often treat the anguish of multitudes as a matter of course.

Even if he had been destitute of every human feeling, yet policy and necessity would have induced Nero to take what steps he could to alleviate the immediate pressure. To create discontent and misery could never have formed any part of his designs. He threw open the Campus Martius, the Monumenta Agrippae, even his own gardens, to the people. Temporary buildings were constructed; all the furniture which was most indispensable was brought from Ostia and neighbouring towns; wheat was sold at about a fourth of the average price. It was all in vain. The misery which it was believed that his criminal folly had inflicted kindled a sense of wrong too deeply seated to be removed by remedies for the past or precautions for the future. The resentment was kept alive by the benevolences and imposts which Nero now demanded, and by the greedy ostentation with which he seized every beautiful or valuable object to adorn the insulting splendour of a palace built on the yet warm ashes of so wide an area of the ruined city.

Nero was so secure in his absolutism, he had hitherto found it so impossible to shock the feelings of the people or to exhaust the terrified adulation of the Senate, that he was usually indifferent to the pasquinades which were constantly holding up his name to execration and contempt. But now he felt that he had gone too far, and that his power would be seriously imperilled if he did not succeed in diverting the suspicions of the populace. He was perfectly aware that when the people in the streets cursed those who set fire to the city, they meant to curse *him*.[1] If he did not take some immediate step he felt that he might perish, as Gaius had perished before him, by the dagger of the assassin.

It is at this point of his career that Nero becomes a prominent figure in the history of the Church. It was this phase of cruelty which seemed to throw a blood-red light over his whole character, and led men to look on him as the very incarnation of the world-power in its most demoniac aspect—as worse than the Antiochus Epiphanes of Daniel's Apocalypse—as the Man of Sin whom (in language figurative indeed, yet awfully true) the Lord should slay with the breath of His mouth and destroy with the brightness of His coming.[2] For Nero endeavoured to fix the odious crime of having destroyed the capital of the world upon the most innocent and faithful of his subjects—upon the only subjects who offered heart-felt prayers on his behalf[3]—the Roman Christians. They were the defenceless victims of this horrible charge; for though they were the most harmless, they were also the most hated and the most slandered of living men.[4]

Why he should have thought of singling out the Christians has always been a curious problem, for at this point St. Luke ends the Acts of the Apostles, perhaps purposely dropping the curtain, because it would have been perilous and useless to narrate the horrors in which the hitherto neutral or friendly Roman Government began to play so disgraceful a part. Neither Tacitus, nor Suetonius, nor the Apocalypse, help us to solve this particular problem. The Christians had filled no large space in the eye of the world. Until the days of Domitian we do not hear of a single noble or distinguished person who had joined their ranks.[5] That the Pudens and Claudia of Rom. xvi. were the Pudens and Claudia of Martial's Epigrams seems to me to be a baseless dream.[6] If the "foreign superstition" with which Pomponia Græcina, wife of Aulus Plautius, the conqueror of Britain, was charged, and of which she was acquitted, was indeed, as has been suspected, the Christian religion, at any rate the name of Christianity was not alluded to by the ancient writers who had mentioned the circumstance.[7] Even if Rom. xvi. was addressed to Rome, and not, as I believe, to Ephesus, "they of the household of Narcissus which were in the Lord" were unknown slaves, as also were "they of Cæsar's household."[8] The slaves and artisans,

---

[1] Dion Cass. lxii. 18.
[2] See Aug. *De Civ. Dei*, xx. 19; Lactant. *Div. Instt.* vii. 16; *De Mort. Persec.* ii. ad fin.; Chrysost. in 2 Thess., *Hom.* iv.; Sulp. Sev. *Hist.* ii. 29; 40, 42; Dial. ii. ad fin.; Jer. in Dan. xi.; Orac. Sibyll. iv. 135—138, v. 362, viii. 1, 153; Verses of Commodianus, in *Spicileg.* of Solesmes, Paris, 1852.
[3] Rom. xiii. 1—7; Tit. iii. 1; 1 Pet. ii. 13. See Tert. *Apol.* 29—33.
[4] 1 Pet. iii. 13—17, iv. 12—19.
[5] Suet. *Dom.* 15.
[6] See *Life and Work of St. Paul*, ii. 569.
[7] Tac. *Ann.* xiii. 32.
[8] Rom. xvi. 11; Phil. iv. 22; *Life and Work of St. Paul*, ii. 105.

Jewish and Gentile, who formed the Christian community at Rome, had never in any way come into collision with the Roman Government. They must have been the victims rather than the exciters of the Messianic tumults—for such they are conjectured to have been—which led to the expulsion of the Jews from Rome by the futile edict of Claudius.[1] Nay, so obedient and docile were they required to be by the very principles on which their morality was based—so far were they removed from the fierce independence of the Jewish zealots—that, in writing to them a few years earlier, the greatest of their leaders had urged upon them a payment of tribute and a submission to the higher powers, not only for wrath but also for conscience' sake, because the earthly ruler, in his office of repressing evil works, is a minister of God.[2] That the Christians were entirely innocent of the crime charged against them was well known, both at the time and afterwards.[3] But how was it that Nero sought popularity, and partly averted the deep rage which was rankling in many hearts against himself, by torturing men and women on whose agonies he thought that the populace would gaze not only with a stolid indifference, but even with fierce satisfaction?

Gibbon has conjectured that the Christians were confounded with the Jews, and that the detestation universally felt for the latter fell with double force upon the former. Christians suffered even more than the Jews because of the calumnies so assiduously circulated against them, and from what appeared to the ancients to be the revolting absurdity of their peculiar tenets. "Nero," says Tacitus, "exposed to accusation, and tortured with the most exquisite penalties, a set of men detested for their enormities, whom the common people called 'Christians.' Christus, the founder of this sect, was executed during the reign of Tiberius by the Procurator Pontius Pilate, and the deadly superstition, suppressed for a time, began to burst out once more, not only throughout Judæa, where the evil had its root, but even in the city, whither from every quarter all things horrible or shameful are drifted, and find their votaries." The lordly disdain which prevented Tacitus from making any inquiry into the real views and character of the Christians is shown by the fact that he catches up the most baseless allegations against them. He talks of their doctrines as savage and shameful, when they breathed the very spirit of peace and purity. He charges them with being animated by a hatred of their kind, when their central tenet was an universal charity. The masses, he says, called them "Christians;" and while he almost apologises for staining his page with so vulgar an appellation,[4] he merely mentions, in passing,

---

[1] Suet. *Claud.* 25.   [2] Rom. xiii. 5.
[3] It is involved at once in the "*subdidit reos*" of Tac. *Ann.* v. 44.
[4] 1 Pet. iv. 14; Jas. ii. 7. There can be little doubt, as I have shown in the *Life and Work of St. Paul*, i. 301, that the name "*Christian*"—so curiously hybrid, yet so richly expressive—was a nickname due to the wit of the Antiochenes, which exercised itself quite fearlessly even on the Roman Emperors. They were not afraid to affix nicknames to Caracalla, and to call Julian Cecrops and Victimarius, with keen satire of his

that, though innocent of the charge of being turbulent incendiaries, on which they were tortured to death, they were yet a set of guilty and infamous sectaries, to be classed with the lowest dregs of Roman criminals.[1]

But the haughty historian throws no light on one difficulty—namely, the circumstances which led to the *Christians* being thus singled out. The Jews were in no way involved in Nero's persecution. To persecute the Jews at Rome would not have been an easy matter. They were sufficiently numerous to be formidable, and had overawed Cicero in the zenith of his fame. Besides this, the Jewish religion was recognised, tolerated, licensed. Throughout the length and breadth of the Empire, no man, however much he and his race might be detested and despised, could have been burnt or tortured for the mere fact of being a Jew. We hear of no Jewish martyrdoms or Jewish persecutions till we come to the times of the Jewish war, and then chiefly in Palestine itself. It is clear that a shedding of blood—in fact, some form or other of human sacrifice—was imperatively demanded by popular feeling as an expiation of the ruinous crime which had plunged so many thousands into the depths of misery. In vain had the Sibylline Books been once more consulted, and in vain had public prayer been offered, in accordance with their directions, to Vulcan and the goddesses of Earth and Hades. In vain had the Roman matrons walked in procession in dark robes, and with their long hair unbound, to propitiate the insulted majesty of Juno, and to sprinkle with sea-water her ancient statue. In vain had largesses been lavished upon the people, and propitiatory sacrifices offered to the gods. In vain had public banquets been celebrated in honour of various deities. A crime had been committed, and Romans had perished unavenged. Blood cried for blood, before the sullen suspicion against Nero could be averted, or the indignation of heaven appeased. Nero had always hated, persecuted, and exiled the philosophers, and no doubt, so far as he knew anything of the Christians—so far as he saw among his own countless slaves any who had embraced this superstition, which the *élite* of Rome described as not only new, but "execrable" and "malefic"[2]—he would hate their gravity and purity, and feel for them that raging envy which is the tribute that virtue receives from vice. Moreover, St. Paul, in all probability, had recently stood before his tribunal; and though he had been acquitted on the special charges of turbulence and profanation, respecting which he had appealed

beard (Herodian. iv. 9; Ammian. xxii. 14). It is clear that the sacred writers avoided the name because it was employed by their enemies, and by them mingled with terms of the vilest opprobrium (Tac. *Ann.* xv. 44). It only became familiar when the virtues of Christians had shed lustre upon it, and when, alike in its true form, and in the ignorant mispronunciation "Chrestians," it readily lent itself to valuable allegorical meanings (Tert. *Apol.* 3; Just. Mart. *Apol.* 2; Clem. Alex. *Strom.* ii. 4, § 18; Bingham, L 1, § 11).

[1] See, on the crime of being "a Christian," Clem. Alex. *Strom.* iv. 11, § 1.
[2] Mala, venefica, exitiabilis, execrabilis, prava, superstitio (Tac. *Ann.* xv. 44: Suet. *Ner.* 16; Plin. *Ep.* 92).

to Cæsar, yet during the judicial inquiry Nero could hardly have failed to hear from the emissaries of the Sanhedrin many fierce slanders of a sect which was everywhere spoken against. The Jews were by far the deadliest enemies of the Christians; and two persons of Jewish proclivities were at this time in close proximity to the person of the Emperor.[1] One was the pantomimist Aliturus, the other was Poppæa, the harlot Empress.[2] The Jews were in communication with these powerful favourites, and had even promised Nero that if his enemies ever prevailed at Rome he should have the kingdom of Jerusalem.[3] It is not even impossible that there may have been a third dark and evil influence at work to undermine the Christians, for about this very time the unscrupulous Pharisee Flavius Josephus had availed himself of the intrigues of the palace to secure the liberation of some Jewish priests.[4] If, as seems certain, the Jews had it in their power during the reign of Nero more or less to shape the whisper of the throne, does not historical induction drive us to conclude with some confidence that the suggestion of the Christians as scapegoats and victims came from them? St. Clement says in his Epistle that the Christians suffered *through jealousy*. *Whose* jealousy? Who can tell what dark secrets lie veiled under that suggestive word? Was Acte a Christian, and was Poppæa jealous of her? That suggestion seems at once inadequate and improbable, especially as Acte was not hurt. But there *was* a deadly jealousy at work against the New Religion. To the Pagans, Christianity was but a religious extravagance—contemptible, indeed, but otherwise insignificant. To the Jews, on the other hand, it was an object of hatred, which never stopped short of bloodshed when it possessed or could usurp the power,[5] and which, though long suppressed by circumstances, displayed itself in all the intensity of its virulence during the brief spasm of the dictatorship of Barcochba. Christianity was hateful to the Jews on *every* ground. It nullified their Law. It liberated all Gentiles from the heavy yoke of that Law, without thereby putting them on a lower level.

---

[1] Under previous Emperors we read of the Jewess Acme, a slave of Livia, and the Samaritan Thallus, a freedman of Tiberius (Jos. *Antt.* xvii. 5, § 7; *B. J.* i. 33, §§ 6, 7).

[2] According to John of Antioch (*Excerpta Valesii*, p. 808), and the *Chronicon Paschale* (i. 459), Nero was originally favourable to the Christians, and put Pilate to death, for which the Jews plotted his murder. Comp. Euseb. *H. E.* ii. 22, iv. 26; Keim, *Rom und Christenthum*, 179. Poppæa's Judaism is inferred from her refusing to be burned, and requesting to be embalmed (Tac. *Ann.* xvi. 16); from her adopting the custom of wearing a veil in the streets (*id.* xiii. 45); from the favour which she showed to Aliturus and Josephus (Jos. *Vit.* 3; *Antt.* xx. 8, § 11); and from the term θεοσεβής, which Josephus applies to her.

[3] Suet. *Ner.* 40. Tiberius Alexander, the nephew of Philo, afterwards Procurator of Judæa, was a person of influence at Rome (Jos. *B. J.* ii. 15, § 1; Juv. i. 130); but he was a renegade, and would not be likely to hate the Christians. It is, however, remarkable that legend attributed the anger of Nero *to the conversion of his mistress and a favourite slave.*

[4] Jos. *Vit.* 3.

[5] Compare what St. Paul says about the virulence of Jewish enmity in 1 Thess. ii. 14—16; Phil. iii. 2. Yet Christianity grew up "sub umbraculo licitae Judaeorum religionis" (Tert. *Apol.* 21).

It even tended to render those who were born Jews indifferent to the institutions of Mosaism. It was, as it were, a fatal revolt and schism from within, more dangerous than any assault from without. And, worse than all, it was by the Gentiles confounded with the Judaism which was its bitterest antagonist. While it sheltered its existence under the mantle of Judaism, as a *religio licita*, it drew down upon the religion from whose bosom it sprang all the scorn and hatred which were attached by the world to its own especial tenets; for however much the Greeks and Romans despised the Jews, they despised still more the belief that the Lord and Saviour of the world was a crucified malefactor who had risen from the dead. I see in the proselytism of Poppæa, guided by Jewish malice, the only adequate explanation of the first Christian persecution. Hers was the jealousy which had goaded Nero to matricide; hers not improbably was the instigated fanaticism of a proselyte which urged him to imbrue his hands in martyr blood. And she had her reward. A woman of whom Tacitus has not a word of good to say, and who seems to have been repulsive even to a Suetonius, is handed down by the renegade Pharisee as "a devout woman"—as a worshipper of God!"[1]

And, indeed, when once the Christians were pointed out to the popular vengeance, many reasons would be adduced to prove their connexion with the conflagration. Temples had perished—and were they not notorious enemies of the temples?[2] Did not popular rumour charge them with nocturnal orgies and Thyestæan feasts? Suspicions of incendiarism were sometimes brought against Jews;[3] but the Jews were not in the habit of talking, as these sectaries were, about a fire which should consume the world,[4] and rejoicing in the prospect of that fiery consummation.[5] Nay, more, when Pagans had bewailed the destruction of the city and the loss of the ancient monuments of Rome, had not these pernicious people used ambiguous language, as though they joyously recognised in these events the signs of a coming end? Even when they tried to suppress all outward tokens of exultation, had they not listened to the fears and lamentations of their fellow-citizens with some sparkle in the eyes, and had they not answered with something of triumph in their tones? There was a Satanic plausibility which dictated the selection of these particular victims. Because they hated the wickedness of the world, with its ruthless games and hideous idola-

[1] θεοσεβής (Jos. *Antt.* xx. 7, § 11). The word means a "monotheist," or proselyte, like σεβόμενος (Acts xiii. 43, xvi. 14, etc.). See Huidekoper, *Judaism at Rome*, pp. 452—469.
[2] As were also the Jews, who were confounded with them. Rom. ii. 22, "Dost thou (a Jew) rob temples?" See *Life and Work of St. Paul*, ii. 202.
[3] Jos. *B. J.* vii. 3, § 2—4.
[4] As St. Peter and St. John did at this very time. 1 Pet. iv. 17; Rev. xviii. 8. Comp. 2 Pet. iii. 10—12; 2 Thess. i. 8.
[5] St. Peter—apparently thinking of the fire at Rome and its consequences—calls the persecution from which the Christians were suffering when he wrote his First Epistle a πύρωσις, or "conflagration." 1 Pet. iv. 12. Comp. 1 Pet. i. 7; Heb. x. 27.

tries, they were accused of hatred of the whole human race.[1] The charge of *incivisme*, so fatal in this Reign of Terror, was sufficient to ruin a body of men who scorned the sacrifices of heathendom, and turned away with abhorrence from its banquets and gaieties.[2] The cultivated classes looked down upon the Christians with a disdain which would hardly even mention them without an apology. The *canaille* of Pagan cities insulted them with obscene inscriptions and blasphemous pictures on the very walls of the places where they met.[3] Nay, they were popularly known by nicknames, like *Sarmenticii* and *Semaxii*—untranslatable terms of opprobrium derived from the fagots with which they were burned and the stakes to which they were chained.[4] Even the heroic courage which they displayed was described as being sheer obstinacy and stupid fanaticism.[5]

But in the method chosen for the punishment of these saintly innocents Nero gave one more proof of the close connexion between effeminate æstheticism and sanguinary callousness. As in old days, "on that opprobrious hill," the temple of Chemosh had stood close by that of Moloch, so now we find the *spoliarum* beside the *fornices*—Lust hard by Hate. The *carnificina* of Tiberius, at Capreæ, adjoined the *sellariae*. History has given many proofs that no man is more systematically heartless than a corrupted debauchee. Like people, like prince. In the then condition of Rome, Nero well knew that a nation "cruel, by their sports to blood inured" would be most likely to forget their miseries, and condone their suspicions, by mixing games and gaiety with spectacles of refined and atrocious cruelty, of which, for eighteen centuries, the most passing record has sufficed to make men's blood run cold.

Tacitus tells us that "those who confessed were first seized, and then on their evidence *a huge multitude*[6] were convicted, not so much on the charge of incendiarism as for their hatred to mankind." Compressed and obscure as the sentence is, Tacitus clearly means to imply by the "confession" to which he alludes the confession of Christianity; and though he is not sufficiently generous to acquit the Christians abso-

---

[1] Tac. *Ann.* xv. 44; *Hist.* v. 5; Suet. *Ner.* 16.
[2] The tracts of Tertullian *De Coronâ Militis* are the best commentary on these sentences.
[3] Tertullian mentions one of these coarse caricatures—a figure with one foot hoofed, wearing a toga, carrying a book, and with long ass's ears, under which was written, "The God of the Christians, Onokoites." He says that Christians were actually charged with worshipping the head of an ass (*Apol.* 16; *ad Natt.* i. 16). The same preposterous calumny, with many others, is alluded to by Minucius Felix, *Octav.* i. 9: "Audio eos turpissimae pecudis caput asini ... venerari." The Christians were hence called *Asinarii*. Analogous calumnies were aimed at the Jews. Tac. *Hist.* v. 4; Plut. *Symp.* iv. 5, § 2; Jos. *c. Apion.* ii. 7.
[4] Tert. *Apol.* 14.
[5] Epictetus, *Dissert.* iv. 7, § 6; Marc. Aurelius, xi. 3, ψιλῇ παρατάξει.
[6] "*Ingens multitudo.*" The phrase is identical with the πολύ πλῆθος of Clemens Romanus (*Ep. ad Cor.* i. 6), and the ὄχλος πολύς of Rev. vii. 9, xix. 1, 6. Tertullian says that "Nero was the first who raged with the sword of Cæsar against this sect which was then specially rising at Rome" (*Apol.* 5).

lutely of all complicity in the great crime, he distinctly says that they were made the scapegoats of a general indignation. The phrase —"a huge multitude"—is one of the few existing indications of the number of martyrs in the first persecution, and of the number of Christians in the Roman Church.[1] When the historian says that they were convicted on the charge of "hatred against mankind" he shows how completely he confounds them with the Jews, against whom he elsewhere brings the accusation of "hostile feelings towards all except themselves."

Then the historian adds one casual but frightful sentence—a sentence which flings a dreadful light on the cruelty of Nero and the Roman mob. He adds, "And various forms of mockery were added to enhance their dying agonies. Covered with the skins of wild beasts, they were doomed to die by the mangling of dogs, or by being nailed to crosses; or to be set on fire and burnt after twilight by way of nightly illumination. Nero offered his own gardens for this show, and gave a chariot race, mingling with the mob in the dress of a charioteer, or actually driving about among them. Hence, guilty as the victims were, and deserving of the worst punishments, a feeling of compassion towards them began to rise, as men felt that they were being immolated not for any advantage to the commonwealth, but to glut the savagery of a single man."[2]

Imagine that awful scene, once witnessed by the silent obelisk in the square before St. Peter's at Rome! Imagine it, that we may realise how vast is the change which Christianity has wrought in the feelings of mankind! There, where the vast dome now rises, were once the gardens of Nero. They were thronged with gay crowds, among whom the Emperor moved in his frivolous degradation—and on every side were men dying slowly on their cross of shame. Along the paths of those gardens on the autumn nights were ghastly torches, blackening the ground beneath them with streams of sulphurous pitch, and each of those living torches was a martyr in his shirt of fire.[3] And in the amphitheatre hard by, in sight of twenty thousand spectators, famished dogs were tearing to pieces some of the best and purest of men and women, hideously disguised in the skins of bears or wolves. Thus did Nero baptise in the blood of martyrs the city which was to be for ages the capital of the world!

[1] Compare Oros. *Hist.* vii. 7, "(Nero) primus Romae Christianos suppliciis et mortibus affecit ac *per omnes provincias* pari persecutione excruciari imperavit; ipsum nomen exstirpare conatus beatissimos Christi apostolos Petrum cruce, Paulum gladio occidit."
[2] Hence the expressions "quaesitissimae poenae" and "crudelissimae quaestiones" (Sulp. Sev. *Hist.* ii. 96).
[3] See, on this *tunica molesta*, Lucr. iii. 1,017; Juv. viii. 235, l. 155, *et ibi Schol.* Sen. *Ep.* xiv. 5, "Illam tunicam alimentis ignium et illitam et textam." Mart. *Spectac. Ep.* v., x. 25; Apul. iii. 9, x. 10; Tert. *Apol.* 15, 50 (sarmenticii . . . semaxii); *ad Mart.* 5; *ad Scap.* 4; *ad Nat.* i. 18, "*incendiati tunicâ.*" Friedländer, *Sittengesch. Roms,* ii. 336.

The specific atrocity of such spectacles—unknown to the earlier ages which they called barbarous—was due to the cold-blooded selfishness, the hideous realism of a refined, delicate, æsthetic age. To please these "lisping hawthorn-buds," these debauched and sanguinary dandies, Art, forsooth, must know nothing of morality; must accept and rejoice in a "healthy animalism"; must estimate life by the number of its few wildest pulsations; must reckon that life is worthless without the most thrilling experiences of horror or delight! Comedy must be actual shame, and tragedy genuine bloodshed.[1] When the play of Afranius called "The Conflagration" was put on the stage, a house must be really burnt, and its furniture really plundered.[2] In the mime called "Laureolus," an actor must really be crucified and mangled by a bear, and really fling himself down and deluge the stage with blood.[3] When the heroism of Mucius Scævola was represented, a real criminal[4] must thrust his hand without a groan into the flame, and stand motionless while it is being burnt. Prometheus must be really chained to his rock, and Dirce in very fact be tossed and gored by the wild bull;[5] and Orpheus be torn to pieces by a real bear; and Icarus must really fly, even though he fall and be dashed to death; and Hercules must ascend the funeral pyre, and there be veritably burnt alive; and slaves and criminals must play their parts heroically in gold and purple till the flames envelope them. It was the ultimate romance of a degraded and brutalised society. The Roman people, "victors once, now vile and base," could now only be amused by sanguinary melodrama. Fables must be made realities, and the criminal must gracefully transform his supreme agonies into amusements for the multitude by becoming a gladiator or a tragedian. Such were the spectacles at which Nero loved to gaze through his emerald eye-glass.[6] And worse things than these—things indescribable, unutterable. Infamous mythologies were enacted, in which women must play their part in torments of shamefulness more intolerable than death. A St. Peter must hang upon the cross in the Pincian gardens, as a real Laureolus upon the stage. A Christian boy must be the Icarus, and a Christian man the Scævola, or the Hercules,

---

[1] Champagny, *Les Césars*, iv. 159.
[2] Suet. *Calig.* 57.
[3] Juv. *Sat.* viii. 187, "Laureolum velox etiam bene Lentulus egit," the actor "was unable *to fly* over the cross." Mart. *Spectac.* vii., "Nuda Caledonio sic pectora praebuit urso. Non falsa pendens in cruce Laureolus Vivebant laceri membris stillantibus artus... In *quo quae fuerat fabula, poena fuit.*" See Suet. *Caius*, 57. Josephus (*Antt.* xix. 1, § 3) alludes to this terrible incident, and so does Tertullian in an obscure but remarkable passage, *adv. Valent.* 14, "nec habens supervo lare crucem... quia nullum Catulli Laureolum fuerit exercitata."
[4] Mart. vii. 8, 21, viii. 30, x. 25; *cf.* θεατριζόμενοι, Heb. x. 33.
[5] The Toro Farnese had been brought to Rome from Rhodes in the days of Augustus, and may have set the fashion for this *tableau vivant* (Plin. xxxvi. 5, 6; Apul. *Metam.* vi. 127; Lucian, *Lucius*, 23; Renan, *L'Antechrist*, 171; Tert. *Apol.* 15; Plut. *De Serâ Num. Vind.* 9: τύρ ἀνιέντες ἐκ τῆς ἀνθινῆς ἐκείνης καὶ πολυτελοῦς ἐσθῆτος; Schlegel, *Philos d. Gesch.* I. ix., p. 332.
[6] "Spectabat smaragdo" (Plin. *H. N.* xxxvii. 57).

or the Orpheus of the amphitheatre; and Christian women, modest maidens, holy matrons, must be the Danaids,[1] or the Proserpine, or worse, and play their parts as priestesses of Saturn and Ceres, and in blood-stained dramas of the dead. No wonder that Nero became to Christian imagination the very incarnation of evil; the Antichrist; the Wild Beast from the abyss; the delegate of the great red Dragon, with a diadem and a name of blasphemy upon his brow.[2] No wonder that he left a furrow of horror in the hearts of men, and that, ten centuries after his death, the Church of Sta. Maria del Popolo had to be built by Pope Pascal II. to exorcise from Christian Rome his restless and miserable ghost!

And it struck them with deeper horror to see that the Antichrist, so far from being abhorred, was generally popular. He was popular because he presented to the degraded populace their own image and similitude. The froglike unclean spirits which proceeded, as it were, out of his mouth[3] were potent with these dwellers in an atmosphere of pestilence. They had lost all love for freedom and nobleness; they cared only for doles and excitement. Even when the infamies of a Petronius had been superseded by the murderous orgies of Tigellinus, Nero was still everywhere welcomed with shouts as a god on earth, and saluted on coins as Apollo, as Hercules, as "THE SAVIOUR OF THE WORLD."[4] The poets still assured him that there was no deity in heaven who would not think it an honour to concede to him his prerogatives; that if he did not place himself well in the centre of Olympus, the equilibrium of the universe would be destroyed.[5] Victims were slain along his path, and altars raised for him—for this wretch, whom an honest slave could not but despise and loathe—as though he was too great for mere human honours.[6] Nay, more, he found adorers and imitators of his execrable example—an Otho, a Vitellius, a Domitian, a Commodus, a Caracalla, an Heliogabalus—to poison the air of the world. The lusts and hungers and furies of the world lamented him, and cherished his memory, and longed for his return.

And yet, though all bad men—who were the majority—admired and even loved him, he died the death of a dog. Tremendous as was the power of Imperialism, the Romans often treated their individual emperors as Nero himself treated the Syrian goddess, whose image he first worshipped with awful veneration and then subjected to the most grotesque indignities. For retribution did not linger, and the vengeance fell at once on the guilty emperor and the guilty city.

---

[1] S. Clem. ad Cor. i. 6, διὰ ζῆλον διωχθεῖσαι γυναῖκες Δαναΐδες καὶ Δίρκαι αἰκίσματα δεινὰ καὶ ἀνόσια παθοῦσαι ἐπὶ τὸν τῆς πίστεως βέβαιον δρόμον κατήντησαν καὶ ἔλαβον γέρας γενναῖον αἱ ἀσθενεῖς τῷ σώματι.
[2] 2 Thess. ii. 3; Rev. xi. 7, xii. 3, xiii. 1, 6, xvi. 13, xvii. 8, 11.
[3] Rev. xvi. 13.
[4] τῷ Σωτῆρι τῆς οἰκουμένης.
[5] Luc. Phars. vii.
[6] Tac. Ann. xv. 74, "Tamquam mortale fastigium egresso."

> "Careless *seems* the Great Avenger: History's pages but record
> One death-grapple in the darkness 'twixt false systems and the Word
> Truth forever on the scaffold, wrong forever on the throne.
> Yet that scaffold sways the future, and behind the dim unknown
> Standeth God within the shadow, keeping watch above His own."

The air was full of prodigies. There were terrible storms; the plague wrought fearful ravages.[1] Rumours spread from lip to lip. Men spoke of monstrous births; of deaths by lightning under strange circumstances; of a brazen statue of Nero melted by the flash; of places struck by the brand of heaven in fourteen regions of the city;[2] of sudden darkenings of the sun.[3] A hurricane devastated Campania; comets blazed in the heavens;[4] earthquakes shook the ground.[5] On all sides were the traces of deep uneasiness and superstitious terror.[6] To all these portents, which were accepted as true by Christians as well as by Pagans, the Christians would give a specially terrible significance. They strengthened their conviction that the coming of the Lord drew nigh. They convinced the better sort of Pagans that the hour of their deliverance from a tyranny so monstrous and so disgraceful was near at hand.

In spite of the shocking servility with which alike the Senate and the people had welcomed him back to the city with shouts of triumph, Nero felt that the air of Rome was heavy with curses against his name. He withdrew to Naples, and was at supper there on March 19, A.D. 68, the anniversary of his mother's murder, when he heard that the first note of revolt had been sounded by the brave C. Julius Vindex, Præfect of Farther Gaul. He was so far from being disturbed by the news, that he showed a secret joy at the thought that he could now order Gaul to be plundered. For eight days he took no notice of the matter. He was only roused to send an address to the Senate because Vindex wounded his vanity by calling him "Ahenobarbus," and "a bad singer." But when messenger after messenger came from the provinces with tidings of menace, he hurried back to Rome. At last, when he heard that Virginius Rufus had also rebelled in Germany, and Galba in Spain, he became aware of the desperate nature of his position. On receiving this intelligence he fainted away, and remained for some time unconscious. He continued, indeed, his grossness and frivolity, but the wildest and fiercest schemes chased each other through his melodramatic brain. He would slay all the exiles; he would give up all the provinces to plunder;

---

[1] Tac. *Ann.* xvi. 13, "Tot facinoribus foedum annum etiam dii tempestatibus et morbis insignivere," etc.; Oros. *Hist.* vii. 7, "Mox (after the martyrdom of Peter and Paul) acervatim miseram civitatem obortae undique oppressere clades. Nam subsequento auctumno tanta Urbi pestilentia incubuit, ut triginta millia funerum in rationem Libitinae venirent."

[2] Tac. *Hist.* i. 4, 11, 78, ii. 8. 95; Suet. *Ner.* 57; *Otho*, 7; Plut. *De Serâ Num. Vind.*; Pausan. vii. 17; Xiphilin. lxiv; Dion Chrysost. *Orat.* xxi

[3] Tac. *Ann.* xiv. 12.

[4] Tac. *Ann.* xiv. 22, xv. 47; Sen. *Qu. Nat.* vii. 17, 21.

[5] Tac. *Ann.* xv. 22.

[6] Suet. *Ner.* 36, 39; Dion Cass. lxi. 16, 18.

he would order all the Gauls in the city to be butchered; he would have all the Senators invited to banquets, and would then poison them; he would have the city set on fire, and the wild beasts of the amphitheatre let loose among the people; he would depose both the Consuls, and become sole Consul himself, since legend said that only by a Consul could Gauls be conquered; he would go with an army to the province, and when he got there would do nothing but weep, and when he had thus moved the rebels to compassion, would next day sing with them at a great festival the ode of victory which he must at once compose. Not a single manly resolution lent a moment's dignity to his miserable fall. Sometimes he talked of escaping to Ostia, and arming the sailors; at others, of escaping to Alexandria, and earning his bread by his "divine voice." Meanwhile he was hourly subjected to the deadliest insults, and terrified by dreams and omens so sombre that his faith in the astrologers who had promised him the government of the East and the kingdom of Jerusalem began to be rudely shaken. When he heard that not a single army or general remained faithful to him, he kicked over the table at which he was dining, dashed to pieces on the ground two favourite goblets embossed with scenes from the Homeric poems, and placed in a golden box some poison furnished to him by Locusta. The last effort which he contemplated was to mount the Rostra, beg pardon of the people for his crimes, ask them to try him again, and, at the worst, to allow him the Præfecture of Egypt. But this design he did not dare to carry out, from fear that he would be torn to pieces before he reached the Forum. Meanwhile he found that the palace had been deserted by his guards, and that his attendants had robbed his chamber even of the golden box in which he had stored his poison. Rushing out, as though to drown himself in the Tiber, he changed his mind, and begged for some quiet hiding-place in which to collect his thoughts. The freedman Phaon offered him a lowly villa about four miles from the city. Barefooted, and with a faded coat thrown over his tunic, he hid his head and face in a kerchief, and rode away with only four attendants. On the road he heard the tumult of the Prætorians cursing his name. Amid evil omens and serious perils he reached the back of Phaon's villa, and, creeping towards it through a muddy reedbed, was secretly admitted into one of its mean slave-chambers by an aperture through which he had to crawl on his hands and feet.

There is no need to dwell on the miserable spectacle of his end— perhaps the meanest and most pusillanimous which has ever been recorded. The poor wretch who, without a pang, had caused so many brave Romans and so many innocent Christians to be murdered, could not summon up resolution to die. He devised every operatic incident of which he could think. When even his most degraded slaves urged him to have sufficient manliness to save himself from the fearful infamies which otherwise awaited him, he ordered his grave to be dug, and fragments of marble to be collected for its adornment, and water and wood for his funeral pyre, perpetually whining, "What an artist to perish!" Meanwhile a courier arrived for Phaon. Nero snatched his despatches out of his hand, and read that the Senate had decided that he should be punished in the ancestral fashion as a public enemy. Asking what the ancestral fashion was, he was informed that he would be stripped naked and scourged to death with rods, with his head thrust into a fork. Horrified at this, he seized two daggers, and after theatrically trying their edges, sheathed them again, with the excuse that the fatal moment had not yet arrived! Then he bade Sporus begin to sing his funeral song, and begged some one to show him how to die. Even his own intense shame at his cowardice was an insufficient stimulus, and he whiled away the time in vapid epigrams and pompous quotations. The sound of horses' hoofs then broke on his ears, and, venting one more Greek quotation, he held the dagger to his throat. It was driven home by Epaphroditus, one of his literary slaves. At this moment the centurion who came to arrest him rushed in. Nero was not yet dead, and, under pretence of helping him, the centurion began to stanch the wound with his cloak. "Too late," he said; "is this your fidelity?" So he died; and the bystanders were horrified with the way in which his eyes seemed to be starting out of his head in a rigid stare. He had begged that his body might be burned without posthumous insults, and this was conceded by Icelus, the freedman of Galba.

So died the last of the Cæsars! And as Robespierre was lamented by his landlady, so even Nero was tenderly buried by two nurses who had known him in the exquisite beauty of his engaging childhood, and by Acte, who had inspired his youth with a genuine love.

But, as we shall see hereafter, his history does not end with his grave. He was to live on in the expectation alike of Jews and Christians. The fifth head of the Wild Beast of the Revelation was in some sort to re-appear as the eighth; the head with its diadem and its names of blasphemy had been wounded to death, but in the Apocalyptic sense the deadly wound was to be healed.[1] The Roman world could not believe that the heir of the deified Julian race could be cut off thus suddenly and obscurely, and vanish like foam upon the water.[2] The Christians felt sure that it required something more than an ordinary death-stroke to destroy the Antichrist, and to end the vitality of the Wild Beast from the Abyss, who had been the first to set himself in deadly antagonism against the Redeemer, and to wage war upon the saints of God.

[1] Rev. xiii. 3, xvii. 11.   [2] Hos. x. 7.

Book II.

ST. PETER AND THE CHURCH CATHOLIC.

CHAPTER V.

WRITINGS OF THE APOSTLES AND EARLY CHRISTIANS.

> Ἁλιεῦ μερόπων
> Τῶν σωζομένων,
> Πελάγους κακίας
> Ἰχθῦς ἁγνοὺς
> Κύματος ἐχθροῦ
> Γλυκερῇ ζωῇ δελεάζων.
> —CLEM. ALEX. *Paed.* iii. *ad fin.*

WHEN we turn from the annals of the world at this epoch to the annals of the Church, we pass at once from an atmosphere heavy with misery and corruption into pure and pellucid air. We have been reading the account given us by secular literature of the world in its relations to the Church. In the First Epistle of Saint Peter we shall read directions which were written to guide the Church in its relations to the world. We have been reading what Pagans said and thought of Christians; in the writings of Christians addressed to each other, and meant for no other eye, we shall see what these hated, slandered, persecuted Christians really were. In place of the turbulence laid to their charge, we shall have proofs of the humility and cheerfulness of their submission. We shall see that, so far from being resentful, they were taught unlimited forgiveness; and that, instead of cherishing a fierce hatred against all mankind, they made it their chief virtue to cultivate an universal love.

But although we are so fully acquainted with the thoughts and feelings of the early Christians, yet the facts of their corporate history during the last decades of the first century, and even the closing details in the biographies of their very greatest teachers, are plunged in entire uncertainty. When, with the last word in the Acts of the Apostles, we lose the graphic and faithful guidance of St. Luke, the torch of Christian history is for a time abruptly quenched. We are left, as it were, to grope amid the windings of the catacombs. Even the final labours of the life of St. Paul are only so far known as we may dimly infer them from the casual allusions of the pastoral epistles. For the details of many years in the life of St. Peter we have nothing on which to rely except slight and vague allusions, floating rumours, and false impressions created by the deliberate fictions of heretical romance.

It is probable that this silence is in itself the result of the terrible scenes in which the Apostles perished. It was indispensable to the safety of the whole community that the books of the Christians, when given up by the unhappy weakness of "traditors" or discovered by the keen malignity of informers, should contain no compromising matter. But how would it have been possible for St. Luke to write in a manner otherwise than compromising if he had detailed the horrors of the Neronian persecution? It is a reasonable conjecture that the sudden close of the Acts of the Apostles may have been due to the impossibility of speaking without indignation and abhorrence of the Emperor and the Government which, between A.D. 64 and 68, sanctioned the infliction upon innocent men and women of atrocities which excited the pity of the very Pagans. The Jew and the Christian who entered on such themes could only do so under the disguise of a cryptograph, hiding his meaning from all but the initiated few in such prophetic symbols as those of the Apocalypse. In that book alone we are enabled to hear the cry of horror which Nero's brutal cruelties wrung from Christian hearts.

But if we know so little of Saint Peter that is in the least trustworthy, it is hardly strange that of the other Apostles, with the single exception of St. John, and—in the wider sense of the word "apostle" —of St. James the Lord's brother, we know scarcely anything. To St. Peter, St. John, and St. James the Lord's brother, it was believed that Christ, after His resurrection, had "revealed the true *gnosis*," or deeper understanding of Christian doctrine.[1] It is singular how very little is narrated of the rest, and how entirely that little depends upon loose and unaccredited tradition. Did they all travel as missionaries? Did they all die as martyrs? Heracleon, in the second century, said that St. Matthias, St. Thomas, St. Philip, and St. Matthew, died natural deaths, and St. Clemens of Alexandria quotes him without contradiction.[2] The only death of an Apostle narrated in the New Testament is narrated in two words, ἀνεῖλε μαχαίρᾳ—"slew with the sword." It is the martyrdom of St. James the Elder, the son of Zebedee.[3] Of St. Philip we know with reasonable certainty that he lived for many years as bishop, and died in great honour at Hierapolis in Phrygia. Eusebius makes express mention of his daughters, of whom two were virgins, and one was married and buried at Ephesus. It cannot be regarded as certain that there has not been some confusion between Philip the Apostle and Philip the Deacon; but there is no reason why they should not both have had virgin daughters, and Polycrates expressly says that the Philip who was regarded as one of the great "lights of Asia" was

---

[1] Clem. Alex. *ap.* Euseb. *H. E.* ii. 1.
[2] Clem. Alex. *Strom.* i. 4. See Döllinger, *First Age of the Church*, p. 137.
[3] He became the patron saint of Spain from the legends about the removal of his body to Iria Flavia. Compostella is said to be a corruption of Giacomo Postolo (Voss). See Cave, *Lives of the Apostles*, p. 150. The Bollandists still retain the legend, first mentioned by Wal. Strabo (*Poem. de XII. Apost.*), that he was martyred there.

one of the Twelve.[1] If we ask about the rest of our Lord's chosen Twelve, all that we are told is of a most meagre and most uncertain character. The first fact stated about them is that they did not separate for twelve years, because they had been bidden by Christ in His parting words to stay for that period in Jerusalem. Accordingly we find that up to that time St. Paul is the only Apostle of whose missionary journeys beyond the limits of Palestine we have any evidence, whereas after that time we find James the Lord's brother alone at Jerusalem as the permanent overseer of the Mother-Church.

We are told that, after the Ascension, the Apostles divided the world among themselves by lot for the purpose of evangelisation,[2] and in the fourth century there was a prevalent belief that they had all been martyred before the destruction of Jerusalem, excepting John. This, however, can have only been an *à priori* conjecture, and there is no evidence which can be adduced in its support.

The sum total, then, of what tradition asserts about these Apostles, omitting the worst absurdities and the legendary miracles, is as follows:—

ST. ANDREW, determining to convert the Scythians,[3] visited on the way Amynsus, Trapezus, Heraclea, and Sinope. After being nearly killed by the Jews at Sinope, he was miraculously healed, visited Neo-Cæsarea and Samosata, returned to Jerusalem, and thence went to Byzantium, where he appointed Stachys to be a bishop. After various other travels and adventures he was martyred at Patræ by Ægeas, Proconsul of Achaia, by being crucified on the decussate cross now known as the cross of St. Andrew.[4]

ST. BARTHOLOMEW (Nathaniel) is said to have travelled to India, and to have carried thither St. Matthew's Gospel.[5] After preaching in Lycaonia and Armenia, it is asserted that he was either flayed or crucified head downwards at Albanopolis in Armenia. The pseudo-Dionysius attributes to him the remarkable saying that "Theology is both large and very small, and the Gospel broad and great, and also compressed."[6]

ST. MATTHEW is said to have preached in Parthia and Æthiopia, and to have been martyred at Naddaber in the latter country.[7] According to St. Clemens, he lived only on herbs,[8] practising a mode of life which was Essene in its simplicity and self-denial.

---

[1] Clem. Alex. *Strom.* iii., p. 448; Polycr. *ap.* Euseb. iii. 31; Dorotheus, *De Vit. et Mort. Apost.*; Isidor. Pelus. *Epp.* i. 447, etc. Metaphrastes and Nicephorus add various fables.

[2] Socrates, *H.E.* i. 19.   [3] Origen *ap.* Euseb. iii. 1.

[4] See Euseb. *H. E.* iii. 1; Nicephorus, *H. E.* ii. 39. In Hesychius *ap.* Photium, *Cod.* 269, is first found his address to his cross. The *Acta Andreae* (Tischendorf, *Act. Apocr.*, p. 105 ff.) are among the best of their kind.

[5] Euseb. v. 10; Sophronius *ap.* Jer. *De Script. Eccl.*   [6] *De Mystic. Theol.* i. 3.

[7] Niceph. *l.c.*; Metaphr. *ad Aug.* 24; Fortunatus, *De Senat.* vii. Various fables are added in Niceph. ii. 41.

[8] *Paedag.* ii. 1.

ST. THOMAS is called the Apostle of India, and is said to have founded the Christian communities in India who still call themselves by his name. But this seems to be a mistake. Theodoret says that the Thomas who established these churches was a Manichee, and the "Acts of Thomas" are Manichean in tendency. Origen says that the Apostle preached in Parthia.[1] His grave was shown at Edessa in the fourth century.[2]

ST. JAMES THE LESS, the son of Alphæus, who is distinguished by the Greek Church from James the Lord's brother, is said to have been crucified while preaching at Ostrakine in Lower Egypt.[3]

ST. SIMON ZELOTES is variously conjectured to have preached and to have been crucified at Babylonia or in the British Isles.[4]

JUDAS, LEBBÆUS, or THADDÆUS, is said to have been despatched by St. Thomas to Abgar, King of Edessa, and to have been martyred at Berytus.[5]

Scanty, contradictory, late, and unauthenticated notices, founded for the most part on invention or a sense of ecclesiastical fitness, and recorded chiefly by writers like Gregory of Tours late in the sixth century, and Nicephorus late in the fourteenth, are obviously valueless. All that we can deduce from them is the belief, of which we see glimpses even in Clemens Alexandrinus and Origen, that the Apostles preached far and wide, and that more than one of them were martyred. It would be strange if none of the Twelve met with such an end in preaching among Pagan and barbarous nations; and that they did so preach is rendered likely by the extreme antiquity and the marked Judæo-Christian character of Churches which still exist in Persia, India, Egypt, and Abyssinia.

But in the silence and obscurity which thus falls over the personal history and final fate of the Twelve whom Christ chose to be nearest to Him on earth, how invaluable is the boon of knowledge respecting the thoughts, and to some extent even the lives, of such Apostles as St. Peter, St. Paul, and St. John, as well as of St. Jude, and St James the Lord's brother, and the eloquent writer of the Epistle to the Hebrews. And the boon is all the richer from the Divine diversity of thought thus preserved for us. For each of these Apostolic writers, though they are one in their faith, yet approaches the hopes and promises of Christianity from a different point of view; each one gives us a fresh aspect of many-sided truths.

Let us imagine what would have been our position if, in the providence of God, we had not been suffered to possess these works, of which the greater number belong to the closing epoch of the New Testament Canon.

The New Testament would then have consisted exclusively of the works of five writers—the four Evangelists and St. Paul.

---

[1] Orig. ap. Euseb. iii. 1. [3] Chrys. Hom. in Hebr. xxvi.
[2] Niceph. ii. 40. [4] Niceph. viii. 30.
[5] Dorotheus, *Vit. Apost.*: Niceph. ii. 40.

The Synoptists, in spite of well-marked minor differences in their point of view, present for the most part a single—mainly the external and historical—aspect of the life of Christ. We find in them a compressed and fragmentary outline of the work of Christ's public ministry, and even this is almost confined to details about one year of His work and one region of His ministry,[1] followed by a fuller account of His Betrayal, Passion, Crucifixion, and Resurrection. In the fourth Gospel alone we have a sketch of the Judæan phase of the ministry, as well as the doctrine of the Logos, and a yet deeper insight into the Nature and Mind of Christ. But, with this exception, we should be left to St. Paul alone for the theological development and manifold applications of Christian truth. And yet in the Acts of the Apostles, and in the Epistles of St. Paul himself, we should have found abundant traces that his view of Christianity was in many respects independent and original. Alike from his own pages, and those of his friend and historian St. Luke, we should have learnt the existence of phases of Christianity, built indeed upon the same essential truths as those which he deemed it the glory of his life to preach, but placing those truths in a different perspective, and regarding them from another point of view. We should have heard the echoes of disputes so vehement and so agitating that they even arrayed the Apostles in a position of controversy against one another, and we should have found traces that though those disputes were conducted with such Christian forbearance on both sides as to prevent their degenerating into schisms, they yet continued to smoulder as elements of difference between various schools of thought. Taking the Corinthian Church as a type of other Churches, we should have found that there was a Kephas party, and an Apollos party, and a Christ party, as well as a party which attached itself to the name of Paul; and even if we admitted that the Corinthian Church was exceptionally factious, we should have learnt from the Epistle to the Galatians, and other sources, that there were Jews who called themselves Christians, and claimed identity with the views of James, by whom the name and work of the Apostle of the Gentiles were regarded not only with unsympathising coldness, but with positive disapproval and dislike. We should have felt that we were not in possession of the materials for forming any complete opinion as to the characteristics of early Christianity. We should have longed for even a few words to inform us what were the special tenets which differentiated the adherents of St. James, and St. Peter, and St. John, and Apollos, from those of the Great Missionary who in human erudition and purely intellectual endowments, no less than in the vast effects of his lifelong martyrdom, so greatly surpassed them all. We should have been ready to sacrifice no small part of classical literature for the sake of any treatise, however brief, which would have furnished us with adequate data for ascertaining

---

[1] See the remark of St. John "the Elder" (*i.e.*, the Apostle) in Papias *ap.* Euseb. *H. E.* iii. 21.

the teaching of Apostles who had lived familiarly with the Lord by the Lake of Galilee; or of some other early converts who, like St. Paul himself, formed their judgment of Christianity with the full powers of a cultivated manhood. We should, indeed, have known how Christianity was taught by one who had been living for years in Heathen communities, whose Jewish training at the feet of Gamaliel had been modified by his early days in learned Tarsus, and still more by his cosmopolitan familiarity with the cities and ways of men; but we should have asked whether the Faith was taught in exactly the same way—or, if not, with what modifications—by a Peter and a John, who had known, as St. Paul had never known, the living Jesus, and by a James the Lord's brother, who spent so many years in the rigid practice of every Jewish observance. We should have been lost in vain surmises as to the growth of heresies. If Marcionism and Antinomianism sprang from direct perversion of the teachings of St. Paul, what was the teaching on which Nazarenes, and Ebionites, and Elchasaites, and Chiliasts professed to found their views? In fact, without the nine books of the New Testament, which will be examined in these volumes, the early history of the Church would have been reduced to a chaos of hopeless uncertainties. We should have felt that our records were grievously imperfect; that only in a unity wherein minor differences were reconciled, without being obliterated—only in the synthesis of opinions which were various, without contrariety—could we form a full notion of the breadth and length, and depth and height of sacred Truth.

Now this is the very boon which the Spirit of God has granted to us. Besides the four Gospels, besides the thirteen Epistles of St. Paul, we have nine books of the New Testament which are the works of five different authors, and every one of these brief but precious documents is marked by its own special characteristics.

1. Earliest, probably, of them all is the book which is unhappily placed last, and therefore completely out of its proper order in our New Testaments, THE REVELATION OF ST. JOHN THE DIVINE. It marks the beginning of the era of martyrdoms. It is in many respects exceptionally precious. It is precious as a counterpart to the Book of Daniel in the Old Testament, and therefore as furnishing us with a splendid specimen of a Christian, as distinguished from a Jewish, Apocalypse. It is precious as showing the effect produced on the thoughts and hopes of Christendom by the first outburst of Imperial persecution. It is especially precious as a Christian Philosophy of History, and as giving a voice to the inextinguishable hopes of Christians even in the midst of fire and blood. And besides all this it is precious as furnishing the earliest insight into the mind of the Beloved Disciple, in a stage of his career before the mighty lessons involved in the Fall of Jerusalem and the close of the old Æon had emancipated him from the last fetters of Judaic bondage.

2. IN THE EPISTLE TO THE HEBREWS, which is being more and

more widely accepted as the work of Apollos, we have a specimen of *Alexandrian Christianity*. Valuable for its singular dignity and eloquence, for the powerful argument which it elaborates, and for the original truths with which it is enriched, it also possesses a very special interest because it gives us a clear insight into the school of thought which sprang from the contact of Judaism and Christianity with Greek Philosophy. Of this Alexandrianism there are but scattered indications in St. John and St. Paul, but it was destined in God's providence to exercise a very powerful influence over the growth and development of Christian doctrine, because it furnished the intellectual training of some of the greatest of the Christian Fathers. Our loss would have been irreparable if time had deprived us of the earliest and profoundest Christian treatise which emanated from the splendid school of Alexandrian Theology.

The remaining seven treatises of the New Testament are known by the general name of the SEVEN CATHOLIC EPISTLES. Various untenable explanations of the name "Catholic" have been suggested; but in the third century it was used in the sense of "encyclical,"[1] and there can be little doubt that these seven letters were so called because they were addressed not to one city, or even to one nation, but generally, to every Christian. In the West they were sometimes called *Epistolae Canonicae*, but this could not have been the original meaning of Catholic, since Eusebius gives the name to the letters of Dionysius of Corinth.[2] Two of these letters—the Epistles of St. James and St. Jude—belong to the Judaic school of Christianity; two others— those of St. Peter—represent the moderate and mediating position of Christians who wished to stand aloof, alike from Paulinists and Judaists, on the more general grounds of a common Christianity; three—those of St. John—represent a phase of thought in which the chief controversies which agitated the first decades of the Church's history have melted into the distance, or have been solved for ever by the Fall of Jerusalem. At that epoch Truth was beginning to be assailed from without by new forms of opposition, or corroded from within by fresh types of error.

As we are about to study these Epistles in detail, we may here confine ourselves to a few general remarks respecting them.

3. THE EPISTLE OF ST. JUDE is the work of a non-Apostolic writer, but of one who was known as brother of St. James the Bishop of Jerusalem, and who evidently resembled his more eminent brother in

---

[1] Euseb. *H. E.* vii. 25.
[2] Euseb. *H. E.* iv. 23; Leont. *De Sect.* 27. Theodoret says: "They are called 'Catholic,' which is equivalent to encyclical, since they are not addressed to single Churches, but generally (καθόλου) to the faithful, whether to the Jews of the Dispersion, as Peter writes, or even to all who are living as Christians under the same faith." The word itself simply means "general." Some scholars have argued that the Fathers use it in the sense of "canonical," but this is a *later* usage. See Ebrard's *Appendix* to his edition of 1 *John*.

intensity of character and vehemence of conviction. His brief letter is interesting from its very peculiarities. It abounds in original and picturesque expressions, and fearlessly utilises both the Jewish *Hagadôth* and the apocryphal literature, with which the writer's training had rendered him familiar. In the passionate vehemence of its denunciations against Gnostic libertinism it reads like a page of Amos or of Isaiah, and is evidently the work of one who, like so many of the early Jewish Christians, had thought it both a national and a religious duty in entering the Church to remain true to the Synagogue. It is a sort of partial and anticipated Apocalypse, but it rests content with isolated metaphors, instead of continuous symbols.

4. The same stern Judaic character, rendered still more unbending by the asceticism of the writer, marks every page of THE EPISTLE OF ST. JAMES. Living exclusively at Jerusalem, accurate as the Pharisees themselves in the observance of the Mosaic Law—a scrupulosity which had gained him his title of "the Just"—he was only called upon "to be a Jew to the Jews," and this he was by nature, by temperament, and by training. In the Synod at Jerusalem, where St. Peter proposed emancipation, St. James—even in assenting—proposes restrictions; and while St. Peter, almost in Pauline language, declares that neither Jew nor Gentile can be saved except "through the grace of the Lord Jesus,"[1] St. James, while holding the same faith, urges the claims of Moses, and follows the indications of the Prophets. St. Peter never mentions "the Law;" St. James never mentions "the Gospel." He accepts it indeed with all his heart, but it still presents itself to him as "the Law," though glorified from "a yoke that gendereth to bondage"[2] into a perfect "law of liberty."[3] In reading St. James we can realise the sentiments of the Mother-Church of Jerusalem, and feel that there is no discontinuity in the great stream of Divine Revelation. For him, and for the Jewish Christians of whom he was the recognised leader, Christianity is not so much the inauguration of the New as the fulfilment of the Old.

5. It is necessary, and even desirable, that there should in all ages be some whose mission it is to develop one special aspect of truth, and to stamp the whole of their religious system with the impress of their own powerful individuality. Such, respectively, were St. Paul and St. James. Even in their lifetime there were some who exaggerated and perverted the special truths which it was their work to teach. After their death there were Marcionites and Antinomians who perverted the doctrines of St. Paul, and there were Ebionites and Nazarenes who falsely claimed the authority of St. James. But happily there are Christians in all ages who, while they only acknowledge a heavenly master, are anxious to accept truth by whomsoever it is presented to them, yet at the same time to strip

---

[1] Acts xv. 11.   [2] Gal. iv. 24.   [3] James i. 25, ii. 12.

it of all mere party peculiarities. Such was St. Peter. He can see the side of truth which either of his great contemporaries represents. He is pre-eminently the Apostle of Catholicity. He had shown in his conduct at Cæsarea that his convictions leaned to the side of the Apostle of the Gentiles; and at Antioch that he could not wholly emancipate himself from the habits induced by lifelong training in the principles of St. James. He was neither able nor willing wholly to shake off the spell of personal ascendency exercised over him alike by the great world-missionary and by the unbending Bishop of Jerusalem. In THE EPISTLES OF ST. PETER we are able to trace the thoughts and expressions of both these great leaders. He dwells with all the energy of St. James on the glory of practical virtue, and with much of the fervour of St. Paul on the distinctively Christian motives and sanctions. But it is no part of his object to follow St. Paul in the logical development and formulation of Christian theology, nor yet to dwell with the exclusiveness of St. James on Christian practice. Even when using language which had been seized upon as the shibboleth of partisans, he strips it of all partisan significance. He was out of sympathy with the spirit which leads to disunion and factiousness by the exclusive maintenance of antagonistic formulæ.

It is interesting to see that the same distinctive peculiarities are continued in later writers of the first and second centuries. In the Epistle of the pseudo-Barnabas we have an exaggerated Paulinism; in the pseudo-Clementines an exaggerated Judaism, which makes a special hero of St. James. St. Peter, standing between both extremes, was claimed by both parties. Basilides, the anti-Judaic Egyptian Gnostic, claimed to have been taught by Glaucias, the interpreter of St. Peter; and another apocryphal work, which uttered strong warnings against Jewish worship, was called "The Preaching of Peter." On the other hand, St. Peter shares, though in a degree subordinate to St. James, the admiration of the Ebionite partisans who wrote the Clementine Homilies and Recognitions. In a less objectionable way, but still with something of exaggeration, Hermas, the author of the famous "Shepherd," reflects the teaching of St. James; while St. Clement of Rome, Catholic, like St. Peter, in all his sympathies, "combines the distinctive features of all the Apostolic Epistles," and "belonging to no party, he seemed to belong to all."[1]

6. There remain THE THREE EPISTLES OF ST. JOHN,[2] which may be regarded collectively as the last utterance of Christian Revelation in the New Testament. They are the more interesting not only on this account, but because they are the work of one who had been exceptionally near to the heart of Christ, and had lived for many years face to face with the great heathen world. They are also the work of one

---

[1] Lightfoot, *Galatians*, p. 315.
[2] I have gone through every fact and every detail of the Gospel of St. John in the *Life of Christ*, and for that reason I do not touch upon it here.

who lived to see mighty changes in the growth and fortunes of the Christian Church. He had perhaps been the only Apostle who had seen Jesus die; he had been last beside the Cross, and first in the empty tomb. As one who had watched the death-bed of the Mother of the Lord, he had been one of the very few depositories of the awful mysteries which it had been given to St. Luke partly to reveal, after they had been pondered for many years in the holy reticence of the Virgin's heart. He had been one of the scattered despairing band who had spent in anguish the awful day in which they knew that Jesus was lying dead, and did not yet understand that He should rise again. For a quarter of a century he was the sole survivor, not only of those who had heard the last discourses of the Lord on the evening of His Passion, but even of any who could say, "That which we have seen and our hands have handled of the Word of Life declare we unto you." But his Epistles have yet a further interest as the writings of one who, in his long and diversified experience, had undergone a remarkable change alike of character and of views; of one who had passed from the Elijah-spirit to the Christ-spirit—from the narrower scrupulosity of a Judaist, living in the heart of the Jewish capital and attending thrice a day the Temple worship, to the breadth and width and spirituality of Christian freedom. We have in the Apocalypse a work of his in the earlier stage of his Christian opinions, when he stood for the first time face to face with the Heathen world in its fiercest attitude of anti-Christian opposition. We have in his Gospel and Epistles the sweetest and loftiest utterances of Christian idealism; the strains, as it were, of Divinest music in which the voice of inspiration died away.

It may perhaps be said that our possession of these treasures—especially of some of them—is disturbed by the growing suspicion as to their genuineness. On this score Christianity has little to fear. Every true and honourable man will regard it as a base and cowardly unfaithfulness to defend as *certain* the genuineness of any book of the Bible of which the spuriousness can be shown to be even reasonably probable. In spite of the conflict which has raged around the Gospel of St. John, we are deeply convinced that the arguments preponderate in favour of those who accept it as the work of the Beloved Disciple. I should find no difficulty in regarding the Apocalypse as being the work of another John if, in spite of some acknowledged difficulties, the Johannine authorship did not seem to be all but incontrovertible. The Epistle to the Hebrews is not a work of St. Paul, but it is pre-eminently worthy of its honoured place in the Canon. The first Epistles of St. Peter and St. John may be said to stand above all suspicion. The Epistles of St. James and St. Jude have less *distinctive* value as parts of the Christian Revelation, but yet have their own inestimable worth, and derive a deeper interest from being the works of "brethren of the Lord." The second and third Epistles of St.

John are almost certainly genuine, but whether they be by the Apostle or not is matter of minor importance, because of their extreme brevity, and because they consist for the most part of recapitulated truths. They are but corollaries to the first Epistle, and contain no doctrine which is not found more fully in the Apostle's other writings. The only one of the seven Catholic Epistles against the genuineness of which strong arguments may be adduced is the Second Epistle of St. Peter, which is in any case the book least supported by external testimony. Its genuineness must be regarded as a question for still further discussion, and the recent discovery of its affinity in some passages to the works of Josephus requires careful attention.[1] In the introduction to each of these Epistles the evidence as to their genuineness is discussed. Many, both in ancient and in modern days, have doubted about some of them. Dionysius of Alexandria and Eusebius, Gaius and Jerome, Erasmus and Cardinal Cajetan, Sixtus Senensis and Luther,[2] Zwingli, Calvin, Œcolampadius, Grotius, and many more, have regarded several of them as being at best deuterocanonical—authentic (if at all) in a lower sense, and endowed with inferior authority; but though the Church of England has shown herself wiser than the Council of Trent in not binding with an anathema the necessary acceptance of the genuineness of every one of them, we have every reason to rejoice that they were admitted by general consent into the Christian Canon.

Enough, I trust, has been urged to show the varied and exceeding preciousness of the writings which we are now about to examine. St. Paul, as has been said, dwells, not of course exclusively, but predominantly, on Christian doctrine, St. James on Christian practice, St. Peter on Christian trials, and St. John on Christian experience;—St. Paul insists mainly on faith, St. James on works, St. Peter on hope, and St. John on love;—St. Paul represents[3] Christian scholasticism, and St. John Christian mysticism;—St. Paul represents the spirit of Protestantism, St. Peter that of Catholicism, while St. James speaks in the voice of the Church of the Past, and St. John in that of the Church of the Future;—St. Peter is the founder, St. Paul the propagator, St. John the finisher;—St. Peter represents to us the glory of power and action, St. Paul that of thought and wisdom, St. James of virtue and faithfulness, St. John of emotion and holiness.[4] Again, to St. James Christianity appears as the fulfilment of the Old Law, to St. Peter as the completion of the old Theocracy, to St. Paul as the completion of the old Covenant, to Apollos as the completion of the old Worship and Priesthood, to St. John as the completion of all the truths which the

---

[1] *V. infra*, pp. 106—8.
[2] Luther was not by any means the only great theologian, either in ancient or modern times, who adopted a subjective test. There were others also who "*den Kanon im Kanon ruckten und fanden.*"
[3] See Schaff, *Hist. of the Church*, 105—110.
[4] See Stanley, *Sermons on the Apostolic Age*, pp. 4, 5.

world possessed.[1] Such generalisations may be too seductive, and may tend to mislead us by bringing into prominence only one special peculiarity of each writer, while others are for the time ignored. Yet they contain a germ of truth, and they may help us to seize the more salient characteristics. Two things, however, are certain :—One is, that in every essential each of the sacred writers held the Catholic faith, one and indivisible, which is no more altered by their varying individuality than Light is altered in character because we sometimes see it glowing in the heavens, and sometimes flashing from the sea. The other is, that in all these writers alike we see the beauty of holiness, the regenerating power of Christian truth.

But among the writers of the New Testament two stand out preeminently as what would be called, in modern phraseology, original theologians. They are St. Paul and St. John. On some of the special differences between them we shall touch farther on. Meanwhile we shall see at a glance the contrast between the dialectical method of the one and the intuitive method of the other, if we compare the Epistle to the Romans with the First Epistle of St. John. The richness, the many-sidedness, the impetuosity, the human individuality of the one, are as unlike as possible to the few but reiterated keynotes, the unity, the sovereign calm, the spiritual idealism of the other. The difference will be emphasised if we place side by side the fundamental conceptions of their theology. That of St. Paul is :—

"But now, apart from the law, the righteousness of God hath been manifested, witness being borne thereto by the law and the prophets; even the righteousness of God through faith in Jesus Christ unto all and upon all them that believe; for there is no distinction : for all sinned, and are falling short of the glory of God, being accounted righteous freely by his grace through the redemption that is in Christ Jesus" (Rom. iii. 21—24).

That of St. John is :—

"Herein is manifested the love of God in us, because he hath sent his only begotten Son into the world, that we might live through him" (1 John iv. 9).

It requires but to read the two formulæ side by side to perceive the characteristic differences which separate the theological conceptions of the two Apostles. It is a rich boon to possess the views of both.

We shall be still more inclined to value this precious heritage of Christian thought when we notice that the least important of these Catholic Epistles stands on an incomparably higher level than any of the writings of the Apostolic Fathers. This will be shown by a glance at the Epistle of St. Clement and the Epistle of Barnabas—writings so highly valued in the Church that the first is found in the Alexandrian Manuscript, and the second in the Sinaitic Manuscript, after the Apocalypse, and both were publicly read in churches as profitable "scriptures."

[1] See Lange, Introduction to Catholic Epistles, *Bibelwerk*, ix.

(1) THE EPISTLE OF ST. CLEMENT is thoroughly eclectic, but the eclecticism is as devoid of genius and originality as an ordinary modern sermon. It consists in a free usage of phrases borrowed promiscuously from each of the great Apostles, rather than in a real assimilation of their views. The piety and receptivity of the writer is very beautiful, but it cannot be said that it is vivified by a single luminous or informing idea.

(a) St. Clement has read St. Paul and St. John, and St. James and St. Peter, and as a pupil of the last he is animated by a genuine spirit of catholicity; but he does not seem to have realised the essential distinctions which separate their writings. The substance of his views is identical with that which we find in St. Peter and St. James, but he clothes them in expressions borrowed from St. Paul. He says with St. Paul, "We are not justified by ourselves, nor by works, but by faith" (c. xxxii.), and he says with St. James, "being justified by works and not by words" (c. xxx.); but he says nothing to bring into harmony the apparent contradictions. His readiness to accept all moral exhortations and all Apostolic phrases acts as a solvent in which the special meaning of these phrases as parts of entire systems is apt to disappear. Three of the sacred writers refer in different ways and for different purposes to Abraham (Rom. iv.; James ii. 21; Heb. xi. 8). In the syncretism of St. Clement the allusions made by all three are mingled in one sentence. Rahab, in St. Clement, is saved by her faith *and by her hospitality*, which is a curious union of James ii. 25 and Heb. xi. 31; and the only original observation which St. Clement adds is the allegorising fancy that the red cord with which she let the spies down from the window indicated the efficacy of the blood of Christ for all who believe and hope in God (*Ep. ad Cor.* xii.). Thus the mechanical fusion of two quotations is ornamented by a loose, poor, and untenable analogy, which enables him to add "prophecy" to the faith and hospitality which distinguished the harlot of Jericho.

(b) So, too, when St. Clement speaks of the Resurrection, we see how immeasurably his theology has retrograded behind that of St. Paul. He does not connect it immediately and necessarily with the Resurrection of Christ, but proves it by Old Testament quotations, and illustrates its possibility by natural analogies, especially by the existence and history of the Phœnix! How much would our estimate of inspiration have been lowered—how loud would have been the scornful laugh of modern materialists—had faith in the Resurrection been founded in the New Testament on such arguments as these! Tacitus, too, believed in the Phœnix; but Tacitus does not refer to the fable of its reappearance by way of founding on it an inestimable truth. We are not comparing St. Clement with Tacitus; we love his gentleness and respect his piety; we are only endeavouring to show how far he stands below the level of St. John and of St. Paul.

(c) But still more striking instances might be furnished of the theological and intellectual weakness of this ancient and saintly writer. He never deviates into originality except to furnish an illustration, and his illustrations, even when they are not erroneous, have but little intrinsic value. The worth of his Epistle consists in its earnest spirit, and in its historic testimony to the canonical Scriptures and to the constitution of the early Church. But how different is its diluted and transitional Paulinism from the force and wealth of the first Epistle of St. Peter!

(2) Nor is it otherwise when we turn to the exaggerated and extravagant Paulinism of THE EPISTLE OF BARNABAS. Here the inferiority is still more marked: it even leads to decadent doctrine and incipient heresy.

(a) The writer has learnt from St. Paul the nullity of the Law as a means of Salvation, but he has not learnt the true and noble function of the Law in the Divine economy. He cannot see that there may be even in that which is imperfect a *relative* perfection. He does not understand the Divine value of Mosaism as God's *education* of the human race. Not content with spiritualising the meaning of the Law, he speaks of its literal meaning in terms of such contempt as almost to compromise the authority of the Old Testament altogether. He ventures to say that the circumcision of the flesh was an inspiration of "an evil angel" (c. ix.). When a writer has gone so far as this, he is perilously near to actual Gnosticism. In his attempt to allegorise the distinction between clean and unclean animals (c. x.) he is seen at his very worst. A single chapter so full of errors and follies, if found in any canonical book, would have sufficed to drag down the authority of Scripture into the dust.

(b) Again, like the writer of the Epistle to the Hebrews, Barnabas —for that may have been his name, though he was not the Apostle—is acquainted with Alexandrian methods of exegesis. But his use of them is indiscriminate and unsatisfactory. The Israelites had been promised a land flowing with milk and honey; Barnabas proceeds to allegorise the promise as follows:—Adam was made of earth; the earth therefore signifies the Incarnation of Christ; milk and honey, which are suitable to infants, signify the new birth. Thus the Old Testament is a prophecy of the New! On this demonstration the author looks with such special complacency that he quotes it as a memorable example of true knowledge (*gnosis*).

(c) Again, the writer of the Epistle to the Hebrews had proved from Scripture that there still remains a Sabbath-rest (*Sabbatismos*) for the people of God. Barnabas connects this with what he calls an Etrurian tradition, and originates the notion that the world is to be burned up in the year 6000 after the Creation. Again, he has learnt the general conception of numerical exegesis (*gematria*) from Jewish and Alexandrian sources, and he is specially proud of pressing Abraham's 318 servants into a mystic prophecy of the Crucifixion, because 318 is represented by *IHT*, of which *IH* stands for Jesus, and *T* for the cross. This is a style of exegesis Rabbinic, but not Christian. No one can read the Epistle of Barnabas after the Epistle to the Hebrews without seeing that the former is not only immeasurably inferior, but that it is *so* inferior as to tremble on the verge of dangerous heresy. Let the reader compare the reference to the Day of Atonement in the Epistle of Barnabas (c. vii.) with that in the Epistle to the Hebrews—let him contrast the numerous errors and monstrously crude typology of the former with the splendid spiritualism of the latter—let him notice how tasteless are the fancies of this unknown Barnabas, and how absurd are many of his statements— and he will see the difference between canonical and uncanonical books, and learn to feel a deeper gratitude for the superintending Providence which, even in ages of ignorance and simplicity, obviated the danger of any permanent confusion between the former and the latter.[1]

We have already seen what the condition of the world was like, let us sum up its points of contrast with the general picture presented by the early Christian Church.

To represent the Christian Church as ideally pure, as stainlessly excellent and perfect, would be altogether a mistake. The Christians of the first days were men and women of like passions with ourselves. They sinned as we sin, and suffered as we suffer; they were inconsistent as we are inconsistent, fell as we fall, and repented as we repent. Hatred and party-spirit, rancour and misrepresentation, treachery and superstition, innovating audacity and unspiritual retrogressions were known among them as among us. And yet, with all their faults and failings, they were as salt amid the earth's corruption; the true light had shined in their hearts, and they were the light of the world. The lords of earth were such men as Tiberius and Caligula, and Nero and Domitian; the rulers of the Church were a James, a Peter, a Paul, a John. The literary men of the world were a Martial and a Petronius; the Church was producing the Apocalypse, the Epistle to the Hebrews, the Gospel of St. John. The art of the world was degraded by such infamous pictures as those on the walls of Pompeii; that of the Church consisted in the rude but pure and joyous emblems scrawled on the soft *tufa* of the catacombs. The amusements of the world were pitilessly sanguinary or shamefully corrupt; those of the Christians were found in gatherings at once social and religious, as bright as they could be made by the gaiety of innocent and untroubled hearts. In the world infanticide was infamously universal; in the Church the baptised little ones were treated as those whose angels beheld the face of our Father in Heaven. In the world slavery was rendered yet more intolerable by the cruelty and impurity of masters; in the Church the Christian

[1] The same result would follow from comparing the Shepherd of Hermas with the Apocalypse. On these writings we may refer to Reuss, *Théol. Chrét.* ii.; Hilgenfeld, *Apost. Väter*; Schwegler, *Nachap. Zeitalter*; Donaldson, *Apostolical Fathers*; Lightfoot, *St. Clement of Rome*; Pfleiderer, *Paulinismus*, ii.; Ritschl, *Altkath. Kirche*.

slave, welcomed as a friend and a brother, often holding a position of ministerial dignity, was emancipated in all but name. In the world marriage was detested as a disagreeable necessity, and its very meaning was destroyed by the frequency and facility of divorce; in the Church it was consecrated and honourable—the institution which had alone survived the loss of Paradise—and was all but sacramental in its Heaven-appointed blessedness. The world was settling into the sadness of unalleviated despair; the Church was irradiated by an eternal hope, and rejoicing with a joy unspeakable and full of glory. In the world men were "hateful and hating one another"; in the Church the beautiful ideal of human brotherhood was carried into practice. The Church had learnt her Saviour's lessons. A redeemed humanity was felt to be the loftiest of dignities; man was honoured for being simply man; every soul was regarded as precious, because for every soul Christ died; the sick were tended, the poor relieved; labour was represented as noble, not as a thing to be despised; purity and resignation, peacefulness and pity, humility and self-denial, courtesy and self-respect, were looked upon as essential qualifications for all who were called by the name of Christ. The Church felt that the innocence of her baptised members was her most irresistible form of apology; and all her best members devoted themselves to that which they regarded as a sacred task—the breaking down of all the middle walls of partition in God's universal temple, the obliteration of all minor and artificial distinctions, and the free development of man's spiritual nature.

CHAPTER VI.

ST. PETER.

'Εκκριτος ἦν τῶν Ἀποστόλων καὶ στόμα τῶν μαθητῶν καὶ κορυφὴ τοῦ χοροῦ.—
CHRYSOST. *in Joann*. Hom. 88.

THE early life of St. Peter cannot here be re-written, because in two previous works[1] I have followed the steps of his career so far as it is sketched in the sacred volume. After his youth as a poor and hardworked fisherman of the Lake of Galilee, we first find him as one of the hearers of St. John the Baptist in the wilderness of Jordan. Brought to Jesus by his brother Andrew, he at once accepted the Saviour's call, and received by anticipation that name of Kephas which he was afterwards to earn, partly by the stronger elements of his character, and partly by the grandeur of his Messianic confession. We have already tried to understand the significance of the scenes in

[1] *The Life of Christ*, 1874; *The Life of St. Paul*, 1879.

which he takes part. We have seen how he was called to active work and the abandonment of earthly ties after the miraculous draught of fishes. We have watched, step by step, the "consistently inconsistent" impetuosity of his character, at once brave and wavering—first brave, then wavering, but always finally recovering its courage and integrity.[1] The narrative of the Gospel has brought before us his attempt to walk to his Lord upon the water; his first public acknowledgment of Jesus as the Christ, the Son of the living God; the magnificent promises which, in his person, the Church received; the subsequent presumption, which his Lord so sternly rebuked; the many eager questions, often based upon mistaken notions, which he addressed to Christ, and which formed the occasion of some of our Lord's most striking utterances; the incident of the Temple contribution; the refusal and then the eagerness to be washed by Christ; the warnings addressed to him; the inability to "watch one hour"; the impetuous blow struck at the High Priest's servant; his forsaking of Christ in the hour of peril; his threefold denial; his bitter repentance and forgiveness; his visit to the Sepulchre; the message which he received from the Risen Saviour; the exquisite scene at morning, on the shores of the misty lake, when Jesus appeared once more to seven of His disciples, and when, having once more tested the love of His generous but unstable Apostle, He gave him His last special injunctions to tend His sheep and feed His lambs, and foretold to him his earthly end.

Similarly we have studied, in the narrative of the Acts of the Apostles, the leading part which he took in the early days after the death of Christ; his speech on the day of Pentecost; his miracles; his journey to Samaria and the discomfiture of Simon Magus; his kindness to St. Paul; his memorable vision at Joppa; his baptism of Cornelius; his bold initiative of living and eating with Gentiles who had received the gift of the Holy Ghost; the dauntlessness with which he faced the anger of the Jerusalem Pharisees; his imprisonment and deliverance, the manly outspokenness of his opinions in the Synod at Jerusalem, when he declared himself unhesitatingly in favour of the views of St. Paul as to the freedom of Gentile converts from the burden of Mosaic observances. At this point—about A.D. 51—he disappears from the narrative of the Acts. From this time forward he was overshadowed—at Jerusalem by the authority of James the Lord's brother, throughout the Gentile communities by the genius and energy of St. Paul. This was naturally due to his intermediate position between the extreme parties of Paulinists and Judaists. Among the scattered Christian communities of the Circumcision he maintained a high authority, although it is probable that Christian tradition has not erred in indicating that even among the Jewish Christians of the Dis-

[1] "Vrai contraste de pusillanimité et de grandeur, condamné à osciller toujours entre la faute et le repentir, mais rachetant glorieusement sa faiblesse par son humilité et ses larmes" (Thierry, *St. Jérôme*, i. 176).

persion St. James still occupied the leading position. All that we can further learn respecting him in Scripture is derived from his own Epistles, and from one or two casual but important allusions in the Epistles of St. Paul. In the Epistle to the Galatians we read the description of the memorable scene at Antioch, which produced upon the Church so deep an impression. Led away by the timidity which so strangely alternated with boldness in his character, St. Peter, on the arrival of emissaries from James, had suddenly dropped the familiar intercourse with Gentiles which up to that time he had maintained. Shocked by an inconsistency of which he would himself have been incapable, St. Paul, the younger convert, the former persecutor, was compelled by the call of duty publicly to withstand the great Apostle, who by his own conduct stood condemned for inconsistency, and had shown himself untrue to his own highest convictions. Further than this, we learn that the name of Peter was elevated at Corinth (A.D. 57) into a party watchword; and that he was engaged in missionary journeys, in which he was accompanied by a Christian sister, who (since we know that he was married) was in all probability his wife. From his own Epistles we learn almost nothing about his biography. Nearly every inference which we derive from them is precarious, even when it is intrinsically probable. He writes "to the elect sojourners of the Dispersion in Pontus, Galatia, Cappadocia, Asia, and Bithynia," but we cannot be certain that he had personally visited those countries.[1] The question whether his letter is addressed to the Jewish or the Gentile converts is one which still meets with the most contradictory, although at the same time the most confident, replies. He sends his letter by Silvanus; but we are not expressly told that this Silvanus is the previous companion of St. Paul. He sends a salutation from "Marcus my son"; but there is nothing to *prove* that Marcus was not his real son,[2] nor have we any certain information that he is referring to St. Mark the Evangelist. In these instances we may, however, accept the general consensus of Christian antiquity in favour of the affirmative suppositions.[3] If so, we see the deeply interesting fact that the chosen friends and companions of St. Peter were also the chosen friends and companions of St. Paul—a fact which eloquently refutes the modern supposition of the irreconcilable antagonism between the two Apostles and their Schools. But when we come to the closing salutation—"The

---

[1] That he had done so is simply an inference from 1 Pet. i. 1. Origen only says, "He *seems* to have preached there" (*ap.* Euseb. iii. 1). See Epiphan. *Haer.* xxvii.; Jerome, *Catal. s. v.* Petrus.

[2] St. Clemens of Alexandria says (*Strom.* iii., p. 448) that he had sons of his own, but their names are not preserved, and they were therefore probably unknown persons. Tradition tells of a daughter, Petronilla (*Acta Sanct.*, May 31).

[3] Some have supposed that an actual son of St. Peter's is meant, but Origen (*ap.* Euseb. *H. E.* vi. 25), Œcumenius, etc., are probably right in supposing that John Mark (Acts xii. 25), the Evangelist, is meant, especially as Papias, Clemens of Alexandria, Irenæus, and others, say that he was the follower, disciple, and interpreter of St. Paul (Euseb. *H. E.* iii. 39, vi. 14, etc.; Iren. *Haer.* iii. 11).

co-elect in Babylon saluteth you," the conclusions of each successive commentator are widely divergent. It is still disputed whether "the co-elect" is a Christian Church or a Christian woman; and if the latter, whether she is or is not Peter's wife; and whether Babylon is the great Assyrian capital or a metaphorical allusion to the great western Babylon—Imperial Rome.

Eminent as was the position of St. Peter,[1] the real details of the closing years of his life will never be known. But Christian tradition, acquiring definitiveness in proportion as it is removed from the period of which it speaks, has provided us with many details, which form the biography of the Apostle as it is ordinarily accepted by Romanists. We are told that he left Jerusalem in A.D. 33, and was for seven years Bishop of Antioch, leaving Euodius as his successor; that during this period he founded the Churches to which his letter is addressed; that he went to Rome in A.D. 40, and was bishop there for twenty-five years, though he constantly left the city for missionary journeys. The chief events of his residence at Rome were, according to legend, his conversion of Philo and of the Senator Pudens, with his two daughters, Praxedes and Pudentiana; and his public conflict with Simon Magus. The impostor, after failing to raise a dead youth—a miracle which St. Peter accomplished—finally attempted to delude the people by asserting that he would fly to heaven; but, at the prayer of St. Peter and St. Paul, he was deserted by the demons who supported him, and dashed bleeding to the earth.[2] During the Neronian persecution the Apostle is said to have yielded to the urgent requests of the Christians that he should escape from Rome; but when he had got a little beyond the Porta Capena he met the Lord carrying his cross, and asked him, "Lord, whither goest thou?" (*Domine, quo vadis?*) "I go to Rome," said Jesus, "to be crucified again for thee." The Apostle, feeling the force of the gentle rebuke, turned back, and was imprisoned in the Tullianum. He there converted his gaoler, miraculously causing a spring to burst out from the rocky floor for his baptism. On seeing his wife led to execution, he rejoiced at her "journey homewards,"[3] and, addressing her by name, called to her in a voice of cheerful encouragement, "Oh, remember the Lord!" He was executed on the same day as St. Paul. They parted on the Ostian Road, and St. Peter was then led to the top of the Janiculum, where he was crucified, not in the ordinary position,

---

[1] See Excursus I., on the Asserted Primacy of St. Peter.

[2] There seems to have been a similar legend about Balaam, dimly alluded to by the LXX. in the words ἐν τῇ ῥοπῇ, Josh. xiii. 22, and in the Targum of Jonathan, Num. xxxi. 8. See Frankl. *Vorstudien*, p. 187. For the whole legend of Simon Magus see Justin. Mart. *Apol.* ii. 69; Iren. *Haer.* i. 20; Tert. *Apol.* 13; Euseb. *H. E.* ii. 14; *Const. Apost.* vi. 8, 9; Arnob. *adv. Gentes*, ii.; Epiphan. *Haer.* xxi.; Sulp. Sev. ii.; Egesippus, *De Excid. Hieros.* iii. 2 (on Egesippus see Herzog, *s. v.* Heg.); Nicephorus, *H. E.* ii. 14; *Acta Petri et Pauli*; Ps. Abdias, *Acta Apost.* From these authors it is taken by Marcossius, *De Haereticis*, p. 444, and the Church historians.

[3] τῆς εἰς οἶκον ἀνακομιδῆς (Clem. Alex. *Strom.* vii.).

but, by his own request, head downwards, because he held himself unworthy to die in the same manner as his Lord.

In the whole of this legend, embellished as it is in current Martyrologies with many elaborate details, there is scarcely one single fact on which we can rely. For instance, the notion that Peter was ever Bishop at Antioch between the years A.D. 33—40 is inconsistent with clear statements in the narrative of the Acts, in which Paul and Barnabas appear as the leaders and virtual founders of that Gentile Church.[1] Again, if he had *founded* the Church of Rome, or had ever resided there *before* A.D. 64, it is inconceivable that neither St. Luke in the Acts, nor St. Paul in his Epistle to the Romans, nor again in the five letters which he wrote from Rome during his first and second imprisonments, should have made so much as the slightest allusion to him or to his work. The story of his collision with Simon Magus is a romance. It is founded on St. Peter's actual meeting with the sorcerer in Samaria, which is developed in the Clementines into a series of journeys from place to place, undertaken with the express view of thwarting this "founder of all the heresies." The legend is partly due to a mistake of Justin Martyr, who supposed that a statue dedicated to the Sabine god Semo Sancus[2] (of whom Justin had never heard) was reared in honour of "Simon Sanctus."[3] With these elements of confusion there is mixed up a malignant Ebionite attempt to calumniate St. Paul in a covert way under the pseudonym of Simon Magus, and to imply that St. Peter was at the head of a counter-mission to overthrow the supposed heretical teaching of his brother Apostle. The notion of this counter-mission is derived from the actual counter-mission of Judaists who falsely claimed the sanction of St. James.[4] The circumstance which suggested the legendary death of Simon in an attempt to fly was the actual death of an actor, who was dashed to the ground at Nero's feet while trying, by means of a flying machine, to sustain the part of Icarus.[5] If the youthful actor who was condemned to make this perilous attempt was a Christian, who would otherwise have been executed in some other way, we may well imagine that Christians would not soon forget an incident which sprinkled the very Antichrist with the blood of martyrs.[6] But it is possible that the legend may rest on small basis of fact. Rome abounded in Oriental thaumaturgists and impostors. Simon may have

---

[1] Acts xi. 19. [2] Ov. *Fast.* vi. 213; Prop. iv. 9, 74, &c.
[3] He was identified with *Dius Fidius*. The inscription was actually found in 1574, in the popedom of Gregory XIII., on an island in the Tiber, as Justin said. Justin, *Apol.* i. 26; Tert. *Apol.* 13; Baronius, *Annal.* ad an. 44; Gieseler, i. 49; Neander, ii. 162; Renan, *Les Apôtres*, pp. 275—277. In this island, now called "The Island of St. Bartholomew," there was a college of *Tridentales* in honour of Semo Sancus (Orelli *Inscr.*, 1860—61).
[4] Acts xv. 24.
[5] On this attempt to fly, see the commentators on Juv. *Sat.* viii. 186; Mart. *Spectac.* vii.; Suet. *Nero*, 12.
[6] "Icarus, primo statim conatu, juxta cubiculum ejus decidit ipsumque cruore respersit, Suet." *l.c.*

been attracted to a city which naturally drew to itself all the villainy of the world, and there he may once more have encountered St. Peter.[1] But if they met at Rome, all the details of their meeting have been disguised under a mixture of vague reminiscences and imaginary details.

The assertion that Peter was Bishop of Rome, but that he constantly left it to exercise apostolic oversight throughout the world, is nothing but an ingenious theory.[2] The statement that he came to Rome in the reign of Claudius, A.D. 42, is first found in the *Chronicon* of Eusebius, nearly three centuries afterwards, and cannot be reconciled with fair inferences from what St. Paul tells us about the Church. As late as A.D. 52, St. Peter was at Jerusalem, and took an active part in the Synod of Jerusalem (Acts xv. 7); and he was then labouring mainly among the Jews (Gal. ii. 7, 9). In A.D. 57 he was travelling as a missionary with his wife (1 Cor. ix. 5). He was not at Rome when St. Paul wrote to that Church in A.D. 58, nor when St. Paul came there as a prisoner in A.D. 61, nor during the years of St. Paul's imprisonment, A.D. 61—63, nor when he wrote his last Epistles, A.D. 66 and 67. If he was ever at Rome at all, which we hold to be almost certain, from the unanimity of the tradition, it could only have been very briefly before his martyrdom.[3] And this is, in fact, the assertion of Lactantius[4] († 330), who says that he first came to Rome in Nero's reign; and of Origen († 254), who says that he arrived there at the close of his life;[5] and of the *Praedicatio Petri*, printed with the works of St. Cyprian.[6] His "bishopric" at Rome probably consisted only in his efforts about the time of his martyrdom to strengthen the faith of the Church,[7] and especially of the Jewish Christians. Indeed, there is much to be said in favour of the view that the Jewish and Gentile sections of the Church in Rome were separated by unusually deep divisions, and possessed their separate "presbyters" or "bishops" for some years. Such a fact would account for some confusion in the names of the first two or three Bishops of Rome. Eusebius—following Irenæus and Epiphanius—says that the first Bishops of Rome were Peter, Linus, Cletus or Anencletus, and Clement.[8] But Hippolytus (A.D. 225) seems to regard Cletus and Anencletus as two different persons, and places

---

[1] As asserted in Justin, *Apol.* L 26, 56; Iren. *contra Haer.* i. 23, § 1; *Philosophumena*, vi. 20; *Constt. Apost.* v.; Euseb. *H. E.* ii. 13, 14, etc.

[2] It was first suggested by Baronius (*Annal.* ad. an. 39, § 25) and Fr. Windischmann (*Vindiciae Petrinae*, p. 112), and hastily adopted by Thiersch (*N. Test. Canon*, p. 104).

[3] This view is now accepted by Roman Catholics like Valesius, Pagi, Baluz, Hug, Klee, Döllinger, Waterworth, Allnatt. See Waterworth, *Engl. and Rome*, ii.; Allnatt, *Cathedra Petri*, p. 114. The Roman Catholic historian Alzog only speaks of the twenty-five years' episcopate as an ancient report (i. 104).

[4] Lactant. *De Mort. Persec.* 2.

[5] Origen *ap.* Euseb. *H. E.* iii. 1.

[6] Cypriani, *Opp.*, p. 139, ed. Rigalt.

[7] Clemens Romanus, third bishop of Rome, speaks even more of St. Paul than of St. Peter (*Ep. ad Cor.* v.).

[8] Euseb. *H. E.* iii. 2, 4, and 21; Iren. *ap.* Euseb. *H. E.* v. 6.

Clement before Cletus; and Tertullian († 218) says that Clement was ordained by St. Peter.[1]

The notion of the Apostle's crucifixion head downwards is derived from a passing allusion in Origen, and seems to contradict an expression of Tertullian.[2] It was possibly suggested by an erroneous translation of some Latin expression for capital punishment. At any rate, it stands condemned as a sentimental anachronism, bearing on its front the traces of later and more morbid forms of piety rather than the simple humility of the Apostles, who rejoiced in all things to imitate their Lord.[3] Those who accept these legends must do so on the authority of an heretical novel, written with an evil tendency, not earlier than the beginning of the third century; or else on that of the apocryphal *Acta Petri et Pauli*, which appeared at a still later date. All that we can *really* learn about the closing years of St. Peter from the earliest Fathers may be summed up in the few words, that in all probability he was martyred at Rome.[4]

That he died by martyrdom may be regarded as certain, because, apart from tradition, it seems to be implied in the words of the Risen Christ to His penitent Apostle.[5] That this martyrdom took place at Rome, though first asserted by Tertullian and Gaius at the beginning of the third century, may (in the absence of any rival tradition) be accepted as a fact, in spite of the ecclesiastical tendencies which might have led to its invention; but the only *Scriptural* authority which can be quoted for any visit of St. Peter to Rome is the one word, "The Church in *Babylon* saluteth you."[6]

If, as I endeavour to show in the Excursus, there is reasonable certainty that Babylon is here used as a sort of cryptograph for Rome, the fair inferences from Scripture accord with the statements of tradition in the two simple particulars that St. Peter was martyred, and that this martyrdom took place at Rome. These inferences agree well with the probability that Silvanus, of whom we last hear in company with St. Paul at Corinth, and St. Mark, for whose assistance St. Paul had wished during his Roman imprisonment, were also at Rome, and were now acting in conjunction with the great Apostle of the Circumcision. The belief that St. Mark acted as the "interpreter" (ἑρμηνευτὴς) of St. Peter may have arisen from the Apostle's ignorance of the Latin language, and his need of some one to be his spokesman during his residence and his legal trial in the imperial city.

---

[1] Tert. *De Praesc. Haeret.* 32.
[2] "Ubi Petrus *passioni dominicae adaequatur*," *De Praesc.* 36.
[3] Neander, *Planting.* p. 377. It is curious to watch the growth of this fiction. It begins with Origen, who simply says that it was done "at his own choice" (ap. Euseb. *H. E.* iii. 1). To this Rufinus adds, "that he might not seem to be equalled to his Lord" (ne exaequari Domino videretur), which contradicts the saying of Tertullian, that "he was equalled to his Lord in the manner of his death." Lastly, St. Jerome says that he was crucified with his head towards the earth and his legs turned upwards, "asserting that he was unworthy to be crucified in the same way as his Lord" (*De Vir. Illustr.* 1).
[4] See Excursus II., on St. Peter's Visit to Rome.   [5] John xxi. 19.
[6] See Excursus III., on the Use of the Name Babylon for Rome,

CHAPTER VII.

SPECIAL FEATURES OF THE FIRST EPISTLE OF ST. PETER.

"Then all himself, all joy and calm,
Though for a while his hand forego,
Just as it touched, the martyr's palm,
He turns him to his task below."—KEBLE.

THE previous chapter has led us to conclude that the First Epistle of St. Peter was written at Rome. The *date* at which it was written cannot be fixed with certainty. The outburst of the Neronian persecution took place in A.D. 64, but it is difficult to suppose that St. Peter arrived accidentally in Rome on the very eve of the conflagration. It seems more probable that he was either brought there as a prisoner, or went to support the Jewish Christians during the subsequent pressure of their terrible afflictions.[1] In that case he wrote the First Epistle shortly before his death, and he must have been martyred in the year 67 or 68, about the same time as his great brother-Apostle, St. Paul, with whom he is always united in the earliest traditions.

That the First Epistle of St. Peter is genuine—a precious relic of the thoughts of one of Christ's most honoured Apostles—we may feel assured. Its authenticity is supported by overwhelming external evidence. The *Second* Epistle, whether genuine or not, is at any rate a very ancient document, and it unhesitatingly testifies to the genuineness of the first. "The First Epistle is," says M. Renan, "one of the writings of the New Testament which are the most anciently and the most unanimously cited as authentic." Papias, Polycarp, Irenæus, Clement of Alexandria, Tertullian, and Origen,[2] all furnish indisputable evidence in its favour.[3] The proof that the writer was influenced by the Epistle to the Ephesians is in accordance with the character of the age, for the early Christians, as was perfectly natural, were in the habit of echoing one another's thoughts. Modern writers

---

[1] St. Paul seems to have been absent from Rome for two full years before his second imprisonment, and during this time the Christians must still have been liable to oppression and martyrdom, even after the first attack upon them had spent its fury. Tertullian asserts that laws were for the first time promulgated against the Christians by Nero, which rendered Christianity a "*religio illicita*" (ad *Natt.* 74; *Apol.* 5; Sulp. Sev. *Hist.* ii. 29, § 3). This is rendered very doubtful by Pliny's letter to Trajan.

[2] See Euseb. *H. E.* iii. 25, 39; iv. 14, v. 8, vi. 25; Polycarp, *Ep. ad Philip.*; Iren. *contra Haer.* iv. 9, § 2; Clem. Alex. *Strom.* iii. 8, iv. 7; Tert. *Scorp.* 12. Besides this, there are many distinct allusions to it in the Epistle of St. Clement to the Corinthians. Little importance, therefore, can be attached to its absence from the Muratorian Canon, and its rejection by Theodore of Mopsuestia.

[3] Keim (*Rom und Christenthum*, p. 194), without deigning to offer a reason, assigns it to the time of Trajan. In this he follows Hilgenfeld.

do exactly the same. The words and thoughts of every writer who makes any wide or serious impression are, consciously or unconsciously, adopted by others exactly as if they were original and independent; and this is true to such an extent that an author's real success is often obliterated by its very universality. The views which he originated come to be regarded as commonplace, simply because all his contemporaries have adopted them. But this was still more the case in days when books were very few in number. The writings of the Apostles are marked by mutual resemblances, and the works of men like Ignatius, and Polycarp, and Clement of Rome, consist in large measure of a mosaic of phrases which they have caught up from their predecessors.

The style of St. Peter in this Epistle resembles in many particulars the style of his recorded speeches. It is characterised by the fire and energy which we should expect to find in his forms of expression; but that energy is tempered by the tone of Apostolic dignity, and by the fatherly mildness of one who was now aged, and was near the close of a life of labour. He speaks with authority, and yet with none of the threatening sternness of St. James. We find in the letter the plain and forthright spirit of the man insisting again and again on a few great leading conceptions. The subtle dialectics, the polished irony, the involved thoughts, the lightning-like rapidity of inference and suggestion, which we find in the letters of the Apostle of the Uncircumcision, are wholly wanting in him. His casual connexions, marking the natural and even flow of his thoughts, are of the simplest character; and yet a vigorously practical turn of mind, a quick susceptibility of influence, and a large catholicity of spirit, such as we know that he possessed, are stamped upon every page. He aims throughout at practical exhortation, not at systematic exposition; and his words, in their force and animation, reflect the simple, sensuous, and passionate nature of the impulsive Simon of whom we read in the Gospels. Even if the external evidence in favour of the Epistle had been less convincing, the arguments on which its authenticity has been questioned by a few modern theologians have been so amply refuted as to establish its authorship with completer certainty.

1. It is not so much a letter as a treatise, addressed to Christians in general. It is mainly hortative, and its exhortations are founded on Christian hope, and on the effects of the death of Christ. It is not, however, a *scholastic* treatise, but rather a practical address, at once conciliatory in tone and independent in character. It may with equal truth be called Pauline and Judæo-Christian. It is Judæo-Christian in its sympathies, yet without any Judaic bitterness. It is Pauline in its expressions, yet with no polemic purpose. In both respects it accords with the character and circumstances of the great Apostle. It is completely silent about the Law, and enters into none of the once vehement controversies about the relation of the Law to the Gospel

or of Faith to Works. There is no predetermined attempt to reconcile opposing parties, but all party watchwords are either impartially omitted, or are stripped of their sterner antitheses.[1]

2. One proof that it was written by St. Peter results from the natural way in which we can trace the influence of the most prominent events which occurred during his association with his Lord.[2] He does not mention them; he does not even in any marked way refer to them; and yet we find in verse after verse the indication of subtle reminiscences such as *must* have lingered in the mind of St. Peter. Christ had said to him, "Thou art Peter, and on this rock will I build my Church," and he speaks of Christ as "a rock," the corner-stone of a spiritual house, and of Christians as living stones built into it. Christ had sternly reproved him when he made himself a stumbling-block, and he sees how perilous it is to turn the Lord's will into a rock of offence,[3] using the two very words which lie at the heart of those two consecutive moments which had been the crisis of his life.[4] When he had rashly pledged his Master to pay the Temple didrachm, our Lord had indeed accepted the obligation, but at the same time had taught him that the children were free; and St. Peter here teaches the Churches that, though free, they were still to submit for the Lord's sake to every human ordinance.[5] Bound by the quantitative conceptions of Jewish formalism, he had once asked whether he was to forgive his brother up to seven times, and had been told he was to forgive him up to seventy times seven; and he has so well learnt the lesson as to tell his converts that "Love shall cover the *multitude* of sins."[6] In answer to his too unspiritual question, "what reward the Apostles should have for having forsaken all to follow Christ," he had heard the promise that they should sit on thrones; and throughout this Epistle his thoughts are full of the future glory and of its "amaranthine crown."[7] He had heard Jesus compare the "days of Noah" to the days of the Son of Man,[8] and his thoughts dwell so earnestly upon the comparison that he uses the expression in a way which unintentionally limits the fulness of his revelation.[9] He had seen his Lord strip off His upper garment and tie a towel round his waist, when, with marvellous self-abasement, he stooped to wash His Disciples' feet;[10] hence, when he wishes to impress the lesson of humility, he is led insensibly to the intensely picturesque expression

---

[1] See Schwegler, *Nachap. Zeitalt.* ii. 22; Pfleiderer, *Paulinism.* ii. 150, E. T.
[2] Matt. xvi. 18; 1 Pet. ii. 4—8. This peculiarity of the Epistle has been worked out and illustrated by no one so fully or with such delicate insight as by Dean Plumptre in his edition of the Epistle in the Cambridge Bible for schools, p. 13, *seq.*
[3] 1 Pet. ii. 8, πέτρα σκανδάλου.
[4] Matt. xvi. 18, ἐπὶ ταύτῃ τῇ πέτρᾳ; 23, σκάνδαλόν μου εἶ.
[5] Matt. xvii. 24—27; 1 Pet. ii. 13—16. [6] Matt. xviii. 22; 1 Pet. iv. 8.
[7] Matt. xix. 28; 1 Pet. i. 5, v. 4. [8] Matt. xxiv. 37.
[9] Compare 1 Pet. iii. 20 with iv. 6.
[10] John xiii. 1—6.

that they should "tie on humility like a dress fastened with knots."[1] Perhaps, too, from that washing, and the solemn lessons to which it led, he gained his insight into the true meaning of Baptism, as being not the putting away the filth of the flesh, but the intercourse of a good conscience with its God.[2] At a very solemn moment of his life Christ had told him that Satan had desired to have him and the other Apostles, that he might sift them as wheat,[3] and he warns the Church of the prowling activity and power of the Devil, using respecting him the word "adversary" (ἀντίδικος), which occurs nowhere else in the Epistles, but more than once in the sayings of the Lord.[4] Again and again on the last evening of the life of Christ he had been bidden to watch and pray, and had fallen because he had not done so; and watchfulness is a lesson on which he most earnestly insists.[5] He had been one of the few faithful eye-witnesses of the buffets and weals inflicted on Christ in His sufferings, and of His silence in the midst of reviling, and to these striking circumstances he makes a very special reference.[6] He had seen the Cross uplifted from the ground with its awful burden, and respecting that cross he uses a very peculiar expression.[7] He had heard Jesus warn Thomas of the blessedness of those who having not seen yet believed, and he quotes almost the very words.[8] He had been thrice exhorted to tend and feed Christ's sheep, and the pastoral image is prominent in his mind and exhortations.[9] Lastly, he had been specially bidden when converted to strengthen his brethren, and this from first to last is the avowed object of his present letter.[10]

3. Again we recognise the true St. Peter by the extreme vividness of his expressions. It has been a unanimous tradition in the Church that the minute details recorded by St. Mark are due to the fact that he wrote from information given him by St. Peter. Picturesqueness is as evidently a characteristic of the mind of St. Peter as it is of the mind of St. Mark. In St. Mark it is shown by touches of graphic description, in St. Peter by words which are condensed metaphors.[11]

4. Such is the close analogy between the thoughts and expressions of the Epistle and those which the Gospel story of the writer would have

---

[1] 1 Pet. v. 5, ἐγκομβώσασθε.
[2] 1 Pet. iii. 21. For the "answer" of the A. V. the Revised Version suggests "interrogation," "appeal," "inquiry," v. infra, p. 75. The verb ἐπερωτᾶν is common in the Gospels, and always means "to ask further," but the substantive does not occur elsewhere in the New Testament.
[3] Luke xxii. 31. Here the *common* danger of the Apostles, "Satan has desired to have *you* (ὑμᾶς), ... but I have prayed for *thee* (σε)," is restored by the Revised Version.
[4] 1 Pet. v. 8; Matt v 25; Luke xii. 58, xviii. 3. [5] 1 Pet. v. 8, seq.
[6] 1 Pet. ii. 20, κολαφιζόμενοι; 23, οὐκ ἀντελοιδόρει; 24, οὗ τῷ μώλωπι αὐτοῦ.
[7] 1 Pet. ii. 24, ἀνήνεγκεν ἐν τῷ σώματι ἐπὶ τὸ ξύλον. V. infra, p. 71.
[8] 1 Pet. i. 8.   [9] 1 Pet. ii. 25, v. 2.   [10] 1 Pet. v. 12.
[11] 1 Pet. ii. 2, "guileless, unadulterated milk;" iv. 4, "outpouring" (excess of riot); iv. 15, "other-people's-bishop" (busybody in other men's matters).

led us to expect. Nor is the resemblance between the speeches of the St. Peter of the Acts and the style of the St. Peter of the Epistle less striking. As in the Acts so in the Epistle, he refers to Isaiah's metaphor of the rejected corner-stone;[1] in both the witness of the Holy Ghost is prominent;[2] in both he speaks of the Cross as "the tree";[3] in both he dwells on the position of the Apostles as "witnesses;"[4] in both he puts forward the death of Christ as the fulfilment of prophecy;[5] in both the Resurrection is made the main ground of faith and hope;[6] in both we find special mention of God as the Judge of quick and dead;[7] in both the exhortation to repentance is based on the fact of man's redemption;[8] lastly, in both, as a matter of style, there is a prevalence of simple relatival connexions, and as a matter of doctrine there is the representation of God as one who has no respect for persons.[9]

5. Is it not, further, a very remarkable circumstance that in the Acts St. Peter, in one of his outbursts of impetuous boldness, ventures to call the Law "a yoke which neither our fathers nor we were strong enough to bear;" and in the Epistle—though he was a Jew, though he was closely allied to St. James in many of his sympathies, though he strongly felt the influence of the Pharisaic Christians at Jerusalem, though he borrows the symbols of the theocracy to a marked extent[10]— does not so much as once mention or allude to the Mosaic Law at all ? Even if any of these peculiarities standing alone could be regarded as accidental, their aggregate force is very considerable; nor do we think it possible that a forger—even if a forger could otherwise have produced such an epistle as this—could have combined in one short composition so many instances of subtle verisimilitude.[11]

6. A very remarkable feature of the Epistle, and one which must have great prominence in leading us to a conclusion about its date, characteristics, and object, is the *extent* to which the writer has felt the influence both of St. James and of St. Paul.[12] No one can compare the

[1] 1 Pet. ii. 7; Acts iv. 11. [2] 1 Pet. i. 12; Acts v. 32.
[3] 1 Pet. ii. 24; Acts v. 30, x. 39.
[4] 1 Pet. i. 8, v. 1; Acts ii. 32, iii. 15, x. 41.
[5] 1 Pet. i. 10; Acts iii. 18, x. 43.
[6] 1 Pet. i. 3, 4, 21, iii. 21; Acts ii. 32—36, iii. 15, iv. 10, x. 40.
[7] 1 Pet. iv. 5; Acts x. 42.
[8] 1 Pet. ii. 24; Acts iii. 19—26. [9] 1 Pet. i. 17; Acts x. 2.
[10] 1 Pet. i. 2 ("sprinkling"), 18—20, ii. 9, 10 (Ex. xix. 5, 6).
[11] To these might be added 1 Pet. i. 13 ("girding up the loins of your mind"), compared with Luke xii. 35; i. 12, "to stoop and look" (παρακύψαι), compared with Luke xxiv. 12; ii. 15, "to put to silence" (φιμοῦν), compared with Luke iv. 35; and the use of the word σκολιὸς (ii. 18), as compared with his use of the same word in his recorded speech (Acts ii. 40).
[12] I pass over as very possibly accidental and independent the few points of resemblance between the language of St. Peter and St. John (cf. 1 Pet. ii. 19, 22 with 1 John i. 7, iii. 3, iv. 11, and 1 Pet. ii. 9 with Rev. i. 6); nor do I think that much importance can be attached to the few coincidences between 1 Pet. and Hebrews (e.g., 1 Pet. i. 2 and Heb. ix. 13; 1 Pet. ii. 2 and Heb. v. 12, etc.). I regard the attempt of Weiss, in his elaborate *Petrinische Lehrbegriff*, to prove the early date of the Epistle, and the indebtedness of St. Paul to its expressions, as misleading and untenable,

number and peculiarity of the identical expressions adduced in the note, without the conviction that they can only be accounted for by the influence of the earlier writers on the later. At this epoch, both among Jews and Christians, there was a free adaptation of phraseology which had come to be regarded as a common possession. That St. Peter has here been the conscious or unconscious borrower may be regarded as certain, alike on chronological and on psychological considerations. If the Epistle was written from Rome, we see the strongest reasons to conclude that it was written later than the Epistle to the Ephesians, and therefore after the death of St. James. The manner in which St. Peter writes shows that he is often accepting the phraseology of others, but infusing into their language a somewhat different shade of meaning. When we consider the extreme plasticity of St. Peter's nature, the emotional impressiveness and impetuous receptivity which characterise his recorded acts; when we remember, too, that it was his habit to approach all subjects on the practical and not on the speculative side, and to think the less of distinctions in the form of holding the common faith, because his mind was absorbed in the contemplation of that glorious Hope of which he is pre-eminently the Apostle,—we find an additional reason for accepting the Epistle as genuine. We see in it the simple, unsystematic, practical synthesis of the complementary—but not contradictory—truths insisted on alike by St. Paul and St. James. St. Peter dwells more exclusively than St. Paul on moral duties; he leans more immediately than St. James on Gospel truths.

7. There is no material difficulty in his acquaintance with these writings of his illustrious contemporaries. Among the small Christian

---

if not as "altogether futile" (Pfleiderer, *Paulinism*. ii. 150). He has found very few followers in his opinion. The resemblances are mainly to the Epistles to the Romans and Ephesians:—

1 Pet. i. 1	Eph. i. 4—7	
1 Pet. i. 3	Eph. i. 3	
1 Pet. i. 14	Eph. ii. 3	
1 Pet. ii. 6—10		Rom. xii. 2
1 Pet. ii. 11		Rom. ix. 25—32
1 Pet. ii. 13		Rom. vii. 23
1 Pet. ii. 18	Eph. vi. 5	Rom. xiii. 1—4
1 Pet. iii. 1	Eph. v. 22	
1 Pet. iii. 9		Rom. xvi. 17
1 Pet. iii. 22	Eph. i. 20	Rom. viii. 34
1 Pet. iv. 1		Rom. vi. 6
1 Pet. iv. 10		Rom. xii. 6
1 Pet. v. 1		Rom. viii. 18
1 Pet. v. 5	Eph. v. 21	

The chief resemblances between St. Peter and St. James will be found in the following passages:—

1 Pet. i. 6—7	James i. 2—4
1 Pet. i. 24	James i. 10
1 Pet. iv. 8	James v. 20
1 Pet. v. 5, 9	James iv. 6, 7, 10

The supposed parallels between the Epistle and those to Timothy and Titus are not real parallels, but arise from similarity of subject (1 Pet. iii. 1, v. 1, *seq*.). There is nothing in these similarities to discredit the authenticity of the Epistle, and the absence of Johannine phrases is another proof of its antiquity.

communities the letters of the Apostles were eagerly distributed. The Judaists would have been sure to supply St. Peter with the letter of the saintly Bishop of Jerusalem; and such companions as Mark and Silvanus, both of whom had lived in intimate relationship with St. Paul, and of whom the former had been expressly mentioned in the Epistle to the Colossians, could not have failed to bring to St. Peter's knowledge the sublimest and most heavenly of the Epistles of St. Paul. The antagonism in which St. James and St. Paul had been arrayed by their hasty followers would have acted with St. Peter as an additional reason for using indiscriminately the language of them both. It was time that the bitterness of controversies should cease, now that the Church was passing through the fiery storm of its first systematic persecution. It was time that the petty differences within the fold should be forgotten when the howling wolves were leaping into its enclosure from without. The suffering Christians needed no impassioned arguments or eager dialectics; they mainly needed to be taught the blessed lessons of resignation and of hope. These are the key-notes of St. Peter's Epistle.[1] As they stood defenceless before their enemies, he points them to the patient and speechless anguish of the Lamb of God.[2] Patient endurance in the present would enable them to set an example even to their enemies; the hope of the future would change their very sorrows into exultant triumph.[3] In the great battle which had been set in array against them, Hope should be their helmet and Innocence their shield.[4]

8. And yet in teaching to his readers these blessed lessons St. Peter by no means loses his own originality. The distinctions between the three Apostles—distinctions between their methods rather than their views—may be seen at a glance. They become salient when we observe that whereas St. James barely alludes to a single event in the life of Christ, St. Peter makes every truth and exhortation hinge on His example, His sufferings, His Cross, His Resurrection, and His exaltation;[5] and that whereas St. Peter is greatly indebted to the Epistle to the Romans, he yet makes no use of St. Paul's central doctrine of Justification by Faith. Thus even when he is influenced by his predecessor's phraseology, he is occupied with somewhat different conceptions. The two Apostles hold, indeed, the same truths, but, to the eternal advantage of the Church, they express them differently. Antagonism between them there was none; but they were mutually independent. The originality of St. Peter is not only demonstrated by the sixty isolated expressions (*hapax legomena*) of his short Epistle, but also by his modification of many of St. Paul's thoughts in accordance with his own immediate spiritual gift. That gift was the $\chi\acute{\alpha}\rho\iota\sigma\mu\alpha$ $\kappa\nu\beta\epsilon\rho\nu\acute{\eta}\sigma\epsilon\omega s$—

---

[1] *Resignation*, 1 Pet. i. 6, ii. 13—25, iii. 1, 9—12, 17, 18, iv. 1—4, v. 6; *Hope*, 1 Pet. i. 4, 12, 13, iv. 6, 7, v. 1, 4, 6, 10, 11.
[2] 1 Pet. i. 19, ii. 22—25. [3] *Joy*, 1 Pet. i. 6, 8, iv. 13, 14.
[4] *Innocence*, 1 Pet. i. 13—16, 22, ii. 1, 2, 11, 12, iii. 13, 16, 21, iv. 15.
[5] 1 Pet. i. 3, 7, 13, iii. 22, iv. 11, 13.

that power of administrative wisdom which made his example so valuable to the Infant Church. It was worthy of his high position and authority to express the common practical consciousness of the Christian Church in a form which avoided party disagreements. The views of St. Paul are presented by St. Peter in their every-day bearing rather than in their spiritual depths; and in their moral, rather than their mystical significance. St. Peter adopts the views of his great brother Apostles, but he clothes them in simpler and in conciliatory terms.[1] And if these phenomena, from their very delicacy, constitute an almost irresistible proof of the genuineness of the Epistle, how decisive is the evidence which they furnish that there was none of that deadly opposition between the adherents of Kephas and of Paul which has been assumed as the true key to the Apostolic history! How certain is it that "the wretched caricature of an Apostle, a thing of shreds and patches, which struts and fumes through those Ebionite romances, would not have been likely to write with thoughts and phrases essentially Pauline flowing from his pen at every turn."[2]

9. It is important and interesting to illustrate still more fully this *indebted yet independent attitude* of the Apostle; this tone at once receptive and original, at once firm and conciliatory, by which he was so admirably qualified to be the Apostle of Catholicity.[3]

i. We see it at once in the language which he uses about *Redemption*. St. Peter, of course, held, as definitely as St. Paul, that "Christ suffered for sin, once for all, the just on behalf of the unjust;"[4] that "He Himself, in His own body, took up our sins on to the cross;"[5] that we were "ransomed with the precious blood as of a lamb blameless and spotless, even of Christ."[6] But divine truth is many-sided and infinite; and whereas St. Paul mainly dwells on the death of Christ as delivering us from the Law, and from the curse of the Law, and from a state of guilt, St. Peter speaks of it mainly as a liberation from actual immorality;[7] a ransom from an empty, traditional, earthly mode of life;[8] a means of abandoning sins and living to righteousness:—and these are to him the consequences which are specially involved in that more general conception that Christ died "to lead us to God."[9] And besides this different

---

[1] 1 Pet. i. 12, 25, v. 12 (comp. 1 Cor. xv. 1).
[2] Plumptre, *St. Peter*, p. 72.
[3] Weiss's *Lehrbegriff* is entirely vitiated by his capricious effort to make out that St. Peter was the original author of the thoughts which he adopted from others.
[4] 1 Pet. iii. 18, περὶ ἁμαρτιῶν . . . ὑπὲρ ἀδίκων.
[5] 1 Pet. ii. 24; on this difficult verse, *vide infra*, p. 91.
[6] 1 Pet. i. 18, 19.
[7] 1 Pet. i. 18, ἐκ τῆς ματαίας ἀναστροφῆς πατροπαραδότου.
[8] 1 Pet. ii. 24, ἵνα ταῖς ἁμαρτίαις ἀπογενόμενοι τῇ δικαιοσύνῃ ζήσωμεν. Mark alike the resemblance to, and the difference from, the words of the discourse which the Apostle had heard from the lips of St. Paul at a moment of deep personal humiliation (Gal. ii. 19, 20), "for I, through the Law, died unto the Law that I might live unto God. I have been crucified with Christ; yet I live." We have in St. Peter the essential Pauline thought without the intensity of the Pauline expression.
[9] 1 Pet. iii. 18; *cf.* Rom. v. 2; Eph. ii. 18; Heb. x. 19.

aspect of the object of the death of Christ, the *means* by which that object is effected are also contemplated from a different point of view. In St. Paul's theology the Christian so closely partakes in the death of Christ that, by that death, the flesh—the carnal principle of all sin—is slain within him;[1] the old man is crucified with Christ, and the new man, the hidden man of the heart, the spiritual nature, lives the life of Christ by mystical union with Him. Now, St. Peter uses expressions which at once remind us of those used by St. Paul, but he uses them with a different scope. He too speaks of "a communion with the sufferings of Christ,"[2] but it is only in the *literal* sense of suffering;[3] and he never distinctly touches on (though he may doubtless assume and presuppose) the mystery of the Christian's identity with, incorporation with, the life and death of the Saviour. Christ's sufferings are set forth as producing their effect by the moral power of example, so that His life of suffering and obedience is as the *copy* over which we are to write, the *track* in which we are to walk; and so we are to be released from sin by the imitation of Christ.[4] "He that hath died," says St. Paul, "hath been justified from sin,"[5] meaning by this that he who by baptism (vi. 4) has been buried with Christ into His death, has also by baptism risen with Him into a new life of communion, in which God's righteousness has become man's justification. St. Paul means, in fact, all the deep truth which he sets forth mystically in Rom. vi. 1—15, and which he explains through the remainder of that chapter by more popular metaphors. Now, St. Peter, in words which are doubtless an echo of St. Paul's language, says that "he who hath suffered in the flesh hath ceased from sin;"[6] but the practical intellect of St. Peter had no resemblance to the deeper genius of St. Paul, and the meaning of *his* words, as developed in the following verses, is simply the truth that the suffering life of the Christian has in it all the blessedness of trial; and that, just as the luxury and surfeit of heathen life (verse 3) is essentially a state of sin, so the trials borne by the Christian warrior who is armed with the mind of Christ, naturally put an end to the seductiveness of sin. St. Paul dwells most on deliverance from *guilt*, St. Peter on deliverance from *sin*. With St. Paul the death of Christ is the means of expiation; with St. Peter it is more prominently a motive of amendment. St. Paul, in Rom. vi. 1—15, writes like a profound theologian. St. Peter, in iv. 1—4, is using the simpler language of a practical Christian. The union between the Christian and the death of Christ, in St. Paul is an *inner* union. In St. Peter the connexion is more outward—a connexion which rather invites our obedience than modifies our inmost nature.[7]

ii. We shall see similar differences in the use of other words. *Faith*,

---

[1] Rom. vi. 12—14, viii. 3; Gal. v. 24; 2 Cor. v. 14.
[2] 1 Pet. iv. 13.   [3] As in Rom. viii. 13.
[4] See Rom. vi. 1; 1 Peter ii. 21, Χριστὸς ἔπαθεν ὑπὲρ ὑμῶν, ὑμῖν ὑπολιμπάνων ὑπογραμμὸν ἵνα ἐπακολουθήσητε τοῖς ἴχνεσιν αὐτοῦ, with the context of these passages.
[5] Rom. vi. 7.   [6] 1 Pet. iv. 1.   [7] See Reuss, *Théol. Chrét.* ii. 300.

for instance, is a prominent word with St. Peter,[1] but neither he nor any other writer of the New Testament uses it in that unique and transcendent sense which is peculiar to St. Paul. With St. Paul, as we have already seen, it comes to mean an absolute *oneness with Christ*.[2] St. Peter, like the author of the Epistle to the Hebrews, and like St. Clement, uses it as "the substance of things which are hoped for—the conviction of unseen realities."[3] It is, in fact, "a confidence in the promises of God."[4] It is hence nearly allied to Hope. In the Epistle to the Romans the main object of faith is God's redeeming favour evidenced by Christ's death ;[5] in St. Peter faith is mainly directed to the future salvation, of which Christ's resurrection is a pledge, and to which His sufferings are a means. And although St. Peter dwells so much on good works, that "to do good" (ἀγαθοποιεῖν) occurs no less than nine times in his Epistle,[6] yet he is not in the least endeavouring to prove any theory of Justification by works, but simply regards good works as St. Paul does—namely, as the natural issue of the Christian calling. Nor, when he speaks of *fear*, in i. 17,[7] is there intended to be any opposition to Rom. viii. 15,[8] any more than there is in 1 John iv. 18.[9] The "fear" spoken of by St. Peter is only a fear of falling away from grace. There is no contradiction between the Apostles, but there is a different gleam in their presentation of the "many-coloured wisdom"[10] of God.

iii. Again, we see a difference respecting *Regeneration* and *Baptism*, and here once more St. Peter's view is predominantly moral and general, St. Paul's is mystic and dogmatic. Regeneration with St. Paul means a new creation, the beginning of a life which is not the human and individual life, but which is "Christ in us." But St. Peter, like St. James, regards this new birth as produced by the living and abiding *word* of God, producing the purification which springs from obedience to the truth, and having as its objects a living hope and a sincere brotherly love.[11] And whereas Baptism is, with St. Paul, the beginning of the new birth, and the communication of the Spirit, with St. Peter, on the other hand—whatever may be the exact meaning of the difficult expression which he uses[12]—it is clear that his thoughts are mainly fixed on the

---

[1] 1 Pet. i. 5, φρουρουμένους διὰ πίστεως ; 7 ; 9, τὸ τέλος τῆς πίστεως, σωτηρίαν ψυχῶν ; 21 ; v. 9, στερεοὶ τῇ πίστει.
[2] See *Life and Work of St. Paul*, ii. 209, *seq.*
[3] 1 Pet. i. 8; Heb. xi. 1; Clem. *Ep. ad Cor.* xxvi., xxvii.; Pfleiderer, *Paulinism*. ii. 140.
[4] 1 Pet. i. 3, 13, iii. 15.   [5] Rom. iv. 25.
[6] 1 Pet. ii. 14, 15, 20, iii. 6, 11, 13, 16, 17, iv. 19.
[7] "Pass the time of your sojourning here in fear."
[8] "Ye received not the spirit of bondage again to fear."
[9] "Perfect love casteth out fear."   [10] πολυποίκιλος σοφία.
[11] 1 Pet. i. 22, 23 ; Jas. i. 18.
[12] 1 Pet. iii. 21, ἐπερώτημα ἀγαθῆς συνειδήσεως εἰς Θεόν. It has been taken to mean (1) "*pledge*," "contract" (ἀρραβών, ἐνέχυρον, Œcum.; *stipulatio*, Luther), as Tertullian calls baptism *obligatio fidei, sponsio salutis, fidei pactio*, but this seems only to be a later Byzantine meaning of the word; or (2) "the *question and answer* of baptism"—the promise to renounce the devil, etc., and so to keep a good conscience ("*Anima non*

moral obligations which enter into baptism as being a type of our deliverance by means of the resurrection of Christ.

10. But while St. Peter brings down, as it were, the transcendental divinity of St. Paul from heaven to earth—from the regions of a sublime theology to those of practical Christian life—while the diversities of gifts imparted by the same Spirit thus meet the individual needs of every Christian—while the contemplation of truth from many different points of view enables us to understand its solidity and perfectness— St. Peter has one doctrine which is almost peculiar to himself, and which is inestimably precious. In this he not only ratifies some of the widest hopes which it had been given to his brother Apostle, if not to *reveal*, at least to *intimate*, but he also supplements these hopes by the new aspect of a much-disregarded, and, indeed, till recent times half-forgotten, article of the Christian creed;—I mean the object of Christ's descent into Hades.[1] In this truth is involved nothing less than the extension of Christ's redeeming work to the dead who died before His coming. Had the Epistle contained nothing else but this, it would at once have been raised above the irreverent charge of being "secondhand and commonplace."[2] I allude of course to the famous passage in which St. Peter tells us (iii. 19, 20) that "Christ died for sins once for all that He may lead us to God, slain indeed in the flesh but quickened in the Spirit, *in which also He went and preached to the spirits in prison, once disobedient, when the long-suffering of God was waiting*,[3] *in the days of Noah, during the preparing of the ark, by entering into which few, that is, eight souls, were brought safe through water*."[4] So far is this from being a casual allusion, that St. Peter returns to it as though with the object of making its meaning indis-

---

la ratione sed responsione sancitur," Tert. *de Resurr. Carn.* 48)—but ἐπερώτημα cannot bear this sense; or (3) joining ἐπερώτημα with εἰς Θεὸν, and taking the phrase ἐπερωτᾶν εἰς in 2 Kings xi. 7 as explaining it—" the inquiry after God of a good conscience ;" or (4) "request to God for a good conscience." Taking ἐπερώτημα in this its natural sense, (the sense it bears in the only passage of the LXX. in which it occurs, *vide* Dan. iv. 14,) I believe this last view to be correct; but if εἰς Θεὸν be taken with συνειδήσις, as in Acts xxiv. 16, then it will be "the *entreaty for a good conscience towards God.*" This, indeed, may seem an inadequate explanation of the saving power of baptism, but so (at first sight) is every other sense which the words will at all bear; and when we remember the practical and non-mystical character of the Apostle's mind, much of the difficulty disappears, and the entreaty involves its own fulfilment. [The Revised Version renders the word "interrogation," and in the margin suggests the alternatives of "inquiry" or "appeal." Archbishop Leighton says, "The word intends the whole correspondence of the conscience with God. . . . The word is judicial, alluding to the interrogation used in law, etc."]

[1] Minor original specialities are "into which things the angels desired to look" (i. 12); Christ, "the chief Shepherd" (v. 4); the presentation of Christ's *sufferings* as an example (ii. 21), etc. See Davidson, *Introd.* i. 423, and for peculiarities of phraseology, *id.* p. 433.

[2] Schwegler.   [3] Leg. ἀπεξεδέχετο.

[4] In my *Mercy and Judgment* (pp. 75—81) I have given (with original quotations) a full history of the exegesis of this passage in the Christian Church. What may be called the *mythological* inferences from it, apart from the blessed truth which it generally indicates, may be found in the Apocryphal Gospel of Nicodemus.

putably plain. When he speaks of the perishing heathen who shall, after lives of sin and self-indulgence, give account to the Judge of quick and dead, he says—"*For, for this cause also, even to the dead was the Gospel preached;*" adding, as though to preclude any escape from his plain meaning, "that they may be judged according to men in the flesh, but may live according to God in the Spirit."[1] Few words of Scripture have been so tortured and emptied of their significance as these. In other passages whole theological systems, whole ecclesiastical despotisms, have been built on the abuse of a metaphor, on the translation of rhetoric into logic, on the ignorance and incapacity which will not interpret words by the universal rules of literary criticism; and yet every effort has been made to explain away the plain meaning of *this* passage. It is one of the most precious passages of Scripture, and it involves no ambiguity, except such as is created by the scholasticism of a prejudiced theology. It stands almost alone in Scripture, not indeed in the gleam of light which it throws across the awful darkness of the destiny of sin, but in the manner in which it reveals to us *the source* from which that gleam of light has been derived. For if language have any meaning, this language means that Christ, when His Spirit descended into the lower world, proclaimed the message of salvation to the once impenitent dead. In the first indeed of the two allusions to this truth, the preaching is formally limited to those who had died in the Deluge. This is due to two causes. St. Peter's mind is full of the Deluge as a *type* of the world's lustration, first by death and then by deliverance, just as baptism is a type of death unto sin and the new life unto righteousness. Also he is thinking of Christ's comparison of the days of Noah to the days of the Son of Man. But it is impossible to suppose that the antediluvian sinners, conspicuous as they were for their wickedness, were the *only* ones of all the dead who were singled out to receive the message of deliverance. That restricted application is excluded by the *second* passage. There the Apostle shows that he had only referred to those who perished in the Deluge as *striking representatives* of a world of sinners, judged as regards men in the flesh, but living as regards God in the Spirit. For, in referring to the judgment which awaits *the heathen*, he attempers the awful thought of their iniquities and of the future retribution which awaited them by saying that, with a view to this very state of things (εἰς τοῦτο) the Gospel was preached to the dead;—in order that, however terrible might be the judgments which would befall their human nature, the hope of some spiritual share in the divine life might not be for ever excluded at the moment of death. Of the *effects* of the preaching nothing is said. There is no dogma either of universalism or of conditional immortality. All details, as in the entire eschatology of Scripture, are left dim and indefinite; but no honest

---

[1] 1 Peter iv. 6.

man who goes to Holy Scripture to *seek* for truth, instead of going to try and find whatever errors he may bring to it as a part of his theological belief, can possibly deny that there is ground here to mitigate that element of the popular teaching of Christendom against which many of the greatest saints and theologians have raised their voices.[1] That teaching rests with the deadliest weight on all who have sufficient imagination to realise the meaning of the phrases in which they indulge, and sufficient heart to feel their awfulness. If Christ *preached to dead men who were once disobedient*, then Scripture shows us that the moment of death does not necessarily involve a final and hopeless torment for every sinful soul. Of all the blunt weapons of ignorant controversy employed against those to whom has been revealed the possibility of a larger hope than is left to mankind by Augustine or by Calvin, the bluntest is the charge that such a hope renders null the necessity for the work of Christ! As if it were not this very hope which gives to the love of Christ its mightiest effectiveness! We thus rescue the work of redemption from the appearance of having failed to achieve its end for the vast majority of those for whom Christ died. By accepting the light thus thrown upon "the descent into Hell," we extend to those of the dead who have not finally hardened themselves against it the blessedness of Christ's atoning work. We thus complete the divine, all-comprehending circuit of God's universal grace! In these passages, as has been truly said, "we may see an expansive paraphrase and exuberant variation of the original Pauline theme of the universalism of the evangelic embassage of Christ and of His sovereignty over the world; and especially of the passage in the Philippians,[2] where all they that are in heaven and on the earth, and *under the earth*, are enumerated as classes of the subjects of the exalted Redeemer."

But alas! human perversity has darkened the very heavens by looking at them through the medium of its own preconceptions; and the clear light of revelation has streamed in vain upon the awfulness of the future. The attempts to make the descent of Jesus into Hades a visit merely to liberate the holy patriarchs, or to strike terror into the evil spirits, are the unworthy inventions of dogmatic embarrassment. The interpretation of Christ's "preaching" as only a preaching of damnation[3] is one of the most melancholy specimens of theological hardness trying to blot out the hope of God's mercy from the world beyond the grave. "It was," as Reuss says, "far better than all that: it was for the living a new manifestation of the inexhaustible grace of God; for the dead a supreme opportunity for casting themselves into the arms of His mercy; and finally, for Christian theologians, so skilful in torturing the letter, and so blind at seizing the spirit, it might have been the germ of a sublime and fruitful conception, if, instead of compressing more and

---

[1] See *Mercy and Judgment*, pp. 16—57.   [2] Phil. ii. 9, 11.
[3] It is needless to say that in the N. T. κηρύσσω has no such meaning, and the parallel passage, iv. 6, has εὐηγγελίσθη. See Clem. Alex. *Strom.* vi. 6.

more the circle of life and light by their formulæ and their anathemas, they would have learnt from the teaching of the Apostle that this circle is illimitable, and that the life-giving rays which stream from its centre can penetrate even the most distant sphere of the world of spirits."

Having thus seen the authenticity, and the characteristics of the first Epistle of St. Peter, we may proceed to ask, What was its object? Clearly it was not meant as a system of theology. Some have supposed that its scope was *directly* conciliatory—that by borrowing alike from St. Paul and St. James, and endeavouring, as it were, to make them both speak with the same mouth,[1] St. Peter wished to calm the controversies which had arisen, and to show that the Christian faith, whether preached by Judaists or Paulinists, was essentially the same. Now there may have been in the mind of St. Peter some such undercurrent of intention. For he was addressing, among others, the Churches of Galatia, which had been the scene of burning controversies; and he may have wished by his silence about the Law, and his omission of such phrases as "Justification by Faith," to show that the essential truths of Christianity might be disengaged from polemical bitterness. There must have been something intentional in this silence, for no one can read the words of St. Paul in Gal. v. 13—

(1) "*For ye were called for freedom, brethren,*
(2) *Only not freedom as a handle for the flesh,*
(3) *But by love serve* (δουλεύετε) *one another*,"

side by side with those of St. Peter, in ii. 16—

(1) "*As free,*
(2) *And yet not using your freedom as a veil of baseness,*
(3) *But as slaves* (δοῦλοι) *of God*,"—

without seeing that the resemblance is more than accidental.[2] The identity of structure, the similarity of rhythm, the echo of the thought, prove decisively that St. Peter had read the Epistle to the Galatians. It could not, therefore, have been without deliberate purpose that, in addressing Galatians among others, he assumes, without the least controversial vehemence, the one startling proposition that faithful Gentiles are the true Jews,[3] an elect race, a holy nation, the true heritage of God, and even the true priesthood,[4] while yet he says no word about Mosaism, or about the terms of communion between Jews and Gentiles. Here, again, we may recognise the exact attitude of Peter as seen in the Acts of the Apostles. He is a sincere and even a scrupulous Jew; yet

---

[1] Reuss, *La Théol. Chrét.* ii. 294.
[2] The quotation is further interesting as being made from an Epistle in which his own conduct is condemned.
[3] 1 Pet. iii. 6.
[4] 1 Pet. ii. 5, οἶκος πνευματικός, ἱεράτευμα ἅγιον; 1 Pet. ii. 9, βασίλειον ἱεράτευμα (cf. מַמְלֶכֶת כֹּהֲנִים, Ex. xix. 5, 6, and LXX.), κ.τ.λ. λαὸς εἰς περιποίησιν (סְגֻלָּה, cf. Acts xx. 28.)

he had been divinely taught that the practices which he might himself continue to adopt as matters of national obligation were in no sense binding on the Gentiles, and that their freedom did not place them in a lower position in the eyes of God, who is no respecter of persons. But though such thoughts may have been in his mind, they did not furnish the motive of his address, which was, as he himself says, essentially hortatory. He wrote to testify and to exhort;[1] to confirm the converts in the truths which they had already learnt from the missions of St. Paul and his companions, and to comfort them under persecution by encouragements, founded on the hopes of which they were partakers, and on the example and effect of the sufferings of Christ.

As in other instances, the question has been raised whether St Peter intended to address Jews or Gentiles;—and, as in other instances, the true answer seems to be—neither class exclusively. The Dispersion of which he is mainly thinking is a spiritual one. He is writing to all Christians in the countries which he mentions.[2] Why he selected the Churches of Asia Minor, and did not include the Churches of Syria, Macedonia, and Achaia, is a question which we cannot solve, seeing that both in Greece and in Syria he was personally known. That he is addressing Gentiles *as well as* Jews cannot be doubted by any unconventional reader;[3] but he regards them as alike pilgrims and sojourners on earth, common members of the ideal Israel, common heirs of the heavenly inheritance.[4] Yet we need go no farther than the first line of his letter, with its two distinctively Jewish expressions of "sojourners" (*Toshabim*) and "the dispersion" (*Galootha*), to show that even to Gentiles he is writing with the feelings and habits of a Jew.

It seems likely that the Epistle was written after the final imprisonment of St. Paul, during whose activity St. Peter would hardly have written to any of the Churches which had been exclusively founded by the Apostle of the Gentiles. The condition of the Churches addressed accords well with such a supposition. He is writing to those who, although their faith was undergoing a severe test, like gold tried in the fire,[5] were yet mainly liable to danger rather than to death. They were

---

[1] 1 Pet. v. 12, παρακαλῶν καὶ ἐπιμαρτυρῶν, κ.τ.λ.

[2] Weiss, in the interests of his arbitrary theory that the letter is one of the earliest documents of Christianity, tries to prove that it was addressed exclusively to Jews. His arguments (*Petr. Lehrbegr.* 115, 116) are entirely inconclusive, and are sufficiently answered in the text. This view has, however, found many supporters in all ages, as Eusebius, Didymus, Jerome, Theophylact, and in modern times Erasmus, Calvin, Grotius, Bengel, etc.

[3] See 1 Pet. i. 14, 18, iii. 6, ii. 9, 10, iv. 3, 4. Many doubtless of these Gentiles had passed into the Church through the portals of the Synagogue. Hence they would find no difficulty in the casual allusions to the Old Testament (i. 15, 16, 23—25, ii. 6, 19, iii. 10, iv. 18, v. 5), which, as Immer remarks (*N. Test. Theol.*, p. 477), are not introduced with any Rabbinic refinements.

[4] 1 Pet. i. 1, iii. 6, v. 9 (*cf.* Heb. xi. 13; Phil. iii. 20; Gen. xlvii. 9; ץ Ps. xxxix. 14); "*nachalath Jehovah*," Jos. xiii. 23, etc. Similarly, Clemens Romanus, though a Gentile, talks of "our father, Abraham."

[5] 1 Pet. i. 7, iv. 12.

exposed to false accusations as malefactors,[1] to revilings,[2] threats,[3] and a general system of terrorism and suffering.[4] Now this is exactly the state of things which must have existed in the provinces after the Neronian persecution. That crisis marked out the Christians for a special hatred above and beyond what they experienced as being, in the eyes of the world, a debased Jewish sect. It even brought into prominence the name of "Christians," which, though invented by the jeering populace of Antioch as early as A.D. 44, had not until this time come into general vogue.[5] It is true that Orosius[6] is the first writer who asserts that the persecution extended "through all the provinces," and there is no authority for the assertion of Tertullian that Nero had made the repression of Christians a standing law of the Empire.[7] Some have attempted to prove that the state of things referred to could only have existed during the persecution of Trajan (A.D. 101),[8] which is of course equivalent to saying that the Epistle is spurious. But, considering that we find the traces of trials at least as severe as those to which St. Peter alludes some time *before* the Neronian persecution had broken out,[9] and in the Apocalyptic letters to the seven Churches of Asia *after* it had broken out,[10] the whole argument is groundless. The members of a sect which was "everywhere spoken against," and for which even the worthiest Gentile writers can find no better epithet than "execrable"— a sect which from the first was supposed to involve a necessary connection with the deadliest crimes[11]—a sect which from the earliest days seems to have been exposed to the insults of the vilest mural caricatures[12]—were certainly as liable in the later years of Nero as they were

---

[1] 1 Pet. ii. 12, 15.   [2] 1 Pet. ii. 23, iii. 9, iv. 14.   [3] 1 Pet. iii. 16, ἐπηρεάζοντες.
[4] 1 Pet. iii. 9, 14, 17, iv. 15, 19. Tacitus counts Christianity among the shameful things (*pudenda*) which flowed Romewards (comp. Rom. i. 16).
[5] See my *Life and Work of St. Paul*, i. 298. Tacitus (*Ann.* xv. 44) uses the word "*Christianos*" with something of an apology. It is well known that in the N. T. it only occurs three times, and always involves a hostile sense (Acts xi. 26, xxvi. 28), as it does in iv. 16.
[6] Oros. vii. 11, "*per omnes provincias* pari persecutione cruciari imperavit." The Lusitanian inscription (Gruter, p. 238; Orelli, 730), which thanks Nero for purging the province of some foreign superstition (novam humano generi superstitionem), is now given up. See Merivale, i. 450; Gieseler, i. 28.
[7] *Ad Natt.* i. 7, "sub Nerone damnatio invaluit." In the martyrologies, we read of martyrs during the Neronian persecution at Milan, Aquileia, Carthage, etc.; and St. John mentions the martyr Antipas by name, at Pergamum (Rev. ii. 13), besides alluding to others (Rev. xvi. 5).
[8] See especially Schwegler, *Nachap. Zeit. II.* 2—29; Köstlin, *Johann-Lehrbegr.* 472 —481; Baur, *First Three Centuries*, i. 133.
[9] For instance, in 1 Thess. ii. 15, iii. 4; 2 Thess. i. 4, iii. 2; Phil. i. 28, 30, etc.
[10] Rev. i. 9, ii. 9, 10, 13, vi. 9, 11, xviii. 24, xx. 4.
[11] Plin. *Ep.* x. 97, "flagitia cohaerentia nomini;" Tac. *Ann.* xv. 44, "quos, per *flagitia* invisos, vulgus Christianos appellabat."
[12] A celebrated graffito of the Palatine, representing an ass on a cross, has been supposed to be a mockery of the Crucifixion. It was found in 1856, and is now in the library of the Collegio Romano. P. Garucci supposes that it was drawn towards the close of the second century. Similar insults to Christians have been found on various gems and wall-inscriptions at Pompeii, etc. See Renan, *L'Antechrist*, p. 40. Merivale, *Hist.* vi. 442. These graffiti and calumnies are alluded to by Tertullian, *Apol.* 16; *ad Natt.* i. 11; Minuc. Felix, *Octav.* ix. 28; Celsus, *ap.* Orig. *c. Cels.* vi. 31.

in the days of Trajan to suffer such troubles as those to which St. Peter alludes.[1] It ought to have been regarded as decisive against the later date thus suggested for the Epistle, that, like all the Epistles in the New Testament, it is anterior to that rapid development of the power of the Episcopate which is so prominent in the earliest of the extra-canonical writings. The Churches of the Spiritual Dispersion are still under the government of Presbyters, and St. Peter addresses them as their "fellow-presbyter." The word "*episkopos*" occurs but once in his letter, and that in its purely general and untechnical signification.[2] Hence the letter is addressed to the converts in general, with only a special message to Presbyters at the end. *Hope* is the keynote of this Epistle. Its main message is, *Endure, submit, for you are the heirs of salvation*.[3]

CHAPTER VIII.

THE FIRST EPISTLE OF ST. PETER.

'Επιστρέψας στήρισον τοὺς ἀδελφούς.—LUKE xxii. 32.

"Habet haec epistola τὸ σφοδρὸν conveniens ingenio principis apostolorum."—GROTIUS.

"Mirabilis est gravitas et alacritas Petrini sermonis, lectorem suavissime retinens."—BENGEL.

"PETER, an Apostle of Jesus Christ"—such is the simple and authoritative designation which he adopts. He does not need to add any of the amplifications of his title, or assertions of his claim to it, which were often necessary to St. Paul, whose apostolic authority had been so fiercely questioned. Nor does he need to adopt St. Paul's practice of associating the names of his companions with his own, although both Mark and Silvanus, so well known to the Asian Churches, were at this time with him in Rome. His dignity as an Apostle was unquestioned.

---

[1] Renan rightly says, "L'épître de Pierre répond bien à ce que nous savons, surtout par Tacite, de la situation des Chrétiens à Rome vers l'an 63 ou 64" (*L'Antechrist*, p. xi.).
[2] 1 Pet. ii. 25, to the Bishop (or Overseer) of your souls.
[3] The letter falls, like most of St. Paul's letters (see *Life and Work of St. Paul*, i. 605, 606) into two great divisions—doctrinal and practical. I. i. 1—ii. 10, the *blessings* of Christians. II. ii. 11—v. 14, the *duties* of Christians. More in detail the outline of the letter is as follows:—(I.) Greeting (i. 1, 2); thanksgiving, intended to console the readers with the living Hope of that future inheritance on which, through God's mercy and Christ's resurrection, they should enter after their brief sorrows on earth—that salvation, to which all prophecy pointed, and into which angels desire to look (i. 3—12); exhortation (α) *to holy living* in hope and obedience (i. 13—17), founded on the price paid for their redemption (18—21); (β) *to brotherly love*, founded on their new birth by the eternal word of God (22—25); and (γ) *to Christian innocence*, as babes desiring spiritual

His words needed no further weight than they derived from his acknowledged position. It is not insignificant that he uses the name which Christ had given him, and uses it in its Greek, not its Aramaic, form. Had he been writing with any *exclusive* reference to the Jewish Christians, it is more probable that he would have used his own name, Symeon, by which James speaks of him to the Church of Jerusalem, or the Aramaic "Kephas," by which St. Paul designates him, because he was so called by the Judaists of Galatia and Corinth.[1]

"To the elect sojourners of the Dispersion of Pontus,[2] Galatia, Cappadocia, Asia, and Bithynia." The Dispersion—in Greek, *Diaspora;* in Aramaic, *Galootha*—was no doubt an essentially literal and geographical expression; but as St. Peter uses the unusual word "sojourners" (*parepidemoi*) in a metaphorical sense for "pilgrims" in ii. 11,[3] he probably uses it in the same sense here, and not in its narrower sense of scattered Jews. The Churches which he was addressing were composed of Jewish and Gentile converts. Many of the latter had doubtless been proselytes. Even those who had been converted direct from heathenism would have been made familiar from the first with the existence of the Old Testament, and with the truth which St. Paul had so powerfully established in his letter to the Galatians, that the converted Gentiles constituted the ideal Israel. Nothing, therefore, is more natural to a Jewish writer than the half-literal, half-metaphorical expression, "the expatriated elect of the Dispersion." The word "elect" marks them out as Christians, being one of the terms by which Christians used to define

---

milk, and as living stones of a spiritual house (ii. 1—10). Then (II.), after a special entreaty to them to abstain from fleshly desires, so as to win their heathen neighbours to glorify God by seeing their honourable mode of life—an entreaty specially applicable to a period when "Christian" was regarded as a synonym of "malefactor" (11, 12), he passes to a second series of exhortations, which have direct reference to the trials by which they are surrounded (ii. 13—iii. 7): namely, to the spirit of submission (α) generally (ii. 13—17); (β) in the position of *servants* (18—20) bearing in mind the meek example of Christ their Redeemer (21—25); (γ) in the position of *Christian women*, who, in meek simplicity, are to imitate Sarah, their spiritual ancestress (iii. 1—6), and (δ) of Christian *husbands* (7). Then follows a *third* series of exhortations (iii. 8—iv. 19), (α) to forgiveness and peaceful self-control as in God's sight (iii. 8—12); (β) to calm endurance of wrongful suffering—again with reference to the example of Christ (13—18), who preached even in Hades to those who were once disobedient (in the days of that deluge from which Noah and his family were saved as we are saved by baptism)—but who is now exalted at God's right hand (19—22); (γ) to the abandonment of the old heathen life, which would bring inevitable judgment (iv. 1—6); (δ) to sobriety, love, hospitality, a right use of gifts, that God may be glorified (7—10); (ε) to the cheerful, innocent, even thankful endurance of sorrow as a normal part of the Christian life (11—16), and one in which, being far less to be pitied than the unfaithful, they might safely entrust their souls to God (17—19). Then follow special exhortations (α) to Presbyters (v. 1—4); (β) to younger members of the Church (5—7); and (γ) to all alike, to watch and strive (9, 10). The Epistle ends with a blessing (10, 11) and a few parting words about Silvanus and the letter of which he is the bearer (12), and greetings (13, 14).

[1] That he wrote in Greek is certain from the style, which is far too animated to be a translation. It is a most narrow view which assumes that St. Peter could not address Gentiles without violating what is called "the Apostolic compact" (Gal. ii. 9).

[2] Hence sometimes known as the Epistle *ad Ponticos* (Tert. *Scorp.* 12).

[3] Ps. xxxix. 13, cxx. 5. Cf. Heb. xi. 13; Judith v. 18; 2 Macc. i. 27. Comp. John xi. 52, and πάροικος in Acts vii. 6, 29.

themselves.[1] Many of them, being Jews by birth, were literal members of "the Dispersion;" all of them were strangers upon earth, exiles from heaven their home, dwelling in Mesech and amid the tents of Kedar. It is natural that the phrases of a Jewish writer should be predominantly Jewish. Even the language of St. Paul, cosmopolitan as were his views, is largely coloured by theocratic images and metaphors belonging to the older dispensation.[2]

There seems to be no traceable significance in the order in which the provinces of Asia Minor—to use a convenient later term—are mentioned. Writing from Rome, he begins with the most distant, Pontus, flinging as it were to its farthest east the net of the fisher of men. The order of the rest, from north-east to south and west, must be due to some subjective accident. The Churches of two of the provinces, Galatia and Asia,[3]—including some so important as Ancyra, Tavium, Pessinus, and the famous Seven Churches—had been founded by St. Paul or his companions. Jews of Pontus and Cappadocia had been present at the great discourse of St. Peter on the day of Pentecost,[4] and these districts contained, among others, such wealthy towns as Tyana, Nyssa, Cæsarea, and Nazianzus. The Churches of Bithynia, which St. Paul had been hindered from visiting by a Divine intimation, were forerunners of the communities to whose simplicity and faithfulness, forty years later, Pliny bore his impartial and memorable testimony in his letter to the Emperor Trajan.

Having thus named the converts whom he meant specially to address, he describes their election as due in its *origin* "to the foreknowledge of God the Father," in its *progress* "to the sanctifying work of the Spirit," and as having for its *end* "obedience, and sprinkling by the blood of Jesus Christ."[5] Thus, no less than St. Paul, he describes each of the Three Persons of the Blessed Trinity as co-operant in the work of man's salvation. In his salutation, "Grace unto you and peace," he follows St. Paul in the comprehensive formula by which he unites the Hellenic greeting of "*joy*," with the Hebrew greeting of "*peace*"—both of them used in their deeper Christian sense,[6] of a "peace" which passeth understanding, and a "joy" which the world could neither give nor take away. From the Book of Daniel, with which he was evidently familiar, he adopts the expression "*be multiplied*," which is

---

[1] 1 Thess. i. 4.
[2] The Galatian Churches, for instance, were largely composed of Gentiles, yet St. Paul's arguments to them are of a Judaic and sometimes even of a Rabbinic character.
[3] Proconsular Asia, which included Mysia, Lydia, Caria, Phrygia, Pisidia, and Lycaonia.   [4] Acts ii. 9. Cf. Jos. *Antt.* xvi. 6.
[5] ῥαντισμῷ, Heb. xii. 24, "Sprinkling," *i.e.*, "Your being sprinkled." The allusion is to the sprinkling of the *people* at the inauguration of the Mosaic Covenant (Ex. xxiv. 8); but there may be also the conception of purifying, as the vessels of the sanctuary were purified by sprinkled blood. Cf Heb. ix. 13, 18—28; Ex. xxiv. 6—8; Lev. xvi. 14 and 19, etc. Any allusion to the Lord's Supper, which Weiss (*Petr. Lehrbegr.* 273) assumes as certain, is more than doubtful.
[6] See my *Life and Work of St. Paul*, i. 580.

found in the letters of Darius and Nebuchadnezzar there recorded[1] (i. 1—3).

Then follows the rich and full thanksgiving, with its comprehensive glance at the future (3—5), the present (6—9), and the past (10—12):—" Blessed be the God and Father of our Lord Jesus Christ,[2] Who according to His great mercy, begat us again[3] to a living hope by the resurrection of Jesus Christ from the dead,[4] to an inheritance incorruptible and stainless and unwithering,[5] which has been reserved in heaven for you,[6]—who by the power of God are being guarded[7] by faith unto a salvation ready to be revealed[8] at the last season. In which thought ye exult,[9] though for a little while at present, if need be, ye have been grieved in various trials, that the tested genuineness of your faith—a far costlier thing than gold which perisheth, and yet is tested by means of fire[10]—might prove to be for (your) praise and honour and glory[11] at the revelation of Jesus Christ; Whom though ye never saw ye love;[12] on Whom—though ye still see Him not—yet believing, ye exult with joy inexpressible and glorified; carrying off as a prize[13] the end of your faith—the salvation of souls.[14] Respecting which salvation the prophets diligently sought and searched, who prophesied concerning the grace which was coming to you;—searching as to what or what kind of season the spirit of Christ in them[15] was indicating, when it testified

---

[1] Dan. iii. 31, iv. 1, vi. 25, whence the Rabbis probably derived it (Wetst. ad Cor.). Cf. Jude 2; 2 Pet. i. 2. [2] Cf. Eph. i. 3.

[3] Ἀναγεννήσας, a word peculiar to St. Peter. But compare ἀπεκύησεν, James i. 18; γεννᾶσθαι ἄνωθεν, John iii. 3; παλιγγενεσία, Tit. iii. 5; πιστεύοντες ἐν Χρ. Ἰησοῦ, Eph. ii. 10.

[4] Here he strikes the key-note of the Epistle, *Hope founded on the Resurrection*; not a *dead*, but an *energising* Hope, such as the Resurrection had wrought in the Apostles by dispelling their despair; a Hope living, life-giving, and looking to life (De Wette), of which the Resurrection was "not only the exemplar, but the efficient cause" (Leighton).

[5] Εἰς. The Hope will end in the fruition of heritage, which is salvation and glory (1 Pet. i. 5, v. 1); ἀμάραντος (Wisd. vi. 12) not the same as ἀμάραντινος in v. 4.

[6] And therefore beyond the reach of danger.

[7] "*Haereditas servata est, haeredes custodiuntur*" (Bengel). Cf. Phil. iv. 7. The MSS. throughout the Epistle vary between "us" and "you," as is so often the case. Here, as in almost every instance, ὑμᾶς is the right reading (א, A, B, C, K, L, etc.), though the E. V. usually adopts "us" and "we." The "you" is characteristic of the Apostolic authority of the teacher.

[8] Draw the curtain at the last time (Jude 18), and the salvation is already there, behind the veil. See 1 Pet. iv. 5, 7.

[9] Here he passes from the future to the *present*. The "salvation" in its completeness is future, the "exultation" (a word characteristically Petrine; cf. 1 Pet. i. 8, iv. 13; Matt. v. 12) is present, and the epithets applied to it are anticipatory only in their *fulness*.

[10] Hermas, *Pastor*, i. 4, p. 440; ed. Dressel.

[11] "Well done, good and faithful servant!" (Matt. xxv. 21).   [12] John xx. 29.

[13] The prize is carried off by anticipation now; in reality hereafter. It is "glory begun below." "The moods of the New Testament converge towards the present."

[14] 1 Pet. i. 6—9. The "salvation" is not from the sorrows and trials of life, but from all sin.

[15] The remark in the Ep. of Barnabas (cap. v.) still remains the best comment on this expression, "The prophets, having their gift from Him, prophesied about Him." St. Peter was not likely to enter into such scholastic refinements as those which separate the idea of "Christ" from that of "the Eternal Son."

beforehand the sufferings which were to fall upon Christ,[1] and the glories that should follow them; to whom it was revealed that not mainly for themselves,[2] but for you they were ministering these things,[3] which have now been proclaimed to you[4] by means of those who preached to you the Gospel by the Holy Spirit sent from heaven;[5] into which things angels desire to stoop and look."[6]

"Therefore, girding up at once the loins of your understanding,[7] being sober, lean with perfect hope upon the grace that is being borne to you in the revelation of Jesus Christ; as children of obedience,[8] not fashioning yourselves in conformity[9] with the former desires in your day of ignorance."[10]

This pregnant exhortation is supported by the motives (i.) of God's holiness (15, 16); (ii.) of the fear due to Him as a Father and impartial Judge (17);[11] and (iii.) of the fact that they were ransomed from their empty traditional mode of life, not by mere corruptible silver and gold,[12] but by costly blood, as of a lamb blameless and spotless, even of Christ;[13] Who was pre-ordained before the world was, but has been manifested at the end of the time[14] for the sake of them who through Him believe on God, who raised Him from the dead, and gave Him glory, so that our faith is also hope towards God.[15]

The exhortation to Hope founded on these motives is followed by an exhortation to sincere and intense Love, as the natural result of the puri-

---

[1] 1 Pet. i. 11, τὰ εἰς Χριστὸν παθήματα.
[2] "As little children lisp and talk of Heaven,
So thoughts *beyond their thoughts* to those high bards were given."
KEBLE.
I insert the word "mainly" after "not" in accordance with a well-known idiom.
[3] See Acts ii. 17, 31, iii. 24.
[4] "You" and "ye" (not "us" and "we," as in the E. V.) are the best authorised readings throughout the Epistle, except in i. 3, iv. 17, and ii. 24 (from Isaiah). This seems to have been St. Peter's method (Acts xv. 7).
[5] Mark the emphatic testimony to the teaching of St. Paul, by whom, directly or indirectly, most of these Churches had been founded.
[6] 1 Pet. i. 10—12. For the word παρακύψαι see James i. 25; Luke xxiv. 12; John xx. 5, 11. Cf. Heb. ii. 16.
[7] Luke xii. 25; Eph. vi. 14.
[8] Cf. τέκνα ὀργῆς, Eph. ii. 3; φωτός, v. 8; κατάρας, 2 Pet. ii. 14.
[9] συσχηματιζόμενοι, Rom. xii. 2.
[10] "Ignorance;" cf. Rom. i. 18; Acts iii. 17, xvii. 30.
[11] εἰ Πατέρα ἐπικαλεῖσθε—"If ye call on Him as 'Father,' Who" etc. Perhaps with reference to the Lord's Prayer. In these verses notice ἀναστροφή, "mode of life," "conversation" in its old sense, used also to render πολίτευμα, "citizenship," in Phil. i. 27. The adv. ἀπροσωπολήπτως occurs here only, but the conception is thoroughly Petrine (Acts x. 34). The "fear" here recommended is not the fear reprobated in 1 John iv. 18; Rom. viii. 15; 2 Tim. i. 7, but "godly fear," φόβος τελειωτικός, awful reverence mixed with love, which "drowns all lower fears, and begets true fortitude" (Leighton).
[12] Notice the Petrine contempt for dross (Acts iii. 6, viii. 20).
[13] With special allusion to the deliverance secured by the Paschal Lamb (Ex. xii. 36); general reference to the whiteness and harmlessness of the Lamb. See *Life of Christ*, i. 143.
[14] 1 Pet. i. 20, ἐπ' ἐσχάτων τῶν χρόνων, אַחֲרִית הַיָּמִים (Gen. xlix. 1).
[15] Or, "so that your faith and hope are in God," who raised Christ from the dead, etc. Acts ii. 22 (i. 13—21).

fication of the soul by the Holy Spirit[1] in the path of obedience; and of that new birth—not by human engendering, but by means of the living word (λόγος) of God, which is not transient, as is the flower of human life,[2] but is an utterance (ῥῆμα) which abideth for ever—"And this is the utterance preached to you as the Gospel."[3]

This is the starting-point to fresh exhortations. There were evidently divisions between the members of the Churches, which led St. Peter to impress on them the duty of fervent love. He proceeds to urge them to lay aside,[4] like some stained robe, all that is ruinous to brotherly union—malice, guile, insincerities, envies, backbitings, which may easily have arisen from such conditions as we have seen existing in the Churches of Galatia.[5] Born again, let them, as new-born babes, desire to be nurtured into perfect growth by the unadulterated spiritual milk,[6] since they knew by tasting that the Lord is sweet.[7] And then, changing the metaphor,[8] he bids them "come to Christ,[9] a living stone, and be built upon Him—as living stones upon a corner-stone—into a spiritual house, a holy priesthood, to offer up[10] spiritual sacrifices acceptable to God by Jesus Christ."[11] The rejection of that precious stone by men, and its choice by God, had long been prophesied.[12] The preciousness of it should belong to those who believed on Him;[13] to the others—"for which they were also appointed"—He should be a stone of stumbling and a rock of offence.[14] "But ye are an elect race, a royal priesthood,[15] a holy nation, a people for

---

[1] Cf. Acts xv. 9, where, however, the verb is καθαρίζω, not ἁγνίζω, as here and in James iv. 8; 1 John iii. 3. (See John xi. 55; Acts xxi. 24.)

[2] ἐξηράνθη ... ἐξέπεσεν, gnomic aorists—*i.e.*, aorists expressive of a general fact. See my Brief Greek Syntax, § 154.

[3] 1 Pet. i. 22—25. The "Logos" of this passage, if it has not yet risen to its Johannine sense, hovers on the verge of it, as in Heb. iv. 12.

[4] Ἀποθέμενοι, 1 Pet. ii. 1.

[5] See *Life and Work of St. Paul*, ii. 129, *seq.*

[6] τὸ λογικὸν (Rom. xii. 1), ἄδολον (1 Pet. ii. 2), γάλα (2 Cor. iv. 2).

[7] Ps. xxxiv. 8, Χρηστός, "sweet" (Aug. *dulcis*, Vulg. *suavis*). Cf. Luke v. 39, vi. 35. Some have supposed a pleasant play of words, founded on itacism, between *chrestos* (sweet) and *Christos* (Christ). See *Life and Work of St. Paul*, i. 301.

[8] There is the same sequence of the same metaphors in 1 Cor. iii. 1, 10.

[9] "Come (προσέρχεσθαι) as true proselytes (προσήλυτοι)." Though St. Peter here uses *lithos*, "stone," not *petra*, he is perhaps thinking of the great promise to himself (Matt. xvi. 18).

[10] ἀνενέγκαι, "to offer once for once" (aor.), (Rom. xii. 1.

[11] Heb. xiii. 15.

[12] Is. xxviii. 16. This citation, divergent from the LXX. in the two same particulars ("I lay in Sion" and "on Him") as in Rom. ix. 33, is a striking instance of the use of that Epistle by St. Peter; ἀκρογωνιαῖον (Eph. ii. 20).

[13] ἡ τιμή, 1 Pet. ii. 7, rendered in E. V. "he is precious." "The honour" is that involved in the ἔντιμον, "honourable" (E. V., "precious"), of the previous verse. For the O. T. reference see Ps. cxviii. 22; Is. viii. 14. (Heb. and Rom. ix. 33.)

[14] See Ps. cxviii. 22; Is. viii. 14; Luke xx. 17, 18; Rom. ix. 32, 33; Matt. xvi. 23. The allusion is to the course of God's earthly dealings, *e.g.*, as Roos says, "If Caiaphas, Judas, etc., had been born in a different century, they could not have acted as they did." There is no decree of reprobation, nor is the future world even alluded to, in εἰς ὃ καὶ ἐτέθησαν. See Acts i. 16. On the whole subject see *Life and Work of St. Paul*, ii. 242—244, 590.

[15] Ex. xix. 6, LXX.

special possession,[1] in order that ye may proclaim the excellence[2] of Him Who called you from darkness into His marvellous light : once not a people, but now a people of God ; once uncompassionated, but compassionated now."[3]

Having thus laid the sure foundations of Hope and Comfort in the great doctrinal truths of Christianity, he devotes the rest of the Epistle to the enforcement of the moral duties which result from our Christian profession.

(1) First comes the appeal *to live purely and blamelessly.*

"Beloved! I beseech you as sojourners and pilgrims to abstain from the carnal desires which make war against the soul,[4] keeping fair your mode of life[5] among the Gentiles, that, in the matter in which they speak against you as malefactors,[6] they may, in consequence of your fair deeds, as they witness them, glorify God in the day of visitation."[7]

(2) A second special duty of Christians in those days was *due respect, in all things lawful, to the civil government.* By Messianic exultation, by eschatological enthusiasms, by the sense of the glory and the dignity of redeemed manhood, by the revealed equality of all men in the sight of Him Who is no respecter of persons, by the conviction of the dwindling littleness of human distinctions in the light of eternal life, they might, if they were not warned, be naturally tempted to a demeanour which would seem contemptuous towards earthly authority. Nay, more ; the fearful spectacle of the power of the world wielded by those who were but too manifest servants of the power of darkness—the sight of Antichrist seated in his infamy upon the world's throne—the daily proof of odious wickedness in high places—the constant expectation of that archangelic trumpet which would shatter the solid globe, and of that flaming epiphany which should destroy the enemies of Christ—might lead them into defiant words and contumacious actions. Occasions there are —and none knew this better than an Apostle who had himself set an

---

[1] εἰς περιποίησιν (Eph. i. 14 ; 1 Thess. v. 9 ; Rev. i. 6 ; Acts xx. 28) ; עַם סְגֻלָּה (Is. xliii. 21 ; Ex. xx. 5).

[2] ἀρετὰς (a rare word, 2 Pet. i. 3), Is. xliii. 20, LXX. ; in Hebr., תְּהִלָּתִי, "my praise" (Is. xlviii. 9).

[3] 1 Pet. ii. 1—10. Lo Ammi and Lo Ruhamah (Hos. ii. 23 ; Rom. ix. 25).

[4] Jas. iv. 1 ; Rom. vii. 23.

[5] ἀναστροφὴ and ἀναστρέφεσθαι occur ten times in 1 and 2 Pet.

[6] At first the Christians were mainly charged with turbulence, moroseness, "*inciviame,*" detestable superstition (Tacitus and Suetonius), and hard obstinacy (Pliny and Marcus Aurelius). The charges of infant murder, cannibalism, and gross immorality (Tert. *Apol.* 16, etc.) belong to a later age, when the Lord's Supper and the Agapae were misunderstood, and, perhaps, when Gnostic sects had really fallen into vile Antinomianism.

[7] 1 Pet. ii. 11, 12. "Day of visitation," when God comes to offer mercy (Gen. l. 24 ; Wisd. iii. 7 ; Luke i. 68, xix. 44), or to judge (Is. x. 3) ; not "when the heathen made judicial inquiry into your conduct" (Œcumen., Bengel, etc.), nor "on the Judgment Day" (Bede). Notice the large-hearted absence of any spirit of revenge. He only desires that the heathen, when they find how base were their calumnies, how cruel their conduct, may be led to glorify God ! No anathemas here. Pliny's celebrated letter to Trajan (*Ep.* x. 98) is the best comment on this passage.

example of splendid disobedience to unwarranted commands[1]—when "we must obey God rather than men." But those occasions are exceptional to the common rule of life. Normally, and as a whole, human law is on the side of divine order, and, by whomsoever administered, has a just claim to obedience and respect. It was a lesson so deeply needed by the Christians of the day that it is taught as emphatically by St. John[2] and by St. Peter as by St. Paul himself.[3] It was more than ever needed at a time when dangerous revolts were gathering to a head in Judæa; when the hearts of Jews throughout the world were burning with a fierce flame of hatred against the abominations of a tyrannous idolatry; when Christians were being charged with "turning the world upside-down;"[4] when some poor Christian slave led to martyrdom or put to the torture might easily relieve the tension of his soul by bursting into Apocalyptic denunciations of sudden doom against the crimes of the mystic Babylon; when the heathen, in their impatient contempt, might wilfully interpret a prophecy of the Final Conflagration as though it were a revolutionary and incendiary threat; and when Christians at Rome were, on this very account, already suffering the agonies of the Neronian persecution.[5]

Submission, therefore, was at this time a primary duty of all who wished to win over the Heathen, and to save the Church from being overwhelmed in some outburst of indignation which would be justified even to reasonable and tolerant Pagans as a political necessity. Nor does St. Peter think it needful to lay down exceptions to his general rule. In his days the letter of Scripture had not yet been turned into a weapon wherewith on every possible occasion to murder its spirit. He could not have anticipated in even the humblest Christian convert that dull literalism which in later ages was to derive from such passages the slavish doctrine of "passive obedience." He felt no apprehension that an unreasoning fetish-worship would fail to see that "texts" of Scripture are to be interpreted, not as rigid and exclusive legal documents, but in accordance with the general tenor of revelation. He was writing to Christians who had not yet invented a dogma about "verbal dictation," which necessitated ingenious casuistry on the one hand, or unreasonable folly on the other, and which turned both into a deadly engine of irresponsible tyranny.

"Submit therefore," the Apostle says, "to every human ordinance,[6] for the Lord's sake, whether to the Emperor as supreme,[7] or to governors,[8] as missioned by him for punishment of malefactors and

---

[1] Acts iii. 19, 31, v. 28—32, 40—42.   [2] John xix. 11.
[3] And yet Volkmar sees in St. Paul the False Prophet of the Apocalypse, mainly because he taught that "the powers that be are ordained of God"!
[4] Acts xvii. 6.
[5] Tertullian and other apologists were greatly aided in their appeals to heathen clemency by referring to such passages as this. See Tert. *Apol.* 29—34.
[6] κτίσιν, lit. "creature." τὰς ἀρχὰς λέγει τὰς χειροτονητὰς ὑπὸ τῶν Βασιλέων, κ.τ.λ. (Œcumen.).
[7] The name "king" was freely used of the Emperor in the Provinces.
[8] Proconsuls, Procurators, Legates, Proprætors, etc.

praise to well-doers; for this is the will of God, that by your well-doing ye should gag[1] the stolid ignorance of foolish persons; as free, yet not using your freedom for a cloak of baseness,[2] but as slaves of God. Honour all men," as a principle; and as your habitual practice,[3] "love the brotherhood. Fear God. Honour the king."[4]

(3) These being the general rules, he applies them first *to domestics*,[5] whether slaves or freemen, bidding them with all fear to be submissive, not only to kindly but even to perverse masters, and that as a matter of conscience[6] even in cases of unjust suffering. "For what kind of glory is it if doing wrong and being buffeted ye shall bear it? but if doing well and suffering ye shall bear it, this is thankworthy with God.[7] For to this ye were called, because Christ too"—Who was also "a servant"[8] —"suffered on your behalf, leaving you a copy,[9] that ye may follow in His track; Who did no sin, nor was guile found in His mouth; Who being reviled reviled not again, suffering threatened not, but gave up[10] to Him Who judgeth righteously;[11] Who Himself carried up our sins in His own body on to the tree,[12] that becoming separated from our sins[13] we should live to righteousness; by Whose bruise we were healed.[14] For ye were as wandering sheep, but ye are now returned to the shepherd and guardian of your souls."[15]

---

[1] φιμοῦν, Deut. xxv. 4, and in the Gospels.

[2] "License they mean when they cry Liberty" (Milton). Calvin speaks of some who "reckoned it a great part of Christian liberty that they might eat flesh on Fridays"!

[3] The first verb is an aor., τιμήσατε. The others are presents, to imply continuance. "All men," see Acts x. 28.

[4] 1 Pet. ii. 13–17.

[5] οἰκέται. The prominence given to this class shows how numerous they were in the early Church, and is an additional proof that St. Peter must be addressing Gentiles as well as Jews. The Jews were rarely slaves, because their religion rendered them almost useless to heathen masters.

[6] Some would here render συνείδησιν, *consciousness*, or cognisance of God (*mitwissen*, not *erwissen*). Cf. Col. iii. 23.

[7] χάρις, as in Luke vi. 32. Cf. חֵן נָקִי Gen. vi. 8.   [8] Is. liii. 9; Acts iii. 13.

[9] ὑπογραμμόν—the letters over which children write. (Clem. Alex. *Strom.* v. 8–50)

[10] παρεδίδου δέ.—the subject is not expressed, but probably the verb has a quasi-middle sense—"entrusted Himself and His cause."

[11] Luke xxiii. 46. The Vulg. reads "injuste," so that there seems to have been a reading ἀδίκως—referring to Christ's submission to Pilate.

[12] I do not think that "He bore" (ἀνήνεγκεν, *tulit et obtulit*) can here have its sacrificial sense (which it has in James ii. 21, Heb. ix. 28, and in the LXX.). Christ is, indeed, the High Priest, and the Cross may be metaphorically described as the Altar (Heb. xiii. 10). But in what possible sense can "sins" be called a sacrifice? The only way to save this sense of ἀνήνεγκεν is to connect ἁμαρτίας very closely with ἐν τῷ σώματι αὐτοῦ, making the *sacrifice* His own body, in which He bare our sins (Isa. liii. 12): "Ita talia peccata nostra ut ea secum obtulerit in altari" (Vitringa). But ἀναφέρω often has its ordinary sense in the New Testament (Mark ix. 2; Luke xxiv. 51, etc.), and there is no sacrificial sense in the verbs *sabal* and *nasa* of Isa. liii. 11, 12. The use of the word "tree" (ξύλον) for "cross" is Hebraic (Deut. xxi. 23; Gal. iii. 13).

[13] ἀπογενόμενοι. This is, however, sometimes an euphemism for "being dead," Hdt. ii. 85 (cf. Rom. vi. 2). "Righteousness is one; sin is manifold."

[14] Is. liii. 5. μώλωπι, "weal."

[15] 1 Pet. ii. 18–25, ἐπίσκοπον. Cf. Ez. xxxiv. 11. Hitherto they had been the other sheep, not of this fold (John x. 16).

(4) But a word was also necessary on the subject of social as well as political submission. *Christian wives* married to heathen husbands might be led to treat them as inferior to themselves. The elevation of their whole sex by the principles of the new revelation might tempt them to extravagances of ornament or demeanour. To them therefore St. Peter extends his exhortations, that, even if (to suppose the worst) any of them be married to heathens who obey not the Word (*i.e.*, the Gospel), they may without word[1] (*i.e.*, by the eloquent silence of deeds) be won by the chaste humility, the "delicate, timorous grace," of wives whose adornment should not consist in elaborately braided hair,[2] golden jewels, or splendid robes, but in the inner soul,[3] in "the incorruptibleness of the meek and quiet spirit, which is in God's sight very precious." It was thus that the holy women of old, hoping Godwards, adorned themselves, submissive to their husbands as Sarah was,[4] whose spiritual children they would prove themselves to be by calm and equable well-doing, and by not living in a state of nervous scare.[5] Christian *husbands* too are to be gentle and considerate to their fellow-heirs of salvation, that no jarring discords might cut short their prayers.[6] What we have said in the first chapter will throw into relief the beauty and wisdom of these exhortations. By the flagrancy of immorality, the frequency of divorce, and the disgust for marriage which prevailed in Rome, we may measure the blessedness of Christian matrimony. The meanest Christian slave who was imprisoned in an *ergastulum*, and would be buried in a catacomb, had no need to envy the splendid misery of a Nero or the pathetic tragedy of an Octavia's life. The life of many a Christian couple in the squalor of a humble slave-cell was unspeakably more desirable than that of the Roman profligates in their terror-haunted palaces.

> "Oh if they knew how pressed those splendid chains,
> How little would they mourn their humbler pains!"

(5) Finally, it was the duty of *all* to be united, sympathising, fraternal, compassionate, humble-minded,[7] requiting good for evil and

---

[1] An interesting *antanaclasis* or intentional variation of meaning, in the use of λόγος which the E. V. has missed. The Christian woman was not to be a preacher in her own house.

[2] 1 Tim. ii. 9. Coins and allusions show how elaborate in this period was the adornment of the hair among women of the world; how many were their jewels, and how extravagant their robes. See *supra*, p. 4.

[3] "The hidden man of the heart"—a striking expression independently borrowed in a different sense (for St. Peter never alludes to "the Christ within us," Gal. iv. 19) from Rom. ii. 29, vii. 22; 2 Cor. iv. 16; Eph. iii. 16. For classical analogies see Plut. *Conjug. Praecept.* 26; and see Clem. Alex. *Paedag.* iii. 4.

[4] Gen. xviii. 12.

[5] On Sarah's spiritual race see Rom. iv. 11; Gal. iii. 7. The word πτόησις, "scare," is probably borrowed from Prov. iii. 25 (LXX.). St. Peter was evidently familiar with the Proverbs.

[6] 1 Pet. iii. 1—7. For ἐκκόπτεσθαι (Rom. xi. 22, etc.), A, B, read ἐγκόπτεσθαι, "be hindered." Cf. 1 Cor. vii. 5.

[7] Leg. ταπεινόφρονες, א, A, B, C

blessing for abuse, as being heirs of blessing. This lesson is enforced by a free citation of David's eulogy of government of the tongue, and of a peaceful disposition as the secret of a blessed life, as well as by the truth that, whether just or evildoers, we live under the eye of God.[1] Who then could harm them if they proved themselves zealots of the good?[2] Let them fear nothing, for there is a beatitude in persecution for the sake of righteousness if the will of God should so decree. Inward holiness,[3] outward readiness to vindicate to every one their grounds of hope with meekness and fear,[4] together with a good conscience, would in the long run make the heathen blush at their insulting and threatening calumnies against the holiness which they accused of criminality. For, contrary to the common opinion of men, it is better to suffer (if such be God's will) *unjustly* than to suffer when we deserve to do so. If we suffer for sins which we have not committed, so did our great Example.[5] "Because Christ also, once for all, suffered for sin, just for unjust, that He may lead you to God; slain in the flesh, but quickened to life in the spirit, wherein also He went and preached[6] to the spirits in prison[7] who once were disobedient when the long-suffering of God awaited[8] in the days of Noah while the Ark was a-preparing; by entering wherein, few, that is, eight souls,[9] were saved through water:[10] which (water, *leg. ŝ*) also as an antitype now saveth you—namely, baptism—(not the putting away of the filth of the flesh, but the entreaty for a good conscience towards God)[11]—by the resurrection of Jesus Christ, who is on the right hand of God, having gone into Heaven,[12] angels and authorities and powers being made subject unto Him."[13]

The general meaning of this passage—Christ's descent into Hades to

---

[1] Ps. xxxiii. 12—16, LXX.
[2] 1 Pet. iii. 13, leg. ζηλωταί, א, A, B, C. On the thought, see a magnificent passage in Chrysostom (*Ep. ad Cyriacum*): "Should the Empress determine to banish me, let her banish me. The earth is the Lord's. If she should cast me into the sea, let her cast me into the sea. I will remember Jonah," etc.
[3] 1 Pet. iii. 15, leg. τὸν Χριστόν, א, A, B, C. "But sanctify the Christ in your hearts as Lord."
[4] 1 Pet. iii. 15. The notion that legal trials are intended by ἀπολογία, and with it the inference that the days of Trajan are alluded to, are excluded by the words "to *every one* that asketh," etc.
[5] 1 Pet. iii. 8—17.
[6] ἐκήρυξεν = εὐηγγελίσατο, "preached the Gospel."
[7] *i.e.*, in Hades. Jude 6; 2 Pet. ii. 4.
[8] 1 Pet. iii. 20. ἀπεξεδέχετο, א, A, B, C, K, &c. The reading ἅπαξ "once for all" of Erasmus and the E. V. is quite untenable.
[9] This indicates the motive of Christ's Descent into Hades. It was *because* few only had been saved from perishing. And this is the view of such Fathers as Clem. Alex. (*Strom.* vi. 6), Origen, Athanasius, Jerome, and even, in his milder moods, Augustine (*Ep. ad Evod.* clxiv.).
[10] Perhaps this means "by water as an instrument," *i.e.*, because the water floated the Ark.
[11] See *supra*, p. 75, note 3.
[12] Cf. 1 Tim. iii. 16. Perhaps, as Dr. Plumptre says, the precious fragment of an early baptismal profession.
[13] 1 Pet. iii. 8—22. Cf. Col. ii. 10—15.

proclaim the Gospel to the once disobedient dead—is to every unobscured and unsophisticated mind as clear as words can make it. Theologians have attempted to get rid of this obvious reference by explaining it of Christ preaching in the person of Noah; or by making "He preached" mean "He announced *condemnation*;" or by limiting "the spirits in prison" to Adam and the Old Testament saints; or by rendering ἐν φυλακῇ "*on the watchtower* of expectation" (!); or by supposing that Christ only preached to those spirits who repented while they were being drowned! These attempts arise from that spirit of system which would fain be more orthodox than Scripture itself, and would exclude every ground of future hope from the revelation of a love too loving for hearts trained in bitter theologies. What was the effect of Christ's preaching we are not told. Some, perhaps, may like to assume that the preaching of Christ in the Unseen World was unanimously rejected by the once disobedient dead, though the mention of their former disobedience seems to imply the inference that they did hearken now. Others can, if they choose, assert that this proclamation of the Gospel to disembodied spirits was confined to *antediluvian* sinners. With such inferences we are unconcerned. "It is ours," says Alford, "to deal with the plain words of Scripture, and to accept its revelations as far as vouchsafed to us. And they are vouchsafed to us to the utmost limit of legitimate inference from revealed facts. The inference every intelligent reader will draw from the fact here announced: *it is not purgatory; it is not universal restitution; but it is one which throws blessed light on one of the darkest enigmas of divine justice:* the cases where the final doom seems infinitely out of proportion to the lapse which has incurred it." On the other hand, we do not press the inference of Hermas and St. Clement of Alexandria by teaching that this passage implies also *other* missions of Apostles and Saints to the world of spirits. We accept the words of Scripture, and leave the matter there in thankful hope.

Thus—continues the Apostle—as a preliminary to His exaltation, did Christ suffer for us, and we should therefore gird on the armour of the same resolve. Suffering (of course *Christian* suffering is implied) is a deathblow to concupiscence. In past times they had perpetrated the will of the Gentiles in "wine-swillings and roysterings,"[1] in lives of wanton excess, and idolatries that violated the eternal law of heaven; and now the Gentiles reviled them in astonishment that they would no longer run with them into "the same slough of dissoluteness."[2] But these Gentile opponents "shall give an account to Him that is ready to judge the living and the dead. For to this end, *even to the dead* was the Gospel preached, that, as regards men, they may be judged in the flesh, but may live as regards God in the spirit."

In the last verse we again encounter the ruthlessness of commentators. "The dead" to whom the Gospel was preached are taken to

---

[1] 1 Pet. iv. 3, οἰνοφλυγίαις, κώμοις.
[2] 1 Pet. iv. 4, ἀσωτίας ἀνάχυσιν

mean something quite different from "the dead" who are to give an account. The dead to whom the Gospel is preached are explained away into "sinners" or "the Gentiles," or "some who are *now* dead." Augustine, as might have been expected, leads the way in one wrong direction, and Calvin in another. Another view—which makes this verse mean that "Christ will judge even the dead as well as the living, because the dead too will not have been without an opportunity to receive His Gospel"—is indeed tenable. To me, however, judging of the feelings of the Apostle, from his boundless gratitude for the opportunities of obtaining forgiveness, and from the love which he inculcates towards all mankind, the connexion seems to be, "The heathen, in all their countless myriads, who seem to be hopelessly perishing around you, will be judged;—but the very reason why the Gospel was preached by Christ to the dead was in order that this judgment may be founded on principles of justice, that they may be judged ($\kappa\rho\iota\theta\hat{\omega}\sigma\iota$) in their human capacity as sinners, and yet may live ($\zeta\hat{\omega}\sigma\iota$) to God as regards the diviner part of their natures;"—if, that is, they accept this offer of the Gospel to them even beyond the grave.[1]

(6) "But the end of all things"—and therefore of calumny and suffering and heathen persecution in this transitory life—"is at hand. Be sound-minded, therefore, and be sober unto prayers, before all things having intense love towards one another, because love covereth a multitude of sins."[2] Then come fresh exhortations to unmurmuring hospitality (so necessary for poor and wandering Christian teachers), and to a right stewardship of God's various gifts for the common benefit to the glory of God through Jesus Christ. They were not to regard the conflagration[3] which was burning among them to serve as their test, as though it were something strange. They ought rather to rejoice because a fellowship in Christ's sufferings would in the same proportion involve a fellowship in His glory. Reproach in the name of Christ is a beatitude. Let none of them suffer as a murderer, thief, malefactor, or intrusive meddler; but punishment for refusing to disown the name of Christian[4] is not a thing for which to blush, but rather to glorify God. It showed them to be, as it were, under the very shadow of the wings of the Shechinah. The time for judgment had come. If it began from the house of God, what would be the end of those who *disobeyed* the Gospel of God? And if the righteous be saved with difficulty, the impious and

---

[1] Analogous elements of thought as to the disciplinary intent of even the severest punishments may be seen in 1 Cor. v. 5; xi. 31, 32.
[2] Prov. x. 12 (cf. xvii. 9), where it is "all sins." James v. 20 quotes the same words, but perhaps in a different sense; not, as here, of love throwing a covering over the sins *of others* by forbearance (cf. 1 Cor. xiii. 5, 6), but of love hiding our own sins from view.
[3] πυρώσει. Were it not that this word occurs in the LXX. of Proverbs (xxvii. 21), a book with which St. Peter shows himself so familiar, we might suppose that he and St. John (Rev. xviii. 9, 18) were reminded of it by the burning of Rome.
[4] Perhaps we should read the ignorant heathen distortion, *Chrestian* (see *Life and Work of St. Paul*, i. 301) with א.

sinner—where shall he appear?[1] So then let even those that suffer commit their lives unto God, as to a faithful Creator, in well-doing.[2]

The remainder of the Epistle is more specific. It is addressed to the elders by St. Peter—as a fellow-elder and witness of the sufferings of the Christ, and therefore also a partaker of the glory about to be revealed. He exhorts them to tend the flock of God[3] among them with willing and self-denying oversight, "not as lording it over their allotted charge,[4] but proving themselves examples of the flock; then, at the manifestation of the chief Shepherd, they should carry off as their prize "the amaranthine chaplet" of the conqueror's glory.[5] The younger, too, were to be submissive to the elders, "yea, all of you, being submissive to one another, tie on humility like a knotted dress,[6] because God arrays Himself against the overweening, but to the humble He giveth grace.[7] Be humbled, then, under the strong hand of God, that He may exalt you in season, casting, once for all, all your anxiety upon Him, because he careth for you. Be sober! watch! because your adversary,[8] the Devil, like a roaring lion, walketh about seeking whom he may swallow up. Against whom take your stand, firm in the faith, knowing that the very same sufferings are running their full course for your band of brethren in the world. But the God of all grace, Who called you unto His eternal glory in Christ Jesus, after you have suffered a little, Himself shall perfect, establish, strengthen, place you on a sure foundation. To Him be dominion for the ages of ages. Amen.[9]

"By Silvanus, your faithful brother, as I esteem him,[10] I write to you

---

[1] Prov. ix. 31. The words "upon earth" of the original Hebrew, show that temporal judgments (as in Matt. xxiv. 22) were prominent in the writer's mind (cf. Jer. xxv. 29). Christians were suffering under the Neronian persecution, but the destruction of Jerusalem and the disintegration of the Roman Empire were not far off.

[2] 1 Pet. iv. 7—19. The latter verses (12—17) are not a repetition of iii. 13, iv. 6, because there the afflictions were spoken of in relation to their persecutors, and here in relation to their own feelings (cf. Matt. v. 11). The μὴ ξενίζεσθε is equivalent to "make yourself at home in," "regard as perfectly natural." In ver. 15, St. Peter seems to have coined the picturesque word ἀλλοτριοεπίσκοποι, "other people's bishops." (The nearest approach to the word is Plato's ἀλλοτριοπραγμοσύνη, "meddlesomeness.") The attempt (Hilgenfeld, Einleit. 630) to render this "informers" (delator), because informers were legally punishable in the days of Trajan (Plin. Paneg. 34, 35), has nothing in its favour. The word is a needful warning against the temptation to a prying religiosity. The ἔρξασθαι of ver. 17, proving as it does that Jerusalem was not yet destroyed, is another death-blow to all hypotheses as to the late date of the Epistle.

[3] ποίμαινε τὰ πρόβατά μου, John xxi. 16.

[4] i.e., their "parishes," not "the clergy."

[5] ἀμαράντινον, not ἀμάραντος, as in i. 4:—

> "Their crowns inwove with amaranth and gold,
> Immortal amaranth. . . . "—MILTON.

not like fading Nemean parsley, or Isthmian pine.

[6] Ἐγκομβώσασθε, Col. iii. 12, Ἐνδύσασθε. Κόμβωμα—"an apron" worn by slaves.

[7] "Humility is a vessel of graces," Aug. Prov. iii. 34.

[8] Matt. v. 25, ἀντίδικος יצר.

[9] 1 Pet. v. 1—11.

[10] Fronmüller (in Lange's Commentary) strangely supposes that this can mean, "I conjecture that you will receive this Epistle by the hands of Silvanus!"

in few words, exhorting, and confirming by my testimony, that this is the true grace of God.[1] In this take your stand!"

"She, who is co-elect in Babylon, saluteth you,[2] and Marcus, my son. Salute one another with a kiss of love. Peace to you all in Christ Jesus. Amen."[3]

CHAPTER IX.

PECULIARITIES OF THE SECOND EPISTLE OF ST. PETER.

"*Petrus magis magisque opus esse statuit admonitione propter ingruentem corruptionem malorum hominum.*—BENGEL."

IN reading the First Epistle of St. Peter, we are reading a book which even a critic so advanced as M. Renan admits to be "one of the writings of the New Testament which is the most anciently and the most unanimously cited as authentic."[4] In turning to the Second Epistle we are met by problems of acknowledged difficulty, and have to consider the claims of a document which the same writer pronounces to be "*certainly* apocryphal," and of which he says that "among true critics he does not think it has a single defender." Such a remark is easy to make; but critics like Schmid, Guericke, Windischmann, Thiersch, Alford, and Brückner, are in learning, if not in genius, as much entitled to decide such a point *ex cathedrâ* as M. Renan, and they, after deliberate examination, do accept the Epistle as genuine, and offer in its defence not a contemptuous dictum, but a serious argument. On the other hand, although it is discourteous and unwarrantable to pronounce the Epistle to be so certainly spurious that nothing but prejudice or ignorance could maintain its genuineness, neither ought its defenders to argue as though any hesitation as to its genuineness was an impious arrangement of the Spirit of God. To say that "there is scarcely a single writing of all antiquity, sacred or profane, which must not be given up as spurious if the Second Epistle of St. Peter be not received as a genuine writing of the Apostle, and as a part

---

[1] This which I have written to you. It is very doubtful whether there is any intention *here* to ratify the orthodoxy of St. Paul's teachings, though all the Epistle shows how deeply the true St. Peter (so unlike the fictitious Peter of the *Clementines*) reverenced them.

[2] 1 Pet. v. 12, στήν, ι͗, A, B.

[3] Ἡ συνεκλεκτή. Some take this to mean "the co-elect lady"—*i.e.*, Peter's wife (cf. 1 Cor. xiv. 5). But surely a Jew would hardly have sent a greeting from his wife—a poor Galilean woman—to all these Churches, or have described her as simply ἡ ἐν Βαβυλῶνι. It is much more natural to understand ἐκκλησία, meaning the *Church* of Rome. It is true that St. Peter has not used that word, even in his salutation, but it might none the less be in his thoughts, just as St. Luke (in Acts xxvii. 14) says αὐτή of the ship, though he has been using the word πλοῖον. On Marcus and Babylon, see *ante*, p. 62.

[4] *L'Antechrist*, p —.

of Holy Writ;"—to assert that we receive it on "the testimony of the Universal Church," which is "the Spouse and Body of Christ enlightened by the Holy Ghost;"—and that if it be "not the Word of God, but the work of an impostor, then, with reverence be it said, Christ's promise to His Church has failed, and the Holy Spirit has not been given to guide her into all truth,"—is to use a style, I cannot say of "argument," but of dogmatising traditionalism, which perilously confuses a thousand separate issues. Such assertions, if listened to, would end in making all criticism impossible, and in reducing all inquiry to mediæval torpor. They can serve no purpose but to damage in many minds the cause of religion. They confound the eternal truths of Christianity with uncertain details. They imperil the impregnable fortress of Revelation by identifying its defence with that of its weakest and most uncertain outposts. To talk of the Second Epistle of St. Peter—if, indeed, it was not the work of that Apostle—as "a shameless forgery," and of its writer as "an impostor," and of his motives as showing "intentional fraud" and "cunning fabrication,"[1] is to use language which only tends to obscure the critical faculty. Such a style of statement is an anachronism. It cannot be said too strongly that it is "inexpedient to encumber the discussion by an attempted *reductio ad horribile* of one of the alternatives."[2]

The question of the genuineness of this Epistle must be regarded as unsettled until the arguments adduced against it by a serious criticism can be met by counter-arguments of a criticism equally serious. Its acceptance cannot be founded upon assertions to which criticism, as such, can pay no heed. That the writing known as the Second Epistle of St. Peter is *canonical*—that for fourteen centuries it has been accepted, and rightly accepted, by the Church as a part of the Canon of Holy Scripture—is not denied. I say *rightly* accepted, because the Church would not have so received it if she had not felt that it was "profitable for doctrine, for reproof, for correction, for instruction in righteousness." But to say that in its present form it is absolutely the work of St. Peter—and that, if not genuine, the Church has "been imposed upon by what must, in that case, be regarded as a *Satanic device*" (!), is to claim a monopoly of the critical faculty which is refuted by every page of the history of exegesis. On all such questions Churches have erred, and may err. The Second Epistle is accepted as St. Peter's *mainly* on the authority of the Church of the fourth century;[3] but the Church of the fourth century had not the least pretence to greater authority, and had a far smaller amount of critical knowledge, than the Church of the nineteenth. The guidance of the Holy Spirit of God was promised not to one age only, but to the Church of all ages, even to the end of the world; but the lessons of

---

[1] Wordsworth, *Introd.*; Fronmüller, § 3.
[2] *The New Testament Commentary* (Ellicott), iii. 437.
[3] It was admitted into the Canon by the Council of Laodicea A.D. 302.

century after century ought to have taught us that guidance into *all necessary spiritual truth* is a very different thing from critical infallibility. Theologians who usurp the right to speak with inspired positiveness on questions which are still unsettled, not only render their own pretensions liable to defeat, but seriously endamage a sacred cause. Nothing has gone farther to shake my conviction of the genuineness of the Epistle than the dangerous plausibility of many of the arguments adduced by its defenders. They have so obviously approached the question with their minds made up beforehand; they have shown themselves so eager to establish a case at all costs; they have treated as so unimportant the absence of that evidence to which in other cases they attach such extreme importance; they have been tempted to use arguments so painfully inconclusive, and to make light of counter-considerations so undeniably strong, that any one who takes the same side with them may well fear lest he too should sink into the advocate, and forget the love of simple truth. The supporters of the Epistle have done far more than its assailants to deepen my own uncertainty whether it can be regarded as the *direct* work of the Apostle.

For what are the facts with which we must start in considering the Second Epistle of St. Peter? Surely common honesty compels us to acknowledge that of all the books of the New Testament it is the one for which we can produce the smallest amount of external evidence, and which at the same time offers the greatest number of internal difficulties.

As regards the *external* evidence, the Epistle is not quoted, and is not *certainly* referred to, by a single writer in the first or second century. Neither Polycarp, nor Ignatius, nor Barnabas, nor Clement of Rome, nor Justin Martyr, nor Theophilus of Antioch, nor Irenæus, nor Tertullian, nor Cyprian, can be proved even to allude to it. It is not found in the Peshito Syriac, nor in the Vetus Itala. It is unknown to the Muratorian Canon. During the first two centuries the only traces of it, if traces they can be called, are to be found in the Pastor of Hermas,[1] and in a recently discovered passage of Melito of Sardis; but even these are of so distant and general a nature that it is impossible to determine whether we should regard them as reminiscences of the language of the Epistle, or accidental approximations to it. But even if we grant *all* the parallels adduced by Dietlein, the concession would be unfavourable rather than otherwise to the genuineness of the Epistle; he ruins his own case by proving too much. For if the writers of the first and second centuries did indeed know the Epistle, it is inconceivable that not one of them should have hinted at the authority which it derived from the name of its author. When we come down to later writers, we find that, in all his learned

---

[1] Hermas, iii. 2; 2 Pet. ii. 20.

works, it is not once alluded to by St. Clement of Alexandria, who even seems to exclude it by the expression, "Peter in *the* Epistle."[1] Origen knew of it, but, since he uses the same expression as St. Clement, seems—when writing accurately—to question its genuineness;[2] although, if we may trust the loose Latin translation of Rufinus, he refers to it as St. Peter's when he alludes to it popularly in a casual quotation. Firmilian († 270), a friend of Origen, is the first person who, in a letter to Cyprian, extant only in a Latin version, refers to it; but neither is this letter beyond suspicion, nor is the reference decisive.[3] Didymus, in a Latin translation of his commentary, calls the Epistle "*falsata*," and says that "it is not in the Canon."[4] Eusebius knew of it, but only recognised one genuine Epistle.[5] It was rejected by Theodore of Mopsuestia, and was still regarded as uncertain in the times of St. Gregory of Nazianzus.[6] It must, therefore, be admitted that the evidence in its favour is exceptionally weak. The First Epistle was almost universally recognised by the ancient Church; the Second was partly controverted, partly ignored—and among those who ignored or rejected it were some Fathers of the greatest learning, and of the keenest critical acumen.

These doubts were so far silenced, that it was on the whole passively accepted by men like Athanasius, Basil, Jerome, and Augustine, and towards the close of the fourth century was declared to be canonical by the Councils of Laodicea (A.D. 363), Hippo (A.D. 393), and Carthage (A.D. 396). But surely this tardy recognition is a suspicious circumstance. If the repeated references to most of the other books of the New Testament Canon by Fathers of the first three centuries be rightly regarded as proofs of their genuineness, then the absence or uncertainty of any reference during the same period must so far be unfavourable. Importance is sometimes attached to fourth century decisions by saying that evidence was then extant which has not come down to us. The proposition might be disputed; but whatever such evidence may have been, it did not remove the doubts which prevailed in the great schools of Alexandria and Antioch, as represented by such eminent scholars as Clement of Alexandria, Origen, and Theodore of Mopsuestia. The intrinsic value of the Epistle, and the growing habit of loosely referring to it as "St. Peter's," would lead to its gradual admission without any further debate, at a period when competent critics were few and far between. St. Jerome did more than any man to hasten the acceptance of

---

[1] Clem. Alex. *Strom.* iii. p. 562, *ed.* Potter. Eusebius (*H. E.* vi. 14) says that Clement, in his *Hypotyposes*, commented both on the acknowledged and the uncertain books of the N. T., not even passing by "The Apocalypse of Peter:" but that can hardly mean this Epistle.

[2] "Peter has left only one generally acknowledged Epistle—perhaps also a second, for this is considered doubtful (ἔστω δὲ καὶ δευτέραν, ἀμφιβάλλεται γάρ)." Orig. ap. Euseb. *H. E.* vi. 25.)

[3] *Epp. Cypr.* 75.

[4] The word which he used was probably νενόθευται, "has been accounted spurious."

[5] Euseb. *H. E.* iii. 25. [6] Greg. Naz. *Carm.* 33, vs. 35.

the Epistle by admitting it into the Vulgate. Yet he was too able not to observe, and too candid not to admit, that it differs from the First Epistle in style, character, and structure of words.[1] Further than this, he tells us that "most men" in his day denied that St. Peter wrote it, "on account of the dissonance of its style with the former." He is the only person in the first four centuries who offers any intelligible theory of that striking divergence. This he does by saying that "from the necessity of things he made use of different interpreters." This is indeed to accept the Epistle as genuine, but with the important modification that it is either a translation from an Aramaic original, or that the *thoughts only* are St. Peter's, while the words belong to some one else. If this be admitted, what becomes of recent attempts to show that the style and phraseology are exactly what we should expect?

It is idle to lay much stress on the fact that no further doubt as to the authorship of the Epistle was expressed during long centuries of critical torpor. During those centuries there was no criticism worth speaking of, because criticism could only register the dictated conclusions of a Church which punished original inquiry as presumptuous and heretical. If any one expressed an independent opinion, however true, the Church and the world combined against him. But the moment that "the deep slumber of decided opinions" was broken by the Reformation—the moment that criticism ceased to be confronted by "the syllogism of violence"—thence the doubts as to the genuineness of the Epistle began to revive. Erasmus, Luther, and Calvin freely express them, and they were shared by Cajetan, Grotius, Scaliger, and Salmasius. In modern times, since the days of Semler, an increasing number of critics have decided against the genuineness of the Epistle, including not only Baur, Schwegler, Hilgenfeld, Mayerhoff, Bleek, Davidson, Messner, Reuss, but even such conservative theologians as Neander, Weiss, and Huther, while Bertholdt, Ullman, Bunsen,[2] and even Lange[3] hold that, though genuine in part, it has been largely interpolated.

The last supposition, which might remove many difficulties, can hardly be accepted. The body of the Epistle must stand or fall as a whole, for it is singularly compact and homogeneous.[4] The writer has stated his twofold object in the last two verses. One of these objects was *warning:* it was that, by being put upon their guard, the readers might not fall away from their firm position through being misled by the error of the lawless. The other object was *exhortation:* "But grow in the grace and knowledge of our Lord and Saviour Jesus Christ." These objects are kept steadily in view, and

---

[1] *Jer. Ep. ad Hedib.* ii. Compare *De Virr. Illustr.* 1.
[2] *Ignatius*, p. 175.   [3] *Apostol. Zeit.* i. 152.
[4] Mayerhoff's remark, that the Epistle is clumsy and illogical, is quite false. See Brückner, *Einl.* § 1; Hofmann, p. 121; Huther, p. 306.

the structure of the letter is more distinctly articulated than that of the First.

The outline of the letter is as follows :—After the greeting (i. 1, 2) the writer enforces his hortatory object by urging the attainment of *full knowledge*, which is the consummation of Christian growth, and the essential of final salvation (3—11). Hence it is his wish to utilise the brief time which remains to him for reminding them of this truth (12—15), a truth of which they might be convinced, because Peter, with others, had been, as it were, an initiated eye-witness of the Transfiguration, and had heard the voice which was then borne from heaven (16—18); and because they all possessed the word of prophecy as a surer witness, to which they would do well to listen as to the voice of inspiration (19—21).

He thus passes quite naturally to the topic of *warning*. False teachers would bring in "sects of perdition," and he describes these false teachers in their successful blasphemies and their certain punishment, like that which fell on the world at the time of the Flood and on the inhabitants of the Cities of the Plain (ii. 1—9); though, as in all such instances, the pious should be delivered (5, 7, 9). None, however, were more deserving of God's vengeance than these impure, disdainful, self-corrupting railers—fools who rushed in where angels feared to tread (10—12), whose vileness and perniciousness are described (13, 14), and whose apostasy resembles that of Balaam (15, 16). After using various indignant images (17), to illustrate their insolence, wantonness, and cunning—which, while it promised liberty, only involved a deadly servitude (18, 19)—he says that their previous knowledge of Christ is the worst aggravation of their horrible apostasy (20, 22).

He is therefore writing once more to remind his readers of previous lessons (iii. 1, 2), and especially to warn them against those scoffers who sneered at the promised coming of Christ (3, 4), and ignored the fact, that as the world had perished by water, so should it hereafter perish by fire (5—7). Let the brethren remember that one day is with the Lord as a thousand years, and that His delays are due to His mercy. But the dreadful day of dissolution should come (8, 9). On this thought he bases the exhortation to them to be blameless, as those who look for new heavens and a new earth, and to make a right use of God's longsuffering, in accordance with the teaching of St. Paul—whose writings they must be careful not to wrest into a wrong sense (10—16). Then into two final verses he compresses his recapitulation of the two chief topics of the letter, together with the final doxology (17, 18).

Such, then—so marked by unity and coherence—is this remarkable letter, which the Church could ill afford to lose, and which is full of impassioned warning and eloquent exhortation. We have seen how weak is the external evidence in its favour; are there any decisive phenomena to which we can appeal by way of internal evidence of its authenticity?

PECULIARITIES OF THE EPISTLE.

That it resembles the First Epistle in the use of some peculiar expressions is certain. The word for "conversation," *i.e.*, general mode of life ;[1] the remarkable word for an eye-witness, which is also the word for one initiated into the mysteries ;[2] the expressions "to carry off as a prize,"[3] "spotless and blameless,"[4] and "to walk in lusts,"[5] are common to both Epistles, and are almost unknown to the rest of the New Testament.[6] If the general style were the same, these would have weight. Their weight is small when we remember (i.) that the writer of the Second Epistle must, on any supposition, have been well acquainted with the First,[7] and when we find (ii.) that the Second Epistle abounds in expressions peculiar to itself, and (iii.) that it is confessedly written in a *style* of marked difference.

The peculiarity of many expressions, of which the majority are unique,[8] must strike the most careless reader of the original. "To acquire faith by lot ;"[9] "to give things which tend to life and piety ;"[10] "to bring in all haste ;"[11] "to furnish an abundant supply of virtue ;"[12] "to receive oblivion ;"[13] "to furnish an abundant entrance ;"[14] "the present truth ;"[15] "to bring in factions of perdition ;"[16] "the judgment is not idle, the destruction is not drowsily nodding ;"[17] "to walk in desire of pollution ;"[18] "to walk *behind* the flesh ;"[19] "to esteem luxurious wantonness in the daytime as a pleasure ;"[20] "eyes full of an adulteress ;"[21] "insatiable of sin ;"[22] "a heart trained in covetousness ;"[23] "the mirk of the darkness ;"[24] "treasured with fire ;"[25] "to fall from their own steadfastness ;"[26] "chains of darkness ;" "to calcine to ashes ;" "to hurl to Tartarus ;" "to blaspheme glories ;" "the heavens shall pass away hurtlingly ;"[27] "the elements being consumed

---

[1] ἀναστροφή, ἀναστρέφεσθαι (1 Pet. i. 15, 18, etc. ; 2 Pet. ii. 7, iii. 11).
[2] ἐπόπτης, ἐποπτεύειν (1 Pet. ii. 3, iii. 2 ; 2 Pet. i. 16).
[3] καμίζεσθαι (1 Pet. i. 9, v. 4 ; 2 Pet. ii. 13).
[4] ἄσπιλοι καὶ ἀμώμητοι (1 Pet. i. 19 ; 2 Pet. iii. 14).
[5] πορεύεσθαι ἐν ἐπιθυμίαις (2 Pet. ii. 10).
[6] To these may be added ἀπόθεσις (1 Pet. iii. 21 ; 2 Pet. i. 14) ; πέπαυται ἁμαρτίας (1 Pet. iv. 1 ; 2 Pet. ii. 12) ; ἄθεσμος (1 Pet. iv. 3, ἀθέμιτος, 2 Pet. ii. 7, iii. 17).
[7] 2 Pet. iii. 1. [8] There are twenty *hapax legomena* in this brief epistle.
[9] λαχοῦσι πίστιν, i. 1. [10] τὰ πρὸς ζωὴν καὶ εὐσέβειαν δεδωρημένης (act.), i. 3.
[11] σπουδὴν πᾶσαν παρεισενέγκαντες, i. 5.
[12] ἐπιχορηγήσατε ἐν τῇ πίστει ὑμῶν τὴν ἀρετήν, 2 Pet. i. 5. [13] λήθην λαβών, i. 9.
[14] ἐπιχορηγηθήσεται ὑμῖν ἡ εἴσοδος, i. 11. [15] ἡ παροῦσα ἀλήθεια, i. 12.
[16] παρεισάξουσιν αἱρέσεις ἀπωλείας, ii. 7.
[17] Τὸ κρίμα οὐκ ἀργεῖ, ἡ ἀπώλεια οὐ νυστάζει, ii. 3.
[18] ἐν ἐπιθυμίᾳ μιασμοῦ πορευομένους, ii. 10.
[19] ὀπίσω, the only passage of the N. T., except Jude 7, where ὀπίσω is not used of a *person*. It has a *special* meaning, and is unlike περιπατεῖν κατὰ σάρκα in Rom. viii. 4.
[20] ἡδονὴν ἡγούμενοι τὴν ἐν ἡμέρᾳ τρυφήν, ii. 13.
[21] ὀφθαλμοὺς μεστοὺς μοιχαλίδος, ii. 14.
[22] ἀκαταπαύστους ἁμαρτίας, ii. 14. Some MSS. (A. B.) have the yet stranger reading ἀκαταπαύστους.
[23] γεγυμνασμένην πλεονεξίαις, ii. 14. [24] ὁ ζόφος τοῦ σκότους, ii. 17.
[25] τεθησαυρισμένοι πυρί, iii. 7. [26] ἐκπέσητε τοῦ ἰδίου στηριγμοῦ, iii. 17.
[27] ῥοιζηδόν, iii. 10. The strange English expression exactly corresponds to the Greek. The only form like it occurs in the LXX. in Cant. iv. 5.

melt away."[1] Such are a few of the striking and even startling phrases which in the course of three short chapters stamp the style with an intense peculiarity. Nothing analogous to these phrases is found in the First Epistle. It may be pleaded that, as in the case of the Epistle to the Colossians, some of these words are due to the new subjects with which the Apostle has here to deal. That answer might be sufficient for three or four of them, but most are of a kind which do not rise from speciality of subject. They show a peculiarity of structure rather than of topic. Some of them are eccentricities of language adopted to clothe conceptions which would have been capable of a perfectly simple and commonplace expression.

Independently of this distinctiveness of verbiage, there is a wide difference between the two Epistles in the general form of thought.[2] This is a fact too obvious to be denied. Obvious as it is to us—for besides minor differences, there is a ruggedness and tautology in the Greek of the Second Epistle very different from the smoothness of the First—this difference of style must have been far more obvious to those to whom Greek was a spoken language, and who were therefore more sensitive than we can be to its delicate refinements. It was pointed out by St. Jerome, and he assigns it as one of the causes which had led to the general rejection of the Epistle.

But it is answered, and again with perfect truth, that the style of a writer differs under differing circumstances. The style of the Epistle to the Ephesians is not the same as that to the Galatians, and both differ from the Pastoral Epistles. The style of St. John's Gospel is very unlike that of the Apocalypse. I grant this to the utmost. I have even insisted upon it, and illustrated it in other instances.[3] But differences of style must not be so wide as to show a difference of idiosyncrasy. They must be accompanied with resemblances of structure; and they must be partially accounted for by a long interspace of years. The difference between the styles of the First and the Second Epistle of St. Peter does not admit of these modifying circumstances; it is deeper than can be accounted for by a difference of mood and object. The Apocalypse and the Gospel of St. John were separated by an interval of perhaps thirty years spent in the most polished cities of Asia. The earlier and later Epistles of St. Paul were divided from each other by many years subjected to the intense influence of ever-varying conditions. But the two Epistles of St. Peter, if both are genuine, must have been written, so far as we can learn, under identical external conditions, and written within a very short time of each other.

For this reason I set aside as irrelevant the instances adduced by the industry of critics to prove that the same writer may adopt different styles. It is true that the style of Plato's Epinomis is inferior to that

---

[1] καυσούμενα τήκεται. [2] This is admitted even by Schott.
[3] See my *Life and Work of St. Paul*, ii. 610.

of the Phædrus; that Virgil's Ciris is unworthy of the author of the Æneid; that the De Oratoribus of Tacitus is marvellously unlike his Annals; that the Paradise Lost is in a loftier key than the Paradise Regained; that the style of Twelfth Night is widely separated from that of Hamlet; that the Racine of the Alexandre is much below the Racine of the Phèdre and Athalie; that Burke on the Sublime and Beautiful is incomparably tamer than Burke's Orations; and that there are marked distinctions between the first and the second part of Goethe's Faust. But these analogies, which might easily be multiplied, do not touch the problem before us. There is not one among them which offers a parallel to the phenomenon of total difference, not only in language, but in thought, presented by two works of the same writer dealing in great measure with the same subjects, and written from the same place, within a very short time of one another. And the differences between the two Epistles go further than this. Many are adduced which I pass over as unimportant. But it is not easy to explain why there should be such and so many variations as those which follow. Thus—(1) In the first the writer calls himself Peter, and in the second Symeon Peter. (2) In the first he writes "to the elect sojourners of the Dispersion;" in the second to those who "obtained like precious faith with us." (3) In the first Christ's descent into Hades is a point of capital importance; in the second, where there would seem to be every reason for such an allusion, no reference is made to it. (4) In the first the writer's mind is full of the Epistles to the Romans and Ephesians, and the Epistle of St. James; in the second, though he makes a special reference to St. Paul, there is scarcely a single thought, and barely two expressions,[1] which can with any plausibility be referred to those two Epistles, and there is only one word[2] which can be derived from St. James. (5) Again, in the first he constantly enweaves without quotation the words of Isaiah, the Psalms, and especially the Book of Proverbs;[3] in the second there is not a single certain quotation, and if ii. 22, iii. 8 be meant for quotations, they are introduced in a wholly different way.[4] (6) Of the first the keynote is *Hope;* of the second, though also written in days of persecution, the leading conception is the totally different one of "*full knowledge.*"[5] (7) In the first our Lord is usually called Christ, or "the Christ," or "Jesus Christ;" in the second the simple title is never used, but He is always called "our Lord," or "our Lord and Saviour Jesus Christ." (8) In the first (a) the Coming of Christ is called "a Revelation;" in the second the "Presence" or "Day of the Lord;"

---

[1] 2 Pet. i. 2, etc., Ἐπίγνωσις (Rom. i. 28, etc.); iii. 15, μακροθυμία (Rom. ii. 4).
[2] 2 Pet. ii. 14; ἀλλάσσοντες, James i. 14.   [3] 1 Pet. i. 7, ii. 17, iv. 8, 18.
[4] It has been supposed that i. 19, "as a lamp shining in a squalid place," is borrowed from 2 Esdr. xii. 42, "Of all the prophets thou only art left us . . . as a candle in a dark place." But so obvious a comparison need not have been borrowed.
[5] This ἐπίγνωσις is made to consist in the knowledge of the Power and Parousia of Christ. See Huther, p. 306.

(β) in the first this Advent is expected as near at hand, while in the second we are warned that it may be indefinitely distant; (γ) in the first Christ's coming is regarded as the glorification of the saints; in the second as the destruction of the world. (9) In the first the sufferings, death, resurrection, and ascension of the Lord are prominent; in the second no allusion is made to them. (10) In the first there is a prevailing tone of sweetness, mildness, and fatherly dignity; the second is, as a whole, denunciatory and severe. Further difficulties have been caused to some minds (11) by the manner in which the writer of the Second Epistle, unlike the author of the First, seems anxious to thrust into prominence his own personality; (12) by the expression "the command of *your* Apostles," in iii. 2; (13) by the manner in which the false teachers seem to be treated of sometimes as future (ἔσονται, ii. 1—3), sometimes as present (ii. 10, 12, 13, 15, 17, &c.);[1] (14) by the growth of a feeling which they consider to be later than the Apostolic age in the allusion to Mount Hermon as "the Holy Mount;" (15) by the unparalleled reference to St. Paul and the apparent placing of his letters on a level with the Scriptures of the Old Testament;[2] and (16) by the curious allusion to "the world standing out of water and amidst water."

(17) But we have not even yet exhausted the list of serious difficulties. An entirely new and very formidable one has just been brought to light by Dr. Abbott. It is nothing more or less than the *certainty* that either the author of the Second Epistle had read Josephus—in which case, of course, he could not have been St. Peter, since the earliest of Josephus's writings were not published till A.D. 75, and the Antiquities not earlier than A.D. 93; or (an alternative which Dr. Abbott does not discuss) that Josephus had read the Second Epistle, which, it must be confessed, is a difficult supposition. One thing is indisputable—namely, that the resemblances between the writer and the Jewish historian *cannot be accidental.*

α. The proof rests partly on single words and phrases, such as "tardiness" applied to the Divine retribution (iii. 9); "to which ye do well if ye take heed" (i. 19); "assuming oblivion" (i. 9); "bringing in besides all diligence" (i. 5); "condemned with an overthrow" (ii. 6); "equally precious"; "*epangelma*" for "promise" (i. 4); "*sesophismenos*" for "cunningly elaborated" (i. 16); and "from of old" (ii. 3). These are not found elsewhere, either in the New Testament or in the Septuagint, or not in the same senses; but they occur in Josephus, often in very similar allusions.

But the proof becomes far more striking when we consider *groups of words*, cases in which several unusual words occur together in similar passages.

---

[1] The same strange phenomenon meets us in the third chapter (iii. 3, ἐλεύσονται; iii. 5, λανθάνει).

[2] These differences might be greatly multiplied. See Davidson, *Introd.* i. 492—494.

Of these there are two most marked instances:—

In the Preface to the Antiquities (§§ 3, 4) Josephus tells us that Moses thought it necessary to consider "*the Divine nature*" (θεοῦ φύσις), without which he would be unable to promote the "*virtue*" of his readers; that other legislators "*followed after myths*," but Moses, having shown that "*God was possessed of perfect virtue*," thought that men should strive after virtue; and that his laws contain nothing derogatory to the "*greatness*" of God.

In this single section, then, there are several very striking expressions, but they occur quite naturally, and betray no deviation from the historian's usual style. It is, however, surprising that we find them occurring as absolutely isolated expressions—*hapax legomena* as far as the New Testament is concerned—in this Epistle. Thus we have "that ye may become partakers of the *Divine nature*" (i. 4), where both the phrase and its context strongly recall Josephus; we have the "*greatness*" (*megaleiotes*) of Christ (i. 16), and in the very same verse "*following after cunningly elaborated* myths." This would alone be sufficient to attract notice; but how much more amazing is the word "*virtue*" applied to God! The word "virtue" in this sense is itself very rare in the New Testament, which uplifts the higher standard of *holiness*. But no one can read that God called us "by His own glory *and virtue*" (for such is the true reading) without something like a start of surprise. We should be struck with the singularity of the expression in any writer; but in Josephus it is at once explained and justified by the context in which it occurs. For Josephus is not making an abstract allusion, but expressly contrasting the Ideal of Virtue in God's revelation of Himself to Moses with the shameful vices which degraded the heathen ideal of their false deities.[1]

But this is not the only group of words.

β. In the last words of Moses (as recorded by Josephus in *Antt.* iv. 8, § 2) there occur no less than eight or nine phrases, some of which either do not occur, or scarcely ever occur, in the New Testament, and some of which are not found even in the Septuagint, but every one of which occurs in this brief Epistle, and some of them in similar collocations.[2]

To me I confess that the evidential force of this fact—and Dr. Abbott informs me that further evidence is forthcoming—seems to be very strong.[3] If, then, the Epistle be genuine, it cannot be questioned

---

[1] 'Ἀρετή only occurs in 2 Pet. i. 3, 5; Phil. iv. 8. In 1 Pet. ii. 9 the plural ἀρεταί is indeed applied to God, but in a very different sense. It there means "excellencies."

[2] They are, τοιάσδε (i. 17); θείας κοινωνοὶ φύσεως (i. 4); "but I think it just" (i. 13); "so long as" (*id.*); "in the *present* truth" (i. 12); "mention" or "memorial" (i. 15); "departure" for "death" (*id.*); "recognising that" (i. 20; iii. 3), and others. Besides these groups of words, we have phrases in 2 Pet. i. 19 and ii. 10, which occur in Jos. *Antt.* xi. 6, § 12, and *B. J.* iii. 9, § 3, but not elsewhere in the N. T. or LXX.

[3] Since these pages have been in the press, Dr. Abbott has published his very interesting discovery in the *Expositor* for January, 1882. Some parts of his second paper are so similar to my own remarks, that I think it right to say that these pages were in print

that it was known to Josephus. Here, however, we are met by the difficulty that the same argument does not apply to the First Epistle, so that once more we have a marked distinction between the two.

(18) Once again, if the Second Epistle of St. Peter be genuine, it was written within a short time of the Apocalypse; yet how different is the tone of the two writings with respect to the Coming of Christ! In the Apocalypse the belief in its immediate imminence "blazes out in its brightest flame, and takes its most concrete form in the idea of the Millennium:" on the other hand, in the Second Epistle of St. Peter, we hear of scoffers, who are already beginning to point out that in their opinion the nearness of the Parousia is a mere delusion, and to ask, "Where is the promise of this coming?" Now, how does the writer meet their objections? Not by thundering forth with yet deeper conviction MARANATHA, but by showing that, as far as human calculations of time were concerned, the coming might be still indefinitely delayed, because with the Lord a thousand years are as one day. There is not another passage in the whole New Testament which implies that the Parousia—for which the early Christians looked with such intense earnestness—so far from being manifested in that very generation, might not take place for even a millennium hence. However we explain the phrase, "Since the fathers fell asleep," the point of view seems to mark an age later than that of the true St. Peter.[1] It seems to point to an epoch in which those who, like the Montanists, still expected the instant close of the age (in another sense than that in which it had already been accomplished by the fall of Jerusalem) were few in number.[2]

The last chapter of the Epistle is devoted to the correction of two errors—namely, (i.) the acceptance of the scoff about the delay in Christ's Second Coming, and (ii.) the misuse of the Epistles of St. Paul. The first error is dealt with at some length (iii. 1—13); the second is dismissed in a few words (15—16). It cannot be said that either of these topics *necessarily* indicates an age later than that of St. Peter. They would, however, have been very suitable to the second century, when even the Fall of Jerusalem—in which men failed to recognise a true Coming of Christ—had not been followed by the expected Advent in flaming fire; and when, as we know, some Gnostic sects, like that of Marcion, were beginning to make a dangerous use of the arguments of St. Paul.

No doubt as regards every one of these difficulties *something* more or

---

before I had read it. Besides the coincidences of phrase, he points out that the allusions to Noah and Balaam in 2 Pet. ii. 5, 8, point to *Hagadôth* found in Jos. *Antt.* i. 3, § 1; iv. 6, § 3.

[1] Even in Justin Martyr's time there was still the expectation of an immediate Parousia (*Dial. c. Tryph.* 80).

[2] See Baur, *First Three Centuries*, i. 247, ii. 45 (E. Tr.). The Montanist view was no doubt that of the primitive Church. See Mr. De Soyre's excellent Essay on Montanism, and Bonwelsch, *Die Nähe des Weltendes*, p. 76.

less possible, probable, or plausible, may be urged. It may be said, for instance, that after St. Peter had written the First Epistle the letter of St. Jude was brought to him, and threw him into such a state of indignant alarm as to alter his whole frame of mind, and to account for many of the differences above mentioned. The non-allusion to Christ's preaching in Hades may be referred to this indignation of mind, and it may be pointed out that St. Peter, if the Second Epistle be genuine, shows the same interest as before in events to which other Apostles have made little or no allusion. The absence or presence of certain marked influences, and modes of quoting Scripture, may be regarded as having in it nothing decisive. The expression "*your* Apostles" may merely mean "St. Paul and those who preached to you." "The Holy Mount," though not a phrase which we should have expected, may be defended on Old Testament analogies,[1] and may hardly involve its modern connotations. The allusion to St. Paul's Epistles may not be to all of them which *we* possess, but only to those, whether lost or extant, which may have been made known to St. Peter by Silvanus or Mark; and doubtless the power of the Holy Spirit was recognised in them from the earliest age. Whether these answers be regarded as sufficient to support the cause in which they are urged, must depend on the feelings of the reader. They mitigate some of the difficulties; few, I think, would pretend to say that they are adequate to remove them all. It must be remembered that objections which might be overruled if they stood alone, may acquire from their number and variety a cumulative force. Nor are *all* these objections easy to meet. The mixture, for instance, of presents and futures in the description of the False Teachers, is a difficulty which has been met by untenable remarks about the "Prophetic style." That St. Jude's Epistle was *prior* to that of St. Peter seems to me an irrefragable conclusion; and if so, it is an unsolved—though I will not say insoluble—difficulty that St. Peter should have described in prophetic futures the teachers whom St. Jude had already denounced as active workers. There is no known reason why he should have mingled predictions of their appearance with traits of their existing physiognomy. If it be urged that St. Peter merely prophesies the worst development of contemporary germs of evil, the answer is that it would be impossible to imagine *anything* more pernicious than the apostates whom St. Jude had scathed with his terrible invective.[2] Before we can acquiesce in these methods of defence let us ask ourselves whether they would have had the least weight with us if no predisposition to side with the popular opinion were

---

[1] Is. xxvii. 13.
[2] Dean Alford and others point out resemblances in this Epistle to the style and phraseology of St. Peter's speeches in the Acts of the Apostles, such as the word "piety" (εὐσέβεια) (Acts iii. 12), "the Day of the Lord" (iii. 10; Acts ii. 20), and a few others. But they seem to me too few and too shadowy for their purpose; nor can we observe in the Second Epistle (with one marked exception, *vide infra*, p. 114) that influence of events narrated in the Gospels on the character and views of St. Peter, which may be so strikingly traced in the First Epistle (*supra*, p. 69, *fg.*).

involved. Would they have been held sufficient to prove the genuineness of a classic treatise, or even of a tract of any of the Fathers?

(19.) But we have not even now exhausted the peculiarities of this weakly-authenticated letter. We have still to consider the extraordinary phenomenon which it presents in its relationship to the short Epistle of Jude. On the facts of this relationship each successive writer comes to a different conclusion; but, after careful consideration and comparison of the two documents, it seems to my own mind *impossible to doubt* that Jude was the earlier of the two writers.[1] If so, the fact that such an Apostle as St. Peter should, without even referring to him by name, have incorporated successively so many of the thoughts and expressions of one who, like St. Jude, was not an Apostle, is yet another extraordinary circumstance. To talk of "plagiarism" would be to import modern notions into the inquiry; and if St. Peter were the borrower, we shall see that he deals with his materials in a wise and independent manner. But as to any further questions which may arise from the relationship of the two writers, we must be content to say that we have no data on which to furnish an answer.

The closeness of the relationship will be seen at a glance by comparing the parallel passages side by side. The characteristics of the "impious persons" of Jude and that of the "false teachers" of St. Peter are identical. Both are marked by those insidious and subterranean methods which seem to be inseparable from the character of religious partisans (Jud. 4; 2 Pet. ii. 1—3); by impious wantonness (*id.*, and Jud. 8; 2 Pet. ii. 10); by denial of Christ (*id.*); by slander of dignities (Jud. 8; 2 Pet. ii. 10); by corruption of natural instincts (Jud. 10; 2 Pet. ii. 12); by greed (Jud. 11; 2 Pet. ii. 14, 15); by pompous assertions and scoffing mockery (Jud. 16—18; 2 Pet. ii. 18, iii. 3). Both are doomed to swift judgment; are described by very similar metaphors; are threatened with the same punishments; are compared to Balaam; and are warned by the example of the Cities of the Plain. But if the two passages are read side by side, it can hardly be denied that the language of St. Jude is the more eloquent and impetuous, while that of St. Peter is the more elaborate and restrained. The burning lava of St. Jude's indignation has evidently poured itself through the secondary channels of a temperament which would probably have been more congenial to its reception at an earlier period. St. Peter, if it be he, catches something of the Judaic fire and heat of his contemporary, but he modifies, softens, and corrects his vehement phrases. His language is but *an echo* of the thunder. He throws the description,

---

[1] The notion of Luther, Wolf, etc., that 2 Peter was the earlier, though still supported by Thiersch, Dietlein, Fronmüller, Hofmann, Wordsworth, &c., is being more and more abandoned. The priority of St. Jude is accepted by Herder, Hug, Eichhorn, Credner, Neander, De Wette, Mayerhoff, Guerike, Reuss, Bleek, Weiss, Wiesinger, Brückner, Huther, Ewald, Alford, Plumptre, Dr. S. Davidson, &c.

[2] Bertholdt and Lange suppose that this chapter was subsequently interpolated into the Second Epistle of St. Peter.

in part at least, into the future, as though to indicate that those against whom he warns his readers have not yet burst into the full blossom of their iniquity.

Travelling through Christian communities as one of "the brethren of the Lord,"[1] St. Jude seems to have come into personal contact with bodies of corrupt, greedy, and subtle Antinomians closely resembling those "Gnostics before Gnosticism" whose appearance had been noted by the prescient eye of St. Paul. Having actually witnessed their baleful influence, he can depict them with startling power and clearness, and he rolls over them peal after peal of Apocalyptic denunciation. St. Peter, now perhaps awaiting his death at Rome, has not personally seen them—not, at any rate, in their worst and most undisguised developments. Startled by the language of St. Jude—such is a perhaps admissible hypothesis—finding that the very words and thoughts and sentences of that brief but strange and powerful letter keep ringing with ominous sound in his memory—in *his* heart too the fire burns and he speaks with his tongue. The mystery of iniquity, he implies, is already working, but he cannot bring himself to believe that it has invaded all the Churches to which he writes, and therefore he predicts even while he is describing, and describes while he predicts. The language of his second chapter seems to show that the author was writing from vivid and even verbal memory of St. Jude's letter, but not with its words, lying actually before him. In some cases he presents the curious but familiar phenomenon of the memory being magnetized rather by the sounds of the words than by the words themselves.[2] Thus from external similarity St. Jude's "sunken reefs" (*spilades*) become "spots" (*spiloi*),[3] and St. Jude's "love-feasts" (*agapai*) become "deceits" (*apatai*). But, besides this, it is evident that both in greater and smaller matters a spirit of conscious modification is at work, both in the way of addition and omission. Where St. Jude speaks of "*clouds* without water," St. Peter, to avoid any scientific cavil—since a cloud without water is a thing not conceivable—speaks of "*wells* without water." Where St. Jude refers to the profanation of the Agapæ St. Peter's allusion is more distant and general. St. Jude in three successive clauses speaks of the fall of the angels through fleshly lusts; of Sodom and Gomorrha as "undergoing a judgment of æonian fire;" of a peculiar form of ceremonial pollution familiar to all who were trained in the Levitic law; of the dispute between Michael the Archangel and the Devil about the body of Moses; and of the corruption of natural and instinctive knowledge. He then proceeds to compare these evildoers to Cain, to Balaam, and to Korah, and after an impassioned outburst of metaphors applies

[1] 1 Cor. ix. 5.
[2] Weiss says that "St. Peter" has here been influenced by the "*wortklang*."
[3] I am aware that some take σπιλάδες to mean the same as σπίλοι, and it is so understood in the ancient versions. See Bishop Lightfoot on *Revision*, p. 137. Dr. Abbott points out (*Expositor*, Feb. 1882, p. 145) that a group of words in this paragraph is also found in Is. lvi. 7—lvii. 5.

to them a prophecy from the apocryphal Book of Enoch. It is instructive to see how the writer of this later Epistle deals with the burning material thus before him. To the fall of the angels he only alludes in the most general manner, excluding all reference to the Rabbinic tradition, which sprung out of inferences from Gen. vi. 2. Omitting St. Jude's allusion to the Israelites in the wilderness, he substitutes a reference to the Deluge. Omitting, perhaps as liable to be misunderstood, the æonian fire of Sodom and Gomorrha, he only says that these cities were reduced to ashes, while he is careful to add, by way of encouragement to the faithful, that Lot was saved. He omits as painful, and to Hellenic readers hardly intelligible, *both* of St. Jude's allusions to certain forms of Levitic pollutions.[1] He omits, as being derived from the apocryphal *Ascension of Moses*, all allusion to the legend about the dispute of Michael and Satan, and even the name of the Archangel, and, in a passage which, apart from the parallel in St. Jude, would be extremely obscure, he gives to the reference a general turn, which, if it conveyed to the readers any distinct conception, would remind them rather of the accuser of the Brethren in the Book of Zechariah. St. Jude, speaking throughout rather of vicious livers than of false teachers, describes them with great clearness as blaspheming in subjects about which they know nothing, and corrupting the knowledge which comes to them instinctively, as it does to animals without reason. The later writer remembers the words "as the animals without reason," but by an ingenious figure of speech, in which the same word serves a double purpose,[2] applies it to compare the *hopeless end* of the false teachers to that of animals. Omitting the instances of Cain and of Korah, but amplifying that of Balaam, which was more germane to his purpose, he tones down the exuberance of St. Jude's rhetoric. Perhaps because he is only writing from impressions without the original manuscript before him, while substituting "wells without water" for "clouds without water," he *adds* the clause "clouds chased by the hurricane." He omits St. Jude's "wandering stars," and yet applies directly to the teachers the powerful metaphor "for whom the gloom of darkness has been reserved for ever." Again, he omits the prophecy of Enoch, probably because it is taken from an apocryphal book; and lastly, he mentions—as a specific instance of the scoffs to which St. Jude only alludes—the mocking questions which were suggested by the delay of Christ's return. I must confess my inability to see how any one who

---

[1] Lev. xv. 16, 17; Jude 8, 23.

[2] This figure of speech is called *antanaclasis*, and consists in the use of the same word twice in different senses in the same passage (see *supra*, p. 92, the note on 1 Pet. iii. 1). Here φθορά is first "destruction," and then "corruption." Compare 2 Pet. ii. 12, "But these, as reasonless animals, creatures of nature (φυσικά), born for capture and *destruction* (φθοράν), blaspheming in things of which they are ignorant (ἀγνοοῦσιν), shall be destroyed in their own *corruption* (ἐν τῇ αὐτῶν φθορᾷ καταφθαρήσονται)," with Jude 10, "These, in all things which they know not (οὐκ οἴδασιν), blaspheme; but all the things which, like the reasonless animals, they know naturally (φυσικῶς), in these they corrupt themselves (φθείρονται)."

approaches the enquiry with no ready-made theories can fail to come to the conclusion that the priority in this instance belongs to St. Jude. It would have been impossible for such a burning and withering blast of defiance and invective as his brief letter to have been composed on principles of modification and addition.[1] All the marks which indicate the reflective treatment of an existing document are to be seen in the Second Epistle of St. Peter. In every instance of variation we see the *reasons* which influenced the later writer. The instances of Cain and Korah did not suit his purpose, which dealt rather with secret corruption than flagrant violence, and with errors of theory than with undisguised revolt. But, had St. Peter written first, there is *no* reason why St. Jude should have omitted so striking and apposite an example as was furnished by the Deluge. It is inconceivable that St. Jude should simply have taken a paragraph of a longer Epistle, have added apocryphal illustrations to it, and flashed lightning into it by a process of reflective treatment. All literary probability decisively shows that the more guarded, more dignified, more exclusively authoritative composition—the one less liable to excite offence and cavil—would be the later of the two. There is nothing absurd in the supposition that a later writer, powerfully moved by the state of things revealed in the letter of St. Jude, should, in a longer and in some respects weightier epistle, have utilised, while yet he modified, that powerful utterance, abandoning its triplicity of structure,[2] and omitting those Hebraic references which would have been a stumbling-block to a wider circle of readers. The notion that St. Jude endeavoured to "improve upon" St. Peter is, I say, a literary impossibility; and if in some instances the phrases of St. Jude seem more antithetical and striking, and his description clearer, I have sufficiently accounted for the inferiority—if it be inferiority—of St. Peter by the supposition that he was a man of more restrained temperament; that he wrote under the influence of reminiscences and impressions; and that he was warning against forms of evil with which he had not come into so personal a contact.

Having now examined—fairly, I trust, and as fully as my limits will allow—the peculiarities of the Epistle before us, and the serious difficulties which lie in the way of our regarding it as the work of St. Peter, I will state one or two of the reasons why, in spite of these difficulties, I cannot regard it as *certainly* spurious. They are mainly three:—

1. First, we must not wholly ignore the similarity in expression and tone of thought between this Epistle and the First,[3] nor the slight re-

---

[1] The genius and fine literary instinct of Herder saw this at once:—"Siehe welch ein ganzer kräftiger, wie ein Feuerrad in sich selbst zurücklaufender Brief: man nehme das Schreiben Petrus dazu, wie es einleitet, mildert, auslässt, &c." So, too, Weiss, Huther, &c.
[2] See *infra*, p. 131.
[3] Words common to both Epistles are "precious" (τίμιος), "abundantly furnish" (ἐπιχορηγεῖν), "brotherly love" (φιλαδελφία), "eye-witnesses" (ἐπόπται), "wantonness"

semblances which it offers to St. Peter's speeches recorded in the Acts.¹ The resemblance of the writer to St. Peter in tone of mind²—as, for instance, in his largeheartedness to the Gentiles,³ in his fondness for the less trodden paths of Biblical illustration and enquiry, and in his tendency to soften instances of doom by the parallel of instances of deliverance—must also be allowed their due weight. Under this head I may refer to the subtle *reminiscences* of the Transfiguration. Of the *appeal* to the Transfiguration as a source of the writer's conviction, it may of course be said that it would naturally occur to any one assuming the name of St. Peter; but the casual subsequent introduction of the word "tabernacle,"⁴ and of the most unusual word for "decease,"⁵ not in any formal connexion with the appeal, but by an inimitably natural association of ideas, has always seemed to me an important item of evidence. To this must be added the little-noticed indication that the Transfiguration probably took place at night, though it is not so stated in the Gospels. This would at once account for the following comparison of the word of prophecy to "a light shining in a squalid place."

2. Another important consideration is the *ancientness* of this Epistle. If we cannot infer this from the vague resemblances to it adduced from passages in the Apostolic Fathers, we may infer it from three circumstances—namely, the want of all *specific* features of later Gnosticism in the heretics here described; the absence of allusions to ecclesiastical organisations; and the absence of any traces of the fall of Jerusalem. As to the first point, is it not certain that a later writer would have aimed his remonstrances at something more distinctly and definitely resembling the heresies of Cerinthus or Ebion, or, later still, of Carpocrates and Valentinus? As to the second point, it is probably better known to us than it was even to many writers in the second century, that there had been a rapid tendency to desynonymize the words "bishop" and "presbyter," and that the consequent development of "episcopal" power was due to the growth of heresy, against which it was designed to be a bulwark.⁶ If, then, the writer of this Epistle was a *falsarius*, writing late in the second century, it is difficult

---

(ἀσέλγεια), "spotless" (ἄσπιλος). In both there is a prominence of the Deluge and of Prophecy. See Plumptre, *Introd.*, p. 75. I have pointed out that in both occurs a specimen of the figure called *antanaclisis* ("word" in 1 Pet. iii. 1, "corruption" in 2 Pet. ii. 12). This has, I believe, escaped the notice of previous inquirers. See *supra*, pp. 92, 112.

¹ This is fully worked out by Prof. Lumby in the *Expositor*, iv. 372—399 and 446—469. But in any case the writer of the Second Epistle would be very familiar with the language of the First. *Differences*, in a question of this kind, furnish a far more serious consideration than identities and resemblances.

² Compare 2 Pet. i. 17, 21; ii. 1, 13; with Acts iii. 12; ii. 2; iv. 24; ii. 15.

³ 2 Pet. i. 1.   ⁴ σκήνωμα. Matt. xvii. 4.

⁵ ἔξοδος, "departure," *i.e.*, death, as in Jos. *Antt.* iv. 812. Wisd. iii. 2.

⁶ In the First Epistle the word *episkopos* only occurs once, and that in its *general* sense of "guardian" (1 Pet. ii. 25), and each Church has only its "presbyters," with whom the Apostle ranks himself (1 Pet. v. 1).

to imagine that he would not have adopted the same tone in reference to this subject as the other writers of his age. As regards the fall of Jerusalem, it may, of course, be said that any reference to it would have betrayed the pseudonymous character of the writer; but I am now only arguing that there are no *traces* of the state of mind produced by the Jewish catastrophe. Is it not probable that a *falsarius* of the ability pre-supposed by this Epistle would have seized the grand opportunity of introducing *as a prediction*, an illustration which would have been in all respects so overwhelmingly apposite? But in any case the end of the Jewish polity was an event so stupendous that no writer dealing with such subjects as those before us could have succeeded in excluding every trace of an occurrence which so radically modified the tone of Christian thought.

3. One more consideration remains, which seems to me of capital importance. It is the superiority of this Epistle to every one of the uncanonical writings of the first and second centuries. If we are to accept the theories of modern critics, that the Epistles of the Captivity, and the Pastoral Epistles, and the Gospel of St. John, and the Second Epistle of St. Peter, are the works of "forgers," then— seeing the indescribable superiority of these writings to all others which saw the light during the epoch at which they are supposed to have been written—we are driven to the extraordinary conclusion that the best strength and brilliancy and spiritual insight of the second century is to be found in its pseudonymous writings! Who will venture to assert that any Apostolic Father—that Clement of Rome, or Ignatius, or Polycarp, or Hermas, or Justin Martyr, could have written so much as twenty consecutive verses so eloquent and so powerful as those of the Second Epistle of St. Peter? No *known* member of the Church in that age could have been the writer; not even the author of the Epistle to Diognetus. Would a writer so much more powerful than any of these have remained uninfluential and unknown? Would one who could wield his pen with so inspired a power have failed to write a line in his own name, and for the immediate benefit of his own contemporaries?

In the face, then, of these counter-difficulties, I see no solution of the problem but the one which St. Jerome indicated fourteen centuries ago.[1] I believe that we may perhaps recognise in this Epistle the opinions, the influence, the impress, direct or indirect, of the great Apostle of the Circumcision. If we cannot find his individual style, if we are faced by many peculiarities, if we miss characteristic expressions, if we recognise a different mode of workmanship, some of these difficulties would be removed by the supposition of a literary amanuensis. The supposition of an Aramaic original, as supported by Mr. King,

[1] "Stilo inter se et charactere discrepant structuraque verborum. Ex quo intelligimus pro necessitate rerum diversis eum usum interpretibus."—*Ep. ad Hedib.* 120, 11.

seems to me untenable.¹ This Epistle is addressed quite as much to Gentiles as to Jews; and even if the Jews of the Dispersion understood Aramaic, the Gentiles did not. This suggestion, moreover, does not remove the most serious difficulties. The Epistle, though it does not show the mastery of Hellenistic Greek possessed by some of the New Testament writers, has yet an energy of its own which excludes the possibility of its being a translation.² I believe there is much to support the conclusion—at which I had arrived before I became aware of the resemblances to Josephus—that we have not here the words and style of the great Apostle, but that he lent to this Epistle the sanction of his name and the assistance of his advice. If this be so, it is still in its main essence genuine as well as canonical, and there is a reason both for its peculiarities and for its tardy reception. On this hypothesis we may rejoice that we have preserved to us both the encouragements addressed to the Church by St. Peter, and his warnings against anti-Christian heresies. These heresies, as we see from the Second Epistle to Timothy, had also occupied a large space in the last thoughts of St. Paul. St. Peter speaks of them mainly in the future, as St. Paul had done, in his farewell to the Ephesian elders at Miletus. It is said that when Charlemagne first saw the ships of the pirate Norsemen he burst into tears, not because he feared that they would give *him* any trouble, but because he foresaw the miseries which they would inflict upon his subjects in the future. So it was with the Apostles. The errors of which others only saw the germ, loomed large on the horizon of their prophetic insight, although it was not until after their death that they assumed their full proportions as the perilous heresies of Gnostic speculation.

CHAPTER X.

THE SECOND EPISTLE OF ST. PETER.

'Ἐν οἷς ἐστι δυσνόητά τινα.—2 Pet. iii. 16.

INSTEAD of following the plan which I have hitherto adopted, of endeavouring to take the reader through each Epistle by explaining and epitomising its general purpose in language which may counteract the deadening effect of over-familiarity, I have thought it best to

---

[1] A translation would not have such a figure as that involved in ii.) use of φθορά (first "destruction," then "corruption") in ii. 12, or such an alliteration as σπυδήτου παραφρονίαν in ii. 16.

[2] "Diese ist fast ohne alle Ausnahme sehr fein Griechisch, voll der freiesten ächt Griechischen Wortstellungen und Satzbildungen," &c.—Ewald, *Sendschr.* ii. 110. It may, however, be best described as the poetic Greek of one who had partly learned the language from the tragedians. The repetitions of words are due to the same sparse but sonorous vocabulary of the amanuensis.

re-translate the whole of this Epistle. I have done so for several reasons. In previous instances I have given a literal version of every passage which was obscure, or specially remarkable, or in which the English Version seemed incorrect, or difficult of apprehension, or dependent on inferior readings. This Epistle has given rise to so many controversies, it is so remarkably compact in its structure, its expressions are so unusual, and sometimes even so astonishing, that I have thought it best to re-translate the whole of it as closely as I could, appending in the briefest form such notes as seemed most necessary. I know that the reader may feel inclined to leave the translation unread, under the notion that he is already familiar with a version not only infinitely more dear to him, but also more euphonious, more smooth, more literary, and (as it will perhaps seem to him) more easy to understand. I would, however, ask him to follow me in this version, because our English Bible, with all its splendid merits, constantly misses the peculiarities of the writer's diction through its besetting fondness for needless variations. My translation, made, I ought to say, before the Revised Version appeared, and with a different object, is meant throughout to be not only a literal version, but also a running commentary.[1]

Symeon[2] Peter, a slave and apostle of Jesus Christ, to those who have obtained[3] a like precious faith with us, in the righteousness of our God and of our Saviour Jesus Christ,[4] grace to you and peace be multiplied in the full knowledge[5] of God and of Jesus our Lord. Seeing that His Divine power hath given us all things that pertain to life and piety,[6] by means of the full knowledge of Him Who called us by His own glory and virtue;[7] by means of which He hath given us His greatest and precious promises,[8] that by their means ye may become partakers of Divine nature, having escaped from the corruption which is in the world in lust. And on this very account, adding all earnestness,[9] abundantly furnish[10] in your faith virtue, and in your virtue knowledge, and in your knowledge self-control, and in your self-control endurance, and in your endurance piety, and in your piety brotherly affection, and in your brotherly affection love.[11]

---

[1] I may perhaps be allowed to remark that, though this book, no less than my *Life of Christ* and *Life of St. Paul*, has been written without the aid which I should have derived from the Revised Version, I find that there is scarcely a single instance in which the corrections I had ventured to make, and the readings which I had selected, were not in accordance with those of the Revisers. The fact that the renderings which I have given are often those which the Revisers place in the margin, may serve to illustrate the exact reproduction of the peculiarities of the original, at which I have always aimed.

[2] Λαχοῦσι, Acts i. 17 (St. Peter).

[3] The adoption of this form at once marks a Hebraist.

[4] "Of our God and Saviour Jesus Christ" would also be grammatical, but see on Tit. ii. 13, *Life and Work of St. Paul*, ii. 553; and the next verse seems to show that the Father and the Son are here meant.

[5] Ἐπίγνωσις, "full knowledge," is the leading word of this Epistle (as "hope" is of 1 Pet.).

[6] Εὐσέβεια. The word only occurs elsewhere in Acts iii. 12 and the pastoral Epistles. Θεῖος, "divine" is peculiar to this Epistle. (Cf. Acts xvii. 29.)

[7] Ἀρετή, here alone of God. In 1 Pet. ii. 9 the word is ἀρετάς, which is quite different. *Leg., ἰδίᾳ δ. καὶ ἀρ.,* א A, C. The writer is fond of using the emphatic ἴδιος (2 Pet. ii. 22; iii. 3, 16, 17; 1 Pet. iii. 15).

[8] As in 2 Pet. iii. 13.

[9] εἰσφέρειν σπουδήν. Jos. *Antt.* xx. 9, § 2.

[10] ἐπιχορηγήσατε. The E. V., "Add to your faith virtue, &c.," is quite untenable.

[11] For these virtues see the first Epistle, where every one of them is mentioned, even the less common words ἀρετή (1 Pet. ii. 9, plur.), φιλαδελφία (1 Pet. i. 22), and γνῶσις (1 Pet. iii. 7).

For these things, when they exist and abound, render you neither idle nor unfruitful unto the full knowledge of our Lord Jesus Christ.[1] For he in whom they are not is blind, wilfully closing his eyes,[2] assuming oblivion[3] of his purification from his olden sins.[4] Wherefore the rather, brethren, give diligence to make sure your calling and election, for by so doing ye shall never stumble.[5] For there shall be richly furnished to you the entrance into the eternal kingdom of our Lord and Saviour Jesus Christ (i. 1—11).[6]

Wherefore I will not neglect to remind you always about these things, though ye know them, and have been firmly fixed in the present truth.[7] But I consider it right, as long as I am in this tabernacle, to arouse you by way of reminder, knowing that swiftly shall come the laying aside of this my tabernacle,[8] as even our Lord Jesus Christ showed me.[9] But I will be diligent, that you may be able[10] even on every occasion after my departure, to make mention of these things.[11] For it was not by following in the track of elaborated myths[12] that we made known to you the power and coming of our Lord Jesus Christ, but by having been initiated,[13] as eye-witnesses, into His Majesty. For having received honour and glory from God the Father when a voice such as this was borne to Him[14] from the magnificent glory,[15] "My Son, my Beloved is this,[16] in whom I am well pleased—"[17] And this voice *we* heard borne from Heaven, when we were with Him in the Holy Mount.[18] And still stronger is the surety we have in the prophetic word,[19] whereunto ye do well if ye take heed[20] as to a lamp shining in a squalid place,[21] until the day dawn, and the morning star arise in your hearts;[22] knowing this first, that no prophecy of Scripture proves to be of

---

[1] Comp. Col. i. 10.
[2] μυωπάζων, one of the numerous *hapax legomena* of this Epistle. There is a gloss ψηλαφῶν, "fumbling his way." If the meaning "short-sighted" (Arist. Probl. xxxi. § 16) be adopted (as in E. V.), it may mean "blind to the far-off heavenly things, able only to see the near earthly things."
[3] Comp. Jos. Antt. ii. 6, § 9.
[4] I.e., by Baptism.—Chrysost., &c.
[5] Ja. ii. 10, iii. 2.
[6] "Furnish knowledge, self-control, &c. (ver. 5), and you shall be rewarded in kind; for so the entrance into Christ's eternal kingdom shall be furnished richly to you."
[7] Ver. 12, ἐν τῇ παρούσῃ ἀληθείᾳ. Cf. Jude 5; Rom. xv. 14; 1 Pet. v. 12.
[8] A mixture of the metaphors of a robe and a building, as in 2 Cor. v. 1 (De Wette).
[9] John xxi. 17, 18 (but of course that was written long afterwards, if the Epistle be genuine):
[10] ἔχειν—δύνασθαι, as in Luke vii. 42
[11] This is the ordinary meaning of μνήμην ποιεῖσθαι. I have already noticed the interesting use of σκήνωμα and ἔξοδος (vide supra, p 114).
[12] μύθοις. See on 1 Tim. i. 4, iv. 7, *Life of St. Paul*, ii. 517; but each commentator guesses differently as to the kind of myths alluded to. The best comment is Jos. Antt. Prœm. § 4: "All other lawgivers *following on the track of their myths*, transferred to the gods the shame of their human sins."
[13] ἐπόπται, a technical word of the Eleusinian mysteries (used in 2 Macc. iii. 30).
[14] ἐνεχθείσης, a most unusual expression, found also in 1 Pet. i. 13. Perhaps it may be explained of the rushing wind accompanying the Bath Kol. Cf. Acts ii. 2. It is analogous to ᾖξι (Is. ix. 8). The Evangelists use γίγνεται, ἔρχεται (Luke ix. 35; John xii. 30).
[15] The glory is "the Shechinah" which uttered the voice (ὑπό).
[16] Ο υἱός μου, ὁ ἀγαπητός μου, א, A, C, K, L. The variations from the Gospel narrative are in favour of the genuineness of the Epistle. "*In whom*," lit. "unto whom."
[17] The sentence is unfinished in the original (*Anakoluthon*).
[18] The inference from this expression, as showing a post-Apostolic date, is not unreasonable, but the epithet may be fairly explained by Jewish conceptions (Ex. iii. 5; Josh. v. 15).
[19] Ver. 19, βεβαιότερον. Why "more sure?" Because wider in its range, and more varied, and coming from many, and bringing a more intense personal conviction than the testimony to a single fact. The reference to prophecy is prominent in both Epistles (1 Pet. i. 11, seq.). Perhaps, too, we may trace the early tendency to underrate the force of individual visions, which we find existing in St. Paul's day (see *Life of St. Paul*, i. 193), and which is so strongly marked in the Clementines (*Hom.* xvii. 13). The "prophetic word" may surely include New Testament as well as Old Testament prophecies (Acts xxi. 10, 1 Cor. xii. 10, 1 Thess. v. 20; 1 Tim. i. 18).
[20] Jos. Antt. xi. 6, § 12, οἷς ποιήσετε καλῶς μὴ προσέχοντες.
[21] αὐχμηρῷ.
[22] The meaning seems to be that the lamp of prophecy will become needless in the full noonday blaze of perfect conviction.

private interpretation.¹ For prophecy was never borne along by will of man, but being borne along by the Holy Spirit, men spoke from God (i. 12—21).

But there rose false prophets also among the people, as also among you shall be false teachers, of a kind² who shall secretly introduce factions of perdition,³ denying even the master that bought them,⁴ bringing upon themselves swift perdition. And many shall follow in the track⁵ of their wantonness,⁶ on whose account the way of the truth shall be railed at.⁷ And in covetousness, with fictitious speeches, shall they make trade of you, for whom, since long ago, their doom idleth not, and their destruction drowseth not.⁸ For if God spared not *angels* who sinned,⁹ but, hurling them to Tartarus,¹⁰ committed them to dens¹¹ of darkness, as reserved for judgment—and spared not the ancient world, but preserved Noah, a herald of righteousness,¹² with seven others, bringing a sudden flood on the world of the impious; and calcining the cities of Sodom and Gomorrha, condemned them with overthrow, having made them a warning for those who should hereafter be impious; and righteous Lot, utterly distressed by the wanton life of these offenders,¹³ He rescued—for by sight and hearing the righteous man, dwelling among them day after day, was torturing his righteous soul with their lawless deeds—the Lord knoweth how to rescue the pious from trial, but to reserve the unrighteous, under punishment, for the day of judgment; and especially those who walk after the flesh in the lust of pollution, and despise dominion. Daring, self-willed, they tremble not when they rail at glories,¹⁴ in cases wherein angels, greater though they are in strength and might,¹⁵ do not bring against them¹⁶ before the Lord a railing judgment.

---

¹ Of the many possible explanations of these wor's, I accept that which makes them mean "that the prophets did not speak by spontaneous knowledge, and spoke more than they could themselves interpret," as where Philo says, "the prophet utters nothing of his own." If his utterance is not his own, his *interpretation* may also well be inadequate. The remark then resembles 1 Pet. i. 10—12. The γίνεται would then mean that history proves the truth of this remark. 'Επιλύσις only occurs in Aquila's version of Gen. xl. 8, and ἐπιλύω means "I explain" in Mark iv. 34. The verb ἐπιλύω occurs in Gen. xl. 8, xli. 12, and the explanation of the thought must be looked for in Gen. xli. 15, 16 (comp. Jer. xxiii. 26). [Since writing this note I see that Dr. Abbott points out that *several* words are here borrowed from the passage in Philo, *Quis Rer. Div. Hær.*, p. 52, viz.: θεοφόρητος, φωσφόρος, ἴδιος, ἀνατέλλει. This seems to be decisive as to the meaning.]

² εἶπτες. The transition from the true to the false prophets, and so to existing false teachers, is very natural.

³ αἱρέσεις. The meaning "heresies" is later (cf. 1 Cor. xi. 19, Gal. v. 20, Tit. iii. 10).

⁴ Peter's mere momentary "denial" at a moment of strong temptation differs wholly from this persistent negation and apostasy. Ἀγοράσαντα—notice the clear expression of Christ's death *for all*. In the participial constructions of this chapter (which I have faithfully reproduced) the sentences sometimes have an unfinished look.

⁵ ἐξακολουθήσουσιν.   ⁶ Leg. ἀσελγείαις, א, A, B, C, K, L. "Lecheries," Wiclyf.

⁷ This furnishes us with an important historical hint. The strange and odious calumnies which were rife from the earliest days against the Christians, originated in the antinomian heresies of Gnostic and other sects in which perverted doctrine led to impure life. See Jer. *Adv. Lucif.*, p. 53; Epiphan. Hær. 23.

⁸ τὸ κρίμα, the sentence of judgment; κρίσις, the act. Νυστάζει, lit. "nods," "dormitat" (Matt. xxv. 5).   ⁹ Gen. vi. 2.

¹⁰ Ver. 4. Ταρταρώσας; a strange classic hapax legomenon. Tartarus is the Hebrew Gehinnom. St. Peter does not follow St. Jude in specifying the traditional sin of the angels; still his allusion is to Jewish tradition. Cf. Book of Enoch v. 16; x. 6; xiv. 4, etc. On such allusions see *Life of St. Paul*, i. 58, ii. 48—51, etc.

¹¹ Leg., σειροῖς. א, A, B, C. Here again St. Peter substitutes a word of similar sound for σειραῖς, "chains," which may have been a variation of memory for Jude's δεσμοῖς. There is, however, an epic daring in the expression "*chains* of darkness;" "*fetter* of darkness" is found in Wisd. xvii. 17.

¹² That Noah was a preacher was a natural Jewish inference (Jos. *Antt.* i. 3, § 1).

¹³ ἀδίκῳ, implying that they violated the most sacred and natural laws.

¹⁴ *Glories*, that is, at "glorious beings."

¹⁵ "Fools rush in, where angels fear to tread."

¹⁶ This can only mean "against glories"—i.e., against angelic dignities even after their fall—and the verse would be perfectly inexplicable without the allusion of Jude to Michael refraining to rail at Satan. He and the fallen angels were δόξαι once, just as they may still be called "angels." Compare Milton's—

"Less than Archangel ruined, or excess
  Of glory obscured."

But these as mere irrational animals, born for capture and destruction,[1] railing in things which they know not, in their own corruption shall be utterly destroyed,[2] suffering wrong as the hire of doing wrong.[3] Thinking that luxuriousness in the day[4] is pleasure, spots[5] and blemishes, luxuriating in their own deceits[6] while they banquet with you, having eyes full of an adulteress,[7] and insatiable of sin, luring with a bait unstable souls, having a heart trained in covetousness, children of malediction! Abandoning the straight path they wandered, following in the path of Balaam the son of Bosor,[8] who loved the hire of wrongdoing, but received a rebuke for his own transgression: a dumb beast of burden[9] uttering a human voice checked the prophet's infatuation. These are waterless springs, and mists driven by a hurricane, for whom the mirk of darkness has been reserved. For uttering inflations of foolishness they lure with a bait[10] in the lusts of the flesh, in wantonness, those who were scarcely[11] escaping them who spend their lives in error,—promising them liberty, though being themselves slaves of corruption.[12] For by whatever any one has been worsted, by that has he also been enslaved. For if, after having escaped the pollutions of the world by full knowledge of the Lord and Saviour Jesus Christ, they are worsted by being again entangled in them, the last things have become worse to them than the first.[13] For it had been better for them not to have fully known the way of righteousness, than, after fully knowing it, to swerve aside from the holy commandment delivered to them. But there has happened to them the fact of the true proverb, "The dog turning to his own vomit," and "A sow that had bathed to its wallowing-place of mire"[14] (ii. 1—22).

This is now, beloved, the Second Epistle I am writing to you, in both of which I am trying to arouse your sincere understanding, by reminding you,— that you may remember the words spoken before by the holy prophets, and the command of the Lord and Saviour, through your Apostles;[15] recognising this first, that there shall come at the end of the days scoffers in their scoffing, walking according to their own lusts, and saying, Where is the promise of His coming? for from the day when the fathers fell asleep[16] all things are

---

Unwilling to adduce Jude's reference to the dispute between Michael and Satan about the body of Moses, which was only recorded by apocryphal writings from Jewish tradition, the writer makes the reference general, so that the reader who was familiar with the Old Testament would rather be reminded of Zech. iii. 1, 2.

[1] "A sacrificial calf ran to Rabbi Judah and wept in his bosom. But "go," he said, "you were created for this purpose" (Babha Metsia, f. 85 a).

[2] The acceptance of Jude's words, and their application in a totally different sense, is very remarkable. St. Jude's language reads like a keen epigram; on the other hand, we have in St. Peter a remarkable play on the two senses of the word φθορά, viz., "corruption" and "destruction" (v. supra, p. 112).

[3] Leg. ἀδικούμενοι, א, B. The common text has κομιούμενοι, "about to carry off," A, C.

[4] I.e., for life's brief day. "Voluptatem aestimantes diei delicias" (Vulg.).

[5] σπίλοι, where Jude has σπιλάδες, "sunken reefs."

[6] ἀπάταις, א, A, C, etc., for Jude's ἀγάπαις, "love feasts" (cf. 2 Thess. ii. 10).

[7] μοιχαλίδος (cf. Rev. ii. 20). But if the reading be right (for μοιχαλίας, א, A) the allusion is uncertain.

[8] St. Paul (1 Cor. x. 8), St. Peter, and St. John (Rev. ii. 14, &c.) alike allude to this false prophet as a type of false teachers in their own day. Bosor, perhaps a Galilean corruption of Beor (בעור), with an intentional assonance (in the Jewish fashion, as in Jerubbesheth, Kir Heres, Baal Zebub, &c., see Life of Christ, i. 456) to Bashar, "flesh."

[9] The New Testament writers, like the LXX., seem to avoid ὄνος (ass), which led to Gentile jeers, and use the more euphemistic ὑποζύγιον.

[10] δελεάζουσιν, as in ver. 14; only found in Ja. i. 14.

[11] Leg. ὀλίγως, A, B, &c.

[12] John viii. 34; Rom. viii. 21; 1 Pet. ii. 16; Gal. v. 13 (Iren. Haer. xxi. 3). An old way with false teachers (Gen. iii. 5). Their argument was, that the Spirit was so supreme and ethereal that indulgence of the flesh could not harm it.

[13] Matt. xii. 45.

[14] Ver. 22, τὸ τῆς παροιμίας, cf. τὸ τῆς σοφῆς, Matt. xxi. 21. The language differs so much from Prov. xxvi. 11 that probably this is merely a current proverb (leg. κύλισμα, א, A, K, L).

[15] "Your Apostles"—i.e., those who first preached to you. Cf. 1 Cor. ix. 2.

[16] Cf. Mal. ii. 17; Ps. xlii. 4. The exact reference to "the fathers" is difficult to determine. It may mean those well known Christian teachers and others (1 Thess. iv. 15) who, like St.

continuing as they now are, from the beginning of creation. For this they wilfully choose to forget—that there were heavens from of old, and earth composed out of water, and by means of water,[1] by the word of God, by means of which (water)[2] the then world being overwhelmed with water perished; but the present heavens and earth by this same word have been stored with treasuries of fire,[3] being reserved for the day of judgment and destruction of impious men. But do not *ye* forget this one thing, beloved, that one day with the Lord is as a thousand years, and a thousand years as one day.[4] The Lord is not tardy concerning His promise as some reckon tardiness, but is long-suffering towards you, not wishing that any should perish, but that all should come to repentance.[5] But the day of the Lord shall be upon us as a thief, in which the heavens shall pass hurtlingly away,[6] and orbs of Heaven, being scorched,[7] shall be dissolved, and the earth and the works in it shall be burnt up.[8] Since, then, all these things are in course of being dissolved,[9] what kind of men ought ye to be in holy ways of life and piety, awaiting and hastening[10] the coming of the day of the Lord, because of which the heavens being set on fire shall be dissolved, and the scorching orbs of Heaven shall be melted?[11] But, according to His promise, we expect *new* heavens and a *new* earth, in which righteousness dwelleth.[12] Wherefore, beloved, since ye expect these things, give diligence, to be found spotless and blameless for Him in peace, and account as salvation the long-suffering of our Lord, even as also our beloved brother Paul, according to the wisdom given to him,[13] wrote to you,[14] as also in all his epistles, speaking in them about these things;—in which are some difficulties which the unlearned and unstable distort, as also the rest of the Scriptures,[15] to their own perdition. Ye, then, beloved, knowing these things

---

James the elder, had died between A.D. 33 and A.D. 68. But it may naturally include the patriarchs and prophets to whom the promise came (Rom. ix. 5). St. Peter refutes this taunt about "*the status quo of the world*" (α) by the deluge of water, which shall be followed by the deluge of fire (5—7); and (β) by the difference between God's conception of time and man's (8—10).

[1] The allusion seems to be to water, as the ὕλη, the matter out of which the world was made (as in Clem. Hom. xi. 24)—the *material* cause of the world, as Thales also thought;—and to water as also the *instrumental* cause (διατελικός) of the world, Gen. i. 6. Cf. Pss. xxiv. 2; cxxxvi. 6.

[2] Gen. vii. 11.

[3] Lit., "treasured with fire," alluding to the subterranean fires. But it may be "treasured up (i.e., reserved) *for* fire." We find the same conception in the Book of Enoch i. 6. See Clem. Alex. Strom. v. 9; Hippol. Ref. Haer. ix. 28.

[4] "The dial of the ages—the *aeoniologism*—differs from the horologe of time."—Bengel, Ps. xc. 4.

[5] His seeming delay is not delay, but mercy and forbearance (*Aufgeschoben nicht aufgehoben*): "*Potius quia aeternus*" (Aug.). See Habbak. ii. 3; Ezek. xviii. 23, xxxiii. 11; Ecclus. xxxv. 2; Heb. x. 37; 1 Tim. ii. 4.

[6] ῥοιζηδόν, one of the Æschylean expressions (τεφρώσας, ταρταρώσας, ὑπέροχκα, λάιλαψ, ζόφος, ὀμίχλη, &c.) of this Epistle.

[7] στοιχεῖα may mean the heavenly bodies, as in Justin Martyr, Apol. ii. 5 (Matt. xxiv. 29). καυσούμενα is first found in Dioscorides, in the sense of feverish.

[8] א, B, K read εὑρεθήσεται, "shall be found." This makes very dubious sense, unless the clause be interrogative. It had occurred to me, before I saw it remarked elsewhere, that it might be some accidental confusion with the Latin *urentur*.

[9] This is the *praesens futurascens*, the grand prophetic present which assumes the progressive realisation of the fixed decree.

[10] Just as the Jews believed that by faithful obedience to the Law they would speed the Advent of the Messiah (see *Life of St. Paul*, i. 65, 66).

[11] Is. xxxiv. 4; Mic. i. 4. [12] Is. xxvii. 16; lxv. 25. [13] 1 Cor. iii. 10.

[14] Even if it is assumed that this can only refer to letters addressed to Asia, we can still refer it to Rom. ii. 4, ix. 2 ("not knowing that the goodness of God is leading thee to repentance"), for it is nearly certain that the Epistle to the Romans was addressed, among other Churches, to Ephesus (see *Life of St. Paul*, ii. 170). The allusion to this Epistle would at once account for the remark that some things in St. Paul's writings were "hard to be understood." The doctrines of Freedom and Justification by Faith were peculiarly liable to ignorant and dangerous perversion, as St. Paul himself was well aware (Rom. iii. 8, v. 20; 1 Cor. vi. 12—20; Gal. v. 13—26). Others explain the reference by 1 Thess. iv. 13—v. 11, &c.

[15] The writings of Christian Prophets, Apostles, and Evangelists would soon acquire a position on the same level as the Old Testament Scriptures. See Rev. xxii. 18, 19.

beforehand, be on your guard, lest, being carried away by the error of the lawless, ye fall away from your own steadfastness. But increase in the grace and knowledge of our Lord and Saviour Jesus Christ, to Whom be the glory both now and unto the day of eternity.[1]

So—abruptly—the Epistle ends. There are no salutations, there is no benediction. The absence of the former is easily understood, because the letter was obviously intended to be Œcumenical in character; and perhaps this, or the indignant agitation which was shaking the heart of the writer, or even that share in the composition which I have supposed to belong to another, may also account for the absence of the blessing. No conclusion, it seems to me, can be drawn from this circumstance, either for or against the genuineness of the letter. But whether it be genuine or not, or genuine only in a partial and secondary sense, no one can read it without a recognition of its power, or without a conviction that the "grace of superintendency" was at work when, in the fourth century, it was finally admitted into the Canon of the Church.[2] We do not possess in it a letter of the intense and touching personal interest which attaches to the Second Epistle of St. Paul to Timothy, because it gives us far less insight into the writer's personal feelings, and because its absolute genuineness is not above suspicion; but if we do not hear in this Epistle, but rather in its predecessor, the last *words* of the great Apostle of the Circumcision, there is at least a reasonable probability that we hear the echo of some of his latest thoughts.

CHAPTER XI.

THE EPISTLE OF ST. JUDE.

'Ιούδας ἔγραψεν ἐπιστολὴν ὀλιγόστιχον μὲν πεπληρωμένην δὲ τῆς οὐρανίου χάριτος ἐρρωμένων λόγων.—ORIGEN (in Matt. xiii. 55).

THE authenticity of the brief but interesting Epistle of St. Jude is more strongly supported by external evidence than that of St. Peter. This circumstance alone tends to establish its priority of origin. It was indeed ranked by Eusebius, as were five of the Catholic Epistles, among the "disputed" books; but it was accepted by Tertullian,[3] Clemens of Alexandria, Origen, Jerome, and Ephraem Syrus, and though absent from the Peshito, is recognised in the Muratorian Canon. This acceptance is the more remarkable, because in the brief space of twenty-five verses it presents so many peculiarities. It startled many Christian

---

[1] "All Eternity in one Day." (Estius.)
[2] I entirely disagree with Dr. Abbott in his very slighting estimate of the value of the Epistle. "In omnibus Epistolæ partibus," says Calvin, "spiritus Christi majestas se exserit."
[3] He is the earliest who mentions it. *De habit. mul.* 3.

readers even in the first three centuries alike by its allusions to strange Jewish legends unauthorised by Scripture, and by its quotation from a book which was acknowledged to be apocryphal. On these grounds, as St. Jerome tells us, most men in his day rejected it, and the triumph of its canonicity over such prejudices can only have been due to the strong reasons for its acceptance. One of those reasons is the absence of any motive for a pseudonym so little known as that of Jude, and one which even in the early Church furnished no certainty as to the identity of the writer. Apocryphal literature was busy from the first with the name of St. Peter;[1] and any one who wished to secure recognition for his own opinions by introducing them under the shadow of a mighty name, would also have had every temptation to give them the weight of authority which they would derive from the name of James, the Bishop of Jerusalem. But there existed no such reason for adopting the name of Jude. The Jude who was believed to have written this Epistle was not one of the Twelve Apostles. He is never expressly spoken of as an Apostle, even in the wider sense. His name is barely mentioned in the New Testament, and only mentioned at all in connexion with the unbelief which he shared with his three brothers during the years of our Lord's ministry, previous to that conversion which, as we may conclude from various indications, was effected by the overwhelming evidence for the resurrection of Jesus from the dead. So little, indeed, is known of St. Jude, that even tradition, which delights to furnish particulars respecting the Apostles and leaders of the early Church, is silent about him. Apart from a few uncertain inferences, no Christian legend, no pious martyrologist, no learned enquirer, can tell us one single particular about the life, the labours, or the death of Jude. The only story in which his name occurs is the one told us by Hegesippus, and preserved in Eusebius. He says that Domitian's jealousy was excited by rumours that some of the earthly family of Him Whom Christians adored as the King of the Universe were still living in Palestine. Prophecies about the advent of the great kingdom which was to take its rise in the East had been prevalent in the days of Nero, and were not entirely set at rest by the elevation of Vespasian to the Empire from the command of the army in Syria. Timid from the sense of his own manifold crimes, Domitian determined to enquire into the matter, and ordered some of these "relations of the Lord," or Desposyni, as they were called, to be brought into his presence. They were grandsons of the "Jude the brother of James" who wrote this Epistle, and when Domitian ascertained that they only possessed a few acres of land, and saw that they filled no higher rank than that of peasants of Palestine, whose hands were horny with daily labour, he dismissed them to their

---

[1] Serapion—τὰ δὲ ὀνόματι αὐτῶν ψευδεπίγραφα . . . παραιτούμεθα (Routh, *Rel. Sacr.* i. 470). Euseb. *H. E.* iii. 3. We know that there was a "Gospel" and an "Apocalypse" of Peter.

homes unharmed and with disdain¹—content with their assurance that the kingdom of Christ was neither earthly nor of this world, but heavenly and angelical.²

I have here assumed that the author of this short Epistle was the person whom he describes himself as being—"Jude the brother of James." That Jude was not one of the Twelve may be regarded as certain. He does not profess to be an Apostle, and speaks of the Apostles as of a class to which he did not belong.³ The only Apostle besides Judas Iscariot who bore that very common name was Judas (the son) of James,⁴ surnamed Lebbæus or Thaddæus. But early tradition says that this Apostle laboured in Syria, and died at Edessa; and if he had been the author, it would be impossible to account for that non-acceptance of his Epistle in the early Syrian Church which is proved by its absence from the Peshito Version.⁵ But, besides this, when the writer calls himself "the brother of James," it is unanimously admitted that he can only mean one James—the James who, after the martyrdom of the son of Zebedee, was universally known throughout the Church—that "pillar" of the Church of Jerusalem who was the undisputed head of Judaic Christianity, and was distinguished as "the brother of the Lord."

I shall not here enter into the disputed question as to who were "the brethren of the Lord," at which I must again glance in speaking of the Epistle of St. James.

All that need here be said is, that Jude, though not an Apostle, was a brother of James, and therefore a brother—or, at least, a brother in common parlance—of the Lord. If it be asked why he does not give himself this title, the simplest answer is that neither does James. Those who had a right to it would be the least likely to employ it. None were so well aware as they that from the moment when Christ began His ministry His whole relations to them and to His Mother had been essentially altered. On more than one occasion, when they aspired to control His actions and direct His movements, He had tried to make clear to them that they must henceforth recognise the Divine mystery of His Being. He had even classed them as children of the world, whom it was therefore impossible for the world to hate as it hated Him.⁶ And if this was the case during His earthly ministry, how infinitely more was it the case after His Resurrection, and when He had

---

¹ Hegesipp. ap. Euseb. iii. 20. They told Domitian that they only had between them about seven acres of land, which they farmed themselves.
² See Routh, Rel. Sacr. 196, and Notes; Fleury, Hist. Eccl. ii. § 52.
³ Ver. 17, 18. ⁴ Luke vi. 16.
⁵ The "Jude of James," who was one of the Twelve (Luke vi. 16; Acts i. 13), is called *a son of* James in Tyndale's, Cranmer's, and Luther's versions, and in the text of the Revised Version.
⁶ John ii. 4 (I have shown, however, in the *Life of Christ*, i. 165, that neither these words, nor the address "Woman!" involved any of the harshness or want of the most delicate reverence which the English translation seems to imply), vii. 7; Luke xi 28; Matt. xii. 50.

ascended to the right hand of the Majesty on High! It was natural that the early Church should speak of those holy men—who, if they were not the sons of the Mother of Jesus, had at any rate been trained under the same roof with Him—as "the brethren of the Lord." It was still more natural that, knowing Him at last, and believing on Him after He had risen from the dead, they should themselves shrink from the adoption of a title which pointed to a partial and earthly relationship, of which they could not but feel themselves transcendently unworthy. As for the later term *adelphotheos*, or "brother of God," which arose to describe this relationship,[1] I believe that St. James and St. Jude would have repudiated it with indignant energy, as arising from a reckless confusion of earthly relationships and Divine mysteries. They could not prevent their fellow-Christians from speaking of them as the "brethren of the Lord," but scarcely even for purposes of identification would they have been willing to use such a title of themselves. Like St. Paul, they must have felt that, though they had known "Christ after the flesh," yet henceforth they knew Him "after the flesh" no more. To have been, in any sense, brothers of Jesus of Nazareth in the humiliation of His earthly life gave them no right to speak of themselves authoritatively as brothers of the Eternal Son of God now sitting on the right hand of the Majesty on High.

On the other hand, nothing was more natural than that Jude should describe himself as "the brother of James." His object was to tell his readers who he was, and how they might distinguish him from thousands of other Jews who bore his name. He was personally unknown to all but a few. If he called himself "the brother of James," his identity would be recognised by all. He would have some influence as a brother of the great "Bishop" of Jerusalem, whose fame had spread through every community of the Christian Church, and whose authority, as a sort of Christian High-Priest, was recognised by the myriads of Jewish Christians[2] who still went up to the Holy City at the great yearly feasts.

Further than this, we only know the single fact that St. Jude was married. This we learn from the curious anecdote of Hegesippus which I have quoted on a previous page. It gives us an interesting glimpse of the simplicity and poverty which continued to the last to be the earthly lot of those who were connected with the Holy Family of Nazareth; and it is the more interesting because it is the last glimpse of them afforded to us by either secular or sacred history. Hegesippus says they lived till the days of Trajan, and perhaps implies that the race of the Desposyni ended with them.[3] This anecdote also accords with

---

[1] It is found in the superscription of the cursive Manuscript *f*, Ἄλλοι ἀδελφόθεοι τάδε ἐπιστέλλουσιν, which also has γράμμα πρὸς Ἑβραίους Ἰακώβου ἀδελφοθέου as a superscription to the Epistle of St. James.

[2] Acts xxi. 20: πόσαι μυριάδες ... Ἰουδαίων τῶν πεπιστευκότων.

[3] Euseb. *H. E.* iii. 20.

the incidental allusion of St. Paul, which, in contradiction to Ebionite traditions, speaks of the brethren of the Lord as being not only married men, but even as travelling about with their wives or Christian sisters on various missions.[1]

In the latter allusion we can see the possibility of circumstances which may have called forth the Epistle of St. Jude. If he travelled as one of the early preachers of Christianity, many years could not have elapsed before he learnt by painful experience that it was possible to accept the profession of Christianity without any participation in the holiness which it required. The imaginative sentiment which dwells with rapture on the supposed perfection of the early Christian Church is one which is cherished in defiance of history and Scripture. Hegesippus[2] says that till the days when Symeon, son of Clopas,[3] was Bishop of Jerusalem, the Church was a virgin, and that then "Thebuthis" began to introduce heresies because he had not been elected bishop. He is, however, probably taking a Hebrew word for a person. True Christians did indeed preach a standard of ideal holiness, and approached that standard in lives more noble and more innocent than any which the world had ever seen. But from the first the drag-net of the Church contained fish both bad and good, and from the first the tares sown by the enemy began to spring up thickly among the growing wheat. Many of the converts had barely extricated themselves from the vices of the heathendom by which they were surrounded.[4] Some openly relaxed into pagan practices.[5] Others, as time went on, betrayed a Satanic ingenuity in making their spiritual freedom a cloak for their carnal lusts.[6] The Epistle to the Corinthians exhibits to us a Church of which the discipline was inchoate and the morality deplorable. The Epistle to the Colossians proves that there had been an influx of gnosticising heresies, which illustrated the fatal affinity of religious error to moral degradation. The Pastoral Epistles show that these germs of sinful practice and erroneous theory had blossomed with fatal rapidity. In the Epistle of St. Jude and the Second Epistle of St. Peter we see perhaps still later developments of these tendencies. The former denounces the atrocities of conduct, the latter the audacities of opinion, which displayed themselves in men who, in the still tentative organisation of Christian discipline, and before the Church had perfected the bulwark of her episcopate, were by the outer world identified with Christians, and had crept in unawares among the faithful. If Jude in

---

[1] 1 Cor. ix. 5. "A sister, a wife," appears to mean, as it is rendered in the Revised Version, "a wife who is a believer."
[2] Ap. Euseb. *H. E.* iv. 22. For "Thebuthis," Rufinus has "Theobutes quidam;" see Routh, i. 237. It may be connected with אבה, and may mean "filth."
[3] Rufinus has *Cleopas.*
[4] This is even more apparent in the original of such passages as 1 Thess. iv. 6 and Eph. v. 3, than it is in the English version, where it is happily obscured by the rendering of πλεονεξία by "covetousness."
[5] See 1 Cor. v. 1—11; 2 Cor. xii. 21.
[6] 1 Pet. ii. 16; Gal. v. 13.

one of his mission journeys came into personal contact with any of these
deadly hypocrites, and was brought face to face with their extending
influence, we can well imagine that one who had lived from childhood
in a home of spotless purity, would have sat down in a flame of zeal to
wrap such infamous offenders in the whirlwind of his wrath. The
anger of a pure-hearted Jew might sometimes burn against the heathen
who knew not God; but here were *Christians*—Christians who claimed
yet loftier privileges than Israel of old, Christians who had received a
grander law and a diviner spirit, Christians who had been admitted into
a holier sanctuary only to become guilty of a more heinous sacrilege!
They were doing the deeds of darkness while they stood in the noonday. They claimed higher prerogatives than the Jew, yet they lived in
viler practices than the Gentile. The fulness of their knowledge aggravated the perversity of their ignorance; the depth of the abyss into
which they had sunk was only measurable by the glory of the height
from which they had fallen.

> "Oh, deeper dole,
> That so august a spirit, shrined so fair,
> Should, from the starry session of its peers,
> Decline to quench so bright a brilliancy
> In Hell's sick spume! Ah me, the deeper dole!"

Filled with the burning indignation which was inspired alike by the Law
and by the Gospel, Jude determined to warn the infant Church against
their perilous influence. It was his object to expose and to denounce
them;—and he did not spare.

But though the intention of the Epistle, as he himself tells us, is thus
distinct, we know nothing of the date at which it was written, or of the
place from which it was sent, or of the Churches to which it was addressed. That it was written in Palestine, and addressed to Corinth or
to Alexandria, are conjectures, which may be correct, but which rest on no
adequate foundation. St. Jude merely addresses his warnings to faithful
Christians. The notion that his letter was dictated by animosity towards
St. Paul or his followers, may be mentioned as a curiosity of criticism. It
is obvious that bad men, whether Paulinists or Judaists, might fall into
grievous aberrations. Truths can always be distorted by headstrong
partisans. There may have been nominal Paulinists—indeed, we know
that there were[2]—who wrested St. Paul's language into the wicked inferences that we may sin in order that grace may abound; and that,
since we are justified by faith, works are superfluous; or even, as we are
told in modern revivalist hymns, that "works are deadly." But that

---

[1] Renan, who accepts many of the theories of the Tübingen School in the fullest
development which they have received at the hands of Schwegler and Volkmar, sees
in the Epistle of St. Jude one of those venomous compositions, full of deadly hatred,
which he supposes to have been circulated through the Judæo-Christian communities by
emissaries of St. James, to counteract the growing influence of St. Paul! See these views
ably criticised by Ritschl, *Studien u. Krit.* 1861, p. 103 *ff.*
[2] Rom. iii. 8; 2 Pet. iii. 15.

Judaists were capable of heresies no less disastrous is proved by the way in which they and their adherents are addressed in St. Paul's Epistles.[1] There is no reason for asserting that the one class are here denounced more than the other; and how little St. Jude was likely to think of St. Paul with bitter feelings is happily, though most incidentally, revealed, not only by the analogous tone of St. Paul's own warnings, but also by the impress of the Epistle to the Romans on the form which St. Jude adopts for his final benediction. We reject the theories of M. Renan and the more extravagant followers of the school of Tübingen, not from any *à priori* views—for we know that in that epoch, as in all others, theological differences were wide and deep, and theological controversies, even between men of the Apostolic age, could be bitter and impassioned[2]—but we reject them because they rest on no foundation, and because they are contradicted by facts of which all can judge.

For purposes of exact comparison with the cognate paragraphs of the Second Epistle of St. Peter, it may be well to translate this letter also in a style more literal than that of our English Version, and then to consider the main problems which it presents. It is only by the aid of a literal translation that the English reader can really estimate the wide divergence of St. Jude's style from the ordinary style of the New Testament writers. In order that all may take in at a glance the affinity between this Epistle and the Second of St. Peter, I have here printed in italics those identical or closely analogous words and phrases which occur in both.

Jude, *a slave of Jesus Christ*, and a brother of James, to them that are beloved in God the Father and have been *kept* for Jesus Christ,[3] being elect, mercy to you, and peace, and *love be multiplied*.[4]

Beloved,[5] in giving *all diligence* to write to you respecting our common salvation,[6] I felt a necessity to write at once[7] exhorting you to fight in protection[8] of the faith once for all *delivered to the saints*. For there *slunk in*[9] certain persons[10] who have *long ago* been fore-described (in prophecy) as doomed for this *sentence*, impious men, changing the grace of our God into *wantonness*,[11] and *denying* the only *Master*, and our Lord *Jesus Christ*.[12] But I desire to *remind* you, *though ye know* all things, once for all,[13] that Jesus,[14] after saving a people from the land of Egypt, secondly *destroyed* such as believed not.[15]

---

[1] Gal. i. 9, v. 12, vi. 12; 2 Cor. xi. 20, &c.
[2] Acts xv. 2, πολλῆς συζητήσεως. [3] See John xvii. 11. [4] Compare Eph. vi. 23.
[5] Only as an opening address in 3 John 2.
[6] Cf. ἰσότιμον πίστιν, 2 Pet. i. 1. Even where the words of the two writers are not identical there is often a close analogy between the meanings which the words express.
[7] γράψαι. The word previously used is γράφειν. The sudden change of tense certainly seems to imply that St. Jude had intended to write a more general letter, but felt compelled by the present necessity to write this immediate warning. [8] ἐπαγωνίζεσθαι, sup.er-certare.
[9] παρεισέδυσαν; cf. 2 Pet. ii. 1, παρεισάξουσιν. Gal. ii. 4; παρεισάκτους, παρεισῆλθον.
[10] τινες and ἄνθρωποι are both depreciative (Gal. ii. 12).
[11] How prevalent was this dangerous possibility we see from 1 Cor. vi. 9—18; 1 John iii. 7—10; 2 Pet. ii.
[12] Or, "our only Lord and Master." א, A, B, C omit Θεόν; but probably (as in Luke ii. 29; Acts iv. 24; Rev. vi. 10, &c.) δεσπότης refers to God, though it is used of Christ in 2 Pet. ii. 1.
[13] I.e., though ye have once for all received all necessary instruction in matters pertaining to salvation.
[14] "Jesus" is the more difficult, and therefore more probable, reading of A, B. It is explained by 1 Cor. x. 4, and the identification of the Messiah with the "Angel of the Lord" (Ex. xiv. 19, xxiii. 20, &c.), and with the Pillar of Fire in Philo.
[15] "Whose carcases fell in the wilderness" (Heb. iii. 17).

And *angels*, those who kept not their own dignity,[1] but abandoned their proper habitation, he hath *kept*[2] *for the judgment* of the great *day* in everlasting *chains under mirky gloom*.[3] Even as *Sodom* and *Gomorrha*, and the cities around them, giving themselves to fornication in like manner with these,[4] and going *after strange flesh*, are set forth as an *example*, undergoing a penalty of eternal fire.[5] Yet, notwithstanding, in like manner, these persons also in their dreamings defile the flesh,[6] and set lordship at naught, and *rail at glories*.[7] But Michael the archangel,[8] when contending with the devil, he disputed about the body of Moses,[9] *dared not*[10] *bring against him a railing judgment*,[11] but said, "The Lord rebuke thee!"[12] But these *rail about such matters as they know not*,[13] and such things as they understand[14] *naturally, like the irrational animals*, in these they *corrupt* themselves.[15] Woe to them, because they

---

[1] Vulg., *principatum*.
[2] τετήρηκεν. I cannot see any intentional play of words here, though it is in contrast with the τοὺς μὴ τηρήσαντας.
[3] ζόφος is the word used by Hesiod of the imprisoned Titans (*Theogon*, 729). Ἀίδιος is stronger than αἰώνιος in the conception of permanence, yet, as we see here, it is used for a limited period, viz., εἰς κρίσιν μ. ἡμ., and in Enoch, to which Jude is referring, we find "Bind them *for seventy generations* under the earth until the day of judgment." (See Enoch xii. 4, xiv. 5, xv. 3, xxi. 10, &c.). I do not think it needful to enter into curious enquiries how these fallen angels, if kept in chains, dwell in the air and go about tempting men (Eph. ii. 2, vi. 12), or whether the tempting spirits are a different class from the fallen angels. See Excursus on the Book of Enoch and Rabbinic allusions of St. Jude.
[4] Clearly "with *these angels*." To refer it to Sodom and Gomorrha as though it were "Even as Admah and Zeboim *like Sodom and Gomorrha*," or "Even as Sodom and Gomorrha, in like manner with these ungodly Christians," is to introduce impossible explanations in order to get rid of St. Jude's plain intimation that he, like the Jews of his day, attributed the fall of the angels to sensuality.
[5] See 3 Macc. ii. 5, where the words are closely parallel ; so, too, ὑπέχειν, unknown to the N. T., is found in 2 Macc. iv. 48. The fire of retribution which destroyed the Cities of the Plain burnt but for a day ; but it is called æonian, or *eternal*, because the smoking ruin of it remains (comp. Wisd. x. 7), and because it is the *fire* of God's retributive wrath which burns eternally against unrepented sin. "Æonian" expresses *quality*, not duration. Libanius uses the same expression, in the same meaning, of the fire which burnt Troy.
[6] See Is. lvi. 10 (LXX.). They are dreamers because they take the substance for the shadow and the shadow for the substance, and their dreamy speculations are mixed up with immoral practices.
[7] What "glories" are meant is very uncertain. Wiesinger and Huther explain it of evil angels, as the context seems to imply. There is no trace of any early sect of heretics (whether in *conduct*, as those spoken of by St. Jude, or in *teaching*, as those spoken of by St. Peter) railing at angels, but rather the reverse (Col. ii. 18). In Enoch vi. 4 we read, "Ye calumniate [God's] greatness;" and in xli. 1, "The sinners who denied *the Lord of glory* ;" and in xlv. 2, "Who deny the Name of *the Lord of Spirits* ;" and in li. 8, "*The splendour of the Godhead* shall illuminate them." But we can hardly imagine that any who *blasphemed* God would be suffered to remain even nominal members of the Christian community. Immorality, however flagrant, would not necessarily exclude them from Churches of which the discipline was lax or weak, as we see not only from 1 Cor. v. 2, but also from the warnings which St. Paul finds it necessary to utter to even faithful communities. We see, however, from 1 Cor. xii. 3 that in the wild abuses of the "Tongues" some even dared to say "Anathema be Jesus!" See my *Life of St. Paul*, ii. 56.
[8] "Archangel" only in 1 Thess. iv. 16 (Dan. xii. 1, LXX.). Michael—"the merciful, the patient, the holy Michael" (Enoch xl. 8)—only in Dan. x. 13; Rev. xii. 7. Origen says that the allusion is taken from an apocryphal book called *The Ascension of Moses* (De Princ. iii. 2). See Rampf, *Der Brief Judæ*. In Targ. Jonath. on Deut. xxxiv. 6 he is the guardian of the grave of Moses.
[9] The Scriptural account of the death of Moses is very simple, but the Jews had many legends about it; especially how he—
"Died of the kisses of the lips of God."
The Angel of Death dared not take his life, and so God drew away his soul with a kiss. One legend was that Satan claimed his body as "lord of matter" (ὡς τῆς ὕλης δεσπόζοντι). Œcumenius says he claimed the body because Moses had murdered the Egyptian.
[10] Why "dared not?" The entire reasoning shows that the answer is "Because of Satan's former greatness." It can hardly be because the language of stern denunciation should never be used, seeing that Jude himself is here using it in the most impassioned form. In the Catena is a strange story that Satan, seeing Moses at the Transfiguration, taunted Michael with the violation of God's oath that Moses should not enter Canaan.
[11] Literally, "dared not bring against him a judgment of railing."
[12] The very words used by the Angel to the Accuser in Zech. iii. 1—3.
[13] This shows that the "railing" of these impious men was employed against spiritual or celestial beings of some kind. We have no materials for entering into further details.
[14] The E.V. does not keep up the distinction between οἴδασι and ἐπίστανται.
[15] See on 2 Pet. ii. 12 *supra*, pp. 111, 120.

went in the *way of Cain*,[1] and *poured themselves forth* in the *error of Balaam for hire*, and perished in the gainsaying of Korah.[2] These are the *sunken reefs*[3] in your *love feasts*,[4] *banqueting with you* fearlessly,[5] *pasturing themselves*;[6] *waterless clouds*,[7] *swept hither and thither by winds*,[8] autumn-withering *trees*,[9] *fruitless*, twice dead,[10] deracinated;[11] wild waves of the sea, foaming out their own shames;[12] wandering stars, *for which the mirk of darkness has been reserved for ever*. Yea, and with reference to them[13] did Enoch, the seventh from Adam,[14] prophesy, saying, "Lo, the Lord came, among his saintly myriads, to execute judgment against all, and to convict all the *impious* about all the deeds of their impiety which they *impiously did*, and about all the hard things which they spake against Him, impious sinners as they are. These are murmurers, blamers of their destiny,[15] *walking according to their lusts ;* and their mouth utters *inflated things*, admiring persons *for the sake of advantage*.[16]

But ye, *beloved*, remember the things *spoken before by the Apostles* of our Lord Jesus Christ, that they used to tell you, that, *in the last time* there shall be *scoffers, walking according to their own lusts* of impieties.[17] These are the separatists,[18] egotistical,[19] not having the spirit. But ye, *beloved*, building up yourselves on your most

---

[1] The allusion to Cain is obviously to the Cain of Jewish *hagadoth*, for St. Jude can hardly be charging these teachers with murder (see Excursus).
[2] "Gainsaying." Heb., Meribah; Numb. xx. 13, "the water of strife" (LXX., ἀντιλογίας).
[3] σπιλάδες, αἱ ὕφαλοι πέτραι, *Etym. Magn.* In 2 Pet. ii. 13, σπίλοι, "spots."
[4] *Agapae* are mentioned under that name in this place alone.
[5] Perhaps συνευωχούμενοι refers to some such insolent selfish greed as that of the rich Corinthians (1 Cor. xi. 21); ἀφόβως, not fearing either the rebukes of Presbyters (who are themselves afraid in poor communities to do their duty) or the consequences which they may bring upon themselves (1 Cor. xi. 30).
[6] Ez. xxxiv. 1, "Woe to the shepherds that feed themselves."
[7] Prov. xxv. 14; "carried about by every wind of doctrine," Eph. iv. 14.
[8] Here St. Peter's "being driven by a hurricane" is the more energetic phrase. The metaphors and expressions are here as Æschylean as St. Peter's, e.g., ἐπαφρίζοντα; cf. Æsch. *Ag.* 1067.
[9] "Spätherbstliche." Grot. *frugiperdas.*
[10] "*Twice dead*," merely a proverbial expression for "utterly dead," as in "*Bis qui cito*," and "*Pro quo bis patiar mori.*"
[11] ἐκριζωθέντα. I take the unique equivalent from Shakespeare —
"Rend and deracinate
The unity and wedded calm of states."
[12] Is. lvii. 20.
[13] Or, "to these also" (as well as to others).
[14] We should say the *sixth*, but the Jews counted inclusively. The only object in mentioning this is the mystic significance of the number seven. Thus the Jews spoke of Moses as the seventh from Abraham; of Phinehas as the seventh from Jacob, &c. In Enoch xli.—xvi. the prophet is sent on a mission to the Fallen Angels. They fell from Heaven to earth, he was exalted from earth to Heaven (Iren. *Haer.* iv. 2, 16). See Excursus, "The Book of Enoch."
[15] μεμψίμοιροι, "blamers of their own lot." Philo, *Vit. Mos.* i. 33, Καὶ πάλιν ἤρξαντο μεμψιμοιρεῖν, "and they began again to blame their lot." Theophrastus, *Eth. Char.* xvii., περὶ μεμψιμοιρίας, "discontent following in the wake of self-indulgence."
[16] θαυμάζειν πρόσωπα, a Hebrew phrase: comp. προσωπολήπτης, Acts x. 34. In Gen. xix. 21, "Lo! I have accepted thee," the LXX. render ἰδού, ἐθαύμασά σου τὸ πρόσωπον. The best comment is in the words of Shakespeare —
"And not a man *for being simply man*
Hath any honour, but honour for those honours
Which are *without him*, as place, riches, favour,
Prizes of accident as oft as merit."
And as to the *cause* which St. Jude assigns for this partiality —
"*Plate sin with gold*
And the strong lance of justice hurtless breaks."
[17] Ἐμπαίκται, Is. iii. 4 (LXX.). Warnings against such apostates, blasphemers, and ungodly men must have occurred often in the teachings of the Apostles (see Acts xx. 29; 1, 2 Thess.; Col. i. ii.; Tim.; Tit.; Rev., *passim*). It seems a most idle argument to refer this prophecy to 2 Pet. iii. 1, 2, and thence to assume the priority of that Epistle!
[18] The word is only found in Arist. *Polit.* iv. 4, § 13. Separatists=Pharisees. But here the Pharisaism is Antinomian and apostate (Hooker, *Serm.* v. 11).
[19] ψυχικοί, "egotistical." If this rendering be not accepted, there is nothing for it but to naturalise the word "psychical" as a translation of this word. It expresses those who live in accordance with the mere natural views of a limited and selfish life. They are not *necessarily* "carnal"—*i.e.*, devoted to the basest fleshly impulses (σαρκικοί)—nor have they become "spiritual" (πνευματικοί). They live the common life of men in simple worldliness, and the slightly expanded egotism of domestic selfishness.

holy faith, praying in the Holy Spirit, keep yourselves in the love of God, awaiting the mercy of our Lord Jesus Christ unto life eternal. And some, indeed, try to convict of error when they dispute with you;[1] and try to save some, snatching them from the fire;[2] and pity some in fear,[3] hating even the tunic that has been *spotted*[4] by the *flesh*.

Now to Him that is able to guard you[5] unstumbling, and to set you before His glory *blameless* in exultation, to the only God[6] our Saviour through Jesus Christ our Lord, be glory, *majesty*, might, and *power* before all the æon,[7] and *now*, and to all the æons. *Amen*.

I. The style of the Greek—which was no doubt the language in which this letter was originally written—is exactly such as we should expect from one to whom Greek was not so familiar as his native Aramaic, but who still writes with a passion which gives force and eloquence to his words. It is the language of an Oriental who knows Greek, partly by reading and partly by having moved among Hellenistic communities, but whose vocabulary is far richer and more powerful than his grammar.[8] The words are Greek words, and sometimes rare, forcible, and poetic; but the whole colouring and tone of thought recall the manner of the Hebrew prophets, in whose writings St. Jude must have been trained during his youth in the humble and faithful house of Joseph at Nazareth.

The most remarkable trace of this Hebraic structure is shown in the extraordinary fondness of the writer for *triple arrangements*. In pausing to tell us that Enoch was the *seventh* from Adam, he at once shows his interest in sacred numbers, and throughout his Epistle he has scarcely omitted a single opportunity of throwing his statements into groups of three. Thus those whom he addresses are sanctified, kept, elect,[9] and he wishes them mercy, love, peace;[10] the instances of Divine retribution are the Israelites in the wilderness, the fallen angels, and the cities of the Plain;[11] the dreamers whom he denounces are corrupt, rebellious, and railing;[12] they have walked in the way of Cain, Balaam,

---

[1] Read for ἐλεᾶτε or ἐλεεῖτε (which spoil the continuity of the structure), ἐλέγχετε, A, C, which can only be fully rendered by "try to convict of error;" διακρινομένους, א, A, B, C, see ver. 9 for the meaning of the word. Elsewhere it means "doubting" (Acts x. 20, Ja. i. 6, &c.).
[2] Zech. iii. 2. "Is not this a brand plucked from the burning?" (Am. iv. 1).
[3] *Leg*. οὓς δὲ ἐλεᾶτε ἐν φόβῳ, א, A, B. The omission of this clause by the E.V. (following K. T. L.) spoils the triple structure. The *first* class of these impious men is to be refuted in argument; the *second* to be saved by vigorous personal influence and exertion; the *third*, which is the most obstinate and degraded class, shun, for fear they should defile and corrupt you; yet pity them in Christian love.
[4] ἐσπιλωμένον (comp. Rev. iii. 4, οὐκ ἐμόλυναν τὰ ἱμάτια αὐτῶν).
[5] αὐτοὺς for ὑμᾶς is the *difficilior lectio*, but as it is only found in A, it may be a mere slip. The doxology evidently recalls Rom. xvi. 25.
[6] The word "wise," omitted in א, A, B, C, &c., is probably interpolated from Rom. xvi. 27.
[7] *I.e.*, "as it was in the beginning."
[8] The number of the *hapax legomena* is remarkable, and some of them are full of picturesqueness and force—*e.g.*, ἐπαγωνίζεσθαι, παρεισέδυσαν, ἐκπορνεύσασαι, ὀπίσω σαρκός, ὑπέχουσαι, φυσικῶς, ἐξεγύθησαν, ἀγάπαις, σπιλάδες, φθινοπωρινά, ἐπαφρίζοντα, πλανῆται, γογγυσταί, μεμψίμοιροι, προσωπα θαυμάζοντες, ἀπταίστους, πρὸ παντὸς τοῦ αἰῶνος, besides others which are only found here and in 2 Peter, or are exceedingly rare in the New Testament. The semi-poetic colouring of these words is a phenomenon often observable in writers who are using a foreign language. "The diction," says Davidson, "is round and full, not neat or easy, but rather harsh. It shows one acquainted with Greek, yet unable to express his ideas in it with ease."—*Introduction to New Testament*, i. 450.
[9] Ver. 1.   [10] Ver. 2.   [11] Vers. 5–7.   [12] Ver. 8.

and Korah;[1] they are murmurers, discontented, self-willed; they are boastful, partial, greedy of gain;[2] they are separatists, egotistic, unspiritual.[3] Lastly, they are to be dealt with in three classes, of which one class is to be refuted in disputation, another saved by effort, and the third pitied with detestation of their sins.[4] But saints are to pray in the spirit, keep themselves in the love of God, and await the mercy of Christ;[5] and glory is ascribed to God before the past, in the present, and unto the farthest future.[6]

Some of these triplets—those, for instance, in the twenty-third and last verses—are missed, in consequence of the adoption by the English Version of inferior readings; but, as regards the rest, even if we might otherwise suppose that some of them were accidental, the recurrence of this arrangement no less than eleven times in twenty-five verses is obviously intentional, or, at any rate, characteristic of the writer's mode of thought. It could not be paralleled from any other passage of Scripture of equal length.[7] It is unlike anything which we should find in classic Greek, and accords with the professed authorship by indicating the Hebraic tinge of the writer's mind. We shall notice hereafter that a similar antithetic balance and rhythmic flow is characteristic of the style of St. John. In both of these sacred writers it is the result of their Semitic origin and Jewish education.

II. But a far more remarkable characteristic of the writer is his fondness for alluding to remote and unrecorded incidents of Jewish tradition. In the brief space of nine verses he introduces current Rabbinic views in a manner to which, in the New Testament, there is scarcely a parallel. He accepts, for instance, the strange notion respecting the fate and fall of the angels through fleshly lusts. Alone of the New Testament writers, except St. John in the Apocalypse, he mentions and names an archangel.[8] He introduces, probably from the apocryphal *Ascension of Moses*[9], a personal contention between this Archangel and the Devil about the body of Moses, to which there is not in Scripture the remotest allusion.[10] He tells us that Michael "did not dare" to bring a "judgment of railing" against the Evil Spirit. He refers to Cain in a manner which seems to imply something more than the murder of Abel. He makes a quotation, which has since been

---

[1] Ver. 11. [2] Ver. 16. [3] Ver. 19. [4] Vers. 22, 23.
[5] Ver. 20. [6] Ver. 25.
[7] There is something which partially resembles it in the half-rhythmic triplets of Eph. v. 14.
[8] In the Apocryphal books and the Talmud we read of seven Archangels—Michael, Gabriel, Raphael, Uriel, Sealthiel, Jeremeel, and Sammael.
[9] 'Ανάληψις Μωϋσέως. See Hilgenfeld, *Mess. Jud.* lxxii. He may, however, be merely introducing the Jewish legend in his own way. (See Lieffert in Herzog. *R. Enc.*, s. v.)
[10] Schüttgen, Meuschen, and others adduce in exact parallel to this, that in the Jalkut Reubeni (f. 43, 3) there is a contest between Michael and Satan about Isaac and the ram. In Hilgenfeld's *Messias Judaeorum*, p. 461, various fragments are quoted of the *Ascension of Moses*, from which the reference was taken. (Orig. *De Princip.* iii. 2, § 1; see, too, Œcumenius *ad loc.*; Cramer's *Catena*, p. 160.)

discovered in a book confessedly apocryphal.¹ How are we to explain these peculiarities? Do they need any apologetic treatment?

There are two ways of treating them, which I shall content myself with stating, leaving every reader of unbiassed mind and fearless sincerity to choose between them.

i. There are many writers who endeavour by various explanations to minimise whatever contradicts their theories of "verbal dictation," and who insist that every allusion which cannot be explained out of the Old Testament must be accepted as a literal fact divinely revealed to St. Jude himself. It would, indeed, be a matter of no small difficulty to accept the Jewish legend that angels fell from their heavenly dignity by sensual impurities with mortal women. Hence these writers interpret the "sons of God" in Gen. vi. 2 to mean men of the righteous race, and they suppose that the "giants" in that passage were the offspring of inter-marriages between the race of Seth and the race of Cain.² They therefore explain St. Jude's allusion as a reference to the expulsion of Satan's angels from Heaven because of their revolt,—a notion very familiar to us from Milton's Epic, but of which there are in Scripture only the dimmest and most disputable traces. They take it as a divinely revealed fact that the body of Moses was really an object of personal contention between the Archangel Michael and the Devil, and they boldly conjecture that Satan desired to seize the body that he might induce the Jews to treat it as a relic to be worshipped.³ Lastly, although the prophecy attributed to Enoch really does occur in almost the same words in the apocryphal book of that name—and although it is certain that the book in whole or in part existed in St. Jude's time— they refuse to admit that St. Jude could have used a quotation from a book confessedly apocryphal, but assume either that he received this particular passage "by independent revelation";⁴ or that it was a genuine prophecy of the antediluvian prophet correctly handed down by tradition for two thousand five hundred years;⁵ or, lastly, that the writer or interpreter of the Book of Enoch borrowed it from St. Jude, and not St. Jude from him.

ii. To others the rare phenomena of the Epistle present no difficulty which requires such a congeries of harsh suppositions—suppositions which, in their opinion, need no refutation, because they rest on no basis. They do not think it necessary to support the authority of this certainly canonical, but as certainly non-apostolic, writer by hypotheses so extraordinary. They know that at this epoch apocryphal literature

¹ Jude 14.
² As was done even by St. Augustine. See, too, Milton, *Paradise Lost*, xii. 580, *seq.*
³ Philippi supposes that the fact was revealed to the disciples, to account for the appearance of Moses on the Mount of Transfiguration. Of what use are such conjectures?
⁴ "Apostolum Henochi verba *ex* singulari divina revelatione habuisse."—Pfeiffer, *Decas*, iv. § 8.
⁵ See "Enoch Restitutus: An attempt to separate from the Books of Enoch the book quoted by St. Jude," by Rev. E. Murray, 1838.

was widely current among the Jews, and that a dense multitude of Rabbinic legends had sprung up around their early literature and history. Many of these are of an absurd and objectionable character, and they see a superintending guidance in the wisdom which excludes all trace of these from the sacred page. Every Jewish Christian, trained in the lore of Palestine, would be familiar with many such Hagadoth; and it was perfectly natural that in writing to his countrymen St. Jude should refer to such beliefs by way of passing illustration, just as St. Paul refers to the traditional names of the Egyptian magicians,[1] and to the legend of the wandering rock.[2]

St. Jude's quotation from the apocryphal Book of Enoch[3] no more stamps the book of Enoch, or the passage quoted from it, as a Divine revelation than do St. James's references to the *Wisdom of Solomon*, or St. Paul's quotations from Epimenides, Aratus, or Menander. From those pagan writers, and even from the last—deeply dyed as he was with the vicious morality of a decadent age—St. Paul quotes without hesitation a religious truth, or moral aphorism, or historical allusion which happens to illustrate his general purpose. It is in no wise strange that St. Jude should make analogous use of the Book of Enoch and the *Ascension of Moses*, which were current among the Hebraists whom he was addressing, and whose views he shared. Some have supposed that he used them because they were accepted by those against whom he is writing, and because any consideration derived from these would have the force of an *argumentum ad hominem*. It seems to be a more natural supposition that he alluded to current conceptions for a particular object, just as all writers do in all ages, without entering into any discussion as to their literal truth.

Such are the conflicting opinions of different commentators. They affect questions which lie in that neutral region of uncertainty where all true Christians should respect their common freedom. They touch on questions of literature and criticism. They hinge upon definitions of inspiration which the Scriptures themselves do not furnish, and which the Church has in consequence withheld. They may be safely left to the influence of time, and the widening thoughts of mankind. All that we need say respecting them is, "Let there be in things necessary unity; in things doubtful liberty; in *all* things charity."

iii. If we ask, lastly, who were the evil-doers against whom the parallel denunciations of St. Jude and the Second Epistle of St. Peter

---

[1] 2 Tim. iii. 8.
[2] 1 Cor. x. 4. See *Life and Work of St. Paul*, i. 48, 638.
[3] The direct quotation is in Jude 14, 15, but there are several other traces of St. Jude's acquaintance with the book; for instance, the pseudo-Enoch, no less than Jude, refers to "wandering stars" (xviii. 14, 16; xxi. 3), and comes near the very remarkable expression "chains of darkness" (Jude 6; 2 Pet. ii. 4, 5; "Bind Azazel . . . cast him into darkness" (xli. 5—7); "Fetters of iron without weight" (liii. 3). Hofmann and Philippi try to prove that the Book of Enoch was written by a Jewish Christian. Locke, Ewald, Weizsäcker, Dillmann, Köstlin, &c., only admit later interpolations of a Jewish book.

were hurled—St. Jude exposing their unnatural wickedness and blaspheming presumption, the Second Epistle dwelling mainly on their corrupting influence and specific faithlessness—the answer is that neither of the sacred writers is dealing with a definite sect, but that the errors and malpractices which they denounce afterwards came to a head in the mysteries of iniquity which characterised *many* sects. These errors contained the germ of the systems which were subsequently known as Antinomian Gnosticism. Very shortly after the period with which we are dealing, the Nicolaitans drew on themselves the indignant anathemas of St. John. The second century saw the rise of other defilers of the Christian name and profession. Such were the Ophites, who lauded the Serpent of Paradise as their benefactor;[1] the blasphemous Cainites, who made their heroes out of all the vilest characters mentioned in the Old Testament;[2] the Carpocratians, who taught licentious communism;[3] the Antitactae, who regarded it as a duty to the Supreme God to violate all the commandments, on the ground that they had been promulgated by His enemy the Demiurgus;[4] the Adamites, who taught men to live like brutes.[5] None of these sects as yet existed *as sects*, but in the wild opinions attributed to Nicolas and Cerinthus we see the seething elements of reckless speculation which sprang from a common fountain, but under the subsequent name of Gnosticism split into the two opposite streams of a reckless immorality and an extravagant asceticism.[6]

[1] Iren. *Haer.* i. 30, § 5.   [2] Epiphan. *Haer.* xxxviii. 2.
[3] Clem. Alex. *Strom.* iii. 2; Theodoret, *Haer.* i. 6.
[4] Clem. Alex. *Strom.* iii. 4.   [5] Epiphan. *Haer.* lii.
[6] ἢ γάρ τοι ἀδιαφόρως ζῆν διδάσκουσιν ἤ, τὸ ὑπέρτονον ἄγουσαι, ἐγκράτειαν (Clem. Alex. *Strom.* iii. 5, § 40).

Book III.

APOLLOS AND ALEXANDRIAN CHRISTIANITY AND THE EPISTLE TO THE HEBREWS

CHAPTER XII.

JUDAISM, THE SEPTUAGINT, AND ALEXANDRIAN INFLUENCES.

"Alexandria . . . vertex omnium civitatum."
Amm. Marcell. xxii. 16.

THE Christian Faith does not centre in a Dogma, or in a Book, but in a Person, and this is the cause and pledge of its essential unity. Its one answer to all who, with the Philippian jailer, ask, "Sirs, what must I do to be saved?" is the answer of Paul and Silas, "Believe in the Lord Jesus Christ, and thou shalt be saved, and thy house." That truth was clearly seen by the writer of the Epistle to the Hebrews, when he began his magnificent sketch of Christian theology with the pregnant words, "God, Who fragmentarily and multifariously of old spake to our fathers by the Prophets, at the end of these days spake unto us by His Son."

But unity does not exclude diversity—nay, more, without diversity there can be no true and perfect unity. Where there is no unity there is distraction, but where there is no diversity there is death. Where the spirits of the prophets are not subject to the prophets—where every man is conscious only of his own invisible consecration—where, as in the Church of Corinth, every one in his fanatical egotism is anxious to shout down the truths revealed to others, that he may absorb the attention of all by his own "tongue," however barbarous, however dissonant, however unintelligible—where it is ignored that amid the diversities of gifts and ministrations there is yet the translucent energy of one and the same Spirit—*there* is confusion, and railing, and irreligious strife. And where, on the other hand, all lips mechanically repeat the same shibboleth for centuries after its significance has been worn away—where the dulness of a self-styled "orthodoxy" has obliterated the many hues of the wisdom of God—where enquiry is crushed under the heel of authority—where, in fact, there can be *no* independent enquiry because all conclusions are dictated beforehand by the tyranny of an usurped infallibility—*there* is uniformity indeed, but therewith corruption and decay. When it is persecution to alter the perspective of a doctrine, and death to leave the cart-rut of a system—when they who question the misinterpretations of Scripture which have been pressed into the service of popular errors, must face the anger of startled ignorance—when there is no life left save the spark which glows in the ashes of the Martyr, or the lamp which flickers in the Reformer's cell—then the caste which has seized the keys of the Kingdom of Heaven may boast indeed of unity, but it is the unity produced by selfishness in the few, and serfdom in the many. The unity so secured is but the stagnancy of the unrippled water, the monotony of the barren sands. It is the unity of the dead plain, "where every molehill is a mountain, and every thistle a forest tree." In this latter condition there is a deadlier peril than in the former. Even discords can be inwrought into the vast sequences of some mighty harmony, but what great music can be achieved with but a single note? Unbroken unanimity may be the boast of a deadening Buddhism, a withered Confucianism, a mechanical Islam; it cannot exist in a free and living Christianity. If it exist at all, it can only be as a uniformity of indifference and ignorance—a uniformity of winter and of night. The uniformity of the noonday is only for the Infinite. For finite beings, if there be any light at all, there must be the colours of the sunset, and the sevenfold lustre of the rainbow, which is only seen when there is rain as well as sun.

> "Only the prism's obstruction shows aright
> The secret of a sunbeam, breaks its light
> Into the jewelled bow from blankest white;
> So may a glory from defect arise."[1]

Hence, as we have seen again and again in the books of the Old Testament, the truth which they reveal comes to us tinged with the individuality of the writers. It comes to us unchanged, indeed, in its essence, because that essence is unchangeable, but still reflected and refracted by the medium through which it has inevitably passed. The Light of Heaven, like the light of day, *can* only reach us through earthly media. The sunlight—lest it should blind us with its brightness—must pass through the atmosphere with its layers of vapour visible and invisible; it must glance from a myriad surfaces; it must fire the mountain tops and blaze upon the sea, and be coloured by the evening clouds. And yet wherever it falls, however it is modified, it is always beneficent—and even more beneficent from the changes to which it is subjected—because it is the sunlight still. And in the same way, to suit our finite capacities, the Light of Heaven also must pass through human subjectivities. It must display blessed varieties of hue, and graduated intensities of radiance, according as it comes to us through the mind of a Moses or of an Isaiah, of a St. James or a St. Paul. But of itself it can never lead astray, because it is light from Heaven. The mystic light which, as Jewish legend tells us, gleamed over the oracular gems of Aaron's breastplate, was ardent now with the azure of the sapphire, now with the deep green of the emerald,

---

[1] Browning.

now with the softer lustre of the amethyst. Even so does the light of inspiration alternately blaze or glow in the fiery heart of the Apostle of the Gentiles, in the loving tenderness of St. John the Divine, in the stern and lofty morality of St. James, the brother of the Lord.

Nor is it otherwise with the truths proclaimed by different communities. Churches, too, have their modifying subjectivity. The Spirit of God that spake of old in the prophets is the Spirit of Christ which speaks in his prophets now. "*Vox quidem dissona, sed una relligio.*" The voices are many, the utterance is one. Churches differ as individuals differ. There were differences of view, differences of perspective, differences of characteristic expression in the Churches of Africa and of Palestine, in the schools of Alexandria and Antioch, in the Churches of the East and of the West. Christianity in all Churches was, and ever must be, in its essence Catholic—one and indivisible; yet Christians shared in all minor matters the varying views of the bodies to which they belonged. There is but one *flock* of Christ, but there are many *folds*. The Christians of Egypt were not absolutely identical in the colour of their theology with those of Ephesus, nor the Christians of Ephesus with those of Rome.

Uniquely great and memorable was the work of the Church of Alexandria. The Christian School of Alexandria was deeply influenced by the views and traditions of the Jewish schools from which it sprang. To those schools it was affiliated by an unbroken course of historical events. I will endeavour, therefore, to furnish here a swift and summary view of the origin and character of ALEXANDRIAN CHRISTIANITY, which may at least serve to render more distinct the special character of the Epistle to the Hebrews.

The Jews, tenaciously as they have always clung to their national peculiarities, have yet shown a remarkable power of adapting themselves, within certain limits, to the civilisation and tone of thought of the age and country in which their lot has been cast. But there has never been any modification of Judaism so remarkable as that which arose in Alexandria when Jewish religion first came into contact with Greek philosophy. Thus did the House of Bondage of their fathers become for the later Jews a School of Wisdom.[1]

If the bringing of East and West into closer contact with each other was one of the main works of Alexander the Great, the deepest mark which he left on the history of the world was his founding of Alexandria. Jewish Hellenism—the utterance of Oriental thought in Greek language, and the interchange of Asiatic and Greek conceptions—was the result of Alexander's conquests, and of the policy which directed them; and this fusion went on more rapidly in Alexandria than in any other part of the Macedonian Empire.

[1] Grätz, *Gesch. d. Juden*, iii. 26.

Alexandria was a city which had the most splendid advantages. The fleets of Asia and Europe met in a commodious harbour, whose entrance was lighted by the Pharos, which has given its name to every lighthouse in the world.[1] Unlike the majority of ancient cities, it was built upon a regular plan, and was magnificently adorned with public buildings and works of art. Its climate was healthy; it was well supplied with pure water by noble aqueducts; its market was a meeting-place for traffickers from every region of the civilised globe. The mixture of various nationalities in an important city always tends to quicken the thoughts of men. Oriental theosophy, Greek culture, philosophic speculations, found their way among the citizens as surely as the sailors of the ships which came to anchor behind the Pharos. Even Theodorus the Atheist was welcomed at the Court of the Ptolemies.[2] Alexandria seethed with intellectual excitement.[3] There was an incessant conflict and rivalry between the Egyptian, Greek, and Jewish elements of the populace, which in later times could barely be kept in order by the rough authority of Roman Proconsuls. But besides the natural sharpening of the intellect which resulted from the contact of opposite religions, the Ptolemies had made it their object to be patrons of literature, and the royal library of Alexandria furnished an unique opportunity for earnest students.

A circumstance which exercised no small influence over the development of Alexandria was the equality of civil rights which the Jews had from the first enjoyed. Alexander the Great had been most favourably impressed by his interview with the high-priest Jaddua.[4] Whatever may be thought of the legendary details of that interview, it is certain that he had spared the Jews from any exactions, and had accorded to them exceptional privileges. His policy was followed by the astute dynasty of the Lagidæ, the famous Ptolemies who ruled at Alexandria for nearly three centuries. Under the fostering care of some of these kings, who understood them better and treated them more wisely than the rival dynasty of Syrian Seleucids, the Jews grew and multiplied in prosperity, as they had multiplied in adversity in the old days of their Egyptian bondage. Before the dawn of the Christian era they had increased to a million, and not only occupied two of the five quarters of Alexandria as their exclusive Ghetto, but were also in possession of the best localities for business in the rest of the city. Their synagogue—the famous Diapleuston, with its seventy gilded chairs, and its size so vast that the signal for the "Amens" of the con-

---

[1] Μέγιστον ἐμπορεῖον τῆς οἰκουμένης (Strabo).
[2] Diog. Laert. II. 102.
[3] Εἰς ἣν καὶ ἡ πανταχόθεν συνέρρει ποτὴς τῶν περὶ φιλοσοφίαν ἐσπουδακότων (Greg. Nyss. Vit. Greg. Thaumat.).
[4] It is an interesting fact—a link between the farther and nearer epochs of antiquity —that Jaddua, B.C. 333, is the latest person (chronologically) who is mentioned in the Old Testament. Nehem. xi. 22; Jos. Antt. xi. 8, § 5.

gregation had to be given by a flag—was the grandest in the world.[1] The management of the harbour-shipping, and of the all-important export of corn, on which Rome depended for its daily bread, was mainly in their hands.[2] Their Sanhedrin was almost as venerable as that of Jerusalem. Their Alabarch was one of the principal persons in the city, and occupied a position of splendid dignity. The Temple of Onias at Leontopolis, while it did not alienate their affections from the Temple at Jerusalem, was a continual source of pride and gratification.[3] So great was the skill of the Alexandrian handicraftsmen that, if any of the finest work was required for the adornment of the Temple at Jerusalem, the Rabbis sent for workmen to Alexandria, as Solomon had done to the Phœnicians in the days of old.[4] The privileges of the Jews had been secured to them under the Roman Empire by the generous edicts of Julius Cæsar and other emperors.[5]

The Jews had been able on more than one occasion to render valuable assistance to the Ptolemies, and especially to Ptolemy Philometor in his struggles against his brother Physkon. It was natural that the Egypto-Grecian kings should desire to know something of the vaunted lore of these remarkable subjects. The Greek Version of the Bible, so famous under the name of the Septuagint, was undertaken for the gratification of Ptolemy Philadelphus, who wished to have a specimen of the Bible in the great library;[6] or, perhaps, as a result of the amicable relations between Ptolemy Philometor and the Jewish philosopher Aristobulus. The House of Lagos must have some of the credit for its production. Whatever may have been the history of this version—which is much obscured by the fictions of Aristeas as to its miraculous origin—the effects which it produced were deep and lasting. The Septuagint was, as the modern Jewish historian quaintly observes, "the first Apostle of the Gentiles." For the first time the heathen of every land were enabled to read and judge for themselves of all that "Moses delivered in his *mystic* volume."[7] The translators of the Greek Bible, whose names are for the most part unknown, rendered two immense, but unconscious, services to the Christianity which was soon to shine upon the world. They disseminated the monotheistic conviction, with the historic revelation on which it was based; and they created the peculiar dialect in which the New Testament was written.

---

[1] See a description of the Diapleuston or Great Synagogue of Alexandria (of which it was said that "whoever had not seen it, had not seen the glory of Israel") in Succah. f. 51, b. There is the usual monstrous hyperbole—*e.g.*, that each of the 71 gilded chairs for the Sanhedrin was worth 21 myriad talents of gold! See Grätz, *Gesch. d. Juden*, iv. 128.
[2] Philo. c. *Flac.* ii. 525 (ed. Mangey).
[3] It seems to have been built about A.D. 150.
[4] Yoma, 38, 1; Grätz, iii. 28.   [5] Jos. *Antt.* xiv. 10, §§ 1—10.
[6] It is said that his attention was called to the subject by the eminent librarian, Demetrius Phalereus.
[7] Juv. *Sat.* xiv. 102. The epithet "*arcano*" seems to be due to the talk of allegorists, who denied that the literal sense was the real sense.

The task of the Apostles and Evangelists would have been far more difficult than it was, if they had not found ready to their hands a dialect which was even more flexible than the pure Greek of the Classics, and a religious phraseology for technical conceptions which had already begun to be widely understood.

The appearance of the Septuagint Version affected the Jews in very different ways. To the Alexandrian Jews, and generally to the Jews of the Dispersion, it furnished an occasion for unmitigated joy. They could now point with pride to the writings of Moses and the Prophets in proof that they too were in possession of a priceless literature. They could show the Greeks that there were Hebrew writers even greater than Pythagoras and Plato, who were the boast of Heathendom. The tenets of their religion became better known, and therefore more respected, wherever Greek was understood. Though Hebrew was now a dead language, and the Jews of Europe and Asia had for the most part forgotten their native Aramaic, they were kept faithful to the laws and institutions of their fathers. Thanks to the labours of "the Seventy," Moses was read in the Synagogues every Sabbath day, and interpreted into a tongue understanded of the people.[1] We cannot, therefore, wonder that the Alexandrian Jews kept the day of the publication of the Septuagint as an annual feast-day, on which they visited, with every sign of rejoicing, the cells on the island of the Pharos in which tradition said that the version had been finished by supernatural aid.

Far different were the views of the stern old Hebraisers—the Hebrews of Hebrews—who taught in the schools of Palestine and Jerusalem. Rejecting the fiction of Aristeas, that the interpreters had been sent to Ptolemy Philadelphus from Jerusalem by the express sanction of the high-priest Eleazar, and scornfully denying that God had shown His approval by granting inspiration to the Translators, they regarded the rendering of their sacred tenets into a profane language as an irreparable misfortune. It had long been forbidden to write the words of the Torah on the skins of unclean animals; surely, they argued, it was a far greater profanation to express them in the accents of a pagan dialect. Was it even *possible* so to express them? Was it possible to place them in the crucible of an unhallowed language and not to evaporate some of their subtlest elements of truth? How could the God of Shem speak in the unblessed accents of Japhet? Was it not certain that, apart from the impossibility of making one tongue express the exact sentiments of another, there would be large room for unfaithful concessions to Greek and heathen prejudices on the part of

---

[1] In the *Life of St. Paul*, i. 369, I have mentioned the interesting fact that from the *Midrash*, or expository sermon delivered by the Apostle, we are enabled to tell with certainty what *Parashah* and *Haphtarah*, or First and Second Lessons, had been read from the LXX. in the Synagogue of Antioch, in Pisidia, on a certain Sabbath more than eighteen centuries ago.

the Translators? As a counter-manifesto to the exultation of the Alexandrian Jews,[1] they kept the day of the publication of the Greek Bible as a Fast, and a day of evil omen as deadly as that on which Israel had danced around the golden calf.[2]

And from their point of view the Rabbis of Jerusalem were more than half right. They had good grounds for being suspicious of what they called the "wisdom of the Ionians."[3] The publication of the Bible in Greek *did* tend to alter the conceptions of the Jews; to widen their tribalism; to prepare the way for Christianity; to throw down the middle wall of partition between them and other nations; to show the absurdity of many of the legends, precedents, and inferential systems which they had based on the isolation of their favourite "texts." But, further than this, there can be little doubt that Judaism, when denuded of the *ism* wherein resided its intense exclusiveness, lost also much of its distinctive character. When the Jews began to recognise that they were not the monopolists of truth, they developed the tendency to underrate the preciousness of the truth which was their special heritage. It was by no means easy to fulfil the aspiration of the learned Rabbi Jochanan Ben Napuchah, who had desired to unite the pallium of Japhet with the tallith of Shem.[4] When in the troubles which burst upon the Alexandrian Jews in the Proconsulship of Flaccus many of them purchased exemption from torture and massacre by apostasy, the religious conservatives of Palestine were strengthened in their conviction that the Jews could never study without peril the literature of the Gentiles. When an old Rabbi was asked at what hour Grecian literature might be studied, he replied that it could only be studied at an hour which belonged neither to the day nor to the night; for God's Law, and that only, ought to be man's meditation both day and night.[5]

Even the Seventy had shown that they either did not sufficiently understand the duty of absolute faithfulness in translators, or that in some instances their sense of the literal meaning of the Sacred Text had been biassed by the spirit of the age in which they moved. Certain it is that they had left traceable indications of their private opinions, and of the tone of thought by which they were surrounded.

In some particulars their variations from the original had been comparatively harmless. If in reading the lists of clean and unclean animals the reader came upon the Greek word *dasupous*, or "rough-footed," when

---

[1] Philo, *Vit. Mos.* ii. 140.
[2] See Frankel, *Vorstudien*, i. 61. In later times Justin Martyr complained that the Jews had falsified the Septuagint by cutting out passages which told in favour of the Christians, such as "Tell it out among the heathen, the Lord reigned *from the tree*" (ἀπὸ ξύλου), Ps. xcvi. 10. See Just. Mart. *Dial.* pp. 169, 170. Tert. *Adv. Marc.* iii. 19. Aug. *Enarratt. in Ps.* p. 714. But the words were probably a Christian gloss.
[3] "*Chokmath Javanith.*" See Derenbourg, *Palest.* p. 361.
[4] See *Life of Christ*, ii. 461; *Life of St. Paul*, i. 37. (Midrash Rabbah on Gen. xxxvi., &c.)
[5] Rabbi Ishmael, arguing from Jos. i. 8. Menachoth, f. 99, 2 (Derenbourg, *Palest.* 361).

he knew that the animal mentioned in the Hebrew was the hare (*arnebeth*), he soon remembered with a smile that, if the courtly translator had rendered the word literally by *Lagos*, the Ptolemies might have seen with disgust that the founder of their dynasty bore the name of an animal which the Jews regarded as unclean! Again, if he found the homely ass (*onos*), on which Moses and the sons of Jair rode, dignified into a prancing steed (*polos*), this might seem to him a simple way of avoiding the scorn which a Greek unfamiliar with the value attached to the ass in Eastern countries would have felt when he read of any eminent person bestriding an animal so humble and so despised.[1] He would have been further amused by finding Keren Happuk, the daughter of Job (Job xlii. 14), whose name means "horn of stibium," turned into "Amalthea's horn;" and by the substitution of Greek for Hebrew proverbs in 1 Kings xx. 11 and Prov. xxiii. 27.[2] Again, the Seventy, in not a few instances, had introduced or implied the legends (Hagadoth) and precedents for inferential rules (Halachoth) which were not only sanctioned in the Rabbinic schools of Jerusalem, but which it was their main occupation to discover and to record. Thus in Deut. xxxii. 8 they had, "He set bounds to the people *according to the number of the Angels of God;*" in Josh. xxiv. 30 they insert that the flint knives used for circumcision in the wilderness had been buried in Joshua's grave; in Ex. xiii. 18 they rendered "harnessed" by "*five abreast;*" in Gen. iv. 4 they added that God "*kindled by fire*" the sacrifice of Abel; in Josh. xiii. 22 they follow the legend which made Balaam, like Simon Magus, fly in the air, until he was dashed down (ἐν ῥοπῇ) by Phinehas; in 1 Sam. xx. 30 they imply that Jonathan's mother was one of the maidens seized at Shiloh; in Num. xxxii. 12 they introduce the belief that Caleb was of Gentile origin.

These were pardonable eccentricities. But there was one important matter of dogma in which the Seventy had shown that they were the children of their own epoch and had deeply imbibed the opinions of the Greek philosophers. The Supreme Being of the Greek philosophers had been a Being infinitely exalted above human imperfections, and therefore a Being absolutely unlimited by human peculiarities. This view of "the Divine" had impressed itself on the philosophising Hellenists of Alexandria. They disliked the simple "*anthropomorphism*" of the earlier Sacred books, and did not wish to represent the God of Israel to the Gentiles as one who was pictured with a body, or who appeared in human form to the eyes of men. Still less was it consonant with Alexandrian prejudice to give literal renderings to those expressions which spoke of God by what is called "*anthropopathy*"—that is, as subject to wrath, repentance, or other human emotions. Yet the "anthropomor-

---

[1] The LXX. were fond of euphemisms, as in their rendering of Gen. xlix. 10; Deut. xxiii. 14; Nah. iii. 5; Is. iii. 17; Job xxxi. 10. They show a little national vanity in small matters in Ex. ii. 1; iv. 6; vi. 12, 15; 1 Sam. xv. 12.

[2] Frankel, *Vorstud.* i. 203.

phism" and "anthropopathy" of the early Scriptural books could only be modified by imperfect or unfaithful renderings;—and of these the translators did not hesitate to be guilty.[1] In Gen. vi. 6 the expression "it repented the Lord," and similar phrases elsewhere, quietly disappear from the Greek Version. In Ex. xxiv. 10 the Elders of Israel are not allowed to see "God," but only "*the place where God stood.*"[2] The falsification of the following words is still more startling. Instead of "Upon the nobles . . . . He laid not His hand; also they saw God," we have the daring change "*Of the elders of Israel not even one perished* (diephonesen), *and they were seen in the place of God.*" Well might the Talmudist[3] charge the Seventy with intentional perversion of the text in this place. In Ex. iv. 16, "Thou shalt be to him for God (לאלהים)" becomes "*Thou shalt be to him the things that relate to God* (τὰ πρὸς τὸν Θεόν)." In Num. xii. 8 the Epiphany to Moses is softened into a vision of the *Shechinah*, or glory. In Num. xiv. 14 it is not Jehovah, but the *Shechinah*, which is seen face to face. In Job xxix. 25, in Ps. xlii. 3, and in many other places, the direct expression "Jehovah" is softened into phrases of which the intention always is to place as many intermediates as possible between the Supreme and man. In Job xix. 26, 27, for "Yet in my flesh I shall see God, Whom I shall see for myself and my eyes shall behold, and not another," we have, "*For these things happened to me from the Lord, which I understand for myself, which my eye has seen, and not another.*" In Job xxxv. 14 "Although thou sayest thou shalt not see Him, yet judgment is before Him, trust thou in Him," becomes "*For the Almighty sees those who do wickedness, and shall save me; be judged before Him.*" In Ps. xvii. 15 the Seventy give us, "*I shall be seen before Him in Righteousness, I shall be satisfied in His glory being seen.*" In Hezekiah's prayer (Is. xxxviii. 11) "I shall not see the Lord, the Lord in the land of the living" is turned into "*I shall not see the salvation of God in the land of the living, I shall not see the salvation of Israel on the earth.*"[4] In Is. ix. 6, "the mighty God" becomes "*an Angel of great counsel.*"

2. This and other tendencies find their illustration in the writings of the Jewish philosopher Aristobulus and in the *Wisdom of Solomon*.[5] Aristobulus, a man of priestly descent, is said to have been the first Jew who studied Greek philosophy, and he was an avowed Peripatetic. Living in the court of Ptolemy Philometor (B.C. 160), he stood in close terms of intimacy with the royal house, and presented the Pentateuch

---

[1] See their versions of Ex. iii. 1; iv. 24; xvii. 16; xxv. 8. They are specially audacious in Ex. xix. 3.
[2] Ex. xxiv. 9—11. Καὶ εἶδον τὸν τόπον οὗ εἱστήκει ὁ Θεός.
[3] Megillah, f. 9, a.
[4] If there is no change in such passages as Amos ix. 1, etc., it is because these are understood as visions only. For a full treatment of the subject see Frankel, *Vorstudien zu der Septuaginta*.
[5] The avoidance of "*anthropomorphism*" and "*anthropopathy*" in the Targums is no less marked. Dr. Deutsch has supplied many instances in his *Literary Remains*, pp. 348—356.

to the King, with a commentary and prolegomena. A fragment of this work, which is sometimes called a *Syngramma* and sometimes *Propephonemena*, is preserved for us by the indefatigable labours of Eusebius,[1] and in this fragment Aristobulus expressly warns the King against a literal understanding of anthropomorphic expressions. If God is spoken of as having hands, arms, feet, and so on, those, he says, must be simply looked upon as pictorial phrases. Where it is said that "God *stands*," the reference is to the fixed order of the universe. The *speech* of God is only to be understood of ultimate causation, for "God spake and it was done." This philosopher appears to have translated the Book of Exodus in the Septuagint Version.

3. The author of the *Wisdom of Solomon* availed himself of the personification of "Wisdom" in the Book of Proverbs as the intermediate agency between God and man which the Alexandrian theosophy required. In this book "Wisdom" plays the part which is assigned to the Logos in the writings of Philo. The dualism—the existence of matter as the source of evil apart from God—of which there is a trace in the avoidance of the term "Creator" by Aristobulus, finds a distinct expression in the *Wisdom of Solomon* when the writer says that God's Almighty hand made the world out of matter without form.[2] In the opinion of the Alexandrians the world was not created out of nothing, but out of the formless chaos, the *Thohû va-bohû* of the second verse of the Book of Genesis. We see, too, in the Book of Wisdom the dislike of the body—that view of it as the fetter and prison rather than the home and temple of the soul—which was afterwards so strongly felt by the Neoplatonists that the philosopher Plotinus is said "to have blushed that he had a body." "The corruptible body," said this eloquent writer, "presseth down the soul, and the earthly tabernacle weigheth down the mind that museth upon many things."[3]

4. The epoch of the Septuagint was characterised by an outburst of Jewish literature of a semi-ethnic character. A poet named Ezekiel dramatised the Exodus; another named Philo wrote an epic on Jerusalem; a third—Theodotus—chose his theme from the story of Dinah and Shechem. Demetrius and Eupolemos wrote history; and the *Story of Susanna* is one of several specimens of Jewish romance. But the name of all the other Alexandrian writers is eclipsed by that of the great Philo, who reproduced Jewish theology for the benefit of Greek and Hellenist philosophers, just as Josephus reproduced Jewish history for the benefit of cultivated Romans. But there is this difference between Philo and Josephus. The astute historian well knew what he was about. He falsifies and colours, and omits and modifies with consummate skill and coolness whenever it suits him, and feels as little scruple in assimilating the Pharisees to the Stoics as he feels in describing the Angel who appeared to the mother of Samson as a handsome

---

[1] Euseb. *Præp. Evang.* viii. 10, xiii. 12. [2] Wisd. xi. 17. [3] Wisd. ix. 15.

youth who kindled the jealousy of Manoah. Philo, on the other hand, wrote with far greater unconsciousness. Unable to read Hebrew[1]—knowing the Sacred books chiefly, if not exclusively, in the Greek Version—having breathed from childhood the atmosphere of Alexandrian speculation—he no doubt considered that he had really grasped the key to the inner meaning of the Scriptures, and that his method of exegesis was the only way to rescue them from philosophic contempt. But it is a great mistake to suppose that he *invented* the philosophic system which is generally known by his name. The main beliefs of that system were —that matter is impure; that God cannot appear under material form, and is therefore invisible; that He chose the Jewish people to receive His revelations; that those revelations can only be interpreted by allegoric methods; that He deals with men solely through the Logos or Word, and the *logoi* or Divine forces; that the body is the source of evil; that the soul is pre-existent; that to gain God's mercy the flesh must be slain, and we must attain to the virtues of resignation, unworldliness, simplicity, faith, hope, and love. But none of these views was absolutely original. He does not announce them as such. He writes as though he were addressing readers who would at once recognise the truth of what he says. His thoughts, apart from many new illustrations, are not peculiar to him, but are found throughout the whole circle of Alexandrian literature.[2] The grounds for this statement will be found in the sketch of the life and writings of Philo, which occupies the following chapter.

CHAPTER XIII.

PHILO, AND THE DOCTRINE OF THE LOGOS.

Σχίδον γὰρ τὰ πάντα ἢ τὰ πλεῖστα τῆς νομοθεσίας ἀλληγορεῖται.
PHILO, *De Josepho.*

AMONG the Jews of Alexandria the family of the Alabarch Alexander had risen to a pre-eminent position. They were of priestly origin, and of wealth so immense that on one occasion Alexander, out of regard to Queen Cypros, found no difficulty in lending to Agrippa I. the great sum of 200,000 drachmæ.[3] At Jerusalem the family was favourably known from the splendid generosity with which the Alabarch had enriched nine gates of the Temple with silver and gold.[4] At Rome they were so much honoured for their integrity that Antonia, the

---

[1] This is clear from his mistakes in explaining simple Hebrew names. See Frankel, *Vorstudien,* ii. 28—41.
[2] To prove this is the object of the second volume of Gfrörer's learned book on Philo, to which I have been much indebted. The author has pointed out that there are in Josephus many traces of similar views.
[3] Jos. *Antt.* xviii. 6, § 3.   [4] *Id., B. J.* v. 5, § 3.

mother of Claudius, made Alexander her steward, and Claudius showed him marked favour. His son, Tiberius Alexander, at the terrible price of apostasy from his religion, rose so high in the Roman service as to be appointed Procurator of Palestine, and, afterwards, Præfect of Alexandria. Of the other two sons, one married Berenice, and died early, the other succeeded his father in the office of Alabarch.[1]

Philo was the brother of this Jewish Crœsus,[2] and therefore the uncle of the three Alexandrian Jews who played so considerable a part in the history of their day. He seems to have passed his life in unbroken prosperity, troubled only by that "inexorable weariness" which is experienced by most men at some period of their lives. He complains somewhat querulously of burdens which might have been lightly borne by those who had been called upon to face severer troubles.[3] He was married, and his wife had so profound an admiration for him that, when asked why she wore no jewels, she answered, in the spirit of the mother of the Gracchi, that "her husband's virtue was her sufficient jewellery."[4] In Philo's single visit to Jerusalem, which fell during the lifetime of Jesus, his priestly birth secured him the privilege of offering sacrifices in the Temple.[5] In the troubles which arose in Alexandria from the brutality of the Greek and Egyptian mob, and the ill-humour of the Præfect Flaccus, he was chosen one of the ambassadors to the Emperor Gaius, and was an eye-witness of the strange scenes of which he has left so vivid a picture in his description of the insane and odious tyrant.[6] He employed his peaceful days in acquiring the knowledge, superficial in character, but encyclopædic in range, which was the fashion of his time; and he threw himself with enthusiasm into the pious task of allegorising Scripture in such a way as to make it speak the language of Greek philosophy, and especially of "the holy Plato" and "the holy community of the Pythagoreans."[7] He was one of those who, under God's Providence, helped to pave the way for Christianity, but that he was not himself a Christian, as early legends assert, is shown by the absence from his writings of every distinctively Christian truth. Judaism sufficed him. In one eloquent passage he argues for the Divine Mission of Moses from the immutability of his legislation amid the numberless vicissitudes of Jewish life, while the works of all other lawgivers had been incessantly modified, abrogated, and swept away.[8]

All the numerous works of Philo may be grouped round four

[1] Jos. Antt. xix. 5, § 1; xx. 5, § 2.
[2] Ibid. xviii. 8, § 1; Gfrörer, Philo, i. 1—7.
[3] De Legg. Spec. ii., ad init. σύνων δ' ὅμως ἀντέχω. (Mangey, ii. 299.) My references to Philo will be made to the folio edition of Mangey (1742), but I generally add the section also.
[4] Fragm. (Mang. ii. 673.)
[5] See Euseb. Praep. Evan. viii. 12; Jer. Cat. Script. Some think that Alexander in Acts iv. 6 was his brother.
[6] In his Legatio ad Gaium, the most popular of his writings.
[7] De Provid. ii. 42: "Quod omnis prob. liber," ad init. Τὸν Πυθαγορείων ἱερώτατον θίασον.
[8] De Vita Mosis, ii. § 3 (Mangey, ii 136).

treatises ; namely, those on the Creation of the world ; on Abraham ; on Joseph ; and on the life of Moses.[1]

I. The first of these—the book on the Creation—and the tracts which touch upon cognate subjects—are an endeavour to bring the Mosaic cosmogony into harmony with the views of Plato in his *Timæus*.[2] Philo keeps in sight two elements of creation: on the one hand a formless chaos; on the other a Being better than all goodness, holier than all holiness, more beautiful than all beauty, of Whom man may know indeed that He *is*, but hardly *what* He is.[3] But how was it possible to bridge over the vast abyss between the two? How, in the words of Plato, could the mortal be woven into the immortal? Philo meets the difficulty partly by the conception of the LOGOS, "the Word" by Whom God created all things ; and partly by the yet lower agencies of "intermediate words"—spiritual entities—angels of all kinds, "thrones, dominations, virtues, princedoms, powers"—who had their share in the work of creation, and by whose existence Philo accounts for the plural "Let us make man." The visible world was not created at once, but there existed in the Divine understanding an eternal determination not to leave Chaos in its formlessness. This determination constituted a spiritual world, which was the archetype and exemplar of the visible. It was the Perfect Idea, of which material existences are the transient and imperfect copy.

II. In the treatises on Abraham and on Joseph, Philo gives the reins to his imagination. The simple narratives of Scripture become, as narratives, almost valueless. They lose their historical beauty and human interest. They become elaborate allegories, through which move a crowd of vapid abstractions. Abraham leaving his country and his kindred and his father's house, is lowered into a sort of typical Stoic departing from the Chaldæa of the sensual understanding to seek the land of pure reason, and turning his back upon desire, and fear, and ambition. He is, in fact, not an Oriental Emir called to inaugurate the era of the chosen people, but a symbol of the soul seeking God. The Chaldees worshipped stars, and therefore the call to Haran was an indication that he was to look, not at the universe, but at himself. Haran means "Holes," and is a symbol of the five senses. Abraham's further wanderings mean that he attains to the knowledge of God. Abram means, according to Philo, "aspiring

---

[1] See Zeller, iii. 2,603 ; Hausrath, *Neutest. Zeitgesch. Die Zeit d. Apost.* 152. Gfrörer divides his writings into four general classes :—(1) Philosophic (*De mundi incorruptibilitate ; Quod omnis probus liber ; De vita contemplativa*) ; (2) Historical (*De mundi opificio ; De vita Mosis ; De Decalogo ; De Monarchiâ ; De Circumcisione ; De legibus specialibus ; De praemiis et poenis*, &c.) ; (3) Allegorising (*Liber Legis allegoriarum ; De somniis*, &c.) ; (4) Political (*Legatio ad Gaium ; Contra Flaccum*) ; Philo i. 7—37.

[2] Hence the oft-quoted proverb, "Either Philo platonises, or Plato philonises." (Suidas, &c.)

[3] St. John, on the other hand, says (i. 3), "Without Him was not even one thing made that hath been made."

father," with an allusion to his star-worship, but Abraham means "father of sound." Sound is like speech, but "father of sound" is like spirit which utters sound.[1] Similarly he says that Sarai means "my rule," and Sarra (= Sarah) "princess;" and that the first name allegorically signifies particular virtue, which is transient; and the second, generic virtue, which is eternal and incorruptible.[2] Thus the grand old patriarch becomes a cold cypher, indicative of mental earnestness; Sarah, the beautiful and passionate Eastern woman, fades into an unsatisfactory symbol for an abstraction. The laughter from which the name of Isaac was derived becomes the joy of the philosopher who has conquered every evil impulse, and entered into the rest of the Eternally Real. And whereas Sarah is Virtue and abstract Wisdom, Hagar represents only the general sciences of grammar, music, geometry, dialectics, and rhetoric! If Jacob comes to a certain place when the sun sets, the statement in the Philonian system is explained by the remarks that the sun is the perceptive faculty, the place is the Divine Word, and Jacob is wisdom attained by training. Hence the only value which that pathetic and deeply instructive story possesses for Philo is the somewhat dreary platitude that man can only grasp the Divine when his natural understanding has set like the sun.[3]

III. In the Life of Moses, Philo is anxious to prove the absurd hypothesis that the Gentiles have learnt their wisdom and philosophy from the Jews, and that Moses was practically the master of Hesiod and Heraclitus, of Plato and Zeno.[4] Here, as everywhere, Philo cares almost nothing for the letter of the Law. He is indeed a faithful Jew, and thinks that the Law should be rigidly observed. Just as we cherish the body as the dwelling-place of the soul, so (he says) ought we to keep the letter of the Law, although its real meaning lies exclusively in the esoteric senses which can be tortured out of it.[5] Circumcision, and the Sabbath, and all the other Mosaic institutions, are but allegories.[6] Even as to the plainest details of jurisprudence, which, in their homely realism, seemed too coarse to form any part of a Divine revelation—such, for instance, as that which punished the immodest interference of women in quarrels—an explanation was forthcoming. The passage is made to mean that every soul has male and female elements, of which the male elements reach forth to the heavenly and the female to the earthly, and that our natural tendency towards the transitory must be flung off.[7] So sincere was Philo in his belief that truth could only be found in

---

[1] Πατὴρ ἐκλεκτὸς ἤχου. *De Cherubim*, i. § 2 (Mang. i. 139).
[2] *De nom. mutat.* § 8, etc. (Mang. i. 591, etc.).
[3] "*Quod a Deo mittantur somnia.*" § xxii. sq. (Mang. i. 638, sq.; Grätz, iii. 295).
[4] *Quis rer. div. haeres* (i. 503, and other passages). See Grätz, iii. 295.
[5] *De Cherubim, ad init.* and *passim*.
[6] *Leg. allegy., ad init.* (Mang. i. 43); *De Josepho*, § 6 (Mang. ii. 46).
[7] *De spec. legg.* (ii. 329); *De circumc.* (ii. 211); Grätz, iii. 297.

these strange paths of exegesis, that he thanked God for having allowed him to be the interpreter who rendered clear the meaning of that which to the mass of men had hitherto been unintelligible.[1] He even tells us that he occasionally fell into ecstasies, in which he was prophetically made aware of profound meanings, which otherwise would have escaped him.[2] Yet, though he thus allegorises everything, his views wholly differ from those of the Epistle of Barnabas. Anything like disrespect for the *letter* of the Law struck him as impious. He delights to point out instances of retribution which fell on the enemies of Israel. He tells of an Alexandrian who, having made himself merry on "the splendid present which the Lord of the world had made to the patriarch Abraham and his wife Sarah, by presenting the one (in Greek) with the letter *alpha* and the other with the letter *rho*," became afterwards mad, as a punishment inflicted on him by Heaven.[3]

The Philonian method is of all styles of exegesis the most arbitrary. But Philo unquestionably did not invent it. Both among Rabbis and Alexandrians it was already in the air. It sprang from the spirit of the times. It was the inevitable result of two beliefs, which would otherwise have come into dangerous collision—the belief in Biblical inspiration, and the belief in Greek philosophy. Alexandrian Jews had to reconcile the letter of the Bible with convictions which could only be deduced from it by allegorising processes. When they had come to believe in Platonic idealism and Pythagorean mysteries— to look on matter as impure, to regard the Divine Being as incognisable, to contemn the body as the source of all evil—they saw no way out of their difficulties except by inventing a Logos as High-priest of the world, and subordinating to him all kinds of powers and spirits, until they had taken the golden reins of external nature out of the hands of God, and transferred them to the charge of intermediate beings.[4]

It may help the reader to understand the method in virtue of which this Judaic philosophy claimed its sole right to exist, if I furnish one or two more specimens of the allegorising inferences which enabled the Alexandrians to make Moses express the thoughts of Plato, and to turn "a religious philosophy" into something which they took for "a philosophic religion." But for these I must refer to the Excursus on "Specimens of Philonian Allegory" at the end of the book.

The doctrine most closely identified with the name of Philo is that of the Logos; and it is sometimes asserted that St. John, and, to a certain extent, the writer of the Epistle to the Hebrews—who, however,

[1] *De spec. legg.* (ii. 300).
[2] *De Cherubim,* § 10 (i. 143): "I once also heard something of still deeper significance from my soul, which is frequently accustomed to be filled with inspiration (θεοληπτεῖσθαι), and to exercise divination (μαντεύεσθαι) concerning things which it does not know."
[3] *De nomin. mutat.* § 8 (Mang. i. 587).
[4] Gfrörer, *Philo,* i. 73.

seems to avoid the use of the actual word—borrowed it from him. It is easy to show that this is far from being an accurate statement of the case.

The word *Logos* has two meanings, Reason and Speech. Philo uses it sometimes in one and sometimes in the other of these senses, but predominantly in the former. When he wishes to distinguish between them, he calls Speech "uttered Reason" (*logos prophorikos*), and Reason "immanent Speech" (*logos endiathetos*). The Reason, he says, is like a fountain, and the utterance flows from it. The seat of the reason is the ruling and spiritual sphere of human nature; the seat of speech is in the vocal organs.[1] Hence "the Divine Logos" is the manifestation of God; and "the Sacred logos" is used for the Scriptures; and the "true logos" is the rule of life, namely, to live in accordance with the highest nature. He uses the plural, "the divine *logoi*," for "the powers of nature." It requires but one step in advance to personify these *logoi*, and identify them with angels. On the other hand, angels are sometimes volatilised into ideas. Hence, in the weakest of its aspects, the philosophy of Philo might be represented by those who dislike it as one of the systems in which "naught is everything, and everything is naught."[2]

But, besides all this, the Logos Himself is again and again directly personified.

(α) He is above all the High Priest. Those who fled to a city of refuge could only return when the High-priest died: which means that as long as the Logos abides in the soul no accidental fault ever can enter into it; but if the Logos dies, *i.e.*, is separated from the soul, a return of the soul to Him is possible even after willing sins. Let us then pray that the stainless High-priest may live in the soul as our judge and conv ncer.[3]

(β) In another passage he compares this high-priestly Logos to a cup-bearer. Commenting on Gen. xl., he says grapes and vineyards sometimes symbolise the joyous absorption of the soul in God, sometimes drunkenness and wickedness. The cup-bearer of Pharaoh is he who feeds his godless master with sensuality; for Pharaoh, who says, "I know not God,"[4] is a type of the godless mind. But the cup-bearer of God is the Sacrificer, the true High Priest, Who receives and distributes the eternal gifts of grace, and pours out the holy vials full of pure wine—that is, Himself.[5] And as the High-priest Aaron was father of Eleazar and Ithamar, so the Logos High Priest is Father of the heavenly *logoi* and powers.

---

[1] *De Vit. Mosis*, iii. § 13 (Mang. ii. 154).
[2] Additional illustration of Philo's views about the Logos will be found in Excursus VII.
[3] *De Profugis* (Mang. i. 563). The allegory is more than usually clumsy.
[4] Philo here seems to confuse the Pharaoh of Joseph with the Pharaoh of Moses (Ex. v. 2).
[5] *De somniis*, ii. (Mang. i. 685 sq.)

(γ) In other passages the Logos is the image of God, the shadow of God, the instrument of all creation, the likeness of God, Who is the archetype of all other things. He is also spoken of as the eldest and the firstborn Son of God;[1] and as an Archangel, and the eldest Archangel, who stands as an intermediate between the Creator and the created. Again, he is the angel that appeared to Hagar; the angel that punished Sodom; the God Who appeared to Jacob at Bethel, and wrestled with him at Peniel; the angel that appeared to Moses in the bush; the pillar of fire which led the Israelites out of Egypt; the angel which appeared to Balaam; the leader of Israel through the wilderness. Melchizedek is a symbol of Him,[2] and so are Noah, and Bezaleel, and Aaron, and Moses.

(δ) By this time the reader will have seen how vague is Philo's conception; how it floats in the air; how the outlines of it are perpetually confused together or melt away. He will see that whether any of the New Testament writers were familiar with Philo, or only with the circle of conceptions in which he moved, the amount to which they are indebted to those conceptions is as nothing compared to the new and immortal life which they breathe into them. In Philo they are, and they would ever have remained, dead philosophic generalisations, founded on loose allegoric methods, and abounding in irreconcilable contradictions. In the New Testament they breathe and stand on their feet as clear, living, and redemptive truths. Philo's misty and ever-changing Logos is an intellectual possession for Judaising philosophers, but is almost inconceivably removed from the Divine Redeemer, the Saviour of all the world. Between the doctrine and method of Philo and that of the Apostles the difference is as wide as that between the living and the dead.

The four words of St. John, "*The Word became flesh*," created an epoch. They tell us more, and are of infinitely more value to us than all the pages and volumes on the subject which Philo and his contemporaries ever wrote. They summarise and concentrate the inmost meaning of the Old Testament revelation and of post-canonical thoughts.[3] They are as a flash of the sword of that Word which cleaves even to the dividing asunder of sword and spirit; a flash which dispels a thousand distorting mists, a sword to cleave the knot of a thousand difficulties, which the Alexandrian philosophy vainly endeavoured to cleave or to unloose.

---

[1] *De ling. confus.* §§ xi., xxviii. (Mang. i. 413, 419).
[2] *Leg. allegg.* iii. § 25 (Mang. i. 102).
[3] Dr. Westcott—who thinks that St. John borrowed the *expression* (not, of course, the *doctrine*) from the Palestinian *Memra* (which always means "word" only), not the Alexandrian *Logos* (which predominantly means Intelligence)—says that St. John's evangelic message is the complete fulfilment of three distinct lines of preparatory revelation—namely, (i.) "the Angel of the Presence" (Gen. xxxii. 24, &c.), (ii.) the "Word," (Gen. i. 1, &c.), and (iii.) "Wisdom" (Prov. viii. 22, &c.).

CHAPTER XIV.
PHILONISM, ALLEGORICAL EXEGESIS, AND THE CATECHETICAL SCHOOL OF ALEXANDRIA.

"All things are double one against another."—ECCLUS. xlii. 24.

"Two worlds are ours; 'tis only sin
Forbids us to descry
The mystic heaven and earth within,
Plain as the sea and sky."—KEBLE.

WE have already seen that St. Paul was acquainted with some of the writings of Philo, or, at any rate, with the ideas which filled the Alexandrian literature of that epoch, and of which Philo was an exponent.[1] We shall learn, farther on, that the author of the Epistle to the Hebrews was deeply imbued not only with the phraseology of the great Alexandrian, but also with the general principles of his theology.[2] But we shall see also how entirely free he is from the defects and weakness, the unreality and the affectations of the Philonian philosophy. There is perhaps no more striking proof of the spiritual gifts of the Sacred writers than the fact that even when they show to the most marked degree the influence of the various forms of lifelong training to which they had been subjected, they rise superior to the errors and limitations of the very systems to which they are indebted.

And yet this "Sapiential literature of Alexandria"—the literature which is represented by the books of Ecclesiasticus and Wisdom and in the writings of Philo—had a great part to play in the development of Revelation. It worthily filled up the interspace between Malachi and the earliest Epistles of St. Paul. The Septuagint created the dialect and phraseology in which the Gospel was to be proclaimed, and the Alexandrian writers, not without heavenly guidance, helped to smooth the path which the early Christian thinkers were to tread. Alexandrianism was too vague, too receptive, too little conscious of the width and depth of the chasm which separates Sacred from Jewish literature; but in its successful endeavour to break down the exclusiveness of Judaism it prepared the way for Christianity as the universal revelation, in which there should be neither Jew nor Greek, neither circumcision nor uncircumcision, barbarian, Scythian, bond nor free.

But, with all its merits, Philonism had obvious defects. The orthodox Rabbis showed their shrewdness when they looked on it with jealousy and suspicion. It was a system of syncretism, and it swarmed

---

[1] See *Life of St. Paul*, i. 642, 643.
[2] It was the observation of this influence that led to the Church legends that Philo for a time embraced Christianity (Photius, *Cod.* cv.), in consequence of having met St. Peter at Rome (Euseb. *H. E.* ii. 17).

with contradictions. It attempted to weld together two dissimilar, if not antagonistic, elements—the letter of Scripture and the Platonic philosophy. The attempt was as unsatisfactory as that of the Schoolmen to form systems which combined Aristotle with the New Testament. Sometimes the philosophic conception was sacrificed to the letter; more frequently the letter was set aside to make room for the philosophy. The allegorical distortion of literal narratives—if it be taken for exegesis—is almost ludicrous. But the Judaisers saw clearly that the method might be so extended as to explain away the whole ceremonial law; and, in point of fact, it *was* so extended. The pride of fancied initiation made some of the Alexandrians despise Levitism just as some of the Gnostics advanced so far in their falsely-called knowledge as at last to despise even the moral law. It is a startling comment on the tendency of Philo's speculations when we find that his nephew was an avowed renegade.

But the author of the Epistle to the Hebrews was not the only Christian writer who had been influenced by the Philonian philosophy. Alexandria became from the earliest days of Christianity the home of a Christian school of thought.[1] The Alexandrian converts were confronted from the first by the same problems, and surrounded by the same influences as their Jewish predecessors. The fact that their teaching was carried on in the midst of Pagans and philosophers—men of wide training and cultivated intellect—rendered it indispensable for them to present Christianity in such a manner as should neither repel their opponents, nor give them an easy victory over ignorant assertions and futile anathemas. From this necessity arose the great catechetical School of Alexandria, which claimed as its founder the Evangelist St. Mark. Its earliest teacher of any fame was the venerable Pantænus, who is always spoken of by his successors with affection and respect. He was followed by St. Clement of Alexandria, many of whose invaluable writings are still preserved to us. Clement was followed by the greatest of all the Fathers, the most Apostolic man since the days of the Apostles, the Father who in every branch of study rendered to the Church the deepest and widest services—the immortal Origen. Origen was succeeded by his pupils Heraclas and Dionysius, to whom succeeded Pierius, Theognostus, Peter Martyr, Arius, and Didymus. This brings us to the fourth century, after which the glory of the school completely died away.

It was the successful effort of these thinkers to prove to the Gentiles that Christianity in no wise shunned the light of reason, but was always ready to come forth into the noon-day, and to meet opponents with a culture equal to their own. They also aimed at checking the Gnostic vanity, which looked down with contempt on

---

[1] ἐξ ἀρχαίου ἔθους. Euseb. *H. E.* v. 10.

the faith of the ignorant, and prided itself on the possession of esoteric mysteries. These were high and worthy ends. But it was no less necessary to show to the zealots of a presumptuous religionism that if God has no need of human knowledge, He has still less need of human ignorance; that a chastened speculation and a Divine philosophy were not only permissible, but necessary in the field of Christian learning; that there was such a thing as an Ethnic as well as a Christian inspiration; and that so far from looking askance on the light which shone outside the Sacred Tabernacle, all Christians should learn to love and welcome it as being a ray from the same inexhaustible orb of glory.[1] The Christian scholars of Alexandria chose as the motto of their school the Greek version of Is. vii. 9, "*If ye believe not, ye shall never understand.*" The words, indeed, are not accurately translated, and are torn from their context. This, however, has been the fate of nine-tenths of the "texts" which have been distorted into the watchwords of party dogmatism; and a misapplication of Scripture is at least pardonable when it is applied to noble purposes, and not (as is so often the case) to burn incense to pride or add fuel to hatred. The saintly Catechists of Alexandria used their motto to imply a twofold truth—namely, that no one could understand the inmost meaning of Judaism who did not accept the Christian revelation; and that no one could advance to the mysteries of the Gospel who did not possess an unsophisticated faith in its initial principles.[2]

In the then stage of Scriptural knowledge the Alexandrian teachers would have found it difficult to defend many parts of the Old Testament without the use of allegory. It was only by allegory that Philo had been able to educe from the Pentateuch the secrets of Greek philosophy. His genius had deepened the conviction that the Scripture was a profound enigma, in which the simple narrative and the obvious moral were all but valueless. But this conviction was not the growth of a day. If the Alexandrian Fathers derived it in part from the influence of Philo,[3] Philo had himself derived it from predecessors who had invented that mystic exegesis which, in its turn, was developed into the system of the Kabbala.

Taking the word *Pardes*, or "Paradise," as their watchword of interpretation, the Kabbalists had declared that every passage of Scripture was capable of a fourfold interpretation, indicated by the letters P R D S. These letters represented the words—

Peshat, or "explanation."
Remez, or "hint."
Darâsh, or "homily."
Sod, or "mystery."

---

[1] See Neander, *Ch. Hist.* ii. 264, etc.
[2] See Bacon, *Nov. Organ.* i. 68, "ut non alius fere sit aditus ad regnum hominis quod fundatur in scientiis, quam ad regnum coelorum, *in quod nisi sub personâ infantis intrare non datur.*" [3] Philo is frequently quoted by Clement and Origen, as also by Eusebius.

In these ways the Rabbis said that the Law could be explained in forty-nine different manners.[1]

PANTÆNUS was the earliest Catechist who gave his adhesion to the allegoric method,[2] and we are told that he applied to the Church what is written of Paradise. CLEMENT vehemently condemns carnal interpretation (σαρκικῶς), and says that nothing should be deduced from Scripture but what is perfectly accordant with the Divine nature.[3] He held that *all* Scriptures, alike of the Old and New Testaments, demanded an allegoric, as well as a literal, interpretation, and he applied to them the passage in the Psalms, "I will open my mouth in parables."[4] He said that the literal sense sufficed for an elementary faith, but that allegory was required for more illustrious knowledge.[5] Thus he explains the furniture of the Tabernacle, and the story of Agar and Sarah, and many other passages, in a way which might have delighted Philo. It was, however, ORIGEN who laid down the express rule that Scripture consisted of the visible and invisible, as man consists of the body and the soul, and that all Scripture, in order to discover the inner soul and spirit, should be interpreted in a threefold sense—historic, moral, and mystic.[6] But he did not quite fling away the literal sense. In proof of its usefulness he appealed to the faith of simple Christians. Nor did he ever proceed to allegory till he had first ascertained, by all the critical aids in his power, the grammatical meaning of the passage on which he was commenting. DIONYSIUS, while still continuing the allegorical method, leaned with greater favour to moral interpretation. PIERIUS followed more closely the guidance of Origen. It was not till the close of the third century that allegory was gradually abandoned by PETER MARTYR, and still later by DIDYMUS, in consequence of the growing influence of the great School of Antioch.[7]

The system continued, however, to be used not only in the Eastern but even in the Western Church. St. Jerome said that to be content with the literal sense of Scripture was "to eat dust like the serpent." The writings of St. Hilary are full of allegorical fancies. He declared it *irreligious* to take literally the natural objects so exquisitely described in Psalm cxlvi. By the "fowls of the air" in Matt. vi. he understands the devils, and by the "cities" the angels. The "two sparrows" which "are sold for one farthing" are sinners whose souls being made to fly upwards sell themselves for trifles. More than one of the Fathers has explained the Mosaic distinction between clean and unclean animals by saying that those which divide the hoof represent those who believe in

---

[1] See my paper on "Rabbinic Exegesis" in the *Expositor*, v. 302.
[2] Athenagoras, who, perhaps, succeeded Pantænus, was not remarkable in any way as an exegete, and he accepted Scripture literally. He paid chief attention to the Prophets, and strangely neglected the New Testament.
[3] *Strom.* ii. 16. [4] Ps. lxxviii. 2. Compare 1 Cor. ii. 6; *Strom.* v. 4; vi. 15.
[5] *Strom.* vi. 15. [6] *Hom. V., in Levit.* § 1; *De princip.* iv. 11.
[7] See Guerike, *De Schola Alex.*, and Vacherot, *Hist. Crit. de l'École d'Alexandrie*, i. 100—303.

the Father and the Son, and those which chew the cud represent those who meditate on God's Law; whereas the unclean animals, which neither divide the hoof nor chew the cud, imply those who neither have faith in God nor study His law. No modern writer can attach the smallest value to such inferences as these. But though the day has come when the allegorical method must be limited to rigid conditions—though it is now regarded as useless for purposes of proof, and only valuable by way of illustration—we must not forget that it once played an important part in the development of doctrine, and that even the Sacred writers have furnished splendid instances of the method in which it may be applied.[1]

CHAPTER XV.

AUTHORSHIP AND STYLE OF THE EPISTLE TO THE HEBREWS.

"De Deo homo dixit et quidem inspiratus a Deo, sed tamen homo . . . . non totum quod est dixit; sed quod potuit homo dixit."—AUG. *Tract. in Joh.* i. 1.

SUCH being, in outline, a history of the great School of Christian philosophy and Christian criticism in Alexandria, we may well be thankful that one of the Sacred Books—while it is the only book of the Canon which emanated from the School of St. Paul—bears the stamp of Alexandrian thought. It thus furnishes one more link of solid gold in the continuity which binds us to the Church of the Jewish Fathers. That is a truly Catholic philosophy which seeks to combine all that is precious and permanent in the wisdom of patriarchs and philosophers, of Hellenists and Hebraists. There ought to be a common sympathy among those who in all nations have loved the Lord, even when they knew Him not: among all who have—by His holy inspiration—thought worthy thoughts respecting the Fatherhood of God and the brotherhood of man.

For all true wisdom is, in its essence, Divine wisdom. There is a light which lighteth every man who is born into the world. Even amid the moral aberrations of heathenism it was granted to some—granted, let us trust, to many—to keep that light unquenched. I know not whether any are still so narrow as to refuse all recognition of inspiration outside the limits of Scripture—any who would still be shocked by the discovery that a Philo, with all his tedious allegorisings and cold abstractions, was yet an appointed minister in influencing the thoughts of an Apollos[2] and a St. John. But if there be any such, let them

---

[1] On modern allegorical systems, as exemplified in Swedenborg, see Möhler, *Symbolik,* p. 589 (ed. 1864).
[2] It will be seen farther on that there are very strong reasons for believing that Apollos wrote the Epistle to the Hebrews. I venture therefore to ask permission to use his name by anticipation, at least hypothetically, in order to avoid cumbrous periphrases.

remember that "*Every* good gift and *every* perfect gift is from above, and cometh down from the Father of lights, with Whom is no variableness nor shadow of turning. A Socrates, a Plato, a Sakya Mouni—these, too, had reared their altars to "the unknown God;" these, too, were enabled to shed some light on the darkness of sin and sorrow, because they had kindled their torches at the Sun of Righteousness, and drawn some sparks of light from the unemptiable fountain of Divine wisdom.[1] If it be a fatal error to cut ourselves adrift from any age in the past history of Christianity—if we shall one day suffer for having disowned our brotherhood with the Church of the Middle Ages, or the Church of the Reformers—so is it also an error to dissever ourselves from *any* in the redeemed brotherhood of man who have taught truth, even if it has been mingled with error, or who have served God, even if it has not been with the service of the Sanctuary. Truth is truth, and it comes from God, whether the speaker be a Balaam or an Elijah, a Caiaphas or a St. John. In the multiplicity of parts and diversity of methods which have characterised the deliverance of the one great Revelation, even the heathen have borne their share. Verses quoted from the Greek poets are to be read on the Sacred page. Philo was deeply influenced by Plato, and Philo in his turn has left on Christian Apostles his own vivid impress. St. Paul did not think it necessary to apologise when he alluded to a homely Latin fable; the risen Lord of Glory did not disdain to address a Greek proverb to His erring saint.

In speaking thus of Ethnic inspiration, I am but reviving—as I have tried to do in other instances—a truth which was firmly held by the greatest thinkers of the Primitive Church, but which, since the days of St. Augustine, has been forgotten or concealed. The primitive doctrine of Inspiration—as held by Justin Martyr, and by the School of Alexandria, who freely appeal to the inspired testimony of "minds naturally Christian"—only resembles the popular doctrine in the use of similar terms, but not in the significance which the terms really bear. The Apologists of the second century, and the philosophic Greek Christians of the third, never hesitated to recognise the truth that the influences of the Spirit are as the wind which bloweth where it listeth, and that the poets and philosophers of the heathen are often the conscious and unconscious exponents of His inward voice. They held with the much injured and much calumniated Montanus, whom Wesley regarded as the best man of his age, that the soul of man is like a lyre, and that it breaks forth into music when its strings are swept by "the plectrum of the Paraclete."

[1] Wisd. vii. 25, 26: "For she (Wisdom) is the breath of the power of God, and a pure influence flowing from the glory of the Almighty; therefore can no defiled thing fall into her. For she is the brightness of the everlasting light, the unspotted mirror of the power of God and the image of His goodness. And *being but one, she can do all things*, and remaining in herself, she maketh all things new; and, *in all ages, entering into holy souls*, she maketh them friends of God and prophets."

In these remarks it may be thought that I have begged the question by assuming that the Epistle to the Hebrews was not written by St. Paul. This, however, is not the case. Even in the recognised writings of the great Apostle there are traces of thoughts which emanated from Alexandria.[1] St. Paul, after his conversion, certainly belonged to that Hagadistic school of Jewish exegesis[2] without which there would hardly have been any room for Philo or for any Hellenist within the narrow limits of Jewish orthodoxy. Philo did something towards breaking down that bristling hedge of technicalities, in the construction of which so many of the Rabbis intensified their Pharisaism, and wasted their unprofitable toil. Paul had been in his early years a student, and perhaps remained a student to the last. There is, therefore, no improbability in the conjecture that he was acquainted with Philo's writings.[3] But even if St. Paul had found room in his large heart for such truths as God had revealed to his philosophic contemporary, not one of his Epistles is coloured with Alexandrian conceptions to anything like the same extent as the Epistle to the Hebrews. Comparative criticism has made it little short of certain that the Epistle to the Hebrews was not written by St. Paul. That science has made gigantic strides since the days of the Fathers. Even if the conclusion had been arrived at in spite of patristic authority, it is established on grounds too sure to be shaken. But in point of fact it is in strict accordance with the tenor of ancient evidence. The continued assertion of the Pauline authorship shows but too plainly to what an extent the manliness of criticism can be benumbed by the paralysis of custom. Adhesion to prejudice is too often mistaken for love of truth.

I shall not stop to show how often, or by what partisans, the external evidence has been mis-stated. One of the most recent commentators, for instance, has prefixed to the Epistle the clause of Origen, that "It is not by haphazard that ancient authorities have handed it down as St. Paul's." He omits to inform us that Origen in the very next word says that "God only knows the truth as to who wrote it," and that though some of his predecessors had held

---

[1] Even Philo appeals to older writings (συγγράμματα παλαιῶν ἀνδρῶν), as did also the Therapeutae. (Tholuck, 79.)
[2] See *Life and Work of St. Paul*, i. 639—642; and Delitzsch, *Commentar. Zum Briefe an die Hebräer*, xxvi., xxvii.
[3] The following passages of St. Paul show familiarity with the Alexandrian author of the *Wisdom of Solomon*:—

2 Cor. v. 1, "The *earthly* house of our tabernacle."
Wisd. ix. 15, "The earthly tabernacle."

Rom. i. 20, "The invisible things of Him . . . are clearly seen, being perceived by the things that are made."
Wisd. xiii. 1, "Who are ignorant of God, and could not out of the good things that are seen know Him that is."

Rom. xiii. 1—7, "There is no power but of God; the powers that be are ordained of God."
Wisd. vi. 1—4, "For power is given unto you (Kings, &c.) from the Lord, and sovereignty from the highest."

See Hilgenfeld, *Einleit*. 223.

it to be St. Paul's, yet the historical tradition (ἱστορία) which had come to him asserted it to be the work of St. Clement or St. Luke. It may be worth while, then, once more to summarise, and to put in its true perspective the evidence of the Fathers.[1]

This evidence may be placed in the Excursus. But we may here most briefly summarise it by saying that in spite of the antiquity and authority of the Epistle no writer of the Western Church in the first, second, or third century, quotes it as St. Paul's; that the first Latin writer who attributes it to St. Paul is Hilary, late in the fourth century; and that in the fifth century both St. Jerome and St. Augustine, though loosely quoting it as St. Paul's, had serious misgivings about its direct genuineness. In the Eastern Church, Pantænus and Clement of Alexandria seem to have set the fashion of accepting the Pauline authorship;[2] but on this subject even Origen felt grave doubts. Eusebius wavered about it, and admitted that the Epistle was accounted spurious by many, but thought that it might perhaps be a translation from an Aramaic original. Even in the Eastern Church it did not meet with unhesitating acceptance as a work of St. Paul.

A Jewish rule, which has found unconscious acceptance in all ages, says that "Custom is Law."[3] But if the Epistle to the Hebrews owes its recognition among the Epistles of St. Paul far more to an unthinking custom than to careful argument, how is it that such a custom arose? The answer is simple. It arose mainly in the Eastern Church from the initiative of Pantænus, and it was only accepted in the Western Church, after considerable hesitation, by the force of example. In both Churches it originated not from trustworthy tradition, but from the superficial acceptance of *prima facie* phenomena. The general theology of the Epistle was Pauline, and the finer differences escaped notice. Many characteristic phrases coincided with those in St. Paul's Epistles, and were current in his school of thought. The allusions at the close of the Epistle led to the careless assumption that they were penned by St. Paul. The observation of similarities is easy to any one; the detection of differences, which, however deep, are yet to some extent latent, is only possible to students who do not rely upon authority and tradition except so far as they are elements in the sacred search for truth. Nothing can more decisively prove the incompetence of a mechanical consensus than the fact that millions of readers have failed to perceive, even in the original, the dissimilarity of style, of method, and of theologic thought, which proves that the same pen could not have written, nor the same mind have originated, the Epistle to the Hebrews and the Epistles of St. Paul.

---

[1] See Excursus viii. on the "Patristic Evidence as to the Authorship of the Epistle to the Hebrews."

[2] See Routh, *Rel. Sacr.* L 472, 480.

[3] כיון נדין

Luther showed his usual insight and robust sense when he saw that Heb. ii. 3 could not have been written by the author of Gal. i. 1, 12. Again, though the author does *not* fall into any *demonstrable* error in his allusion to the details of Temple worship in vii. 27, ix. 3, 4, x. 11—yet he goes to the verge of apparent inaccuracies, against which St. Paul, who was familiar with the Temple service, would surely have guarded himself. In reading the Epistle to the Hebrews we are in contact with the mind of a great and original writer of the Apostolic age, whose name escaped discovery till modern times.

It is hardly worth while to quote later authorities. They can have no effect but to impose upon the ignorant. They simply float with the stream. They are uncritical, and therefore valueless. When such writers as Clement of Alexandria and Origen in the Eastern Church, and Jerome and Augustine in the Western Church, had made timid concessions to the custom of popularly quoting the Epistle as St. Paul's, it was natural that later writers should follow their example. Gradually, by the aid of conciliar decrees,[1] prevalent assumption hardened into ecclesiastical conviction. The result of the evidence may be summed up by saying that, as far as the evidence of antiquity is concerned, loose conjecture tended in one direction and genuine criticism in the other. It is astonishing that any one should attach importance to the conventional allusions of writers who neither discussed nor considered the question. That this or that Father of the fourth or fifth century introduces a quotation from the Epistle with the words "St. Paul says" is of no more consequence than when this or that clergyman announces a lesson or a sermon from "the Epistle of St. Paul to the Hebrews." Such "patristic authorities" are, for any *critical* purpose, not worth the paper on which they are written. The acceptance of a current view by a writer who has not examined the question has no evidential weight, even if that author be an Athanasius or a Theodoret.

But among thoughtful writers who really turned their attention to the matter the old doubts on the subject were by no means extinguished. In the Western Church the Epistle was not publicly read to the same extent or on the same footing as the others, even at the close of the fourth century. The assertion that it was written by St. Paul was sometimes accompanied with modifications, in the fifth century. It had never been commented on by any Latin writer as late as the sixth. In the seventh, Isidore of Seville records that many still attributed it, at least in part, to Barnabas or Clement "because of the discrepancy of style." Even in the ninth it is entirely omitted by the Codex Boernerianus (G), and only appears in a Latin translation in the celebrated

---

[1] The first Synod which used the Epistle to the Hebrews as Pauline was that of Antioch, A.D. 264, which was summoned to correct the errors of Paul of Samosata. It is placed tenth among St. Paul's Epistles by the Council of Laodicea, A.D. 364 (*Can.* 60). This canon appears to be genuine (Wieseler, i. 23), though not above suspicion. (Credner, *Gesch. d. Kanon*, 21 *fg.*)

F, the Codex Augiensis. But long before the ninth century, and for centuries afterwards, the science of criticism was forgotten. St. Thomas of Aquinum, in the thirteenth century, repeats the old objections in order to refute them by the old arguments; but all doubt on the subject was lulled to sleep by the spell of ecclesiastical infallibility. Then came the reviving dawn of the sixteenth century, when "Greece rose from the dead with the New Testament in her hand." At that epoch even Roman Catholic writers like Ludovicus Vives and Cardinal Cajetan ventured to point out the uncertainty which had been felt by Origen, Jerome, and even Augustine. Erasmus, while confessing his willingness to accept any certain definition of the Church on the subject, yet quotes some of the Fathers to show the absurdity of the pseudo-orthodoxy which condemned a man as "plusquam heretical" if he doubted about the authorship of this Epistle. His own opinion was that St. Paul did not write it.[1] Luther calls attention to its style, and quotes various passages[2] to show that it *could* not have been written by St. Paul or by any Apostle. While speaking of it with admiration as "a strong, mighty, and lofty Epistle," he considers that its Scriptural method indicates the authorship of Apollos, and says that at any rate it is the work of "an excellent apostolic man."[3] Calvin, again—while, like some of the Fathers, he *popularly* quotes it as "the Apostle's"—says that he cannot be induced to recognise it as St. Paul's because it differs from him in its style and method of teaching, and because the writer speaks of himself as a pupil of the Apostles,[4] a thing very alien from St. Paul's custom.[5] Melancthon never quotes it as St. Paul's. The Magdeburg Centuriators denied that it was his. Grotius and Limborch and Le Clerc supposed it to have been written by St. Luke, Apollos, or some companion of St. Paul.

Then for a time the tyranny of indolent custom began once more to reassert itself. During the seventeenth century, and long afterwards, especially in England, no one, without incurring dislike or suspicion, could hint, even apologetically, at any doubt as to whether the translators of the English Bible were in the right when they headed the Epistle with the superscription, "The Epistle of Paul the Apostle to the Hebrews."[6] But since the time of Semler (1763) many eminent writers

---

[1] "Quod ad sensum meum attinet, non videtur illius esse, ob causas quas hic reticuisse praestiterit."—Erasm. *Opp.* vi. 1024.

[2] ii. 3; vi. 4, *seq.*; x. 26, *seq.*; xii. 17.

[3] He only gives it precedence over the Epistles of James and Jude. "Lutherus eam simpliciter rejicit atque ita fere sentiunt Lutherani."—Gerhard († 1637), *Comment.* p. 10.

[4] Heb. ii. 3.

[5] Gal. i. 11—15; ii. 6; 1 Cor. ix. 1; xi. 23; Eph. iii. 2, &c. See Calvin, *ad. Heb.* ii. 3; xii. 13.

[6] "St. Paul saith in the twelfth chapter of the Hebrews" (Office *for the Visitation of the Sick*). "Marriage is commended of St. Paul to be honourable of all men" (Heb. xiii. 4), (Office *Form for the Solemnisation of Matrimony*). Such accidental allusions are in no sense authoritative. This is exactly a question on which Councils and Churches are very fallible, and have no authority beyond that which they derive from the study and research of their individual members. These *obiter dicta* have no more weight in proving

have practically set the question at rest by furnishing the results of that close examination, which prove, not only that St. Paul was not the actual *writer* of the Epistle—a fact which had been patent even in the days of Origen—but that it is not even indirectly due to his authorship. The phraseology has been passed through a fresh mint, and the thoughts have been subjected to the crucible of another individuality.

It will, therefore, serve no purpose to heap up words and phrases which are common to the author and to St. Paul.[1] Many, indeed, of those which have been adduced belong to the current coin of Christian theology. Those that *are* distinctively Pauline only prove a point which every one is ready to concede, that the writer had adopted much of the Apostle's teaching, and had been deeply influenced by his companionship. It is this very fact which throws into relief the positive dissimilarities. The more we read such books as Mr. Forster's *Apostolical Authority of the Epistle to the Hebrews*, "the closer," says Alford, "becomes the connexion in faith and feeling of the writer of the Epistle and St. Paul, but the more absolutely incompatible the personal identity; the more we perceive all that region of thought and feeling to have been in common between them which mere living together, talking together, praying together would naturally range in; but all that region wherein individual peculiarity is wont to put itself forth, to have been entirely distinct.

Again, it is vain to talk about difference of subject or difference of aim as furnishing any explanation of these dissimilarities. We have writings of St. Paul on all kinds of topics, and at all ages of his mature life; and though the style of a writer may vary in different moods, as the style of St. Paul in the Epistle to the Ephesians differs from that in the Pastoral Epistles, yet every style retains a certain stamp of individuality. Now, the differences between the Epistle to the Hebrews and the Epistles of St. Paul are differences which go down to the roots of the being. That the same pen should have been engaged on both is a psychological impossibility. The Greek is far better than the Greek

---

the Pauline authorship than the insertion of 1 John v. 7 in the English Version has weight in deciding on the authenticity of that passage. On such matters the Church of the seventeenth century was less qualified to decide than the Church of the nineteenth; and if the learned divines of the Church were now called upon for an opinion, the preponderance against the Pauline authorship would be overwhelming. To use such casual allusions as though they were decisive, in this and similar discussions, is one of the most unworthy—and therefore, alas! one of the commonest—forms of the *reductio ad horribile* and the *mentum ad invidiam*.

[1] Some of these may be seen collected by Tholuck and Bishop Wordsworth in their introductions to the Epistle, as also in the editions of Stuart and Forster. Any one will see at a glance the large sifting they require. I subjoin some of the most striking—1 Thess. i. 3, "unceasingly making mention of your work of faith and labour of love;" Heb. vi. 10, "*God is not unjust to forget your work and love;*" Rom. xii. 18, "if possible, being at peace with all men;" Heb. xii. 14, "*Follow peace with all.*" Compare also Heb. xiii. 18 with 2 Cor. iv. 2; Heb. x. 30 with Rom. xii. 19; Heb. ii. 10 with Rom. xi. 36; and Heb. xiii. 20 with Rom. xv. 33.

of St. Paul.[1] St. Paul is often stately and often rhetorical, and sometimes writes more in the style of a treatise than of a letter; but the stateliness and rhetoric and systematic treatment of the Epistle to the Hebrews in no way resemble his. The form and rhythm of its sentences are wholly different. Paul is often impassioned and often argumentative, and so is the author of the Epistle to the Hebrews; but the passion and the dialectics of the latter furnish the most striking contrast to those of the former. The writer cites differently from St. Paul;[2] he writes differently; he argues differently; he thinks differently; he declaims differently; he constructs and connects his sentences differently;[3] he builds up his paragraphs on a wholly different model. St. Paul is constantly mingling two constructions, leaving sentences unfinished, breaking into personal allusions, substituting the syllogism of passion for the syllogism of logic. This writer is never ungrammatical; he is never irregular; he is never personal; he never struggles for expression; he never loses himself in a parenthesis; he is never hurried into an anacoluthon.[4] His style is the style of a man of genius who thinks as well as writes in Greek: whereas St. Paul wrote in Greek, but thought in Syriac. The writings of both have the indefinable stamp of distinction; but the distinction of Apollos is marked by a less burning passion, and a more absolute self-control. The notion that the Epistle is a translation may be set aside. It only arose from a desire to save the Pauline authorship while accounting for the glaring differences of style. The fact of its acceptance by writer after writer[5] shows that criticism had little to do with deciding on the peculiarities of the letter. The quotations from the Septuagint even where it differs from the Hebrew, the structure of the sentences, and even the use of the *two*

---

[1] This does not exclude Hebraisms, because *lexical* Hebraisms (such as πληρούμενος, αίωνυμένη μέλλουσα, ἁγιάζειν, σάρξ καὶ αἷμα, κ.τ.λ.) were inwoven into the theological language of Christianity; but the majority of the *grammatical* "Hebraisms" in Prof. Stuart's list are not Hebraisms at all, or are reminiscences of Old Testament expressions (see Tholuck, *Komment.* 26—30). Bleek and Tholuck select six special peculiarities of style—1. The constant use of πᾶς, "all;"; 2. The intransitive use of καθίζειν, "sit" (i. 3, viii. 1, etc.); 3. The use of ἐάνπερ, "even though," where St. Paul always uses εἴγε, "if at least;" 4. ὅθεν, in the sense of "wherefore;" 5. εἰς τὸ διηνεκές, "to perpetuity;" and εἰς τὸ παντελὲς (Heb. vii. 3, 10, 25, etc.) for St. Paul's πάντοτε, "always," which is not a good Greek word; 6. The use of παρὰ and ὑπὲρ after comparatives.

[2] He follows the LXX., and usually the *Alexandrian* form of it, even where it differs from the Hebrew (i. 8, 9, ii. 7, x. 5—7, 30, 37—38, xi. 21, xiii. 5); whereas St. Paul often reverts to the Hebrew, and his citations agree with the *Vatican* MS. of the LXX. See this demonstrated by Bleek, *Der Brief an d. Hebr.* 338, seq.; Tholuck, *Komment.* 55. And he introduces his quotations all but invariably, not by "as it is written," "the Scripture saith," or "David so saith," but by "He saith," or "the Holy Spirit *or* God saith *or* beareth witness," etc. (i. 5, 6, iii. 7, 15, iv. 3, 4, v. 5, vi. 14, vii. 14, 21, viii. 5, 8, etc.).

[3] Γάρ, τοιγαροῦν, καὶ γάρ, τοίνυν, διό, ἀλλὰ οὐ (ii. 16 and iii. 16); εἶτα (xii. 9); δήπου (ii. 16). See Bleek, i. 330.

[4] How totally unlike St. Paul's rugged impetuosity is the calm and masterly grasp over the grammar in the splendid paragraph of xii. 18—24, in spite of its double parentheses! St. Paul would have made shipwreck of the grammar in such a sentence.

[5] Eusebius, Jerome, Theodoret, Euthalius, Œcumenius, Theophylact, etc., and down to Thomas Aquinas.

senses of the word *diatheke*, are sufficient to prove that the letter was written in Greek. A translation may be very able, but it can never bear upon its surface such marks of originality as we find in this Epistle. Its eloquence belongs to the language in which it is composed.[1] It is as unlike the eloquence of the LXX. translators when they are rendering into Greek the promises and denunciations of the Hebrew prophets as it is possible to conceive. It is full of paronomasiæ and plays of words which could have had no meaning or parallel in Hebrew.[2] It abounds in words which, while they have not the startling life of St. Paul's— while they are neither half-battles nor "creatures with hands and feet" —are yet terse, beautiful, and essentially Greek.[3] It could not have been a version from an Aramaic original. If then the Greek be the Greek of the original author, it is wholly unlike St. Paul's Greek. It was not in St. Paul's nature to be, as this writer is, "elaborately and faultlessly rhetorical." St. Paul, as I have shown elsewhere, has his own style of rhetoric, breathless, impetuous, bursting out like a lava stream of spontaneous passion. But never under any circumstances does St. Paul use rhetoric for its own sake. Never does he look out for expressions which shall merely please by their own sonorous majesty. Never does he indulge in the balanced equilibrium of euphonious clauses. His expressions are never leisurely. The movement of this author is that of an Oriental sheikh with his robes of honour wrapped around him; the movement of St. Paul is that of an athlete girded for the race. The rhetoric of this writer, even when it is at its most majestic volume, is like the smooth flow of a river amid green fields; the rhetoric of St. Paul is like the rush of a mountain torrent amid opposing rocks.

The idiosyncrasy of the writer is seen in his fondness for amplitude and rotundity of expression. Where St. Paul uses "reward" (*misthos*) his ear requires "recompense of reward" (*misthapodosia*); where St. Paul would have been content with the word "blood" (*haima*) he requires "shedding of blood" (*haimatecchusia*); where St. Paul has "oath" (*horkos*) he uses the fuller and rounder *horkomosia*. St. Paul thrice employs the expression "sitting at the right hand of God;" this writer, perhaps also with a touch of the Alexandrian dislike of anthropomor-

---

[1] Thus Philastrius (*Haer.* 89) says of some, "In eā (epistolā) quia rhetoricē scripsit, sermone plausibili, inde non putant esse ejusdem apostoli." The emphatic and sounding uses of the hyperbaton in vii. 4 (the position of ὁ πατριάρχης) could not be paralleled in St. Paul; nor the strikingly effective collocation of words in the very first sentence, in xii. 1, 2, ix. 11, 12, etc.

[2] i. 1, πολυμερῶς καὶ πολυτρόπως; ii. 5—8, ὑπέταξεν ... ἀνυπότακτον ... ὑποτεταγμένα; v. 8, ἔμαθεν ἀφ' ὧν ἔπαθεν; v. 14, καλοῦ τε καὶ κακοῦ; ix. 8, ἐπὶ βρώμασιν καὶ πόμασιν; xiii. 14, μένουσαν ... μέλλουσαν; ix. 15, διαθήκη (in two senses, "a covenant" and "a will"); vii. 39, μετάσχηκεν ... προσέσχηκεν; x. 29, ἡγησάμενος ... ἡγιάσθη; xi. 9, παρῴκησεν ... κατῴκησεν; xiii. 2, ἐπιλανθάνεσθε ... ἔλαθον; and many instances of plays on compound words (ii. 8, vii. 23, 24, viii. 7, 8, ix. 28), besides numerous rhetorical assonances (vii. 19, 22, x. 29, 34, 38, 39, etc.).

[3] i. 3, ἀπαύγασμα; xii. 1, εὐπερίστατος; v. 2, μετριοπαθεῖν.

phism, thrice amplifies it into sat[1] "on the right hand of the *Majesty in the highest*," or "on the right hand of *the throne of God*," or "on the right hand of *the throne of the Majesty in the heavens*." St Paul speaks of Christ as "the image of God," this writer as "the effulgence of the glory and impress of the hypostasis of God."[2] All this arises from his love for "musical euphony." On the other hand, St. Paul rarely speaks, as this writer usually does, of our Lord as "Jesus," or "the Lord," or "Christ," but rather of "our Lord Jesus Christ," and "Christ Jesus our Lord."[3] The variation is remarkable, but is due to the fact that as time went on the names "Christ" and "Jesus" became to all Christians so connotative of the supreme exaltation as no longer to need that addition or description which had become familiar to the earlier converts.

CHAPTER XVI.

THEOLOGY OF THE EPISTLE TO THE HEBREWS.

> "Oh, that I knew how all Thy lights combine,
> And the configurations of their glorie,
> Seeing not only how each verse doth shine,
> But all the constellations of the storie."
>
> G. HERBERT.

BUT the importance of all these differences, great as it is, sinks into insignificance when we consider the deep distinctions which exist between the *theological conceptions* of St. Paul and those of the writer of the Epistle to the Hebrews. There is, it need scarcely be said, no contradiction, any more than there is a contradiction between the theology of St. Paul and St. John; but there is a dissimilarity so marked that, as St. Paul could not have written the Epistle to the Hebrews without a radical change of style and individuality, so neither could he have written it without completely shifting the perspective and the inter-relations of the truths which he habitually taught. These facts are so interesting, so convincing, so intrinsically important, and so frequently overlooked, that they deserve the reader's most careful consideration.

(1.) That the writer was of the *School* of St. Paul we have said already, and accordingly we find him dwelling on three cardinal topics of the Pauline theology, namely (1) the contrast between Judaism and Christianity, (2) the saving efficacy of faith, and (3) the re-

---

[1] Καθίζειν, "to sit," is intransitive in Heb. i. 3, viii. 1, x. 12, xii. 2. In St. Paul it is always transitive, "to seat."
[2] See Alford, IV. i. p. 79.
[3] These compound forms occur sixty-eight times in St. Paul, and even "our Lord Jesus" only once in the Hebrews.

demptive work of Christ. But the fourth great topic of St. Paul's teaching—namely, the Universality of the Gospel as offered to all men, and to the Gentile in no less degree than to the Jew—is conspicuously absent in the Epistle to the Hebrews.

"*The people*" is to our author repeatedly, and, so far as this Epistle is concerned, exclusively, the Chosen People.[1] The Gentiles are ignored. The word "Gentiles" does not occur in the Epistle; and the writer speaks as though there were no such thing as a pagan in the world.[2] No one, surely, can refuse to recognise this phenomenon, or will think that it is sufficiently explained by saying that the Epistle is "addressed to the Hebrews." That might account for the absence of any *discussion* of the relations between the two unfused, and even half-discordant, elements of the Christian Church; but St. Paul, with whom the offer of salvation to the Gentiles was the most essential element of "his Gospel,"[3] could not have excluded every allusion to them, however remote. Had he done so by way of deference to Jewish prejudices, it would have been a concession altogether unworthy. That this writer accepted the call of the Gentiles we do not dispute; had he not done so he could not have been, as he so evidently was, a friend and adherent of the great Apostle. But it was not a topic of which his thoughts were full to overflowing, as were the thoughts of St. Paul. It was not a truth for the sake of which he had spent, amid combat, calumny, and persecution, the best years of his life. His thoughts were so exclusively occupied with the Hebrews, that he even speaks of the Incarnation as a taking hold not of humanity, but of Abraham's seed.[4] It is, perhaps, this circumstance which has robbed us of that enquiry into the position of Heathenism in the Divine economy, which would not only have had an intense interest, but would have completed for us the now imperfect scheme of what may be called the philosophy of historic religion.

But while the writer of the Epistle to the Hebrews had evidently embraced the views of St. Paul, how differently does he handle the three great themes which he has in common with his predecessor! His whole Epistle deals with *the relations between Christianity and Judaism*, but it is doubtful whether, at earlier stages of the controversy, St. Paul would have thought it expedient to adopt his line of argument. It is one which was in itself admirably suited to pacify the furious indignation of his Jewish opponents; but rougher and sterner work had to be done before it could be profitably employed. Jewish ex-

[1] Ὁ λαός, v. 3; vii. 5, 11, 27; viii. 10; ix. 7, 19; x. 30; xi. 25. See especially ii. 17; iv. 9; xiii. 12. In this sense the writer (as we should have supposed, *à priori*) is a Jewish Christian; but he is a Jewish Christian of a large and liberal type, and he does not utter one word which is antagonistic to the great spiritual conceptions of St. Paul. He dwells emphatically on the imperfection of Judaism (ἀσθενές . . ἀνωφελές); places Abraham below Melchizedek; does not dwell on Christ, either as the Jewish Messiah, or as the Son of David; and places the attainment of salvation in faithful endurance, not in obedience to the Law. [2] See Reuss, *Théol. Chrét.* ii. 289.
[3] Eph. iii. 4—8. [4] See ii. 16.

clusiveness had taken refuge in what they regarded as the impregnable fortress of Levitism; and it was necessary to batter down that fortress with many a rude shock of argument before the Apostle could pause to show the beauty and past usefulness of its walls and towers. Similarly there can be no question that the Papacy had in its day rendered magnificent services to the cause of civilisation; but it is scarcely from the Reformers that we should have expected a demonstration that it did so. It was their appointed task to show the dangerous elements which, in the sixteenth century, had rendered it necessary to emancipate mankind from its oppressive sway. There is force and truth in the arguments of De Maistre, but it was not a Luther who could be expected to originate them.

The specific character of the argument cannot be more briefly described than by saying, as we have said already, that it is Alexandrian. It is not only Alexandrian in its learning and culture,[1] but has its bases in the Alexandrian theosophy, and appeals for support to the allegoric method of Alexandrian exegesis.[2] St. Paul was no stranger to that method; but his approaches to it are distant and external. They are of the nature of literary reminiscences. They tinge the phraseology rather than sway the entire conception. They are such as had flowed from Alexandria into the field of Palestinian thought. On the other hand, the Alexandrianism of the author of the Epistle to the Hebrews is that of one who had been trained in the system, and whose whole theology is influenced by the conceptions which he has thence acquired.

I will try to make this clear.

α. We have already touched upon the exclusive regard paid to the Chosen People. The writer's thoughts are absorbed in the Hebrews. It is the same with Philo. His cosmopolitan interests and encyclopædic training had made him familiar with Roman institutions and Greek culture; yet everything appears to him in the light of Hebraism. Moses is to him the ultimate source of all wisdom. Philo was as ardently convinced as the fiercest of the Zealots that Israel is the leader of the Gentiles, and that to Israel belongs the future of the world. Israel is to the nations as the Pillar of Fire, wherein the Logos, or some other Divine minister, led their fathers in the wilderness. Israel, with his Temple and his laws, is the priest to pray and intercede for the seventy nations of mankind. The souls of the Israelites are of a higher order than those of the heathen. To Philo the Messianic kingdom means mainly the assembling of the Dispersion by some new and personal manifestation of the Logos.[3] To him

---

[1] Instances will be frequently found in the notes to the following pages. See also Excursus IX. "The Epistle to the Hebrews and the writings of Philo."
[2] iv. 1—10; vii. 1—17; ix. 1—10; x. 1—10.
[3] For these allusions see Philo, *Vita Mosis*, Opp. ii. 104, 107, 124, 126, 155 (ed. Mangey); and Hausrath, *Die Zeit d. Apost.* 181.

Judaism means Philosophy, but he still regards it as the absolute religion. Similarly, to the writer of this Epistle Christianity is but the fulfilment of Judaism. He sees in all mankind the undeveloped germs of the ideal Hebrew.

β. Another marked trace of the writer's Alexandrianism is his method of treating Scripture. To him, as to Philo, it is pregnant with *latent* meanings. Its silence is divinely significant, and is indeed as important for instruction as are its utterances. On two passing and isolated allusions to Melchizedek, allusions separated from each other by an interval of nine centuries, he builds a theological system of unequalled grandeur. That system receives strong support from the import and omen of names. It is partly built on the fact that certain circumstances are *not* mentioned in the Sacred narrative. Similarly, from the absence of any reference to the death of Cain, Philo infers the deathlessness of evil in mortal life. He calls Sarah "without mother" because the name of her mother is not recorded. So, to the writer of this Epistle, the mystic splendour of Melchizedek is enhanced by the circumstance that he is "without father, without mother, without recorded genealogy."

γ. But again and again, in peculiar phrases and pregnant hints, we see how much the writer has benefited from the study of Philo. If his main argument turns on the Priesthood of Christ, and His *sinless* Priesthood, we cannot forget that Philo too has called the Logos a High Priest, an "image of God," and "first-born of God," and has spoken of his having "no participation in sin."[1] Philo as well as St. Paul has contrasted the milk and the solid food of religious instruction. If Apollos speaks of Christ's sitting on the right hand of God to make intercession for us, Philo too has spoken of the Logos as "a Priest of the Father of the Universe;" as "an Advocate to obtain both forgiveness of sins and a supply of all good;" as "the boundary between created things and the Creator;" as "an intercessor for mortality in its longings after the incorruptible, and an ambassador from the Lord of all to that which is His subject." These are but some of the memorable ways in which, by God's gradual education of mankind, Alexandrian Judaism was enlightened to create forms of thought of which Christianity could make use in proclaiming the Gospel of the Incarnation, and in basing it upon the utterances of the Old Testament Scriptures.[2] But we must again be reminded how vast is the superiority of the Christian faith to the Philonian philo-

---

[1] *De profugis*, 20: ἀρχιερεὺς ... ἁμαρτημάτων ἀμέτοχος.
[2] Among phrases common to the writer and to Philo, but unknown to St. Paul, we may mention—δήπου, τοσοῦτο .. ὅσον, the interchange of meanings between "covenant" and "testament" in *diatheke*, φωτίζειν, γινώσκεσθαι, μετριοπαθεῖν, ἀμήτωρ. There is a remarkable parallel between Heb. x. 29 and Philo, *De profug.*, "For if those who abuse mortal parents are led to death, *of what punishment must we think them worthy* who venture to blaspheme the Father and Maker of all things?" Such striking terms as "to sin willingly" and "prayers and supplications" are also common to both

sophy. The Logos of Philo has to be removed from any direct contact with matter by an endless number of intervening Powers; the forms in which He is represented are so self-contradictory, that we never know whether he is to be regarded as a Person or an Idea. And Philo is still so far entangled in Jewish particularism that he is unable to understand the universal prophecies of the Old Testament. His Logos is at the best a Jewish deliverer, and is infinitely far from being the Saviour of the World.

5. But the still closer comparison of a few of the most memorable passages of the Epistle with the words and thoughts of Philo will show that the author is indebted to him to an extent to which St. Paul's writings furnish no parallel.

(i.) Take, for instance, the memorable opening passage. He speaks of Christ as "*the effulgence of God's glory.*" Philo had spoken of God as the "archetypal brightness," and of the Logos as a "sunlike brightness," and the Book of Wisdom had spoken of Wisdom as "the effulgence of everlasting light."—He calls the son "*the stamp and impress of God's substance.*" Philo speaks of the word of man as "the stamp of divine power," and of the Logos as "the stamp of the seal of God."—He says that the Son "*upholds all things by the utterance of His power.*" Philo speaks of the Logos as "bearing all things that are."—He says, "*By whom also He made the worlds.*" Philo says that "the instrument (*organon*) of creation was the Word, by Whom it was set in order," and that "the Word is the image (*eikon*) of God, by Whom the whole universe was fashioned."[1]

(ii.) Again, take Heb. iv. 12, 13: "*For living is the Word of God, and active, and more cutting than any two-edged sword, and piercing even to the division both of soul and spirit, both of joints and marrow, and quick to discern the thoughts and intents of the heart.*" In this passage the writer evidently has in his mind the thoughts of Philo and of the Book of Wisdom. Philo compares the Word to the flaming sword of Paradise; he speaks of the "fire and knife" of Abraham as being used "to cut off and consume his still adherent mortality." He calls the Word "the cutter of all things," and says that "when whetted to the utmost sharpness it is incessantly dividing all sensuous things." He compares it to the midmost branch of the golden candlestick, as being the cutter or divider of the six faculties of the human soul. Similarly the author of Wisdom compares God's Almighty word to a sharp sword leaping down from earth to Heaven.[2]

(iii.) Again, this Epistle is remarkable for several passages which express with uncompromising sternness the hopeless condition of willing and determined apostates. Those passages (vi. 4—8; x. 26—29; xii. 16, 17) are in some respects unique in Scripture, and they furnished a stronghold to the heretics of the religiosity which delights in hatred.

---

[1] *De monarchia,* ii. § 5 (Mang. i. 47, 106—162, etc.).
[2] See Excursus IX. *Quis rer. div. haer.* (Mang. i. 491, 503, 506).

That they do not sanction such perversions we shall see further on; but we find something very analogous to them in a passage of Philo[1] which is almost apostolic in its solemnity, where he describes the irreparable loss sustained by that soul which refuses to submit itself to the discipline of the Logos and which overpasses the limits of fitting humility. "Such a soul," he says, "will not only be widowed in respect to all true knowledge, but will also be cast out. Once unyoked and separated from the Logos, she will be cast away for ever, without possibility of returning to her ancient home."[2]

After instances so striking, it will be needless to do more than to point to two of the most fundamental conceptions in the entire Epistle.

1. One of them is the Melchizedek Priesthood of Christ. In his whole treatment of the subject, the writer adopts the method and the thoughts of Philo. Philo speaks of the "Just King," as holding "a self-acquired, self-taught priesthood," which—building solely on the *silence* of Scripture—he describes as having been bestowed on him without merit or work. He directly compares him to the Logos in the words, "The Logos, *who is shadowed forth by Melchizedek*," is "priest of God the Most high." Philo also speaks of the Logos as "the great High Priest."[3]

But here again, as throughout the Epistle, the writer shows himself superior to Philo. With Philo allegory is everything, and the literal narrative almost nothing. With Apollos the literal narrative is accepted, and the typology is confined within rational limits, not pushed into absurd details. He does not say, as Philo does, that Melchizedek brought forth the nourishment for the soul which the Ammonites and Moabites would not do, because the Ammonites are the children only of perception, and the Moabites of mind.[4]

2. But there is a yet more fundamental Alexandrianism in his mode of thought, and one which requires a fuller examination.

It had been a main object of St. Paul to dissuade the Jews from clinging to Judaic observances as a means of salvation; to prevent their enforcement upon the Gentiles; and to convince the Gentiles that they were abrogated and null. He does this by a dialectic method, in which he proves to the Jews that Mosaism was but a transient, imperfect, relative dispensation, having no absolute value, but only intended to lead men by an unsatisfied yearning, or rather to drive them with the scourge of an awakened conscience, to a diviner and an eternal faith.

---

[1] *Legg. alleg.* iii. (Mang. i. 119; δυσκλπιστίαν μετὰ πολλῆς ἀνίας ἐτᾶται κ.τ.λ.).
[2] Delitzsch, on Heb. vi. 4. On the resemblance between this Epistle and Philo, see Excursus X., and consult Carpzov, *Sacr. Exerc. in Ep. ad Hebr. ex Philone*, 1750; Lösner, *Observ. in N. T. ex Philone*; Bleek, i. 399, f. 9; Tholuck, 78, f. 9; Gfrörer, *l.c.*; Dähne, *Alex. Religionsphilos.* i.
[3] *De Somn.* § 38 (Mang. i. 653).
[4] Tholuck points out that in the Hagadoth about the infancy of Moses the writer is nearer to Josephus (*Antt.* xv. 563) than to Philo.

To him the Law is neither Promise nor Fulfilment, but a stern though necessary discipline which had been interposed between the two. Moses, in the Apostle's view, was by no means the supreme chief of the Hebrew race, but a personage of secondary importance in comparison with Abraham. The fiery Law of Sinai, so far from being, as the Rabbis said, the one thing for the sake of which the universe had been created,[1] was deposed into complete subordination. St. Paul placed it immeasurably lower than the promise to Abraham, and showed that it sank into insignificance before the Gospel of Christ. Hence the contrast between the Law and the Gospel is, for St. Paul, a contrast between Command and Promise, between Sin and Mercy, between Works and Faith, between Curse and Blessing, between the threat of inevitable Death and the gift of Eternal Life. Apollos, on the other hand, treats of the contrast only as a contrast between Type and Reality. The polemical aspect of the question has disappeared. The Circumcision controversy, the question about meats,[2] the proofs that the Gentiles were not to be under Levitic bondage, are matters that have no existence in his pages. He does not say one word about that opposition of Faith and works which occupy so many chapters of St. Paul. Election, Regeneration, the Rejection of Israel, the difference between the physical and the spiritual seed of Israel, are absent from his treatise. He only alludes even to Repentance and to the Resurrection to class them among the "elements" which he may safely pass by.[3] To St. Paul Judaism was represented by a Law which enforced, by one universal menace, its impossible exactions; it was a dispensation of wrath which revealed to man that he was naturally under the curse of God. Christianity, on the other hand, was represented by a Deliverance, a Reconciliation, a Free Grace, which men were forced to seek as a refuge from a doom which their troubled consciences declared to be deserved. This Epistle views the two religions under an aspect entirely different. It sees in Judaism *not so much a Law as a System of Worship*, of which Christianity was the antitype and fulfilment. Both writers arrive at the same conclusion, but they do so by different routes, and from different premisses. St. Paul represents Mosaism as a cancelled servitude; this writer as an incomplete satisfaction. To St. Paul the Levitic system was a discipline which had been rendered superfluous; to this writer—to whom by anticipation I will again ask permission to give the name of Apollos—it was a symbol which had become nugatory. To St. Paul the Law was a bond, of which Christ had nailed the torn fragments to His Cross; to Apollos Judaism was a scaffolding within which

---

[1] See the Introd. to Delitzsch's Commentary on the Epistle, and Kitzur Sh'lh, *f.* 7, 2 (Hershon's *Talm. Miscell.* p. 331). Avoda Zara, *f.* 3, 1. Shabbath, *f.* 89, 1. Pesachim, *f.* 54, 1, etc.

[2] There is a passing allusion to the distinction of meats in xiii. 9, but only as it affected the Jews, and with no reference to its present obligatoriness or non-obligatoriness either for them or for the Gentiles.

[3] vi. 1.

the true Temple had been built, a chrysalis from which the winged life had departed. St. Paul looked on Mosaism as a broken fetter, his follower regarded it as a vanished shadow. To St. Paul the Law was abrogated because it consisted of "beggarly elements;" to Apollos it was annulled because the Priesthood on which it depended had become weak and profitless. Both regarded Christianity as far more ancient than Judaism—but it was so to St. Paul because he saw in it the fulfilment of a Promise, and to Apollos because he saw in it the realisation or an archetype. St. Paul's proof hinges on the threat which lay by implication in the words: *He that doeth them shall live by them;* the argument of Apollos rests on the command to Moses: "*See that thou make all things after the pattern showed thee in the Mount.*" St. Paul proves the independence of Christianity by referring to Abraham; Apollos by referring to Melchizedek. The Jewish ritual was to Apollos a material something between the Divine Idea and its partial realisation by Christians on earth until they passed to its absolute realisation in Heaven. Hence, "the Epistle to the Hebrews is a thoroughly original attempt to establish the main results of Paulinism upon new presuppositions and in an entirely independent way."[1] We may add that this way, being more comprehensible, was of the extremest importance. It was clearer to the Gentiles because it did not involve the transcendental heights of St. Paul's fervid mysticism. It was more easily accepted by Jews because it gave a less violent shock to their prejudices. It soothed the wounded pride of Levitism, by recognising it as part of an unbroken continuity.[2] The Jew was less likely to cling with frantic patriotism to the traditions of his fathers if he could be persuaded that Christianity was not in opposition to them, but might be regarded as a progress beyond them, an evolution out of them, a nearer approximation to the Eternal Substance of which they were the acknowledged but evanescent shadow.[3]

And yet how effective the argument was! The Temple seems to rise before us in all the splendour of its most imposing ceremonial. We see the Ark and the Cherubim and Aaron's budding rod, and the

---

[1] Pfleiderer, *Paulinism.* ii. 53.

[2] This may be illustrated from the writer's treatment of Revelation. Here again we find the *argumentum a minori ad majus*. The Revelation to the Jews (πάλαι) was in all respects a genuine revelation (i. 1 ; ii. 2; iii. 9; iv. 12; xii. 19, etc.), but the Instrument of the Christian Revelation was higher and greater (i. 1; ii. 3)—One far above angels, far above Moses, far above Aaron; and he spoke not in terror, as on Sinai, but in mercy, as by the Galilean Lake (xii. 18—21; iii. 7; iv. 1, etc.)

[3] The whole subject has been well treated by Baur (*Church History*, I., pp. 114—122, E.T.) and by Pfleiderer, *Paulinismus*, Kap. ix.), to whom I am much indebted. Baur says (p. 118)—"The distinction between the two views may be said to be that the tendency of St. Paul's is *ethical*, that of this Epistle *metaphysical*." There is nothing in this Epistle so startling to the Jew as St. Paul's remark that the Law was given "for the sake of transgressions" (Gal. iii. 19); but what Apollos sees in the Law is mainly its *negative* relation to Christianity. The *Priesthood*, not the Law, is with him the essential thing, and as to the Law, he merely says that when there is a change in the one there must be a change in the other (vii. 12).

golden pot of manna, and the curling wreaths of incense. We hear the trumpets blow, and see the Levites in their white tunics on the marble steps, and the High Priest in his golden and jewelled robes. And while the Jew is exulting in all this gorgeous and significant ritual, it is by one wave of a wand reduced to a shadow, a picture, a transient symbol of that by which it is all to be done away!

For the main section of the Epistle is occupied with the proof that Christ is the true Priest, who continues indeed the Aaronic priesthood, but supersedes it by reverting to a higher type; that Judaism is but an inchoate and imperfect Christianity. The difference between the two systems is quantitative rather than qualitative, though quantitative in an almost infinite degree. The ancient novice, when initiated into the mysteries, used to exclaim, ἔφυγον κακόν, εὗρον ἄμεινον, "I fled the bad, I found the better." But to revert from Christianity to Judaism was the worst kind of apostasy—it was to fling away the better from a deliberate preference for the worse.[1]

The author (as we have seen) found his fruitful thought of a pre-existent Ideal in the Alexandrian philosophy. That philosophy had sprung up from seed which Plato had sown in the rich soil of Semitic monotheism. To the school of Philo, as to that of Plato, earth was—

> "But the shadow of Heaven, and things therein,
> Each to the other like more than on earth is thought."[2]

To them—and they found sanction for their views in Holy Writ—the world of *phenomena* was but the shadow of a world of *noumena*. The things seen and temporal were dim copies of things unseen and eternal. The visible universe is a faint adumbration of the archetypal, and it is only Divine in so far as it answers to the Great Idea of its Creator.

The Jews had begun to study Greek philosophy, and to see that

> "All knowledge is not couched in Moses' Law,
> The Pentateuch, or what the Prophets wrote:
> The Gentiles also know, and write, and teach
> To admiration, led by Nature's light."

The spirit of Judaism had been kindled afresh by a breath of secular inspiration. They had begun to recognise in the nobler tones of heathen literature the voice of that eternal Sibyl who "in all ages entering into holy souls makes them sons of God and prophets, and speaking things simple and unperfumed and unadorned reaches through ten thousand years by the aid of God."[3] Familiar with the *Timaeus*, Philo made his entire system depend on the existence of a Κόσμος νοητὸς,

---

[1] Hence the constant recurrence of κρείττων ἐλπίς, κρείττων διαθήκη (vii. 19, 22); διαφορωτέρα λειτουργία (viii. 6); μείζων καὶ τελειοτέρα σκηνὴ (ix. 11); κρείττονες θυσίαι, ἐπαγγελίαι (ix. 23). It might almost be said that πόσῳ μᾶλλον, "how much more," is the key-note of the argument (ix. 14; x. 29)—the *argumentum a minori ad majus*.

[2] "Der Sinnenwelt ein Schatte ist der Geistwelt" (Mahomed, a Persian poet, quoted by Tholuck, 135).

[3] Heraclitus.

or World of Ideas, of which the Mosaic system was a *copy*. He learnt from Scripture that the worlds were made by the Word of God, and he regarded the ideal world as being the sum total of the concrete developments of this Infinite Logos. As St. John identifies the Logos with Christ, so the author of this Epistle identifies the Ideal World with the kingdom of Heaven, and the kingdom of Heaven with perfected salvation. And thus the conception—transplanted from the atmosphere of philosophy into that of religion—acquires new life. It is no longer a transcendental abstraction: it gives form and expression to a living hope.

We might, perhaps, suppose that there is a trace of the same conception in the language of St. Paul about "the heavenlies" in the Epistle to the Ephesians;[1] but St. Paul merely uses the expression as a moral appeal, and not as the basis of a theological system. In the Epistle before us the whole argument is made to turn upon it. Levitism is but a sketch in outline, a rough copy, a quivering shadow of the things in Heaven, which are supersensuous, invisible, immaterial, immovable, eternal.[2] This æon is but an imperfect realisation of the future æon.[3] The Tabernacle was made after the pattern of a Divine Temple,[4] and Christianity *is* that Temple. The superiority of Christianity to Judaism is shown to consist in this, that Judaism is earthy and sensuous, Christianity supersensuous and ideal. But the Christianity of this world is itself but a *closer* copy, a *truer* realisation of the perfect kingdom beyond the grave. Hence the kingdom of Heaven is both present and future. It is a salvation subjectively enjoyed, not yet objectively realised.[5]

(1.) From this different way of handling the relation of Christianity to Judaism there arises incidentally a remarkable difference between the aspect presented by the Christian Hope in this writer and in St. Paul. St. Paul says, "We were saved by our Hope."[6] The salvation is secured, yet Hope is necessary, because here we groan in the mortal body. There is in us a "psychological dualism"—a disintegrated individuality—flesh struggling against spirit, and spirit against flesh, although the spirit is winning a progressive victory, and gradually asserting its sole pre-eminence. The Christian *receives* the Sonship, but he still awaits its perfect fruition.[7] He looks forward

---

[1] Eph. i. *passim*; and Heb. viii. 5; ix. 23.
[2] ὑπόδειγμα, viii. 5; σκίαν, ix. 1; ix. 23; xi. 1, 3; xii. 18, 27; παραβολὴ, ix. 9; ἀντίτυπα, ix. 24; as opposed to ὁ τύπος, or τὸ τέλειον, or τὰ ἀληθινὰ, or αὐτὴ ἡ εἰκών. The world of phenomena (αὐτὴ ἡ κτίσις) is described as visible (τὸ βλεπόμενον, xi. 3), capable of being shaken (τὰ σαλευόμενα, xii. 27), tangible (xii. 18), but the archetypal world is the "House of God" (x. 21); "the genuine Tabernacle" (viii. 2); "the city which has the foundations" (xi. 10); our true "fatherland" (xi. 14); the unshakeable kingdom" (xii. 28); "the heavenly Jerusalem" (xii. 22). [3] Heb. ii. 5; vi. 5.
[4] Thus the Jews said that "An Ark of fire, and a Table and Lampstand of fire, came down from Heaven to Moses as patterns, and that Gabriel, clothed as a workman, showed Moses how to make them."—(Menachoth, *f.* 29, 1.)
[5] Heb. xii. 28; vi. 4, 5.
[6] Rom. viii. 24: τῇ γὰρ ἐλπίδι ἐσώθημεν. [7] *Ib.* υἱοθεσίαν ἀπεκδεχόμενοι.

to the resurrection as his final deliverance from the assaults of the fleshly principle, after which he will be in possession of a spiritual body. In the Epistle to the Hebrews we read nothing of this fierce struggle. Constantly as the author speaks of the future life, he says nothing about the Resurrection, except to mention it among the elementary subjects which he does not mean to discuss. But Hope is necessary, because the state in which we live is but a shadow of the state wherein we shall be. In this view we can only realise the future by exultant anticipation and inward evidence.[1] Hope is not fruition. Here the ship still tosses on the turbid waves, but yet it is held by a sure and steadfast anchor, of which the golden chain passes out of our sight in that aerial ocean beyond the veil;—and the unseen links of that chain are held by the hand of Christ, Who has gone before us there.[2] It remained for St. John to say and to show still more clearly and comfortably that he that hath the Son *hath* life—that this *is* eternal life. In him Hope melts into actual fruition. The future becomes one with the present. The chasm between the two is bridged over by the highest utterance of revelation, that "the Word became flesh."

(2.) So far, then, we have seen that the Epistle to the Hebrews differs theologically from the writings of St. Paul by its marked Alexandrianism. But this is not the only difference. FAITH is prominent alike in the Epistle to the Hebrews and in St. Paul, but it is presented under a changed aspect. The terminology is in part identical, the accentuation of meaning is not the same. The writer uses St. Paul's phrases, but he applies them to truths seen under a different light. To St. Paul Faith meant the essence of the Christian life. Ultimately it meant the unity of the spirit of man with the Spirit of God—the life in Christ—the identity of the life of Christ with the life of the Christian. The life of faith in St. Paul is the realised immanence of Christianity, "Christ in me." This is the *form* of faith in his writings, and its *object* is the life, the death, the resurrection of his Lord. Now, often as faith is spoken of in this Epistle, the form and the object of it are different. Its *form* is " the substance of things hoped for, the conviction of things invisible."[3] The *object* of it is neither the Person of Christ,[4] nor the death of Christ,[5] nor the resurrection of Christ,[6] but it is trust in the word of God, and the entrance into that unseen world whereinto Christ has preceded us.[7] Not that the faith of this writer sinks into a Chiliastic expectation. It is the *present* approximation to future perfectness.

---

[1] Heb. vi. 4, 5; xii. 28.   [2] Heb. vi. 19.
[3] xi. 1. On the meaning of ὑπόστασις and ἔλεγχος, see *infra*, on Heb. xi. 1. "Der Begriff der πίστις ein anderer ist, nämlich nicht so wohl die *fides specialis in Christum* als die *fides generalis* in das unsichtbare (Ideale) Heil." Immer, *Neu-Test. Theol.* p. 403.
[4] Rom. iii. 22; Gal. ii. 20; Eph. i. 15; Col. i. 4, etc.
[5] Rom. iii. 25; Gal. ii. 20.
[6] Eph. *passim*; 1 Cor. xv. etc. Christ's resurrection is only once alluded to by Apollos, Heb. xiii. 20, and that but passingly.
[7] vi. 1; xi. 1, 2, 4, etc. He does not speak of πίστις Ἰησοῦ Χριστοῦ or ἐν Χριστῷ Ἰησοῦ

It is confidence in the promised rest, founded on approach to God,[1]—analogous to the belief of the old heroes and Patriarchs, but more perfect and less distant,[2] and evinced by endurance.[3] Faith in St. Paul is oneness with Christ; in this writer it has Christ for its *example*. It is not the instrument of justification, but the condition of access. It is used in a sense more easily intelligible, and therefore more likely to be widely accepted. It is "Christ for us" rather than "Christ in us." Hence faith, as treated in this Epistle, becomes very closely allied with "endurance to the end."[4]

(2) β. There is a similar difference observable in the use of the word RIGHTEOUSNESS. St. Paul's use of the word is peculiar. The main dogmatic thesis of the Epistle to the Romans—"justification by faith"—is an illustration of the method whereby the subjective righteousness of God can become the objective righteousness (or justification) of man. To this dogma the letter before us does not allude, and *Dikaiosunê* is confined to its original meaning of simple "righteousness." For that state which St. Paul calls "justification" this writer has a different word. The words "imputed righteousness" nowhere occur in him. Righteousness with him is not a condition bestowed on man by God as a result of the work of Christ, but, as in James, it is faith manifested by obedience, and so earning the witness of God.[5] Thus the word *Dikaiosunê* is stripped of judicial accessories,[6] and the results of a life of obedience based on faith are expressed by the terms "purification," "sanctification," "perfectionment."[7] In other words, "righteousness" is not to this writer "the Divine gift which faith receives"—the white robe put into the outstretched hands; but it is "the human condition which faith produces,"[8] the inheritance which man acquires.[9]

Here, again, there is no contradiction of St. Paul, who carefully guards himself against Antinomian misconceptions, and who shows that where faith is there works must be, just as where sunlight is there warmth and light must be. But though there is no contradiction, there is marked divergence. The identity of phraseology does but serve to bring into prominence the underlying differences. Even when the author quotes the famous verse of Habakkuk, "The just shall live by faith," or, as he more probably wrote, "*My* just man shall live by faith," he applies it in a manner which is not the same as that of St. Paul. Each of the three words of the text has a different shade of meaning. By

---

[1] xi. 10.   [2] x. 34; xi. 40; xii. 22, 28.
[3] x. 35—39.
[4] xi. 1; xii. 1, τοιγάρουν . . . δι᾿ ὑπομονῆς τρέχωμεν. So Philo defines Faith as "a bettering in all things of the soul which has cast itself for support on the Author of all things" (*De Abrahamo*, ii. 39).
[5] ἐμαρτυρήθη εἶναι δίκαιος, xi. 4, 5.
[6] Δικαιόω occurs twenty-eight times in St. Paul; not once in this Epistle.
[7] ἁμάζειν, ἁγιάζεσθαι, ii. 11; x. 10, 14, 29; xiii. 12. Compare ῥαντίζειν, ῥαντισμός, x. 22, 29; xii. 24 (1 Pet. i. 2).
[8] xi. 33, διὰ πίστεως εἰργάσαντο δικαιοσύνην.
[9] xi. 7, δικαιοσύνης ἐγένετο κληρονόμος. See Pfleiderer, ii. 86,

"the just" St. Paul means "he who has been justified;" by "faith" he means "union with Christ;" by "shall live" he means "enter into the spiritual life." The use of the text by Apollos comes nearer to its original significance in the old Jewish prophet, which was that "the upright man should be preserved from ruin by his fidelity."[1] How any careful reader with such facts before him can persist in maintaining that St. Paul wrote the Epistle to the Hebrews, must remain one of the strangest problems of theological criticism.

(3.) Once more, without the smallest *contradiction* between the CHRISTOLOGY of St. Paul and that of the Epistle to the Hebrews, we can trace in the latter the speciality of Alexandrian influences. The conception of the Eternal Christ, as One Who was far above all angels, is the same as in the Epistle to the Colossians, but the expressions used of Him are even stronger. In the Epistle to the Hebrews Christ is not only the Image of God, as He is in St. Paul,[2] but also, as in the Book of Wisdom,[3] "the effulgence of His glory, and the impress of His substance;" and is not only, as in St. Paul, the Instrument of creation, but also the upholder of all things by the word of His power. In this respect Apollos stands midway between St. Paul and St. John. The word *Logos*, as directly applied to Christ, seems constantly to be in his mind, but he does not actually use it. And yet in his first chapter,[4] and elsewhere,[5] he transfers directly to Christ the attributes of the Logos of Philo.[6] And by so doing he produced a deep effect. In the Apocalypse, also, Christ appears as the Logos and the High Priest. In its exalted conception of our Lord's Divinity, and in the development of His highpriestly functions,[7] the Epistle to the Hebrews exercised an influence upon the Church which perpetuated its value long after any proof of the superiority of Christianity to Judaism had been rendered needless by the inexorable demonstrations of History.

(4.) And the REDEMPTIVE WORK of Christ is also looked at from a slightly different standpoint, both in its nature and its results. In St. Paul the decree of God and the passivity of Christ are mainly dwelt

---

[1] Hab. ii. 4; Rom. i. 17; Heb. x. 38. See my *Life and Work of St. Paul*, ii. 181; Pfleiderer, *Paulinism*. ii. 89; Weiss, *Petrin. Lehrbegr.* 527.

[2] εἰκὼν τοῦ Θεοῦ τοῦ ἀοράτου, Col. i. 15; iii. 12; 2 Cor. iv. 4.

[3] Wisd. vii. 25, 26. Noack suggested an ingenious theory, that the Book of Wisdom was written by Apollos before his conversion. This theory has been worked out by Dean Plumptre in the *Expositor*, i. 327, 348, 400—435. He adduces the words common to Wisdom and the Epistle, such as πολυμερῶς, ἀπαύγασμα, ὑπόστασις, θεράπων, τόπος μετανοίας, βεβαίωσις, ἔκβασις, and many more; shows the connection of both books with Philo; points to parallel passages like Heb. iv. 12 and Wisd. xviii. 22; shows that Clement of Rome used both books; illustrates the sonorous style of both, the fondness for compounds, for unusual words, and for an accumulation of epithets; and calls attention to the fact that the two books are mentioned in juxtaposition by Irenaeus (Euseb. *H. E.* v. 26), and nearly so in the Muratorian Canon.

[4] Heb. i. 1—4.

[5] iv. 12, 13.

[6] *De Somn.* (Mang. i. 633, τὸ μὲν γὰρ παραδειγμα ὁ πληρέστατος ἦν αὐτοῦ Λόγος φῶς.)

[7] It is reproduced in Clem. Rom. *ad Rom.* 36, 58, and referred to in the *Martyrdom of Polycarp*, and the *Testament of the Twelve Patriarchs*.

upon, and His death is regarded from its most mysterious aspect as being an expiatory sacrifice to redeem mankind from the curse of the Law; but in the Epistle to the Hebrews Christ is not only the passive victim, but the sacrificing priest.[1] The result of His willing sacrifice of Himself is the purification of man's conscience from the sense of guilt,[2] and the sanctification of man's life by a new relation towards God. Guilt had rendered us impure before God. The Jews of old were replaced in a condition of Levitical purity, partly by sacrifices, partly by a sprinkling of blood. We are rendered spiritually pure from the defilement of a tormenting conscience by the death of Christ for us once for all, and by the sprinkling of our consciences with His Blood. The point of view from which Christ's death is here regarded is not the identity of the Christian with Christ, but the passing through the veil into the Holiest—the approach to Christ, and through Christ to God. Even when he is dwelling directly on the death of Christ, the author scarcely ever uses any phrase which can be interpreted as intimating that it was an expiation which was necessary to manifest that God was righteous although He forgave sin.[3] The reason which he assigns for the abstract *necessity* of Christ's death is that a testament can only come into force after the death of the testator.[4] This reason, taken alone, explains so small a part of the matter, and so completely leaves out of sight the *sacrificial* death of Christ, and bears so slightly on the analogy of the ancient sacrifices on which he has so long been dwelling, that we are almost driven to infer that the writer supposed his readers to be aware of the explanation of this mystery furnished by St. Paul, and therefore deemed it needless to develop it further. This is the more remarkable, because whereas the author speaks even more strongly than St. Paul of the majesty of the Eternal and Pre-existent Christ, he yet dwells more distinctly than St. Paul on the moral and human side of the life of Christ—His prayers and tears, His anguish, His holy fear, His perfectionment through suffering.[5] He contents himself with the general expression that there was a moral fitness in its being thus ordained.[6] But while we can have no doubt that he accepted the truth which St. Paul had taught,[7] we can see how natural it was for one who had been

---

[1] Geiger has argued that this conception came from the Sadducees, and therefore that the writer must have once been a Sadducee. There is nothing to be said in favour of this view, and much against it. See Matt. xxii. 23, and Acts xxiii. 8, compared with Heb. vi. 2; xi. 35; i. ii. *passim*.
[2] The two words most frequently used are καθαρισμός, καθαρίζειν, as in ix. 13, 14; x. 2, 22, &c.; and ἁγιάζειν, ii. 11; x. 10, 14.
[3] As in Rom. iii. 25; Gal. iii. 13; 2 Cor. v. 21.   [4] Heb. ix. 15–22.
[5] ii. 10; iv. 15; v. 8; vi. 20; vii. 2, 10; xii. 2.
[6] ἔπρεπεν ἡμῖν, vii. 26.
[7] That he does so is clear from such expressions as ἀπολύτρωσις, ix. 15; αἱματεκχυσία, ix. 22; ἱλάσκεσθαι, ii. 17; ὅπως ὑπὲρ παντὸς γεύσηται θανάτου, ii. 9. But these expressions make it only the more remarkable that he nowhere touches on the *reason* for these necessities—the rationale of this reconciliation. He says that Christ was offered and man was cleansed, but he nowhere develops any theory of vicarious satisfaction to explain the fact. (Köstlin, *Johann Lehrbegr.* 435.)

trained in Alexandrian notions to accept it without being led to dwell upon it; to leave it as an insoluble mystery; to feel a difficulty in speaking of "reconciliation," or of any apparent contrast between God's retributive wrath and His reconciling love. That which only *could* be expressed in anthropomorphic, and therefore in imperfect metaphors, was least calculated to attract the genius of Alexandrian elucidation. We are not surprised that an Alexandrian should reverently leave this on one side, as being the mysterious element in Christ's sacrifice which is to us incomprehensible. He does not therefore touch on the satisfaction of God's justice, but on another aspect of Christ's death—namely, the annihilation of the power of the Devil.[1] He is content to declare, without further discussion, that Christ's death is man's purification. He "leaves a gap between the means and the end."[2] He dwells more on Christ the Sanctifier than on God the Justifier.[3] He speaks of Christ's sufferings as the appointed pathway of His perfection, and of the following of His example as the appointed means of our being perfected.[4] Scarcely touching on St. Paul's words "ransom," "reconciliation," "justification," he teaches that Christ, by His suffering and death, performed once for all the work of an Eternal High Priest—offered that sacrifice of Himself which purges the consciousness of man from its sense of guilt, and, as our forerunner and standard-bearer, flung open the heavenly sanctuary, the archetypal world, wherein man, purified from guilt, can enter into the Presence of God—in hope and humble access now, in beatific vision hereafter behind the veil.[5]

(5.) In seizing upon PRIESTHOOD and SACRIFICE, rather than on the

---

[1] Compare Col. ii. 14, 15. Both writers use the word "ransom," because *as regards man* Christ's death has the effect of a ransom paid. But neither of them touch on the question, "*To whom* is the ransom paid?" And with good reason: because that question is an invasion of the secrets of the Deity. When men insist on trying to answer it, they (1) either draw out a doctrine of the Atonement which represents God in a light which utterly shocks the moral sense, or (2) infer, as was taught by theologians for a thousand years, that the person to whom the ransom was paid was—the Devil! Such a notion would have been abhorrent to the Alexandrian monotheism; and that the notion of a "warfare or lawsuit" between Christ and Satan should for so many hundred years have formed a constant element of Church teaching respecting the mystery of the Atonement, from Augustine to Anselm, is one of the many historic facts which should abate the towering pretensions of an inferential theology.

[2] x. 14.

[3] See Davidson, *Introd.* ii. 245.

[4] ii. 9, 10; xii. 6—11; v. 9; τελείωσις, "perfectionment," is a characteristic word of this Epistle, and it seems to include both "justification," "sanctification," and "glorification."

[5] vi. 20; x. 20. It will be seen, then, that points in which the writer is not distinctively Pauline are, (1) the prominence of τελείωσις rather than of δικαίωσις; (2) the conception of Christ less as the Crucified and Risen than as the sympathetic High Priest; (3) the conception of approach to Him (προσέρχεσθαι πρός) rather than of mystic union with Him (Immer, *Neu-Test. Theol.* p. 403). (4) St. Paul's quotations are introduced by γέγραπται γάρ or καθώς γέγραπται, etc. (2 Cor. vi. 16, 17; Rom. ix. 15; 2 Cor. vi. 2; Gal. iii. 16), those of this Epistle are introduced by "God" or "the Holy Ghost" (iii. 7; x. 15) "saith" or "witnesseth" (Heb. ii. 6; vii. 17; x. 15). (5) He holds more closely to the LXX. and the readings now found in *Cod. Alexandrinus*, whereas St. Paul follows those now found in *Cod. Vaticanus* (Bleek).

Law, as the central point of his treatment, the writer showed his deep knowledge of Jewish feeling. Not only do the regulations respecting worship occupy the greater part of the Book of Leviticus, but, as we shall see further, the imagination of the people had almost concentrated itself upon priestly functions, and especially upon the Great Day of Atonement. A glance at the Talmud will show how large a part Priesthood occupied in the thoughts of every Jew. Thus we are told of the priests that their descent from Aaron was the badge of exclusive privilege;[1] that in the faithful days of the first Temple each High Priest enjoyed an average of 23 years of office;[2] that when he was admitted to service he was inspected by the Sanhedrin, and if there was so much as a mole on his body he was dressed in black and dismissed;[3] that even if priests were unworthy, no one was to think evil of them;[4] that if a priest was found to be Levitically unclean while performing the Temple service, his juniors might at once drag him out of the Temple and brain him with clubs.[5] The very garments of the priests were not only used to make wicks for the great candlestick,[6] but were regarded as so holy that they had the faculty of atoning for sin—the tunic for murder, the ephod for idolatry, the girdle for evil thoughts.[7] One passage will still further show their estimation: "So long," says the tract Gittin,[8] commenting on Ezek. xxi. 26, "as there is a diadem on the head of a priest, there is a crown on the head of every man. Remove the diadem from the head of the high-priest, and you take away the crown from the head of all the people."

(6.) There is yet another point on which we may seize as marking the difference between the writer and St. Paul. It is perhaps an accident that he uses a phrase—"to Him *that made Him*" (iii. 2)[9]—which, though capable of perfectly simple explanation, yet lent itself with so much facility to the misinterpretations of heresy that it acted as one of the causes which delayed the general acceptance of the Epistle by the Church. But it is no accident that the writer in three passages (vi. 4 —8; x. 26—31; xii. 16, 17) uses language of such unconditional sternness that it was seized upon with avidity by those who held the uncompromising tenets of the Montanists and Novatians. No such passages are to be found in St. Paul's Epistles. The fulness of almost universal hope which marks the outbursts of emotional eloquence in his epistles, shows that such language could hardly have been used by him without large qualification. It is true, as I have shown in dealing with those passages, that they lend no real sanction to the conclusions which have been built upon them; and that, if they did, they would stand in

---

[1] Berachoth, f. 29, a.
[2] Yoma, f. 9, a.
[3] Yoma, f. 19, a.
[4] Kiddushin, f. 70, b.
[5] Sanhedrin, f. 81, b.
[6] Shabbath, f. 21, a.
[7] Zevachim, f. 88, b.
[8] Fol. 7, a. These and other passages are quoted in Mr. Hershon's *Talmudic Miscellany*, p. 107.
[9] See the note on this passage.

flagrant contradiction to other passages of Scripture. I believe that the real thoughts of the writer would have coincided with those of St. Paul; but the use of language which lends itself to perversion with so much facility is yet another mark that his idiosyncrasy differs from that of the great Apostle.

If, then, there be these marked differences between the aspect of the same great Christian verities as viewed from the standpoint of St. Paul's individuality and that of the writer of this Epistle, it is idle to pretend any longer that St. Paul was the author. The differences are there. No one can any longer overlook them. And if the differences are there, it is clear that the ancient guesses about an amanuensis who used the thoughts of St. Paul, but expressed them in his own language, fall to the ground.[1] We are, therefore, studying the work of another writer of the Apostolic age, who thought for himself, and who wrote in his own manner. The inspiration of the Holy Spirit was not a mechanical dictation, which makes a man the pen rather than the penman of sacred utterance, and obliterates the plainest landmarks of human idiosyncrasy. It is a positive gain to us that we have here the treatise of a great follower of the Pauline school of thought—a school which was so completely overshadowed by the mighty genius of the Apostle of the Gentiles that it scarcely produced a single other writer of remarkable eminence.[2]

CHAPTER XVII.

WHO WROTE THE EPISTLE TO THE HEBREWS?

"Auctor Epistolae ad Hebraeos quisquis est, sive Paulus sive *ut ego arbitror* Apollo."—LUTHER, *ad Gen.* xlviii. 20.

"Quis porro eam composuerit non magnopere curandum est. . . Sed ipsa dicendi ratio et stilus alium quam Paulum esse satis testantur."—CALVIN.

IF the author—and by author I do not mean merely the amanuensis, but the actual originator of this Epistle—were not St. Paul, who was it? I have already indicated my belief that it was Apollos, and it is now necessary to furnish the grounds, both positive and negative, for that all but certain conclusion.

The author does not adopt the invariable practice of St. Paul by

[1] Schwegler supposes that the writer tried to pass for Paul (*Nachap. Zeit.* ii. 304), and was amply refuted by Köstlin, *Theol. Jahrb.* 1853, p. 420; 1854, p. 437.
[2] The notion of Hase, that the Epistle is by a Nazarene heretic and addressed to Nazarenes, though partially favoured by Ritschl (*Altkathol. Kirche* (second edition), p. 159), needs no further notice (see Hilgenfeld, *Einleit.* 359). Every sober enquirer now acquiesces in the opinion that the Epistle represents Pauline views, but coloured by Alexandrian influences, and leaning to the Jewish-Christian standpoint, so far as this was possible to any follower of St. Paul. (See Baur, *Three Christian Cent.* i. 115, seqq.)

beginning his Epistle with a greeting in his own name, although it is clear that he meant his readers to know, both from the Epistle itself and through the bearer of it, who he was; nor is his treatise full of that rich element of personality which lends to St. Paul's Epistles so indefinable a charm. But yet, from the Epistle itself we see certain broad facts.

(1.) The writer was a Jew, for he writes as though Heathendom were practically non-existent.

(2.) He was a Hellenist, for he exclusively quotes the Septuagint version, even where it diverges from the original Hebrew.[1]

(3.) He had been subjected to Alexandrian training, for he shows a deep impress of Alexandrian thought, and quotes from Alexandrian manuscripts of the Septuagint, without pausing to question the accuracy of the renderings.[2]

(4.) He was a man of great eloquence, of marked originality, of wide knowledge of the Scriptures, and of remarkable gifts in the application of Scripture arguments.

(5.) He was a friend of Timotheus, for he proposes to visit the Jewish Churches in his company.

(6.) He was known to his readers, and writes to them in a tone of authority.

(7.) He was not an Apostle, for he classes himself with those who had been taught by the Apostles.[3]

(8.) The Apostle by whom he had been taught was St. Paul, for he largely, though independently, adopts his phraseology, and makes special use of the Epistle to the Romans.[4]

(9.) He wrote before the destruction of Jerusalem, and while the Temple services were still continuing.

(10.) It is doubtful whether he had ever been at Jerusalem, for his references to the Temple and its ritual seem to apply, not, indeed, to the Temple of Onias, at Leontopolis,[5] but mainly to the Tabernacle as described in the Septuagint version of the Pentateuch.

Further than this we have no data[6] on which to decide the question

---

[1] In one remarkable passage (x. 30) he follows St. Paul (Rom. xii. 19) in a variant quotation of Deut. xxxii. 35.

[2] See Bleek, i. 357, and Heb. ii. 3; Köstlin, *Theol. Jahrb.* 1853.

[3] Heb. ii. 3. Any one who chooses to explain away the obvious meaning of this verse in the interests of the Pauline authorship, by talking of "*anakoinosis*" or "*sunkatabasis*," must do so. But those technical words are here inapplicable, and the supposed parallels too illusory to need refutation. Serious readers will see how impossible it is that such a phrase should have been used (and that to Jewish readers!) by one who had written such passages as Gal. i. 1, 12; 2 Cor. xi. 24, xii. 12; Eph. iii. 2, 3, etc.

[4] *V. infra*, p. 190.

[5] See Wieseler, *Untersuchung über d. Hebr.* A great deal too much has been made of the suggestion. Philo only recognised *one πατρῷον ἱερόν*, and the Jews of Egypt never dreamt of looking on the Temple of Onias in the same light as the Samaritans looked on Mount Gerizim, namely, as a rival shrine to the one Temple, to which they sent their yearly offerings. The conjecture of Wieseler ought, therefore, to be finally dismissed. See the decisive remarks of Grätz, *Gesch. d. Juden*, iii. 31—34, 412.

[6] The allusion in x. 34 has no bearing on the authorship.

of his identity: but we may fairly assume that we should find in the New Testament the name of any friend and companion of St. Paul of sufficient authority, learning, and genius, to have been the author of so remarkable an Epistle. Now, the only known companions of St. Paul who would in any way fall under this description were Aquila, Silas, Titus, Barnabas, Clement, Mark, Luke, and Apollos,[1] and accordingly several of these were conjecturally designated as the authors, or part authors, in ancient days. Assuming, as we are entitled to do, that it was one of these, the only way to decide between them will be by a process of elimination.

The claims of some of them may be dismissed at once.

1. AQUILA, for instance, could not have been the author; for the fact that he is constantly mentioned with his wife, and even after her, shows that his personality must have been somewhat insignificant,[2] and that his wife was superior to him in energy.

2. TITUS could not have been the author, for he was a Gentile.

3. There is nothing to be said in favour of the authorship of SILAS,[3] especially as he seems to have been not a Hellenist, but a Jew of Jerusalem.

4. Tertullian, in his usual oracular way, attributes the Epistle to BARNABAS, but he seems to have done so by an unsupported conjecture.[4] The Epistle is incomparably superior to the Epistle of Barnabas, with its exaggerated Paulinism; but that Epistle is not by the Barnabas of the New Testament, and is not earlier in date than A.D. 110.[5] The "Apostle" Barnabas, as a Levite, would more probably have described the Temple at Jerusalem *as it then was*, and if he had possessed the natural ability to compose such a treatise as this, he would not have been so immediately thrown into the shade by St. Paul from the very beginning of his first missionary journey.[6] His claims have received but little support, and he would have been indeed unfortunate if a false

---

[1] Timotheus is, of course, excluded by xiii. 23.
[2] Acts xviii. 18; Rom. xvi. 3; 2 Tim. iv. 19.
[3] Only held by Böhme and Mynster. The former supposed that the Greek of 1 Peter was also by Silvanus, and that it resembled the Greek of this Epistle.
[4] Tert. *De pudicit.* 20: "Exstat enim et Barnabae titulus ad Hebraeos." Perhaps he had heard of an "Epistle of Barnabas," and confused this letter with it. The claims of Barnabas are maintained by Camerarius, Twesten, Ullmann (*Stud. u. Krit.* 828), Thiersch (*Comment. Hist. de Ep. ad Hebr.* 1847)—who, however, thinks that the Epilogue was by St. Paul—and Wieseler (*Chronol.* p. 504, and *Untersuchung über den Hebräerbrief*, 1861). Wieseler speaks of Tertullian's assertion as the only authentic tradition on the subject. His arguments about the position of the Epistle in the Peshito, etc., seem to me to be very inconclusive. Thiersch supposes that the Epilogue may have been written by St. Paul, and so too Delitzsch (arguing from xiii. 8). Renan also inclines in favour of Barnabas (*L'Antechrist*, p. xvii.). In the Clementine Homilies (i. 9), Barnabas (and not St. Mark) appears as the founder of the Church of Alexandria.
[5] See Harnack, in Herzog, *s. v.* Barnabas, and the article by Heberle in the old edition. Hefele also (*Patr. Apost.*) has shown how impossible it would have been for the *Apostle* Barnabas to see in the Jewish ceremonies mere foolish carnal mistakes about things which God had intended to be understood spiritually.
[6] Bp. Wordsworth (*Introd.* p. 362) adds that Epiphanius, as a Cyprian Bishop, might have been supposed to know the work of a fellow-Cypriot.

Epistle was attributed to him, and his real Epistle, which was so far superior, assigned to another.

5. St. Clement's claims, though mentioned by several of the Fathers,[1] may be set aside, because we have one genuine Epistle from his hands, and—independently of differences of view—that letter is sufficient to show that he had not the capacity to write the Epistle to the Hebrews. Besides this he quotes from the Epistle to the Hebrews as though it were of co-ordinate authority to the rest of Holy Scripture, which he certainly could not have done in the case of any writing of his own.[2]

6. St. Mark has never been seriously suggested as the possible author, because his Gospel presents no points of analogy to this Epistle either in style or sentiment. Further than this, it is probable that he also was a Jew of Jerusalem, and his connexion with St. Peter was closer and more permanent than his connexion with St. Paul.

7. St. Luke, though often suggested as the *scribe* of the letter[3]—on the hypothesis that the *thoughts* came directly from St. Paul—could not possibly have been the author. It is true that in the Gospel and the Acts we frequently find words and idioms which occur in this Epistle.[4] That is a phenomenon which is not difficult to explain in the case of two writers who had passed through the same kind of training, and had lived, perhaps, in each other's company, and certainly in close contact with the mind and teaching of St. Paul. But in spite of these resemblances the style and the tone of the Epistle to the Hebrews differ essentially from those of St. Luke. Balanced rhetoric and majestic periods are nowhere found in the writings of the Evangelist, and it is psychologically difficult to believe that a writer whose prevailing tone of mind was tender and conciliatory should have written passages of such uncompromising sternness as those which occur in Hebrews vi. 4—8; x. 26; xii. 27. In these passages the sternest Montanists exulted, and they were used as bulwarks of the Novatians in their refusal to re-admit the lapsed to Baptism or the Lord's Supper; but they have always raised a difficulty

---

[1] *E.g.*, Origen (τ. *infra*, Excurs. VIII.), Euthalius, Eusebius (*H. E.* iii. 18), and Jerome. The view is accepted as probable by Erasmus and Calvin. Almost the only modern writer who maintains this view is Riethmayer (*Einleit.* p. 681).

[2] It is strange that Euthalius (A.D. 460) should say τοῦ γὰρ καὶ σώζει τὸν χαρακτῆρα, though it is true enough that many of the sentiments resemble each other (μὴ πόρρω τὰ ἐν ἑκατέροις τοῖς συγγράμμασι νοήματα καθεστάναι, Euseb. *H. E.* iii. 38). But the resemblance is merely due to direct plagiarism, while the difference in strength and originality is immeasurable.

[3] Clemens Alex., Origen, Grotius, Hug, Stier, Guerike, F. Delitzsch, Ebrard, Bisping, Wieseler, Renan.

[4] Clemens Alex. observes on the general resemblance of style (τὸν αὐτὸν χρῶτα) between the Epistle and the Acts. The parallels are tabulated by Lünemann in his edition of the Epistle, and are constantly referred to by Delitzsch and Ebrard. Among them are εὐλαβεῖσθαι, εἰς τὸ παντελές, ἡγούμενος, ἀρχηγός (used of Christ, Acts iii. 15, v. 31; Heb. ii. 10, xii. 2), μαρτυρούμενος, παροξυσμός, μέτοχος. They are, however, of no decisive importance. See Richm. *Lehrbegriff*, p. 886, note. Moreover, St. Luke more closely followed St. Paul's theological views and expressions (ἡ εἰς Χριστὸν πίστις, δικαιοῦσθαι ἐξ Ἰησοῦ, etc., Acts xiii. 39; Luke xviii. 14) than this writer does. See *supra*, cap. xvi.

in the minds of those who reject the ruthless dogma that there is no forgiveness for post-baptismal sin.[1] Apart from these considerations, it appears to be almost certain that St. Luke was a Gentile Christian,[2] and there is much ground for the tradition which describes him as a Proselyte of Antioch. He could not, therefore, have written this Epistle. It may be regarded as an axiom that it could not have been written by any one of Gentile birth.

8. If, then, the writer was neither St. Paul nor any of these, we are led by the exhaustive process to consider the claims of APOLLOS, and we at once find not only that none of those objections can be urged against him which are fatal to the claims of the others, but also that he meets in every one of the ten particulars the requirements of the problem. He was a Jew; he was a Hellenist; he was an Alexandrian; he was a friend of St. Paul and had been deeply influenced by his teaching; he could not have been specially familiar with the Temple ritual; he was remarkable for originality; he was an attractive orator; he was a powerful reasoner; he was a man of great personal authority; he taught with so much independence, that St. Paul formally recognised his gift of maturing and preserving the germs of truth which he himself had sown.[3] Had St. Paul and St. Luke deliberately designed to point out a man capable of writing the Epistle to the Hebrews, they could not have chosen any words more suitable to such an object than those by which they actually describe him as a Jew, an Alexandrian by birth, an eloquent man, and mighty in the Scriptures, fervent in spirit, who, after having been carefully taught the way of the Lord, "began to teach accurately the things concerning the Lord," and powerfully confuted the Jews out of the Scriptures.[4] Even in minor matters we trace the same congruence between Apollos and the writer of this Epistle. We are told that he was originally acquainted only with the baptism of John, and this writer places the "doctrine of baptisms" among the rudiments of Christian teaching.[5] We are told that "he began to speak with confident boldness in the Synagogue," and this writer has a high estimate of confident boldness as a virtue which the Christian should always retain.[6] Lastly, we see in Apollos the rare combination of a dislike of prominence with a remarkable power of oratory. This is exemplified in his refusal of the invitation of the Corinthians, some of whom so greatly admired his culture and oratory that they preferred his teaching even to that

---

[1] Even the Novatians did not exclude the hope that God would forgive post-baptismal sins. Acesius, a Novatian bishop, said that "those who had sinned a sin unto death" could not be indeed admitted to the Christian mysteries, ἐλπίδα δὲ τῆς ἀφέσεως ... παρὰ τοῦ Θεοῦ ἐκδέχεσθαι (at the Council of Nice; Socr. *H. E.* i. 10).
[2] Col. iv. 11—15. See my *Life of St. Paul*, i. 480.
[3] Some of these peculiarities in the mind and manner of Apollos are illustrated by the allusions to the partisans who used his name in Corinth (1 Cor. iii.).
[4] Acts xviii. 24—28, xix. 1; 1 Cor. iii. 4—6.
[5] Acts xviii. 26; Heb. vi. 2.
[6] παρρησιάζεσθαι, Acts xviii. 26; τὴν παρρησίαν, x. 35; iii. 6.

of St. Paul. In that generous refusal he displayed the very feeling which would have induced him to suppress all personal references, even when his readers were perfectly well acquainted with the name and antecedents of him who was addressing them.

It is stated as an insuperable objection to this theory that the Church of Alexandria retained no tradition that this Epistle was written by their brilliant fellow-countryman. But although Apollos was an Alexandrian by birth and by training, it does not follow that he had lived in his native city,[1] and as he had left the city before he became a Christian, he may have been a stranger to the Alexandrian Christians. We do not hear a word about the Epistle in that Church until a century after it was written. At any rate, this difficulty is not so great as that which arises from the supposition that the Epistle was the work of St. Paul, and yet was not recognised as such for some centuries by the Western Church, and only partially and hesitatingly by the Eastern Church.[2] For there would be every temptation to attribute the work to the Apostle, and none to associate it with the name of Apollos, which, except in one or two Churches, seems to have been but little known.[3]

It is not a decisive objection to the Apollonian authorship that no one is known to have suggested it before Luther. We have seen that in the early centuries the Epistle was only assigned to this or that author by a process of tentative guesswork. Those who saw that St. Paul could not have been the actual author often adopted one of the arbitrary hypotheses, that it is a translation, or that the sentiments and the language were supplied by different persons. The self-suppression of Apollos resulted in the comparative obscurity of his work, and the Fathers, having nothing but conjecture to deal with, fixed upon names every one of which was more generally familiar than that of the eloquent Alexandrian. And if it be strange that the name of Apollos should not have been preserved by the Church to which the letter was despatched, we may account for this by the absence of superscription, and by the fact that it was only addressed to the Jewish section of that Church. This much may be said with certainty, that if it were not written by Apollos, at any rate the evidence which points to him as its author is more various and more conclusive than that which can be adduced to support the claims of any one else. It is a greater

---

[1] The reading of D (the *Codex Bezae*) in Acts xviii. 24 (ἐν τῇ πατρίδι) may be a mere conjecture.
[2] The last paragraphs are more in the style of St. Paul than any of the rest; and even in modern times this has led Thiersch and others into the opinion that, though the body of the Epistle was not written by him, yet he adopted it as his own, and wrote the last chapter with his own hand. The suggestion is untenable, but the superficial grounds on which it rests were sufficient to lead many, in uncritical days, to assume that the whole Epistle was written by the great Apostle of the Gentiles.
[3] The passages on which we can alone depend for our knowledge of Apollos are Acts xviii. 24—28; 1 Cor. iii. 4—6; xvi. 12 (comp. Rom. xvi. 3; 2 Tim. iv. 19); Tit. iii. 13.

testimony in his favour that his name, when once suggested by a flash of happy intuition, should have been accepted, with more or less confidence, by an ever-increasing number of trained and careful critics of all schools,[1] than that it should not have occurred to the less laborious and penetrating examination of writers in the early centuries. To suppose that even an Origen or a Jerome—much less an Augustine—subjected the Epistle to that minute comparative study, word by word and line by line, which it has since received from writers like Bleek and Tholuck, and in its theological aspect from Delitzsch, Riehm, Ebrard, Reuss, and Pfleiderer, is to ignore facts. The decision of the future will be that it was either written by Apollos or by some writer who is to us entirely unknown.

As to the date of the Epistle, our only clue is furnished by the certainty that it was written before the destruction of Jerusalem in A.D. 70, and by the allusion to the liberation of Timotheus.[2] Had it been written after the fall of Jerusalem, the arguments of the writer might have been stated with tenfold force. The author of the Epistle of Barnabas, for instance (4, 16), is able to treat very differently a similar line of reasoning. The destruction of Jerusalem came like a Divine comment on all the truths which are here set forth. It is no answer to this difficulty that Josephus,[3] the Mishna, the Gemara, the Epistles of Barnabas,[4] and Clement,[5] and Justin Martyr,[6] continue to speak of the Temple worship in the present tense after the City and Temple had been destroyed.[7] In the Epistle to the Hebrews we are dealing not with a figure of speech,[8] but with the structure of an argument. A writer who could argue as in Heb. x. 2, without adding the tremendous corroboration which his views had received from the Divine sanction of History, could not have written the Epistle at all.

The allusion to Timothy is too vague to admit of any certain conclusion being founded upon it. It is probable that Timothy obeyed the summons to come immediately to Rome which he had received from St. Paul,[9] and that in the then exacerbation of the imperial government against the Christians he so far shared in the peril of the great Apostle as to have been thrown into a prison. He may have been subsequently set free because of the harmlessness of his character and the lack of evidence against him. If so, this Epistle must have been written soon after the year of St. Paul's death, at the end of A.D. 67, or the beginning of A.D. 68. This date suits well

---

[1] Luther, Osiander, Le Clerc, Heumann, L. Müller, Semler, Ziegler, Dindorf, Bleek, Tholuck, Credner, Reuss, Rothe, Feilmoser, Lutterbeck, Guerike, De Wette, Lünemann, Alford, Kurz, Davidson, Plumptre, Moulton. A few writers—*e.g.*, R. Köstlin, Moll, Ewald, Riehm—think that the name of the author is undiscoverable.
[2] Heb. xiii. 23.   [3] Jos. *Antt.* vii. 6, §§ 7—12; *c. Apion*, i. 7; ii. 8, 23.
[4] *Ep. Barnab.* 7.   [5] Clemens Rom. i. 40.   [6] *Dial. c. Tryph.* 107.
[7] This argument is used by Keim (*Jesu von Nazara*, i. 148, 636), who, with Volkmar (*Rel. Jesu*, 388) and Holtzmann (in Schenkel's *Bibellexicon*), tries to bring down the date of the Epistle to the persecution of Domitian.
[8] See Hilgenfeld, *Einleit.* 381.   [9] 2 Tim. iv. 9, 21.

with the allusions which indicate that the first generation of Christians had already passed, or was rapidly passing, away.

It was addressed to Jewish Christians exclusively—to Jews by birth, who, though they had been converted,[1] were in imminent danger of apostasy, and who had been subjected to persecution, which was not, however, so severe as to have led to many martyrdoms.[2] If we could assume that the last four verses were a special postscript to some particular Church, it might be supposed that the letter was rather intended as a treatise in which Jews were addressed in the abstract;[3] but even then it must have been sent in the first instance to at least one Church.

i. That this was not the Church of Jerusalem[4] is all but certain. It is true that the Mother Church might have been specially interested by all that the writer says; but the saints of Jerusalem would have been hardly likely to welcome a letter from a Hellenist, which only quoted from the Septuagint, and which was written in Greek. Moreover, it cannot be said of them, in any ordinary sense, that "they had not yet resisted unto blood;" nor were they in a position to minister to the saints,[5] being themselves overwhelmed in the deepest poverty; nor would it be likely that no allusion should have been made to the fact that some of them must have actually heard the words and witnessed the sufferings of Christ; nor would any of St. Paul's companions have been entitled to address them in the tone of authority which the writer adopts; nor were the Christians of Palestine specially interested in Timothy. A Paulinist in the position of Apollos could not have ventured to reproach the Church of the earliest saints in such words of severe and authoritative rebuke for their ignorance and childishness as occur in Heb. v. 11—14. This passage is alone sufficient to show the unlikelihood that the "Hebrews" addressed are the Palestinian Christians.[6]

ii. CORINTH, which would otherwise be naturally conjectured, is

---

[1] Heb. ii. 3, 4; iv. 14; v. 11; vi. 1; viii. 1; x. 19, etc. Comp. Acts vi. 1. Hase supposes that it was addressed to a group of Palestinian Nazarites; Stuart, that it was written by St. Paul to Cæsarea; Boehme, that it was sent to Antioch.

[2] Wieseler (*Untersuchung*, ii. 3, *seq.*) has conclusively proved that the term "Hebrews" need not be confined to Palestinian Jews. (See 2 Cor. xi. 22; Phil. iii. 5.) Josephus originally wrote his "Jewish War" in Aramaic, yet he tells us it was meant for Jews all over Asia (see Tholuck, *Hebr.* p. 97). Moreover, it is far from certain that the superscription πρὸς Ἐβραίους is genuine. From the Muratorian Canon we might suppose that in another inscription it was called "to the Alexandrians."

[3] So Euthalius thought: πᾶσι τοῖς ἐκ περιτομῆς πιστεύσασιν Ἐβραίοις. Delitzsch is therefore mistaken when he says that it was the *unanimous* ancient opinion that it was addressed to Judæa.

[4] τοῦ δὲ οὖσιν ἐπιστέλλειν; ἐμοὶ δοκεῖ ἐν Ἱεροσολύμοις καὶ Παλαιστίνῃ, Chrysost. *Prooem in Hebr.*; and so, too, Theodoret. This is the view of Bleek, De Wette, Tholuck, Thiersch, Delitzsch, Lünemann, Riehm, Ebrard, Lange; but the notion is being readily abandoned. It sprang from the Greek Fathers, and it is a mistake to suppose that it is necessitated by the title "the saints" (1 Cor. vi. 1; 2 Cor. i. 1; viii. 4, &c.).

[5] Heb. vi. 10.

[6] Ebrard supposes that it was meant for Christian neophytes at Jerusalem, who were rendered anxious by being excluded from the Temple worship.

excluded by the allusion (ii. 3) which points to a Church founded by one of the original Twelve Apostles.

iii. ALEXANDRIA[1] would have seemed probable, and has in its favour the dubious allusion of the Muratorian Canon; but Timothy had no relations with Alexandria, and (which is a far more serious objection) it is unlikely that a Church like that of Alexandria would have forgotten the authorship of a letter by one of their own countrymen, if it had been in the first instance addressed to them.[2]

iv. If our conjecture about Timothy's imprisonment be correct, it could not have been addressed to ROME, which otherwise has many considerations in its favour.[3] It was well known to St. Clemens of Rome, and some of the allusions of the Epistle might suit the Neronian persecution. On the other hand, the tortures spoken of are somewhat distant in time (τὰς πρότερον ἡμέρας, x. 32), and the Roman Church more than any other *had* resisted unto blood.[4] We have no hint in the New Testament that Apollos ever visited Rome; and a writer addressing the Jews of that city, and familiar with the Epistle to the Romans,[5] would hardly have ignored the existence of the Gentiles. Again, although this hypothesis would indeed account for the conviction of the Roman Church that the Epistle was not written by St. Paul, it would be difficult to explain why Clement, who knew the Epistle—and who, if it had been sent to the Roman Church, must from the nature of the case have known the name of the writer—handed down no tradition on the subject. If we must single out one Church as the probable recipient of the letter, it would be the Jewish portion of the Church of EPHESUS, where both Apollos and Timotheus were well known, and in which they had both laboured.

---

[1] Heb. ii. 3. See Dean Plumptre's argument in the *Expositor*, i. 428—432, that it is addressed to Christian ascetics connected with Alexandria. The notion that it was addressed to Alexandria is adopted by Schmidt, Bleek, Credner, Volkmar, Köstlin, Bunsen (*Hippolytus*, i. 365), Hilgenfeld, Ullmann, Schleiermacher, and Wieseler (*Chron.* 496).

[2] Schleiermacher, *Einleit.* 445; Ad. Maier, *Hebr.* 4. If ἐν τῇ πατρίδι, the reading of D in Acts xviii. 25, is correct, Apollos had been converted in Alexandria. Hilgenfeld (*Einleit.* 357) gets over the difficulty by supposing that it may have been addressed as a *private* letter to one *section* of the Church.

[3] It was suggested by Wetstein (*N. T.* ii. 386), and supported at length by Holzmann (Bunsen's *Bibelwerk*, viii. 432; *Stud. u. Krit.* 1859), Kurtz, Renan, and Alford (*Introd. to Hebrews*). It is the view of Eichhorn, Schulz, Baur, Holtzmann, &c. Ewald thinks it may have been written to—Ravenna! Wilibald Grimm fixes on Jamnia; Hofmann on the Jewish section of the Church at Antioch.

[4] This expression must surely refer to martyrdom (since αἷμα is used so often of the Blood of Christ, Eph. ii. 13; Rev. vi. 10, &c.), as μέχρις θανάτου does. 2 Macc. xiii. 14; Phil. ii. 8. The context also points to this meaning, and not to a pugilistic metaphor. It cannot be regarded as certain that ἐκβάσιν in xiii. 7 means martyrdom.

[5] The following are some of the parallels between the Epistle to the Hebrews and that to the Romans:—

Rom. xii. 1—21.	Heb. xiii. 1—6; x. 30.
xiv. 7.	xiii. 9.
xv. 33.	xiii. 20.

In Heb. x. 30 there is a quotation which agrees neither with the Hebrew nor the LXX, of Deut. xxxii. 35, but is also found in Rom. xii. 19, ἐμοὶ ἐκδίκησις, ἐγὼ ἀνταποδώσω.

The place *from* which the Epistle was written can only be a matter of guess, since there is nothing to indicate it, and least of all the expression "they of Italy" in xiii. 24. That clause, as we shall see, is quite vague. It may equally well imply that the Epistle was written in Italy, or in any Church in which there happened to be a few Italian Christians.

We hear of Apollos for the last time in the Epistle to Titus (iii. 13), where we find that he was expected in Crete during the course of some missionary journey. At that point he disappears from Christian history; but he will, as we believe, speak to the Church to the end of time in the eloquent teachings of the Epistle to the Hebrews.

CHAPTER XVIII.

THE EPISTLE TO THE HEBREWS.

" . . . Nihil interesse cujus sit, cum ecclesiastici viri sit, et quotidie, ecclesiarum lectione celebretur."—JER. *Ep.* 129, *ad Dardanum.*

"Das ist eine starke, mächtige, und höhe Epistel."—LUTHER.

"Of this ye see that the Epistle ought no more to be refused for a holy, godly, and catholic than the other authentic Scriptures."—TYNDALE.

SECTION I.

THE SUPERIORITY OF CHRIST.

" Christus vincit, Christus regnat, Christus imperat."—*Inscription on Obelisk at Rome.*

HAVING now examined all that can be ascertained respecting the author of the Epistle, and the circumstances in which it originated, we are more in a position to follow the outline of its teachings. The writer's main object was to prevent the Jewish Christians from apostatising under the stress of persecution, by convincing them that they would find in the finality and transcendence of the Christian Faith a means of perfection and a path of blessedness which the shadow of their old ceremonial Judaism could never afford. This end he achieves by a comparison between Christianity and Judaism under the double aspect of (1) the *Mediators* between God and man, by whom they were respectively represented, and (2) the *nature of the blessings* which they were calculated to impart.

Of those five familiar divisions—greeting, thanksgiving, didactic nucleus, resultant moral application, final salutations and benedictions —which constitute the normal structure of the Epistles of St. Paul, the first two are entirely wanting. The writer begins with the statement of his thesis, that God has given to the world by His Son the complete and final revelation of His will. Christians were taunted by Jews as apostates from Jehovah and renegades from Moses, who had abandoned the Law which had been delivered by the mediation of Angels, and had proved faithless to the Aaronic priesthood; they were told that by accepting as their Messiah a crucified malefactor they had forfeited all the blessings and promises of the Old Covenant. It is the object of the writer, FIRST, to convince them, with many an interwoven warning, that, on the contrary, Christ, as the Son of God, is above *all* mediators and *all* priests, and the sole means of perfect and confident access for all men to the Holy Sanctuary of God's Presence. He therefore proves that Christ is ABOVE ANGELS,[1] and that this supremacy was in no sense weakened by His earthly humiliation, which was the voluntary and predestined necessity whereby alone He could have effected His redeeming work; that He is ABOVE MOSES by His very nature; ABOVE JOSHUA, because He leads His people into their true and final rest; like Aaron in being called of God and in being able to sympathise with men, but ABOVE AARON, first because His Priesthood is eternal and not hereditary, and next because He is personally sinless, and thirdly because His Priesthood was established by an oath, and most of all because of the incomparable benefits resulting from it. He is only to be paralleled by the mysterious MELCHIZEDEK, the kingly Prince of Peace, anterior and superior to Aaron, springing from another tribe than that of Levi, and belonging to an earlier and loftier dispensation than that of Sinai. He is at once the unchangeable Priest and the sinless sacrifice. And this change of Priesthood involves a change of the Law, and the introduction of a New Covenant, and an entrance into the true archetypal sanctuary which God made and not man.

Having thus in the first eight chapters shown the superiority of Christ to all those to whom was entrusted the dispensation of the Mosaic Covenant, he proceeds, SECONDLY, in the ninth and tenth chapters, to show the vast superiority of this New Covenant as the fulfilling of the shadowy types and symbols of the Mosaic Tabernacle, and as having rendered possible—not by the impotence of repeated animal sacrifices, but by the blood of Christ once offered—a perfect purification from sin. Under the New Covenant as under the Old there is sin and the need of expiation, and therefore in the New Covenant as in the Old there is a Temple, a Sacrifice, and a High Priest—only that these are not temporary, but eternal; not human, but Divine.[2]

On the basis of this double comparison of the two covenants as regards their *agents* and their *results* he passes, (1) into exhortations to confidence and steadfastness in that faith of which he records the many memorable triumphs; (2) into warnings against the awful peril of apostasy and

---

[1] "Messiah is greater than the Patriarchs, Moses and the Ministering Angels."—*Yalkut Chadash*, f. 144, b (Schöttgen). I am also referred to *Yalkut Shimoni*, pt. 2, f. 53, 3: "He shall be exalted above Abraham and shall be extolled above Moses, and shall be more sublime than the Ministering Angels."

[2] See Reuss, *Théol. Chrét.* ii. 274.

willing sin; and (3) into practical inculcations of duties both general and special, ending with a few brief personal messages, and a single word of benediction.

The keynotes of the Epistle are the phrases, "BY HOW MUCH MORE" (ὅσῳ μᾶλλον), and "A BETTER COVENANT" (κρείττων διαθήκη).

In one grand sentence, eminently original in its expressions, and pregnant with thoughts which would be capable of almost indefinite expansion, the writer states the thesis on which he intends to base his warnings against the peril and folly of retrogression into an imperfect and abrogated dispensation.

"God, who in many portions[1] and in many manners[2] of old[3] spake to the fathers in the prophets[4] at the end of these days[5] spake unto us in His Son, whom He appointed Heir of all things, by whom also He made the world;[6] who being the effulgence[7] of His glory, and the stamp of His substance,[8] and sustaining all things by the utterance of His power,[9] after making purification of sins,[10] sat on the right hand of the Majesty in high places,[11] having proved Himself by so much better than the angels as He hath inherited a more excellent name than they."[12]

In this powerful Introduction, of which the opening words alone are a marvellously instructive summary of the religious history of the world before Christ,[13] it declares the dawn of the last æon of God's earthly dispensations, by setting forth the supremacy of the Son of God over all created things, and the finality of His redemptive work. Apart from the stateliness and artistic balance of the language, we find in these three verses no less than *six* expressions which occur only in this Epistle,[14] and at least *nine* constructions[15] which, even when not rare in

---

[1] Not giving at once a final and perfect revelation, but revealing Himself part by part—lifting the veil fold by fold (1 Cor. xiii. 9, ἐκ μέρους προφητεύομεν).
[2] By promises, types, sacrifices, Urim, dreams, voices, similitudes, prophets specially commissioned.
[3] Malachi, the last of the Old Testament prophets, lived B.C. 320.
[4] ἐν, like the Hebrew בְּיַד. Cf. 1 Sam. xxviii. 6; Matt. ix. 34.
[5] Compare ix. 26. A recognised Messianic expression, Dan. viii. 17; xii. 13. The "last days" date from Christ's Advent. They are the *Acharith hayamim*, the καιροὶ διορθώσεως and the συντέλεια τῶν αἰώνων. With them ends the former dispensation (the *Olam hazzeh*, the αἰὼν οὗτος), and begins the *Olam habba*, or the μέλλων αἰών. The "last days" (Jas. v. 3) are to be ended by "the last crisis" (καιρὸς ἔσχατος, 1 Pet. i. 5; 1 Tim. iv. 1), after which come "the rest" and "the sabbatism;" but the "last hour" has begun (1 John ii. 18).
[6] *Lit.* "The ages," Hebr. *Olamim*; but in this Epistle it means "the Universe," being used in its Rabbinic and post-Biblical sense. as in xi. 3, "by faith we believe κατηρτίσθαι τοὺς αἰῶνας;" v. *infra* ad loc. Cf. Tobit xiii. 6; 1 Tim. i. 17; Col. i. 5; John i. 3—10.
[7] Cf. Wisd. vii. 26. Philo, *De Mund. Opif.* i. 35. "Light of (ἐκ) Light."
[8] In Philo, *De Monarch.* ii. p. 219, the Logos is compared to a seal-ring.
[9] Col. i. 17; Eph. vi. 10. Similarly Philo calls the Logos δεσμὸς τῶν ἁπάντων.
[10] E, K, L, M, Syr., Copt., Æthiop., &c., add δι᾽ ἑαυτοῦ, "by His own act." This is in any case involved in the *middle* voice φαινόμενος. In "purification" there may be a glance at *Yom Hakkippurim*, the Day of Atonement, ἡμέρα τοῦ καθαρισμοῦ. (Ex. xxix. 36, LXX.)
[11] The old "Ubiquitarian" controversy, as to whether "the right hand of God is *everywhere*," is now as dead as hundreds of other theological controversies once waged with much dogmatic bitterness.   [12] Namely, the title of "Only-begotten Son."
[13] The paronomasia of the first words, and the general style of the sentence, ought to have been sufficient to prove, on the very threshold, that the Epistle is not a translation.
[14] Ἅπαξ λεγόμενα, as far as the New Testament is concerned. πολυμερῶς, πολυτρόπως, ἀπαύγασμα, χαρακτήρ, μεγαλωσύνη, διαφορώτερον.
[15] πάλαι, λαλήσας, ἐπ᾽ ἐσχάτου τῶν ἡμερῶν τούτων, φέρων (in this sense), καθαρισμὸν τῶν ἁμαρτιῶν, ἐν ὑψηλοῖς, τοσούτῳ . . . ὅσῳ, κρείττων (in this sense), διαφορώτερον παρά.

themselves, occur nowhere in St. Paul, together with others which occur but once in all his thirteen Epistles.

The manner in which the writer here introduces his subject is not only full of majesty, but it also goes straight to the point. In a tone which reminds us of the Christology of the Epistles to the Colossians and Ephesians he sets forth the supreme exaltation of Christ as Light *of* (i.e., *from ἐκ*) Light and very God *of* very God[1]—as the enthroned exalted Purifier from sin. He specifies particularly his superiority to ANGELS. The necessity for doing this points not so much to those seductive influences of Essene speculation against which St. Paul argues in his Epistle to the Colossians—for here there seems to be no danger of the *worship* of Angels—but rather to the Judaic boastings that their fiery Law was uttered by the mediation of Angels on Mount Sinai, and must therefore be superior to any teaching of man. The exaltation of Angels was, both at this period and long afterwards, a tendency of Jewish thought. In the fourth book of Esdras we find many speculations about the greatness of Gabriel, Uriel, Michael, Raguel, Raphael, the starry and the sleepless ones.[2] In the almost contemporary Epistle of Clemens of Rome[3] the argument is again expanded and enforced. It was necessary, therefore, to show that Christ was not a mere man whom it was idolatry to adore, but that he was above all the heavenly Principalities and Powers ; and even more than this—that men themselves, by virtue of Christ's work, were more concerned than Angels in the æon of future glory. That Jesus was the Christ and the Son of God, he does not need to prove, because he is writing to those who had accepted Him as their Messiah ; but it was necessary to show that this Messiah was Divine, and that even the angelic heralds of Sinai[4] shrank into insignificance in comparison with His eternal and final work.

This he proceeds to prove in the remainder of the chapter by that Scriptural method which was to the Jews more conclusive than any other, and with which the writings of St. Paul have already made us familiar. He does so in a mosaic of magnificent quotations from the second, the ninety-seventh, the forty-fifth, and the hundred-and-second Psalms, and from Deuteronomy and the Second Book of Samuel.

"For to which of the angels said He ever, My Son art thou ; to-day have I begotten thee ?[5] And again, I will be to him a Father, and he shall be to me a Son ?[6]

---

[1] It is strange that the great majority of clergymen, in reading the Nicene Creed, should still say, "God of God, Light of Light"—which is surely quite meaningless—instead of "God *of* God, Light *of* Light."
[2] See *Supernat. Relig.* i, 93.
[3] Clem. *ad Cor.* 36.
[4] Apollos gives no sanction to Philo's distinction that the Ten Commandments were uttered by the immediate voice of God, and the rest of the Law by angels.
[5] Ps. ii. 7; on its Messianic interpretation compare Rom. i. 4; Acts xiii. 3. Kimchi and Rashi testify to this being the ancient view. The whole clause must be taken together, for angels are called sons in Job i. 6; Dan. iii. 25; and in LXX. (A) Ps. xxix. 1; Deut. xiv. 1, etc. "To-day"—a part of "God's Eternal now."
[6] 2 Sam. vii. 14; Philo, *Legg. Allegg.* iii. 8. The allusion is perhaps to the Incarnation.

CHRIST ABOVE ANGELS.

And when He, again,[1] bringeth the firstborn into the habitable world, He saith, And let all the Angels of God worship Him.[2] And of the Angels He saith, Who maketh His Angels winds, and His ministers a flame of fire;[3] but to the Son, thy throne, O God,[4] is for ever and ever. And the sceptre of rectitude is the sceptre of thy[5] kingdom. Thou lovedst righteousness, and hatedst lawlessness; therefore did God, thy God, anoint thee with the oil of exultation above thy fellows.[6] And thou, O Lord, in the beginning didst found the earth, and the heavens are the work of thy hands. They shall perish, but thou remainest. And they all shall wax old as doth a garment, and as a mantle shalt thou roll them up,[7] and they shall be changed; but thou art the same, and thy years shall not fail.[8] But to which of the angels has He said at any time, Sit at My right hand until I make thine enemies a footstool of thy feet?[9] Are they not all ministrant spirits,[10] sent forth for service for the sake of those who are about to inherit salvation?"[11]

This mode of argument, by Scriptural quotation, has been made a needless stumbling-block, on the ground that some of the passages here adduced in proof of Christ's exaltation were originally addressed to David and Solomon, and had a directly historical reference. That such passages did really have such a primary reference no fair reasoner is likely to deny; but to assert that they had such a reference *only* is to repudiate an interpretation which they may obviously bear, and which had been attached to them by the nation among whom they originated for centuries before, as well as for centuries after, the coming of our Lord. Let us take these quotations in order. No one will question that the second Psalm was originally a song of trust and anticipated triumph in times of gathering war; that the words of 2 Sam. vii. 14 were, in the first instance, addressed to Solomon; that in Psalm xcvii. 7 (if that be source of the quotation), or in Deuteronomy xxxii. 43—the song of Moses—the "Elohim" are bidden to worship God; that the forty-fifth Psalm was an epithalamium for Solomon, or one of his successors; that in Ps. cii. 25 the "O Lord" does not exist in the

---

[1] If the "again" merely introduces a new quotation, as in i. 5, ii. 13, iv. 5, etc., there is no difficulty except the very strange misplacement (hyperbaton). But it seems better to apply it prophetically to the Final Advent, though I have left the translation ambiguous, as the original is.

[2] Ps. xcvii. 7 (cf. Deut. xxxii. 43). The LXX., the Syriac, and the Vulgate, render *Elohim* by "angels," as in Ps. vi l. 6, etc.; the Chaldee, by "all who worship idols."

[3] Ps. civ. 4. Both ἀγγέλους and πνεύματα are dubious; ἀγγέλους means either "messengers" or "angels"; πνεύματα either "winds" or "spirits." The context shows that the *latter* meanings are intended *here*. In the original the *context* seems to demand an inversion, *i.e.*, "He maketh the winds His messengers, the flaming fire His ministers"—but *grammatical* considerations make this difficult to accept. See Perowne, *The Psalms*, ii. 229, 237. Further, the Rabbinic notion was that the angels could "clothe themselves with the changing garment of natural phenomena," and be changed into wind and flame (Wetst. and Schöttgen, *ad loc*).

[4] Ps. xlv. 6, 7.   [5] Or "His kingdom," א.

[6] Here all the ancient versions render *Elohim* as a vocative; moderns render it "Thy Divine throne," as 1 Chron. xxix. 23. The Jews have never doubted its Messianic interpretation, and the Chald. Paraphrast on ver. 3 was, "Thy beauty, O King Messiah, is greater than that of the Son of men" (Schöttgen). See Perowne, i. 357.

[7] ἀλλάξεις, א, D, read ἀλλάξεις, as in Hebrew and in the Alexandrian MS. of the LXX, which this Epistle generally follows.

[8] Ps. cii. 25. Although "O Lord" (Κύριε) is not in the original, a Christian, writing to Christians who accepted Christ as the Messiah, might quote these verses in a Messianic application, especially as he has already said, "By whom also He made the world."

[9] Ps. cx. 1. The fact that this Psalm was prominently used by our Lord without dispute in a Messianic sense shows incontestably that in the Priest-King after the order of Melchisedek all readers, Jewish as well as Christian, would at once accept a type of the Messiah.

[10] They render service (λειτουργία) to God, and aid (διακονία) to men.

[11] Heb. i. 5—14.

Hebrew, and that the words are addressed to Jehovah; that even the hundred-and-tenth Psalm must have had a contemporary and historic meaning. And this being so, if any one were to adduce these citations as a proof of the supremacy of Jesus Christ over the angels to one who began by denying altogether the Messianic import of the Old Testament, the arguments could not have any weight until this method of applying the Old Testament had been justified. But to pass through these preliminary reasonings was in this case needless. Apollos is arguing with the Hebrews, and arguing with them on admitted principles. Those Hebrews were Christians. He had no need to begin by proving to them that Jesus was the Messiah. That part of his work had been mightily accomplished many years before. It would have been necessary only for unconverted Jews, whom he is not addressing. But even Jews, if they were once convinced on this point, would have been compelled to accept his further arguments. Their whole religion was ultimately resolvable into a Messianic hope, and their whole method of Scriptural study was Messianic application. It was an accepted rule of their interpretation that everything which the Prophets had spoken they had spoken of the Messiah. Calvin, in his great commentary, thinks it sufficient to say that the New Testament writers make a pious use of such passages by infusing into them a new meaning.[1] But no Jewish scribe or Christian Apostle would have regarded himself as making a strained use of these quotations. To such readers the passages derived their chief importance from the prophetic meaning which had always been assigned to them. The Christological application cannot, and is not meant to, disturb the historical foundation of such passages; but mystical extensions of the language, and inferential deductions from it were in the inmost nature of things perfectly tenable, and constituted indeed, the very essence of Jewish exegesis.

But it may be said that, however conclusive this method of argument and citation may have been to the Jews, it cannot be so to ⸺ It would be useless and dishonest to ignore that such a remark natural. The objection was felt so strongly even by Cardinal Cajeta that he says, "It is not quite becoming that so great an Apostle shou use an argument in a matter of so much importance."[2] My reply that the argument can and ought to be, if not logically conclusive, y full of weight and instruction to us. It may be that the whole resu of our training, and our entire method of criticism lead us to atta more exclusive import to the primary application of the Old Testamen and not to allow its full force to the Messianic presentiment whic largely moulded the language of Scripture. Yet how is it possible fc us to deny that the Jews had read these texts in a Messianic sense fo ages before Christ was born, and in many instances continue so t

---

[1] "Piâ deflectione ad Christi personam accommodat" (Calvin, in Eph. iv. 8). He calls thi method of application ἀναξερῃασία.
[2] "Minus decet in tantâ re tantum Apostolum uti tali argumento." Comment. (ap. Tho luck, 66).

accept them? Is it not further true that these utterances *have* received a fulfilment such as was attributed to them, and a fulfilment more universal and magnificent than was ever anticipated by those who received or those who uttered them? Is it not true that Jewish literature is the embodiment of Jewish religion; that the very heart and soul of Jewish religion was the Messianic faith; and that in Christ that Messianic faith has found its most glorious accomplishment? A pious Jewish interpreter might carry a modern critic with him when he said that much of the language of the Old Testament respecting the ideal Man—the ideal Jashar—the ideal Israel—the ideal seed of David and of Abraham, COULD only find its true and full meaning in the promised Messiah. The very name *Adam*, said the Rabbis, involves the names *Adam, David, Messiah*; so that the mystery of Adam is the mystery of the Messiah.[1] The Rabbinic *Midrash* on Ps. civ. 1 is that God lent "glory" to Moses, and "honour" to Joshua; but, according to Ps. xxi. 6, he meant to lend *both* to King Messiah. The New Testament quotations are all based on the principle, nowhere more powerfully expounded than in this Epistle, that the New Testament is latent in the Old, and the Old is laid open in the New—that both are but parts of one system of Divine ideas, moments in the course of one progressive revelation.

With the extent to which the Old Testament writers themselves realised the force of their own utterances we are not immediately concerned. "Their words meant more than they." The Spirit who, entering into their holy souls, made them Sons of God and Prophets, gave them the large utterance which has reached over three thousand years, and of which the final consummation is yet afar. The grandeur of prophecy did not consist in mechanical predictions, but in the Faith which enabled the Chosen People to support with unflinching allegiance the cause of right, and in the Hope which burned with unquenchable brightness even in the depths of universal gloom.

But when we have given their fullest weight to these considerations, we must still admit that the tendency of our exegesis is different from that of the Jews. We find in this and other Epistles a style of Scriptural application which comes home with less force to us than it did to its earlier readers. We must, however, remember that this mode of argument was once both necessary and convincing, although to us, with the widening knowledge of centuries, it is no longer indispensable. The argument from some of the Messianic Psalms is undoubtedly to be taken into account among the other evidences of Christianity. If there are other Psalms which can be regarded as having no such evidential value, except to those who accept the ancient methods of interpretation—if the prophetic evidence appeals to us with less force than of old—the Historic evidences of Christianity have, on the other hand, been incomparably strengthened. Different methods of argument appeal with

[1] Nishmath Chajim, f. 152 b.

varying force to different ages. This is nothing more than we should have expected from the fact that God never willed to reveal at once the whole mystery of His dispensations. His revelations (as we have just been told) come to us gradually like the dawn—fragmentarily and multifariously—in many portions, in many ways.

SECTION II.

A SOLEMN EXHORTATION.

Having thus proved the superiority of Christ to Angels, the writer pauses for a word of warning.

"On this account we ought more abundantly to pay heed to the things heard, lest perchance we should drift away from them.[1] For if the word uttered by means of angels[2] proved stedfast, and every transgression and neglect[3] received a just recompense of reward, how shall we[4] make good our escape[5] if we neglect so great a salvation? which, having begun to be uttered through the Lord, was ratified to us by them that heard,[6] God attesting it with them by signs and portents, and various powers, and distributions of the Holy Spirit, according to His will" (ii. 1—4).

After this exhortation the thread of argument is resumed, and he proceeds to show that this destined supremacy of man over Angels was foretold in the Scriptures, and has been fulfilled in Jesus. He won supreme glory by willing suffering, in order to share the trials of those whom He is to sanctify and lead to glory as sons of God. This brotherhood of man with Christ is illustrated by passages from Ps. xxii. and Is. viii., and the chapter concludes with a pregnant summary of the reasons why it was—from the human point of view—necessary that Christ should condescend to incarnation and death. It was that he might bring to nought the lord of Death, and liberate men from the lifelong terror of death—it being His aim to aid men and not angels, and to be made like men that He might show the sympathy of the Infinite with the finite by actually sharing in their trials and their life.

"For not to angels did He subject the age to be,[7] respecting which we speak,

---

[1] παραρρυῶμεν, 2nd aor. subj. pass. of παραρρεῖν. Cf. Prov. iii. 21, LXX., υἱὲ μὴ παραρρυῇς . . . ἐμὴν βουλήν. It is the opposite of τηρεῖν. "Lest peradventure we fleten away" (*Wiclif*). "Let them slip" first appears in the Genevan Bible of 1560.
[2] Acts vii. 53; Gal. iii. 19; Deut. xxxiii. 2; Ps. lxviii. 17; Jos. *Antt.* xv. 5, 3. See on these Angels at Sinai my *Life and Work of St. Paul*, ii. 149. The prominence given to the angelic mediators of the Law is still more observable in the Talmud, the Targums, the Midrashim, etc.; and in the tract "Maccoth" we are informed that the only words actually spoken by God were the First Commandment. [3] παράβασις, sins of commission; παρακοή, of omission.
[4] "The child owes a deeper debt than the servant." [5] ἐκφευξόμεθα.
[6] St. Paul would never have written thus. He always insists most strongly on the independence of his call, his revelation, and his gospel (Gal. i. 1, &c.).
[7] Heb. vi. 5. In the Old Testament the "Age to be" is the Messianic Age. But when the Messianic Age had dawned—when this "future age" (*olam habba*) had become "present" (*olam hazzeh*)—then Christians were still led to look forward to yet another "future age." The *olam habba* is the Christian dispensation, in its *present* existence here, which involves its *future* perfectionment. The *olam hazzeh*, or "this Age" (αἰὼν οὗτος), might be applied to the period before the destruction of Jerusalem, regarded in its Jewish, Heathen, and *imperfect* Christian aspect; and the "present world," in *this* sense, *was* subjected to angels (Deut. xxxii. 8, LXX., "according to the number of the angels of God;" Dan. x. 13, 20, 21; Tobit xii. 15). In point of fact, the horizon of the "Age to be" is one which must ever fade before us until we reach the end of *this* Age, and of all things.

THE WORK OF CHRIST.

But one somewhere[1] testified, saying, What is man[2] that thou rememberest him? or the son of man, that thou lookest upon him? Thou loweredst him a little in comparison to the angels;[3] with glory and honour thou crownedst him; all things didst thou subject beneath his feet. For in subjecting the universe to him, He left nothing unsubjected to him; but now we see[4] not yet the universe subjected to him, but we look upon[5] Him who has been for a little time made low in comparison of angels—even Jesus—on account of the suffering of death, crowned with glory and honour,[6] in order that by the grace of God[7] He may taste death[8] on behalf of every man. For it became Him, for whose sake are all things, and by whose means are all things—in bringing many sons to glory—to perfect by means of sufferings the Captain[9] of their salvation. For the Sanctifier and they who are being sanctified are all from one, for which cause He is not ashamed to call them brethren, saying, I will declare thy name to my brethren, in the midst of the Church will I sing praise to thee.[10] And again, I will put my trust in Him; and again, Lo, I and the children which God gave me.[11] Since then the children have shared in blood and flesh,[12] He Himself also similarly partook in the same things, in order that by means of death He may render impotent him that hath the power of death, that is the devil,[13] and may set free those who by fear of death through their whole life were subjects of slavery. For assuredly[14] it is not angels whom He takes by the hand, but it is the seed of Abraham whom He takes by the hand.[15] Wherefore it behoved Him[16] in all respects to be made like to His brethren, in order that He may prove Himself merciful, and a faithful high priest

---

[1] This vague method of quotation is found also in Philo and the Rabbis. Generally, each quotation is referred to "God" or "the Holy Spirit," but that method could not be here adopted, because God is addressed.

[2] אֱנוֹשׁ—man in his humiliation and weakness.

[3] Heb. *Elohim*. [4] ὁρῶμεν. [5] βλέπομεν.

[6] On the connexion of the Crown with the Cross, compare Phil. ii. 5—11 ("via crucis, via lucis").

[7] The reading χωρὶς Θεοῦ ("without God," or "except God," now only found in MSS. 53 and 67) was found by Origen in some MSS. (ἐν τισιν ἀντιγράφοις), and by Jerome ("absque Deo, in quibusdam exemplaribus"). Theodore of Mopsuestia spoke with contempt of the reading χάριτι, as meaningless; but χωρὶς seems to be either an accidental misreading of χάριτι, or a marginal gloss on τὰ πάντα ("might taste death for everything except God"). (Cf. 1 Cor. xv. 27.) The Nestorians, however (and even St. Ambrose and Fulgentius), interpreted it, "might, apart from *His Divinity* (i.e., in His human nature only), taste death." If accepted, it can only mean "that He may taste death for every being. God excepted" (1 Cor. xv. 27). Drs. Westcott and Hort (Greek Test. ii. 129) regard it as a Western and Syrian reading which sprang from an accidental confusion of letters.

[8] A common Semitic metaphor, from the notion that death gives a cup to drink. In the Arabian poem "Antar" we find, "Death gave him a cup of absinth by my hand."

[9] ἀρχηγόν (Acts v. 31). In Acts iii. 15 it means "the Leader" in the sense of "the Author" or "Originator." Comp. xii. 2, *Herzog ihrer Seligkeit* (Luther).

[10] Ps. xxii., a typico-prophetic Psalm (Matt. xxvii. 46). It is headed in our Hebrew Bibles, "On the hind of the dawn," which the Midrash Tehillin explains to mean, "On him who leaps—as a stag—and brightens the world in the time of darkness" (Mic. vii. 8). R. Chija explained it of the *gradual redemption* of Israel.

[11] The verse continues, "Behold I and the children which God gave me (viz., Mahershalal-hashbaz and Shearjashub), *are for signs and for wonders in Israel from the Lord of Hosts* (Is. viii. 18). The names of those two sons ("Speed-plunder-haste-spoil" and "A remnant shall remain") were symbolical, as also was their whole position. It indicated the relation of the chosen part of the people towards God. These texts are not (in our sense of the word) *proofs*, but only symbols and illustrations.

[12] This (as in Eph. vi. 12) is the order in A, B, C, D, E, M.

[13] Compare Phil. ii. 9: "He humbled Himself, becoming subject to death, &c." The Devil has the power of death, not as Lord, but as executioner. (Cf. John viii. 44, ἀνθρωποκτόνος ἀπ᾽ ἀρχῆς; Rev. xii. 10). Wisd. ii. 24, "By the envy of the Devil death entered into the world." The Jews called Sammael the "Angel of Death," and he was the Devil (Eisenmenger, p. 821).

[14] Δήπου (*opinor*) in Classic Greek has a semi-ironical tinge. It occurs nowhere else in the New Testament or LXX., but is common in Philo.

[15] Sc., "to help and rescue" (Matt. xiv. 31, etc.; cf. viii. 9). Wisd. iv. 11, "Wisdom . . . . takes by the hand those that seek her." By the "seed of Abraham" there can be no doubt that the writer means Jews, because throughout the whole Epistle he has them exclusively in view; but of course he did not for a moment dream of *excluding* the spiritual Israel.

[16] The obligation is involved in the *purpose* of Christ's assimilation to man.

in things that relate to God, to expiate the sins [1] of the people. For in that sphere wherein [2] He suffered by being Himself tempted, He is able to succour them that are being tempted" (ii. 5—18).

Having thus introduced the word "High Priest," he might have proceeded at once to the proof of the nature and superiority of Christ's High Priesthood, which is the central idea of the Epistle. But he was arguing with Jews who raised Moses to a pedestal of almost Divine eminence, in their enthusiasm for his work as a mediator between God and their nation.[3] It was desirable, therefore, to pause and show that Christ was superior not only to the angels by whose *instrumentality*, but also to Moses by whose immediate *agency*, the Law was delivered to Israel. In doing this he follows the lines of his previous demonstration. He has shown that the angels were but "ministering spirits," and that the Son is, in His very nature, more exalted than they (i. 5—14); and then, after a few words of exhortation (ii. 1—5), he has proved that in Christ our human nature is also to be elevated above the angels in the "future age" or true Messianic kingdom (ii. 6—16), since Christ as our High Priest took part in that nature (ii. 17, 18). He now proceeds to show that Christ is higher than Moses, inasmuch as the Son is higher than the minister (iii. 1—6); and then, after another exhortation (iii. 7—19), that the future belongs to Christ, and not to Moses, because Christ achieved the work of bringing Israel into the promised rest, a work which Moses had left imperfect (iv. 1—13). The angels had come in the name of God before Israel, and Moses had come in the name of Israel before God; the High Priest came in the name of God before Israel, wearing the name Jehovah on the golden *petalon* upon his forehead, and in the name of Israel before God, bearing the names of their tribes on the oracular gems upon his breast. Christ is above the Angels,

---

[1] ἱλάσκεσθαι, "to expiate" or "propitiate." It is never connected with "God," or "the wrath of God," either in the LXX or N.T., because, as Delitzsch says, man must not regard sacrifice as an act by which he induces God to show him grace; just as it is nowhere said that Christ's sacrifice propitiated *God's wrath*, as though that sacrifice had in any way anticipated God's own gracious purpose (see Rom. iii. 25; Eph. ii. 10). It represents the Hebrew *Kippeer*, "to cover." Comp. Ecclus. iii. 3, "whoso honoureth his father *maketh* an *atonement for his sins*;" 3), "Alms *maketh an atonement* for sins;" xx. 28 and xxxiv. 19, "Neither is he pacified for sin by the multitude of sacrifices."

[2] The E.V. renders ἐν ᾧ "in that"—*i.e.*, "forasmuch as,"—like the Hebrew *ba-asher*; but it is more simple to make it mean, "in that particular wherein." Comp. vi. 17; Rom. viii. 3.

[3] This will be seen at once by a few extracts from the Talmud about Moses. They may be found in Hamburger's *Wörterb.* and Mr. Hershon's *Genesis*:—

"Three things did Moses ask of God: (1) He asked that the Shechinah might rest upon Israel; (2) That the Shechinah might rest upon none but Israel; and (3) That God's ways might be made known unto him. And all these requests were granted."—(Berachoth, f. 7, a.)

"The soul of Moses, our Rabbi, embraced all the souls of Israel, as it is said, Moses was equivalent to all Israel" ("Moses our Rabbi" is in Hebrew, by Gematria, = 613, which is the numerical value also of the Hebrew words for "Lord God of Israel").—(Kitzur sh'lu, p. 2.) Hershon, *Miscellany*, p. 324.

"The Angels asked the Holy One, Blessed be He .... Why did Moses and Aaron die, who fulfilled the whole Law? He answered, 'There is one event to the righteous and the wicked.'"—(Shabbath, f. 55, b.)

"Moses' face was like the sun, Joshua's like the face of the moon" (Num. xxvii. 27).—(Bava Bathra, f. 75, a.)

"All the Prophets saw through a dim glass, but Moses saw through a clear glass."—(Yevamoth, f. 49, b.)

"Fifty gates of understanding were created in the world; all but one were opened to Moses."—(Rosh Hashanah, f. 21, b.)

as Son of God and Lord of the future world, and is not only the messenger of God to men, but as High Priest is the propitiatory representative of men before God. The distinctive exaltation of Christ above Angels and above Moses as regards His mediatorial work, rests in His High-Priestly office—a truth which is stated in that hortatory form which continually asserts itself throughout these two chapters.[1]

"Wherefore,[2] holy brethren,[3] partakers of a heavenly calling,[4] contemplate the Apostle[5] and High Priest of our profession, Jesus, as faithful to Him that made Him (such),[6] as also Moses was faithful in all His house.[7] For He hath been deemed worthy of more glory than Moses, in proportion as He who established the house hath more honour than the house. For every house is established by some one, but He who established all things is God. And Moses indeed was faithful in all his house, as a servant, for a testimony to the things which were to be afterwards spoken;[8] but Christ as a Son over His (God's) house, whose house are we" if we hold fast the confidence and ground of boasting of our hope firm unto the end"[10] (iii. 1—6).

Then follows a powerful appeal to faith and faithfulness,[11] founded on the exhortation in the ninety-fifth Psalm, to hear God's voice "to-day,"[12] and not to harden the heart against Him,[13] as the Israelites had

---

[1] This parallelism of structure between chapters iii., iv. and i., ii., is well drawn out by Ebrard:—

I. Christ higher than ministering spirits (i. 5—14.)
Exhortation (ii. 1—5).
He raises humanity above angelhood (ii. 6—16).
For He was our High Priest (ii. 17, 18).

II. Christ higher than Moses, because the Son is higher than the servant (iii. 1—6).
Exhortation (iii. 7—19).
In Him Israel has entered into rest (iv. 1—13).
Thus He is also our High Priest (iv. 14—16).

[2] Ὅθεν—i.e., Since we have such a helper. Ὅθεν (ii. 17; viii. 3) is never once used in the Epistles of St. Paul (though once in a speech, Acts xxvi. 19), and only elsewhere in 1 John ii. 18.

[3] A mode of address never once used by St. Paul.

[4] "Heavenly," because *from* heaven and calling *to* heaven.

[5] Ἀπόστολον, because "sent from the Father" (ἀπεσταλμένον παρὰ Πατρός), as the High Priest was sometimes regarded as a messenger (*Sheliach*) from God (John x. 36); sent by God as an Apostle to us; going from us as a High Priest to God; and, therefore, most strictly a Mediator. The title is referred to by Justin Martyr, *Apol.* i. 12 and 63, where he says that the Word of God is called an angel, because He announces (ἀναγγέλλει), and an Apostle because He is sent (ἀποστέλλεται).

[6] The expression "To Him that made Him" (τῷ ποιήσαντι αὐτόν), which might be taken superficially to indicate that Christ was a *created being*, caused the genuineness of the Epistle to be suspected (Philastr. *Haer.* 89). But even if this sense were necessary, it would merely refer to Christ's human birth (*corporalis generatio*, Primasius), as Athanasius understood it. It cannot possibly refer (as Bleek and Lünemann suppose) to His Eternal generation, though they rightly urge that ποιῶ, with an accusative, usually means to create or make. It is simpler to understand it, "Who made Him an Apostle and High Priest." Compare 1 Sam. xii. 6 (ὁ ποιήσας τὸν Μωυσῆν); Mark iii. 14; Acts ii. 36, "God made Him Lord and Christ." So the Greek Fathers understood it: τί ποιήσαντι; ἀπόστολον καὶ ἀρχιερέα (Chrys.); ποίησιν . . . τὴν χειροτονίαν κέκληκεν (Theodoret).

[7] An allusion to Num. xii. 7. His (*i.e.*, God's) House.

[8] "By Christ" (Deut. xviii. 15).

[9] "How we ought to walk in the *House of God*, seeing that it is *the Church* of the Living God" (1 Tim. iii. 15). "Ye are the temple of God" (1 Cor. iii. 16).

[10] The "firm unto the end" is omitted in B.

[11] The διό of iii. 7 refers on to the βλέπετε of ver. 12, the intervening words being a long parenthesis.

[12] The Hebrew of Ps. xcv. 6 rather is, "O that ye would hear His voice;" but this ejaculatory wish is often rendered in the LXX. by ἐάν (cf. Ps. cxxxviii. 19).

[13] Remarkable, as Bleek observes, because it is the only place where *man* is said to harden his own *heart*, which is usually ascribed immediately to God (Ex. vii. 8, and *passim*; Is. lxiii. 17; Rom. ix. 16). Man is usually said to stiffen his neck (Deut. x. 16, etc.) or back (2 Kings xvii. 14). But we have "but since some hardened themselves" (ὡς δέ τινες ἐσκληρύνοντο), Acts xix. 9.

done at Massah and at Meribah,[1] which had resulted in God's oath that they should not enter into His rest.[2] The "to-day" of the Psalm, repeated by David five hundred years afterwards, showed that the "to-day" of God's offered mercy had not been exhausted in the wilderness,[3] God had offered "a rest" to His people, but through unbelief they had failed to enter into it (iii. 7—19).[4] "Let us then fear," he says, "lest haply, though a promise is still left us of entering into His rest, any one of you should seem to have failed in attaining it.[5] For indeed we too, just as they, have had a Gospel preached to us, but the word of hearing benefited not them, since they had not been tempered in faith with them that heard it."[6]

"For we who believed are entering into that rest." This he proceeds to prove by the argument that God has long ago entered into *His* rest after the worlds were made; and it had been evidently intended that some men should enter that rest of God. Since, then, those who had first heard the glad tidings of promise had *not* entered into God's rest, as a punishment for their disobedience, the promise was repeated ages afterwards. For again, after so long a time, God had in the Psalm of David used the limiting term "to-day."[7] Clearly, therefore, Joshua[8] had not led Israel into any real or final rest. If he had done so the promise of rest would not have needed to be renewed.[9] There still remains, then, a Sabbath-rest for the people of God. For any Christian who entered into his rest (by death) ceased from his labours, as God ceased from His own labours.

---

[1] The writer follows the LXX. in rendering it "In the embitterment," as though the Seventy had here read "Marah" for "Meribah." In Ex. xvii. 1—7 they render it *Loidorēsis*, or "Reproach." Massah and Meribah were two different places (Num. xx. 1—13).

[2] Num. xiv. 28—30.

[3] "Few things in the Epistle," says Dr. Moulton, "are more remarkable than the constant presentation of the thought that Scripture language is *permanent, and at all times present*." As regards the forty years in the wilderness, it is remarkable that forty years was also the period between the Crucifixion and the Fall of Jerusalem, and that according to Rabbi Akhiva the years of the Messiah were to be forty years (Tanchuma, f. 79, 4). So, too, R. Eliezer, referring expressly to Ps. xcv. 10 (Sanhedr. f. 99, a). The word "always" in ver. 10 is not in the original, but is either due to loose citation (for, as Calvin says, "Scimus apostolos in citandis testimoniis magis attendere ad summum rei quam de verbis esse solicitos"), or to some slight difference of reading. The "if they shall enter" is a Hebraism for "they shall not enter" (cf. var. 18). It is really due to a suppressed apodosis (Mk. viii. 12).

[4] In ver. 10 he says "with this generation" (א, A, B, D, M) for the "that" of the LXX.—no doubt intentionally (compare Matt. xxiii. 36; xxiv. 34). In ver. 15 ὑπόστασις is "confidence," as in Ps. xxxviii. 7, "My sure hope (LXX. ὑπόστασις) is in Thee."

[5] The δοκῇ is used by a sort of litotes to suggest to the conscience of each a stronger term. Ebrard renders it "lest any of you think that he has come too late for it," which is a perfectly tenable rendering, but unsuitable here, because the object is warning against presumption, not encouragement against despair.

[6] This is a strange expression, and the reading συγκεκραμένους in the E.V. is certainly much simpler; but it is for that very reason suspicious when we find συγκεκραμένους in A, B, C, and συνκεκερασμένους in M. The meaning will then be, as in the text, that the Word did not profit the rebellious Israelites because they were not blended with Joshua and Caleb in their faith. Westcott and Hort suspect the possibility of the reading τοῖς ἀκουσθεῖσιν, or even of Noesselt's conjecture τοῖς ἀκούσμασιν.

[7] iv. 4, εἴρηκε, "He (God) hath said"—a method of citation not once used in St. Paul's Epistles.

[8] iv. 8. The unfortunate rendering "Jesus" in this verse might seem as if it were expressly designed to perplex ignorant readers.

[9] iv. 8, οὐκ ἂν περὶ ἄλλης ἐλάλει, "He would not have been speaking of another day." The imperfect is in accordance with the writer's habit of seeing things in their ideal continuity.

"Let us, then, be earnest to enter into that rest, that no one fall into the same example of disobedience. For living[1] is the word of God,[2] and effectual, and keener than any two-edged sword, and cleaving through even to the severance of soul and spirit, of joints and marrow,[3] and a discerner of the thoughts and conceptions of the heart. And there is not a created thing unseen in His presence, but all things are naked and laid prostrate[4] to His eyes. To whom our account must be given."[5]

SECTION III.

THE HIGH PRIESTHOOD OF CHRIST.

Then follows the transitional exhortation to the long proof and illustration of the following chapters.

"Having, then, a great High Priest who has passed through the heavens—Jesus, the Son of God—let us hold fast our confession. For[6] we have not a High Priest who cannot sympathise with our weaknesses, but one who has been tempted in all respects just as we are, apart from sin. Let us approach, then,[7] with confidence to the throne of grace, that we may receive mercy, and may find grace for a seasonable succour" (iv. 14—16).

The predominance of the thought of Christ's High Priesthood in the mind of the writer has already been shown, not only by the two last verses, but by his two previous allusions to it. In ii. 17 he had said by anticipation that it was necessary for Christ to take a human, not an angelic, nature from the moral necessity for His being made like unto His brethren, "that He might be a merciful and faithful High Priest in things pertaining to God." In iii. 1 he had solemnly invited his

---

[1] "*Living* oracles" (Acts. vii. 38).
[2] Clearly not here the personal Logos in St. John's sense, though many Fathers and divines, who wrote far more from the theological than from the critical point of view, have so understood it. No doubt that meaning may lie in the background, but if so, the writer has purposely left it in the background; for again and again such a usage seems to be hovering on his lips, and yet he does not actually adopt it. It was left for the inspired genius of St. John to adopt the term "THE WORD" into the theology of Christianity, and in adopting it to glorify every previous and analogous usage of it (*vide infra*, p. 512). The word of God is here the written and spoken word of God, of which again and again the writer shows that he has a most vivid perception as a living reality; there may also be a sort of semi-personification. The comparison was also familiar to Philo, as in *Quis rer. div. hæres*, § 27: "Thus God having whetted that Word of His which cutteth all things, divides the shapeless and unformed essence of all things." It is clear from the context that the passage was known to the writer, for Philo also speaks of the Word as penetrating even to things called invisible, and separating the different parts of the soul. We find the same figure in Ps. lvii. 5, etc.; Rev. i. 16; Wisd. xviii. 15, 16. "Thine Almighty Word leaped down from heaven . . . . and brought thine unfeigned commandment as a sharp sword, and standing up filled all things with death."
[3] That is, the Word of God pierces not only the natural soul, but also the Divine Spirit, and even to the very depths of these. "*Animâ* (ψυχῇ) *vivimus, spiritu* (πνεύματι) *intelligimus*," Primas. Μερισμοῦ may mean the "joint" or "articulation." It should be observed that while the expressions recall those of Philo, the application of them is wholly different.
[4] τετραχηλισμένα. The word has been rendered, (1) "seized by the throat and overthrown;" (2) "bent back by the neck, like malefactors" (Bleek, etc.); (3) "flayed" (Chrys.), or "anatomised" (by the Priest in his μωμοσκοπία, or inspection of victims), or "manifested" (Hesych., Phavorin), or "sacrificed" (Theodoret). But "*laid prostrate*" is almost undoubtedly the right meaning, since the word is constantly used in that sense by Philo.
[5] Heb. iv. 11—13. This may also be, as in the E.V. (more generally).—"with whom we have to do." It would be very lame to make it mean "with reference to whom we are speaking" (as in v. 11).
[6] [And we may do this with perfect confidence], "for"—the "for" anticipates an objection (occupat objectionem," Schlichting).
[7] προσέρχεσθαι is a favourite word with this writer (vii. 25, x. 1, 22, xi. 6, xii. 18—22), though only found once in St. Paul (1 Tim. vi. 3), and then in an entirely different sense, "take heed." We have, however, "access" (προσαγωγή) in Eph. ii. 18, iii. 12.

hearers to the contemplation of Christ as our High Priest. It had been necessary for him to pause for a moment to show that Christ was greater even than Moses, and to invite his readers by a solemn appeal to strive to enter into that rest which some of those whom Moses led out of Egypt had failed to attain. The true rest which Moses had promised was a rest typified by the Sabbath-rest of God. It pointed far beyond the possession of Canaan to the *final* rest which remaineth for the people of God. CHRIST'S HIGH PRIESTHOOD is a pledge to us of a grace by which that rest may be obtained.

We thus reach the very heart of the Epistle, for the development of this topic occupies nearly six chapters.

First he lays down two qualifications which must be found in every High Priest, namely,—

i. That he must be able to sympathise with men by participation with them in their infirmities (v. 1—3, comp. ii. 17); and,

ii. That he must not be self-called, but appointed by God (4—10).

That Christ possessed the first of these qualifications was self-evident, and had indeed been expressly stated (comp. ii. 17).

That He possessed the second he proves by a reference to His eternal Sonship (Ps. ii. 7) and His Melchizedek Priesthood (Ps. cx. 4).

He then pauses once more during a somewhat long digression to express his sorrow that their spiritual dulness and backwardness made it needlessly difficult for him to illustrate these deep truths (v. 11—14). He therefore urges them to more earnest endeavours after Christian progress (vi. 1—3), partly by an awful warning of the danger of relapse from truth (4—8), and partly by encouragements derived from the activity of their Christian benevolence (9, 10) and the immutable certainty of the promises of God (11—18). These inspire a hope founded on this Priesthood of our Lord (19, 20), which was a Priesthood not merely Aaronic, but transcendent and eternal after the order of Melchizedek.

Having thus cleared away every preliminary consideration, and raised them by his warnings and exhortations to a state of mind sufficiently solemn for the consideration of the subject, he proceeds to show that in many most important particulars the Priesthood of Melchizedek was superior to that of Aaron; namely—

i. Because it is eternal, not transient (vii. 1—3).

ii. Because even Abraham acknowledged the superior dignity of Melchizedek, by paying tithes to him and receiving his blessing (4—10).

iii. Because the Priesthood of Melchizedek is recognised in the Psalms as loftier than that of Aaron,—which implied a change in the Priesthood, and therefore in the Law (11, 12). This is confirmed by the fact that the Lord sprang from the tribe of Judah, not from that of Levi (13, 14); and from the fact that the Melchizedek Priesthood, being eternal, could not be connected with a Law which perfected nothing (15—19).

iv. Because the Melchizedek Priesthood was founded, as the Aaronic never was, by an oath (20—22).

v. Because the Levitic priests died, but Christ abideth for ever (23—25).

He then pauses to dwell for a moment on the eternal fitness of Christ's Priesthood to fulfil the conditions which the needs of humanity require; and proceeds to show that as Christ's *Priesthood* is superior to that of Aaron, so is His *Ministry* more excellent as belonging to a better Covenant (viii. 1—6). This is mainly proved by the fact that a *new* Covenant—and therefore a *better* Covenant—had been distinctly prophesied and promised (7—13).

The superiority of this second Covenant is shown by a comparison of the ministry of the High Priest entering the Holy of Holies on the Day of Atonement with that of Christ passing into the Heavens. The Levitical High Priest entered the Holiest Place but once a year. He had to do this year after year; he offered for his own sins as well as for those of the people; his sacrifices could not cleanse his conscience; his whole service stood merely in connexion with rites and ceremonies of a subordinate character. But, on the other hand, CHRIST (i.) entered, not a symbolic tabernacle, but the Heaven of Heavens; (ii.) He entered it once for all, and for ever; (iii.) He had no need to make any offering for His own sins, being spotless; (iv.) He entered through His own blood, which (v.) was eternally efficacious for the purging of the conscience from dead works; and (vi.) His whole ministration had to do with abiding realities, not with passing shadows (ix. 1—14). Then, led by the double meaning of the word *diathēkē*, which means both "testament" and "covenant," he shows that the blood of Christ was necessary to sanctify the new Covenant, and was efficacious even for the redemption of transgressions under the old (15—22), and that His one Death has wrought an all-sufficient expiation (23—28). He concludes the argument by contrasting the impotence of the Levitic sacrifices to perfect those who offered them—an impotence attested by their incessant repetition—with the one sacrifice offered by the willing obedience of Christ (x. 1—10). Christ's sacrifice issued in His eternal exaltation, after He had perfected the new Covenant in which constant sacrifices are no longer needful, because by the one sacrifice is granted the Forgiveness of Sin (11—18).

Such, in barest outline, is a sketch of the great argument of the Epistle, and we can see at once how powerfully it must have appealed to the intellect and conscience of an enquiring Jew. The sweeping proofs which St. Paul had furnished of the nullity of the Law under the new Christian dispensation, and of the secondary, parenthetic position which it had always occupied in the designs of God, might sway the reason of a Hebrew reader, but they tended to shock his most cherished prejudices. He would hail an argument which did not involve so apparently absolute a disparagement of the system under which he had been brought up.

For, in this new method of Christian argument, even while he enjoyed the glory of the substance he was permitted to admire the beauty of the shadow; he could joyfully see that even in the passing type there had always been a prophecy of the eternal antitype.

Let us now look at this great section in closer detail, and with an effort to understand not only the general bearing of the Epistle, but its separate paragraphs; and let us try in passing to remove any difficulties which may arise from the expressions or the arguments which the writer adopts.

Having spoken of the boldness with which we may approach the Throne of Grace, because of the High Priesthood of Christ, he gives the two conditions of Priesthood, namely, (i.) a power to sympathise, and (ii.) a special call.

(i.) "For every High Priest, being taken[1] from among men, is appointed on behalf of men in things relating to God that he may offer both gifts and sacrifices[2] on behalf of sins,[3] being able to deal compassionately[4] with the ignorant and erring, since he himself also is encompassed with moral weakness; and because of this very weakness[5] he is bound, as for the people so also for himself, to offer sin-offerings[6] (v. 1—3).

(ii.) "And no one takes this honourable office for himself, but on being called by God as even Aaron was.[7] So even the Christ[8] glorified not *Himself* to be made a high priest, but he [glorified Him] who said to Him, Thou art my Son; to-day have I begotten thee.[9] As also in another place He saith, Thou art a priest for ever after the order of Melchizedek;[10]—Who, in the days of his flesh,[11] having offered up

---

[1] Λαμβανόμενος, "being (as he is) chosen."

[2] This may be one of the writer's sonorous amplifications, for no distinction can here be made between δώροι and θυσίαι. In accurate Greek they differ, and the latter means "slain beasts;" but in the LXX. they are used indiscriminately (παρὰ δὲ τῇ γραφῇ ἀδιαφόρως κεῖνται, Theophylact). The writer may, however, have been thinking of the incense and meat-offerings of the Day of Atonement when he says δώρα, or of free-will offerings.

[3] ὑπέρ, *i.e.*, to make atonement for (ii. 17).

[4] Properly, "to show *moderate* emotion." Μετριοπαθής was the word used by the Peripatetics, and was invented by Aristotle (Diog. Laert. v. 31) to express the right state of mind, as against the Stoics, who demanded of their "sage" a complete suppression of emotion (ἀπάθη). The word is used both by Philo and Josephus of moderating passion. Here the context shows that it means "reasonable compassion" (μετριοπαθής . . . συγγιγνώσκων ἐπιεικῶς, Hesych.).

[5] δι' αὐτήν (א, A, B, C, D).

[6] See Lev. iv. 3; ix. 7, etc. The first confession of the High Priest on the Day of Atonement was—"O do Thou expiate the misdeeds, the crimes, and the sins wherewith I have done evil and have sinned before Thee, I and my house."

[7] Ex. xxviii. 1; Num. xvi.—xviii.: "God Himself judged Aaron worthy of this honour" (Jos. Antt. iii. 8, § 1; and contrast Num. xvi.; 2 Chron. xxvi. 16—21). See Bammidbar Rabba, § 18 (in Schöttgen), where Moses brings this fact as a reproach against Korah. The Highpriests of the day, when this Epistle was written, were alien Sadducees not of high-priestly lineage, who bought and sold, and transferred from one to the other, and generally degraded the office, being originally mere nominees of Herod. They belonged "to certain obscure persons who were only of *priestly* origin," not descendants of Aaron (Jos. Antt. xx. 10, § 5). For their characteristics see the Talmudic quotations in my *Life of Christ*, ii. 330, 342, and *infra*, p. 313. But it is doubtful whether the writer means to hint at this state of things. As an Alexandrian, living in Hellenistic communities, it would not be brought prominently under the notice of Apollos, especially as these Boethusim, etc., had now held the office for more than half a century.

[8] The true "anointed Priest."

[9] The Sonship, in the writer's argument, involves the proof of His Divine call to the Priesthood.

[10] "A priest upon his throne" (Zech. vi. 12); κατὰ τάξιν, al-dibhrathi, after the office, or place (Ps. cx. 4). The Jews said that the "two anointed ones" ("sons of oil") in Zech. iv. 14 are Aaron and Messiah, and argued from Ps. cx. 4 that Messiah was the dearer to God. They always accounted the Psalm to be Messianic, and the Targum of Jonathan began, "*The Lord said to his Word.*"

[11] σαρκὸς here means His "Humanity."

supplications and entreaties to Him who was able to save him out of death, with strong crying and tears,[1] and having been heard because of his reverential awe,[2] Son though he was, learnt his obedience from the things which He suffered,[3] and, after being perfected,[4] became to all those that obey Him the cause of eternal salvation, saluted by God a high priest after the order of Melchizedek[5] (v. 4—10).

"Now, respecting Melchizedek, what we have to say is long, and is difficult to explain to you, since ye have become dull in your hearing.[6] For, indeed, though ye ought to be teachers as far as *time* is concerned,[7] ye again have need that some one teach you the rudiments[8] of the beginning of the oracles of God, and ye have sunk to the position of those who need milk and not solid food.[9] For every one who feeds on milk is inexperienced in the word of righteousness,[10] for he is an infant. But solid food pertains to the fullgrown—to those who by virtue of their habit have their organs of sense trained to discrimination of good and evil[11] (v. 11—14).

"Leaving, then, the earliest principles of Christian teaching,[12] let us be borne along towards full growth, not laying again the foundation of repentance from dead works,[13] and of faith towards God, of the doctrine of ablutions[14] and laying on of hands,[15] and of resurrection of the dead, and of æonian judgment.[16] And this let us

---

[1] Not mentioned in the Gospels in the Agony at Gethsemane, but absolutely implied.

[2] εἰσακουσθεὶς ἀπὸ τῆς εὐλαβείας. Ἀπὸ may certainly mean "for," "because of," as in Luke xix. 3 : οὐκ ἠδύνατο ἀπὸ τοῦ ὄχλου; xxiv. 41, ἀπιστούντων ἀπὸ τῆς χαρᾶς. Comp. John xxi. 6; Acts xii. 14; xxii. 11 (οὐκ ἐνέβλεπον ἀπὸ τῆς δόξης), etc ; Εὐλάβεια (which in the N. T. occurs only at xii. 28) is "reverent fear," as opposed to terror and cowardice. Zeno defined it as "reasonable shrinking" (εὔλογος ἔκκλισις) and as being the opposite of fear, and says that the wise man might εὐλαβεῖσθαι but never φοβεῖσθαι. Demosthenes contrasts the εὐλαβὴς with the δειλός. The E. V. is therefore correct, and the meaning of this interesting passage is quite clear. It is a bulwark against the heresies which never will see or allow the perfect *Humanity* of Christ, as well as His true *Divinity*. The attempts to avoid this meaning by rendering it "was heard by Him whom He feared" (comp. Gen. xxxi. 42), or "was heard (and so delivered) from that which he feared," are merely due to theological bias. Both renderings are absolutely untenable. The rendering of the E. V. is that of *all the Greek Fathers*, and the meaning of εὐλάβεια excluded every other (see Trench, *New Test. Synonyms*, § x.). The εἰσακουσθεὶς may refer to the Angel who strengthened Him in consequence of His prayer (Luke xxii. 43), or to His absolute triumph over death and Hades.

[3] "Son," *i.e.*, not "a Son" (for then there would have been no stress on His "learning obedience"), but "*the* Son of God." ἔμαθεν . . . ἔπαθεν, one of the commonest of ancient paronomasias (Herod. i. 207; Æsch. *Ag.* 170; and often in Philo). Theodoret called this expression hyperbolical, and Chrysostom seems surprised by it; and Theophylact goes so far as to call it unreasonable. But "the things that He suffered" have a reference far wider than to the Agony. Still there is no doubt that passages like these increased the hesitancy in receiving the Epistle.

[4] "Perfected" in His *mediatorial* relation, ii. 10.

[5] Comp. Philo, *Opp.* i. 653; ἐν ᾧ (κόσμῳ) καὶ Ἀρχιερεὺς ὁ πρωτόγονος αὐτοῦ Λόγος.

[6] This passage also was perhaps known to Justin Martyr (*Dial. c. Tryph.* 33).

[7] The expression shows that the Epistle was written somewhat late—to those who had long been converts.

[8] Gal. iv. 3.   [9] 1 Cor. iii. 1, 2.

[10] Apparently a general phrase for the Gospel. The word *Tsedakah* in Hebrew has a wider range of meaning than "Righteousness."

[11] Clearly not "right and wrong," but here referring to doctrines—the power to "discriminate the transcendent" (Rom. ii. 18), to distinguish between excellence and inferiority in matter of truth. The phrase is a Hebrew one, *Yada tobh va-rā* (Gen. ii. 17, etc.).

[12] *Leaving* such principles—not, of course, in the sense of neglecting or forgetting them, but in the sense of making an advance beyond them.

[13] Repentance was the *first* and earliest lesson of the Gospel (Mark i. 15). Dead works—works of the Law (ix. 14; Rom. ix. 32), which have no inherent life in them (*Article XIII.*).

[14] Jewish ablutions (ix. 10) the Jewish converts to Christianity might still retain and explain in a more spiritual sense. *Baptismos* is never used for Christian Baptism (*baptisma*).

[15] For healing (Mark xvi. 18, etc.), for ordination (Acts vi. 6, etc.), for confirmation (Acts viii. 17, etc.).

[16] The αἰώνιος expresses the quality of the κρίμα as referring to the future world. Undoubtedly this sentence is surprising. The τελειότης towards which we are to be carried along is evidently connected in the writer's mind with the doctrine of Christ's High Priesthood, as typified by that of Melchizedek. It seems strange that he should rank this Gnosis as so *great* an advance beyond the doctrines of faith, repentance, and the resurrection, which both St. Paul and we regard as being of such primary importance. See, however, Riehn, *Lehrbegriff der Hebräerbriefs*, 763, f. 9. The writer means, "These truths you know, or ought to know, thoroughly by this time; but your special danger is apostasy to Judaic formalism,

do if God permit. For as to those who have been once for all enlightened,[1] and have tasted of the heavenly gift,[2] and become partakers of the Holy Spirit, and have tasted the excellence of the word of God,[3] and the Powers of the Future Age,[4] and who have fallen away[5]—it is impossible again to renew them to repentance, while they are crucifying to themselves the Son of God afresh, and putting Him to open shame. For land which has drunk the rain which often cometh upon it, and which is producing herbage suitable for those for whose sake it is also being tilled, partakes of blessing from God; but that which produces thorns and thistles is rejected, and near a curse, the end of which is for burning.[6]

"But, beloved, we are convinced of the better alternative about you,[7] and things akin to salvation,[8] even though we do thus speak. For God is not unjust to forget in a moment [9] your work and love which ye showed towards His name in having ministered to the saints, and yet ministering.[10] But we long for each of you to show the same earnestness with the view to the full assurance of your hope until the end,[11] that ye may prove yourselves not sluggish,[12] but imitators of those who by faith and patient waiting inherit the promises. [And I say who *inherit* the promises] for God, when He promised to Abraham, since He could not swear by any greater, swore by Himself,[13] saying Verily,[14] blessing I will bless thee, and multiplying I will multiply thee. And so, by waiting patiently, he obtained the promises. For men indeed swear by the greater, and to them the oath is an end of all contradiction for confirmation.[15] On which principle,[16] God wishing to show more abundantly [17] to

and you would be beyond the reach of this peril if you were capable of grasping the truths which I shall now set forth." He does not *disparage* these elementary truths, though they were all common to Christianity *with the older Covenant*.

[1] ἅπαξ is a favourite word of the writer, occurring more frequently in this Epistle than in all the rest of the New Testament. *Photismos* became (probably in consequence of this passage) the regular phrase for baptism (Just. Mart. *Ap.* i. 62; Chrysostom, etc.). Here it has the more general sense.

[2] It is impossible to be certain as to the definite meaning of this expression. It probably means "remission" or "regeneration." It is not easy in this passage to see a clear distinction between γεύσασθαι with the genitive (δωρεᾶς) and the accusative (ῥῆμα).

[3] This phrase is also indefinite, but from a parallel passage of Philo (*De profug.* vi. 25) it probably means the Divine teaching of the Gospel. The writer may here have used the accusative with γεύσασθαι because the genitive would have caused a confusion with Θεοῦ. On the gifts in general comp. ii. 3, 4.

[4] Compare with this expression Philo, *De proem. et poen.* (*Opp.* i. 428, ed. Mangey). "This is he who has quaffed much pure wine of God's benevolent power, and banqueted upon sacred words and doctrines." The "powers of the future æon" (*i.e.*, of the *Olam habba*) may be foretastes of its glory, or, as Chrysostom says, "the earnest of the spirit."

[5] Comp. ii. 1; iii. 12; x. 26, 29.

[6] vi. 1—8. See *infra*. These strong warnings against apostasy (comp. x. 26—31; xii. 15—17) are a special characteristic of this Epistle. Their general meaning is, that for deliberate and defiant apostasy there is no remedy provided. They are involved in the strong expression of St. Paul, "God is not mocked" (Θεὸς οὐ μυκτηρίζεται, Gal. vi. 7), and may be compared with Matt. xii. 31, 32, 43—45; 1 John v. 16. It must be borne in mind that a rare insolence and wretchedness of sin must be involved in such expressions as "trampling down the Son of God" and "insulting the spirit of grace."

[7] τὰ κρείσσονα. [8] The opposite to ἐγγὺς κατάρας in ver. 8.

[9] ἐπιλαθέσθαι—forget in a single act. "Labour" (κόπου) is omitted in the best MSS., and is probably added from 1 Thess. i. 3.

[10] For the phrase see Rom. xv. 25. The "saints" at Jerusalem (Gal. ii. 10; 1 Cor. xvi. 1) were too poor to minister to others, and this is one indication that the letter was not sent to them.

[11] To show the same earnestness in advancing to perfection as they had shown in ministering to the saints.

[12] That ye may not become as "sluggish" (νωθροί) in Christian progress as ye *have* become in spiritual knowledge (ver. 11).

[13] In this passage we again find an almost unmistakable reference to Philo, *De Legg. Alleg.* iii. 72: "Having well confirmed His promise even by an oath . . . for thou seest that God sweareth not by another—for nothing is superior to Himself—but by Himself, Who is the best of all."

[14] The MSS. vary between εἰ μή, εἰ μήν, ἦ μήν; but the three readings mean much the same. εἰ μή, a literal rendering of the Hebrew אִם לֹא, may have led to the variations.

[15] Comp. Philo, *Quod a Deo mittantur somnia* (*Opp.* i. 622), and there are very similar passages in *De Abrahamo* (*Opp.* ii. 39).

[16] ἐν ᾧ. [17] "More abundantly" than if He had not sworn.

the heirs of the promise the immutability of His purpose, intervened with an oath[1] that by means of two immutable things,[2] in which it is impossible for God to lie,[3] we may have a strong encouragement who fled for refuge to grasp the hope set before us.[4] Which we have as an anchor of the soul,[5] secure and firm, and passing to the region behind the veil,[6] where a forerunner on our behalf entered—Jesus—having become a High Priest for ever after the order of Melchizedek" (vi. 9—20).

The earlier sections of this passage are easy to understand. We see at once that a High Priest who was not of like feeling with ourselves—one who had no capacity for suffering, and therefore no power of sympathy—would be a most imperfect representative of his fellow-men, on whose behalf he has to stand in the presence of God. Nor is it difficult to understand the importance which the writer attaches to a Divine calling to the Priesthood. Of the Divine calling of Christ he furnishes a twofold proof,—the one, that it was involved in the eternal Sonship, which he illustrates by Psalm ii. 7; and the other, that He is addressed as a Priest after the order of Melchizedek in Psalm cx. 4. As both Psalms were fully acknowledged to be Messianic, the cogency of these references would not be disputed. He adds a few words of profound interest to show that Christ's eternal Priesthood was perfected first by the sufferings which He endured for our sakes, and then by His glorification. He regards the whole life of Christ as a part of the work wherein God glorified Him to be an Eternal Priest. The main work of that Priesthood was infinite self-sacrifice; for the sake of which, in the days of His flesh, He not only emptied Himself of His glory, but laid aside for a time every claim as the co-eternal and co-equal Son,[7] in order to become a man with men; to dwell in man's house of clay; to have a human soul; to entreat and supplicate and cry to His heavenly Father with tears both in Gethsemane and on the Cross. And He was heard, because of the glory of the infinite self-abnegation involved in this humble awe. In this passage, as elsewhere, the writer furnishes the most inestimable proof that Christ's High Priesthood has the qualification derived from perfect human sympathy. He also gives us a stronghold of assurance to resist the Apollinarian heresy which, with irreverent reverence, denies the true humanity of Christ, and has often been as dangerous to the Church as Arianism itself. Neither that heresy, nor

---

[1] Made his oath intermediate between Himself and Abraham. In Berachoth, f. 32, a, Moses says to God, "Hadst Thou sworn by Heaven and Earth I should have said They will perish, and therefore so may Thy oath; but as Thou hast sworn by Thy great name, that oath shall endure for ever."
[2] Namely, His word and His oath (Gen. xxii. 17). The Targums have not "By Myself," but "By My word have I sworn."
[3] "Nothing is impossible with God, except to lie" (Clem. Rom. 27).
[4] A metonymy for "the object of our Hope set before us as a prize."
[5] In very early times the Anchor was the emblem of Hope. πολλῶν ῥαγεισῶν ἐλπίδων, μιᾶς τυχών (Æsch. Ag. 488).
[6] "Nostram ancoram mittimus ad interiora coeli, sicut ancora ferrea mittitur ad inferiora maris." "Christ hath extended to us a Hope from Heaven, as a rope let down from the throne of God, and again reaching from us to the inmost Heaven and the seat of God" (Faber Stapulensis). "The veil," Ex. xxvi. 31—35.
[7] Phil. ii. 6: "He counted not equality with God a thing at which to grasp."

the Monothelite heresy, which denies to our Lord a human will, can find a moment's admission so long as this passage and the early chapters of St. Luke retain their places in Holy Writ. The fact that some of the Fathers were startled by this passage is an additional indication of its importance to the Christian Church. Theodoret ventures to say that since Christ manifested His obedience not *after*, but *before*, His suffering, the expression that "He learned obedience by the things which He suffered" is a hyperbolical expression.[1] Theophylact goes even farther, and says that Paul (for he traditionally accepts the Pauline authorship), "for the benefit of his hearers, used such accommodation as obviously to say some unreasonable things."[2] Had these Fathers sufficiently borne in mind that Christ was "perfectly man" as well as "truly God" they would not have used so free a style of criticism. And it might have been better for the Church if they had been less ready to claim a right to use this "accommodation" themselves, and less ready to attribute it to the Apostles.[3]

The digression that follows does not in the least resemble what has been called St. Paul's habit of "going off at a word." This writer does not go off at a word at all. Nothing less resembles being "hurried aside by the violence of his thoughts." His method is precisely the opposite of this. Instead of yielding to the impulse of a strong emotion, as St. Paul does, he prepares himself in the most leisurely and deliberate manner for an argument of consummate skilfulness and power. That argument was wholly original in its development, and he therefore endeavours to stimulate the spiritual dulness of his readers. By a powerful mixture of reproach, warning, and encouragement, he arouses them to the moral and intellectual effort without which it is impossible for us to grasp new truth.

He is about to give them not the milk which was necessary for infants—for beginners in Christ's teachings[4]—but solid food, such as was only fitted for mature understandings.[5] In their present condition—long as was the time since their conversion—they were incapable of receiving it; but he encourages them to hope that they would become capable, if they were sincere and earnest, in their desire for Christian progress.. He bids them, therefore, dismiss for the present the subjects which had engaged their attention when they were catechumens. In those days they had been occupied with the initial steps of religious knowledge. It was not his present purpose—it ought to be quite unnecessary now—to remind them once more of such rudimentary truths as the difference between faith and works; the distinction between

---

[1] The special objection only arose from Theodoret's failure to recognise that the word "suffered" applies not only to the Agony in Gethsemane and on the Cross, but to the whole life of the Saviour.
[2] See *supra*, p. 207, *note*.
[3] See note on "Accommodation" in my *Mercy and Judgment*, p. 296.
[4] The young Rabbinic neophytes used to be called thinokôth (תינוקות), "sucklings." Comp. Philo, *De Agric.*, Ἔτι δὲ νηπίοις μὲν ἐστὶ γάλα τροφή, κ.τ.λ.
[5] Comp. 1 Cor. iii. 1, 2.

Jewish ablutions and Christian Baptism; the meaning of imposition of hands; the truths of the resurrection of the body and the sentence of the world to come. They could not need such teachings as this—unless, indeed, they were in danger of apostasy. Of the peril of such apostasy he gives them a most solemn warning.

And here at once we find ourselves launched on a sea of controversy which has been age after age renewed. The originality of the writer's mind constantly shows itself in expressions and modes of thought which occur in him alone.

1. First of all the word "enlightened" acquired at a very early age the technical sense of "baptised," so that "enlightenment" (*photismos*)[1] was a recognised synonym of baptism, though it referred directly not to the outward sign, but to the thing signified. Hence the sterner schismatics of the early Church deduced from this passage the duty of finally excluding the weak from Church communion by refusing absolution to those who once had lapsed into apostasy or flagrant sin.[2] This was equivalent to the assertion that "all sin willingly committed after baptism is unpardonable." The fact that the use of "enlightenment" for "baptism" did not exist before this passage was written, but is derived from it, is at once sufficient to set aside the cogency of their inference, which was, it is needless to add, diametrically opposed to the practice and teaching of Christ and His Apostles, and is justly condemned by our Church in her 16th Article.

2. This hard dogma was also rightly rejected by the Fathers, who, following the example of Christ and the Apostles,[3] never closed the door of repentance even to the most flagrant sinners. From this passage, however, they deduced the unlawfulness of administering a second time the rite of Baptism—a right conclusion indeed, but one which rests on other grounds than those which this passage affords.

3. But while these ancient controversies are practically set at rest, we have not yet heard the last of that which raged between Calvinists and Arminians on the "indefectibility of grace."

a. Both sides tampered with the plain meaning of the words. The expression "when they have once fallen away" was fatal to the theories of the Calvinists, who held that those who were regenerate were also elect, and *could never fall away*.[4] It has been often supposed that the

---

[1] The φωτίζεσθαι is equivalent to the "receiving full knowledge of the truth" in x. 26. The word also occurs in 2 Cor. iv. 4, "the illumination of the Gospel of the glory of the Christ." In the LXX. φωτίζειν is "to teach" (Judg. xiii. 8; 2 Kings xii. 2). Similarly in the Fathers ἀνακαινίζειν is "to rebaptise."
[2] See Tert. *De pudicit.* 20; Epiphan. *Haer.* lix., μετὰ τὸ λουτρὸν μηκέτι ἐλεεῖσθαι δύνασθαι τὸν παραπεπτωκότα; Euseb. *H. E.* vi. 43; Ambrose, *De Poenit.* ii. 2, etc.; Pearson, *On the Creed*, Art. x; and the Dp. of Winchester on Art. xvi. This attempt to insist upon a transcendental perfection arose from the conviction, held by Montanists, though not by them exclusively, that the end was imminent. The rule of the Novatians was μὴ δέχεσθαι τοὺς ἐπιτεθυκότας εἰς τὰ μυστήρια (Socrates, *H. E.* iv. 28).
[3] 2 Cor. ii. 7, 10; vii. 12.
[4] The reader will be reminded of what was said by the dying Cromwell. He asked his chaplain a question as to "the indefectibility of grace." "Was it possible for any one who had

rendering of the English Version, "*if* they shall fall away," is an attempt to get rid of this inference. That it is a mistranslation of the most obvious kind is undeniable, since the Greek participle is in the *past* tense; but, if the history of it be traced through various versions of the Bible, it seems not to have been due to a Calvinistic bias, but to be a perfectly honest mistake, derived from other sources. Calvin himself was far too great a scholar to defend his view by such a rendering. He adopted the different method of attempting to weaken the force of the previous expressions, and to argue that when the writer spoke of those "who tasted of the heavenly gift, and were made partakers of the Holy Ghost, and tasted the good word of God and the powers of the future world," he did not mean "true and sincere believers," but only 'the reprobates who had but *tasted, as it were, with their outer lips* the grace of God, and been irradiated by some sparks of His Light.' He tried, in fact, to exaggerate the literal meaning of the word "taste," so as to imply that it meant nothing more than an *inkling* of Christian truth. It will be seen at once that such an argument is not to explain Scripture, but to explain it away. Extravagant literalism has been even more fatal to exegesis than extravagant allegorising.

β. But the Calvinists had no monopoly in the distortion of the plain meaning of the sacred words. That error belongs, alas! to all sects and all religious partisans alike. Arminians, who were unwilling to admit that in this life the door of repentance and of hope could ever be closed to any sinner, stumbled at the word "impossible," and actually rendered it (as in some ancient Latin manuscripts) by the word *difficile*, "difficult." The doctrine on behalf of which they thus twisted words to suit their own meaning may, indeed, be amply supported, but it must not be supported by such an untenable procedure. "Impossible" has a very different meaning from "difficult," and it is clear that the writer lays down quite distinctly that, when those who have received spiritual illumination and shared in Divine gifts deliberately apostatise, it is *impossible* to renew them to repentance, seeing that they are—or, as the words may perhaps be rendered, *so long as* they are—crucifying afresh, to their own ruin, the Son of God. He does not say that this *has* occurred in the case of the Hebrew Christians; nay, he expresses his conviction that it has not. He does not even say that it *can* occur. He only says that, *when it occurs, and so long as it lasts*, renewal is impossible. There can be no *second* "Second Birth."

4. On the other hand, his words must not be forced and tortured into conclusions which do not fall within the scope either of his language or of his hypothesis. All that he has here in view is the agency of men —the teaching and ministry of the Church; he is neither speaking nor

---

once been in a state of grace to fall away from it?" When his chaplain answered in the negative, Cromwell replied that in that case he was happy, for he felt sure that once he had been in a state of grace.

thinking of the omnipotence of God. It is impossible in the highest degree for a camel to go through the eye of a needle;[1] but what is impossible with men is possible with God.[2] And, indeed, the marked change of tenses in this passage is not without its significance. He says that it is impossible to renew to repentance those who *have* fallen away, *crucifying as they are* the Son of God. The change from the past to the present implies a continuous, as well as an insolent apostasy. It implies the case of those who cling deliberately to their sins.[3] While this continues, how can there be any hope of renewal? The condition of such men, so long so it continues unchanged, precludes all possibility of the action of grace. It is impossible at once "to be pardoned" and to retain the offence. If, said the Jewish Rabbis, a man has merely touched a creeping thing, the smallest drop of water suffices for his Levitic purification; but if he keeps the unclean thing purposely in his hand, an ocean of ablutions will not make him clean. It is impossible to save willing offenders in the sense in which *man* may "save" his brother (1 Tim. iv. 16); but nothing is impossible to God.

5. It will be seen, then, how little this passage lends itself to the violent oppositions of these old controversies. Nor, again, has it much bearing on the too curious speculations in which some have indulged about the sin against the Holy Ghost, and the unpardonable sin.[4] That there is a sin which shall not be forgiven, either in this or the future age—that there is "a sin unto death," for the forgiveness of which we are not bidden to pray—that the last state of a backslider or an apostate may be worse than the first[5]—we learn from other passages of Scripture. That a daring and willing apostasy—a deliberate return from light to darkness, and from the power of God to Satan—must be the most perilous of all conditions, and therefore must very nearly approach to those awful sins, is clear from the nature of the case, since like "the doing despite to the spirit of grace" (x. 29) it seems to close against itself the very door of salvation.[6] We must neither turn the text into "a rack of despair" nor into "a pillar of carnal security." If by the expression "on their falling away" he meant to describe *every* fall into mortal sin, then, as Luther says, his words would contradict "all the Gospels,

---

[1] Matt. xix. 26; Mark x. 27; Luke xviii. 27. That the words must be understood in their literal sense, and that neither can κάμηλος mean "rope," nor "the eye of a needle" mean "the side-gate of a city," I have shown in a paper in the *Expositor* (Vol. iii. 169).

[2] So St. Ambrose (*De poenit.* ii. 3): "Quae impossibilia sunt apud homines, possibilia sunt apud Deum, et potens est Deus quando vult donare nobis peccata, etiam quae putamus non posse concedi."

[3] ἀνασταυροῦντας ἁμαρτανόντων, x. 26.

[4] See *infra* on 1 John v. 16.

[5] 2 Pet. ii. 20; Luke xi. 26.

[6] A writer who was not thinking of the Epistle to the Hebrews has said, in touching on only one little aspect of the consequences of apostasy, that "When the Christian falls back out of the bright hope of the Resurrection, even the Orpheus song is forbidden him; not to have known the hope is blameless: one may sing, unknowing, as the swan or Philomela. But to have known and fall away from it, and to declare that the human wishes which are summed in that one—'Thy kingdom come'—are vain! The Fates ordain that there shall be no singing after that."—Ruskin, "Fiction, Fair and Foul" (*Nineteenth Century*, Aug. 1880).

and all the Epistles of St. Paul." But he is speaking only of predetermined and wilful apostasy, and irrevocable Divine dereliction;[1] such as is described in that passage of Isaiah[2] where the Prophet speaks of renegades passing through the land hardly bestead, and hungry, and fretting themselves, and looking upwards only to curse their King and their God, and seeing nothing but dimness and anguish when they look downwards. Beyond this we cannot go. The various modern discussions which have risen out of these mysterious passages do not seem to have been consciously present to the writer's mind. He is speaking to a very different class from those whom Jesus warned about the sin against the Holy Ghost. He is speaking to Hebrew Christians, and pointing out to them with awful faithfulness the fact that they were becoming spiritually stagnant, and that stagnancy ends in corruption. To return to their dead works after the heavenly enlightenment—to abandon the eternal substance for the transient shadow—to go back from the finished sacrifice of Christ to the beggarly elements of the Law, was a peril which they were beginning to incur, but from which he felt convinced that they would be saved in time. Nor could he have chosen any words better fitted than these to arrest the degeneracy which he already saw and deplored.

A less voluminous controversy has arisen out of the writer's comparison of the backsliding, or rather the apostate, Christians to waste and worthless land.

α. The test of sincerity is fruitfulness. The field that has drunk the rain from heaven, and bears thirty, sixty, or a hundredfold, is a field which God has blessed. But the field on which the rain falls and the sun shines in vain, and which only brings forth weeds wherewith the mower filleth not his hand, nor he that gathereth the sheaves his bosom, has been tested and found profitless, like the clay ground between Succoth and Zeredatha.[3] Of such land he says that it is "nigh to a curse." Doubtless he has in mind the older curse—which yet the mercy of God mitigated into something not far from a blessing—"Cursed is the ground for thy sake. Thorns also and thistles shall it bring forth to thee."[4] But yet the form of his expression surely shows how far are his thoughts from the awful dogma of final reprobation. "See," says St. Chrysostom, "how much consolation his words involve! He says '*near* a curse,' not '*a curse.*' But he who has not yet fallen into a curse, but has got *near* it, will also be able to get afar from it. If then we cut out and burn up the thorns, we shall be able to enjoy the unnumbered benefits, and to become approved, and to share in the blessing."

β. Yet *the end* of such waste soil is "for burning." Some have thought that even in this burning there is implied, not hopeless

---

[1] Von Oettingen and Delitzsch refer to the case of Spira (see Herzog, Real. Encykl., s.v.).
[2] Is. viii. 21. [3] 2 Chron. iv. 17. [4] Gen. iii. 18.

destruction, but a method of improvement. Such a method was well known to Roman agriculture. "Often, too," says Virgil, "hath it been of use to fire barren fields, and to burn the light stubble with crackling flames; whether it be that so the lands acquire hidden strength and fattening nurture, or that so every distemper is baked out of them by fire, and the useless moisture sweats out, or that the heat opens out more paths and secret apertures through which sap may come to the tender plants."[1] It may be doubted whether the writer was familiar with this agricultural practice, or its supposed utility. It is more likely that he was thinking of scorched and waste wildernesses like that "Burnt Phrygia" with which he must have been familiar, or of regions like the Solfatara, or of the smoke rising from the fields of Sodom, where "the whole land is brimstone and salt, and burning, that it is not sown, nor beareth, nor any green groweth therein."[2] He is not describing the actual fate in store for any of his readers; he is illustrating by a passing metaphor the ultimate destiny of those who deliberately reject God—of those who, having sinned willingly against light and knowledge, continue hardened in defiant impenitence. Such, for instance, would be the position of those Jews who, having once known Christ, so far apostatised from Him as to adopt the current names of scorn by which He was described in the Jewish cryptographs—to speak of Him as "Absalom" or "the Hung," or to turn the form of His name into an anagram of malediction.[3] If the ground which God gives us to till produces only thorns and thistles, we must, as St. Chrysostom says, cut up and burn them. We must "break up our fallow ground, and not sow among thorns."[4] We shall then be able "to enjoy unnumbered blessings and to become approved." The evil produce of the soil must be consumed that the soil may be saved for better purposes, just as the bad work of a workman must be burned while the workman shall be saved so as by fire. But if the work of the workman be always and continuously bad, he is rejected; and if a soil brings forth nothing but things rank and gross in nature, it must itself be scathed with fire. The metaphor acquires a fuller significance if we think of the Jews to whom it was addressed, and remember that, but a few years afterwards, their beloved city was trodden under foot by its enemies, and their Holy Temple was given to the devouring flame.

But he proceeds to tell them that he has a conviction that they, his Christian readers, have adopted the better course, and will inherit the better lot. He did not doubt that they were heirs of salvation, though he used this language. "Their work, their alms, and all their good endeavours" furnished a proof of this; for God is just, and God

---

[1] Virg. *Georg.* i. 84, seq. See, too, Plin. *H. N.* xviii. 39, 72.
[2] Deut. xxix. 23.
[3] See *Life of Christ*, ii. 452. [By *notarikon*, *Jemach Shemo Vezichro*, "May his name and memory be blotted out."]
[4] Jer. iv. 3.

does not forget. They had ministered to the saints; they were still doing so, though, perhaps—as he seems to hint with delicate kindness—with less zeal than before. He exhorts them not to show themselves remiss, but with all zeal to work out their salvation to the end, and so by faith and endurance to enter into that heritage which was pledged to them not only by the word but by the oath of God. However severe, therefore, their afflictions had been, they might rest upon a sure hope. The little boat of their lives was being tossed by many a storm, yet it was safe, for it was moored by an anchor which could never slip its hold. That anchor was not fixed even on the rock of any earthly sea, but the hawser which held it passed out of sight behind the veil of Heaven; and in that heavenly sanctuary ONE had entered as a forerunner on their behalf. HE would see that the anchor held; He would keep guard over the promised hope,—the High Priest for ever after the order of Melchizedek.

SECTION IV.

THE ORDER OF MELCHIZEDEK.

In those words, the writer, with great literary skill, resumes the allusion which he had introduced in v. 10, and had left unexplained in order to prepare them for his argument by the exhortation of these intermediate verses. But now that he has stimulated them to a loftier range of spiritual attainments by warning them of the peril of apostasy, and by encouraging them to perseverance in good works, he can proceed with a surer step to develop the truths which were best fitted to emancipate them from their temptation to relapse.

"For this Melchizedek, king of Salem, priest of God most high,[1] who met[2] Abraham returning from the slaughter[3] of the kings and blessed him,[4] to whom also Abraham apportioned a tithe of all,[5] being first by interpretation King of righteousness,[6] and then also King of Salem, which is King of peace; without father, without mother, without lineage,[7] having neither beginning of days nor end of life, but having been likened to the Son of God[8] remaineth a Priest for perpetuity" (vii. 1—3).

This comparison of the Priesthood of Christ to that of Melchizedek occupies so cardinal a position, that we must pause over this passage if we are to form any true conception of the meaning of the Epistle.

---

[1] King and Priest, Zech. vi. 13 (Serv. ad Æn. iii. 80). See the subsequent remarks for further notes on this passage.
[2] The true reading is ὅς, not ὁ (א, A, B, D, E, K). The construction is an anakoluthon.
[3] κοπῆς, from κόπτω, "I cut." Comp. Josh. x. 20 (LXX.).
[4] Philo (De Abraham. § 40) says that Melchizedek "sacrificed for Abraham the offerings of victory.
[5] I.e., of all his spoils.   [6] V. infra.
[7] Ἀγενεαλόγητος, which occurs here only, cannot mean "without descent" (see ver. 6), though, misled by this error, Ignatius (Ep. ad Philad.) reckons Melchizedek among those who have led a celibate life.
[8] This expression not only refers to Ps. cx. 4, but speaks of Melchizedek as a Divinely appointed type of Priesthood, which he is not recorded to have either received from any ancestors, or transmitted to any successors.

Let us first endeavour to clear up the separate expressions.

All that we know historically respecting Melchizedek is contained in two verses in the Book of Genesis (Gen. xiv. 18, 19).

We are there told that when Amraphel, king of Shinar, with three allies, made war on Bera, king of Sodom, and his four allies, and defeated them, they carried away the plunder and captives of the Cities of the Plain. Among these captives was Lot, whose goods they had also seized. Abraham, arming his three hundred and eighteen servants, and assisted by the Amorite chiefs Mamre, Aner, and Eshcol, pursued the victors to the neighbourhood of Damascus, defeated them, rescued their prisoners, and recovered the spoil. On his return the king of Sodom went out to thank and greet him, and met him "at the valley of Shaveh, which is the king's dale." "And Melchizedek king of Salem brought forth bread and wine: and he was the priest of the most high God.[1] And he blessed him, and said, Blessed be Abram of the most high God, possessor of heaven and earth: and blessed be the most high God, which hath delivered thine enemies into thy hand. And he gave him tithes of all."

If we first take the narrative as it stands, we observe that it is not stated that Melchizedek went out to meet Abraham, as it is stated of the king of Sodom. It is, however, a natural inference that he did so, and we see from the reference of the writer of the Epistle that such was part of the Jewish tradition on the subject. The place of meeting is uncertain. Shaveh has never been identified, nor is anything known of the King's dale.[2] The name Melchizedek may mean "king of righteousness"—a rendering found in the Targums,[3] and here introduced perhaps with reference to Is. xxxii. 1, where it is said of the Messiah, "Behold a king shall reign in righteousness."[4] It may also mean "righteous king," as it is rendered in Josephus[5] and Philo.[6] It is a name closely analogous to Adonizedek, which means "Lord of righteousness" or "justice," and is a natural name for an Eastern king whose chief function in time of peace was that of a judge. Adonizedek is called king of Jerusalem,[7] but Melchizedek is called king of Salem. It has been a disputed point for centuries whether by Salem is meant Jerusalem or not.[8]

That this king of a Canaanite city should be "a priest of the most high God" is an interesting circumstance. Attempts have been made to

---

[1] The union of Royalty and Priesthood was regarded as peculiarly sacred. "Rex Anius, rex idem hominum Phœbique sacerdos" (Virg. Æn. iii. 80).
[2] Josephus calls it Πεδίον βασιλικόν (Antt. i. 10, § 2). There is nothing to identify it with "the King's dale" in which Absalom built himself a pillar. Even if it be the same "King's dale" it may have been in the tribe of Ephraim, if the reading of 2 Sam. xiii. 23 be right; but there, instead of "beside Ephraim," there is a various reading, "the Valley of Rephaim."
[3] In Bereshith Rabba, f. 42, c, it is said that Tsedek was a name of Jerusalem, as is implied in Is. i. 21. "Righteousness lodged in it." Aben Ezra makes Melchizedek mean "King of a righteous place."
[4] Compare Is. ix. 6; Zech. ix. 9; Mal. iv. 2; 1 Cor. i. 30.
[5] Antt. i. 10, § 2; B. J. vi. 10; ὁ τῇ πατρίῳ γλώσσῃ κληθεὶς βασιλεὺς δίκαιος.
[6] Leg. Allegg. iii. 25.
[7] Josh. x. 3.
[8] See Excursus X., "'Salem' and Jerusalem."

explain it away. The Hebrew phrase for the most high God is *El Eliôn*, and it appears that the Phœnicians also had a god to whom they gave the title of Eliôn, or The Highest.[1] Nothing, however, can be clearer than that Moses intended the word to be understood in its fullest sense of the True God.[2] Nor is there any excuse for being incredulous about the fact, for, when we remember the longevity of the patriarchs, it is probable that the worship of God would have been preserved in some families. And the *primary* intention of the sacred historian in mentioning this incident may have been a desire to do honour to this kingly priest, whose dignity was recognised with such deep reverence by Abraham himself, that he accepted his solemn blessing, and gave him a tithe of his spoils.

It was natural that a circumstance so remarkable should attract the attention of the Jews, and that they should see something memorable in the priesthood of a king who enjoyed his sacerdotal dignity so many centuries before the days of Aaron, and who had been treated with so much honour by their great ancestor himself. Hence it was also natural that the Hebrew poet in the 110th Psalm,[3] in prophesying of a Prince and Deliverer who was the type of the Messiah, should say, "The Lord sware, and will not repent, Thou art a priest for ever after the order of Melchizedek." The Messianic interpretation of this Psalm was never disputed."[4] If it had been, nothing would have been easier for the Jews than to set aside the question about David's son and David's Lord which our Lord propounded to them, and which they expressed their inability to solve.[5] But even the Targum of Jonathan renders the first verse of this Psalm by "The Lord said to His Word."

But when Melchizedek was thus elevated into a type of the Messiah, the brief notice respecting him was studied with the minutest scrutiny, and mysteries were supposed to lurk in every word. Thus so simple a circumstance as his bringing forth to Abraham bread and wine is in Bereshith Rabba explained by Rabbi Samuel Bar Nachman to mean that he taught to Abraham the ordinances of the High Priesthood, the bread being a type of the shewbread, and the wine of libations. Other Rabbis, referring to Prov. ix. 5—"Come eat of my bread, and drink of the wine which I have mingled"—say that Melchizedek explained the Law to Abraham. These, it is obvious, are mere fancies of a fantastic exegesis bent on seizing every opportunity to proclaim the eternity of the Levitic dispensation. Yet multitudes of Christian writers, imbued with the spirit which *will* see in Scripture more than Scripture

---

[1] Philo Bybl. ap. Euseb. Præp. Ev. i. 10. A trace of this title (elonim velonoth) is perhaps discoverable in the Poenulus of Plautus.
[2] Though this is the earliest occurrence of the name, it is found frequently in the Pentateuch and Psalms. Abram repeats it with "Jehovah" in ver. 22.
[3] In the title, Ps. cx. is called "A Psalm of David;" the LXX. call it "An ode to the Assyrian."
[4] Comp. Zech. vi. 13, where, of the High Priest Joshua (Jeshua in Ezra and Neh.) as a type of the Messiah, it is said, "He shall be," or perhaps, "There shall be," a priest upon his throne."
[5] Matt. xxii. 44.

sanctions, make this simple act of hospitality a sacerdotal oblation, and argue (with Bellarmine) that it was the one characteristic of his Priesthood.[1] But that the bread and wine were not typically intended is clear from the silence of the Epistle. Had the application been legitimate, a point so germane to the writer's purpose could not have been passed over without notice, especially as Philo, who has very similar views respecting Melchizedek, ventures to say that on this occasion he did offer a sacrifice for victory—*ἐπινίκια ἔθυε*.[2] What an opportunity for powerful argument would have been furnished if Apollos could have said that Melchizedek's sacrifice was not an offering of victims in the Jewish fashion, but was an offering which prefigured the Christian oblations of bread and wine! Of such a sacrifice he does not say a word. Whatever may have been the acts in which the priesthood of Melchizedek consisted, Apollos does not mention sacrifice among them. He does not so much as allude to the bread and wine—much less does he imply that it was an Eucharistic offering.

But he touches on other points which seem to enhance the dignity or mysteriousness of Melchizedek by saying that he was "fatherless, motherless, without pedigree, having neither beginning of days nor end of life."

His method of illustration, like that of which St. Paul occasionally made use, is Rabbinic in its general character, but not fantastic or inadmissible. He takes a Scriptural fact as it stands, and merely shows its typical value. It is, however, this passage which has originated so many untenable conjectures about Melchizedek, and which has been made an excuse for most strange hypotheses. Such discussions would never have arisen if we had been more familiar with the way of handling Scripture which had become prevalent at Alexandria, and was perpetuated for centuries in the later schools of Tiberius and Babylon.

Of course, if the words be taken literally, they can have but one meaning. One who had neither father, nor mother, nor ancestors, neither beginning of days nor end of life, could not be a human being at all. Accordingly Melchizedek has been regarded by some commentators, even of this century, as "the Angel of the Presence," the "Captain of the Lord's Host," "the Divine Angel of the Lord," the Second Person of the Ever Blessed Trinity, the Jewish "Shechinah" and Metatron,[3] who continually appeared to the Fathers under the Old Testament dispensation. Cunæus even refers to this incident

---

[1] On this perversion see Waterland, *Works*, v. 165; Jewel, *Reply to Harding*, art. xvii.; and on the other side, Jackson, *On the Creed*, ix., § ii. 10.
[2] *De Abrahamo.*
[3] Metatron is a Talmudic word of foreign origin, perhaps a rude hybrid of μετὰ θρόνιος, or "sharer of the Throne." He was the chief of the four Angels who were "Masters of Wisdom." He stands in a subordinate relation to God, but to him are attributed many of the works of the "Angel of the Presence,"—a sort of Pre-incarnate Messiah (see Hamburger, s.v.).

in explanation of our Lord's words to the Jews, "Your father Abraham rejoiced to see my day, and he saw it and was glad." Marcus Eremita mentions a sect which believed Melchizedek to be "God the Word, previous to incarnation."[1]

Others, again, thought that Melchizedek was the Holy Spirit.[2] This was the opinion maintained in an anonymous work—probably written by the deacon Hilarius—which St. Jerome received from Evagrius, and which led him to an elaborate study of what had been written on this question, which even in his day was eagerly debated. He found that Origen and Didymus believed Melchizedek to be an angel, and that the Jews supposed him to be Shem, the son of Noah,[3] who—as they showed by calculation—might have survived till the days of Abraham.[4] It is hard to see why, in that case, he should not have been introduced by his own name. Yet this hypothesis satisfied Lyra, Cajetan, Melancthon, and even Luther and Selden. Others again, with about as much justification, suppose that he was Ham. Calmet regards him as a re-appearance of Enoch. Nork, with hardly less absurdity, discovers in him the Phœnician god Sydik, or Saturn![5]

I unhesitatingly follow those who reject these idle hypotheses, and who hold with Hippolytus, Eusebius of Cæsarea, and other Fathers, as well as the ablest recent commentators, that Melchizedek was neither more nor less than what Moses tells us that he was—namely, Melchizedek, a Priest and King of the little Canaanite town of Salem, to whom, because he was a worshipper of the True God, Abraham paid tithes, and from whom he received a blessing.[6] His importance was purely typical; his *personal* importance was very small. It is amazing that any one familiar with Rabbinic exegesis should hesitate for a moment in coming to this conclusion. In the Alexandrian School especially, the habit of allegorising had been carried so far as to imperil, and even obliterate, the plain sense of the sacred narrative. The allegorists saw or imagined mysteries in the silence of Scripture no less than in its simplest circumstances, and even in the numerical values and methods of writing its letters. The writer of this Epistle, familiar with the works of Philo, adopts the Alexandrian method in arguing with those by whom it would be regarded as specially cogent. But

---

[1] Epiphan. *Hær.* lv. 7; Ambrose, *De Abraham.* i. 3. All these opinions and quotations are diligently collected by Bleek.

[2] Epiphan. *Hær.* lxvii. 3. This wild theory was maintained by the sect of Melchisedekites (see Dorner, i. 515).

[3] Rabbi Jochanan Ben Nuri says: "The Holy One—blessed be He!—took Shem, and separated him to be a priest to Himself, that he might serve before Him. He also caused His Shechinah to rest with him, and called his name Melchizedek, Priest of the Most High, and King of Salem."—*Avodath Hakkodesh*, Pt. iii. c. 20; *Nedarim*, f. 32, b.

[4] Thus in two of the Targums—though not in that of Onkelos—we find the gloss "Malka Zedika, who was Shem bar Noah." But as far as the Epistle to the Hebrews is concerned, it is enough to say that (1) Shem is not ἀγενεαλόγητος; his lineage is recorded; (2) that Canaan was in the territory of Ham (see Deyling, *Obs. Sacr.* ii. 73; Bochart, *Phaleg.* ii. 1; Jackson, *On the Creed*, Bk. ix.). This opinion of the Jews, though embraced by Luther, Lightfoot, etc., seems to have been post-Christian.

[5] Nork, *Bibl. Mythol.* i. 154.

[6] See Cave, *Lives of the Apostles*, xxii. This is the view of Josephus (B. J. vi. 10).

he neither abuses the method nor carries it to untenable extremes. He sees that the suddenness with which Melchizedek is introduced into the sacred story, and the subsequent silence respecting him, are reasons for regarding him as a Divinely-appointed *type* of the Messiah. The Book of Genesis, as Bishop Wordsworth says, casts on him a shadow of eternity; gives him a typical eternity. But he expressly treats of him as a type, and a *type only*, of One whose "office was incomparably beyond that of the legal Economy"—his person greater, his undertaking weightier, his design more sublime and excellent, his oblation more meritorious, his prayers more prevalent, his office more durable than even any whose business it was to intercede and mediate between God and man.[1] Had Melchizedek been the Metatron, or the Pre-incarnate Messiah, he would *not* have been a type, but the Divine Son Himself; he would not have been *likened to* Christ, but would have *been* Christ. All the conjectures respecting him were excusable in times when the peculiarities of Semitic thought were little known; but now that the history of exegesis is better understood, such suggestions can only be ranked among obsolete mistakes.

For there are abundant instances to prove that such phrases as "fatherless, motherless, without pedigree," were used, not only in Rabbinic Hebrew, but even in Classical Greek and in Latin, of those whose parents and ancestry were simply *unrecorded*. Thus Ion, in the tragedy of Euripides, calls himself "motherless" when he supposes himself to be the son of a slave-woman;[2] and Scipio addressed the mongrel crowd in the Forum as people "who had neither father nor mother;"[3] and Horace speaks of himself as "sprung from *no* ancestors."[4] Similarly we find in Bereshith Rabba that "a Gentile has no father,"[5] *i.e.*, the father of a proselyte is of no account in Jewish pedigrees. The Jewish priests were obliged to keep the most careful genealogies, and some families were for ever excluded from the priesthood in Ezra's days because they could not produce adequate proof of their priestly descent.[6] And not only must they be able to produce the names of their fathers and their ancestry up to Aaron, but, further, their marriages were regulated by the most rigid restrictions.[7] It was remarkable to the Jews of Ezra's day that Melchizedek should be introduced *as a priest*—and as a priest of such striking dignity—while not a word is said of his father or mother, or ancestors, or birth or death.[8] In the mystic treatment of Scripture by the Talmudists, arguments are drawn from this silence. Thus, from the non-mention of Cain's death in Scripture, Philo draws the lesson that evil never dies among the human race. The very vague-

---

[1] Cave, l.c. [2] *Ion*, 850. [3] Cic. *de Orat.* ii. 64.
[4] Hor. *Sat.* i. 6, 10. [5] f. 18, b.
[6] Ezr. ii. 61, 62; Nehem. vii. 63, 64. [7] Lev. xxi. 7, 13, 14.
[8] "The Melchizedek of human history has, indeed, died; but the Melchizedek of sacred history lives without dying, fixed for ever *as one who lives* by the pen of the sacred historian, and thus stamped as a type of the Son, the ever-living Priest" (Delitzsch). "He is simply an otherwise unknown king, whose meeting with Abraham is, however, in the history of redemption, of the greatest historical and typical importance" (Moll).

ness in which this grand figure of Melchizedek is left, although he is the first who in Scripture is called a priest, makes him better suited to stand as the type of one who was endowed with an eternal priesthood. The words of the writer taken literally are applicable to Jesus alone,[1] and are only applicable to Melchizedek in the secondary and metaphorical sense which I have explained. He stands on the page of Scripture as an eternal priest, because Scripture witnesses alike to his priesthood and his life without an allusion to the abrogation of the one or the close of the other.[2] If any harshness still remains, it is removed by the consideration that in the mind of the writer the type and the antitype are so simultaneously prominent that the language which refers to the one is mingled with that which is more strictly applicable to the other. To ignore these facts, and to regard Melchizedek as a Divine being, still alive as a priest, though he only occurs in a single clause of a simple historic narrative,[3] is to apply to Scripture the methods of explanation which reduce it to an insoluble enigma, and which subject the souls of unbiassed readers to a strain which it was never intended that they should bear. Any one who helps to rescue the Holy Book from these extravagances of superstitious letter-worship renders to faith a service for which he may be rebuked by contemporary ignorance, but which will bear good fruit in future times.

"But observe,"[4] he continues, "how great was this man to whom even Abraham gave a tithe out of his best spoils[5]—he, the patriarch.[6] And those of the sons of Levi who receive the priestly function,[7] have commandment to tithe the people according to the law[8]—that is, their brethren, sprung though they are from the loins

---

[1] The word "without mother" might seem inapplicable, and would be inapplicable if the Church had ever sanctioned the title *Theotokos* applied to the Virgin Mary; but, as Theodoret rightly observes, "as God, He has been begotten of the Father alone."

[2] Alford thinks it "almost childish" to suppose that the writer meant no more than that the life, death, etc., of Melchizedek are not recorded; and therefore he regards him as a Divine being about whom we are not to be wise above what is written, and about whom we are not called upon to enquire further! It is not "almost," but "quite" childish to pretend to interpret Scripture by ignoring the plain peculiarities of the language and method of thought among those by whom it was written. And the misapplied text about "not being wise above what is written" is usually degraded into an excuse for *being* wise above what is written—to the extent, sometimes, of utter superstition.

[3] Josephus simply calls him "a chief of the Canaanites."

[4] The proper difference between ὁρῶ, "I see," and θεωρῶ, "I observe" (though it is not always kept in common usage), is given by Phavorinus, who says that ὁρῶ is applied to bodily, and θεωρῶ to spiritual, insight.

[5] ἀκροθίνια, derived from ἄκρος and θίς, properly means "what is taken from the top of the heap," but it is used for "the first fruits of τὰ ἶλα" and sometimes, apparently (according to Hesychius and Phavorinus), for "spoils" generally.

[6] The position of ὁ πατριάρχης is very forcible, and the oratorical style of the writer evidently makes him fond of these sounding collocations. The use of the Ionicus a minoris ("⏑⏑--") to end the sentence makes the word still more prominent. A whole argument about the grandeur of Abraham is thus condensed into one emphatic word. Comp. Acts vii. 16, 43; xxviii. 31; Gal. iii. 1.)

[7] Aristotle defines this word ἱερατεία as meaning "the care concerning the gods" (Pol. vii. 8). It seems to be a little more specific than ἱερωσύνη.

[8] A needless difficulty has been made of this expression because the Priests did not directly receive tithes from the people, but only from the Levites, who paid them a tithe of what they received as tithes (Numb. xviii. 22, 23, 26; Neh. x. 38). Hence Biesenthal proposes to read Λευίν for λαόν. But (a) the Priests might take these tithes directly, as Jewish tradition said that they did in the days of Ezra (Yevamoth, f. 86, b; Bechoroth, f. 4, a); and (β) the expression is a general one—"qui facit per alium, facit per se." The question, as Dr. Moulton says, is not one of emolument, but of position, and the Priests stood alone in receiving tithes and paying none.

of Abraham; but he whose descent is not derived from them hath tithed Abraham, and hath blessed[1] the holder of the promises. Now, beyond all dispute, that which is inferior is ever blessed by the superior. And in this case dying men[2] receive tithes; but in *that* case he of whom it is testified that he lives,[3] And, so to speak, by means of Abraham, even Levi, who receiveth tithes, hath been tithed; for he was still in the loins of his father when Abraham met him" (vii. 4—10).

The argument of this passage is the superiority of Melchizedek's priesthood to that of Aaron in seven particulars:—

(i.) Because even Abraham gave him tithes.

(ii.) Because even the yet-unborn Levi may be said to have paid tithes in the person of Abraham.

(iii.) Because it is the superior who gives the blessing, and Melchizedek blessed Abraham.

(iv.) Because the Aaronic priests die, but Melchizedek stands as a type of undying priesthood.

(v.) Because the permanence of his Priesthood implied the abrogation of the whole Law on which the Levitic Priesthood was grounded.

If there was a transference of the Priesthood there was necessarily also a transference of the Law. Had there been in the Levitic Law any power of perfectionment, what need would there have been for a different priest[4] to rise of whom it was expressly said, not that he was "after the order of Aaron," but that he was "after the order of Melchizedek"? And "our Lord,"[5] in whom was fulfilled the Type of Eternal Priesthood, *was a different* Priest, seeing that He has sprung[6] from a different tribe than that of the Aaronic priests—namely, the royal but non-priestly tribe of Judah.[7] Christ is a Priest, not in accordance

---

[1] The perfects express the absolute and permanent fact.
[2] *I.e.*, men under the liability to die, as in the well-known lines—
"He preached as one who ne'er should preach again,
And as a dying man to dying men."
[3] We know nothing of the death of Melchizedek; so far, therefore, as the page of Scripture is concerned, he always lives. The argument is analogous to that which I have already mentioned, derived by Philo from the absence of any mention of the death of Cain in Scripture. To a writer addressing those who in the Rabbinic Midrashim heard daily specimens of similar applications, nothing would be more natural than to argue that the absence of all mention of the death of Melchizedek made him, in yet another respect, an eternal type of Christ. The difference between his method and ours is not in the point *of view*, but only in *the method of statement*. Writing in these days we might argue thus: The Psalmist says that God had sworn that the Priest-king, the Messiah, of whom he is prophesying, should be "a priest for ever after the order of Melchizedek." We learn from the Book of Genesis that the Priesthood of Melchizedek was one of such high dignity as to be recognised even by the Patriarch Abraham; and in this respect, as well as in its magnificent and untransmitted independence, it is evidently spoken of as superior to the Aaronic Priesthood. And it is also a type of the Messianic Priesthood, because just as Christ was eternal and superior to all earthly relationships, so on the page of Scripture Melchizedek stands without father, mother, or descent, and with no record of human birth or human death. This is all condensed by the writer of the Epistle into such expressions as those in the text.
[4] ἕτερος, "a different," not merely ἄλλος, "another."
[5] This passage is memorable as being the *first* in which this expression—now so familiar and universal—is applied to Christ. It marks an advance in the growth of Christianity.
[6] ἀνατέταλκεν, a word almost invariably used of the sunrise (Mal. iv. 2; Is. lx. 1; Luke xii. 54; 2 Pet. i. 19), though also of the springing of plants (Zech. iii. 1; vi. 12; Jer. xxiii. 5, where the LXX. render "the Branch" by Ἀνατολή; and Is. xliv. 4; Ezek. xvii. 6).
[7] The writer does not touch on the doubt which hung over the High Priesthood of his time. If his readers were Palestinian Jews, they at least, and probably all Jews, would be quick to catch the fresh force which was added to his arguments by this circumstance. Those Sadducean

with "the law of a fleshen commandment"—*i.e.*, with the transitory system which was hedged round with the limitations of earthly relationships[1] but in accordance with the power of that indissoluble life[2] which is indicated by the swearing of the oaths that He should be "a priest for ever after the order of Melchizedek." From the change, then, of the Priesthood we infer nothing less than the disannulment of the preceding commandment[3] because of its weakness and unprofitableness—(for the Law perfected nothing)—and the introduction of a better hope, by means of which we draw nigh to God.[4]

(vi.) It was superior because it was founded on the swearing of an oath,[5]—namely, that of Psalm cix. 4—which was not the case with the Levitic priests. "Of so much better a covenant"[6] hath Jesus become a surety.[7]

---

hierarchs had been introduced by Herod. They were of priestly, but it was far from certain that they were of high-priestly, descent (Jos. *Antt.* xx. 10; xv. 3, § 1). Philo, who was himself of Aaronic descent, uses the expression ἀρχιερεὺς ψευδώνυμος (*Opp.* ii. 246, Mangey).

[1] Neither this writer nor St. Paul would have called the Law "carnal" (σαρκικός), a term which he expressly disclaims (Rom. vii. 14). The true reading is σαρκίνης (א, A, B, C, D, etc.; 1 Cor. iii. 1; 2 Cor. iii. 3), as here explained.

[2] The balance and rhythm of the original (*paris'sis, paromoiosis*) are characteristic of this writer, but not of St. Paul. Instances of this style may no doubt be found in St. Paul's Epistles, because, as I have shown in my *Life of St. Paul* (i. 627), he had probably had some initial training in the rhetorical schools of Tarsus, and there is scarcely a single figure of speech or technical method of construction which he does not sometimes use. But they are not *characteristic* of him; they do not enter into the very heart of the periodic structure which he naturally adopts. If I may use a current distinction, St. Paul is often *rhetorical*—*i.e.*, he writes with a passion which finds natural expression in the most forcible figures of speech; but he is scarcely ever *oratorical*—*i.e.*, he never *studies* the form of his sentences with a view to pleasing or satisfying the ear. He does not habitually adopt a stately, sounding, and impressive style. Now, the writer of this Epistle is scarcely ever impassioned; he is never quite swept away by the force of his own feelings, as St. Paul repeatedly is; and he is always oratorical—it was evidently natural to him to adopt such expressions and such a periodic structure as fill and gratify the ear, while at the same time they give impressiveness to the arguments which he is endeavouring to enforce. I have always insisted (see *Life of St. Paul*, ii. 601, 610) on the necessity of making the fullest allowance for the change of style which may be caused by the different moods, or circumstances, or objects of an author at different ages of his life; but no author can continuously adopt a style which is alien to the characteristics of his own temperament; and to me it is only necessary to read the Epistle to the Hebrews side by side with any Epistle of St. Paul to feel more and more strongly that it is *impossible* that the two should have emanated from the same mind.

[3] He does not venture on the s'rong word ἀθέτησις, "disannulment," till he has, so to speak, prepared his way for it by the much milder word "*metathesis*"—"transference," or "alteration," in ver. 12.

[4] vii. 11—19. The E. V. in the latter verse follows a bad punctua'ion of the Greek. The word ἐπεισαγωγή is not the nominative of ἐτελείωσεν, but of γίνεται—"there takes place a cancelling of the previous commandment and a superinduction of a better hope."

[5] The writer uses the sounding word ὁρκωμοσία as being statelier and more impressive than ὅρκος.

[6] The E. V. here renders διαθήκη by "testament." Now διαθήκη is the Greek equivalent of "*berith*," as in Baal Berith ("the Lord of the Covenant") in Judg. ix. 4; and *berith* is rendered by the LXX. διαθήκη, and by our version "covenant," at least 200 times. In fact, in the Old Testament the word *can* have no other meaning, for the Romans invented the "will," and the Jews knew nothing of testamentary bequests. It is certain, then, that any Jew reading this passage, and familiar with the LXX., would take the word to mean "covenant," and not "testament." The Vulgate uses "testamentum," because in Classic Greek διαθήκη often has this meaning; but, as Dr. Moulton remarks, it seems clear from such passages as Ps. lxxxiii. 5 that St. Jerome used it in a wider sense than that of "will." It is from the influence of the Vulgate that we get our phrase "the Old and New Testaments." There is happily nothing misleading or erroneous in the term, but there can be little doubt that St. Paul, from the translation of whose expression the term is derived (2 Cor. iii. 6), meant "Old Covenant," and not "Old Testament." What the meaning of the word is in ix. 15—17 we shall see in the notes to that passage.

[7] vii. 20, 21. As Eternal Priest, he is a pledge (Ecclus. xxix. 15) of the validity of the New Covenant (ver. 25; see viii. 1).

(vii.) It was superior because the Levitic priests were necessarily many, requiring to be constantly replenished to fill up the ravages made in their ranks by death; but His Priesthood, because of His Eternal permanence, is intransmissible; whence, also, He is able to save to the uttermost those who through Him approach to God, seeing that He ever liveth to intercede for them.[1]

Having thus in seven particulars proved how far superior was the Melchizedek Priesthood of Christ to the Levitic Priesthood, and having incidentally introduced the important truth that this transference of Priesthood involved the abrogation not only of Leviticism, but of the whole Mosaic system, he adds a weighty summary of all that he has said about Melchizedek as a Type of Christ, into which, in his usual skilful manner, he introduces the vein of thought which he proceeds to develop in the three following chapters:—

"*For,*" he says—and this "*for*" clinches the whole argument by showing the moral fitness which there was for the disannulment of the old imperfect Priesthood, and the introduction of a better hope—"for such a high priest even became us—holy,[2] harmless,[3] undefiled,[4] separated from sinners,[5] and made loftier than the heavens; who hath not daily necessity,[6] even as those high priests have, first on behalf of his own sins to offer sacrifices, then on behalf of the sins of the people: for this He did once for all in offering up himself. For the law appoints human beings who have infirmity as high priests; but the utterance of the oath, which was *after* the law, appoints a Son, perfected[7] for ever more" (vii. 26—28).

[1] vii. 22—25. Comp. Is. lix. 16, and a passage in Philo on the mediation of the "Eldest Word" (Quis rer. div. haer. Opp. i. 501, ed. Mangey).
[2] Ps. xvi. 10; Acts ii. 27; חָסִיד—"holy" as regards God.
[3] Blameless as regards man.
[4] Comp. ix. 4; 1 Pet. i. 19; Lev. xxi. 17.
[5] The High Priest was in a general sense "separated" (Lev. x. 10; xxii. 2; 1 Chr. xxiii. 13; Jos. Antt. iii. 12, § 2), but he was more specially separated for the week before the Day of Atonement (Yoma, f. 2, a).
[6] If this is interpreted to mean that the High Priest offered sacrifices *daily*, the expression taken literally is inaccurate; for, normally, the High Priest only offered sacrifices once a year, as the writer seems to have been well aware (ix. 25; x. 1, 3). Various ways have been suggested for meeting the difficulty; *e.g.*, (a) that "daily" means "one fixed day every year"; or (β) "often," since it appears that the High Priest *might*, if he chose, offer sacrifices on other occasions (Lev. vi. 19—22; Jos. B. J. v. 5, § 7), or might be represented by one of his sons; or that the expression is, as Bengel says, "indignabunda hyperbole."—But if the expression refers either to the daily meat-offerings—the "*Mincha*"—(Ex. xxix. 38—42; Lev. vi. 13—16, 20; Ecclus. xlv. 11), or to the morning and evening sacrifices in which he might, if he chose, take part, there can be no question that these, so far as we can find any trace in the Law, had nothing to do with the expiation of sins. On the other hand, the High Priest might, if he chose, offer the daily incense, which was regarded as partly expiatory (Lev. xvii. 11, 12). "We are taught," says the Talmud, "that incense atones" (Num. xvii. 12), the silent smoke atoning for slanders spoken in a whisper (Yoma, f. 44. a). Some, again, have supposed that it was a custom for the High Priest to take part in daily expiatory sacrifices, in the Temple of On as at Leontopolis, in Lower Egypt, and that the writer is thinking of this Temple—a conjecture of the most baseless kind. It is certain that Philo uses the same expression exactly, for he speaks of the High Priests "offering on each day prayers and sacrifices" (*De Spec. Legg.* § 23; see, too, in the Talmud, Chagigah, ii. 4; Pesachim, f. 57, a). It may, however, be doubted whether there is any inaccuracy in the mind of the writer, for he possibly means that "Christ had no need to offer sacrifices for daily sins, as the High Priests had year by year to offer a sacrifice for the sins which they daily committed.
[7] Ver. 5, 6, 9; ii. 10; Pss. ii. cx. The rendering "consecrated" (in our version) is taken from Lev. xxi. 10; Ex. xxix. 9, but is much less appropriate.

SECTION V.

THE DAY OF ATONEMENT.

It is evident that in this passage the thoughts of the writer are passing from Melchizedek to the Levitic High Priest in his grandest function on the Day of Atonement. The ideal of his whole position on that day was that he should be free from every ceremonial pollution as a type of his freedom from every stain of sin and wrong. In order to represent as fully as possible this ideal cleanness, he had to be accompanied, and kept awake all the previous night, and had on the day itself to submit to five washings and ten purifications. The Day of Atonement was so memorable in its symbolism—it stirred so intensely the hopes or fears of the people—it was supposed to be attended by so many supernatural omens, on the presence or absence of which the whole welfare of the people depended during the ensuing year—the anxiety caused by any accident which impaired the due ceremonies was so extreme—that the Jews regarded no precaution as extravagant which could ensure the due performance of the requisite ceremonial. It was a shock to the feelings of the whole nation when, on one occasion, the High Priest Ishmael Ben Phabi had been incapacitated from his functions because, in spite of all the long and elaborate endeavours to make his legal cleanliness complete, he had after all become ceremonially unclean, and had been compelled to depute his Sagan to perform the most memorable of his yearly duties. In this instance the pollution had arisen because he had been conversing with the Arab ethnarch Hareth (Aretas), and a speck of the Emir's saliva had touched the High Priest's beard. It was impossible, therefore, by any amount of lustrations or isolation to secure so small a matter as the *ceremonial* cleanness of the High Priest for even one day in all the year; but Jesus was morally, in inmost reality, and for all eternity, that which the human Priest could not be even ceremonially, even in semblance, even for a single day—the sinless offerer of one all-sufficient offering for the sins of all the world.

Having exhausted the comparison of the Priesthood of Christ with that of the Levites, the writer proceeds to a comparison of their respective ministrations, which continues to chap. x. 18.

"But the chief point in all we are saying is this:[1] Such is the High Priest whom we have, who sat on the right hand of the Majesty in the heavens,[2] a minister of the sanctuary[3] and of the genuine tabernacle[4] which the Lord

---

[1] The context shows that κεφάλαιον here cannot mean "summary," for it is by no means a summary, and it also adds fresh particulars. The word is here used in its proper classical sense of "chief point" (Thuc. iv. 50; vi. 16). Dr. Field would render it, "Now to crown (or sum up) our present discourse" (*Otium Norvicense*, iii. 141).

[2] On this sonorous amplification see *ante*, p. 234, n. The ἐκάθισεν seems to be a mark of emphatic pre-eminence (comp. x. 11, 12).

[3] This is probably the meaning of τῶν ἁγίων here as elsewhere in this Epistle (ix. 8, 12, etc., x. 19, xiii. 11), and not "of the saints" (Œcumenius) or "of holy things."

[4] The ideal Archetypal (ἀληθινός) Tabernacle is not only real (ἀληθής), but the perfected

pitched, not man. For every High Priest is appointed to offer both gifts and sacrifices; whence it is necessary that this High Priest also have something which he may offer.[1] Now, if he were upon earth, he would not be a priest at all,[2] since there are priests already who offer the gifts according to the law[3]—the priests who serve an outline and shadow of the heavenly things; even as Moses when about to complete the tabernacle has been Divinely admonished[4]—for See, he says, that thou make all things[5] according to the pattern[6] shown thee in the mount. But now he has obtained a better ministration in proportion[7] as he is also a mediator[8] of a better covenant—one which has been constituted upon better promises.[9] For had that first covenant been faultless,[10] no place would have been sought for a second "(viii. 1—7).

But—as he goes on to argue—place *has* been sought for a second, and this is sufficiently demonstrated by the passage of the Prophet Jeremiah[11] in which, by way of blame[12] to his countrymen, he says, that the days should come when Jehovah would accomplish[13] for Israel and Judah a NEW Covenant, unlike the one which He made for their fathers in the day when He took them by the hand to lead them forth from Egypt—and that because they did not abide in His Covenant, therefore He rejected them.[14] But in the coming days the covenant which He would make would be marked by three great blessings, which were but partially understood by a few of the most enlightened under the Old Covenant—namely, the writing of the Law not on granite slabs, but on their hearts;[15] the immediate knowledge of God by all without human

---

reality of its material counterpart (comp. ix. 24, x. 22; John i. 9). To see in this Tabernacle "the glorified body of Christ" is to give it here too special a meaning.
[1] Namely the Blood of His own finished sacrifice (ix. 14).
[2] Not even a Priest, much less a High Priest.
[3] The present tenses, here as elsewhere, seem to show decisively that the Epistle was written before the fall of Jerusalem.
[4] κεχρημάτισται. The use of the perfect is due to the writer's mode of regarding everything which has been said in the Bible as a present actuality (iv. 9, etc.). For the meaning of the word itself see Luke ii. 26; Acts x. 22; Matt. ii. 12, 22.
[5] Ex. xxv. 40. In the Hebrew and LXX. it is simply "make *it*," not "*all things*;" but this remarkable variation is due to Philo (*De Leg. Alleg.* iii. 33).
[6] It seems to be a very idle enquiry whether this pattern was something real, or only an idea, so that the Tabernacle was "a shadow of a shadow," or only a vision. These are questions which would not so much as occur either to Moses or to the writer, and are in any case otiose because incapable of being decided. The notion that there is in Heaven a real Tabernacle of which that erected by Moses was an exact counterpart—"a fiery ark, and a fiery candlestick, and a fiery table," which descended from Heaven for Moses to see—is mere Rabbinic letter worship and superstition, founded on an abuse of the most ordinary principles of human language.
[7] This method of stating results by proportions is found in other passages of this Epistle (i. 4, iii. 3, vii. 22).
[8] A mediator between God and man, as the Introducer of the New Covenant. Philo applies the same term to Moses (comp. Gal. iii. 19, 20; 1 Tim. ii. 5).
[9] *Better* promises, because, as Theodoret says, the promises of the Mosaic dispensation—a land flowing with milk and honey, multitudes of children, etc.—were mostly temporal, but the new dispensation promised the kingdom of Heaven and Eternal Life.
[10] Whereas it *was* "weak and unprofitable" (vii. 18).
[11] Jer. xxxi. 31—34 (comp. Ezek. xxxvi. 25—27). It forms, says Delitzsch, "the third part of the third trilogy of the three great trilogies into which the prophecies of Jeremiah may be divided." The reference evidently is to the days of the Messiah.
[12] The object of μεμφόμενος is not expressed, but probably it is αὐτοῖς. Comp. 2 Macc. ii. 7.
[13] συντελέσω is used for the less emphatic διαθήσομαι of the LXX., as a rendering of the Hebrew phrase, "to cut a covenant" (כרת ברית).
[14] In our E. V. it stands (Jer. xxxi. 22, although "I was a husband to them" (lit. "a lord," as in Hos. ii. 16; comp. Jer iii. 14; Is. liii. 4). But the quotation is from the LXX., which either follows a different reading (גָּעַלְתִּי), or takes another meaning of the verb בָּעַלְתִּי, which is perhaps tenable, as Kimchi asserts.
[15] viii. 8—13. Even the Rabbis, in their moments of saner exegesis, anticipated a day when the Law should cease to be. This they inferred from Deut. xxxi. 21. R. Bechai, on this verse, argues that the Law "shall be forgotten" when "the evil impulse" (the *yetser ha-rá*) ceases to exist.

intervention; and the final pardon of sins. Such was to be the New Covenant which God promised. The fact that He called it "new" was a making the existing dispensation old,[1] and the fact of its being thus regarded as "old" showed that it was hastening to final decay—that the decree of dissolution had been passed upon it.

After this digression the writer resumes the subject on which he had touched in viii. 6—the superiority of the *ordinances of ministration* in the New Covenant over those which had been appointed in the Old. He wishes to prove, above all, the transcendent efficacy of Christ's high-priestly atonement as compared even with the most solemn sacrifices and the most sublime ceremonial of Jewish worship. To this he hastens as to the very heart of his subject, not pausing to explain any minor details of the Jewish sanctuary and its service, though these had a deep interest for him, and he would have been as admirably fitted as Philo himself to bring out the allegoric meaning of every shadowy type of the Mosaic dispensation. This, however, would have been impossible in a letter, and would have dissipated the attention of his readers, which he wished to concentrate on one central consideration. If he could but convince them that "Christ was the end of the Law"—that by His sacrifice all other sacrifices had been rendered needless—that His resurrection and ascension robbed of all its meaning the splendid ceremonial of the Day of Atonement, which was the crowning event of the Jewish year—then it would be impossible for them to relapse into Judaism out of any admiration for the ordinary routine of its liturgical appliances.

"To resume, then, even the first (covenant)[2] had its ordinances of public worship,[3] and its sanctuary—a worldly one.[4] For a tabernacle was established; the outer one, in which is[5] the lampstand,[6] and the table, and the setting forth of the shewbread[7]—which is called the holy place.[8] But behind the second veil[9] was the

---

[1] This is the same argument as in vii. 11, etc.
[2] There can be no reasonable doubt that "Covenant" (διαθήκη) and not "Tabernacle" (σκηνή), as in our text, is the proper word to supply with ἡ πρώτη. It is true that σκηνή is read by the Coptic Version and one or two cursive MSS., probably from the mistaken supposition that πρώτη means "first," and not "outer," in ver. 8. But the author has been thinking all along of two Covenants, not of two Tabernacles, and the Heavenly Tabernacle as in no sense a second Tabernacle, but the first in order as in pre-eminence.
[3] ix. 1; *Leitourgia*; hence our "liturgy." The classic meaning of the word was a public service rendered to the State.
[4] Κοσμικόν—i.e., "visible," "material," "temporary," in contrast to the one which was not of this world. The notion of Schöttgen and Bp. Middleton that Κοσμικόν is a Rabbinic expression for "furniture" is mistaken.
[5] I supply "is" and not "was," because the writer uses the present (λέγεται, εἰσίασιν, etc.), in accordance with the vivid presentment to his imagination of everything mentioned in Scripture, as though it were eternally existent. (See on vii. 6—8, etc.)
[6] Ex. xxv. 31—37. The writer is thinking throughout of the Mosaic Tabernacle, not of the Temples of Solomon or Herod. In Solomon's Temple there were ten lampstands (1 Kings vii. 49). In the second Temple there was only one (1 Macc. i. 21; iv. 49; Jos. Antt xii. 7, § 6).
[7] The table has no importance except for the shewbread, or "Bread of the Face" (of God), rendered by the LXX. "Loaves of the setting forth" (see Gen. xxv. 23—30; Lev. xxiv. 5—9). There were ten of these acacia-wood tables overlaid with gold in Solomon's Temple (2 Chr. iv. 8, 19).
[8] Probably ἅγια, "Holy (places)," neut. pl.; not ἁγία, fem. sing. He uses the generic name.
[9] The curtain called *Parocheth* hung between the Holy Place and the Holiest (Ex. xxvi. 31—35): the other curtain, called *Mâçâk* (Ex. xxvi. 36, 37), hung before the Tabernacle door. The LXX. in some places call both these curtains καταπέτασμα, and in other passages use κάλυμμα or ἐπίσπαστρον for the outer one. Philo also in one place (*Vit. Mos.* iii. 9) calls the outer one κάλυμμα. The Rabbis often speak of two curtains between the Holy and the Holiest Place.

tabernacle which is called the Holy of Holies,[1] having a golden incensor,[2] and the ark of the covenant overlaid on all sides with gold, in which are a golden pot holding the manna, and the rod of Aaron which budded, and the tables of the covenant; and above it the cherubim of glory overshadowing the propitiatory, respecting which things I cannot now speak generally" (ix. 1—5).

We must follow the example of the writer in not being tempted to linger over the facts upon which he here slightly touches. Doubtless, had he been able to expand the symbolism of the Tabernacle he would have elucidated points which are still dark to us. We are, however, able to see something of the meaning of the Holiest Place, with the few things which it contained. It was always shrouded in darkness, except for the moment when the High Priest lifted the curtain to enter its awful precincts. No window or opening of any kind admitted into it a single ray of light, and the interior was only visible to the High Priest in the crimson gleam of the thurible from which rose the clouds of fragrant incense. But in the Ark, containing the granite slabs on which were carved the Ten Words of Sinai—with the Propitiatory above it[3] and the "Cherubim of glory"[4] bending over it, we cannot fail to recognise an emblem of all that is highest and best in Creation upholding the throne of the Eternal, and rapt in adoring contemplation of that Moral Law which is the revelation of His will.

It is, however, to be borne in mind that what the writer says of the furniture of the Temple is applicable primarily to the Tabernacle, and, only in a lower degree, to the Temple of Solomon. As an Alexandrian, he had no personal knowledge of the ritual, but derived his views from the Pentateuch. To the Herodian Temple of his own day, and even to the Temple of Zerubbabel, his description is not applicable. In the Holiest Place of the later Temple there was nothing.[5] The Ark had disappeared at the time of the Babylonian captivity. When Pompey, nearly a hundred years before, had, to the horror of the Jews, profanely forced his way into the inmost shrine, he had been amazed to find that

---

[1] with a sort of lobby—a space of a cubit's breadth—between them, called the *Tarkesis*. The derivation of the word is much disputed. Some connect it with the Greek τάραξις, "confusion." Because the builders were "confused" as to whether it belonged to the Holy Place or the Holiest; and there are other conjectures equally improbable. The fact itself is more than doubtful. As to the *Paroketh*, or Inner Veil, the Rabbis said that it was a hand-breadth thick, woven of 72 cords each 24 strands thick; that it was 40 cubits long, and 20 wide; that it took 300 priests to draw it, etc. (Chullin, f. 90, b).

[2] Ἅγια ἁγίων, like the Latin *Sancta Sanctorum*, is a literal rendering of the Hebrew *Kodesh hak-Kodashim*, for which one version uses "Most Holy," or "the Holy Place." In Solomon's Temple it was called "the Oracle."

[3] See *infra*. I use this word in order not to prejudice the question as to whether it means Thurible or Altar of Incense.

[4] The word ἱλαστήριον, "propitiatory," is a rendering of the Hebrew *cappóreth*, which means a "covering." It is translated "mercy seat" in our version from the notion that it implied the covering of sins, and the LXX. selected the word ἱλαστήριον, or ἐπίθεμα, to represent it, because upon it was sprinkled the blood of the propitiatory offering.

[5] The expression means much more than "glorious Cherubim." It no doubt means the Cherubim which bear on their wings the Glory of God, the Shechinah or Cloud of Light which was the symbol of His Presence (Hag. ii. 7—9; Meuschen, p. 701). Even the Jews spoke of the passage in Ezekiel which describes the Cherubim as "the chariot," and it was a favourite passage with the Kabbalists.

[6] Jos. B. J. v. 5, § 5; ἔκειτο δὲ οὐδὲν ὅλως ἐν αὐτῷ.

there was nothing whatever—*vacua omnia!* The mass of native rock on which the Ark had once stood—called by the Rabbis "the stone of the foundation"—alone was visible. The absence of everything else perhaps originated the notion that the Jews worshipped "nothing except clouds and the Deity of Sky," just as the living creatures which formed part of the Cherubim may have helped to give currency to the old ignorant Pagan slander that they worshipped an ass.

Two questions are raised by this brief glance at the furniture of the Tabernacle, which we are bound to examine because they affect the accuracy of the Epistle, and have been supposed to bear on the question of its authorship.

I. Of these the minor question is, Has not the writer fallen into a mistake in saying that the Ark contained not only the Tables of the Law, but also the golden pot of manna,[1] and Aaron's rod that budded? Speaking of Solomon's Temple, the First Book of Kings (viii. 9)[2] says that "there was nothing in the Ark save the two tables of stone, which Moses put there at Horeb;" and in Ex. xxv. 16, 21; xl. 20, we are told that he put "the testimony" into the Ark. Neither in those passages, nor in Deut. x. 2, 5, are we told that he put anything besides.[3] But in Ex. xvi. 33, 34, Moses is bidden to lay up a pot of manna, and in Num. xvii. 10, to lay up Aaron's rod which budded, "*before* the testimony," and "*before* the Lord." Since these expressions are not defined, it is obvious that they may have been interpreted to mean either *in* the Ark or in front of it. It is idle to contend that there would have been no room for them inside the Ark when we have no indication as to the size of the tables of stone. In these small matters much was left to the discretion of the High Priests. The statement of the Book of Kings only applies to Solomon's Temple, and since the writer of this Epistle is not thinking of Solomon's Temple, but only of the Tabernacle, he may be following a trustworthy tradition in stating that these memorials had in former days been placed inside the Ark. They might have been removed when the Ark was hurried from place to place in the troublous times of the Judges—lest the frailer objects should have been

---

[1] The word rendered "pot" is στάμνος. It seems to mean a jar with a tapering base. The Palestine Targum calls it "earthen," but Jewish tradition always spoke of it as made of gold, and the epithet "golden" is added by the LXX. in Ex. xvi. 33, as also by Philo. Perhaps a golden pot was substituted for the earthen one in Solomon's Temple. It contained one "omer" of manna, which was the daily portion for each person (Ex. xvi. 16, 32).

[2] Comp. 2 Chr. v. 10.

[3] The Talmud says the tables of stone were "*six* handbreadths long, six broad, and three thick" (Nedarim, f. 38, a), and they weighed, according to the Targum of Palestine, 40 seahs. But the Talmudic estimate is probably very excessive. The Talmud says further that the broken Tables, as well as the new ones, were stored up in the Ark—which Rashi inferred from Deut. x. 2 (Bernchoth, f. 8, b; Kethuboth, f. 104, a)—and also the Roll of the Law, written by Moses (Bava Bathra, f. 14, a). As to the disappearance of the Ark, they say that Josiah hid it because of Deut. xxviii. 36, and this they inferred from 2 Chr. xxxv. 3 (Yoma, f. 52, b). But "the foundation-stone" was supposed still to remain three inches above the soil. A priest who, by the condition of the plaster, conjectured the spot in the wood-store where the Ark was hidden, died immediately; and once when a priest was in the wood-store, he happened to drop his chopper on the spot above where it was hidden, whereon fire sprang forth and consumed him. The stone on which it had rested was believed to be (like the *omphalos* at Delphi) the centre of the world (see Hershon, *Talmudic Miscellany*, etc.).

broken to pieces by the slabs of stone. Nothing was farther from the intention of the Rabbis than the desire to vindicate the accuracy of the Christian writer who directed against them so powerful a polemic; yet Rabbi Levi Ben Gershom, Abarbanel, and others, testify to the existence of the tradition which is here followed.[1] There is, therefore, no necessity for the theory of Michaelis that the "*in which*" is the mistake of some one who was translating the Epistle into Greek from the Aramaic original. There is still less room for the suggestion of Danzius and others, supported by expressions which are not at all parallel, that "*in which*" can mean "*together with* which." It would be better to acknowledge a difficulty than to remove it by such desperate expedients. In this case there is no difficulty. In the Temple of our Lord's day there was no Ark at all;[2] in the Temple of Solomon the manna-pot and the rod were probably placed in front of the Ark; but in the Tabernacle of the Wilderness there can be little doubt that these objects were actually inside the Ark, as the writer says.

II. But it is asserted that he made a mistake in saying that the "*thumiaterion*" was in the Holy of Holies. The word which he uses is rendered "censer" in our version.[3] It does not occur[4] in the Greek version of the Pentateuch, where the "altar of incense" is called τὸ θυσιαστήριον θυμιάματος (Ex. xxxi. 8; Luke i. 11). But the LXX. use it in 2 Chron. xxvi. 19; Ezek. viii. 11, and in both of these places it means "censer." The Rabbis assert that the High Priest used on all other days a silver censer, but a golden one on the Day of Atonement.[5] On the other hand, in Philo and Josephus the word *thumiaterion* means the "altar of incense," and this might be called "golden," though in reality it was only of acacia-wood overlaid with gold.[6] Considering how deeply the author is influenced by Philo, and also that in the Hellenistic Greek of his day—from Josephus to Clemens of Alexandria—the word is used for the "altar of incense," it is most probable that this is here the meaning. But since both "censer" and "altar of incense" are closely connected with the ceremonies of the great Day of Atonement, of which the writer is here thinking, we cannot come to any positive decision as to which of the two he meant.

But now occurs the further difficulty—Were *either* of these objects in the Holiest Place?

a. As regards the *censer*, if that be the meaning here intended, it may have been kept in the Holiest, and, though we cannot corroborate the assertion from other sources, the writer may be following a correct Jewish tradition in saying that it was. Or, again, the name may have

---

[1] See Wetstein, ad loc. The reader will find a full discussion of these particulars in Prideaux's *Connection*, i. 138.
[2] Yoma, v. 2; Surenhusius, *Mishna*, ii. 239.
[3] And in the Vulgate, Syriac, Arabic, and Æthiopic; and the word is so understood by Theophylact, Anselm, Thomas Aquinas, Grotius, Wetstein, Bengel, Reland, Stier, &c.
[4] Except as a various reading.
[5] Yoma, iv. 4.
[6] In Solomon's Temple it was of cedar-wood.

been given to some permanent golden censer-stand in the Holiest Place on which the High Priest placed the small brazier or shovel-shaped basin (*machettah*, LXX. *pureion*) which he carried with him when he stood before the Ark on the Day of Atonement.

β. As regards the *altar of incense*, if we assume that to be the meaning of the word, there is no question that it was *not* in the Holiest. No tradition ever asserted, nor could have asserted, that it was. If the writer meant that it was, he then made a mistake which even in an Alexandrian Jew would be almost inconceivable, and as to which Philo, with whose writings he was so familiar, would have set him right.[1] But it may be fairly argued that he did *not* mean to say that the incense-altar was *inside* the Holiest Place. If he did, why does he go out of his way to vary the expression? He tells us that the manna-pot and the rod were "*in* the Ark," but he only says that the Holiest Place "*had*" the *thumiaterion* and the Ark, and we cannot assert that the change of phrase is due to the rhetorical desire for variation. The phrase "having" may therefore be adopted to apply not only to the Ark which was inside the Holiest, but also to the altar which, though not actually inside, was close outside the veil, and was intimately associated with the Holiest, not only in the use to which it was put, but also by the express language of Scripture. On the Day of Atonement, when the Veil was drawn, the altar of incense might be said, in the strictest sense, to *belong to* the Holiest Place.[2]

"Since then these things have been thus arranged, into the outer tabernacle the priests enter continually in the performance of their ministrations;[3] but into the inner, once in a year,[4] the High Priest alone, not without blood, which he offers on his own behalf and for the ignorances[5] of the people;[6] the Holy Spirit signifying this, that the entrance into the Holiest had not yet been manifested, while yet the

---

[1] Philo, *De vict. off.* § 4.

[2] See Excursus XI. "The Altar of Incense and the Holiest Place." If this view be correct, and certainly it cannot be disproved—the ἔχουσα will be equivalent to the Hebrew לְ, in the sense of "belonging to," in 1 Kings vi. 22 ("the altar which was לַדְּבִיר to the Oracle").

[3] Num. xviii. 7. The ordinary priestly duties were to offer sacrifice, burn incense, and light the lamps. No priest might enter the Holiest, except the Sagan, and then only in most exceptional circumstances; but the High Priest might perform any of the ordinary functions if he chose. The graduated sanctity of the rest of the Tabernacle—which gave its special awfulness to the Holiest—was remarkable. In the Temple all might enter the outmost court; all Jews the second court; all males the third; priests alone, in their robes, might enter the first chamber; the High Priest alone, in his robes, might enter the shrine (Jos. c. *Apion*, ii. 8).

[4] Undoubtedly the High Priest must actually have entered into the Holiest three times (Lev. xvi. 12—16), if not four times (Yoma, v. 2; vii. 2), on the Day of Atonement (the 10th of Tishri)—viz. (1) with the incense; (2) with the blood of the bullock offered for his own sins; (3) with the blood of the goat offered for the sins of the people; and (4) to remove the censer. But these entrances were practically only one, as they were but parts of one grand ceremony. There was no need of pragmatic accuracy when this would be at once understood by every reader. On such matters the ancients, and especially Semitic writers, cared much less than the moderns for pedantic exactness.

[5] No doubt ἀγνοήματα is used generally to include sins and errors of all kinds (v. 2, 3; vii. 27; Ex. xxxiv. 7).

[6] I have rendered the Greek literally, but no doubt ὑπὲρ ἑαυτοῦ means "for his own sins," and, as we learn from Lev. xvi. 6, 11, for those of his house. The confession of the High Priest was made in the following terms: "And now, O Lord, I have sinned, and done iniquity, and trespassed before Thee. I pray, therefore, O Lord, cover my sins and iniquities and trespasses, wherein I have sinned, offended, and trespassed against Thee!"

outer Tabernacle stands [1]—which outer Tabernacle is a parable for the present time, in accordance with which (parable) [2] both gifts and sacrifices are offered, such as are not able as far as conscience is concerned to perfect the worshipper; [3] seeing that they consist only in meats and drinks, and divers washings [4]—being ordinances of the flesh, imposed (only) till the season of reformation" [5] (ix. 6—10).

"But Christ having appeared, a High Priest of the good things to come, [6] through the greater and more perfect Tabernacle, not made with hands, that is, not of this (visible) creation [7] nor even by means of the blood of bulls and goats, but by means of His own blood, entered once for all into the Holiest Place, obtaining for us eternal redemption. [8] For if the blood of goats and bulls, [9] and the ashes of a heifer sprinkling the defiled, [10] sanctifies to the purity of the flesh, how much more shall the blood of the Christ, [11] who through an eternal Spirit [12] offered Himself without blemish [13] to God, purify your conscience from dead works [14] to serve the living God?" [15] (ix. 11—14.)

"And on this account"—i.e., because of the greatness of His work—"He is a mediator of a *new* covenant, that,—when death had occurred for the redemption of the transgressions under the first covenant—they who have been called may receive the promise of the eternal inheritance. For where there is *a testament* it is necessary that there should be legally involved the death of the testator. For *a testament* is of force in the case of the dead—since is there any validity in it when the testator lives?" [16] (ix. 15—17.)

---

[1] The outer Tabernacle was the place of the priests in general, who might not penetrate further. "Stands"—the present is used in accordance with the general idiom of the Epistle. See *supra*, p. 202, n. The writer throws himself vividly into the past, and so he conceives of all the contemplated arrangements as still existing.

[2] Leg. καθ' ἥν; A, B, D, etc.

[3] The "parable," or typical meaning, of the Tabernacle and its service is this: The object of the gifts and sacrifices is to obtain entrance into God's presence; but since the Holiest is not opened by them, the result is not obtained; which shows that the worshippers, so far as their inmost hearts are concerned, are not perfected.

[4] Meats (Ex. xii.; Lev. xi.; Num. vi.); drinks (Lev. x. 9; Num. vi. 3); divers washings (vi. 2; Ex. xix. 10, 11; xxix. 4; Lev. xv. 8; xvii. 5; xxii. 5). See on both classes of observance the teaching of Christ (Mark vii. 1—15).

[5] ix. 6—10. It is not meant that the system of sacrifices was useless, but only that in themselves—and apart from the grace of God which might be imparted by their faithful use—they could not give perfect ease and peace, or gain admission for the worshipper into the presence of God. There is probably a slight sense of painful burden in the word ἐπικείμενα (comp. Acts xv. 10). The "reformation" (διορθώσεως) is that prophesied by Jeremiah (see viii. 7—12). Various other ways of translating this clause have been suggested, but the one which I have adopted seems to me so much the more correct that I do not mention others.

[6] In B and D we have the reading "good things that have come" (γενομένων).

[7] Comp. viii. 2. But *here* it seems best, with Chrysostom and many of the Fathers, to understand this Tabernacle, through which Christ passed, of His Human Nature (ἐσκήνωσεν, John i. 14; comp. ii. 19; xiv. 10; Col. ii. 9). Of the other explanations the best is perhaps that of Bleek, De Wette, Lünemann, etc., who understand it of "the lower heavens" (comp. iv. 14). Moll renders διὰ "by means of;" κτίσις may mean "building," on the analogy of κτίζω, but in that case ταύτης must mean "vulgar," "ordinary"—*quae vulgo dicitur* (Field, *Otium Norvicense*, iii. 142).

[8] Λύτρωσιν, "ransom," with its cognate words, occurs in ver. 15 and xi. 35; Matt. xx. 28; Luke xxi. 28; xxiv. 21; 1 Tim. ii. 6; Tit. ii. 14; 1 Pet. i. 18. The metaphor applies only to the effects of the Redemption as regards man, whom it sets free from the bondage of sin. So little is the notion of its *Divine* side dwelt upon, that it is never said to whom the ransom is paid, and for many centuries the Church in general held the strange and grievous notion that it was paid to Satan.

[9] Lev. xvi.

[10] See Num. xix. 9 (comp. xii. 24). Thus, in this verse he refers, by way of example, to the two most significant ceremonies of the Jewish Law.

[11] The blood of Christ was the *true* fountain opened for sin and for uncleanness (Zech. xiii. 1).

[12] Probably His own Spirit is intended—"per ardentissimam caritatem a Spiritu Ejus aeterno profectam" (Œcolamp.). If we explain it of the Holy Spirit, we must refer, by way of parallel, to such passages as Matt. xii. 28; Luke xi. 20.

[13] The word used by the LXX for sacrificial victims (comp. 1 Pet. i. 19).

[14] Comp. vi. 1. Here the expression has possibly a slight reference to the dead things which caused pollution under the Levitical Law. The writer does not here attempt to explain the mystery of the efficacy of Christ's blood, which is indeed, on the *Divine* side, inexplicable; he only dwells on it as a revealed fact—in its effects for us.

[15] ix. 11—14. For the expression "living God" see Deut. xxv. 2ff.

[16] ix. 15—17. The μήποτε is most simply explained by regarding the clause as a question.

We must pause for a moment to examine the meaning of the last two verses. A voluminous controversy has arisen about them, because we seem to be almost compelled to alter the translation "*covenant*," which throughout the Epistle has been the only tenable rendering of *diathêkê*, and—in these two verses only—to substitute for it the rendering *testament* or *will*. This has seemed to many commentators a great difficulty. In the quotation from Jeremiah (xxxi. 31—34), which plays so important a part in the argument of the Epistle, διαθήκη *must* mean "covenant," and this meaning must be retained in the following verses even as far as verse 15. It may well seem extraordinary that in the very next verses (16 and 17), and these alone, the different sense—which is the *classical* sense of the word—should be introduced. After these two verses the word evidently reverts to its normal sense. For the Old Dispensation alluded to in verse 20 was indeed "a covenant," but could only be called a "testament" by a remote analogy. Yet, if on these grounds we resist the concession of a new meaning in the two verses before us, we have to reconcile with plain facts the statement, that "when there is a *covenant* there must also be of necessity the death of him who made it." This is attempted by arguing that in verse 15 the death spoken of is the death of Jesus; that the new covenant was "a covenant in Christ's blood (1 Cor. xi. 25); and that no covenant could be established without the death of sacrificial victims (Gen. xv. 9, 10; Ps. l. 5), in which the death of the covenanter is *implied* (φέρεσθαι),[1] either as a *punishment* if he should break the compact, or as involving a total change—a sort of death—as regards the past or the future. We should then be obliged to render verse 17 by "a covenant is of force *over dead victims*," and to regard Jesus as both the mediator and maker of the covenant. Thus the death of the covenanter becomes a sort of ideal conception—an imaginative realisation of the supposed significance of the sacrifices over which the compact is made.

However ingeniously these arguments may be stated, they attach to the writer's words a very vague and unnatural sense. I see no alternative but to suppose that the writer *does* in these two verses introduce a sort of side light from the classical meaning of the word *diathêkê*, which he has elsewhere been using in the ordinary Hellenistic sense.[2] These two verses do not belong to the essence of his argument. He is comparing the Old with the New dispensation, and the old with the new Priesthood. In the Old the High Priest entered the Holiest with the blood of bulls and goats; in the New, Christ, as our Redeemer, passed with His own blood into the immediate presence of God. In both dispensations there was a purifying and propitiatory shedding of blood.

---

[1] Perhaps the word may be rendered "be proved or established"—*constare*.
[2] How completely the illustration is an *obiter dictum* appears from this—(1) that he does not even touch upon the fact that Christ did not merely die, but died a violent and shameful and agonising death; and (2) does not pause to co-ordinate the two senses of *diathêkê*, or (3) explain the very distant analogy between the *necessity* of a death when there is a "will," and the (very different) sacrifice of victims when there is a covenant."

In developing this argument the writer passingly recalls another illustration. The word which he is using has two recognised senses.¹ A *diathêkê* in the sense of a "covenant" involved the necessity for the death of sacrificial victims; a *diathêkê* in the sense of a "will" involved the necessity for the death of the testator; and he avails himself with perfect simplicity of this second meaning. To call this a Hellenistic play on words, or a specimen of sophistry, or a proof of feeble logic, is a mistaken method of criticism. The writer is not furnishing any *proof* of the necessity for Christ's death. If he were, he would have had to prove why the Christian Dispensation must be regarded as a *diathêkê*, which it is unnecessary for him to do. He is writing to those who have already accepted the truth of Christianity, and to whom, therefore, the necessity for Christ's death transcends the need of proof. He is comparing two dispensations, of which his readers are convinced that both have come from God, and his sole object is to prove the superiority of the latter. By the double sense of the word he is reminded, in passing, that death is the condition of inheritance by *testament*, just as death is the efficient cause of purification by *covenant*. "The same death which purifies us from guilt makes us partakers of the kingdom of glory; the same blood which cleanses us from sin seals the testament of our inheritance." It requires but a slight development of the literary sense to see that if, in carrying out his comparison, he could illustrate it by a momentary reference to another meaning of the word with which he is dealing, he is only adopting a method which might be used by any writer, whether ancient or modern.²

We may now resume the thread of the argument, which we will here translate, because of the extreme importance of this section of the Epistle.

"Whence"—*i.e.*, because a "covenant" and a "testament" alike involve the idea of death; a *covenant* being ratified by the death of victims, and a *testament* involving the death of the testator—"not even the first covenant has been inaugurated ³ apart from blood. For when every commandment according to the Law had been spoken by Moses to all the people, taking the blood of the calves and the goats, with water and scarlet wool and hyssop, he sprinkled both the book itself and all the people,⁴ saying, 'This is the blood of the Covenant which God (Heb. Jehovah) commanded in regard to you.'⁵ And the Tabernacle, and all the vessels of the

---

¹ ברית (diathêkê) in the Talmud certainly means "a will," and is said also to be used in the sense of *Berith* ("covenant"). It is of course only the Greek word *diathêkê*, though R. Obad. de Bartenora offers an astonishing Hebrew derivation for it (see McCaul, *ad loc.*). Originally (Deut. xxi. 16) the Jews knew nothing about "wills," but they learnt the use of them from the Romans.

² Philo similarly alludes to the two senses of the word (*De Nom. Mutat.* § 6). Alford compares the term "New Testament" itself as bearing two meanings—a "book," and a "will." No one would accuse an English writer of sophistry or feeble logic if, in speaking of the Book, he introduced a passing illustration from the other meaning of the name by which the Book is called.

³ ἐγκεκαίνισται—another of the perfects which, with the presents, are so characteristic of the writer. He regards every ordinance of Scripture either as representing a permanent fact, or as still continuing its past existence. The Alexandrian word ἐγκαινίζω is used by the LXX. (Deut. xx. 5; 1 Kings viii. 63), and means to "handsel." Hence the name "Encaenia," for the feast of the "Dedication" (John x. 22).

⁴ Ex. xxiv. 3—7. The book of the Covenant was Ex. xx. 22; xxiii. 33. See *infra*, p. 237.

⁵ πρὸς ὑμᾶς—*i.e.*, for me to deliver to you. In the LXX. for "this is the blood," we have the more literal rendering, "behold (הנה) the blood." Böhme and others suppose that the varia-

ministration, did he likewise so sprinkle with the blood,[1] and, speaking generally,[2] all things are purified with blood according to the Law, and without bloodshed[3] remission does not take place. It is necessary, then, that the outlines[4] of the things in the heavens be purified with these, but the heavenly things themselves[5] with sacrifices better than these.[6] For not into a material sanctuary did Christ enter—a (mere) imitation of the ideal[7]—but into the Heaven itself, now to be visibly presented before the face of God for us. Nor yet did He enter Heaven that He may often present Himself there as the High Priest enters into the Holiest year by year with blood not his own—since it would then have been needful[8] for Him often to suffer since the foundation of the world; but now, once for all, at the consummation of the ages[9] has He been manifested[10] for the annulment of sin by the sacrifice of Himself. And, inasmuch as it is appointed for men once only to die, and, after this judgment,—so also the Christ, having been once for all offered to bear[11] the sins of many,[12] shall, a second time, apart from sin,[13] appear, to those who wait for Him, for salvation "[14] (ix. 18—28).

It is worth while to notice, in passing, the familiarity of the writer

tion is due to a reminiscence of the words of Christ in inaugurating the Last Supper, as recorded in Luke xxii. 20. The writer substitutes 'commanded' (ἐνετείλατο) for the διέθετο of the LXX. The Hebrew as usual has "cut" (כרת)

[1] This was on another and later occasion, not recorded in Scripture, but implied in Ex. xl.
[2] There were a few exceptions (see Ex. xix. 10; Lev. v. 11—13; xv. 5; x-i. 26, 28; xxii. 6; Num xxxi. 22—24). Σχεδόν is only used elsewhere in Acts xiii. 44; xix. 26.
[3] De Wette and others render αἱματεκχυσια, "pouring out of blood," at the foot of the altar (Ex xxix. 16; 2 Kings xvi. 15; 2 Chron. xxix. 22, LXX.). But the pouring out of the blood is secondary; it is the *shedding* of the blood which is of chief importance, and the meaning seems to be decided by Luke xx.i. 20, "This cup is the new covenant in my blood which is being shed for you;" and (Lev. xvii. 11), it is the blood that maketh an atonement for the soul, ' whence the Rabbinic rule: "No expiation except by blood"—אין כפרה אלא בדם (Yoma, f. 5, b). The famous passages of the Prophets (Hos. vi. 6; Isa, i. 1 '—17, etc.) are directed not against the use of sacrifices, but against their abuse.
[4] ὑποδείγματα (iv. 11; viii. 5). They were "copies" (*Abbilden*), not "patterns" (*Urbilden*).
[5] What is meant by "the heavenly things?" The notion that the phrase means "the new covenant" (Chrys, Œcumen.), or "the church" (Theophyl.), or ourselves as heirs of heaven (Tholuck), are only suggested to avoid the difficulty of supposing that heaven can need any purification. But the best proof that this natural meaning is the true one may be seen in Job iv. 18, "His angels He charged with folly."
[6] The plural is merely generic.
[7] The Ideal is that which is actual and eternal; the uncreated archetype as contrasted with the hand-made antitype. The word ἀντίτυπος is found only in 1 Pet. iii. 21. The better sanctuary is some proof that there was a better *sacrifice*. It is an argument from the *effect* to the *cause*.
[8] ἔδει. On this idiom, see Winer, § 41. [9] Comp. Matt. xiii. 39, 40, 49; xxiv. 3; xxviii. 20.
[10] ἐμφανισθῆναι. This *emphanismos* is the actual vision face to face (Ex xxxiii. 13). The E.V. makes no difference between ἐμφανισθῆναι (ver. 24), πεφανέρωται (ver. 26), and ὀφθήσεται (ver. 28).
[11] Isa. li 1, 12. The sense may be "to take away" in the Hebrew.
[12] Of course this does not mean that He did not bear the sins of *all*, as is again and again stated in Scripture; but "many" is used as the antithesis of "few." Once for all, *One* died for all, who were (quantitively) many. (See *Life of St. Paul*, ii. 216.) Christ may be said both to offer Himself (v. 14), and to be offered (ver. 28), just as He is said to deliver up Himself for us (Eph. v. 2), or to be delivered for us (Rom. iv. 25).
[13] Not merely "without sin" (which would be ἀνίρ), but "apart from all connexion with sin" (comp. vii. 26), either in the form of temptation (iv. 15) or burden (2 Cor. v. 21). At His first appearance also Christ was "without sin," but He was not "apart from sin," for He was tempted like as we are; and He was made sin for us; but at His second coming He shall have triumphed over sin, and taken it away (Dan. ix. 24, 25; Isa. xxv. 7--9).
[14] ix. 18—28. In this, as in so many other cases, it is remarkable how evidently the sacred writers, as a rule, avoid dwelling on the more terrible features of the Second Advent. "How shall He be seen?" says St. Chrysostom. "Does He say, as a Punisher? He did not say this, but the bright aspect." Their normal conception of the returning Christ was not the wrathful avenging figure of Michael Angelo, with His right hand uplifted as He turns away from His interceding mother, to drive the lost myriads of humanity in dense herds before Him, but the Deliverer bringing glory and salvation to all His children. It is not that they exclude the other notion altogether (x. 27; 1 Thess. iv. 16; 2 Thess. i. 8), but they do not love to dwell on it. The parallelism of these two verses is as follows:—Man dies once, and then is judged; the Christ died once for man, and shall return to be (he might have said "the Judge," but he does say, "the Saviour of those who look for Him."

with the Jewish Hagada and Halacha—that is, with the unrecorded circumstances which Jewish tradition added to the History or to the Ceremonial Law of the Sacred Books. In this chapter there are five or six references to one or the other. He has already said (1) that the pot of manna was of gold, and (2) that it and the rod of Aaron were in the Ark; and (3) that there was a close connexion between the altar of incense and the Holiest Place. In these latter verses he mentions (4) that Moses purified the people with the blood of the goats (which may be presumed to have been among the burnt-offerings mentioned in Ex. xxiv. 5); (5) that the sprinkling was done with water, scarlet wool, and hyssop (perhaps on the analogy of Ex. xii. 22, Num. xix. 6, Lev. xiv. 4—6, etc.); (6) that the Book of the Covenant was sprinkled as well as the people—perhaps from the Hagada that the book was lying on the altar when Moses sprinkled it (Ex. xxiv. 7); and (7) that on a subsequent occasion he sprinkled the Tabernacle and all its furniture. The latter circumstance is mentioned by Josephus.[1] It was probably done when Moses (Ex. xl. 9, 10) anointed the Tabernacle and its implements with holy oil. By a similar sprinkling Aaron and his sons were consecrated to their sacred functions (Lev. viii. 30), and the altar was touched with blood to hallow it for use. These seven references to the traditional lore of the Rabbis incidentally mark the writer as an accomplished "pupil of the wise."

But far more important is the general scope of this chapter as proving the unapproachable superiority of Christ's priesthood over that of the sons of Aaron.

If any one desired to contemplate the Levitical high priesthood in its grandest phase—to realise its antiquity, its sacredness, the splendour of its ministrations, and the awful sense of responsibility with which its representative was bound to fulfil its functions—he would naturally have turned his thoughts to the great Day of Atonement—that "Sabbath of Sabbatism"—which was the most memorable day of the Jewish year. It was the day of expiation for the sins of the whole people, and was observed as a perfect Sabbath.[2] It was the one fast-day of the Jewish calendar.[3] It was emphatically "*the* day." The seventy bullocks prescribed for sacrifice during this week were supposed to be an atonement not for Jews only, but for the seventy nations of the world.[4]

It was supposed that on New Year Day (Tishri 1) the Divine decrees are written down, and that on the Day of Atonement (Tishri 10) they are sealed,[5] so that the decade is known by the name of "Terrible

---

[1] *Antt.* iii. 8, § 6. On the whole passage see especially Bleek's Commentary. Philo, *De Vit. Mos.* iii. 18 (Opp. ii. 157, ed. Mangey) is referred to, but he does not make this statement.
[2] Lev. xvi. 31: שבת שבתון.
[3] The bi-weekly fasts of the Pharisees in the days of Christ were a later invention. (See *Life of Christ*, i. 340.)
[4] Succah, f. 55, b.
[5] Rosh Hashanah, f. 16, a.

Days," and "the Ten Penitential Days." So awful was the Day of Atonement that we are told in a Jewish book of ritual that the very angels run to and fro in fear and trembling, saying, "Lo, the Day of Judgment has come!" It was not until that day that the full pardon was granted which repentance had insured.[1] On that day the year of Jubilee was proclaimed. On that day alone the people came early to the synagogues and left them late.[2] On that day alone, they said, Satan has no power to accuse, for Ha-Satan by numeration (Gematria) is 364, which means that on the one remaining day of the year he is forced to be silent.[3] To die on the eve of that day was a good omen.[4] It was supposed to be the day on which Adam had sinned and repented; on which Abraham was circumcised; on which the latter tables had been given to Moses.[5] It was supposed by some to secure pardon for most sins even *without* repentance, and indeed, according to Rabbi Judah Hakkodesh, for all sins except apostasy.[6] The Gentiles are said to have committed a fatal and suicidal error in destroying the Altar, because it made atonement even *for them*, which was now impossible.[7] Three books, it was said, are opened on New Year's Day—one for the perfectly wicked, one for the perfectly righteous, and one for the intermediate class. The first are sealed to death, and the second to life; the fate of the third is suspended till the Day of Atonement.[8]

Nothing could exceed the solicitude with which the High Priest was prepared for the sacred functions of the day. Seven days before it came he was removed from his own residence to the chamber of the President of the Sanhedrin, and he appointed a Sagan, or deputy, to act for him in case of his being incapacitated by any Levitic impurity. When the Elders of the Sanhedrin had read over to him the duties of the day, they said, "My Lord High Priest, read for thyself, read for thyself; perhaps thou hast forgotten, or never learnt it." On the day before, he was taken to the east gate, and with bullocks, rams, and lambs, actually before him, was instructed what to do. Towards the dusk of the last evening he was only allowed to eat little, lest he should be sleepy. Then he was handed over to the senior priests, who swore him in, and said, "My Lord High Priest, we are the ambassadors of the Sanhedrin, and thou art our

---

[1] Yoma, f. 85, b; f. 86, a (Lev. xvi. 3)). The reader will find a deeply interesting account of the Day of Atonement compiled from the Talmud (especially *Yoma*) in Hamburger, s.v. *Versöhnung*, and Mr. Hershon's *Treasures of the Talmud*, 89—114.
[2] Megillah. f. 23, a.
[3] For this they quoted Ps. lxviii. 28; Rosh Hashanah, f. 16, b.
[4] Kethuboth, f. 103, b.   [5] Bava Bathra, f. 121, a.
[6] Kerithoth, f. 7, a; Shevuoth, f. 13, a; Yoma, f. 86, a.
[7] Succah, f. 55, b. These and the preceding passages have been collected by Mr. Hershon in his interesting Talmudic *Miscellanies*.
[8] This information was furnished by Elijah the Tishbite to Rav Judah, and he proved it by Gematria as above (Yoma, f. 20, a). This treatise of the Talmud is devoted to the Day of Atonement. It is one of the earliest, and was written by Simeon of Mizpeh, a contemporary of Gamaliel the First (Derenbourg, p. 375, who refers to Peah, if. 6; Yoma, 14, b).

ambassador, and we adjure thee by Him who dwells in this house that thou wilt alter nothing that we have told thee." Then they parted, he and they both weeping; they because they suspected he was a Sadducee, and the penalty for wrongful suspicion was scourging; and he because they suspected him.[1] During the night, if he was a learned man, he preached or read to others; if not, they preached or read to him. The books read to him were Job, Ezra, Chronicles, and Daniel. If he became drowsy, the younger priests filliped their fingers before him, and said, "My Lord High Priest, stand up and cool thy feet upon the pavement." Thus they kept him engaged till the time of sacrifice, lest by chance any accidental defilement should spoil his propitiation. And so important was his ceremonial purity that if he was found performing the sacred duties in a state of defilement, the junior priests might drag him into the Hall of Paved Squares and brain him with clubs.[2] It may be safely said that, to the imagination of a Jew, the most solemn moment of the year was that in which the High Priest in his white robes stood alone before the Presence of God in the Holy of Holies; and that the proudest and gladdest moment of the year was that in which, awe-struck but safe, he came forth from the Holy Place in his golden garments to bless and to dismiss the forgiven worshippers.[3]

To the Mosaic ritual the Jews added many legendary particulars. They said, perhaps with reference to Isa. i. 18, that round the horns of the scapegoat which was to be "for Azazel," and round the neck of the goat "for Jehovah," was tied a tongue of scarlet cloth, and that if the ceremonies of the day were accepted by God, then this tongue of scarlet was turned to white. They also asserted that, in order to secure that the scapegoat should not, with fatally evil omen, wander back to the congregation, it was sent by the hands of a trusty person to Zuk, some cliff in the wilderness, down which it was hurled backwards and killed.[4] The later Rabbis, echoing perhaps the mournful traditions of the last days of Jerusalem, told how, in the time of Simeon the Just, the lot for the Lord always fell on the right-hand[5] goat, and the tongue of scarlet always turned white; but forty years before the destruction of the Temple—a date which closely corresponds with the death of Christ—the lot did not fall on the right, nor the crimson cloth turn white, nor a light burn in the west. And the doors of the Temple opened of themselves, so that R. Jochanan Ben Zaccai rebuked them, and said, "O Temple, Temple, why art thou dismayed? I know thy end will be to be destroyed, for

[1] Yoma, f. 2, a; 18, a, b; 19, b. In the Herodian Temple the ark and mercy-seat were only supposed to be present. The sprinklings were made towards the stone of the foundation.
[2] Sanhedrin, f. 81, b.
[3] Further details of the ceremony of the Day of Atonement will be found in Excursus XII., "Ceremonies of the Day of Atonement."
[4] Yoma, f. 66, a. There is no such provision in the Law. "Zuk" was to be 12½ miles from Jerusalem. See Hershon's *Treasures of the Talmud*, ch. vii.
[5] Lev. xvi. 8—10.

Zechariah, the son of Iddo, hath foretold concerning thee, 'Open thy doors, O Lebanon, that the fire may devour thy cedars.'"[1]

They also regarded the function of the High Priest on this day as one of extreme peril. In his various confessions he had to pronounce ten times the Sacred Tetragrammaton—the ineffable name of Jehovah. The injunction never to enter the Holiest except on that one day of all the year had been laid on Aaron after the sudden death which had avenged the presumptuous irreverence of his two eldest sons, Nadab and Abihu; and the Jews said that if the High Priest entered the Holiest *five* times instead of the four which were actually necessary, he was slain by the wrath of God.[2] They even believed that many High Priests had perished on that day for neglect of the details which they swore to observe. During the whole ceremony the High Priest was alone in the Tabernacle. No Priest, until it was completed, was allowed to enter even into the Holy Place.[3] Hence the people, standing in the Court of Israel, waited with intense solicitude the reappearance of the High Priest through the outer veil. After his last entrance into the Holiest, he prayed in the Holy Place; and it was a special custom to make the prayer a short one, both from the awfulness of the solitude and in order that the apprehensions of the people might not be too painfully kindled by any long delay.[4]

Now the writer of the Epistle shows his fairness of spirit by taking this great ceremonial as his point of comparison, in order to give every advantage to the priesthood of which he wishes to prove the inferiority. He might have touched—a smaller man certainly would have touched—on the sacerdotal functions in their meaner, more trivial, more repellent aspect; but instead of this he takes the Aaronic Priesthood in the crown and flower of its loftiest ritual, and strives to warn the Christian converts from the peril of retrograding, by showing how the work and person of Christ transcends these seductive, but transitory and unsatisfying splendours. If the ritual of this day was, after all, a nullity, how great a

---

[1] Zech. xi. 1; Yoma, f. 29, b. Since the due fulfilment of the ceremonies of this great day has for 1,800 years been impossible to the Jews, the reader may be interested to see the melancholy folly into which its splendid ordinances have degenerated in the hands of the Polish Jews. It is now observed by what is called "the Atonement of the Cock." Since, in one passage of the Talmud, Gever (גבר) is used, not for "man," but for "cock" (Yoma. f. 20, b), modern Rabbis have invented the substitution of a cock for a man (Temurath Gever begeveri), and this custom has become a law according to the rule "custom is as law." Fowls, and especially white cocks, are in great request on that day, as indicating that though the sins of the man who kills it be as scarlet, they shall be white as snow. The legs of the cock are tied, and holding them in his hand, the Jew repeats the customary prayer. Then he swings the cock round and round his head with the words, "This is my substitute (Chalaphathi), my commutation (Temarathi), my atonement (Kapparathi)." Then the cock's neck is wrung, it is dashed on the ground, and its throat is cut, so that it undergoes (in a sense) the four Mosaic capital punishments of strangling, stoning, beheading, and burning. I borrow these, among other interesting particulars, from the *Jewish Herald* for July, 1890.

[2] Maimonides in Surenhusius, *Mishna*, ii. 239. See Lev. xvi. 2, 13. In the evening the High Priest gave a banquet to his friends to commemorate his safety. Perhaps it was the awe inspired by the ceremony which made the Sadducean High Priests of our Lord's day so willing to hand the office from one to another. See *Life of Christ*, ii. 342; Derembourg, 231 sq.

[3] Lev. xvi. 17.

[4] Yoma, iv. 7 (Surenhusius, *Mishna*, ii. 231). See Excursus XIII, "Impressions left on the Mind of the Jews by the Ceremonies of the Day of Atonement."

nullity must be the other Levitical details! These High Priests were but provisional. From Aaron downwards their dignity had been dwarfed and overshadowed by the mysterious grandeur of Melchizedek. They were but priests; He who came to cancel their prerogatives was, like His antitype, a King as well as a Priest. They are for a time; He is for ever. They are but links in a long succession, each with many predecessors, each transmitting his office to his posterity; He stands alone, preceded by none, with no successor. They were established by an ordinance of Moses; He by the oath of God. They were sinful; He is innocent. They weak; He all powerful. They had to offer "daily" sacrifices; He offered Himself once for all. They serve a Tabernacle which is but a copy and shadow of the True; He is a Minister of the Immaterial, the Ideal Tabernacle, Eternal in the Heavens. Their dispensation is declared to be Old; His is prophesied of as New and founded on better promises. They died and passed away; He sits for ever at the right hand of God still to make intercession for His people.

Further, the fact that even the Priests might not enter into the Holiest stamped with imperfection their whole ministration. The restriction proved that the priesthood could not perfect the worshipper as to his inmost life, since it was unable to lead him into the Presence-chamber of God. The whole Dispensation of which their ritual formed a part was necessarily provisional, consisting as it mainly did in matters relating to meats and drinks and washings—human ordinances, only imposed as preparatory to the season of their final rectification. The High Priest did indeed enter the Holiest with the blood of bulls and goats; but it was an exceptional privilege, not a right of continual and fearless access. The fact that it was necessary for him to make an atonement year after year, showed how little permanent was the effect of even that most solemn purification. And though he entered with awful precautions, so conscious were the people for whom he sacrificed that he was but a weak and sinful man, that they awaited his return in trembling suspense, lest by some sin or error he should provoke the wrath of God. Yet this was the system, this the central act of the system, to which Christians, heirs of privileges so infinitely greater, were looking back with longing glances—to which some of them were even tempted to apostatise or retrogress! And what a retrogression! They were looking back to their petty Levitism, while Christ, the Mediator of a new, of a better, of a final dispensation—Christ, Whose death had made valid His Testament, Whose blood had a real and not a symbolic efficacy[1]—had died for all, and having died—not many times, but once for all, not as one of a long line, but Alone for all—not for Himself, be-

---

[1] The following passages illustrate the Jewish belief that there was "no remission without blood":—
"Abraham was circumcised on the Day of Atonement; and on that day God looks annually on the blood of the covenant of the circumcision as atoning for all our iniquities" (Yalkut Kadash, f. 121, b).
"R. Eliezer asked, 'For whose benefit were the seventy bullocks intended?' (Num. xxix.

cause He did not need it—not as a sinful man, but as the sinless Son of God—not with the blood of calves and goats, but with His own blood—had entered not into a secondary and imitative tabernacle of perishable gold, but into one greater and more precious, and not made with hands! And so, passing for ever into the Immediate Presence of God, He had opened a way thither for all, obtaining an eternal redemption. And having thus with His own blood purified, not the earthly shadows of things, but even the heavenly things themselves, He would, at the consummation of the Ages, appear for salvation to those who were awaiting Him with feelings not of terror but of hope; He would appear, not as a sinful man, not even as bearing the sins of men, but apart from all sin, as the Everlasting Victor over all sin, with death and every other enemy laid prostrate beneath His feet.[1]

SECTION VI.

A RECAPITULATION.

It only remained for the writer to sum up his argument, which he does in the first eighteen verses of the following chapter. In these he dwells mainly on Christ's voluntary offering of Himself in obedience to the will of God, which he illustrates from Ps. xl. 6, 7;[2] on the one act of Christ's Redemption as contrasted with the many Levitic sacrifices;[3] and on Christ's finished work in accordance with the great prophecy of Jeremiah,[4] which he has already quoted.[5] And thus the leading thoughts of the argument are brought together in one grand finale, just as in the finale of a piece of music all the hitherto scattered elements are united in an effective whole.[6]

"For the Law having a shadow[7] of the good things to come,[8] not the very form[9] of the things—they can never,[10] with the same sacrifices, year by year, which they offer continuously, perfect (vii. 11, xi. 9) them that draw nigh (vii. 26). Since, in

---

12—36). The answer is, 'For the seventy nations of the Gentile world, to atone for them. . . . Woe to the Gentile nations for their loss and . . . they know not what they have lost; for as long as the Temple existed the Altar made Atonement for them; but now who is to atone for them?'" (*Succah*, f. 55, b).

[2] See Jeremy Taylor's *Life of Christ*, iii. § 15. "He was arrayed with ornaments more glorious than the robes of Aaron. The crown of thorns was his mitre, the cross his pastoral staff . . . and his flesh rased and chequered with blue and blood instead of the parti-coloured robe."
[3] x. 1—10.   [4] x. 11—14.   [5] See viii. 8—12; Jer. xxxi. 33, 34.
[6] x. 15—18.   [6] Delitzsch.
[7] viii. 5 (comp. Col. ii. 17): ἅ ἐστι σκιὰ τῶν μελλόντων, τὸ δὲ σῶμα τοῦ Χριστοῦ.   [8] ix. 11.
[9] For other uses of the word, see 2 Cor. iv. 4, where Christ is called the εἰκὼν of God. "*Umbra* in Lege; *Imago* in Evangelio; *Veritas* in Coelo," S. Ambrose in Ps. xxxviii. (see 1 Cor. xiii. 12).
[10] The best supported reading seems to be δύνανται, and all the more because it is the more difficult reading, א, A, C. But with this reading, the passage becomes an anakoluthon, and the κατ' ἐνιαυτόν (if we accept the rendering of the E. V.) is very strangely placed (hyperbaton). To avoid this difficulty some explain it thus:—"They (the priests) can never, year by year, with the same sacrifices which they offer continuously, make them that draw nigh perfect." The meaning will then be that the priests cannot by the sacrifices of the Great Day of Atonement—which are after all but the same sin-offerings as they offer daily—perfect the worshippers. Yet another way of taking the words is to separate the κατ' ἐνιαυτόν ταῖς αὐταῖς by commas, and render "can never perfect the comers by the sacrifices which they offer, which are the same year by year." So Bleek and De Wette. But after all it is not impossible that δύνανται may be a mere clerical error.

that case, would they not have ceased to be offered, because the worshippers, purified once for all, would have had no more consciousness of sins? But in these sacrifices there is a calling to mind of sins year by year;[1] for it is impossible for the blood of bulls and of goats to take away sins.[2] Therefore, on entering into the world He saith,[3] 'Sacrifice and offering thou wouldest not,[4] but a body didst thou prepare for me,[5] whole burnt offerings and sin-offerings thou approvedst not. Then I said, Lo, I have come (in the roll of the book it has been written concerning me[6]) to do, O

---

[1] See v. 3, and note on vii. 27. Here again, we find a striking resemblance to Philo, who speaks of the sacrifices providing "not an oblivion of sins, but a reminding of them" (*De Vict. Off.*, and *De Vit. Mos.* iii.) And again (*De plant. Noe*), he calls attention to Num. v. 15, where Moses speaks of the meat-offering of jealousy as being "a memorial meat-offering *bringing iniquity to remembrance*." The fact that the oft-repeated sacrifices thus *reminded* the worshipper of sins, and pointed daily to the means of their removal, and exercised his obedience in offering them, was the justification of their existence, although they were intrinsically without efficacy.

[2] Impossible that sacrifices should have this efficacy in themselves; they can only possess it *per accidens*, by faith, and because of the special grace of God attached to them. Even the Talmudists saw and said that the Day of Atonement itself was no remedy for, no expiation of, the willing sin which constantly defers repentance (Yoma, viii. 9).

[3] This remarkable quotation comes from Ps. xl. 6, 7. It is probably a Psalm of David, and although this passage is typically Messianic, other parts of the Psalm (*e.g.* ver. 12) are almost exclusively personal. But yet the "He saith" means "Christ saith," because the words of David apply in a deeper and truer sense to Him.

[4] "Thou carest not for slain beast and bloodless oblation." This is one of the many memorable utterances of the Prophets, which show that they had been led to feel the nullity of sacrifices regarded as mere outward acts, and the vast superiority of a spiritual worship. It specially resembles 1 Sam. xv. 22, and anticipates the grand thoughts of Isaiah (i. 11—17); Jeremiah (vi. 20; vii. 21—23); Hosea (vi. 6); Amos (v. 21—24); and, above all, Micah (vi. 6—8). Philo in a beautiful passage (*De plant. Noe*) shows how well he had caught the spirit of these prophetic passages, when he warns against the ignorant superstition which confounded the offering of sacrifices with the practice of piety, and against the fancy that sacrifices alone will cleanse from moral guilt. He adds that God accepts the innocent even when they offer no sacrifice, and delights in fireless altars round which the virtues dance.

[5] A remarkable variation of the LXX. from the Hebrew text, which literally is "*Ears hast thou digged for me.*" How did this variation arise? (i.) One supposition is that the LXX. followed a different reading, but this is now generally abandoned, as the attempts to alter the Hebrew text have been unsuccessful; and all other versions render the clause literally, showing that they had the present Hebrew text. (ii.) Nor is it very probable that the text of the LXX. is corrupt, though Usher and others have very ingeniously supposed that ΚΑΤΗΡΤΙΣΑΣΩΤΙΑ has got changed partly by homœoteleuton, and partly by mistaking ΤΙ for Μ, into ΚΑΤΗΡΤΙΣΑΣ ΣΩΜΑ; and the reading ὠτία is actually traceable in some manuscripts. (iii.) It is, however, more probable that the LXX. use their phrase as a sort of Targum, a way of explaining a Hebrew allusion which they perhaps thought would be unintelligible to Gentile readers. The next question is, How did they arrive at this sense? (α) A favourite explanation is, that the Hebrew expression alludes to the custom of boring the ear of a slave if he chose to remain in servitude (Ex. xxi. 6; Deut. xv. 17), so that the bored ear would be a sign of willing obedience. But the verb means rather "digged" than "bored" (as in Ex. xxi. 6), and if this explanation were true we should expect "ear," not "ears." (β) It seems much more likely that the phrase "digging the ears," refers to opening the ears so that the soul may hear and obey—a metaphor found both in 1 Sam. xv. 22, and in Is. l. 5: "The Lord hath *opened the ear for me*, and I was not *rebellious*" (comp. Is. xlvii. 8). The meaning of the Psalmist will then be "thou hast revealed to me," or "caused me to hear so as to obey." The antithesis of the four clauses in the two verses of the Psalm is then perfect:—

"Slain beast and bloodless oblation thou desiredst not.
But mine ears thou diggedst.
Burnt-offering and sin-offering thou requiredst not,
Then said I, 'Lo! I have come to do thy will.'"

In the first clauses of each distich we have the sacrifices for which (comparatively, or in themselves) God does not care; in the second clauses the obedience for which He does care (see McCaul's *Messiahship of Jesus*, p. 162). In this sense then, the rendering of the LXX., though not a translation, is an intelligible, though somewhat bold, paraphrase, the "body" apparently meaning "the form of a slave" (comp. Phil. ii. 7; Rev. xviii. 13). Finding the rendering in the LXX., believing it to represent the true sense of the original (as it does), and also seeing it to be eminently illustrative of his subject, the writer naturally adopts it. The suggestion of an ancient writer that it was he who altered the reading of the LXX. must be unhesitatingly rejected. The word "holocausts," or whole burnt-offerings, occurs here alone in this Epistle. They were the emblem of *entire* self-consecration (while the meat-offerings were eucharistic, and the sin-offerings expiatory). But the holocaust was valueless without the self-sacrifice of which it was the symbol

[6] κεφαλίς is properly the knob (*umbilicus*) of the roller on which the vellum was rolled. The LXX. chose it to represent the Hebrew *Megillah*. The writer probably did not stop to ask what

God, 'Thy will.'[1] Saying as above, 'Sacrifices and offerings and whole burnt offerings, and sin offerings, thou wouldest not, nor even approvedst (the which are offered according to the Law),[2] then He has said, 'Lo, I have come to do Thy will.' He takes away the first (namely, sacrifices) 'that He may establish the second' (namely, the Will of God). 'By which will we have been sanctified by the offering of the body (vs. 8, Rom. xii. 1) of Jesus Christ once for all.'

"And every High Priest,[3] indeed, standeth daily ministering, and offering often the same sacrifices, of a kind which are never able to strip away sins.[4] But He, after offering one sacrifice for sins for ever, sat down at the right hand of God (vii. 27, viii. 1), henceforth awaiting until His enemies be placed as a footstool for His feet.[5] For by one offering He hath perfected (vii. 11, 25) for ever those who are in the way[6] of sanctification.[7]

"But the Holy Spirit also testifies to us. For after having said, 'This is the covenant which I will make with them after those days,' saith the Lord,[8] giving My Laws on their hearts, and upon their understandings will I inscribe them—and their sins and their iniquities will I remember no more. Now where remission of these is, there is no longer offering for Sin.'"[9]

Those last words are the triumphant close of the argument. If the forgiveness, the removal, the obliteration of sin, has been obtained, the object of all expiatory offerings has been accomplished, and they are rendered not only needless, but harmful—harmful as involving a faithlessness to Christ's finished work. If offerings are no longer admissible, there is an end of the Aaronic Priesthood; and if of the Priesthood, then also of the Law, which was based upon its existence; and if of the Law, then of the entire Old Dispensation. But if the Dispensation, which had long been depreciated by the voice of prophecy as "old," was now utterly vanishing away, this could only be because, in accordance with that same sure word of prophecy, the New had been inaugurated. And the New was an abrogation of the Old, because it was as the substance to the shadow, as the picture to the sketch.

---

book *David* was thinking of, because his mind is solely occupied with the Messianic application in which "the book" would be the whole Old Testament (Luke xxiv. 27). The words of the Psalm may mean "in the roll of the book it is prescribed to me," or as Gesenius and Ewald take it, "I am come with the volume of the book which is written for me." ἐν κεφαλίδι cannot mean "in the chief part" (Luther), or "in the beginning." David alludes to the writings of Moses, or possibly to the unwritten book of God's purposes (Ps. cxxxix. 16). The writer has omitted the words "I delight," before "to do Thy will." The sacred writers never aim at verbal accuracy in their quotations, since they did not hold any slavish and letter-worshipping theory of verbal inspiration. They hold it sufficient to give the general sense.

[1] x. 1—10 (comp. 1 Thess. iv. 3). [2] The τὸν is omitted in א, A, C.
[3] ἀρχιερεὺς (A, C.); ἱερεὺς, א, D, E, K, L (B. ends at καθαιρεῖ, in ix. 14). As to the daily offerings of the High Priest, see vii. 27, but the supposed difficulty may have led to the various reading. The "standeth" is emphatic. In the inner court none were allowed to sit, and the Levites are described as "standing before the face of the Lord."
[4] "To strip away"—sin being like a close-fitting robe (see on xii. 1).
[5] See i. 13; Ps. cx. 1.
[6] τοὺς ἁγιαζομένους; literally, "those who are being sanctified" (ii. 11). Sanctification is continuous, never instant and complete; but in the perfect sacrifice of Christ lies the germ of certain ultimate perfectionment for the believer (comp. τοὺς σωζομένους, Acts ii. 47).
[7] x. 11—14.
[8] The quotation is from Jer. xxxviii. 33, 34 (comp. viii. 10—12). To avoid the somewhat harsh form of the clause, the words ὕστερον λέγει, "Then He saith," are added before vi. 7 as the apodosis to μετὰ τὸ εἰρηκέναι. They are found in the Philoxenian Syriac, and were placed by Dr. Paris in the margin of the Cambridge Bible of 1762. There is no MS. or MS. authority for them, except the cursive 37. Others make these words "Saith the Lord," in ver. 16, prospective, and so the true apodosis. The question is not very important, being merely one of continuity of style.
[9] x. 15—18.

It was founded on better promises; it had an Eternal High Priest; it needed no renewal; it looked with confidence to the fulfilment of illimitable hopes; it rejoiced in the admission into God's Presence, by virtue of the finished sacrifice and endless intercession of its King and Priest, its Divine Saviour and everlasting Lord.

To this conclusion the whole Epistle has been leading up. In the first six chapters, with many hortative and illustrative digressions, the writer has made good his opening words, that "God had in these last days revealed Himself to us in His Son." This he has done by showing Christ's superiority to angels, the mediators of the Old Covenant (i. 5, ii. 18), and to Moses, the appointed Lawgiver (iii. 1, iv. 16). Then, after showing the way in which Christ fulfilled the qualifications of High Priesthood, as a High Priest after the order of Melchizedek (v. 1—10), he enters on the solemn strain by which he designs to prepare the thoughts of his readers for due attention to his central argument (v. 11—vi. 20). That argument falls into three parts, namely—

(A) The superiority of Melchizedek's Priesthood, and therefore of the Priesthood of Christ, to that of Aaron in many particulars (vii. 1—28).

(B) The superiority of the ordinances of Christ's New Dispensation to those of the Old (viii. 1—ix. 28), with special reference to the ceremonies of the Day of Atonement.

(c) The final recapitulation and summary of the conclusions which he has set forth (x. 1—18).

SECTION VII.

A THIRD SOLEMN WARNING.

The main work of the writer is finished. He has set before the recent converts from Judaism incontrovertible reasons for holding fast that which they have received, and for not abandoning the better for the worse, the complete for the imperfect, the valid for the inefficient, the archetype for the copy, the Eternal for the evanescent. It only remains for him to supplement the weight of reasoning by solemn warning and appeal. And this he does, first by an exhortation to faith, partly in the form of encouragement (x. 19—25), partly of warning (26—31); next, by a magnificent historic illustration of what faith is (xi.); lastly, by fervent exhortations to moral steadfastness and the holiness of the Christian walk (xii. 1—xiii. 19), ending by a few affectionate words of prayer and blessing.

The first burst of exhortation I proceed to translate, both because of its special solemnity and because it offers some difficulties of illustration and peculiarities of reading. The translation is offered not by any means as preferable to other versions, but as written with special objects. My aim is to follow (sometimes silently) what seems to me to be the best text; to avoid pages of discussion by only giving results; and to keep as nearly as possible to the form of the original Greek. In the notes I merely offer what seems to me to be most necessary for the elucidation of the text in the briefest form into which I can compress it.

"Having, then, confidence, brethren, in the blood of Jesus[1] for our entrance into the holies—(an entrance) which He inaugurates for us as a fresh and a living road,[2] through the veil, that is His flesh[3]—and (having) a Great Priest[4] (set) over the House of God, let us approach with sincere heart, in full assurance of faith, having our hearts sprinkled from an evil conscience, and our body washed with pure water.[5] Let us hold fast the confession of our Hope[6] unwavering, for faithful is He who promised.[7] And let us consider one another for provocation[8] to love and good works, not deserting the assembling of ourselves together,[9] as is the custom with some,[10] but encouraging one another, and so much the more as ye see the day approaching.[11]

For if we sin willingly[12] after the receiving of the full knowledge of the truth,[13] there is no longer left a sacrifice for sins, but a certain fearful expectance of

---

[1] These words go best with παρρησία (comp. Eph. iii. 12). It cannot be accurately said that we enter God's presence with the blood of Jesus, but He with His own blood (vi. 20; ix. 12).

[2] "New," ix. 8, 12; "Living," not in the sense of "life-giving" (Grotius, etc.), or "enduring" (Chrysostom), or "real," but because "He who liveth" is Himself the Way (John xiv. 6).

[3] As the veil hung between the Holy and the Holiest, so for a time the veil of Flesh, i.e., of suffering humanity, was the way through which Christ entered into the Holiest (see vi. 20); and His laying aside that veil of Flesh, and so, as it were, passing through it into Heaven, was symbolised by the rendering of the Parôketh (see on chap. ix. 3), Matt. xxvii. 51.

[4] See iv. 14. By "a great Priest" (cohen gadôl, Lev. xxi.) is meant not only a High Priest, but "a Priest upon His throne," as in Zech. vi. 11—13.

[5] Comp. Ezek. xxxvi. 25. The meaning is, "with our hearts sprinkled, as it were, with the blood of Christ (xii. 24; ix. 14; 1 Pet. i. 2), and so cleansed from a conscience which has become depraved, and our whole beings cleansed in the waters of baptism" (Eph. v. 26; Tit. iii. 5; 1 Pet. iii. 21), just as the Jewish priests were sprinkled with blood (Ex. xxix. 21; Lev. viii. 30), and bathed (Ex. xxx. 20; Lev. viii. 6; xvi. 4) before they could enter the Holy Places; ἐρραντισμένοι . . . λελουμένοι, "sprinkled . . . washed, once and for ever." For all Christians are priests (Rev. i. 5, 6).

[6] See vi. 11, 18, 19. Here, by a very singular oversight, our version has "the profession of our *faith*." We have "Faith" in ver. 22; "Hope" here; and "Love" in ver. 24. In this, as throughout the Epistle, we recognise the friend and pupil of St. Paul (1 Cor. xiii. 13; 1 Thess. i. 3; Col. i. 4, etc.).

[7] See vi. 13; xi. 11; xii. 26; 1 Thess. v. 24; 1 Cor. i. 9.

[8] Παροξυσμός is generally used in a bad sense, like "provocation;" and perhaps he uses the word because there had been among them a *paroxusmos* of hatred and not of love.

[9] Namely, in Christian gatherings for worship and Holy Communion. Ἐπισυναγωγή is only found in 1 Thess. ii. 1, and Delitzsch thinks that the word is here selected to avoid the Jewish συναγωγή; for the Jews also were stringent in requiring this duty (Berachoth, f. 8, a).

[10] In this neglectfulness he saw the dangerous germ of apostasy.

[11] x. 19—25. The day is the Last Day when Time, as counted by days, shall end (1 Cor. iii. 13). That Day, as regards the Old Covenant, came within a few years of this time at the fall of Jerusalem, which was God's judgment on the Judaism which refused to recognise its own Divine annulment. And that Day of the Lord was "the bloody and fiery dawn" of the Last Great Day (Matt. xvi. 28; xxiv.; Luke xvii.).

[12] The whole of this striking clause of warning closely resembles the passage on vi. 4—8, where see the notes. It contemplates not the ordinary sins and shortcomings of human frailty (ἀσθένεια . . . ἀγνοοῦντες . . . πλανώμενοι, v. 2), which may be forgiven upon repentance, but the last extreme of deliberate and self-chosen wickedness in those who say, "Evil, be thou my good," and who thus close the door of repentance against themselves, by passing from the spiritual life into impenitent and determined apostasy; and it contemplates this state as continued till "the Day" comes. The warning is against tendencies so perilous that they might end in a state of sin which deliberately despised and rejected its Saviour.

[13] Ἐπίγνωσις—not a mere historical knowledge of the truth, but some advance in that knowledge—a recognition of the truth at once theoretical and practical. He is speaking, not of lip-Christians, but of converts who lapse into "wretchlessness of unclean living." The passage has nothing directly to do with the Novatian dispute about the possibility of a second baptism. Nor does it say that the sinner has exhausted the infinitude of God's forgiveness, but only that there is no other sacrifice for sin left for him except that which he has willingly rejected.

PERIL OF APOSTASY.

judgment,[1] and a jealousy of fire which is about to devour the adversaries.[2] Any one who set at nought Moses' Law is without compassion put to death on the testimony of two or three witnesses; of how much worse vengeance,[3] think yo, shall he be deemed worthy who has trampled under foot the Son of God, and considered the blood of the Covenant wherewith he was sanctified a common thing, and insulted the Spirit of Grace?[4] For we know Him who said Retribution is Mine; I will repay, saith the Lord;[5] and again, The Lord shall judge His people.[6] Fearful is it to[7] fall into the hands of the Living God" (x. 19—31).

"But recall the former days[8] in which, after being enlightened,[9] ye endured much struggle of sufferings, partly by being made a public spectacle[10] in reproaches and afflictions, and partly by becoming partakers with those who were thus treated. For indeed ye sympathised with the prisoners,[11] and ye accepted with joy the plundering of your possessions,[12] recognising that ye have *yourselves*[13] as a better

---

[1] The τις is intensive.

[2] See Is. xxvi. 11. He personifies the fire, because the same thought is in his mind which he expresses in xii. 29. Perhaps, too, he is referring to such passages as Ps. lxxix. 5, "Shall thy jealousy burn like fire?" (Ezek. xxxvi. 5, etc.). The fire of God's wrath is that which was soon to devour the whole existence of Judaism. The New Testament writers are often alluding primarily to these consequences with none of those further allusions which have been introduced into the interpretation of their language.

[3] Deut. xvii. 2—7, where the sin to be punished is idolatry. This is the only passage in the New Testament where τιμωρία—which properly means retributive or vindictive punishment—is used of God. The word "punishment" is elsewhere κόλασις, which properly means "remedial punishment." It must be borne in mind that (1) it is here applied to the worst, deadliest, and most impenitent apostates; and (2) that its immediate reference is to the Day of Christ's coming, which was so close at hand in the temporal overthrow of the Jewish polity (Ewald, *Sendschr. an d. Hebr.* p. 122).

[4] It is clear that no more violent extremity of sin—no nearer approach to the unpardonable sin, the sin against the Holy Ghost—can be described than that which is contemplated in these verses. By "a common thing" may be meant either "unclean" (Vulg., Luther, etc.) or "of no specific value (Theophyl., etc.).

[5] He quotes this text to show that his warnings are founded on Scripture warrant. The reference is to Deut. xxxii. 35, but it exactly follows neither the Hebrew (To me [is] vengeance and recompense") nor the LXX. ("in the day of retribution I will requite"). It *is* exactly identical with St. Paul's citation of the same verse in Rom. xii. 19, especially if "saith the Lord" is here genuine (which is, however, omitted by א, D, and several versions and Fathers). An argument has been drawn from this fact that St. Paul must be the author of the Epistle to the Hebrews, but this argument is untenable, because (1) it is universally admitted that the writer was a friend and follower of St. Paul, and familiar with his phraseology and method of thought; (2) he may very possibly have had the Epistle to the Romans in his hands, especially as in xiii. 1—6 he shows traces of Rom. xii. 1—21 (see Alford, *Introd.* p. 71); and (3) the quotation in this very form, or one which nearly resembles it, seems to have been current in the Jewish schools, for it is found in the Targum of Onkelos. The reference to Deuteronomy shows that he is thinking mainly of *national* punishments.

[6] The primary sense of these words in Deut. xxxiii. 36, "The Lord will deliver His people as a righteous Judge;" but judgment involves both acquittal and condemnation, and the deliverance of the Jews meant the overthrow of their enemies.

[7] Here again the *stern* aspect of "falling into the hands of God" is given—the aspect which it bears "for the apostate and covenant-breaker" who has deliberately rejected and defiled God. For the penitent sinner there is another aspect. David, expecting and bowing to just punishment, yet says (1 Chr. xxi. 13), "Let *me fall now into the hand of the Lord;* for very great are His mercies: but let me not fall into the hand of man." And the son of Sirach, referring to the same passage, says (Ecclus. ii. 18), "We will fall into the hands of the Lord, and not into the hands of men; for as His majesty is, so is His mercy." Some would render it of "a *living* God" (comp. iii. 12); and this may be right, because there is a silent reference to Deut. xxxii. 40.

[8] Here, as in vi. 9—12, he passes from warning to encouragement, and bids them imitate their former and better selves.

[9] This word is not a mere synonym for "when ye were baptised" (see on vi. 4).

[10] The same metaphor as in 1 Cor. iv. 9; xv. 32.

[11] The common reading is τοῖς δεσμοῖς μου, "with my chains;" and this has been one of the circumstances which have led to the identification of the author with St. Paul. But this reading may easily have crept in from Col. iv. 18; Phil. i. 7, etc., and δεσμίοις, "with the prisoners," is the reading of A, D, the Vulgate, Syriac, and Coptic versions, St. Chrysostom, etc., and is strongly supported by xiii. 3. It also suggests fewer historical difficulties.

[12] There is a very striking parallel in Epictetus—"I became poor at Thy will, yea and gladly."

[13] I here follow the very striking and beautiful reading of א, A, which suggests the same great spiritual truth as ver. 39 and Luke ix. 25, xxi. 19. If ἐν ἑαυτοῖς, the very ill-supported

possession and an enduring. Fling not away, then, your confidence, since it has[1] a great recompense of reward. For ye have need of endurance, in order that, by doing the will of God, ye may win the promise. For yet but a very, very little while,[2] He who cometh will have come, and will not tarry.[3] 'But my righteous one shall live by faith,' and 'if he[4] draw back my soul approveth him not.' But we are not of defection unto perdition, but of faith unto the gaining of the soul"[5] (x. 32—39).

We are not of defection unto perdition—we do not belong to the party of those who have passed over the verge of apostasy, to the ruin of their souls; "but we are of FAITH to the salvation of the soul." What, then, is Faith?

SECTION VIII.

THE GLORIES OF FAITH.

By his mention of the word FAITH in this climax of exhortation, the writer, with the skill of a great orator, prepares the way for the enumeration of the heroes of faith in the next chapter. And this muster roll of the elders of the Jewish Church is by no means intended only as a series of good examples. It serves a more powerful end. It shows the Jewish converts, who were in danger of relapsing into their old bondage, that there was no painful discontinuity in their religious life; no harsh break between their present hopes and the past history of their race. The past was not discarded and disgraced; it was fulfilled and glorified. So far from being dissevered from the gracious lives of the Patriarchs, and the splendid zeal of the Prophets, they were infinitely nearer to them as Christians than they could have been as Jews. They were in possession of the mystery on which the elders had gazed with longing eyes, and were better able

---

reading of our text, be followed, the true translation will even then be, not (as in our version) "knowing in yourselves that," but "knowing that you have in yourselves," i.e., in your own hearts, or omitting the ἐν with A, D, E, K, L, "for yourselves." The "in Heaven" must in any case be omitted as a gloss (א, A, D, etc.).

[1] ἥτις, quippe quae.
[2] μικρὸν ὅσον ὅσον. This forcible phrase is borrowed from LXX Is. xxvi. 20.
[3] The quotation is an adaptation of the words of Hab. ii. 3, 4. For a fuller consideration of it, as it occurs in Gal. iii. 11, Rom. i. 17, see my *Life of St. Paul*, i. 369. The μοῦ ("my just man") is weakly supported by MS authority, being only found in א A; but the fact that it is not found in the two citations by St. Paul makes it more probable that it is genuine here. In the original it is "*the vision*" which will soon come. The Rabbis said that into this one precept as to the saving nature of faith, Habakkuk has compressed the 365 negative and the 248 positive precepts of the Law, which David had reduced to 11 (Ps. xv. 1—5), Isaiah to 6 (Is. xxxiii. 15), Micah to 3 (Mic. vi. 8), Isaiah again to 2 (Is. lvi. 1), and Amos, as well as Habakkuk, to 1 (Amos v. 4) (*Maccoth*, f. 23, b; f. 24, a).
[4] "If he," i.e., "if my just man." The E. V. inserts "if any man," but this is not warrantable, and as it is only found in the Genevan Version, there is some reason to fear that this is one of the very rare instances in which our translators have yielded to the temptation of dogmatic bias. But the belief that "the just" may fall back runs throughout the Epistle. There is not in it a single trace of the notion of "indefectible grace," or of "final perseverance."
[5] For this word ὑποστείληται see Acts xx. 20, 27; Gal. ii. 12. In these words the LXX. diverge widely from the Hebrew, which means "Behold his soul is lifted up, it is not upright in him"—words which seem to refer to the haughty Chaldean invader. The word rendered "faith" means, in the language of the Prophet, primarily "faithfulness."

than their unconverted brethren to understand the inmost heart of their fathers. Physical descent and identity of worship could not enable them to know the meaning of the faith displayed in the ante-Diluvian, the Patriarchal, and the Mosaic days. But Faith in Christ was the sunlike centre of all the types, and symbols, and sacrifices, and promises which constituted the religion of the Chosen People until Christ came.

What, then, is faith?

It is nowhere defined in Scripture, and the famous words with which this chapter opens are not so much a definition as a description. They are not a definition, for they do not, as St. Thomas Aquinas says, indicate the essence of Faith. They tell us what Faith *does*, rather than what it *is*—its *issues*, rather than its nature. "Faith," the writer says, "is the basis of things hoped for,[1] the demonstration of objects not seen."[2] This is what faith is in its results. It furnishes us with a foundation on which our hopes can securely rest, and with a conviction that those things exist which are not earthly or temporal, and which, therefore, we cannot see. Faith itself—not in the highest Pauline sense, but in its more usual sense[3]—is the spiritual power by which we are enabled to occupy this sure foundation, and arrive at this firm persuasion. It is the hand stretched forth into that Holiest Place which is as yet hidden from us by the veil of sense—the hand which can hold the spiritual gifts of God with so sure a grasp that it can never be deprived of them. To the eye of Faith the unseen and the eternal are more real than the things seen and temporal. To the heart of Faith hopes are as actual as realities, and heavenly promises are more precious than earthly possessions. To the eyes of the unilluminated heart the region in which Faith lives and moves is a dark cavern

---

[1] ὑπόστασις. This word "*hypostasis*" occurs only in 2 Cor. ix. 4; xi. 17 ("confident boasting"); Heb. i. 3 ("substance"); iii. 14 ("confidence"). Here it has been variously understood to mean (1) the "substance," in the metaphysical sense; that unseen substance in which all properties of a thing cohere; that which "*stands under*" all the visible or sensible qualities of a thing—its essence; that, therefore, which alone gives it reality. Thus among others Theophylact, who calls it the οὐσίωσις τῶν μήπω ὄντων καὶ ὑπόστασις τῶν μὴ ὑφεστώτων, and Ewald ("*Bestand in dem was man hofft*"). It would thus mean the cause of the subjective reality of things hoped for; or, as Dr Moulton says, "the *giving substance* to them;" or (2) "*confidence*"; or (3) as understood by Luther, Grotius, Bleek, Delitzsch, De Wette, Ebrard, Lünemann, etc., "*foundation*." This latter rendering seems to me the best. It is true that it is not the meaning of the word in iii. 14, nor i. 3, and the LXX. use it for "standing" in Ps. lxix. 2 (see Dante, *Paradiso*, xxiv. 52—81). St. Jerome says that this clause "breathes somewhat of Philo," who similarly speaks of "faith as dependent on a gracious hope, and regarding things not present as being indubitably present," and as "the fulness of excellent hopes . . . the lot of happiness . . . the sole genuine and secure blessing."

[2] If we could render the word "inward conviction," it would give a more forcible sense, and perhaps this is implied, though the word usually bears the more objective meaning of "demonstration." The use of the word πραγμάτων in this clause seems to imply that Faith not only makes Hope seem to rest on a basis of actual fruition, but also demonstrates the existence of the immaterial as clearly as though it were material. Ewald renders it, "Es ist aber Glaube . . . Beweis für Dinge welche man nicht schauet."

[3] For the distinctions in the meaning of Faith, see supra, p. 172, and my *Life of St. Paul*, ii. 198, sq. Here the writer uses the word, not in its specifically Christian sense (Gal. ii. 16; iii. 26; Rom. iii. 24), but in its general Old Testament sense of faithfulness resulting from trust in God (Gen. xv. 6, etc.), as also sometimes in St. Paul (2 Cor. v. 7; Rom. viii. 24—25). In this sense it is the hope which, without seeing, holds the ideal to be the real (Immer, *Neu. Test. Theol.* p. 413).

where nothing is even visible, much less can anything be beautiful; but Faith carries in her hand a lamp, kindled with light from Heaven, and wherever she moves an atmosphere of light is shed around her, and under every ray of it the streets and walls of the New Jerusalem seem to flash as with innumerable gems.

It was then a great encouragement and safeguard for these recent converts to know that it was by Faith that the elders[1] obtained a good report—that they, too, had to walk by Faith, and not by sight, and that the object of Faith was the same then as now, with this only difference, that then it was dim and unrevealed, but now was made fully manifest. For the object of the faith of the righteous—even from the days in which it had been promised in Paradise that the seed of the woman should break the serpent's head—was none other than the Christ. To the ancients He had been known solely under the guise of type and shadow, but now He was set forth to all as the brightness of the Father's glory and the express image of His person.

But, before beginning his list of worthies, he says,

"By faith we perceive that the ages[2] have been established by the utterance of God,[3] so that not from things which appear hath that which is seen come into being[4]" (xi. 4).

It is a mistake to regard this verse as incongruous with those which follow, or as introducing a different line of illustration from them. On the contrary, it strikes the keynote of all faith. Faith can only take its origin from the belief in God as the Creator of the Universe, and of the very substance from which the material Universe is made, so as to exclude all semi-Manichæan conceptions of the Eternity of Matter. We cannot believe in Christ, the end of our Faith, nor can we in any way understand His work, until we have learnt to believe in God as the Infinite Creator of all things visible and invisible. And this belief was, from the dawn of Humanity, the foundation of all holiness. Like the

---

[1] By the elders is not meant merely "the ancients," but the Zekênim, the greatest and best men of past ages (Is. xxiv. 22, etc.). "One who is in truth an elder is regarded," says Philo, "not in distance of time, but in worthiness of life" (De Abraham. § 46).

[2] See Philo, De Monarch. ii. p. 823; Leg. allegg. iii. p. 79; De Cherub. i. p. 162 (ed. Mangey), where the Logos is the Instrument of Creation, οἱ αἰῶνες, עולמים ("the ages"), is the world regarded in its history, regarded as existing in time. It differs from "the Universe" (κόσμος), which is the world regarded in its material aspect (see the quotation from the Talmud in Gesenius, Thes. II. 1056). This expression, therefore, includes the moral government of the world, as well as its creation (see i. 2); "the invisible, spiritual, and permanent potencies of the phenomenal world which owe their origin to the Son of God" (Möll).

[3] It is hardly to be doubted that the writer means no more here than that "God spake, and it was done" (λέγων ἅμα ἐποίει—Philo, De Sacr. Abel et Cain, § 18). Had he meant to imply that God created the world by the Divine Logos, he would have used the word λόγῳ, not ῥήματι, especially as the LXX. use it in Ps. xxxii. 6. Even in iv. 12, it is more than doubtful whether Logos bears its technical sense.

[4] I read τὸ βλεπόμενον with א, A, D, E. The wording of the phrase and its meaning may seem harsher than the rendering of the E. V., but it is the only rendering of which the order of the Greek admits, and the meaning is that "the visible world did not derive its origin from anything phenomenal"—in other words, that there was no pre-existent matter from which God made the world—not even the wild waste, "thohu va-bohu," of the chaos mentioned in Gen. i. 2. The meaning then, is practically identical with 2 Macc. vii. 28 (reading ἐξ οὐκ ὄντων). "I beseech thee, my son, look upon the heaven and earth, and all that is therein, and consider that God made them of things that were not."

first chapter of Genesis, the verse is meant to exclude from the region of faith all Atheism, Pantheism, Dualism, or Polytheism, and to fix the soul on the thought of the One True God.

Then he begins to adduce his handful of illustrations—"plucking, so to speak, only the flowers which stand by his way, and leaving the whole meadow full to his readers."[1] And he first culls examples from the antediluvian days to show that the Faith which Christ required was analogous to the Faith which had worked in every holy soul since the world began.

It was by faith, then, that Abel offered to God a sacrifice which was "more than that of Cain,"[2] and was borne witness to as being Righteous[3] —since God bore witness respecting his gifts, and so, by his faith, he though dead yet speaketh.[4] It was by faith that Enoch was removed hence,[5] because he had that faith both in God's Being and in His Divine government of the world, without which it is impossible to please Him. By faith Noah built the Ark, and became an heir of the Righteousness which is according to faith.[6] By faith Abraham, when called by God,[7] left his home in Ur of the Chaldees to wander as a nomad Sheikh in a land not yet his own, awaiting the city that hath the foundations[8] whose architect and framer was God.[9] By faith even Sarah[10] became a mother of him from whom sprang people numberless as the sand along the lip of the sea.[11] The death of all these resembled

---

[1] Delitzsch. The chapter falls into five groups of instances:—(i.) Antediluvians (4—6); (ii.) from Noah to Abraham (7—13). Then follows a general reflexion (13—16); (iii.) Abraham and the Patriarchs; (iv.) from Moses to Rahab; (v.) summary reference to later heroes and martyrs down to the time of the Maccabees (32—40).

[2] Ver. 4. πλείονα παρὰ Κάϊν (comp. iii. 3; Matt. vi. 25). The exact point in which the sacrifice of Abel was superior to Cain's is left uncertain, though not difficult to conjecture.

[3] By God's approval of his sacrifice (Gen. iv. 4). He is called "righteous" in Matt. xxiii. 35; 1 John iii. 12.

[4] Primarily, an allusion to "the voice of his blood" (Gen. iv. 10), as seems probable from xii. 24, but hardly excluding the wider sense, in which it is so often quoted, of "speaking by his example." Another reading is λαλεῖται (D), "is spoken of"; but here, again, the writer seems to be thinking of a passage of Philo, where he says that "Abel—which is most strange—has both been slain, and lives," which he deduces from Gen. iv. 8—10 (Opp. i. 200, ed. Mangey)

[5] xi. 5, μετετέθη; lit., "he was transferred" (Gen. v. 24).

[6] Noah is called Righteous (tsaddîk, δίκαιος) in Gen. vi. 9; and, as Philo observes, he is the first to whom the title is given in Scripture. He is mistaken in making the name Noah mean righteous (Leg. alleg. iii. 24). The "righteousness according to faith," is a very Paulinesounding phrase, though St. Paul never actually uses it. He uses, however, "the righteousness of faith" (Rom. iv. 13). The phrase could hardly have been used by one unfamiliar with St. Paul's terminology; but the writer shows his own marked individuality by applying both words, "Righteousness" and "Faith," in a sense by no means identical with that of St. Paul, but strongly marked with his own views (see supra, pp. 172, 173).

[7] Ver. 8. I read καλούμενος with most uncials. If, however, ὁ κ. be the right reading (א A, D), the meaning can only be "he who was called Abraham," with a reference to the change of his name from Abram. This is by no means impossible (so Theodoret). The faith of Abraham was one of the commonest topics of eulogy and dissension in the Rabbinic schools.

[8] Ver. 10. Not Jerusalem (Ps. xlvi. 5; lxxxvii. 1; Rev. xxi. 10), but "the Jerusalem above" (xii. 22; xiii. 14). The same thought and expression occurs often in Philo.

[9] Philo in several places speaks of God as the Architect (τεχνίτης) of the world; and this is one of the resemblances of this Epistle to the Book of Wisdom (Wisd. xiii. 1).

[10] Even Sarah, though once she laughed.

[11] Dr. Field seems to think that καὶ αὐτὴ Σάρρα may be a gloss: for (L) ἔτεκεν is not found in א A, D; (ii.) from the reference to Abraham in Rom. iv. 8; (iii.) because καταβολή properly applies to the male.

their lives, for they all died in accordance with faith, not having received the (fruition of the) promises made to them,[1] but having seen that fruition from afar, and greeted it,[2] and acknowledged that human life is but a sojourn in an alien country.[3] Such language showed clearly that they were looking for a fatherland; and this was not the land which they had left, for, had this been all, they could easily have returned to it. But they were yearning for a better—a heavenly country; and because they were thus homesick their Father was not ashamed of them, not ashamed to be entitled their God (Gen. xvii. 7; xxvi. 24; xxviii. 13, etc.), for He prepared for them a city.

Then, returning to Abraham, he dwells on the faith he showed in the willingness to offer up his son, his only son, whom in *will* he so absolutely sacrificed that, typically speaking,[4] he received him back only from the dead. By faith Isaac blessed Jacob and Esau, even respecting things future.[5] By faith Jacob on his death-bed blessed each of the sons of Joseph,[6] and bowed his head to God as he leaned over the top of his staff.[7] By faith Joseph felt so sure that God would fulfil His promises that he bade the children of Israel carry back his bones with them from Egypt to the Promised Land.[8] By faith Amram and Jochebed, the parents of Moses, struck with his beauty,[9] fearlessly hid him for three months. By faith Moses when he grew up, undazzled by the rank and splendour of the Egyptian throne,[10] turned away his eyes to the great reward, deli-

---

[1] They had received the promises in one sense ($\dot{\epsilon}\kappa o\mu i\sigma a\nu\tau o$), but not in another ($o\dot{v}\ \lambda a\beta\acute{o}\nu\tau\epsilon s$.) See ix. 15.

[2] See Gen. xlix. 19; John viii. 56.

[3] Gen. xxiii. 4; xlvii. 9; 1 Chron. xxix. 15; Ps. xxxix. 12, etc.

[4] Ver. 19. Elsewhere in the Epistle $\delta\theta\epsilon\nu$ means "for which reason." The meaning of the words $\dot{\epsilon}\nu\ \pi a\rho a\beta o\lambda\tilde{\eta}$ has been much disputed. (1) Some take it to mean "unexpectedly" (as in Polybius. i. 23. $\pi a\rho a\beta\acute{o}\lambda\omega s$), or "in bold venture," on the analogy of $\pi a\rho a\beta\acute{a}\lambda\lambda\epsilon\sigma\theta a\iota$—"to undertake a *daring risk*." (2) Luther erroneously follows the Vulg. in rendering them "for a type" (in *parabolam*, *zum Vorbilde*). There is, however, no doubt that it must mean (3) "in a figure," as in our E. V. But the question then arises how he can be said to have received Isaac back "in a figure," and not in reality? Omitting untenable conjectures, it may mean either "as a type of the resurrection," or be taken as a qualification of the "received him from the dead." Isaac was, "*figuratively speaking*, dead" when Abraham received him back. The form of expression is unusual, but the Jewish analogies seem to show that this is the meaning here. (See the passages quoted by Wetstein—in one of them—Pirke Eliezer, § 31 —it is said that Isaac did actually die; and see Rom. iv. 17—19).

[5] Esau too was blessed. He got the lower life that he desired, though the true rendering of Gen. xxvii. 39 is not as in our Version, but "Behold, thy dwelling shall be away from the fatness of the earth, and *away from* the dew of blessing."

[6] See Gen. xlviii. 14, 17—20.

[7] This seems to refer, not to the blessing of Ephraim and Manasseh, but to Gen. xlvii. 31. In our version it runs, "And Israel bowed himself upon his bed's head." The LXX. and Peshito render it as here, "upon the top of his staff;" and the strange rendering of the Vulgate, "He (Jacob) adored the head of his (Joseph's) staff," has led to the wildest vagaries of conjecture, and to the defence of image-worship from this passage! the main variation of rendering arises only from the fact that the LXX., Vulgate, and Peshito, understood the word to be *matteh*, "staff," not *mittah*, "bed," as they understood it two verses later (Gen. xlvii. 2). Jacob was lying in bed; but, getting up to take the oath from Joseph, supported his trembling limbs upon "the staff," which was a memorable type of his pilgrimage (Gen. xxxii. 10), and, at the end of the oath, bowed his head over his staff in sign of thanks and reverence to God.

[8] Gen. l. 26; Ex. xiii. 19; Josh. xxiv. 32.

[9] Acts vii. 20, "fair to God." His Divine beauty seemed to them a sign of something remarkable. See Philo, *Vit. Mos.* (*Opp.* ii. 82).

[10] "The son of a daughter of Pharaoh," *i.e.*, the son of a princess. The reference is to the Jewish legend, which was peculiarly rich in details about Moses. It is not recorded in Scripture, though it is implied. Comp. Luke iv. 5, 6.

berately preferring to share in the reproach of the Christ[1] with God's suffering people. By faith, with his eyes still steadfastly fixed on the *unseen* King, he braved the wrath of Pharaoh, and led his people out of Egypt.[2] By faith he celebrated[3] the Passover and the sprinkling of blood that the Destroyer of the firstborn might not touch them. By faith the Israelites crossed the Red Sea as through dry land. It was by their faith that the walls of Jericho fell. It was faith[4] which led Rahab, the heathen harlot,[5] to receive their spies. And after these many examples of heroic faith exhibited in many particulars—Abel, Enoch, Noah—Abraham, Sarah, Isaac, Jacob, Joseph, the parents of Moses—Moses, the Israelites, Rahab—what need was there to continue[6] the glorious enumeration, and go through the deeds of Gideon, Barak, Samson, Jephthah, David, Samuel, and the Prophets—

"Who, through faith subdued kingdoms, wrought righteousness,[7] obtained promises,[8] stopped the mouths of lions,[9] quenched the power of fire,[10] escaped the edges of the sword,[11] were strengthened out of weakness,[12] became mighty in war, drove back the armies of the aliens.[13] Women received their dead by resurrection,[14] and others were broken on the wheel,[15] not accepting the offered deliverance, that they may obtain a better resurrection.[16] Others again bore trial of mockings and scourgings,[17] aye, and further of chains and imprisonment; [18] they were stoned,[19] were sawn asunder,[20] were tempted,[21] died by slaughter of the sword.[22] They went about in sheepskins and goatskins, being destitute, afflicted, tormented—of whom

---

[1] See xiii. 13; 2 Cor. i. 5; Col. i. 24. "The reproach which Christ had to bear in His own person, and has to bear in that of His members" (Bleek). There is probably a reference to Ps. lxxxix. 50, 51. Comp. Phil. iii. 7—11.
[2] This clearly alludes to the Exodus. If it alluded to his flight into Midian, it would require some violence to harmonise it with Ex. ii. 14. It is true that for the moment Pharaoh consented to the Exodus, but it was only in wrath and fear, and it was certain that he would pursue them.
[3] For the perfect see ver. 17, and the notes on iv. 7, ix. 8, x. 9, x. 29, etc.
[4] It is equally true, in another sense, that it was by works. Jas. ii. 25.
[5] The word is to be understood literally (Matt. i 5), and its retention is a proof of the faithfulness of the sacred narrative, even in matters most likely to wound the national sensibilities of the Jews. The Targum softens it down into Pundakitha=πανδοκευτρία, cauponari ", "innkeeper," and Bruno most arbitrarily renders it "idolatress."
[6] The phrase, "time will fail me," is found also in Phil) (De somn.).
[7] A proof that the writer never dreamt, any more than St. Paul did, of an inoperative faith.
[8] The allusion is to the promises of victory, etc., of Josh. xxi. 45, etc. (Comp. ver. 13, 39).
[9] Dan. vi. 23 ; Judg. xiv. 6; 2 Sam. xvii. 34; xxiii. 20.
[10] Dan. iii. "the burning fiery furnace."
[11] 1 Sam. xviii. 11; xix. 10, 12; 2 Kings iv. 14; etc., etc.
[12] Samson, David, Hezekiah, Isaiah, Jeremiah, Ezra, etc.
[13] These two clauses seem to refer to the Maccabees.
[14] 1 Kings xvii. 22, 23; 2 Kings iv. 35—37.
[15] This is the technical meaning of the word, and is probably intended here, if the reference is to 2 Macc. vi. 18—30, and vii.
[16] Not a resurrection like that of the Shunamite and the woman of Sarepta. See 2 Macc. vii. 9—36.
[17] 2 Macc. vii. 7—10; 1 Macc. ix. 26; Jos. Antt. xii. 5, § 4.
[18] 1 Macc. xii. 19; and in the Old Testament, Micah; 1 Kings xxiii. 26; Jer. xxxii. 23; etc.
[19] See 2 Chron. xxiv. 20—22 ; Matt. xxiii. 35—37. Tradition said that Jeremiah was stoned.
[20] Isaiah was perhaps sawn asunder. (See Yevamoth, f. 49 b; Sanhedrin, f. 103 b; Hamburger, Talm. Wört. s.v. Jesaia.)
[21] Comp. Matt. xxiv. 51. As the prophet from Judah was by Jeroboam, 1 Kings xiii. 7. If the reading be correct, it can only imply that the temptation to apostatise was the most cruel of afflictions (comp. Acts xxvi. 11; *Life and Work of St. Paul*, i. 172). But ἐπρήσθησαν, "they were burned," would be a probable conjecture if there were the slightest variation in the MSS. Comp. Philo, *in Flacc.* 20, where he tells us that some Jews of Alexandria were burned alive. (See 2 Macc. vi. 11.)
[22] 1 Kings xix. 10; Jer. xxvi. 27; 1 Macc. ii. 38; 2 Macc. v. 26.

the world was not worthy—wandering in deserts and mountains, and caves and the clefts of the earth.[1] And these all, being borne witness to by their faith, received not the promise,[2] since God provided something better concerning us,[3] in order that they may not, apart from us, be perfected"[4] (xi. 33—40).

SECTION IX.

FINAL EXHORTATIONS.

He can now resume with added force his final exhortation to faithful endurance. They are running a race, they are fighting a battle, but they are not alone. They are successors of the old saints, united with them in sympathy, but endowed with even richer blessings, and inspired with more glorious hopes.

"Wherefore let us also, since we have on all sides around us so great a cloud of witnesses (to the faith),[5] laying aside every weight[6] and the closely-clinging sin,[7] let us run with patience the race set before us, gazing earnestly on the leader[8] and perfecter of our faith, Jesus, who for the joy set before him endured a cross, despising shame, and has sat down on the right hand of the throne of God. For compare yourself with him who hath endured such contradiction at the hands of sinners against himself,[9] that ye be not weary by fainting in your souls. Not yet unto blood did ye resist in your struggles against sin,[10] and yet ye have utterly forgotten the encouragement which discourseth with you as with sons, My Son, despise not the training of the Lord, nor faint in being corrected by Him: for whom the Lord loveth He traineth, yea, He scourgeth every son whom He accepteth.[11]

---

[1] Judg. vi 2; 1 Kings xviii. 4, 13; xix. 8, 13; 1 Macc. ii. 23, 29; 2 Macc. v. 27; vi. 11; x. 6; Matt. xiv. 10.

[2] See ix. 15. If this be the right reading, we must suppose a contrast between general promises (xi. 33) and the one great final promise. But A reads "promises," and this is followed by some of the Fathers. (Comp. vi. 15.)

[3] Matt. xiii. 17; 1 Pet. i. 10, 11. [4] 1 Thess. i. 10; Rev. xxi. 3, 4.

[5] "A cloud," i.e., a dense multitude, like "a cloud of foot-soldiers," in Hom. *Il.* iv. 274; Herod. viii. 109; and comp. Is. lx. 8. Since patience was the characteristic of the faith of all these elders, he exhorts to patience (ὑπομονή), which Christ also showed (ὑπομείνας τὸν σταυρόν).

[6] As an athletic technicality the word meant "superfluous flesh," such as was reduced by training (Galen, Hippocrates).

[7] εὐπερίστατον occurs here alone in Greek literature. The meanings which have been suggested are (1) "circumventing," "hemming in on all sides;" (2) "easily avoidable" (comp. περιίστασο, 2 Tim. ii. 16; Tit. iii. 9); (3) "much-applauded," in the sense of "surrounded by spectators;" (4) "easily-besetting." This last is one of the senses approved by St. Chrysostom and many others (e.g., Erasmus, "tenaciter inhaerens;" Bp. Sanderson, "quae nos arcte complectitur;" Wiclif, "that standeth about us"), and involves the metaphor of a closely-fitting robe (στατὸς χιτών, "a close tunic"), which also seems to be suggested by ἀποθέμενοι. (Comp. Eph. iv. 22; Col. iii. 9.)

[8] Ἀρχηγόν. See Acts iii. 15, "the Prince of life;" v. 31, "a Prince and a Saviour;" *infra*, p. 312; Is. xxx. 4 (LXX). Whether, as Riehm and others think, the idea is involved of Jesus also "setting forth and manifesting faith in its perfection" is a very doubtful "afterthought of theology."

[9] א, D. E have ἑαυτούς, "sinners against themselves."

[10] "Unto blood" may either be the technical pugilistic expression ("an athlete can bring no great courage to a contest who has never had blood drawn"—"*qui nunquam suggillatus est*," Sen.); or, more probably, means, "there have as yet been no actual martyrdoms among you." The use of the aorist seems to imply a slight reproach—"ye resisted not unto blood, but gave way to the attack." Until we have any grounds for reasonable certainty as to the Church to which this Epistle was addressed, the phrase can hardly be used as an argument in settling the date at which it was written. Certainly in Rome and in Jerusalem there had been martyrdoms before any date which is at all probable for its composition.

[11] Philo comments on the same passage (Prov. iii. 11, 12) in much the same strain (Opp. i. 544). The quotation is from the LXX., with slight variations. It agrees with the Hebrew, except that "faint in being corrected" is in the Hebrew "loathe not his correction." The Vat. MS. of the LXX. has ἐλέγχει, "rebukes" or "chastens," for παιδεύει, "trains" (see Rev. iii. 19). In the last clause, for "scourgeth every son," etc., the Hebrew has "even as a father the son in whom he delighteth." Probably the LXX. read ולאב for יכאב.

Endure with a view to your training,[1] since God is dealing with you as with sons" (xii. 1—7).

He continues the illustration of God's Fatherhood by human fatherhood. The father who nobly and wisely loves his child will not spoil him by suffering him to grow up in headstrong wilfulness, but will punish him when punishment is needful, and the father does not thereby lose, but rather increases, his son's reverence for him. How much rather shall we subject ourselves to the Father of our spirits?[2] The punishment of earthly parents is only for the brief days of their authority, and there mingles with it an element, if not of caprice, yet of the possible errors of human opinion. God corrects us only for our good, that we may partake of His holiness. Now the sterner side of training is never immediately pleasurable; but men enjoy its fruits afterwards in the peace of moral hardihood and serene self-mastery. He urges them to straighten into vigour the relaxed hands and palsied knees, and to make straight tracks for their feet,[3] that lameness may not be quite put out of joint,[4] but may rather be cured.

"Pursue peace with all,[5] and the sanctification without which no man shall see the Lord; looking carefully lest there be any one who is falling short of the grace of God—lest any root of bitterness[6] springing up trouble you, and by its means the many be defiled—lest there be any fornicator,[7] or scorner, like Esau, who for one meal sold his own birthright.[8] For ye know that afterwards, when he was even

---

[1] The best reading seems to be εἰς, not εἰ (א, A, D, K, L, etc.).

[2] This is the most natural meaning of τῷ Πατρὶ τῶν πνευμάτων, especially when we compare it with Num. xvi. 22, "the God of the spirits of all flesh." And this seems to have originated the expression among Rabbinic writers (v. Wetstein and Schöttgen, ad loc.). Others take it to mean "the Father of spiritual life" (the Author of χαρίσματα, or Divine graces), or "of the spirit-world," i.e., "of angels," etc. But it would not then be a direct antithesis to "fathers of our flesh." To draw any inference here about the verbal controversy (as it seems to me) between Creationists—those who consider that the human soul is in each birth distinctly created—and Traducianists—those who think that it is derived in the way of natural birth—is perfectly futile.

[3] xii. 13. Καὶ τροχιὰς ὀρθὰς ποιήσατε τοῖς ποσὶν ὑμῶν is an unintentional hexameter. These are metrical accidents. The metaphor is borrowed from Prov. iv. 26. The fact that, beside this hexameter, there are two distinct iambics (ver. 14, 15)—
οὗ χωρὶς οὐδεὶς ὄψεται τὸν Κύριον,
Ἐπισκοποῦντες μή τις ὑστερῶν ἀπο,
and one half-iambic, ἵνα μὴ τὸ χωλὸν ἐκτραπῇ (ver. 13) and a bad pentameter (ver. 26)—though the rhythms are evidently unintentional—shows the elaboration and oratorical finish and stateliness of the style.

[4] ἐκτραπῇ. I have given the technical sense of the word (luxari); and the familiarity of the writer with St. Luke's language, and, in all probability, with St. Luke himself, makes it not unlikely that he may have learnt a technical term or two from intercourse with "the beloved physician." Possibly, however, the word may have its ordinary sense of "be turned out of the way." 1 Tim. i. 6; v. 15; 2 Tim. iv. 4.

[5] Ps. xxxiv. 10; 1 Pet. iii. 11.

[6] xii. 15; Deut. xxix. 18, "a root that beareth gall and wormwood," or, as in margin, "a poisonful herb." The mention of "gall" has led to the untenable conjecture that we should read ἐν χολῇ here as in the LXX; but the Alexandrine MS. of the LXX has ἐνοχλῇ. See Exc. IX.

[7] xii. 16. Since the word here can hardly mean "idolator" (Chrys., Calvin, Grotius, De Wette, Bleek, etc.), and would be too strong to apply to Esau on account of his heathen marriages (Gen. xxvii. 35; xxviii. 8), we must suppose that the writer follows the Jewish tradition, as Philo also does, in which Esau was represented as a man of impure life. They applied to him the expression in Prov. xxviii. 21. If it mean apostasy from Jewish privileges (Tholuck, Ebrard, Riehm), then his πορνεία in abandoning Judaism is compared with the πορνεία of now returning to it (Riehm, p. 155, f. 9).

[8] ἑαυτοῦ, א, A, C.

anxious to inherit the blessing, he was rejected: for he found no opportunity for repentance—though he sought it [*i.e.*, the blessing] earnestly with tears"[1] (xii. 14—17).

Then comes the great outburst of triumphant comparison in which he closes this, his main exhortation against the imminent peril of apostasy—

"For ye have not come to palpable and enkindled fire,[2] and to darkness and gloom, and storm, and sound of trumpet, and voice of utterances (ῥημάτων), which they who heard deprecated, entreating that no further discourse (λόγος) should be addressed to them, for they could not bear what was being enjoined, 'and if a beast touch the mountain it shall be stoned;' and (so fearful was the pomp of the vision) —Moses said, 'I am terrified and trembling'[3]:—but ye have approached Sion, mountain and city of the Living God, the heavenly Jerusalem, and to myriads of angels, to a festal assembly and church of the Firstborn enrolled in Heaven,[4] to a Judge, the God of all, and to the spirits of just men who have been perfected, and to Jesus, Mediator of a new covenant,[5] and to a blood of sprinkling, which speaketh

---

[1] xii. 14—17. The general tenor of the warning is, Do not despise your birthright, lest hereafter you should be unable to recover it when you feel the bitter consequences of the loss. If this clause means that Esau desired to repent, and no chance of repenting was allowed him, it runs counter to the entire tenor of Bible teaching. Hence the τόπος μετανοίας (comp. Wisd. xii. 10) must mean, like its Latin equivalent, "*locus poenitentiae*," not merely an opportunity for repentance, but a chance of so changing his mind as to avert the fatal consequences. "It does not mean," says Theodore of Mopsuestia, "that he did not obtain pardon of sins on repentance, for that he was not in any way asking; but that it was never possible for *the blessing* to be given him again." "His tears were tears of remorse for the earthly consequences, not tears of spiritual sorrow (2 Cor. vii. 10). They sprang from the *dolor amissi*, not the *dolor admissi*; from the *dolor ob poenam*, not the *dolor ob peccatum*" (Wordsworth). Hence, though we cannot accept the favourite view of many modern commentators (Beza, Ebrard, Tholuck, etc.) that the words mean "an opportunity of a change of mind *in his father*," we must either (1) give to μετάνοια some less special sense than that of "repentance," which it usually bears; or (2) put the clause in a parenthesis, and take it to mean that, as a fact, Esau never repented, which is rendered more probable by the Targum on Job, which says: "All the days of Esau the ungodly they expected that he would have repented, but he repented not;" or (3) we must suppose that it means "he found no opportunity of repentance *of such a kind as would reverse the consequences of his profane levity*, and win him back the blessing." If we take this last view, the "though he sought it" may mean "*this kind of* repentance;" if not, we have no alternative but to understand "it" of "the blessing." It is perfectly true that there is thus a difficulty either in the construction of the sentence, or in the meaning given to μετάνοια; and some may prefer to say that the passage merely expresses the hopeless condition, *humanly speaking*, of the hardened and defiant apostate, like vi. 4—8; ii. 3; x. 26—31; xii. 25. But if any one rejects all these ways of removing the difficulty, he is left with a statement which will ever furnish its best stronghold to that guilty despair which is antagonistic to all that is best and most precious in the Gospel of Love. It was the abuse of this passage by the Montanists and Novatians to justify their refusal of absolution to those who fell into sin after baptism which tended to the discrediting of this Epistle in the Western Church.

[2] xii. 18. This rendering may surprise the reader; but ὄρει is omitted by א, A, C, and some of the best versions, and this view is adopted by Bengel, Delitzsch, Tischendorf, Davidson, Moulton, etc. See Ex. xix. 18; xx. 12; Deut. iv. 12. The words may, however, mean "that [mountain] which is material (or 'that is being groped for' (Wordsworth); comp. Lk. x. 21; LXX.) and burned with fire."

[3] In speaking of this terror of Moses at Sinai, the writer follows the Hagada, unless he can be supposed to refer to Deut. ix. 19. In Shabbath, f. 88, b, Moses exclaims, "Lord of the Universe, I am afraid lest they (the angels) should consume me with the breath of their mouths." The same tradition of Moses' terror is found in Midrash Koheleth, f. 69, 4, and in Zohar. In Ex. xix. 16 it is said that "all the people trembled." Similarly, in Acts vii. 32 we are told the unrecorded fact that Moses trembled on seeing the burning bush (Ex. iii. 6).

[4] I will not here enter into the voluminous controversy which has arisen as to the punctuation of these words, or the *exact* significance which the writer attached to the expression "church of the first-born enrolled in heaven," because I do not think that any certain conclusions can be arrived at. I take the μυριάσι with ἀγγέλων, because of Deut. xxxiii. 1, 3; Ps. lxviii. 17; Dan. vii. 10; and I suppose the "Church of the first-born enrolled in heaven" to be the Church of Christ, the heir of the spiritual Jacob, while the Jews had forfeited their spiritual birthright. (Luke x. 30; Rev. iii. 5; xiii. 8; xx. 15; Phil. iv. 3. Comp. Ex. iv. 22, xix. 1—6, with 1 Pet. ii. 9; and see xiii. 8.)

[5] Διαθήκη νέα, as distinguished from the commoner epithet καινή, implies not only that it is "recent," but that it is "young" and "strong."

something better than that of Abel.¹ Take heed that ye do not decline to listen to Him that speaketh. For if *they* escaped not by refusing him who spake on earth, far more shall not we, who are turning away from Him who is from Heaven.² Whose voice shook the earth then,³ but now He hath promised, saying, 'Again, once for all will I shake not only the earth, but also the Heaven.'⁴ Now this 'again once for all' indicates the removal of the things that are being shaken, as of things which have been made in order that things which cannot be shaken may remain.⁵ Wherefore since we are receiving a kingdom which cannot be shaken, let us cherish thankfulness, and thereby let us serve God acceptably with holy awe and fear. For, indeed, our God is a consuming fire" ⁶ (xii. 18—29).

In this, then, was to be their great encouragement to Faith and Patience. The Dispensation which they were now enjoying was infinitely richer in blessing, infinitely less surrounded with elements of terror, than that under which had lived those elders of whose steadfast endurance he had just been telling them. In the culminating point of that Dispensation God had spoken to the Israelites of old, not from heaven, but from the flaming and earthquake-riven peak of the desert mountain. His voice had come with a sound so awful from the dark storm and careering fire as to force from them the entreaty that God would speak to them no more, except through the voice of their lawgiver. Even that great lawgiver had almost recoiled in terror from the awful splendour of the scene. To the mountain itself the Israelites had not dared to approach, for they had been told to set a fence around it, so as not even to touch its border, and if even an animal touched it they were to stone it, or pierce it with a dart. They stood, therefore, afar off, and Jewish legend told how at the utterance of each commandment they recoiled twelve miles, till the ministering angels brought them back.⁷ But now the True Israel—they who had accepted the Messiah and King of Israel—had come near, and that with perfect boldness, to another and a heavenly hill, where there were angels indeed in myriads, but not surrounded with attributes of terror; where they would be admitted into the peaceful and blessed communion which united the

---

¹ See ix. 13; x. 22; xi. 4; xiii. 12. "The blood of Abel demanded vengeance, that of Christ remission" (Erasmus). It is curious that, according to Jewish legend, the dispute between Cain and Abel had reference to the question whether God was a judge or not, which, Selden says, was even found in some editions of the Hebrew Pentateuch (*De jur. natal.*). One interpretation of the plural "bloods" in Gen. iv. 10 was that his "blood was sprinkled on the trees and stones" (Surenhus. *Mishna* iv. 229).

² Chrysostom, etc., understood Moses to be meant by him that uttereth sacred words on earth. He who speaks from heaven is Jesus. But the contrast evidently is between the voice that spoke on Sinai and that which appeals to us from the heavenly Sion. It is not a contrast between the *speakers*, but between the places from which they spoke, involving as it did the vast difference between the inferior and the superior revelation. The speaker may be regarded as the same, for even the Jews always said that the speaker at Sinai was Michael=the Shechinah=the Angel of the Presence (Isa. lxiii. 9), or of the Covenant (Mal. iii. 1).

³ See Ex. xix. 18; Judg. v. 4; Ps. cxiv. 7.

⁴ Hagg. ii. 6, 7. The words literally mean, "Yet once it is, a little while." Comp. Luke xxi. 26.

⁵ The words may also be rendered, "The removing of the things that are being shaken, as of things which have been made in order that the things not shaken may remain."

⁶ xii. 18—22. The quotation is from Deut. iv. 24 (comp. ix. 3), and gives a reason why our love of God should be mingled with holy awe and fear. The best reading is μετὰ εὐλαβείας καὶ δέους, although δέος occurs nowhere else in the New Testament.

⁷ See McCaul's *Old Paths*, pp. 202—205.

saints on earth to those in heaven ; and where it was the Voice of the Son of God Himself which invited them to enter the immediate Presence of God their Loving Judge. If, then, the neglect of that voice from Sinai had brought down its own terrible consequences, how much more inexcusable would it be, how much more terrible, to neglect and despise the voice which now called to them in tones of infinite tenderness ! The earth had trembled at Sinai ; the sure word of prophecy had declared that it should be shaken once again. But there was one thing which could never be shaken, and that was the Kingdom of God into which they had entered. Let that thought be to them one of thankfulness and godly reverence, lest forfeiting the blessings into which they had been freely admitted, they should find that the Fire of Love was no less terrible to purge and punish than had been that of Sinai to their fathers ! [1]

The last chapter of the Epistle consists of notices and exhortations, such as the writer considered to be necessary for the Church whose members he is addressing. He urges them to a continuance of their brotherly love.[2] He tells them not to forget hospitality, a virtue which was so indispensable for the happiness of the poor brethren who found themselves in strange towns.[3] It was a virtue for which the ancient Christians were celebrated even among the heathen,[4] and the writer reminds them how by the exercise of hospitality some of the elders (like Abraham and Lot and Manoah and Gideon) had even entertained angels unawares.[5] He bids them be mindful of prisoners, as being themselves Christ's prisoners,[6] and of all in distress, liable as they were, while still in the body, to similar sufferings.[7] He bids them in all respects to honour marriage, and to keep undefiled the marriage bed, since God will judge the unclean.[8] He warns them against covetousness,[9] and encourages them to contentment by the blessed promise that

---

[1] Comp. x. 27, 28, 30.
[2] vi. 10 ; x. 32, 33. Comp. Rom. xii. 10 ; 1 Thess. iv. 9 ; 1 Pet. i. 22. Perhaps the neglect, by some, of Christian gatherings, had tended to disunion (x. 25).
[3] 1 Pet. iv. 8, 9 ; Rom. xii. 13 ; Tit. i. 8 ; 1 Tim. iii. 2. Comp. Berachoth, f. 63, b, and many passages in Hershon's *Treasures of the Talmud*, chap. x.
[4] Lucian, *De mort. Peregr.* 16 : "Their principal lawgiver has inspired in them the sentiment that they are all mutually brethren." Julian (Ep. 49) says that ἡ περὶ τοὺς ξένους φιλανθρωπία has been the chief element of success in the spread of their ἀθεότης.
[5] Comp. Matt. xxv. 35. The writer had doubtless read Philo's *De Abrahamo* (Opp. ii. 17) : "I know not what excess of happiness and blessedness I should ascribe to the household wherein angels deigned to be introduced to men, and to share their gifts of hospitality."
[6] 1 Cor. vii. 22 ; 2 Cor. ii. 14 ("who leadeth us in triumph"). Lucian, in his curious tract on the Death of Peregrinus, dwells on the extraordinary tenderness of Christians for the Confessors in prison. This incidental notice shows the courage and endurance which a Christian was called on to display in these times of persecution.
[7] Calvin takes ἐν σώματι to mean "the body of the *Church*"; but the words standing alone could not bear such a meaning. Here, again, we might be prepared to see a reminiscence of Philo, who says, ὡς ἐν τοῖς ἑτέρων σώμασιν αὐτοὶ κακούμενοι, "as being yourselves afflicted in the persons of others" (*De spec. legg.* § 30). But the meaning clearly is, "as being yourselves liable to suffer."
[8] The warnings may have been equally needed by Essenes, who disparaged marriage (1 Tim. iv. 3), and by Antinomians, who made light of unchastity (Acts xv. 20 ; 1 Thess. iv. 6 ; xii. 16).
[9] For a similar juxtaposition of covetousness and uncleanness see 1 Cor. v. 10 ; vi. 9 ; Eph. v. 3, 5 ; Col. iii. 5 ; and here the very idiom (ἀφιλάργυρος ὁ τρόπος· ἀρκούμενοι) is identical with that of St. Paul (Rom. xii. 9 : ἡ ἀγάπη ἀνυπόκριτος· ἀποστυγοῦντες). It need hardly be added that this is no proof whatever of the Pauline authorship. It is quite clear throughout the Epistle

God would never leave nor forsake them,[1] a promise which gave them an impregnable security against all assaults of man. He bids them bear in memory their leaders who had passed away [2]—leaders who once spoke to them the word of God, "whose faith imitate, contemplating the issue of their Christian walk."[3]

And since those leaders had ever preached Christ, Who *is* the Word of God—(though here again the term is not *directly* applied to Him)— he warns them once more of their tendency to be seduced by the haughty boasts and privileges of Judaism, or by any which would lead them to relapse into the religion from which they had been converted.

"Jesus Christ is the same yesterday, and to-day, and for ever.[4] Be not swept away[5] by various and strange teachings. For it is a beautiful thing[6] to be established in heart by grace,[7] not by meats, in which they who walked were not benefited.[8] We have an altar,[9] wherefrom they have no license to eat who serve the tabernacle.[10] For the bodies of those animals, the blood of which is carried by the High Priest into the holy place, are burned outside the camp. Therefore Jesus also, that he may sanctify the people by his own blood, suffered without the gate.[11] Let us then go forth to him outside the camp, bearing his reproach.[12] For we

---

that the writer has lived in close communion with St. Paul, and a writer of such intense originality as St. Paul stamps his thoughts and idioms on the minds of his associates. These similarities only force into more prominent relief the marked individuality of the style of the present writer.

[1] "He hath said." "He," as in the Talmud, means God (אמר הוא). The exact words, "I will never leave thee nor forsake thee," do not occur in the Old Testament, though they are so quoted by Philo (*De confus. ling.* § 32). The expression may be taken from 1 Chr. xxviii. 20; Deut. xxxi. 6, 8; or (more probably) Josh. i. 5.

[2] *If* the letter was addressed to Palestine, these leaders would include such men as St. Stephen and St. James the brother of St. John.

[3] The word ἔκβασιν ("outcome") occurs only in 1 Cor. x. 13, where it is rendered "escape." The word here may imply their death (on the analogy of ἔξοδος, 2 Pet. i. 15; Luke ix. 31, and ἄφιξις, "departure," Acts xx. 29). It means that they were faithful to the end (see Wisd. ii. 17).

[4] Mal. iii. 6 ; Jas. i. 17.

[5] "Being swept away (περιφερόμενοι) by every wind of teaching" (Eph. iv. 14).

[6] Ver. 9, καλὸν.

[7] Its meaning is that our security should rest on God's grace, not on Levitical rules and distinctions about meats and drinks, which had been profitless to the Jews, who attached so much importance to them. On the extent to which these questions agitated the modern Church, and their bearing on daily life, see *Life of St. Paul*, i. 264 ; and comp. ix. 10 ; Rom. xiv. ; Col. ii. 16—23 ; 1 Tim. iv. 3 ; and Gal. vi. 12, 13. No doubt the Jews appealed to the eternal Pharisaism of the human heart, and said to the Christian converts, "We live Jewish-wise ; you have degraded yourself into living Gentile fashion (ἐθνικῶς, Gal. ii. 14) ; you neglect the Kashar ; you feed with those who are defiled by eating of the unclean beast."

[8] x. 29 ; xiii. 15, 28. [9] Namely, "the Cross." See *infra*.

[10] The connexion is not quite obvious at first sight, but seems to be as follows :—He has said that "matters of meat" had been found unprofitable (vii. 18, 19), and is perhaps reminded of the boasted Jewish privilege of partaking of the sacrifices (1 Cor. ix. 13), which was of course no longer possible for Christians whom the Jews had excommunicated. So far, then, the Christians may have felt, and may have been taunted with, their loss. But the writer reminds them that *their* sacrifice was analogous to the highest and most solemn of all the Jewish sacrifices— those offered on the Day of Atonement. Now of these neither the priests nor any of the Jews might eat (Lev. iv. 12 ; vi. 30 ; xvi. 27). The bodies of these victims were burnt without the camp, just as our Divine Victim suffered outside the city gate. Now of *our* altar, of *our* sacrifices, we may eat (John vi. 51—56). We are bidden spiritually to eat His flesh, and drink His blood. But of *this* altar, of *this* sacrifice, they who serve the Tabernacle (see viii. 5) may not eat. We, therefore, are better off than they. Let us then go forth to Him out of the old city which rejected Him and the old dispensation—which refused to recognise its own annulment ; let us bear His reproach, that we may also enjoy the blessings which He offers.

[11] His suffering without the gate (Matt. xxvii. 32) corresponded to the sacrifice of the victim, and the burning of its body ; the sanctification of His people by the blood of this sacrifice, with which He has passed into the heavens, corresponds to the sprinkling of the blood by the high priest in the holiest place.

[12] Matt. v. 10—16 ; Luke vi. 22. The Jews treated them as outcasts and apostates, but they were to remember that they were citizens not of the doomed city (Matt. xxiv. 2), but of the city

have not here an abiding city, but we are seeking further for that which is to come. Through him, then, let us offer up a sacrifice of praise[1] continually to God, that is the fruit of lips which confess to His name.[2] But forget not beneficence, and free-sharing of your goods, for with such sacrifices God is well pleased"[3] (xiii. 8—16).

This passage, like multitudes of others in the Holy Scriptures, has been pressed into modern controversies with which it has no connexion. The whole context shows that the word "altar" is here secondary, incidental, and metaphorical. The passage is highly compressed, and is so allusive, that we should hardly be able to understand it apart from the tenor of the argument which has occupied the main part of the Epistle. I have endeavoured in the note to explain its meaning. Here I may, perhaps, add a general paraphrase. Do not forget the rulers of your Church who have ended consistent lives by holy deaths. Imitate their faith. They are gone, but the object of their faith is deathless and unchangeable. Jesus Christ is the same yesterday, to-day, and for ever. Be then steadfast in the immutable truth of His doctrine. Do not be swept away by gusts of everchanging opinion—particularly those of the Jewish Halachists, who spend their whole lives in torturing strange inferences out of Levitic regulations. The meats and drinks with which this science of the Halachah is mainly occupied have been proved by the experience of ages to be in themselves profitless (vii. 18, 19). It is not scrupulosity about ceremonial minutiæ, but it is the grace of God which is the real stay and security of the spiritual and moral life. When they speak about these distinctions of clean and unclean meats— doubtless your priestly antagonists taunt you with their privilege of partaking of many sacrifices, such as the sin-offerings and trespass-offerings, and wave-offerings, and doves—a privilege which you, priests though you are to God (1 Pet. ii. 5; Rev. i. 6; xx. 6), may share no longer. Be it so. Still our case is far superior to theirs. For of their greatest and most significant sacrifices, those offered on the Day of Atonement, even their High Priests could not partake. The blood of those victims was sprinkled on the mercy seat, their bodies were burnt without the camp. Since, then, the Jewish priests were forbidden to eat of the type, how could they have license to eat of the antitype? But we, too, have our great sacrifice, and we *may* eat of it, and it is "food indeed." It is the sacrifice of Him Who was offered without the

that hath the foundations which were not material but built by God. Possibly in this "reproach" there may be a passing allusion to the fact that those who burnt the bodies of the Atonement-victims outside the camp, were ceremonially unclean; but far more to the fixed Jewish conception that he who was crucified was "accursed of God" (Deut. xxi. 22, 23). (See *Life of St. Paul*, ii. 77, 148.)

[1] See Lev. vii. 12; Pss. xliv. 23; cxvi. 17. The Jews had a very remarkable saying that in the days of the Messiah all other sacrifices should cease, but that the sacrifices of praise (Jer. xvii. 26) should never cease.

[2] Is. lvii. 19, "I create the fruit of the lips." Hos. xiv. 3; (lit., our lips, as calves); but as the next verse says, we must (unlike the Jews of old, Is. xxix. 13—21; Ezek. xxxiii. 21) offer to God the sacrifices of well-doing, as well as of praise, and thank Him with our lives as well as with our lips (Matt. xv. 1—9).

[3] xiii. 8—16. On this beneficence and participation of earthly goods see Rom. xii. 13; 2 Cor. ix. 13; 1 Tim. vi. 18.

gate, whose blood is sprinkled to sanctify His people, and to sanctify even the heavenly places (ix. 12—28); and on that sacrifice we may live by perpetual sustenance. He was rejected; He was thrust outside the city to be offered up. Let us go forth to Him, bearing His reproach. If we leave the city of our affection, we are at the best but strangers and sojourners there, and we are going forth to the Heavenly and the Eternal City. That earthly city will be shaken; the Heavenly City is one of those things which can never be shaken, and will remain. Let us then offer our thankofferings to Him. Those thankofferings are not the bullocks enjoined by the Levitic Law (Lev. vii. 12); they are "the bullocks of our lips," and those thankofferings will be acceptable if we offer therewith the thankofferings of holy lives.

It will be seen, then, that what is prominent is the sacrifice, and our sustenance thereby. No prominence is given to the altar on which the sacrifice is offered. It is, so to speak, *extra figuram*. If in the mind of the writer any significance was attached to the "altar," it could only be explained as THE CROSS, as it is understood by St. Thomas Aquinas and the Roman Catholic Este, no less than by De Wette and Bleek. It was on the altar of burnt-offering that the Jewish victims were slain; it was on the Cross that our great High Priest perfected once and for ever the offering of Himself. The Cross, then, is the altar, not the *material* Table of the Lord. What the writer had in mind was the feeding on Christ in the heart by faith; living not on His flesh, which, materially considered, profiteth nothing, but on His words, which are spirit and life, and of which they who rejected Him neither might nor could eat. The "eating of the flesh of Christ and drinking His blood" was the symbol—far commoner, far less strange, far more directly intelligible to any one familiar with Jewish habits of thought and expression than it is to ourselves—of that close union with Him whereby "He that sanctifieth and they that are being sanctified are all of one," and whereby it is not we who live, but Christ in us. The Victim Lamb has been once offered (ix. 25—28), but after a heavenly and spiritual manner we may feed upon Him, and so be partakers of the Altar until we see Him face to face.[1]

Then follows an exhortation to obey and be subject to their leaders,[2] who watched sleeplessly for their souls as men who would have to give an account, so that they might give their account with joy, and not with groaning, which would be "unprofitable" for them—a euphemistic

---

[1] Whether it is desirable or not to speak of the Lord's Table as an altar is a question of very secondary interest. Certainly there would not be the smallest objection to doing so if the meaning of the term was never perverted in support of false and superstitious conclusions. But even Baxter said that it is no more improper to call the Lord's Supper a sacrifice (as was constantly done in the ancient Church), than it is "to call our bodies, and our alms, and our prayers, sacrifices." "And the naming of the Table an altar, as related to this representative sacrifice, is no more improper than the other." (*Christian Institutes*, i. 304, quoted by Wordsworth. Baxter applies this passage *directly* to sacramental communion.)

[2] The emphasis laid on this injunction perhaps hints at tendencies to self-assertion and insubordination. In the importance given to the position of these leaders we see the gradual growth of episcopal powers.

way of saying that it would be for their deep disadvantage. Then he asks them for their prayers, adding a profession of conscientious sincerity, such as St. Paul also had to make on more than one occasion.[1] And he begs for these prayers in the hope that they might bring about a speedier restoration of the writer to their society.[2]

"But the God of Peace[3] who brought up from the dead[4] that Great Shepherd of the sheep, our Lord Jesus,[5] by virtue of the blood of an eternal covenant,[6] stablish you in every good work so that ye may do His will, doing that in you,[7] through Jesus Christ, which is well-pleasing before Him, to whom be the glory which is His for ever.[8] Amen.

"But I beseech you, brethren, bear with the word of my exhortation.[9] For indeed I have written to you briefly.[10] Ye know[11] that our brother Timothy has been set free, with whom, if he come soon, I will see you. Salute all your leaders and all the saints. The Italians salute you. Grace be with you all. Amen." xii. 13–25.)

The last clauses have been pressed into the discussion of the authorship of the Epistle, but they are too vague to give any real clue. All that we learn from the allusion to Timothy is that he had been detained, probably in prison, but that now he had been liberated, and that it was the intention of the writer to visit in his company the Church to which he was writing, if Timothy came sufficiently soon. There is not the slightest clue as to where Timothy or the writer were at the time when the letter was written. Even the inferred imprisonment of Timothy is uncertain, for the word used of him (ἀπολελυμένον), though used of liberation from prison (Acts iii. 13, iv. 21), is also used of official, and even of ordinary, dismissal on any errand or mission (Acts xix. 41, xxiii. 22).[12] It is, however, as I have already said, a reasonable conjecture that Timothy obeyed with all speed the urgent summons of St. Paul in his second letter, and either arrived in time to

---

[1] Acts xxiii. 1; xxiv. 16; 1 Cor. iv. 4; Gal. i. 13, πεπείσμεθα, ᾐ A, C, D; Acts xxvi. 26, πεποίθαμεν; Gal. v. 10; Phil. i. 25; ii 24. It is probable that some would look with suspicion, and even with angry denunciation, at the spiritual freedom in all matters of form which was claimed and exercised by the school of St. Paul. These concluding sentences of the Epistle greatly resemble those of St. Paul, and were probably a common feature in letters of his friends. See Col. iv. 3; 1 Thess. v. 25.
[2] Phil. 22. The circumstances that hindered him may have been of a special character ("but Satan hindered us," 1 Thess. ii. 18); we cannot at all conjecture what they were.
[3] xiii. 14; Rom. xv. 33; xvi. 20; Phil. iv. 9; 1 Thess. v. 23, etc.
[4] The only allusion to Christ's Resurrection in this Epistle (comp. vi. 2; xi. 35; Rom. x. 7).
[5] Zech. ix. 11; Is. lxiii. 11.
[6] ix. 15–18; Ex. xxiv. 8.
[7] εἰς τὸ ποιῆσαι . . κοινὸν . . ἐν ὑμῖν (comp. Phil. ii. 13, ὁ ἐνεργῶν ἐν ὑμῖν καὶ τὸ θέλειν καὶ τὸ ἐνεργεῖν).
[8] Gal. i. 5.
[9] Acts xiii. 15. A courteous apology, lest he should seem to have adopted a tone of authority which he did not possess.
[10] Acts xv. 20; xxi. 25; διὰ βραχέων = δι' ὀλίγων; 1 Pet. v. 12: "paucis pro copiâ rerum et argumenti dignitate" (Bengel). 'Ἐπιστολή is the epistolary aorist, which may be idiomatically represented in English either by "I write" or "I have written." He adds "briefly" to show that he had had no space for lengthened apologies, or for anything but a direct and compressed argument and appeal. Possibly, however, this allusion to the brevity of his letter is given as a reason why they should bear with it. "Since you see that I have not troubled you at any great length."
[11] Or "know." It cannot mean "Pay friendly regard to."
[12] Even Chrysostom, Theophylact, and Œcumenius, felt no certainty that ἀπολελυμένον meant "freed from prison."

be present at the martyrdom of the Apostle or soon afterwards. The Church in Rome was then suffering from the Neronian persecution, and any one who came to Rome as a prominent Christian, and as a devoted friend of the greatest Christian teacher, would have been little likely to escape suspicion and arrest. If so, we are unable even to conjecture the circumstances to which he owed his acquittal. Perhaps his comparative youth and the unobtrusive timidity of his character may have worked in his favour. But if these conjectures are true, he must have been set free at Rome, and this would be a proof that the Epistle to the Hebrews was written to some other place. The data are, however, too slight to furnish any ground on which to build; and when Ewald ventures, from these hints, to conjecture that the letter may have been addressed to a Christian community at Ravenna, he might have conjectured a hundred other places with just as much, and just as little, probability.

Nor can anything be deduced from the salutation which the writer sends. His words literally translated are, "Those from Italy salute you."[1] If we give to these words the sense which they ordinarily bear, they must mean "the Italians," just as "The scribes from Jerusalem" mean "Jerusalemite scribes" (Matt. xv. 1), and "those from Cilicia" mean "Cilicians" (Acts vi. 9), and "the Jews from Thessalonica" mean "Thessalonian Jews" (Acts xvii. 13), and "the Jews from Asia" mean "Asiatic Jews" (Acts xxi. 27). But there is nothing to show where these Italians were residing, or what interest would be felt in their salutation by the purely conjectural Church to which the letter is addressed.

The subscription to the Epistle in the Alexandrine manuscript is, "It was written to the Hebrews from Rome." That in the Moscow Manuscript (κ) and in the Syriac and Coptic Versions is, "It was written to the Hebrews from Italy by Timotheus," and this is adopted in our received text. Both subscriptions are destitute of authority, and the latter is in plain contradiction with what we should infer from the allusion to Timothy in the letter itself. It would be interesting to us to know more of the history of the letter, but this is no longer discoverable. Like Melchizedek, it has been said, the letter is ἀπάτωρ, ἀγενεαλόγητος, without known father or lineage. None the less it will always remain as a priceless possession to the Church. Its eloquence, its enthusiasm, its loftiness of conception, would alone suffice to stamp it as a remarkable work; but its highest value lies in the force and originality of its whole train of reasoning. No Epistle even of St. Paul was so well calculated to win the unconverted Hebrews, or when they had embraced Christianity, to save them from their temptation to succumb under the force of grievous persecution, and to find refuge once more from the reproach of Christ in the Synagogue of their fathers.

[1] See supra, p. 191.

For no writer had ever yet developed with such grace and power the thought that the New Dispensation was not the ruinous overthrow, but the glorious fulfilment of the Old; that the Christian, so far from being robbed of that viaticum of good examples which had been the glory of Judaism, could feed upon them with a deeper sympathy; that the Temple and the whole Levitic ritual, so far from being scornfully flung aside by the follower of Jesus, did but shine with a new splendour in the light of that revelation which, for the first time, shed on them a blaze of more glorious significance. To retrograde into Judaism after the study of this Epistle would indeed be to go back into the darkness from the noonday. But yet this conclusion was brought home both to the Jew and to the Jewish Christian so gently, so considerately, so skilfully, so gradually, that the reader was drawn along as by a golden chain of irresistible reasoning, without one violent wrench of his prejudices, or one rude shock to his lifelong convictions. The golden candlestick of the Church to which these words were addressed must, indeed, have been burning dim if the tendency of any of its members to flag or to apostatise—to prefer Moses to Christ, and the Temple to the true Church of the firstborn—was not checked for ever by arguments which enabled them to see their true position in the light of such inspired and inspiring wisdom.

Book IV.
JUDAIC CHRISTIANITY.

CHAPTER XIX.
"THE LORD'S BROTHER."

"No man having drunk old wine desireth new, for he saith, 'The old is excellent.'"—LUKE v. 39.

WE now pass to yet another phase of Christianity—neither Pauline nor Alexandrian, but distinctively Jewish. Of this phase—the type of Christianity which prevailed with unbroken continuity in the Holy City until its destruction, and was afterwards maintained among the Nazarenes—we have a magnificent specimen in the Epistle of St. James.

But before we can understand this Epistle, or enter with intelligent sympathy into the truths which it was its mission to proclaim, it will be essential for us to discover by whom it was written.

Now, all the clue which the author gives us as to his identity is by calling himself "James, a slave of God and of the Lord Jesus Christ."

But, unfortunately, the same name and the same description is equally applicable to others. The name thus Anglicised is, in reality, that of the old Hebrew patriarch Jacob,[1] the father of the Twelve Patriarchs who gave their names to the Tribes of Israel. That "Syrian ready to perish"[2]—the wretched supplanter who ultimately reached the moral grandeur of a Prince with God—was what the Greeks would have called the Hero Eponumos of the Jewish nation. Hence the name Yakoob was as common in Palestine in our Lord's day as it is to this day in many parts of the East. There was among the Jews a remarkable paucity of personal names, and the fact that persons, and even groups of persons, had the same names, is but of little importance in defining their identity, particularly when they belong to kindred families. The name of James gives us as little clue to a man's identity as would the name William in England, or Mohammed in Egypt.

Now, in the little Galilean group of early disciples we find no less than six persons so called. These are—

1. James, the son of Zebedee, brother of John (Matt. iv. 21; Mark i. 19; Luke v. 10).

2. James, the son of Alphæus (Matt. x. 3; Mark iii. 18).

---

[1] In Hebrew, Yakoob; in Greek, Ἰακωβος; Spanish, Iago; Portuguese, Xayme; French, Jacques and Jamé; Scotch, Hamish. See the Introduction to my friend Dr. Plumptre's excellent edition of the Epistle in the *Cambridge Bible for Schools.*

[2] "A Syrian ready to perish was my father" (Deut. xxvi. 5).

3. James, mentioned with Joses (*i.e.*, Joseph), Simon, and Judas as one of the "brothers" of Jesus (Matt. xiii. 55, xxvii. 56; Mark vi. 3).

4. James "the little," brother of a Joseph, and son of a Mary (Mark xv. 40) who, as we find from John xix. 25, was the wife of Clopas.

5. James, the "Bishop" of Jerusalem, "the Lord's brother" (Gal. i. 19), who plays a leading part in the Acts of the Apostles (Acts xv. 13, xxi. 8), and held a position of high authority in the early Church (1 Cor. xv. 7; Gal. i. 19, ii. 9).

6. James, the brother of Jude (Jude 1).

There cannot be the least reasonable doubt that these six, who are referred to under this name, are in reality three.

For James, the son of Alphæus (No. 2), is rightly identified with the son of Mary (No. 4), who from his diminutive stature is called "the little."[1] This is intrinsically probable, and is confirmed by the fact that Clopas is only the Greek transliteration of the Hebrew Chalpai, which, in the universal Jewish fashion, was further Grecised, for use among the Gentiles, into the classical name Alphæus.

And James, "the Lord's brother" (No. 3), is, beyond doubt, the first "Bishop" of Jerusalem (No. 5) and the brother of Jude (No. 6).

And both of these were probably first cousins to each other, and to the third James, the son of Zebedee. The question then arises (1) Which of these three is the author of the Epistle? And this question is inextricably mixed up with the further question (2) Is the son of Alphæus the same as the first "Bishop" of Jerusalem? And this question really depends for its solution on the question, Who were our Lord's brethren? or, in other words, are we, by the term "brethren," to understand His cousins? But we have then further to ask, If the Apostle, the son of Alphæus, is *not* the same as the "Bishop" of Jerusalem, the Lord's brother, which of the two wrote this Epistle—the Apostle or the Bishop?

It might have been thought that the question of authorship was set at rest so far as the son of Zebedee is concerned. For—

α. Not a single ancient author ever thought of attributing the Epistle to him.

β. He was the first martyr of the Twelve Apostles, and since his martyrdom took place in the reign of Herod Agrippa I., A.D. 44, fourteen years after the Ascension,[2] the Epistle, if written by him, would be the earliest work of the entire canon. The allusions of the Epistle, and the state of circumstances which it describes as existing in the Church, are incompatible with this supposition. Setting aside for the present the question whether it was meant to be a polemical answer to those who misinterpreted or exaggerated the views of St. Paul, it is clear on other

---

[1] This is the meaning of the word μικρὸς in Luke xix. 3 (Zacchæus, "little of stature").
[2] Acts xii. 2.

grounds that it could not have been written so early as A.D 44. For it is addressed to the twelve tribes of the Dispersion, and until the missionary labours of St. Paul, Christianity had not spread to the Jews throughout the world. Even those of Asia Minor, as well as those of Greece, heard the name of the Lord Jesus for the first time from his lips. The doctrine of "justification by faith," in that distinctive form which alone rendered it liable to perversion,[1] had never been previously preached by any Christian teacher. It found its great exponent in the Apostle of the Gentiles, and its elaborate development in the Epistles to the Galatians and Romans. And, not to dwell on other points, the whole tone of the letter shows that it is addressed to Churches which were liable to fall into a slumbering Christianity, and not to Churches which were feeling the glow of their first love. Respect of persons, for instance, had already grown up in these Jewish-Christian communities. These reasons have been so strongly and universally felt that not one of the Fathers has imagined that this letter was written by the son of Zebedee, the first Apostolic martyr. The only authority, if the name "authority" can be given to such a careless mistake, is to be found in a single Latin manuscript of the ninth century. The MSS. of the Peshito version, do, indeed, attribute it to "James the Apostle;" but it is idle to interpret this to mean James, the son of Zebedee, when it is far more probable that the term was meant to describe James, the son of Alphæus; or (if not) that the term Apostle—in accordance with the *less* specific use of it in the Apostolic age[2]—is meant to describe the general dignity of James, the Lord's brother.

It is therefore to be regretted that so baseless a theory should have been supported by an English commentator in one of the latest editions of this Epistle.[3] The arguments which he adduces are entirely inconclusive. The supposed improbability that one of the inner circle of Apostles should have passed away without any written memorial of his teaching, would be worth nothing as an argument even if the death of the son of Zebedee had not occurred at so early an epoch. The supposed resemblances to the teaching of John the Baptist are of the most general character; they might occur equally well in *any* Christian writer,[4] and might be illustrated by many other parallels. Moreover, it is more than doubtful whether James, the son of Zebedee, had ever been a disciple of the Baptist. It is implied that he was not with the little group of disciples who were with the Baptist at Jordan when they first heard the call of Christ. The resemblances of the Epistle to the Sermon on the Mount would be accounted for equally well if the writer were the son of Alphæus. They do not require the theory that the writer heard the sermon, since they might have been derived from intercourse with St. Matthew, or from a perusal of the

---

[1] 2 Pet. iii. 15.   [2] Andronicus, Junias (Rom. xvi. 7).
[3] By the Rev. F. T. Bassett (Bagsters, 1876).
[4] Jas. i. 22, 27; ii. 15, 16, 19, 20; v. 1—6 (comp. Matt. iii. 8—12; Luke iii. 11).

outlines which perhaps formed the original nucleus of the Gospels.[1] But even if they did involve the certainty that the author of the Epistle had personally heard Christ's gracious words, there is not the least unlikelihood that James the Lord's brother may have been seated, as well as the son of Zebedee, amid that listening throng. The notion that the phrase "The Lord of Glory" renders it probable that the writer had seen the Transfiguration is an argument so fragile and so far fetched[2] that it could only be dictated by despair of more valid indications. Vain-glory, rivalry, and self-seeking, may have existed in the Apostolic band, and the son of Zebedee may himself have shared in these frailties, as he did in a vehement intolerance which savoured rather of the Elijah-spirit than the spirit of Christ;[3] but it is surely strange to adduce the warnings against these faults, and the reference to Elias, as conferring any probability on a theory which otherwise has nothing in its favour. The inferences drawn from the parallelism of some passages to the First Epistle of St. Peter,[4] and to the great eschatological discourse of our Lord, are as much overstrained as the others. They do not confer on this hypothesis any claim to serious attention, and it may be regarded as finally dismissed.

2. There is more to be said for the claim of the son of Alphæus.[5] That is supported by the ancient theory that the son of Alphæus was, in fact, the same person as the Bishop of Jerusalem.[6] Beyond this theory, however, it has nothing in its favour. For this "James the little," or "James, the son of Alphæus," is to us a name and nothing more. Not one incident is narrated of him; not one utterance is attributed to him in the Gospels; not one fact is preserved respecting him by any tradition older than those recorded, or accepted, or invented, by Nicephorus in the fourteenth century.[7] It is inexcusable to argue *à priori*, as Lange does, that the son of Alphæus *must* be James, "the Lord's brother," and Bishop of Jerusalem, because the assumption is highly improbable that James, the son of Alphæus, should, in so short a time, have vanished from the stage past all tracing, without being

---

[1] It seems to be doubtful whether the word *logia* in the well-known passage of Papias means "discourses;" but in any case discourses of our Lord must have been early committed to writing by some of the disciples.

[2] It was a common and well-known Jewish designation with reference to the Shechinah. Compare "cherubim of glory," Heb. i. 3; ix. 5; Acts vii. 2; Eph. i. 17, *supra*, p. 229.

[3] Luke ix. 54.   [4] See *supra*, p. 72.

[5] To argue that "James, the Lord's brother," *must* have been one of the Apostles, from Gal. i. 19; 1 Cor. xv. 7, is to ignore the commonest facts of the Greek language Even *if* in these passages he were identified with, not excluded from, the number of the Apostles, they would prove nothing; for James, the Bishop of Jerusalem, was an Apostle just as much as Barnabas or Paul.

[6] In the Apostolical Constitutions (ii. 55) James, the son of Alphæus, is especially distinguished from the Lord's brother.

[7] Nicephorus (*H. E.* ii. 40) says that he preached in South-west Palestine, and was ultimately crucified at Ostracine, in Lower Egypt. See Cave, *Lives of the Apostles*, and *supra*, p. 48.

thought worthy of having even his death noticed by Luke, the historian, and that there should suddenly have sprung up some non-apostolical James, who actually occupied a prominent position among the Apostles." The instance of Philip might be alone sufficient to show the futility of the argument; for Philip the deacon springs into extreme prominence in the Acts of the Apostles without any further mention of Philip the Apostle. When Lange says, further, that it is "purely inconceivable" that James, "a recently-converted non-Apostle," should have been acknowledged so early as a man of Apostolical authority, it is strange that he should regard as "purely inconceivable" what was an actual fact in the cases of Barnabas and Paul. When he adds, "If anything, it is still more inconceivable that the names of three real Apostles (James, Simon, Jude) should have been extinguished without all trace by the names of three non-Apostles," he is making capital out of an identity of names which is not of the smallest significance. For that the prominence of every one of the twelve, except Peter and John, was from the first obliterated, so far as our Scriptural record is concerned, by the names of others who were not among the original twelve, is proved by the New Testament itself, and by every trace of early Church history. And as for the names James, Simon, Jude, it is as certain that no one could have taken a walk through the streets of Jerusalem without meeting dozens, perhaps scores, of people who bore one or other of those names, as it is that you would meet scores of people who bore the names of John, George, and Thomas, in a walk through London streets. The fact is, that of the twelve Apostles the majority are only known to us as names, sometimes undistinguished by a single incident. We know less of the son of Alphæus than of any one among their number. We are told the name of his father and of his mother, and nothing more.

His father was Alphæus, who, as we have seen, was the same as Clopas (John xix. 25; Matt. x. 3).[1] It is usually asserted that he cannot be the Cleopas to whom our Lord appeared on the road to Emmaus (Luke xxiv. 18), because that name is an abbreviated form of Cleopater, whereas Cleopas, or Chalpai, is a Hebrew name, of which Alphæus is the current assonance adopted for intercourse with the Gentile world. But it is as little improbable that this disciple may have had both names, as that Judas should have been called both Lebbæus and Thaddæus. However this may be, we know nothing more of Alphæus except that the name of his wife was Mary, and that his other sons were Matthew and Thomas. "Jude of James" would be yet another son, if we could be sure that it meant "brother of James." In the absence, however, of any evidence to the contrary, it is more natural to take it to mean "*son* of James."

But was the Mary who was the wife of Alphæus a sister of the

[1] The R. V. has Cleophas, which only comes from late Latin MSS.

Virgin Mary?[1] This has been inferred from John xix. 25, where the punctuation which some would adopt is, "there stood by the cross of Jesus his mother, and his mother's sister Mary, the wife of Clopas, and Mary Magdalene." But, apart from the authority of the Peshito, which inserts "and" before Mary, it is now generally accepted that by this verse *four* women are intended, namely—(1) The Virgin Mary; (2) her sister Salome, who being St. John's mother is left unnamed by his delicate reserve; and the two other Marys, namely—(3) the wife of Clopas, and (4) Mary of Magdala.

Is it, then, the case that Alphæus, or Clopas, was the brother of St. Joseph, and therefore (legally) the uncle of our Lord? The suggestion is supported by the testimony of Hegesippus.[2] It may be true or not; but that the sons of Alphæus were our Lord's "brothers" is only a conjecture of Jerome, made in the interests of an ecclesiastical hypothesis. His authority gave it currency, and consequently a rash conjecture, treated even by its author as unimportant, became the favourite theory of the Western Church.[3]

A still later afterthought—planted upon this groundless conjecture, like a rootless stalk on a thin soil—is the guess that Alphæus died early, and left all his sons to be supported by his brother Joseph; that they thus became legally Joseph's sons, and can thus be called "the brethren of the Lord."

These are hypotheses invented to support a conception of which no trace is discoverable in Scripture, and which is mixed up with many aberrations of Essenian and Gnostic asceticism. All that we know about James the Apostle is that he was a son of Alphæus, and that he was called "the little." All that we can reasonably conjecture is that he was "a cousin of the Lord."

3. It may be regarded as certain, in accordance with ancient tradition,[4] and with the best of modern opinions, that the author of the Epistle is the "Bishop of Jerusalem," and the "brother of the Lord."

But is he *identical with* the son of Alphæus? There seems to have been a confused notion among some ancient writers that he was, and this view is accepted by many modern commentators, among whom I may mention Lange and Bishop Wordsworth.

The identification is, however, only possible to those who hold, in despite of the plain evidence of the Synoptists, and still more of

---

[1] In the paucity of Jewish names, and the commonness of the name Mary, there is no decisive objection to this view from the fact that, in this case, two sisters would have borne the same name. No doubt such instances are rare, but I have found several in ancient and modern history.

[2] *Ap.* Euseb. *H. E.* iv. 22.

[3] Thus in the Church of England July 25th is dedicated to the Son of Zebedee, and May 1st to St. Philip and St. James; and since part of the Epistle of St. James is read on that day, it is clear that "the son of Alphæus" is identified with "the brother of the Lord." In the Greek Church they are distinguished—October 9th is dedicated to the son of Alphæus, and October 23rd to the brother of the Lord.

[4] Euseb. *H. E.* ii. 23; Jer. *De Virr. Illustr.* 2.

St. John, that our Lord's "brethren" were among the number of His Apostles. For if James, the Lord's brother, was indeed the same person as the son of Alphæus, then Jude also, and, according to some, Simon too, and Matthew, and perhaps Thomas, were "brethren of the Lord," since they, too, were sons of Alphæus. So that we shall have this singular phenomenon—that whereas four only of our Lord's "brethren" are mentioned by name, viz., James and Joseph and Judas and Simon, *three* out of these four were Apostles, and certainly one, if not two *other* sons of Alphæus were also Apostles; and yet we are expressly told that "*neither did His brethren believe in Him.*"[1] An attempt is made to get rid of this plain contradiction by saying that His brethren had not "the resigned obedience of faith," so that in the same sense it might have been said that neither Peter, nor Thomas, nor even the Blessed Virgin, believed on Him![2] And this theory is (ostensibly) to be built on the notion that it is "inconceivable" that a James, a Simon, and a Jude, should have been Apostles, and yet that there should have been another James, another Simon,[3] and another Jude who became distinguished in the Church. There is, however, nothing inconceivable, nothing about it even improbable. There were hundreds, and even thousands, who, at this epoch, bore those names. Even among the twelve Apostles there were two Simons, two Jameses, and two Judes; among the handful of those first connected with Christianity there were nine Simons, three Jameses, six Josephs, and four Judes; and in the very narrow circle of early disciples there were five Marys.[4] Any one, therefore, who considers this identity of names to be "purely inconceivable," must be extremely limited alike in his power of imagination[5] and in his knowledge of facts.

I hold it, then, as certain that James, the Bishop of Jerusalem, and "the Lord's brother," was *not* the same person as the Apostle, the son of Alphæus.[6] The latter was one of the Twelve; the former was one of those who up to a late period in the life of Christ "did not believe on Him."

But having advanced thus far, it is almost impossible to avoid saying one word more on the question of the Lord's brethren— (1) Were they, as Helvidius thought, the sons of Joseph and Mary? or (2) were they, as Jerome fancied, the adopted nephews of Joseph?

---

[1] John vii. 5.
[2] Lange, *Introd.* § ii. 1, and in Herzog's Cyclopædia, *s. v.* Jacobus.
[3] Tradition, as preserved by Hegesippus (*ap.* Euseb. iv. 23), says that Simon, son of Clopas, succeeded James as Bishop of Jerusalem because he was our Lord's cousin (ἀνέψιος).
[4] (1) The Virgin; (2) the wife of Clopas; (3) Mary Magdalene; (4) Mary of Bethany; (5) Mary, mother of John Mark.
[5] Hegesippus says, ἐστὶ πολλοὶ Ἰάκωβοι ἐκαλοῦντο.
[6] This denial of their identity has the powerful support of Gregory of Nyssa, *De Resurr. Orat.* ii.; Chrysost. *in Matt. Hom.* 5; and Jerome (who, however, wavers) *in Isai.* xvii., and *in Gal.* i. 19.

or (3) were they, as Epiphanius argued, sons of Joseph by a previous or (4) as Theophylact suggests, by a Levirate marriage?

Now, on this question I have no desire either to dogmatise or to press my own opinion; but I will endeavour once more, in the fewest and simplest words, to indicate the inference to which the Gospels seem to point. And in doing so I shall dwell on two considerations, which, in spite of the enormous mass of literature upon the subject, have been all but universally neglected.

The inference, whether correct or not, to which the language of the Evangelists would naturally lead us, certainly is that "the Lord's brothers" were the children of Joseph and Mary, born in holy wedlock after the birth of Christ. Can any one honestly say that such is not, at least, the *prima facie* conclusion which every reader would draw from the Gospel allusions and the Gospel narrative?

In the very first chapter of the Gospel we are told that "Joseph took unto him his wife, and knew her not until she brought forth her son, her firstborn, and called his name Jesus." Now would not the aorist "took unto him" (παρέλαβε) in connexion with the imperfect tense "knew her not" (ἐγίνωσκεν), to say nothing of the words "her son, her firstborn,"[1] naturally lead us, in any ordinary case, to conclude that Joseph and Mary lived together in wedded union after the birth of Jesus, and that children were born to them?

Of course the verse is not in itself decisive. Instances may be adduced in which an action is said *not* to have happened *until* a certain time, and yet is not thereby asserted to have happened after the lapse of the fixed period. Other instances may be quoted in which the word "firstborn" does not *necessitate* a belief in the birth of subsequent children. Proofs to this effect were adduced by Bishop Pearson, and have been repeated by hundreds since. But this much may be affirmed —that if it had been a heresy to deny the Perpetual Virginity of the Blessed Virgin—(as St. Augustine and others have tried to hint, in accordance with the fatal tendency of theologians to brand as heretical everything that does not coincide with their own inferences)—then the Evangelists would not have gone out of their way to use an exceptional idiom, which seemed to countenance such a heresy. They would, on the contrary, have been anxious to avoid language which could not but lead ordinary readers to understand them in the very sense which (in that case) they would have most wished to exclude.

And yet so little anxiety do they show under this head, that, without so much as a single exception, *every* phrase they use, and *every* incident they record, tends directly to confirm an error which, if it be an error, they could again and again have rendered impossible by a single line of explanation, or even by a single word;—nay, even

---

[1] The words "her first-born" are omitted in א, B, Z, etc., and must be regarded as uncertain.

using correct and accurate expressions instead of others which, if it be necessary to believe in the Perpetual Virginity, were, strictly speaking, inaccurate and incorrect. If it were indeed "heretical," as was asserted by third and fourth century dogmatists, to doubt whether Scripture taught the Perpetual Virginity of the Virgin, could any expressions have been more unfortunately conducive to heresy than such a verse as Matt. xiii. 55, "Is not His mother called Mary? and His brethren James, and Joses, and Simon, and Judas?"

a. For, to take first, the theory of St. Jerome, if these brethren of Jesus were in reality His *cousins*, what answer can be given to the question, *Why did not the Evangelists call them so?* Certainly not that they had no word expressive of that meaning. Such words were ready to their hands in the Greek *anepsioi*, or *sungeneis*—"cousins" or "kinsmen"—or in very common periphrases.[1] With such terms they were perfectly familiar. If James, and Joses, and Simon, were habitually called "*brothers*" when they were only "*cousins*," it can only be said that they were needlessly and systematically misnamed.

But, it is said, the Hebrews used terms of relationship very vaguely, and, in accordance with their usage, our Lord's cousins would quite normally have been called His brethren.

Now, although this assertion has been repeated by writer after writer down to our own day, it is quite untenable.[2] There are four senses of the word "brethren." (1.) There is the *general* sense in which it is applicable to all mankind. (2.) There is the narrower sense in which it is applied to men of the same race, nation, or creed, or to dwellers in the same town. (3.) There is the still narrower sense in which it is applied to all members of the same kin or family. And all these being metaphorical senses, there is (4.) *the only proper and literal sense* in which it means the sons of the same, or of one of the same, parents.[3] Now certainly the term "brethren" might have been applied

---

[1] ἀνέψιος, Col. iv. 10 (incorrectly rendered "sister's son"); συγγενής, Luke i. 36; ii. 44; xiv. 12; John xviii. 26, etc.

[2] I insisted strongly on this point in an article on the word "Brethren," in *Smith's Dictionary of the Bible*, nearly twenty years ago; but, so far as I am aware, the point has never been noticed, and the objection never answered. One of the latest popular editors of the Epistle of St. James can still repeat, "that in Holy Scripture there are four senses of brotherhood, namely, of blood, of tribe, of nation, and of friendship, and *the three last of these will all apply to the case in point*." To talk thus is to ignore the dictates of common sense. We might just as well argue that any two persons who, through four different historical records, were invariably called "brothers," were perhaps only Freemasons, who are often called "brethren." The source of this mistake (as of so many others) seems to be St. Augustine, *Evang. Tract.* in. S. Jo. xxviii. 3: "Consanguinei Virginis Mariae fratres Domini dicebantur. Erat enim consuetudinis Scripturarum appellare fratres quoslibet consanguineos et cognationis propinquos."

[3] When Bishop Wordsworth and others speak of the words "brother" and "sister" in the New Testament being used for "cousin" "in the Hebrew sense," on what basis does this strange generalisation rest? *In the New Testament there is not a single instance of such a usage.* In the Old Testament (i.e. in a literature which spreads over a thousand years) the Hebrew word אָח is used *twice only* in a loose general sense. In every other instance (not *metaphorical*) it has its proper meaning. The sacred writers usually mean what they say.

emotionally, or metaphorically, or loosely, or on any special occasion, to the Lord's cousins, or He may so have addressed them by way of affection.[1] But to assert that "cousins" could be called "brothers" in ordinary prose, time after time, throughout a perfectly plain and simple history, with no hint whatever that they were *not* "brothers" in the everyday sense, and always in connexion with the *actual* mother of Him whose "brothers" they are called—and not seldom when His mother with these "brothers" appear together on the scene with a desire to check, or control, or dictate to their Divine kinsman—is to assert something for which no analogy is to be found either in Semitic or any other literature in the whole world. No language could be contented with the use of terms habitually misleading. In this case such a form of speech would not only be misleading, but could only be termed a direct encouragement to views which theologians have attempted to represent as all but heretical. That John and James, the sons of Zebedee, were first-cousins of our Lord may now be regarded as a nearly certain conclusion. If, on the common theory, His *other* cousins who "did not believe on Him," are *always* called His "brethren," how comes it that this term is never once, or by any chance applied to these first-cousins who *did* believe on Him, and of whom one was His specially-beloved disciple? But to refute the Hieronymian theory again—though there will probably be found commentators to repeat it till the end of time—can only be regarded as a slaying of the slain; like the soldier in Ariosto,[2] it goes on fighting without being aware that it is dead.[3]

The whole theory sprang from a notion that it would be derogatory to the dignity of the Virgin, or of our Lord, that she should subsequently have become a mother of children born in ordinary wedlock. Such a theory, I freely admit, might better accord with our *à priori* conceptions. But can we venture to hold it if the natural interpretation of so many Scripture passages seems to point the other way? The only text which has ever been quoted from the whole range of Scripture in favour of the Aciparthenia, or Perpetual Virginity, is Ezek. xliv. 2. It is—"This gate shall be shut and shall not be opened, and no man shall enter in by it, because the Lord the God of Israel hath entered by it; it shall be shut." But to quote such a verse in these days as possessing any controversial value on this question is an insult to common sense. If such allusions can be so applied, then we can prove anything whatever. Can it be called anything short of a deplorable Kabbalism to make such a use of

---

[1] This is unlikely, because He never so addressed even John, the disciple whom He loved.

[2] "Il pover' uom che non sen era accorto
Andava combattendo, ed era morto."
Orland. Innam.

[3] St. Jerome quotes no tradition in its favour; speaks of it very waveringly; and finally (*Ep. ad Hedibiam*) seems to abandon it, or at least to regard it with complete indifference. It had served the purpose of exalting Virginity when he wrote against Helvidius in A.D. 383; but twenty-three or more years later (A.D. 406) he had ceased to regard it as important. See Lightfoot, *Galatians*, p. 248.

a description of the Eastern Gate of the Prophet's mystic Temple, into which "the Prince" was to enter by "the porch," and in which he was to sit "to eat bread before the Lord"? If such perversions of Scripture were permissible, it would then be quite fair to say of the Bible—

> "Hic liber est in quo quaerit sua dogmata quisque
> Invenit et pariter dogmata quisque sua."

The belief in the Aeiparthenia—of which there is no trace in the Church for centuries—had its origin in two tendencies, both perilous, both unscriptural. The one—the tendency to exalt the Virgin to superhuman dignity—is markedly ignored, and even discountenanced, in Scripture. The other—the tendency to disparage the wedded state, and to exalt celibacy into a counsel of perfection—is not only discouraged in Scripture, but had its root in dangerous heresies, and runs counter to the express and repeated teachings of Holy Writ.

Every Christian will feel that the Mother of the Lord ought to receive the deepest honour and reverence. She was highly favoured, and could not have been thus selected out of the myriads of the human race to be the mother of the Saviour without the possession of conspicuous gifts and graces. Yet, as though with definite purpose, she is left in the depths of her almost unbroken seclusion and reserve. In some of the few instances in which this silence respecting her is broken, she is by no means singled out for special commendation. After the return of Joseph and Mary with the child Jesus to Nazareth, she is only mentioned or alluded to on six or seven occasions. One of these was when she and Joseph lost Jesus, and finding Him in the Temple, she addressed Him in words of sorrowing and almost reproachful wonder, and understood not His reply.[1] Another was when, at Cana, in answer to her faint suggestion that He should work a miracle, He said to her, "Woman, what have I to do with thee?"[2] A third—and perhaps a fourth—was when she came with His brethren—who "did not believe on Him"—to seek Him,[3] and even, as St. Mark tells us, "to lay hold on Him,"[4] thinking that His enthusiasm, which they could neither measure nor understand, was getting the better of Him. On that occasion, as though with the express view of discouraging every attempt to exalt His relatives after the flesh, He exclaimed, as He looked round on those who were sitting about Him, "Behold my mother and my brethren!" And, again, when a woman of the multitude exclaimed, in a burst of emotion, how blessed His mother must be, His public reply had been, "Yea, rather, blessed are they that hear the word of God and keep it."[5] We catch but one more glimpse of the Virgin. Seeing her as she stood beside the cross, our Lord said to St. John, "Behold thy mother," and to her, "Woman, behold thy son."[6] After this her name

---

[1] Luke i. 50.
[2] Matt. xii. 46; Mark iii. 31: Luke viii. 19.
[3] Luke xi. 28.
[4] John ii. 4.
[5] Mark xi. 21.
[6] John xix. 26.

occurs for the last time in Scripture in the passing mention of the fact that she, with His brethren—unbelievers in Him no longer—was present in the gatherings of the faithful disciples for purposes of prayer and supplication, which filled up the period between the Ascension and the Day of Pentecost.[1] On which of these notices can we found the dogma of the Aeiparthenia or of the Immaculate Conception?

But, it will be said, our Blessed Lord consigned her to the care of His beloved disciple, and not to the care of His "brothers." That circumstance needs no explanation St. John was the Virgin's nephew. He was nearer and dearer to Jesus, in accordance with his own express declaration, than any of His brethren were. They were absent from the cross;[2] St. John was present. They had been absent from Him all the darker and more troubled phases of His ministry; St. John had accompanied Him through them all. They had not been at the Last Supper; St. John had then leaned his head upon His breast. They had not been with Him at Gethsemane; St. John had been one of the chosen three. They had addressed Him dubiously, almost reproachfully, on the occasion of His going to the Feast of Tabernacles;[3] St. John had been His chief companion. The Lord, as He Himself bore testimony, had been no prophet "*in His own house*," any more than in His own country. His brothers, therefore were less suited than St. John to care of that precious charge. And further than this, we have reason to infer three facts about St John's position which were not applicable to theirs, and which, besides the sweetness and nobleness of his nature and his dearness to Jesus, made him exceptionally suited to give a home to the suffering Mother. One was that he had a home in Jerusalem, which they had not; another, that his circumstances were more prosperous than theirs, which would have enabled him to feel no burden in undertaking the support of Mary; a third, that he alone had powerful friends at Jerusalem, which might enable him to render her position more secure than it could have been in the lodgings of struggling Nazarenes. On any hypothesis, the Virgin was removed to another home; she lived no longer with those brothers of the Lord with whom up to this time she had always been associated.

To what lengths the tendency to exalt, beyond all warrant of Scripture or reason, the dignity of the Blessed Virgin has led, we have seen even in our own age, in the adoption of the dogma that she was born sinless. There is no further need to dwell upon this tendency. But the notion of the Aeiparthenia was aided by the growth of erroneous views respecting the supposed degradation, or comparative unworthiness, of marriage.

---

[1] Acts i. 14.
[2] It cannot be said that this is an *argumentum ex silentio*; for (1) as this is the only place in the Gospels after the visit to the Temple in which the Virgin alone is mentioned without the brethren, this is a clear indication that they were not with her; and (2) the whole tenor of the narrative leads us to believe that but few of our Lord's relatives or followers stood beside His cross, and that those few are all mentioned.
[3] John vii. 1—10.

It is assumed that the Virgin would have been dishonoured by subsequent motherhood. Where is there any Scriptural or other warrant for such a notion? It may be certainly affirmed that such a notion was unknown alike to the Jews and to the early Christians.[1]

And in the view of all those who regard holy wedlock as *no* stain and *no* disparagement, but as a sacred and blessed institution, the Virgin-mother is in no way lowered from that high blessing which she received from the annunciation of the angel by receiving the after-blessing of sons and daughters, a blessing which cometh from God alone.[2] And so far is the Divine dignity of the Son of God from being lowered by such a circumstance—in that human humiliation which was to Him the appointed path of his perfectionment[3]—so far was it from being derogatory to Him to live in the same house with "brothers" and "sisters," the children of His mother, that, on the contrary, there is something inexpressibly beautiful and consoling in the thought that He, too—as part of that sympathy with us, which was one of the great qualifications for a High Priesthood which could be touched with a feeling of our infirmities—knew to the full the dignity, the happiness, the innocence, the holiness of family life. Such a life—the deep and helpful love of brothers and sisters bound together in a common bond of resistance against the perils, of consolation amid the trials, of joy in the happiness, of the world—is one of the most beautiful and sacred spectacles which earth can offer. It forms yet one more link of union between us and our Saviour, if He shared with us this, as well as every other relationship of life in which it was possible for Him to share at all. If I held the common sentiment that the Virgin would have been *dishonoured* by the ordinary family relationship—if I shared the Apollinarian tendency to obliterate as much as possible all traces of those things which our Lord had in common with an ordinary human life—then I, too, might be tempted to succumb to the force of those sentiments which in this matter have led so many to interpret the Gospels in a non-natural sense. But I hold it to be a paramount duty to interpret Scripture by what it says, and not by our own fancies as to what it *ought* to say. I also hold that our Lord came to ennoble and glorify our human nature in all its normal conditions, and that all His teaching is opposed to notions of ceremonial as apart from moral sanctity, and to all Gnostic, or Manichean, or Essene, or monastic fancies. He never breathed one word to exalt the celibate over the wedded life, and to attribute to that age the glorification of the celibate *in* the wedded life is an immense anachronism. I am unable to accept the arguments which still lead so many to turn the word "brothers" into "cousins," or to borrow apocryphal

---

[1] 1 Tim. iv. 3; Col. ii. 18—23; 1 Cor. vii. 5 (on which see *Life of St. Paul*, ii. 70). And for Jewish opinion see Bava Bathra, f. 116 a; Pesachim, f. 113 b; Nedarim, f. 64 b; Kiddushin, f. 29, b; Yevamoth, ff. 62, 63, as quoted by Hamburger, etc.
[2] Even Tertullian, in spite of his glorification of celibacy, seems to have held the same view as Helvidius.
[3] Heb. ii. 10.

fictious to help out a theory of married relationship known to the traditions of mediævalism, unknown to the Scriptural simplicity of Jewish family life.

These, then, are the considerations which, to my mind, give the main force to what is called the Helvidian theory—the theory that the Lord's "brothers and sisters" really were the children of His mother.[1] It is really no theory at all, but an acceptance of what the Gospels seem to say. I regard it as possible—nay, even as probable—that the sons of Alphæus, of whom two or more were Apostles, were, like the sons of Zebedee, the first cousins of Jesus; but I do not believe they were ever called His "brothers."[2]

2. There is, however, yet another theory, which is more plausible than that of St. Jerome, and which may be accepted by any who can be satisfied with such evidence as is adduced for it. It is the theory which Bishop Lightfoot has called the Epiphanian, because it seems to be first definitely maintained by Epiphanius,[3] A.D. 367. This is the theory that "the Lord's brethren" were the children of Joseph by an earlier marriage. It is adopted by Theophylact under the form that they were his children by a Levirate marriage with the widow of his brother Clopas. Modern writers, again, have regarded them as adopted nephews, whose father was dead. These variations show that we are in the region of conjectural tradition rather than of traditional evidence. But the *general* notion that "the brethren" were children of Joseph and not of Mary derives such support as it may from the Apocryphal Gospels. They show what was a popular belief in the second and third centuries. That they show nothing more will, I suppose, be conceded by every one; and the measure of value which we are to attach to such popular belief is shown by the monstrous and even abhorrent fictions in which these Apocryphal Gospels abound. A support which comes from a source so radically tainted is not one on which we can rely. In fact, St. Jerome contemptuously dismisses this theory under the name of *deliramenta apocryphorum*—"apocryphal ravings." These fictions originated the notion that Joseph was an old man, and that he had sons who were grown up when Jesus was born. One of the oldest of these Apocryphal Gospels is the Protevangelium of James,[4] which, however, either blunders in saying that Joseph had no daughter,[5] or does not hold to the Perpetual Virginity. The Gospel of pseudo-Matthew calls James

---

[1] It is accepted by Neander, Blom, Meyer, Stier, Alford, Schaff, etc.
[2] The well-known story of the Desposyni (*supra*, p. 123) obviously accords far better with the view that our Lord's brethren were, in the Helvidian sense, His brothers, than with any other.
[3] Bishop Lightfoot has rendered a great service in correcting the error that the Papias who is quoted (Mill, *Mythical Interpretation*, p. 291) in support of the Hieronymian theory, is Papias of Hierapolis. He is a Papias not of the second, but of the eleventh century.
[4] See, too, the Gospel of Joseph, and the Arabic Gospel of the Infancy.
[5] Mark vi. 3.

"the first-born son of Joseph,"[1] which does not in any way decide the question; and the story which, in common with the Gospel of Thomas, it tells about James being bitten by a viper, and healed by Jesus, seems to be a confused echo of a story which, in distorted forms, was current in the Rabbinic schools.[2]

Such is the evidence for this Epiphanian theory. Its first respectable support comes at the close of the fourth century, and its earlier traces are only found embedded in worthless and pernicious forgeries. If there are any who consider such evidence sufficiently strong to overthrow the apparently straightforward indications of the Gospel, and the other difficulties on which I have here touched, I have no desire to combat their opinion. What I must myself regard as proven is, that James, the author of the Epistle, was not the son of Alphæus, and therefore was not one of the Twelve Apostles. Whether we embrace the view of Epiphanius, or that of Helvidius, is not a religious question. It is a question of literature and of criticism. It is the question whether we are to interpret the Gospels by their apparent meaning, or to correct them by imagined fitnesses, and by the confused combinations of apocryphal forgers. It is the question above all of the view which we take of the married life—whether, with some of the Essenes and many of the Gnostics, we regard it as involving something essentially impure, and therefore derogatory to the honour of the Virgin as the Mother of our Lord;—or whether we regard it as a holy mystery, which is so far from having in it any touch of earthly defilement, that it is deliberately, and again and again adopted as a type of the union between God and holy souls, between Christ and His spotless Church. Whichever view we adopt, we shall indeed be justified in stating the arguments which have led us to our conclusion; but to advance them with courtesy, and to hold them in perfect charity, will be a Christian duty, from which no amount of zeal and no intensity of conviction can for a moment hold us excused.

---

[1] How purely arbitrary were the inventions about the relationships of the Holy Family appears from the genealogical details furnished in this apocryphal writing, which may be thus tabulated:—

Joachim = Anna = Cleophas (by a second marriage).
| |
= Joseph = The Virgin Mary. Mary = Alphæus.
| |
James, Joseph, Judas, Simon. Philip and James the Little.

[2] Avodah-Zarah, f. 27 b.

CHAPTER XX.

LIFE AND CHARACTER OF ST. JAMES, THE LORD'S BROTHER.

"Thy Nazarites were purer than snow."—LAM. iv. 7.

IT is one of the signs of the inimitable truthfulness and power of Scripture, that again and again, by a few simple touches, it enables us to realise the character of those of whom it speaks. There are many whose lives, as recorded in Holy Writ, would only occupy two or three verses, whom, nevertheless, from the inspired power with which they are delineated, we are enabled to represent to ourselves in their distinctest personality. Still more is this the case when we also possess some of their utterances and writings. And such a picture we can paint of St. James, first Bishop of Jerusalem, one of the "brothers of the Lord."

Even of his childhood and training we can form some conception. Whether he were a half-brother or only a step-brother of Jesus, tradition and Scripture alike tend to show that he was brought up with brothers and sisters in the lowly home at Nazareth. Joseph was but a village carpenter, and, as tradition says, by no means a skilful one. A carpenter at an outlying Galilean village must of necessity have been poor. But there is an immense chasm between poverty and pauperism. The circumstances of Eastern life take away all the sting from the condition of the industrious poor. The wants of life are there reduced to their simplest elements. There is no wasteful luxury, no extravagant display. A little bread, a few dates, a spring of water, a humble cottage, a single change of raiment, are enough to support the honest labourer in dignity and contentment; and these he can earn with ease and certainty. Where there is no envy in the heart, where restlessness and ambition are under due control, such a state of life is not only tolerable—it is endowed with special elements of happiness. There must, we may be sure, have been many who sat around our Lord as they listened to the Sermon on the Mount who could understand from happy personal experience the beatitudes pronounced upon the poor who were also poor in spirit.

It will be needless to touch once more on that course of a Jewish boy's education which I have already described in the Lives of Christ and of St. Paul. We know how the Scriptures of the Old Testament formed the very staple of a boy's training in every genuine Israelitish family, how the children began to learn them at five and continued the study until manhood, only adding to them the teachings of the Scribes[1]

---

[1] Judah Ben Temah in *Pirkê Avoth*, v. 21: "At five the Bible, at ten the Mishnah, at thirteen the commandments, at fifteen the Talmud, at eighteen marriage, at twenty trade, at thirty full vigour, at forty maturity, at fifty counsel," etc.

Those teachings, under the two forms of Halachoth and Hagadoth—the one mainly consisting of ceremonial rules, the other of imaginative legends—were first collected in the second century by Rabbi Judah the Holy (Hakkodesh), into the Mishnah.[1] In the course of centuries they grew, by the constant accretions of the Gemara, until they now fill the twelve folio volumes of the Jewish Talmud. We cannot, of course, tell with any certainty how much of the teaching existed at the beginning of the Christian era; but the essence of Jewish teaching at that day consisted in the repetition of precedents and opinions, and a large body of these precedents and opinions are attributed to Hillel and Shammai, and other great Rabbis partly contemporary with, partly anterior to, the days of Christ. Again, how much of this teaching was likely to penetrate into the families and schools, if schools there were, of the despised Galilean village, is a matter of still greater uncertainty. But the discourses of Christ show that He was familiar with the conceptions which lay at the heart of the Rabbinic system;[2] and when He came to an open rupture with the Pharisees of Jerusalem, He showed His intensest disapproval of the spirit which identified their ritualistic observances and stereotyped formulæ with true religion. The language of St. James shows that, in later days, at any rate, he had accepted the truths which the Lord had taught. Until the time of his conversion he may have held the Pharisaic traditions in higher estimation. The essence of Pharisaism consisted in the extravagant exaltation of the Law, in its ceremonial no less than in its moral elements, and in the endless developments of pedantic scrupulosity into which its regulations had been expanded. The object of these developments was to enclose the Law in a hedge of separatism,[3] out of which no Jew could break without threats of excommunication, and into which no Gentile could force his way with any promise of advantage, unless he accepted the seal of the covenant, abandoned his Gentile antecedents, and became a Proselyte of Righteousness. Whatever may have been the earlier opinions of St. James, he ultimately learned to regard even the Levitic Law as a yoke too heavy for Gentiles to bear;[4] and he lived to teach the Jews of the Dispersion that the only ritual which was pure and undefiled before God was the ritual of Christian tenderness, the activity of Christian love.[5]

But whether he had been trained or not in the traditional expansions of Judaic scholasticism, we know that he was a rigid adherent of the Mosaic Law, and a faithful maintainer of the Levitical worship. His father Joseph[6] is characterised by St. Matthew as "a just man."

[1] Rabbi Judah the Holy was born about A.D. 130 and died A.D. 190.
[2] Matt. xxiii. 16—22, 25; Mark vii. 5—13; &c.
[3] From this word—*perishuth*—the name Pharisee is derived.
[4] Acts xv. 10, *seqq*. He listened without protest to the startling language of St. Peter, who also said that it was too heavy for "our fathers."
[5] Jas. i. 26, 27.
[6] Joseph was his father on the "Epiphanian" hypothesis as much as on the Helvidian.

This word conveys to Jewish ears a more definite meaning than it does to ours. It means not only that he was fair and honourable and upright, as we see that his conduct was in every incident of Christ's nativity and infancy in which he bore a part, but also that he made it his special study to meet all the requirements of the Mosaic Law. A "just man" was one who gave tithes; who went to the yearly feasts; who kept the one yearly fast; who was scrupulous in the observance of the Sabbath; who attended the Synagogue; who used the prescribed prayers; who observed the rules of Levitic purification; who reverenced the great Rabbis; who wore fringes and phylacteries; who made a constant study of the commandments, the precepts, the judgments, the testimonies, the Law, the word, the will of the God of the Covenant of his fathers.[1] To be a just man, according to the Jewish ideal, was to be "a Hebrew of the Hebrews," to walk in all the commandments and ordinances of the Lord blameless.[2] And this was the aim of the Holy Family. Not only did Joseph go up to Jerusalem to the Feast of the Passover, but Mary accompanied him, though, in consequence of the fatigue and the perils of the journey, it was deemed unnecessary, and what the Schoolmen would have called "a work of supererogation," for women to accompany their husbands.[3] It is certain, then, that St. James was educated in an atmosphere of rigid Judaism, perhaps not untinged with that fervid patriotism and unbounded appreciation of the privileges of the Jewish people which was characteristic of the Galileans,[4] and which, unless duly controlled, might easily degenerate into fierce fanaticism and haughty exclusiveness.

But in St. James these tendencies assumed the nobler form of a morality which was not only energetic, but even stern in its holy severity. He had grown up amid men and women of beautiful and simple natures—among those whose souls wore, "when they looked without, the glow of sympathy; when they looked within, the bloom of modesty." Of his other brothers we know nothing, but we trace the same characteristic features in the mind of his brother St. Jude. May we not suppose that "steady love of good and the steady scorn of evil" may have been intensified in their minds to a rare degree by their intercourse with ONE Who was holy, harmless, undefiled, and separate from sinners? Perhaps we may trace one result of that intercourse in the intense belief showed by St. James in the efficacy of prayer. The duty and blessedness of prayer occupies no small part in the teaching of his Epistle;[5] and he speaks of it as one who had learnt the lesson from the Lord Jesus.[6] In this, and in all respects, must not the presence of the

---

[1] Ps. cxix; Matt. i. 19; Luke xviii. 12. [2] Luke i. 6.
[3] Such had been the decision of Hillel.
[4] Jos. *Antt.* xviii. 1, § 6; *Vit.* 19, and passim, *B. J.* iii. 3, § 2.
[5] See i. 5; iv. 2, 3, 8; v. 13--18.
[6] Compare the above passages with Matt. v. 44; xvii. 21, etc.

Son of God in that humble household of Nazareth have exercised a spell which could not but create in the hearts of good men a horror of vice even deeper than that which such natures would spontaneously derive from the training of righteous parents, and from their exclusive study of Holy Books?

In the writings both of St. James and St. Jude we find an intimate familiarity with the books of Scripture. The Bible had been their main library. In St. James we can even trace the portions of Scripture which had the deepest charm for him, and the impression which they had left upon his mind. He alludes to Abraham, to Rahab, to Elijah; he refers to the Pentateuch, to the Psalms, to Isaiah, and to the Prophet Amos. On a passage of the latter Prophet he founded the main argument of the speech which had so vast an influence on the spread of Christianity, and he echoes his views in two passages of the Epistle.[1] But the Old Testament writers whose spirit he had most fully imbibed are those whose teachings bear on that practical wisdom which the Jews called *Chokmah*. They held, and held truly, that they were in possession of a moral "wisdom" which was the peculiar heritage of their race. It was not a "philosophy;" it was too little systematic, too much founded on practical experience and intuitions which transcended proof, to correspond to the ordinary meaning of that term. But the Hebraising Jews valued it so exclusively that they looked with unwise suspicion, and even with ignorant contempt, upon Greek and Roman lore.

Now the Jewish "wisdom" bore far more on conduct than on speculation. With this kind of wisdom the Epistle of St. James is largely occupied.[2] There is no book of the Hagiographa to which he more frequently refers than the Book of Proverbs.[3] He has evidently caught his *tone* from the Prophets of his nation; but the *lessons* which he deemed to be of the highest importance are those lessons of "wisdom for a man's self" which recorded the long results of experience in the terse apophthegms of Solomon and of the school which he had founded.

But St. James had not studied the Scriptures only. It is not certain that our Lord ever alludes to the Apocrypha, though there are one or two passages in which it is possible that he does so. But both St. James and his brother St. Jude show a marked familiarity with apocryphal writings. St. Jude, as we have seen, makes a direct quotation from the apocryphal Book of Enoch, and alludes to other circumstances which he could only have derived from apocryphal tradition. In other words, St. Jude was in great measure what the Rabbis would have called a Hagadist, or one who dwelt on allegory, legend, and historical story more than on the legal precedents of the Halachah.

---

[1] Amos ix. 12 (Acts xv. 17), ii. 7, v. 12 (Jas. v. 4).   [2] i. 5–8; iii. 13–17.
[3] See *infra*, p. 318.

There are no such legendary allusions in St. James; but, on the other hand, he shows a surprising fondness for the two best books of the Old Testament Apocrypha—the books of Ecclesiasticus and Wisdom. To these books he makes no less than thirteen references in the short compass of five chapters. These allusions, strange to say, are more numerous and definite than those which he makes to any of the books of the Old Testament. The reader will have an opportunity of estimating this fact by a reference to the parallels which I have mentioned farther on. It has been reckoned that he alludes more or less directly to the Book of Job six times, to the Book of Proverbs at least ten times, to the Book of the "Wisdom of Solomon" at least five times,[1] but to the Book of Ecclesiasticus—"the Wisdom of Jesus the son of Sirach"—more than fifteen times.[2] It requires but a glance at his Epistle to see that what has influenced him most of all is the Sermon on the Mount, to which he has some fourteen allusions; but he has used its teaching to breathe new life into the beautiful though apocryphal treatise of the Son of Sirach, on which it is evident that he had deeply meditated. The fact is the more striking because in other respects St. James shows no sympathy with Alexandrian speculations. There is not in him the faintest tinge of Philonian philosophy; on the contrary, he belongs in a marked degree to the School of Jerusalem. He is a thorough Hebraiser, a typical Judaist. All his thoughts and phrases move normally in the Palestinian sphere. This is a curious and almost unnoticed phenomenon. The "Sapiental literature" of the Old Testament was the *least* specifically Israelite. It was the direct precursor of Alexandrian morals. It deals with mankind, and not with the Jew. Yet St. James, who shows so much partiality for this literature, is of all the writers of the New Testament the least Alexandrian and the most Judaic.

But there is another fact about St. James which goes far to account for his position, his character, and the tone which he adopts, and which also throws an interesting light on the views of Joseph and of the Holy Family. It is that he was—if we may accept the testimony of Hegesippus, which is in this instance intrinsically probable—a Nazarite from the womb.[3] Joseph was called a "just man" in the sense which I

---

[1] If any further evidence should ever throw probability on the ingenious theory of Dean Plumptre that the Book of Wisdom was written by Apollos before his conversion to Christianity, it would be an interesting circumstance that there should have been these intellectual affinities between the head of Jewish Christianity and the great disciple of the Apostle of the Gentiles.

[2] The Talmud places among those "who have no portion in the world to come" (the *olam habba*) "those who read the books of outsiders" (ספרי החיצונים); and Rav Yoseph said "*that it was unlawful to read the Book of the son of Sirach*" (Sanhedrin, f. 100 b). On the other hand, it is referred to with respect in Yevamoth, f. 63 b.

[3] The sketch of St. James by Hegesippus is preserved in Euseb. *H. E.* ii. 23. Grätz has no ground for his assertion (*Gesch. d. Juden.* iii. 250) that St. James was in these particulars a representative of the Church; but I cannot agree with Mr. Sorley (*Jewish Christians*, p. 18) that the sketch is unworthy of credit, for it is confirmed by many incidental allusions in the Acts and Epistles.

have already explained; it was probably to the vow of the Nazarite
that St. James owed his title of "the Just." The close of the Jewish
age was an age of vows. The gathering of the eagles which were
beginning to flap their fierce wings over the Holy Land awakened
anguish and terror in the hearts of the Jews.[1] In the spirits of many
of them, and not least in those of brave and hardy Galilæans, the
sense of peril kindled a flame of patriotism which showed itself in wild
revolt.[2] In those who were unprepared for these movements—who did
not hear the call from Heaven, which in the form of prophetic sanction
or manifest opportunity would alone have justified an appeal to the
sword—the sorrow of political extinction found its sure consolation in
the Law of God. The beauty and purity of that Law had kindled the
rapturous delight of the exile who wrote the 119th Psalm. In that
golden alphabet of Hebrew faithfulness he found a compensation for
every earthly trial. It was the desire to preserve that Law intact
which, amid manifold aberrations, formed the nobler side of Pharisaism.
In faithfulness to that Law—which he at last learnt to regard from the
Christian standpoint as "a Law of Liberty"—St. James found the
highest meaning of his life. To obey it in the most open manner
became the vow of his life. A people suffering under oppression learns
to value the force which is derivable from sacred vows. In vows the
age of the Judges had found a spring of enthusiasm which helped them
to win deliverance. The instances of St. John the Baptist and St.
James—not to mention the Essenes or Banus the Pharisee[3]—show us
that in the days of Roman oppression the Jews were once more learning
the same lesson.[4]

As a Nazarite St. James would be regarded as holy even from
infancy. The vow was one which devoted him to the cause of God.
He never tasted wine or strong drink. He never ate any animal food.
No razor had ever come upon the long locks which streamed over his
shoulders. He never anointed himself with oil.[5] Although he must
have constantly practised the ablutions which were an essential part of
Levitic rule, he never allowed himself the effeminate luxury of the
bath, which had been borrowed from the soft customs of Ionia.[6] The

---

[1] See 2 Esdras xi. 45.
[2] The name "Galilean," though not, as has been erroneously said, almost identical with "Zealot," yet in common use denoted a certain amount of disaffection to the Roman Government (Matt. xxvi. 69; Mark xiv. 70; and Jos. B. J. iii. 3, § 2, etc.).
[3] Jos. Vit. 2.   [4] See Ewald, Gesch. Volks Israel, ii. 517.
[5] See Hegesippus, ap. Euseb. H. E. ii. 23. This may be regarded as irreconcilable with the directions given in James v. 14; but the use of oil *medicinally* is very different from its use as a *luxury*.
[6] Βαλανείῳ οὐκ ἐχρήσατο. Some have been rather horrified by the expression of Hegesippus that St. James "never used the bath." But it must not for a moment be supposed that St. James approved of that revolting notion of "the holiness of dirt" which seems to have found a place in the minds of some of the hermits. The expression "the bath" seems to me to have a technical meaning, so that it might be said even of an Essene, in spite of his daily ablutions in cold water (Jos. B. J. ii. 8, § 5), that "he did not use the bath." See Schwegler, *Nachapost. Zeitalt.* i. 141.

scrupulous cleanliness of Levitism, which arose from its abhorrence of defilement from any creeping thing, led him always to wear robes of pure white linen, because woollen substances could not be kept so absolutely clean. This would indicate a scrupulosity even greater than that of the Priests, for they ordinarily wore woollen garments,[1] although they might only be clad in linen while performing their sacred functions. The Nazaritism of St. James is a circumstance of great moment in the explanation of his life and character. It added strength to his personal influence. There are traces in Scripture that the Nazarites were regarded with peculiar pride. They were looked upon as endowed with health and beauty, as well as holiness. "Thy Nazarites," says Jeremiah,[2] "were purer than snow, they were whiter than milk, they were more ruddy in body than rubies, their polishing was of sapphire." They may even have been admitted into some of the functions which were otherwise confined to the tribe of Levi. It cannot indeed be true that "because he was a Nazarite" St. James was allowed, like the High Priest, to enter the Holiest once a year. In making that statement Epiphanius[3] probably mistakes the remark of Hegesippus[4] that he was admitted into the Sanctuary (εἰς τὰ ἅγια). And this may be true. For if we read of Rechabites who were "scribes" and "singers," and were allowed "to stand before the Lord" in the service of the Sanctuary, though they were of Kenite blood,[5] the same was more likely to be true of Nazarites, especially if, like St. James, they were of priestly kin and of Davidic descent. At any rate, the Nazarites were pledged champions of Mosaic institutions,[6] and signs are not wanting that the vow of the Nazarite had been adopted by other members of the circle who were connected with the earthly home of Jesus.[7]

In the case of St. James, as in that of his kinsman John the Baptist, this life-long vow helps to account for the tone of prophetic authority and fiery vehemence in which he speaks. May it not also account for "the little rift within the lute"—the gradual severance, if not alienation, from Christ of His earthly "brethren" which is traceable in the Gospels? It is probable that there was no disturbance of harmony so long as Jesus continued to live in the home of His childhood, and to work with the other members of His family as "the Carpenter of Nazareth." On the Divine instructiveness of that long epoch of seclusion—on the eloquence with which that silence teaches us some of the best and most necessary lessons of life—I have dwelt elsewhere.[8] We

---

[1] Lev. xvi. 4; Ezek. xliv. 17.　　[2] Lam. iv. 7.
[3] Epiphan. *Haer.* xxix. 4; lxxviii. 13.　　[4] Hegesippus, *ap.* Euseb. *H. E.* ii. 23.
[5] On the Rechabites see 2 Kings x. 15, 23; Jer. xxxv.; 1 Chron. ii. 55; Ps. lxxi., *inscr.*; and the allusion of Hegesippus to the Rechabite priest, *ap.* Euseb. *H. E.* ii. 23.
[6] Hence, perhaps, in part, the title borne by St. James of *Obliam*, or "bulwark of the people" (*Ophel am*), which Hegesippus confusedly says is "defence of the people, and righteousness."
[7] Thus we are told of St. Matthew—who, being a son of Alphæus, was perhaps a cousin of St. James—that he only ate vegetables. (Clem. Alex. *Paed.* ii. 1.)
[8] See my *Life of Christ*, i. 80–104.

may well believe that those early years at Nazareth were exceptionally peaceful and blessed. But when the Lord's hour was come there fell a shadow between Him and those with whom He had been brought up. He went to be baptised of John in Jordan. He returned with a body of youthful disciples, of whom one was His first cousin, and who were subsequently joined by other relatives. But His brethren did not join that cluster of young men in all their glowing enthusiasm whom Jesus gathered round Him as the fresh garland of His ministry. He left His home: they stayed in it. They must have heard many a rumour of Him before He re-appeared in His native village. Of the secret of His birth, shrouded in awful reticence by the awe-struck humility of their mother, it may be that they had not heard. They had seen Him grow up as one of themselves, living in obscure poverty, toiling at a humble trade. Could they approve of the astonishing boldness with which—usurping, as it might seem to them, the functions of the greatest Priests, or the most learned Rabbis, and even endangering the position of His countrymen with Herod, and with the Romans—He had swept the courts of the Temple clear from the crowd of chaffering traffickers? If such conduct showed a noble zeal, how could they approve of such a violation of all custom—such a disregard of all patriotic prejudices—as was indicated by His stay among the detested Samaritans? And how intense must have been their astonished disapproval when, in the Synagogue of Nazareth, they heard Him—Him with Whom they had all grown up side by side— proclaim Himself to be the promised Messiah of the Great Prophecy of Isaiah! His expulsion from Nazareth—the narrow escape from the death for "blasphemy" which His infuriated townsmen wished to inflict upon Him—the consequent disturbance of all their hitherto peaceful relations with their neighbours[1]—the necessity, arising from this disturbance, which compelled the whole family to migrate from a town endeared to them by so long a residence, and by so many associations—these and other circumstances must all have come upon them as heavy trials—trials which had arisen from the claims and the conduct of Him Whom men called their brother. All these circumstances would tend to produce the want of perfect cordiality to which our Lord alluded when He said that " a Prophet is not without honour except in his own country, and *among his kinsmen and in his own house.*"[2]

At first, however, they did not venture to interfere. With their strong Levitic prejudices, they must have heard with disapproval of His disparagement of the "traditions of the fathers;" of His indifference to the Oral Law; of His neglect of Levitic rules when He touched a

---

[1] "Is not this the son of Mary, and the brother of James, and Joses, and Judas, and Simon? and are not his sisters here with us?"—Mark vi. 3.
[2] Mark vi. 4; Matt. xiii. 57; Luke iv. 24; John iv. 44. The last words are omitted, perhaps out of respect for the feelings of the Lord's brethren, by the two later Evangelists.

corpse or a leper; of His graciousness to the poor woman, whose slightest contact involved ceremonial pollution; of His eating with unwashen hands; of His annulment of the distinction between clean and unclean meats; of His not observing the two weekly fasts; of the way in which He set at nought the common rules about the observance of the Sabbath. But the awe which He inspired hushed the voices which would otherwise have risen in remonstrance. It was only when the path of the "Prophet of Nazareth" seemed to darken—only when they found that He was arraying against Himself, first the disapprobation, then the indignant hatred, of all those on whom they looked with the deepest veneration—that they thought it a duty, if possible, to control His actions. It is difficult for us to realise how profound was the respect with which the humbler Jews looked up to the Priests, the Sanhedrists, the Pharisees, the Teachers of the Law. The titles which the Rabbis so eagerly accepted, the tone of contempt which they adopted towards those who were not initiated into their system, the insolence with which they depreciated all who did not belong to their little clique, had gradually led the mass of the Jews to accept these teachers at their own estimate, and to obey their decisions with almost abject humility. It was inconceivable to them how one of the people should dare to scorn the wisdom, to set aside the authority, to defy the injunctions of their idolised theologians. It startled them that He should denounce as blind guides and pernicious hypocrites the men whom they had been accustomed to regard as little Ezras or Simeons—as "uprooters of mountains"—as "glories of the Law"—as men of whom the least was "worthy that the Shechinah should rest upon him."[1] They, too, were inclined to repeat, "Is not this the carpenter?" In the sixteenth century men marvelled at the audacity of the German monk who dared to breathe defiance against the immemorial majesty of the Papacy, and to brave the opposition of a compact ecclesiasticism. But the courage of Luther was as nothing to what Jews who did not accept the Divine mission of Jesus must have considered to be the daring of the Nazarene, who cared nothing for the threats of the Scribes and Pharisees who had been despatched from Jerusalem to watch his movements. How could one who "had never learnt letters," and knew nothing of what passed for "theology"—gaze without quailing on those broad phylacteries, and listen without reverence to that micrology of erudition? Was it not amazing that He should dare to teach with personal authority, and without any reference to the precedents and technicalities of men who had actually listened to Shammai and to Hillel! The brethren of Jesus could only attribute such conduct to an enthusiasm which seemed to be getting beyond His own control. They imagined that the Spirit of the Prophet was no more subject to the Prophet. *They said, "He is beside Himself."* Fortifying their interference with the presence of His mother,

---

[1] The Rabbis, like the mediæval schoolmen, were distinguished by such flattering titles as "the glory of the Law," "the Holy," &c.

they went in a body to the skirts of the vast crowd which he was addressing at Capernaum, and sent a message that they wished to speak with Him. It was an act of which they themselves were as yet incapable of understanding the immense irreverence. It was time that James and Judas should be taught, as Mary had been gently taught even at the wedding-feast of Cana, that for Him the bond of earthly relationships was transcended for ever. Stretching out His hand to His disciples, He said, "Behold My mother and My brethren! For whosoever shall do the will of My Father in Heaven, *he* is My brother, and sister, and mother."[1]

Yet even this repudiation of their interference—this rebuke, so distinct yet so gentle, of the presumption which relied on fleshly kinsmanship—was not effectual to silence finally the remonstrances of His "brethren." Once more—and this time they were unable to bring Mary with them—they ventured to proffer their advice to Jesus; ventured, not obscurely, to intimate their disapproval of His conduct, and their rejection of His highest claims.[2] The burst of unpopularity which had followed His discourse at Capernaum about the Bread of Life—the discourse in which He had checked the false Messianic enthusiasm excited by the feeding of the five thousand—rendered His position more and more isolated. So great was His peril that, though the Feast of Tabernacles was at hand, He could not go publicly to Jerusalem. It was at this sad crisis that His brethren came to Him, and said, with impatient perplexity, "Depart hence, and go into Judæa, that Thy disciples also"—not merely these few Galilæans, but those who have believed on Thee in Jerusalem and Judæa—"may behold the works that Thou doest; for no man doeth anything in secret"—as Thou art now practically doing—"and seeks to be publicly acknowledged.[3] If Thou doest these things"—and though the words are not a denial of His work they are at least a cold and hesitating acknowledgment—"it Thou doest these things, manifest Thyself to the world." This forward and ungracious speech, in which they ostentatiously separate themselves from His disciples, is accounted for by the remark of the Apostle, "For even His brethren were not believers on Him."[4] Their belief, such as it was, was neither permanent nor deep. They may have given to His claims a general acceptance,[5] but their faith was lacking in energy and depth. Had it not been so, they would never have aspired to control His actions. Once more His calm words involved a deep reproof: "My opportunity has not yet come: *your* opportunity is always ready. The world cannot hate you; but Me it hateth, because I bear witness concerning it that its deeds are evil. Go ye up unto the feast. I do not mean yet to go up unto this feast, because my opportunity is not yet fulfilled." Accordingly He did not go up to the feast publicly, or

---

[1] Matt. xii. 49, 50.
[2] John vii. 1—10.
[3] John vii. 4: ἐν παρρησίᾳ εἶναι.
[4] Ver. 5: οὐδὲ γὰρ οἱ ἀδελφοὶ ἐπίστευον εἰς αὐτόν.
[5] Such as is expressed by πιστεύειν τινι, but not by πιστεύειν εἰς.

with them, or as one who went to observe it; He only appeared in the Temple suddenly in the midst of it. But what a severance between Himself and them the words reveal! How marked is the emphasis of the contrasted pronouns? How unmistakably do His words imply that *they* belonged as yet to the world of Judaism and Pharisaism; to the world which hated Him; to the world in which *they* were in no sort of peril, but which was seeking to take *His* life. *They* were members of the religious world; they sided with the dominant parties; they walked in the odour of sanctity; they were breathing the beatitude of orthodox benediction. *His* was the isolation and the persecution of the Prophet—of the Prophet who awoke the deadliest of all forms of hatred—the hatred of professional partisans; the hatred which must ever be the meed of those who are not afraid to pluck off the mask of the hypocrite, to startle the slumbers of a false orthodoxy, and to expose the insincerity of a false pretence.

In the four Gospels we do not again hear of the brothers of the Lord. They were not with Him during the last scenes; they were not at the Last Supper; they were not in the Garden; they drew no sword for Him; they did not follow Him to the Hall of Caiaphas; they did not defile themselves for the feast by entering the Prætorium; they did not stand beside the Cross; they did not, so far as we know, visit with sorrowing gifts His tomb.

Yet, strange to say, when next we meet with them they have thrown themselves heart and soul into the struggling fortunes of the Church! It is after the Ascension. The Eleven have returned from the Mount of Olives, and go to the Upper Room, which is their regular place of meeting in Jerusalem; and in that Upper Room are not only the Eleven, but also Mary the mother of Jesus and His brethren.[1] From that moment as a body they disappear, and we hear no more of either Joses or Simon. But Jude lived to travel as a Christian missionary, and to write the Epistle which bears his name; and James lived to furnish the nearest approach to a bishop which is to be found in the Apostolic age, and to be for twenty years a main pillar of the persecuted Church.

Whence came this marvellous change?

We have no account of it; we have no means of even conjecturally explaining it, unless the explanation lies in three words of the Apostle Paul. In his relation of the appearances of Christ after His Resurrection he says that he was seen of Kephas, then of the Twelve, then of more than five hundred brethren at once; "*then He was seen of James.*"[2] That this James means the Lord's brother, the head of the Church in Jerusalem, is clear, because when the Epistle was written the son of Zebedee was dead, and the son of Alphæus was unknown to Gentile Christians. They knew but of one James, the one whose authority was so highly venerated, and the only one whom

---

[1] Acts i. 14.   [2] 1 Cor. xv. 7: ἔπειτα ὤφθη Ἰακώβῳ.

St. Paul mentions by name. Three, and three alone, were singled out to be separate eye-witnesses of the appearances of the risen Christ on earth. One was the leader of the Apostolic band, the repentant Kephas; another was she who loved much, whose love made her last at the cross and earliest at the tomb; the third was the brother of the Lord.

Not a single further detail is added in Scripture respecting the appearances to Kephas and to James. But in the Gospel of the Hebrews—the most ancient and trustworthy of the apocryphal Gospels —we find the striking story that James had bound himself by an oath that from the hour when he had drunk of the Lord's cup he would neither eat nor drink until he should see him risen from the dead. "Now the Lord, when He had given the cloth (*sindon*) to the servant of the priest, went to James and appeared to Him, and said after a while, 'Bring hither a table and bread;' and He took bread, and blessed it, and brake it, and gave it to James the Just, and said to him, 'My brother, eat thy bread now, for the Son of Man hath risen from among those that sleep.'"[1] There are several circumstances here which show us indeed that we are in the region of the Apocryphal, for James was not present at the Lord's Supper, and there did not exist among the Apostles—in spite of all that Jesus had told them—any expectation of the Resurrection. Indeed, so far from the belief creating the conviction, we are expressly told of the incredulous astonishment with which they received the first Easter tidings. But though there may be some confusion in these details, there is nothing improbable, nothing which is unlike St. James's character, in the main facts of the tradition. That he loved the Brother with whom he had lived at Nazareth for thirty years we cannot doubt. Although he may have been unconvinced at first of His Divine claims, though he may even have yielded to doubts respecting His Messiahship, yet one into whose heart had sunk so deeply the lessons of sentence after sentence from the Sermon on the Mount could not have regarded Him as other than a great prophet from the earliest days of his public ministry. All his personal affection may have been stirred to its lowest depths by the knowledge of what He had suffered. His nascent and imperfect belief may have been greatly strengthened by the events which accompanied the Crucifixion, and which made so deep an impression not only on the awestruck Jews, but even on the heathen centurion. It is therefore far from impossible that when he heard the first reports of His resurrection, the subsequent intelligence that He had been actually seen—and not only by Mary of Magdala, but by Kephas, and by the Twelve, and by five hundred brethren at once—he may have bound himself by the not uncommon *cherem*, or ban, which the tradition records. He was a Nazarite, and bound by a general vow; he would

---

[1] Jer. *De Virr. Illustr.* 2.

now make a *special* vow neither to eat nor drink until he too had seen the Lord—until he had been thus thoroughly convinced that all which yet remained of his past doubts was wrong and vain. However this may be, we know on the testimony of St. Paul that a special vision was vouchsafed to him. We know further from sacred history that he became thenceforth, until his martyrdom, a faithful shepherd of souls, a tower of defence to the Church of Christ in the Holy City.

Seven or eight years elapse before we again hear of him,[1] and then it is merely a passing allusion to the fact that St. Paul saw him in Jerusalem, three years after his conversion, when he had been forced to fly for his life from Damascus. All the brethren at first—and therefore James among them—received the new convert, who had lately been so terrible an inquisitor, with fear and suspicion. When the generosity of Barnabas had rescued his friend from this painful isolation, Peter was the earliest to hold out to him the right hand of fellowship, and from that time James seems also to have received him with kindness.[2] Even then St. James appears to have held some authoritative position in the Church, though he is distinguished from the Apostles. Since no other Apostle except Peter is mentioned, we may infer that they were not at Jerusalem at that moment. Indeed, the whole Church had been scattered by the storm of persecution which had been directed by Paul himself.

Six more years elapse before, in A.D. 44, we again meet with the name of James. In that year Herod Agrippa I., in trying to sustain the politic *rôle* of a national king, had taken the readiest method of pleasing the Jews by harassing the Christians. He had accordingly seized James the son of Zebedee, and put him to death. The selection of the elder son of Zebedee for a victim shows either that the burning zeal was still unquenched which in old days had earned for him and his brother John the surname of Sons of Thunder, or that he was at that time regarded as the leader in the Church at Jerusalem. Why that position was assigned to him rather than to Peter we can only conjecture. It may have been owing to his position, or to his connexion with Jerusalem, or to the fact that as the son of Salome he was the near relative of his Lord. No sooner had he been executed than, seeing the delight which the Jews had taken in his execution, Herod proceeded further to seize Peter. The angelic deliverance of Peter from prison thwarted the king's murderous designs; and when Peter went at once to the house of Mary the mother of John Mark, to remove the anxious fears of the assembled brethren before his flight from Jerusalem, he ended his hasty narrative with the words, "Tell *James* and the brethren these things."[3]

The expression shows that James the Lord's brother had succeeded the son of Zebedee as the chief person in the mother Church. The

---

[1] About A.D. 38. [2] Gal. i. 18, 19. [3] Acts xii. 17.

twelve years had now elapsed during which, according to a probable tradition, the Apostles had been bidden to stay at Jerusalem before they scattered far and wide to preach the Gospel to all nations.[1] The stationary superintendence of the little body of Christians in the head-quarters of Jewish fanaticism was felt to be a position which belonged less fitly to any of the Twelve than to one who, though he might in the less technical sense be called an Apostle, was not one of the chosen witnesses to whom had been entrusted the evangelisation of all the world.

To James, therefore, the Lord's brother—not only *because* he was the Lord's brother, but because of the force of his character and influence—fell naturally and at once the office of Bishop of Jerusalem.[2] The appointment was eminently wise, and as Jerusalem was yearly visited at the great feasts by hundreds of thousands of pilgrims, of whom multitudes were Christians,[3] this position at once gave to the Lord's brother an immense authority. He became a pillar of the Church;[4] and if it had been in the power of any one even at the eleventh hour to win over the people of the Ancient Covenant, he would have achieved the task. The shadow of an awful mystery clung about him as the earthly brother of Him Whose true Divinity as the Eternal Son of God was brought home more deeply by the Holy Spirit to the hearts of the disciples as year after year passed by. And this awe of his personality, enhanced among the Jews by his Davidic descent, was increased by the stern sanctity of his character. This was he—so men whispered, and we catch the echo of their whispers centuries afterwards—"who is wont to go alone into the sanctuary, and is found prostrate in prayer, so that his knees have grown hard and worn like a camel's because he is ever kneeling and worshipping God, and asking forgiveness for the people."[5] "This is the righteous one." "This is *Obliam*, the bulwark of the people." "He is even allowed," they said, "like the high priest, to wear on his forehead the *petalon*, the plate of gold on which is inscribed Holiness to the Lord." The latter notion is probably a symbolic expression translated into a fact,[7] for there is no trace that such a privilege was accorded to any one, even if he were, as James may have

---

[1] Clem. Alex. *Strom.* vi. 5, § 43, quoting the *Kerugma Petrou*; and Apollonius, ap. Euseb. *H. E.* v. 18.
[2] Clemens (ap. Euseb. *H. E.* ii. 1) says that he was appointed bishop by Peter and the two sons of Zebedee. Hegesippus says: διαδέχεται δὲ τὴν Ἐκκλησίαν μετὰ τῶν ἀποστόλων ὁ ἀδελφὸς τοῦ Κυρίου Ἰάκωβος, κ.τ.λ. It is amazing that Jerome should have ventured to render this "Suscepit Ecclesiam Hierosolymæ *post apostolos* frater domini Jacobus." It means "*with* the Apostles," and shows that James was not one of the Twelve.
[3] In Acts xxi. 20 we find the startling expression, "Thou beholdest, brother, *how many myriads* (πόσαι μυριάδες) there are of Jews who have believed."
[4] Gal. ii. 9.   [5] Euseb. *H. E.* ii. 23.
[6] Epiphan. *Haer.* xxix. 4; lxxviii. 13.
[7] As is the case with the similar story told by Polycrates about St. John (Euseb. *H. E.* v. 24).

been, of Aaronic as well as of Davidic origin.[1] But it is not incredible that James may, as a Nazarite, have been allowed to share in some of the priestly privileges.[2] In any case, these stories must indicate that he was held in exceptional reverence, for legends only gather round the names of the greatest, just as it is only the loftiest mountain-tops to which the mists most densely cling. And every indication with which we are furnished shows that he was providentially fitted to give one last chance to all who would accept salvation, whether in the Jewish capital or amid the Twelve Tribes of the Dispersion. From the whole character of his views he would speak to them in a voice more acceptable than that of any other man.

In the narrative of the anger which arose at Jerusalem when the news arrived that Peter, not content with baptising Gentile proselytes, had actually lived in their houses and eaten with them, the name of James is not mentioned. Nor, again, are we told that St. Paul saw him in his hurried and unimportant visit, in the year of Peter's imprisonment, to carry alms from the Gentile Christians at Antioch to their suffering brethren, the "saints" of Jerusalem.[3] But five years later, about A.D. 50, when Paul and Barnabas went up a second time to Jerusalem for the settlement of the great question which was then agitating the Church, we again see St. James as the most prominent figure in that memorable Synod. The question whether the Gentiles were or were not to be circumcised—was one on the decision of which hung the entire future of Gentile Christianity. It involved the whole relation of the Gentiles to the Mosaic Law. I have elsewhere so fully entered into its bearing, and into the circumstances of the scene at which it was decided, that I must be content to refer to what I have there said.[4] But I may here repeat that the whole weight and responsibility of the decision rested with St. James, and that he rose on this occasion to a height worthy of his parentage and of his character. In the face of all the prejudices of his life—rising superior to the views of all the Rabbis, his predecessors and contemporaries—ignoring the wrathful murmurs and fanatical arguments of the Pharisaic Zealots, he decided in an opposite sense to what seems to have been expected of him. He, the Righteous—he, the Bulwark of Judaism—he, the priestly Nazarite, to whom, Christian though he was, even Jews looked up with reverence—he, who was so rigidly accurate an observer of all the precepts of legal righteousness—he, the very man whose name and authority had been claimed by the Judaic emissaries who had troubled the Church of Antioch by their insistance on legal scrupulosity and Jewish particularism—he, whose name they afterwards abused in counter-missions to undo the teaching of St. Paul—he gave his voice in favour of the liberal view! Never, perhaps, did a result so awful in its responsibility depend

---

[1] Mary was related to Elizabeth.
[2] See *supra*, p. 286. Dean Plumptre refers to Maimonides, *Moreh Nevochim*, iii. 43.
[3] Acts xi. 30; xii. 25. [4] See *Life and Work of St. Paul*, i. 405—408.

on the wisdom of any single man. The assembly of Jewish Christians in the Holy City, seething with intense excitement,[1] hung on the lips of their Bishop, as, in the hush of awe inspired by his person and character, he rose, with the long locks of the Nazarite streaming over his white robes, to close the discussion in which so many fierce passions had been aroused. The Pharisees had been insisting on the Law—the Law of Moses—the sacred, irrevocable, fiery Law of Sinai, for the sake of which they thought the very world had been created—the Law which the Saviour had Himself said that He came not to destroy, but to fulfil—nay, which He had personally fulfilled—nay, respecting which He had openly declared that no jot nor tittle of it should ever pass away. Who had the power to say that this Law which God had uttered from the rolling fire, with the sound of a trumpet amid myriads of angels—who should dare to say that any portion of it was special? that any utterance of it was evanescent? Who would dare to argue that it was meant for Jews only, and that it need not be adopted by proselytes, and that it had not been intended for all the world? Could even the Bath Kol itself, the voice from Heaven,[2] supersede its universal sacredness, or absolve, were it but one Gentile, from so much as the position of a phylactery or the colour of a fringe? Did not tradition say that all the souls even of nations yet unborn had been summoned to the awful mountain to hear that Law delivered? And be it remembered that these arguments were being uttered at Jerusalem, in the midst of, and to the knowledge of, a madly fanatical population—uttered, as it were, in the audience of those long centuries of Sacred history to which every tower and pinnacle of the Holy City was bearing witness—uttered by men who were not only Pharisees, but Christians. And let it be further remembered that every argument which they were urging was one addressed as it were in shorthand to the impassioned prejudices of the majority of the hearers; anticipated almost before its utterance by their quick and excited sensibility; weighted with the emphasis of those lifelong convictions, which come to be identified with the very essence of religion. Against this mighty current of obstinate Judaism, Paul, the once fierce Inquisitor and Persecutor—Paul, the hated renegade of the Sanhedrin—Paul, who had his share in the death of the proto-martyr—Paul, the suspected teacher of heathen customs which were the subversion of legal righteousness—Paul, and even Barnabas, tainted, as many of these Pharisees would have thought, by intercourse with "the enemy,"—would have struggled in vain. One tower of strength the wiser and larger-hearted party possessed in the advocacy of Peter; but Peter himself, though he adduced irresistible

---

[1] Acts xv. 2.
[2] See the memorable story in the Talmud, where the Rabbis repudiate even the testimony of the Bath Kol against one of their Halachoth. "It is not mysterious voices," said Rabbi Joshua, "but the majority of the Sages which ought alone to decide questions of doctrine" (Bava Metzia, f. 59 b). See my paper on "Christ and the Oral Law" in the *Expositor*, (v. 233).

proofs of a Divine sanction for what he had done, had barely been able to justify, at Jerusalem, the isolated baptism and admission into fellowship of a single pious proselyte. The question now at stake was not the treatment of an individual case, but the obligations of the whole Gentile world. Was the coming of the Jewish Messiah to be the annulment of the Jewish Law, the obliteration of all that was most distinctive in the Jewish Church? Was the triumph of Israel to involve its national effacement? Such were the questions which led to a storm of passionate dispute. But meanwhile, before the convening of this deeply-moved assembly, the result of which was to be fraught with consequences so momentous, Paul and Barnabas had, with consummate wisdom, secured the adhesion of the three great pillar-Apostles. Peter was already with them in heart; but Peter's impulsive and yielding temperament might have been little able to stand alone against the rushing tide of fanaticism if he had not been supported by the authority of John and James. But John was won by the clear signs that God had been with the heroic missionaries, and that the Holy Spirit had set His seal on all their work. And when James also was convinced—when even *his* practical wisdom had grasped the truth, which was the last which the Holy Spirit made perfectly clear to the minds of the Early Apostles—the greatest victory ever achieved by Gentile Christianity was won. The fiery speech of St. Peter might only have fanned the prejudices of the Jewish Christians into a fiercer flame. Even to the striking narratives of Paul and Barnabas they listened in unconvinced silence. They attached chief importance to the original Apostles and witnesses.[1] Their hopes were in James. And James arose to dash those hopes to the ground. He referred to the narrative of "Symeon;" he passed over in silence the speeches of Barnabas and Paul; but then —appealing to the words of a prophet who was a Nazarite like himself —with his "*Therefore I decide*," he settled the question.[2] And his decision was that the Gentiles were to be admitted into the Christian Church on the footing of proselytes of the Gate, and were not to be burdened with any requirements beyond the simple and easy rules of the Noachian Dispensation. I have pointed out elsewhere how many points of discussion were still left undecided by this decree; how local and how transitory was its authority; how completely, in Churches outside the limited circle to which the letter was addressed, St. Paul set aside its authority. I have also shown how openly the implied contract was also broken by those who were most hostile to the Apostle of the heathen, and who, appealing too often to credentials furnished by St. James, sophisticated St. Paul's feeble converts and undid his toilsome work. But, meanwhile, James himself, with worthy firmness and true

---

[1] See *Clem. Hom.* xix. 17.
[2] Acts xv. 19. Two resemblances have been observed between the speech and the Epistle—(1) The epistolary greeting, χαίρειν (*infra* p. 326); and (2) ἀδελφοί, ἀκούσατε (Acts xv. 13; Jas. ii. 5).

wisdom from on high, had conceded the whole question at issue. When the principle had been thus once conceded, it was, from the nature of the case, conceded for ever. The details could be safely left to future adjustment as they were seen by the light of circumstances. No one who called himself a Christian, whether Jew or Gentile, could really dispute a rule which had been laid down by the concurrent authority not only of Paul and Barnabas and Peter, but even of the Beloved Disciple and of the Brother of the Lord. But myriads of Jewish Christians remained secretly unpersuaded, until the destruction of Jerusalem, like a lightning-flash from heaven, dispelled their perplexities by the Divine logic of events.

Years again pass by, and we have but incidental references to the name of James. It is clear that if James was satisfied as to the right of St. Paul to act as he had done, many of his adherents were not. In violation of the whole spirit of the synodical compact, they insisted on maintaining a rigid line of distinction between Jews and uncircumcised Gentiles; and their presence at Antioch was so successful in reawakening the terrors of a fancied unorthodoxy that Peter himself once more wavered, and even Barnabas was led away with the dissimulation which followed the arrival of these "certain from James." It is not necessary once more to write the history of that bitter quarrel which nearly rent asunder the unity of the early Church, and which it took a full century to heal. It is enough to say that the habits and convictions of a lifetime can never be lightly, and rarely with completeness, laid aside. Although St. James had shown on the one great occasion a noble liberality, yet his sympathies were to the last with the Jewish Christians. As the head of their party and the exponent of their views, he could never have felt in entire accord with the Apostle of the Gentiles. Hence his memory was fondly cherished by all Judaisers, and the Ebionites claimed his special patronage.[1] Peter was too wide in his sympathies, too free from narrowness and prejudice, to be the chosen leader of so intensely Judaic a sect. The Nazarenes also, who were Judaists but not heretical, looked up to James with the highest reverence. In the Church of Jerusalem he was succeeded by Symeon son of Clopas, who is said to have suffered martyrdom, at the age of 120, in the reign of Hadrian. Every one of the next thirteen Bishops was of the Circumcision.[2] The first Gentile Bishop was Marcus (A.D. 137), who presided over the Church when some of the Christians had returned from Pella to Jerusalem, then called by its new name of Ælia Capitolina.

That St. James continued to the last to be swayed by the thoughts and traditions of his earlier life may be asserted without any blame to

---

[1] In the pseudo-Clementine Homilies and Epistles he, and not Peter, is elected to the rank of supreme and universal Bishop. One Ebionite romance, the *Anabathmoi Iakobou*, went so far as to describe his ascension into Heaven. Epiphan. *Haer.* xxx. 16.
[2] Euseb. iv. 5.

him. It is only what we see every day. The saints of God, who will be very near and very dear to each other in Heaven, are on earth separated by bitter prejudices, by party shibboleths, by mutual misunderstandings, by the almost grotesque misrepresentations in which they mutually indulge. The Holy Spirit of God was with St. Paul, and with St. James, and with each of the Apostles, dividing to each man severally as He would. But there was a diversity of gifts and graces in accordance with the individuality of each; nor did the Holy Spirit bestow on any one of them an infallible wisdom or a perfect sinlessness. "Even a Paul," as St. Chrysostom says, "was still but a man." It is surely one of the heresies of modern times, one of the faithless misconceptions which alter the central meaning of Christianity, to suppose that the Holy Spirit, who was promised for all time, was with the Apostles and is not with us. He is with us. He is with all who seek Him. But as it is alien from the possibilities of earthly life that His indwelling Presence should make us perfect or all-wise, so neither did it make them perfect or all-wise. They were mortal men, not angels. They were liable to inconsistencies, and they fell into errors. It is, I think, an unmistakable inference, both from the hints which we find in the Acts of the Apostles and from the silence of that book in other places, that St. James and St. Paul felt but little congeniality towards each other. They differed in sympathies and in temperament. No lives could be more diverse than those of these two great servants of God. St. Paul was constantly traversing Europe and Asia in long journeys, living in heathen cities, crossing and recrossing the Mediterranean, brought into daily contact with the rich though unsanctified culture of the grandest nations of antiquity, seeing the works and learning the thoughts of many men. It was impossible for him to retain the Jewish standpoint when, by the wisdom of Providence, his mind had been enlarged by such influences and such knowledge. It forced upon him, in a way far different from that of theoretical assent, the conviction of God's fatherhood over the family of man. In the light of Christ's command to gather all mankind into the fold of His Church, the promises and prophecies which ran throughout the whole Old Testament flashed into new significance. The training which St. Paul had received from God's Holy Spirit, that he might become a true "vessel of election" to win the Gentiles unto Christ, shifted, as it were, the centre of gravity of his whole theological system. Theologically, as well as geographically, he was now aware that it was but a fiction of Rabbinism to regard Jerusalem as the centre of all the earth. The one thing which imperilled the conversion of the world was the attempt to force on the neck of the Gentiles a yoke of observances which they were unable to bear. It was impossible for St. Paul to dwell on the symbolism which gave to the Law its true splendour. What *he* had to enforce was its deathful, its menacing, its elementary aspect as a curse and a bondage. He was driven in the earnestness of controversy to use such expressions as "weak and beggarly elements," which we cannot imagine that St. James could under any circumstances have brought himself to use. We can hardly wonder if a polemic so unsparing produced feelings of intense exasperation. The Rabbis applied to their hedge of Levitic Halachôth the expression of the Book of Ecclesiastes (x. 8), "Whoso breaketh down a hedge a serpent shall bite him." St. Paul broke down that hedge in every direction—it was the duty and object of his life to do so—and he was bitten in consequence by the "offsprings of vipers." They whose work it is to win multitudes to Christ, to show religion in all its width and attractiveness, to make it wear a winning aspect in the eyes of all who love mercy and culture, have always aroused the alarmed antagonism of more timid natures.[1]

But the life and training of St. James, and consequently to a great extent the colour of his opinions, were the reverse of cosmopolitan. So far as we know, he never left Jerusalem after the Ascension. All that he learnt of the outer world was the glimpse of it which he received from intercourse with the Paschal pilgrims who came from "the Dispersion" with all their thoughts full of Jerusalem, and of Jerusalem alone. There was nothing in such intercourse to decrease, rather there was everything to intensify, the feelings of the Jew as to the grandeur and importance of his own privileges. Now the cause and substance of those privileges lay in the institutions which God had given him, and even more in the ceremonial Law, with its service and Priesthood, than in the moral law, which—in its great outlines—was common to the Jew with all mankind. A Christian Jew might concede that these institutions were not obligatory on the Gentile, at any rate to their full extent; but it was almost impossible for him to realise that they had become needless and insignificant shadows for himself also. They had been delivered from Sinai by the voice of God speaking out of the fire. How, then, could they become obsolete? Who had repealed them? When had they been annulled? Had any prophet greater than all the prophets reduced to a dead letter so much of the Levitic Books? Had Christ done so? There were those who argued that implicitly He *had* done so; but was the implicit and the inferential a sufficient warrant for the abrogation of that which was positive and Divine? Could it, moreover, be said with certainty that Christ had even implicitly set aside the Mosaic Law which He said He had come not to destroy, but to fulfil? If St. Paul appealed to the guidance of the Holy Spirit, others too, who thought that they had the Spirit of God, did not feel so sure as to their warrant for neglecting or undervaluing what was to them the certain revelation of 1,500 years ago.

Least of all could it be expected that one like St. James—a Hebrew of Hebrews, the son of a "just" man, and one whose own title of "the Just" was a testimony to the faithfulness of his observances, a Nazarite

---

[1] "Above all, let us not make the doors of the Church bristle with razors, and pitchforks, and bundles of thorns" (H. Peyrreyve to Père Lacordaire).

"holy from his mother's womb,"—would readily embrace such views. If he did, would not the Temple in which he worshipped, the vows in which he took part, the Holy Place in which he was permitted to kneel, the sacrifices which he offered, the streets of the city which he trod, the very robe he wore, bear daily witness against him? No doubt the Gentiles, if they chose, might be contented with the Noachian precepts; and the question as to the relative position of Jews and Gentiles, and of proselytes of the Gate in comparison with proselytes of Righteousness, might be left in abeyance. But to St. James Jerusalem was the joy of the whole earth, the City of the Great King. To him "the people" meant the Chosen People, and the rest of the world was, in comparison, as nothing.[1] It had not been elected for exceptional blessings. It stood in a wholly inferior relation towards God. If such were not the views of St. James, they were the views of many of those Priests and Pharisees by whom he was surrounded, and with whom he lived in friendship. Many of these were only so far Christians that they recognised in Christ a Divine Messiah. They were Jews *as well as* Christians, and by the whole bent of their lives they were Jews first and Christians afterwards. To many of them, as we see from the New Testament, it was the strongest temptation of their lives to waver halfway between Judaism and Christianity, on the verge of apostatising into the former. It was not so with St. James. His heart was sure, his affections fixed, his soul anchored on the rock of Christ. He was a Christian first, a Jew afterwards, although his Epistle shows that it was the moral rather than the dogmatic side of Christianity which most absorbed his thoughts. But a man is insensibly affected by intercourse with those around him; and every circumstance around St. James was of a kind to deepen in his eyes the sanctity of Judaism. Those about him, often without his sanction, and sometimes in defiance of his wishes, did not scruple to make use of his name to discountenance the views of St. Paul. It was the position of St. James as the head of the Judaising Christians which made his name so dear to the Ebionites.[2] They were glad to attribute to *him* that bitter antagonism to the teachings of St. Paul which was true only of those who usurped his name. This is why, in the spurious Epistle of Peter prefixed to the Clementine Homilies, Peter is made to exalt the Law against the attacks of "the enemy," and none are regarded as full Christians but those who are devout and *circumcised*. This is why "James, the slave of the Lord Jesus Christ," becomes in the dedication of the Epistle of the pseudo-Clemens, and in the Liturgy of James, not "the Lord's brother," but *Adelphotheos*, "the brother of God." He is spoken of,

---

[1] Rabbis used to talk of all the world except Judea as *chootsah-la-arets*, "outside the land."

[2] The "Ascent of James," the "Witness," and the "Protevangelion of James" were Ebionite writings. There are imitations of the Epistle of St. James in the Clementine Homilies, iii. 1, 17, 54, 55; viii. 7; xix. 2 (*Ep. Clem. ad Jac.* 15).

with the pompous inflation of a later sacerdotalism, as "the Lord James," "the prince of bishops, Apostles, and martyrs," "the bishop of bishops, who rules Jerusalem, the Holy Church of the Hebrews."[1] He is the Archbishop of Jerusalem, who, sending about even the greatest of the Apostles, at his own behest[2] despatches St. Peter to withstand Paul, "the enemy," thinly disguised in the person of Simon Magus. He stands seven days on the steps of the Temple witnessing (as though against the teaching of this "enemy"!) that Jesus is the Christ. In the Clementine Recognitions,[3] Peter—with pointed reference to the remark of St. Paul that he needed no letter of recommendation (2 Cor. iii. 1)—is made to give solemn warning to the Church to test false Apostles, and "to trust *no* teacher who has not brought a testimonial" (as we may call it) "from James or from his successor; because, unless any one has gone up to Jerusalem and there been approved as being a teacher fit and faithful to preach the word of Christ, he is not by any means to be received." Such were the dreams and extravagances and ambitions and calumnies of party theology in the days of the Ebionites. Most of this Ebionising exaltation of Judaic episcopacy is the nonsense of an heretical and malignant ecclesiasticism, savouring of the elements which have ever been the corruption of all that is pure and sound and simple in the Church. But it bases its fictions upon circumstances which at one time did really exist, although to a much less extent than this. It had its root in the real differences between Judaic and Pauline Christianity. A passionate contest did really occur between those who wished to maintain intact and those who wished to annul the Levitic Law; and there may have been a want of heart-felt union between the leaders of the Church of Jerusalem and the great founder of the Church of the Gentiles. The state of circumstances which I have here sketched finds a striking illustration in the advice given by St. James and his elders, in A.D. 58, on the occasion of St. Paul's fifth and last visit to Jerusalem, when they recommended him to take a part in helping some poorer brethren to bring to due conclusion a temporary vow. That vow, with all its Levitic ceremonials, involved circumstances which could not but have been painful to St. Paul; and the recommendation, though given in all sincerity as a supposed means of averting a collision between Jews and Christians, produced the most disastrous consequences for many years.[4]

---

[1] The forged letter of St. Peter in the Clementines is addressed "To James, the Lord and Bishop of the Holy Church," who is described as being at the head of a college of seventy Presbyters. The letter of pseudo-Clemens describing the martyrdom of St. Peter is addressed "To James the Lord, and Bishop of Bishops, who rules the Holy Church of the Hebrews in Jerusalem, and all the Churches everywhere established by the Providence of God," etc. See too *Recogn.* i. 43.
[2] *Recogn.* i. 44, 68, 73.   [3] *Recogn. Clem.* iv. 35; *Hom.* xi. 35.
[4] See this fully explained in my *Life of St. Paul*, ii. 295—306. The Nazarite vow might be taken for a longer or shorter period, and one who undertook it for a period only was called "a Nazarite of days" (see Amos ii. 11, 12; 1 Macc. iii. 49). St. Paul's vow at Cenchreae may, or may not, have been of this character (Acts xviii 18).

From that time forward we lose sight of St. James in Scripture; but we gain one more glimpse of him in Jewish history and Christian tradition five years afterwards, in the year of his martyrdom, A.D. 63.

Respecting this martyrdom, Josephus tells us that it was due to Ananus, or Annas—or, to give him his true name, Hanan—the younger, who in that year was High Priest, the last of the high-priestly sons of the "Annas" of the Gospels. Hatred against Christ and Christians had already led the house of Hanan to imbrue their guilty hands in the blood of Christ and of St. Stephen, to approve of the murder of James the son of Zebedee, and to endeavour to procure the assassination of St. Paul. The same unrelenting animosity now hurried the younger Hanan, a man of violent and imperious temper, into a fresh crime. He seized a sudden opportunity to put to death the Lord's brother, and so to strike one more blow at the Christian Church. Festus, whose justice had saved the life of St. Paul, and who was one of the most honourable of the Roman procurators of Judæa, had died after a brief government of two years. Albinus was appointed as his successor, and before he arrived there was a little interval during which Judæa was only under the distant supervision of the Legate of Syria. Agrippa II. was absent from Jerusalem. At such a time a bold and cruel Sadducee like this High Priest might easily induce the Sanhedrin to stretch their authority, and exercise a power of inflicting capital punishment which had ceased strictly to belong to them. He hoped that this irregularity would be either unnoticed or condoned by the Romans, who were very tolerant of what was done in the interests of any legally-permitted religion, and who would not be likely to interfere with an execution which had no political significance. Inspiring the Sanhedrin with his own audacity, Hanan induced them to arrest James and other leading Christians, and to have them stoned. The charge brought against them was doubtless blasphemy, for it was impossible to charge James at any rate with "transgressing the Law." Perhaps, if James had been as much hated as St. Paul was, no more would have been said. But James, at Jerusalem, like Ananias at Damascus, was profoundly honoured by Jews no less than by Christians. He, too, was "a devout man according to the law, having a good report of all the Jews which dwelt there."[1] It was not merely the converts to Christianity, but "some of the most equitable in the city, and those who were most accurate in their knowledge of the Law," who were grieved at this wanton murder of the saintly Nazarite. They were determined to protect such citizens from the insolence of a blood-stained house, and they laid their complaints before Agrippa II. This king had heard the defence of St. Paul before Festus, and was capable of taking a fairer view of Christianity than that which was deemed politic by his astute and unprincipled father. They also

---

[1] Acts xxii. 12.

complained to the new Procurator, who was now on his way from Alexandria to Jerusalem. The consequence was that Albinus (A.D. 63) wrote to Hanan a stern rebuke for his illegal violence, and Agrippa II. felt that he might, without danger to his own popularity, expel him from the High Priesthood, though he had only held it for three months.[1] We can see from this brief narrative that the cruelty of the younger Hanan was only part of a bold plan to restore the waning influence of the Sadducean priesthood. Those who, by informing against him, defeated his purpose and drove him from his office, were evidently Pharisees.[2] The Pharisees were never actuated by the same animosity against the Judæo-Christians as the Sadducees. Judaic Christianity leaned to the views of Pharisaism. Sadducees like the Beni-Hanan naturally hated it on this ground, and all the more because the many Pharisees who had by this time embraced the faith were believers in the Resurrection of Christ, and were therefore extreme opponents of the very negation which was most characteristic of the Sadducean sect. Hanan is perhaps the proud young priest, who, on reproaching his father for conformity to Pharisaic practices while he had lived all his life in the profession of Sadduceism, received the answer that only at the price of such hypocrisy could their priestly position be maintained at all.[3] If so, we see that he was exactly the sort of person who would have taken the initiative in a Sadducean conspiracy.

Hegesippus supplements the narrative of Josephus by giving a more detailed account of the martyr's death.[4] He says that James won over many of the Jews to Christianity by his testimony to Jesus as being the Door of the Sheepfold, the Way of Life, until the multitude of conversions aroused, as it had done twenty-five years earlier, the angry attention of the Scribes and Sanhedrists. They accordingly sent him a deputation from their "Seven Sects" to ask him, "Who is the Door of Jesus?"[5] He answered, "that Jesus was the Saviour;" and by this testimony he again won so many converts that a tumult arose, from the fear that all the people would be won over to look for the coming of Christ. Accordingly they once more sent him a deputation, acknowledging his "righteousness," and the reverence with which they regarded him, and the strong influence which he held over the people, but entreating him to stand upon the pinnacle of the Temple on the day of the Passover, and persuade "all the tribes" and the Gentiles "not to be led

---

[1] Joshua, son of Damnaeus, was appointed in his place, but was soon superseded by Joshua Ben Gamala, who bought the office by an enormous bribe, offered by his wife, Martha, a daughter of Boethus.
[2] Jos. *Antt.* xx. 9, § 1.
[3] *Tosefta Joma*, c. 1; Geiger, *Urschrift*, 112; Derenbourg, *Palest.* 104.
[4] Hegesippus wrote, he tells us, when Eleutherus was Bishop of Rome, A.D. 174—189 (Euseb. iv. 22).
[5] The phrase may mean "Which is the door of which Jesus spoke?" (John x. 7, 9), or "What is the Door which leads to Jesus?"

away concerning Jesus." The rest of the story may be told in the quaint style of the old writer itself:—

"The Scribes and Pharisees, then, who have been previously mentioned, set James on the pinnacle of the Temple, and cried to him and said, 'Just one! whom we ought all to obey, since the people is wandering after Jesus the Crucified, tell us, Who is the Door of Jesus?' And he answered in a loud voice, 'Why do ye ask me again about Jesus the Son of Man? He both sits in the heavens on the right hand of the Mighty Power, and He will come on the clouds of heaven.' And when many had been fully assured, and were glorifying God at the witness of James, and saying, 'Hosanna to the Son of David!' then again the same Scribes and Pharisees began to say to one another, 'We did wrong in affording such a testimony to Jesus. Come, let us go up and cast him down, that they may be afraid, and not believe him.' And they cried out, saying, 'Oh! oh! even the Just has gone astray!' and they fulfilled the Scripture written in Isaiah, 'Let us away with the Just, for he is inconvenient to us.' (Is. iii. 10?) Therefore they shall eat of the fruit of their own deeds. They went up, therefore, and flung down the Just, and said to one another, 'Let us stone James the Just.' And they began to stone him, since he did not die from being flung down, but turned and knelt on his knees, saying, 'I entreat Thee, O Lord God! O Father! forgive them, for they know not what they do.' But while they were thus stoning him, one of the Priests, of the sons of Rechab, a son of the Rechabites to whom Jeremiah the Prophet bears witness, cried out, saying, 'Cease! what are ye doing? The Righteous One is praying for you?' But one of them, one of the fullers, lifting up his club with which he used to beat out clothes, brought it down on the head of the Righteous One. So he bore witness; and they buried him on the spot, beside the Sanctuary.[1] He was a true witness to Jews and Greeks that Jesus is the Christ. Immediately afterwards Vespasian besieged them." Eusebius quotes Josephus for the statement that the destruction of Jerusalem fell on the Jews in punishment for his murder; but he exaggerates the remark in the *Antiquities*, unless he is quoting from passages of Josephus no longer extant.[2] The episcopal chair of St. James was, we are told, long preserved at Jerusalem as a relic.

Such is the story of Hegesippus, mixed up, no doubt, with legendary particulars, and consisting in part of a cento of Scripture phrases,[3] but

---

[1] *Ap.* Euseb. *H. E.* ii. 23 (quoting from the fifth book of the Hypomnemata). See, too, Epiphan. *Haer.* ii. 1 (where he quotes from Clemens Alexandrinus); lxxvii. 13, 14; Abdias, *Apost. Hist.* vi. 15. Kern's objection (*Tübingen Mag.*, 1835) to the genuineness of the Epistle of St. James, because Hegesippus does not happen to mention it, is surely insufficient.

[2] He says that Josephus, in his 18th book, "openly confesses that Jerusalem had been destroyed because of the murder of James the Apostle." Josephus, in *Antt.* xx. 9, § 1, only says that his murder offended the most equitable citizens.

[3] Matt. xxvi. 64; Luke xx. 21; Gal. ii. 6; Luke xxiii. 34.

bearing some marks of genuineness in the picture it presents of the estimation in which James was held, of his eminently prayerful character, of his courage, holiness, and devotion to the Law, and of the sympathy which he excited among those who like himself were partial Nazarites. And looking at his whole career in the light which was thrown upon it by later history, we cannot but see how merciful was the Providence which placed him in that sphere of labour, and made him what he was. If there was any voice to which even a remnant of Israel would listen, it was the voice of James. He venerated their Law, he observed their customs, he loved their nation, he attended their worship with scrupulous devotion. There are traces even in the Talmud of the deep influence which he exercised. There, among the chief *Minim*, or "heretics"—which is the ordinary Talmudic name for Christians—we constantly hear of a certain Jacob (*i.e.* James) of Kephar Zekania, who works supernatural cures in the name of Jesus son of Pandera. One of the stories about him is that Ben Dama, nephew of Rabbi Ishmael, was bitten by a serpent, and James coming to him, offered to cure him after the fashion of the Nazarenes. Rabbi Ishmael forbade any recourse to such methods. "Suffer me," said Ben Dama, "to prove from the Scripture that this is lawful;" but before his proof was ready he died. "Happy Ben Dama," said his uncle, "in that thy soul hath departed hence, and that thou hast not broken through the hedge of the wise," quoting Eccles. x. 8, "He who breaketh through a hedge a serpent shall bite him."[1] Another story of him is that he was met by Rabbi Eliezer in the street of Sepphoris, and gave to the Rabbi a Halacha, or legal decision, which pleased him, on Deut. xxiii. 19. But when Eliezer repeated this, he got into trouble by being accused of sympathy with the Christian heretics.[2] Whether these and other anecdotes have in them any truth or not, they at least show the importance of St. James's position in the traditional recollections of the Jews.

It was one of the wild legends of the Jews, which yet hid beneath it a meaning even deeper than they imagined, that before the city fell the Shechinah had gone to the Mount of Olives, and for three years had pleaded with the people of Jerusalem in vain. The Shechinah, the Metatron, the Divine Son, the effulgence of God's glory, had indeed pleaded and had vanished; but in the teaching of St. James there was still left the echo of that tender patriotism in which He had bewailed the obduracy of guilty Jerusalem. Yet even to this human voice of the fellow citizen whom they reverenced, and who had not kindled their burning hatred by any denunciation of the things wherein they trusted, they would not listen. When they murdered the just observer of the Law, they filled to the brim the cup of their iniquity. It was at about

---

[1] Midrash Koheleth, i. 8 (in Wünsche's *Biblioth. Rabbinica*, p. 15).
[2] See Wünsche, p. 14; Grätz, iv. 47; Derenbourg, *Palest.* 359. The chronological difficulties go for nothing in the looseness of the Talmud as to such matters.

this very time that a strange fanatic, who bore the common name of Jesus, appeared in Jerusalem, at the Feast of Tabernacles, and began to make the streets resound with the melancholy cry—

"Woe to the city! woe to the Temple! A voice from the east! A voice from the west! A voice from the four winds! A voice against Jerusalem and the Temple! A voice against bridegroom and bride! A voice against the whole people!"

Annoyed and alarmed by his cries, the people complained of him. The unresisting offender was secured and brought before the Procurator Albinus, but he would answer no question; even the horrible scourging to which he was subjected, until his bones were laid bare, wrung from his lips no other cry than "Woe, woe to Jerusalem!" Unable to extort any answer from him, they released him as a monomaniac; and every year for seven years, at the great yearly feasts, he traversed the city with his wailing cry, answering to no man either bad or good, but whether beaten or kindly treated uttering no word but "Woe!" At last, during the siege, he suddenly exclaimed, "Woe, woe to me also!" and a stone from a Roman catapult laid him dead.

The blood of St. James, shed by priests and Zealots, stained the Temple court at Jerusalem, in the year A.D. 63. Three years had not elapsed before the marble floor of the Temple swam with the blood of more than eight thousand Zealots, who stabbed each other in internecine massacre. Hanan, the prime mover in the martyrdom, perished miserably. He was seized by the Idumeans, murdered, and his corpse was flung out naked to dogs and beasts.[1] Six years had not elapsed before priests, swollen with hunger, were seen madly leaping into the altar flames.[2] Seven years had barely elapsed before city and Temple sank into charred and blood-stained heaps, and the place, the nation, the ritual of Judaism were for ever swept away.

"Though the mills of God grind slowly, yet they grind exceeding small;
Though in patience long He waiteth, yet He surely grindeth all."

---

[1] The eulogy which Josephus pronounces on the younger Hanan in his *Jewish War* (iv. 5, § 2), where he attributes to his death the precipitation of the ruin of Jerusalem, is quite inconsistent with the severe remarks which he applies to him in the *Antiquities* (xx. 9, § 1). But when he had any purpose to serve, Josephus was not in the least to be trusted.

[2] Hegesippus says that he was martyred the year before the siege of Jerusalem; but this does not agree with the date of the Procuratorship of Albinus, and the deposition from the Priesthood of the younger Hanan (Jos. *Antt.* xx. 9, § 1).

CHAPTER XXI.

CHARACTERISTICS OF THE EPISTLE OF ST. JAMES

Γίνεσθε δὲ ποιηταὶ λόγου.—Jas. i. 22.

Of the canonicity of the Epistle of St. James there can hardly be a reasonable doubt, and there is strong ground for believing it to be authentic. It is true that Origen is the first who ascribes it to St. James, and he only speaks of it as an Epistle "currently attributed to him."[1] Clemens of Alexandria, though he wrote on the Catholic Epistles, does not appear to have known it.[2] Tertullian, from his silence, seems either not to have known it, or not to have accepted it as genuine. It is not mentioned in the Muratorian Fragment. It is a curious fact that even in the pseudo-Clementines it is not directly appealed to. It is classed by Eusebius among the Antilegomena,[3] but he seems himself to have accepted it. Theodore of Mopsuestia rejected it. On the other hand, there can be little doubt, from the occurrence of parallels to its phraseology, that it was favourably known to Clemens of Rome, Hermas, Irenæus, and Hippolytus. Jerome vindicated its genuineness against the opinion that it was forged in the name of James.[4] It is quoted by Dionysius of Alexandria; and it has the important evidence of the Peshito in its favour. Thus, the Syrian Church received it early, though it was not till the fourth century that it was generally accepted by the Greek and Latin Churches. Nor was it till A.D. 397 that the Council of Carthage placed it in the Canon. On the other hand, the Jewish-Christian tendencies of the Epistle, and what have been called its Ebionising opinions, agree so thoroughly with all that we know of James and the Church of Jerusalem, that they form a very powerful argument from internal evidence in favour of its being a genuine work of the "Bishop" of Jerusalem. Suspicion has been thrown on it because of the good Greek in which it is written, and because of the absence of the essential doctrines of Christianity.[5] On the first difficulty I shall touch later. The second is rather a proof that the letter *is* authentic,

---

[1] Orig. *in Joann.* xix. If we could trust the translation of Rufinus (*e.g., Hom. in Gen.* xxvi. 18), in other parts of his commentaries he spoke of it as St. James's, and even called it "the Divine Epistle."

[2] Cassiodorus says that he wrote upon it, but "Jude" ought to be read for James (see Westcott, *On the Canon,* p. 353). Eusebius only says that Clemens in his *Outlines* commented even on disputed books: "I mean the Epistle of Jude, and the rest of the Catholic Epistles, and that of Barnabas," &c.

[3] νοθεύεται (Euseb. ii. 23).

[4] *De Virr. Illustr.* 2. It must, however, be admitted that Jerome's remark is somewhat vacillating.

[5] See Davidson's *Introd.* i. 303.

because otherwise, on this ground, and on the ground of its apparent contradiction of St. Paul, it would never have conquered the dogmatic prejudices which were an obstacle to its acceptance. The single fact that it was known to St. Peter, and had exercised a deep influence upon him, is enough to outweigh any deficiency of external evidence.[1]

In this Epistle, then, St. James has left us a precious heritage of his thoughts, a precious manual of all that was purest and loftiest in Jewish Christianity. Having passed into the Church through the portals of the Synagogue, and having exulted in joyous obedience to a glorious law,[2] the Hebraists could not believe with St. Paul that the Institutions of Sinai had fulfilled no loftier function than that of bringing home to the human heart the latent consciousness of sin. They thought that the abrogation of Mosaism would give a perilous licence to sinful passions. St. James also writes as one of those who clung fast to the prerogatives of Israel, and could not persuade themselves that the coming of the Jewish Messiah, so long expected, would have no other national effect than to deprive them of every exclusive privilege, and place them on the same level as the heathens from whom they had so grievously suffered. Further than this, his letter shows some alarm lest a subjective dogmatism should usurp the place of a practical activity, and lest phrases about faith should be accepted as an excuse, if not for Antinomian licence, at least for dreamy indifference to the duties of daily life. St. James keenly dreaded a falling asunder of knowledge and action.[3] His letter might seem at first sight to be the most direct antithesis to the Epistles of St. Paul to the Galatians and the Romans, and to reach no higher standpoint than that of an idealised Judaism which is deficient in the specific elements of Christianity. It does not even mention the word Gospel. The name of Jesus occurs in it but twice. Nothing is said in it of the work of Redemption. Even the rules of morality are enforced without any appeal to those specific Christian motives which give to Christian morality its glow and enthusiasm, and which occur so repeatedly in the Epistles of St. Paul, St. Peter, and St. John. "*Be ye doers of the word,*" he says, "*not hearers only.*"[4] "*Who is wise among you? Let him show forth his works with meekness of wisdom.*"[5] "*Adulterers and adulteresses, know ye not that the friendship of the world is enmity with God?*"[6] "*Take the prophets, my brethren, as an example of suffering and of patience.*"[7] "*Go to now, ye rich, weep and howl.*"[8] Is it possible to deny that there is a difference between the tone of these appeals and such as "*I have been crucified with Christ.*"[9] "*But I say walk in the Spirit.*"[10] "*The love of Christ constraineth us.*"[11] "*We were buried with Him by baptism unto death . . . so let us also walk in newness of life.*"[12] "*As he who called*

---

[1] See *supra*, p. 71.   [2] Ps. cxix. *passim*.   [3] Wiesinger, *Einl.* p. 42.
[4] i. 22.   [5] iii. 13.   [6] iv. 4.   [7] v. 5.   [8] v. 1.
[9] Gal. ii. 20.   [10] Gal. v. 16.   [11] 2 Cor. v. 14.   [12] Rom. vi. 4.

you is holy, so become ye holy."[1] *"This is the message which ye heard from the beginning, that we love one another."*[2] It was the presence of such peculiarities which made Luther take up his hasty, scornful, and superficial view of the Epistle. "On that account," he said, "the Epistle of St. James, compared with them (the Epistles of St. Paul), is a veritable straw-Epistle (*recht strohern*), for it lacks all evangelical character."[3] "This Epistle of James, although rejected by the ancients,[4] I praise and esteem good withal, because it setteth not forth any doctrine of man. . . . . But to give my opinion, yet without the prejudice of any one, I count it to be no Apostle's writing, and this is my reason: first, because, contrary to St. Paul's writings and all other Scriptures, it puts righteousness in works," on which account he thinks that its author was merely "some good, pious man," though in other places he seems to think that it was written by James the son of Zebedee.[5] It was, perhaps, hardly strange that Luther, who did not possess the clue by which alone the apparent contradictions to St. Paul could be explained, should have arrived at this opinion. To him the letter seemed to be in direct antagonism to the truth which had wrought his own conversion, and which became powerful in his hands for the overthrow of sacerdotal usurpation and the revival of religious faith. But this unfavourable opinion of the Epistle lingered on. It is found in the Magdeburg centuriators and in Ströbel, who said that, "no matter in what sense we take the Epistle, it is always in conflict with the remaining parts of Holy Writ." On similar grounds Erasmus, Cajetan, Grotius, and Wetstein, hesitated to accept it.[6] Such views are untenable, because they are onesided. We shall consider afterwards the alleged polemic against St. Paul; and in judging of the Epistle generally we must bear in mind its avowedly practical character, and the entire training of the writer and of those to whom it was addressed. The purpose for which it was written was to encourage the Jewish

---

[1] 1 Pet. i. 15.   [2] 1 John iii. 11.
[3] Preface to New Testament of 1524, p. 105.
[4] This is hardly a fair account of the history of the Epistle and its reception into the Canon.
[5] In 1519, he calls it "wholly inferior to the Apostolic majesty" (in the seventh Thesis against Eck); in 1520, "unworthy of an Apostolic spirit" (*De Captiv. Babylon.*). In the *Postills* he says it was written by no Apostle, and is "nowhere fully conformable to the true Apostolic character and manner, and to pure doctrine." In his preface to the Epistle in 1522 (*Werke*, xiv. 148), he speaks almost contemptuously. "He" (St. James), he says, "has aimed to refute those who relied on faith without works, *and is too weak for his task in mind, understanding, and words*, mutilates the Scriptures, and thus directly (*stracks*) contradicts Paul and all Scripture, seeking to accomplish by enforcing the law what the Apostles successfully effect by love. Therefore, I will not place his Epistle in my Bible among the proper leading books." Nor did he ever, as is sometimes asserted, retract these opinions. His *Table Talk* shows that he held them to the last, and considered St. James irreconcilable with St. Paul (*Colloq.* lxix. 4). See the quotation, *infra*, p. 355). Archdeacon Hare (*Mission of the Comforter*, ii. 815) rightly says that "Luther's words cannot always be weighed in jewellers' scales."
[6] The objections of Schleiermacher, De Wette, Reuss, Baur, Schwegler, Ritschl, Davidson, etc., are based on critical and other grounds.

Christians to the endurance of trial by stirring them up to a brighter energy of holy living. And in doing this he neither urges a slavish obedience nor a terrified anxiety. If he does not dwell, as assuredly he does not, on the specific Christian motives, he does not at any rate put in their place a ceremonial righteousness. His ideals are the ideals of truth and wisdom, not of accurate legality. The Law which he has in view is not the threatful law of Moses, which gendereth to bondage, but the royal Law, the perfect Law of liberty, the Law as it was set forth in the Sermon on the Mount. He is the representative, not of Judaism, but of Christian Judaism—that is, of Judaism in its transformation and transfiguration. A book may be in the highest sense Christian and religious without using the formulas of religion and Christianity. The Book of Esther is a Sacred book, a book of the inspired Canon, and a book justly valued, though it does not so much as mention the name of God. The bottom of the ocean is always presupposed as existent though it be neither visible nor alluded to. And, as we shall see later on, there are passages in the Epistle of St. James which involve the deepest truths of that Christian faith of which he avows himself a humble follower, although it was not his immediate object to develop the dogmatic side of Christianity at all. If some of the weightiest Christian doctrines are not touched upon, there are, on the other hand, more references to the discourses of Christ in this Epistle than in all the others put together.[1]

If we could be certain of the date of the Epistle, and of the characters whom St. James had chiefly in view, some light would doubtless be thrown on these peculiarities. But on these subjects we are unfortunately in doubt. Amid the differing opinions respecting the date, I side with those who look upon the Epistle as one of the later, not as perhaps the earliest, in the Canon. One or two facts seem to point in this direction. On the one hand, the Epistle could not have been written after the year A.D. 63, because in that year St. James was martyred. On the other hand, the condition and wide dissemination of the Churches to which it is addressed; the prevalence of the *name* Christ instead of the *title* "the Christ";[2] the growth of respect for persons as shown in distinction of seats; the sense of delay in the Second Coming,[3] and other circumstances, make it necessary to assume that many years had elapsed since the Day of Pentecost. Further, it seems probable that some of St. James's allusions may find their explanation in a state of political excitement, caused by hopes and fears which, perhaps, within a year or two of the time when it was written, broke out in the wild scenes of the Jewish revolt. Lastly, it seems impossible to deny that although St. James *may* have written his arguments about faith and works[4] without having read what had

---

[1] See Döllinger, *First Age of the Church*, p. 107 (tr. Oxenham).
[2] ii. 7. [3] v. 7, 8. [4] ii. 21—26.

been written on the same subject by St. Paul,[1] and in the Epistle to the Hebrews, still his language finds its most reasonable explanation in the supposition that he is striving to remove the dangerous inferences to which St. Paul's doctrine of justification by faith was liable when it was wrested by the unlearned and the ignorant.[2] If so, the Epistle cannot have been written more than a year or two before St. James's death, since the date of the Epistle to the Galatians is A.D. 57, and that of the Epistle to the Romans A.D. 58. It has been urged against this conclusion that if it had been written later than the so-called "Council of Jerusalem" in A.D. 50, it must have contained references to the great dispute about the obligations of circumcision. But the circumcision question, fiercely as it was debated at the time, was speedily forgotten; and it must be borne in mind that St. James is writing exclusively to Jews. Again, it has been urged that the trials to which he alludes must have been the persecutions at Jerusalem, in which Saul and Herod Agrippa I. were respectively the chief movers. But persecution in one form or other was the chronic trial of Jewish as well as of other Christians. To refer to the existence of deep poverty as a sign that the Epistle was written about the time of the general famine of A.D. 44 is to rely on a very shadowy argument, since famines at this period were by no means unfrequent, and poverty was the permanent condition of the saints at Jerusalem. I therefore disagree with the views of Neander, Alford, and Dr. Plumptre, who argue for the early date; and I agree with those of De Wette, Bishop Wordsworth, and many others, who fix the date of the Epistle about the year A.D. 61.[3]

If, however, the date of the Epistle be uncertain, we have no uncertainty about the place where it was written. That is undeniably Jerusalem. When once settled in that city, St. James, with the natural stationariness of the Oriental, seems never to have left it. Its Temple and ritual would have had for him a strong attraction. The notion of writing the Epistle may have partly originated from the

---

[1] It is not necessary to assume in consequence that "Apostolical Epistles were transcribed by the hundred and circulated broadcast"; or that "copies of what was written for Rome or Galatia would be at once despatched by a special courier to the Bishop of Jerusalem" (Plumptre, p. 42). The Church of Jerusalem was kept well acquainted with the movements and tenets of St. Paul, and any of the Passover pilgrims from Asia Minor might have informed James of the drift of the Apostle's arguments, and of some of his more striking expressions, even if he could not procure a copy of a complete Epistle.

[2] Baur says (*Ch. Hist.* p. 128), "It is impossible to deny that the Epistle of James presupposes the Pauline doctrine of justification." He admits that "it may not be aimed directly against the Apostle himself," but says that, if so, "its tendency is distinctly anti-Pauline." Nevertheless, both St. Paul and St. James might, in the sense in which they were alone intended, have interchanged each other's apparently antagonistic formulæ. See *infra*, pp. 356—359.

[3] Eusebius (*H. E.* ii. 23; iii. 11) gives A.D. 69 as the date of St. James's death, apparently because Hegesippus said that the siege happened "*immediately*" afterwards." But if the narrative of Josephus is correct, St. James could not have been killed *later* than A.D. 63. This is the date given by Eusebius in his *Chronicon*.

circumstance that the Jewish high priest sent missives from the Holy City, which were received with profound respect throughout the length and breadth of the Dispersion. Similarly, the first bishop of the metropolis of Christianity was one to whom every Jewish Church might naturally look for advice and consolation. The physical allusions in the Epistle to oil, and wine, and figs, to salt and bitter springs, to the Kauson, or burning wind of Palestine, and, above all, to the former and the latter rain, show that the letter was despatched from Jerusalem. Some have supposed that it was written at Joppa; but this is only a precarious inference from the allusion to the life of the shore and the traffic in the harbour, the fish and the wonders of the sea.[1] There can, at any rate, be no doubt that it emanated from Palestine.

In this Palestinian origin I see an explanation of some of the phenomena of the Epistle. We see, for instance, why it is that St. James seems to be speaking sometimes to Jews and sometimes to Christians, sometimes to all the Churches of the Dispersion and sometimes almost exclusively to the Churches of Judæa. The difficulty vanishes when we remember the position of the writer. He is addressing "the Twelve Tribes of the Dispersion." It was a sufficiently wide range—wider than that of any one of the Epistles. It included Parthians, and Medes, and Elamites, dwellers in Cappadocia, Galatia, Pontus, Asia, Phrygia, Pamphylia, Egypt, the parts of Libya about Cyrene, strangers at Rome, Cretes and Arabians, Jews and proselytes.[2] But of the varying conditions of these widely-scattered communities he could know almost nothing. He could have no information about them except such as he might now and then derive from the general talk of some Passover pilgrim. He addresses them, indeed, as a "Christian high priest wearing the golden mitre" might have done, or as a sort of ideal *Resh Galûtha*, or "Prince of the Captivity," might have addressed his fellow-countrymen in later days.[3] But he could only speak on topics which he might infer to be necessary because he saw that they were necessary for the Syrian Churches, with whose trials and temptations he had an exclusive familiarity. His remarks, for instance, about the conduct of the rich, and the bearing of the poor towards them, have created the greatest perplexity. These rich men, whose arrogance is described as so outrageous, were they Jews, Christians, or Gentiles? I think that I find an explanation of his allusions in conduct which he saw daily taking place under his own eyes. The Jewish Church at Jerusalem was at that time governed by a clique of aristocratic Sadducees. They were men of immense

---

[1] James i. 6; iii. 4; iv. 13 (Hausrath, *N. Test. Zeitg.* 1, § 5).
[2] Acts ii. 9—12. The reader will find a sketch of the character of the Jewish Dispersion, and of the events which led to it, in my *Life of St. Paul*, i. pp. 115—125.
[3] The Jews of the Dispersion in Babylonia were called "the Gola," or "Deportation," and they enjoyed a sort of independence under a ruler of their own choice known as the *Resh Galûtha*. See on his office, Etheridge, *Hebr. Lit.* 151, *seq.*

wealth, which they increased by violent and dishonest exactions. Profoundly hated by the people, they were yet kept secure in their positions by the close understanding which they usually preserved with the Herods and the Romans. Outwardly, therefore, they were treated with abject reverence, and in spite of the curses, not loud but deep, which were secretly uttered against them, and which were soon to burst in vengeance upon their heads, they were able to exercise an almost uncontrolled authority. When we read side by side the denunciations hurled by St. James against the tyrannous greed and cruel insolence of the rich, and the eight-fold and thrice-repeated curse of the Talmud[1] against the blood-stained and worldly hierarchs who disgraced the mitre of Aaron, it will be seen, I think, that these passages of the Epistle sprang, at least in part, from the indignation with which the Christian bishop had witnessed the conduct of the detested Boethusim and Beni-Hanan. To their vengeance he at last succumbed, and under their avarice and worldliness the Jews of that day vainly struggled. St. James says:—

"Do not rich men oppress you, and draw you before the judgment seats? Do they not blaspheme that worthy name by the which ye are called?"[2]

And again—

"Go to now, ye rich men; weep and howl for the miseries that shall come upon you. . . . Behold the hire of the labourers which have reaped down your fields, which is of you kept back by fraud, crieth. . . . Ye have lived in pleasure in the earth, and been wanton; ye have nourished your hearts as in a day of slaughter; ye have condemned and killed the just, and he doth not resist you."[3]

It is obvious that these remarks could not apply to the treatment of the poor by the rich throughout all the Ghettos and Christian communities of the world. In the infant Churches, during the whole of the first century, there were "not many rich."[4] The few wealthy and noble Gentiles who were converted were so far from being able to wield such a tyranny as St. James describes, that, in the gatherings of the converts they might be under the spiritual supervision of presbyters and "bishops" who occupied no higher earthly rank than that of slaves. Moreover, no Christian could have dared to "blaspheme"—that is, to speak injuriously of the name of "Christian" or of "Christ." But St. James is not thinking exclusively of Christian communities. He is writing of things which were on the horizon of his daily life. Read what the Talmudists say of the priestly families by which he was surrounded, and his allusions at once become explicable. For thus in the tract Yoma (f. 9, a) we find:—

"What is meant by Ps. x. 27, 'The fear of the Lord prolongeth days, but the years of the wicked shall be shortened'? The first clause

---

[1] Pesachim, 57, a; Tosefta Menachoth; Derenbourg, Palest. 233; Geiger, Urschrift, 118.
[2] Jas. ii. 6.
[3] v. 1—6.
[4] 1 Cor. i. 26.

alludes to the 410 years of the first Temple, during which period there were but eighteen high priests. But '*the years of the wicked shall be shortened*' is illustrated by the fact that during the 426 years of the second Temple there were more than 300 high priests in succession. So that deducting the forty years of Simon the Righteous, and the eighty of Rabbi Jochanan, and the ten of Ishmael Ben Phabi, it is evident that not one of the remaining high priests lived to hold office for a whole year."[1] The supposed fact is unhistorical, but the remark shows in what low estimation these later hierarchs were held.

Again, in the tract Pesachim (57, *a*) we find one of several repetitions of the famous malediction on those priestly families:—

> "Woe unto the family of Boethus,
> Woe to their bludgeons!
> Woe to the house of Hanan,
> Woe to their viper hissings!
> Woe to the family of Canthera,
> Woe to their libels!
> Woe to the family of Ishmael Ben-Phabi,
> Woe to their blows with the fist!

"They are themselves chief priests, their sons are treasurers, their sons-in-law captains of the Temple, and their servants strike the people with their staves."

Again, we are told that the Vestibule of the Temple uttered four cries—"Depart hence, sons of Eli, who defile the Temple of the Eternal! Depart, Issachar of Kephar Barkaï, who only carest for self, and profanest the victims consecrated to Heaven!" And again: "Open, ye gates, let Ishmael Ben Phabi enter, the disciple of Phinehas (son of Eli), to do the duties of high priest; open, let John, son of Nebedæus, enter, the disciple of gluttons, to gorge himself with victims."[2]

Tales of these priests—their luxury, their gluttony, their simony, their avarice, their atheism—long lingered in the hearts of the people. They told how this Issachar, in his fastidious insolence, had had silk gloves made to prevent the soiling of his hands while he sacrificed; of the calves which John, son of Nebedæus had devoured, and the tuns of wine which he had drunk; how Martha, daughter of Boethus, had bought the priesthood for her husband Joshua, son of Gamala, for two bushels of gold denarii, and had carpets spread from her house to the Temple when she went to see him sacrifice; how the house of Hanan deliberately raised the price of doves, in order to make gain out of the poor, till they were liberated from this tyranny by Gamaliel, the grandson of Hillel; how Eliezer Ben Charsom went to the Temple in a robe which had cost 20,000 minæ, and which was so transparent that the other priests forbade him to wear it.[3] Even Josephus bears witness to

---

[1] Hershon, *Talm. Miscell.* p. 107. All insolent priests were supposed to be descended from Pashur, the son of Immer. Kiddushin, f. 70 *b*. (id. p. 244).
[2] Pesachim, *l.c.*, and Kerithoth, 28, *a*.
[3] Yoma 35, *b*. See Raphall, *Hist. of Jews,* ii. 370; Grätz, *Gesch. de Juden,* iii. 321; Derenbourg, *Palest.* p. 233, *seqq.*, and my *Life of Christ,* ii. 330—342, where the original references are given.

the ruthless extortion and cruelty with which they defrauded the inferior priests of their dues until they were almost reduced to the verge of starvation.[1] In the section which follows his account of the murder of James, he says that the greedy procurator Albinus cultivated the friendship of Joshua, the high priest, and the other chief priests, and joined with them in robbing the threshing-floors by violence, and that for this reason some of the priests died from inability to recover the tithes which were their sole means of sustenance.

But, while he thus alluded to the state of things in Jerusalem, there can be no doubt that St. James mainly intended to address Christians. Otherwise he would have added some explanation of his simple title, "James, a servant of God and of the Lord Jesus Christ."[2] Nor could he otherwise have said, "My brethren, have not. the faith of our Lord Jesus Christ, the Lord of Glory, with respect of persons;"[3] nor again, "Be patient, therefore, brethren, unto the coming of the Lord."[4] How is it, then, that the Epistle contains none of the rich and advanced Christology of many other Epistles? that the allusions to *specific* Christian doctrine and motive are so rare? How is it that the word "gospel" does not once occur in it? that Christianity is still viewed under the aspect of Law, though truly of an idealised and royal Law? that the general tone of appeal is much more like that of John the Baptist than that of St. Paul, St. Peter, and St. John? How is it that next to the moral parts of the Sermon on the Mount, St. James is most frequent in his references to books of apocryphal wisdom, written by unconverted Jews? How is it that there are whole sections which might have been written by an Epictetus or a Marcus Aurelius? I think that the reason, and the only reason, which can be given, is that while he is *writing* in the first instance to Christians, he is *thinking* to a great extent of Jews. The Christians were few, the Jews many. He has begun by saying that he is writing to the Twelve Tribes of the Dispersion, and he meant his letter to be delivered primarily to the Christians among them. But the Christians whom he has in view were *also* Jews. He does not even allude to the Gentiles. The converts whom he addresses had never thought of deserting the ceremonies, or abandoning what they imagined to be the exclusive privileges of the chosen seed.[5] And he was himself a Jew, living among Jews, and living in all respects as a Jew of the strictest orthodoxy, reverenced even by many who regarded his belief in Christ as a mere aberration—a mere excrescence on his Judaic devotion. It was from Jews, not from Christians—it was because of accuracy in

---

[1] Jos. *Antt.* xx. 8, § 8; 9, § 2. [2] i. 1. [3] ii. 1.
[4] v. 7. See other distinctively Christian allusions in i. 18 : "Of His own will begat He us by the word of truth;" ii. 7 : "Do they not blaspheme that worthy name by which ye are called?" v. 6 : "Ye condemned and killed the Just;" v. 14 : "Anointing him with oil in the name of the Lord."
[5] We have observed the same phenomena of a sort of dual consciousness as to the readers whom he is addressing in St. Paul's Epistle to the Romans. See *Life and Work of St. Paul*, ii. 168, 169.

Jewish observances, not for strictness of Christian morality—that he had received the surname of "the Just." Let it be borne in mind that, alike amid Jews and Gentiles, the distinction between the Jew and the Christian was infinitely less wide in the first generation after Christ's death than it afterwards became. St. Paul, even after he had written the Epistles to the Romans and Galatians, did not hesitate to exclaim before the assembled Sanhedrin, "Brethren, I am a Pharisee, a son of Pharisees," and to reduce the whole question between him and them to a question of believing in the Resurrection. As a Nazarite, as an heir of David, as having priestly blood in his veins, as one whose faithfulness was known to all the dwellers in Jerusalem, and to all who visited it, as a Jew who walked in all the commandments and ordinances of the Law blameless, James might well consider it his duty to address words of warning and exhortation, primarily indeed to the Christian Churches of Judæa, but through them to all his countrymen. To him the Church is still not only Ecclesia (v. 14), but the Synagogue (ii. 2)— a word which even the writer of the Epistle to the Hebrews seems purposely to avoid, but which was used exclusively by the Ebionites.[1] When alluding to the object of faith, he speaks not of Christ, but of "One God" (ii. 19). He warns against swearing by the heaven and by the earth (v. 12), which we know from the Gospels (Matt. v. 33) to have been common formulæ of Jewish adjuration. He saw in Jews the catechumens of Christianity, and in Christians the ideal Jews. The fact is, that alike in the real and in the traditional St. James we see the traces of views which distinguished three parties of Jewish Christians in the first century, and which continued to exist in three classes of Jewish Christians in the second. Like St. Paul and like the Nazarenes, he did not insist on the observance of Mosaism by the Gentiles, yet, like the milder Ebionites, he appears to have leaned—or, at any rate, his followers leaned—to the belief that even for Gentiles they might be of great importance; and, like the Essene or ascetic Judaists, he personally adopted the rigid practices which may have been to him a valuable training in self-discipline, but which the Colossian and other heretics regarded as constituting a legal righteousness. To us the name "Jewish Christian" may seem almost an oxymoron—a juxtaposition of contrary terms. We see with St. Paul—whose opinions had been the result of special Divine training—that between the bondage of ceremonialism and the freedom of Christianity—between the righteousness of legal ordinances and justification by faith—there is a profound antithesis. But it was impossible that it could wear this aspect to the early Christians. We view the matter after nineteen centuries of Christian experience; they were the immediate heirs of nineteen centuries of Jewish history.

But while in the first line of his letter St. James testifies to his own

---

[1] Epiphan. *Haer.* xxx. 18.

faith, he must have known that his words would be received with respect by genuine Hebrews, and that it would be useless to enforce the lessons which he wished to impress upon *all* his countrymen by appeals distinctively Christian. His whole nation was in a state of wild tumult; swayed by passion and worldliness; indulging in the fierce language of hatred, fanaticism, and conceit; becoming godless in their tone of thought; relying on the orthodoxy of Monotheism; careless and selfish in the duties of life; forgetful of the omnipotence of prayer. And the Christians whom he is addressing, being Jews, participated in these dangers. He wished to make the Christians better Christians, to teach them a truer wisdom, a purer morality. He wished to make them better Christians by making them better Israelites; and he wished to convert the Israelites into being worthier members of the commonwealth of Israel before he could win them to become heirs of the covenant of the better promise. If we bear these circumstances in mind, if we also remember that his letter is not intended for a dogmatic treatise, but for the moral exhortation of one to whom the Law means the rule of life as Jesus had taught it, we shall be better able to judge of the rashness which has only condemned or slighted this Epistle because it has failed to understand the true purpose of the writer.

Again, to grasp the full meaning of St. James, we must appreciate the passionate earnestness of one whose ideal is too stern to admit of any compromise with the aims and pleasures of the world.

i. Critics have spoken of the *Essenism and the Ebionism* of the Epistle. But although "help and mercy" were special duties of the Essene, and though St. James "writes mercy upon his flag," there is no trace that he was an Essene. Doubtless he sympathised with many of the views of that singular body. Any Essene might have spoken just as St. James does about oaths, and riches, and merchandise, and the virtue of silence, and the duty of checking wrath;[1] but so might any Christian who had studied, as St. James had studied, the precepts of the Sermon on the Mount. The later Ebionites represented Judaism when it had passed into heresy. The views and tendencies of the early Christians in Jerusalem, before they had been modified by the teachings of experience, were only Ebionite in a sense perfectly innocent. In these views and tendencies St. James shared, but he did not fall into the extravagant exaggeration by which they were subsequently caricatured.

ii. Some, again, have seen in the expressions of St. James an *Orphic colouring;* but of this we require much stronger proof than the phrases "the engrafted word," or "the wheel of being" (iii. 6), even though those phrases may be illustrated by parallels in the writings of Pytha-

---
[1] Comp. Jas. i. 19; ii. 5, 13; iv. 13; v. 12; with Josephus, *Bell. Jud.* II. 8, 6, and Philo, *Quod omnis prob. lib.*, § 12 (Hilgenfeld, *Einleit.* p. 539).

goreans.[1] Undoubtedly, however, we find a peculiarity of the Epistle in the extreme frequency of the parallels between its language and that of other writers. These are so numerous that I have no space to write them out at length, but no careful reader can entirely miss them.[2] They show how strong was the originality which could absorb influences from many different sources, and yet maintain its own perfect independence. In this respect the Epistle of St. James differs remarkably from the Epistle of St. Clemens of Rome. St. James, even while he borrows alike from Jewish prophets and from Alexandrian theosophists, fuses their language into a manifesto of Judaic Christianity by the heat and vehemence of his own individuality. He strikes lightning into all he borrows. St. Clemens is far more passively receptive. He has the amiable and conciliatory catholicity which leads him to adopt the moral teaching of all schools; but he has none of the individual force which might have enabled him to infuse into what he has borrowed an individual force.

iii. The *style* of St. James, as compared with his tone of thought, presents the singular combination of pure, eloquent, and even rhythmical Greek, with the prophetic vehemence and fiery sternness of the Hebrew prophet. The purity of the Greek idiom has been made a ground for doubting the genuineness of the Epistle.[3] But the objection is without weight. Palestine—even Galilee—was in those days bilingual. James had probably spoken Greek from his birth. He would therefore find no difficulty in writing in that language, and his natural aptitude may have given him a better style than that of many of his countrymen.[4] But even if not, what difficulty is there in the supposition that St. James, like St. Peter, employed an "interpreter,"[5] or adopted the common plan of submitting his manuscript to the revision of some accomplished Hellenist? The thoughts, the order of them, and the tone

---

[1] The hexameter in i. 17 (where the word δώρημα is unknown to the N. T. in this sense), and the expression "Father of lights" have been suspected of being borrowed from Alexandrian sources. For the latter see Dan. viii. 10.

[2] Every chapter will furnish parallels to passages in the *Sermon on the Mount* (see Matt. v. 3, 4, 10—12, 22, 24, 33—37, 48; vi. 14, 15, 19, 24; vii. 1—5, 7—12, 21—23) and the eschatological discourse (Mark xiii. 7, 9, 29, 32). For the very remarkable and close parallels to the *Book of Ecclesiasticus*, comp. i. 5, 8—12, 13, 19, 23, 25; iii. 5, 6, respectively with Ecclus. xx. 15; xli. 22; i. 28; xv. 11; v. 11; xx. 7; xii. 11; xiv. 23; xxviii. 10, 19 (especially in the Greek). For parallels to the *Book of Wisdom*, comp. Jas. i. 10, 11, 17, 20; ii. 21; iv. 14; v. 1—6, with Wisdom ii. 8; v. 8; vii. 17—20; xii. 16; x. 5; v. 9—14; ii. 1—24. For parallels to the *Book of Proverbs*, comp. i. 5, 6, 12, 19, 21; iii. 5; iv. 6; v. 20, respectively with Prov. iii. 5, 6; xxiii. 34; iii. 11; Eccl. v. 2; Prov. xxx. 12; xvi. 27; iii. 34; x. 12. Many more might be added, but the student who will verify these references for himself will see how fully the points mentioned in the text are proved.

[3] *E g.*, De Wette asks, How could James write such good Greek?

[4] Incomparably better, for instance, than that of St. John in the Apocalypse.

[5] St. Mark and a certain Glaucias are both mentioned as "interpreters" of St. Peter. Of the latter—claimed as an authority by the Basilidians—nothing is known; but St. Mark may have acted as "interpreter" to St. Peter rather when he needed Latin at Rome than when he wrote in Greek.

in which they are expressed, are exactly such as we should have expected, from all that we know of the writer. The *form* of expression may easily have been corrected by any literary member of the Church of Jerusalem. But the accent of authority, the noble sternness, the demand for unwavering allegiance to the laws of God—even the poetic parallelisms[1]—are all his own. When Schleiermacher speaks of "much bombast" in the Epistle, and describes the style as being "in part ornate, in part clumsy," it is because he criticises it from a wrong standpoint. It is like Voltaire criticising Æschylus or Shakspeare. It is due to the application of Hellenic canons to Semitic genius. The style of St. James is formed on the Hebrew prophets, as his thoughts are influenced by the Hebrew gnomologists. He has nothing of the Pauline method of dialectic; he is never swept away, like St. Paul, by the tide of his own impassioned feeling. His moral earnestness glows with the steady light of a furnace, never rushes with the uncontrolled force of a conflagration. The groups of thoughts follow each other in distinct sections, which never interlace each other, and have little or no logical connexion or systematic advance. He plunges *in medias res* with each new topic; says first in the plainest and most straightforward manner exactly what he means to say, and enforces it afterwards with strong diction, passionate ejaculations, rapid interrogatives, and graphic similitudes. He generally begins mildly, and with a use of the word "brethren," but as he dwells on the point his words seem to grow incandescent with the writer's vehemence.[2] In many respects his style resembles that of a fiery prophetic oration rather than of a letter. The sententious form is the expression of a practical energy which will tolerate no opposition. The changes—often apparently abrupt—from one topic to another; short sentences, which seem to quiver in the mind of the hearer from the swiftness with which they had been launched forth; the sweeping reproofs, sometimes unconnected by conjunctions,[3] sometimes emphasised by many conjunctions;[4] the manner in which the phrases seem to catch fire as the writer proceeds; the vivid freshness and picturesque energy of the expressions;[5]— all make us fancy that we are listening to some great harangue which has for its theme the rebuke of sin and the exhortation to righteousness, in order to avert the awfulness of some imminent crisis. The power of his style consists in the impression which it leaves of the burning sincerity and lofty character of the author.

iv. For these reasons it is almost impossible to write an *analysis* of the Epistle. The analysis is only a catalogue of the subjects with which

---

[1] Bishop Jebb, *Sacred Literat.* p. 273.
[2] As specimens of his method in these respects see ii. 1—13; iv. 11, 12.
[3] Asyndeton, or absence of conjunctions, Jas. v. 3—6.
[4] Polysyndeton, or multiplicity of conjunctions, Jas. iv. 13.
[5] What the ancient critics call δεινότης. St. James is a perfect autocrat in the use of words. He abounds in *hapax legomena*, or expressions either not found elsewhere or not in the New Testament. These are mentioned in the notes.

it deals.[1] Writing to those who are suffering trials, he exhorts them to endurance, that they may lack nothing (i. 1—4). But if they lack wisdom, they must ask God for it, and desire it with whole-heartedness (5—8). The enemy of whole-heartedness is often worldly wealth, and he therefore tells them how blessed poverty may be, and how transitory are riches (9—11). Since poverty is in itself a trial, he shows the blessedness of enduring the trials which come from God. But there are trials which, while they come in the semblance of trials from God, have their origin in lust and their end death (12—15). It is only the good and perfect gifts which come from God; above all, the gift of our birth by the Word of Truth (16—18). Let them in meekness and in purity live worthily of that Word of Truth (19—21); let them be doers, and not mere hearers of it (22—25); let them learn to distinguish between external service and the true ritual of loving unselfishness (26, 27).

Then passing to some of their special national faults, he first sternly rebukes the respect of persons, which was contrary to Christ's ideal, and a sin against the perfect law of liberty (ii. 1—13). It is, perhaps, because he saw the origin of this selfish arrogance and abject servility in the reliance which they placed on a nominal orthodoxy, that he enters into the question about faith and works, to show that the former, in his sense of the word, is dead, and therefore valueless without the latter (14—26).

Then he powerfully warns them against the sins of the tongue in passion and controversy (iii. 1—12); and, to show that the loudest and angriest talker is not therefore in the right, he draws a contrast between true and false wisdom (13—18).

The source of the evils on which he has been dwelling is the unbridled lust which springs from worldliness. They need humility, and the determination to fight against sin, and sincere repentance (iv. 1—10), which will show itself in an avoidance of evil speaking (11, 12), and in a deeper sense that their life is wholly in God's disposing hands (13—17).

---

[1] Ewald arranges it in *seven* divisions, followed by *three* shorter paragraphs :—
i. 2—18. On trials.
i. 19—27. How we ought to hear and do God's Word.
ii. 1—13. Right behaviour in general.
ii. 14—26. The relation between Faith and Works.
iii. 1—18. Control of the tongue is true wisdom.
iv. 1—12. The evils of strife.
iv. 13—v. 11. Perils of the rich, and duty of endurance with reference to the coming of Christ.
(i.) v. 12. The sinfulness of needless oaths.
(ii.) v. 13—18. The power of prayer, especially in sickness.
(iii.) v. 19, 20. The blessing of converting others.
The reader will perhaps think some of the divisions somewhat artificial, especially as Ewald himself describes them. But there is nothing surprising in the general fact that a Jewish Christian should arrange his work with some reference to numerical symmetry; and Ewald points out that the number *three* prevails in ii. 19, iii. 15, and the number *seven* in iii. 17.

After this he bursts into a strong denunciation of the rich who live in pride, oppression, and self-indulgence (v. 1—6), while he comforts the poor, and counsels them to patience (7—11). Then he warns against careless oaths (12), gives counsels for the time of sickness (13—15), advises mutual confession of sins (16), dwells once more on the efficacy of prayer, as shown in the example of Elijah (16—20), and ends somewhat abruptly with a weighty declaration of the blessedness of converting others.

v. If it be asked what is the one predominant thought in the Epistle, its one idea and motive, the answer seems to be neither (as some have supposed) the blessedness of enduring temptation—though this is very prominent in it;[1] nor a polemic against mistaken impressions respecting justification by faith, though that occupies an important section;[2] nor an Ebionising exaltation of the poor over the rich, though the rich are sternly warned;[3] nor a contrast between the friendship of the world and the enmity of God.[4] Each of these topics has its own weight and importance, but to bring any of them into *exclusive* prominence is to confuse the general with the special. The general object, as is shown again and again, is to impress the conviction that Christian faithfulness must express itself in the energy and action of loving service.[5] "Temptations," indeed, occupy a large share in his thoughts, but he wished his readers to try against them the "expulsive power of good affections." The ritualism of active love and earnestness in prayer are with him the means of perfection.[6]

vi. It is this object which gives to the Epistle its controversial aspect. St. Paul says that a man is justified by faith; St. James, that he is justified by works; but St. James is using the word "faith" from the standpoint of Jewish realism, not of Pauline ideality. With both of these Apostles the Law is an inward, not an outward thing; a principle of liberty, not a yoke of bondage; a word of truth; a living impulse of fruitful activity implanted in man.[7] Seeing the danger of doctrinal formalism, St. James writes to counteract its unpractical tendencies, and to furnish us—from the standpoint, indeed, of Jewish Christianity, but still of an enlightened, liberal, and spiritualised form of it—the delineation of the Christian as he ought to be, "as a perfect man in the perfection of the Christian life, which can only be properly conceived as a perfect work." And from this point of view his letter was

---

[1] Jas. i. 3 and 4, ὑπομονή; 12, μακάριος ἀνήρ, ὅς ὑπομένει; v. 7, μακροθυμήσατε οὖν, ἀδελφοί . . . μακροθυμῶν; 8, μακροθυμήσατε καὶ ὑμεῖς; 10, ὑπόδειγμα λάβετε . . . τῆς μακροθυμίας; 11, ὑπομένοντας.

[2] ii. 10—26.

[3] ii. 1—7; iv. 1—10; v. 1—6.

[4] iv. 4, 5 (1 J. ii. 15—17), and he opposes special forms of worldliness in i. 2—15; ii. 1- 4; iii. 1—18; iv. 13, 14.

[5] i. 4, 22; ii. 14—26; iii. 13—17; iv. 17; etc.

[6] St. James dwells on this word, i. 3, 25; iii. 2; v. 4; "Tout dans l'écriture est l'idéal" (Ad. Monod). He speaks of prayer in i. 5; iv. 2, 3, 8; v. 13—18.

[7] λόγος ἔμφυτος. Jas. i. 21.

a valuable contribution to the formation of a Catholic Christianity. There is nothing harshly intended in its statement of the counter-aspect of the truth which St. Paul had proclaimed. St. Paul would himself have rebutted the one-sided distortion of his views; and he who opposes one-sided tendencies always does a useful work. It is a duty of Catholic Christianity to adjust one truth with another, and to place apparent contraries in their position of proper equilibrium.[1] It is inevitable—it is even desirable—that men should approach truth from many points of view. We can only hope to gain completeness of vision by combining their separate results. It is certain that we ourselves shall be more inclined, by temperament and training, to dwell on one aspect of truth than we shall on others. Yet it is not therefore necessary that we should become party men. It is possible to insist upon party truths without being tainted by party spirit. There existed at least three marked parties in the early Christian Church—the parties of Jewish, of Alexandrian, and of Pauline Christianity. There were many Christians who would not identify themselves with any of these parties, but who aimed at being many-sided, conciliatory, catholic. Now St. James stood at the head of the party of Jewish Christians, though his followers thrust him more prominently into this position than he would have himself desired.[2] But if we would see the depth of difference which separates him from the Jewish Christians to whom the party-view was everything, and the common Christianity was, by comparison, as nothing, we shall be able to judge of it by reading his Epistle side by side with the poisonous innuendoes and rancorous calumnies of the pseudo-Clementines. *Their* polemic consisted in secretly maligning the views and character of the Apostle of the Gentiles. The polemic of St. James issued in the delineation of the moral character of a Christian man. The party controversialists only fostered mutual hatred and opposition; St. James drew so noble a picture of Christian faithfulness that, as has well been said, "a Church which lived in sincere accordance with his lessons would in no respect dishonour the Christian name."

In proceeding to examine the Epistle of St. James, we shall do so with deeper interest if we bear in mind that it is yet another appeal of a great Christian writer to Jews and Jewish Christians shortly before the final destruction of their separate nationality. St. Paul had shown them the eternal superiority of the new to the old covenant. St. Peter had shown them how Christianity was the true kingdom, the royal priesthood, the theocratic inheritance. Apollos, in the Epistle to the Hebrews, had furnished them with a masterly proof that Christians had the true priesthood, which could alone admit any man into the heavenly sanctuary. St. James calls them to obey the royal Law, the law of

---

[1] See the few but weighty remarks of Baur, *Ch. Hist.* pp. 128—130, though he unfortunately denies the genuineness of the Epistle.
[2] Acts xv. 24, "to whom we gave no such commandment."

liberty. Thus they had been shown by St. Paul and Apollos that the rejection of Christianity, or apostasy from it, was the rejection of, or apostasy from, grace to sin—from the substance to the shadow. St. Peter had warned them against murmuring and faithless impatience; St. James sternly sets before them the perils of insincerity and double-mindedness. And the common message of all is that Jews who had embraced the faith of Christ should hope and endure, and be faithful unto the end.

vii. In one respect the Epistle is unique. Alone of the twenty Epistles of the New Testament, it begins with no benediction, and ends with no message of peace.[1] We might, perhaps, see in this fact a reflexion of the unbending character of the writer. He was a man who in many respects stood alone, and whose manner it was to say what he had to say without formula or preamble, in the fewest and simplest words. The times demanded sternness and brevity. They resembled the days which had called forth the sixfold woe of Isaiah[2] on greed, and luxury, and unbelief, and pride, and injustice, and the reversal of moral truths; and which had forced him to end those woes with the denunciation of terrible retribution. Hollow professions of religion, empty shows and shadows of faith, partiality and respect of persons, slavish idolatry of riches, observance of some of God's commandments, together with open and impious defiance of others; arrogant assumption of the office of religious teaching without due call and authority; encouragement and patronage of those who set themselves up to be spiritual guides; sins of the tongue; evil speaking against man and God; envying and strife; factions and party feuds; wars and fightings; adulteries; pride and revelry; sordid worldliness and presumptuous self-confidence; a Babel-like building-up of secular plans and projects, independently of God's will, and against it; vainglorious display of wealth; hard-heartedness towards those by whose industry that wealth is acquired; self-indulgence and sensuality; an obstinate continuance in that temper of unbelief which rejected and crucified Christ; "these," as we see from this Epistle, "were the sins of the last days of Jerusalem; for these she was to be destroyed by God; for these she *was* destroyed; and her children have been scattered abroad, and have now been outcasts for near two thousand years. . . . Amid such circumstances, St. James, the Apostle and Bishop of Jerusalem, wrote this Epistle—an Epistle of warning to Jerusalem—the last warning it received from the Holy Spirit of God. He thus discharged the work of a Hebrew Prophet and of a Christian Apostle. He came forth as a Christian Jeremiah and a Christian Malachi. A Jeremiah in denouncing woe; a Malachi sealing up the roll of Divine prophecy

---

[1] This might be said also of the First Epistle of St. John; but that Epistle—even if we do not accept the view that it was sent to accompany the Gospel—has no epistolary address, and is more of the nature of a treatise than an Epistle.
[2] Is. v. 1—30.

to Jerusalem ; and not to Jerusalem only, but to the Jews throughout the world, who were connected with Jerusalem by religious worship and by personal resort to its great festal anniversaries. The Epistle of St. James is the farewell voice of Hebrew prophecy."[1]

CHAPTER XXII.

THE EPISTLE OF ST. JAMES.

"Christianorum omnis religio sine scelere et macula vivere."—LACTANTIUS.

"What a noble man speaks in this Epistle! Deep unbroken patience in suffering! Greatness in poverty! Joy in sorrow! Simplicity, sincerity, firm direct confidence in prayer! . . . How he wants action! Action! not words, not dead faith!"—HERDER.

As we have now learnt all that we can about the author of the Epistle, and the circumstances under which he wrote, we shall be in a better position to understand rightly his solemn teaching.

"JAMES, a slave of God and of the Lord Jesus Christ,"[2]—such is the title which he assumes, and the only personal word in his entire Epistle.[3] It was a simple title, and yet in his eyes, as in those of the other Apostles, nobler than any other badge which he could adopt, for they all felt that they were "bought with a price." He will not call himself an Apostle, because in the highest technical sense he is not an Apostle, since he is not one of the Twelve.[4] He had no need of any such title to command the attention of Christians, among whom he exercised unquestioned authority, and it was not a title which would be recognised among the unconverted Jews, whom he also desired to address. Nor, again, will he call himself "a brother of the Lord." That was a claim which was thrust into prominence on his behalf by others, but it is not one which he would himself have approved. It reminded him, perhaps painfully, of the wasted opportunities of those

---

[1] Bishop Wordsworth, whom I quote the more gladly because I dissent widely from his exegetical views.
[2] This and ii. 1 are the only passages in which the names "Jesus" or "Christ" occur, but by no means the only *references* to Him. See *supra*, p. 315. Bengel says that it might have looked like pride if he had seemed to speak too much of Jesus after the flesh. The real solution of the matter lies in the object and character of the Epistle. He does not, indeed, mention Christ in his speech (Acts xv. 14—21); but that was brief and purely special. The wording of ii. 1, and the association of Jesus with God the Father in this verse, clearly shows that to St. James the Lord was not the ψιλὸς ἄνθρωπος of the Ebionites; nor would James have called himself "a slave" of any mortal man. See *Christologie*, i. 95.
[3] ὑπὲρ πᾶν δὲ κοσμικὸν ἀξίωμα . . . τὸ δοῦλοι εἶναι Χριστοῦ καλλωπιζόμενοι τοῦτο γνώρισμα ἑαυτῶν βούλονται ποιεῖσθαι (Œcumen.); Rom. i. 1; 2 Pet. i. 1, etc.; 1 Cor. vi. 20; vii. 23.
[4] "The thirteen Apostles were appointed by the Lord; St. James, St. Clemens, and others by the Apostles" (*Apost. Constt.* ii. 55).

years in which he had not believed on Him; nor could he forget with what marked emphasis the Lord Jesus, from the beginning of His public ministry, had set aside as of no spiritual significance the claims of fleshly relationship. Of the risen, of the glorified, of the Eternal Christ, he was in no sense "the brother," but "the slave."[1] I cannot imagine that he would have listened without indignation to the name conferred on him by the heated partisanship of those who in after days called him "the brother of God." The name would have shocked to its inmost depths the feeling which every Jew imbibed from the earliest training of his childhood respecting the nothingness of man and the awfulness and unapproachable majesty of God. He was, in a secondary and carnal sense, a half-brother of Jesus in His earthly humiliation; but he must have learnt from the words of the Lord Himself that this kinsmanship in the flesh could hardly redeem from unconscious blasphemy a name so confusing, so unwarrantable, and so unscriptural, as "brother of God." In the only sense in which the word could have any meaning, every faithful Christian was in all respects as much "a brother of God" as he. That he was, in common parlance, "a brother of Him who was called the Christ," there was no need for him to mention. It was a fact known to every Jew of the Dispersion who visited Jerusalem at the yearly feasts, and it even stands as a description of St. James on the indifferent page of the Jewish historian.

"To the twelve tribes that are in the Dispersion,[2] giving them joy."[3] The ten tribes had, as a body, been indistinguishably lost among the nations into whose countries they had been transplanted;[4] but there were probably some communities, and certainly many families, which had preserved their genealogy, and still took pride in the thought that they belonged to this or that tribe of ancient Israel.[5] And the nation never lost the sense of its ideal unity. The number "twelve" was to the Jews a symbolic number. "*Three*" was to them the sacred number, the number of spirit, the number of the life that is in God; "*four*" was the number which symbolised Divine Providence; "twelve" (4 × 3) was the number of Heavenly completeness, the number of the consummation of the Kingdom of God.[6] Hence St. Paul also speaks of "the *dodekaphulon*,"[7] our "twelve-tribed nation,"

---
[1] Rom. i. 1; 2 Pet. i. 1; Jude 1.
[2] See *Life and Work of St. Paul*, i. 115, *seq*. The word *Diaspora* occurs in John vii. 35; 1 Pet. i. 1; and in the LXX of Ps. cxlvi. 2; Deut. xxviii. 25.
[3] See *infra* p. 326.
[4] Dean Plumptre points out that the first appearance of the fiction that the Ten Tribes were somewhere preserved as one body is in 2 Esdr. xiii. 39—47, where the author says that, in the determination to keep their own statutes, "they took this counsel among themselves, that they would leave the multitude of the heathen, and go forth into a farther country, where never mankind dwelt." The Talmud recognises their entire dispersion. Thus Rabbi Ashe said, "If a Gentile should betroth a Jewess, the betrothal may not now be invalid, *for he may be a descendant of one of the Ten Tribes*, and so of the seed of Israel" (Yevamoth, f. 16, b). Again, "the Ten Tribes will never be restored (Deut. xxviii. 25) . . . so says R. Akhiva" (Sanhedrin, f. 110, b).
[5] E.g., the widow Anna, who was of the tribe of Asher.
[6] See Herzog, *Real. Encycl.*, *s. v. Zahlen*; Lange, *Apocalypse*, Introd., § 6, a.
[7] Acts xxvi. 7.

and St. John, in the Apocalypse, echoes in various forms[1] the conception of the Elect of the Twelve Tribes in Heaven which had been involved in the promise of Christ, "Ye also shall sit upon twelve thrones judging the Twelve Tribes of Israel."[2]

It is a curious and undesigned coincidence that this letter, and the encyclical letter from the Church of Jerusalem, of which St. James was the main author, are the only two Christian letters in the New Testament which begin with the greeting "giving them joy."[3] It was distinctively the Greek salutation. The Jewish was *Shalôm*—"Peace."[4] St. Paul, wishing to combine in his salutations all that was most blessed alike in ethnic and in spiritual life, combines the two national methods of salutation in his χάρις καὶ εἰρήνη, "grace and peace," which in his pastoral Epistles is tenderly amplified into "grace, mercy, and peace."

I have here rendered the word by "giving them joy"[5] because it forms the transition to the opening passage, "My brethren, count it all joy." This mode of transition by the repetition of a word—which is technically known as *duadiplosis*—is very characteristic of this Epistle, and forms, in fact, the writer's ordinary method of passing from one paragraph to another.[6] The remainder of the chapter—the phraseology of which I will endeavour to elucidate in the notes, and the general bearing in the text—runs as follows:—

"Count it all joy,[7] my brethren,[8] when ye suddenly fall into varied temptations,[9] recognising that the testing of your faith[10] works endurance; but let endurance have a perfect work,[11] that ye may be perfect and complete, lacking nothing[12] (i. 2—4).

---

[1] 12 tribes; 24 elders; 12,000 of each tribe; 144,000 of the followers of the Lamb, etc. The latter number is so far from being narrowly restrictive, that it stands for a number ideally complete.

[2] Matt. xix. 28; Rev. vii. 5—8.

[3] Acts xv. 23, χαίρειν. The word also occurs in the Greek letter of Claudius Lysias to Felix (Acts xxiii. 26), and in that of Antiochus in 2 Macc. ix. 19. Its recurrence here is one of the undesigned coincidences between this letter and the account given of St. James in the Acts.

[4] Is. xlviii. 22; lvii. 21, where *Shalom* is rendered χαίρειν by the LXX.

[5] Comp. 2 John 10, 11. The absence of any opening benediction may be due to the general character of the letter.

[6] Thus we have ver. 1, χαίρειν; ver. 2, χάραν, ὑπομονήν; ver. 3, ἡ δὲ ὑπομονή; ver. 4, λειπόμενοι; ver. 5, εἰ δέ τις λείπεται; ver. 6, μηδὲν διακρινόμενος· ὁ γὰρ διακρινόμενος, etc.; and so throughout.

[7] πᾶσαν χαράν, *merum gaudium*, *eitel Freude*. Comp. Luke vi. 22, 23; Acts v. 41; Col. i. 24.

[8] The perpetual recurrence of this word shows that the wounds which St. James inflicts are meant to be the faithful wounds of a friend.

[9] περιπέσητε of sudden accidents, as ληστὰς περιέπεσεν, Luke x. 30; περιπεσόντες δὲ εἰς τόπον διθάλασσον. The word ποικίλος literally means "many-coloured." Comp. ἐπιθυμίαις ποικίλαις, 1 Tim. iii. 6. The word "temptations" includes all forms of trial: Luke xxii. 28; Acts xx. 19. Persecution was rife at this time: 1 Thess. ii. 14; Heb. xi. 32, 33.

[10] Verse 3, τὸ δοκίμιον ὑμῶν τῆς πίστεως. St. Peter (1 Pet. i. 7) uses the same phrase, and the coincidence can hardly be accidental.

[11] Matt. xxiv. 13—ὁ δὲ ὑπομείνας εἰς τέλος σωθήσεται.

[12] "The work of God," says Alford, "in a man *is* the man." The word τέλειος is a favourite one with St. James (i. 3, 4, 17, 25; iii. 2), borrowed doubtless from the words of our Lord (Matt. v. 48; xix. 21). 'Ολόκληρος is also used by St. Paul (1 Thess. v. 28), and means "well regulated in every part" (Acts iii. 16). Philo and Josephus use it for *unblemished* sacrificial victims.

"But if any one of you lacks wisdom,[1] let him ask from God, who giveth to all simply[2] and upbraideth not,[3] and it shall be given him[4] (5).

"But let him ask in faith,[5] nothing doubting,[6] for he that doubteth is like a wave of the sea wind-driven[7] and tossed about. For let not that person think that he shall receive anything[8] from the Lord—a double-minded man,[9] unsettled in all his ways[10] (6—8).

"But let the humble brother glory in his exaltation, but the rich in his humiliation,[11] because as the flower of the grass he shall pass away.[12] For the sun ariseth with the burning wind, and drieth the grass, and its flower fadeth away, and the beauty of its aspect perisheth;[13] so also shall the rich man fade away in his goings[14] (9—11).

"Blessed is the man[15] who endureth temptation, for when he has been approved he shall receive the garland of the life[16] which He promised[17] to those who love Him[18] (12).

"Let no one who is being tempted say, 'I am being tempted from God.' For

---

[1] "Wisdom" with St. James is evidently that practical wisdom which surpasses knowledge (γνῶσις), because it not only knows truth, but acts upon that knowledge (*Etym. Magn.*). Comp. iii. 15—17; 1 Cor. xii. 8; Col. ii. 3.

[2] ἁπλῶς. So in Rom. xii. 8 we are bidden to grow in "simplicity."

[3] The meaning of this expression is best seen from Ecclus. xx. 15, where it is said of the fool, "He giveth little, and upbraideth much; he openeth his mouth like a crier; to-day he lendeth, and to-morrow he will ask. Such an one is to be hated of God and man;" Id. xli. 22, "After thou hast given, upbraid not" (μὴ ὀνείδιζε). The "*approbatio beneficii*" (Ter. Andr. i. 1)—i.e., the casting in the teeth of others what we have done for them—is a vice of all ages.

[4] See 1 Kings iii. 11, 12, "Because thou hast asked this thing (wisdom), behold, I have done according to thy word," Luke xi. 13; Ecclus. vii. 10, "Be not fainthearted when thou makest thy prayer." We see here that by "faith" St. James means undivided confidence in God.

[5] See v. 15; Matt. xxi. 22, "All things whatsoever ye ask in prayer, *believing*, ye shall receive."

[6] Διακρινόμενος, Matt. xxi. 21, "If ye have faith and doubt not (μὴ διακριθῆτε) ye shall do only the miracle of the fig-tree, but," &c.; Rom. iv. 20, Abraham οὐ διεκρίθη τῇ ἀπιστίᾳ. "When faith says 'yes' and unbelief says 'no,'" says Huther, "to doubt (διακρίνεσθαι) is the union of 'yes' and 'no,' but so that 'no' is the weightier. The deep-lying ground of it is pride." Dean Plumptre quotes from Tennyson—

"Faith and unfaith can ne'er be equal powers,
Unfaith in aught is want of faith in all."

[7] ἀνεμιζομένῳ καὶ ῥιπιζομένῳ. The words occur here only, and κλύδων ("billow") only in Luke viii. 24; but we have the metaphor in Is. lvii. 20; Eph. iv. 14. The words well express the state of tumultuous excitement which preceded the Jewish War.

[8] That is, "any special answer to prayer."

[9] Ἀνὴρ δίψυχος. "The man who has two souls in conflict with each other." This striking expression occurs only at iv. 8. Rabbi Tanchum (f. 84) on Deut. xxvi. 17 gives a close parallel, "Let not those who pray have two hearts, one directed to God, one to something else." Comp. 1 Kings xviii. 21; Ps. xii. 2, "a double heart" (lit. "a heart and a heart"); Ecclus. i. 28, "Come not unto the Lord with a double heart;" Is. ii. 12, "Woe be to . . . the sinner that goeth two ways;" Matt. vi. 24, "No man can serve two masters." The passage is imitated in "The Shepherd of Hermas" (*Mandat.* ix.).

[10] Ἀκατάστατος. A classical expression (again) found only in St. James (iii. 8). Comp. Is. liv. 11, "tossed with tempest;" Ἀκαταστασία, iii. 16; Luke xxi. 9; 1 Cor. xiv. 33, &c. It is one who "never continueth in one stay" (Job xiv. 2).

[11] For the different views taken of this verse see *infra*, p. 330. Καυχάσθαι is literally "to boast." Rom. ii. 17, etc.

[12] For the metaphor, specially suitable to the brief life of flowers in the scorching heat of Palestine, see Is. xl. 6, 7; Ps. cii. 15; Job xiv. 2; 1 Pet. i. 24; Wisd. ii. 12, "Let us crown ourselves with rosebuds before they be withered;" riches are no "unwithering inheritance" (1 Pet. i. 4) as the kingdom of God is.

[13] The aorist tenses show us the whole story, so to speak. The καύσων is usually taken to mean the *kadim*, or simoom, as in Jonah iv. 8; the "east wind" of Ezek. xvii. 10; xix. 12; "the wind of the Lord from the wilderness" of Hos. xiii. 15; but may mean merely "scorching heat;" Matt. xx. 12; Luke xii. 55.

[14] Μαρανθήσεται only in Wisd. ii. 8 and Job xv. 30 (LXX.). πορείαις is the best-supported reading, and alludes, perhaps, to travels for purposes of gain, etc. (iv. 13). (A, πορίαις, "gettings.")

[15] ἀνήρ—"*non mollis nec effeminatus sed vir*" (Thos. Aquin.).

[16] There is no special reference to athletes (Ps. xxi. 3; Rev. ii. 10; Wisd. v. 16).

[17] The "He" (as in א, A, B) is more emphatic than if he had inserted "the Lord," and seems to show how early the Talmudic method of reference had begun.

[18] Amor parit patientiam (Bengel).

God is out of the sphere of evils,[1] and Himself tempteth no one, but each is ever tempted when he is being drawn forth[2] and enticed by his own desire.[3] Then the desire, having conceived, bears sin; but sin, when full grown, brings forth death (13—15).[4]

"Be not deceived, my brethren beloved. Every good giving and every perfect gift[5] is from above, descending from the Father of the Lights,[6] with whom there is no varying nor shadow of turning.[7] Because He willed it, He brought us forth by the word of truth that we might be in some sense[8] a first fruit of His creatures[9] (16—18).

"Ye know,[10] my brethren beloved. But let everyone be swift to listening, slow to speaking,[11] slow to wrath. For the wrath of a man (ἀνδρὸς) worketh not the righteousness of God. Therefore laying aside all filthiness and superfluity of malice, receive in meekness the implanted word which is able to save your souls.[12]

---

[1] ἀπείραστος occurs here only. It means (1) "untempted," and (2) "one who does not tempt." Luther follows the Vulgate in understanding it to mean "does not try evil men" (intentator malorum est), or "is not a tempter of yvell things" (Wiclif); but this St. James has said already. It seems to mean "has nothing to do with evil things," and therefore cannot tempt men to evil. Œcumenius quotes a heathen saying, "The Divine neither suffers troubles nor causes them to others." "Why, then, is it said that God did tempt Abraham in Gen. xxii. 3?" That means that He tried Abraham, not from evil motives to an evil end, but from good motives to a good end" (Aug.).

[2] Prov. xxx. 13 (LXX.). The word may be used of "dragging a prey to land," as in Hdt. ii. 76, and so we might take the metaphor to be one from fishing. The word δελεαζόμενος may also mean "enticing with a bait," as in 2 Pet. ii. 14, 18; Xen. Mem. ii. 1, § 6. But the further expansion of the metaphor shows that he is thinking of the enticement of the harlot Sense (Prov. vii. 16—23), to which in classical and Hellenistic usage the words are equally applicable (Hom. Od. π. 294; Arist. Polit. v. 10; Testam. XII. Patriarch. p. 702); and especially Plutarch's De Ser Num. Vindict.; "the sweetness of desire, like a bait (δέλεαρ), entices (ἐξέλκει) men."

[3] "No man taketh harm but by himself;" "passion becomes to each his own God;" "sua cuique Deus fit dira cupido" (Virg. Æn. ix. 185).

[4] Milton expands the metaphor into an allegory in Par. Lost, ii. 745—814. Lange points out the varying expressions of the New Testament: "Sin brings forth death" (James); "death is the wages of sin" (Paul); "sin is death" (John).

[5] This forms in the original a perfect hexameter, except that the last syllable of δόσις is lengthened—

πᾶσα δόσις ἀγαθὴ καὶ πᾶν δώρημα τέλειον.

On these metrical phrases see note on Heb. xii. 14. δώρημα only occurs in Rom. v. 16. "From above" (John iii. 3, 7, 31; xix. 11). Bishop Andrewes, in two sermons on this text, says the δόσις ἀγαθὴ refers to the gifts of eternal life; the δώρημα τέλειον the treasures laid up for us in eternity.

[6] By "the lights" is meant probably "the heavenly bodies," as in Ps. cxxxvi. 7; Jer. iv. 23, called by Gen. i. 14 φωστῆρες, which is metaphorically applied to Christians (John v. 35; Phil. ii. 15). The "Father" then means the Creator (comp. Job xxxviii. 28. "Hath the rain a father?") Some explain it of angels and spirits, and of Him who is the "Light of the world" (John ix. 5). But the question is not what meaning the words may be made to include, but what meaning they originally had.

[7] The words are curious—παραλλαγὴ ἢ τροπῆς ἀποσκίασμα. The first word is a hapax legomenon in the New Testament (but see 2 Kings ix. 20, LXX.), and has been understood to be a technical term of astronomy, like parallax. But in Epictet. i. 14 it merely means "change," even in an astronomical sentence; and Plotinus speaks of "a change (παραλλαγὴ) of days to nights." It seems, however, to have a semi-technical connexion with astronomy. Ἀποσκίασμα is also a hapax legomenon, and τροπαὶ ἡλίου means "the solstices" (see Job xxxviii. 33). Here, however, there seems to be a general allusion to the changes and revolutions of the sun, moon, and stars (Wisd. vii. 17—19), as compared with the sun which never sets. Comp. 1 John i. 5, "God is light, and in Him is no darkness at all;" Ps. cxxxix. 11.

[8] ἀπαρχήν. The τινα shows that he is using a new metaphor.

[9] On the great theological importance of this verse—all the more noticeable because the Epistle is predominantly practical—see infra, p. 333.

[10] The true reading seems to be ἴστε, A, B, C (Heb. xii. 17; Eph. v. 5). Its very abruptness probably caused the variations of the MSS.

[11] Ecclus. v. 11: "Be swift to hear . . . . and with patience give answer;" "Thou hast two ears and one mouth" (Rückert). Œcumenius here quotes the proverb that "no one ever repented of having been silent," and every one will be reminded of the proverb, "Speech is silvern, Silence is golden" (Prov. xiii. 3, etc.; Eccl. v. 2)—Philo has the phrase, "slow to benefit, swift to injure." The Jews were ever "slow to hear" (Heb. v. 11; x. 25).

[12] It is able, for it is a power of God (Rom. i. 16). Without it they are unable, whether by outward works (as Pharisees said) or by determination of will (as Sadducees said) to be saved. On ἔμφυτος, see p. 331.

But prove yourselves doers of the word, and not hearers only, misleading yourselves (Col. ii. 4; Luke xi. 28). For if any one is a hearer of the word, and not a doer, this person is like a man[1] contemplating the face of his birth in a mirror. For he contemplated himself, and has gone away,[2] and immediately forgot what kind of person he was. But he who has stooped down to gaze[3] into a perfect law, the law of liberty,[4] and has stayed to gaze,[5] proving himself not a hearer who forgets, but a doer who works, he shall be blessed in his doing[6] (19—25).

"If any one fancies that he is 'religious'[7] while he is not bridling his tongue (iii. 2, 3), but is deceiving his own heart, this man's religious service is profitless. A religious service pure and undefiled[8] before our God and Father is this—to take care of orphans and widows in their affliction (Ex. xxii. 22—24; Acts vi. 1), to keep himself unspotted from the world"[9] (26, 27).

I have broken the chapter into brief sections to indicate as far as possible the transitions of thought. Special difficulties of expression are, I hope, sufficiently elucidated in the appended notes, and the very literal translation will show what I believe to be the best reading and construction. But there are one or two general points in the chapter which require notice.

i. It will be observed that St. James begins at once with the subject of temptation, using the word in its broadest sense of all forms of trial. It includes both outward persecution—from which the Churches of scattered Jews, whether converted or unconverted, were always liable, from the common hatred which Pagans felt for them—

---

[1] ἀνδρί. Some have referred the term to the comparative carelessness of *men* in looking at mirrors (1 Cor. xiii. 12; Wisd. vii. 26; Ecclus. xii. 12), but it is doubtful whether St. James intends any special distinctiveness in the word (see vers. 8—12).

[2] ἀπελήλυθεν, *perf.* The tenses make the image more graphic.

[3] The true meaning of the word will be seen by a reference to Luke xxiv. 12—"Stooping down and looking in"; Ecclus. xiv. 23; John xx. 5, 11; 1 Pet. i. 12 (see the note on that verse). Doubtless St. James thought, in passing, of the Cherubim bending down over the Ark as though to gaze continually on the revelation of God's will in the moral law. See on this word Coleridge (*Aids to Reflection*), p. 15, "A more happy and forcible word could not have been chosen to express the nature and ultimate object of reflection."

[4] "Legum servi sumus ut liberi esse possimus" (Cic.). We have seen already that St. James's ideal of the Law is not that of Moses (Acts xv. 10; Gal. v. 1, but comp. Ps. xix. 8—11), but that of the Sermon on the Mount (ii. 8; v. 12; John viii. 32), the law of the Spirit (Rom. viii. 2), the law of faith (Rom. iii. 27).

[5] Notice the antithesis, παρακύψας, παραμείνας, οὐκ ἀκροατὴς ἐπιλησμονῆς, as against κατενόησεν, ἀπελήλυθεν, ἐπελάθετο.

[6] "Ut ipsa actio sit beatitudo" (Schneckenburger).

[7] θρησκεία means ritual service, external observance; "gay religions, full of pomp and gold" (Acts xxvi. 5), which (as we see from Col. ii. 18, the only other place where the word occurs in the New Testament) have a perpetual tendency to degenerate into superfluous and self-satisfying human ordinances (ἐθελοθρησκεία), and even, to use the bold coinage of a later writer, ἐθελοπερισσοθρησκεία. It is the peril and disease of the externally virtuous—vice corrupting virtue itself into pride and intolerance. Hence the θρῆσκος is one who plumes himself on his outward service. This paragraph illustrates the "slowness to speak," as the last did the "swiftness to hear." Obtrusiveness in talk is a natural consequence of a spurious religion.

[8] The Jewish notion of defilement was very different (John xviii. 28; Lev. v. 3, and *passim*; comp. Ecclus. xxxv. 14). For "the fatherless and widows" (where "respect of persons" is also alluded to), and for the general thought, compare Mark vii. 20—23; Luke xi. 40.

[9] St. James would feel this duty all the more keenly, and would feel that *this*, and not the performance of outward religious duties, was what God really desired, because the day had been when he too was of the world, for which reason the world which hated Christ had not hated him (John vii. 7). By "the world" is here meant everything in the world, and in the worldly life which tempts to sin (1 Tim. vi. 14). With this thought compare John xvii. 15; 1 Tim. v. 22. With the general thought of the paragraph comp. Ecclus. xxxv. 2: "He that requiteth a good turn, offereth fine flour; and he that giveth alms, sacrificeth praise." The same thought is found both in Scripture (Deut. x. 12; Ps. xl. 7; xxi. 17; 1 Sam. xv. 22; Mic. vi. 6—9; Hos. vi. 6; xii. 6, etc.) and in heathen writers.

and those inward temptations which are often closely connected with outward circumstances. St. James shows his readers how to turn these temptations into blessings, by making them a source of patient endurance, and so using them as the fire which purges and tests the fine gold. For the Christian should aim at such perfection[1] (i. 2—4).

ii. Now for perfection he needs wisdom[2] most of all; and if he lacks this wisdom he has only to ask for it from One whose gifts are absolute and gracious (i. 5).

iii. Yet it is useless to ask without faith in Him to whom the petition is addressed, and without faith that it will be granted. Such faithless prayers can only arise from a wavering disposition, a want of stability, a want of whole-heartedness, a dualism of life and aim (i. 6—8).

iv. Then comes an apparently sudden transition of exhortation to rich and poor.[3] That the transition was not so sudden in the mind of the writer is shown by his connecting particle. "The man of two souls," he says, "is restless in all his ways; *but* let the humble brother rejoice." The unexpressed connexion seems to be, "Now, what is the cause of this spiritual distraction and instability? Does it not arise from worldliness? Well, *ye cannot serve God and Mammon.* If, then, any brother be poor and humble, let him rejoice in his exaltation. For if he take it rightly his earthly humiliation is his true dignity. He is enjoying the beatitude of poverty. It is something like the thought expressed so tersely by our great philosopher,[4] "Prosperity is the blessing of the Old Testament, Adversity is the blessing of the New" (i. 9).

v. "But the rich," he adds, "in his humiliation." The meaning of these words is not clear. It has even been supposed by some that the words "rich" and "poor" are used in this Epistle in a metaphorical sense.[5] Another discussion turns on the question whether by "the rich" we are here to understand rich Christians, or rich Jews and Gentiles. I feel convinced that the words are to be understood in their primary meaning. As I have already explained, St. James is not thinking of Gentiles at all, and is drawing no marked

---

[1] The Christian aims at "endurance," not at "apathy," as the Stoic did. His endurance has "a sublimer origin, a milder character, a greater duration, a more glorious fruit." (Van Oosterzee).

[2] The history of the next few years shows how deeply the Jews needed this wisdom. "Wisdom is justified of her children" (Matt. xi. 19);— and she abode not at Jerusalem, but with the Christians who fled in time to Pella.

[3] So in Shemoth Rabba (§ 31, f. 129) we find, "Blessed is the man who stands in his temptation; for there is no man whom God does not try. He tries *the rich*, to see if they will open their hands to the poor; He tries *the poor*, to see if they will not murmur," etc.

[4] Lord Bacon.

[5] Lange thinks that by "the brethren of low degree" are meant Jews and Jewish Christians, and by the rich the Gentiles; for, he says, the rich Jews have always been kind to the poor. I think I have already met this difficulty. It is surely extravagant to say that "the rich man with a gold ring and splendid garment denotes the proud Ebionitish Jewish Christian *proud of his ring of the Jewish Covenant* (!), while the poor man, with a vile garment, describes the Gentile Christian" (*Introd.* p. 27). This is to introduce into New Testament exegesis fancies borrowed from Lessing and Swift.

distinction between Jews and Christians. A further question is, are we to understand this phrase hortatively in the sense of "but let the rich man boast in his humiliation," or as a contrast, "but the rich man rejoices or glories in that which is in reality his humiliation"?[1] In the one case it is an exhortation to the rich man as to what he *ought* to do; in the other a censure upon him for what he *does*. Neither interpretation is without difficulty, but on the whole the meaning seems to be that worldliness, with the temptations which it brings, is full of dangers. Poverty and riches stand in God's estimation in reverse positions. Humble poverty is true wealth. Pampered wealth is real poverty.[2] Let the poor brother glory in the beatitude of poverty; it is a gift of God. The rich brother, then, is worse off, is in a worse position, than he—his riches are his humiliation in the heavenly order, for they are a temptation to which he is only too liable to succumb; they tend to make him more of a worldling, less of a Christian. Such views belong to the so-called Ebionitism of St. James. But the opinions of the Ebionites were due to the falsehood of extremes. Neither is wealth in itself a sin, nor poverty in itself a virtue. They are conditions of Life in which God has placed us, each liable to its own, and each to *different* temptations. But as regards those days—perhaps as regards all periods—riches were liable to severer temptations than poverty. In the teaching of St. James we recognise, not the exaggerations of Ebionitism, but the impression left by the sermons and parables of Christ[3] (i. 10).

vi. And the reason why the rich brother should glory in the humiliation which the world regards as his enviable superiority is that reason which Isaiah had so exquisitely expressed, and to which St. Peter also refers.[4] It is the transitoriness of riches.[5] Often, even in this brief life, they make themselves wings and fly away. But they must always pass away with the fading flower of life; not even the poorest fragment of them can be held by the relaxing hand of death. Is that a condition to glory in, which Christ showed to be surrounded with peril, and which must soon become like a withered blossom in a dead man's hand? (i. 11).

vii. But whether our trial comes in the form of wealth or of poverty it becomes a beatitude if it works in us the spirit of patient endurance. And here it is necessary for St. James to introduce a strong caution.

---

[1] This would resemble Phil. iii. 19, "whose glory is in their shame." Compare the saying of Pascal about man—"Gloire et rebut de l'Univers, s'il se vante, je l'abaisse; s'il s'abaisse, je le vante."
[2] Matt. v. 3.
[3] Matt. xxiii. 12; Luke xiv. 11; xviii. 14. The commoner view of the clause is "Let the rich man rejoice when he is humiliated by the 'spoiling of his goods'" (Heb. x. 34). But (1) this loss of wealth happens only to a few. (2) He is throughout addressing "rich men," who are in the full flower of their prosperity.
[4] Is. xl. 6; 1 Pet. i. 24 (comp. Matt. vi. 30; xiii. 26).
[5] Some refer the passage chiefly to reverses in life. "The rich man, overtaken by judgment, perishes in the midst of his doings and pursuits, as the flower, in the midst of its blessings, falls a victim to the scorching heat of the sun" (Huther).

The word which he has used for temptation is capable of two meanings—trial in the sense of a difficult and painful test—*adversa pati;* and trial in the sense of strong impulse to sin (*malis ad defectionem sollicitari*). In the first sense it comes from God; it is a part of His providential ordering of our lives. In the second sense it by no means comes from God.[1] When a man pleads, as men have so often done, that "God has made them so;"[2] or that "the flesh is weak," or that "God for a moment deserted them;"[3] when they say that they have done wrong because they could not do otherwise;[4] when they contend that each man is practically no better than an automaton, and that his actions are the inevitable—and therefore irresponsible—result of the conditions by which he is surrounded—they are transferring to God the blame of their misdoings. "The foolishness of man perverteth his way, and his heart fretteth against the Lord."[5] The doctrine of fatalism is but a poor and false excuse for crime.[6] When passively accepted it paralyses every nerve of moral effort; when it takes the form of materialism, and poses as the final result of science, it lays the axe at the root of every motive by which men rise to the dignity of free and moral beings. Men become the children of God by obedience to His laws, resulting not from necessity, but choice. And so St. James gives the true genesis of sin. It springs from lust—desire—the *yetser-ha-râ*, or evil impulse, which plays so large a part in later Jewish literature. This is to each soul the harlot-temptress which draws him forth from the safe shelter of innocence, entices him, and bears the evil offspring of committed sin. But the bad genealogy ends not there. Sin, too, grows to maturity, and the offspring of her incestuous union is death (i. 12—15).

viii. No, God is not the author of evil; it is only every *good* gift which comes from Him. "God is always in the meridian."[7] He dwells in the φῶς ἀνέσπερον, in the light whereof there is no eventide, the sun whereof knows no tropic. No darkness can flow from the fountain of that unchanging Sun, which is not liable to the parallax and eclipses of

---

[1] The history of temptation, says Bede, is (1) Suggestion; (2) Delight; (3) Consent. Suggestion is of the enemy, delight and consent from our own frailty. If the birth of a wrong action follows the delight of the heart, the enemy leaves us as a victor, and we are liable to death. "Lust is the mother of sin, sin the mother of death, the sinner the parent of both" (Macknight).
[2] St. Paul deals with this question—"Why doth He yet find fault? For who hath resisted His will?" (Rom. ix. 19).
[3] "Seems there any recess? It is we forsake Him; not He us (Jer. ii. 17.)" (Bishop Andrewes.)
[4] The unhappy Henry II., shortly before his death, passionately exclaimed to God, "Since Thou hast taken from me the town I loved best . . . I will have my revenge on Thee too. I will rob Thee of that thing Thou lovest most in me" (see Green's *Hist. of Engl.* I. p. 181). There can be little doubt that St. James had in his mind a magnificent passage of Ecclus. xv. 11—17, "Say not thou, '*It is through the Lord that I fell away:*' for thou oughtest not to do the things that He hateth. Say not thou, 'He hath caused me to err,' for He hath no need of the sinful man . . . He hath set fire and water before thee: stretch forth thy hand unto whether thou wilt. Before man is life and death, and whether him liketh, shall be given him."
[5] Prov. xix. 3.
[6] It was familiar to St. James, for, as Josephus says, it was a doctrine of the Pharisees (*Antt.* xviii. 1, § 3 ; *B. J.* ii. 8, § 14).
[7] Wetstein.

the heavenly bodies which He has made.¹ And then, in one singularly pregnant clause which—although in this respect it stands somewhat isolated—shows how little the practical tendency of the author was dissevered from deep dogmatic insight, he tells us of God's *most* perfect gift to us. He tells us that we need a new life; that God by one great act has bestowed it upon us; that this act sprang from his own free will and choice;² that the instrument of this new birth was the word of truth,³ the Divine revelation of God to man, which, of course, requires faith in them that hear it; that the result of this new birth is our dedication as "the first-fruits of a sacrificial gift"⁴ which shall only be completed with the offering up of all God's creatures. Thus in one brief sentence he concentrates many solemn truths, and even by the one word, "of His own will" (βουληθείς), he repudiates alike the dangerous fatalism of the Pharisees, and the arrogant assertion of the Sadducees that salvation lies within the power of our own unaided will (i. 16—18).

ix. They know this; but let them apply it—let them listen to this word of truth, hearing more, speaking less, wrangling not at all. Passionate fanaticism does not help forward God's righteousness. It deceives itself when it brings into God's service that impure mixture of human evil.⁵ The Gospel is meant to be used for our own sanctification, not to be abused to quarrelsomeness with others. God's word, implanted in the heart,⁶ is powerful to save, but the condition of its power is its meek reception. It requires steady, earnest contemplation, not a mere hasty passing gaze. There were many, both Jews and Christians, who were absorbed in outward service⁷—who were content

---

¹ "Though the lights of heaven have their parallaxes, yea 'the angels of heaven He found not steadfastness in them' (Job. iv. 18); yet for God, He is subject to none of them. He is '*Ego sum qui sum*' (Ex. iii. 14), that is, saith Malachi, '*Ego Deus et non mutor*' (Mal. iii. 6). We are not what we were a while since, what we shall be a while after, scarce what we are; for every moment makes us vary. With God it is nothing so. He is that He is; He is and changeth not" (Bishop Andrewes, Serm. iii. 374; John viii. 58).

² God is the cause of His own mercy. "Unde sequitur naturale esse Deo benefacere" (Calvin). See John i. 13; 1 Pet. i. 23. βουληθείς, "voluntate amantissimâ, liberrimâ, purissimâ, foecundissimâ" (1 John i. 13; 1 Pet. i. 3). Ἀπεκύησεν, the antithesis to the ἀποκύει of sin, in ver. 17, "Ipse Deus Patris et matris loco est" (Bengel) (Rom. viii. 15; Gal. iii. 26; 1 Pet. i. 23).

³ John xvii. 17, "Sanctify them by Thy truth. Thy word is Truth." 1 Pet. i. 23, "Having been born again by the word of the Living God." It is the equivalent to the Gospel (2 Tim. ii. 15; Eph. i. 13). "The lying word of the serpent has corrupted us, but the true word of God makes us good again" (Luther). Here and elsewhere, some (*e.g.*, Athanasius) give to "the Word" its specific Johannine sense, and interpret it of Christ, the Divine Logos. No doubt it may be made to bear this meaning in this and many other passages; but as this letter was addressed to the Jews of the Dispersion, of whom many had no Alexandrian training or Alexandrian sympathies, the question is (1), Would they so have understood it? and, therefore, (2) Did St. James intend it so to be understood?

⁴ "First-fruit" (see Lev. xxiii. 10; Deut. xxvi. 2; 1 Cor. xv. 22; xvi. 15; Rev. xiv. 4). Christ is the true first-fruit, and 'then we in Him (Rom. viii. 19—22). See a valuable note of Wiesinger, who was the first to call due attention to the depth and importance of this verse.

⁵ "Purius sine ira fit" (Bengel). There is always a germ of the atheistical in the heat of fanaticism (Nitsch), as in Jonah's, "I do well to be angry." Lange observes that Simeon and Levi, the ancestors of the Jews in fanaticism, were disapproved by Jacob (Gen. xxxiv. 49), but afterwards upheld as patterns (Judith ix. 20).

⁶ Perhaps an allusion to the Parable of the Sower, and so parallel with Matt. xiii. 23. The word ἔμφυτος only occurs in Wisd. xii. 10. In classic Greek it means also "*innate*," but this does not furnish so simple a meaning, though it may be compared with such passages as Col. ii. 16, "as ye have received Christ, so *walk* ye in Him."

⁷ See Dr. Mosley's admirable sermon on the Pharisees. "Qui crassiora vitia exuerunt, huic morbo sunt ut plurimum obnoxii" (Calvin).

with endless ablutions and purifications, and not with what is true, pure, unspotted, and undefiled; who made long prayers, and yet devoured widows' houses. But all service is fruitless if it does not lead a man to refrain from bitter words. The only pure and perfect ritual is active love,[1] and a freedom from "the contagions of the world's slow stain."[2]

He proceeds, in the second chapter, to rebuke the respect of persons,[3] the worldly partialities, which are so alien to "the faith of our Lord Jesus Christ, the Lord of the glory."[4] That faith teaches before all things the Fatherhood of God and the brotherhood of man. Since in God's sight all are equal—since in the eye of His Church the greatest princess is but "this woman," and the proudest emperor but "this man" —was it not most unworthy to thrust oppressive disparities into prominence in a wrong place by ushering the gold-ringed man[5] in the bright dress into the best seat in the synagogue,[6] while they made the squalidly dressed pauper[7] stand anywhere, or thrust him down into a seat on the floor. When ye acted thus, "did ye not *doubt* in yourselves,[8] and did ye not show wicked reasonings as judges?" It shows *doubt* to act as though Christ had never promised His kingdom to the poor, rich in faith;[9] and wicked reasonings to argue mentally that the poor *must* be less worthy of honour than the rich. It is the evil schism in the heart which leads to this evil judgment in the life. And was not this a strange method of judging, when it was the rich who played the lord over them, dragged them into law-courts,[10] and blasphemed the

---

[1] Comp. Tobit i. 16, 17.
[2] "The outward service (θρησκεία) of ancient religion, the rites, ceremonies, and ceremonial vestments of the old law, had morality for their substance. They were the letter of which morality was the spirit; the enigma of which morality was the meaning. But morality itself is the service and ceremonial (*cultus exterior*, θρησκεία) of the Christian religion" (Coleridge, *Aids to Reflection*, Aph. xxiii.).
[3] Curiously enough the Talmud says, "God is a respecter of persons," Num. vi. 26 (Berachoth, f. 20, 2).
[4] Lit. "of our Lord Jesus Christ, of the glory." Bengel takes the two words in apposition —"ut ipse Christus dicatur, ἡ δόξα, Gloria." The Shechinah was a Jewish name for the Messiah, but it is better, as in the E. V., to understand it as "the Lord of the glory" (comp. John xvii. 5). The title here implies the utter obliteration, by comparison, of petty earthly distinctions.
[5] The ostentation of gold rings was a fashion of this epoch, and Roman fops wore them even inconveniently large (Juv. Sat. i. 28, 30; Mart. xi. 60), six on each finger. Lucian (Somn. 12) speaks of wearing sixteen heavy rings. "All fingers are loaded with rings" (Plin. H. N. xxxiii. 6).
[6] "A synagogue" is, on the whole, the best supported reading (א, B, C). The passage is not a mere rebuke to "sexton rudeness." It illustrates faithless partiality by a common instance, and this desire for prominence was largely developed among the Jews (Matt. xxiii. 6). Christians probably used Jewish synagogues (as St. Paul did) as long as they were permitted to do so.
[7] No doubt "gold rings" and squalid apparel (Zech. iii. 3, 4; Rev. xxii. 11) may be used symbolically, but to understand this passage as an allegory of Jewish exclusiveness towards the Gentiles (as Lange does), is very far-fetched. Notice the picturesque antitheses—
You—sit—here—honourably (near the coffer which held the Law).
You—stand—there—under my footstool (out of sight and hearing, near the door).
Even in courts of law the Jewish rule was that (to show the perfect impartiality of the law) both suitors, whether rich or poor, should sit, or both stand.
[8] διεκρίθητε. "Doubt" is the ordinary meaning of διακρίνομαι, as in i. 6; and there is no reason to change it here into "make differences, or judge," etc. (Matt. xxi. 21; Acts x. 20; Rom. iv. 20, etc.).
[9] Matt. v. 3; Luke vi. 20.
[10] Acts vii. 12; xvii. 12; xviii. 5; xix. 33.

fair name by which they were named?[1] It were nobler to fulfil the royal law,[2] "Love thy neighbour as thyself," and so to treat all, whether rich or poor, with equal courtesy. Not to act thus is sin. They must not regard such sin as unimportant. There is in God's law a uniform solidarity, and one God made all the law. To break one commandment is to break all,[3] for it is to violate the principle of obedience, just as "it matters not at what particular point a man breaks his way out of an enclosure, if he is forbidden to go out of it at all."[4] Every separate commandment has the same Divine source. The sum total of all commandments is that law of liberty[5] by which we shall be judged. That judgment shall be merciless to the merciless.[6] And then he adds, with an emphasis all the more forcible from its brevity and abruptness: "Mercy"—whether in the heart of God or of man—"glories over judgment"[7] (ii. 1—13).

The passage that follows is the famous passage about justification by works:—

"What is the advantage, my brethren, if any say that he has faith, but hath not works?[8] Is the faith able to save him?[9] But if a brother or sister be naked, and lacking the day's food, and one of you should say, 'Go in peace;[10] warm yourselves and feed yourselves,' but ye give them not the necessaries of the body, what is the advantage?[11] So also faith, if it have not works, is dead in itself.[12] Yea, some one

---

[1] Literally "which was invoked over you" (Deut. xxviii. 10, etc.; Jer. xiv. 9; Am. ix. 12; Heb. xi. 16), i.e., the name of Christ. Christians were called οἱ Χριστοῦ (1 Cor. iii. 23). Nominal Christians, however rich, could hardly have ventured to "blaspheme," or "speak injuriously of," the name of Christ. St. James must be passing in thought to rich Jews, Sadducean oppressors, etc. (Acts iv. 1, 6, v. 17), though he may include the conduct of rich Christians which caused Christ's name to be blasphemed among the Gentiles, as the Jews caused God's name to be (Rom. ii. 24; comp. 2 Sam. xii. 14).
[2] A royal law, because the best of all laws—a king of laws. "Love is the fulfilment (πλήρωμα) of the Law" (Rom. xiii. 10).
[3] "He who observes but one precept, secures for himself an advocate (Parklit, or Paraclete), and he who commits one sin procures for himself an accuser" (Pirke Avoth, iv. 15).
[4] "A garment is torn though you only take away one piece of it; a harmony in music is spoiled if only one voice be out of tune" (Starke).
[5] St. James is thinking of the free service of the will to Christ's pure moral law, not of the law "which gendereth to bondage," and enforces incessant restrictions on unwilling souls (Gal. iv. 10, 24), which was a yoke which neither they nor their fathers had been able to bear (Acts xv. 10). [6] Matt. vii. 1.
[7] This is a great law of the moral kingdom. It applies alike to God and to men. 'Tis mightiest in the mightiest. It is the reason why Christian universality is better than Judaising exclusiveness; why the geniality, love, and brightness of the Gospel is better than the gloomy hatred of the Talmud; why tolerance is better than the Inquisition; why philanthropy is nobler than sensual egotism (see Lange, p. 78).
[8] Comp. οὐ γὰρ ὠφελήσει τινα τὸ λέγειν ἀλλὰ τὸ ποιεῖν ἐκ παντὸς οὖν τρόπου καλῶν ἔργων χρεία (Clem. Hom. viii. 7).
[9] Not if it be the faith that St. James has in view, which is here merely a theoretically orthodox belief, not a vital faith. Such a faith cannot save such a man. Vital faith carries in itself the animating principle from which works must emanate. The whole argument is aimed at those Antinomians who said, "If you have faith, it matters little how you live" (Jer. in Mich. iii. 5).
[10] Such a parting benediction would, without some accompanying help, be as incongruous a mockery as Claudius's reply of "Avete vos" to the gladiators' "Morituri te salutamus" (Judg. xviii. 6; 2 Kings v. 19; Luke vii. 50; viii. 48). Similarly, Plautus has "Of what use is your benevolent language if your help is dead?" (Epidic. i. 2, 13).
[11] St. James uses an illustration of what faith leads to, which he borrows from the teaching of Christ (Matt. xxv. 35—45).
[12] Just as the compassion is dead and useless if it be that of—

"The sluggard Pity's vision-weaving tribe,
Who sigh for wretchedness yet shun the wretched,
Nursing in some dalicious solitude
Their dainty loves and slothful sympathies"—(Coleridge.)

may say[1] [quite fairly], 'Thou hast faith and I have works. Show me thy faith without the works'—which you cannot do—' and I,' who do not pretend to believe in the possibility of such a faith, 'will,' very easily, 'show thee my faith by my works'" (ii. 14—18).

Assuming that the Solifidian—the believer in the possibility of an abstract faith which can show no works as an evidence of its existence—is thus refuted, St. James proceeds to refute him still farther :—" Thou believest that God is one."[2] It was the proud boast of the Jew, who among all the nations of antiquity, gloried in being a monotheist.

"Excellent so far; the demons also believe and shudder.[3] But wilt thou recognise, O vain man,[4] that faith apart from works is idle?[5] Abraham, our father—was he not justified by works, when he offered up Isaac his son upon the altar?[6] Dost thou see that faith wrought with his works,[7] and by works the faith was perfected?[8] And the Scripture was fulfilled which says,[9] ' But Abraham believed God, and it was reckoned unto him for righteousness, and he was called the Friend of God.'[10] Ye see that by works a man is justified, and not by faith only.[11] But likewise also Rahab, the harlot,[12] was she not justified by works, when she received the messengers,

so faith is dead and useless if it do not work by love. " No spirit, if no work (Spectrum est, seu spiritus); a flying shadow it is; a spirit it is not, if work it do not. Having wherewith to do good, if you do it not, talk not of faith, for you have no faith in you if you have wherewith to show it and show it not " (Bp. Andrewes).

[1] 'Ἀλλ' ἐρεῖ τις, is something in St. Paul's manner (1 Cor. xv. 35; Rom. ix. 19). The interlocutor is not here, however, an objector, but a Gentile Christian, who makes a perfectly true criticism of the worthlessness of an idle orthodoxy (see Tert. De Poenit. 5). "Faith," says Luther, "is the mother who gives birth to the virtues as her children." And St. Paul presses the same truth quite as clearly as St. James (Rom. ii. 13).

[2] Σὺ, emphatic; thou, as distinguished from the heathen. The Jews had learnt Credere Deum, and Credere Deo, but not (according to St. Augustine's distinction) Credere in Deum. This shows that St. James is thinking of some sort of verbal orthodoxy, not of specific Christian faith. The Unity of God was the very first and most important belief of Judaism. The first line of the Talmud begins with discussing it; it was daily repeated in the Shemá (Deut. vi. 4), to which, as to all their observances, the Jews attached most extravagant virtue. Thus they said that the fires of Gehenna would be cooled for him who repeated it with attention to its very letters. To this they attached Hab. ii. 4. All the fine things which they called hapardés (פרדס), the " Garden," or " Paradise," turned on the Unity of God. Akhiva was supremely blessed because he died uttering the word " One " (see infra, p. 352).

[3] This unique and unexpected word (φρίσσουσι, horrescunt) comes in with great rhetorical and ironic force. It explains the horror of physical antipathy. For the fact, see Matt. viii. 29; Mark ix. 20, 26. " The sarcasm lies in the fact itself. Formally, it only flashes out in the splendid καί" (Lange).

[4] The Hebrew רֵקָא, Ráca (Matt. v. 20). Some think that this objurgation is aimed at St. Paul! Apostles did not speak of each other in the language of modern religious controversy (See Pirke Avoth, i. 17).

[5] ἀργή, B. C.

[6] St. Paul does not refer to this act, which is indeed only alluded to in Heb. xi. 17 (and Wisd. x. 5), but to the faith which Abraham had shown forty years before.

[7] " Operosa fuit non otiosa " (Calvin).

[8] "Faith aided in the completion of the work, and the work aided in the completion of the faith " (Lange). "His faith was completed, not that it had been imperfect, but that it was consummated in the exercise " (Luther).

[9] Says elsewhere, Gen. xv. 6 (before the sacrifice of Isaac).

[10] Is. xli. 8. In Gen. xxv. 9, this clause seems to have occurred in some readings (Ewald, Die Sendschreiben, ii. 225). Abraham is still known through the East as El Khalil Alah ("the Friend of God "), and hence Hebron is called El Khalil. Dean Plumptre points out the curious fact that the title occurs neither in the Hebrew nor in the LXX., and is first applied to Abraham by Philo (De resip. Noe, c. 11).

[11] St. Paul had adduced Abraham as a proof of justification by faith, not by legalism. St. James adduces him as an example of justification by the works which spring from faith, not by orthodoxy.

[12] This second example is chosen because he wishes to prove the unity of faith in Jews and Gentiles, by two examples of faith manifested by works. Abraham was a man, a Hebrew, a Prophet; Rahab a woman, a Canaanite, a harlot; yet both were justified (i.e., shown to be righteous in the moral sense) by works which sprang from their faith (Heb. xi. 31).

and hastily sent them forth by another way? For even as the body apart from the spirit is dead, so also faith apart from works is dead."¹

Leaving the theology of this remarkable passage for subsequent discussion,² in order not to break the thread of the Epistle, we proceed to the next chapter.

It was natural that those who had seized a Shibboleth, of which they neither fathomed the full depth nor even rightly understood the superficial meaning, should endeavour to force it upon others with irate, obtrusive, and vehement dogmatism. This "itch of teaching," this oracular egotism, is the natural result of vanity and selfishness disguising themselves under the cloak of Gospel proselytism. With all such men words take the place of works, and dogmatising contentiousness of peace and love. Therefore he warns them against being many teachers³—self-constituted ministers—"other peoples' bishops"⁴—persons of that large class who assume that no incompetence is too absolute to rob them of the privilege of infallibility in laying down the law of truth for others. "My brethren, do not become many teachers,⁵ being well aware that we (teachers) shall receive a severer judgment than others," since our responsibility is greater than theirs. "For in many respects we stumble, all of us."⁶ Speech is the instrument of all teachers. If any man stumbles not in word, he is a perfect man,⁷ able to bridle also the whole body. Sins of speech are so common, the temptations to them are so universal, that there can be no question of the perfect wisdom and self-control of him who has acquired an absolute immunity from these. For how great is the power of the tongue! how evil its depravity, untameableness, and duplicity! It is like the little bridles which rule the horse, like the little helms that steer the great ships. It is like the spark which kindles a conflagration in the forest.⁸ Yes, the tongue—

---

¹ ii. 19—26.
² See *infra*, pp. 349—361.
³ Any authorised person might speak, either in the synagogue or the early Christian assembly (1 Cor. xiv. 28—34). The ordinary readers and preachers were not clergy at all. The eager seizure of a party watchword would be likely to lead to mere prating.
⁴ ἀλλοτριοεπίσκοποι (1 Pet. iv. 15).
⁵ Matt. xxiii. 8—10. "But be not ye called Rabbi, for one is your guide—even Christ; but all ye are brethren." "Love the work, but strive not after the honour of a teacher" (Pirke Avoth, i. 10).
⁶ St. James would no more have thought of claiming immunity from sin than St. Paul (Phil. iii. 12) or St. John (1 John i. 8) did. When Schleiermacher condemned this passage as "bombast," he condemned the equally strong language of many great moralists of all ages. And it must be remembered that St. James was living in the Jerusalem of A.D. 60. There was not more backbiting then than there now is, but good men felt its evil more strongly. They did not take an interest in it, let it lie on their tables, subscribe to its dissemination. Compare the language of the Son of Sirach (xxviii. 15—26): "Many have fallen by the edge of the sword, but not so many as have fallen by the tongue. ... Strong cities hath it pulled down; well is he that hath not passed through the venom thereof. ... The death thereof is an evil death; the grave were better than it. ... Such as forsake the Lord shall fall into it; and it shall burn in them and not be quenched; it shall be sent unto them as a lion, and devour them as a leopard." For Jewish views, even of the Talmudists, see Schoettgen.
⁷ "By thy words thou shalt be justified" (Matt. xii. 37). See the great sermon on this text by Barrow.
⁸ Both these metaphors are common in classical writers (Soph. *Antig.* 332, 475), and both occur in the hymn of Clemens of Alexandria (*Pedag. ad finem*). "Quam lenibus initiis quanta incendia oriuntur" (Sen. *Controv.* v. 5). "ΥΛη is here probably "a wood," not "material." The setting on fire of forests by sparks furnished similes even in Homer's days (Hom. *Il.* ii.

that world of injustice—is a fire. It inflames the wheel of being,[1] and is ever inflamed by Gehenna.[2] It is the sole untameable creature—a restless mischief brimmed with deathful venom.[3] Therewith we bless the Lord and Father, and therewith we curse the human beings who have been made after His likeness.[4] Is this inconsistency anything short of monstrous?[5] Is it not like a fountain bubbling out of the same fissure the bitter as well as the sweet? Can a tree produce fruits not its own?[6] Can the salt water of a cursing tongue produce the sweet water of praise? (iii. 1—12).

These sins of the tongue among Jews and Christians sprang in a great measure from the obtrusive rivalries, the contentious ambitions to which he had alluded in the first verse. Never have they been extinct. Party spirit has always been a curse and disease of every religion, even of the Christian. The formulas of Christian Councils have been tagged with anathemas; Te Deums have been chanted at Autos da Fé. And because this factiousness shows an absence of true wisdom amid the pride of its imagined presence, he proceeds to contrast the false and the true wisdom. True wisdom, true understanding,[7] is shown by a course of life spent in meekness, which is the attribute of wisdom.[8] For a man to boast of wisdom when his heart is full of bitter emulation and party spirit is a lying vaunt. The wisdom of which he thus boasts is not, at any rate, the heavenly wisdom of the Christian, but earthly, animal,[9] demon-like. The wisdom which evinces itself in party spirit leads to unhallowed chaos and every contemptible practice. "But the wisdom from above is first pure,[10] then peaceful, reasonable, open to persuasion,

---

455; xi. 115; Virg. *Georg.* ii. 303: "et totum involvit flammis nemus"); but St. James is more likely to have adopted it from Philo (*De migr. Abr.* p. 407). μεγαλαυχεῖ (ver. 5) occurs only in Philo.

[1] iii. 6, τὸν τροχὸν τῆς γενέσεως (comp. Eccl. xii. 6). It is a phrase of uncertain meaning, perhaps "the orb of creation"—hardly " the rolling wheel of life" (ἀνακυκλήσις, see Windet. *De Vita funct.*), though Anacreon uses that expression, and the Syriac here has, "it turneth the course of our generations, which run as a wheel" (comp. Sil. Ital. iii. 6, "rota volvitur aevi").
[2] Comp. Pss. lii. 2—5; cxx. 3, 4; Prov. xxvi. 27: "*there is as a burning fire;*" (Ecclus. v. 14; xxii. 24, "As the vapour and smoke of a furnace goeth before the fire, so reviling before blood").
[3] Hermas, who has several references to this Epistle, says (*Pastor.* ii. 2): "Backbiting is a wicked spirit, and a restless demon" (comp. Ps. cxl. 13).
[4] Even in fallen man, "*remanet nobilitas indelebilis*" (Beng.). He still retains sparks (*scintillulae*, Confess. Belg. 14) of the heavenly fire, though "very far gone from original righteousness" (Art. ix.).
[5] The word χρή occurs here alone in the New Testament or the LXX. The word which they use for "ought" is δεῖ, which expresses moral fitness. "Praise is not seemly in the mouth of a sinner" (Ecclus. xv. 9).
[6] Matt. vii. 16, 17. The metaphor both of this and the next verse show a marked local colouring.
[7] "Who is wise (*chakam*) and intelligent (*nabhon*) amongst you?" (Deut. i. 13; iv. 6; Eph. i. 8; Col. i. 9). The ἐπιστήμων is one who understands and knows; the σοφός is one who carries out his knowledge into his life. "Knowledge comes, but wisdom lingers" (Tennyson). (Job xxviii. 12.)
[8] Ps. l. 16—20.
[9] ψυχικός (see Jude 19); ψυχικοί, πνεῦμα μὴ ἔχοντες. "Soulish"—*i.e.*, sensuous—living only the natural animal life, and therefore *unspiritual*. This wisdom is earthly, because it avariciously cares for the goods of earth (Phil. iii. 19); animal, because it is under the sway of animal lusts (1 Cor. ii. 14); demon-like, because full of pride, egotism, malignity, and ambition, which are works of the devil (1 Tim. iv. 1).
[10] "Pure," *i.e.*, chaste, consecrated, free from admixture of carnal motives. Even out of this strong condemnation of contentious dogmatism, the universal misinterpretation of Scripture has extorted an excuse—nay, an argument—for intolerance. But the wisdom is only said to be

full of mercy and good fruits, without vacillation,[1] without hypocrisy. . . . But the fruit of righteousness is ever sown in peace by those who work peace" (ii. 13—18). Thus we see that with St. James, no less than with St. Paul, St. Peter, and St. John, love, peace, mutual respect, mutual toleration, is the highest form of wisdom, and is a far truer sign than a contentious and bitter orthodoxy that he who has it has reached to the highest ideal of the Christian character.

But how strong are the feelings of St. James on this subject! It was a period of turmoil and contention within and without the fold.[2]

"Whence," he asks, "come wars, and whence fightings among you? Is it not from hence, from your pleasures that militate in your members?[3] Ye desire and have not. Ye murder[4] and envy and are not able to obtain. Ye battle and ye war, and ye receive not because ye ask not for yourselves. Ye ask and receive not because ye ask ill for yourselves that ye may squander it in your pleasures. Adulteresses![5] know ye not that the friendship of the world is enmity against God? Whosoever, then, prefers to be a friend of the world, establishes himself as an enemy of God. Or deem ye that it is vainly that the Scripture saith, 'The spirit which He made to dwell in us jealously yearneth over us?'[6] But" (because of this jealous love for us) "He giveth greater grace. Wherefore He saith God arrayeth Himself against the haughty, but giveth grace to the humble"[7] (iv. 1—6).

i. This passage is in several respects remarkable. First, we cannot but feel surprise at such a picture as this. Wars, fightings, pleasures

---

"*first* pure," because "purity" describes it *inward essence*, and the other epithets its outward manifestations. "Peaceable" (Matt. v. 9), "reasonable," *i.e.*, "forbearing" (1 Tim. iii. 3), "open to persuasion" (Vulg. *suadibilis*), or perhaps "winning its way by gentleness." Seven qualities of wisdom—seven colours of the Divine rainbow—all blended into the one "Light of the world." The phrase "the wisdom from above" is common in the Talmudic writings, where it is attributed to Adam, Enoch, Solomon, etc.

[1] ἀδιάκριτος, one of St. James's frequent *hapax legomena*. It is better to interpret it by the ordinary sense of διακρίνομαι, "to doubt." The E. V. follows Luther in rendering it "without partiality." Bengel says, "Non *facit discrimen* ubi non opus est." Lange, "unsectarian," "not Separatist," *i.e.*, not Pharisaic. There is force in his remark that the epithet would naturally refer to social conduct, and have some relation to ἀνυπόκριτος. If so, we may render it "not partial," or "censorious." "Being ἀδιάκριτος it does not spy out motes in a brother's eye; and being ἀνυπόκριτος, it does not hide the beam in its own" (Wordsworth, who adds that "this beautiful picture of true wisdom may be placed side by side with that of charity portrayed by St. Paul, 1 Cor. xiii.). Comp. Ecclus. i. 1—11, "All wisdom cometh from the Lord, and is with Him for ever . . . Wisdom hath been created before all things, and the understanding of prudence from everlasting. The Word of God Most High is the fountain of wisdom . . . She is with all flesh, according to His gift, and He hath given her to them that love Him."

[2] See *infra*, Chapter XXXI., on the Last Days of Jerusalem.

[3] "For in truth nothing else except the body and its desires causes wars, and seditions, and battles" (Plato, *Phædo*, p. 66, c).

[4] Some conjecture φθονεῖτε, "ye grudge;" but the reading is probably right, and *means* "ye murder," not "ye *wish* to kill," etc. See below.

[5] Μοιχαλίδες! (the μοιχοὶ is omitted by א, A, B). The *feminine* word is explained by the common Old Testament metaphor for idolatry (Isa. liv. 5; Jer. ii. 12; Ezek. xvi. 32). Hence in the New Testament γεννὰ μοιχαλίς (Matt. xii. 39; xvi. 4; 2 Cor. xi. 2); and the strange expression of 2 Pet. ii. 14, "having eyes *full of an adulteress*" (see note there).

[6] See *infra*, p. 341. πρὸς φθόνον, not "against envy" (Luther), but the phrase seems to be adverbial, like πρὸς βίαν, πρὸς ἡδονήν, etc. ἐπιποθεῖ never means "lusteth," as in E. V., but expresses warm tenderness (2 Cor. ii. 9; Phil. i. 8). This seems to be the only tenable translation. I may mention one other version, which is to make πνεῦμα an accusative—"God yearns jealously for the spirit which He placed in us, and gives us greater grace." Yet another way (but inconsistent with the usage of the phrase ἡ γραφὴ λέγει) is to break the clause into two questions—"Do ye fancy that the Scripture speaketh vainly? Doth the Spirit, which He planted in us, lust to envy?" (I see that this is accepted by the Revised Version, with the other renderings in the margin.)

[7] Prov. iii. 34; 1 Pet. v. 5; Clem. Rom. c. 30.

that are ever setting out as it were on hostile expeditions,[1] disappointed desires, frustrate envy and even fruitless murder to supply wants which would have been granted to prayer—then, again, prayers utterly neglected or themselves tainted with sin because misdirected to reckless gratification of pleasure, and because ruined by contentiousness[2] and selfishness—all this spiritual adultery, the divorce of the soul from God to the love of the world—is this indeed a picture of the condition of Christian Churches within thirty years of the death of Christ? Again, I see no possible solution of the difficulty except in the twofold answer— partly that St. James is influenced by the state of things which he saw going on around him in Judæa, and partly that he is drawing no marked line of distinction between Jews and Christians in the communities which he is addressing.[3] And this being so, there was certainly in the Palestine of that day an ample justification for every line of the dark delineation. Alike among priests and patriots there was a fierce and luxurious greed. Strifes about the Law were loud and violent.[4] Even in the days of our Lord, while the tree of Jewish nationality was still green, and not dry, as it had now become, the very Temple had been polluted into a brigands' cave.[5] The dagger of the assassin was often secretly employed to get rid of a political opponent. A bloodthirsty spirit had possessed itself of the once peaceful nation. Righteousness had once dwelt in their city, but now murderers. Men like Barabbas had become heroes of the people. Men like Theudas, and Judas, and the Egyptian impostor, were crowding the horizon of the people's life, and found no difficulty in leading after them 4,000 men or even murderers. Zealots had increased in numbers and in recklessness. Bands of robbers were the terror of every district which offered them hopes of plunder. Assassins lurked in the streets, and mingled unnoticed in the dense throngs which crowded the Temple courts at the great annual festivals.[6] Sects were arrayed in bitter envy against sects, and all were united in burning hatred against their Roman conquerors. It became in popular estimation a pious act—an act which even High Priests could hail and bless—for *sicarii* to bind themselves under a curse to waylay and massacre an enemy.[7] The fury of fanatical savagery assumed the guise of patriotism. False Christs and false prophets abounded and flourished, but "Stone him," and "Crucify him," and "Away with him," and "He is not fit to live," were cries into which

---

[1] iv. 1, στρατευομένων.
[2] St. Peter saw no less clearly (1 Pet. iii. 7) that quarrelsomeness is fatal to prayer.
[3] It is a weighty remark of Lange (ad loc.) that "James put this Epistle into the hands of the Jewish Christians that it might influence all Jews, as it was a missionary instruction to the converted for the unconverted, and the truly converted for the half-converted."
[4] St. Paul (Tit. iii. 9) applies to these the very word of St. James, "legal battles" (μάχα νομικαί). There were the struggling sects of Pharisees, Sadducees, Essenes, Herodians, Samaritans, etc. Laurentius says—"Non loquitur Apostolus de bellis et caedibus, sed de mutuis dissidiis, litibus, jurgiis, et contentionibus." Doubtless of these—but of actual struggles also.
[5] σπήλαιον λῃστῶν, Matt. xxi. 13. Comp. Mark xv. 7; Acts xxi. 38.
[6] See Jos. B. J. ii. 1, 23; iv. 10; vii. 31; Antt. xviii. 1.
[7] Acts xxiii. 12.

men were ready to burst at a moment's notice against those whose thoughts had been enlightened to believe in the Son of God.

Besides all this, the world and the interests of the world assumed a complete preponderance in the thoughts of all men; the fear of God seemed to have been banished into the far background of life. Could such men pray at all? Yes, and long prayers and loud prayers in the Temple courts and at the corners of the streets at the very time when they were devouring widows' houses, and making their proselytes ten-times-worse children of Gehenna than themselves. There is literally no end to the anomalies of prayers. Rochester went home to pen a pious prayer in his private diary on the very day that he had been persuading his sovereign to commit an open sin. Cornish wreckers went straight from church to light their beacon fires, and Italian brigands promise to their saints a share in the profits of their murders.[1] This "Italian piety" is the terrible state of moral apostasy against which St. James speaks with all the impassioned sternness of one of the old prophets. Like Amos, who had, no less than himself, been both a peasant and a Nazarite, he raised his indignant voice against the luxury and idolatry of the Chosen People. It is in the love of the world that he sees the source of all these enormities, and it is against this love of the world, arrayed in the golden robe of the hierarchy, and wearing "Holiness to the Lord" upon its forehead—it is against this tainted scrupulosity and mitred atheism that he speaks trumpet-tongued.

ii. But besides these remarks on the general purport of the chapter, we must notice his unidentified quotation. The English version renders it "*the spirit that dwelleth in us lusteth to envy.*" The correct version, according to the best reading, is probably as I have given it, "The spirit, which He made to dwell in us, yearneth over us jealously." The meaning, then, is that the guilt of worldly unfaithfulness is enhanced because the Spirit of God, which he hath given us, longs with a jealous fondness that we should pay to God an undivided allegiance, a whole-hearted friendship; and for that reason He gives us greater grace—greater because of His yearning pity and love.[2] But where does this passage occur in Scripture? Doubtless from the library of the writers of the Old Covenant, which forms our Old Testament, we can produce analogies, more or less distinct, to the general meaning of this utterance,[3] but nowhere do we find the exact words. Only two solutions are therefore possible—(1) St. James may be quoting from some lost book, or

---

[1] Plumptre, p. 89.
[2] Here, as elsewhere, I have not thought it worth while to trouble the reader with masses of "explanations," which torture out of the words the most impossible senses by the most untenable methods. Beza, Grotius, etc., make it mean "the spirit of man has a natural bias to envy," but *invidi* cannot bear this sense, nor that given by Bede, Calvin, &c., "Is the Spirit (of God) prone to envy?" nor that of Bengel, "the Spirit lusteth against envy." There is much less objection to the view of Huther, Wiesinger, etc., "He (God) yearns jealously over the Spirit which He has placed in us, and gives greater grace" (*supra*, p. 339).
[3] It has been variously referred to Gen. vi. 3, 5; Num. xi. 29; Ezek. xxiii. 25; xxxvi. 27; Deut. v. 9; xxxii. 10, 11; Ps. cxix. 20; Prov. xxi 10; Cant. viii. 6; Ecclus. iv. 4; Wisd. vi. 12, 23.

some apocryphal book—like the *Testament of the Twelve Patriarchs*. The suggestion is rendered less unlikely by the references which he makes in this Epistle to other apocryphal books,[1] and by the fact that his brother, St. Jude, quotes from the book of Enoch.[2] We must in that case understand the words ἡ γραφή in a lower sense than that which we attribute to the Scripture. Or (2) he may be adopting the method, not unknown to the Scripture writers and to early Fathers, of concentrating the meaning of several separate passages into one terse summary.[3] In that case the word "saith" will have to be understood generically to mean, "Is not this the sense of Scripture?" If we adopt this solution, we must suppose that the passages alluded to are such as Gen. vi. 3, "My spirit shall not always strive with men;" or Deut. xxxii. 11, where God describes His love for Israel under the image of an eagle covering her young in the nest, and bearing them on her wings, and where in the Septuagint this very verb *epipothei*, or "yearns over," occurs; or, again, Ezek. xxxvi. 27, "I will put My spirit within you." The difficulty cannot yet be considered to have been removed, but other methods of solving it are far less probable than the two to which I have here referred.

iii. Having thus shown their dangerous condition, he urges them, with strong exhortation, which reminds us of the tone of Joel, to submission, moral effort, resistance of the devil,[4] the earnest seeking of God, and deep humiliation of soul,[5] which might lead God to interfere on their behalf.

iv. Then, with a repetition of the word "brethren," which shows that his rebukes are being uttered in the spirit of love, he warns them once more against evil-speaking as a sin which is averse to the humility which he has been urging on them, since it rises from an imaginary superiority. It arrogantly usurps the functions of God, who is the one true Judge, because He alone stands above the Law on the behests of which we are not capable of passing any final judgment.[6]

v. Passing to another sin, he strongly condemns the braggart self-confidence[7] and sensual security with which, like the Rich Fool in the Parable, men make gainful plans for the future without any reference to God, or to His provident ordering of our lives, or to the fact that life itself

---

[1] Ecclesiasticus and Wisdom. Similarly the writer of the Epistle to the Hebrews makes distinct references to the Books of Maccabees (xi. 37, 38).
[2] Jude 14.
[3] We find similar condensed quotations in John vii. 33, 42; Matt. ii. 23; and perhaps Eph. v. 14. Dean Plumptre quotes from Clemens Romanus (c. 46) the curious passage, "It has been written, 'Cleave to the saints, for they who cleave to them shall be sanctified.'"
[4] This is one of the few places in the New Testament where διάβολος occurs. "The devil," says Hermas (Past. ii. 12), "can wrestle with us, but cannot throw us; if, then, thou resist him, he will be conquered, and flee from thee utterly ashamed." (Matt. iv. 1—11.")
[5] He uses the striking word κατήφεια—"downcastness of face"—which occurs nowhere else in the New Testament. He is thinking of the outward manifestations as the signs of the inward humiliation.
[6] "Nostrum non est judicare, praesertim cum exsequi non possumus" (Bengel). "To offer to domineer over the conscience," says the Emperor Maximilian, "is to assault the citadel of heaven."
[7] iv. 16. ἀλαζονεία only in 1 John ii. 16: "Ye boast in your vain-glorious presumptions."

is—or rather that *they* themselves are—but as a fleeting mist.[1] They *knew* in their hearts that they ought not to speak thus. If they thought for a moment their consciences would condemn them for thus ignoring all reference to God, and this was a plain proof that it was sin[2] (iv. 13—17).

vi. Then in language full of prophetic imagery and prophetic fire, meant to terrify men into thoughts of repentance, but not by any means as Calvin too characteristically said, *absque spe veniae*—" apart from hope of pardon "—he bursts into terrible denunciation of the rich, which shows how much his thoughts had dwelt upon their arrogant rapacity.

"Go to now, ye rich, weep, howling[3] over your miseries that are coming upon you. Your riches are rotted, and your garments have become moth-eaten. Your gold and your silver is rusted through and through,[4] and the rust of them shall be for a witness to you,[5] and shall eat your flesh[6] as fire. Ye treasured up in the last days.[7] So the pay of your labourers, who reaped your fields, the pay kept back by fraud, cries aloud from you,[8] and the cries of the reapers have entered into the ears of the Lord of Sabaoth.[9] Ye luxuriated on the earth and waxed wanton, ye fattened your hearts in a day of slaughter.[10] Ye condemned, ye killed the just man. He doth not resist you[11] (v. 1—6).

---

[1] Job vii. 7; Ps. cii. 3; Wisd. v. 9—14. The best reading is ἀτμίς γάρ ἐστε, " for ye are a vapour," B, and the Syriac and Æthiopic versions (and practically A, K, for ἔσται must be due to Itacism). " Pulvis et umbra *sumus* " (Hor.). But St. James turns the transitoriness of life to an opposite lesson from that of the Epicureans (Hor. Od. 1, 9 ; 1 Cor. xv. 32).

[2] " There shall no harm happen unto me " (Ps. x. 6); " I shall die in my nest " (Job xxix. 18). For a Jew to talk thus, as if there were no God, or as though He took no part in the concerns of life, was to run counter to the central thought of their whole dispensation. A sense of God's nearness was the one thing which more than all others separated the Jews from other races as a chosen people. To abnegate this conviction in common talk was to show a practical apostasy. The Rabbinists also felt this. In *Debharim Rabba*, § 9, a father at his son's circumcision produces wine seven years old, and says, " With this wine will I continue for a long time to celebrate the birth of my new-born son." That night Rabbi Simeon meets the Angel of Death, and asks him " why he is wandering about." " Because," said Asrael, " *I slay those who say, We will do this or that, and think not how soon death may overtake them.* The man who said he would drink that wine often shall die in thirty days." From this verse and from 1 Cor. iv. 19, " I will come quickly to you, *if God will*," has come the common phrase, " *Deo volente*."

[3] Only in Isa. xiii. 6; xiv. 31; xv. 3; xxxiii.; Ezek. xxxvii. The language must be judged from the standpoint of prophetical analogies in Isaiah, Amos, etc., and also in Matt. xxiii., Rev. xviii. And the warnings, like all God's warnings, are hypothetical (Jonah iii. 10; Jer. xviii. 7—10).

[4] v. 2. The perfects are *prophetic* perfects; they express absolute certainty as to the ultimate result. Κατίωται is another ἅπαξ λεγόμενον (except Ecclus. xii. 11), as are σέσηπεν (Ecclus. xiv. 19) and σητόβρωτα in this verse. Gold and silver do not rust, but the expression is perfectly intelligible (Isa. i. 22, " Thy silver has become dross ").

[5] " In their tarnish and consumption you may see a picture of what will come on you." " Magna vanitas ! thesaurisant morituris morituris " (Aug.).

[6] τὰς σάρκας (plur.) has been taken to mean " your bloated bodies," etc., but occurs in Lev. xxvi. 29, etc.

[7] There was much worldly prosperity and ostentatious legalism at this epoch. Some take ἐν ταῖς ἡμέραις ἐθησαυρίσατε—" your treasury of gold is in reality a treasury of fire."

[8] " From you," i.e., from your hands or treasures. Ecclus. xxxiv. 22, " He that taketh away his neighbour's living slayeth him, and he that defraudeth the labourer of his hire is a bloodshedder " (comp. Gen. iv. 10; Deut. xxiv. 14, 15; Jer. xxii. 13; Mal. iii. 5). The rendering of the E. V., " kept back by you," is also tenable. The tract Succah (f. 29, b) gives four reasons why the avaricious lose their goods, which are (1) *because they keep back the pay of their labourers*; (2) because they neglect their welfare; (3) because they shift burdens upon them; (4) because of pride.

[9] The form of expression (used by no other New Testament writer, except in a quotation, Rom. ix. 29) is characteristically Judaic. The LXX. rendering is mostly παντοκράτωρ. See Bp. Pearson *On the Creed*, Art. I.

[10] Like cattle grazing in rich pastures on the day that they are doomed to bleed (Theile); Ezek. xxxiv. 1—10.

[11] Hos. iv. 17 ; 2 Tim. ii. 24; Isa. liii. 7. This makes the conclusion of the clause far more striking than the proposed renderings, " Does he not set himself in array against you ? " or " bring the armies against you ? "

"Be patient, therefore, brethren, until the coming of the Lord.[1] So the husbandman awaiteth the precious fruit of the earth, being patient over it until he receive the early and latter rain.[2] Be patient then, ye also, stablish your hearts because the coming of the Lord is near" (v. 7, 8).

vii. Here again we ask, Of whom is the Prophet thinking? Were there indeed, in those early days of Christianity, any—still more, could there have been *many*—who correspond to this picture of voluptuous and fraudful wantonness, which had forgotten God and was so cruel and false to men? Surely St. Paul gives us the answer when he says, "Consider your calling, brethren. Not many of you are wise after the flesh; not many mighty, not many noble"[3]—and therefore certainly not many rich—"are called." In those early congregations of slaves and sufferers there was little to attract, there was everything to repel, the ordinary multitude of the wealthy. In those days the truth of the Lord's words was seen, "How hardly shall they that have riches—how hardly shall they who trust in riches—enter into the Kingdom of Heaven." The "deceitfulness of riches" became very manifest, and the "woe unto you that are rich" was seen in its full meaning. Rich men, indeed, there were in the Church, as there had been since Nicodemus and Joseph of Arimathæa brought their costly spices to the tomb; for St. Paul in one of his latest Epistles could give a charge to the rich not to be arrogant, and not to trust in the uncertainty of riches.[4] But considering what a Christian had in those days to suffer, is it conceivable that any of the few rich men who had ventured to bear the reproach of the cross would have lived the haughty, greedy, oppressive life of the men on whom St. James here hurls his unsparing denunciation? So strongly has this difficulty been felt that some, once more, see in "the rich" only a symbol of the proud, haughty, exclusive, self-satisfied religionist;[5] but though the words "rich" and "poor" may not be confined to their literal senses—yet certainly the literal sense is not excluded. Once more, I see the explanation of his passion, the moving cause of his righteous menaces, in the conduct of the leading classes at Jerusalem—the gorgeously clad Herodians, the aristocratic Sadducees. The extracts from the Talmudists which I have given on a previous page describe their conduct, and will show what bitter need there was for the language which St. James employs.

Nor is Josephus less emphatic.

"About this time," he says, "King Agrippa gave the high priesthood to Ishmael Ben Phabi. And now arose a sedition on the part of the chief priests against the priests and the leaders of the multitude at Jerusalem. Each of them gathered around himself a company of the boldest innovators and became their leader. And when they came into

---

[1] This must be a reference to *Christ's* coming.
[2] The former in winter, the latter in spring (Deut. xi. 14; Jer. iii. 3; v. 24; Joel ii. 23).
[3] 1 Cor. i. 26.
[4] 1 Tim. v. 17.
[5] Comp. Rev. ii. 9; iii. 17; and see 1 Sam. ii. 8; Ps. lxxii. 13; Amos ii. 6; Luke i. 52, 53; vi. 20; etc.

collision they both abused each other and flung stones. There was no one to keep them in awe, but all these things went on with a high hand as though in a city where there was anarchy. And such impudence and audacity seized the chief priests that they even dared to send slaves to the threshing-floors to seize the tithes due to the priests. And it happened that some of the priests died of want from being deprived of their sustenance, so completely did the violence of the seditious prevail over all justice."[1]

viii. And if these words of St. James were addressed to Jews and Jewish Christians about the year A.D. 61, how speedily were his warnings fulfilled, how terribly and how soon did the retributive doom fall on these wealthy, luxurious tyrants! A few years later Vespasian invaded Judæa. Truly there was need to howl and weep when, amid the horrors caused by the rapid approach of the Roman armies, the gold and silver of the wealthy oppressors was useless to buy bread, and they had to lay up, for the moth to eat, those gorgeous robes which it would have been a peril and a mockery to wear. The worshippers at the last fatal Passover became the victims. The rich only were marked out for the worst fury of the Zealots, and their wealth sank into the flames of the burning city. Useless were their treasures in those "last days," when there was heard at the very doors the thundering summons of the Judge! In all their rich banquets and full-fed revelling they had but fattened themselves as human offerings for that day of slaughter! The Jewish historian here becomes the best commentator on the prophecies of the Christian Apostle.

ix. "*Ye condemned, ye murdered the just.*" The aorist tenses of the original may point equally well to some single act, or to a series of single acts; and "the just man" was a title of every devout and faithful Israelite. The present tense, "he doth not resist you"—so abruptly and pathetically introduced—seems to show that St. James is alluding to a general state of things. In the delivery of Christ to the Gentiles the Jewish Church had slain "that Just One;"[2] and since His death they had consented to the murder of His saints in the stoning of Stephen, and the beheading of James, the son of Zebedee. But in the scantiness of the records of the early Church of Jerusalem there is too much reason to fear that there was a crowd of obscurer martyrs.[3] And Christ suffered, as it were, again in the person of His saints. When they were murdered, He was, as it were, led once more to unresisted sacrifice. And now St. James himself bore pre-eminently the title of "the Just." His words might seem to have been prophetic of his own rapidly-approaching fate, while yet they tacitly repudiate the title by which he was called, to confer it on Him who alone is worthy

---

[1] Jos. *Antt.* xx. 8, § 8. He repeats the same complaints against Joshua, son of Gamala, in xx. 9, § 2.
[2] Acts vii. 52.
[3] Acts xxvi. 10. "When they were condemned to death," says St. Paul, "I gave my voice against them."

of it. But the state of things which he is describing was by no means isolated. It had been already described at length in the language of a book which also belonged to this epoch, and with which St. James has more than once shown himself to be familiar.

"For the ungodly said . . . Come on therefore, let us enjoy the good things that are present; and let us speedily use the creatures as in youth. Let us fill ourselves with costly wine and ointments, and let no flower of the spring pass by us; let none of us go without his portion of our voluptuousness—*let us oppress the poor righteous man* . . . for that which is feeble is found to be nothing worth. Let us lie in wait for the righteous. He professeth to have the knowledge of God, and he calleth himself the child of the Lord. He was made to reprove our thoughts. We are esteemed of him as counterfeits. He pronounceth the *end of the just* to be blessed, and maketh his boast that God is his father. Let us examine him with despitefulness and torture, *that we may know his meekness and prove his patience*. Let us condemn him with a shameful death, for by his own saying he shall be respected" (Wisd. ii. 6—20).

x. But all such warnings proved vain. Nay, it is probable that they only precipitated the fate of the speaker, and that he, like other prophets, felt the vengeance of those whose unrepented sins he so unsparingly denounced.[1] When the priests had murdered James the Just, not resisting them, but praying for them, the day for warning had passed away for ever, and over a guilty city and a guilty nation History pronounced once more her awful verdict of "Too late."

"Ye condemned, ye murdered the just. *He resisteth you not*."[2] "And thus," says Wiesinger, "we have, as it were, standing before us the slain and unresisting righteous man, when, lo! the curtain falls. Be patient, brethren, wait!" The coming of the Lord for which they had to wait was not far distant. The husbandman had to wait in patience, and often in disappointment, for the early and latter rain. Let them learn by his example. But since the Judge was standing already before the doors,[3] let them, that they might escape His condemnation, not only bear with patience the afflictions of persecutors, but also abstain from murmuring at each other's conduct.[4] It was patience that they needed most; patience with one another, patience under external trials. As an example of that patience, let them take the prophets, and let the Book of Job[5] remind them that in the end God ever vindicates his attributes of compassionate tenderness.[6]

---

[1] Hegesippus, ap. Euseb. ii. 23; Origen, c. Cels. i. 48; Jer. De Virr. Illustr. ii.

[2] Comp. Amos v. 12: "They afflict the just . . . . therefore the prudent shall keep silence in that time."

[3] Some have fancied that the question tauntingly asked of St. James in the story of his martyrdom in Hegesippus—"Which is the door of Jesus?"—had reference to this saying of his; as though they would ask, "By which door will Christ come to judge?"; but it more probably refers to John x. 7—9 (see Gieseler, Ch. Hist. § 31).

[4] A clear reference to Matt. vii. 1 (μὴ στενάζετε κατ' ἀλλήλων); lit., "groan not against one another." The E. V. "grudge," once meant "murmur" (see Ps. lix. 15); "he eats his meat without grudging" (Shakesp. Much Ado, iii. 4, 90).

[5] Here alone referred to in the New Testament, though quoted in 1 Cor. iii. 19, and by Philo, De Mutat. Nom. xxiv.

[6] v. 9—11. Others interpret "Ye have seen the end of the Lord," to mean, "Ye saw the death of Christ," as in 1 Pet. ii. 22—25; πολύσπλαγχνος is yet another unique expression for εὔσπλαγχνος (Eph. iv. 32; 1 Pet. iii. 8). οἰκτίρμων occurs in Ecclus. ii. 13; Luke vi. 36.

xi. His task is now done, but he adds a few needful admonitions. Let them avoid all rash and needless oaths, and be simple in their affirmations.[1] Let them be more fervent in prayer.

"Is any one among you in affliction? Let him pray. Is any cheerful? Let him sing praise. Is any sick among you? Let him summon the elders of the Church, and let them pray over him, anointing him with oil[2] in the name of the Lord,[2] and the prayer of faith shall save the sick man, and the Lord shall raise him (from his bed of sickness, Acts ix. 34).[4] Even if he shall have committed sin, it shall be remitted him. Confess then to one another[5] your transgressions, and pray for one another, that ye may be healed.[6] Much availeth the supplication of a just man, when it worketh with energy. Elias was a man of like passions with us,[7] and he prayed earnestly that it might not rain, and it rained not upon the earth three years and six months.[8] And again he prayed, and the heaven gave rain, and the earth brought forth her fruit."[9]

The leading idea of this passage, which Lange most needlessly allegorises, is the efficacy of Christian prayer. The course which St. James recommends in cases of sickness is natural and beautiful, and in the small numbers of the Christian communities could be easily followed. It is the advice of which the entire spirit is carried out in our service for the Visitation of the Sick. We no longer, indeed, anoint with oil, because we do not live in Palestine or in the first century.[10] The therapeutic means of one climate and age are not necessarily the best to be adopted in another, but prayer belongs to all

---

[1] Comp. Matt. v. 35, 36. Jews (unlike Christians, alas!) were not likely to take God's name in vain. "That ye fall not into judgment"; the reading εἰς ὑπόκρισιν, gives a worse sense, and is not well supported.

[2] A common Eastern therapeutic, as we see from Isa. i. 6; Mark vi. 13; Luke x. 34; Jos. B. J. i. 33, § 5; Antt. xvii. 6, § 5. It was also used by Romans (Pliny, H. N. xxxi. 47). The use of oil for bodily healing is retained by the Eastern Church.

[3] That is, of Christ (Matt. xxviii. 19; Acts ii. 38; iii. 16; iv. 10; 1 Cor. i. 13—15).

[4] "Nisi nempe aliter ei suppeditat ad aeternam salutem" (Grotius). In the first Prayer-book of Edward VI. the anointing was accompanied by the prayer: "Our Heavenly Father vouchsafe for His great mercy (*if it be His blessed will*) to restore to thee thy bodily health." The prayer will not be thrown away; it will be answered as is best for us and the sufferer. How much connexion this has with Extreme Unction (of which with an anathema the Council of Trent commanded it to be understood) may be seen from the fact that extreme unction is forbidden, except in cases in which recovery seems quite hopeless.

[5] In the manipulation of this text by Cornelius à Lapide, "to one another" becomes "to a priest" ("frater fratri confitemini, puta sacerdoti"). Confession in sickness is also enjoined in the Talmud (Shabbath, f. 32, a).

[6] "When Rabba fell sick he bade his family publish it abroad, that they who hated him might rejoice, and that they who loved him might intercede with God for him" (Nedarim, f. 40, a). "The wise men have said, No healing is equal to that which comes from the Word of God and prayer" (Sepher Ha Chayim).

[7] Acts xiv. 15.

[8] Luke iv. 25. This period (42 months, 1,260 days—comp. Rev. xi. 3) was mentioned by the Jewish tradition (Yalkut Simeoni), and is perfectly consistent with fair inferences from 1 Kings xviii.

[9] v. 13–18. Thus the prayer of Elijah was one of mercy as well as one of judgment. Dean Plumptre thinks that St. James may have had in mind the sudden burst of rain after drought which fell in answer to prayer after the troubles caused by the attempt of Caligula to set up his statue in the Temple (Jos. Antt. xviii. 8, § 6). Analogous to this is the story of the Thundering Legion (Euseb. H. E. v. 5; Tert. Apol. 5), and the well-known story of Mr. Grimshaw. Hegesippus says of James himself, that it was supposed by the people that he caused rain to fall by his prayers.

[10] "Things which were practised and prescribed by Christ Himself and His Apostles are not of perpetual obligation unless they are conducive to an end which is of perpetual necessity."—Bp. Wordsworth, who instances feet-washing (John xiii. 14) and the Kiss of Peace (1 Thess. v. 26; 1 Pet. v. 14).

countries and all times, and the mutual confession of sins is often helpful. We must always distinguish between the letter and the spirit, the accidental adjunct and the eternal principle. If this passage has been perverted into the doctrine and practice of extreme unction regarded as a sacrament,[1] and of sacramental confession to a priest, it has only shared the fate of hundreds of other passages. There are few prominent texts on which the tottering structures of purely inferential dogmas have not been reared. Thus do men build upon Divine foundations the hay and stubble of human fancies. And if the passage has thus been perverted in one direction by the growth of sacerdotalism, it has been perverted in another by the fanaticism of ignorance. Because the promises of healing given by St. James are unconditional, it has been assumed by some poor fanatics that no one need ever die, as though death, in God's good time, were not man's richest birthright, and as though every good man's prayer for any earthly blessing was not in itself made absolutely conditional on the will of God.[2] But neither for extreme unction, nor for sacramental confession, nor for sacerdotal absolution,[3] nor for fanatical extravagance, does this passage afford the slightest sanction. Such inferences are only possible to the exegesis which takes the sound of the words, and not their true meanings. The lessons which we must here learn are lessons of the blessedness of sympathy, and of holy intercourse, and of the humble confession of sin, and, above all, of prayer, at *all* times, but most of all in times of sickness. Our faith, too, may find encouragement in the efficacy of prayer for the achievement of results which even transcend the ordinary course of nature. In enforcing this faith by the example of Elijah,[4] St. James does so on the express ground that, saint though he was, and prophet though he was, he was no supernatural being, but one " of like passions " with ourselves.

xii. Then, in one last weighty word, comes the solemn close of the Epistle.

" My brethren, if any one among you wander from the truth, and one convert him, know that he who has converted a sinner from the error of his way shall save a soul from death, and shall cover a multitude of sins " (v. 19, 20).

He has spoken many words of warning and condemnation against the worldliness, the violence, the forgetfulness of God, which were but too prevalent among Jewish and Christian communities, and he has

---

[1] Anointing with oil was provided for in the first Prayer-book of Edward VI., " if the sick man desire it " ; but as no *miraculous* results can follow, and as oil is not specially valuable in our climate as a means of healing in *all* diseases, it was wisely dropped in the Prayer-book of 1552 (see Jer. Taylor's Preface to *Holy Dying*).
[2] Œcumenius, on the other hand, has no warrant for confining the reference of the verse to miraculous healings in the days of the Apostles (the χάρισμα ἰαμάτων, 1 Cor. xii. 9).
[3] Even Cardinal Cajetan admits, with perfect frankness: " Haec verba non loquuntur de Sacramentali Unctione extremae unctionis—nec hic est sermo de confessione sacramentali."
[4] It is implied in 1 Kings xviii. 42, seq., that Elijah prayed for rain. It was the Jewish tradition that he also prayed for the drought, but Scripture does not say so. He announced it (1 Kings xvii. 1).

given many an exhortation to patience, and dehortation from iniquity. But this last word is a word to those who were most faithful, and is meant to stimulate them to the best and most blessed of all duties—the endeavour to help and save the souls of others. No reward could equal that of success in such a task.[1] To hide as with the gracious veil of penitence and forgiveness the many sins of a sinner was a Christlike service, and he who was enabled to render it would share in the joy of Christ. And may not the thought be at least involved that in covering the sins of another he would also be helping to cover his own—that he who waters others shall be watered also himself?[2]

And there, as with a seal affixed to a testament,[3] he ends. He would leave that thought last in their minds, and would suffer neither greetings nor messages to weaken the force of the injunction, or the supremacy of the blessing by which he would encourage them to its fulfilment. "*Insigni doctrinâ, velut colophone epistolam absolvit.*"[4]

CHAPTER XXIII.

ST. JAMES AND ST. PAUL ON FAITH AND WORKS.

"Thy works and alms and all thy good endeavour
Staid not behind, nor in the grave were trod;
But, as Faith pointed with her golden rod,
Followed thee up to joy and bliss for ever."—MILTON.

OUR sketch of the Epistle of St. James cannot conclude without a few words on the famous passage in which, it has been supposed, the Bishop of Jerusalem deliberately contravenes and argues against the most characteristic formula of the Apostle of the Gentiles.[5]

---

[1] Ps. xxxii. 1, 2; lxxxv. 2; Neh. iv. 5; Prov. x. 12; 1 Pet. iv. 8. "He commends the correspondence of brothers from its *result*, that we may more eagerly devote ourselves to it" (Calvin). A faint analogy occurs in Yoma, f. 87, a, "Whoever leads many to righteousness, sin is not committed by his hand."

[2] "Whosoever destroyeth *one* soul of Israel, Scripture counts it to him as though he had destroyed the whole world; and whoso preserveth one soul of Israel, Scripture counts it as though he had preserved the whole world" (Sanhedrin, f. 37, a). R. Meyer said—"Great is repentance, because for the sake of one that truly repenteth, the whole world is pardoned (Hos. xiv. 4)" (Yoma, f. 86, b). How much wiser and more controlled is the language of St. James!

[3] Herder. [4] Zuinglius.

[5] I have consulted the treatment of this subject by Luther, Bengel, Jer. Taylor (Sermon iii. "*Fides formata*"), Barrow (*Sermon on Justifying Faith*), De Wette (whose note is quoted in Alford, *ad loc.*), Hare (*Vindication of Luther*), Bishop Lightfoot, Plumptre, Dean Bagot, Wordsworth, Ewald, Lange, Pfleiderer, Baur, Wiesinger, Huther, Schaff, Reuss, Immer (*N. Test. Theol.*), Meander, and other writers.

Let us first place side by side the passages which are in most direct apparent contradiction:

"... *if Abraham were justified by works*, he hath whereof to glory, but not before God" (Rom. iv. 2). "*Therefore being justified by faith*, we have peace with God through our Lord Jesus Christ" (Rom. v. 1). "By grace are ye saved *thro' faith ... not of works*, lest any man should boast" (Eph. ii. 8, 9). "*Therefore we conclude that a man is justified by faith without the deeds of the law*" (Rom. iii. 28).	"*Was not Abraham our father justified by works* when he had offered Isaac his son upon the altar?" (Jas. ii. 21). "What doth it profit, my brethren, though a man say he hath faith, and have not works? *Can the faith save him?*" (Jas. ii. 14). "... *Faith, if it hath not works, is* dead, being alone" (Jas. ii. 17). "Ye see, then, *how that by works a man is justified, and not by faith only*" (Jas. ii. 24).

It is hardly strange that the opposite character of these statements should have attracted deep attention, and of late years there have been two distinct views respecting them.

(1.) One is that the passages involve a real and even intentional contradiction.[1] Baur, while holding that St. James meant to oppose the formulæ of St. Paul, or of his School, yet speaks with moderation. He believes that St. James's arguments were not so much meant to be polemical as corrective of misapprehensions, and therefore that they were dictated by the true spirit of catholic unity. Others, however, and notably the advanced members of the Tübingen School, regard the Epistle as a bitter manifesto of Judaising Christians against the Paulinists.[2] The research and insight of Baur led him to a real discovery when he pointed out the importance of the contest between the Judaisers and the Paulinists. Those who pushed his views to an extreme were prepared to sacrifice the entire historical credibility of the Acts of the Apostles in order to make out that St. James and St. Paul, or at least their immediate followers, hated each other with irreconcilable opposition. They thought, in fact, that in the Clementine Homilies, with their strong animus against St. Paul, they had discovered the true key to the early history of the Church. They attributed to the Apostles themselves heretical slanders which they would have rejected with astonished indignation. They think that three of the Apostles—St. James, St. John, and St. Jude—were Judaists, who not only took an impassioned part in the controversies which were excited by the actions of St. Paul, but have even recorded their abhorrence of his views upon the Sacred page. In their opinion, it is St. Paul at whom St. James is aiming one of the bitterest terms of Hebrew condemnation when he exclaims, "But art thou willing to recognise, *O empty person*,[3] that faith without works is dead?" The Epistle of St. Jude becomes,

---

[1] Luther, Cyril Lucar, Ströbel, Kern, Baur, Schwegler, Renan.

[2] The notion that Jas. iii. 13—18, and the praise of the wisdom which is "earthly, unspiritual, demoniah," is a reflection on 1 Cor. ii. 14, 15 (Hilgenfeld, *Einleit.* 536) is very baseless.

[3] רֵיקָא, Raca.

in their view, a specimen of the "hatred-breathing Epistles" which were despatched to the Jewish Churches by the heads of the Mother Church in Jerusalem, to teach Christians not only to repudiate, but to denounce the special "Gospel" of the Apostle of the Gentiles. According to their interpretation, St. John, the Apostle of Love, hurled forth against his great fellow-Apostle yet fiercer execration, and, in " cries of passionate hatred," described him as a False Apostle, a Balaam, a Jezebel, the founder of the Nicolaitans, and a teacher of crime and heresy. They, therefore, regard the addresses of the Apocalypse to the Seven Churches as manifestoes directed by a Judaist against the very Apostle by whose heroic labours those Churches had been founded.[1] The falsehood of this hypothesis has long been demonstrated. It only furnishes an illustration of the ease with which a theory, resting on a narrow basis of fact, may be pushed into complete extravagance. That St. Paul and St. James approached the great truths of Christianity from different points of view; that they did not adopt the same phrases in describing them; that they differed about various questions of theory and practice; even that they stood at the head of parties whose mutual bitterness they would have been the first to deplore—is clear from the Acts of the Apostles, and still more clear from scattered notices in the Epistles of St. Paul. But it is quite common for the adherents of great thinkers to exaggerate their differences, and fail to catch their spirit. Whatever may have been the tone of the Jerusalem Pharisees towards Gentile Christians who paid no regard to the ceremonial Law, we have the evidence of St. Paul himself,[2] as well as of public records of the Church, that between him and the other Apostles there reigned a spirit of mutual respect and mutual concession. The view, therefore, that St. James was trying, in the approved modern fashion, to "write down" St. Paul, may be finally dismissed.

(2.) The other view, which has recently been maintained by Bishop Lightfoot,[3] is that St. James is not thinking of St. Paul in any way; that his expressions have no reference to him whatever; and that he is only occupied with controversies which moved in an entirely different world of ideas. Now it is, I think, sufficiently proved that this view is *possible*. Evidence has been adduced to show that the question of faith and works was one which had been long and eagerly debated in the Jewish Schools, and that the names of Abraham, and even of Rahab,[4] as forming two marked contrasts, had constantly been introduced into these discussions. It is not, therefore, true to say that St. James *must* be thinking of St. Paul. The "Solifidianism" of the Jews consisted in an exclusive trust in their Monotheism, their descent from

---

[1] Renan, *St. Paul*, p. 367.
[2] Gal. ii. 9; Acts xv. 13—21; xxi. 17—25.
[3] *Galatians*, pp. 152—162. This is the view of Schneckenburger, Theile, Neander, Schaff, Theirsch, Hofmann, Huther, Lange, Plumptre.
[4] That Rahab was prominent in Jewish thought we see from Matt. i. 5.

Abraham, their circumcision, and their possession of the Law.[1] Justin Martyr alludes to Jews who, "although they were sinners, yet deceived themselves by saying that, if they knew God, He would not impute sin to them."[2] If, then, the early date of the Epistle could be otherwise demonstrated, the question as to any designed opposition between the two Apostles would fall to the ground, and we should only have to show whether it is possible to reconcile independent statements which at first appear to be mutually exclusive. It is so important to establish this fact—so important to prove that whatever be the date of the Epistle, St. James *may* be refuting the notion of *a* justification by faith which is not that described by St. Paul, but a blind Judaic trust in privileges and observances—that it will be worth while to show from the Talmud how prevalent these views were in the Jewish world.

α. Thus, as regards *Monotheism*, we find that in repeating the Shemâ, or daily prayer, "Hear, O Israel, the Lord our God is one God" (Deut. vi. 4); "whosoever prolongs the utterance of the word One (*echad*) shall have his days and years prolonged to him" (Berachoth, f. 13, *b*).

When Akhiva was martyred by having his flesh torn from him, he died uttering this word "One;" and then came a Bath Kol, which said, "Blessed art thou, Rabbi Akhiva, for thy soul and the word One left thy body together" (id. f. 61, *b*).

β. Again, as regards *circumcision*:

"Though Abraham kept all the commandments, including the whole ceremonial law" (Kiddushin, f. 82, *a*), "still he was not *perfect* till he was circumcised" (Nedarim, f. 31, *b*).

"So great is circumcision, that thirteen covenants were made concerning it" (Nedarim, f. 31, *b*).

Many Jews relied less on their observances than on their possession of special privileges.

γ. As regards their *national position*, they said that God had given to Israel three precious gifts—the Law, the land of Israel, and the world to come;[3] that all Israelites were princes,[4] all holy,[5] all philosophers, "full of meritorious works as a pomegranate of pips,"[6] and that it was as impossible for the world to be without them as to be without air.[7] They even ventured to say that "All Israelites have a portion in the world to come, as it is written, And thy people are all righteous, they shall inherit the land" (Is. lx. 21). (Sanhedrin, f. 90, *a*).

"The world was created only for Israel: none are called the children of God but Israel: none are beloved before God but Israel" (Gerim, 1).

δ. In fact, on the testimony of the Talmud itself, *externalism* had triumphed in the heart of the Jewish Church. The High Priests, though they were, according to the best Jewish testimony, shameful examples

---

[1] Matt. iii. 9; John viii. 33; Rom. ii. 17—20; and compare Jer. vii. 4.
[2] Just. Mart. *Dial.* § 141.   [3] Berachoth, f. 5, *a*.   [4] Shabbath, f. 57, *a*.
[5] Shabbath, f. 86, *a*.   [6] The Machzor for Pentecost.   [7] Taanith, f. 3, *b*.

of greed, simony, luxury, gluttony, pride, and violence, were yet quite content with themselves if they were rigorists in the minutiæ of Levitism instead of examples of ideal righteousness. In the tract Sota (47, *b*) there is a bitter complaint that moral worth was disregarded, and no regard paid to anything but external service. In another tract (Yoma 23, *a*) we are told that outward observance was more highly esteemed than inward purity, and that murder itself was considered venial in comparison with a ceremonial defilement of the Temple.[1] St. James was daily familiar with this spectacle of men who, living in defiance of every moral law, yet thought to win salvation by the easy mechanism of ceremonial scrupulosity. Against such mechanical conceptions of holiness his Epistle would have told with great power.

(3.) But believing as I do, on other grounds, that the Epistle was written shortly before St. James's death, it becomes difficult to suppose that St. James's argument in favour of "justification by works" bears *no relation whatever* to the great argumentative Epistles in which St. Paul had established the truth of Justification by Faith. And while I freely concede that the question of faith and works was frequently discussed in the Jewish Schools, and with special reference to the life of Abraham, there is not, I think, sufficient evidence that the doctrine had ever been so distinctly formulated, and certainly it had never been so fully and powerfully discussed, as it was in the Epistles to the Romans and Galatians.[2] If we are right in supposing that St. James wrote his Epistle about the year 61 or 62, then some years had elapsed since St. Paul had sent forth these great Epistles. Considering that emissaries, who came from Jerusalem—who came ostensibly from James—who boasted, though not always truly, of his sanction and authority—who carried with them letters which, if not written by him, were written by leading personages in the Church of which he was the Bishop—had penetrated into many of the communities founded by St. Paul, and had half-undone his work by reducing his converts to the legal bondage from which he had set them free—it becomes almost inconceivable that St. James, even if he had not seen copies of one or other of those Epistles, should not at least have been familiar with the general drift of views which had become notorious wherever the name of Christ was preached. Now, the teaching of St. Paul was intensely original. It was not easy for any one to grasp its full meaning; and it was quite impossible for any hostile and prejudiced person to understand it at all. To many, educated in the absorbing prejudices of Judaism, his opinions about the Law would have appeared dubious. Their indignation would have been

---

[1] For the various Talmudic quotations see Grätz, iii. 321, 322, and the works of Schöttgen, Meuschen, Eisenmenger, Hershon, Hamburger, etc. No less than fourteen of the Treatises of the Talmud, both Mishna and Gemara, have now been translated into French by Moïse Schwab.

[2] "Und sicher kann man nicht leugnen dass die vom Apostel Paulus aufgestellte Lehre über dem Glauben zu dieser Abhandlung die nächste Veranlassung gab" (Ewald, *Die Sendschreiben*, ii. p. 198).

kindled by the fiery and almost contemptuous boldness of some of the expressions which he wrote and published, and which he must therefore have frequently let fall in the heat of controversy. In the Church of Jerusalem it is hardly likely that the dialectics of St. Paul were lovingly or patiently studied. St. James himself is our witness to the fact that there, and throughout the Ghettos of the world, the views of the great missionary were systematically misrepresented. To the ordinary Jewish Christian he was known as one who constantly taught "*apostasy from Moses,*" as one who "*forbad*" not only Gentiles, but "all Jews," to circumcise their children, and "to walk according to the customs."[1] As regards Jews, the charge was false. St. Paul never interfered with them; and since he himself kept the general provisions of the Law as a national duty—greatly as, to him, they must have lost their significance—we have every reason to suppose that he would have advised any Jew who consulted him to do the same. But any lie, however often refuted, is good enough for party-spirit; and no amount of explanation, however simple and sincere, will prevent the grossest misrepresentations of opinion from being used for their own purposes by religious partisans. Further than this, it is not only possible, but probable, that some of St. Paul's followers *did* misinterpret his characteristic expressions, did make a bad and even dangerous use of them. We might easily imagine that this would be the case, because every day shows us how easy it is, first to turn any expression into a watchcry, then to empty it of all significance, and finally to use it in a sense entirely alien from that in which it was originally used. Here again, we are not left to conjecture. We have the express testimony of the second Epistle of St. Peter that there were those who wrested the difficult parts of St. Paul's Epistles, as they did also the rest of the Scriptures, *to their own perdition.* Now, if it be merely snatched up as a formula—without an earnest desire to understand it, without the thought which was necessary to see it in its proper perspective—there is no expression more liable to be perverted than St. Paul's characteristic formula of "Justification by Faith." In his sense of the words it is one of the deepest and most essential truths of Christianity; but in his sense only. And he had used both words, "Justification" and "Faith" in meanings which made them parts of one great system of thoughts. It is owing to this that his words have been constantly misunderstood, and are to this day deplorably misinterpreted. To this day there are some who use expressions so objectionable as "works are deadly." There were even in the days of the Apostles, as there have been since, Nicolaitans and other Antinomians, who, on the claim of possessing faith, have set themselves in superiority to the moral law, and asserted a licence to commit all ungodliness. Now, if St. James had come across such men, or had been told of their existence, or had even met with Jewish Christians who, without understanding St.

[1] Acts xxi. 21.

Paul's teaching, were perplexed by the ignorant repetition of the formula which was selected to represent it, would there have been anything derogatory to the character of St. James, or unworthy of his position, in the endeavour to refute the perversions to which this formula was liable? Is it not a high service to expose the empty use of any expression which has been degraded to the purposes of cant and faction? Would not St. Paul have rejoiced that such a task should have been performed? Would he not have performed it himself, if circumstances had led him to see that it was needful? It is, indeed, improbable that he would in that case have used all the expressions which St. James has used; but his pastoral Epistles are sufficient to prove that he would have cordially concurred with him in his general opinion. I believe, then, with many of the Fathers, that St. James wrote this passage with the express intention of correcting false inferences from the true teaching of St. Paul;[1] and that, though there is no contradiction between them, there is a certain antithesis—a traceable difference in the types of dogma which they respectively adopted.[2]

If the arguments of St. James had been intended for a refutation of St. Paul himself, they would have been singularly ineffectual. They do not fathom the depths of his meaning; they deal with uses of his words which are more superficial and less specifically Christian. A polemical argument must, as such, be a failure if every word which the writer says could be adopted by the person against whom he is writing. It is only as the correction of onesided and erroneous *inferences* from St. Paul's teaching, drawn by honest ignorance or circulated by hostile malice, that the argument of St. James has a value, which the Church of all ages has rejoiced to recognise.

But setting aside the question of *conscious* opposition between the views of the two Apostles, as one which lies outside the range of proof, we have to ask the far more important question, How is their language reconcilable with the truth of God? How can it be said with equal confidence

"Ye are saved *through* faith .... *not of works*" (Eph. ii. 8, 9),
and
"Ye see ... that *by works a man is justified*, and *not by faith only*" (James ii. 24)?

And here I must entirely differ from Luther in the view that the two statements, in the senses intended by their authors, are irreconcilable.[3] The reconciliation is easy when we see that St. James is

---

[1] This is the view adopted by Bp. Bull in his *Harmonia Apostolica*.
[2] So Schmid, Wiesinger, etc.
[3] Luther says: "Plures sudarunt in Epistolâ Jacobi ut cum Paulo concordarent ... sed minus feliciter, *sunt enim contraria*, 'fides justificat' 'fides non justificat'—qui hæc rite conjungere potest, huic vitam meam imponam, et fatuum me nominare permittam" (*Colloq.* ii. 202). Ströbel, in a review of Wiesinger, says, "No matter in what sense we take the Epistle of St. James, it is always in conflict with the remaining parts of Holy Writ."

using all three words—Faith, Works, Justification—in a different sense to different persons, with different illustrations, under different circumstances; and when we find, further, that St. James, in other passages, insists no less than St. Paul on the importance of faith; and St. Paul, no less than St. James, on the necessity of works.

i. For by *Faith* St. Paul never means dead faith (*fides informis*) at all. He means (1), in the lowest sense of the word, general trust in God (*assensus, fiducia*);[1] then (2) self-surrender to God's will;[2] in its highest and most Pauline sense—the sense in which he uses it when he speaks of "Justification by Faith"—it is self-surrender which has deepened into sanctification; it is a living power of good in every phase of life; it is *unio mystica*, a mystical incorporation with Christ in unity of love and life.[3] But this application of the word was peculiar to St. Paul, and St. James does not adopt it. He meant by faith in *this* passage a mere theoretical belief—belief which may exist without any germinant life—belief which may stop short at a verbal profession of Jewish orthodoxy—belief which does not even go so far as that of demons—belief which, taken alone, is so inappreciable in value that he compares it to a charity which speaks words of idle comfort and does not give.[4]

ii. Again, by *Works* the two writers meant very different things. St. Paul was thinking mainly of those works which stood high in the estimation of his Jewish opponents; he meant the works and observances of the Levitical and ceremonial Law—new moons, sabbaths, sacrifices, ablutions, meats, drinks, phylacteries, and so forth;—or, at the very highest, works of ordinary duty, "deeds of the Law," untouched by emotion, not springing from love to God. He did *not* mean, as St. James did, works of love and goodness done in obedience to the royal law,[5] those works which spring from a true and lively faith, which *must* spring from it, which it is as impossible to sever from it as to sever from fire its light and heat.[6]

iii. And, finally, the sense of the word *Justification* in St. Paul moves in a higher plane than that in which it is used by St. James. St. Paul uses the word in a special, a technical, a theological sense, to express the righteousness of God, which, by a judgment of acquittal, pronounced once for all in the expiatory death of Christ, he imputes to guilty man. St. James uses the word in the much simpler sense of our being declared and shown to be righteous—not indeed, as many have

---

[1] Rom. iv. 18; as in Heb. xii. 1. [2] Rom. x. 9; Phil. iii. 7.
[3] Rom. xii. 5; Phil. i. 21; 1 Cor. vi. 17. See *Life and Work of St. Paul*, ii. 188—193; Pfleiderer, *Paulinismus*, § 5; Baur, *Paul*. ii. 149; *Neue Test. Theol.* i. 176.
[4] In other passages "faith" connotes somewhat more than this, namely, trust in God (i. 5; v. 15).
[5] Jas. i. 25; ii. 12.
[6] If St. Paul attaches to "*works*" a lower meaning than St. James, St. James attaches to "*faith*" a lower meaning than St. Paul; but there can be no confusion about the results, because each writer uses the words in senses which he makes perfectly clear.

said, before men only[1]—but righteous before God, as those whose life is in accordance with their belief.[2] St. Paul speaks of the justification which begins for the sinner by the trustful acceptance of his reconciliation to God in Christ, and which attains its perfect stage when the believer is indeed "in Christ"—when Christ has become to him a new nature and a quickening spirit. St. James speaks of the justification of the believer by his producing such works as are the sole possible demonstration of the vitality of his indwelling faith.[3]

Briefly, then, it may be said that the works which St. Paul thinks of are the works of the Law, those of St. James the works of godliness; that St. Paul speaks of deep and mystic faith, St. James of theoretic belief; that St. Paul has in view the initial justification of a sinner, St. James the complete justification of a believer.[4]

iv. In accordance with this view, although both Apostles refer, for illustration of their views, to the life of the Patriarch who lived so many centuries before the delivery of the Law, they do *not* refer to the same events in his life. St. Paul illustrates his position by Abraham's belief in God's promise that he should have a son, when against hope he believed in hope.[5] St. James, taking the life and the faith of Abraham, so to speak, "much lower down the stream," shows how Abraham, many years afterwards, was justified as a believer, justified by works, when he gave the crowning proof of his obedience by the willingness to slay even his only son and the heir of the promise.[6] It is obviously as true to say that Abraham in that act was (in the ordinary meaning of the

---

[1] This common explanation (Calvin, Grotius, Baumgarten, etc.) is quite untenable. There is not a word in St. James to indicate that he is only thinking of justification before men; and the notion that he is, is refuted by ver. 14.

[2] As our Lord also said, "By thy words thou shalt be justified" (Matt. xii. 37); and St. Paul himself, in Rom. ii. 13, "the *doers* of the law shall be *justified*." Had this sentence occurred in St. James, how eagerly would it have been seized upon as a flat contradiction of Rom. iii. 20, "Therefore, from the works of the law shall *no* flesh be justified before Him." But if the same author can thus in the same Epistle use the same word in different senses, what difficulty can there be in supposing that this may be done by *different writers*, without any hostile intention?

[3] "To justify" (δικαιοῦν צדק) has in the Bible two meanings: (1) "To pronounce the innocent righteous in accordance with his innocence" (Ex. xxiii. 7; Prov. xvii. 15; Is. v. 23; Matt. xii. 37, etc.); (2) to make righteous, or lead to righteousness (Dan. xii. 31; Is. liii. 11; and Rom. *passim*). In St. James true faith is imputed as righteousness, but justification follows works as the proof of true faith (Lange).

[4] "Works," says Luther, "do not make us righteous, but cause us to be declared righteous" (Luke xvii. 9, 10).

[5] Rom. iv. 3, 9, 22; Gen. xv. 6.

[6] Jas. ii. 23; Gen. xxii. 12. See Huther *ad loc.* A remarkable Talmudic story tells us that Satan slandered Abraham before God, saying that God had given him a son when he was a hundred years old, and he had not even spared a dove for sacrifice. God answers that Abraham would not spare even his son if required. So God said, "Take now thy son" (*as if a king should say to his bravest warrior, Fight now this hardest battle of all*), "for fear it should be said that thy former trials were easy." "I have two sons," answered Abraham. "*Take thine only son.*" "Each," he answered, "is the only son of his mother." "*Take him whom thou lovest.*" "I love them both." Then God said, "*Take Isaac.*" Abraham obeyed, and on the way Satan met him, and tried to make him murmur. Abraham answered, "*I will walk in mine integrity*" (Sanhedrin, f. 89, b).

words) justified by faith, as that he was justified by works. He was justified by faith, because nothing but his faith could have led him to such perfect endurance in the hour of trial; he was justified by works, because, without his works, there could have been no proof that his faith existed. Faith and works, in this sense, are, in fact, inseparably intertwined. There cannot be such works without faith; there cannot be such faith without works. It is really the same thing to say that a man is (in one or other of the senses of the word) justified by such a faith as must from its very nature issue in good works, or by such works as can only issue from a true and lively faith. Nor is it surprising (as we have seen) that the question should be illustrated by the example of Abraham, whose life and faith were constantly discussed in their minutest particulars by the Jewish Rabbis, and who was asserted to have not only been saved by faith, but to have observed even the oral commandments centuries before they were delivered.[1] If St. James also takes the instance of Rahab, this does not involve a necessary reference to the remark in the Epistle to the Hebrews, that she, too, was saved by faith. For the example of Rahab was also greatly discussed in the Jewish schools, and for her faith and works it was said that no less than eight prophets, who were also priests, had sprung from her, and that Huldah, the prophetess, was one of her descendants.[2]

v. And the superficial contradiction between the Apostles vanishes to nothing when we bear in mind that St. Paul is dealing with the vain confidence of legalism, St. James with the vain confidence of orthodoxy. St. Paul was writing to Gentile Churches to prevent them from being seduced into trusting for salvation to the adoption of external badges and ceremonials, or to good deeds done in a spirit of servile fear. St. James is arguing either with Jewish bigots who thought that a profession of Monotheism and a participation in Jewish privileges[3] would save them; or with mistaken Paulinists who had snatched up a formula which they did not understand, and who thought that justification could be severed from sanctification—that a saving faith was possible without the holiness of an accordant life. St. Paul is contrasting faith in Christ with works of the Law; St. James is contrasting a dead unreal faith with a faith which evidences its reality by holy works. St. Paul's arguments were meant to overthrow the vain confidence of the Pharisee[4]: St. James's tell equally against the Jew who pillowed his hopes on fruitless orthodoxy, and the Antinomian who identified saving faith with barren profession.

For, lastly, there is no difficulty in showing that both as regards faith and works the Apostles, however much their expressions may differ, were substantially at one.

---

[1] Yoma, f. 28, b; Kiddushin, f. 82, a.
[2] Matt. iii. 9.
[3] Meggillah, f. 14, b.
[4] Comp. Acts xiii. 39.

(i.) Thus as regards FAITH, St. James says in this very chapter:—
"And the Scripture was fulfilled which saith, And *Abraham believed God*, and it was reckoned to him for *righteousness*"[1] (ii. 23).

And St. Paul quotes the same verse in the same words (Rom. iv. 3), with the introduction "What saith the Scripture?"

So little does St. James exclude faith, that he speaks of "the testing of faith" as working out that "endurance" which is the appointed path of perfectionment (i. 3); he urges the duty of prayer offered in unwavering faith as the means of obtaining Divine wisdom (i. 6); he describes Christianity as being the "holding the faith of our Lord Jesus Christ the Lord of the Glory" (ii. 1); he speaks of the poor as being heirs of the Kingdom because they are rich in faith (ii. 5); he implies the absolute necessity of faith co-existing with works—working with them, receiving its perfection from them (ii. 22, 26), and does not imagine the possibility of such works as he contemplates except as the visible proofs of an invisible faith.

(ii.) And exactly as St. James neither ignores nor underestimates faith, so neither does St. Paul ignore nor underestimate the value and necessity of good WORKS. He speaks of God as "being able to make all joy abound in us, that having in all things always all sufficiency (αὐτάρκειαν) we may abound unto every good work" (2 Cor. ix. 8). He speaks of good works as the appointed path in which we are predestined to walk (Eph. ii. 10). He describes the walking "in every good work, bearing fruit," as being the worthy walk, and the walk which pleases God (Col. i. 10). He prays that the Lord Jesus may stablish the hearts of His converts in every good word and work (2 Thess. ii. 17). He devotes a practical section in every Epistle to the inculcation of Christian duties and virtues (Rom. xii.—xvi.; 1 Cor. xvi.; 2 Cor. ix.; Gal. v. 6; Eph. v., vi.; Phil. iv.; Col. iii., iv., &c.). He devotes the almost exclusive exhortations of his very latest Epistles to impress on all classes of his converts the blessedness of faithful working (1 Tim. ii. 10, v. 10, vi. 18; 2 Tim. iii. 17; Tit. ii. 7—14, iii. 8). Nay, more, in the very Epistle of which the central idea is Justification by Faith, he does not scruple to use the word justification in the less specific sense of St. James, and to write that "*the doers of the Law shall be justified*"[2]—a sentence which St. James might have adopted as his text. Both Apostles would have freely conceded that (in a certain sense) faith without works is mere orthodoxy, and works without faith mere legal righteousness.

Surely after these proofs that for all practical purposes the Apostle of the Gentiles and the Bishop of the Circumcised are fundamentally at

---

[1] "Magnum opus sed ex Fide" (Aug. on Ps. xxxi.). Ewald briefly says, "Faith is the first and most necessary thing; this is here also taken for granted throughout; but it must prove its existence by corresponding works, otherwise man cannot obtain Divine justification and final redemption" (*Die Sendschreiben*, ii. 199).

[2] Rom. ii. 13.

one—that they agree in thought, though they differ in expression, or at least that their minor differences are merged in a higher unity—it is unjustifiable to speak as though, on this subject at any rate, there was any bitter controversy between them. They approached the truths of Christianity from different sides; they looked at them under different aspects; they lived amid different surroundings; they were arguing against different errors; they used different phraseology. The antithesis between them only lies in regions of literary expression; it in no way affects the duty or the theory of the Christian life. There is not a word which St. Paul wrote on those topics which would not have been accepted after a little explanation by St. James, though he might have preferred to alter some of the expressions which St. Paul employed. There is not a word which St. James wrote on them which—when explained in St. James's sense—St. Paul would not have endorsed. It is true, as St. Paul wrote, that we are "justified by faith;" it is true, as St. James wrote, that "we cannot be justified without works." Amid the seeming verbal contradictions there is a real agreement. Both Apostles held identical views respecting the will of God, the regeneration of man, and the destiny of the redeemed.[1] The ideal which each accepted was so nearly the same, that St. James's brief sketch of the Wisdom from above might be hung as a beautiful companion picture to St. Paul's glorious description of Heavenly charity. Both would have agreed, heart and soul, in the simple and awful moral truth of such passages as these:—

"So speak and so do as they who shall be judged by the law of liberty." (Jas. ii. 12.)

"Faith apart from works is dead, by itself." (Jas. ii. 17, 26.)

"The work of each shall become manifest, for the day shall reveal it." (1 Cor. iii. 13.)

"God shall give to each according to his works." (Rom. ii. 6—10.)

"We must all be made manifest before the judgment-seat of Christ that each may obtain the things done by the instrumentality of the body, with reference to the things he did, whether good, or evil." (2 Cor. v. 10.)

Both, again, would have accepted heart and soul such language as that of St. John, in which these superficial discrepancies are finally reconciled—"If we say that we have fellowship with Him and walk in darkness, we lie, and do not the truth" (1 John i. 6);—or as that of St. Paul himself in the very Epistle in which he first worked out the sketch of his great scheme, and in the three different conclusions to his own favourite and thrice-repeated formula:—

"For in Christ Jesus neither circumcision availeth anything nor uncircumcision,"—

But, "Faith working effectually by means of love." (Gal. v. 6.)

But, "A new creature." (Gal. vi. 15.)

But, "An observance of the commandments of God." (1 Cor. vii. 19.)

---

[1] See *supra*, pp. 328, 333, the note on Jas. i. 18.

Had St. Paul written, as Luther wrote for him, that man is justified "by Faith *only*"—had he been in this sense a Solifidian—then there would have been a more apparent contradiction between him and St. James. But what St. Paul said was, "Therefore we reckon that a man is justified *by faith*, apart from the works of the Law" (Rom. iii. 28), and it was Luther who ventured to interpolate the word "alone"—the "word *alone*," as Erasmus calls it—"stoned with so many shoutings"— ("Vox *sola* tot clamoribus lapidata"). In St. James's sense of faith this would have indeed been open to the contradiction (ii. 24) "Not by faith alone" (οὐκ ἐκ πίστεως μόνον). But even had St. Paul used the word "alone" he would have said what is true in his sense of the words, and in the sense in which they are adopted in the Articles of our Church. His words only become untrue when they are transferred into the different senses in which they are used by his brother Apostle.[1]

In this, as in so many other cases, we may thank God that the truth has been revealed to us under many lights; and that, by a diversity of gifts, the Spirit ministered to each Apostle severally as He would, inspiring the one to deepen our spiritual life by the solemn truth that Works cannot justify apart from Faith; and the other to stimulate our efforts after a holy life by the no less solemn truth that Faith cannot justify us unless it be the living faith which is shown by Works. There is, in the diversity, a deeper unity. The Church, thank God, is "*Circumamicta varietatibus*"—clothed in raiment of many hues. St. Paul had dwelt prominently on Faith; St. Peter dwells much on Hope; St. John insists most of all on Love. But the Christian life is the synthesis of these Divine graces, and the Works of which St. James so vehemently impresses the necessity, are works which are the combined result of operative faith, of constraining love, and of purifying hope.[2]

[1] See Article IX., and on it Bishop Forbes, Bishop Harold Browne, etc.
[2] See an excellent tract on St Paul and St. James by Dean Bagot.

Book V.

THE EARLIER LIFE AND WORKS OF ST. JOHN.

CHAPTER XXIV.

ST. JOHN.

> "For life, with all it yields of joy and woe,
> And hope and fear—believe the aged friend—
> Is just our chance of the prize of learning love,
> How love might be, hath been indeed, and is."—
> BROWNING, *A Death in the Desert.*

"AND recognising the grace given to me, James, and Kephas, and John, who are thought to be pillars, gave to me and Barnabas the right hand of fellowship, that we to the Gentiles, but they to the circumcision'"—

So wrote St. Paul to the Galatians, in one of the passages of the New Testament, which—apart from the Gospels—has a deeper personal interest, and which throws more light on the condition of the Church in the days of the Apostles than any other.[2] It is an inestimable privilege to the Church that we possess writings of each of these three Pillar-Apostles—as well as of that untimely-born Apostle on whose daring originality they were inclined to look with alarm, until he had fully set forth to them that view of the Gospel which was emphatically "*his* Gospel,"[3] and which he had learnt "neither from men nor by the instrumentality of man."[4] We are thus enabled to see the Gospel in the fourfold aspect in which it appeared to four men,—each specially enlightened by the Spirit of God, but each limited by individual conditions, because each received the treasure in earthen vessels. The minds of men inevitably differ. The individuality of each man—his subjectivity—his capacity to receive truth—his power of expressing it —all differ. Hence the truths which he utters, since they are uttered in human language, must be more or less differentiated by human peculiarities, and hence arises a gracious and fruitful variety, not a perplexing contradiction. Had the Apostles been bad men, had there been in their hearts the least tinge of spiritual or moral falsity, the pure stream of truth would have been corrupted by evil admixtures; but since they were sincere and noble men, the individuality with

---

[1] Gal. ii. 9.   [2] Gal. i. 11—ii. 21.
[3] "My Gospel," 1 Cor. xi. 23. τὸ εὐαγγέλιον ὃ κηρύσσω (Gal. ii. 2).
[4] Gal. i. 1, οὐκ ἀπ' ἀνθρώπων οὐδὲ δι' ἀνθρώπου, 1 Cor. xi. 23; xv. 3.

which the style and method of each is stamped, so far from being a loss to us, is a peculiar gain. No one man, unless his powers had been dilated almost to infinitude, would have been able to set forth to myriads of different souls the perfection of many-sided truths. It was a blessed ordinance of God which enables us to hear the words of revelation spoken by so many noble voices in so many differing tones.

We see from St. Paul's allusion, that twenty years after the Resurrection[1] the three Pillar-Apostles, at the date of his conference with them, were at Jerusalem, and were still regarded as the chief representatives of Jewish Christianity. But their Judaic sympathies were felt in very different degrees. St. James represents Christianity on its most Judaic side—spiritualising its morals, but assuming rather than expounding its most specific truths. He wrote exactly as we should have expected a man to write who was a Nazarite, a late convert, a Bishop of the Church at Jerusalem, a daily frequenter of the Temple, a man in the highest repute among the Jews themselves, a man who, for more than a quarter of a century, lived in the focus of the most powerful Judaic influences. He was the acknowledged leader of those converts who were least willing to break loose from the Levitic law and the tradition of the fathers. St. Peter, on the other hand, became less and less a representative of the narrower phase of Judaic Christianity—more and more, as life advanced, the Apostle of Catholicity. The vein of timidity which, in his natural temperament, was so strangely mixed with courage—the plasticity which gave to his conduct a Judaic colouring so long as he was surrounded by the elders at Jerusalem, or by emissaries who came from James to Antioch—caused him to be long regarded by the converted Jews (undoubtedly against his will) as a party leader. Yet he was among the earliest to see the universality of the Gospel message, and he flung himself with ardour into the support of St. Paul's effort to emancipate the Gentiles from Levitic observances. And when he began his missionary journeys, his thoughts widened more and more until, as we find from his Epistle, he was enabled to accept unreservedly the teachings of St. Paul, while he divests them of their antithetical character, and avoids their more controversial formulæ. When we combine the teaching of St. James and St. Paul, we find those contrasted yet complementary truths which were necessary to the full apprehension of the Catholic Faith in its manifold applicability to human needs. St. Peter occupies an intermediate and conciliatory position between these two extremes—more progressive than St. James, less daringly original and independent than St. Paul. But to utter the final word of Christian revelation—to drop, as it were, the great keystone, which was still needed to complete and compact the wide arch of Truth—was reserved as the special glory of the Beloved

---

[1] About A.D. 52.

Disciple. And this was the crowning work of that old age which, as a peculiar blessing to the Church of Christ, was probably prolonged to witness the dawn of the second century of the Christian Church.[1]

But in St. John too we see that growth of spiritual enlightenment which made his life an unbroken education. In his latest writings we find a deeper insight into the truth than it would have been possible for him to attain before God had "shown him all things in the slow history of their ripening." The "Son of Thunder" of the Synoptic Gospels had the lessons of many years to learn before he could become the St. John who in Patmos saw the Apocalypse. The St. John who saw the Apocalypse had *still* the lessons of many years to learn, and the fall of Jerusalem to witness, before he could gaze on the world from the snowy summit of ninety winters, and become the Evangelist of the fourth Gospel, the Apostle of Christian Love.

And yet the days of St. John were not divided from each other by any overpowering crisis, but were, from first to last,

"Bound each to each by natural piety."

In the life of St. Paul the vision on the road to Damascus had cleft a deep chasm between his earlier and later years. The *character* of the Apostle retained the same elements, but his *opinions* were suddenly revolutionised. Paul the Apostle could only look back with an agony of remorse on the thoughts and deeds of Saul the Inquisitor. Like Augustine and Luther, he is a type of the ardent natures which are brought to God and to the service of the truth by a spasm of sudden change. But St. John was one of those pure saints of whom the grace of God takes early hold, and in whose life, as in those of Thomas à Kempis and Melancthon, "reason and religion run together like warp and woof to weave the web of a holy life." To him, from earliest days, the words of the poet are beautifully applicable—

> "There are those who ask not if thine eye
> Be on them; who, in love and truth,
> Where no misgiving is, rely
> Upon the genial sense of youth:
> Glad hearts! without reproach or blot,
> Who do thy work, and know it not;
> Oh, if through confidence misplaced
> They fail, thy saving arm, dread Power! around
> them cast."

Never, perhaps, was a more glorious destiny reserved for any man, or a destiny more unlike what he could have conceived possible, than that which was awaiting the Apostle, when he played as a boy beside his father's boat on the bright strip of sand which still marks the site of Bethsaida. His father was Zabdia or Zebedee, of whom we know

---

[1] Qui in secreta divinae se nativitatis immergens *ausus est dicere quod cuncta saecula nesciebant*, "In principio erat verbum" (Jer. *in Isa.* lvi. 4).

nothing more than that he was a fisherman sufficiently well-to-do to have hired servants of his own.[1] He was thus in more prosperous circumstances than his partner Jonas, the father of Peter and Andrew. His wife was Salome, sister of the Virgin Mary. The fact that she was one of those who ministered to the Lord of her substance, and also bought large stores of spices for His grave, are additional signs that Zabdia and his wife were not poor. Their sons were James and John, who were thus first cousins of our Lord according to the flesh.[2]

We catch no glimpse of John till we see him among the disciples of the Baptist on the banks of the Jordan. We are told, however, that in his manhood he appeared to the learned Sanhedrists of Jerusalem to be a "simple and unlettered" man.[3] Doubtless the term which they actually used was the contemptuous *am-haarets*, a technical expression far more scornful than its literal translation, "people of the land."[4] It is clear, therefore, that he had never been what they called "a pupil of the wise," and had not been trained in that cumbrous system of the Oral Law which they regarded as the only learning. It was well for him that he had not. The Rabbinism of that day was nothing better than a system of scholastic pedantry, impotent for every spiritual end, like many another vaunted system of purely verbal orthodoxy, yet tending to inflate the minds of its votaries with the conceit of knowledge without the reality. Of such learning it might well be said, in the words of Heraclitus, that "it teaches nothing."[5]

On the other hand, we see from St. John's own writings that he was a man of consummate natural gifts, and that he had been so far well educated as to be acquainted with both Greek and Hebrew,[6] of which the latter was not an ordinary acquirement even of well-educated Jews. Apart from his unequalled capacity for the reception of spiritual grace, his natural gifts appear in his deep insight into the human heart; in the dramatic power with which by a few touches, he sets before us the most

---

[1] Mark i. 20.
[2] Nicephorus and others rightly call Zebedee ἰδιοναύκληρον, "an independent fisherman with a ship of his own." What St. Chrysostom (*Hom.* i. *in Joann.*) says of the extreme poverty and humility of his lot (οὐδὲν πενιχρότερον οὐδὲ ἀτελέστερον, κ.τ.λ.) is rhetorical exaggeration (see Lampe, *Prolegomena*, p. 5). The Lake of Galilee was extraordinarily rich in fish, some of which were regarded as great delicacies, and—like the *coracinus*—were extremely rare. The trade in fish at Tiberias, Sepphoris, Tarichese, and especially at Jerusalem, was so active that a leading fisherman like Zabdia must have been almost rich.
[3] Acts iv. 13. A man was called a mere ignoramus (*am-haarets*) even if he knew the Scriptures and the Mishna, but had never been one of the "pupils of the wise" (*Thalmidi hachakamim*). If he knew only the Scriptures, he was called "an empty cistern" (*bōr*) (Wagenseil, *Sota*, p. 517). The *idiōtēs* is one who is no authority on a subject (see Orig. *c. Cels.* i. 30). Augustine calls the Apostles "ineruditos . . . non peritos grammaticae, non arinatos dialectica, non rhetorica inflatos" (*De Civ. Dei*, xxii. 5).
[4] For the meaning and associations of this word see Dr. McCaul. *Old Paths*, pp. 458–464.
[5] πολυμαθίη οὐ διδάσκει (Heracl.).
[6] The quotations of St. John in the Gospel are not always taken direct from the LXX., but are sometimes altered into more direct accordance with the Hebrew (xix. 37; vi. 45; xiii. 18).

vivid conception of the most varied characters; in his style, apparently so simple yet really so profound—a style supremely beautiful, yet unlike that of any other writer, whether sacred or profane; and above all, in the fact that he was a fit and chosen vessel for that consummate truth —the Incarnation of the word of God. That truth, while with one swift stroke it summarised the speculations of Alexandrian theosophy, became in its turn the starting-point for the most sacred utterances of all Christian thinkers till the end of time.

His native Galilee was inhabited by the bravest and truest race in Palestine.[1] They were remarkable for faithfulness to their theocratic nationality. They detested and were ashamed of alike the Roman dominion and the Herodian satrapy which was its outward sign. Their temperaments were full of an enthusiasm which easily caught fire. The revolt of Judas of Galilee against the registrations of Quirinus showed the indignation with which Galileans contemplated the reduction of the Holy Land to the degraded position of a Roman Province. The watchword of that uprising was that the Chosen People should have "no Lord or master but God." Wild and hopeless as the insurrection was, and terribly as it was avenged, its failure was so far from quenching the spirit of patriotism by which it had been instigated, that it was not difficult for the sons of Judas long years afterwards[2] to fan the hot embers into flame.[3] The revolt of Judas took place when St. John was about twelve years old—the age at which a Jewish boy began to enter on the responsibilities of manhood. It was impossible that an event which produced so widespread an agitation should have failed to leave an impression on his memory. His sympathies must have been with the aims, if not with the acts, of the daring patriot. In both the sons of Zebedee we trace a certain fiery vehemence, and this it was which earned for them from the Lord the title of "Boanerges."[4] It is probable that they shared in some of the views which had once actuated their brother Apostle, the Zealot Simon.[5]

If the home of Zebedee was in or near Bethsaida, his two sons must have grown up in constant intercourse with Philip and Andrew and Peter, and with his cousins, the sons of Alphæus, and with Nathanael of the not-far-distant Cana. Whether he ever visited the home of the Virgin at Nazareth, and saw the sinless youth of Jesus, and the sternly legal faithfulness of "His brethren," we do not know, but in any case we can see that he enjoyed that best of training which consists in being

---

[1] Jos. *Antt.* xviii. 1, § 1, 6; *B. J.* ii. 8, § 1. [2] A.D. 8 of our era.
[3] In A.D. 47 and A.D. 66.
[4] Boanerges, "*Bent-regesh*" (Mark iii. 17). No doubt the title was earned by the fire and impetuosity of their nature; not because they were, as Theophylact say, "mighty heralds and divines" (Theophyl. in *Mark* i.; Epiphan. *Haer.* 73; Cyrill. Alex. *ad Nestor.* 1). For a multitude of the guesses about a matter perfectly simple, see Lampe, *Prolegom.* 24—30.
[5] Luke vi. 15, Kananite=Zealot. The Zealots formed the "extreme left" division of the Pharisees politically, as the Essenes did religiously.

brought up in the midst of sweet and noble natures, and in the free fresh life of a hardy calling and a beautiful land. And what most of all ennobled the aspirations of these young Galileans was that, with perfect trust in God, they were waiting for the consolation of Israel— they were cherishing the thought which lay at the very heart of all that was best and deepest in the old Covenant—the hope that the promised Messiah at length would come.

We are not told a single particular about his early years. We first see him—evidently in the prime of early manhood—as a disciple of the Baptist.[1] He does not mention himself by name, because in his Gospel he shows a characteristic reserve. But there never has been a doubt that he is the disciple who was with St. Andrew when they heard from their Master the words which were to influence their whole future life. The Baptist had received the deputation which the Sanhedrin had sent to inquire into his claims, and had told them that he was not the Christ, nor Elijah, nor "the Prophet." On the next day he saw Jesus coming towards him on His return from the temptation in the wilderness. Then first he said, "Behold the Lamb of God which taketh away the sins of the world!" and testified that he had seen the Spirit descending from heaven like a dove, and it abode upon Him. Again, the next day, fixing his eyes on Jesus as He walked by, he exclaimed, "Behold the Lamb of God!" At once the two disciples followed Jesus. Turning and gazing on them as they followed, He said, "What are ye seeking?" Giving Him the highest title of reverence they knew, the simple Galileans answered, "Rabbi, where stayest thou?" He saith to them, "Come and see." They came and saw. It was now four in the evening, and they stayed with Him that night.

That brief intercourse sufficed to convince them that Jesus was the Christ. The next morning Andrew sought his brother Simon, and with the simple startling announcement, "We have found the Messiah," led him to the Lord.

It is not mentioned that St. John sought his brother, and it is clear that the elder son of Zebedee was not called to full discipleship till afterwards on the Sea of Galilee. It was from no difference in character that James did not, so far as we know, become a hearer of the Baptist. He was earning his daily bread as a fisherman, and may have found no opportunity to leave the Plain of Gennesareth. I have ventured elsewhere to conjecture the reason why St. John was able to seek the ministry of the Baptist though his brother was not.[2] He had some connexion with Jerusalem, and even had a home there.[3] We find

---

[1] Ecclesiastical tradition says that he was called "*adolescentior*," and even "*puer*." Paulin. Nol. *Ep.* 51. Ambros. *Offic.* ii. 20, § 101. Aug. c. *Faust.* xxx. 4. Jer. c. *Jovin.* i. 26.

[2] See *Life of Christ*, i. 144.

[3] John xix. 27. "From that hour the Disciple took her to his own home" (εἰς τὰ ἴδια).

an explanation of this in the fact that the fish of the Lake of Galilee were largely supplied to Jerusalem, and nothing is more probable than that Zebedee, as a master fisherman, should have sent his younger son, at least occasionally, to the Holy City to superintend what must have been one of the most lucrative branches of his trade. If so, it would have been easy for St. John to reach in less than a day the banks of Jordan, and to listen to the mighty voice which was then rousing Priests and Pharisees as well as people from their sensual sleep.

The teaching of the Baptist appealed to the sternest instincts of his youthful follower. Its lofty morality, its uncompromising denunciations, its dauntless independence must have exercised a strong fascination over the young Galilean. It made him more than ever a Son of Thunder. It has been said of John the Baptist that he was like a burning torch—that the whole man was an Apocalypse. In the Apocalypse of him who was for a time his disciple, we still seem to hear echoes of that ringing voice, to catch hues of earthquake and eclipse from that tremendous imagery.

The question here arises whether St. John was or was not unmarried. The ancient Fathers are fond of speaking of him as a "virgin." As early as the pseudo-Ignatius we find an address to "Virgins," *i.e.*, celibates, with the prayer, "May I enjoy your holiness as that of Elijah, Joshua the son of Nun, Melchizedek, Elisha, Jeremiah, John the Baptist, the Beloved Disciple, Timothy, Evodius, and Clemens." Nothing corresponding to this praise of "virginity" is found either in the Scripture or in the earliest Fathers, for "the virgins" of Rev. xiv. 14, and "those who have made themselves eunuchs for Christ's sake" of Matt. xix. 12, are expressions which, when taken in the sense which was familiar to the Jews themselves, convey no such exaltation of the unwedded life.[1] Tertullian, however, in his book "On Single Marriage," calls St. John "*Christi spado*," and St. Jerome, filled with his monastic *gnosis* on this subject, says that "when St. John wished to marry his Lord restrained him."[2] Similar testimony is repeated by St. Augustine, Epiphanius, and others, but it only seems to have been derived from the "Acts" of Leucius. Apart from direct evidence, all the customs of the Jews make it extremely improbable, and St. Paul tells us that "*the rest of the Apostles*" as well as Kephas were married.[3] The notion of his celibacy was strengthened by the erroneous misreading of a superscription to his

---

[1] See the passages of Zohar quoted by Schöttgen, p. 159.
[2] Tert. *De Monogamia*, 17; Epiphan. *Haer.* lviii.; Jer. *c. Jovinian.* 1, 14, and is proleg. Joann., Praef. in Matt., ad Is. lvi. 4; Aug. c. Faust. xxx. 4. The virginity of St. John became a commonplace with the Ecclesiastical writers. See Chrysostom, *De Virg.* 82 (*Opp.* i. 332), Ps.-Chrysostom (*Opp.* viii. 2, 246, ed. Montfaucon) where Peter is a type of σεμνογαμία, and John of παρθενία. Ambrose, *De Inst. Virg.* viii. 50. The belief originated in the *Acts* of Leucius. See Zahn, *Acta Joannis*, c. ciii.
[3] 2 Cor. xi. 2, on which Ambrosiaster remarks "omnes Apostoli, excepto Johanne et Paulo uxores habuerunt."

first epistle which is itself erroneous. Augustine in one place quotes 1 John iii. 2, as occurring in St. John's letter "*to the Parthians*,"[1] and he is followed by Idacius Clarus, and (according to Bede) by Athanasius. But as there are also traces of its having been called "*a letter to Virgins*," it has been supposed that *Parthos* is a mistaken contraction for *parthenous*, or *vice versâ*. But even if St. John had thus written a letter to "virgins," it would not be a necessary inference that he was himself unmarried, or even that "virgins" and celibates were equivalent terms.[2]

The first call of St. John on the banks of Jordan was not the final call. St. John accompanied Jesus to the marriage feast of Cana in Galilee, and saw Him manifest forth His glory. Then, during the early ministry of Jesus in Southern Judæa, the little band of brethren seem to have resumed for a time their ordinary avocations.

It was on the Lake of Galilee, after the miraculous draught of fishes, that there came to him the decisive call—"Follow Me." He obeyed the call. With his brother he left his father Zebedee and the boat, and the hired servants—left all, and followed Jesus. Of Zebedee we hear no more. It is probable that he died soon afterwards; for in the bright year of the Galilean ministry, before Jesus was driven to fly northward, and to wander through semi-heathen districts, we find Salome, the mother of James and John, among "the women who ministered unto Him of their substance."

The Apostles whom the Lord gathered finally around Him before the Sermon on the Mount fall into three groups of four, of which the first and most privileged consisted of Andrew, Peter, James, and John; of these again the last three were the most chosen of the chosen.[3] Alone of the Apostles they were permitted to witness the Raising of Jairus's Daughter, the Transfiguration, and the Agony in the Garden. And of these three again the nearest and dearest was John. Of both Peter and John it might have been said that they, more than all the rest, were disciples whom Jesus loved as personal companions[4]; but St. John alone—not with a claim of vainglory, but with the simple testimony of truth—has indicated to us unmistakably, yet with dignified reserve, that he was the disciple whom Jesus loved and honoured with the affection of high esteem.[5] St. Peter was the more prominent as the champion of the Christ; St. John was the closer friend of Jesus.[6]

---

[1] *Est. Praef. in* 1 *John.*
[2] Another cause of this belief was the fancy that our Lord specially approved of St. John's celibacy, and that this also was the reason why the Virgin was entrusted to his care. Zahn, *Acta Joannis*, p. 201, seqq.
[3] Ἐκλεκτῶν ἐκλεκτότεροις (Clem. Alex.).
[4] In John xx. 2 we have the expression ἔρχεται πρὸς Σίμωνα Πέτρον καὶ πρὸς τὸν ἄλλον μαθητὴν ὃν ἐφίλει ὁ Ἰησοῦς. From the change of term (ἐφίλει, not as in other places, ἠγάπα), and from the structure of the sentence, Canon Westcott (*ad loc.*) infers, with much probability, that Peter is here included in the description.
[5] ἠγάπα, xiii. 23; xix. 26; xxi. 7, 20.
[6] St. Peter has been called Φιλόχριστος, St. John Φιλοιήσους.

And we see in his Gospel the *proof* that he was so. The Synoptists witness faithfully to external events. St. John gives a far more inward picture. He writes as one to whom it had been granted to know something of his Master's inmost thoughts.[1]

And yet this high honour, this distinguishing personal affection, arose from no faultless ideality in his character. The youth with whom Italian art has made us familiar—the youth of unearthly beauty, with features of almost feminine softness, with the long bright locks streaming down his neck, and the eagle by his side, is not the St. John of the New Testament: he is neither the St. John of the Synoptists and the Apocalypse, nor of the Fourth Gospel and Epistles—but is the one-sided idealisation of Christian painters.[2] Jesus loved him because of his warm affections, his devoted faithfulness, his glowing zeal, his passionate enthusiasm; not because his character as yet approached perfection. The young St. John had very much both to learn and to unlearn. He participated in the faults of fretfulness, impatience, emulous selfishness, ambitious literalism, want of consideration, want of tenderness, dulness of understanding, and hardness of heart, which, as the Gospels so faithfully tell us, were common to all the disciples.[3] Nay more, it is remarkable that, in nearly every instance in which he is brought into prominence, either singly or with his brother, it is in connexion with some error of perception or fault of conduct. He had to *unlearn* the exaggeration of the very tendencies which gave to his character so much of its human charm. He had to learn lessons of tolerance, lessons of mercy, lessons of humility, which perhaps it took him his whole life to understand in all their fulness as falling under the one law of Christian love.

1. Thus on one occasion a selfish dispute had arisen among the Apostles as to which of them should be the greatest.[4] Our Lord rebuked it by taking a little child and saying, by way of consolation as well as by way of reproof, "Whosoever shall receive this little child in My name receiveth Me."[5] The conscience of St. John seems to have smitten him as he listened to the tender and moving lesson, and with an ingenuous impulse he confessed to having taken part in conduct which now struck him as a fault. "Master," he said, "we saw one in Thy name trying to cast out the demons, and we prevented him, because he does not follow with us." To prevent him had been a natural impulse of sectarian pride and ecclesiastical jealousy. The man was not an

---

[1] See John vi. 6, 61, 64: ᾔδει γὰρ ἐξ ἀρχῆς κ.τ.λ. ἐνεβριμήσατο τῷ πνεύματι καὶ ἐτάραξεν ἑαυτόν, xi. 33; xiii. 1, 3, 11, 21. ἐταράχθη τῷ πνεύματι, xviii. 4; xix. 28, etc.
[2] Pictures of St. John existed in early days among the Carpocratians. See the fragments of Leucius in Zahn, p. 223.
[3] Matt. xv. 16; xvi. 6—12; John xii. 16; Mark ix. 33; Luke ix. 49; xxii. 24; xxiv. 25, etc.   [4] Luke ix. 49; Mark ix. 38.
[5] An old tradition, mentioned by Hilary, seems strangely to have said that St. John was the boy to whom Jesus pointed in order to rebuke the ambition of the disciples. See Zahn. *Acta Joannis*. p. cxxxiv.

Apostle, nor even a professed disciple; what right had he thus, as it were, to steal the credit of miracles which belonged to the Lord only, and which He had delegated to none but His genuine followers?" "Who," St. John may have thought, "is this unknown exorcist, who thus encroaches on *our* privileges?" and so, with other Apostles, he had disowned the man, and peremptorily forbidden him.[1] It was an impulse somewhat similar to that which made Joshua exclaim, "O my lord Moses forbid them," when he heard that Eldad and Medad were prophesying in the camp. Instantly and nobly the great law-giver had answered, "Enviest thou for my sake? Would God that all the Lord's people were prophets, and that the Lord would put His spirit upon them."[2] So now came at once the answer, the spirit of which in two thousand years Christians have hardly begun to learn, "Prevent him not! for he who is not against us, is on our side."

2. But, once again, John and his brother James had needed a stern and public lesson. They had been taught that sectarian jealousy is alien from the heart of Christ; they had now to learn that religious intolerance and cruel severity are violations of His spirit. They had to learn, or *begin* to learn, the lesson—of which (once more) nineteen centuries have failed to convince the self-styled representatives of Churches —that violence is hateful to God.[3]

The incident occurred at the beginning of the Lord's great public journey from Galilee to Jerusalem, when He now openly assumed the dignity of the Messiah, and was accompanied not only by His disciples, but by a multitude of followers, all—like Himself—pilgrims on their way to the Holy City. The first village which lies between the borders of Galilee and Samaria, at the foot of the Hills of Ephraim, is the pleasant village of En Gannim, or the "Fountain of Gardens," then, as now, inhabited by a rude and fanatical community. The numbers of his retinue, and the fact that He was now about to enter on the territory of Samaria, made it necessary to send messengers before Him to provide for His reception. It was not always that the Galileans ventured to take the road through Samaria, for the intense exacerbation between Jews and Samaritans constantly showed itself by collisions between Samaritans and Passover pilgrims. Still this road was taken sometimes by the festival caravans, and it may be that our Lord was willing to test whether the memory of His previous stay among the Samaritans would secure for Himself and His followers a friendly welcome. But one of the numberless quarrels which were constantly arising had made the Samaritans more than usually hostile. Violating the rule of hospitality, though it is the very first rule of Eastern life, the villagers of En Gannim refused to receive the Messianic band.

It was a flagrant wrong thus to dismiss a weary and hungry multitude at the foot of the frontier hills, at a distance from other villages,

---

[1] Luke ix. 49. ἐκωλύσαμεν.   [2] Num. xi. 38.   [3] Βία ἐχθρὸν Θεῷ.

and at the beginning of their sacred pilgrimage. But besides this it was an undisguised insult, a refusal, open as that of the Gadarenes, to admit the now public claims of Him who asked their courtesy. Instantly the hot spirit of the sons of Zebedee took fire. It was in this very country that Elijah, to avenge a much smaller wrong, had called down fire from Heaven.[1] Had not the time arrived for One greater than Elijah to vindicate His majesty, and to revive by some signal miracle the drooping spirits of His followers? "And on seeing it, His disciples James and John said, Lord, willest Thou we should bid fire to descend from heaven, and consume them, as even Elijah did?" What wonder, it has been said, "that the Sons of Thunder should wish to flash lightning?" But how significant are the touches of character even in these few words, "Willest Thou that *we*—"! They want to take part in the miracle themselves. *They*, too, have been insulted in the person of their Lord. They have an uneasy sense that calling down fire from heaven does not quite accord with the character of Him who "went about doing good," but they are ready to undertake the task for Him. Yet, even in expressing the wish, they felt a little touch of shame. Is not such conduct vindictive and impatient? Well, at least, their excuse is ready—"*as Elijah did.*" They can shelter themselves behind a great name. For their earthly wrath they can adduce a Scripture precedent. They have "a text" ready to consecrate their personal resentment. Alas! had it been in their power to make the heavens blaze they would but have furnished another instance of the crimes which have been committed or excused in the name of Scripture. What is it that we learn from remorseless persecutions, bitter hatreds between those who bear the common name of Christian—from the atrocities of the Inquisition, from savage crusades, from brutal witch-murders, from the fires of Smithfield and of Toledo, from the condonation and even the approval of mere assassins, from medals struck in honour of massacres of St. Bartholomew, from sermons preached amid the agonies of martyrs, from the slanders and calumnies weekly used to write down imaginary opponents by those who think that in the hideous forms of their fanaticism they are doing God service?—what do we learn from these most miserable and blood-stained pages of ecclesiastical controversy, but that

> "In religion
> What damnèd error but some sober brow
> Will bless it and approve it with a text,
> Hiding the grossness with fair ornament"?

But the lesson of all Scripture is that, though the Elijah-times may require the Elijah-spirit, yet the Elijah-times have passed for ever, and that the Elijah-spirit is not the Christ-spirit. For Christians, at any rate, it is written, bright and large, over every page of the New Testa-

---

[1] 2 Kings i. 9—14.

ment, that "the wrath of man worketh not the righteousness of God."¹ And how full of instruction is Christ's reproof! He does not stop or stoop to argue. He does not unfold the hidden springs of selfishness and passion which had caused their fierce request. He does not dispute their Scripture precedent. He does not point out that texts *must* be misused if they be applied to exacerbate human hatreds born in the inflation of religious vanity. He does not reproach them for the indifference to the agony of others which lay in the words, "Willest Thou we should bid fire to descend from Heaven and *consume them!*" No; but, turning round, He rebuked them, and said, "Ye know not—ye— of what spirit ye are.² For the Son of Man came not to destroy men's souls, but to save." His words were brief and compassionate, because, in their error, flagrant as it was, there was still a root of nobleness. Their zeal for the Lord, their love of His person, their impassioned estimate of the heinousness of any insult directed against Him—these were the salt of good motives which saved their conduct from being entirely evil. Where they erred was in the fancy that love to Him can be rightly shown by fury and vengeance against those whom they deemed to be His enemies; and that it was His will that any should perish rather than come to repentance. It was a lesson, for all ages, of infinite tenderness and infinite tolerance; a lesson which during these long centuries theologians and religious parties and partisans have for the most part failed to learn. Of old, when it was permitted them, they resorted to chains and stakes; now that the secular weapons have been struck out of their grasp, they shoot out their arrows, even bitter words. And they take this to be religion,—this to be the sort of service which Christ approves!

3. Once again in the Gospels the sons of Zebedee come into separate prominence, and once again they appear as disciples who have misunderstood Christ's promises, and but imperfectly learnt His lessons. The incident occurred at one of the most solemn moments of His life. From the plots and excommunications of His enemies, with a heavy price on His head, He had taken refuge in deep obscurity in the little town of Ephraim. There he remained for some weeks between the death of Lazarus and the Passover,³ until from the summit of the conical hill on which the little town was built, He could see the long trains of Galilean pilgrims streaming down the Jordan valley on their

---

¹ The needfulness of the lesson becomes even more clear when we find St. Ambrose (in Luke ix. 54, 55) deliberately defending the Apostles: "Nec discipuli peccant, qui legem sequuntur," etc. How greatly do we all need to offer the prayer—

"Let not this weak unknowing hand
Presume Thy bolts to throw,
And deal damnation round the land
On each I judge my foe."

² Luke x. 55. οἶον πνεύματός ἐστε ὑμεῖς. Both the expression of the word ὑμεῖς and its position make it extremely emphatic.

³ John xi. 54.

way to Jerusalem. Then He knew that He could join them and proceed at their head to the Holy City. He set forth to what He foresaw would be His death of agony and shame. As seems to have been common with Him, He walked alone, and in front, while the Apostles followed in a group at some little distance behind Him. But on this occasion the majesty of His purpose seems so to have clothed His person with awe and grandeur—He seemed to be so transfigured by the halo of Divine sorrow, that—as we learn from St. Mark—in one of those unexplained references which he doubtless borrowed from the reminiscences of St. Peter—the disciples as they walked behind Him were amazed and full of fear.[1] From His look and manner they felt instinctively that something more than usually awful was at hand. Nor did He leave them long in doubt as to what it was. He beckoned them to Him, and in language more definite and unmistakable than ever before, He revealed to them not only that He should be betrayed, and mocked, and scourged, and spit upon, but even the crowning horror that He should be *crucified*—and then that, on the third day, He should rise again.

It was at that most inopportune moment that Salome came to Him with her two sons, James and John, worshipping Him, begging Him to grant them something. The facile mother was but the mouthpiece for the ill-instructed ambition of her sons. Relying on her near relationship to Him, on her services in His cause, on His known regard for them both, on His special affection for one of them, they wanted thus to forestall the rest, and to secure a special and personal blessing for themselves. They wanted thus, and finally, to settle the dispute, which had so often risen among the half-trained Apostles, as to which of them should have the precedence, which should be the greatest among them. Yet we must not think that their motive was altogether earthly in its character. It was not *all* selfishness; it was not *mere* ambition—at any rate, not vulgar selfishness, not ignoble ambition. In the strange complexity of human motives there was doubtless a large admixture of these impurer elements, and there was also a complete ignorance as to the nature of the approaching end. But there was also a loving desire to be nearest to Jesus, one at His right hand, one at His left. They had thought of material power and splendour in their interpretation of His promises. *His* thoughts had been of the cross, theirs were of the throne. In their ignorance they had asked for the places which, seven days afterwards, were occupied in infamy and anguish by two crucified robbers. Oh, fond, foolish mother! oh, too presumptuous sons! the kingdom of Heaven is not as ye think. It is not a place for ambitious precedence and selfish rivalries. Not there do Michael and Gabriel contrast the respective value of their services, or compete as to which shall do "the maximum of service on the minimum of grace." There the

---

[1] Mark x. 32.

success of each is the joy of all, and the glory of each the pride of all. Nor is there, as ye vainly imagine, any favouritism, any private partiality, any acceptance of men's persons with God and with His Christ. All are alike the children of His impartial mercy—"all equally guilty, all equally redeemed." With Him many of the first shall be last, and many of the last first, and many whom their brethren would altogether exclude shall be heirs of His common heaven, and many who, on earth, figured as saints, and great divines, shall be far below the peasants and little ones of His kingdom—and, alas! here on earth, how many, glorying in themselves, have delighted in anathemas and misrepresentations—

> "Who there below shall grovel in the mire,
> Leaving behind them horrible dispraise!"

But once more, because the request was not *all* selfish or *all* ignoble, and because in true hearts deeper lessons spring from loving forbearance than from loud rebuke, Jesus gently said to them, "Ye know not"— again, "*Ye know not*," for it was ignorance, not badness, from which their errors sprang—"Ye know not what ye are asking for yourselves. Can ye drink the cup which I am about to drink, and be baptised with the baptism wherewith I am being baptised?"[1] They say to Him, "We can." And He saith to them, "My cup indeed ye shall drink, and with the baptism wherewith I am being baptised shall ye be baptised; but to sit on My right hand and on My left is Mine to give to those only for whom it has been prepared by My Father."[2] In that bold answer, "*We can!*" had flashed out all the true nobleness of the sons of Zebedee. For the answer of Jesus had by that time partially undeceived them. It had shown them the mistaken nature of their chiliastic hopes. They saw that the blessing for which they had asked had been, so far as things earthly were concerned, a primacy of sorrow; that the only passage to Christ's throne of glory lay through the endurance of suffering; that to be near Him was—as the oldest Christian tradition quoted some of His unrecorded words—to be "near the sword and near the fire:"[3]—and yet they had not shrunk. Whatever the price was, they were ready to pay it. To be near Him was worth it all.

And the punishment of their fault came in part and at once in the indignant disapproval of their fellow Apostles. The other disciples, too, had *their* chiliastic hopes; they wanted *their* thrones and their prerogatives; and all that had been selfish and unworthy in this attempt of the Sons of Thunder to wring, as it were, from private influence or private kinsmanship an exclusive privilege, aroused a strong counter selfishness. Doubtless the voice of Judas was loudest in the complaint that this was

---

[1] The Fathers speak of the triple baptism in water, by the Spirit, and in blood.
[2] Matt. xx. 23.
[3] ὁ ἐγγύς μου ἐγγὺς τοῦ πυρός (Didymus *in* Ps. lxxxviii. 8).

a mean attempt to steal from others their fair share of a private advantage; that it was "just what might have been expected of Salome and her sons."[1] But instantly the Lord healed the rising feud. He called them all round Him. He taught them that arrogant lordship and domineering despotism[2] were the characteristics of Gentile self-assertion. "Not so shall it be among you. But whosoever wills to become great among you shall be your servant; and whosoever wills to become first of you shall be slave of all. For even the Son of Man came not to be ministered unto, but to minister, and to give His life a ransom for many."

Yet the fault and the rebuke of which St. John had had his share in no ways alienated from him the affection of his Lord. We see him again at the last supper, and he is leaning on Christ's breast. It is from this that he gains his title in the early Church of "the bosom disciple."[3] Although he does not mention his own name, he is himself the describer of the incident. Jesus and the Twelve are reclining at the quasi-paschal meal. Our Lord is in the centre of the couch leaning on His left arm. At His right, in the place of honour, was perhaps Peter, or perhaps—as an office-bearer of the little band—the traitor Judas. At his left, and therefore with his head near the breast of Jesus, is reclining "the disciple whom Jesus loved." The anguish of the soul of Jesus wrung from Him the groan, "Verily, verily, I say to you that one of you shall betray Me." The words fell very terribly on the ears of the Apostles. They began to gaze on one another with astonishment, with perplexity, almost with mutual suspicion.[4] They thought that if any one knew, John knew the secret; and supposing that Jesus had whispered into his ear the fatal name which He would not speak aloud, St. Peter, catching his eye by a sign, whispered to him, "Tell us who it is of whom He speaks?"[5] John did not indeed know the traitor's name, but leaning back his head with a sudden motion, so as to look up in the face of Jesus,[6] he said, "Lord, who is it?" Then Jesus whispered, "It is that one for whom I shall dip the sop, and give it him." He dipped the piece of bread in the common dish, and gave it to Judas. Then Satan entered into him, and he went forth into the night. Relieved of the oppression of that painful presence, Jesus began those Divine discourses which it was granted to John alone to preserve—so "rarely mixed of sorrows and joys, and studded with mysteries as with emeralds."

We see John once again, with Peter and James, in the Garden of Gethsemane sleeping the sleep of sorrow and weariness, when it had

---

[1] Matt. xx. 24, οἱ δέκα ἠγανάκτησαν περὶ τῶν δύο ἀδελφῶν.
[2] Mark x. 42, κατακυριεύουσιν . . . κατεξουσιάζουσιν.   [3] ὁ ἐπιστήθιος
[4] John xiii. 22, ἀπορούμενοι περὶ τίνος λέγει.   [5] B, C, L.
[6] John xiii. 25, ἐπιπεσών, not "leaning" (ἀνακείμενος), as in the E. V., but *suddenly changing his posture*. The οὕτως, which is read in B, C, E, F, etc., is a vivid touch of reminiscence, describing the actual posture as in iv. 6.

been better had he kept awake; and then we see him showing no greater courage than the rest when "all the disciples forsook Him and fled."

> "'What should wring this from thee?'—ye laugh and ask;
> What wrung it? Even a torchlight and a noise,
> The sudden Roman faces, violent hands,
> And fears of what the Jews might do! Just that,
> And it is written 'I forsook and fled.'
> There was my trial, and it ended thus."[1]

But if he was one of those who fled, he was the earliest of all to rejoin his Lord. Braving the multitude, and the peril, and the shame, he at once returned from his flight, and followed the group who, under the traitor's guidance, were leading Jesus bound to the joint palace of Hanan and Caiaphas. He even ventured to enter the palace with those who were guarding the Prisoner.[2] He gained admission because he was known to the High Priest. It is unlikely that this has anything to do with the fact that he had some distant affinity with priestly families,[3] or with the strange and probably symbolical tradition that, in his old age at Ephesus, he wore the *petalon* or golden plate which marked the mitre of High Priesthood.[4] Nor is it easy to imagine how a Galilean fisherman should have known anything personally of these wealthy Sadducean aristocrats, with whom he had not a single thought or a single sympathy in common. To me it seems probable that he knew Hanan and his household only in the way of his business, and I see in this incidental notice a fresh confirmation of my conjecture that the duties of this business obliged him sometimes to reside at Jerusalem.

And thus the beloved disciple stayed with Christ during the long hours of that night of shame and agony. He was doubtless an eye-witness of all that he narrates respecting Peter's denial, and the scenes which took place before Annas, Caiaphas, and Pilate. He saw Jesus—with the murderer by his side—standing on the pavement, wearing the crown of thorns, and the purple robe, dyed a deeper purple with His blood. He heard the Jews prefer to Him Barabbas as their favourite, and Tiberius as their king. He heard the bursts of involuntary pity and involuntary admiration which wrung from the half-Christianised conscience of the cruel governor the exclamations, "Behold the man!" "Behold your king!" He saw Him bear His cross to Golgotha; and saw Him crucified; and saw the two brigands occupying the places for which he and James had asked so ignorantly, at His right hand and at His left.

---

[1] Browning, *A Death in the Desert.*
[2] John xviii. 15, "went in with Jesus."
[3] The Virgin Mary was a kinswoman of Elisabeth, who was the wife of a leading priest; and, therefore, the sons of Zebedee, through their mother, must have had some priestly connexions.
[4] Euseb. *H. E.* v. 24, quoting Polycrates.

Four women stood beside those crosses. They were the mother of Jesus; Salome, His mother's sister; Mary, the wife of Clopas, perhaps another sister; and Mary of Magdala. With them, alone apparently of all the Apostles, stood St. John. No other disciple, except standing in a group afar off, was present during those awfully agonising, those supremely crushing moments which seemed to dash into indistinguishable ruin all their hopes, and to give an almost fiendish significance to the taunts of priests and mob. Let us recognise the heroism, the faith, the endurance which enable the three Maries, and Salome, and her son, to stand gazing at a scene which must have made the sword pierce their souls with unutterable agony. Let us see in it the proof that if Salome and John had indeed looked to share with him a pre-eminence of blessedness, they were not ashamed to stand beside Him in the hour of His humiliation, and in the Valley of the Shadow of His Death.

And even in His hour of agony, His kingly eye was on them. To them were addressed the second, perhaps the first words which He uttered after the actual elevation of His cross.[1] "Seeing then His mother and the disciple standing by, whom He loved, He said to His mother 'Woman, behold thy son!' Then He saith to the disciple, 'Behold thy mother!'" Very few words, but there was compressed into them a whole world of meaning and of tenderness! And what can appear less strange than that to St. John was entrusted that precious charge? True that Christ had "brethren;" but apparently they were not there; or, if they were there, it was only among "the many" who stood "beholding from afar"—the many whose love was not at that moment strong enough to overcome the horror and the fear. But John was there—almost His earliest disciple; whom He loved most; who believed on Him unreservedly; who was akin to Him; whose mother was the Virgin's sister; who was rich enough to undertake the charge; whose natural character, at once so brave and so loving, fitted him for it; who had powerful friends; who was probably the only Apostle and the only relative of Jesus who had a home at Jerusalem, where, in the bosom of the infant Church which Christ had founded, it was fitting that the Virgin should henceforth dwell. "And from that hour that disciple took her into his own home."[2]

"*From that hour;*"—he felt probably that the Virgin had witnessed as much as human nature could sustain of that awful scene.

---

[1] The prayer for His murderers seems to have been breathed when the hands were pierced, and before the cross was uplifted (Luke xxiii. 34). The omission by B, D, etc., may be due to some lectionary arrangement, but is surely insufficient to throw doubt on its genuineness, since it is found in ℵ, A, C, F, G, etc. We cannot tell whether the promise to the converted robber was spoken before or after those words to His mother and St. John.

[2] The tradition to which the Fathers refer as "*ecclesiastica historia*" (probably derived from the *Acts* of Leucius) assign another reason. "Cujus privilegii sit Joannes, immo *Joannis Virginitas*; a domino virgine mater virgo virgini discipulo commendatur" (Jer. c. *Jovin.* i. 26). δῆλον ὅτι Ἰωάννη διὰ τὴν παρθενίαν (Epiph. *Haer.* lxxviii. 10; Paulinus of Nola, *Ep.* 51, etc.). See Zahn, p. 206.

There would be no rescue; no miracle. Jesus would die—would die, as He had said, upon the cross. The Virgin had suffered enough of agony; she had received her last farewell; it needed not that she should witness the deepening anguish, the glazing eye, the horrible *crurifragium* which probably awaited Him. The Beloved Disciple took her to his own home.

But he must himself have returned to the cross, for he tells us expressly and emphatically that he was a personal eye-witness of the last scenes. He was standing by when the soldiers broke the legs of the two robbers to hasten their deaths, which otherwise might not have happened till after two more days of lingering agony. He was close by the cross when, seeing that Jesus was already dead, a soldier gashed His side "with the broad head of his lance," and "immediately there came out blood and water"[1]—to be for all the world the mystic signs of imparted life and cleansing power. "And he that hath seen hath borne witness, and his witness is true, and he knoweth that he saith things that are true that ye also may believe." That witness was to be henceforth the work of his life;—the winning over of men to that belief was to be henceforth the main end of all he did and all he wrote.[1] And to that incident, narrated by him alone of the Evangelists, he refers with special emphasis in the Epistle which enshrines his final legacy to the Church of God.

How long the Apostle stood to the Virgin in the place of a son we do not know. She is mentioned in the New Testament but once again, when we see her united in prayer and supplication with the other holy women and the Apostles, and with the "brethren of the Lord," now at last fully converted by the miracle of the Resurrection. After that slight notice she disappears not only from Scripture history, but from early tradition. It was unknown, even as far back as the second century, whether she died in Jerusalem, where the tomb of the Virgin is now shown, close to Gethsemane:[3] or whether, after more than eleven years had elapsed, she accompanied St. John to Ephesus, and died and was buried there.[4]

The subsequent glimpses which we obtain of St. John in Scripture are not numerous. He does not once appear alone, but always in conjunction with St. Peter, and for twenty years and more he does not seem to have manifested any independent or original action. On the morning of the Resurrection he was with St. Peter, when they two were the first who received from Mary of Magdala the startling tidings

---

[1] John xix. 34, λόγχῃ ... ἔνυξεν. [2] xix. 35; xx. 30.
[3] This supposed tomb was unknown for at least six centuries. Nicephorus, in the fourteenth century—from whom has been derived such a mass of entirely untrustworthy tradition—says that she died at Jerusalem, aged fifty-nine (*H. E.* ii. 3).
[4] Epiphan. *Haer.* lxxviii. 11. This was asserted in a synodical letter of the Council of Ephesus, A.D. 431. It seems, however, to be very unlikely, for had she died at Ephesus *her* grave would have been even more likely to be pointed out than the grave of John.

that the tomb was open and empty. Instantly they ran to visit it. The swift step of St. John, who was the younger of the two, outran Peter; and as he stood stooping and peering into the darkness he saw that Jesus was not there, and caught only the white gleam of the linen clothes. But when Peter came to the place, no awe, no danger of Levitical pollution, could restrain his impetuous eagerness. He would see all, know all. Instantly he plunged into the dim interior, and stood gazing on the scene which presented itself.[1] The shroud which had swathed the body lay there; the napkin lay rolled up in a place by itself. As they went home together, the Divine *necessity* that Jesus should rise from the dead dawned first with full conviction upon their minds.

Once more we see St. John separately and as a distinct figure in his own Gospel. He was with the Eleven on that first Easter evening when Jesus appeared to them in the closed upper room, and said, "Peace be with you," and showed them His hands and His feet, and breathed on them, and said, "Receive ye the Holy Ghost." He was with the Twelve when Jesus again appeared to them on the next Sunday, and Thomas was convinced. Then for a little time the Appearances of the Risen Lord seem to have been intermitted. Driven to earn his daily bread, Peter proposed to resume the fishing, which had for so long a time been abandoned. Thomas and Nathaniel, James and John, and two other disciples accompanied them. They toiled all night; but they caught nothing. But when day began to dawn,[2] Jesus stood suddenly upon the beach. They, however, did not recognise Him in His glorified body,[3] and in that unexpected place, as He stood with His figure looming dimly through the morning mist. He said to them, "Children, have ye anything to eat?" They answered, "No." Then He bade them cast the net on the right side of the ship, and immediately they were not able to drag the net into the boat for the multitude of fishes. The meaning of the sign flashed at once upon the soul of the disciple whom Jesus loved. He said to Peter, "*It is the Lord!*" Instantly Peter had snatched up his fisher's coat, and plunged into the sea to swim to land. More slowly the rest followed in the little boat,[4] dragging to land the net full of one hundred and fifty-three fishes, which they were unable to haul into their ship. When they got to land they saw there a charcoal fire with a fish broiling on it, and a loaf beside it, as one may often see now when the poor Fellahin are fishing in the Sea of Galilee. Jesus bade them bring some of their fish, and share in the morning meal. They dared not ask Him, "Who art Thou?" knowing that it was the Lord. Jesus brought them the bread and the loaf, and they broke their fast. Then, after the meal, there took place that deeply touching interview

---

[1] John xx. 6, εἰσῆλθεν . . . θεωρεῖ.
[3] John xx. 14; Luke xxiv. 37.
[2] John xxi. 4, γινομένης.
[4] xxi. 8, πλοιαρίῳ.

in which Jesus bade the now-forgiven and deeply-repentant Peter to feed His little lambs, and to feed and tend His sheep,[1] and prophesied to him the martyr-death that he should die. Peter, as he turned away, caught sight of John, who was following them, and with sudden curiosity asked, "Lord, but this man—what?"[2] "If I will him to abide while I am coming,[3] what is it to thee? Follow *thou* Me." The expression was misunderstood, as those of the Lord so often were. It led to the mistaken notion among the brethren that that disciple was not to die. It is to remove that erroneous impression that he relates the incident. It is clear from his language that he did not even then, in extreme old age, understand its complete significance, because Christ had never revealed the secrets about the time and manner of His coming. But his correct version of the misquoted words did not prevent the continuance of the error. Even when he was dead, legend continued to assert that he was living in the grave, and that his breath gently heaved the dust.[4]

CHAPTER XXV.

LIFE OF ST. JOHN AFTER THE ASCENSION.

"Æterna sapientia sese in omnibus rebus maxime in humanâ mente, omnium maxime in Christo Jesu manifestabit."—SPINOZA, *Ep.* xxi.

AFTER this St. John is mentioned but thrice, and alluded to but once in the New Testament.

i. He is enumerated among the eleven Apostles who were gathered in the Upper Room with the rest of the little company of believers after the Ascension, and who were constantly engaged in prayer and supplication.[5]

ii. He was going up with Peter to worship in the Temple at three o'clock in the afternoon—one of the stated hours of prayer—when Peter healed the lame man, and afterwards addressed the assembled worshippers, whose amazement had been kindled by that act of power. This great address—in which, as we infer from Acts iv. 1, St. John took some part—was interrupted by the sudden arrest of the Apostles. They were seized in the sacred precincts by the dominant Sadducees—the priests and the captain of the Temple. As it was now evening the two Apostles

---

[1] xxi. 15, βόσκε τὰ ἀρνία μου; 16, ποίμαινε; 17, βόσκε τὰ πρόβατά μου.
[2] xxi. 21, Κύριε, οὗτος δὲ τί; Vulg. *Domine, hic autem quid?*
[3] See Canon Westcott's note on this expression (*Speaker's Comm. ad loc.*).
[4] St. Augustine (*in Joh.* cxxiv. 2) seems to have been half inclined to accept this strange and unmeaning legend on the testimony of grave people who imagined themselves to have witnessed it!
[5] Acts i. 13

were thrown into prison. Next morning they were haled before the Sanhedrin which gathered for their trial in the imposing numbers of all its three constituent committees. The accused, according to the usual custom, were set in the midst of the semicircle and sternly interrogated. The two Apostles—Peter again being the chief spokesman—gave a bold and noble testimony, from which the Sanhedrists recognised the two facts that "they had been with Jesus," and that they were simple and unlettered persons. The Pharisees from the whole height of their ignorance looked down on them as "no theologians." Their Galilean dialect, and their obvious unacquaintance with Rabbinic learning, inclined the Sanhedrin to despise them. On the other hand, they were perplexed by the presence and witness of the lame man who had undeniably been healed. They therefore remanded the Apostles while they held a discussion among themselves. In spite of the severity for which the Sadducees were notorious, they did not feel justified on this occasion in doing anything more than threatening them with worse consequences if they ventured to preach again in the name of Jesus. The Apostles gave them frank warning that such threats must be in vain, since it was a plain duty to obey God rather than man. Afraid, however, of exciting a tumult among the people, who, up to this time, sided heartily with the Christians, and were glorifying God for the recent miracle, the Sanhedrin were forced to content themselves with renewing their threats, and they set the Apostles free.

The return of Peter and John to the assembled brethren was followed by a song of triumphant gladness, and by another outpouring of spiritual influences. During these earlier scenes of Christian history there is no doubt that St. John lived mainly at Jerusalem—though he may have made short excursions to places in Palestine. He must have lived through the short period during which the Church adopted the experiment of community of goods; must have heard of, or witnessed, the terrible fate of Ananias and Sapphira; and must have shared in the outburst of supernatural power, followed by multitudes of conversions, which marked the early energy of St. Peter. He was arrested with the other Apostles in a fresh alarm of the priestly party, and thrust into the public prison. Having been delivered in the night by an angel, at the dawn of the next day they were once more led before the startled Sanhedrin. This time they were arrested without violence, for the priests feared a violent intervention of the people on their behalf. Stung, however, to madness by the firm attitude of the Apostles, who, to the remonstrances of the High Priest, answered by their spokesman St. Peter that they were bound to refuse obedience to the murderers of their Lord, the Sanhedrin seriously debated whether they should put them all to death, and were only saved by the wise counsel of Gamaliel from the commission of that fatal crime. They determined, however, to scourge the Apostles; and then first St. John knew what it was to suffer disgrace and bodily anguish for his Lord. But that anguish failed of its intended purpose. The Apostles rejoiced that they were deemed worthy to suffer shame for His name, and daily in the Temple preached the good news of Jesus Christ.

iii. Then followed the appointment of the Seven; the preaching and martyrdom of St. Stephen; the scattering of all the Church except the Apostles, in consequence of the fierce persecution of Saul the Pharisee; the work of Philip in Samaria; the journey of St. Peter and St. John to confirm the new converts, and the stern encounter with Simon Magus.[1] After this the two friends travelled through Samaria, preaching in many of the villages. Perhaps En Gannim was one of those villages, and by that time St. John had learnt the meaning of the rebuke "Ye know not—ye—of what spirit ye are." He saw then why Jesus had rebuked the evil wish to call down fire from heaven and consume them all. Then, too, he learnt what Jesus meant when He had said to them by the well of Jacob, "Lift up your eyes and gaze on the fields, because they are white unto harvest already. . . I sent you to reap that wherein ye have not toiled. Others have toiled, and ye have entered into their toil."[2]

iv. After this the name of St. John disappears entirely from the Acts of the Apostles. We cannot tell what view he took at first of the bold conduct of Peter in admitting to baptism a Gentile soldier and his household—in "going in to men uncircumcised and eating with them." We can only feel sure that Peter's conviction would—in the close union which had ever subsisted between them—have gone far to help his own. By the time when he wrote the Apocalypse he had learned to look upon the Gentiles as true and equal members of the Church of God.[3]

It was four or five years after the conversion of Cornelius[4] that Herod Agrippa I. seized James, the elder brother of John, and put him to death with the sword. We are told so little of St. James, the son of Zebedee, that we do not know by what bold deed or burning word he had provoked his doom. We may judge with what mingled feelings of anguish and exultation St. John would witness or hear of the murder of the elder brother with whom he had spent his life. St. James was the first martyr of the Apostles. How vast were to be the changes in the Church and in the world during the long half century before John passed away to join his brother—the last survivor of that high and glorious band! But, doubtless, he was in some measure prepared for this lengthening of his life. In that memorable scene on the misty lake at early morning Jesus had spoken to Peter of martyrdom; to John He had spoken only of tarrying while He was coming. It is as though He had said, "Let finished action follow me, shaped by the example of My passion; but let contemplation, now

---

[1] Acts viii. 14.   [2] John iv. 35–38.
[3] On the much disputed question whether in the Apocalypse the Gentiles are placed on a footing of absolute equality with the Jews, see Gebhardt, *Doctrine of the Apocalypse*, pp. 180–194.   [4] A.D. 44.

commenced, abide until I come, to be perfected when I have come."[1] "The one Apostle," says Canon Westcott, "is the minister of action, whose service is consummated by the martyrdom of death; the other is the minister of thought and teaching, whose service is perfected in the martyrdom of life."

v. The name of St. John occurs but once in the thirteen Epistles of St. Paul. Perhaps in the early years of St. Paul's stormy ministry the two would not have been naturally drawn together. They would be separated in part by the memories of "the great persecution,"[2] of which Saul had been the most furious agent, and in which John may have lost many friends. They would be still more separated by deeply-seated differences of character. St. John, as we have said, was wholly unlike the effeminate pietist of Titian's or of Raphael's pictures. We have seen that there was within him a spring of most fiery vehemence. Yet, so far as we can judge, this passion was not often or easily aroused. None could have written as St. John wrote who had not thought long and deeply; and the slight part which he is recorded to have taken in the history of the Church during the first twenty-five years of its existence shows that he was either absorbed in the care of the Virgin, or that he was living a life of meditation and devotion. This was almost necessitated by the atmosphere of persecution which was continuously breathed by the Church of Jerusalem. But St. John must have been naturally inclined to a quiet and contemplative life. Men of very opposite temperaments are not readily drawn together, and there must have been much in the almost feverish energy of the Apostle of the Gentiles which would not at once win the sympathies of the beloved disciple. Besides this, the glimpse which we are allowed to see of John shows him still devoted to the outward life of the Jewish system. He was a daily worshipper in the Temple at the stated hours of prayer, and remembered, even to his last days—though with ever-widening vision and ever-deepening insight into the meaning of the words—that "salvation was from the Jews." One, therefore, who loved peace as he loved it—one who could only be prepared by the training of experience for the immense development which the Church was to undergo from its earlier conditions in the days of Galilee—one who as a mystic lived in the absorbing realisation of a Divine idea—would hold aloof from the loud questions which began to agitate the Church, and almost unconsciously would feel inclined to shrink from him who stirred them up. It is easy to conceive that to one trained as John had been in the intensest feelings of nationality, and in the most absolute devotion to the Law, the characteristics of St. Paul were not attractive. Paul's breadth and cosmopolitanism, his emancipation from Judaic prejudices, his vehement dialectics, his irresistible personality, his daring expressions, the independence of his course of action, the bitter feelings which he kindled in

---

[1] Aug. *in. Joh.* cxxiv. 8.   [2] Acts. viii. 1, μέγας διωγμός.

the hearts of men among whom John lived, and whom he could not but respect—all tended to prevent any close union between the two. When Saul first returned from Damascus an ardent and controversial convert, St. John seems to have been absent from Jerusalem.[1] At any rate, St. Paul did not see him, either on that occasion or on his subsequent visit to convey to the elders the alms of the Gentiles at Antioch. But on the occasion of the third visit of St. Paul to Jerusalem with Barnabas, in order to settle the question—so momentous to the future of the Church—whether or not the yoke of circumcision, and therewith of all Levitism, was to be laid on the necks of the Gentiles—St. Paul tells us that St. John *was* at Jerusalem as one of the Three Pillar-Apostles, and that he met him in conference. I have elsewhere described that most important scene in the history of the world. St. John was at that time by conviction a fervid Jewish Christian. He was living with and acting with the Jewish Christians, side by side with St. Peter, who at Jerusalem conformed to all their usages. Both of them—though all three "were held to be pillars"—were overshadowed by the commanding personality of the Lord's brother, St. James, the Bishop of Jerusalem. Between the first reception of the delegates from Antioch and the stormy meeting in which the question was debated, St. Paul, with the consummate statesmanship which was one of his intellectual gifts, had privately secured the assent of the three leaders of the Church to his views and proposals. All three were convinced; all three gave to him and Barnabas the right hands of fellowship; all three recognised their mission to the Gentiles. Nay, they not only *recognised* this mission, but formally handed it over to the care of those who had hitherto been its all but exclusive ministers. They made to Paul and Barnabas but two requests—both most readily granted: the one that they should themselves be left undisturbed in the ministry of the circumcision; the other that the needs of the poor saints at Jerusalem should not be overlooked in the wealthier Churches of the Gentiles. The fact of this mutual recognition—this interchange of Christian pledges in a spirit of friendship—is the best answer to the dreams of those who would persuade us that St. John, in the Apocalypse, condescended to attack St. Paul himself, as well as his followers, in language of unmitigated hate.

This seems to have been the only occasion—at any rate, it is the only one known to us—on which there was any meeting between the Beloved Disciple and the Apostle of the Gentiles. St. John took no part in the great debate. He seems to have shrunk from everything which bore any resemblance to noisy publicity. On this occasion he left the speaking to St. Peter and St. James, only supporting their concession by his vote and silent acquiescence. His was not the temperament which delights, as did that of St. Paul, in ruling the stormy elements of popular assemblies. In the earlier days, when he and Peter worked together in close

---

[1] Gal. i. 19.

communion, it is Peter who on every occasion comes forward as the chief speaker. Yet we must not infer from this that the relation of John to the elder Apostle was at all like that which subsequently arose between Paul and Barnabas. In the first missionary journey Paul took the lead by virtue of his superior intellect and more vigorous energy. He was, in human estimate, the abler and greater of the two. It was not so with St. Peter. His, doubtless, was the readier, the more practical, the more oratorical ability; but, judging by their writings, we should again say that in human estimate St. John's was the profounder and more gifted soul. But his sphere was by no means the sphere of daily struggles and controversies—

> "Greatest souls
> Are often those of whom the noisy world
> Hears least."

We can think of St. John in the cave at Patmos; we cannot fancy him addressing a yelling mob on the steps of Castle Antonia. His was to be a very different, yet a no less necessary work. It was his to be guided by the Spirit through the education of outward circumstances to truths deeper, richer, more comprehensive, more final than it had been granted even to St. Paul to set forth.

From this time we lose sight of St. John in Holy Scripture, so far as any external record or notice of him is concerned. All our further knowledge respecting the outward incidents of his life is reducible to the fact that when he wrote the Apocalypse he was "in the isle that is called Patmos, because of the word of God and the testimony of Jesus Christ." But, meagre as is this one personal fact, we learn much respecting him from early tradition, and from the precious legacy of his own writings. From these sources we are able to trace the Apostle in his advance towards Christian perfection—in the expansion of his enlightened intellect, in the deepening of his universal love.

It will be better to separate the story of his remaining years as it is handed down to us by early tradition, from the proofs furnished by his own writings of his gradual growth in the wisdom and knowledge of the Lord Jesus Christ. Yet tradition helps us to realise the conditions under which the beautiful but partial dawn which we witness on the banks of Jordan and the shores of Galilee broadened at last into the perfect day.

Many details of his history are left in the deepest obscurity. During a period of at least eighteen years we neither know where he lived nor what he did. In the New Testament we lose sight of him in A.D. 50, at the date of the Synod of Jerusalem; we do not meet with him again till we find him in the isle called Patmos, in A.D. 68.

Perhaps some readers may feel surprise that the latter date should be given with any confidence. It was the general belief of antiquity that his residence in Patmos was owing to his banishment. Even this has been disputed, on the ground that it is only an inference from his expression that he was there "because of the word of God and because of the testimony of Jesus Christ." These words have been interpreted by some to mean that he retired from Ephesus to the seclusion of the rocky islet in order to concentrate his mind on the thoughts and visions which were being revealed to him. There are, however, no certain grounds for setting aside the old tradition. It furnishes the most natural interpretation of his language, and well accords with his saying that he was "the companion" of those to whom he was writing, "in their tribulation, and in the kingdom and endurance of Jesus Christ." But the date of this banishment, if banishment it were, is most variously conjectured. Epiphanius[1] says that it took place in the reign of Claudius; Theophylact and the superscription of a Syrian MS. say that it was in the reign of Nero. Irenæus,[2] Jerome,[3] and Sulpicius Severus[4] agree that it was in the reign of Domitian, and Eusebius in his *Chronicon* places St. John's banishment in the fourteenth year of that reign;[5] Dorotheus places it in the reign of Trajan. On the other hand, Clemens of Alexandria[6] and Tertullian[7] do not venture to name the particular Emperor, and Origen[8] observes that St. John himself is silent on the subject. But—as I hope to show hereafter—there can be no reasonable doubt respecting the date of the Apocalypse, and therefore none as to St. John's stay in Patmos, if, as I myself believe, he was the author of that book. That he was the author is the all but unanimous testimony of antiquity from the days of Justin Martyr to those of the great Fathers of the third century, and it is, I believe, the inference to which the book itself most decisively points. The notion that it was written either by John the Presbyter, or by the Evangelist John Mark,[9] requires for its support far weightier and more decisive evidence than any which modern ingenuity has even attempted to provide.

Of this hiatus of eighteen years in the life of the great Apostle tradition has very little to tell us, and what it does tell us is of no value. That he left Jerusalem is certain, and he probably left it for ever. This may have been at the end of the twelve years during which, as tradition says, Jesus had bidden His Apostles to stay in the Holy City;[10] but, more probably, it was at a much later period. What were the circumstances which induced him to leave his own home,[11] we cannot tell, but it may have been the result of that terrible combat between Romish oppression and Jewish exasperation which arose during the Procuratorships of

---

[1] *Haer.* li. 33. [2] Iren. c. *Haer.* v. 30, 3.
[3] *De Virr. Illustr.* 9. [4] *Sacr. Hist.* ii. 31.
[5] *H. E.* iii. 18; xx. 23; and *Chron.* He says he returned from exile in the reign of Trajan.
[6] *Quis Div. Salv.* 42. [7] *De Praescr. Haer.* 36.
[8] *Comm. in Matt.* iii. p. 719.
[9] Baza, *Proleg. in Apoc.*; Hitzig, *Ueber Joh. Markus*, 1843.
[10] Apollonius, ap. Euseb. *H. E.* v. 18; Clem. Alex. *Strom.* vi. 5, quoting from the *Praedicatio Petri.* [11] τὰ ἴδια, John xix. 27.

Albinus and Gessius Florus. We have seen that the agitation which affected the minds even of Christian Jews had given occasion to the warnings of the Bishop of Jerusalem that "a man's wrath worketh not the righteousness of God." The death of the Virgin,[1] the murder of "the Lord's brother"—perhaps precipitated by his own stern rebukes—the meditated flight of the Christians to Pella—the actual outbreak of the Jewish war,—any of these may have been St. John's motive for thus changing the settled habits of his life. Perhaps by this time, when a race of young men was growing up around him to whom the Crucifixion was but a tale which they heard from the lips of their fathers, he may have been led to the conviction that the day of Jerusalem had passed away for ever, that Jewish obduracy had finally hardened itself against the message of the Gospel. Any peace which the Church of Jerusalem had enjoyed had been owing to the famines, and political troubles, which had diverted the attention of the Jews from the Christians to the desperate struggle against the encroachments of the Romans and their Herodian nominees. Perhaps it had been due, to an even greater degree, to the legal "righteousness" of St. James, his faithfulness to all Jewish traditions, his conciliatory and respectful attitude towards the Mosaic Law. But the death of James seemed to open a new chapter in the history of the Mother Church. Simon, son of Alphæus, another kinsman of Christ according to the flesh, was chosen to succeed him. St. John may have felt that his work at Jerusalem was now finished; that his thoughts had ripened; that his labours were needed in wider regions of the mission-field. Of this we are sure—that he would leave himself to be guided in all the main decisions of his life by the influence of the Holy Spirit of God.[2]

Two common legends account for his presence in Patmos by a supernatural deliverance from martyrdom. It is said that he was plunged into a caldron full of boiling oil at the Latin gate of Rome, and so far from suffering, only came out of the caldron more vigorous and youthful than before.[3] Another story, frequently represented in Christian art, says that an attempt was made to kill him by a poisoned chalice, but

---

[1] Nicephorus, *H. E.* ii. 42. There is nothing to be said for the conjecture of Baronius and Tillemont that the Virgin accompanied St. John to Asia. οὐδαμοῦ λέγεται ὅτι ἐπηγάγετο μεθ᾽ ἑαυτοῦ τὴν ἁγίαν παρθένον (Epiphan. *Haer.* lxxviii. § 11). This statement was made at the Council of Ephesus (Labbe, *Concil.* iii. 547).

[2] He may even have stayed in Jerusalem till Nero sent Vespasian to suppress the Jewish revolt (Luke xxi. 20; Jos. *B. J.* ii. 25; Euseb. iii. 5). One tradition says that on leaving Jerusalem he went and preached to the Parthians. It rests on such very shadowy foundation that it may safely be set aside (see Lampe, p. 48, and *supra*, p. 368). Even if there were not some strange error in St. Augustine's reference to this Epistle as being written "to the *Parthians*" (*Quaest. Evang.* ii. 19), his writing to them would not prove that he had preached among them, and there is no trace that he did.

[3] Tert. *de Praescr. Haer.* 36, "in oleum igneum demersus, nihil passus est." Jer. *adv. Jovin.* i. 26, and *in Matt.* xx. 23; Origen, *in Matt., Hom.* 12. Baronius says truly enough of Tertullian that he was so credulous that he would snatch up any old woman's story with avidity (*Annal.* A.D. 201). On these two legends see the various references in Zahn, *Acta Joannis*, cxvii.–cxxii.

that "it was rendered harmless when he signed over it the sign of the cross, and the poison fled from it in the form of a little asp."[1] The silence of Irenæus, Hippolytus, Eusebius, Chrysostom, Sulpicius Severus, and many others is alone sufficient to prove that these are unauthorised fables.

But these legends bring us face to face with the question, Was St. John ever at Rome ? It is true that the legends furnish no conclusive evidence, and that there is no authentic trace of St. John's visit to Rome in the history of the Roman Church.[2] On the other hand, there is throughout the Apocalypse so intensely vivid a realisation of the horrors of the Neronian persecution, and the wickedness of the agents by which it was brought about, that we feel strongly inclined to believe that the visions of that book reflect the terrible experiences of an eye-witness. St. John may have reached Rome as St. Peter and St. Paul did, either as an Evangelist or as a prisoner, during the final spasms of that dreadful movement which first caused the blood of martyrdom to flow in rivers. In any case the Apocalypse is the echo of a harp whose perturbed strings have been smitten by fierce and bloodstained hands, and then have been swept by the mighty wind of inspiration. St. John did not indeed perish as did his brother Apostles during those years of horror, but the legends of the poisoned cup and the boiling oil may be dim reflections of the narrowness of the escape which ended in what was (perhaps erroneously) believed to be his deportation to a rocky island, and his condemnation to toil as a labourer in its quarries.[3]

We must, however, be content to remain in ignorance as to the causes of his presence in Patmos. The tone of his letter to the Seven Churches speaks of an intimate knowledge of their circumstances, and the possession of an unquestioned authority over them. He must have resided in Asia Minor before we find him at Patmos, and the attempt to prove that his connexion with Ephesus is apocryphal must be pronounced to have egregiously failed. That attempt, first made by Lützelberger, in 1840, has been seriously followed up by Keim, in 1867,[4] and by the Dutch theologian Scholten, in 1871,[5] but it surely shows "the very intemperance of negation." Not only Baur, and Strauss,

---

[1] Augustine, *Soliloq.*; Isidor. Hispalensis, *De Vit. et Mort. Sanct.* 73; Ps. Abdias, *Hist. Apost.* v. 20 (Fabric. *Cod. Apocr.* ii. 575); Cave, *Lives of the Apostles.* Papias tells the same story of Joses Barsabbas, and it may be allegorically deduced from Mark xvi. 18.

[2] It is curious that in the Latin translation of the *Journeys of the Divine* (περίοδοι) by the Pseudo-Prochorus (*Bibl. Patr.* 1677), an attempt is made to fix his martyrdom at Rome. The MS. was found in the library of the monastery of St. Christodulus in Patmos. See Zahn, *Acta Joannis,* p. 191. Tischendorf, *Act. Apocr.* 266—271. Hippolytus exclaims "Tell me, blessed John, what didst thou see and hear about Babylon?" *De Christ. et Antichrist.* 36.

[3] Victorinus and Primasius say that he was "in *metallum* damnatus." There are no mines in Patmos, but *metallum* may mean "a stone-quarry." It was not one of the islands usually selected for deportations.

[4] Keim, *Jesu von Nazara,* i. 161—167; iii. 44—45.

[5] Scholten, *Der Apost. Joann. in Klein-Azie* (Leyden).

and Renan, but even the most advanced followers of the Tübingen school, such as Schwegler, Zeller, and Volkmar, admitted the cogency of the evidence for a fact which till the last ten years has been universally accepted. The notion that the Apostle John was mistaken for the Presbyter John—if ever there was such a person—is wholly baseless. Even if we accept the wild conjecture that the Apocalypse is by John Mark the Evangelist or by the supposed Presbyter John—conjectures which crumble to nothing before the first serious examination—it results from the whole manner and phraseology of the book that the writer *meant* himself to be regarded as the Apostle. And such being the case, it is equally clear that his residence in Asia Minor is assumed as a thing well known to all readers of the book. It would have been absurd for a forger to start with an assumption which, if false, would at once have proved that he was not the person he pretended to be. Even if we set aside the authority of such men as St. Clemens of Alexandria,[1] and Origen,[2] the fact that St. Polycarp, in A.D. 160,[3] who had actually seen and heard the Apostle, appeals to his authority for the Eastern custom of keeping Easter on Nisan 14, ought alone to be decisive. Polycrates, in A.D. 190, who as Bishop of Ephesus was a man likely to be well informed, made the same appeal,[4] as also did St. Irenæus in his letter to Florinus.[5] When we remember the statement of St. Irenæus that as a boy (about A.D. 150) he had heard from the mouth of Polycarp, Bishop of Smyrna, and many other elders, many memorable things about John, the Lord's disciple, who, as a successor to St. Paul, lived in Ephesus, wrote the Revelation and the Gospel, and died at a great age in the reign of Trajan,[6]—does it not require an extraordinary stretch of credulity to suppose that he made a confusion between John the Bosom-friend of the Lord, the beloved Apostle and Evangelist, the immortal survivor of the Apostolic choir, and a "nebulous presbyter," whose very existence is problematical? And who can believe that when Polycrates ranks John with the Apostle Philip as "the two great stars of Asia,"[7] he is thinking only of this dubious presbyter? Eusebius does indeed in one place (iii. 39) infer from a well-known passage that Papias had been a personal hearer of Aristion and John the Presbyter, and *not* of John the Apostle. In the style of Papias, so inartificial and inexact, it cannot be regarded as certain that this is his meaning; but even if it is, the inference drawn from this, that St. John had not lived in Asia, has no weight against

---

[1] Clem. Alex. *Quis Div. Salv.* § 42, and *ap.* Euseb. iii. 23.
[2] Orig. *in Gen.* (Euseb. iii. 1, 1).
[3] Tert. *De Praescr. Haer.* 32; Jer. *De Virr. Illustr.* 17; *Chron. Pasch.* p. 252. Waddington places the martyrdom of Polycarp in 154 or 155.
[4] *Ap.* Euseb. v. 18, 24. (Comp. *Haer.* III. iii. 4.)   [5] Euseb. v. 20, 24.
[6] Surely this testimony more than outweighs the mere *silence* of Ignatius (ad *Eph.* 12; *ad Trall.* 5).
[7] *Ap.* Euseb. *H. E.* iii. 31. I believe, with Renan, that the Philip intended was the Apostle not the Deacon.

the clear statements of Polycarp and Irenæus. It has never been doubted that Cerinthus taught in Asia, and from the first the Church has, in many ways, connected the names of Cerinthus and St. John. By a strange fatality the writings of St. John were actually attributed to Cerinthus (*against* whom they were perhaps written) by the Alogi, who denied the doctrine of the Logos.[1] A scholar so accomplished as Dionysius of Alexandria, in expressing his doubts about the Apocalypse, thinks it worth while to record the legend that Cerinthus had written it, and fraudulently prefixed to it the name of John.[2] But even if it should be proved that the Apocalypse was not written by John, it still bears decisive testimony to the belief that he was the acknowledged head of the Christians of Asia.

Relegating to the Excursus[3] the intricate inquiry as to the *identity* of the Apostle with John the Presbyter, we may here be allowed to assume that the belief of the Church—unquestioned for nineteen centuries—is still to be accepted. It is not difficult to discover why St. John should have fixed his new home in the famous capital of Proconsular Asia. The Church in that city was large and flourishing. It stood at the head of many Churches of great importance. The position of the city as an emporium of the Mediterranean made it an eminently favourable centre for missionary labours. The Christians of Asia were liable to severe temptations, and had long been tried by the influx of various errors. Everything called for the presence of St. John. St. Paul was imprisoned, if not dead, and had, at any rate, bidden farewell to Ephesus for ever.[4] The other Apostles were scattered or dead. The Church, largely composed of Judaising Christians, naturally looked for the support of an Apostle from Jerusalem. St. John was alone available for the work: nor is it impossible that he may have felt all the more need to obey the call because, like St. James, he may have been aware of the danger which arose from the perversion of St. Paul's teaching by Gnostic and Antinomian heresiarchs, who were ever mixing it up with alien elements borrowed from Greek or Eastern speculation.

That St. John's individual leanings long continued to be in favour of the Judaists is proved by the impression which he left upon the minds of those with whom he had lived;[5] as well as by the countenance he gave to the Quartodecimans, who kept the Passover on the 14th of

---

[1] Epiphan. *Haer.* li. 3. The other Fathers are unanimous—Chrys. *Praef. in Ephes.*; Theod. Mops. *Procem. in Cat. Patr.*; Tert. *c. Marc.* iv. 5.
[2] Ap. Euseb. iii. 28.
[3] See Excursus, "St. John in Ephesus."
[4] Acts xx. 25, 38.
[5] *E.g.*, by the story that he was a priest (ἱερεύς) wearing the high-priestly mitre, Ex. xxviii. 36 (Polycr. *ap.* Euseb. v. 24). But it must be borne in mind that St. John regarded all Christians not only as priests, but as high priests (i. 6; xx. 6; and ii. 17, where the mystic stone seems to be analogous to the Urim and Thummim which were put inside the ephod). The word "mitre of the faith" is used metaphorically in *Test. XII. Patr.* iii. 8.

Nisan. It is proved most of all by the general tone of the Apocalypse, which, amid many resemblances, differs so widely from that of the Gospel and Epistles. That the Apocalypse was written many years before the Gospel and Epistles ought to be regarded as a certain conclusion. The difference of style alone—apart from the deeper differences on which I shall dwell hereafter—is sufficient to prove it. The Greek of the Gospels and Epistles, though Hebraic in the structure of its sentences, is yet perfectly smooth and correct. It is the Greek of one who had long been familiar with the language. But the Greek of the Apocalypse is so ungrammatical and so full of solecisms as to be the worst in the entire Greek Testament. Now it is natural that St. John, after so many years in which he had spoken little but Aramaic, should write Greek imperfectly; and that he should subsequently gain power in writing Greek by residence in heathen cities and among a Greek-speaking population. But it is inconceivable that he should have written the Gospel and Epistles in pure Greek, and then, after years of familiar practice, should have come to write the language incomparably worse. The attempts to explain the difference of style by the peculiarities of Apocalyptic writings are impossible after-thoughts, wholly inadequate to account for the phenomena. But besides this, without the invention of a moral miracle, we cannot regard it as possible that, by writing the Apocalypse after the Gospel, St. John could have gone back from clear thought to figures, and have reduced the full expression of truth to its rudimentary indications.[1]

Perhaps it needed nothing less than the fall of Jerusalem to teach to St. John, as it taught to most Jewish Christians, that though Judaism had been the cradle of Christianity it was not to be its grave. Their intense belief in the symbolism of the Mosaic worship, their identification of faithfulness and orthodoxy with obedience to the Levitic law, were opinions so inveterate that nothing could shake them save that visible interposition which, when Christianity was fairly planted in the world, rendered *impossible* the fulfilment of Mosaic ordinances. The extreme Judaisers had so long encouraged themselves in the belief that St. Paul was a dangerous, if not a wicked, teacher, that they could not be convinced that after all they had been immeasurably inferior to him in insight, until their eyes were opened by the catastrophe which closed the order of the old ages, and which was the First Coming of Christ. St. John, of course, would not have agreed with these Judaisers in their extreme views, but no one can read his Gospel and Epistles, written some time after the destruction of Jerusalem, without seeing how much his knowledge of the truth had been widened since he wrote the Apocalypse in the days when the Holy City had not as yet been made a heap of stones.

It has been said, and with scarcely any exaggeration, that the

---

[1] On this subject see Canon Westcott, *Introd. to Gospel*, p. lxxxvi.

Apocalypse is of all the books in the New Testament the most intensely Jewish, and the Fourth Gospel the least so. In the Apocalypse "Jew" is a term of the highest honour; in the Gospel it usually describes the enemies of Jesus, the Pharisees and Priests. Yet these differences are capable of explanation, and we must remember that they are found in connexion with close resemblances. Even in the Gospel there is no higher eulogy than "an Israelite indeed, in whom is no guile."

We must be content to remain in uncertainty as to the chronology of this part of St. John's life, and as to the circumstances which took him to Ephesus.[1] We may, however, be sure that his residence alike in the rocky islet and in the thronged Ionian capital were very fruitful in his divine education. In Ephesus he saw—perhaps for the first time—the wicked glittering life of a great Gentile city, with its merchandise not only of fine linen, and purple and scarlet, and vessels of ivory and precious wood, and amomum, and incense, and wine, and horses, and chariots,—but also of "*slaves, and souls of men.*" There, on the centre of the western coast of Asia Minor, he could, as from a beacon-tower, look back over the plains and valleys watered by the Hermus and Mæander, and while he kept watch over all the Churches of Asia, his voice could sound like a trumpet of God over the Isles of Greece, and westward to the great cities of Greece and Italy, and Gaul and Spain.[2] Amid that busy scene, with its harbour thronged with the sails of the civilised world, and its Temple frequented by nations of worshippers, there could have been little time for contemplation in the midst of the work which life in such a city entailed upon a Christian Apostle. But in his retirement at Patmos, whether voluntary or compulsory, he would have leisure for peaceful thought. Patmos, with its strangely shattered configuration, is little more than a huge rock, and it can never have had many inhabitants. In its grotto of La Scala, on its bare hills, by its projecting promontories, as he sat alone— with man distant from him, but God near—he could meditate in undisturbed devotion. He might naturally pass into mystic ecstacy, as he sat under some grey olive and looked up in prayer to the glow of heaven, or gazed on the silent expanse of the sea, which under the burning sun gleams so often like a sea of glass mingled with fire. No outward circumstances could have been more providentially ordered to bring out his noblest faculties than the interchange of a life spent "amid the madding crowd's ignoble strife," with one spent in seclusion and solitude, wherein he could commune with his own thoughts and hear the voice of God speaking to him, and be still.[3]

---

[1] A legend preserved by the author of the *Life of Timotheus*, of which some extracts are furnished by Photius, says that he was shipwrecked on the coast of Ephesus during the Neronian persecution. It is also mentioned by Simeon Metaphrastes, *Vit. Joh.* 2 (Lampe, *Proleg.* p. 46).

[2] Magdeb. *Eccl. Hist. Cent.* ii. 2 ; see too Chrysost. *Hom.* i. *in Johan.*

[3] "Patmos ressemble à toutes les Îles de l'Archipel : mer d'azur, air limpide, ciel serein, rochers aux sommets dentelés, à peine revêtus par moments d'un leger duvet de

The history of Patmos itself throws no light on this interesting subject. It is scarcely alluded to by any ancient author, which is the more surprising because it furnished a convenient point at which vessels could touch on their way from Ephesus to Italy. It is only mentioned incidentally by Pliny and Strabo,[1] and there seem to be no adequate grounds for Renan's assertion that in the first century it was very populous. A sterile rock, about eighteen miles in circumference,[2] can never have been important. We have no mention of its being used for the deportation of criminals, and when St. John says that he was there "for the word of God and the testimony of Jesus," the phrase is indecisive. Patmos was, indeed, so completely in the highway of the Icarian sea, and its port was so convenient, that it would not, under ordinary circumstances, have suited the object for which islands were selected as places of exile. It is curious that the pseudo-Prochorus, in his *Periodoi*, says nothing about any banishment to Patmos, and does not even mention the Apocalypse, but says that St. John went there to write his Gospel. We can trace no special influences of the scenery on his mind, unless it be in the mention of "a burning mountain in the midst of the sea," which may be a reminiscence of the then active volcano of Santorin, the ancient Thera.[3]

CHAPTER XXVI.

LEGENDS OF ST. JOHN.

Δεῖ δὲ καὶ παραδόσει χρῆσθαι. οὐ γὰρ πάντα ἀπὸ τῆς θείας γραφῆς δύναται λαμβάνεσθαι.—EPIPHAN. *Haer.* lxi. 1.

No account of St. John would be complete without some estimate of the many legends which cluster round his later years. We may say at once that some of them, if true at all, belong—in spirit at any rate—far more to the epoch in which he wrote the Apocalypse than to that in which he wrote the Gospel.

---

verdure. L'aspect est nu et stérile ; mais les formes et la couleur du roc, le bleu vif de la mer, sillonnée de beaux oiseaux blancs, opposé aux teints rougeâtres des rochers sont quelque chose d'admirable" (Renan, *l'Antéchrist*, p. 376). "Silent lay the little island before me in the morning twilight. Here and there an olive breaks the monotony of the rocky waste. The sea was still as the grave. Patmos reposed in it like a dead saint ... John—that is the thought of the island. The island belongs to him; it is his sanctuary. The stones speak of him, and in every heart he lives" (Tischendorf, *Reise in's Morgenland*, ii. 257 ; see too Ross, *Reisen auf griech. Inseln*, ii. 123, and Guérin, *Descr. de l'Ile de Patmos*, 1856). It consists of three masses of rock united by narrow isthmuses.

[1] Strabo, x. p. 488; Pliny, *H. N.* iv. 12 ; Thuc. iii. 23.
[2] Tournefort, *Voy. du Levant*, i. 168. In his time there were only 300 inhabitants. See on Patmos, Stanley's *Sermons in the East*, p. 230.
[3] Pliny, *H. N.* iv. 12, § 23 ; Sen. *Qu. Nat.* ii. 26 ; vi. 21. But it is just as easy to suppose that St. John may have sailed past Stromboli in going to Rome.

1. One of the best-known of these tells us that once at Ephesus he was entering into one of the great public baths (thermæ), when he was informed that Cerinthus was in the building. Thereupon he instantly turned away, exclaiming, "Let us fly, that the thermæ fall not on our heads, since Cerinthus, the enemy of the truth, is therein."[1] In another version of the anecdote, given by Epiphanius, the name of the mythical Ebion[2] is substituted for that of Cerinthus, and this variation happily serves to throw great doubt on a story which is still quoted with applause by religious partisans, because it is supposed to furnish a sanction for violent religious animosities. We catch, indeed, in this story the old tone of the passion and intolerance of the Son of Thunder, at a period of his life when we might have hoped, from other indications, that he had climbed to that region "where above these voices there is peace." Cerinthus was a Jewish Christian, and the earliest of the Christian Gnostics. He was one of those who believed in two principles, making a distinction between God and the Demiurgus or Creator.[3] Further than this, he was one of the founders of Docetism, in that form of it which spoke of "Jesus" as being a mere man, on whom "Christ," the Son of the Most High God, had descended at His baptism in the form of a dove, leaving Him again at the moment of His crucifixion. We can understand how abhorrent such views would be to St. John; how they would run counter to his inmost and most precious convictions. But in the idly superstitious notion that the thermæ must therefore necessarily fall and crush the heretic, we could only trace (were the story true) the spirit which had once wished to perform Elijah-miracles of fire—the spirit of one who forgot for the moment that Christ came to save, not to destroy—that God maketh His sun to shine upon the evil and upon the good, and sendeth His rain upon the just and upon the unjust.[4]

There is another reason for *hoping* that this favourite story of religious hatred is a fabrication. It was not the usual custom of Jews to frequent the public baths. They could hardly do so without ren-

---

[1] Iren. *c. Haer.* iii. 3; Euseb. *H. E.* iii. 28; iv. 14; Theodoret, ii. 3; Nicephorus, iii. 30. Besides the original authorities here quoted, I may refer to Lampe (*Proleg.* 68), Krenkel (*Der Apostel Johannes*, pp. 21—32), and Stanley (*Sermons on the Apostolic Age*).
[2] Epiphan. *Haer.* xxx. 24.
[3] Iren. *c. Haer.* i. 25; Hippol. *Philosoph.* vii. 33.
[4] "A man," said the Rabbis, "should not wade through water, or traverse any dangerous place, in company with an apostate, or even a wicked Jew, lest he be overtaken in the same ruin with him" (*Kitzur Sh'lah*, f. 10, *b*). This is not the spirit of Eph. v. 7, or Rev. xviii. 4, which forbids, not the ordinary intercourse of life, which St. Paul expressly told his converts that he did *not* mean to forbid (1 Cor. v. 10), but participation in the *sins* of others. It is more like the heathen notion—

"Vetabo qui Cereris sacrum
 Vulgarit arcanum sub isdem
   Sit trabibus, fragilemve mecum
 Solvat phaselon," etc.

By entering the same baths, St. John would certainly not have been supposed by any human being to make himself a "partaker of the evil deeds" of Cerinthus (2 John 10, 11).

dering themselves liable to the grossest insults. Further, the baths were almost invariably adorned with statues, and it would have been strange indeed if those statues were not sometimes those of heathen deities. The iconoclasm of the Jew made such places detestable to him, and it was thought an instance of reprehensible laxity when the younger Gamaliel entered a bath which contained one of the common statues of Aphrodite.[1] Then, too, the Ionian baths were thought to be very luxurious. We are told that for this reason they were never used by St. James.[2] Epiphanius also asserts that St. John "used neither bath nor oil."[3] Cerinthus was surely not worse than thousands of bad Christians and worse Pagans—Pagans dyed in every extreme of vice—whom St. John would be quite sure to encounter if he went to public baths at all. Strange to say—heretical as were the speculations of Cerinthus—he is actually asserted by one ancient writer to have been the author of the Apocalypse. That conjecture is absurd, but it surely shows that Cerinthus—who, in virtue of his restless and impressionable nature, has thus become "the spectre of St. John"—could not have been so flagrantly wicked as to render it dangerous to be under the same roof with him! The story is surrounded by difficulties, and I for one am glad to dismiss it from my memories of the holy Apostle, as an anachronism in the history of his life, and wholly unworthy of the later period of his career. If there be any truth in it, it can only be regarded as an expiring flash of that old intolerance which Christ had reproved; or, again, any slight basis of truth in it may be reducible to the utterance of a strong metaphor by way of expressing marked disapproval.[4] In that case the Apostle would not have meant it to be taken literally and *d'un trop grand sérieux*. That it was so taken is due to Polycarp—through whom we get the story third-hand in Irenæus—and of Epiphanius, who repeats it fourth or fifth-hand, and tells it wrongly. Polycarp, who would not notice Marcion in the streets, and when challenged as an acquaintance replied—not surely in the true Christian spirit, which is peaceable and meek and gentle—"Yes, I know thee, the first-born of Satan;" Irenæus, who tells these stories with approval; Epiphanius, who spent his credulous age in hunting for heresy in the dioceses of wiser men and better saints than him-

---

[1] *Avoda Zara*, f. 44, b. The excuse which the Rabbi made, "that the statue was a mere appendage of the bath," showed more good sense than the impetuous conduct ascribed to the Apostle.

[2] Iren. c. *Haer.* v. 33. [3] Epiphan. *Haer.* lxxviii. 14.

[4] Epiphanius, though glad to retain the story, is puzzled by the visit to the baths, and thinks that it must have been a quite unusual, providential visit; that he must have gone "compelled by the Holy Spirit" (ἠναγκάσθη ὑπὸ τοῦ ἁγίου Πνεύματος), to give him an opportunity for the valuable anathema! Baronius (*Annal.* ad A.D. 74) thinks to reconcile Epiphanius with Irenæus by the suggestion that perhaps *both* Cerinthus and Ebion (!) might have been in the bath, a conjecture which Ittigius (*De Haeresiarchis*, p. 58) approves. See on the story generally, Lampe, *Proleg.* p. 69. I am sorry that Holtzmann should say (Schenkel, *Bib. Lex. s. v. Joh. d. Apost.*) "Diese Tradition ist von allen . . . die glaubwürdigste," assigning as his reason its accordance with the character of St. John.

self—would not have been likely to soften the features of an anecdote which had an evil effect even on the saintly mind of John Keble, and is but too dear to the *odium ecclesiasticum*.[1]

2. Another curious story was current in the Churches of Asia long after the Apostle's death. It rests upon the authority of Papias,[2] who professes to have heard it from Polycarp and others, who had heard it from St. John. It is as follows:—"The Elders who had seen John, the disciple of the Lord, related that they heard from him how the Lord used to teach about those times, and to say, 'The days will come in which vines shall spring up, each having ten thousand stems, and on each stem ten thousand branches, and on each branch ten thousand shoots, and on each shoot ten thousand clusters, and on each cluster ten thousand grapes, and each grape when pressed shall give five-and-twenty measures of wine. And when any saint shall have seized one cluster, another shall cry, "I am a better cluster, take me; through me bless the Lord."' And he used to add, 'These things are believable to believers.' And when Judas the traitor did not believe, and asked, 'How will such products be created by the Lord?' the Lord said, 'They shall see who shall come to those times.'"[3]

What are we to make of this strange story? It comes to us only fifth-hand, in a free Latin translation of a passage of Papias; and Papias, on whose authority it rests, was generally looked on as a weak and credulous person. To make it still more suspicious, it is found also in the Apocalypse of Baruch. As to its right to belong to the *agrapha dogmata*, or unrecorded sayings of Christ, two suppositions alone are possible—either that it rests on no foundation, or that it is due to an unintelligent literalism which has mistaken some bright symbol used by our Lord in the genial human intercourse of His happier hours. He may have been speaking with His Apostles of the festal anticipations which, in the common notions of the people, were mingled with their Messianic hopes; and in touching on their true aspect—the aspect which, for instance, makes the wedding festival a picture of the Lord's kingdom—He may have used some such words in the half-playful irony which marks some of the finer shades of His familiar language. Perhaps He may only have meant to expose the carnal notions of Jewish chiliasm, which appear again and again in the teaching of the Rabbis. If so, St. John—fond at that time, as the Apocalypse

---

[1] Dean Stanley (*Sermons on the Apostolic Age*, p. 273), to show how stories do not lose by repetition, quotes the purely imaginary sequel of the story in Jeremy Taylor (*Life of Christ*, xii. 2), that the bath *did* fall down, and Cerinthus was crushed in the ruins! Jeremy Taylor, however, was not the inventor of this story. It is first found in the *Elenchus Haeresium*, by Prateolus ("*De suo addit Prateolus*, etc., at apud primitivae ecclesiae auctores altum est de hac re silentum" (Ittigius, *Haeresiarch.* p. 58).

[2] On Papias see the Excursus on "John the Presbyter."

[3] Iren. *Haer.* v. 33, 3; Euseb. *H. E.* iii. *ad fin.*; Routh, *Rel. Sacr.* p. 9. Grabe rightly observes that the narrative must be reckoned among the μυθικώτερά τινα and ξένας παραβολάς, which Eusebius charges Papias with recording.

shows, of material symbolism—may, with due oral explanation, have repeated some of His words. A literal-minded hearer like Polycarp may have repeated the tale on the authority of St. John, while he robbed it of all the *nuances* which alone gave it any beauty or significance.[1] It would become still more prosaic and material in the writings of a commonplace reporter, and the last traces of its real bearing might easily evaporate in the loose translation and paraphrase of Irenæus.

In this point of view the story has a real value. It shows us that we can only attach a modified credence to any report intrinsically improbable, even when it comes to us attested by one who professes to have known at least two of the Disciples of the Lord.[2] If the anecdote be based upon fact at all, it has come to us so reflected and refracted through the medium of a weak mind as to have lost its real significance. Experience shows that a story told second-hand, even by an honest narrator, may be so tinged in the narrator's subjectivity as to convey an impression positively false. We are thus obliged to discount the tales and remarks for which Irenæus refers us to the authority of "the Elders,"[3] by whom he seems chiefly to mean Papias and Polycarp. Now Eusebius does not hesitate to say that Papias was a source of error to Irenæus and others who relied on his "antiquity." When Irenæus says that the "Pastor of Hermas" is canonical; that the head of the Nicolaitans was the Deacon Nicolas; and that the version of the LXX. was written by inspiration;—we know what estimate to put on his appeals to apostolic tradition. But there is one instance of mistake or credulity even more flagrant. The whole Christian world unites in rejecting the assertion that our Lord was fifty years old when he died, although Irenæus asserts it on the authority of "elders who received it from the Apostles."[4] If in these particulars Irenæus followed too hastily the credulous Papias, he may have derived the harsher elements of the story about Cerinthus from the aged Polycarp. The *accentuation* of that dubious anecdote is what we should expect from the old man whose way of expressing disapproval of heresy was not to refute it, but indignantly to stop his ears. The description of the passion and vehemence of Polycarp given by Irenæus in his fine letter to Florinus exactly resembles the conduct attributed to St. John. Irenæus says that if Polycarp had heard the views of Florinus, "I can testify before God that the blessed and apostolic elder, crying out loud, and stopping his ears, and *exclaiming in his usual fashion*, 'Oh, good God,

---

[1] So Eusebius says of Papias that he failed to understand the apostolic traditions which he received, τὰ ἐν ὑποδείγμασι πρὸς αὐτῶν μυθικῶς εἰρημένα μὴ συνεωρακότα (*H. E.* iii. 39).

[2] Namely, Aristion and "the Presbyter John." Renan needlessly conjectures that the true reading of Papias in this passage is ἅ τε Ἀριστίων καὶ ὁ πρεσβύτερος Ἰωάννης οἱ τοῦ Κυρίου μαθηταὶ [μαθηταί] λέγουσι (Euseb. iii. 39).

[3] "Audivi a quodam *Presbytero*; quidam ante nos dixit; ὑπὸ τοῦ κρείττονος ἡμῶν εἴρηται," etc. See his forms of quotation, collected in Westcott, *On the Canon*, p. 80.

[4] See for these opinions Iren. I. 26; ii. 22; iii. 21; v. 30, § 2.

to what times hast thou kept me alive, that I endure such things!' would have fled away from the place in which he had been sitting or standing when he had heard such words." Here we have indeed the story of St. John and Cerinthus in all its distinctive features! But how ineffectual and how little Christ-like is such a method of meeting error! How widely does it differ from the calm reasoning, and *" Ye therefore do greatly err,"* of the Divine Master! Neither Papias nor Irenæus are safe authorities for stories like these. Papias has evidently fallen into some confusion, and Irenæus has probably mixed up his reminiscences of Polycarp with Polycarp's reminiscences of St. John.[1]

3. Far different is another story related for us at full length by Clemens of Alexandria, and worthy in every respect of the great Apostle. We may assume that it rests on some foundation, because it is full of touches which could not easily have been invented. It shows St. John to us in the full tide of his apostolic activity, appointing and reproving bishops, visiting and directing Churches, and yet finding time to care for individual souls, loving the young, and willing to brave any danger in order to rescue them from temptation. I will tell it mainly in the words of St. Clemens himself.[2]

"But that you may be still more confident, when you have thus truly repented, that there remaineth for thee a trustworthy hope of salvation, hear a legend—nay, not a legend but a true narrative—about John the Apostle, handed down and preserved in memory. When, on the death of the tyrant, he passed over to Ephesus from the island of Patmos, he used to make missionary journeys also to neighbouring Gentile cities, in some places to appoint bishops, and in some to set in order whole Churches, and in some to appoint one of those indicated by the Spirit. On his arrival then at one of the cities at no great distance, of which some even mention the name, ... he saw a youth of stalwart frame and winning countenance and impetuous spirit, and said to the bishop, 'I entrust to thee this youth with all earnestness, calling Christ and the Church to witness.' The bishop accepted the trust, and made all the requisite promises, and the Apostle renewed his injunctions and adjurations. He then returned to Ephesus, and the Elder taking home with him the youth who had been entrusted to his care, maintained, cherished, and finally baptised him. After this he abandoned further care and protection of him, considering that he had affixed to him the seal of the Lord as a

---

[1] Euseb. *H. E.* v. 20. See some excellent remarks in Lampe's *Prolegomena*, pp. 67—71.
[2] *Quis Div. Salv.* c. 42. Perhaps the life of Apostolic journeyings, of which this story furnishes a trace, may show that even if Timothy was "bishop" of Ephesus there would have been no conflict between his functions and the Apostolic duties of St. John. But we do not know whether Timothy returned to Ephesus or not after the visit to Rome, which we may assume that he made at the urgent summons of St. Paul (2 Tim. iv. 9). The notion of a double succession of bishops—of the circumcision and of the uncircumcision—which is mentioned in the *Apostolic Constitutions* (vii. 16), does not agree with the indications of the Apocalypse.

perfect amulet against evil. Thus prematurely neglected, the youth was corrupted by certain idle companions of his own age, who were familiar with evil, and who first led him astray by many costly banquets, and then took him out by night with them to share in their felonious proceedings, finally demanding his co-operation in some worse crime. First familiarised with guilt, and then, from the force of his character, starting aside from the straight path like some mighty steed that seizes the bit between its teeth, he rushed towards headlong ruin, and utterly abandoning the Divine salvation, gathered his worst comrades around him, and became a most violent, blood-stained and reckless bandit-chief. Not long afterwards John was recalled to the city, and after putting other things in order said, 'Come now, O Bishop, restore to me the deposit which I and the Saviour entrusted to thee, with the witness of the Church over which thou dost preside.' At first the bishop in his alarm mistook the meaning of the metaphor, but the Apostle said, 'I demand back the young man and the soul of the brother.' Then groaning from the depth of his heart and shedding tears, 'He is dead,' said the bishop. 'How and by what death?' 'He is dead to God! For he has turned out wicked and desperate, and, to sum up all, a brigand; and now, instead of the Church he has seized the mountain, with followers like himself.' Then the Apostle, rending his robe and beating his head, with loud wailing, said, 'A fine guardian of our brother's soul did I leave! Give me a horse and a guide.' Instantly, as he was, he rode away from the Church, and arriving at the brigands' outposts, was captured without flight or resistance, but crying, 'For this I have come. Lead me to your chief.' The chief awaited him in his armour, but when he recognised John as he approached, he was struck with shame and turned to fly. But John pursued him as fast as he could, forgetful of his age, crying out, 'Why, my son, dost thou fly from thine own father, unarmed, aged as he is? Pity me, my son, fear not; thou hast still a hope of life. I will give account to Christ for thee, should need be. I will willingly abide thy death; the Lord endured the death on our behalf. For thy sake I will give in ransom my own soul. Stay! believe! Christ sent me.' But he on hearing these words first stood with downcast gaze, then flung away his arms, then trembling, began to weep bitterly, and embraced the old man when he came up to him, pleading with his groans, and baptising himself afresh with his tears, only concealing his right hand. But the Apostle pledging himself to win remission for him from the Saviour by his supplications, kneeling before him, covering with kisses even his right hand as having been cleansed by repentance, led him back to the Church, and praying for him with abundant prayers, and wrestling with him in earnest fastings, and disenchanting him with various winning strains, he did not depart, as they say, till he restored him to the bosom of the Church, affording a great example of true repentance, and a great badge of renewed birth, a trophy of visible repentance, when in the close of the age the angels receive those who are truly penitent into heavenly habitations, radiantly rejoicing, hymning their hymns, and opening the heavens."[1]

4. Other traditions may be briefly mentioned. One beautiful story rests solely on the authority of the monk Cassian (A.D. 420), and is far too late and unsupported to have any authentic value.[2] It is yet in many respects characteristic. It tells us that St. John, in his hours of rest and recreation, used to amuse himself by playing with a little tame partridge. On one occasion a young hunter, who had greatly desired to see him, could hardly conceal his surprise, and even his disapproval, at finding him thus employed. He doubted for a moment whether this could indeed be the last survivor of the Apostles. "What is that thing which thou carriest in thy hand?" asked St. John. "A bow," replied the hunter. "Why then is it unstrung?" "Because," said the youth, "were I to keep it always strung it would lose its spring, and become useless." "Even so," replied the aged saint, "be not offended at this my brief relaxation, which prevents my spirit from waxing faint."

The beauty of the anecdote lies far less in the common illustration of the bow which is never unbent, than in the old man's tenderness for the creatures which God had made. The Jews were remarkable among the nations of antiquity for their kindness to dumb animals. Even Moses had taught careless boys not to take the mother bird when they took the young from their nest, and had meant to inculcate the lesson of mercy in the thrice-repeated command: "Thou shalt not seethe the kid in its mother's milk." It is a beautiful Rabbinic legend of the great legislator that once he had followed a lamb far into the wilderness, and when he found it, took it into his arms, saying, "Little lamb, thou knewest not what was good for thee. Come unto me, thy shepherd, and I will bear thee to thy fold." And God said, "Because he has been tender to the straying lamb, he shall be the shepherd of my people Israel." Another Talmudic story will show how much the Jews thought of this duty. Rabbi—the title given by way of pre-eminence to Rabbi Judah Hakkodesh, the compiler of the Mishna—was a great sufferer. One day a calf came bellowing to him, as though to escape slaughter, and laid its head on his lap. But when Rabbi pushed it away with the remark, "Go, for to this wast thou created," they said in heaven, "Lo! he is pitiless; let affliction come upon him." But another day his servant, in sweeping the room, disturbed some kittens, and Rabbi said, "Let them alone; for it is written, 'His tender mercies are over all His

---

[1] The *Chronicon Alexandr.* mentions Smyrna as the city. Rufinus, in adding that John made the youth a bishop, seems to be mistaking the meaning of κανίστηοι τῇ Ἐκκλησίᾳ. If, however, the story be well attested, it is strange that no use should have been made of it in the controversies against Tertullian and the Montanists.

[2] Cassian, *Collat.* xxiv. 21. The twenty-four *Collationes* of Cassian are prefixed to the works of John Damascene. See Zahn, p. 190.

works.'" Then they said in heaven, "Let us have pity on him, for he is pitiful."[1]

> " He prayeth well who loveth well
> Both man, and bird, and beast,
> He prayeth best who loveth best
> All things, both great and small;
> For the dear God who loveth us,
> He made and loveth all."

5. The tradition that St. John lived in Ephesus the life of a rigid ascetic, eating no animal food, having the unshorn locks of a Nazarite, and wearing no garments but linen, has little to recommend it. It rests solely on the authority of Epiphanius, who wrote three centuries after St. John was dead. No hint of it is found in the writings of those who had conversed with friends and pupils of the great Apostle. But when the possibility of Apostolic labours and journeyings was over, he doubtless led a life of peaceful dignity, not indeed, except in metaphor, as " a Priest, wearing the golden frontlet,"[2] but as a beloved and venerated old man whose lightest words were treasured up because he was the last of living men who could say, " I have seen the Lord."

6. The unsupported assertion of Apollonius, that he had raised a dead man to life at Ephesus,[3] may be passed over without further notice; as also may be the assertion that he was, in the Apocalyptic sense, "a virgin."[4] The expression of St. Paul in 1 Cor. ix. 5,[5] at least gives some probability to the belief that all the Apostles were, like St. Peter, married men.

7. One more tradition has met with almost universal acceptance.[6] It is that when St. John "tarried at Ephesus to extreme old age, and could only with difficulty be carried to church in the arms of his disciples, and was unable to give utterance to many words, he used to say no more at their several meetings than this:—' Little children, love one another.' The disciples and fathers who were there, wearied with hearing always the same words, said, 'Master, why dost thou always say this?' 'It is the Lord's command,' was his worthy reply; ' and if only this be done, it is enough.'"[7]

---

[1] Bava Metsia, f. 85, a.
[2] Polycr. ap. Euseb. iii. 31, ὃς ἐγενήθη ἱερεὺς τὸ πέταλον πεφορεκώς. Hegesippus affirms the same thing of James (ap. Euseb. ii. 23). Epiphanius (Hær. xxix. 4) appeals to the authority of Clemens in favour of this legend (ἀλλὰ καὶ τὸ πέταλον ἐπὶ τῆς κεφαλῆς ἐξὸν αὐτῷ φέρειν) (comp. id. lxxviii. § 13).
[3] Apollon. ap. Euseb. v. 18; Sozomen. vii. 26.
[4] Rev. xiv. 4 (see Life of St. Paul, i. 80; Tert. De Monogam. "Joannes .. Christi spado;" Ambrosiaster on 2 Cor. xi. 2; and in the Pistis Sophia, and Apocalypse of Esdras (Fabricius, Cod. Apocr. II. 585).
[5] " As the rest of the Apostles."
[6] Lessing has touched on this story in his Testament des Johannes, as Herder has told the story of the Ephesian robber in his Der gerettete Jüngling.
[7] "Beatus Joannes Evangelista cum Ephesi moraretur usque ad extremam senectutem, et vix inter discipulorum manus ad ecclesiam deferretur, nec posset in plures vocem verba contexere, nihil aliud per singulas solebat proferri collectas, nisi hoc

8. We cannot with certainty name those with whom he was familiar during the closing epoch of his life. We only know that, according to the unanimous testimony of antiquity, Polycarp was his friend and hearer.[1] There is less certainty about Ignatius, Papias, and Quadratus.[2]

9. Respecting the death of St. John we are left in the completest darkness. Two words—ἀνεῖλε μαχαίρᾳ, "slew with the sword"—suffice to record the martyrdom of his elder brother;[3] not one word tells us how the last, and in some respects the greatest, of the Apostles passed to his reward. It is only a very late and worthless rumour which says that he was killed by the Jews. From the silence of all the early Fathers as to this supposed martyrdom, we may assume it for certain that, so far as they knew, he died quietly at Ephesus in extreme old age. His grave was shown at Ephesus for several centuries, and the legend, before mentioned, that the dust was seen to move with the breathing of the great Apostle, as he lay in immortal sleep, arose from the awe with which it was regarded.[4] But the age which he attained—far surpassing, if some of our accounts are true, the ordinary three score years and ten[5]—only deepened the impression that he would not die till

---

'FILIOLI, DILIGITE ALTERUTRUM.' Tandem discipuli et fratres qui aderant, taedio affecti quod eadem semper audirent, dixerunt: 'Magister, quare semper hoc loqueris?' Qui respondit dignam Joanne sententiam: 'Quia praeceptum Domini est, et si solum fiat, sufficit" (Jer. *in Gal.* vi. 10).

[1] Iren. ii. 3, and *ap.* Euseb. v. 20; Euseb. iii. 36; Jer. *Chron.* A.D. 101; *de Virr. Illustr.* 17; Suidas, *s. v.*; and Tert. *de Praescr. Haer.* 32.

[2] Ignatius is said to have been a hearer of St. John, in Jer. *Chron.* A.D. 101. The question about Papias is touched upon in the Excursus on "John the Presbyter." Quadratus is mentioned by Eusebius and Jerome. Prochorus and Bucolus are mentioned by later writers of no authority.

[3] Acts xii. 2.

[4] See *supra*, p. 381; Polycrates, *ap.* Euseb. *H. E.* iii. 31, 39; v. 24; Jer. *de Virr. Illustr.* ix.; Aug. *Tract.* 124, *in Joann.* "Assumat in argumentum quod illic terra sensim scatere et quasi ebullire perhibetur atque hoc ejus anhelitu fieri" (Niceph. *H. E.* ii. 42; Zahn, p. 205).

[5] According to Isidore Hispalensis (*De ortu et obitu*, 71), he lived to the age of eighty-nine. But if he lived till the reign of Trajan (Iren. *c. Haer.* ii. 225; Jer. *de Virr. Illustr.* ix., *adv. Jovin.* i. 14) he must have been nearly ninety-eight. The *Chronicon Paschale* says he lived one hundred years and seven months, and pseudo-Chrysostom (*de S. Johan.*) that he lived to one hundred and twenty; as also Suidas *s. v.* Ἰωάννης, and Dorotheus (Lampe, p. 92). In the ninth century a writer named Georgius Hamartolos quotes the authority of Papias, "who had seen him," for the statement in the second book of his *Words of the Lord*, that John was "put to death by the Jews." On the other hand, (i) Polycrates (*ap.* Euseb. iii. 31, v. 20), Irenaeus (*Haer.* ii. 22, § 5), and Tertullian (*de Anim.* 50) speak of his having died a natural death, which they certainly would not have done if there had been any tradition of his martyrdom; and (ii) the epithet "martyr" was only applied to him in consequence of the legends about the caldron of oil (Tert. *Praescr. Haer.* 36) and the poison cup ("Acts of John," Fabricius, *Cod. Apocr.* i. 576), as well as with reference to his banishment to Patmos (Origen, *in Matt.* xvi. 6 and *Rev.* i. 9). Keim most erroneously says (*Jesu von Nazara*, III. 44) that Herakleon, the Valentinian, quoted by Clemens of Alexandria (*Strom.* iv. 9, § 73), asserted that the only Apostles who had not suffered martyrdom were Matthew, Thomas, and Philip. But, in the first place, Herakleon added "Levi, and *many others*," of whom, therefore, John may have been one; and, secondly, he is speaking not of martyrdom at all, but of various kinds of "confession," one of which is "confession by the

Christ returned. He did not die till Christ had returned, in that sense of the "close of the aeon" to which His own words and that of His Apostles often point; but legend said that he had been taken alive to Heaven like Enoch and Elijah,[1] and that sometimes he still wandered and appeared on earth.[2] So prevalent were such notions as to his immortality, even during his lifetime, that in the appendix to his Gospel he thought it necessary to point out the erroneous report of the words of Jesus from which they had been inferred.

He died, as his brother had died, unnoticed and unrecorded, but he will live in his writings till the end of time, to teach and bless the world. "His body is buried in peace, but his name liveth for evermore. The people will tell of his wisdom, and the congregation will show forth his praise."[3]

CHAPTER XXVII.

GENERAL FEATURES OF THE APOCALYPSE.

> "Volat avis sine meta,
> Quo nec vates, nec propheta
> Evolavit altius.
> Tam implenda quam impleta
> Nunquam vidit tot secreta
> Purus homo purius."—*De S. Joanne.*

MILTON has spoken of the Apocalypse as "the majestic image of a high and stately tragedy, shutting up and intermingling her solemn scenes and acts with a sevenfold chorus of hallelujahs and harping symphonies."[4] In this aspect of the book—though the notion of its dramatic form must be rejected—we may perhaps be content with the arrangement which places it as the last book of Holy Writ. But the whole

---

voice in the presence of authorities," and certainly John had made such a "confession" (Acts iv. 13, 19). Even Scholten gives up the value of this testimony and that of Georg. Hamartolos (see Wilibald Grimm in Hilgenfeld's *Zeitschr.* (1874), p. 123). His loosely Hamartolos quotes may be seen in the same passage (which was first discovered by Nolte, *Tüb. Quartalschr.* 1862, and is quoted in Hilgenfeld's *Einleit.* p. 399), from his reference to Origen, who does *not* say that St. John was *martyred* in our sense of the word, but only that he was banished to Patmos. Nor can any counter-inference be drawn from a rhetorical passage of Chrysostom, *Hom. in Matt.* lxv.

[1] Tert. *de Anima*, 50. Obiit et Johannes, quem in adventum domini remansurum frustra fuerat spes. Ps.-Hippolyt. *de Consummat. Mundi.* Photius Myriobybl. Cod. 229. The notion that he revised the Canon is quite baseless, nor is it worth while to do more than mention the story of his having degraded the Presbyter who forged the Acts of Paul and Thecla (Jer. *de Virr. Illustr.*; Tert. *de Baptismo*). See, for all legendary particulars about his death, Zahn, *Acta Joannis*, cvii. sqq., 200 sqq.

[2] As in the famous legends of his appearance to Theodosius (Theodoret, *H. E.* v. 24), to Gregory Thaumaturgus (*Vit. d. Greg. Nyss.*), and to Edward the Confessor and the English pilgrims, which is represented on the screen of the Confessor's Chapel in Westminster Abbey; and of his appearance to James IV. before the battle of Flodden.

[3] Ecclus. xliv. 14, 15.   [4] *Reasons of Church Government.*

weight of evidence now tends to prove that it is *not* the last book in chronological order; that it was written nearer the beginning than the end of St. John's period of apostolic activity amid the Churches of Asia;[1] that the last accents of revelation which fall upon our ears are not those of a treatise which, though it ends in such perfect music, contains so many terrible visions of blood and fire, but are rather those of the Gospel which tells us that the "Word was made flesh," and of the Epistle which first formulated the most blessed truth which was ever uttered to human hearts—the truth that "God is Love."[2]

And if this conclusion be correct, it is impossible to say how much we lose—what confusion we introduce into the divine order—by neglecting the indications of chronology. Chronological sequence is always of the utmost importance for the right understanding of what a writer says. We are always liable to judge of him erroneously if we intermingle his writings, and put those messages last which he delivered first. It is impossible to say how much the difficulty in understanding the mind of St. Paul has been increased for ordinary readers by the unfortunate arrangement—an arrangement made on the most haphazard and unintelligent principles—which obliterates the lessons which would naturally spring from the right arrangement of his Epistles. It is a subject of

---

[1] Modern criticism tends more and more to the conclusion that the Apocalypse is a genuine work of the Apostle St. John. Even Baur and Zeller regard it as one of the most certainly authenticated of the Apostolic writings. The Alogi at the close of the second century rejected it only on internal grounds, and their judgment is of no importance. Gaius (circ. 200) appears to attribute it to Cerinthus. Dionysius of Alexandria (A.D. 247) was inclined, on grounds of style, to assign it to some other John, but speaks of it with reverence. Eusebius wavers about it, placing it among the spurious books in one passage, and among the acknowledged books in another. Cyril of Jerusalem († 386) deliberately excludes it from the Canon. The Council of Laodicea (A.D. 381) omits it. Amphilochius, in his *Iamb. ad Seleucum*, says that "most" regard it as spurious. Junilius, even in the sixth century, says that among the members of the Eastern Church it was viewed with great suspicion. Theodore of Mopsuestia († 429) never cites it. Theodoret († 457) alludes to it very slightly. It is not found in the Peshito. The Nestorian Church rejected it. It is not mentioned in the sixth century by Cosmas Indicopleustes. Nicephorus (ninth century) in his *Chronographia* omits it. Even in the fourteenth century Nicephorus Callistus, while accepting it, thinks it necessary to mention that some held it to be the work of "John the Presbyter," regarded as a different person from "John the Apostle." But, on the other hand, these adverse views are to some extent accounted for by dislike to the difficulty and obscurity of the book (διὰ τὸ ἀσαφὲς αὐτῆς καὶ δυσέφικτον καὶ ὀλίγοις διαλαμβανόμενον καὶ νοούμενον), and by the dangerous uses to which it was often turned (μηδὲ συμφέρον εἶναι τοῖς πολλοῖς τὰ ἐν αὐτῇ βάθη ἰοντάν, Prol. to MS. 224). Dislike to chiliastic fanaticism, as well as obvious critical difficulties, also led to its disparagement in many quarters. The *positive* evidence in its favour is very strong. It was accepted by Papias, Justin Martyr, Dionysius of Corinth, Hermas, Melito of Sardis, Theophilus of Antioch, Apollonius, and Irenæus, the Canon of Muratori, and the Vetus Itala, in the second century; by Clemens of Alexandria and Origen in the third; by Victorinus of Pettau, Ephræm Syrus, Epiphanius, Basil, Hilary, Athanasius, Gregory of Nyssa, Didymus, and Ambrose, in the fourth. Besides this, the internal evidence, in spite of differences and difficulties, is too clear to be overlooked, and too subtle to have been forged.

[2] It is hardly worth while to mention the Apocryphal writings attributed to St. John, such as the one on the Descent from the Cross, on the Death of the Virgin Mary, etc. See Lampe, *Prolegomena*, p. 131; Fabricius, *Cod. Apocr. N. T.* pt. iii. p. 200.

regret that the Revisers of the Authorised Version did not render a permanent service by placing them in that sequence which is now ascertained with certainty as regards the four several groups into which they fall, and which is known with approximate certainty respecting almost every one of the separate Epistles. How is it possible for any one to enter into the real working of St. Paul's mind—the effects produced upon his thoughts by years of Divine education—who is led to infer that he wrote the two Epistles to the Thessalonians *after* he had written not only those to the Romans and Galatians, but even after those to the Philippians, Colossians, and Ephesians? It is to be hoped that the day will come when the obstinacy of custom will no longer prevent the correction of these conventional misplacements. But even graver misapprehensions result from the misplacement of the writings of St. John. Their present arrangement is due to suppositions, which lead to endless difficulties. It confuses the value of precious lessons, and paves the way for grievous errors. Some may think it an exaggeration to say that this closing of the Holy Book with the Apocalypse has not been without grave consequences for the history of Christendom; but certainly it would have been better both for the Church and for the world if we had followed the divine order, and if those books had been placed last in the Canon which were last in order of time. Had this been done, our Bible would have closed, as the Book of God to all intents and purposes *did* close, with the gentle and solemn warning of the last Apostle—" Little children, keep yourselves from idols."

This, then, is the order which we here shall follow. In the Apocalypse the New Testament seems to be still speaking in the voice and in the tones of the Old Testament. In trying to see something of the meaning of the Apocalypse, we shall see the mind of St. John when he first emerged from the overshadowing influence of St. James and the Elders of Jerusalem; when, from the narrowing walls of the metropolis of Judaism, he passed forth into the Christian communities which had grown up in the heathen world. We shall see how he wrote and what he thought while under the guidance indeed of God's Holy Spirit, but before he had profited by his thirty last years of continuous education, and while yet he was but imperfectly acquainted with the language in which his greatest message was to be delivered. The Apocalypse was written before he had witnessed the Coming of Christ and the close of the Old Dispensation, in the mighty catastrophe which, by the voice of God in history, abrogated all but the moral precepts which had been uttered by the voice of God on Sinai. The moral conceptions of the Gospel transcend the symbolism of visions, and the kabbalism of numbers. We do not pass from the purest and most etherial region of thought to dim images of plague and war, foreshadowed by fire-breathing horses and hell-born frogs. When we have grasped the abstract and absolute forms in which the Gospel and the Epistles set forth to us the eternal conflict of life with death, and light with darkness, we have learnt higher and deeper lessons than when we gaze on the material symbols of scarlet dragons and locust-horsemen, and the warring of Michael with the devil and the beast.

A few words from one of our latest and best students of the writings of St. John, though not written with this purpose, may serve to show what we lose by our customary reversal of the proper order.

"In the Apocalypse," says Canon Westcott, "the thought is of an outward coming for the open judgment of men; in the Gospel, of a judgment which is spiritual and self-executing. In the Apocalypse, the scene of the consummation is a renovated world; in the Gospel, the Father's House. In the former, the victory and the transformation are from without, by might, and the 'future' is painted in historic imagery; in the latter, the victory and the transformation are from within, by a spiritual influence, and the 'future' is present and eternal. . . . . The Apocalypse gives a view of the action of God in regard to men in a life full of sorrow, and partial defeats and cries for vengeance; the Gospel gives a view of the action of God with regard to Christ, who establishes in the heart of the believers a presence of completed joy. . . . In a word, the study of the Synoptists, of the Apocalypse, and of the Gospel of St. John in succession, enables us to see under what human conditions the full majesty of Christ was perceived and declared, not all at once, but step by step, and by the help of the old prophetic teaching." [1]

SECTION I.

DATE OF THE APOCALYPSE.

But before we enter on the difficult task of attempting to see the significance of the Apocalypse, we must once more pause to cast a glance over the condition of the world at the time when it was written.

The chief obstacle to the acceptance of the true date of the Apocalypse, arises from the authority of Irenæus. Speaking of the number of the Beast, and repeating those early conjectures which, as I shall show elsewhere, practically agree with what is now known to be the true solution, he remarks that he cannot give any positive decision, since he believes that, if such a solution had been regarded as necessary, it would have been furnished by "him who saw the Apocalypse. For it is not so long ago that *it* (the Apocalypse) was seen, but almost in our generation, towards the close of the reign of Domitian." Three attempts have been made to get rid of this evidence. Guericke proposes to take "*Dometianou*" as an adjective, and to render the clause "near the close of the Domitian rule," *i.e.*, the rule of *Domitius Nero*.[2] But the absence of the article on which he relies gives no support to his view, and no scholar will accept this hypothesis, though he may admit the possibility of some *confusion* between the names Domitius and Domitian.[3] Others

---

[1] Introd., pp. lxxxv.–lxxxvii. [2] Guericke, *Einleit. ins N. Test.* p. 285.
[3] This is the view of Niermeyer.

again make the word ἑωράθη mean "*he, i.e.*, St. John, was seen," since no nominative is expressed. Now Irenæus, in the same passage and elsewhere, dwells so much on the fact of testimony given by those who had seen John face to face, that we cannot set aside this suggestion as impossible.[1] It has the high authority of Wetstein. Again, the Latin translator of Irenæus renders the verb not "*visa est*," "the Apocalypse was seen," but "*visum est*," "the Beast (τὸ θηρίον) was seen." The language is, unfortunately, ambiguous, and as, in uncritical times, it would naturally be understood in what appears to be the most obvious sense, it is not surprising that St. Jerome follows the supposed authority of Irenæus in dating the Apocalypse from the later epoch. Eusebius says that St. John was banished to Patmos in the reign of Domitian, but, even if he be not misunderstanding the meaning of Irenæus, his evidence goes for little, since he leant to the view that the Apocalypse was written by John the Presbyter, and not by the Apostle. But the authority of Irenæus was not regarded as decisive, even if his meaning be undisputed. Tertullian places the banishment to Patmos immediately after the deliverance from the caldron of boiling oil, and Jerome says that this took place in the reign of Nero.[2] Epiphanius says that St. John was banished in the reign of Claudius, and the earliest Apocalyptic commentators, as well as the Syriac and Theophylact, all place the writing of the Apocalypse in the reign of Nero. To these must be added the author of the "Life of Timotheus," of which extracts are preserved by Photius. Clemens of Alexandria and Origen only say that "John was banished by the tyrant," and this on Christian lips may mean Nero much more naturally than Domitian.[3] Moreover, if we accept erroneous tradition or inference from the ambiguous expressions of Irenæus, we are landed in insuperable difficulties. By the time that Domitian died, St. John was, according to all testimony, so old and so infirm that even if there were no other obstacles in the way it is impossible to conceive of him as writing the fiery pages of the Apocalypse. Irenæus may have been misinterpreted; but even if not he might have made a "slip of memory," and confused Domitian with Nero. I myself, in talking to an eminent statesman, have heard him make a chronological mistake of some years, even in describing events in which he took one of the most prominent parts. We cannot accept a dubious expression of the Bishop of Lyons as adequate to set aside an overwhelming weight of evidence, alike external and internal, in proof of the fact that the Apocalypse was written, at the latest, soon after the death of Nero.[4]

---

[1] μαρτυρούντων ἐκείνων τῶν κατ' ὄψιν Ἰωάννην ἑωρακότων (Iren. *ad Haer.* v. 30).
[2] Tert. *De Praescr.* 36, Jer. *c. Jovin.* i. 26.
[3] See Epiphan. *Haer.* li. 12 and 33; Andreas on Rev. vi. 12; Arethas on Rev. vii. 1—8; Syriac MS. No. 18; Theophylact. *Comment. in Joann.*
[4] This result is now accepted, not only by Lücke, Schwegler, Baur, Züllig, De Wette, Renan, Krenkel, Bleek, Reuss, Réville, Volkmar, Bunsen, Düsterdieck, etc., but also by such writers as Stier, Neander, Guericke, Auberlen, F. D. Maurice, Moses Stuart, Niermeyer, Desprez, S. Davidson, the author of *The Parousia*, Aubé, etc.

For the sole key to the Apocalypse, as to every book which has any truth or greatness in it, lies in the heart of the writer; and the heart of every writer must be intensely influenced by the spirit or the circumstances of the times in which he writes. His words are addressed in the first instance to his living contemporaries, and it is only through them that he can hope to reach posterity. Now, if there was ever any book which bears upon every page the impress of reality—the proof that it is written in words which came fresh and burning from the heart, and passed fresh and burning into the hearts of others—that book is the Apocalypse. "Without tears," says Bengel, "it was not written; without tears it cannot be understood." It comes to us with tenfold force when we remember the tumult of emotions with which the small and persecuted communities of early Christians found themselves in direct antagonism to the Roman Empire, as well as to the Jewish religion. Could any powers more venerated and more portentous than these be ever banded together to crush a nascent faith? The Apocalypse is not in the least a book of dim abstractions, of fantastic enigmas, of monstrous symbols. It had a very definite object, and a very intelligible meaning for all who had been trained in familiarity with the strange form of literature to which it belongs. The single phrase of Tertullian —"Sub Nerone damnatio invaluit"—goes far towards giving us a clue to the meaning of the Apostle. John writes as a Christian prophet would be likely to write who may have seen a Peter crucified and a Paul beheaded.[1] The book is a rallying cry to the Christian warriors who might seem liable to be trampled to the earth in irremediable defeat.

The book has been persistently misunderstood. Herder might well ask, "Was there a key sent with the book, and has this been lost? Was it thrown into the Sea of Patmos, or into the Maeander?" Intolerance, ignorance, sectarian fierceness, the sanguinary factiousness of an irreligious religionism, the eternal Pharisaism of the human heart, have made of it their favourite camping-ground. Others have been driven into a natural but irreverent scorn of it, because they turn with disgust from the degradation to which it has been subjected by fanatical bigotry. But when rightly used, it is full of blessed instruction, and it would never have been discredited as it has been if its own repeated assertions and indications had not been ignored. Instead of seeking out the meanings which must have made it precious to its original readers, as, in great part at least, to all loving and humble Christian hearts, men have wandered into the quagmire of private interpretations after the *ignis fatuus* of religious hatred. God has revealed Himself in the history of the Church and the World, but this manifestation of God in history has been hopelessly confused by an attempt to make it correspond with

---

[1] The remarkable expression, "And I saw the souls of them that had been *beheaded* (πεπελεκισμένων) for the testimony of Jesus" (Rev. xx. 4), may (as Ewald thinks, *Gesch.* vi. 618) point especially to the death of St. Paul. "Beheading" was the form of death adopted for Roman citizens.

symbols with which it has no connexion. The surest and deadliest injury to which the Apocalypse can be subjected is to treat it as a sort of anticipated Gibbon, or a controversial compendium of ecclesiastical disputes. Its symbols have become plastic in the hot hands of party factiousness, but under such manipulations they have been rendered unintelligible to the eyes of truth and love.

Happily these "theological romances"[1] of Apocalyptic commentary have had their day. Like a thousand other phantoms of exegesis, they are vanishing into the limbo of the obsolete. They may linger on for a time, like spectres not yet exorcised, but they are doomed to disappear for ever in the broadening light of a sounder knowledge.

The Apocalypse had its immediate origin in two events which happened at this period of the life of St. John. One was the Neronian persecution. The other was the outbreak of the Jewish war. It was not until these events were over, it was not until their Divine teaching had done its work, that a third and more gradual event—the development of Gnostic teaching in the form of new Christologies—called forth in its turn the Gospel and the Epistles of St. John as the final utterance of Christian revelation.

Unless we study these events there is no chance of our understanding the writings of St. John. Those writings, like all the Books of Scripture, are indeed full of sacred lessons for every humble heart. The comprehension of such lessons—which, after all, are the best and deepest—require nothing but the spiritual enlightenment of a pure and truthful soul. But the historical and critical knowledge of a book demands other qualifications; and it has been a fatal mistake of Christians to claim infallibility for their subjective convictions, not only in matters of religious experience, but in questions of history and criticism, respecting which they may be quite incompetent to pronounce an opinion of any value.

We have already seen what manner of man Nero was. The spectacle of such a man seated on the Imperial throne of the heathen world accounts for the abhorrence which he inspired as a living impersonation of the "world-rulers of this darkness."[2] We have also seen the origin and history of the Neronian persecution, and the circumstances which connected it with the burning of Rome. For the history of these events we must refer back to the earlier portion of the volume. But we must remind the reader that the Apocalypse of St. John can only be rightly read by the lurid light which falls upon it from the Burning City—under the horrible illumination flung by the bale-fires of martyrdom upon the palace and gardens of the Beast from the abyss.

A great French artist has painted a picture of Nero walking with his lictors through the blackened streets of Rome after the conflagration.

---

[1] Moses Stuart.   [2] Eph. vi. 12.

He represents him as he was in mature age, in the uncinctured robe with which, to the indignation of the noble Romans, he used to appear in public. He is obese with self-indulgence. Upon his coarsened features rests that dark cloud, which they must have often worn when his conscience was most tormented by the furies of his murdered mother and his murdered wives. Shrinking back among the ruins are two poor Christian slaves, who watch him with looks in which disgust and detestation struggle with fear. The picture puts into visible form the feelings of horror with which the brethren must have regarded one whom they came to consider as the incarnate instrument of Satanic antagonism against God and against His Christ—as the deadliest and most irresistible enemy of all that is called holy or that is worshipped.

Did St. John ever see that frightful spectacle of a monster in human flesh? Was he a witness of the scenes which made the circus and the gardens of Nero reek with the fumes of martyrdom? We have already observed that tradition points in that direction. In the silence which falls over many years of his biography, it is possible that he may have been compelled by the Christians to retire from the menace of the storm before it actually burst over their devoted heads. St. Paul, as we believe, was providentially set free from his Roman imprisonment just in time to be preserved from the first outburst of the Neronian persecution.[1] Had it not been for this, who can tell whether St. Paul and St. John and St. Peter might not have been clothed in the skins of wild beasts to be torn to pieces by the bloodhounds of the amphitheatre? or have stood, each in his pitchy tunic, to form one of those ghastly human torches which flared upon the dark masses of the abominable crowd? But even if St. John never saw Rome at this period, many a terrified fugitive of the "vast multitude" which Tacitus mentions must have brought him tidings about those bloodstained orgies in which the Devil, the Beast, and the False Prophet—" that great Anti-Trinity of Hell "—were wallowing through the mystic Babylon in the blood of the martyrs of the Lord.

Supposing that St. John had written an apocalyptic book at this time, is it not *à priori* certain that these events, and the appalling figure of the Antichrist who then filled the world's eye, would have been prominent in such a book? Do not contemporary events and contemporary persecutions figure in every one of the numerous Apocalypses in which Jews and Christians at this epoch expressed their hopes and fears? Is it not a matter of certainty to every reasonable man, that the Apocalypse must be interpreted by laws similar to those which regulate every other specimen of that Semitic form of literature to which it avowedly belongs? Does not the fact that the anticipated Antichrist of Daniel is the persecutor Antiochus Epiphanes, make it in the highest degree probable that the incarnate Antichrist of St. John is the persecutor Nero?

[1] See my *Life of St. Paul*, ii. 604—607.

The Neronian persecution, then, was one of the two events which awoke in Christian hearts those thundering echoes of which the Apocalypse of St. John is the prolonged and perpetuated reverberation. The other event was the outbreak of the Jewish war and the siege of Jerusalem. If we succeed in fixing the date of the Apocalypse, we shall be able to know what was the exact condition of the Empire and of the Holy Land, of Judaism, Heathendom, and Christianity— of the world and of the Church of Christ—when St. John saw and wrote.

But while the date may be fixed with much probability, it cannot be fixed with certainty. All that can be asserted is that the book was written before the destruction of Jerusalem, and the burning of the Temple. This is clear from the beginning of the eleventh chapter. The Temple is there spoken of as still standing, in language which closely resembles, and indeed directly refers to, the language of our Lord in his great Eschatological discourse. Such language, and the whole sequel of it, would have been unreal and misleading if, at the time when it was penned, nothing remained of the Temple and city of Jerusalem but heaps of bloodstained stones. But though Jerusalem was not yet taken, there are signs that the armies had already gathered for her anticipated destruction, and that the whole length of the land had been deluged and drenched with the blood of its sons. We cannot tell the exact year in which the Christians—warned, as Eusebius says, "by a certain oracle given to their leaders by revelation;" or, as Epiphanius tells us, "by an angel"[2]—left the doomed and murderous city and took refuge across the Jordan, in the Peræan town of Pella.[3] There can be little doubt that their flight took place before the actual blockade of Jerusalem by Titus, and probably in A.D. 68. It seems to be alluded to in Rev. xii. 14. Now the first threatening commotions in Judæa began in A.D. 64, shortly after the fire of Rome. The actual revolt burst forth at Cæsarea in A.D. 65. Vespasian was despatched to Judæa by Nero during his visit to Greece in A.D. 66. He arrived in Palestine early in A.D. 67. The years 67 and 68 were spent in suppressing the brave resistance of Galilee and Peræa. Nero died in June, 68. Political uncertainties caused a suspension of the Roman

---

[1] Euseb. *H. E.* iii. 5 (κατά τινα χρησμὸν κ.τ.λ.). Probably the leading Presbyters of the Church pointed out that the signs of the times indicated by our Lord, as He sat two days before His death on the Mount of Olives (Matt. xxiv. 15, *seq.*), now clearly required obedience to His warning.

[2] Epiphan. *De Mensuris*, 15. In *Haer.* xxix. 7, he refers directly to the command of Christ. Jerusalem might be said to be "circled with armies" (Luke xxi. 20), long before its actual circumvallation by Titus.

[3] Which might well be described as in "the mountains." Pella is in a lofty position, and is on one side surrounded by precipices. It was the nearest city to Jerusalem which was at once safe and neutral. Though a free city, it had placed itself more or less under the protection of Agrippa II., and by so doing had severed its fortunes from those of the Jews. By their flight to this town, the Jewish Christians cast in their lot with the opponents of Jewish fanaticism. It was one of the steps in that Divine education which showed them that the days of Mosaism and of the synagogue were past.

measures during the year 69, but when Vespasian felt himself secure of the throne, in A.D. 70, he sent Titus to besiege Jerusalem. The siege began early in March, 70, and was brought to its terrible conclusion in August of the same year.

But there are two passages, Rev. xiii. 3, and xvii. 10, 11, which might seem to give us the very year in which the book was written. The former tells us about the Wild Beast, and how "one of his heads was smitten to death and his deathstroke was healed;" the other, explaining the previous symbols, tells us that the seven heads of the Beast "are *seven kings;* the five are fallen, *the one is,* the other is not yet come." Now we shall see hereafter, with perfect certainty, that the Wild Beast, and the wounded head of the Wild Beast, are interchangeable symbols for Nero. The five "kings" then can be no other than Augustus, Tiberius, Gaius, Claudius, and Nero. The reckoning of the "kings"[1] from Augustus is the natural reckoning, and is the one adopted by Tacitus. If Suetonius begins his Twelve Cæsars with the life of Julius, the greatest of them all, the reason is that he wishes to give an account of the Cæsarean family, and of the *hero eponymus* who raised them to the summit of earthly power.[2] So far then it might be regarded as certain that Galba is the sixth emperor, and therefore that the Apocalypse was written between June, 68, when Nero committed suicide, and January, 69, when Galba was murdered. And since the news of Galba's successful rebellion could not have been known without a little delay, we might fix the date of the Vision in the summer or autumn of A.D. 68.

This is, indeed, the all but certain date of the book. We have already seen reason to set aside the notion of its having been written in the reign of Domitian, as due partly to the mistake of Irenæus,[3] and partly to idle repetition and idle inference. It is not, however, *impossible* that Vespasian and not Galba may have been regarded by the Apostle, no less than by others, as having been in reality the sixth emperor. Galba, Otho, and Vitellius passed like phantoms across the imperial stage. The Sibyllist dismisses them in the single line—"After him three kings shall be destroyed by one another."[4] They neither belonged to the old imperial family, nor did they found a new one. Between them they barely covered the space of a year and a half. It is true that they are spoken of as "Cæsars" both by Tacitus and Suetonius, though Vitellius refused the name. But when Vespasian succeeded the murdered Vitellius, at the end of A.D. 69, it was believed that the

---

[1] "Kings" was a common title for the Roman Emperors in the Eastern provinces (see Ewald, *Gesch.* vi. 604, *seqq.*).
[2] "*Imperator*" was a title which Julius Cæsar bore, in common with Cicero and other private persons. He never was "Princeps." The last private Imperator was Junius Blaesus, in the reign of Tiberius.
[3] The Commentary of Andreas, Bp. of the Cappadocian Cæsarea, in the fifth century, rightly says, in contradiction of Irenæus, that it was supposed to have been written before A.D. 70.
[4] *Orac. Sib.* v. 35.

Flavian dynasty would be secure and lasting, and the fashion arose of regarding the reigns of Galba, Otho, and Vitellius as a mere "*rebellion of three military chiefs*."[1] If this were the view of the seer, the date of the Apocalypse would be brought down to A.D. 70. The earlier date accords better with his own indications.

The tension of feeling caused by the tremendous conflict of the Antichrist against the Saints must have been still further strained by the imminent destruction which seemed to threaten the existence of the Jewish race. To minds already glowing with expectations of the Coming of Christ, and the close of the ages, the signs of the times must have worn a portentous aspect. The sunset sky of the ancient dispensation was red and lowering with the prophecy of storm. The "woes of the Messiah"—the travail throes of the Future Age—the pangs which were to accompany the new birth of the Messianic kingdom—were already shaking the world. There were wars and rumours of wars. There were famines and earthquakes. The Church had barely passed through the anguish of the great tribulation. Christians had realized what a tremendous thing it was to be "hated of all men," and to be treated as the offscourings of the world. Hundreds of martyrs had been baptized in blood. The name of "Christian" was regarded as the synonym of malefactor; and all the world hated Christians on the false charge that Christians hated all the world. Many were faltering in the faith; many had proved false to it. Even within its sacred fold many regarded each other with suspicion and hatred. There were false Christs and false Prophets. The powers of heaven were being shaken. Suns and moons and stars—from Roman Emperors down to Jewish Priests—were one after another waxing dim, and shooting from their spheres. Clearly the day must be at hand of which the Lord had said that it would come *ere that generation passed away*, and that all the things of which He had spoken would be fulfilled. Men were not expecting it. They were eating and drinking, as in the days of Noah, marrying and giving in marriage, drinking with the drunken, and beating their servants in all the security of greed, in all the insolence of oppression. But none the less were the powers of vengeance nursing the impatient earthquake, and a belief in the eternal laws of morality was alone sufficient to make every Christian feel that the fiat had gone forth—

> "ROME SHALL PERISH! write that word
> In the blood that she hath spilt:
> Perish hopeless and abhorred,
> Deep in ruin as in guilt."

---

[1] The language of Suetonius is very remarkable, and certainly lends some sanction to the views of those who regard Vespasian as the sixth Emperor. He says, "*Rebellione trium principum et caede incertum diu et quasi vagum Imperium suscepit firmavitque tandem gens Flavia*" (*Vesp.* 1).

[2] This is the term used not only by the Rabbis, but also by the Evangelists, ἀρχὴ ὠδίνων (Matt. xxiv. 8; Mark xiii. 8). It is a rendering of the Hebrew *Chebelî hammeshîach*. (See Hos. xiii. 14; Isa. xxxvii. 3; Mic. iv. 9; v. 2, &c.)

The fields were white for the harvest, the grapes were purple for the vintage of the world. The carcases of a corrupt Judaism and a yet corrupter heathendom seemed already to be falling in the wilderness; and on the distant horizon were visible the dark specks which the seer knew to be the gathering vultures of retribution, which should soon fill the air with "the rushing of their congregated wings."

SECTION II.

THE REVOLT OF JUDÆA.

"Conquest, thy fiery wing their race pursued,
Thy thirsty poniard blushed with infant blood."
HEBER.

On the whole the Jews had borne with reasonable patience, for nearly a hundred years, the odious yoke of the Herods and the Romans. The volcano of their fanaticism was, indeed, only slumbering; and every now and then such events as the rebellion of Judas of Galilee, or the bold teaching of the Pharisee Matthias Ben Margaloth, or some turbulent movement of the Zealots, or some secret assassination by the Sicarii, proved to the Procurators that it was not extinct. The affair of the Standards, and of the Gilt Votive Shields, and of the Corban Money, under the rule of Pilate—the fierce persistency with which the Jews braved death by the sword or by famine, rather than admit the desecration of their Temple by the Colossus of Caligula—showed the Romans that they were walking over hot lava and recent ashes. The rise of false Messiahs under Fadus, the seditious movements in Samaria under Cumanus, the spread of brigandage under Felix, the establishment of a sort of *vehmgericht*, which carried out by murder its secret decrees, the quarrels between Agrippa and the Jews under Festus about the wall of his palace, the avarice of Albinus (A.D. 63), and the manner in which he allowed the disgraceful factions of rivals in the High Priesthood to assail each other unchecked, all tended to precipitate the end. But though the Jews and the Romans felt for each other a profound hatred, there was no overt rebellion till the days of Gessius Florus, who was appointed Procurator in A.D. 65. Under the best of circumstances the administrative customs of the Romans were odious to the Jews, and although the Romans were anxious to extend to them the utmost limits of a contemptuous tolerance, yet they looked upon the conduct of the Jews as so unreasonable, so fanatical, so unworthy of ordinary human beings, that they were in a state of perpetual exasperation. The Jews, in return, regarded the Romans as the impersonation of brutal violence, infamous atheism, and impure greed. In the Talmud, and in the Books of Esdras and Enoch, we see how they loathed their political rulers. The arrogance of Jewish exclusiveness constantly betrayed itself in language which showed that they regarded

Gentiles as worthless,[1] and even Proselytes as little better than a blotch on the health of Israel.[2] On the other hand, Tacitus shows us how a grave Gentile historian could describe the Jews as no people at all, but the mere scum and offscouring of peoples, the descendants of a horde of leprous slaves, devoted to execrable superstitions, degraded by ass-worship, and animated by phrenetic hatred of all nations except themselves. The mutual aversion of Semites and Aryans thus finds ample illustration in the literature of both.

Between such elements there could be no deep or lasting peace, least of all when the Jews were so seething with Messianic expectations that even the Gentiles had come to believe that some one from the East was to be Master of the World. The Romans afterwards explained this prophecy as applicable to Vespasian; but Suetonius tells us that the Jewish revolt was due to their understanding it in a Messianic sense.[3] The air, too, was full of prodigies. A great writer has said that the most terrible convulsions of nature have often synchronised with the political catastrophes.[4] However this may be, it is certain that events are often influenced by the effect produced on the imagination by strange portents or uncommon appearances. The tension of men's minds among the heathen made them notice or imagine all sorts of prodigious births, storms, inundations, comets, showers of blood, earthquakes, strange effects of lightning, abnormal growths of trees, streams of meteorites.[5] In Jerusalem men told how, at the Passover of A.D. 65, a mysterious light had gleamed for three hours at midnight in the Holiest Place; how the enormous gates of brass, which it required the exertions of twenty men to move, had opened of themselves, and could not be closed; how, at Pentecost, the priests had heard sounds as of departing deities, who said to each other, "Let us depart hence;"[6] how

> "Fierce fiery warriors fought upon the clouds,
> In rank and squadron, and right form of war,
> Which drizzled blood."

"Every one," says Renan, "dreamed of presages; the apocalyptic colour of the Jewish imagination tinged everything with an aureole of blood."

It seems to have been the wicked object of Gessius Florus—the last of the Procurators of Judæa—to bring these elements of rebellion to a

---

[1] *Bava Kama*, f. 113, b; *Sanhedrin*, f. 59, a; *Sopherim*, 15; *Rosh Hashanah*, f. 2; &c. These, and other similar passages, may be seen translated in Dr. McCaul's *Old Paths*, Hershon's *Treasures of the Talmud*, etc.
[2] "The following three are attached to each other—proselytes, slaves, and ravens." (*Pesachim*, f. 113, b). Rabbi Chelbo said, "Proselytes are as injurious to Israel as the scab" (see my *Life of St. Paul*, i. 606).
[3] Suet. *Vesp.* 4. "Percrebuerat Oriente toto vetus et constans opinio esse in fatis ut eo tempore Judeâ profecti rerum potirentur. Judaei ad se trahentes rebellarunt" (Jos. B. J. vi. 5, § 4 ; Tac. *Hist.* v. 13).
[4] Niebuhr.   [5] Suet. *Vesp.* 5.
[6] Jos. *B J.* ii. 22, § 1 ; vi. 5, § 21 ; Tac. *H.* v. 13, and in the Talmud.

head.[1] Though he owed his appointment to the friendship of his wife, Cleopatra, with Poppæa, who, if not a proselyte, was very favourable to the Jews, it seems as if he took every step with the intention of escaping from legal enquiries into his own administration, by maddening the Jews into acts which the Romans would regard as irreparably criminal. The legions of Palestine were not purely Roman. They were recruited from the dregs of the provincials, especially from the Syrians of Cæsarea and the Samaritans of Sebaste, two places in which the Jews were regarded with special antipathy.[2] At Cæsarea the population was half Jewish, half Greek and Syrian. Nothing but the Roman authority prevented these hostile nationalities from flying at each other's throats. In A.D. 66 Nero settled their rivalries by giving the precedence to the Greeks and Syrians. A Greek immediately built a wall so close to the Jewish synagogue that the Jews had hardly room to pass. The young Jews assaulted the workmen, and John, a Jewish publican, gave Florus the immense bribe of eight talents to prohibit the continuance of the building. Florus accepted the money, and, without taking any step, went to Sebaste. The next day, being the Sabbath, some worthless Greek, in order to insult the Jews, turned up an earthen pot near the door of the synagogue, and began to sacrifice birds upon the bottom of it. This was intended to be a parody on Lev. xiv. 4, 5, and therefore an allusion to the old calumny that the Jews were a nation of lepers.[3] The Jews flew to arms, and since the Roman Master of the Horse could not quell the tumult, they carried off their sacred books to Narbata. When John and twelve of the leading Jews went to Sebaste to complain to Florus, he threw them into prison. As though this was not enough, he sent to Jerusalem, and demanded seventeen talents from the Corban treasury for the use of the Emperor. This was more than the Jews could tolerate. They not only refused the demand, but heaped reproaches upon the Procurator. He set out for Jerusalem, with a body of horse and foot, to enforce his requisition; and when the people came forth to pay him the customary compliment of receiving him with a shout of joy, he ordered his cavalry to drive them back into the city. Next day, with outrageous insolence, he refused every apology which was offered him, demanded the surrender of those who had reproached him, and scourged and crucified some of the Jewish publicans, though they held the rank of Roman knights. In these disturbances 3,600 Jews were slain. Even then the chief citizens tried to calm the people, and to hush the voice of their natural lamentations. But Florus now bade them all go out and welcome with a shout of joy two cohorts which were advancing from Cæsarea. To these cohorts he

---

[1] "Duravit tamen patientia Judaeis usque ad Gess. Florum . . . . sub eo bellum ortum." (Tac. *H.* v. 10).
[2] "Ekron shall be rooted up" (Zeph. ii. 4). "This is Cæsarea, the daughter of Edom (Rome)" (*Megillah*, f. 6, a).
[3] See Jos. c. *Apion.* 1. 25; Tac. *H.* v. 4.

had given the brutal order not to return the shout, and to fall on the Jews, sword in hand, if they showed any signs of dissatisfaction. A tumult naturally arose, and many of the defenceless Jews were massacred or crushed to death. Next day the people were in open revolt. They drove back Florus from the Temple into Antonia, and demolished the covered way, down which it had been the custom of the Roman soldiers to rush when any disturbance arose in the Temple. After these acts pardon was impossible, and Florus, having effected his infamous purpose, retired to Cæsarea, leaving only a single cohort in the Castle of Antonia.

The principal Jews, with the Queen Berenice, then went to complain of Florus to Cestius Gallus, the Legate of Syria. He sent Neapolitanus and Agrippa to Jerusalem to make enquiries, and Agrippa sincerely tried to save the people from rebellion. They were willing to make every concession except that of continuing to obey Florus. When Agrippa urged them to do this, they pelted him with stones, and drove him from the city.

The revolt continued. Though occasioned by the tyranny of Florus, it was inspired by Messianic hopes.[1] The strong fortress of Masada was seized by the Zealots,[2] and the Roman garrison was put to the sword. Eleazar, captain of the Temple, refused to permit any sacrifices for the Emperor. The loyal party, aided by 3,000 Batanean horsemen, sent them by Agrippa, could only command the upper city, and this was stormed after a few days by the Zealots and Sicarii, who burnt the palaces of Agrippa, Berenice, and the High Priest Ananias. Two days after—on July 5, A.D. 66—they took the tower of Antonia, and though they had sworn to let the Roman garrison depart, they massacred the whole cohort with the exception of their head centurion, Metilius, who basely purchased his life by accepting circumcision. The High Priest Ananias was dragged out of his place of concealment, a sewer of the Asmonæan Palace, and was murdered. By the end of September, 66, Jerusalem was in the hands of the rebels. The Romans in the strong fortress of Machærus capitulated. Cypros was taken. In five months the whole of Palestine—Judæa, Peræa, Galilee, and even Idumæa—was in open rebellion against the Roman Empire.

Then began that internecine war of races—that horrible "epidemic of massacre"—which is unparalleled in the whole of history. The rebellion failed chiefly because of the hatred with which the Jews had inspired the Syrians. In Cæsarea the Greeks and Syrians attacked the Jews, and massacred them to the number of 20,000; while Florus seized the few that had escaped, and sent them to the galleys. The

---

[1] Jos. B. J. vi. 5, § 4. Josephus and Tacitus are almost our sole authorities for the history of the revolt. Grätz (Gesch. d. Juden. iii. 331—414) and Derenbourg (Hist. de Tal. 255—302) add a few particulars gleaned from the Talmud.

[2] The Zealots (Kannaîm) were the fiercest and most unscrupulously reckless of the national party. They were chiefly Galilæans. Simon the Apostle was a Kananite—i.e., a Zealot.

Jews avenged themselves by massacring the Syrians in Philadelphia, Heshbon, Gerasa, Pella, Scythopolis, and other towns; and by laying waste with sword and fire every city and village which they could seize in Decapolis, Gaulonitis, Samaria, and the maritime plain. The Syrians took fearful reprisals at Ascalon, Ptolemais, Tyre, Hippo, and Gadara. The madness spread even to Alexandria. The Præfect at that time was the apostate Jew, Tiberius Alexander, a nephew of Philo. The quarrel broke out when the population were assembled in the huge wooden amphitheatre. Insulted by the Greeks, the Jews hurled stones at their adversaries, and seized torches to set fire to the amphitheatre, and involve the whole population in destruction. Unable to stop them in any other way, Tiberius let loose 17,000 soldiers upon them, and 50,000 Jews were slain. Before the year was ended, there was another horrible plot of massacre at Damascus, and 10,000 Jews, unarmed and defenceless, were shamefully butchered by their fellow-citizens. Early in the next year, the streets of Antioch also were deluged with Jewish blood.

Cestius Gallus now marched southward with Agrippa, at the head of a considerable force, to quell the rebellion. Conflagration and massacre marked his path. Zabulon, Joppa, Narbatene, Mount Asamon, Lydda, were the scenes of various tragedies. In October he arrived at Gibeon. Though it was the Sabbath, the Jews, with whom intense zeal supplied the place of skill and discipline, rushed to encounter him, and killed 515 men, with the loss of only twenty-two on their own side, while the rear of the Romans was harassed by Simon Bar Giora. Of the ambassadors sent by Agrippa to appeal to the Jews, one was killed, the other wounded. All hope of peace being now at an end, on October 30, Cestius advanced to Scopus, at the north of Jerusalem, seized Bezetha, fired the timber market, and drove the rebels within the second wall. If he had shown the least courage and resolution, he might now without difficulty have taken the city by assault, and ended the war, for large numbers of the peaceful citizens were ready to open the gates to him. His irresolution and cowardice frustrated their plans. Even when he was on the verge of success, he so unaccountably sounded a retreat, that the Zealots, in a fury of reviving hope, chased him first to Scopus, thence to Gibeon, and finally inflicted upon him a desperate defeat at the famous path of Bethhoron, over which, in old days, Joshua had uplifted his spear to bid the sun "stand still upon Gibeon, and thou moon in the valley of Ajalon." Cestius left 5,300 footmen and 380 horsemen dead upon the field, lost an eagle, and, flying to Antipatris, left behind him the military engines which the Jews afterwards turned to such good account against the besiegers of Jerusalem. The sheep, as in the Book of Enoch, were now armed to do battle against the wolves. The Legate died soon after, weary of a life which had suffered so severe a shame.

The defeat of Cestius took place in November, 66. When the news of it reached Nero in Greece, even the supreme folly and disgrace of his daily proceedings did not prevent him from realising the gravity of the crisis. He saw that an able general was necessary to recover the country, which he had been taught by soothsayers to regard as his future Empire.[1] He had such a general in Vespasian, whose humble origin and plebeian surroundings secured him from jealousy. Vespasian was then in disgrace, for having gone to sleep or yawned while Nero was singing. When the messenger came to announce his elevation to the post of commander-in-chief of the Judæan legions, Vespasian thought that he was the bearer of a death-warrant from the imperial buffoon. But accepting the proffered command, he at once took vigorous measures, and was ably seconded by Titus, his son.

Meanwhile—though it was clear from the first that the revolt was foredoomed to defeat, and that the rebels would drag nation and city and Temple to destruction—even serious citizens were swept away by the tide of frenzied enthusiasm. They may have thought that the only way to control the revolt was to range themselves at the head of it. The city was placed under the younger Hanan and Joseph Ben Gorion. The country was divided into military districts. Gamala and Galilee were assigned to the protection of the historian Josephus.

It was on him, and the forces under his command, that the first shock of battle fell. Vespasian had formed the plan of conquering the country in detail, and of driving the defeated population southwards in disorderly masses towards Jerusalem, where he hoped that famine would expedite the work of war. He started from Antioch in March, A.D. 67. Then once more began the bath of blood for the hapless race. Josephus, though he displayed both genius and courage, and was the nominal general of "more than 100,000 young men," was hindered by want of cavalry, and hampered by the rashness, treachery, and opposition of followers, from whom his very life was often in danger. Gadara was the first city to fall. There, as well as in the surrounding villages, men, women, and children were indiscriminately slain. For forty-six days Josephus defended Jotapata. On the forty-seventh it was betrayed. Forty thousand Jews had fallen in the siege; 1,200 were made prisoners: the city was committed to the flames. At Ascalon 10,000 Jews were slaughtered. At Japha 27,000 were killed, and the women and children were sold into slavery. On Mount Gerizim many Samaritans perished of thirst, and 11,600 fell before the soldiers of Celearis. At Joppa, 8,400 had been slain by Cestius and the city burnt. But a number of fugitives had ensconced themselves in the ruins, and were living by piracy and brigandage. These Jews fled to their ships before the advance of the Roman soldiers. Next morning a storm burst on them, and, after a frightful scene of despair, 4,200 were drowned, and their

---

[1] Suet. (*Ner.* 40): "Spoponderant tamen quidam destituto ei ordinationem Orientis, nonnulli nominatim *regnum Hierosolymorum.*"
[2] So he says (*B. J.* ii. 20, § 6); but perhaps his numbers would bear dividing by ten at least, and his items (*id.* § 8) seem only to amount to 65,350.

corpses were washed upon the shore. Tarichææ was a strongly-fortified city on the shores of Lake Tiberias. It was taken by Titus, and 6,000 Jews dyed with their blood the waters of that crystal sea. Titus had promised safety to the inhabitants, but in spite of this 2,200 of the aged and the young were massacred in the Gymnasium; 6,000 of the strongest were sent to Nero to dig through the Isthmus of Corinth; and 30,400 citizens of this and neighbouring cities, including some whom Vespasian had given to Agrippa, were sold as slaves.

After this dreadful experience, nearly the whole district submitted to the conqueror. Gamala, however, still resisted. It was deemed impregnable by its citizens, since it was built at the top of a mountain, accessible only by one path, which was intersected by a deep ditch. Agrippa besieged it for seven months in vain. Then Vespasian invested it. Pressed by hunger, of which many died, some of the citizens climbed down the precipice, or escaped through the sewers. At last, aided by a storm, the Romans took it on October 23, A.D. 67. Once more there was a fearful slaughter. Two women alone escaped; 4,000 were slain in the defence; 5,000 flung themselves down the precipices; all the rest —even the women and children—were cut to pieces or thrown down the rocks.

Mount Tabor, which Josephus had fortified, still held out. Placidus drew away some of its defenders by a feigned flight, and the rest were driven to surrender from want of water. We are not informed of the number of the slain.

Giscala, the native city of the Zealot John, was the last to succumb. John fled from it with his adherents, and in the pursuit of them by the troops of Titus, 6,000 women and children were slain.

After this the Roman generals led their troops into winter quarters, postponing the siege of Jerusalem till the following year. But this respite brought no peace to the miserable and polluted city. John of Giscala, escaping to Jerusalem, excused his flight by saying that it was not worth while to defend other cities so long as the Jews possessed such a stronghold as Jerusalem, which the Romans, unless they made themselves wings, could never reach. By such boastings he fired the audacity of the young and the fanatical. Brigandage increased on all sides, and the Zealots were guilty of such atrocities that many preferred to throw themselves on the mercy of the Romans. By night and by day, openly and in secret, murder, pillage, and every form of crime raged in the Holy City. The rich and noble were seized in multitudes on the false charge of treachery, and were put to death, partly to get rid of their authority, partly to plunder their goods. For the purpose of humiliating the priests, it was pretended that the High Priest ought to be chosen by lot, and they thrust into the venerable office a poor peasant who was totally ignorant of the necessary duties. Hanan the Younger, a man of great courage and of high authority, because he and his family had long been the wealthiest and most eminent of the High Priests, made one more attempt to rouse the wretched citizens against this brutal tyranny, which, in the name of religion and patriotism, was guilty of the most awful crimes. To the last, and to the utmost of his power, he was true to the traditional policy of his house, which was so to act that "the Romans might not come and take away their place and nation."[1] It was for this reason only that he had so far yielded as to give an apparent sanction to the revolt. But he was as little able to stay the shocks of the subsequent earthquake as Mirabeau or Lafayette to stem the course of the French Revolution. When these tremendous outbreaks have fairly begun, their issues always belong to the most violent. The Zealots were the Montagnards of the Jewish revolt. John of Giscala, while he swore a most solemn oath that he was faithful to the party of moderation, betrayed all their plans to the Zealots. A combat ensued, in which the party of Hanan succeeded in driving the Zealots into the inner courts of the Temple. Then, at the instigation of John, the Zealots introduced 3,000 Idumeans into the city, by sawing through the bars of the city gates, on a night of such violent storm that they were not heard or suspected. The Idumeans, once admitted, began to massacre the people. When their presence was discovered, a wild wail of terror rang through the night, and many of Hanan's party flung themselves in despair from the walls and porticos of the Temple. The massacre was continued in the city. Zealots and Idumeans scourged and tortured the most eminent citizens, and murdered the wealthy Zachariah, the son of Baruch, under circumstances of peculiar brutality.[2] They not only killed Hanan the Younger, and Jesus son of Gamala, but, with unheard-of ruthlessness, stripped naked the bodies of these venerable priests, and flung them forth unburied to be devoured by dogs and jackals.

The scenes enacted at Jerusalem during this year, A.D. 68, and the year following, may perhaps be faintly paralleled by the worst orgies of the Reign of Terror, but far exceeded them in stark and irredeemable wickedness. The Idumeans, says Josephus, "fell upon the people as a flock of profane animals, and cut their throats." It was not long before they were so gorged with plunder, so sated with blood, so sick of their own brutalities, that with a qualm of self-disgust they expressed repentance, opened the prisons which they had themselves filled, and leaving the city, joined Simon, the son of Giora. But the Zealots did not pause for a moment in their work of horror. They murdered Gorion, and Niger of Perea, and every noble citizen that was left. They sold to the rich permission to fly, and murdered all who attempted to escape without bribing them. Vespasian and his soldiers were glad to look on and see

---

[1] John xi. 48—50; xviii. 14. Josephus, with his usual untrustworthiness where he had any purpose to serve, directly contradicts himself as to the character of Hanan (B. J. iv. 3, § 7; Vit. 39).

[2] In Matt. xxiii. 35, "Son of Barachias," is probably an ancient but mistaken gloss (see my Life of Christ, ii. p. 246, n.).

these infatuated wretches do the work of their Roman enemies. Mercy seemed to be dead. All the streets of the city, all the roads about the city, were heaped with unburied corpses, which putrefied in the sun. Brigands and sicarii raged uncontrolled, and the Zealots, who had seized Masada, attacked the town of Engedi, murdered more than 700 women and children, pillaged the town, and terrorised the whole coast of the Dead Sea.

Such was the state of things when the campaign reopened in the spring of 68. The first task of Vespasian was to seize Gadara. At Bethennabris there was another slaughter. Placidus pursued the fugitive Jews to Jericho. It happened that at this time the Jordan was in flood. Such multitudes were drowned that the river and the Dead Sea were filled with corpses, as the Sea of Galilee had been after the siege of Tarichea. Thirteen thousand were left dead upon the field; 2,200 were taken prisoners. Every other Perean town which offered resistance was taken. Those who took refuge in boats on the Dead Sea were chased and slain. On the eastern bank of the Jordan, Machærus alone remained in the hands of the rebels.

The reader may now understand something of the force of the expression in the Apocalypse, that when the vintage of the land was trodden, the blood without the city rolled in a torrent, bridle-deep, for a distance of 1,600 furlongs.[1] The length of the Holy Land, from Dan to Beersheba, is 139 miles; but over a still larger area, from Tyre—nay, even from Damascus—in the north, to Engedi in the south, the whole country had been scathed with fire and drowned in blood. The expression of the Seer would hardly seem an hyperbole to one who had seen the foul red stains which had polluted the silver Lake of Gennesareth; the Jordan choked with putrefying corpses; even the waves of the Dead Sea rendered loathlier than their wont with the carcases of the countless slain. No one could witness, no one could think of those unsparing massacres without having his eyes dimmed, as it were, with a mist of blood. "For seven years," says the Talmud, "did the nations of the world cultivate their vineyards with no other manure than the blood of Israel."[2]

But in truth when we read the Jewish annals of these years, we never seem to have reached the cumulus of horrors. It was in vain that—even after he seemed to have drawn round Jerusalem his "circle of extermination"—Vespasian was called away from the scene. He arrived at Jericho on June 3, A.D. 68, but his attention was at once diverted into an entirely different direction. Vindex revolted from Nero on March 15; Galba on April 3; the Prætorians revolted on June 8; on June 9 Nero committed suicide. Vespasian had been flattered by dreams and prognostications of future Empire, to which his ears were always open. Up to this time, however, he had not com-

[1] Rev. xiv. 19, 20.   [2] Gittin, f. 57 a.

mitted himself, and he now sent Titus with Agrippa to salute Galba as his legitimate Emperor. Before they arrived, the news came that on January 2, A.D. 69, Vitellius had been proclaimed Emperor by the legions of Germany, and that on January 15 Galba had been murdered, and Otho proclaimed by the Prætorians. Vespasian was not prepared to acknowledge either Otho or Vitellius. He paused in his warlike operations to watch the course of events. But the doomed and miserable land, and the yet more doomed and miserable city, were far from profiting by this respite. It seemed as if the Zealots were now drunken with blood and fury. Simon, son of Giora, had got together an army of slaves and cut-throats, and was spreading terror far and wide. He conquered the Idumeans, and desolated their country with fire and sword. He repelled an attack of the Zealots, and drove them back into Jerusalem. When, by a stratagem, they had captured his wife, he seized all who came out of the city, cut off their hands, sent them back, and threatened to treat every one of the citizens in the same way, if his wife were not restored to him. Power was given to the mystic rider of the Red Horse, says St. John, "to take peace from the earth, and that men should slay one another."[1] Civil war raged within and without the city with such fury, that the Romans almost appeared in the guise of friends. All who attempted to fly from Simon were murdered by John; all the fugitives of John were murdered by Simon. At last, in despair at the tyranny of John, the people admitted Simon within the walls. The only difference was that they had now two tyrants instead of one. John and his Zealots were confined to the Temple, and were the fewer in number; but from its height and impregnable position they were enabled to make sallies, and to hurl down upon their enemies, from the captured engines of the Romans, a perfect hail of missiles. In the incessant collision between the hostile factions, all the houses in the neighbourhood of the Temple were burnt down. It was surrounded by a chaos of blackened ruins, in which unburied corpses bred pestilence in the summer noon. Not only the streets, but even the courts and altar of the Temple constantly swam in blood. Priest and pilgrim mingled their blood with their sacrifices, smitten down by balistæ or catapults as they stood beside the altar. Their feet were soiled, so that they polluted every corner of the holy precincts with steps encrimsoned by the uncleansed pools of gore, which told the tale of daily slaughter. Every semblance of performing the rites of religion was reduced to the most monstrous mockery. It was impossible that men could breathe this reeking atmosphere of blood and crime, in which every brain seemed to reel with the hideous intoxication, without a total collapse of the moral sense. At the very time that the Zealots were representing themselves as the God-protected champions of a cause the most sacred in the

[1] Rev. vi. 4.

world, they had become so dead to every precept of religion, that, putting on the robes and ornaments of women, decking their hair, painting underneath their eyes, but carrying swords under their gay female apparel, they plunged headlong into such nameless obscenities, that it seemed as if the city had become not only a slaughter-house, and a robbers' cave, but a very cage of unclean beasts, fit only to be taken and destroyed. "How is the faithful city become an harlot! It was full of justice! Righteousness lodged in her, but now murderers."[1] Very early, amid these scenes of horror, it must have been evident to the little Christian community that "the abominable wing that maketh desolate"[2] was standing in the Holy Place, which was now more shamelessly defiled than any shrine of Moloch or Baal Peor. Well might they recognise that the city which was known as "the Holy, the Noble," was "spiritually called Sodom and Egypt, where also their Lord was crucified."[3]

Thus horrible was the aspect of the world—politically, morally, socially, even physically—during the months in which the Apocalypse was written. *Physically* men seemed to be tormented and terrified with catastrophes and portents. "Besides the manifold changes and chances of human affairs," says Tacitus, "there were prodigies in heaven and on earth, the warnings of lightnings, and the presages of the future, now joyous, now gloomy, now obscure, now unmistakable. For never was it rendered certain by clearer indications, or by more deadly massacres of the Roman people, that the gods care nothing for our happiness, but do care for our retribution."[4] In Rome a pestilence had carried off tens of thousands of the citizens. A disastrous inundation of the Tiber had impeded the march of Otho's troops, and encumbered the roads with ruins.[5] In Lydia an encroachment of the sea had wrought fearful havoc. In Asia city after city had been shattered to the dust by earthquakes.[6] "The world itself is being shaken to pieces," says Seneca, "and there is universal consternation."[7] Comets, eclipses, meteors, parhelions, terrified the ignorant, and were themselves the pretexts for imperial cruelties.[8] Auroras tinged the sky with blood. Volcanos seemed, like Vesuvius, to be waking to new fury.[9] *Morally*, the state of the Pagan world was such as we have seen. It was sunk so low that, in the opinion of the Pagan moralists of the Empire, posterity could but imitate and could not surpass such a virulence of degradation. The state of the

---

[1] Isa. i. 21. [2] Dan. ix. 27; xi. 31; xii. 11; Matt. xxiv. 15; Mark xiii. 14.
[3] Rev. xi. 8. [4] Tac. *H.* i. 3. [5] Tac. *H.* i. 86.
[6] Eusebius (*Chron.* A.D. 17) mentions Ephesus, Magnesia, Sardis, Ægae, Philadelphia, Tmolus, Apollonia, Dia, &c. In the third book of the *Sibyllines* (iii. 337—366) many others are mentioned.
[7] Sen. *Nat. Qu.* vi. 1. [8] Suet. *Ner.* 36. [9] Tac. *Ann.* xv. 22.

Jewish world is revealed alike in the Gospels, in the Talmud, and in the writings of Josephus. It may suffice to quote the opinion of the latter that his own generation in Judæa was the wickedest that the world had seen, and that if the avenging sword of the Romans had not smitten Jerusalem with God's vengeance, the very earth must have opened to swallow up her iniquities. *Socially*, we see how desperate was the condition alike of Jews and Pagans, in St. Paul, St. James, and Josephus on the one hand, and in Tacitus, Suetonius, and the Satirists on the other. *Politically*, the whole Empire was in a state of agitation. That the sacred sun of the Julii should set in a sea of blood seemed an event frightfully ominous, while, owing to the obscurity which hung about the death of Nero, and the very small number of those who had seen his corpse, and the prophecies which had always been current about his complete restoration, not only was there a universal belief that he would return, but as early as the end of A.D. 68 a false Nero gained many adherents, and caused wide-spread alarm.[1] The election of Galba by the legions of Spain seemed to divulge a secret full of disaster—the fact that an Emperor could be created elsewhere than at Rome. Emperor after emperor died by suicide or by the hands of assassins.

> "In outlines dim and vast
> Their fearful shadows cast
> The giant forms of Empires on their way
> To ruin;—one by one
> They tower, and they are gone—"

The Romish world and the Jewish world were alike rent by civil war. There were banquets in the reign of Nero at which seven emperors and the father of an eighth—for the most part entirely unrelated to one another—might have met under the same roof, namely, Nero, Galba, Otho, Vitellius, Vespasian, Titus, Domitian, Nerva, and the elder Trajan;[2] and five of these, if not six, died violent deaths. Every general of the smallest eminence became ambitious to raise himself to "the dread summits of Cæsarian power."[3] Vindex, Nymphidius, Galba, Vitellius, Vespasian, Claudius Macer in Africa, Fonteius Capito in Germany, Betuus Chilo in Gaul, Obultronius and Cornelius Sabinus in Spain, were all seized with the vertigo of this ambition; while the generals who helped their various attempts—such as Cæcina, Valens, Mucianus, Antonius Primus—became themselves the objects of jealousy and suspicion. More than once the soldiers had serious thoughts of murdering all the senators, in order to keep the whole government of the world in their own hands.[4] Almost alone among the crowd of military chieftains, Virginius stood superior to these dreams of usurpation, and when he died peacefully, full of years and honours,

---

[1] Suet. *Ner.* 40, 57.
[2] Renan, *L'Antéchrist*, p. 481.
[3] See Merivale, *Hist.* vi. 374.
[4] Tac. *H.* i. 80; Dion Cass. lxiv. 9.

he deserved the proud epitaph which he engraved upon his tomb, that he, when Vindex was defeated,[1] "claimed the Empire not for himself but for his country."[1] The fatal results of consular ambition might be seen on the field of Bedriacum. There the very roads were obstructed with the mounds of the dead, and the massacre was all the more deadly because Romans could not be sold as slaves, so that no one on either side was tempted to pause from slaughter in the hope of booty. After a desperate hand-to-hand conflict between Romans and Romans, which heaped the field with an almost incredible number of the slain,[3] "the soldiers fell sobbing into one another's arms, and all denounced in common the wickedness of civil war." Amid portents so threatening and scenes so terrible, it is not strange that the hearts of men should have been failing them for fear. There had been for many years an all but universal impression that the days of Rome were numbered. It had probably originated from the expectations of Jews and Christians, and is found again and again in the Sibylline books.[4] In Dion. Cassius we read that a proverb was prevalent that when thrice three hundred years had passed, or in the beginning of the tenth century since Rome was founded, she should perish.[5] It was even sung as a song in the streets, that after thrice three hundred years internal sedition should destroy the Romans; and at a later period, the line "Last of the descendants of Æneas, a matricide shall reign," was on everybody's lips. "Rome shall be ruins," says one of the Sibyllists, writing long before the Apocalypse. The calculations of that Jewish form of Kabbalism which was known as *Gematria*—or the substitution of numerical values for words—led the writers of the Sibyllines to notice that the numerical value of the letters of Rome was 948, and they therefore prophesied that in that year Rome should be destroyed.[6] They thought that Nero would awake from the dead to accomplish this vengeance, and that "dark blood should mark the track of the Beast."[7] The Sibyls, says Lactantius, "say openly that Rome shall perish, and that by the judgment of God."[8] The topic of them all is, in prophetic language, "The burden of Rome."

And amid all these evils—these multiplied signs of the approaching end—the "woes of the Messiah" afflicted the Church also. Two of the greatest cities of the world—Rome, the spiritual Babylon; Jerusalem, the spiritual Sodom—had drunk deep of the blood of the prophets and saints of Christ. Nor had the guilt of such murders been confined

---

[1] "Hic situs est Rufus, pulso qui Vindice quondam,
Imperium asseruit non sibi sed patriæ."—(Plin. *Ep.* vi. 10.)
[2] Tac. *H.* ii. 44.
[3] Dion Cassius (lxiv. 10) mentions the fearful but most improbable total of 400,000 (τέσσαρες μυριάδες). Tacitus (*H.* ii. 44) calls it a *strages*.
[4] *Orac. Sibyll.* ii. 15, 19; iii. 46—59; vii. 111—112, etc.
[5] Dion Cass. lvii. 18; lxii. 18.
[6] 'Ρώμη =100+800+40+8=948. (*Orac. Sib.* viii. 147.)
[7] *Id.* 157. [8] Lactant. *Div. Inst.* vii. 15.

to them. "Through all the provinces" it seemed as if Satan had come down having great wrath, as knowing that his time was short. Many a nameless martyr in the various cities of the Empire had been added to that "vast multitude" who, in the Neronian persecution, had suffered their baptism of blood. Yet even persecution from without had not secured the Church from the growth of deadly heresies within. Every one of the Apostles had been driven to utter words of sternest warning against teachers who, while they called themselves Christians, were guilty of worse than heathen wickedness—who turned the grace of God into lasciviousness, and made their liberty a cloak for evil lives. Thus alike the Jewish and the heathen world, each at the nadir of their degradation and impiety, were bent upon the destruction of Christ's little flock; and even into that little flock had intruded many who came in sheep's clothing, though inwardly they were ravening wolves.

Such were "the signs of the times" during the course of these awful years in which St. John found himself on the rocky isle "that is called Patmos,"[1] and uttered his prophecies respecting the past, the present, and the immediate future. In those prophecies we see the aspect of the age as it presented itself to the inspired mind of a Christian and an Apostle; and we can compare and contrast it with the aspects which it presented to heathens like Tacitus and Suetonius, or to Jews like Josephus and the authors or interpolators of the Books of Enoch and Esdras. It is true that our want of familiarity with Apocalyptic symbols which were familiar to the Jewish Christians of that epoch, seems at first to give to many of the Apostle's thoughts an unwonted obscurity. But, on the one hand, the obscurity does not affect those elements of the book which we at once feel to be of the most eternal import; and on the other, we are only left in the dark about minor details which have found no distinct record in history. Let any student compare the symbols of the Apocalypse with those of Joel, Isaiah, Ezekiel, Zechariah, and Daniel; let him then see how those symbols are applied by the almost contemporary writers of such Jewish Apocalypses as the Book of Enoch, the Fourth Book of Esdras, and the Vision of Baruch; let him meditate on the conditions of the age in the particulars which we have just been passing in review; lastly, let him bear in mind the luminous principle that the Apocalypse is a stormy comment upon the great discourse of our Lord on Olivet, as it was being interpreted by the signs of the times, and he will read the Vision of the Apostle with a freshness of interest and a clearness of apprehension such as he may never previously have enjoyed. He will then see in it, from first to last, the words "Maran atha! the Lord cometh."

---

[1] The expression militates against the notion of Renan, that Patmos was at this time populous and well known.

He will recognise that the contemplated Coming was first fulfilled in the catastrophe which closed the Jewish dispensation, and the inauguration of the last age of the world. He will find that the Apocalypse is what it professes to be—an inspired outline of contemporary history, and of the events to which the sixth decade of the first century gave immediate rise. He will read in it the tremendous counter-manifesto of a Christian Seer against the bloodstained triumph of imperial heathendom; a pæan and a prophecy over the ashes of the martyrs; "the thundering reverberation of a mighty spirit," struck by the fierce plectrum of the Neronian persecution, and answering in impassioned music which, like many of David's Psalms, dies away into the language of rapturous hope.

And thus we shall strive to overcome that spirit of dislike to the Revelation of St. John which has existed in so many ages. We have already seen that this dislike existed among the Alogi,[1] and that it finds expression in the remains of the Presbyter Gaius, Dionysius of Alexandria, and Eusebius of Cæsarea. In later ages the disinclination to accept its authenticity found more or less open expression in the writings of Erasmus, Calvin, Zwingli, Luther, Œcolampadius, Bucer, Carlstadt, as well as in those of Scaliger, Lowth, Schleiermacher, Goethe, and many others. This alienation from the book arose in the ancient Church from the abuse of it by the fanaticism and narrowness of the Chiliasts; in the modern Church from the Hellenic taste which took offence at its Judaic imagery, and from the discredit which it has suffered at the hands of rash, uncharitable, and half-educated interpreters. Even the most reverent inquirers have pronounced it to be unintelligible.[2] Such views of it can only be removed by a reasonable, a charitable, and—at least within broad limits—a certain exegesis.

---

[1] The Alogi were those who rejected the doctrine of the Logos, and therefore the writings of St. John. The name of this obscure sect, which had its headquarters at Thyatira, seems to have been invented by Epiphanius:—ἐπεὶ οὖν τὸν Λόγον οὐ δέχονται . . . ἄλογοι κληθήσονται (*Haer.* li. 3). They attributed the Apocalypse to Cerinthus, declaring that a book about seals, trumpets, etc., was unworthy of an Apostle, and saying that he addressed a Church in Thyatira, when there was no Church in Thyatira.

[2] Dionysius of Alexandria says that the Alogi spoke with positive scorn (χλευάζοντες) of the Apocalypse, and that some, before his day, not only rejected it, but criticised it chapter by chapter to demonstrate its illogical character, and denied that it could be a Revelation, seeing that it had been covered with so dense a veil of non-intelligibility. They, like Gaius, attributed it to Cerinthus. Junilius tells us that the Eastern Church had great doubts about it. "*Fateor multa me in ejus dictis saepissime legendo scrutatum esse nec intellexisse,*" says Primasius, even in the sixth century. St. Gregory of Nyssa (*Opp.* ii. 44. ed. Paris) quotes from the Apocalypse as a writing of St. John, ἐν ἀποκρύφοις . . . δι' αἰνίγματος λέγοντος, but this expression does *not* necessarily mean that he regarded it as deutero-canonical. Jerome, in the fourth century, said that the book had as many mysteries as words (Ep. liii. *ad Paulinum*), and Augustine admitted that it was full of obscurities, due in part to its repetition of the same events with different symbols, and in part to the absence of definitive clues. "*Et in hoc quidem libro obscure multa dicuntur . . . et pauca in eo sunt ex quorum manifestatione indagentur caetera cum labore, maxime quia sic eadem multis modis repetit*" (Aug. *De Civ. Dei,* xx. 17). Nicolaus Collado (*Methodus,* 1584) dwells on the same peculiarity (see Düsterdieck, p. 17). "*Apocalypsim fateor me nescire exponere juxta sensum literalem; expunat cui Deus concessit,*" wrote

For if indeed the Apocalypse were the kind of treatise which it has become in the hands of controversialists from the Abbot Joachim downwards—if it were a synopsis of anticipated Church history, ringing with the most vehement anathemas of sectarian hatred, and yet shrouded in such ambiguity that every successive interpreter has a new scheme for its elucidation—if it were a book in which only Protestants could take delight because it is supposed to express the intensest spirit of denunciation against the errors of a Church which, whatever may be its errors, is still a sister Church—then it might be excusable if the spirits of those who seek peace and ensue it, and who look on brotherly love between Christians as the crown of virtue and the test of true religion, should turn away from the book with a sense of perplexity and weariness. They could never gain much comfort and edification from any pulpit in which

> "A loud-tongued pulpiteer,
> Not preaching simple Christ to simple men,
> Announced the coming doom, and fulminated
> Against the scarlet woman and her creed.
> For sidewise up he flung his arms, and shrieked
> 'Thus, thus with violence,' as though he held
> The Apocalyptic millstone, and himself
> Were that great Angel—'thus with violence
> Shall Babylon be thrown into the sea.
> Then comes the end.'"[1]

There are few of us who would find much music in such "loud-tongued anti-Babylonianisms" as these. The blind fumes of party hatred can only distract and lead astray. The spirit of the Inquisition, even when it is found in Protestants, is essentially anti-Christian. It is a scorpion-locust out of the abyss. But when we put ourselves in the position of the Seer, and grasp the clues to his meaning which he has himself furnished—when we accept his own assurance that he is mainly dealing with events which were on the immediate horizon—when, lastly, we discount the Oriental hyperboles which, in fact, cease to be hyperbolical if they be understood in their normal usage, then for the first time we begin to understand

---

Cardinal Cajetan (*Opp.* v. 401). Zwingli said he took no account of it: "*Dann es ist ein biblish Buch ist*" (*Werke*, ii. 169). Tyndale wrote no preface to the Apocalypse. Luther calls it "a dumb prophecy." He says, "*Mein Geist kann sich, in das Buch nicht stricken, und ist mir Ursach genug dass ich sein nicht hoch achte dass Christus darinnen weder gelehrt nach erkannt wird.*" Gravina says, "*Mihi tota Apocalypsis valde obscura videtur, et talis cujus explicatio citra periculum vix queat tentari.*" Quite recent commentators have held similar language. "*Ein Buch von dem man ganze Capitel nach Ausdrückung von einigen Tropfen saft als leere Schalen beiseite-legen muss*" (De Wette). "No book of the New Testament has so defied all attempts to settle its interpretation" (Bloomfield). "I cannot pretend to explain the book; I do not understand it" (Adam Clarke). "No solution has ever been given of this part of the prophecy" (Alford). "*Deutero-kanonische Dignität kommt ihr zu, aber nicht weniger*" (Düsterdieck).

[1] Tennyson (*Sea Dreams*). "*Totum hunc librum . . . spectare praecipue ad describendam tyrannidem spiritualem Romani papatus et totius cleri ejus*" (Nic. Collavio, ap. Düsterdieck, p. 48).

the Apocalypse in all its passion and grandeur, as it was understood by those for whom it was written. We no longer expect to find in it the Saracen conquests, or the Waldenses, or the French Revolution, or "the rise of Tractarianism." We are soothed by its heavenly consolations and inspired by its inextinguishable hopes. When read in the light of events then contemporary, it rolls with all its thunder and burns with all its fires. Over the guilt of Jerusalem, over the guilt of Rome, it hurls the prophecy of inevitable doom. Around the diadem of Nero and the hydra-heads of Paganism in its hour of tyranny and triumph it flashes the sure wrath of heaven.[1] But, like all prophecy, it has "springing and germinal developments." It is the defiance uttered by true Christianity for all time against the tortures, the legions, the amphitheatres, the fagots, the prisons, the thumbscrews, the falsehoods, the inquisitions of that demoniac spirit of persecuting intolerance, which, whether it uses the asp-poison of slander or the sword of murder, is never so irreligious as when it vaunts its zeal for God. Though he wrote in the hour of seeming ruin, such is the passionate intensity with which the Seer pours forth the language of victory, that it seems as though the hand which he has dipped in the blood of the martyrs flames like a torch as he uplifts it in appeal to the avenging heavens. And since the truths which he utters become needful at the recurrence of every similar crisis—and most of all when the execrable weapons of tyranny are grasped by the reckless hands of sectarian bitterness—the Apocalypse has ever been dearest to God's true saints at the hour of their deepest trials. It ceases then to be a great silent sphinx, reading its eternal riddle at the gate of Scripture, and devouring those who fail to answer it; it becomes a series of glorious pictures, wherein "are set forth the rise, the visible existence, and the general future of Christ's kingdom, in figures and similitudes of His First Coming, to terrify and to console."[2]

There have been three great schools of Apocalyptic interpretation:—
1. The Præterists, who regard the book as having been mainly fulfilled.
2. The Futurists, who refer it to events which are still wholly future.
3. The Continuous-Historical Interpreters, who see in it an outline of Christian history from the days of St. John down to the End of all things. The second of these schools—the Futurists—has always

---

[1] The use of the word "diadem" of the Roman Emperor in this book is made much of by the commentators, who try to overthrow the sure results of recent exegesis. They urge that Caligula alone of the Cæsars ever attempted to wear a diadem, as distinguished from a crown or wreath; that Julius Cæsar refused a diadem; that Sulpicius Severus is mistaken when he describes Vespasian as wearing one; and that the first Emperor who boldly assumed this badge of Oriental autocracy—a purple silken fillet, embroidered with pearls—was Diocletian. Meanwhile this imposing array of arguments crumbles at a touch. When Antony offered the diadem to Julius, he betrayed the secret as to the real character of Imperial power. Orientals in the provinces both thought and spoke of the Emperors as "Kings," though such a name would have horrified the Romans; but Oriental kings wore diadems, and therefore the Oriental symbol of the Roman Emperor was the diadem. [2] Herder

been numerically small, and at present may be said to be non-existent. The school of Historical Interpreters was founded by the Abbot Joachim early in the 13th century, and was specially flourishing in the first fifty years of the present century.[1] The views of the Præterists have been adopted, with various shades of modification, by Grotius, Hammond, Le Clerc, Bossuet, Eichhorn, Hug, Wetstein, Ewald, Herder, Zullig, Bleek, De Wette, Lücke, Moses Stuart, Davidson, Volkmar, Krenkel, Düsterdieck, Renan, and almost the whole school of modern German critics and interpreters. It has been usual to say that the Spanish Jesuit Alcasar, in his *Vestigatio arcani sensus in Apocalypsi* (1614), was the founder of the Præterist School, and it certainly seems as if to him must be assigned the credit of having first clearly enunciated the natural view that the Apocalypse, like all other Apocalypses of the time, describes events nearly contemporaneous, and is meant to shadow forth the triumph of the Church in the struggle first with Judaism and then with Heathendom. But to me it seems that the founder of the Præterist School is none other than St. John himself. For he records the Christ as saying to him when he was in the Spirit, "Write the things which thou sawest, and THE THINGS WHICH ARE, and the things which are about to happen (ἃ μέλλει γίνεσθαι) after these things." No language surely could more clearly define the bearing of the Apocalypse. It is meant to describe the contemporary state of things in the Church and the world, and the events which were to follow in immediate sequence. If the Historical School can strain the latter words into an indication that we are (contrary to all analogy) to have a symbolic and unintelligible sketch of many centuries, the Præterist School may at any rate apply these words, ἃ εἰσίν, "THE THINGS WHICH ARE," to vindicate the application of a large part of the Apocalypse to events nearly contemporary, while they also give the natural meaning to the subsequent clause by understanding it of events which were then on the horizon. The Seer emphatically says that the future events which he has to foreshadow will occur *speedily* (ἐν τάχει,)[2] and the recurrent burden of his whole book is the nearness of the Advent (ὁ καιρὸς ἐγγύς). Language is simply meaningless if it is to be so manipulated by every successive commentator as to make the words "speedily" and "near"

---

[1] There are two schools of the interpreters who make the Apocalypse a prophecy of all Christian history. The school of Bengel, Vitringa, Elliott, etc., make it mainly a history of *the Church*. Another school regards it more generally, and less specifically, as an outline of Epochs of the History of *the world* and the great forces which shape it into a Kingdom of God. To this latter school belong Hengstenberg, Ebrard, Auberlen, etc.

[2] Comp. ταχύ (Rev. ii. 5, 16; iii. 11; xi. 14; xxii. 20). It is curious to see with what extraordinary ease commentators explain the perfectly simple and unambiguous expression "speedily" (ἐν τάχει), to mean any length of time which they may choose to demand. The word "*immediately*," in Matt. xxiv. 29, has been subject to similar handling, in which indeed all Scripture exegesis abounds. The failure to see that the Fall of Jerusalem and the end of the Mosaic Dispensation was a "Second Advent"—and *the Second* Advent contemplated in many of the New Testament prophecies—has led to a multitude of errors.

imply any number of centuries of delay. The Præterist method of interpretation does not, however, interfere with that view of prophecy which was so well defined by Dr. Arnold. This is the view of those who have been called the "spiritual" interpreters. It admits of the *analogical* application of prophecy to conditions which, in the cycles of history, bear a close resemblance to each other. It applies to all times the principles originally laid down with reference to events which were being then enacted, and starts with the axiom of Bacon, that divine prophecies have steps and grades of fulfilment through divers ages.[1] All that is really valuable in the works of the Historical Interpreters may thus be retained. No importance can be attached to their limitation of particular symbols, but the better part of their labours may be accepted as an illustration of the manner in which the Apocalyptic symbols convey moral lessons which are applicable to the conditions of later times.

But, apart from St. John's own words, it cannot be conceded that the central conception of the Præterist exegesis is a mere novelty of the 17th century. On the contrary, we can trace from very early days the application of various visions to the early Emperors of Pagan Rome. Thus Justin Martyr believed that the Antichrist would be a person who was close at hand, and who would reign three and a half years.[2] Irenæus also thought that Antichrist, as foreshadowed by the Wild Beast, would be a man; and that "the number of the Beast" represented *Lateinos*, "a Latin."[3] Hippolytus compares the action of the False Prophet giving life to the Beast's image, to Augustus inspiring fresh force into the Roman Empire.[4] Later on, I shall furnish abundant evidence that a tradition of the ancient Church identified Nero with the Antichrist, and expected his literal return, just as the Jews expected the literal return of the Prophet Elijah. St. Victorinus (about A.D. 303) counts the five dead Emperors from Galba, and supposes that, after Nerva, the Beast (whom he identifies with Nero) will be recalled to life.[5] St. Augustine mentions a similar opinion.[6] The Pseudo-Prochorus, writing on Rev. xvii. 10, says that the "one head which *is*" is meant for Domitian. Bishop Andreas, in the fifth century, applies Rev. vi. 12 to the siege of Jerusalem, and considers that Antichrist will be "as a king of the Romans." Bishop Arethas, on Rev. vii., implies that the Apocalypse was written before the Jewish War. The fragments of ancient comment which we possess cannot be said to have much intrinsic value; but, such as they are, they suffice to prove that the tendency of modern exegesis approaches quite as nearly to the earliest traditions as that of the Historic School. It is a specially important fact that St. Augustine, as well as many others, recognised the partially *retrogres-*

---

[1] *De Augment. Scient.* ii. 11.
[2] *Dial. c. Tryph.* p. 250.
[3] Iren. *Haer.* v. 25.
[4] *De Antichristo*, p. 6.
[5] "Bestia de septem est quoniam ante ipsos reges Nero regnavit."
[6] *De Civ. Dei*, xx. 19.

sive and iterative character of the later visions, and thereby sanctioned one of the most important principles of modern interpretation.[1] The internal evidence that the book was written before the fall of Jerusalem has satisfied not only many Christian commentators, who are invidiously stigmatised as "rationalistic," but even such writers as Wetstein, Lücke, Neander, Stier, Auberlen, Ewald, Bleek, Gebhardt, Immer, Davidson, Düsterdieck, Moses Stuart, F. D. Maurice, the author of "The Parousia," Dean Plumptre, the authors of the *Protestanten-Bibel*, and multitudes of others no less entitled to the respect of all Christians.

If, however, the reader still looks with prejudice and suspicion on the *only* school of Apocalyptic exegesis which unites the suffrages of the most learned recent commentators in Germany, France, and England, I hardly know where he is to turn. The reason why the early date and mainly contemporary explanation of the book is daily winning fresh adherents among unbiassed thinkers of every Church and school, is partly because it rests on so simple and secure a basis, and partly because no other can compete with it. It is indeed the only system which is built on the plain and repeated statements and indications of the Seer himself, and the corresponding events are so closely accordant with the symbols as to make it certain that this scheme of interpretation is the only one that can survive. A few specimens may suffice to show how completely other systems float in the air.

Let us suppose that the student has found out that in viii. 13 the true reading is "a single eagle," not an angel; but, whether eagle or angel, he wants to know what the symbol means. He turns to the commentators, and finds that it is explained to be the Holy Spirit (Victorinus); or Pope Gregory the Great (Elliott); or St. John himself (De Lyra); or St. Paul (Zeger); or Christ Himself (Wordsworth). The Præterists mostly take it to be simply an eagle, as the Scriptural type of carnage—the figure being suggested not by the resemblance of the word "woe!" ("*ouai*") to the eagle's screams, but by the use of the same symbol for the same purpose by our Lord in His discourse about the things to come.[2]

But this is nothing! The student wishes to learn what is meant by the star fallen from heaven, in ix. 1. The Historical School will leave him to choose between an evil spirit (Alford); a Christian heretic (Wordsworth); the Emperor Valens (De Lyra); Mohammed (Elliott); and, among others, Napoleon (Hengstenberg)!

The confusion deepens as we advance. The locusts are "heretics" (Bede); or Goths (Vitringa); or Vandals (Aureolus); or Saracens (Mede); or the mendicant orders (Brightman); or the Jesuits (Scherzer); or Protestants (Bellarmine).

The same endless and aimless diversity reigns throughout the entire works of the Historical interpreters; none of them seems to satisfy any

---

[1] *De Civ. Dei*, xx. 17.   [2] Matt. xxiv. 28.

one but himself. The elaborate anti-papal interpretation of Elliott—of which (to show that I am far from prejudiced) I may mention, in passing, that I made a careful study and a full abstract when I was seventeen years old—is all but forgotten. Mr. Faber admits that there is not the least agreement as to the first four trumpets among writers of his school, and he rightly says that "so curious a circumstance may well be deemed the opprobrium of Apocalyptic interpretation, and may naturally lead us to suspect that the true key to the distinct application of the first four trumpets has never yet been found."

Not that this school leaves us any better off when we come to the seven thunders. They are seven unknown oracles (Mede); or events (Ebrard); or the seven crusades (Vitringa); or the seven Protestant kingdoms (Dunbar); or the Papal Bull against Luther (Elliott).

The two wings of the great eagle in xii. 14 are the two Testaments (Wordsworth); or the eastern and western divisions of the Empire (Mede, Auberlen); or the Emperor Theodosius (Elliott).

The number of the Beast—which may be now regarded as *certainly* intended to stand for Nero—has been made to serve for Genseric, Benedict, Trajan, Paul V., Calvin, Luther, Mohammed, Napoleon—not to mention a host of other interpretations which no one has ever accepted except their authors.[1]

It is needless to multiply further instances. They might be multiplied almost indefinitely, but their *multiplicity* is not so decisive of the futility of the principles on which they are selected, as is the *diversity of results* which are wider than the poles asunder. What are we to say of methods which leave us to choose between the applicability of a symbol to the Holy Spirit or to Pope Gregory, to the Two Testaments or to the Emperor Theodosius? Any one, on the other hand, who accepts the Præterist system finds a wide and increasing consensus among competent inquirers of all nations, and can see an explanation of the book which is simple, natural, and noble—one which closely follows its own indications, and accords with those to be found throughout the New Testament. He sees that events, mainly contemporary, provide an interpretation clear in its outlines, though necessarily uncertain in minor details. If he takes the view of the Spiritualists, he may at his pleasure make the symbols mean anything in general and nothing in particular. If he is of the Historical School he must let the currents of Gieseler or Gibbon sweep him hither and thither at the will of the particular commentator in whom he for the time may chance to confide. But if he follows the guidance of a more reasonable exegesis, he may advance with a sure step along a path which becomes clearer with every fresh discovery.

But I cannot leave this subject of Apocalyptic interpretation

---

[1] The majority of guesses which have the least seriousness in them point to Rome, the Roman Empire, or the Roman Emperor.

without repeating my conviction, that the *essential* sacredness and preciousness of the book lies deeper than the primary or secondary interpretations of its separate visions. Whatever system of exegesis we adopt—whether we suppose that St. John was indicating to the Churches of Asia the influence of Mohammed, Hildebrand, and Luther centuries later—whether he was foreshadowing events of which they could not have the remotest comprehension, or events with which they were immediately and terribly concerned—he is, at any rate, dealing on the one hand with awful warnings, and on the other with exceeding great and precious promises. His teaching is needful for our education in the ways of God. It will be well for every Christian to take it deeply to heart. Amid endless diversities, here at any rate is a point respecting which all true Christians may be cordially agreed.

It is admitted by every unbiassed critic that Apocalyptic literature is inferior in form to the Prophetic. The Jews themselves have marked their sense of this by excluding the Book of Daniel from the prophetic canons, and placing it among the Hagiographa. Apocalypses belong, as a rule, to later ages and less vivid inspiration. Why then, it may be asked, did St. John choose this form of utterance? The answer is simple. It was, first, because it was in this form that his inspiration came to him; it was in this form that his thoughts naturally clothed themselves. It was, next, because the Apocalypse was the favourite form of the prophetico-poetic literature of this epoch, with which many instances had made his readers familiar. But lastly, and perhaps chiefly, it was from the dangers of the time. An Apocalypse, by the very meaning of the term, implies a book which is more or less cryptographic in its contents. Hence in every Apocalypse—in the Books of Esdras, Enoch, and Baruch, no less than in St. John—there are for us some necessary difficulties in the details of interpretation which perhaps did not exist for contemporary readers. But if anything were obscure to them, this was more than compensated by the resultant safety. No danger incurred by the early Christians was greater than that caused by the universal prevalence of political spies. If one of these wretches got possession of any Christian writing which could be construed into an attack or a reflexion upon their terrible persecutors, hundreds might be involved in indiscriminate punishment on a charge of high treason (*laesa majestas*), which was then the most formidable engine of despotic power. St. Paul, writing to the Thessalonians even so early as A.D. 52, had found it necessary to speak of the Roman Empire and of the Emperors Claudius or Nero in terms of studied enigma.[1] St. Peter, making a casual allusion to Rome, had been obliged to veil it under the mystic name of Babylon.[2] Even Josephus has to break off his explanation of the Book of Daniel with mysterious suddenness rather than indicate that the fate of the Roman

---

[1] 2 Thess. ii. 3—12.   [2] 1 Pet. v. 13.

Empire was there foreshadowed. Concealed methods of allusion are, for similar reasons, again and again adopted in the Talmud. St. John saw in Nero a realisation of Antichrist; but it would have been fatal to whole communities, perhaps to the entire Church, if he had openly committed to writing either the indication of Nero's character or the prophecy of his doom. He could only do this in the guise of Scriptural and prophetic symbols, which would look like meaningless rhapsodies to any Gentile reader, but of which, as he was well aware, the secret significance was in the hands of those for whom alone his revelation was intended. It may be laid down as a rule, to which there is no exception, that the commentator who approaches the Apocalypse without the fullest recognition of the fact that in its tone and in its symbols it bears a very close analogy to a multitude of other Apocalyptic books, both Jewish and Christian, is sure to go utterly astray. But if he knows the symbols and their significance, not only from the Old Testament but also from seeing how the imagery of the Old Testament was applied in the first century to contemporary events, he will be prepared to see that to the original readers of the Apocalypse, at any rate, the book had and could have but one meaning, and that the intended meaning is still partially discoverable by those who do not read its visions through the ecclesiastical veil of unnatural and fantastic hypotheses.

CHAPTER XXVIII.

THE APOCALYPSE.

"Apocalypsis Johannis tot habet sacramenta quot verba. Parum dixi pro merito voluminis. Laus omnis inferior est."—JER. *ad Paulin.*

IN the superscription of the Apocalypse found in some of the cursive manuscripts, St. John is called by the title of "the Theologian," or, as it is rendered in our version, "the Divine." It was a title borne by the highest order of priests in the Temple of the Ephesian Artemis, as appears from inscriptions discovered by Mr. Wood at Ephesus. It is, however, unlikely that St. John bore the title in his own day, or that it was intended to contrast him with the local and pagan hierarchy. It was more probably due to the grandeur of his witness to Christ as the Divine Logos. It is remarkable that only one great Christian writer has shared it with him—the large-hearted St. Gregory of Nazianzus. The true Theology is the glorious mother of all the sciences, and differs infinitely from the narrow and technical pedantry which has in modern times too often usurped the exclusive name. It would have been well for the world if it could have rescued the term from the degradation to which it has been subjected by Pharisaism and self-assertion. Theology would have received the honour of all mankind if it had not so often mistaken verbal minutiæ for divine essentials, if its self-styled votaries had caught something of the love and something of the loftiness of the Beloved Disciple of Galilee and the eloquent Patriarch of Constantinople.

SECTION I.

THE LETTERS TO THE SEVEN CHURCHES.

To write a full commentary upon the Apocalypse, or to enter into the numerous questions to which it gives rise, would be impossible in the space at my disposal. All that I can hope to do is to give a rapid outline of its contents, and, so far as ascertainable, of its probable meaning in those parts of its symbolism which are capable of explanation, or which do not at once explain themselves.

After the Prologue,[1] the main sections of the book are arranged in accordance with the number Seven, which is the most prominent among the symbolic numbers with which the book is filled. Thus we have :—

Prologue, i. 1—8.
1. Letters to the Seven Churches of Asia, i. 9—iii. 22.
2. The Seven Seals, iv.—vii.
3. The Seven Trumpets, viii.—xi.
4. The Seven Mystic Figures, xii.—xiv.[2]
5. The Seven Vials, xv.—xvi.
6. The Doom of the Foes of Christ, xvii.—xx.
7. The Blessed Consummation, xxi.—xxii. 7.

The Epilogue, xxii. 8—21.[3]

---

[1] The Vision takes place on "the Lord's Day," which probably means neither "Easter Day," nor the "Day of Judgment," but "Sunday." It is the earliest use of the expression, but furnishes no proof at all of the later date assigned to the Apocalypse.

[2] I borrow this ingenious suggestion from the author of the "*Parousia*," a book full of suggestiveness, although I disagree with the author in its limitation of the Apocalyptic horizon mainly to Jerusalem. The Seven Mystic Figures are :—(1) The Sun-clothed Woman ; (2) The Red Dragon ; (3) The Man-child ; (4) The First Wild Beast from the Sea ; (5) The Second Wild Beast from the Land ; (6) The Lamb on Mount Sion ; (7) The Son of Man on the Cloud.

[3] Ewald divides the book into three main sections of seven members each :—The Seven Seals (iv.—vii.); the Seven Trumpets (viii.—xi. 14); the Seven Vials, with the group of associated Visions (xi. 15—xiv. 3), which are divided into three members; (xi. 15—xiv. 20; xv.—xviii.; xix.—xxii. 5). He thinks that the book has an Introduction in four parts; Preface and Dedication in seven parts (ii., iii.); and a Conclusion in three parts. Volkmar's division is into two main parts :—(I.) The Announcement of the Judgment (i.—ix); (II.) The Achievement of the Judgment (x.—xiv.). The subordinate parts are :—Prologue (I. 1—7); (1) First Vision (i. 8 – iii.); (2) Second Vision, the Seals (iv.—vii.); (3) Third Vision, the loud Declaration of God's Judgment (viii., ix.); (4) Fourth Vision, the Introductory Judgment (x.—xiv.); (5) Fifth Vision, Avenging Justice (xv., xvi.); (6) Sixth Vision, the overthrow of the World-Power, or Rome (xvii., xviii.); (7) Seventh Vision, the Completion of the Judgment (xix.—xxi.); Epilogue.—Whatever division of the book be adopted, it will be seen at once that it is constructed in a very artificial manner, and dominated by the numbers

The Seven Churches addressed in the person of their Angels[1] are :—

EPHESUS, the Church faithful as yet, but waxing cold.
SMYRNA, the Church faithful amid Jewish persecutions.
PERGAMUM, the Church faithful amid heathen persecutions, but liable to swerve into Antinomianism.
THYATIRA, the Church faithful as yet, but acquiescent under Antinomian seductions.
SARDIS, the Church slumbering, but not past awakenment.
PHILADELPHIA, the Church faithful and militant.
LAODICEA, the Church unfaithful, proud, lukewarm, and luxurious.[2]

The letters to these Seven Churches are normally sevenfold, consisting of: 1. The address; 2. The title of the Divine Speaker; 3. The encomium; 4. The reproof; 5. The warning; 6. The promise to him that overcometh; 7. The solemn appeal to attention. These elements are, however, freely modified. Two Churches—Smyrna and Philadelphia—receive unmitigated praise. Two—Sardis and Laodicea—are addressed in terms of unmitigated reproof. To the three others—Ephesus, Pergamum, and Thyatira—is awarded a mixture of praise and blame.

The Angel of the Church of Ephesus is praised for "having tried them which called themselves Apostles, and they are not,[3] and having found them false," and also for hating the works of the Nicolaitans. The Angel of the Church of Smyrna is praised for faithfulness amid "the reviling of them which say they are Jews and are not, but are a synagogue of Satan." The Angel of the Church of Pergamum is blamed because he has there "some who hold the teaching of the Nicolaitans, and the teaching of Balaam, who taught Balak to cast a

---

seven, three, and four. Seven is the mystic number of peace, expiation, and the covenant between God and man. Three is the signature of the Deity. Four is the number of the world and created things. Ten = 1 + 2 + 3 + 4, indicates completeness. On the symbolism of numbers, see Bähr, *Symbolik.* i. 187, etc. Herzog. *Real. Encycl. s. v.* Zahlen; Lange, *Revelations*, Introd. § 6, etc.

[1] The Angels cannot be the Bishops, for even if the Domitianic date of the Apocalypse be accepted, episcopacy had not even then attained to such proportions, and if the Ancients had supposed the Bishops to be meant, they would have adopted this title in speaking of them. Probably the title implies the Genius of the Church, ideally represented as a Responsible Head, or Guardian of it; just as Daniel idealises the Angels of the nations (Dan. x. 20, 21; xii. 1).

[2] The number seven is ideal. It is idle to suppose that there were no Churches at Tralles, Hierapolis, Laodicea, etc. The book is pervaded by the number seven (i. 4; iv. 5; vii. 1; viii. 2; x. 3; xii. 3; xv. 1; xvii. 9, 10, etc.). It should be observed that the *sacred* numbers are throughout parodied by the anti-sacred numbers.

[3] Men (Dean Plumptre says) of the Hymenæus, Alexander, and Philetus type (1 Tim. i. 20; 2 Tim. ii. 17). In the days of Nero there were still false teachers, who called themselves "Apostles" (2 Cor. xi. 13, 14). It is tolerably certain that there were none in the days of Domitian. Hippolytus (recently discovered in an Arabic translation) says that they were "Judaisers *from Jerusalem,*" and certainly no such agents were at work so late as A.D. 95.

stumbling-block before the children of Israel, to eat things offered to idols, and to commit fornication." The Angel of the Church of Thyatira is blamed for "suffering the woman Jezebel[1] to seduce my servants to commit fornication and to eat things sacrificed to idols." The Angel of the Church of Philadelphia is promised the victory " over the synagogue of Satan, of them which say they are Jews and they are not, but do lie."

Little is known about the special characteristics of the heresies here alluded to. It would hardly be necessary to notice the wild guesses respecting them but for the increasing confidence of the assertion that these expressions are aimed at St. Paul or his followers. St. Paul is supposed to be the chief of the heresiarchs, and the leader of those who falsely claimed to be Apostles.[2] In other words, we are to believe that the virtue of the Ephesian Church consisted in casting forth the doctrines and adherents of its glorious founder—of the Apostle who had there faced martyrdom, who had there "fought with beasts," who had won the passionate affection of the first presbyters, who had toiled there with infinite devotion for more than two years, admonishing them night and day with tears, and with his own hands ministering to their necessities. The whole theory is monstrous. The tone of deep respect in which the Asiatics Polycarp and Irenæus speak of St. Paul is alone sufficient to overthrow it. St. Paul himself had warned his Churches against "false Apostles." They did not, of course, pretend to be of the number of *the Twelve;* neither did St. Paul. The notion that St. John jealously excludes St. Paul by saying that on the Twelve foundation stones of the New Jerusalem were the names of the "Twelve Apostles of the Lamb," is the idlest extravagance. St. Paul's Apostolate was neither from men, nor by means of men. Unless the calm and definite testimony of St. Luke is to be set aside for the fictions of nameless heretics, the Twelve, and St. John among them, had expressly sanctioned St. Paul's Apostolic claim, had given him their right hands of fellowship, had recognised his equality, had found no fault with his teaching, had sanctioned his independence in his own wide sphere of toil, had even appealed to him for sympathy and assistance in the support of their poor. Polycarp was the hearer and devoted admirer of St. John. If St. John had been actuated by a fanatical horror of St. Paul's teaching, would Polycarp have spoken of the Apostle as "the blessed and glorious Paul?"[3]

As for the Nicolaitans, we know of no excuse for regarding them

---

[1] Or, "thy wife Jezebel," A, B, g, Andreas, etc. Dean Blakesley precariously identifies Jezebel with the Hebrew sibyl Sambetha, who was worshipped at Thyatira (Smith's *Dict. Bibl. s. v.* Thyatira). If "thy wife" be the true reading, it presents a curious parallel to the state of the Philippian Church in the days of Polycarp. In his letter to the Philippians (ch. xi.), he speaks of the wife of one of the Presbyters, named Valens, who was guilty of much the same wickedness as this "Jezebel."
[2] See Volkmar, *Commentar zur Offenb.* pp. 79, *seqq.*
[3] Polyc. *Ep. ad Philip.* 3.

as Paulinists, even if we admit the absurd notion that Nikolaos, which means "*conquering* the people," is a Greek translation of Bileam, which is precariously rendered "*corrupting* the people."[1] The conduct of Balaam, and the traditional teaching of the Deacon Nicolas,[2] would have been at least as abhorrent to St. Paul as to St. John. He has himself again and again denounced such impure and Antinomian tenets, in language as powerful as and more profoundly reasoned than that of the Apocalypse. He has even drawn the same warning illustration from the example of Balaam.[3] To say that in any sense, literal or allegorical, he or any one of his *genuine* followers ever seduced Christians to fornication, whether in the form of tampering with idolatry, or thinking lightly of uncleanness, is to affix a wanton calumny on one of the purest of the saints of God. If it be true that any Christians distorted to their own perdition, or to that of others, his doctrine of Christian liberty, he was himself the first to utter his warning against such perversions. Nor did he, directly or indirectly, induce men to eat "meat offered to idols." In cases where the conscience was in no way wounded by doing so—in the instance of those who were firmly convinced that an idol is nothing in the world—where the meat was innocently bought in the open market, or eaten in the ordinary intercourse of social life—in those carefully limited circumstances he had taught, and rightly taught, that the matter was one of pure indifference. If in saying, "I will lay on you none other burden," St. John meant (as Renan says) that those had nothing to fear who kept the concordat arranged at the Synod of Jerusalem (Acts xv.), it is strange to overlook that this very concordat had only been won by the genius, the energy, and the initiative of St. Paul. But so far from "casting a stumbling-block" in the path of others, he had, on the contrary, always maintained, as his Lord had done before him,[4] that the casting of stumbling-blocks—which he expressed by the very same word as St. John—is the deadliest of crimes against Christian charity,[5] and that it would be better to eat no meat of any kind while the world lasted than to cause a weak brother to offend.

---

[1] Gesenius and Fürst explain the name to mean "Not of the People," *i.e.*, a foreigner. Vitringa makes it mean "lord of," and Simonis "*destruction* of the people." In no sense is it an equivalent of Nikolaus.

[2] On Nicolas, see my *Life of St. Paul*, i. 133. There is no absolute proof that the heretic was the Deacon, but Irenæus (*Haer.* i. 26; iii. 11) and Hippolytus (*Haer.* vii. 36) supposed him to be so. Clemens of Alexandria (*Strom.* ii. 20; iii. 4) tells a dubious story that when he was accused of jealousy of his beautiful wife, he disproved the charge in a very strange and unseemly way. He is the reputed author of the rule that "we must *abuse* the flesh" (ὅτι δεῖ παραχρῆσθαι τῇ σαρκί), which might convey the innocent meaning that stern self-denial was requisite to repress evil passions. The verb was, however, capable of the meaning "use to the full," and possibly some may have founded on this phrase the wicked inference that criminal passion should be cured by unlimited indulgence. See Ewald, *Gesch.* vii. 172.

[3] 1 Cor. x. 7, 8.

[4] Matt. xviii. 6, 8, 9; Mark ix. 43—47.

[5] 1 Cor viii. 13; x. 32; 2 Cor. xi. 29; Rom. xiv. 21.

Again, to suppose that because St. John (Rev. ii. 24) reflects severely on those who talked of "knowing *the depths of Satan*," he must necessarily be uttering a malignant sneer against St. Paul, who had spoken of "the Spirit searching all things, yea, even *the depths of God*,"[1] is to use a style of criticism which builds massive systems upon pillars of smoke. The utmost which we could infer would be that false teachers had distorted and parodied the expression of St. Paul. The single grain of truth in the whole hypothesis is that St. John speaks in a more sweeping and less limited way than St. Paul about eating "meats offered to idols." It was natural that it should be so, both because St. John's Judaic training had given him a deeper instinctive horror of even the semblance of participation in idolatry, and also because he was writing at a later date and in days of persecution, in which the act itself had acquired a more marked significance. Had St. Paul been writing under the same circumstances as St. John, he would have spoken no less strongly on the sin of a cowardly conformity. To eat of idol offerings in cases where no mistaken inferences could be drawn from doing so, was perfectly innocent; but it became a very different thing to eat of them in days, like those of the Neronian persecution or those of Justin Martyr, when to do so meant to be indifferent to the sin of idolatry. This attempt to represent the Apostles as actuated by a burning animosity against each other, and a determination to "write each other down," as though they were contributors to modern religious newspapers, is a total failure. It is time it were dismissed. When the Apostles differed from each other—as we know, from the Acts of the Apostles and the Epistle to the Galatians, that they sometimes did— it was only in the spirit of mutual respect and affection in which Luther differed from Melancthon, and Bossuet from Fénélon.[2]

The false Jews, the false Apostles, the Nicolaitans, the Balaamites, were immoral sectarians, whether Judaic or anti-Judaic, against whom St. Paul had beforehand warned his Churches, very much as St. John has done, and against whom every one of the sacred writers has lifted up his voice. To admit that St. John could have written such railing accusations against his glorious brother Apostle, is to imply that he was unworthy to be an Apostle, or a sacred writer at all. It is to degrade him at once to the level of modern partisans. The early Christians had not yet been taught that religion consisted in breathing the atmosphere of faction, slanderousness, and hate. There were some, even then, "who preached Christ of contention, supposing to add affliction to St. Paul's bonds," and they would have been well qualified to write anonymous articles of unfair and unchristian depreciation. But they incurred a stern censure from the lips of Christ's Apostle. Such

[1] 1 Cor. ii. 10; comp. Rom. xi. 33.
[2] Luther, as a friend reminds me, is sometimes a little severe upon "Philippianus," and Bossuet admitted that he had sometimes argued in opposition to Fénélon without naming him.

orthodoxy is heterodoxy; such religion is irreligion; such Christianity is worse than heathendom, and is no Christianity at all.

We reach the culmination of these exegetic absurdities when we find Volkmar also identifying the Second Wild Beast from the Land, and the False Prophet of Rev. xiii. and xvii., with St. Paul!

Writers of the Tübingen School were so enchanted with their discovery that the struggle between Jewish and Pauline Christianity was longer and more permanent than had been supposed, that they exaggerated the significance of the second century calumnies against St. Paul. They forgot that the Clementines were heretical, and that these Ebionite attacks were, after all, subterranean and pseudonymous. As for the *grounds* on which St. Paul is identified with the False Prophet —namely, because in writing to the Romans[1] he taught loyal obedience to the powers that be as being "ordained of God"[2]—Volkmar surely forgets that the teaching of St. Paul on this subject was the normal teaching of all the Apostles, of all the early Christian Fathers and Apologists, nay, more, of the Lord Jesus Himself. St. Peter—writing in the days of Nero—writing, in all probability, during the Neronian persecution, had not only said "Honour the king," but even "Submit yourselves unto every ordinance of man for the Lord's sake, *whether it be to the king as supreme*, or unto governors, as unto them that are appointed by him for the punishment of evil doers, and for the praise of them that do well." And as to the Divine authority of heathen government, St. John himself records in his Gospel how our Lord said to Pilate, "Thou couldest have no power at all against me, *except it were given thee from above.*"[3] Indeed, such teaching was so obviously based on common sense and common duty, that even after the destruction of Jerusalem—even in the days when detestation of the Gentiles had been reduced to something like a system—Rabbi Chanina used to say, "Pray for the established government, for, but for it, men would devour each other."[4]

SECTION II.

THE SEALS.

After the letters to the Seven Churches begins the more definitely Apocalyptic portion of the book. The Apostle hears a voice bidding him ascend to heaven, and see things which must come to pass after these things. Instantly, in an ecstasy, he sees a throne in heaven, encircled by an emerald rainbow, whereon was seated One whose lustre was as a jasper and a sardine. Round the throne were twenty-four enthroned elders, representing the Patriarchs of the redeemed Church of both dispensations, arrayed in white and crowned with gold. Out of the throne came an incessant rolling of thunders and voices, and a stream of light-

---

[1] Rom. xiii. 1—7.
[2] John xix. 11.
[3] 1 Pet. ii. 13, 14—17.
[4] Mechilta on Exod. xix. 1.

nings; and before it there burned, as with the flame of seven lamps, the sevenfold Spirit of God. Before the Throne flowed a glassy sea of crystal brightness, and about it were the fourfold cherubim, six-winged and full of eyes, symbols of all that is most perfect in creation, hymning the perpetual Trisagion, and joining in the endless liturgy of prayer and praise. On the right hand of Him who sat on the throne was a book, seven-sealed, and written within and without. In answer to the appeal of an angel, none is found worthy to open the book but the Lion of the Tribe of Judah, who is also the Lamb that was slain. When He has taken the book there is a fresh outburst of universal triumph and blessing, in which even those join who are "under the earth."[1]

i. The Lamb opens one of the seven seals, and one of the Immortalities cries with a voice of thunder, "Come!"

Instantly there springs forth a *white* horse, bearing a rider with a bow in his hand, to whom a crown is given, and who goes forth conquering and to conquer. It is a symbol of THE MESSIAH riding forth to victory, but armed only with a bow to smite his enemies, not as yet in close conflict, but from afar.[2]

But the coming of the Messiah was to be ushered in by the woes which are the travail-pangs of a new dispensation.

ii. The Lamb opens the Second Seal, and the second Immortality cries "Come!"

Instantly a *fiery* horse—a horse red as blood[3]—leaps forth,—whose rider is armed with a great sword. It is the symbol of WAR. To him it is given to take peace from the earth, and that—as in the fierce conflicts between Otho and Vitellius, between Vitellius and Vespasian, between the Jews and the Romans, between John of Giscala and Simon —men should slay one another in internecine and civil discord. It was an epoch of wars and massacres. There had been massacres in Alexandria; massacres at Seleucia; massacres at Jamnia; massacres at Damascus; massacres at Cæsarea: massacres at Bedriacum. There had been wars in Britain, wars in Armenia, wars in Gaul, wars in Italy, wars in Arabia, wars in Parthia, wars in Judæa. Disbanded soldiers and marauding troops filled the world with rapine, terror, and massacre. The world was like an Aceldama, or field of blood. The red horse and its rider are but a visible image of the words of our Lord—"For nation shall rise against nation, and kingdom against kingdom;" and "Ye shall hear of wars and rumours of wars, which things are the beginning of the birth-throes."[4]

---

[1] Verse 13, comp. Phil. ii. 10. With the vague numbers of the numberless multitude comp. Dan. vii. 10.
[2] Comp. xix. 11. Both Victorinus, in his commentary, and Tertullian (*de Cor. Mil.* 15) understand the Rider of the White Horse to be Christ. The white horse is a sign of victory (Virg. *Æn.* iii. 537). The symbol of the bow is, perhaps, derived from Ps. vii. 13, xlv. 6.
[3] 2 Kings iii. 22, συρρὰ ὡς αἷμα.
[4] Matt. xxiv. 4, 7. For corroborative authorities see Jos. *Antt.* xviii. 9, § 9; xix. 1,

iii. The Lamb opens the Third Seal, and the third Immortality utters the word "Come!"

Instantly a *black* horse leaps forth. Its rider is unarmed, but holds in his hand a balance; and by way of explanation a voice is heard from among the four Immortalities saying, "A chœnix of wheat for a denarius, and three of barley for a denarius." The rider is FAMINE. A chœnix was less than a quart, and was the minimum allowance for a day's food,[1] yet it was to cost a whole day's wages;[2] and a third of the same price was to be given for even so coarse a grain as barley—a food to which Roman soldiers were only degraded by way of punishment. Thus wheat and barley were to rise to twenty times their usual price, to the infinite distress of men.

> "He calls for Famine, and the eager fiend
> Blows poisonous mildew from his shrivelled lips,
> And taints the golden ear."[3]

It was an epoch of constant famines. The dependence of Rome and Italy upon Alexandria for corn caused bitter and constant distress. In the reign of Claudius the famine and its accompanying prodigies had been deemed an omen, and only fifteen days' food had been left in Rome.[4] About this very time, A.D. 68—in the midst of Nero's impotent buffooneries—the people, already burdened by famine prices, were nearly maddened by the discovery that a ship from Alexandria, which had been mistaken for one of the famous wheat-ships, had a lading of sand with which to strew the amphitheatre.[5] The overflow of the Tiber, early in the reign of Otho, caused, as Tacitus says, famine among the common people, and a scarcity of the commonest elements of life.[6] It was the deliberate object of Vespasian to cause famine and dissensions at Rome by stopping the supplies of provisions, nor did he let the corn-ships sail till only ten days' supply was left in the city.[7] In Jerusalem, during the final state of siege which was now rapidly approaching, the anguish and horror of the famine were unspeakable. Josephus tells us that many sold their all for a single chœnix of wheat if they were rich, of barley if they were poor, and shut themselves up in the inmost recesses of their houses to eat it raw; and that many had to undergo unspeakable tortures to make them confess that they had but one loaf of bread, or so

---

§ 2; *B. J.* ii. 17; x. 18 (where he says that "a terrible disturbance prevailed throughout Syria, and every city had been divided into two camps"); Tacitus and Suetonius *passim*.

[1] Herod. vii. 187; Diog. Laert. viii. 18.

[2] Matt. xx. 2; xxiv. 7; Mark xiii. 7; Tac. *Ann.* i. 1. In Sicily, in the days of Cicero, twelve *Chœnixes* of *wheat* could be bought for a denarius (Cic. *Verr.* iii. 81), and therefore thirty-six of barley. [3] Cowper.

[4] Tac. *Ann.* xii. 43: "frugum egestas et orta ex eo fames." Suet. *Claud.* 18, "*assiduae sterilitates*." (Comp. Jos. *Antt.* iii. 15, § 3.)

[5] Suet. *Ner.* 46.

[6] Tac. *H.* i. 86: "fames in volgus, inopia quaestus, et penuria alimentorum" (Suet. *Otho*, 8). [7] Tac. *H.* iii. 48; iv. 52.

much as a handful of barley meal.[1] Terribly—both in Italy and in Judaea—did the fearful rider of the black horse do his appointed work! He is a visible symbol of the Lord's words—"There shall be famines . . . . in divers places."[2]

But the third Immortality added the strange words, "And the oil and the wine hurt thou not." Oil and wine are not necessaries but luxuries. It is as though he had said, "In the wild anguish of famine let their pangs be aggravated by having the needless accessories of abundance." So it was—strange to say—in both the places on which the Seer's eye is mainly fixed, Jerusalem and Rome. In Jerusalem, while myriads were starving, John of Giscala and his Zealots had access to the sacred stores of *wine and oil* in the Temple, and wasted it with reckless extravagance,[3] and Simon's followers were even hindered from fighting by their perpetual drunkenness. In Rome immense abundance of wine was a frequent concomitant of extreme scarcity of corn. So marked was the evil, that Domitian endeavoured to secure by edict the diminution of the vineyards, and the devotion of wider areas to the cultivation of cereals for human food.[4]

iv. The Lamb opens the Fourth Seal. The fourth Immortality utters his solemn "Come!"

Instantly a *livid* horse leaps forth. His rider is DEATH; and HADES follows to receive the prey. They usher in a crowd of calamities over a quarter of the earth—sword, and famine, and pestilence, and wild beasts. Sword and famine had done part of their work; pestilence and the increase of wild beasts naturally follow them. God's four sore judgments usually go hand in hand.[5] Christ had already said of these days that there should be famines and pestilences, as well as wars and rumours of wars. Apart from the inevitable prevalence of wild beasts in places where the inhabitants are thinned and weakened by calamity, an incredible number of human beings were yearly sacrificed to wild beasts in the bloody shows of the amphitheatres, not only at Rome but throughout all the provinces. Lions and tigers were literally fed with men.[6] A pestilence at Rome carried off 30,000 in a single year.[7] At Jerusalem there was from these combined causes "a glut of mortality" almost incredible. It was calculated that upwards of a million perished in the siege, and Mannæus, son of Lazarus, told Titus that even before the Romans encamped under the walls, he had seen 115,880 corpses carried through one single gate.[8]

v. The Lamb opens the Fifth Seal.

Immediately under the golden altar of incense before the throne are

[1] Jos. *B. J.* v. 10, § 2.   [2] Matt. xxiv. 7.
[3] Jos. *B. J.* v. 13, § 6; 1, § 4.   [4] Suet. *Dom.* 7.
[5] Ezek. xiv. 21; Matt. xxiv. 6, 8; Mark xiii. 7, 8.
[6] Hence one of the wild plans of revenge which chased each other across the brain of Nero on his last day of life, was to let loose upon the people the wild beasts of the amphitheatre. Suet. *Ner.* 43: "urbem incendere feris in populum immissis."
[7] Suet. *Ner.* 39; Tac. *Ann.* xvi. 13.   [8] See Jos. *B. J.* v. 12, § 3; 13, § 7.

seen the souls of the "great multitude" who had perished "for the word of God and for the testimony which they held,"¹ some at Jerusalem, some in the provinces, but most of all in the Neronian persecution at Rome. They are impatiently appealing for vengeance and judgment.² Hero after hero had fallen in the Christian warfare. Apostle after Apostle had been sent to his dreadful martyrdom. St. Peter had been crucified; St. Paul beheaded; St. James the Elder beheaded; St. James, the Bishop of Jerusalem, hurled down and beaten to death; hundreds of others burnt, or tortured, or torn to pieces in the gardens of Nero and in the Roman circus; yet no deliverer flashed from the morning clouds. How long, oh Lord, how long! When all the world is arrayed against Thy saints, must not deliverance assume the inevitable guise of temporal vengeance?—White robes are given them, and they are bidden to wait till the number of the martyrs is complete, till their brethren who are still on earth shall have fulfilled their course.³ They are those of whom Christ had prophesied when He said "Then"—after the "beginning of sorrows"—"shall they deliver you up to be afflicted, and shall kill you." The time had come for judgment to begin at the throne of God. Meanwhile the fire of olden prophecy was re-kindled for their inspiration, and they found that the more they were trodden down the more did they feel the conviction of glorious triumph and the exultation of inward peace. They who have an invisible King to sustain them, and a John to utter His messages, may brave the banded forces of secular despotism and religious hatred— and may stand undismayed between a Zealot-maddened Jerusalem and a Neronian Rome. If the judgment began with Christians, what should be the end of those who obeyed not the Gospel of God?⁴

vi. The Lamb opens the Sixth Seal.

Instantly there are all the signs which usher in a Day of the Lord. The darkened sun, the lurid moon, the showers of meteors, the shrivelling heavens, the terror with which men call on the rocks and mountains to fall on them and hide them, are the metaphors of vast earthly changes and catastrophes. At first sight it might well seem as if they could describe nothing short of the final conflagration and ruin of the globe. But there is not one of these metaphors which is not found in the Old Testament prophets,⁵ and in them they refer in every instance to the destruction of cities and the establishment of new covenants, or

---

¹ Rev. vi. 9; vii. 13; xvii. 6; xx. 4.
² This has been variously excused by different commentators. "Non haec odio inimicorum," says Bede, "pro quibus in hoc saeculo rogaverunt, orant, sed amore aequitatis." Bengel explains their impatience as zeal for the truth and holiness of the Lord (comp. Ps. lxxiv. 19; Luke xviii. 7, 8).
³ Comp. Enoch civ. 1—3. "Ye righteous, . . . your cries have cried for vengeance . . . *wait with patient hope.*" See too Gen. iv. 10; Job xvi., xix.; Is. xxvi. 21; 2 Esdras xv. 8, etc. ⁴ 1 Pet. iv. 17.
⁵ See Is. ii. 12, 19; xiii. 10; xxxiv. 3, 4; l. 3; lxiii. 4; Jer. iv. 23—26; Ezek. xxxii. 7, 8; Joel ii. 10, 31; iii. 4, 15; Hos. x. 8; Nah. i. 6; Mal. iii. 2, etc. The extent to which the Apostle borrows the phrases of the Old Testament may be seen by taking

to other earthly revolutions. Not only had our Lord adopted these vivid Oriental symbols to describe the signs of His coming in the fall of Jerusalem, and the close of the old æon, but he had expressly said that "*this generation shall not pass away until all these things be fulfilled.*"[1] It is clear, therefore—as nearly every school of interpreters has seen—that they are but a description, in the language of Eastern poetry and metaphor, of an age terrified alike by political crises and physical calamities. Such a description accords exactly with the reality. In the sudden collapse of the deified line of the Julii, who had governed them for four generations, the Romans saw an omen which seemed to threaten the world with destruction.[2] There reigned everywhere an universal terror.[3] Throughout the length and breadth of the Roman Empire, but most of all in Judæa, in the midst of the violent revolutionary movements which marked the day, men's hearts were failing them for fear.[4]

vii. Then, before the opening of the Seventh Seal, there is a pause. The Angels of the winds had been bidden to prevent their ravages[5] until the servants of God are sealed upon their foreheads by the Angel from the sunrising. The seal is doubtless the cross of baptism, just as in Ezekiel (ix. 4, 6) those alone are to be spared from slaughter who have "the sign Thau,"—that is the cross—upon their foreheads.[6] A purely ideal number are sealed—namely, twelve times twelve thousand—twelve thousand from each of the twelve tribes. The tribe of Dan is alone omitted, probably because it had almost disappeared from the annals of Israel.[7] Besides these, the seer beheld an innumerable multitude of every nation, and all tribes and peoples and tongues, arrayed in white and with palms in their hands. One of the elders tells him[8] that these are they who came "out of *the* great tribulation"—that is, the Neronian persecution—and have washed their robes and made them

---

Rev. i. 12—17, and comparing it phrase by phrase with Zech. iv. 2; Dan. vii. 13; x. 5; vii. 9; x. 6, 11, 12; Is. xlix. 2; Ezek. xliii. 2.

[1] Matt. xxiv. 29—34.   [2] See Tac. *H.* i. 11.
[3] Luke xxiii. 36.
[4] Here, if any one believes that the Apocalyptic symbols are infinitely plastic, he may hold with Godet that the seals foreshadow "*all* the wars, *all* the famines, *all* the persecutions, *all* the earthquakes, etc., which the earth has seen or will see until the last scene for which the trumpets give the signal."
[5] Among other things they are forbidden "to hurt *any tree*," vii. 1 (comp. ix. 4). The Jews felt deeply the destruction of all the trees in the neighbourhood of Jerusalem during the Jewish War. Rabbi Yochanan said, "The Holy One—blessed be He—will in future replace every acacia which the heathen have taken away from Jerusalem." He supported this by Is. xli. 19, saying that "the wilderness" (Is. lxiv. 10) was meant to indicate Jerusalem (Rosh Hashanah, f. 23, a).
[6] The ancient form of the letter Thau was +
[7] It is not worth while to repeat all the idle conjectures about this point. The Targum of Jonathan on Ex. xvii. 8 represents Dan as "a sinner from the beginning"—a tribe thoroughly idolatrous (see Ewald, *Gesch.* i. 490). Simeon is omitted in Deut. xxxiii., and Dan in 1 Chron. iv. After 1 Chron. xxviii. 22 it is not mentioned. Levi is here counted as one of the tribes, because *all* the Lord's true people are now priests.
[8] Cf. Zech. iv. 4, 5.

white in the blood of the Lamb. The whole company are "the elect gathered together from the four winds, from one end of heaven to the other."[1] The 144,000 seem to represent the ideal Israel. The "numberless multitude," which is almost the identical expression used of the Neronian martyrs alike by Tacitus and by Clemens Romanus,[2] are those who have died for the truths of Christ, whose souls St. John has already seen in shadowy throngs beneath the altar.

viii. We still await in dread expectation the opening of the Seventh Seal. But when it is opened there is a pause of terrified astonishment, a silence for half an hour in Heaven, as though the dwellers in Heaven drew their breath in anguish of expectation. It is like the awful pause before the hurricane, when we hear "the destroying Angels murmuring together as they draw their swords in the distance," and "the questioning in terrified stillness of the forest leaves which way the wind shall come." For hitherto the judgments of the earth have only been seen in Heaven by the shadowy images of those who went forth for their accomplishment; but now are to be seen the very judgments themselves. There are seven Angels[3]—

> "The Seven
> Who in God's presence, nearest to His throne
> Stand ready at command, and are His eyes
> That run through all the Heavens, and down to the earth
> Bear His swift errands."

To these angels are given seven Trumpets to blow the signals of doom.[4] The results that follow the blast of these seven trumpets practically form the issue of the breaking of the Seventh Seal. But the troubles which follow are neither definite, nor continuous, nor rigidly historical. They closely resemble those which have followed at the opening of the Sixth Seal, only that these trumpet calamities affect a third, and not a fourth, part of the earth.[5] They indicate the widening spread and deepening intensity of judgment; and although it is not possible to point out in chronological sequence the exact events which they describe in hyperbolic symbolism, they resemble those signs in the sun, the moon, the stars, and the sea by which the Lord on the Mount of Olives had shadowed forth the troubles of the approaching end. The language is also coloured by reminiscences of the Plagues of Egypt.[6] Further, it must be borne in mind that to the eye of the seer the outlines of time are indistinct, and there is a commingling of the events of the present

---

[1] Matt. xxiv. 31.   [2] ὄχλος πολύς, "*ingens multitudo.*"
[3] See Tobit xii. 15; Dan. x. 13; Zech. iv. 10. The names are given differently in the Book of Enoch, the Targum of Jonathan, and other sources (see Gfrörer, *Jahrb. d. Heils*, i. 361).
[4] Comp. 1 Cor. xv. 52; 4 Esdr. v. 3; Matt. xxiv. 31.
[5] The "third part" is evidently a general expression, as in Zech. xiii. 9. It probably indicates the Roman Empire (ix. 18; xii. 6).
[6] See Luke xxi. 25.

and the immediate past with those of the instantly anticipated future. The repetition of the vision of judgment in various forms is one of the recognised Hebrew methods of expressing their certainty. The same general calamities are indicated by diverse symbols. Let it not be supposed that there is anything novel in this view. On the contrary, it is found as far back as the close of the third century, in the most ancient of all the extant Scholia on the Apocalypse—those by St. Victorinus of Pettau, who was martyred in the days of Diocletian.[1] He regards the visions as mainly retrogressive and iterative. "The phials," he says, "are a supplement of what he said of the trumpets. We must not regard the mere order of the statements, for the Holy Spirit, after he has advanced to the end of the latest time, often returns to the same time again, and supplies all which was before partially stated." And just before this passage, he says, "that though the seer repeats by the vials (what had been implied by the trumpets) this does not imply a repetition of the fact, but is a twofold statement of a single decreed event." There is fair reason to suppose that Victorinus derived this valuable, and by no means obvious, principle of interpretation from early, and perhaps from Apostolic tradition.

SECTION III.

THE TRUMPETS.

Before the seven Angels sound, another Angel, standing at the altar, mixes abundant incense in a golden censer with the prayers of the saints. Some at least of these prayers are represented as having been a unanimous cry for speedy vengeance. In answer to these, the Angel takes the censer, fills it with fire from the altar, and hurls it upon the earth, which echoes back its crashing fall in thunderings, lightnings, voices, and earthquakes. Such thunderings and lightnings and earthquakes were, according to Tacitus and Suetonius, characteristic of the epoch. I have already quoted the solemn language in which Tacitus summarises the manifold calamities of this very period.[2] Speaking of the day on which Galba adopted Piso—Jan. 10, A.D. 69—he says that the day was foul with rain-storms, and disturbed beyond natural wont with thunders, lightnings, and the *threats of heaven*"[3]—omens which he blames Galba for neglecting. Speaking a few years earlier, he observes that "never had the storms of lightning flashed with more frequent violence;"[4] and this he mentions among the prodigies which were the indication of imminent calamities. In Asia, where St. John

---

[1] See Aug. *De Civ. Dei*, xx. 14. So too Andreas, Corn. à Lapide, Vitringa, Bengel and many commentators of all schools, including writers so unlike each other as Bossuet, Ewald, De Wette, and Reuss, on the one hand, and Elliott, Wordsworth, and Hengstenberg, on the other.

[2] Tac. *H.* i. 3. It had long been customary to connect such phenomena with political events (Cic. *De Div.* i. 18; Suet. *Aug.* 94).

[3] Tac. *H.* i. 18.

[4] Tac. *Ann.* xv. 47.

was writing, the era might well be called the era of earthquakes. "Nowhere in the whole world," says Solinus, "are earthquakes so constant and cities so frequently overthrown." They are referred to again and again by all the writers and historians of the age.[1]

i. Then the first Angel sounded. Hail followed, and fire mingled with blood, and a third part of the surface of the earth, with its grass and trees, was scorched up.[2] They are but the beginning of the worse hail (xvi. 21) and fire (xx. 9) and blood (xiv. 20) which are to follow. They point to years of burning drought and rains of blood,[3] and to disastrous conflagrations, such as those at Lyons, Rome, and Jerusalem, and to fierce storms of hail—such as so often destroy in a few hours the vineyards of Lombardy—and to scenes of human bloodshed. And we must once more remind the reader that these storms and prodigies, so far from being peculiar to the Apocalypse, or understood in a peculiar significance, are referred to in very similar terms and explained in a very similar way by other Christian, Heathen, and Jewish writers. Speaking of the earthquake of A.D. 63, Dion Cassius, reflecting the impression of contemporaries, calls it the "greatest that had ever happened." Can we be surprised if, in a book which reads like a hundredfold reverberation of older prophecies, the contemporary phenomena are depicted in the same imagery as that which had been used in their day by the Prophets of Judah and Israel to describe the calamities which were then happening before their eyes? Is the language of St. John about contemporary calamities anything like so hyperbolical as that in which the Prophet Joel had described the ravages produced by a plague of locusts? It is only to the tamer and colder imagination of Teutonic races that such terms sound hyperbolical if applied to anything short of the final consummation.

ii. The second Angel sounds, and something which resembles a burning mountain is flung down into the sea, and the third part of the sea is turned into blood, and the third part of the fish die, and the third part of the ships is destroyed. The image is original. St. John may have derived this terrific picture of "a burning mountain cast into the sea" either from seeing the lurid flashes that leap up night and day from the cone of Stromboli, which he may have passed in a voyage to Rome,

[1] Dion Cass. lxvi. 23—24; Jos. *Antt.* xv. 5, § 2; *B. J.* l. 19, § 3; iv. 4, § 5; Tac. *Ann.* ii. 47; iv. 13; xii. 43—58; xiv. 27; Sen. *Qu. Nat.* vi. 1; Suet. *Tib.* 74, *Ner.* 20; Juv. *Sat.* vi. 411; *Carm. Sib.* iii. 471; Strabo, xii. 8, § 16, etc. Seneca exclaims, "How often have the cities of Asia, how often those of Achaia, fallen by one shock! How many towns in Syria, how many in Macedonia, have been devoured! . . . . Often have the ruins of whole cities been announced to us" (*Ep.* 91).

[2] See Ex. ix. 22; Joel ii. 3. The reference to the destruction of trees in the Apocalypse may be due to the terrible destruction of the trees and the vegetation of Palestine in the Jewish War, especially round Jerusalem; a destruction from which it has never recovered. The "third part" may, as we have seen, vaguely correspond to the Roman Empire.

[3] Liv. xxxix. 46; and often mentioned among Roman portents. Dion Cassius (lxiii. 26) mentions such a rain in A.D. 68, and says that "the blood"—really a natural phenomenon, which happened at Naples so late as 1869—discoloured even the streams.

or more probably from seeing on the horizon, as he gazed from Patmos, the dense smoke vomited from the burning island-mountain of Thera, the modern Santorin. The notion of seas and rivers turned into blood by way of punishing the guilty is well known to the imagery of the Prophets and Apocryphal writers.[1] The language is obviously that of daring symbolism. Taken literally, the fall of the burning mountain resembles no event ever seen or known in the history of the world. Taken metaphorically, it may be meant to depict great calamities connected with the sea and ships, deaths by drowning and massacre which "incarnadined the multitudinous seas." The times of Nero furnished abundant instances. Such were the inundation which devastated the coasts of Lydia, and the destruction of fleets, and the waves reddening with the blood of men, as at Joppa, and on the coasts of the Dead Sea, and on the Lake of Galilee. At Joppa, "the sea was bloody a long way, and the maritime parts were full of dead bodies; and the number of bodies that were thus thrown out of the sea was four thousand two hundred."[2] At Tarichese "one might see the Lake of Galilee all bloody, and full of dead bodies . . . and the shores were full of shipwrecks and of dead bodies all swelled, and as the dead bodies were inflamed by the sun they putrefied and corrupted the air, insomuch that the misery was not only an object of commiseration to the Jews, but to those that hated them and had been the authors of that misery . . . and the number of the slain was six thousand five hundred."[3] Considering, however, that in no age of the Church has there been any accepted identification of the scenes thus pictured, it must always remain uncertain whether the seer meant to point to any very definite events. His object may have been to express in imaginative emblems broad general circumstances and conditions of warning and judgment.

iii. The third Angel sounded, and a great star called Absinth "fell upon the third part of the world's waters, and made them so bitter that men died of them." Here again we are in the abstract region of apocalyptical imagination tinged by reminiscences of the Plagues of Egypt. Alike the result and the agency by which it is accomplished are indefinite. As stars are the images of rulers, and fallen stars of rulers flung down from heaven,[4] the symbol may dimly express the bitterness and terror caused by the overthrow of Nero and the ominous failure of the Julian line. The details of the image may have been suggested by the wicked habit of poisoning the waters of which an enemy was to drink. The Romans excused their cruelty at Jerusalem by asserting that the springs and fountains had been poisoned by the Jews;

---

[1] Wisdom xi. 6, 7.   [2] Jos. *B. J.* iii. 9, § 3.   [3] Jos. *B. J.* iii. 10, § 9.
[4] "How art thou fallen from heaven, oh Lucifer, Son of the Morning!" (Is. xiv. 12).
[5] As a specimen of the strange diversities of interpreters, I may mention that Bossuet understands the fallen star of heretics generally; N. de Lyra applies it to Arius and Macedonius; Luther thinks that it represents——Origen! Mede understands it of Romulus Augustulus; Grotius of "that Egyptian"; Herder of the Zealot Eleazar; others of Gregory the Great!

iv. The fourth Angel sounded, and the third part of the sun and moon and stars, and day and night are smitten;[1] in other words—in accordance with the recognised imagery of Apocalypse and Prophecy—ruler after ruler, chieftain after chieftain of the Roman Empire and the Jewish nation was assassinated and ruined. Gaius, Claudius, Nero, Galba, Otho, Vitellius, all died by murder or suicide; Herod the Great, Herod Antipas, Herod Agrippa, and most of the Herodian Princes, together with not a few of the leading High Priests of Jerusalem, perished in disgrace, or in exile, or by violent hands. All these were quenched suns and darkened stars. It must be again borne in mind that all the events thus symbolised are not meant to be *consecutive*. Although progressive, they are analogous to, or even identical with, those already described. The plagues of the trumpets are but the deadlier form of the plagues indicated by the seals; and in the vials the same woes reach their consummation. So far, therefore, as the effects of the fourth Trumpet are meant to be historical, and not a general echo of our Lord's great discourse about the Last Things, they allude, like those of the sixth Seal, to political perils and revolutions in the Roman Empire, which were the special characteristic of that epoch, and of which every comet and every eclipse and every unusual tempest was believed to be a threatening sign.[2]

v. The trumpets are broken into divisions of four and three. To prepare for the remaining three, a single eagle[3] flies in the mid region of Heaven, screaming with loud cry a triple "Woe!" by reason of the Angel trumpets which were yet to sound. The eagle denotes carnage;—"where the slain are there is she."[4] The massacres of these years stained, as we have seen, both the land and sea. The furrows of earth were red with slaughter; the waves were dyed with blood.

The fifth Angel sounds, and a star falls to earth, to whom is given the key of the abyss. He opens the abyss, and in the issuing smoke which dims the air comes forth a host of scorpion-locusts, which are forbidden to hurt the grass or green things or trees, but are bidden, for a space of five months, to torment without killing all who have not the seal of God on their forehead. These scorpion-locusts resemble war-horses, with crowns like gold, with the face of men, the hair of women, the teeth of lions; they have breastplates as of iron, and the sound of their wings is like the sound of chariots, or of horses charging to battle. The anguish they inflict makes men desire to die;[5] and their king is called Abaddon, Apollyon, or the Destroyer.

[1] Matt. xxiv. 29.
[2] Stars are the well-understood Scripture symbol for persons in authority (Gen. xxxvii. 9; Jer. iv. 23; Ezek. xxxii. 7, 8; Isa. xiii. 9, 10, 17). The symbol is a natural one. Similarly, Shakspere tells us how—
"Certain stars shot madly from their spheres
To hear the sea-maid's music."
[3] Rev. viii. 13. ἀετοῦ, א, A, B, &c. [4] Hos. viii. 1.
[5] Jer. iii. 8: "Death shall be chosen rather than life, by all them that remain of this evil family."

The fallen star may again be meant for Nero; but on the whole I agree with those who see in this vision a purely demoniac host. The fallen star will then be Satan, of whom the Lord said, "I saw Satan as lightning fallen from heaven."[1] The abyss is pre-eminently the abode of "demons."[2] It is their speciality to cause torment.[3] They are as appropriately symbolised by scorpion-locusts as by frogs.[4] Christ had specially prophesied that "this wicked generation" should be more grievously afflicted by demons. As time went on, Rome and Jerusalem —the two places typically prominent in the mind of the writer—were becoming more and more "a habitation of demons, a hold of every unclean spirit, a cage of every unclean and hateful bird."[5] In Rome the loose, disbanded soldiery and the scum of the forum had degraded society to the lowest levels of infamy. The city had become a foul pool, into which every polluted river had poured its dregs. In Jerusalem, according to the emphatic testimony of Josephus, never since the beginning of the world had there been any generation more prolific of wickedness. Stier says, "that in the period between the Resurrection and the Fall of Jerusalem the Jewish nation acted as if *possessed by seven thousand demons*. The whole age had upon it a stamp of the infernal."[6]

Whether in this general picture of the host of hell swarming out of the abyss, there is any direct allusion to the Idumeans, Zealots, and Sicarii stinging themselves to death with untold anguish, like scorpions encircled by a ring of fire; or, again, to the tumults, bloodshed, and agonies of Rome, the frequency of suicide, and the many tales of those who seemed to long for death in vain—cannot be affirmed. The description of the scorpion-locusts evidently recalls the Egyptian Plague, and the language of Joel, and the fanciful allusions to locusts which abound in the songs and proverbs of the East.[7] The five months may point to the summer period, which is the time of locust plagues.[8]

---

[1] Luke x. 18. The Book of Enoch is full of good and evil angels, who are spoken of as stars (Enoch xviii. 13; xxi. 3, etc.).
[2] Luke viii. 31.   [3] Matt. xv. 22.
[4] Rev. xvi. 13. Renan may be right in saying that the notion of frogs and locusts coming from the abyss, may have been partly suggested by the actual phenomena of the Solfatara, or some similar district.
[5] Rev. xviii. 2.   [6] *Reden Jesu*, ii. 187.
[7] Locusts are called "*cavaletti*" in Naples. Hermas (*Vis.* iv. 1) sees "a great beast . . . . and fiery locusts coming out of his mouth," which appears to be (*Vis.* iv. 3) "the type of the great tribulation which is to come." Compare Claudian's description—

"Horret apex capitis; medio fera lumina surgunt
Vertice; cognatus dorso durescit amictus.
Armavit natura cutem dumique rubentes
Cuspidibus parvis multos acuere robores."—(*Epigr.* xxxiii.)

[8] Bochart, *Hierozoic.* ii. 495; Plin. *H. N.* ix. 50; "*latent quinis mensibus.*" If any one desires to see once more the endless guesses of interpreters, I may mention that Bede explains the "five months" of human life, because we have five senses; the scorpions are heretics. Vitringa makes the five months mean 150 years—the time of Gothic domination. Calovius explains them of the prevalence of Arianism. Bengel makes them mean 79½ years—the time of the Jewish afflictions in Persia in the sixth

But two circumstances seem to show that we are here dealing not with human avengers but with invisible demons of the air. One is that their leader is the Demon Destroyer; the other is that Christians, and Christians only, are expressly exempted from their power to hurt.

vi. Two woes yet remain. A voice is heard from the horns of the golden altar, bidding the sixth Angel loose the four Angels which are bound at the great river Euphrates,[1] who were prepared for the due time, to slay the third part of men. Immediately there ride forth *two hundred million horsemen*, breathing fire and smoke, on lion-headed steeds, armed with breastplates as of fire, jacinth, and brimstone. With their flames and their amphisbæna-stings they slay the third part of men;—and yet the rest do not repent.[2]

It is probable that the facts which loom large and lurid through this blood-red mist of Apocalyptic symbols are the swarms of Orientals who gathered to the destruction of Jerusalem in the train of Titus,[3] and the overwhelming Parthian host which was expected to avenge the ruin of Nero. It was a popular belief that he was still living; that he had taken refuge in the East; or that in any case Tiridates, who greatly admired him, or Vologeses, whose relations with him were very amicable, would bring him back with a whirlwind of triumphant horsemen.[4] These great Eastern Empires took deep and dangerous interest in the affairs of Rome. "Vologeses, King of the Parthians," says Suetonius, "had sent ambassadors to the Senate about the renewal of amity, and earnestly made this further request, that the memory of Nero should be held in honour. In my youth, twenty years after, when a false Nero had arisen, his name was so popular among the Parthians that he was strenuously assisted and with difficulty given up."[5] Both Suetonius and Tacitus relate that Vologeses offered to assist Vespasian with forty thousand mounted archers.[6] One of the circumstances which most deeply aroused the indignation of Titus against the Jews was that they had sent embassies for assistance to their kinsmen beyond the Euphrates.[7] In the *Sibylline Oracles* and in the *Ascension of Isaiah* we find distinct and repeated allusion to some

---

century. Hofmann refers to the five sins; and Züllig to the time of the Deluge (Gen. vii. 24). Some consider that Apollyon meant Napoleon. Bullinger explains the locusts of the monks; Bellarmine of the Protestants; and so on. And this is "*Exegesis!*"

[1] These four bound angels have never been explained. Some refer them to the Angel princes of the Assyrians, Babylonians, Medes, and Persians. Some to the four Roman stations on the Euphrates. Bound angels would recall to St. John's readers the notion of evil spirits. Comp. Tobit viii. 3; Matt. xii. 43—45.

[2] "Et gravis in geminum surgens caput amphisbæna." (Luc. *Phars.* ix. 719).

[3] Jos. *B. J.* iii. 1, § 3; 4, § 2. Four kings—Antiochus, Sohemus, Agrippa, and Malchus—contributed archers and horsemen. The latter, who was an Arabian Prince, sent 5,000 archers and 1,000 cavalry.

[4] See Suet. *Nero*, 13, 30, 47, 57; *Carm. Sib.* iv. 119—147; v. 93, and *passim;* viii. 70, etc.

[5] Comp. Tac. *H.* l. 2.

[6] Tac. *H.* iv. 51; Suet. *Vesp.* 6.   [7] Jos. *B. J.* vi. 6, § 2.

expected catastrophe from the realm of Parthia.[1] The metaphor will then closely resemble that of Jer. li. 27, "Cause the horses to come up as *rough caterpillars;* prepare against her the nations with the Kings of the Medes." These vaticinations do not belong in the least to the essence or heart of the Apocalypse. They are but passing illustrations of the great principles—the hopes and warnings—which it was meant to inculcate. Warriors from the Euphrates had their share in the siege of Jerusalem; and though Parthian horsemen did not sweep down from the East at that time against pagan Rome, yet in due time vengeance did fall on her, and in due time the countless hosts which swarmed from beyond the Euphrates may well be said to have destroyed a third of men, and yet to have left the rest impenitent for their crimes.

SECTION IV.
AN EPISODE.

Then follows another pause.

A mighty Angel arrayed with cloud, and with a rainbow encircling a sunlike face, descends from Heaven. His feet are like pillars of fire, and he sets one on the land and one on the sea.[2] A little open book is in his hand, and when he speaks in his lion-voice seven thunders utter their voices. But the seer is forbidden to write, and it is, therefore, absurd to conjecture what they uttered. Then the Angel, lifting his right hand to Heaven, swears by the Almighty Creator that no further time shall intervene, but that at the trumpet-blast of the seventh Angel the mystery of God shall be finished.[3] The seer is bidden to take the book and eat it. In his mouth it is sweet as honey; in his belly it is bitter. He is then bidden to prophesy again concerning many peoples, nations, tongues, and kings.

This magnificent episode tends to deepen and heighten the expectation of what the seventh Trumpet is to bring. The incident of eating the roll is also found in Ezek. ii. 9; iii. 3,[4] and the command to seal up

---

[1] "Towards evening war will arise, and the great fugitive of Rome (Nero) will raise the sword, and *with many myriads of men ride through the Euphrates*" (*Carm. Sib.* iv. 116, *seq.*). In the fifth book of Sibylline verses Nero is called "the dread serpent," who though vanquished would return, and give himself out as God (*Id.* v. 93, and *passim*). Nero is the "godless king," and murderer of his mother, of the Vision of Isaiah, who shall be destroyed after 1,335 days. Jerome on Dan. i. 28, says that many Christians expected the return of Nero as Antichrist.

[2] Since, in xi. 3, he says, "I will give power to my witnesses," we may perhaps see in this mighty Angel a representation of the Son of God. The descriptions correspond with those of the first (i. 15) and fourth Angel (iv. 3); see too Dan. xii. 1. Nic. de Lyra supposes that the Angel is meant for the Emperor Justinian; Luther, for the Pope; and Bede, for St. John himself! But it is worse than useless to record the vagaries of Apocalyptic interpretation.

[3] This is a reference to vi. 11, where the souls of the martyrs are bidden to rest, "still a little time."

[4] Comp. Jer. xv. 16, "Thy words were found, and I did eat them." The contents of the roll were sweet in anticipation, because he had hoped to read in them the perfect conversion of Jerusalem; but were bitter when their real import was known.

the "utterance" of the seven thunders resembles those given to Daniel, in Dan. viii. 26; xii. 4—9. The general meaning seems to be that much of the future is to be left in deep mystery, and that the messages yet to be delivered are of mingled import, sweet with consolations, yet bitter with awful judgments. The little book is intended to contain the issues of the seventh Trumpet. They are as yet undeveloped. Much of the vision hitherto has referred to the past. It has explained the meaning of the signs in the physical and political world which pointed to the Coming Judgment. It has made clear to believers that the woes which had shaken and were still shaking the earth were the beginning of the Palingenesia. What the seer has now to foreshadow is the Coming Dawn itself.

His first warning prophecies are addressed to the Jews. The judgments of the first six Seals affect the fourth part of all men alike—Christians, Jews, heathens. Before the opening of the seventh Seal, the servants of God—that is, all the members of the Christian Church—are sealed upon their foreheads. The judgments of the first six Trumpets affect, therefore, only the Jews and the heathens. But now, before the actual sounding of the seventh Trumpet, the Jews are won to God (xi. 13). St. John, like St. Paul, sees that it is only "in part" that "blindness hath befallen Israel," and only "until the fulness of the Gentiles be come in." Consequently the judgments of the first six Vials, though they extend over the whole earth, fall only upon the heathen. The seventh Vial brings upon all the unconverted the final judgment.

So that before the seventh Trumpet sounds the seer is bidden to measure the Temple, and altar, and worshippers with a measuring reed,[1] exclusively of the court which has been given over to the Gentiles, who are to trample down the Holy City for forty-two months—*i.e.*, three and a half years.[2] During these twelve hundred and sixty days, the Two Witnesses are to prophesy in sackcloth. They resemble the two olive trees and the two lamp-stands of the Temple.[3] With fire from their mouth they can destroy their enemies.[4] They can shut up the Heavens and smite the earth with plague. When their testimony is over, the Wild Beast out of the abyss shall kill them. Their dead bodies shall lie for three and a half days in the streets of Jerusalem, the spiritual Sodom [5] and Egypt, where their Lord was crucified. Men of all nations

---

[1] Ezek. xl.; Zech. iv.
[2] Dan. viii. 13; 1 Macc. iii. 45, 51; iv. 60; Luke xxi. 24. "Jerusalem shall be trodden down of the Gentiles, until the times of the Gentiles be fulfilled." The period 3½ years, 42 months, or 1,260 days (the half of seven years), is often found in Scripture in connexion with judgments. Dan. vii. 25 (Antiochus Epiphanes rages for "a time, times, and half a time"); ix. 27 (the oblation ceases for half a week); xii. 7, 11; comp. Luke xxi. 24; James v. 17 (time of drought at Elijah's prayer).
[3] Zech. iv. 3, 11.
[4] 2 Kings i. 10; Jer. v. 14; Ecclus. xlviii. 1. "Then stood up Elias the Prophet as fire, and his word burned like a lamp."
[5] Jerusalem (Sodom); Isa. i. 10; iii. 9: Jer. xxiii. 14; Ezek. xvi. 48, 49. There may

shall rejoice over their corpses,[1] and will not suffer them to be buried.[2] Then the breath of life from God shall enter into them. To the terror of all they shall stand upon their feet,[3] and at the bidding of a voice from Heaven shall ascend in cloud. Then a great earthquake, in which seven thousand shall perish, shall shake down a tenth of the city. The rest of its inhabitants repent in their terror, and give glory to the God of Heaven.

Every item of the symbolism, as will have been seen from the references, is borrowed from ancient prophecy: and yet neither in its details nor in its general import is the vision clear. There neither is nor ever has been in Christendom, in any age or among any school of interpreters, the smallest agreement, or even approach to an agreement, as to the events which the seer had in view.

What is the object of the measuring? Judging from Ezekiel and Zechariah, we should say that it is for construction and preservation; but in other passages the "stretching out of a line," or "setting a plumb-line," or "measuring with a line," are emblems of punishment or destruction.[4] As both destruction and preservation follow, the question is not easy to answer.

Again, is the seer now dealing with more or less definite history, whether contemporary or impending, or are the limits of past, present, and future obliterated in illustrating the Divine principles of the Eternal Now?

Again, does the vision refer to the actual Jerusalem, or to Jerusalem as an emblem of the whole Jewish race?

Once more, who are the Two Witnesses? Were there during the siege of Jerusalem, or during the general epoch of its imminent doom, two witnesses for God and for Christ, who in their characteristics recalled Moses and Elijah? Or are Moses and Elijah themselves symbolically described? Was the seer thinking of St. John the Baptist and our Lord?[5] or of the two Christian martyrs, James the son of Zebedee and James the Bishop of Jerusalem? or of two Christian witnesses of whom no history is recorded?[6] or of the murder of men like Zechariah, son of Berachiah? or is he indeed only thinking of Enoch and Elijah,[7] according to the almost unanimous tradition of the Early Church?[8] Or, again,

---

be a passing allusion to the detestable crimes of the Zealots, as recorded by Josephus, B. J. iv. 6, § 3.

[1] Congratulations of the enemies of God. Heb. viii. 10, 12; Esth. ix. 19, 22.
[2] 1 Kings xiii. 22; Isa. xiv. 18; Tobit i. 17.
[3] Ezek. xxxvii. 10.
[4] Lam. ii. 7, 8; Isa. xxxiv. 11; Amos vii. 6, 9; 2 Sam. viii. 2; 2 Kings xxi. 12, 13.
[5] Matt. xvii. 9—13. [6] Compare Rev. xi. 3 with Acts i. 8.
[7] In the Gospel of Nicodemus, Enoch says of himself and Elijah, "We are to live until the end of the world; and *then we are to be sent by God to resist Antichrist, and to be slain by him, and after three days to rise again, and to be caught up in clouds to meet the Lord*" (Gosp. Nicod. ii. 9).
[8] As preserved in the Commentary of Andreas, Bp. of Cæsarea in Cappadocia (comp. Gospel of Nicodemus xxv.). The view derives some sanction from Luke xvi. 31; and the Transfiguration, Matt. xvii. 3.

widening the symbol of Jerusalem to apply to the whole Jewish and Christian Church, is he thinking of St. James and St. Peter? or even of St. Peter and St. Paul as the two most illustrious victims of the Neronian persecution? None of these guesses are certain; and perhaps the same may be said of a solution which has sometimes occurred to me, that the Two Witnesses represent Jewish and Gentile converts to the Church. Is the description of their unburied corpses and subsequent ascension a symbol of the true fulfilment of their prophecies, the vindication of the truths they taught, the posthumous honours paid to their memories? Are we to understand the vision literally, or ideally, or allegorically? None can tell us; and who shall say?

Lastly, in the earthquake and the overthrow of a tenth part of the city, and the resultant terror and repentance, are we to see a picture of the anticipated results from the rapidly approaching siege of Jerusalem, or do they shadow forth the fate of the besieged, and the effect of their awful judgment upon the minds of their co-religionists throughout the world?[1]

These questions have never been satisfactorily answered, and perhaps never will be. We must be content to leave them in the half-light in which the uncertainty of nineteen Christian centuries has left them hitherto. There are no two writers of any importance who even approximately agree in the interpretation of the symbols. Those symbols were probably coloured not only by the language of the Old Testament, but by actual events in the siege. Such, for instance, was the terrific storm, the bursts of rain, the earthquake, "the amazing concussions and bellowings of the earth," during which the Idumeans were admitted, and in which Josephus says that "the whole system of the universe seemed to be in disorder."[2] In the subsequent massacres, the outer Temple—that is, the Court of the Gentiles—"was all overflowed with blood," and eight thousand five hundred corpses lay about its precincts. The insults to the unburied witnesses recall for a moment the fate of the younger Hanan and the priest Jesus, whose bodies were "cast out naked and unburied to be the food of dogs and wild beasts," but whose reputation was so thoroughly vindicated in the eyes of their countrymen, that Josephus pronounces a high eulogy upon them, and attributes the final doom of the city to the guilt incurred by their murderers.[3] The three and a half years, again, correspond with the actual length of the siege, together with the special horrors by which it was preluded. On the other hand, we know of nothing which corresponds to the fall of only the tenth part of the city, or to any repentance on the part of its inhabitants. Every interpretation seems to be beset with insuperable difficulties. No one school of commentators has been more successful than its rivals in furnishing an historical solution. May

---

[1] Doubtless the imagery is coloured by reminiscences of the events mentioned in Matt. xxvii. 51; xxviii. 2.
[2] Jos. *B. J.* iv. 5, § 5.
[3] *Ibid.* iv. 5, § 2.

not this be a sign that no exact historical counterpart to these symbols was contemplated by the seer, and that he is only moving in the region of ideal anticipation in order to use material symbols as the vehicle for eternal principles? He who has learnt the lesson, "not by power nor by might, but by my Spirit, saith the Lord of Hosts;" he who feels that the downfall of Evil and the ultimate triumph of Good has all the certainty of an inevitable law;—he who is waiting for the consolation of the spiritual Israel and the gathering of all nations into one flock under one shepherd at the Coming of the Lord,—he, it may be, has learnt more of the inner spirit and essential meaning of the Apocalypse than if he followed all the flickering lights of Exegesis which have led men into the marshes of rival fictions from the days of St. Victorinus down to the present time.

It has been often asserted that St. John meant to indicate the preservation of the Temple, in accordance with the general expectation and what was believed to be the express wish of Titus. But he does not say so. The measuring-rod may have been, as we have seen, a mark of coming overthrow. There is indeed an absolutely fatal argument against the notion that St. John anticipated that the Temple would be preserved. It is that our Lord on Olivet, in the very discourse on which the Apocalypse is an expanded and symbolic commentary, had declared without the least ambiguity, and in exact accordance with the result, that of that Temple not one stone should be left upon another. St. John indicates the conversion of the Jews, not the deliverance of Jerusalem.

But all that we cannot understand of St. John's symbolism belongs—the very failure of the Christian world in any age to understand it is a sufficient proof that it belongs—to the secondary, the subordinate, the less essential elements of the book. It must always be more than doubtful whether, in the very small fraction of the book which touches on the yet earthly and historic future, St. John intended to deal with specific vaticinations. At any rate, the meaning and literal accomplishment of such vaticinations is irrevocably lost for us, and, in point of fact, has never been known to any age of the Church—not even to the earliest, not even—so far as our records go—to Irenæus, the hearer of Polycarp, or to Polycarp, the hearer of St. John. What we *can* see in the whole vision of the Holy City and the Two Witnesses, is a prophecy of the ultimate conversion of the vast mass of Israel, and the final triumph of Christian testimony over every opposing force; further than this, there is nothing to be found in any commentary but fancy and guess-work, and arbitrary combinations, which may seem irrefragable to those who indulge in them, but which have not succeeded in convincing a handful of readers.

Then, at last, the seventh Angel sounds. There is a shout of jubilee in Heaven, because the kingdoms of the world have become the kingdom of our Lord and of His Christ. The Jews are now converted

There remains nothing but the judgment of the Gentiles and the Coming of Christ in the close of the æon. The earthly Temple has at last disappeared. In the Heaven is seen the Temple of God, open even to the Holiest Place, to which there may now be universal access at all times, through the Blood of Christ.

SECTION V.

THE WILD BEAST FROM THE SEA.

But, as though to compensate for the uncertain idealism of the last Vision, the meaning of the next Vision is retrospective, and, in its main outlines, perfectly clear.

A woman, arrayed with the sun, with the moon beneath her feet, and a crown of twelve stars around her head, brings forth a man-child. A huge scarlet dragon, with ten horns and seven diademed heads, whose tail sweeps after it the third part of the stars to the earth,[1] stands before her to devour the child the moment it is born, since the child is to rule the nations with a rod of iron. But the child is snatched up to the throne of God, and the woman flies into the wilderness, where she is to be nourished for 1,260 days.

All agree as to the interpretation. The star-crowned woman is the ideal Church of Israel.[2] The child she brings forth is a symbol, partly of the Messiah, partly of the Christian Church.[3] The scarlet dragon is an emblem of Satan, with the attributes of the world-power, as specially represented by the Roman Empire—of which a dragon was one of the later insignia. A dragon or serpent (for between the two words there is no real distinction) was also the apt inspirer for an Emperor who was believed to wear as an amulet a serpent's skin, and whose life, according to popular legend, had been saved by a serpent when he was an infant in the cradle.[4] Its seven heads and ten horns are seven Emperors[5] and ten Provincial Governors. But no power of legions, no violence of martyrdoms, can slay the infant Church of Christ. The Mother Church, the Church of Jerusalem, which, as it were, rocks the cradle of Gentile Christianity, is saved alike from Idumeans and Zealots, and the Roman armies which advance to besiege the Holy City. She flies to the mountains; to the wilderness; to the secure and desolate region of Pella, in which town, on the edge of the deserts of Arabia,[6]

---

[1] Dan. viii. 10 (of Antiochus Epiphanes).   [2] Isa. lxvi. 7, 8.
[3] The narrative is doubtless coloured by the perils and escapes of the Infant Christ (Matt. ii. 11—15).   [4] Suet. *Ner.* 6.
[5] The "seven" may include Julius Cæsar; or, excluding him, may include Otho. In the days of Julius, however, the name *Imperator* had not acquired its exclusive significance, and he never had the title of Princeps. Apocalyptic symbolism, dealing in mystic numbers, does not greatly trouble itself with these minor details. Thus the seven heads of the Beast serve alike to symbolise seven hills and seven emperors. The Dragon is at once Satan and the representative of Satan—the Empire of Pagan Rome.
[6] Josephus says of Peræa, "Its eastern limits *reach* to Arabia" (*B. J.* iii. 3, § 3). Pella is now Tabakát Fahil.

at an early period of the impending siege, the Christians took refuge, in accordance with their Lord's command.[1] They thus escaped the horrors of the three and a half years which elapsed between A.D. 67, when Vespasian began his dreadful work in Judea, and September, A.D. 70, when the city and Temple perished in blood and flame.

The attempts of the dragon are practically foredoomed. Michael and his Angels have warred against him, and flung him down to earth. There is no place for him in heaven as an accuser of the brethren, because the blood of the Lamb and the blood of the martyrs prevails against him. His great wrath must be confined to earth, and that only for a little time.[2]

He rages against the sun-clad woman, but she escapes from him into the wilderness, with the two great eagle-wings of divine protection.[3] There may have been, and doubtless was, an attempt to pursue and murder the flying Christians. We know that desertion from the city was checked by the most violent measures. Had any details of the flight to Pella been preserved to us, we should understand what is exactly meant by the dragon vomiting out of his mouth water as a river that she might be swept away, and by the earth helping her and swallowing the river. When Vespasian sent Placidus to chase the Jewish fugitives from Gadara, they were stopped by the swollen waters of the Jordan, and being compelled to hazard a battle, were driven in multitudes into the river, and 15,000 of them perished.[4] It is very probable that some such obstacle may have impeded the flight of the Christians, and that while they were enabled to escape safely by some manifestation of special Providence, many of their pursuers perished in the swollen stream.

The next Vision is not only plain, but must henceforth be regarded as so certain in its significance as to furnish us with a *point de repère* for all Apocalyptic interpretations. It is the Vision of the Wild Beast from the Sea; and beyond all shadow of doubt or uncertainty, the Wild Beast from the Sea is meant as a symbol of the Emperor Nero. Here, at any rate, St. John has neglected no single means by which he could make his meaning clear without deadly peril to himself and the Christian Church.

He describes this Wild Beast by no less than *sixteen* distinctive marks, and then all but tells us in so many words the name of the person whom it is intended to symbolise.

These distinctive marks are as follows:—

1. *It rises from the sea;*—by which is perhaps indicated not only a

---

[1] Matt. xxiv. 16; Luke xxi. 21.
[2] Comp. Luke x. 18. "I beheld Satan as lightning fallen from heaven," John xii. 31. "Now is the judgment of this world, now shall the prince of this world be cast out" (comp. 1 John iii. 8).
[3] For eagles' wings as the symbol of the Divine protection, see Ex. xix. 4; Deut. xxxii. 11.   [4] Jos. *B. J.* iv. 7, § 5.

Western power, and therefore, to a Jew, a power beyond the sea,[1] but perhaps especially one connected with the sea-washed peninsula of Italy.[2]

2. *It is a Beast like one of Daniel's four Beasts*, but more portentous and formidable. Daniel's four Beasts were the Chaldean lion, the Median bear, the Persian panther, and the Beast of Greek dominion, of which the ten horns represent the ten successors of Alexander,[3] and the little horn represents Antiochus Epiphanes. St. John's Beast being the all-comprehensive Roman power, is a combination of Daniel's Beasts. It is a panther, with bear's feet and a lion's mouth. It has seven heads,[4] which indicate (in the apparently arbitrary but perfectly normal vagueness of Jewish apocalyptic symbolism) both the seven hills of Rome and seven kings.[5] The Beast is a symbol interchangeably of the Roman Empire and of the Emperor. In fact, to a greater degree than at any period of history, the two were one. Roman history had dwindled down into a personal drama. The Roman Emperor could say with literal truth, "*L'État c'est moi*." And a Wild Beast was a Jew's natural symbol either for a Pagan kingdom or for its autocrat. When St. Paul was delivered from Nero, or his representative, he says quite naturally that "he was delivered out of the mouth of the lion" (2 Tim. iv. 17; comp. Heb. xi. 33). When he is alluding to his struggles with the mob and their leaders at Ephesus, he describes it as "fighting with wild beasts" (1- Cor. xv. 32). When Marsyas announced to Agrippa I. the death of Tiberius, he did so in the words, "*the lion* is dead."[6] Princes, as well as kingdoms, had been described under the same symbol by the Old Testament prophets.[7] Esther, in the Jewish legends, was said to have spoken of Xerxes as "the lion." Lactantius speaks of Nero as a *tam mala bestia*.[8] But, besides all these reasons, which made the symbol so easily intelligible, Renan may be right in conjecturing that there was yet another. It was that, on an occasion which was exceptionally infamous even for Nero, he had been *disguised as a wild beast, and in that disguise had been let loose from a cage* and personated the furies of a tiger or panther.[9]

---

[1] In the *Sibylline Oracles* (iii. 176) the beast rises "from the Western sea." In 2 Esdras xi. 1 the Eagle (Rome) comes *from the sea*.

[2] Such is the not improbable conjecture of Ewald. From xvii. 15 we might explain it of "the peoples, and multitudes, and nations, and tongues," over which Rome ruled. In Shabbath, f. 56 b, we are told that when Solomon married Pharaoh's daughter, Gabriel thrust a reed *into the sea*, and of the mud formed an island, on which Rome was built.

[3] The Diadochi, as they were called. See Grote, xii. 362.

[4] Comp. *Orac. Sibyll.* iii. 176, where also the many-headed beast is Rome.

[5] Rev. xvii. 9, 10.

[6] Jos. *Ant.* xviii 6, § 10.

[7] Ezek. xix. 1—9.

[8] The Sibyllists call Nero "the Beast." *De Mort. Persec.* 2.

[9] *L'Antéchrist*, p. 175. Suet. *Ner.* 29. I am told that to this day, in the Had Gadyo, which the Jews of Germany use at the Passover, their old persecutors are compared to various animals.

3. *This wild beast of Heathen Power has ten horns*, which represent the ten main provinces of Imperial Rome.[1] It has the power of the dragon—that is, it possesses the Satanic dominion of the "prince of the power of the air."

4. *On each of its heads is the name of blasphemy*. Every one of the seven "kings," however counted, had borne the (to Jewish ears) blasphemous surname of Augustus (*Sebastos*, "one to be adored"); had received apotheosis, and been spoken of as *Divus* after his death; had been honoured with statues, adorned with divine attributes; had been saluted with divine titles; and in some instances had been absolutely worshipped, and that in his lifetime, with temples and flamens—especially in the Asiatic provinces.

5. *The diadems are on the horns*, because the Roman Proconsuls, as delegates of the Emperor, enjoy no little share of the Cæsarean autocracy and splendour; but—

6. *The name of blasphemy* (for such is the true reading) *is only on the heads*, because the Emperor alone receives divine honour, and alone bears the daring title of "Augustus."

7. *One of the heads is wounded to death,*[2] *but the deadly wound is healed.* If there could be any doubt that this indicates the violent end, and universally expected return of Nero—or, which is the same thing for prophetic purposes, of one like him—that doubt seems to be removed by the parallel description of the 17th chapter, where we are told that of the seven kings of the mystic Babylon—

8. *The five are fallen, the one is, the other is not yet come;* and "the Beast that thou sawest was, and is not, and is about to come out of the abyss;" "the Beast that was and is not, even he is an eighth, and is of the seven."[3] Can language be more apparently perplexing? Yet its solution is obvious. No explanation worth the name has ever been offered of this enigma except that which makes it turn on the widespread expectation that Nero was either not really dead, or that, even if dead, he would in some strange way return. Only two or three slaves and people of humble rank had seen his corpse. All of these, except one or two soldiers and a single freedman of Galba, had been his humble adherents. It seemed inconceivable that after a hundred years of absolutism the last of the deified race of Cæsars should thus disappear like foam upon the water. The five kings are Augustus, Tiberius, Gaius (Caligula), Claudius, and Nero. Since the seer is

---

[1] Ten horns, as in Dan. vii. 24. There they are the Diadochi; here the provinces of Italy, Achaia, Asia, Syria, Egypt, Africa, Spain, Gaul, Britain, Germany (Renan, *L'Antechrist*, p. 13). The history of this troubled epoch amply justifies the additional touch of description in which, later on, they, in conjunction with the Beast (*i.e.*, the Provincial Governors and Generals, together with the Emperor), hate the harlot (*i.e.*, the City of Rome, and the *Senatus Populusque Romanus*), and devour her flesh, etc. Again and again in the civil disorders Rome was brought by Emperors and Proconsuls to the verge of ruin and despair.

[2] Just as the eagle's head (Nero) in 2 Esdras xi. 1, 36.

[3] Rev. xvii. 8, 10, 11. In ver. 8 the true reading is καὶ παρέσται.

writing in the reign of Galba, the fifth king (Nero) was, and is not; Otho, the seventh king, was not yet come. When he came, which could not be long delayed, for Galba was an old man—he was to reign for a short time, and then was to come the eighth, who, it was expected, would be Nero again, one of the previous seven, and so both the fifth and the eighth. For, strange to say, Nero still lived in the regrets alike of Romans and of Parthians.[1] Since Rome is the great city (xvii. 18), and the ten horns its provincial governors—"kings who had received no kingdom as yet" (xvii. 12)[2]—it seems difficult even to imagine any other explanation of symbols which it is quite clear that the Apostle *meant* to be understood, and which he assumed *would* be understood, since otherwise they would have been useless to his readers. But, after he has thus all but told us in so many words whom he means, the seer continues the hints by which he describes the characteristics of the Beast. He says that—

9. "*All the earth wondered after the Beast.*" In that day men rejoiced in the omnipotence of evil, and did homage to it in its concrete form. The Roman plebs had become "sottish, licentious, gamblers;" and one who was more gigantically sottish than themselves had become their ideal.[3] The best comment on this particular may be found in the description of Tacitus of the manner in which all Rome, from its proudest senators down to its humblest artisans, poured forth along the public ways to receive with acclamations the guilty wretch who was returning from Campania with his hands red with his murdered mother's blood.[4]

10. That the world "*worshipped the dragon, who gave his power to the Beast*," would be a natural Jewish way of indicating the belief that the Pagan world, when it offered holocausts for its Emperor, was adoring devils for deities.[5]

11. The cries of the world, "*Who is like unto the Beast? who is able to make war with him?*" sound like an echo of the shouts "Victories Olympic! victories Pythian! Nero the Hercules! Nero Apollo! Sacred one! The One of the Æon," *i.e.*, unparalleled in all the world! with which Dion Cassius tells us that he was greeted by the myriads of the populace, when, with the crowns of his 1,800 artistic triumphs, he returned from his insane and degraded perambulation of Greece.

12. "*The mouth speaking great things and blasphemies*" is the mouth which was incessantly uttering the most monstrous boasts and preten-

---

[1] Suet. *Ner.* 49, 50, 57; Tac. *H.* l. 2, 78; ii. 8; Dion Cassius, lxiv.; and Dio. Chrysost. *Orat.* xxi. 10.
[2] *As yet*—but several of them were to do so in the course of the next few years. This completely disposes of the supposed refutation of the views here maintained on the plea that the Roman Emperors did not wear *diadems*. The ten horns are kingdomless kings (*i.e.*, Provincial Governors), and yet even these *horns* are diademed (xiii. 1).
[3] Maurice, *Revel.* p. 238.
[4] Tac. *Ann.* xiv. 13; Dion Cass. lxi. 16; Suet. *Ner.* 39.
[5] 1 Cor. x. 20.

sions,[1] declaring that no one before himself had the least conception of what things an Emperor might do, and of the lengths to which he could go; the mouth which ordered the erection of his own colossus, 120 feet high, adorned with the insignia and attributes of the sun.[2] As for his blasphemies, Suetonius tells us that he was an avowed and even contemptuous atheist—"religionum usquequaque contemptor."[3]

13. "*Power was given him to act*[4] *forty-two months.*" The exact significance of this mystic number, which is also described as 1,260 days (xi. 2; xii. 6), and as "a time, times, and half a time" (xii. 14), is variously explained. The simplest explanation is that it refers to the time which elapsed between the beginning of Nero's persecution in Nov., 64, and his death in June, 68, which is almost exactly three and a half years.

14. "*It was given him to make war with the saints, and to overcome them,*" for it was he who began the terrible era of martyrdom, and put "a vast multitude" to death with hideous tortures on a false accusation.[5]

15. "*Power was given him over all kindreds, and tongues, and nations.*" Of the representatives of the world-powers in that day, Greece received him with frantic adulation, Parthia was in friendly relations with him, and Armenia, in the person of Tiridates, laid its diadem before his feet.[6] Even Herod the Great, though himself a powerful king, had been accustomed to talk of the "Almighty Romans."

16. All "*the inhabitants of the earth, except the followers of the Lamb, worshipped him.*" This, as we have seen, was literally true of the Emperors, both in their lifetime and after their death. At this dreadful period the cult of the Emperor was almost the only sincere worship which still existed.[7]

Then follow two verses (xiii. 9, 10) which do not bear directly upon the symbol. They are either a prophecy of retribution given for the consolation of the suffering saints,[8] or, if we take what seems on the whole to be the more probable reading, they are a declaration that the

---

[1] The "mouth speaking great things" of Antiochus Epiphanes, in Dan. vii. 8, 25, never uttered half such monstrous boasts as that of Nero.
[2] Pliny, *H. N.* xxxix. 7; Suet. *Ner.* 30—32; Dion Cass. lxvi. 15; Mart. *Spectac.* i. 1, *Ep.* i. 71. It required twenty-four elephants to drag it away in the reign of Hadrian. Spart. *Hadr.* 19.
[3] *Nero*, 56. The first object of his veneration was the Syrian goddess "hanc mox ita sprevit ut urinâ contaminaret."
[4] xiii. 5. ποιῆσαι, can hardly mean "to continue" as in the English version. It must mean "to act," "to do what he will;" and, if so, the addition of ὃ θέλει in א is at least a correct gloss.
[5] Tac. *Ann.* xv. 44.
[6] Tac. *Ann.* xiv. 26; Suet. *Ner.* 13.
[7] See Boissier, *La Religion Romaine*, i. 122—208. Augustus disliked all personal worship, and insisted that his cult should be joined to that of Rome. But Caligula claimed to be worshipped in person (Suet. *Cal.* 21), and Nero received *apotheosis* in his lifetime. Tac. *Ann.* xv. 74.
[8] Perhaps an allusion to Nero's supposed death and flight.

saints must indeed suffer, but that their sufferings should be endured in faith and patience.[1]

In these paragraphs, then, we have sixteen hints as to who and what is intended by the Apocalyptic Wild Beast, and it is undeniable that *every one of these directly points to Rome and Nero.* They point so directly to Rome and to Nero that it is difficult to conceive how the writer could have expressed his meaning *less* enigmatically, if he adopted at all that well-understood literary method of Jewish Apocalypses which was enigmatical in its very nature.[2] The most remarkable indication that Nero is mainly intended is that it is exactly in the *most* enigmatical particulars that the resemblance is most close. He was mortally wounded, and yet (according to the then belief, which is here adopted for purposes of description, and which was symbolically though not literally true) the wound was *healed;* and he was a fifth king who was, and is not, and yet (so St. John indicates him by the popular belief) should be once more the eighth king, and one of the seven.[3] If we had not the perfectly simple clue to what what was indicated by this strangely riddling description, we might give up the interpretation as insoluble; but the clue is preserved for us, not only by Jewish Talmudists,[4] and Pagan historians and authors, such as Tacitus,[5] Suetonius,[6] Dion Cassius,[7] and Dion Chrysostom;[8] but also by Christian fathers like St. Irenæus,[9] Lactantius,[10] St. Victorinus, Sulpicius Severus,[11] and the Sibylline books;[12] and even by St. Jerome,[13] and by St. Augustine.[14] Nothing can prove more decisively than these references that for four centuries many Christians identified Nero with the Beast. An Eastern kingdom had long been promised to him by soothsayers.[15] The author of the *Ascension of Isaiah* says that Beliar shall descend from the sky in the form of man, an impious king, the murderer of his mother (*i.e.*, in the form of Nero).[16] So, too, Commodianus, in the third century, talks of

---

[1] Rev. xiii. 10.
[2] How strange were the symbolic devices of Apocalyptists we see in the 8th Book of the Sibyllines, where Hadrian is described as "having a name like that of a sea" (the Hadriatic), and is called "the wretched one," because of the resemblance of his name (Ælianus) to the Greek *eleeinos* (*Orac. Sib.* viii. 52, 59).
[3] It was believed that he would return from the *East*, by the aid of Parthians, among whom he was thought to have taken refuge.
[4] The tract Gittin, quoted by Grätz, *Gesch. d. Judenth.* vol. iv. p. 203.
[5] Tac. *Hist.* ii. 8. [6] Suet. *Ner.* 57, et ibi Casaubon.
[7] Dion Cass.; Xiphilinus, lxiv. 9; see Zonaras, *Ann.* xi. 15—18. The expectation was most current in Asia Minor, and Nero's thoughts were incessantly turned to the East by astrologers, etc. Tac. *Hist.* ii. 95; *Ann.* xv. 36; Suet. *Ner.* 40—47.
[8] Dion Chrysost. *Orat.* xxi. (i. p. 504, ed. Reiske: "Even now all desire him to live, and most persons think that he is still alive.")
[9] Iren. *l.c.* [10] Lactant. *De Mort. Persec.* 2.
[11] Sulp. Sever. *Hist. Sac.* ii. 28. "It is the current opinion of many that he is yet to come as Antichrist." This was written A.D. 403.
[12] *Sibyll.* v. 33; viii. 71. [13] Jer. *In Dan.* xi. 28.
[14] Aug. *De Civ. Dei*, xx. 19, 3. "Unde nonnulli ipsum (Neronem) resurrecturum et futurum Antichristum suspicantur, alii vero nec occisum putant sed subtractum potius."
[15] Suet. *Ner.* 40. [16] *Ascens. Is.* iv. 2—11.

Nero being raised from the under-world.[1] Nay, more, we can appeal to the earliest extant Greek commentary on the Apocalypse—that of Andreas, Bishop of the Cappadocian Cæsarea, who says that "the king of the Romans shall come as Antichrist to destroy" the four kingdoms of Daniel. It would have been strange that the Christian world should have felt any doubt that Nero is intended, if all history did not show the extent to which dogmatic bias—which only resorts to Scripture in order to find there its own ready-made convictions—has dominated for centuries over simple and straightforward exegesis. But as though to exclude *any possibility of doubt* about the matter, St. John, after all these clear indications, has all but told us in express words the name of the man whom he means by his Antichrist and Wild Beast—by this deified yet slain and to-be-resuscitated murderer of the saints. He does so in the last verses of the chapter. They furnish a *seventeenth* detail, in which the indications of the seer point immediately and distinctly to the worst of the Roman Emperors.

17. "Here is wisdom," he says (chap. xiii. 18); or, as he expresses it in chap. xvii. 9, "wisdom is needed to grasp the meaning of my symbol;" or, perhaps, as Ewald understands it, "this is the sense— whoever has wisdom will understand it thus." "Let him that hath understanding count the number of the Beast; for *it is the number of a man.*" In other words, he tells us that he now intends to *indicate numerically* the name which he dared not actually express. A Jew or Jewish Christian would at once be aware that he now intends to give an instance of one of the forms of that Kabbalistic method, of which traces are found even in the ancient prophets, and which was known to the Rabbis as *Gematria—i.e.*, Geometry, or the numerical indication of names.[2] Gentile Christians were not so familiar with this method;[3] but we see from Irenæus that they could easily have got the general clue from their Judaic brethren, to whom the Apocalypse is mainly ad-

---

[1] Commodian. *Instr.* 41.

[2] For an account of Gematria, and numerous illustrations of it, I may refer to my paper on Rabbinic Exegesis in the *Expositor* for 1877, vol. v. Similarly among Egyptian mystics the God *Thouth* was spoken of by the cypher 1218. On the Gnostic gems the word Abraxas is used as isopsephic to Meithras (the sun) because the letters of both names = 325.

[3] It was, however, by no means unknown to educated Greeks under the name of *isopsephia*. For instance, they called verses *isopsephics* when their letters made up numerically the same sum. In the Anthology we find an epigram which begins—

"One, hearing the words Demagoras and Plague (Loimos), which are of equal numerical value"—

which he could test in a moment, since, in Greek letters, Demagoras is—

$$4 + 1 + 40 + 1 + 3 + 70 + 100 + 1 + 200 = 420$$
$$\Delta\ \text{A}\ \text{M}\ \text{A}\ \Gamma\ \text{O}\ \text{P}\ \text{A}\ \Sigma$$

and Loimos (Plague) is—

$$30 + 70 + 10 + 40 + 70 + 200 = 420$$
$$\Lambda\ \text{O}\ \text{I}\ \text{M}\ \text{O}\ \Sigma$$

There are isopsephic inscriptions in the *Corpus Inscr. Græc.* 3541–3546. (*See* Aul. Gell. xiv. 14.)

dressed.[1] There was not much danger of a secret being betrayed which might cost the life of any one who mentioned it, and at the same time imperil the whole community. What St. John says in effect is: "I shall now give you the name of the Wild Beast in its *numerical value*. You have heard many specimens of this method, so that you can apply it in this instance, though I warn you that it may give you some difficulty." He evidently *intended* some of them to find out the number of the Beast, which was also the number of a man, while he pointed out that there was *one* unexpected element in the particular solution. If it had been merely a name in the numerical value of its *Greek* letters there would have been so little difficulty about it that any ordinarily educated reader might have discovered it after a few trials. He would only have to find out what living men there were who had the dozen or more attributes which the seer had given to the Beast, and whose names, counted by the value of the letters, made up the number of 666. As there was scarcely *any* other living person to whom the Apocalyptic description could apply, Nero's was probably the first name which a Jewish Christian reader would have tried. And here he would have been at once baffled. In Greek letters he would have found that *Nerōn* made $50 + 5 + 100 + 800 + 50 = 1005$. If he tried Neron Kaisar, it would only make $1005 + 332 = 1337$. Almost every combination which he tried would fail, and very possibly he would give up the task in despair, with the thought that he did not possess the requisite "wisdom," though he may have solved many such problems in Sibylline or similar books. Thus, in the Sibylline books, the poet indicates the name Jesus, in Greek Ἰησοῦς, by saying that it is a word which has 4 vowels and 2 consonants, and that the whole number is equivalent to 8 units, 8 tens, 8 hundreds—*i.e.*, 888 (Ἰησοῦς $= 10 + 8 + 200 + 70 + 400 + 200 = 888$), and no Greek-speaking Christian would have had any trouble in solving the riddle. Since, however, all the other indications pointed so clearly to Rome and Nero, the Greek Christian reader might very naturally have hit upon "Latinus" (Λατεινὸς $= 30 + 1 + 300 + 5 + 10 + 50 + 70 + 200 = 666$) as a sort of general indication of Rome and "a Latin man." This accounts for the prevalence of this explanation among the Fathers, beginning with St. Irenæus, who may have heard it from St. Polycarp, who had seen St. John in his old age.[2] These early Christian writers were, so to speak, on the right track; yet with "Latinus" they could hardly have been quite satisfied. It is a vague adjective, and the names *Latium* and *Latinus* had long been practically obsolete. If this were indeed the

---

[1] The Sibyllist describes Nero as the Emperor whose sign is 50, "*a fearful serpent who shall cause a grievous war.*" N, the initial letter of Nero, $= 50$. I have already referred to the fancy of Barnabas about Abraham's 318 servants as represented by ΙΗΤ, and so a sort of symbol of Jesus on the Cross. Similarly in Tertullian (*Carm. adv. Marc.* iii. 4), the victory of Gideon's 300 is connected with the fact that $300 = $ T, the sign of the Cross: "Hoc etiam signo praedonum stravit acervos."

[2] Iren. *Adv. Haer.* v. 30; Hippolyt. *De Christo*, p. 26.

solution, they might have put down its vagueness to intentional obscurity. We can hardly conceive what care a Jewish writer had to take if he touched in any respect unfavourably upon the imperial power in those days of *delators* and *laesa majestas*.¹ Josephus was in high favour, first with Poppæa and then with the Flavian dynasty; at Rome he was so great and influential that he probably had the honour of a statue in the imperial city :²—yet he stops abruptly in his explanation of the prophecies of Daniel, with a mysterious hint that he does not deem it prudent to say more.³ This evidently was because he feared that, if he touched on any explanation of the work of destruction wrought by the "stone cut without hands," he might seem to be threatening future ruin and extinction to the Roman Empire; and to do this went beyond his very limited daring. It was perhaps the complete unsatisfactoriness of the solution "*Lateinos*" which made some Christians, as Irenæus further tells us, try the name *Teitan*, which also gives the mystic number 666 (*Teitan* = 300 + 5 + 10 + 300 + 1 + 50 = 666), and which has the additional advantage of being a word of six letters. In this instance also ingenuity was not very far astray; for Titan was one of the old poetic names of the Sun, and the Sun was the deity whose attributes Nero most affected, as all the world was able to judge from seeing his colossus with radiated head, of which the substructure of the base still remains close by the ruins of the Colosseum.⁴ The mob which greeted him with shouts of "Nero-Apollo!" were well aware that he had a predilection for this title.

On the whole, however, the Greek Christians must have remained a little perplexed, a little dissatisfied, and must have been inclined to say, with some of the Fathers,⁵ that only time could reveal the secret; or else to believe that perhaps there was more than one solution. They must, however, have known what was *meant*, even if the exact equinumeration of any words which they could hit upon did not entirely satisfy them. And this was the general condition in which the secret remained in the early Christian Church. At any rate there stood the strange number before them.

$$\chi\xi\varsigma'$$

The very look of it was awful. The first letter was the initial letter of the name of Christ. The last letter was the first double-letter (*st*) of the Cross (*stauros*). Between the two the Serpent stood confessed with its writhing sign and hissing sound.⁶ The whole formed a triple re-

---

¹ See Tac. *Ann.* iii. 38, iv. 50; *Hist.* i. 77; Suet. *Ner.* 32 :—"tum ut lege majestatis, facta dictaque omnia, quibus modo delator non deesset tenerentur."
² Juv. *Sat.* i. 130.
³ Jos. *Antt.* x. 10, § 4: "Daniel did also declare the meaning of the stone to the king; *but I do not think proper to relate it.*"
⁴ What was meant by the guess *Euanthas* is uncertain. Could it be an allusion to the "aurea caesaries" which grew down over Nero's neck?
⁵ Irenæus, v. 30.   ⁶ Rev. xii. 9, xx. 2.

petition of 6, the essential number of toil and imperfection; and this numerical symbol of the Antichrist, 666, stood in terrible opposition to 888—the three perfect 8's of the name of Jesus.

But Jewish readers—and, as we have said, it was to Jewish readers that the Apocalypse was primarily addressed—would find none of the difficulties which perplexed their Gentile fellow-Christians. The Apostle had warned them that the solution did not lie so much on the surface as was usual in similar enigmas. Every Jewish reader, of course, saw that the Beast was a symbol for Nero.[1] And both Jews and Christians regarded Nero as also having close affinities with the serpent or dragon. That Nero was intended would be as clear to a Jew as that Babylon meant Rome, though Rome is never mentioned. He would not try the name Nero Cæsar in Latin, because *isopsephia* (which the Jew called *Gematria*) was almost unknown among the Romans, and their alphabetic numeration was wholly defective. He might try Νέρων Καῖσαρ in Greek, but it would not give him the right number. Then, as with a flash of intuition, it would occur to him to try the name *in Hebrew*.[2] The Apostle was writing as a Hebrew, was evidently thinking as a Hebrew.[3] His solœcistic Greek was sufficient to prove that the language was unfamiliar to him, and that all persons of whom he thought would primarily present themselves to his mind by their Hebrew designations. This, too, would render the cryptograph additionally secure against the prying inquisition of treacherous Pagan informers. It would have been to the last degree perilous to make the secret *too* clear. Accordingly, the Jewish Christian would have tried the name as he *thought* of the name—that is *in Hebrew letters*. And the moment that he did this the secret stood revealed. No Jew ever thought of Nero except as " *Neron Kesar*," and this gives at once—נרון קסר = 50 + 200 + 6 + 50 + 100 + 60 + 200 = 666.[4]

Jewish Christians were familiar with enigmas of this kind. They occur even in the ancient Prophets after the days of Jeremiah, and are

---

[1] The Sibyllists had already spoken of Caligula as Beliar (*Carm.* iii. 63), and as a serpent. The stories of the serpent which had crawled from Nero's cradle, and of his serpent-amulet (*v. supra*, p. 461) would add significance to the symbolism.

[2] I am not sure that a Jew would not have tried Hebrew letters at once. A Talmudic scholar wrote to tell me that my number for Rome (*supra*, p. 427) was wrong, because he had tried it in Hebrew letters. It had not occurred to him to try it in Greek letters!

[3] See the startling Hebraism in the Greek of Rev. i. 4, and comp. Rev. ix. 11; xvi. 16.

[4] The name was so written in Jewish inscriptions. See Ewald, *Die Johann. Schriften*, ii. 203; Buxtorf. *Lex Rabbin. s.v.* The name Cæsarea appears in the Talmud as קסרין. Renan mentions the remarkable fact that the name for Antichrist in Armenian is *Neren* (ii. 23). Ewald found that Josippon writes the name קסר. The secret has been almost simultaneously re-discovered of late years by Fritzsche in Halle, by Benary in Berlin, by Reuss in Strasbourg, and by Hitzig in Heidelberg. See Bleek, *Vorlesungen*, 292 ff.; Krenkel, *Der Apostel Johannes*, 88; Volkmar, *Offenbarung*, 18 and 214. Ewald was only prevented from making the discovery in 1828 by the assumption, which he afterwards found to be erroneous, that Cæsar must be spelt in Hebrew with a *yod*. He therefore conjectured " Cæsar of Rome " (קסר רום) (*Johann. Schrift.* ii. 263).

found in the Old Testament Scriptures.[1] The Jewish Christians could not have hesitated for a moment in the conclusion that in the Hebrew name of Nero the solution of the riddle stood revealed. The Jews were remarkable for reticence, and men are specially liable to keep their secrets to themselves when they involve matters of life and death. Many methods and secrets of Rabbinic exegesis, though of great value, have remained unrevealed by Jews to Christians, simply because the jealous exclusiveness and haughty prejudice of that singular race —feelings which, it must be confessed, have been due in no small degree to the brutality of their enemies—make them indifferent to the religious views of others. It is, therefore, by no means remarkable that the Asiatic Judaists, who first read St. John's Apocalypse, did not betray what they must have recognised to be the name which exactly corresponded with the number of the Beast. They might be pardoned if they were reluctant to place their lives and the very existence of their churches at the mercy of Gentile brethren, of whose prudence and fidelity they could not in every instance be perfectly secure. Enough, however, may have escaped them to put others in the right direction; and, as far as the *general* understanding of the Apostle's meaning was concerned, it mattered very little whether the guessed solution was *Lateinos*, or *Teitan*, or *Neron Kesar*, since all three words were but varying forms of the same essential thing. All the earliest Christian writers on the Apocalypse, from Irenæus down to Victorinus of Pettau[2] and Commodian in the fourth, and Andreas[3] in the fifth, and St. Beatus in the eighth century, connect Nero, or some Roman Emperor, with the Apocalyptic Beast.

If any confirmation could possibly be wanting to this conclusion, we find it in the curious fact recorded by Irenæus that, in some copies, he found the reading 616. Now this change can hardly have been due to *carelessness*. The letters χξϛ´ were so singular, even in their external form, that no one would have been likely to alter them into χιϛ´ or 616.[4] But if the above solution be correct, this remarkable and ancient variation is at once explained and accounted for. A Jewish Christian, trying his Hebrew solution, which would (as he knew) defend the interpretation from dangerous Gentiles, may have been puzzled by the *n* in Neron Kesar. Although the name was so written in Hebrew,

---

[1] Thus in Jerem. li. 41, "Sheshach" stands for "Babel," by the transmutation of letters known as Atbash (a subspecies of what the Rabbis call *Themourah* or "change"); and in li. 1, "*they that dwell in the midst of them*," means the Chaldæans (lebâ kamai = Kasdim); and in Isa. vii. 6, Tabeal, by another sort of Themourah, gives us the name of Remaliah. See my Paper in the *Expositor*, v. 375.

[2] "Hunc ergo—sc. Neronem—suscitatum Deus mittet regem dignum dignis et Christum qualem meruerunt Judaei" (Vict. Pett. *in Apoc.* xiii.).

[3] ὃν κρατήσει ὁ Ἀντίχριστος ὡς Ῥωμαίων βασιλεὺς ἐλευσόμενος (Andr.).

[4] ἑξήκοντα δέκα ἕξ. is the reading of the Codex Ephraemi. Irenæus appeals for the correctness of the reading 666 not only to all the good and ancient MSS., but to the direct testimony of those who had seen St. John (μαρτυρούντων αὐτῶν ἐκείνων τῶν κατ᾽ ὄψιν τὸν Ἰωάννην ἑωρακότων).

he knew that to Romans, and Gentiles generally, the name was always Nero Cæsar, not Neron. But Nero Kesar in Hebrew, omitting the final *n*, gave 616, not 666; and he may have altered the reading because he imagined that, in an unimportant particular, it made the solution more suitable and easy.

One objection will be made at once to this solution. Nero, it will be said, never did return. The belief in his return, though it showed an obstinate vitality, was a mere chimæra. St. John could not have enshrined in his Apocalypse what turned out to be but a popular mistake.

Such an objection is entitled to respect, but it imports *à priori* considerations into a plain matter of exegesis. This belief about Nero's return *did* prevail in the Christian, no less than in the Pagan, world. It is found again and again in the Sibylline books, and in later Christian writers. In the Pagan world it led to the success of more than one false Nero. It is probable that one of these was making himself extremely formidable in the very region in which St. John was writing, and at that very time.[1] In the Christian world the belief was still existent, three centuries later, that Nero would return in person as the future Antichrist. The vividness of the contemporary belief must be measured by its extraordinary permanence.

We have no right, then, to frame our interpretation of Scripture by our theories respecting the character and limits of how it ought to be written. Our duty is, on the contrary, to discover its interpretation, and to be guided by this to the true theory of its claims. When we study the meaning of a passage, our sole and our solemn aim should be to get at the real meaning, and not to repudiate or to gloss over that meaning in obedience to subjective convictions. We should not conceal from ourselves that to *get rid* of a plain explanation because it does not at once fall in with our ready-made dogmas is a dishonesty which, in the language of the Book of Job, is a form of "lying for God." God's own rebuke to Job's three friends was meant to teach mankind for ever that truth and charity are infinitely more sacred than either conventional orthodoxy or traditional exegesis.

In reality, however, this question is not one which in any way affects the dignity of revelation. St. John uses the common belief, as he might have used any other contemporary fact, or any other contemporary notion, merely to help him in the elaboration of his symbol, and to enable him to point out the person whom he is describing. The arrangement of the symbolism affects in nowise the truth of the great *principles* which he reveals. The Divine hopes and consolations of which the Apocalypse is full, the priceless lessons in which it abounds, are not in the slightest degree affected by the circumstance that he depicts the Neronian Wild Beast in the colours which every other historian, whether secular or sacred, would have used for his delineation.

---

[1] Tac. *H.* i. 2; ii. 8; Suet. *Ner.* 57; Zonaras, xi. 15, 18, etc.

But farther, be it observed that, even if this detail of Nero's personal return had been meant to be in any way essential to the general prediction, it was, with singular exactness, symbolically fulfilled. Although Nero had not (as was popularly supposed) taken refuge among the Parthians, and never was restored by their aid, as was the common expectation of that day, yet such an anticipation is not directly involved in the Apocalypse, and in any case does not belong to its essential meaning. Every successive Antichrist has shown the Neronian characteristics. If the prophecy of the return of Elijah the Prophet was adequately fulfilled in the ministry of John the Baptist, the prophecy of the returning Nero was adequately fulfilled in Domitian, in Decius, in Diocletian, in many a subsequent persecutor of the saints of God. Allegory is only susceptible of allegoric interpretation; and in the person of Domitian, as we shall see further on,[1] the prophecy of Antichrist in the person of *Nero redivivus* may be regarded as having been almost literally, and in every sense symbolically, fulfilled. I am well aware that even recent English commentators have done their best to treat this view of the Apocalypse with suspicion and contempt, to treat it as unworthy of their modern theory of "verbal dictation." Let them beware lest in so doing they be haply found to fight against God, and lest, in their attempts to force upon Christendom their private interpretations of prophecy, they only succeed in bringing all prophecy into suspicion and contempt.[2]

SECTION VI.

THE SECOND BEAST AND THE FALSE PROPHET.

But if Nero be the Wild Beast from the sea, who is the Wild Beast from the land? If Nero be, in the parallel passages, the death-wounded yet unslain *head* of the Beast, who is the False Prophet which wrought the signs before him?

Our great difficulty in answering this question arises from the fact that not the lightest breath of tradition upon the subject has been preserved in the first two centuries. The earliest suggestion is furnished by Victorinus at the close of the third. All commentators alike, Præterist, Futurist, Continuous-Historical, and Allegorical, with all their subdivisions, have here been reduced to manifest perplexity, and have been forced to content themselves with explanations which do violence to one or more of the indications by which we must be guided.

What are those indications?

They are mainly given in Rev. xiii. 11—17, and are as follows:—

1. I saw another wild beast coming up out of the earth.

---

[1] See *infra*, pp. 482, 483.
[2] See some wise remarks of Ewald, *Johann. Schrift.* ii. 15.

2. And he had two horns like unto a lamb.
3. And he spake as a dragon.
4. And he exercised all the authority of the first Beast in his sight.
5. And he maketh the earth to worship the first Beast whose death-stroke was healed.
6. And he doeth great signs which it was given him to do in the sight of the Beast, that he should even make fire to come down from heaven upon the earth by reason of the signs which it was given him to do in the sight of the Beast, saying to them that dwell on the earth that they should make an image to the Beast who hath the stroke of the sword and lived.
7. He gives breath to the image of the Beast, and makes it speak.
8. He causes the execution of those who will not worship the image of the Beast.
9. He makes men of all ranks and classes receive a stamp on their right hand or their forehead.
10. He prevents all who have not the mark of the Beast (his name and the number of his name) from buying and selling.

The only additional clue is that in the parallel description of Rev. xix. 20 he is described under another aspect as "the False Prophet that wrought the signs in the sight of the Beast wherewith he deceived those that had received his mark and worshipped his image."

Now in trying to discover the meaning of the symbol, we may again pass over the countless idle guesses of those who have endeavoured to torture the Apocalypse into a prediction of the details of all subsequent Christian history. With these guesses we are not concerned. They have, as a rule, only been adopted by the individual commentators who suggested them. Nothing, we may be sure, was further from the mind of the writer than a desire to gratify the fantastic curiosity of eighteen centuries of Christians as to events yet future which they have been always unable to foresee, or even subsequently to recognise. The resemblance of Nero to Antiochus Epiphanes as the personification of savage enmity to the people of God in the book of Daniel, is enough to suggest the certainty that in the case of the second Beast, as in the case of the first, the seer has primarily in view some contemporary person or phenomenon.

Setting aside many conjectures, which I have fully examined elsewhere,[1] that the Second Beast is meant for Balbillus of Ephesus, or Tiberius Alexander, or Josephus, or Gessius Florus, three conjectures alone seem to me to be worthy of special consideration:—

I. One is suggested by Victorinus of Pettau (A.D. 303). He thinks that by this Wild Beast and False Prophet is meant the Roman Augurial system.

There is in this suggestion much probability, and we may point out

[1] In the *Expositor* for Sept. 1881.

in passing that Victorinus in the third century, no less than Irenæus in the second, saw that the Apocalypse moved in the plane of contemporary events. The early mention of this solution may have been due to some echo of still more ancient tradition. Certain it is that, in appearing to identify the Second Beast with the "False Prophet" (xvi. 13; xix. 20; xx. 10), St. John lends some sanction to this view. The influence exercised by *Chaldæans, Mathematici, Astrologers, Magi, Augurs, Medici, Prophets, Casters of Horoscopes, Sorcerers, Dream-interpreters, Sibyllists*[1]—Oriental charlatans of every description, from Apollonius of Tyana and Alexander of Abonoteichos down to Peregrinus—is a phenomenon which constantly meets us in the Age of the Cæsars. They appeared in Rome more than two centuries before Christ. Ennius mentions them with contempt.[2] As early as B.C. 139, they had been ordered to quit Italy in ten days. In B.C. 33 they had again been banished by the Ædile M. Agrippa. Augustus and Tiberius had also directed severe edicts against them.[3] But they held their ground.[4] Tacitus calls the edict of Claudius "severe and ineffectual." We see, both from Tacitus and from the anecdotage of Suetonius, that almost every Emperor felt and indulged in some curiosity about these divinations. Tiberius reckoned the "Chaldæan" Thrasyllus among his intimate friends.[5] Poppæa, the wife of Nero, had "many" of them in her household.[6] Nero had his Balbillus;[7] Otho his Ptolomæus;[8] Vespasian his Seleucus;[9] Domitian his Ascletarion.[10] Agrippina depended on Chaldæans for the favourable hour of Nero's usurpation.[11] There is scarcely one of all the Emperors whose history had not some connexion or other with auguries, prophecies, and dreams.[12] In the reign of Nero these prognosticators were brought into special prominence,[13] because the restless and tortured conscience of the Antichrist was constantly seeking to pry into futurity. It is remarkable that they especially encouraged his Oriental dreams, and that some of them even went as far as to promise him the empire of Jerusalem.

It has, however, been generally felt that the institution of Prophets was not so prominent even in Nero's reign as to admit of our applying to it the ten definite indications of the Apocalyptic seer. False prophets were hardly in any sense a *delegate* and *alter ego* of the Emperor. There is at least a probability that as one person is specially

---

[1] Σιβυλλισταί. Plutarch, *Marius*, 42. See Tac. *Ann.* xii. 52; *Hist.* i. 22, ii. 62; Suet. *Tib.* 36, *Vitell.* 14; Juv. *Sat.* vi. 542.
[2] Cic. *De Div.* i. 58.
[3] See Val. Max. i. 3; Dion Cass. xlix. 1; Tac. *Ann.* ii. 27, 32; iii. 22; iv. 58; vi. 20.
[4] Tac. *Ann.* xii. 52.
[5] Tac. *Ann.* vi. 21.
[6] Tac. *Hist.* i. 22.
[7] Suet. *Nero*, 36.
[8] Suet. *Otho*, 4; Tac. *Hist.* i. 22, 23.
[9] Tac. *Hist.* ii. 8.
[10] Suet. *Domit.* 15.
[11] Tac. *Ann.* xii. 68.
[12] Suet. *Jul. Caesar*, vii. 61; *Octav.* 94; *Tiber.* 16; *Calig.* 57; *Otho*, 4; *Titus*, ii. 9; *Domit.* xiv. 16. For Nero, see Tac. *Ann.* xiv. 9.
[13] Suet. *Ner.* 34, 36, 40. Plin. *H. N.* xxx. 2.

pointed to by the symbol of the Beast, so one person is intended by his False Prophet.

II. More, on the whole, is to be said in favour of the view that the Second Beast, or False Prophet, is SIMON MAGUS. In one direction he corresponds with remarkable closeness to the symbols. His baptism gave him a certain lamb-like semblance to Christianity, while his gross deceptions were the voice of the serpent. Christian tradition, which may well be founded on facts, has much to say about his pretended miracles, and two classes of those miracles are of the very character here indicated. It is said, for instance, that the Second Beast makes fire come down upon the earth. Now among the miracles of Simon we are told that one was to appear clothed in flame.[1] It is said that the Second Beast animates an image of the Beast, and Simon is expressly said to have made statues move, so that he may well have also pretended to make them speak.[2] If he attempted this imposture at all he is more likely to have applied it to the statue of the Emperor —" the image of the Beast "—than to any other. All that would have been needed was a little machinery and a little ventriloquism. If the Middle Ages were deceived by winking Madonnas and glaring crucifixes it must have been equally easy to delude the Roman mob by moving statues. Further, it was at Rome that Simon displayed his magic powers, and they are said to have been exercised with the immediate object of winning influence over Nero. In this the legend declares that he entirely succeeded, and that his influence was wielded to induce the Emperor to persecute and massacre the Christians. These features appear not in one, but in many authors,[3] and though the sources from which we now derive this information are exceedingly dubious, there is nothing improbable in the supposition that Simon Magus did find his way to Rome—the reservoir, as Tacitus says, into which all things infamous and shameful flowed[4]—and did there endeavour to win dupes by the same magical arts which had gained him so many votaries among the simple Samaritans.[5] If we suppose that he dazzled the mind of Nero, and that he was one of those men of Jewish race, who, with Aliturus and Josephus, taught Nero and his servants to discriminate between Jews and Christians, and to martyr the latter while they honoured the former, then in Simon Magus the Second Beast of the Apocalypse—especially in the attributes

---

[1] Arnobius (*Adv. Gent.* ii. 12) speaks of Simon being precipitated from a fiery chariot. Augustine (*Haer.* i.) says that he professed to have come to the Apostles in fiery tongues. Nicephorus says that he pretended to pass through fire unhurt.
[2] Clem. *Recogn.* iii. 47. "I have made statues move about."
[3] Justin Mart. *Apol.* ii. p. 69; Tertull. *De Anim.* 34; *De Praescr. Haer.* 37; Sulp. Sev. *Hist. Sacr.* ii. 42; Clem. *Hom.* ii. 34; iv. 4; *Recogn.* ii. 9; iii. 47, 57; *Constit. Apost.* vi. 9; Epiphan. *Haer.* xxi. 5; Arnob. *Adv. Gentes,* ii. 12; Ambros. *Hexaem.* iv. 8, § 33; Cyrill. *Catech.* 6; Ps. Egesipp. *De excidio Hieros.*; August. *Serm.* iii. de SS. Petro et Paulo; Nicephorus Callistus, *H. E.* ii. 27.
[4] Tac. *Ann.* xv. 46; v. *supra,* p. 64.
[5] Acts viii. 11.

of a False Prophet—would stand revealed. It is true that the Pagan historians are silent about him and his doings; but the events themselves had no political significance, and lay outside their sphere. They belong to the history of the Church not of the State.[1] And Victorinus seems to be referring to Simon Magus when, with reference to the signs wrought by the False Prophet, he says that "the *Magi* do these things even to this day by the help of the banished Angels."

III. We now pass from what may be called the ecclesiastical and the religious fields of conjecture to the political. It must be remembered that it is as it were only by an afterthought that the Second Beast is called the False Prophet. May we not look for him in another region of Roman life?

There is, I think, much to be said in favour of Hildebrandt's suggestion[2] that by the False Prophet, or the "Second Beast from the land," is meant Vespasian. Let us apply to him the ten indications which the seer has furnished.

1. Being a "*wild beast*" it is à priori probable that he will belong to the heathen world. He rises "from the earth" or "from the land." If we take the former rendering it may point to his taking his origin, as an important power, not from the sea, or any sea-washed peninsula like Italy, whence Nero had sprung, but from the vast continent of Asia; *i.e.*, the growth of his power is connected with the East. If the words be rendered "*from the land*," they then apply to Judæa. Now both Jews[3] and Pagans[4] were struck with the fact that Vespasian, as Emperor, "went forth from Judæa," and they connected his rise in that country with many prophecies then current, not only in the East, but among the Romans themselves—prophecies which were familiar to more than one of the Cæsars, and had exercised no small influence on their aims and actions.

2. He had *two horns like unto a lamb*. There is hardly one of those who have been suggested as answering to the False Prophet to whom this description in any way applies. To Vespasian it *does* apply in a remarkable manner. His nature and his language, as compared with those of a Caligula and a Nero, were absolutely mild. He was indeed as indifferent to the blood and misery of a hostile people as all the Romans, were; but there was nothing naturally ferocious and sanguinary in the character of this worthy bourgeois.[5] Now since the *ten horns* of the

---

[1] I have already mentioned that Justin's mistake about a statue to him as a god was dispelled in 1574, when the inscription to the Sabine god, Semo Sancus, was found in the place which he mentions; v. *supra*, p. 64.
[2] Hilgenfeld's *Zeitschr*. 1874.   [3] Jos. B. J. vi. 5, § 4.
[4] Suet. *Vesp.* 6.
[5] Josephus boasts of the generosity of Vespasian as something extraordinary (*Antt.* xii. 3, § 2). His natural kindness, and freedom from hatred and revenge, are freely admitted, and may account for his external semblance to "a lamb" in the Apocalyptic symbol. Suetonius says that from the beginning to the end of his reign he was "*civilis et clemens*" (*Vesp.* 11); that he bore all kinds of opposition in the gentlest manner (*lenissime*, c. 13); and that he neither remembered nor revenged injuries (c. 14). But

first beast are ten provincial governors—ten powers which are, primarily, a source of his strength—we should expect that the *two horns* also indicated persons, and especially persons more or less imperial in their functions, in whose existence lay the strength of the Lamb-like Beast. And this was the exact position of Vespasian. His force lay in the fact that he had *two sons, both of them men of mark* : Titus, the conqueror of Judæa, who kept the allegiance of the army firm for him while he was awaiting his actual accession to power ; Domitian, who headed his party in Rome. But for their assistance his cause could not have prospered so decisively, and both of them succeeded to the empire after his death.[1]

He spake as a dragon or *serpent*, that is, he used the language generically of Paganism, and specifically of subtle and deceptive invention. The allusion may be to circumstances which were better known to St. John than to us ; but, meanwhile, whether it be generic or specific, there is sufficient evidence that it is appropriate in a sketch of the rise of Vespasian, and corresponds with the serpentine wisdom and caution with which his designs were carried out.

4. He is a *visible delegate of*, and responsible to, the first Beast. This applies better to Vespasian than to any one. The first outbreak of the Jewish war took place while Nero was indulging in his frantic follies of æstheticism in Greece, A.D. 66. He instantly despatched Vespasian to suppress the rebellion. To a general so placed it would have been an easy matter to revolt against the blood-stained actor who then afflicted the world. But as long as the Emperor lived, Vespasian, though not a favourite of Nero, remained conspicuously faithful.

5. And he *made the earth worship the first Beast*, whose death-stroke was healed. To enforce subjection to Nero, who even in his lifetime was "worshipped" as a god, was the express object of Vespasian's mission to the East. Moreover, it must be borne in mind that by the Wild Beast is meant the Roman Empire in general as well as Nero; and Rome was worshipped as a goddess in many of the provinces.[2]

6. It might seem an impossibility that any Roman general should

---

St. John, a Jew by birth and a true patriot, saw with Jewish eyes the inner wild-beast nature of the man. He would be little likely to share in the renegade admiration of Josephus for the general who, like his son, caused such myriads of Jews—

"To swell, slow by the car's tall side,
The stoic tyrant's philosophic pride ;
To flesh the lion's ravenous jaws, and feel
The sportive fury of the fencer's steel ;
Or sigh, deep-plunged beneath the sultry mine,
For the light airs of balmy Palestine."

St. John's estimate of him is that of the Rabbis, who narrated that he died in frightful torments ; and that of the 2nd book of Esdras, that he ruled "with much oppression" (2 Esdr. xi. 32).

[1] Titus and Domitian are probably the two heads on each side of the central head of the eagle in 2 Esdr. xi. 30, and ver. 35 may allude to the belief that Domitian poisoned Titus.
[2] On the apotheosis of Emperors, often even in their lifetime, see Suet. *Octav.* 59 ; *Tiber.* 40 ; *Claud.* 2 ; *Calig.* 22, 24 ; *Vesp.* 9 ; Tac. *Ann.* i. 10, 74 ; iv. 15, 37 ; xiv. 31, etc., and *supra*, p. 4.

have pretended *to work signs*, still more that there could be anything in his history which could be specifically described as a bringing down fire from heaven. It happens, however, that Vespasian is the one Roman—the only Roman in high places, *the only Imperial delegate*—to whom such language will apply. *His visit to Alexandria was accompanied by signs and wonders*, which obtained wide credence. Not only had the Nile risen in a single day higher than it had ever done before, but Vespasian was believed to have worked personal miracles.[1] He had anointed with spittle the eyes of a blind man, and restored his sight; before a full assembly he had healed a cripple; and he had shown a remarkable example of second sight.[2] We do not indeed read that he had called down fire from heaven; but that expression may be metaphorical of the fire and sword with which he scathed and devastated Palestine, and we *can* see the circumstance which may have given shape to the image. It represents the False Prophet as a pseudo-Elias, and there was a circumstance which might well have suggested a sort of antithesis between the two. Vespasian had visited Carmel, and had received a remarkable communication from "the god Carmelus" (evidently intended for Elijah),[3] who, though not worshipped under the form of any image, had there an altar which was regarded as peculiarly sacred. This god Carmelus had given him an oracle, which, even in the version of Suetonius, reminds us strongly of Dan. xi. 36, namely, that "everything which he had in his mind should prosper, however great it was."[4] As a "*fulmen belli*," and as the supposed recipient of a favourable oracle from Elijah, Vespasian, in his brilliant successes at the beginning of the Jewish war, might well be said, in the style of writing which constantly mingles the symbolic and the literal, to have flashed fire from heaven upon the enemies of the Beast.

7. He *gives breath to the image of the Beast and makes it speak*. Whether in this instance again we have some allusion to the story of a magic wonder current in that day we cannot tell. All that we know is that Vespasian would certainly enforce homage and reverence from the conquered Jews to the statues of the Emperor,[5] which Nero was specially fond of multiplying, and which the Jews regarded with peculiar abhorrence.[6] In the *Ascension of Isaiah* it is made a characteristic of Nero that "he shall erect his statue in all cities before his face."[7] Since Simon Magus pretended to animate statues with life, there may have been a rumour that something of the kind had taken place in Judæa. If not, the metaphorical meaning—the reanimation of the Roman power in Palestine, which the successful revolt of the Jews had for a time extinguished—is quite sufficient to meet the language of the seer.

[1] Dion Cass. lxvi. 8; Suet. *Vesp.* 7. [2] Tac. *Hist.* iv. 82.
[3] Ritter, *Erdkunde*, viii. 705. Carmel is now called Mar Elyas.
[4] Suet. *Vesp.* 5; Tac. *Hist.* ii. 78. [5] Jos. *Antt.* xviii. 8, § 1.
[6] "The image of the beast is clearly the statue of the Emperor."—*Milman*.
[7] *Ascens. Isa.* iv. 11; Lactant. ii. 7.

DOINGS OF VESPASIAN. 481

8. The *putting to death of those who will not worship the image of the Beast*—the slaughter, banishment, and sale into slavery of all who refused to accept the imperial authority, reverence the imperial images, and accept the imperial coinage, is a circumstance which will explain itself. It is a symbolic condensation of all that had already occurred in the Jewish war at Ascalon, at Sepphoris, at Gadara, at Jotapata, at Gerasa, at Japha, Joppa, Tarichesæ, Giscala, Gamala, and throughout the whole north and west of Palestine.

9. *He stamps men of all ranks* and classes, high and low, rich and poor, *with the image of his Beast*, and the number of his name. This detail, which only applies in the loosest possible manner to any of the others who have been regarded as the antitypes of the False Prophet, suits Vespasian very closely. It exactly describes his natural conduct in giving his soldiers the brand of their service,[1] and exacting from all classes the oath of allegiance, making them swear " by the genius of Cæsar"—first of Nero, then of Galba.

Lastly, 10. *The forbidding all to buy and sell who have not got the mark of the Beast*, seems to be a very natural reminiscence of one of Vespasian's most remarkable acts. When Nero was dead, and Galba murdered, and Otho also had committed suicide after the terrible battle of Bedriacum, neither Vespasian nor his soldiers felt inclined to obey the imbecile rule of the glutton Vitellius. Vespasian accepted his own nomination to the Empire by the legions of Mucianus as well as by his own soldiers, and he hastened to make himself master of the occasion by establishing his headquarters at Alexandria. Any ruler who had hold of Alexandria could command the allegiance of Egypt, and the lord of Egypt could always put his hand upon the very throat of Rome. For if the corn ships did not sail from Alexandria the populace of Rome was starved. Accordingly, the first thing which Vespasian did was to *forbid all exports* from Alexandria. That stern edict was felt throughout the Empire. The object of it was to starve Rome into an absolute acceptance of his "mark of the Beast," *i.e.*, his imperial claim. It was entirely successful. Galba, Otho, and even Vitellius, were regarded as isolated military usurpers; Vespasian, the Wild Beast's delegate, the Wild Beast's miraculous upholder, mounted the Wild Beast's throne, and like him became one of the seven heads, and wielded the power of the ten provincial horns—once rebellious—now subdued; often inimical to the harlot-city, but always faithful to the Roman Empire.[2]

To me these circumstances, which I have drawn out in my own way, but of which the original discovery is due to Hildebrandt, seem to be nearly decisive. My only doubt is whether, in that subtle interchange of ideas which marks all symbolic literature, St. John *may not have mingled two conceptions* in his description of the Second Beast.

---

[1] See Ronsch, *Das N. T. Tertullians*, p. 702.
[2] Rev. xvii. 12, 13, 16, 17.

If so, I should feel no doubt that the subordinate monster was meant to *combine* the features observable in the position and conduct of Simon Magus, as the False Prophet and Impostor who supported Nero at Rome, and of Josephus the False Prophet who embraced the cause of Vespasian in Palestine, with that of Vespasian himself as a two-horned Wild Beast maintaining the power of Rome in the Holy Land. The composite character of such a symbol presents no difficulty. It closely corresponds with known apocalyptic methods — and certainly in this instance if the Second Wild Beast and False Prophet be regarded as a composite symbol (as is suggested by the alternative description), I think that I have here offered a closer approximation to every one of the requirements of the imagery than I have found in the pages of any other interpreter.

Lastly, to revert for one moment to the return of the Antichrist in the person of Nero, it is—as I have said—in apocalyptic and Oriental style amply fulfilled in the reign of Domitian. If Galba, Otho, and Vitellius, be omitted from the list as mere transitory usurpers who would hardly be regarded as Emperors at all, then Nero the fifth Emperor *did* reappear, *not indeed in person but in symbol*, in the eighth Emperor, Domitian.[1] Even Titus was regarded as likely to be a coming Nero.[2] The Jews were very far from looking upon him as the *amor et deliciae humani generis*. It is probable that Sulpicius Severus may be preserving for us the testimony of Tacitus when (ii. 97) he attributes to Titus the thoroughly Neronian and Antichristian purpose of uprooting both Christianity and Judaism in one and the same stroke. This purpose, if he ever had it, he did not live to carry out. But Domitian, at any rate, was, like Nero, an open persecutor of Christianity. Tertullian not only sets him side by side with Nero, but even calls him "a fragment of Nero, so far as his cruelty was concerned," and a sub-Nero.[3] In Domitian the Christians saw the legend of *Nero redivivus* symbolically and effectively if not literally fulfilled.

So great was the resemblance between him and his blood-stained prototype that the common nickname of Domitian in Rome was "*the bald Nero.*" "Titus," says Ausonius, "was fortunate in the shortness of his rule: his brother followed him, whom his Rome called 'a bald Nero;'"[4] and Juvenal talks of the time when "the last Flavius was rending the half-dead world, and Rome was enslaved to *the bald Nero.*"[5] The identification of the spirit of Domitian with that of Nero was also familiar to Christian historians. Eusebius says that towards the close of his reign Domitian established himself as a successor of Nero's

---

[1] The Eight would then be Augustus, Tiberius, Gaius, Claudius, Nero, Vespasian, Titus, Nero again in the form of Domitian; so that Nero was, and is not, and yet was to recur: he was at once the fifth and the eighth.

[2] "Denique propalam *alium Neronem* et opinabantur et praedicabant" (Suet. *Tit.* 7).

[3] Tert. *Apol.* 5; *De Pall.* 4.

[4] Auson. *Monost. de Ord. XII. Imp.* 11, 12.   [5] Juv. *Sat.* iv. 34, 35.

hatred to God and hostility against Him.¹ It was natural to St. John to symbolise Nero as "the Wild Beast," and the very same term (*immanissima bellua*) is applied by Pliny to Domitian.² Tacitus even draws a parallel between the two to the advantage of Nero.³ Both showed the wild beast nature, but the ferocity of Domitian was more cruel and more innate. In him the death-wounded Antichrist was once more restored to life.

SECTION VII.
THE VIALS.

We have now passed in review all the more difficult Apocalyptic visions. A great part of the remainder of the Book is occupied with scenes which require but little comment, and convey directly their own great lessons. First, we have the glorious vision of the Lamb upon Mount Zion with the redeemed and virgin multitude. Then three Angels fly in rapid succession through the mid region of heaven. The first bears in his hand an eternal gospel which must be preached to every nation, tribe, tongue, and people before the end.⁴ The second cries out in prophetic anticipation, "Fallen, fallen is Babylon the Great." A third utters an awful warning to the Gentiles who worship the Beast and receive his mark. Then a Voice proclaims the blessedness of the dead who die in the Lord from henceforth, and immediately afterwards there appears on a white cloud one like unto the Son of Man, wearing a golden crown and grasping a sharp sickle. Then follows the harvest of the elect, and the vintage of the wrath of God, which seems to take place in the valley of Jehoshaphat,⁵ and of which the imagery is tinged by reminiscences of the terrible Jewish War, with its deluge of rolling blood⁶—rolling 200 miles, or, roughly, the whole length from Tyre to Rhinocolura, from north to south of the Holy Land.⁷

Then, after an episode of resplendent triumph and thanksgiving in heaven, seven Angels, arrayed in precious stone,⁸ pour out their vials of wrath upon the heathen world.⁹ Like the plagues of the first four

---

¹ τελευτῶν τῆς Νέρωνος θεοσχθρίας τὸ καὶ θεομαχίας διάδοχον ἑαυτὸν κατεστήσατο (Euseb. *H. E.* iii. 17). ² *Paneg.* 48.
³ Tac. *Agric.* 45 : "Nero tamen subtraxit oculos, jussitque scelera non spectavit."
⁴ Matt. xxiv. 14.
⁵ Rev. xiv. 20 ; Isa. xvii. 5 ; lxiii. 1—6 ; Joel iv. 2, 11—14 ; Mic. iv. 13 ; Hab. iii. 12.
⁶ Isa. lxiii. 3 ; comp. Enoch xcviii. 3 : "The horse shall wade up to his breast, and the chariot shall sink to his axle in the blood of sinners." So too Silius Italicus (iii. 704) speaks of "flammam exspirare furentes cornipedes, *multoque fluentia sanguine lora.*"
⁷ Jerome, *Ep. ad Dard.* states this at 160 miles ; but the deluge of blood began to roll from a point far north of Tyre.
⁸ Leg. λίθον, A, C, Vulg., and some MSS. known to Andreas. Comp. Ezek. xxviii. 13 (πάντα λίθον χρηστὸν ἐνδέδεσαι), "Every precious stone was thy covering" (see Westcott and Hort, *Greek Test.* ii. *ad loc.*, and compare Milton's—
"His vaunting foe
Though huge, and in a rock of diamond armed ").
⁹ Ezek. xxii. 31 ; Zeph. iii. 8.

trumpets, they affect the earth, and the sea, and the rivers,[1] and the heavenly bodies, the seat of the Beast, and the river Euphrates, and they are ended by the terrible phenomena of storm and earthquake. They are again but a vivid picture of the repeated signs in the sun, and the moon, and the stars, the distress of nations with perplexity, the sea and waves roaring, men's hearts failing them for fear, and the shaking of the powers of heaven, of which Christ had prophesied.[2] At the outpouring of the sixth Vial, the Euphrates is metaphorically dried up to prepare for the invasion of the kings of the East; and out of the mouths of the Devil, the Beast, and the False Prophet come three frog-like spirits of demons working miracles which gather the heathen kings to the great battle of Har-Magedon—a symbol of satanic opposition gathering to a final head, and meeting with its final overthrow.[3]

The seventh Angel pours out his vial on the air. There are thunders and a mighty earthquake. The great city (Jerusalem) is divided into three; the cities of the Gentiles fall; Rome—the mystic Babylon—comes into remembrance before God for vengeance; islands and mountains flee away, and there is a mighty plague of hail. We seem here to be in a region beyond the limits of history; but we can see that the images were in part suggested by that remarkable epoch of earthquakes which affected especially the cities of Asia, and by the three camps occupied by the army of Titus, and the three factions which occupied the three regions of Jerusalem—Simon in Bezetha, John in the Upper City, Eleazar in the Temple, and tore it to pieces with their internecine fury.

Then the great harlot city (Rome) drunken with the blood of the Neronian martyrs, is judged. Her judgment comes in part from the ten horns, which should have been the source of her strength, but which hate her, and eat her flesh, and burn her with fire. Part at least of the symbol corresponds with the horrors inflicted upon Rome and the Romans in the civil wars by provincial governors—already symbolised as the horns of the Wild Beast, and here characterised as kings yet kingdomless. Such were Galba, Otho, Vitellius, and Vespasian. Vespasian and Mucianus deliberately planned to starve the Roman populace;[4] and in the fierce struggle of the Vitellians against Sabinus and Domitian, and the massacre which followed, there occurred the event which

---

[1] Comp. Wisd. xi. 15—16; xvi. 1, 9; xvii. 2, seqq.
[2] Luke xxi. 25, 26. We have already seen that the practical identity of the seals, trumpets, and vials was known by tradition even to the earliest commentators; v. supr. pp. 430, 434, 453.
[3] The hill and plain of Megiddo were the scenes of great battles. They are in the Plain of Jezreel, the battlefield of Palestine (Judg. v. 19; 2 Kings xxiii. 29; Zech. xii. 11). Hence Ewald's conjecture that Har-Magedon is a cypher for Rome the Great (Ha Romah Haggedolah) is needless. Otherwise we might see here another instance of Gematria, for *Har-Magedon* and *Romah Hagedolah* are both = 304.
[4] Jos. B. J. iv. 10, § 5.

sounded so portentously in the ears of every Roman—the burning to the ground of the Temple of the Capitoline Jupiter, on December 19th, A.D. 69.[1] It was not the least of the signs of the times that the space of one year saw wrapped in flames the two most hallowed shrines of the ancient world—the Temple of Jerusalem and the Temple of the great Latin god. The Jews were not alone in interpreting these events of the final dissolution of the Empire. Josephus saw, in the establishment of the Flavian dynasty, "the unexpected deliverance of the fortunes of Rome from ruin;"[2] Tacitus looked on the year A.D. 68 as one which threatened to be the final year of the Roman commonwealth.[3] The Apocalyptist of *II. Esdras* says of the Eagle, in which he symbolises Rome, "Thou hast afflicted the weak, thou hast hurt the peaceable, thou hast loved liars, and hast cast down walls of such as did thee no harm; therefore appear no more, O Eagle! nor thy horrible wings, nor thy wicked feathers, nor thy malicious heads, nor thy hurtful claws, nor all thy vain body." (2 Esdr. xi. 42—46.) The author of the *Book of Baruch* says of Rome, the city which afflicted Jerusalem, "Fire shall come upon her from the Everlasting, long to endure; and she shall be inhabited of devils for a great time" (Bar. iv. 35).

The next chapters are occupied by the mingled wail and pæan over the doom of fallen Babylon, which is echoed in heaven.[4] The armies of heaven ride forth after the Word of God, and the fowls of the air are summoned to feed on the flesh of kings and captains slain in impious battle. The Beast and the False Prophet are cast into the Lake of Fire, and their followers are slain by the sword of the heavenly Rider. Satan is bound for a thousand years, and the Millennium of the Saints begins.[5] When the thousand years are ended, Satan is to be loosed to gather all the heathen, Gog and Magog,[6] to the final battle against God, after which he shall be flung to join the Beast and the False Prophet in the Lake of Fire. The great White Throne is set. The dead are judged. There is a new heaven and a new earth. Glowing with gold and gems,[7] the New Jerusalem descends out of Heaven from God,[8]

---

[1] Tac. *H.* iii. 83; Jos. *B. J.* iv. 11, § 4.   [2] Jos. *B. J.* iv. 11, § 5.
[3] Tac. *H.* i. 11.
[4] The expressions throughout chapters xvii.—xviii. are almost entirely borrowed from the ancient prophets (Isa. xiii., xxiii., xxiv., &c.; Jer. xvi., xxv.; Ezek. xxvi., xxvii.; Amos vi. 5—7.
[5] A literal millenarianism has been generally condemned by the Catholic Church. Victorinus and the earliest commentators understood the 1,000 years to have begun at the Incarnation. Origen and most of the Fathers understood it spiritually and metaphorically.
[6] Barbarian nations from the North (Ezek. xxxviii., xxxix.). Abarbanel on Jer. xxx. calls them nations from the East.
[7] Derived from Is. liv. 12; and comp. Yalkut Shimeoni, f. 54, a.
[8] The Rabbis inferred from Ps. cxxii. 3, that there was "a Jerusalem above (Taanith, f. 5, a); and Rabbi Johanan says, "The Holy One will bring precious stones and pearls, each measuring 30 cubits by 30, and after polishing them down to 20 cubits by 20, will place them in the gates of Jerusalem" (Bava Bathra, f. 25, a). Again, "The Jerusalem of this world is not as the Jerusalem of the world to come. The former is open to all;

through whose streets flow, bright as crystal, the River of the water of life, and there is no Temple there, nor light of moon nor sun, for the Lord God gives them light; and there shall be no more curse.[1] The book ends with that which is the burden of the whole—Yea! I come quickly. And the seer answers, as all Christians have ever answered, Amen! Come Lord Jesus![2]

And thus the whole book, from beginning to end, teaches the great truths—Christ shall triumph! Christ's enemies shall be overcome! They who hate Him shall be destroyed; they who love Him shall be blessed unspeakably. The doom alike of Jew and of Gentile is already imminent. On Judæa and Jerusalem, on Rome and her Empire, on Nero and his adorers, the judgment shall fall. Sword and fire, and famine and pestilence, and storm and earthquake, and social agony and political terror, are nothing but the woes which are ushering in the Messianic reign. Old things are rapidly passing away. The light upon the visage of the old dispensation is vanishing and fading into dimness, but the face of Him who is as the sun is already dawning through the East. The new and final covenant is instantly to be established amid terrible judgments; and it is to be so established as to render impossible the continuance of the old. Maranatha! The Lord is at hand! Even so come, Lord Jesus! *Mane nobiscum Domine, nam advesperascit!*

CHAPTER XXIX.

THE FALL OF JERUSALEM.

" The Lord, whose fire is in Zion, and His furnace in Jerusalem " (Isa. xxxi. 9).
" What was the cause of the destruction of the Second Temple, seeing that the age was distinguished for the study of the laws? . . . It was *groundless hatred* " (Yoma, f. 9, *b*).

THERE is no need to dwell upon the last days of Jerusalem. Very little can be added to the horrible story beyond what is to be read by every one in the pages of Josephus.[3] It is true that Josephus has effectually

---

to the latter (Rev. xxi. 5) none shall go up but those who are ordained to enter" (*id.* 75, *b*). As to its height (Rev. xxi. 16) the Rabbis say that God will place it on the summits of Mounts Sinai, Tabor, and Carmel (Isa. ii. 2). [1] Zech. xiv. 11.

[2] The solemn curse against any one who adds to, or takes from, the book, was not uncommon in days when literary forgery and interpolation was remarkably common. Thus Irenæus ended one of his books with the words:—"I adjure you, copyists of this book, by the Lord Jesus Christ, and by His glorious coming to judge the quick and the dead, that you compare and carefully correct your copy by this exemplar, and likewise place this adjuration in your copy " (*Opp.* i. p. 821, ed. Stieren). A similar passage is found at the end of Rufinus's prologue to his version of Origen's *De Principiis* (see Huidekoper, *Judaism at Rome*, p. 289).

[3] For modern narratives derived from him, see F. de Sauley, *Les Derniers Jours de Jerusalem*, 1866; Milman, *Hist. of Christianity*, vol. iii.; Merivale, *Hist. of the Romans*, ch. lix.; Ewald, *Gesch.* vi. 696—812.

blackened his own memory. It would have been well for him if he had only written the *Antiquities* and the *Dialogue against Apion.* In his *Jewish War*, and, above all, in his autobiography, he stands confessed as a false, heartless, and designing renegade. The man who, standing in sight of the ruins of Zion and the blackened area on which had shone the Holy of Holies, complacently tells us how Titus gave him other lands in Judæa, because those which he had possessed near Jerusalem had become useless; the man who gloatingly recounts the honours heaped upon him by the conquerors who flung thousands of his brave countrymen to the wild beasts, and sold tens of thousands more into brutal misery; the man who, in the sumptuous palace which he owed to his conqueror, could detail without a sob the extermination of his people; the man who could gaze with complacent infamy on the triumph which told of the destruction of his nation's liberty, and could look on while the hallowed vessels of the Sanctuary were held aloft before a Pagan populace by bloodstained hands; the man who in youth haunted the boudoir of Poppæa, and in old age hung about the antechambers of Domitian; the man who pursued with posthumous hatred of successful treachery the brave though misguided patriots who had held it a glory to die for Jerusalem—must stand forth till the end of time in the immortal infamy which his own writings have heaped upon himself.[1] We cannot be surprised that all the patriots of his nation hated him, and tried to disturb his base prosperity and "gilded servitude." No one trusts the words of Josephus where he has the least interest in palming off upon us a deception. But he had no particular reason to misrepresent the general facts of the awful and heroic struggle in which for a few months he bore a part. And since the writings of Justus of Tiberias and Antonius Primus have perished, as well as the latter part of the *History* of Tacitus, Josephus becomes our sole guide. The Talmud has almost nothing to tell us. In it we look in vain for the names of John, or Simon, or Eleazar. We only see a dim glimpse of flames and assassination, and ruin, mixed up with curious legends and tales of individual agony.[2]

In April, A.D. 70, Titus, with a force of 80,000 legionaries and auxiliaries, pitched his camp on Scopus, to the north of the city. Besides the 2,400 trained Jewish warriors who defended the walls, the city was thronged with an incredible number of Passover pilgrims, and of fugitives from other parts of Judæa. Feats of heroic valour were performed on both sides, and the skill of the besiegers was often checked by the almost insane fury of the besieged. Fanatically relying on the visible manifestation of Jehovah, while they were infamously violating all His laws, the Zealots rejected with insult every offer of terms. At last Titus drew a line of circumvallation round the doomed city, and

---

[1] See Derenbourg, p. 264, and n. xl.; Grätz, iii. 365, *seq.*, 386, 411; Salvador, *Hist.* ii. 467; De Quincey, *Works*.
[2] Derenbourg, pp. 266, 282—288. Some of the stories which Josephus recounts of himself are transferred in the Talmud to the celebrated Rabbi Yochanan Ben Zakkai.

began to crucify all the deserters who fled to him. The incidents of the famine which then fell on the besieged are among the most horrible in human literature. The corpses bred a pestilence. Whole houses were filled with unburied families of the dead. Mothers slew and devoured their own children. Hunger, rage, despair, and madness, seized the city. It became a cage of furious madmen, a city of howling wild beasts, and of cannibals—a hell![1] For the first time for five centuries, on July 17, A.D. 70, the daily sacrifices of the Temple ceased for want of priests to offer them. Disease and slaughter ruthlessly accomplished their work. At last, amid shrieks and flames, and suicide and massacre, the Temple was taken and reduced to ashes. The great altar of sacrifice was heaped with the slain. The courts of the Temple swam deep in blood. Six thousand miserable women and children sank with a wild cry of terror amid the blazing ruins of the cloisters. Romans adored the insignia of their legions on the place were the Holiest had stood. As soon as they became masters of the Upper City they only ceased to slay when they were too weary to slay any longer. According to Josephus, it had been the earnest desire of Titus to preserve the Temple, but his commands were disobeyed by his soldiers in the fury of the struggle. According to Sulpicius Severus, on the other hand, who is probably quoting the very words of Tacitus, Titus formed the deliberate purpose to destroy Christianity and Judaism in one blow, believing that if the Jewish root were torn up the Christian branch would soon perish.[2] The tallest and most beautiful youths were reserved for the conqueror's triumph. Of those above seventeen years of age multitudes were doomed to work in chains in the Egyptian mines. Others were sent as presents to various towns to be slain by wild beasts or gladiators, or by each other's swords in the provincial amphitheatres. The young of both sexes were sold as slaves. Even during the days on which these arrangements were being made, 11,000 perished for want of food; some because their guards would not give it to them, others because they would not accept it. Josephus reckons the number of captives taken during the war at 97,000, and the number of those who perished during the siege at 1,100,000. The

---

[1] Renan, *L'Antechrist*, 507.

[2] "Alii *et Titus ipse* evertendum templum imprimis censebant, quo plenius Judaeorum et Christianorum religio tolleretur. Quippe has religiones licet contrarias sibi, iisdem tamen auctoribus profectas; radice sublata stirpem facile parituram" (Sulp. Sev. *Sacr. Hist.* ii. 30, § 6, 7). He had access both to the lost part of the *Historiae* of Tacitus, and also to the work of Antonius Julianus, *De Judaeis*. The latter, who was one of Titus's council of war, wrote with far less biassed motives than Josephus, who is not to be trusted when he had anything to gain by disguising the truth. Dr. Bernays, of Breslau, believes that Sulpicius Severus is quoting Tacitus in the sentence quoted above. Grätz (iii. 403) contemptuously rejects this suggestion, on the ground that Titus could scarcely have heard of the Christians. But Titus saw a great deal of Josephus and of Agrippa II., and there are signs that Josephus knew a good deal more about Christianity than he ventures to say, and that Agrippa had not been uninfluenced by the arguments of St. Paul (see Derenbourg, p. 252). On the other hand, Ewald thinks that this assertion as to the purpose of Titus is weakened by the repetition of it in the case of Hadrian:—"existimans se Christianam fidem loci injuria" (*i.e.* by profaning the site of the Temple) peremturum" (Sulp. Sev., *Sacr. Hist.* ii. 31, § 3; Ewald, *Gesch.* vi. 797).

numbers who perished in the whole war are reckoned at the awful total of 1,337,490, and the number of prisoners at 101,700; but even these estimates do not include all the items of many skirmishes and battles, nor do they take into account the multitudes who, throughout the whole country, perished of misery, famine, and disease. It may well be said that the nation seemed to have given itself "a rendezvous of extermination." Two thousand putrefying bodies were found even in the subterranean vaults of the city. During the siege all the trees of the environs had been cut down, and hence the whole appearance of the place, with its charred and bloodstained ruins, was so completely altered, that one who was suddenly brought to it would not (we are told) have recognised where he was. And yet the site had been so apparently impregnable, with its massive and unequalled fortifications, that Titus freely declared that he saw in his victory the hand of God.[1] From that time all Jews on seeing Jerusalem rend their garments and exclaim, " Zion is a wilderness, Jerusalem a desolation. Our holy and beautiful house, where our fathers praised Thee, is burned with fire, and all our pleasant things are laid waste."[2]

It was to this event, the most awful in history—"one of the most awful eras in God's economy of grace, and the most awful revolution in all God's religious dispensations"[3]—that we must apply those prophecies of Christ's coming in which every one of the Apostles and Evangelists describe it as *near at hand*.[4] To those prophecies our Lord Himself fixed these three most definite limitations—the one, that before that generation passed away all these things would be fulfilled;[5] another, that some standing there should not taste death till they saw the Son of Man coming in His kingdom;[6] the third, that the Apostles should not have gone over the cities of Israel till the Son of Man be come.[7] It is strange that these distinct limitations should not be regarded as a decisive proof that the Fall of Jerusalem was, in the fullest sense, the Second Advent of the Son of Man which was primarily contemplated by the earliest voices of prophecy.

And, indeed, the Fall of Jerusalem and all the events which accompanied and followed it in the Roman world and in the Christian Church,

---

[1] It is curious to contrast the pious, gentle, and amiable Titus of Josephus, and the "Love and darling of the human race" of Roman historians, with "Titus the Bad" (Ha-rashá), or "the Tyrant," of the Talmudists. Their well-known legend tells that, being caught in a terrible storm, and getting safe to land, he defied God, Who, to punish him, sent a little gnat (יתוש), which crept up his nostrils into his brain, and caused him incessant and sleepless anguish. At his death it was found to be "as big as a bird, and to have a beak and claws of steel" (Bereshith Rabba x.; Tanchuma, 62, a, etc.). It may be imagined how patriotic Jews felt towards *Titus Flavius* Josephus. The name on which he prided himself would be to them a veritable "brand of the Beast."
[2] Isa. lxiv. 10, 11; Moed Katon, f. 26, a.
[3] Bp. Warburton's *Julian*, i. p. 21.
[4] Acts ii. 16—20, 40; iii. 19—21; 1 Thess. iv. 13—17; v. 1—16; 2 Thess. i. 7—10; 1 Cor. i. 7; x. 11; xv. 21; xvi. 22; Rom. xiii. 11, 12; Phil. iii. 20; iv. 5; 1 Tim. iv. 1; 2 Tim. iii. 1; Heb. i. 2; x. 25, 37; James v. 3, 8, 9; 1 Pet. ii. 7; 2 Pet. iii. 12; 1 J. ii. 18.
[5] Matt. xxiv. 34. [6] Matt. xvi. 28. [7] Matt. x. 23.

had a significance which it is hardly possible to over-estimate. They were the final end of the old Dispensation. They were the full inauguration of the New Covenant. They were God's own overwhelming judgment on that form of Judaic Christianity which threatened to crush the work of St. Paul, to lay on the Gentiles the yoke of an abrogated Mosaism, to establish itself by threats and anathemas as the only orthodoxy. Many of the early Christians—and those especially who lived at Jerusalem—were at the same time rigid Jews. So long as they continued to walk in the ordinances of their fathers as a national and customary duty, such observances were harmless; but it is the inevitable tendency of this external rigorism to usurp in many minds the place of true religion. In every Church, as we see from most of the Catholic epistles, as well as in those of St. Paul, the Judaists asserted themselves, and won over the devoted adherence of the multitude, which is ever ripe for the slavery of rigid dogmas and narrow forms. It required the whole force of St. Paul's inspired and splendid genius to save Christianity from sinking into an exclusive sect of repellent Ebionites. No event less awful than the desolation of Judæa, the destruction of Judaism, the annihilation of all possibility of observing the precepts of Moses, could have opened the eyes of the Judaisers from their dream of imagined infallibility. Nothing but God's own unmistakable interposition—nothing but the manifest coming of Christ—could have persuaded Jewish Christians that the Law of the Wilderness was annulled; that the idolised minutiæ of Levitism could no longer claim to be divinely obligatory; that the Temple, to which so many myriads had resorted from every region of the world, as to a common refuge, where they found peace and forgiveness and holy thoughts and joyous hopes,[1] had been smitten to the ground as though by flashes of God's own avenging fire; that the sacrifices, of which Philo had so recently said, "they are being offered even until now, and they shall be offered for ever,"[2] had been finally, decisively, and, by the direct action of Divine Providence, annulled. It was absurd to imagine that salvation could in any way depend on obedience to a law to which obedience had been rendered impossible by God's own decree. The facts, so terrible to Jewish imagination, that the steps of the profane had carried their bloody footprints into the Holiest, where only the High Priest could enter once a year; that the unclean hands of Gentiles had been laid on the golden altars; that the sacred rolls of the Torah, for which any Jew would have been ready to die, had been carried captive, for every profane eye to gaze upon, along the streets of Edom and Babylon—were but symbols of the yet deadlier fact that henceforth that Law could not be kept, nor the Paschal lamb slain, nor the ceremonies of even the Great Day of Atonement any longer observed. Judaism, a religion of which the Temple was the most essential centre,

---

[1] Philo, *De Monarchia* (Mangey, ii. 223).
[2] *Id., Leg. ad Gaium* (Mangey, ii. 569).

of which sacrifices were the most essential element, became a religion without a temple and without a sacrifice. It became no longer possible for even the most Pharisaic of sacerdotalists to talk as though the very universe depended on ceremonies and vestments, or on the right burning of the two kidneys with the fat.

Christian historians rightly appreciate the significance of the event. The Temple, says Orosius, was overthrown and done away with, because it could no longer serve any good or useful object, since now the Church of God was vigorously germinating throughout the world.[1] When, in A.D. 120, Ælia Capitolina was built by Hadrian on the ruins of Jerusalem, and Christians were allowed free access to it, while no Jew was suffered to approach it, the Church of the Circumcision was practically at an end. "Up to that time," says Sulpicius Severus, "almost all Christians in Judæa observed the Law while they worshipped Christ as God; but it was the result of God's ordinance that henceforth the slavery of the Law should be taken away from the freedom of the Church."[2] The Church of Ælia Capitolina was no longer prevalently Judaic; nay more, in a mission to Hadrian it formally severed itself from the Jews. For the first time, in A.D. 137, it selected as its bishop Marcus, an uncircumcised Gentile."[3] The event significantly proved that even in Judæa the future destinies of the Christian Church were in no further danger of falling into the hands of either Ebionites or Nazarenes.[4] The Church then emancipated itself finally and for ever from the trammels of the Synagogue.

No one was more deeply influenced by this event than St. John. A full quarter of a century elapsed between the ripe manhood when he wrote the Apocalypse and the old age in which he wrote the Gospel and Epistles. The colouring and spirit of the Apocalypse are clearly Judaic; but we see alike in the advanced Christology,[5] and in the recognition of the equality of the redeemed Gentiles,[6] and in the absence of any Temple in the New Jerusalem, how far St. John was removed from the heresies of those Jewish Christians to whom Christ was no more than the Jewish Messiah, and Christianity no more than an engrafting of their belief upon an otherwise unchanged Pharisaism. And yet, though the Gospel and Epistles are identical with the Apocalypse in essential doctrines—though the thought of Christ as the Victim Lamb is prominent in both—we see how wide is the difference which separates them; how much calmer is the style, how

---

[1] "Ecclesia Dei jam per totum orbem germinante, hoc (templum) tanquam effoetum et vacuum nullique usui bono commodum arbitrio Dei auferendum fuit" (Oros. vii. 9).
[2] Sulp. Sev. H. S. ii. 31.
[3] Euseb. H. E. iv. 6; Grätz, Gesch. d. Juden. iv. 183.
[4] "The furious persecutions and massacres of Christians by the False Messiah Bar Cochba (A.D. 132—134), which first thoroughly opened the eyes of the Pagan world to the difference between Jews and Christians, were due alike to the rejection of his claims by the Christians, and their refusal to join in his revolt" (Grätz, Gesch. iv. 154, 457).
[5] Rev. iii. 14; v. 13; xix. 13; xvii. 14; xix. 16; etc.
[6] Rev. vii. 9.

much deeper the revelation, contained in the later writings; how the light which had dawned so brightly upon the Apostles in the Church of Jerusalem had shone more and more unto the perfect day. The Gospel and Epistles contain the same truths as the Apocalypse,[1] but the symbols are spiritualised. Jerusalem, even as a symbol, no longer occupies the foreground of his thoughts, and positive Judaic ordinances sink into insignificance in comparison with the knowledge of God which is eternal life. The Apocalypse is mainly occupied with the awfulness of retribution: The Gospel and Epistles are dominated by the ideal of love.

Unless these considerations be admitted in their fullest extent, it becomes impossible to maintain that writings so different, even amid their partial similarities, could have come from the same hand. It is true that in the Apocalypse we have a material eschatology, and in the later writings a spiritual consummation. It is true that the Apocalypse is an expression of Judaic Christianity, and that the Gospel and Epistles are not. It is true that the points of contrast which they offer are more salient than their resemblances. It is even true that both could never have existed *simultaneously* in the same mind. In the Apocalypse the symbols of Heaven itself are mainly Jewish and Levitical, and in the Gospel the evanescence and annulment of such forms is clearly proclaimed. In the Apocalypse the elements of Divine wrath are mainly depicted in phraseology borrowed from the old prophetic images; in the later writings God is depicted almost exclusively in the attributes of compassion and love. In the Apocalypse Christ is the Lion of the Tribe of Judah, the ruler who, with a rod of iron, shall dash the nations in pieces like a potter's vessel; in the Gospel He is the Good Shepherd who layeth down His life for the sheep. In the later writings there are no wars and collisions—no acts of awful vengeance at which the saints look on with exultation; but the world is something wholly apart from the kingdom of the saints, and that kingdom is spiritual and in the heart. In the Apocalypse the Antichrist is a bloodstained Roman Emperor; in the Epistles there are many antichrists, and they are forms of speculative error. In the Apocalypse there are two resurrections, both physical, one before, one after, the Millennium; in the Gospel the first and chief resurrection is that from the death of sin to the life of righteousness. In the Apocalypse Heaven is wholly a future splendour; in the Epistles it is already a living and present realisation of God's presence in the heart. The Apocalyptist consoles the Christian sufferer with the hope of what he shall be; the Evangelist with the knowledge of what he is.[2]

How, then, it may be asked, can the Evangelist and the Seer of Patmos be one and the same person?[3]

---

[1] As even Baur admits (*Three Christian Centuries*, i. 154).
[2] See Reuss, *Hist. de la Théol. Chrét.* ii. 564—571.
[3] Ewald says with his usual positiveness, "Sie ergibt sich je genauer man sie nach

They are one and the same, but divided from each other by nearly a quarter of a century—by more than twenty years of divine education and broadening light. Many of these differences arise from the dealing with truths which are indeed widely diverse, but which yet are equally true, and which are necessary to complement each other. Many of them may be summed up and accounted for in the single remark that the Apocalypse *is* an Apocalypse, and that it was written amid the throbbing agonies of the Jewish War and after the bloodstained horrors of the Neronian persecution. At that time St. John still belonged in training and sympathy to the Church of the Circumcision. The Gospel and Epistles, on the other hand, were written after long residence among Gentiles, when the whole perspective of the Apostle's thoughts had been altered by the flood of divine illumination cast alike upon the Old and the New Covenant by the fulfilment of Christ's own prophecies of His coming. After the fall of Jerusalem He had established His kingdom upon earth by closing for ever the Jewish dispensation.

Nor must it be forgotten that amid all the differences which separate these writings there are many subtle similarities in the temperament of the writer, in his phraseology and in his theological standpoint. In both we have the prominent conception of Christ as the Lamb of God;[1] in both—and in them alone—He is called—"The Word." In both we read of the "Living Water." In both we find the recognition of the priority in time of the Jew and of the admission of the Gentiles. Both books give prominence to the prophecy of Zechariah (xii. 10), "they shall look upon me whom they have pierced," and both in their reference to this verse diverge in the same way from the LXX. No careful student of St. John's writings can fail to see that in many respects, and in relation to many doctrines, an identity of essence underlies the dissimilarity of form.[2] Not one of the Johannine books could be spared from the sacred canon without manifest and grievous loss; all of them are rich in truths which are necessary to make us wise unto salvation.

---

allen Seiten hin untersucht . . . desto gewisser als von einem ganz andern Schriftsteller und als nicht vom Apostel verfasst" (*Johann. Schriften*, ii. 1).

[1] In the Gospel ἀμνός, in the Apocalypse ἀρνίον. It has been ingeniously suggested that ἀρνίον may have been chosen as physiologically equivalent in sound to θηρίον.

[2] For a most satisfactory proof of this, see Gebhardt, *Doctrine of the Apocalypse* (E. Tr., Clark, Edinb., 1878). Isolated resemblances are Rev. ii. 2; John xvi. 12 ("cannot bear"); Rev. ii. 3; John iv. 6 ("faint"); angels and saints "in white" (ἐν λευκοῖς, Rev. iii. 18; John xx. 12); effects of "anointing" (Rev. iii. 18; 1 John ii. 20). Besides these there are other verbal resemblances, such as τηρεῖν λόγον, or λόγους (Rev. iii. 8, 16; xxii. 7, 9, etc.; John viii. 51; 1 John ii. 5); ποιεῖν ψεῦδος, or ἀλήθειαν (Rev. xxii. 15; 1 John i. 6); αἵματα (? B, etc.) (Rev. xviii. 24; John ii. 13); "He that is true" (Rev. iii. 7, xix. 11; John i. 14, xiv. 6; 1 John v. 20); and the common peculiar usage of the words ἀληθινός, βροντή, δαιμόνιον, ἰβραιστί, ἐκκεντεῖν, ὄψις, πορφύρεος, σκηνοῦν, σφάττειν, etc. On the other side see, among others, Düsterdieck, pp. 73—80; Ewald, *Johann. Schriften*, ii. 52, 53, 61, 62.

CHAPTER XXX.

THE GROWTH OF HERESY.

.... ὃς ἄρα μέχρι τῶν τότε χρόνων παρθένος καθαρὰ καὶ ἀδιάφθορος ἔμεινεν ἡ
'Εκκλησία.—HEGESIPP. *ap.* Euseb. *H.E.* iii. 32.

"La fumée qui obscurcit le Soleil c'est à dire l'hérésie."—BOSSUET.

THERE were, as I have said, three great events which deeply influenced the last and most active period in the life of St. John—the Neronian persecution, the fall of Jerusalem, and the growth of Heresy. The two former events, which were sudden and overwhelming, woke their tremendous echoes in the Apocalypse. The third event was very gradual. We find traces of it in the letters to the Seven Churches, but it had a still deeper influence on the Gospel and the Epistles, which were the inestimable fruit of the Apostle's ripest years. According to the tradition of the Church, they were especially written to combat heresy, not by the method of direct and vehement controversy, but by that noblest of all methods which consists in the irresistible presentation of counter truths.

The word "heresy," though it is used in the Authorised Version to translate the *hairesis* of the New Testament, has not the same meaning. The word was not originally applied in a bad sense. In classic Greek, for instance, it merely meant a choice of principles, a school of philosophy or of thought.[1] In the New Testament it comes to mean "a faction," and the sin condemned by the word is not the adoption of erroneous opinions, but *the factiousness of party spirit.*[2] It was, however, perfectly natural that it should come to mean[3] a wrong choice, a false system. For Christianity, being a divine revelation, involves a fellowship and unity in all essential verities, and he who gives undue preponderance to his own arbitrary conceptions, he who allows to subjective influences or traditional errors an unlimited sway over his interpretations of truth, becomes a heretic. And in this sense many are heretics who most pride themselves on their vaunted catholicity; for the source of all heresies is the spirit of pride, and the worst of all heresies is the spirit of hatred. The word "heretic" has indeed been shamefully abused. It has again and again been applied in a thoroughly heretical, and worse than heretical manner, to the insight and inspiration of the few who have discovered aspects of truth hitherto unnoticed, or restored old truths by the overthrow of dominant perversions. A

---

[1] Sext. Empir. i. 16; Cic. *ad Fam.* xv. 16, 3.
[2] It only occurs in Acts v. 17; xv. 5; xxiv. 5, 14; xxvi. 5; xxviii. 22; 1 Cor. xi. 19; Gal. v. 20; 2 Pet. ii. 1.
[3] See Neander, *Ch. Hist.* ii. 4.

Church can only prove its possession of life by healthy development. Morbid uniformity, enforced by the tyranny of a dominant sect, is the most certain indication of dissolution and decay. Since Christianity is manysided, the worst form of heresy is the mechanical suppression of divergence from popular shibboleths. Every great reformer in turn, every discoverer of new forms or expressions of religious truth, every slayer of old and monstrous errors, has been called a heretic. When a new truth could not be refuted, it was easy for the members of a dominant party to gratify their impotent hatred by burning him who had uttered it; and though religious partisans can no longer commit to the flames those who differ from them, it is as true in our days as in those of Milton, that—

> " Men whose faith, learning, life, and pure intent
> Would have been held in high esteem by Paul,
> Must now be called and printed ' heretic '
> By shallow Edwards and Scotch what-d'ye-call."

But the real heretics were, in most cases, the supporters of ecclesiastical tyranny and stereotyped ignorance, by whom these martyrs were tortured and slain. He, and he only, is, in the strict and technical sense of the word, a heretic, who denies the fundamental truths of Christianity, as embodied in the catholic creeds which sufficed to express the doctrines of the Church in the first four centuries of her history. But we are taught by daily experience that it is possible to hold catholic truth in an heretical spirit, and heresy in a catholic spirit. By the fraud of the devil many a Catholic has acted in the spirit of an infidel; and, by the grace of God, many a heretic has shown the virtue of a saint. As for the existence of diversity in the midst of general unity, it is not only inevitable, but, in our present condition of imperfection, it is the only means to secure a right apprehension of truth. Christianity may be regarded in two aspects—as a law of life and as a system of doctrines. But neither was the law of life laid down in rigid precepts nor was the plan of salvation set forth in dialectics. Men may be pure and true Christians, though their holiness reveals itself in manifold varieties of form; they may be in faithful and conscientious communion with the Catholic Church, though the inevitable differences of individuality lead to different modes of apprehending the essential Gospel. All that is indispensable is that their varieties of opinion should be subordinate to one divine unity, and that their mode of life under all differences should express some aspect of the one divine ideal.

The *moral* fibre of bitterness, from which all heresies spring, is one and the same. Whether they result from the blind and tyrannous unanimity of corrupt Churches, or the wide self-assertion of opinionated individuals, they owe their ultimate origin to the pride and ambition of the heart. But the *intellectual* sources of heresy were manifold. It was produced by the contact of Christianity with Heathenism and with

Judaism, and was especially derived from the forms of philosophy which had sprung up in the bosom of both religions.

The Gentiles, as a rule, hated the Mosaic Law, and looked on Christianity as the antagonist of Judaism, rather than as its dissolution and fulfilment. The Jews, on the other hand, saw in Christianity only an accretion to the Law of Moses, and clung to the most rigid letter of institutions which Heathenism despised. Hence, amid the numberless ramifications of heretical sects which disturbed the Church of the first century, and which were massed together under the vague and often inappropriate name of Gnosticism, some were Judaic and some were anti-Judaic.

1. To the Jewish sects we have aleady alluded. They may be classed under the two heads of Nazarenes and Ebionites.

We have been obliged again and again to notice that the earliest decades after the Ascension were marked by a severe struggle between the views of Judaising and of Gentile Christians. St. James, the head of the Judaisers, had nevertheless adopted the views of St. Peter as regards the freedom of the Gentiles, and while he continued to be a blameless observer of the Mosaic Law, he gave full tolerance to all converts from Paganism who did not violate the Noachian precepts. This was the decision of the Synod at Jerusalem. But the party who wrote upon their banners the name of the Bishop of Jerusalem went much further. It was one of the main works of St. Paul's life to counteract their surreptitious methods of strangling the growth of true Christianity by insisting that all Gentiles must be circumcised, and must observe the entire Levitic Law. It was in the ranks of these Judaists that there arose that imminent danger of apostasy against which they had received such solemn warnings in the Epistle to the Hebrews, and the Epistle of St. James himself; it was from their ranks also that there arose the two sects of Ebionites and Nazarenes.

It may well be thought strange that the most definite existence of these Jewish Christian sects falls in the era *after* the Fall of Jerusalem, when it might have been deemed impossible for any one to retain the opinion that God had intended the Jewish Law to be eternally obligatory. But prejudice, fortified by custom, is almost ineradicable. Judaism, when robbed of all power to observe its ritual, took refuge in its Law, regarded as a separate and ideal entity. The disease, uncured even by the amputation of its chief limb, fastened itself with unabated virulence on the vital organs. The Mosaic Law assumed in the minds of Talmudists the place of God Himself, and by the Law they meant not morals but Rabbinism, not the Decalogue, but the Halacha. When Pope says that in some of the discussions of the *Paradise Lost*—

> "In quibbles angel and archangel join,
> And God the Father turns a school divine,"

he was using the broadest satire; but his words are applicable in their most literal sense to the teachings of the Rabbis, who arrogantly usurped the exclusive name of *Hachakamîm,* or "the Wise." They represent God as Himself a student of the Torah. They disputed whether God Himself did not wear phylacteries.[1] They represent Heaven as a great Rabbinic school in which there are differences of opinion about the Halacha. On one occasion, they assert there was a dispute in the celestial academy about the minutiæ of a Levitic decision, and as the Deity took one view while the angels took the opposite, it became necessary to summon the soul of Rabbi Bar Nachman. To him consequently the Angel of Death is despatched. The Rabbi is asked his opinion, and gives it on the side of the Almighty, who is represented—with a *naïveté* astonishing in its blasphemous arrogance—as highly pleased with the result of the discussion ![2]

If then the Jews could still find space for the practice and idealisation of their Levitism when scarcely one of its directions could be carried out—if almost without an effort the schools of Jamnia and Tiberias and Pumbeditha could transform their theocracy into a nomocracy, and their theology into a Levític scholasticism, we are hardly surprised to find that the influence of old traditions was sufficiently strong, and especially within the limits of the Holy Land, to keep alive the spirit of Jewish Christianity. Far on into the fourth, and perhaps even down to the fifth century, there continued to be not only "*Genists,*" or Jews by race, and "*Masbotheans,*" who observed the Jewish Sabbath, and "*Merists,*" who kept up a partial observance of the Jewish Law,[3] but also organised Christian sects who although they were excluded from the bosom of the orthodox Church, had a literature of their own—the ancient counterpart of the modern "religious newspaper"—and not only maintained their ground, but even displayed a wide-spread and proselytising activity.

α. The NAZARENES, as a distinctive sect, were the Jewish Christians who did not remove from Pella when—if we may accept the ancient tradition—the fugitive Church of Jerusalem returned to Ælia Capitolina,[4] which no Jew was allowed to enter. But they existed much earlier, and are to be regarded less as deliberate heretics than as imperfect, narrow-minded, and unenlightened Christians. Epiphanius calls them "Jews, and nothing else;"[5] but since they accepted the Epistles of St. Paul, and acknowledged the true divinity of Christ,[6] we may set aside his uncharitable description of them. If, as is probable, their views are represented by the *Testament of the Twelve Patriarchs,* we can see that while they clung with needless tenacity to the obsolete and the abrogated, this was only the result of limited insight and national custom. Their re-

[1] Bab. Berachoth, 6 a, 7 a (p. 240, Schwab).   [2] Babha Metzia, 86, a.
[3] Hegesippus, ap. Euseb. *H. E.* iv. 22.   [4] Neander, *Ch. Hist.* i. 475.
[5] Epiphan. *Haer.* xxx. 9.
[6] They are said, however, to have denied His Præ-existence (Euseb. *H. E.* iii. 27), but we may class them with the τὸν Ἰησοῦν ἀποδεχόμενοι of Origen (*c. Cels.* v. 61). The reason why the early allusions to them are contradictory, is because the opinions of these "subdichotomies of petty schisms" were doubtless ill-defined.

version to the religion of the Patriarchs, as representing a purer and more absolute religion than the Levitic system, is distinctly Pauline, and they honestly accepted the faith of Christ.[1] It has been inferred from passages of this book that they held the view that Jesus only became a Divine Being at His baptism, but the expressions used seem to be at least capable of a more innocent and orthodox interpretation.[2]

b. The EBIONITES, on the other hand, were daringly heretical. They rejected altogether the writings of St. Paul,[3] and pursued his memory for some generations with covert but virulent calumny. They insisted on the necessity of circumcision and the universal validity of the Law. They regarded Christ as a mere man, the son of Joseph and Mary, justified only by his legal righteousness.[4] To these views some of the Ebionites—who died away as an obscure sect on the shores of the Dead Sea—superadded ascetic notions and practices which they seem to have borrowed from the Essenes.[5] Hence, in all probability, was derived their name of Ebionites, from the Hebrew word *Ebion*, "poor." The error that there was such a person as Ebion was due to Epiphanius, who calls him a "successor of Cerinthus."[6] The assertion that they were called "paupers" because they thought "meanly and poorly" of Christ, was merely a way of turning their name into a reproach.[7] The ELCESAITES, or followers of Elxai, who were Ebionites with Essene and Gnostic admixtures, were never more than a small and uninfluential sect.

By the time when St. John wrote his Gospel and Epistles, the question of circumcision, and all the most distinctively Judaic controversies, had ceased to be discussed. They had, at any rate, lost all significance for the Church in general. The Nazarenes and Ebionites had at best but a local influence. Even the Nicolaitans are charged, not with heresy, but with immoral practices, and with teaching indifference to idolatry by the ostentatious and indiscriminate eating of meats offered to idols.[8] This tendency to Antinomianism was the natural result and the appropriate Nemesis of that extravagant legal rigorism to which the Judaists strove to subjugate the Church.

2. The two heresiarchs who came into most dangerous prominence

---

[1] See Neander, *Ch. Hist.* ii. 19—21; Mansel, *Gnostic Heresies*, pp. 123—128; Lightfoot, *Galatians*, pp. 298—301; Ritschl, *Altkath. Kirche*, pp. 152, seq.
[2] *Test. XII. Patr.*, Levi, 18; Simeon, 7.
[3] Orig. c. *Cels.* v. ad fin.
[4] Hence Marius Mercator calls them Homuncionitae (*Refut. anath. Nestor.* 12), and Lactantius *Anthropiani* (*Instt.* iv. ad fin.).
[5] Tert. *De Carn. Christi*, 14; *De Praescr.* 33, 48; Philastr. *Haer.* 37; Aug. *de Haer.* 16.
[6] *Dial. c. Lucifer.* 8; Ps. Tert. *Append. de Praescr.* 48.
[7] Euseb. *H. E.* iii. 27.
[8] On the Nicolaitans see notes on Rev. ii. 6, 14, 15. An account of them, taken from Iren. *Haer.* i. 27, iii. 11; Euseb. *H. E.* iii. 29; Epiphan. *Haer.* xxv. 1; Clem. Alex. *Strom.* ii. 20, iii. 4, will be found in Ittigius, *De Haeresiarchis*, l. 9, § 4; Mosheim, *De rebus Christ.* ii. 69. They, like other sects, are charged with cloaking licentious habits under specious names (Clem. Alex. *Strom.* iii. 4; *Constt. Apost.* vi. 8; Ignat. *Ep. ad Trall.* and *ad Philad.*).

in the Apostolic age are SIMON MAGUS and CERINTHUS. If any credit can be given to the vague and much-confused traditions as to their tenets, it is clear that those tenets, at least in their germ, were strongly and directly condemned in several of the Epistles.

a. Of SIMON MAGUS, "the hero of the romance of heresy," little is known which is not legendary. In the Acts of the Apostles[1] we find him in the position of a successful impostor in Samaria, where the whole population, amazed by his sorceries, accepted his assertion that he was "the Power of God which is called Great." He was baptised by Philip, but proved the hollowness of his religion by being guilty of the first act of the sin which from him is called "simony"—he endeavoured "to purchase the gift of God with money." According to the high authority of Justin Martyr—who was himself a Samaritan—Simon was a native of Gitton in Samaria.[2] Josephus, in calling him a Cypriote (if he be speaking of the same person), may have confused Gitton with Citium in Cyprus.[3] Felix made use of his iniquitous agency in inveigling from her husband the Herodian princess Drusilla.[4] He is the subject of many wild and monstrous legends. He is said to have been a pupil of a certain Dositheus, and to have fallen in love with his concubine Luna (Selene or Helena). When Dositheus wished to beat him he found that the stick passed through his body as through smoke.[5] The "sorceries" which he practised are said to have consisted in passing through mountains and through fire, making bread of stones, breathing flames, and turning himself into various shapes. With the money that he offered to St. Peter he purchased as his slave and partner a woman of Tyre named Helena.[6] Hence his followers are called by Celsus Heleniani. Irenæus says[7] "that he carried this woman about with him, calling her his first Conception (Ennoia) and the mother of all things. Descending to the lower world, she had produced the angels and powers by which the lower world was made, and had been by them imprisoned and degraded. She had been Helen of Troy, and in her fallen condition was "the lost sheep," whom he had recovered. He himself, though not a man, became a man to set her free. His adherents, he declared, had no need to fear the lower angels and powers which made the world, but they might live as they pleased, and would be saved by resting their hopes on him and on her. Later on he is said to have gone to Rome, and to have met with his end in an attempt to fly, which was defeated by the prayers of St. Peter and St. Paul.[8]

[1] Acts viii. [2] Just. Mart. *Apol.* i. 26.
[3] Jos. *Antt.* xviii. 5; xx. 7, § 2. Euseb. *H. E.* ii. 13.
[4] See *Life and Work of St. Paul,* ii. 341.
[5] *Constt. Apost.* vi. 8; Clem. *Recogn.* ii. 31.
[6] Clem. *Recogn.* ii. 31; Niceph. *H. E.* ii. 27.
[7] Iren. *Haer.* i. 23; ii. 9, and comp. Hippol. *Ref. Haer.* vi. 19; Tert. *De Anima,* 34; Epiphan. *Haer.* xxv. 4; Theodoret, *Haer. Fab.* i. 1.
[8] Hippolytus says that he was buried—promising to rise again (*Ref. Haer.* vi. 26).

It is clear that Simon Magus was not only a heresiarch, but also a false Christ or antichrist. His notions were partly Jewish and Alexandrian. Philo had spoken of "Powers" of God, of which the greatest was the Logos. According to Jerome, Simon used to say, " I am the word of God, I am beautiful, I am the Paraclete, I am the Almighty, I am the all things of God;"[1] and Irenæus says that he spoke of having appeared to the Jews as the Son, to the Samaritans as the Father, and to the Gentiles as the Holy Spirit. Hippolytus gives an account of his opinions from a book called *The Great Announcement* (*Apophasis Megale*), which, though it can hardly be his, may be supposed to express the views of his followers. The views there stated resemble those of the later Gnostics and Kabbalists. The " Indefinite Power" is described as Fire and Silence. This Fire has two natures, the source respectively of the Intelligible and the Sensible Universe. The world was generated by three pairs of roots or principles—namely, Mind and Consciousness, Voice and Name, Reasoning and Thought; and the Power in these roots is manifested as "he who stands," or who shall stand—by which he seems to mean himself as the perfect man. It is clear that in these roots we see the germ of the Gnostic Aeons and the Kabbalistic Sephiroth—the object of which, like that of every Gnostic system of emanations, was to separate God as far as possible from man and from matter. The inmost conception of Gnosticism is contradicted—its very basis is overthrown—by the words of St. John's Gospel, "The Word became flesh."

b. The name of CERINTHUS is less mixed up with fantastic legends: but the accounts given of his views are full of uncertainty and contradiction, and seem to show that he was one of those who " wavered like a wave of the sea," and was tossed about by every wind of doctrine. Thus it is that he mixed up Millenarianism and other Judaic elements with fancies which were afterwards developed by the most anti-Judaic Gnostics.[2] Thus, too, he has been credited with the authorship of the Apocalypse, though, in accordance with early Church tradition, he was the very teacher against whom the later writings of St. John were specially aimed.[3]

Of his personal life scarcely anything is known. It is conjectured that he must have been a Jew by birth, but he had evidently been

---

As to *this* legend—which (as we have seen) may have sprung from the attempt of an actor taking the part of Icarus (Suet. *Ner.* 12)—Irenæus, Tertullian, and Eusebius are silent. It is found in Arnobius, *adv. Gent.* ii. 12, and with many varying details in the *Apostolic Constitutions* (vi. 9); Ambrose (*Hexaem.* iv. 8); Sulp. Severus (ii. 41); Egesippus (*De Excid. Hierosol.* iii. 2), etc., as well as in Cedrenus, Nicephorus, Glycas, etc. I have already alluded to the mistake which led Justin Martyr to suppose that he was worshipped at Rome (*Apol.* 11, 69, 91; Tert. *Apol.* 13).

[1] Jer. *in Matt.* xxiv. 5.

[2] The assertion of Philastrius (*Haer.* 36) and Epiphanius (*Haer.* xxviii. 2) that he was the person who stirred up the dispute about circumcision at Jerusalem (Acts ix. 1) is an unchronological guess.

[3] Jer. *Cat. Script.* 9, and so too Irenæus, etc.

trained in Egypt,[1] and he certainly taught in Asia. The name *M*erinthus, which is sometimes given him, is probably a nickname, since the word means "a cord." But even his date is uncertain. He is usually believed to have taught in the old age of St. John; but Tertullian places him after Karpokrates, who did not flourish till the reign of Hadrian, A.D. 117.

His errors, as noticed by Irenæus,[2] are as follows:—

(1). He declared that the world was made by a Virtue or Power far inferior to the Essential Divinity.

(2). That the human Jesus was not born of a virgin, but was the son of Joseph and Mary, and that he only differed from men in supreme goodness.

(3). That the Divine Christ only descended upon Jesus at His baptism;[3] and—

(4). That, when Jesus suffered, the Divine Christ flew back into His Pleroma, being Himself incapable of suffering.[4]

Besides these errors, he is said to have regarded Jesus as a teacher only, not as a redeemer; to have rejected the Epistles of St. Paul; and to have sanctioned the practice of being baptised for the dead.

Even from these glimpses we can see that he did not exactly deny the Divinity of Christ. The first who is said to have done this was Theodotus of Byzantium.[5] But Cerinthus was evidently actuated by the Gnostic desire to remove as far as possible the notion of any contact, much more any intercommunion, between God and Matter. Now, the Christian doctrine of the Incarnation cut at the root of the Alexandrian and Gnostic fancies that Matter was evil, and that God was so infinitely removed from man that he could hold no immediate communion with him. It was the fatal system of Dualism which led to so many heresies. It was the cause of Ebionism, which denied Christ's Divinity altogether; of Docetism, which maintained that the body of Jesus was purely phantasmal and unreal;[6] and it probably lay at the base of Nestorianism, which lost sight of the indivisible union of the human and the Divine in the one God-man. Cerinthus, like

---

[1] Hippolyt. *Ref. Haer*. vii. 33; Theodoret, *Haer. Fab.* ii. 3.
[2] *Haer.* i. 26.
[3] This view was afterwards elaborated by Bardesanes. Valentinus, on the other hand, taught that the body of Christ was celestial, but merely passed through the Virgin without partaking of her nature.
[4] Epiphanius and Theodoret repeat this testimony of Irenæus, and say that Cerinthus attributed the miracles of Jesus to Christ, whom he represented as identical with the Holy Spirit. Jesus was to Cerinthus only "the earthly Christ," or "the Christ below" (ὁ κάτω Χριστός), while the Divine Christ was "the Christ above" (ὁ ἄνω Χριστός).
[5] Euseb. *H. E.* v. 28.
[6] Clemens of Alexandria (*Strom*. iii. 13) ascribes the invention of Docetism to Julius Cassianus, A.D. 173, but it is clear that the germs of it existed long before, and are even found, as Hippolytus says (*Ref. Haer*. vi. 14), in Simon Magus. It was taught in the Apocryphal Gospel of Peter (Euseb. *H. E.* vi. 23), which was perhaps forged by Leucius, a disciple of Marcion, about A.D. 140. The Docetae were also called Phantasiasts and Opinarians.

other Gnostics of Egyptian training, denied the hypostatic and eternal union of the two natures in Christ. He taught that Christ alone was the Son of God, and that until His baptism, and at His crucifixion, Jesus was an ordinary man. In the one pregnant expression of St. John, he "loosed" or "disintegrated Jesus."[1]

Views essentially similar to these are found in all the Gnostic systems.[2] They all sprang from speculations about the origin of evil, and about the method of bridging over the chasm between absolute and finite being. Since they identified evil with matter, they led at once to a Manichean dualism; and it was only by inventing elaborate series of hermaphrodite pairs of æons or emanations that they could imagine any communication of God's will to man.[3] They were all influenced by the Platonised Judaism of Philo[4] and the Alexandrians, as well as by Persian and other Oriental elements of thought.[5] But the deadliness of their system revealed itself in many and in opposite forms. It exalted an imaginary knowledge above a pure and unsophisticated faith. It mistook a terminology for a creed. It confused a manipulation of words with a removal of difficulties. It puffed up its followers with an inflated sense that they were an intellectual aristocracy, possessed of an esoteric teaching which elevated them far above their simple brethren. The doctrine of the inherent evil of matter, and the confusion of "the body" with "the flesh," drove the Gnostics either into an extravagant asceticism, which destroyed the body without controlling it, or into Antinomian license, which destroyed it in the opposite way by shameful self-indulgence. This they excused either on the plea that to the true Gnostic the spiritual was everything, and that anything which his body did was of no moment, since it did not affect his true self; or by arguing that the moral law was only the work of the evil or inferior Demiurge.[6] In both extremes they confused the true nature of sin, turned religion and morality into curious

---

[1] See *infra*, p. 557.

[2] The name Gnostic—"one who knows"—was first adopted by the Naassenes or Ophites, "alleging that they alone knew the depths" (Hippol. *Haer.* v. 6). Irenæus (*ap.* Euseb. *H. E.* iv. 7), calls Karpokrates "the father of the heresy which is called that of the Gnostics" (comp. *id. Haer.* i. 25, 6; see Lipsius, *Gnosticismus*, p. 48). The original sources for the history of Gnosticism are to be found in Irenæus (*adv. Haereses*), Tertullian (*adv. Marcionem, De Praescr. Haereticorum*, and *Scorpiace*), Epiphanius (*adv. Haereses*), and passages of Clemens Alex. and Origen, and Hippolytus *Philosophumena*. For modern treatises, see Beausobre (*Hist. du Manichéisme*), Matter, *Hist. du Gnosticisme*), Burton (*Inquiry into Heresies of the Apostolic Age*), Mansel (*Gnostic Heresies*), and Baur (*Die Christ. Gnosis*). See too Milman, *History of Christianity*, ii. 68; Robertson, *Ch. Hist.* i. 31; Neander, *Ch. Hist.* ii. 82; Gieseler, *Ch. Hist.* i. 114; Burton, *Bampt. Lect.* iv., etc. Later treatises are Ad. Harnack, *Quellen d. Gesch. d. Gnost.* (1873); Lipsius, *Quellen d. ält. Ketzergesch.* 1875.

[3] So Plato, in the *Timaeus*, said that it was the function of the subordinate gods "to weave the mortal to the immortal."

[4] "Haereticorum patriarchae philosophi" (Tert. *adv. Hermog.* 8); "Plato omnium haereticorum condimentarius" (*De Anim.* 23).

[5] Some of the Gnostics referred to Zoroaster. Porphyr. *Vit. Plotin.* 10.

[6] Clemens Alex. (*Strom.* iii. p. 529) points out that they taught extravagant asceticism (ὑπέρτονον ἐγκράτειαν), or moral indifferentism (ἀδιαφορὼς ζῆν).

questions, placed salvation in systems of metaphysics, and by vain speculation and verbal analyses lost sight of the practical answer which Christianity had given to all the deepest problems of human life.

These errors existed in their germs from a very early period. We often hear the voice of St. Paul raised in warning respecting them, especially in the Epistles to the Colossians and Ephesians, and in the later Epistles. Against their Antinomian developments we have the strong denunciations of St. Jude. But St. John lived at a time when they had acquired a more definite consistency. He saw and he declared that all of them began or ended with a denial of Christ, or with errors as to His nature. He discountenanced alike their exaggerated spirituality and the carnality into which it passed. He erected a bulwark against them all in those inspired words which contain the essence of all the truths which are most precious to Christianity, and which form the Prologues of his Gospel and First Epistle. He regards them all as forms of Antichrist. He who denies that Jesus is the Christ the Son of God—in other words, who asserts, as Cerinthus did, that the historical Man Jesus was not in the fullest sense Divine—is an Antichrist in a far different sense than Nero was, and yet in a true sense. St. John tells us this in his usual way, both positively and negatively.[1] He tells us that Jesus is the Christ, and the son of God, and that the Divine Eternal Being tabernacled in human flesh.[2] He says, in every possible form of words, that Jesus is Christ; that Christ is Jesus; that Jesus is Divine—that Jesus is not a separate being from the Son of God, but indistinguishable from Him. The Gnostics made the Divine "come and go to Jesus like a bird through the air," but St. John testifies throughout Gospel and Epistles, as he had also done, though with less absolute distinctness, in the Apocalypse, that the Divine became Human, and dwelt in our Humanity indivisibly.[3] The Eternal Son of God not only filled the whole person of Jesus, which is Himself, but also filled all believers—who are born of God, not of "the will of the flesh." He fills all life and death and resurrection with Divine life and glory. Yet while thus protesting alike against Psilanthropia—the Ebionite doctrine that Christ was a mere man—and against Docetism, and against the Dualistic theories of incipient Manichees, and against all severing of the Person of Jesus into a Man who is not God, or a God who refuses to be a man—he at the same time makes it clear that he does not identify religion with orthodoxy, but places true religion in love to God shown by love to man. The self-satisfaction of a supercilious orthodoxy which might at any time soar into Pharisaic asceticism, or sink into reckless immorality, is confronted with the assurance—Oh that in all ages the Christian Church had better understood it, and taken it more deeply to heart!—that "he who saith I know God, and

[1] 1 John ii. 18, 22; iv. 3, 15; v. 1, 10.
[2] 1 John iv. 2, 3; 2 John 7.
[3] See Keim, *Jesu von Nazara*, Introd. II. ζ.

keepeth not His commandments," were he ten-times-over orthodox in his asserted knowledge, is yet "a liar, and the truth is not in him;"[1] and that "he who loveth not, knoweth not God; for God is love."[2]

CHAPTER XXXI.

LATER WRITINGS OF ST. JOHN.

"Sumtis pennis aquilæ et ad altiora festinans de Verbo Dei disputat."—Jer. *ad Matt., Proem.*

"Transcendit nubes, transcendit virtutes coelorum, transcendit angelos, et *Verbum in principio* repperit."—Ambros. *Prol. in Luc.*

APART from its own beauty and importance, the Epistle of St. John derives a special interest from the fact that it is the latest utterance of Apostolic inspiration. It is addressed to Churches which by the close of the first century had advanced to a point of development far beyond that contemplated by St. Paul in his earlier Epistles. Many of the old questions which had raged between Judaisers and Paulinists had vanished into the back-ground. The Gospel had spread far and wide. It had become self-evident that nothing could be more futile than to confine those waters of the River of God in the narrow channels of Jewish particularism. The fall of Jerusalem had illuminated as with a lightning flash the darkness of obstinacy and prejudice. It had proved the inadequacy of the Pharisaic ideal of "righteousness," and the ignorance of the system which proclaimed itself to be the only orthodoxy. The liberty for which St. Paul had battled all his life long against storms of hatred and of persecution, had now been finally achieved. St. John himself had advanced to a standpoint of knowledge far beyond that of the days when he had lived among the Elders of the Church which was dominated by the views and example of St. James. He had learnt the full meaning of those words of the Lord to the woman of Samaria, that the day should come in which men should worship the Father neither on Gerizim or in Jerusalem but everywhere, and acceptably, if they worshipped in spirit and in truth. On the other hand, new and dangerous errors had arisen. Christianity had come into contact with Greek philosophy and Eastern speculation. Men were no longer interested in such questions as whether they need be circumcised; or to what extent their consciences need be troubled by distinctions between clean and unclean meats; or whether they were to place the authority of James or Kephas above that of Paul; or what was the real position to be assigned to the gift of tongues; or whether

---

[1] 1 John ii. 4.   [2] 1 John iv. 8.

the dead in Christ were to lose any of the advantages which would be granted at His second return to the living. All such questions had received their solution in the Epistles of St. Paul. Christians as a body were by this time fully acquainted with his arguments, and acquiesced in them all the more unhesitatingly because they had been stamped with irrefragable sanction by the course of History. All men could see the rejection of the once chosen people. Far different were the questions which now agitated the minds of Christian thinkers. They were questions of a more abstract character, relating above all to the nature of Christ. Was He, as the Ebionites maintained, a mere man? Was He, as Cerinthus argued, a twofold personality, the Eternal Christ and the sinless Jesus, united only between the Baptism and the Crucifixion?[1] Or, was He, again, as the intellectual precursors of the Docetæ were beginning to suggest, a man in semblance only—who had but lived in the phantasm of an earthly life? Nay more, men were beginning to speculate about the nature of God Himself. Could God be regarded as the author of evil? Must it not be supposed, as the Manichees subsequently argued, that there were two Gods—one the supreme and illimitable Deity belonging to regions infinitely above "the smoke and stir of this dim spot which men call earth," the other a limited and imperfect Demiurge? Again, what was the relation between these questions and the duties of daily life? Christians were free from the Law; that was a truth which St. Paul had proved. But was there any fundamental distinction between the authority on which rested the ceremonial and the moral law? Might they not regard themselves as free from the rules of morality, as well as from the routine of Levitism? Was not faith enough? If men believed rightly on God and on His Son Jesus Christ, would He greatly care as to how they lived? So argued the Antinomians, and many of them were prepared to carry their arguments from theory into practice. Such, then, were the errors which it became the special mission of St. John to counteract.

But he does not counteract them controversially. The method of Pauline dialectics was entirely unsuited to his habit of mind. That method in its due time and place was absolutely necessary. It met the doubts of men in the intellectual region in which they had originated. It broke down their objections with the same weapons by which they had been maintained. But when that work was done there was another way to bring home the truth to the conviction of the universal Church. It was by witness, by spiritual appeal, by the statement of personal experience, by the lofty language of inspired authority. Hence the method which St. John adopts is not polemical but irenical. He overthrows error by the irresistible presentation of counter truths. In the Gospel, as Keim says, he counteracted heresy thetically, in the

---

[1] Iren. *Haer*. xi. 7. "Qui autem Jesum separant a Christo et impassibilem perseverasse Christum, passum vero Jesum dicunt . . ."

Epistles antithetically; in other words, in the Gospel he lays down positive truths, in the Epistles he states those truths in sharp contrast with the opposing errors. To those who moved in the atmosphere of controversy " difficulties " loomed large and portentous all around the doctrines of the Church. St. John dealt with those difficulties from a region so elevated and serene that to all who reached his point of view they shrank into insignificance. At the heights whence he gazed men might learn to see the grandeur of the ocean, and to think little of the billows, and nothing of the ripples upon its surface. Hence it has been a true Christian instinct which has assigned to St. John the symbol of " the eagle," in the four-fold cherub of the Gospel-chariot. The eagle which sails in the azure deep of air " does not worry itself how to cross the streams." Dante, in the *Paradiso*, showed no little insight when he called him " Christ's own eagle," and when he describes the outlines of his form as lost in the dazzling light by which he is encircled. " The central characteristic of his nature is intensity—intensity of thought, word, insight, life. He regards everything on its divine side. For him the eternal is already. . . . . He sees the past and the future gathered up in the manifestation of the Son of God. This was the one fact in which the hope of the world lay. Of this he had himself been assured by the evidence of sense and thought. This he was constrained to proclaim: 'We have seen and do testify.' He had no laboured process to go through; he saw. He had no constructive proof to develop; he bore witness. His source of knowledge was direct, and his mode of bringing conviction was to affirm." [1] His whole style and tone of thought is that of "the bosom disciple." [2]

Thus then the one consummate truth which St. John had to offer to the gathering doubts and perplexities of all unfaithful hearts was the Incarnation of the Divine. This is the central object of all faith. This is the one counteraction of all unbelief.

And by the manner in which he set forth this truth—by this presentation to the world of " the spiritual Gospel " [3]—he at once obeyed the Divine impulse of inspiration which came to him, and met the natural wishes which the Church had earnestly expressed. The tradition which records that he was urged to write his Gospel by the Elders and Bishops of the Church,[4] is one which has every mark of probability. The generation of the Apostles was rapidly passing away. St. John had now long exceeded the ordinary limits of human age. The day would very soon

---

[1] Westcott, *St. John*, p. xxxv.
[2] This title (ὁ ἐπιστήθιος) was given to St. John as early as the second century. It is found (ὁ ἐπὶ τὸ στῆθος τοῦ Κυρίου ἀναπεσών) in Polycrates, Bp. of Ephesus (see Routh, *Rel. Sacr.* i. 15, 37, 370) and Iren. *c. Haer.* iii. 1, 1.
[3] Clem. Alex. *ap.* Euseb. *H. E.* vi. 14.
[4] " Impelled by his friends " (Clem. Alex. *l.c.*). The legend is, that on being requested to write the Gospel, he asked the Ephesian elders to join him in fasting, and then suddenly exclaimed, as if inspired, "In the beginning was the Word" (Jer. *de Virr. Illustr.* 29). Irenaeus only says that he was asked to write the Gospel (*Haer.* iii. 1).

come when not a single human being could say of the Lord "I saw." But *he* could still say this; he had not only seen and heard and gazed upon and handled the Word of Life, but had even been the beloved disciple of the Son of Man. The facts of the life of Jesus had been recorded by the three Synoptists. What the world now needed was some guide into the full and unspeakable significance of those facts. Who was so fit to give it as St. John, nay, who besides him was even capable of giving it with authority? He had hitherto written nothing but the Apocalypse. The Apocalypse had indeed depicted the glory of the Eternal Christ, but it was a book of peculiar character; it was full of symbols; it was difficult of interpretation; it was based on the imagery and prophecies of the Old Testament; it was full of storm and stress. It was the Book of Battle, the Book of the Wars of the Lord; it portrayed the struggles of the Church with the hostile forces of the Jewish and Gentile world; and its celestial visions were interposed between scenes of judgment,

"As when some mighty painter dips
His pencil in the hues of earthquake and eclipse."

There were, morever, many Christian doctrines on which the Apocalypse did not touch, and, above all, it had been written before that Divine event which had evidently been the beginning of a new epoch in the history of Christianity. In the final removal of the candlestick of Judaism, the Christian Church had rightly seen the primary fulfilment of those prophecies which had spoken of the Immediate Coming of the Lord.

To all the living members of the Church, that stupendous event had set the seal of God to the revelation of the New Covenant. It was the obvious close of the epoch which had begun at Sinai. It was the extinction of the Aaronic in order to establish the Melchizedek Priesthood. It had rendered the system of Jewish sacrifices impossible, in order to show that the one true sacrifice had now once for all been offered. It had been the burning desecration of the sin-stained Temple in order that men might see in the Church of God the new and spiritual Jerusalem which had no need of any temple therein, because the body of every true believer was the spiritual temple of the one God. But to St. John especially that event had come as with a burst of light. It had been, perhaps, the greatest step since the death of Christ in that education for the sake of which his life had been so long preserved. The oral teaching of the Apostle must have been sufficient to show that the gradual revelation which had so long been going on within him had now reached its fulness. The light which had begun to pulse in the Eastern sky over the banks of Jordan had shone more and more towards the perfect day. Was this teaching to be lost to the world for ever? Was it only to be entrusted to the shifting imperfections of oral tradition? Was it to be but half apprehended by the simplicity, or misrepresented by the limitations, of such men as Papias and Irenæus? How little had the

Synoptists detailed respecting the Judæan ministry of which St. John so often spoke! They had not recorded the earliest call of the disciples nor the raising of Lazarus, nor the washing of the Apostles' feet. They had reported some of the public sermons of Jesus, but they had not preserved any memorial of such private discourses as that to Nicodemus and the woman of Samaria, or as those Divine farewells delivered at the Last Supper. Nor, again, had they spoken of Christ's præ-existence; nor had they used that title of "the Word," which was now so frequently on the lips of St. John, and to which he gave such pregnant significance; nor did they furnish a final insight into the two natures in the one Person of the Son of Man.

It was true, indeed, as the Elders and Bishops who urged their request upon St. John would at once have admitted, that as regards the divinity and atoning work of Christ, the knowledge of the Church had been greatly widened and systematised by the teachings of St. Paul. He had brought into clear light the truth that Jesus was not only the Messiah of the Jews, the Prophet, Priest, and King, but that He was the Incarnate Son of God, the eternal Saviour of the World; that only by faith in Him could we be justified; that the true life of the believer is merged in absolute union with Him; and that because He has risen we also shall rise.

Yet none could have listened to St. John in his latter years without feeling that, while he accepted the doctrines of St. Paul, he had himself, in the course of a longer life, enjoyed more of that teaching which comes to us from the Spirit of God in the lessons of History. Whilst he gave no new commandment, and had no new revelation to announce, he yet stamped with the impress of finality the great truths which St. Paul had taught. There is not a single doctrine in the writings of St. John which may not be found implicitly and even explicitly in the writings of St. Paul; and yet—to give but two instances out of many—the Church would have been indefinitely the loser had she not received the inheritance of sayings so supreme, so clear, and so final as these of St. John,—

"*The Father sent His Son to be the Saviour of the world,*" and

"*We are in Him that is true, even in His Son Jesus Christ. This is the true God and eternal life.*"[1]

No one, again, had yet uttered such clear words respecting the Divinity and Humanity indissolubly yet distinctly united in the Person of Christ as those which are contained in the Prologue to the Gospel and the opening address of the Epistle and which are concentrated in the four words, "*The Word became flesh.*" No one had so briefly summarised the Atoning and Mediatorial work of Christ, as, "*He is the Propitiation*[2] *for our sins, and not for ours only but also for the Whole World!*"

Indeed, as they listened to the white-haired Apostle, men must have

---

[1] 1 John v. 20.   [2] 1 John ii. 2; ἱλασμός, a unique expression of St. John.

felt that there was something in his manner of exposition which tended to remove all difficulties, to solve all apparent antinomies. Take, for instance, the apparent contradiction between the terms used by St. Paul and St. James as to Righteousness by Faith and Righteousness by Works. Would it not cease to be a difficulty—was not the controversy lifted to a higher region—when they heard such words as, "*He that doeth righteousness is righteous, even as He is righteous,*" in connexion with, "*Whoso keepeth His word, in them verily is the love of God perfected, and every one that doeth righteousness is born of Him;*" and, "*Behold what and how great love God hath given us that we should be called the children of God*"? Or, again, if men felt the difficulties which rise from the forensic and sacrificial aspects of the Atonement, how would they feel that the forgiveness in the Court, and the cleansing in the Temple, was simplified when it was mingled with the thoughts of the perfection of our sonship in union with the Son of God, and indicated in terms so sublimely final as,

"*If we say that we have no sin we deceive ourselves, and the truth is not in us. But if we confess our sins, God is faithful and just to forgive us our sins and to cleanse us from all unrighteousness*"?

The expressions of the New Testament which describe the privileges of the Christian estate fall into three classes, of which one revolves around the word Righteousness; another round the word Sonship; a third around metaphors expressive of Sacrifice. Now let the reader study the First Epistle of St. John, from ii. 29 to iii. 5, and he will find the order there—Righteousness (ii. 29), Sonship (iii. 1), Sanctification (iii. 2—5); but the three are one. The terms of the Court, the Household and the Temple confirm and illustrate each other. Jesus Christ—the Righteous, the Son of the Father, the Holy One—presides, in the glory of His holiness, over all and over each.[1]

CHAPTER XXXII.

THE STAMP OF FINALITY ON THE WRITINGS OF ST. JOHN.

"Aquila ipse est Johannes, sublimium prædicator, et lucis internæ atque aeternæ fixis oculis contemplator."—AUG. *in Joh., Tract.* 36.

IT is in ways like these—by the use of expressions at once larger and simpler, more comprehensive and more easily intelligible; expressions which transcend controversy because they are the synthesis of the complementary truths which controversy forces into antithesis—that St. John, the last writer of the New Testament, in traversing the whole

[1] I owe this thought to Dr. Pope's excellent Introduction to his translation of Haupt's *First Epistle of St. John*, p. xxxi.

field of Christian theology, sets the seal of perfection on all former doctrine. This is exactly what we should have desired to find in the last treatises of inspired revelation. And one remarkable peculiarity of his method is that he indicates the deepest truths even respecting those points of doctrine on which he does not specifically dwell. Thus, he does not dwell on the explanation (if the term may be allowed) of Christ's atonement; he does not offer any theory as to the reason for the necessity or efficacy of Christ's death; yet he involves all the teaching of St. Paul and of Apollos in the words, that "Christ is the propitiation for our sins and for the whole world," and that "the blood of Jesus Christ cleanseth us from all sin." He does not use the words "mediator between God and man," but he sets forth, with a clearness never before attained, that our mediator *is* God and Man. He does not contrast God's love with His justice, but he shows that love and propitiation were united in the antecedent will of God. He does not work out the details of Christology, but he so pervades his Gospel and Epistle with the thought that "the Word was God," and that "without Him was not anything made that was made,"[1] as to produce a Christological impression, sublimer even than that which we derive from the Epistles to the Ephesians and the Colossians. He does not dwell on the sacraments, and yet in his few words on the witness of the Water, and on the Bread of Life, he brings out their deepest significance. He does not develop the reasons for the rejection of the Chosen People after the grandeur of their past mission; but he illustrates both no less fully than the Epistles to the Romans and the Hebrews, when, in his Gospel, he contrasts, step by step, the unbelief of the Jews with the faith of the disciples, and yet records the expression of Christ's eulogy "an Israelite indeed." He records Christ's saying to the Woman of Samaria, that salvation—the salvation of which all the Prophets had spoken—was from the Jews;[2] and, in his own words, he writes of Christ's coming to the Jews as a coming to "His own people and His own house."[3] Once more, St. John nowhere enters into any formal statements about the Triune God; yet in whose writings do we see more fully than in his the illustration of St. Augustine's saying, "*Ubi amor ibi Trinitas*," when we hear him say that "God is Love," and that "God is Light;" and that in Christ was Light, and that Light was the Life of Men; and that all Christians have an unction from the Holy One, and that the Holy Spirit is the Spirit of Christ?

But there are three points in the last writings of St. John which more especially stamp his teaching with the mark of finality.

1. The first of these is the new and marvellous light which he throws on the Idea of Eternity.

The use of the word *aionios*, and of its Hebrew equivalent, *olam*,

---

[1] "These words, taken in their widest significance, constitute the signature of the Johannæan writings" (Haupt). [2] John iv. 22, ἡ σωτηρία ἐκ τῶν Ἰουδαίων ἐστίν.
[3] John i. 11, οἱ ἴδιοι . . . τὰ ἴδια. Comp. John xix. 27.

throughout the whole of Scripture, ought to have been sufficient to prove to every thoughtful and unbiassed student that it altogether transcends the thoroughly vulgar and unmeaning conception of "endless." Nothing, perhaps, tends to prove more clearly the difficulty of eradicating an error that has once taken deep and agelong root in the minds of "theologians" than the fact that it should still be necessary to prove that the word eternal, far from being a mere equivalent for "everlasting," *never* means "everlasting" at all, except by reflexion from the substantives to which it is joined; that it is only joined to those substantives because it connotes ideas which transcend all time; that to make it mean nothing but time endlessly prolonged is to degrade it by filling it with a merely relative conception which it is meant to supersede, and by emptying it of all the highest conceptions which it properly includes. I am well aware that this truth will, for some time, be repeated in vain. But, once more, I repeat that if by *aionios* St. John had *meant* "endless" when he speaks of "aeonian life," there was the perfectly commonplace and unambiguous word *akatalutos*, used by Apollos in Heb. v. 6, and there were at least five or six other adjectives or expressions which were ready to his hand. But the Life which had been manifested, which he had seen, to which he was bearing witness, which stood in relation to the Father, and was manifested to us,[1] was something infinitely higher than a mere "endless" life. The life—if mere living be life—of the most doomed and apostate of the human race—the life even of the devil and his angels—is an "endless" living, if we hold that man and evil spirits are immortal. But by qualifying the divine life by the epithet "eternal" (*aionios*) St. John meant, not an endless life (though it is also endless), but a *spiritual* life, the life which is in God, and which was manifested by Christ to us. By calling it *aionios* he meant to imply, not—which was a very small and accidental part of it—its unbroken continuance, but its ethical quality. The life is "endless," not because it is the infinite extension of time, but because it is the absolute antithesis of time; and *aionios* expresses its internal quality, not as something which can be measured by infinite tickings of the clocks, but as something incommensurable by all clocks, were they to tick for ever. The horologe of earth, as Bengel profoundly expresses it, is no measure for the *aeonologe* of heaven. The meaning of "eternal" ought long ago to have been vindicated from its popular degradation. St. John is the last of all Scripture writers who uses it; he alone of all Scripture writers defines it; and he makes it consist not in idle duration, but in progressive knowledge. In defining it, he says that it is the gift of Christ, "and that the eternal life is this, that they may know Thee the only true God, and Him whom Thou sendest, even Jesus Christ."[2]

[1] John i. 2.
[2] John xvii. 2, 3. Literally "that they may be learning to know"—not so much the possession of a completed life as of a life which is advancing to completion.

For thus we see at once, that, in the mind of St. John eternal life is an antithesis *not* to the temporal, but to the Seen;¹ that it is not a life which *shall be*, but one that, for the believer, now IS: that "every one who beholdeth the Son has—not shall have, but *has*—eternal life;"² that "he who hath the Son, *hath* the life" here and now; and that one of the objects why St. John wrote at all was that they might know that they had it.³ He who will lay aside bigotry and factiousness and newspaper theology, and will sincerely meditate on these passages, will see how unfortunate is the antique and vulgar error as to the meaning of this word. If a man be incapable of seeing this, or unwilling to admit it, for such a man reasoning is vain.⁴

2. Another mark of finality is St. John's teaching about the LOGOS, or WORD. In the Epistle he enters into no details or description respecting the nature and Person of the Logos; and yet—in accordance with that peculiarity of his method which we have already noticed—the doctrine of the Logos, as the source of all life, is the fundamental matter and pith of the Epistle.⁵ This, we may remark in passing, is one of the indications that the Epistle was a didactic accompaniment of the Gospel. But in the use of the Logos as a distinct name of Christ St. John stands alone. Other Apostles—St. Paul, St. James, and, above all, the writer of the Epistle to the Hebrews—seem to hover on the verge of it; but they do not actually use, much less do they insist on it; and when they approach it they are thinking always of the Divinity more than of the Humanity—of the glorified, Eternal Christ, and not immediately of the man Christ Jesus. Other writers, again, both Hebrew and Hellenistic, had employed terms which bore some resemblance to it, but not one had infused into it the significance which makes it a concentration of the Johannine Gospel. Philo had repeatedly dwelt on the term, and surrounded it with Divine attributes; but Philo knew not the Lord Jesus, and in Philo the Logos is surrounded with associations derived from the Platonic and Stoic philosophies. The Targums had used the words *Meymra* (מימרא) and *Debûra* (דבורא), which could indeed only mean "the Word;" but in these the use had been intended simply to avoid the rude anthropomorphism of early Hebrew literature, and to make God seem more distant rather than more near. Alike the Alexandrians and the Targumists would have read with a shock of astonishment and disapproval that utterance which St. John puts in the very forefront of his Gospel, as containing its inmost essence, and as solving all the problems of the world, that "the *Logos*

---

¹ John iv. 14, 36; vi. 27; xii. 25.   ² iii. 36; v. 24; vi. 40, 47, 54.
³ 1 John v. 13, 14.
⁴ I should not use language so positive if I had not furnished the most decisive and overwhelming proof of my position in *Mercy and Judgment*, pp. 391—405. Of that proof another generation will be able to judge. From the false and fleeting criticisms of to-day, I appeal once more to a diviner standard. I exclaim again with Pascal, "*Ad tuum, Domine Jesu, tribunal appello.*"
⁵ See Haupt, p. 4.

became *flesh.*" It was a truth far beyond anything of which they had dreamed, that the Word—who was in the beginning, who was with God, who was God, by whom all things were made, in whom was life, which life was the light of man—that this Word was in the world, came to His own people and His own home, and was by most of them rejected—that this WORD BECAME FLESH, and tabernacled among us, and we beheld His glory, a glory as of the only begotten from the Father, full of grace and truth. To make such a use of the word Logos was to slay those conceptions which lay at the heart of the Alexandrian theosophy with an arrow winged by a feather from its own breast. It was to adopt the most distinctive watchword of the Philonists in order to overthrow their most cherished conceptions.

3. I see yet another mark of Finality in what St. John says of GOD, and especially in the First Epistle. It is not indeed possible to make the whole analysis of the Epistle turn on the three great utterances—definitions we dare not call them, yet approximations to some description of the Essence of Him who is Divine—that God is Righteous, that God is Light, and, above all, that God is Love. But I regard it as a most blessed fact, that words so full of depth and blessedness should occur in what is practically, and perhaps literally, the latest utterance of Holy Writ.

"GOD IS RIGHTEOUS," and therefore He hates all unrighteousness in others, and there can be no unrighteousness in Him. Unrighteousness, masking itself as righteousness—unrighteousness putting on as its disguise the flaming armour of religious zeal—unrighteousness in the form now of persecution, now of violence, now of scholastic orthodoxy, now of depreciation, unfairness, and slander—has been again and again represented as doing Him service. But because He is righteous He hates it. Whether it take the form of Inquisitorial cruelty or of anonymous falsehood, all violence is hateful to Him. Lying for God is to God an abomination, even when the lie claims to be a shibboleth of His most elect. Want of candour, want of gentleness, want of forbearance, are unhallowed incense which does but pollute His altar. Notions that represent Him as a God of arbitrary caprice, treating men as though they were nothing but dead clay, to be dashed about and shattered at His will—notions which represent His justice as something alien from ours, and those things as good in Him which would be evil in us—notions which imagine that in His cause we may do evil that good may come—those idols of the School are shattered on the rock of the truth that God is Righteous.

"GOD IS LIGHT."[1] Notions that represent Him as taking pleasure in man's blind and narrow dogmatism, self-satisfied security, and bitter

---

[1] Rabbi Simon Ben Jehosadek asked R. Samuel Ben Nachman "from what the light was created?" He answered, in a whisper of awe, "God wrapped Himself in light as in a garment, and caused its bright glory to shine from one end of the world to another" (Bereshith Rabba, ch. iii.).

exclusiveness—as making His chosen and His favoured ones not of earth's best and noblest, but of the wrangling religionists who claim each for his own party the monopoly of His revelation—as though one could love the dwarfed thistles and the jagged bents better than the cedars of Lebanon—these idols of the fanatic, idols of the sectarian, idols of the Pharisee, are shattered by the ringing hammerstroke of the truth that God is Light.

GOD IS LOVE. The words do not occur in the Gospel, and yet they are the epitome of the Gospel, and the epitome of the whole Scriptures, and the epitome of the history of mankind; and as such they are a standing protest against all that is worst and darkest in many of the world's schemes of inferential theology. God is Love—not merely loving, but Love itself. The notions, therefore, which would represent Him as living a life turned towards self, or folded within self, caring only for His own glory, caring nothing for the endless agonies of the creatures He has made, predestining them by millions to unutterable torments by horrible decrees, regarding even the sins of children as infinite, "drawing the swords on Calvary to smite down His only Son" —these idols of the Zealot, idols of the Calvinist, idols of those who think that they by their wrath can work the righteousness of God, and that they "can deal damnation round the land on each they deem their foe"—these idols of the Inquisitor, idols of the persecutor, idols of the intolerant ignorance of human infallibility, idols of the sectarian newspaper and the religious partisan, are dashed to pieces by the sweeping and illimitable force of the truth that God is Love.

And, therefore, those three final utterances of Revelation will become more and more, we trust, the protection, the emancipation, the precious heritage of all mankind; they will be the barrier against wicked persecutions, against unjust calumnies, against savage attacks of sectarian hatred. They are as a charter of Humanity against the misrepresentations of religion by misguided Infidelity—against its no less perilous perversion by the encroachments and usurpations of religious hatred and religious pride.

4. We may see a last mark of finality in the *simplification* of the ultimate essential elements of Christian truth which we find in St. John. In reading St. Paul we are at once struck with the richness and variety of the terms and phrases which he has introduced into the statement of Christian dogma. St. John, on the other hand, moves in the sphere of a few ultimate verities. St. Paul is like a painter who works out his results by the use of many colours, and with an infinitude of touches; St. John produces the effect which he desires by a few pure colours and a few sweeping but consummate strokes. St. Paul is discursive, St. John intuitive. St. Paul begins with man, St. John with God. In other words, St. Paul passes from anthropology to theology, and St. John moves chiefly in the purely theologic sphere. St. Paul reasons most respecting the *righteousness* of God and how it

becomes the justification of man; St. John's aim is to show the nature of Eternal *Life*, and how man participates therein. Hence the different tone of their moral teaching. The aim of St. Paul is human and practical, and he dwells incessantly on Faith, Hope, and Charity. St. John's Divine idealism is mainly occupied with the abstract conceptions of Love, and Life, and Light. St. Paul is pleading with men as they are, and building them up into what they should be. St. John assumes that the Christians to whom he writes are resting with him in the full knowledge of Christ. The Churches of St. Paul are full of disturbing elements; the Church which St. John mentally addresses is the true and inner Church, which has no new doctrine to learn, which has received the unction from the Holy One, and which is separated by an unimaginable abyss from the world and from its own false members.[1] St. Paul is ever yearning for an ultimate fraternity of all men, a universal and absolute triumph of the work of redemption; St. John fixes his eyes on the Perfect Church and the Perfect Christian, with whom the virulence of evil and the ultimate destiny of evil seem to have no immediate concern.[2]

5. Now we cannot suppose that these blessed and mighty thoughts occurred for the first time on St. John's written page. They must have been previously expressed in his oral teaching. And would it have been strange if—after having heard so much about the Life of Christ, so much about His nature and person, so many of His discourses, so many applications of the truth of His Gospel to meet every phase of moral temptation and philosophic difficulty—the Bishops and Elders came to St. John to urge him, before he died, to set forth his testimony to the world in writing? At first he shrank from so solemn a task out of humility.[3] But on their still pressing him, "Fast with me for three days," he answered—so runs the deeply-interesting tradition preserved for us in the Muratorian fragment—"and let us tell one another[4] any revelation which may be made to us severally (for or against the plan). On the same night it was revealed to the Apostle Andrew that John should relate all in his own name, and that all should review his writing." "And then," says St. Jerome, in his allusion to this tradition, "after the fast was ended, steeped with inspired truth (*revelatione saturatus*), he indited the heaven-sent preface, '*In the beginning was the Word.*'"[5]

---

[1] 1 John ii. 20; iii. 14; v. 15.
[2] See the able essay, "*Paul et Jean*," in Reuss, *Théol. Chrét.* ii. 572—600.
[3] Epiphan. *Haer.* li. 12, διὸ ὕστερον ἀναγκάζει τὸ ἅγιον πνεῦμα παραιτούμενον . . . ἐπ συλάβειαν καὶ ταπεινοφροσύνην. Comp. Euseb. iii. 24 (ἀναγκαῖς), and Jer. *Prol. in Matt.* ("*Coactus* ab omnibus paene tunc Asiae episcopis," etc.).
[4] This seems to be the meaning of *alterutrum*, as in the Vulg. of James v. 16 (Westcott, *Hist. of Canon*, p. 527; *St. John*, p. xxxv.).
[5] Jer. *Comm. in Matt.* Prol. Comp. Clem. Alex. ap. Euseb. *H. E.* vi. 14. But see Basnage, viii. 2, § 6. This was afterwards improved into the story that he wrote the whole Gospel impromptu (αὐτοσχεδιαστί), and that his autograph, in letters of gold, was preserved in the Church of Ephesus (see Lampe, *Proleg.* p. 171).

Such, then, having been the origin of the Gospel, it supplies us with a certain clue to the origin of the Epistle. A mere glance at the two writings shows that, on the one hand, there is the closest possible connexion between them, and that, on the other hand, the Gospel was the earlier of the two.[1] For the Gospel contains the more explicit, the Epistle the more allusive and concentrated expressions. The Gospel is intelligible by itself; the Epistle would hardly be intelligible without some previous instruction to explain its phraseology. The Gospel shows us how various expressions originated; the Epistle adopts, generalises, and applies them. The Gospel furnishes us with a history, inspired throughout by certain immanent ideas; the Epistle assumes those ideas to be known, and points out their practical bearing. The Gospel deals with the manifestation of the Word in the flesh as an event which the Evangelist has actually witnessed in all its phases; the Epistle shows how that event bears on the errors which were beginning to creep into the Church, and on the lives of its individual members.

We may therefore safely conclude that the Epistle has distinct reference to the Gospel; but we may also infer that they were published together, or in very close succession. The Epistle implies that the truths of the Gospel are known to the reader with all the freshness of recent study. It is based upon them as though they would be already prominent in the reader's mind. This is explicable if we suppose that the one treatise accompanied the other, and it would also account for the absence of salutation and benediction, which would only partially be accounted for by the encyclical character of the Epistle. The Epistle is most easily understood if we suppose it to be addressed not only to the Churches of Asia, whom the Apostle may have had primarily in view, but to all readers of the Gospel. The external proof of this is indeed insignificant; but it is sufficiently established by internal probability. If we may accept with reasonable confidence the tradition that the Gospel, as well as the Apocalypse, was written in Patmos and published in Ephesus, the same tradition will apply to the Epistle also.[2] And this would be a further light on the absence of salutations.

---

[1] The reader will find the proof of this placed visibly before him if he will study the parallels between the Gospel and the First Epistle of St. John, as gathered (among others) by Canon Westcott, in his edition of the Gospel. There are no less than thirty-five such passages, and it may be seen at a glance that they are neither borrowed nor imitated, but independently introduced in the way which would be most natural in two works written by the same author. More than half of the parallels are drawn from the last discourses (John xii—xvii.). To me it seems clear that the Epistle represents the later, less developed, and more allusive form of expression. Reuss says that the Gospel is needed as a commentary on the Epistle; but it is at least equally true to say that the Epistle is needed as an application of the Gospel. It is clear that both gain indefinitely when they are read together. St. Clemens implies that the Epistle was written after the Gospel, for he says that "the Epistle begins with a spiritual proem, *following that of the Gospel*, and in unison with it" (*Adumbratt.* p. 1009).

[2] Patmos was within a day's reach of Ephesus, and if St. John had already felt that the loneliness of the island was suitable to meditation, he might have been led to retire thither once more while he was meditating on his last and greatest work.

Patmos is a small and rocky island, with few inhabitants. It is doubtful whether it had any Christian community within its narrow limits; but even if it had, such a community would be all but wholly unknown, and could hardly bo regarded as an organised Church.

6. The only supposed clue as to the readers to whom the Epistle was addressed is the curious statement of St. Augustine, in one single passage, that it was written "to the Parthians." It is clear that this is either a misreading, or a blunder. If, however, it be a misreading, all the conjectural emendations of it have been quite unsuccessful. Hug's supposition, that it crept in by mistake from the superscription of the Second Epistle, "*pros parthenous*," "to Virgins," will be considered farther on.[1]

7. The supposition that the Apostle wrote in Patmos well accords with the whole *tone* of the Epistle. It was written evidently at a time when the Church was not under the stress of special persecutions.[2] Dangers and sufferings are not alluded to; there are no trumpet-calls to courage or endurance. This period of peace may have been due to the crushing destruction which had now fallen on the Jewish nationality; for, as we are again and again informed, both in history and in Scripture, the deadly animosities of the Gentiles were in the early days stirred up for the most part by Jewish hatred.[3] Now in the Epistle there is no distinct reference either to Jews or Gentiles. All the old questions between the Church and these two great masses of mankind have sunk out of sight. The controversies as to the relations which should subsist between Jewish and Gentile converts within the limits of the Church itself are regarded as settled. In the eyes of St. John there are but two great existing communities, and those are not Jews and Gentiles, but the Church and the world. The severance between them is complete and absolute. In this respect, as in so many others, the Epistle recalls the last discourses of our Lord. In them, too, the hatred of the world means that of the Jew no less than that of the Gentile. But this hatred is here calmly assumed without being dwelt upon. There is no complaint respecting it. Not a word is said as to its origin; not a hint is breathed as to its issues. The world is not even spoken of as a source of special temptation, or as a sphere for

---

[1] See *infra*, on the Second Epistle.

[2] This would point to some date after the reign of Nero (A.D. 54–68). We see further that it must have been written, as the Gospel was, after the destruction of Jerusalem (A.D. 70), and either before the persecution of the Christians in A.D. 95, during the reign of Domitian (A.D. 91—96), or between that date and the persecution of the Christians in the reign of Trajan (A.D. 98). Ewald (*Die Johann. Schriften*, i. 471) suggests A.D. 90 as a probable date. Canon Westcott says that the Gospel may be referred to the last decennium of the first century, and even to the close of it (*St. John*, p. xl.). This view is supported both by early tradition and by the fact that (1) the Gospel assumes a knowledge of the substance of the Synoptic narratives; (2) it deals with later aspects of Christian life and opinion than these; (3) it corresponds with the circumstances of a new world (*id.*, pp. xxxv.—xl.).

[3] Acts xvii; 1 Thess. i. 14—16, ii. 15; Phil. iii. 2; etc. See, too, the remarks of Justin in his *Dial. c. Tryph.*

missionary activity. It is simply set on one side as a satanic kingdom, a kingdom of darkness and of death, with which it is impossible to conceive that the Christian should have anything to do. But such a view is little possible to one who lives in the hearts of great cities, and is in daily struggle with hostile forces from without. It would be far more possible to the contemplative recluse in some secluded retirement than to the toiling Apostle in the streets of Sardis or Ephesus.

8. Yet there *are* dangers which St. John evidently contemplates. They are dangers from heresy and from antichrists; dangers not arising from attacks of the world outside the Church, but from developments of the world within it. The perils which the Christians have to encounter are perils from those who themselves profess the faith; from wolves—clad in sheep's clothing; from Satan—disguised as an angel of light. What St. John dreads is not flagrant wickedness and open blasphemy, but "false types of goodness," and "false types of orthodoxy." Such perils had existed from the very earliest days in which the Church was a Church at all; but now, in the pause from outward assault, they were assuming subtler and more seductive forms. In one shape or other, in their moral or their intellectual aspects, every Apostle has lifted up against them his warning voice. St. Paul had been obliged, even weeping, to warn his converts against false teachers; St. Peter, St. Jude, St. James, had "burst into plain thunderings and lightnings" against them. Far different is the tone of St. John. That they are greatly in his thoughts is evident. Nay, since he frequently refers to their several tenets, since in two passages he expressly names them,[1] since the very last words of his Epistle refer to them,[2] it is clear that it was one of his primary objects to protect the Church from their insidious teachings. Yet how instructive is the tone in which he speaks about them! It is calm, not tumultuous or agitated. It leads to the establishment of positive truth, not to anathemas against negative errors. It does not betray the least touch of anxiety. What St. John has to teach is the nature of eternal life; its concentration in the Word; its communication to the world. The passages about the antichrists might even be omitted without materially affecting the structure of the Epistle. Here again we find not only the stamp of finality, on which we have already dwelt, but an indication of the circumstances under which St. John was writing. He is not in the thick of the battle. His soul is not harrowed by daily watching the ravages of error. Removed from the scene of conflict, living in daily meditation on the truth, in daily communion with God, he can write in the tone of serene joy, of sovereign conviction. It is the peculiarity which we have already noticed in St. Paul's Epistle to the Philippians. The keynote of that letter is joy. In the prison, amid general desertion, left face to face with God, St. Paul seems as if the one thought which inspires his whole being is,

[1] 1 John ii. 20—26, iv. 1—6.   [2] 1 John v. 21.

"Rejoice in the Lord always: again I will say Rejoice." It is the same with St. John. He speaks with the composure which befits the last of the Apostles, the composure of a man who knew the certainty, who had witnessed the victories of the faith. "The unique consciousness which an Apostle, as he grew older, could carry within himself, and which he, once the favourite disciple, had in a peculiar measure; the calm superiority, clearness, and decision in thinking on Christian subjects; the rich experience of a long life steeled in the victorious struggle with every unchristian element; and a glowing language lying concealed under their calmness, which makes us feel intuitively that it does not in vain commend us to love, as the highest attainment of Christianity—all this coincides so remarkably in this Epistle, that"—in spite of its purely impersonal character and the lofty delicacy with which, as in the Gospel, the writer retires into the background, unwilling to speak of himself—"every reader of that period, probably without any further intimation, might readily determine who he was."[1] In its "unruffled and heavenly repose, it appears to be the tone not so much of a father talking with his beloved children, as of a glorified saint speaking to mankind from a higher world. Never in any writing has the doctrine of heavenly love, of a love working in stillness, a love ever unwearied, never exhausted, so thoroughly proved, and approved itself, as in this Epistle."[2]

CHAPTER XXXIII.

CHARACTERISTICS OF THE MIND AND STYLE OF ST. JOHN.

"Columba sancta Ecclesia est; quae duas alas habet per dilectionem Dei et proximi."—A. DE ST. VICTORE.

THE effect which the Epistle thus produces upon us is due partly to the habit of St. John's mind, partly to the peculiarities of his style.

1. One great peculiarity of his mind—on which we have already incidentally touched—is his *contemplativeness*—what has been sometimes, but not very accurately, called his mysticism. It was the invariable tendency of his mind in these his later years to live and move in the region of abstract thought. The abstractions are, however, by no means treated *as* abstractions, but rather as facts and experiences of life. In St. John we see yet another illustration of the fundamental distinction between the Nominalist and the Realist—the Nominalist who regards abstract terms as representing nothing but the generalisations of the mind out of concrete presentments, the Realist who regards

[1] Ewald, *Die Johan. Schriften*, L 431.   [2] *Id. ib.*

them as representing those eternal ideas which are the only absolute realities. St. John is entirely a Realist. It has been truly said of him that "*Universalia ante rem*" is the principle of all his philosophy. With him Ideas—Light, Darkness—Truth, Falsehood—are not mere concepts, but are the actual reality, the principles of life out of which all individual things emerge. In his point of view Mankind, the individual man, the particular action, only exist as the Idea prescribes. The Idea, indwelling in them, moulds them as a law, by virtue of which all that belongs to them is fashioned. Thus, to St. John, history is the invisible translated into the visible.[1] In the Gospel it is shown how the ideas have been introduced into this earthly life; in the Epistle how the life of the individual may be modified in accordance with them.[2] Thus once more we see how every thought which St. John utters depends upon his doctrine of "the Word made flesh." The Divine ideas of which he speaks—Truth, Life, Light—are realities, and the only realities, because they are inherent in the Logos. They are in men only because He is in men, and they are the only Life, the only Light, the only Truth. The Gospel shows how, by the manifestation of the Logos on earth, the fulness which was in Him is imparted to us; the Epistle speaks throughout of our personal appropriation of this fulness and the way in which it is expressed in Christian lives.

2. But all this at once accounts for another of his characteristics—namely, the sovereign calm of the Apostle's tone. In this region of the Idea there is no room for jarring conflicts. He is building the superstructure, not laying the foundation. He is reminding, not instructing. He is perfecting, not commencing. He is stating, not arguing. He is delivering a solemn homily, not conducting an embittered controversy. He can appeal to his readers, as those who know;[3] as those whose sins have been forgiven; who have an unction from the Holy One;[4] who already believe;[5] to whom the new commandment can be represented as the old. And this is the reason why his defensive polemics can take the form of positive instruction. He can teach true Christians to conquer heresy by the expulsive power of right affections. He can invigorate their interior life as the best means of strengthening their outward warfare. The multiplication of antichrists was a serious danger, but the Churches would be less likely to succumb to it if he could inspire them with the victorious tranquillity with which he himself regarded all dangers, as he looked forth on the troubled sea from the haven of his island rest.

3. A third secret of St. John's power lies in his *style*. It is a style absolutely unique, supremely original, and full of charm and sweetness. Under the semblance of extreme simplicity, it hides unfathomable

---

[1] Haupt, pp. 376, 377.
[2] "The Gospel seeks to deepen faith in Christ, the Epistle sets forth the righteousness which is necessary to faith, and only possible to faith" (Hoffmann).
[3] 1 John ii. 12–14.   [4] 1 John ii. 20, 27.   [5] 1 John v. 13.

depths. It is to a great extent intelligible to the youngest child, to the humblest Christian; yet to enter into its full meaning exceeds the power of the deepest theologian. Thus, St. John remarkably exemplifies the definition that genius is "the heart of childhood taken up and glorified in the powers of manhood." In his Gospel and Epistles the artless ingenuousness of a child is intimately blended with the deep thoughtfulness of a man. But the style, by its very characteristics, would be ill suited to controversy. It is not syllogistic, like that of St. Paul; nor rhetorical, like that of the author of the Epistle to the Hebrews. It is rather contemplative, "noting the substance of the thoughts without marking the mutual relations of the thoughts themselves."[1] The logic moves, as has been said, in circles rather than straight onwards.[2] The sentences are ordinated by simple conjunctions, not subordinated to each other by final particles. The periods are *paratactic*, not syntactic. The particles, as in Aramaic, are few.[3] Hence, though the Greek is pure, in so far that it is free from solecisms, it is as unlike Greek as possible in its periodic structure. There is scarcely a single oblique sentence throughout St. John's Gospel. Often the sentences follow each other without any conjunction between them, and only by taking up again the chief word in the previous clause. But under the appearance of incessant repetitions the thought is still constantly advanced. "The still waters," as Herder says, "run deep, flowing along with the easiest words, but the profoundest meaning." The thoughts are pressed home in the simplest fashion of Aramaic idiom by being expressed first positively, then negatively.[4] They gain further from the numerical symmetry of the clauses into which they are thrown.[5] The same word occurs again and again as the leading

---

[1] Braune calls it "the dialectics of contemplation."

[2] Düsterdieck. Tholuck had already given to St. John's style the epithet "cycloidal." Renan admits that the style has "fervour, and occasionally a kind of sublimity, but withal something inflated, unreal, obscure—an utter want of *naïveté*."

[3] Ebrard, *Introd.* He points out that the sentences are often joined by καί, when St. Paul would have used δέ or γάρ. St. John constantly makes use of *anaphora*, i.e., the introduction of a new sentence by the repetition of a word which has just been used. Erasmus excellently describes it: "Dicendi genus ita velut ansulis ex sese cohærentibus contextus, nonnunquam ex contrariis, nonnunquam ex similibus, nonnunquam ex iisdem subinde repetitis . . . ut orationis quodque membrum semper excipiat prius, sic ut prioris finis initium sit sequentis."

[4] St. John seems to "think in antitheses." It is his manner "to construct the matter of a positive idea out of its combination or contrast with its opposite." By a curious variation of style, for which it is not easy to account, we have conditional sentences ("if we walk," "if we say," "if we confess"), in the first section of the Epistle (i. 6; ii. 8), and participial construction ("he that loveth," "he that saith") afterwards.

[5] There is an interesting specimen of this numerical concinnity of expression in ii. 9–11, where, in steady progression, the first verse has *one* predicate: "He who saith that he is in the light, and hateth his brother" (α) "is in the darkness even still." The second verse has *two* predicates: "He who loveth his brother" (α) "abideth in the light," (β) "and there is no stumblingblock in him." The third verse has *three* predicates: "But he who hateth his brother" (α) "is in the darkness," (β) "and walketh in the darkness," ( ) "and knoweth not whither he goeth, because the darkness blinded his eyes." The symmetry is so absolute in its musical flow and rhythmic balance that even the double clause of the *last* line corresponds to the double clause of the *first*.

word of an entire section until it becomes impressive by the very monotony of its iteration. It is like a stone flung into a smooth lake, round which the ripples widen to the shore in concentric circles. No style could be worse to imitate. In feeble hands it would deserve the charges of weakness, tautology, senility, which have been so idly made against it. On the other hand, no style could better suit the character of a mind absorbed in heavenly contemplation;—of a mind filled with conceptions of a depth so inexhaustible that words, however often repeated, failed to convey the fulness of meaning with which they were charged.

4. But—to revert to the characteristics of St. John's later teachings—it must not be supposed that St. John has no sternness in him. Had such been the case he could not have been the Son of Thunder. Probably the natural character of no man had ever been so softened and ennobled as his had been by the long years of Christian suffering and Christian education; yet the elements of the natural character remained. The essence of St. John's temperament, the foundation of his teaching, in these his later years, was love; but where there is an intense and perfect love there must also be hatred of all that most offends and injures love; not hatred of men—that becomes impossible—but hatred of all that degrades men into beasts or devils. It is impossible not to feel that there is an accent of intense severity—of a severity even more intense than that of St. James—in such words as,

"*He that doeth sin is from the Devil, because the Devil sinneth from the beginning.*" "*Every one who abideth in Him sinneth not; every one who sinneth hath not seen Him, nor even known Him.*" "*Every one who doeth not righteousness is not from God, nor he who loveth not his brother.*"[1]

How does such language accord with Christ's unbounded love to sinners, to publicans, to harlots, even to Pharisees? How is it reconcilable with the paternal tenderness, the overflowing love, the gentle tolerance, which breathes through the rest of the Epistle? How is it in unison with certain and universal Christian experience? How is it consistent with St. John's own gentleness to most flagrant offenders! How can it be left side by side with language so apparently contradictory to it as that which urges God's children to confess their sin, and even lays it down that,

"*If we say that we have no sin, we deceive ourselves, and the truth is not in us.*"[2]

Does not the only solution lie in the fact that here, too, St. John is moving in the regions of the ideal, and that every sin is, in its ultimate issue, in its final nature, Satanic? As children of God we cannot sin, and children of God we are. We are so by His gift,[3] we must become so by our own act. In so far as we by our own choice are sinners, so

---

[1] 1 John iii. 4—10.   [2] i. 8—10.   [3] iii. 1.

far we are not children of God; and if, at the last day—if, in the general and unerring sentence of judgment pronounced upon us—we are declared to be in a state of *permanent and willing sin*,[1] then, in spite of the imparted gift of sonship, we are children of the Devil. The *ideal* of our position as children of God is the impossibility to sin; and a nearer and nearer approximation to this ideal is required of us in actual life. But if to the very end we fall very far short of that ideal, and so might be driven to despair, St. John himself has saved us from any such despair by his previous sayings that if we confess our sins God will forgive them,[2] and that if any man sin we have an Advocate with the Father, Jesus Christ the righteous, and He is the propitiation for our sins.[3]

5. The personal question indeed remains. "*If we say that we have fellowship with Him, and walk in the darkness, we lie.*" "*He who doeth sin is of the Devil.*" "*If any one come to you and bring not this teaching, receive him not into your house, and give him no greeting.*"[4] Are those the accents of the Apostle of Love? Does not St. John by such expressions and such advice reopen the floodgates of party railing, ignorant zeal, malignant persecution, bitter intolerance? So, at any rate, those have thought who forget that *hatred* of any kind is the essential note of the world. Those very "texts" have been seized with avidity by the fierce party-spirit which all the Apostles alike so unhesitatingly denounce as godless and anti-Christian. Heated controversialists have revelled in the imaginary licence to set aside all the precepts of Christian love which breathes from every page of the New Testament in order that they may, with these texts, bless and approve with sober brows the very sin which is never more deadly or more inexcusable than when it shamelessly intrudes into the sphere of religious life. All that can be said is that such partisans wrest these, as they do also the other Scriptures, to their own perdition. These phrases, rightly understood, belong to that sphere of the Ideal and the Abstract in which St. John moves, but in which those do not move who pervert his meaning in order to undo the teaching which he loved best. No texts in Scripture can authorise any man to hate and persecute those who teach the truths which he in his ignorance regards as heresy. St. John's words do not confer on persecuting zeal the attribute of infallibility. They do not exempt religious differences from the realm of Christian charity. If they did, they would have to be themselves overruled as proofs of weakness, because in that case

---

[1] The force of the present tenses, and the alleviation which they introduce into the force of the sentences, must not be overlooked. [2] i. 9.
[3] ii. 12. We may remark in passing that this word "propitiation" (ἱλασμός) (here and in iv. 10) is one of the very few which introduce into the Epistle conceptions which are not directly touched upon in the Gospels. Another is χρίσμα, the "unction" of the Holy One, in ii. 20, 27. Another is the application of the name Paraclete ("Advocate") to Christ (ii. 1), though this is indeed involved in John xiv. 16.
[4] See *infr* to the remarks on this passage.

they would run counter to the best and holiest teachings of him who uttered them. Religious persecution, religious intolerance, religious hatred, are not religious, but irreligious, even if St. John be distorted into their defence. If he did indeed defend them—as he does not—his plea could only be due to the still lingering traces of the Elijah spirit: it could only be ranked with the conduct of St. Carlo Borromeo, who, after tending the plague-stricken with the gentleness of a saint, persecuted those whom he regarded as heretics with the fury of an Inquisitor. The Apostle and Evangelist of Love would have destroyed the very essence of his own divinest work if he had meant—as I believe he never meant—to gratify the meanest and fiercest champions of party in the indulgence of exactly those forms of hatred which have ever been the most virulent, the most ignorant, the most hateful, and the most intense.

6. I will mention only one more characteristic of this rich and profound Epistle, which is, that though it is ethical and didactic, it does not resemble the treatment of ethics by any other of the Apostles. Here, again, the manner of the writer finds a fresh illustration. Other Apostles enter into many details, touch on many successive duties. Not so St. John. In his view two words enclose the whole cycle of moral conceptions. Those two words are Righteousness and Love. Both words have their roots in the Divine. God is righteous. God is love. Therefore man must be righteous towards God, and must manifest that righteousness by love towards the brethren. Even these broad conceptions are lost in others still broader—namely, those of Light and Truth. God is Light, and therefore every sin partakes of the nature, and belongs to the realm, of darkness. God is True—i.e., Real—and therefore all sin partakes of the nature of unreality and falsehood. All details, all special applications are involved in this. He who does the truth, he who walks in the light, he who does righteousness, he who confesses the name of Jesus Christ, he who loves his brother—he has eternal life. He will therefore need no instruction as to outward and individual acts.[1] For him even the Church and the Sacraments, and all ecclesiastical questions of organisation and ritual, may, in St. John's manner, be passed over as "silent presuppositions." He is forgiven; he is cleansed; he is a son of God. His faith in the Divinity of Christ is transposed into life, and his life in Christ deepens his faith in Christ's Divinity. The two are inextricably interlaced. A righteous life is the result of faith, and faith is deepened by a righteous life.[2] He who denies Christ, he who "severs Christ," is of the Devil, and belongs to the lie, the world, the darkness. Thus St. John moves

---

[1] See ii. 27. Hence the constant words οἴδατε (ii. 20; iii. 5, 15), οἴδαμεν (iii. 2, 14; v. 15, 18, 19, 20), γινώσκομεν (ii. 5, 18; iii. 19, 24; iv. 6, 13; v. 2), ἐγνώκαμεν (iii. 16; iv. 16), ἐγνώκατε (ii. 13, 14), γινώσκετε (ii. 29; iv. 2), δοκιμάζετε (iv. 1). Thus the thought that they already know the truth of what he is saying recurs some thirty times. Οἶδα represents knowledge generally; γινώσκω represents "recognition," experiential knowledge.
[2] Braune (in Lange's *Bibelwerk*), Introd. § II.; Hofmann, *Schriftbeweis*, p. 337.

"Scindit iter liquidum celeres neque promovet alas."

CHAPTER XXXIV.

OBJECT AND OUTLINE OF THE FIRST EPISTLE OF ST. JOHN.

> "Sed Joannes alâ binâ
> Caritatis, aquilinâ
> Formâ fertur in divina
> Puriori lumine."—ADAM DE ST. VICTORE.

AFTER these considerations we shall, I trust, be better prepared to understand St. John's object in the Epistle, and how it bears on the circumstances in which the Epistle was written. We shall be better able to understand that it is a coherent whole, and that its purpose is worked out in continuous development.

As to the object, we can have no doubt, because St. John tells it to us quite distinctly in the first four verses. It was to set forth to his readers his witness respecting the Word of Life, in order that he and they might have fellowship with one another in their common fellowship with the Father and with His Son, and that in consequence of this their joy may be full. He expresses the same object in other terms at the end of the Epistle, when he says, "These things I have written to you that believe on the name of the Son of God, that ye may know that ye have eternal life."[1] In pursuing this object he shows that there can be no fellowship with God without righteousness, rooted in faith and manifested by love; and that the Christian not only *ought* to live such a life, but *does* so, because he is born of God. Thus does St. John refute the antichristian lie which was already prevalent. He would empty these souls of falsehood by filling them with truth. He writes in order that, by fellowship with one another and with God and His Christ—by perfected joy, by assured confidence in their present possession of eternal life—the seductions of the teaching of antichrists may become impossible to souls filled with Christian love.

An analysis of the Epistle, such as may serve to show that it is not merely aphoristic, is perfectly possible. When Calvin spoke of it as containing "doctrine mixed with exhortation;" when Episcopius

---

[1] v. 13. The reading of B is here most probably correct, and the source of the other variations—ταῦτα ἔγραψα (epistolary aorist) ὑμῖν ἵνα εἰδῆτε ὅτι ζωὴν ἔχετε αἰώνιον, τοῖς πιστεύουσιν εἰς τὸ ὄνομα τοῦ υἱοῦ τοῦ Θεοῦ. Compare the closely-analogous description of the object of the Gospel in John xx. 31.

said that "the method of treatment was arbitrary, and not bound to rules of art;" they had missed its meaning. The art is concealed, but it is consummate. The method is unique, but it is most powerful. It is an entire mistake to speak of the Epistle as "incoherent," as a congeries of scattered remarks about the Divinity of Christ, about the blessings of adoption, about love, and as "briefly touching on other things also, such as being on our guard against impostors, and such matters."[1] Schmid, Oporinus,[2] Bengel, and the other scholars who first endeavoured to prove its consecutive and systematic character, rendered a real servive to biblical theology. The student who reads it in the light of some well-considered scheme, will gain more advantage from it than others, even if details of his scheme be untenable. It is, for instance, very tempting to arrange the Epistle under the three heads which are suggested by the three great thoughts that God is Light, God is Righteous, God is Love. I myself tried hard to do so in first studying the Epistle. But though these great utterances throw some light on the order of thought, it is evident that they are not the pivots of arrangement in the mind of the writer.[3] Nor, again, is it possible to analyse the Epistle, as Bengel endeavoured to do with reference to the doctrine of the Trinity, an attempt into which that great theologian was misled by his acceptance as genuine of the verse about the Three Heavenly Witnesses. There is, indeed, as we shall see, a remarkable triplicity in the subordinate divisions, due to the Hebraic training of St. John, and to the rhythm and symmetry of the sacred idioms with which he was familiar. Bengel, of course, rightly saw that the Epistle falls at once into the three divisions of

   Exordium, i. 1—4.
   Treatment of the Subject, i. 5—v. 12.
   Conclusion, v. 13—21.

But the unreality of his other divisions arose from his attempting to analyse the Epistle in the interests of an *à priori* conception instead of following step by step its own indications. The reason why it is so difficult to analyse, is the extreme richness and fulness of the thoughts, and the manner in which they interfuse each other. I said just now that the leading words of St. John—words expressive of some inexhaustible and abstract idea—might be compared to stones thrown into a lake, which raise around them a far-spreading concentric ripple;

---

[1] "*Doctrinam exhortationibus mistam continet . . . sparsim docendo et exhortando varius est*" (Calvin).

[2] Joachim Oporin, in a Göttingen programme. "*De constanter tenenda communione cum Patre et Filio—i.e., Joannis Ep.* i. *nodis interpretum liberata,* etc.," 1741. Some have called the Epistle *aphoristic*, which is a misleading term if meant to exclude the notion of a definite plan. The idea seized upon by Oporin is certainly the leading one of the Epistle. So too Lücke—"As the ground and root of all Christian fellowship is the fellowship which each has with the Father and the Son in faith and love, so this latter necessarily unfolds and exhibits itself in that former."

[3] Huther, who, in his first edition, in Meyer's *Commentary*, adopted an analysis on this plan (at De Wette's suggestion), abandoned it in his second edition.

but of this Epistle it would be even truer to say that word after word exercises its influence over the surface, and that the innumerable ripples which they create overflow and are influenced by each other, so that the concentric rings of thought are broken and interlaced.[1] Hence it is probable that no analysis will be accepted by any careful student as final or unobjectionable in all its details. Let each perform the task as he thinks best; but for myself I can find no analysis so helpful and thorough as that which has been indicated by one of the latest, and by far the profoundest, expositor of the epistle, Eric Haupt.[2] In giving it, however, I must remind the reader that we do not pretend to imply that St. John, in writing the Epistle, had any such scheme definitely before him, but only that, in the development of the great central thoughts which he desired to impress upon his readers, one general object dominated through all the separate passages, and coloured the particular expressions.

INTRODUCTION, i. 1—4.

A. The main theme—Eternal Life manifested by the Word.
B. Certain assurance of this as an irrefragable truth;—the object of setting it forth being that it is the ground and root of Christian fellowship with God and with one another.

A. ETERNAL LIFE, i. 5—v. 5.

I. The evidence that it has been communicated to us by the Word is *Walking in the Light*, which must show itself—

1. Towards God—in the form of sinlessness (i. 6—ii. 2).
   α Sinlessness is effected positively by redemption through Christ's blood (i. 5—7).
   β Negatively, by forgiveness of past sin (i. 8—10).
   γ Hortative recapitulation (ii. 1, 2).

---

[1] I find that Huther has expressed exactly the same thought under a completely different image. He says that in St. John's style "the leading thought is like a key-note, which he strikes and causes to sound through the derivative thoughts until a new key-note is struck that leads to a new key."

[2] Generally speaking, throughout this and my former books on the New Testament, I have, I trust, shown that my line of thought is always independent; that I have tried in each instance to think and to judge for myself, *nullius addictus jurare in verba magistri*. It is right, however, to say that in the exegesis of the First Epistle of St. John I have been guided to an unusual extent by the admirable treatise of Haupt. I have not always agreed with him. At times he seems to me to be over-subtle. I do not always accept his views of scholarship. But though I have also studied the views of many other editors—Huther, Düsterdieck, Ebrard, Braune, Alford, Wordsworth, Reuss, etc.—I have not found in any one of them the depth and insight of this little-known writer. I have, therefore, been *specially* indebted to him, and desire thus generally to express my obligation. From Reuss I have gained scarcely any help. His treatment of the Johannine writings in his *Théologie Johannique* seems to be decidedly poor, and far inferior to his treatment of the Epistles of St. Paul. Nor have I learnt much from the wordy obscurity of Braune.

2. Towards the brethren—as brotherly love (ii. 3—13).
 α Keeping God's commandments is union with God (ii. 3—5).
 β Love as the new commandment (ii. 6—11).
 γ Hortative encouragement (ii. 12—14).
3. By utter severance from the world.
 α No fellowship with the world or with Antichrist (ii. 15—19).
 β Security by means of the unction from the Holy One (ii. 20—26).
 γ Recapitulation (27).

II. If we possess Eternal Life we have confidence, because we have been born of God (ii. 28—v. 5).

1. The evidence of this sonship is seen in action (iii.).
 α Towards God it is evidenced by doing righteousness (iii. 1—10).
 β Towards the brethren, by love (iii. 11—18).
 γ Recapitulation (iii. 19—23).
2. The source of this sonship is the reception of the Spirit of God.
 α The confession of Christ through the Spirit saves us from false Spirits (iv. 1—6).
 β Human love is a reflection of the Divine, and is derived from the Spirit (iv. 7—12).
 γ Recapitulation (iv. 14—16).

Retrospective conclusions:—when the Divine birth is thus manifested in action (iii.), which may be traced back to the Spirit (iv. 1—6), then we have the perfect confidence of sonship, and may stand unabashed in the Day of Judgment (iv. 17, 18).

III. Final Illustrations.

A. LOVE AND FAITH.
 α The Idea of Love embraces love both to God and to the brethren (iv. 19—21).
 β The Idea of Faith involves love both to God and to the brethren (v. 1—3).
 γ And also involves Victory over the world (v. 4, 5).

B. ASSURANCE THAT THE WORD IS THE GIVER OF ETERNAL LIFE.
 i. Because it is founded on the certain witness of God (v. 6—9).
 ii. And this witness is echoed from within (v. 10—12).

C. CONCLUSION.
 α The substance of Eternal Life, as consisting of Faith in Christ, and confidence, and intercessory love (v. 13—17).

β The signatures of the child of God (v. 18—20) in the threefold knowledge that he is sinless, that he is from God, that he is in Christ.

γ Emphatic conclusion, showing the practical aim of the Epistle.[1]

I have inserted this formal analysis of the Epistle into the text, and not placed it in a note, because of its great importance, and because it illustrates to no small extent the characteristics of St. John's method, and the colouring of his thoughts. Some may be inclined to look on it with suspicion, from the very fact of its prevailing triplicity; and no doubt this might be justly regarded as unfavourable to its reception if we pretended to imply that St. John drew up beforehand any outline of this definite division. Had he done so, it would at once have stamped his Epistle with formalism of statement and want of spontaneity. But this is not the case. The triplicity is entirely unintentional. It is so little insisted on, that some of the sections, and especially the minor divisions which I have not here pointed out, fall into pairs. The detection of this involuntary triplicity and duality of statement does not arise from any *à priori* determination to find it, but results naturally from careful study of the Epistle step by step. The very same peculiarity is observable in the Gospel. Any one who analyses it sees at once that there is scarcely one, either of its main or its minor divisions, which does not fall into double or triple parts. This was pointed out by Luthardt, and may be seen by a glance at Canon Westcott's analysis of the Gospel, though he does not expressly allude to it. As to the Epistle, "the order and symmetry which pervade all, down to the minutest details, only show how clearly and sharply the Apostle was accustomed to think, and that, in consequence of an inherent sense of order, his thoughts grouped themselves with facility in a definite way."

The genuineness of the Epistle may be regarded as beyond all suspicion. It was known to and quoted by Papias (A.D. 140).[2] There are unmistakable allusions to it in the Epistle to Diognetus (A.D. 117), in the Epistle of the Churches of Lyons and Vienne (A.D. 177), and in Polycarp's letter to the Philippians.[3] It was often quoted by Irenæus.[4] There can be little doubt that the testimony of the Muratorian fragment (circ. A.D. 170) is in its favour.[5] It is translated in the Peshito; is constantly quoted by the Fathers of the third century;

---

[1] It would only confuse the reader to give the analysis of Hofmann, Ebrard, Huther, etc. Ewald adopts three divisions, i. 1—ii. 17; ii. 18—iv. 6; iv. 7—v. 21. Dusterdieck, closely followed by Alford, who gives his analysis at length, divides as follows—Exordium, i. 1—4; two main sections, i. 5—ii. 28; ii. 29—v. 5; a double conclusion, v. 6—13, 14—21.

[2] Euseb. *H. E.* iii. 39, κέχρηται . . . μαρτυρίαις ἀπὸ τῆς Ἰωάννου προτέρας ἐπιστολῆς.

[3] Polyc. *ad Philipp.* 7. This quotation constitutes a strong proof of genuineness.

[4] Euseb. *H. E.* v. 8; Iren. *c. Haer.* iii. 16, 5, 7.   [5] See *infra*.

is ranked among the *Homologoumena* by Eusebius,[1] and is said by St. Jerome to have been accepted by all true Churchmen.[2] This external evidence combines so overwhelmingly with the internal, that we are not surprised to find that from the days of Marcion[3] (about 140) and the Alogi[4] down to the days of Joseph Scaliger, the Epistle has been received with unquestioning reverence.[5] The notion that it shows signs of senility is the superficial conclusion of careless and prejudiced readers. The endeavour of Baur to find Montanism in the Epistle, and that of Hilgenfeld to prove that it is a forgery of the middle of the second century, need be no further debated, because they have found scarcely any followers. And even Hilgenfeld spoke of the writer as "a great independent thinker," and called his Epistle, not as Baur had done, a "weak imitation" of the Gospel, but a "splendid type" of it.[6] The notion that such Epistles as this, and the Epistles to the Ephesians and Colossians, and the Pastoral Epistles, could have been second-century forgeries, is refuted by the entire literature of that century, whether authentic, or anonymous, or pseudonymous. That literature is of a character incomparably more feeble, and is animated by a spirit incomparably less divine.

Some have preferred to regard this Epistle as a theological treatise, or a religious homily; but the form which it assumes, and the direct addresses with which it abounds, show that it really was intended as an encyclical letter, addressed neither "to Parthians" nor "to Virgins,"[7] but to the Churches of Asia, with which the Apostle was most familiar. The conclusions which have here been indicated may be considered certain:—namely, that it was written towards the close of the first century; and—which is a deeply interesting and suggestive circumstance—that it was, in some instances at least, accompanied by copies of the Gospel to which it is closely related in its tone of thought, and to which it served as a practical commentary.

---

[1] Euseb. *H. E.* iii. 24, 25.
[2] Jer. *De Virr. Illustr.* 9. It is quoted by Clemens Alexandrinus (*Strom.* ii. 66; iii. 32, etc.), Tertullian (*c. Marc.* v. 16; *c. Prax.* 15, etc.), Cyprian (*Ep.* 28, etc.), and pseudo-Chrysostom (*in Matt.* xxi. 23) says, ἅπαντες εἶναι Ἰωάννου συμφώνως ἀντεφώναντο.
[3] Marcion either did not know or rejected the writings of St. John.
[4] τάχα δὲ καὶ τὰς Ἐπιστολάς, συνᾴδουσι γὰρ αὗται τῷ Εὐαγγελίῳ καὶ τῇ Ἀποκαλύψει (Epiphan. c. *Haer.* li. 34).
[5] The isolated exception of Cosmas Indicopleustes in the sixth century is hardly worth mentioning, for his remark is evidently made in great ignorance of the subject. He foolishly observes that "the majority" regarded the Catholic Epistles as not being the writings of the Apostles; ἀλλ' ἑτέρων τινῶν πρεσβυτέρων ἀφελεστέρων.
[6] Hilgenfeld, *Das Evang. und die Briefe Johannis,* 1849.
[7] Thus γράφω occurs seven times, ἔγραψα six times, ὑμῖν, ὑμεῖς, etc., thirty-six times, τεκνία, παιδία six times, ἀγαπητοί six times, etc. The unconstrained style, the hortatory tendency, the informal transitions, all point to its epistolary character.
[8] This is the view of Michaelis, Augusti, Hug, Thiersch, Ebrard, Haupt, etc.

CHAPTER XXXV.

THE FIRST EPISTLE OF ST. JOHN

"Ubi Amor, ibi Trinitas."—S. AUG.

"Locuturus est multa, et prope omnia de caritate."—S. AUG. *Expos. in Ep. Johann.*

"The main substance of this Epistle relates to love."—LUTHER.

"Put off thy shoes from off thy feet, for the place whereon thou standest is holy ground."—*Ex.* iii. 5.

SECTION I.
ETERNAL LIFE.

"THAT which was from the beginning, which we have heard, which we have seen with our eyes, which we gazed upon, and our hands handled,[1] concerning the Word of Life; and the Life was manifested,[2] and we have seen it, and are witnessing and announcing to you[3] that Life—even that Eternal Life which was with the Father, and was manifested to us. That which we have seen and have heard we announce to you also, that ye also may have communion with us; and indeed our communion is with the Father, and with His Son, Jesus Christ.[4] And these things we write,[5] that your joy may be fulfilled" (i. 1–4).

We have here the introductory theme of the whole Epistle. It should be compared with the golden prologue of the Gospel to which it is so closely analogous, and the knowledge of which it assumes.[6] Though St. John seems to be labouring with the desire to express a truth too great for the power of his language to utter, the clause, so

---

[1] Luke xxiv. 39 : ψηλαφήσατέ με καὶ ἴδετε. The word would be the strongest possible refutation of Docetic error. In Ignat. ad Smyrn. 4, 5, our Lord says to Peter after His Resurrection, "Take, handle me, and see that I am not a bodiless spirit" (δαιμόνιον ἀσώματον); "and immediately they took hold of Him and believed, convinced by His flesh and His Spirit."

[2] By "the life" is here meant the Absolute Life, ἡ αὐτοζωή, ἡ πηγάζουσα τὸ ζῆν (Schol., John i. 4).

[3] The reading of μ is καὶ ἀπαγγέλλομεν καὶ ὑμῖν.

[4] The Holy Spirit is not mentioned, because He is *in* us, rather than *with* us (2 Cor. xiii. 13).

[5] "There are two species of testimony—announcement and writing. Announcement lays the foundation : writing builds the superstructure" (Bengel).

[6]
JOHN i. 1.	1 JOHN i. 1, 2.
Ἐν ἀρχῇ ἦν ὁ Λόγος καὶ ὁ Λόγος ἦν πρὸς τὸν Θεόν.	ὃ ἦν ἀπ' ἀρχῆς . . . (ἡ ζωὴ) ἥτις ἦν πρὸς τὸν Πατέρα.
Ver. 4.	
ἐν αὐτῷ ζωὴ ἦν καὶ ἡ ζωὴ ἦν τὸ φῶς τῶν ἀνθρώπων, καὶ τὸ φῶς ἐν τῇ σκοτίᾳ φαίνει.	περὶ τοῦ λόγου τῆς ζωῆς . . . ἡ ζωὴ ἐφανερώθη . . . καὶ ἐφανερώθη ἡμῖν.
Ver. 14.	
καὶ ἐθεασάμεθα τὴν δόξαν αὐτοῦ.	ὃ ἐθεασάμεθα.

Others of the ideas found in the prologue of the Gospel occur elsewhere in the Epistle. Thus compare—

i. 1, "The Word was God."   v. 20, "This is the true God."
i. 9, "There was the true light."   ii. 8, "The true light already shineth."
i. 12, "To become children of God."   iii. 1, "That we should be called children of God."
i. 13, "Born . . . . of God."   v. 1, "Begotten of God."
i. 14, "The Word became flesh."   iv. 2, "Jesus Christ is come in the flesh."
i. 18, "No man hath seen God at any time."   iv. 12, "No man hath beheld God at any time."

This opening clause of the Epistle resembles that of the Epistle to the Hebrews in the absence of name and greeting, but the majestic beginning of that Epistle is more rhetorical and less emotional.

far from being, as Calvin said, "abrupt and confused," is to the highest degree pregnant with clear and majestic thought. It compresses into a few lines a world of meaning, while at the same time it is steeped in the deep emotion of the writer.

What he has to announce—for he only uses the plural as one of the Apostolic witnesses—is not the Word, but something respecting Him—namely, that He is the source from which all life streams. In hearing and seeing Him, the Apostles had heard and seen this inward significance of His Person and of His acts by the immediate perceptions of sense; and in gazing on and handling Him, as they all did, and Thomas especially, after His resurrection, they had learnt, by yet fuller investigation, that He is indeed the Conqueror of Death and the Source of Life. And this Life of His was "from the beginning," so that the announcement of it is as though he were now inspired to write a new Book of Genesis, but one which dated backwards to a yet earlier—nay, to an absolute eternity. Thus the "from the beginning" of the last book of the Bible repeats, but in even deeper tones, the "in the beginning" of the first book. The one speaks of the Incarnation, the other testifies to the Eternity, of Him by whom the worlds were made.

The prœm of the Gospel declared that "the Word became flesh," because in the Gospel St. John is treating of Christ's person; but in the Epistle he says, "the Life was manifested," because he is about to deal, not directly with His Person, but with the influence which flowed from it—namely, life. And the quality of that life is that it is eternal, *i.e.*, spiritual, supratemporal, Divine, seeing that ($\eta\tau\iota s$) it stands in immediate relation to ($\pi\rho\grave{o}s$) the Father, and was only manifested to man, in its priority and fulness, when Christ appeared. This was the Life which the Apostles had seen, to which they bore witness as true, which they were communicating to the world, and of which the assurance could be derived from their testimony. And the aim of the announcement is to establish a fellowship between the witnesses and those who received their witness; for indeed this fellowship is, in reality, a fellowship with God and with Christ. If it be asked how it could be St. John's object to *establish* a fellowship which they possessed already, the simple answer is one which applies to all the writings of the Apostles. They wrote to Christians, who were indeed, as Christians, ideally perfect, but in whom the ideal was as yet very far from having become the real. Ideally they were saints and perfect: in reality they were struggling with daily imperfections, and had not by any means attained the measure of the fulness of the stature of Christ. They were, therefore, far from that fulness of joy which was their proper heritage.[1] The Eternal Life which they possessed was as yet but in the germ.

[1] Comp. John xv. 11; xvii. 3; Phil. ii. 2. "Quorum gaudium tu ipse es. Et ipsa est beata vita gaudere ad te, de te, propter te" (Aug. *Conf.* x. 22). "The peace of reconciliation, the

"And this is the message[1] which we have heard from Him, and are announcing to you, that God is Light, and there is not in Him any darkness of any kind. If we say that we have fellowship with Him, and are walking in the darkness, we lie, and do not the truth. But if we walk in the Light, and He is in the Light,[2] we have fellowship with one another,[3] as the blood of Jesus, His Son, cleanseth us from all sin"[4] (i. 5—7).

Into those words, GOD IS LIGHT, St. John compresses the substance of his message, and utters one of those great final truths, which, since they cannot be transcended, mark the close of revelation. It is not introduced abruptly or disconnectedly, but it requires a knowledge of the Gospel to see its force. There, too, and in the same order, we have—First, the Word (i. 1), then Life (i. 4), then Light (i. 5); and there we see that the Light is the highest manifestation of the Life in relation to men; so that the epitome of the Gospel and the epitome of the Life of Christ, as regards the world, is this—that the Light shineth in darkness, and the darkness comprehended it not. But, when man receives the Life *as* Light, he also reflects it, and so becomes a child of Light.[5] In these words, therefore, as in "God is Love," St. John sums up all the meaning of his Gospel, although in the Gospel itself neither of the two expressions occurs. Yet Christ is there called Light, because He is one with the Father, and because He manifested the Father as Light. "I," He said, "am the Light of the world."[6]

But what is the *meaning* of this final revelation that God is Light? The only answer which we can give is that, of all existing things, not one is so pure, so abstract, so glorious, so beneficent, so incapable of stain or admixture, as earthly light; and earthly light is but an analogue of the Light which is immaterial and Divine.

> "Hail, Holy Light! offspring of heaven firstborn,
> Or of the Eternal co-eternal beam.
> May I express thee unblamed? since God is Light,
> And never but in unapproached Light
> Dwelt from eternity: dwelt then in thee,
> Bright effluence of bright essence uncreate;
> Or, hear'st thou rather, pure ethereal stream,
> Whose fountain who shall tell? Before the sun,
> Before the heavens, thou wast."

---

blessed consciousness of sonship, the happy growth in holiness, the bright prospect of future completion and glory, all these are but details of that which is embraced by one word, Eternal Life." (Düsterdieck).

[1] 'Ἀγγελία (not ἐν.), A, B, K, L, etc.
[2] One of the many passages in which there is close affinity between the thoughts of St. John and St. Paul (see Eph. iv. 25; v. 8, 9, 11—14). We can only walk in the light (Isa. ii. 5), coming into it out of darkness; but the essence and element of God's Being *is* in the Light (φῶς οἰκῶν ἀπρόσιτον).
[3] μετ' ἀλλήλων (א, B, etc.), and not μετ' αὐτοῦ (A), is the better reading. "Christian fellowship is then only real when it is in fellowship with God" (De Wette). "Nisi in bonis amicitia esse non potest" (Cic.).
[4] Col. i. 20; Eph. i. 7; Heb. ix. 14. Christ's blood, applied by Faith, becomes our Justification, and is also the purifying medium of our sanctification. The verse, as Bp. Wordsworth points out, refutes many heresies—*e.g.*, that of Cerinthus, that Jesus was not the Christ (reading Χριστοῦ); that of the Ebionites, that He was not the Son of God; that of the Docetae, that the Christ did not really die; that of the Novatians, who denied pardon to deadly sin after baptism; that of the Antinomians, who denied the necessity of moral obedience.
[5] John viii. 12.   [6] John i. 4; iii. 19; viii. 12.

St. John, as is usual with him, follows the positive statement by a negative one, which strengthens and adds to it—"in Him is no darkness whatever." The words furnished an answer, if such were needed, to Manichean dreams; and they introduce the truth that it must be the duty of the Christian TO WALK IN LIGHT, which is the same thing as to live in God. We are surrounded with elements of darkness; but we are not to love it, nor to love the world, which is the sphere of its extension; we are to pass from it, by heart-repentance, into the region of Light, which is the kingdom of God. If we have not done so, and yet profess fellowship with God, our life is a lie. In that case "we lie;" and to this positive he adds the negative, "and we do not the truth." The clause illustrates his manner. It is not a mere antithesis of positive and negative, but the addition of a stronger and partially new clause, after the fashion of Hebrew parallelism. For the word "truth" means something much more than that purely relative conception which we ordinarily attach to the word. We must seek the meaning of it in such expressions as St. Paul's "obeying the truth,"[1] and the words of Jesus, "I am the Truth."[2] It means absolute reality. The Gnostic dreamer—the professing Christian who talks about union with God and yet is walking in darkness, who wilfully deceives himself, who shrinks in hatred from the revealing light—not only says that which is false, but leads a life which is entirely false and hollow and unreal—a life of semblance and of death. But if we walk in the light, then our fellowship in light is perfected, and we are cleansed from all sin. In other words, we are sanctified by the blood of Jesus. His blood has won our justification—the forgiveness of our actual sins; His blood—that is, "His power of life working its effects and ruling within us"—is our sanctification from all sin. And to be forgiven, and cleansed, is to have fellowship with one another and with God.

"If we say that we have no sin, we mislead ourselves, and the Truth is not in us.[3] If we confess our sins,[4] faithful[5] is He and Righteous, that He should forgive us our sins, and cleanse us from all unrighteousness.[6] If we say that we have not sinned, we make Him a liar, and His Word is not in us" (i. 8—10).

The denial of sin, the assertion of our independence and perfection, is a radical abandonment of honesty. There can be no reality, and, therefore, nothing akin to the Divine,[7] in the man who makes such an

---

[1] Rom. ii. 8; 2 Thess. i. 8.   [2] John xiv. 6.
[3] The connexion is that we all need to be thus cleansed by the Blood of Christ (Iren. <i>Haer.</i> i., vi. 20). It is at least doubtful whether there is any special allusion to Gnostic Antinomian Perfectionists.
[4] Of course St John means confession springing from true contrition (James v. 16).
[5] True to His Nature and Promise (1 Cor. i. 9; x. 13; 1 Thess. v. 24, etc.).
[6] "In the background lie all the details of the Redemption" (Alford). "All sin, original and actual" (Bengel). "Si te confessus fueris peccatorum est in te veritas, nam ipsa veritas lux est. Nondum perfecte splenduit vita tua, quia insunt peccata: sed tamen jam illuminari coepisti quia inest confessio" (Aug.).
[7] In the tract Sanhedrin (f. 64, a), there is a story that for three days the Israelites wrestled with the Evil Impulse (<i>Jetser-hara</i>), and said that God had permitted this Evil Impulse, that

assertion, whether it be dictated by haughty self-sufficiency as to our own virtues, or by Antinomian denial that sin is exceedingly sinful. But with consciousness of sin begins the hope and possibility of amendment. When sin is confessed with real contrition to God, and, if needful, to men, then—because God is God, and is, therefore, faithful to His own nature, and because, as a Righteous Judge, He judges uprightly—it is the very object of His righteousness that He should remit our past sins,[1] and renew our whole nature. A denial on our part of past sin gives the lie to all His revelation, and proves that His Word is not in us.

Having thus illustrated the truth that to have fellowship with God is to walk in the Light, and that this involves our deliverance, alike from the *principle* of sin by redemption, and from the *guilt* of sin by forgiveness, he sums up in these words:—

"My little children,[2] these things I write to you that ye may not sin: and if any one have sinned,[3] we have an Advocate[4] to the Father, Jesus Christ, as Righteous. And He is a propitiation for our sins, but not for ours alone, but also for the whole world"[5] (ii. 1, 2).

The personal address, "my little children," shows the warmth and earnestness of this recapitulation. The aim of all that he has said is that the Christian should not sin; but if that deliverance be impossible in its ideal fulness, if we do fall into sins of infirmity, still, even then —if only we are on our guard that such sins never so master and possess our lives that we walk in darkness—we need not despair.[6] The best of all is not to sin; but if we cannot attain to this, there is a propitiation for sin, by which—an Advocate for us to the Father, by whom—we may gain the blessedness of the unrighteousness forgiven,

---

men might gain a reward by overcoming it. Thereupon a letter dropped from heaven, on which was the word "Truth." Rabbi Chanina said, "From this we may see that the *Seal of the Holy One is Truth.*"

[1] ἵνα ἀφῇ κ.τ.λ. "In this one particle (ἵνα) lies the most comprehensive and the highest witness of God's love that it is possible to conceive" (Haupt, p. 50).

[2] Tradition has also preserved this expression as a favourite one of St. John in his old age.

[3] ἐάν τις ἁμάρτῃ. Si quis peccaverit (Vulg.).

[4] The word is used in this sense in the letter of the Churches of Lyons and Vienne (Euseb. H. E. v. 1), where a young Christian—Vettius Epagathus—after begging to be heard in defence of the martyrs, himself received the martyr's crown—παράκλητος Χριστιανῶν χρηματίσας, ἔχων δὲ τὸν Παράκλητον ἐν ἑαυτῷ—"being called the Advocate of the Christians, but having the Advocate in himself." On this word Canon Westcott (on St. John xiv. 16) has one of those exhaustive notes, which are so valuable as tending to a final settlement of uncertain questions. The word is only found in the New Testament here, and in John xiv. 16, 26; xv. 26; xvi. 7, where it is rendered Comforter. The double rendering dates from Wiclif, followed by Tyndale and other versions, except that the Rhemish, following the Vulgate, uses Paraclete in the Gospel (Luther has in the Gospel "Tröster," and here "Fürsprecher"). The Latin Fathers use the words *Paracletus, Advocatus, Consolator;* and Tertullian (once), *Exorator.* The English word means not "Comforter" in the modern sense, but "Strengthener." ("Comfort is that by which in the midst of all our sorrows we are *comfortati*—i.e., strengthened," Bp. Andrewes.) The form of the word is passive; in Classical Greek it means Advocate. It is used in this sense by Philo and the Rabbis and early Christian writers. The meaning in this passage is clear, and the use of the word in the sense "Consoler" by the Greek Fathers seems only to be a secondary application (Westcott, l. c.). It was necessary for St. John to dwell on the truth that Christ was our only Advocate in churches given to Angel worship (Col. ii. 18; 1 Tim. ii. 5).

[5] "Thou, too, art a part of the whole world: so that thine heart cannot deceive itself, and think the Lord died for Peter and Paul, but not for me" (Luther).

[6] "Sed forte surrepit de vita humana peccatum. Quid ergo fiet? Jam desperatio erit? Andi:—si quis, inquit peccaverit," etc. (Aug.).

of the sin covered. That Advocate[1] is righteous in His nature and a propitiation by His office, so that, in and through Him, we can be acceptable to God.[2] The word "a propitiation" (*hilasmos*) is peculiar to St. John, occurring only here and at iv. 10. It is therefore in the Septuagint that we must look for its meaning, and there it is used as the translation of *Kippurim*, "the Day of Atonement,"[3] just as the corresponding verb to "propitiate," or "make a propitiation for,"[4] is the standing version of *kipper*. It is therefore a sacrificial metaphor, and points to the same series of thoughts which we have already examined in the Epistle to the Hebrews. The word itself stands in close relation to the word *hilasterion*,[5] or mercy-seat, which—sprinkled with the blood of atonement, and dimly seen in the darkness through the clouds of incense—was a type of the means whereby man may stand redeemed and accepted in the presence of God. The emblem and the expression belonged to the Jewish ritual; but, as St. John here adds, Christ's atonement was not only for Jews, not only for believers, but for the whole world. "Wide as was the sin, so wide was the propitiation."

With the third verse of the second chapter, begins a second section in illustration of the fundamental theme—the *manner*, namely, whereby "walking in the light," as a proof that we have eternal life, is evidenced. It is evidenced, as we have hitherto seen, by sinlessness—that is, by forgiveness from the past guilt of sin (i. 8—10), and deliverance from its present power (i. 5—7). But this is a proof that we are walking in the light with reference *to God*. The Apostle now proceeds to illustrate how such a walk is evidenced *towards men*, and this occupied the section ii. 3—14. In the first paragraph of this section he tells us that it is thus evidenced by keeping God's commandments (3—5); in the second, he proceeds to define all God's commandments as being summed up essentially in one, namely in walking as Christ walked, which (as the whole accompanying Gospel would have already made clear to his readers) was to walk in love, since love is the epitome of this life.[6] This section, then, is an illustration of our "fellowship with one another," as the last was of our "fellowship with the Father, and the Son Jesus Christ;" and thus the two together are meant, directly and consecutively, to promote the object which he has already placed in the forefront of his Epistle—union with one another and with God.[7]

And since critics have ventured to talk so superficially and irreverently of St. John's tautology and senility, and the loose, inconsequential structure of his Epistle, as though it were (as Caligula said

---

[1] Advocate (as we have seen), not Comforter, is perhaps always the right rendering of Παράκλητος. The word has been adopted by the Talmudists by simple transliteration (פרקליט), and only in *this* sense. This is the only passage in which the title is directly given to the Son, but it is *indirectly* given to Him in John xiv. 16, "I will send you *another* Comforter." Further, St. John generally regards and speaks of the Paraclete as the Spirit of *Christ*.
[2] "The righteousness of Christ stands on our side, for God's righteousness is in Jesus Christ, ours" (Luther). [3] כִּפֻּרִים [4] ἱλάσκεσθαι.
[5] Rom. iii. 25 (see *Life and Work of St. Paul*, ii. 209), and see *supra* on Heb. ix. 5.
[6] John xiii. 34, 35. 1 John iii. 1. [7] See I. 3.

of the style of Seneca)[1] a mere "rope of sand," it may be well to set visibly before the reader a proof of the extreme coherence and symmetry which mark its structure. It may serve to show that when these rude critics fancied that they "understood his ignorance," they were, as critics so often are, merely "ignorant of his understanding." If the reader will open his Bible and refer to the paragraphs i. 5—10 and ii. 3—11, he will find that they present the close and symmetrical parallelism which is indicated below.

CHAPTER i. 5.	CHAPTER ii. 3.
Subsection α—	Subsection α—
General statement.	General statement.
Ver. 6—	Ver. 4—
Negative supposition, and two condemnatory conclusions.	Negative supposition, and two condemnatory conclusions.
Ver. 7—	Ver. 5—
Positive supposition, and two declarations.	Positive supposition, and two declarations.
Subsection β—	General statement, ver. 6—8.
Three opposed sentences, ver. 8, 9, 10.	Three opposed sentences, ver. 9, 10, 11.

The symmetry is not slavishly artificial, but it is a very marked characteristic of a careful and meditative style.

"And in this we recognise that we have learnt to know Him, if we keep His commandments. He that saith, I have learnt to know Him, and keepeth not His commandments, is a liar, and in him the Truth is not. But whosoever keepeth His Word, of very truth in him the love of God has been perfected. By this we learn to know that we are in Him" (ii. 3—5).

"To know God" is not merely to know that He *is*. In St. John's sense it is to have *full* knowledge of Him[2]—that is, to receive Him into the heart. And *thus* to know Him is to walk in the light, which we cannot be doing if we are not keeping His commandments. Here, then, is a test for us as to whether we know Him or not, a test as to our Fellowship with Him. St. John has already told us (i. 6) that

If we say that we have fellowship with Him,
And walk in darkness,
    (α) We lie, and
    (β) Do not the truth :
and here, in closest parallel, but in stronger form, he tells us
He that saith, I have learnt to know Him
And keepeth not His commandments,
    (α) He is a liar, and
    (β) The truth is not in him.

---

[1] The shrewd, though more than half-insane Emperor, said that Seneca's style was "commissiones merus" ("mere display"), and "arena sine calce" "sand without lime."
[2] The word ἐπίγνωσις, however, so common in St. Paul and in 2 Peter, is not used by St. John.

But he who keepeth God's word—the words of Him who was the Word, and whose words are spirit and life[1]—is truly Christ's disciple. That word, whether as the personal Logos or as His announcement, is essentially "Love;" and, therefore, in him who keeps God's word the "love of God" has been perfected. Such a man has in himself, as the pervading influence of his life, the love which is in God—for "God is love."[2] The thought is exactly the same as that expressed by St. Paul, in the Ephesians, where, in the only passage in which he bids us be imitators of God,[3] he tells us to "walk in love, even as Christ loved us." But though the fundamental thought is the same, it is set forth by St. John in a more developed, a more penetrative, and a more final manner. The words, "herein we learn to know that we are in Him," are a recapitulation, but one which adds to the emphasis with which a truth so important is announced, and serves to perfect the symmetry between this section and the corresponding one in the last chapter.

In the next paragraph St. John gives the central thought, to which he has been drawing nearer and nearer—namely, that the ideal unity of God's commandments is found in brotherly love; and that this, therefore, is the true manifestation of "walking in the light," as expressed towards our brethren in the world.

"He that saith that he abideth in Him, ought himself also to walk even as He walked. Beloved, I write not a new commandment to you, but an old commandment which ye had from the beginning. That old commandment is the word which ye heard. Again a new commandment I write to you;[4] a thing which is a living reality in Him and in you; because the darkness is passing away, and the real Light is already shining. He that saith that he is in the Light, and hateth his brother,[5] is in the darkness even still. He that loveth his brother abideth in the Light, and there is no stumbling-block in him.[6] But he who hateth his brother is in the darkness, and in the darkness he walketh, and knoweth not where he goeth,[7] because darkness blinded his eyes" (ii. 6—11).

The verb used in the first verse of the clause expresses yet another stage of fellowship with God—not only *knowing* Him (verse 3), or *being* in Him (verse 5), but *abiding* in Him. But the stronger word is only used to express a development in the conception of obedience—

---

[1] John viii. 31.   [2] 1 John iv. 16.   [3] Eph. v. 1, 2.

[4] The whole passage is explained in the accompanying comment. It will be seen that I reject the explanation of the commandment as *new*, (1) because continually renewed (Calv.); or (2) "given *as though* it were new" (Neander); or (3) as unknown before Christ came. The commandment is "old" as dating from the beginning of Christianity; new if we look back to all previous ages. See Düsterdieck and Haupt.

[5] By "brothers" St. John means in the first instance "Christians," but obviously he means to include those wider senses which Christ gave to the word "neighbour." In his method of regarding all conceptions in their ideal and absolute nature, he only contemplates "love" and "hatred," and nothing intermediate. "Ubi non est amor, odium est: cor enim non est vacuum" (Bengel).

[6] "He," says Bengel, "who hates his brother is a stumbling-block to himself, and runs against himself and against everything within and without; he who loves has a smooth journey." See John xi. 9, 10. "If any man walk in the night he stumbleth, because the light is not in him." The man who walks in the light does not "set up the stumbling-block of his iniquity before his own face" (Ezek. xiv. 3).

[7] "It nescius in Gehennam, ignarus et caecus praecipitatur in poenam" (Cyprian).

"A NEW COMMANDMENT."

the walking as Christ walked. To do this is a moral obligation following necessarily from the profession of constant union with God. The earnest address, "Beloved," prepares us for some emphatic announcement. St. John has to explain the identity of "walking as Christ walked" with a commandment which is at once old and new. The new and the old commandments are not two different commandments, but one and the same—namely, the commandment which they received from the beginning of their Christian life. It is an old commandment, not only (though that is true) because it is found even in the Old Testament—for the letter is addressed to the Gentiles; but because it is as old as the whole message of the Gospel to them—"the entire word about the personal Word" which they received in the Apostolic preaching. But if Love was thus, even to these Gentile Christians, an old commandment, seeing that they had heard it all along, in what sense was it new? We might be left—as St. John's readers would have been —merely to conjecture the answer, if the Epistle had not depended upon a knowledge of the Gospel. But turning to the Gospel we find the new commandment there, and also the occasion on which our Lord delivered it. In that sweet and solemn discourse which He uttered after He had washed His disciples' feet, and which was intended to explain that act of sovereign condescension, He said, "A new commandment I am giving to you, that ye love one another; as I loved you that ye also love one another. In this shall all recognise that ye are my disciples, if ye have love for one another."[1] All readers of the Epistle in reading the phrase, "a new commandment," would be at once reminded of the passage which, in all probability, they had just read in the Gospel, and would see the analogy between "walking as Christ walked," and "loving as Christ loved." Again and again, both in parables and in direct exhortation, Christ had bidden them love one another, and yet the commandment *became* a new commandment with reference to the time and the manner in which it was then delivered. For, on the one hand, He had never before bidden them to love *as He loved*, and, on the other, His act in washing their feet had set brotherly love in a light entirely new. It was an act of love, altogether exceptional and transcendent, as St. John in the Gospel had emphatically pointed out.[2] For the Lord Himself had called attention to its import in the question, "Do ye recognise the meaning of what I have done to you? I gave you an example, that as *I* did to *you*, so ye also should ever do."[3] I was an act of love in its supremest energy—an *instantia elucescens* of love which could not be surpassed. All His previous acts of love had been the loving acts of One infinitely above them—of one whom they called, and who was, their Teacher and Lord. *This* was an act done as though He were their minister and slave. All other acts had been acts which as it were, He *must* have

---

[1] John xiii. 34, 35. [2] xiii. 1. [3] xiii. 12, 15

done in accordance with His nature; which if he had *not* done, He would not have reflected the perfectness of His own nature. But this was not an act which could have been expected; it was an act supremely astonishing; it arose, not as it were from the law of any moral obligation, but from love acting as an immeasurable impulse. This, then, is the love which furnishes the essence of the new commandment: not that love only which must ever be the first rule of Christian exhortation, but the love which ever advances to perfectionment,[1] and so works out the perfect joy into which it was one of the Apostle's objects to lead his readers.

When he proceeds to say that this new commandment is—is already —a "true thing," as being alive in *them*, as it was in Christ, we might perhaps be once more driven to ask, "What, then, is the necessity for impressing it upon them?"[2] The answer, as before, is one which applies to every one of the Epistles. It is a question which meets us at every turn in the Epistles of St. Paul, where there is so often so glaring a contrast between what Christians *ought* to be, and are asserted ideally to be, and what they really are. Christians can only be addressed as Christians, as having entered into the hopes of Christians, as enjoying the privileges of Christians, as being Christians not only in name but in deed and in truth. If then they were Christians they were "in Christ"; and if they were in Christ they were walking as He walked, and therefore walking in love. The love which was a real thing in Him was necessarily also a real thing in them. St. John could not address them as though they were *not* that which, as the very meaning of their whole lives, they were professing to be. And, indeed, that is the reason which he gives. The Love, he says, which is the new commandment, is a verity in Him and in you, because ye are children of the Light, and therefore the darkness is passing away. For all who were truly in Christ, that darkness must soon have passed away altogether; for not only was "the night far spent, and the day at hand,"[3] but the night was actually over, and the day had dawned. The very Light—Christ who is the Light—was shining already; shining not only in them but in the world. For the world is the universal realm of darkness, but in Him the Light is concentrated in its very essence and fulness.[4]

And then very plainly the Apostle furnishes them with a *test* of their professions. Love, he tells them, is the sign whether or not the Truth is in them, whether or not they are in the Light, whether or not they are walking as Christ walked. And the energetic severity of his moral nature appears here also in his stern antithesis of love to hatred, as though there were no possible intermediate between them. When we consider all that is involved in the word "brother," the idea of mere indifference in such a relationship becomes

---

[1] Heb. vi. 1.
[2] See *supra*, p. 532.
[3] Rom. xiii. 12.
[4] John i. 4—9.

impossible. If there be not the essence of love, there can only be the essence of hatred. He, therefore, that professes to be in the light and yet hates his brother is in the darkness—belongs to the world and not to the Kingdom of Heaven—however long he may have called himself a Christian. But he who loves will never cause another to stumble, can never therefore incur that grievous sentence which Christ pronounced on those who wilfully lead others into sin. The man who hates his brother has the permanent sphere of his life in the darkness. The light of the body is the eye; and since the eye of such a man is evil, his whole body is full of darkness. He stumbles through life along a road of which he does not know the goal.

These two illustrative paragraphs are closed, as is the case in the first section of the Epistle (ii. 1, 2), by a hortatory conclusion,[2] which falls into the rhythm so natural to St. John—

"I write to you, my little children,[3] because[4] your sins have been forgiven you for His name's sake:
"I write to you, fathers, because ye have learnt to know Him who is from the beginning:[5]
"I write to you, young men, because ye have conquered the evil one:
"I wrote[6] to you, little children,[7] because ye have learnt to know the Father:
"I wrote to you, fathers, because ye have learnt to know Him who is from the beginning:
"I wrote to you, young men, because ye are strong,[8] and the Word of God abideth in you, and ye have conquered the wicked one"[9] (ii. 12—14).

In these words we have a six-fold appeal, of which the first three clauses are introduced by the present, "I write," and the last three by the aorist, "I wrote." This aorist might be rendered in English by the perfect, "*I have written*," since it was the tense used by epistolary idiom to represent a letter regarded as a whole. The first question to be settled is whether the Apostle has in view three different ages of life. If so, it is certainly strange that he should place "fathers" between "little children" and "young men." From his use of "little children" in other parts of the Epistle,[10] to express *the whole body of Christians*,

---

[1] Matt. xviii. 6. [2] See analysis, *supra*, p. 527.
[3] τεκνία, addressed to all Christians, as in ver. 1; iii. 18; iv. 4; v. 21; John xiii. 33. It is only found in St. John.
[4] That ὅτι here means "because," and not "that," is proved by ver. 21.
[5] "Alii juvenes corpore, vos *fide*" (Bengel).
[6] ἔγραψα (א, A, B, C, L, Syriac, Coptic, Æthiopic, Arabic), not γράφω, seems to be the true reading in this verse. It is very difficult to say why the tense is altered; possibly only for emphasis, like the formula "we decree and have decreed." The attempt to refer it only to the part of the Epistle already written, while γράφω points to what follows, is untenable and against usage. Both words refer to the whole Epistle. It is, however, curious that up to this point γράφω has occurred seven times, whereas ἔγραψα is used six times in the rest of the letter.
[7] παιδία seems to differ in no sense from τεκνία. See ver. 18; John xxi. 5. Perhaps the change is merely for the sake of literary form and variety. Τεκνία may be a little more personal and affectionate, and so be represented, as Bishop Wordsworth says, by "my little children."
[8] "Fitque valens juvenis neque enim robustior aetas Ulla" (Ov. *Met.* xv. 208). ἰσχυροί (Luke xi. 21; Heb. xi. 34).
[9] In all these appeals the strongest warning is involved in the loftiness of the assumed ideal.
[10] ii. 1, 28.

there can be little doubt that this is his meaning here. If so, in the first of each three clauses he is exhorting Christians as a body, and in the latter two he is specially speaking to the two classes into which Christians of that day might most generally be divided, namely, "fathers" and "young men." Indeed, to address "little children" *as such* would have been alien to the habits of that age, nor would little children have understood the language here addressed to them. He says to the Christians generally that their sins have been forgiven them, because, as we have had repeated occasion to see, every address to Christians "must *presuppose* Christianity in the hearers, and yet *teach* it." Hence he addresses the fathers of the Churches, whether in a literal or an ideal sense, as having attained to the true knowledge of the Eternal Father; and the young men as having won a secure and tranquil mastery over temptation. After due time the young man's conquest will lead to the father's knowledge. The general identity in meaning of the second three with the first three clauses makes it somewhat difficult to account for the change of tense. Both phrases, "I write" and "I wrote," refer to this letter; the first as expressing the writer's present purpose, the other mentally glancing at it as a completed whole. The two together give a greater emphasis to his exhortations,[1] and are, perhaps, meant by way of introduction to the following section of the Epistle:—

"Love not the world,[2] nor yet the things in the world.[3] If any man love the world, the love of the Father is not in him;[4] because everything that is in the world, the desire of the flesh, and the desire of the eyes,[5] and the braggart vaunt of life,[6] is not from the Father, but is from the world. And the world is passing away, and the desire of it. But he who doeth the will of God abideth for ever. Little children, it is the last hour,[7] and as ye heard that Antichrist[8] is coming, even now antichrists in numbers have come into being, whence we recognise that it is the last hour.[9] From us they went forth, but they were not of us, for had they been of

---

[1] "A scribo transit ad scripsi; non temere; scilicet verbo scribendi ex praesenti in praeteritum transposito immisit commonitionem formosissimam" (Bengel).
[2] "God loved the world" (John iii. 16) with Divine compassion, as its Creator; we are not to love it with base desire. We are not to set our affections either on its material seductions, or on those human corruptions which mark its ruined condition.
[3] All kinds of sinful living, thinking, and demeanour (Ebrard). "Vulgata consuetudo hominum, res corporeas unice appetentium" (Semler).
[4] "Contraria non sunt simul" (Bengel).
[5] "Desire" (ἐπιθυμία) is coupled (always subjectively, *i.e.*, the desire *of*, not *for*) with "the heart" (Rom. i. 24), "the body" (Rom. vi. 12), and "mankind" (1 Pet. iv. 2, etc.). Desires are called "worldly" (Tit. ii. 12) and "fleshly" (1 Pet. ii. 11). By the "desire of the flesh" is meant every form of wrong or excessive lust. By the "desire of the eyes" is meant the sphere of selfishness, envy, covetousness, hatred, and revenge (Ebrard). Thus in the *Testament of the Twelve Patriarchs*, one of the seven "spirits of deceit" is the "spirit of seeing, with which desire is produced."
[6] Similarly, while speaking of luxurious extravagance, Polybius (vi. 5, 7) says—ἡ περὶ τὸν βίους ἀλαζονεία καὶ πολυτέλεια. Chrysostom calls it "the inflation (τύφος) and outward splendour (φαντασία) of worldly life." "Libido sentiendi, sciendi, dominandi" (Pascal).
[7] All Christians felt that the fall of Jerusalem was the close of an æon. It was a coming of Christ. They all felt that after that He might finally come to judgment at any time. "Ultimum tempus, in quo sic complentur omnia ut nihil supersit praeter ultimam Christi revelationem" (Calvin; 1 Cor. xv. 22; 2 Cor. v. 1, sq.; 1 Thess. iv. 15, sq.).
[8] "Antichrist" is a word peculiar to St. John in the N. T. (ii. 18, 22; iv. 3; 2 John 7). These are the only passages in which the word occurs. Strange to say, it is not once used in the Apocalypse.
[9] 2 Tim. iii. 1, sq.

us they would have abode with us; but (they went out) in order that they may be manifested that all are not of us"[1] (ii. 15, 19).

With this clause begins the third section of St. John's illustrations as to the nature and meaning of "walking in the light." As the very name of the Light reminds us of the darkness, which is its opposite; and as God's kingdom is the sphere of Light, so the world is the realm of darkness. He, then, who would walk in the Light must enter into the meaning of this severance. He must not love the world, nor the things which enter into the ideas of the world. Those things are defined under their ethical aspect. They are the objects of sensual desire in all its forms. They are the things which tend to the gratification of the flesh—that is, of our whole lower and animal nature —everything which tends to foster and stimulate the sins of gluttony, drunkenness, and impurity in all their many forms and gradations. They are the things which gratify the desire of the eyes—all that tends to the sins of intellectual selfishness and slothful æstheticism.[2] They are the braggart vaunt of outward life—all that tends to the sins of vulgar ostentation, egotistic pride, intellectual contempt, which spring from regarding life, not in its divine and spiritual (ζωή), but in its earthly and external aspect (βίος).[3] In St. John's language, therefore, the world (kosmos) does not mean the physical universe, which does indeed deserve the name of "order," by which it is described,[4] but the world regarded in its ethical sense, that is, a world disordered by the unrestrained prevalence of sinful forces, the world fettered in the bondage of corruption.[5] He bids us not to love this world—to have no esteem and affection for it—for two reasons. First, because such love cannot proceed from God, but from that evil principle which is the source of all vain and vile desires; and next, because the world is but a fleeting show, and the desires which it inflames can have but an instant's gratification. On the other hand, he who makes the will of God the law of all his actions, abides for ever. And it is the property of love to bind us closely to that which we love; if we love the earth we are earthly; the love of God makes us divine.[6]

Then from the general warning against the world he descends to its special manifestation in the form of anti-Christian error, which he introduces with the address of fatherly tenderness, "Little children, it is the last hour." The world and its desire is passing away now, it has not long to last. The final dispensation has begun. There will not be, there cannot be, any new dispensation. How long *this* æon is

---

[1] The οὐ πάντες might mean "none," as οὐ πᾶσα σάρξ means "no flesh" in Rom. iii. 20, but it is simpler to explain the passage as a mixture of two constructions, "that they may be manifested as not belonging to us," and "that it may be manifested that all (i.e. all who nominally belong to us) are not of us." [2] Matt. vi. 22.
[3] βίος, mere "living"—the psychic, animal, sensuous life, as in iii. 17. ἐν σαρκὶ βιώσαι, 1 Pet. iv. 2.
[4] "Quem κόσμον Graeci nomine ornamenti appellaverunt" (Plin. H. N. ii. 3).
[5] Rom. viii. 19, 20.
[6] "Amor habet vim uniendi; si terram amas terrenus es, si Deum divinus" (Gerson).

to last neither St. John knew nor any man, not even the angels in heaven. With reference to all previous æons *this* is the final æon. At its close there will be the new heaven and the new earth. And potentially this æon is already complete. With the manifestation of the Word in flesh its whole development was condensed into its first moment. It may linger on for a thousand years, for a thousand years is with the Lord as one day; but "it has already advanced to the top of its development, and therefore hastens to its end." And one sign of that ever-approaching end—ever approaching however long delayed—is the existence already of many Antichrists. Whether the many were yet to be concentrated into one monstrous development of intense personal wickedness, St. John does not say. The word Antichrist, which St. John alone uses, may mean either "*rivals* of Christ," i.e., pseudo-Christs (Matt. xxiv. 5, 11), or "*enemies* of Christ;"[1]—either those who try to pass themselves off as Christs, or those who set themselves in open array against Him. An Antichrist may take the semblance of a Nero or of a Simon Magus, of a Priest or of a Voltaire. St. John enters into no details because his readers had already heard that Antichrist cometh. This must refer to his own oral teachings, or those of other Apostles, for he tells us afterwards that by "Antichrists" he means those who deny the Incarnation (iv. 3), or who deny the Father and the Son (ii. 22). This form of Antichrist is not described either by Daniel, or by St. Paul in his Man of Sin. If, in 2 Thess. iii. 4, the expression of St. Paul may admit of some sort of analogous interpretation, it certainly could not have been assumed by St. John that the brief letter to a Macedonian Church would already have pervaded the whole of Asia.[2]

Nevertheless, the prevalence of these Antichrists, of whom St. John had orally spoken, was the direct fulfilment of the weeping prophecy of St. Paul, in his farewell to the Ephesian Elders, "that after his departure grievous wolves would enter among them, not sparing the flock, and that *from among their own selves* men would arise, speaking perverted things to drag away disciples after them." The very danger to the Church lay in the fact that this anti-Christian teaching arose out of her own bosom. The Antichrists did not openly apostatise from the Christian body; they corrupted it from within. They still *called* themselves Christians; had they really been so, they would have continued to be so. But their present apostasy was a manifestation of the fact that they never had been true Christians, and that not all who called themselves Christians are such in reality.

---

[1] The preposition ἀντί is used in both senses in compounds—either (1) "instead of" or (2) "opposed to." Thus we have (1) ἀντιβασιλεύς, "a viceroy;" ἀντίθεος, "a demi-god;" ἀνθύπατος, "a proconsul," etc.; and (2) ἀντιφιλόσοφος, "an enemy to philosophers;" ἀντιμαχητής, "an opponent;" ἀντικάτων, a book "against Cato." Had St. John meant "a rival of Christ," he would have used *pseudochristos*, as he uses *pseudo-prophetes*. The Fathers, both Greek and Latin, understood the word *normally* to mean "contrarius Christo" (Aug.), "Christi rebelles" (Tert.). See Trench, *Synonyms of the New Testament*, p. 145. See Hurd's *Sermons on Prophecies respecting Antichrist, and Prejudices against the Doctrine*. [2] Acts xxi. 29, 30.

THE SPIRIT'S UNCTION.

But if there be these dangers from within—if the Christianity of the *lips* is consistent with anti-Christianity of life—if walking in the light is nevertheless wholly incompatible with any fellowship with the world, as manifested in this or any other form of anti-Christianity— how is the Christian to be secured? That is the question which, in the next section, St. John proceeds to answer.

"But ye have an unction from the Holy One, and ye know all things.[1] He that confesseth the Son hath also the Father. I have not written unto ye because ye know not the truth, but because ye know it, and because no lie is of the truth. Who is the liar but he that denieth Jesus is the Christ? This is the Antichrist; even he that denieth the Father and the Son; whosoever denieth the Son the same hath not the Father; he that confesseth the Son hath the Father also. *Ye*—what ye heard from the beginning, let it abide in you. If that abide in you which ye heard from the beginning, ye also shall abide in the Son and in the Father. And this is the promise which He promises to us—Eternal Life.

"These things wrote I to you concerning those who mislead you. And ye—the unction[2] which ye received from Him, abideth in you, and ye have not need that any man teach you, but as the unction itself teacheth you concerning all things,[3] and is a true thing and not a lie; and even as it taught you, abide in it" (ii. 20—27).

Here then is the Christian's security—an unction from the Holy Spirit, an outpouring of the Holy Spirit by which we are anointed to be Kings, and Priests, and Prophets,[4] even as Prophets,[5] Priests, and Kings were anointed of old. We are anointed by the same chrism as was Christ Himself, and therefore can discern between Christ and Antichrist. This was the Lord's promise that His Holy Spirit should lead us into all truth, and therefore separate us, by His consecration, from the region of darkness, from the world, its errors, and its lusts. And this is why St. John need not dwell on a multitude of particulars, or track the various ramifications of deceit. For he is not writing to Jews or to Gentiles, but to Christian men, whom he needs only to remind that they belong to the sphere, not of lying semblances, but of the Eternal and the Real. They are already "in the light;" he does but need to remind them to abide therein. Now, for a Christian to deny that Jesus is the Christ, stamps him as radically untrue. He must have ceased to be "in Christ" by that denial; he must have left the kingdom of heaven for the world, the light for the darkness, the Real for the illusory. And to deny the Son is to deny the Father, since only by the Son has the Father been made known. These stern, disconnected sentences, falling like hammer strokes on the heart of the

---

[1] "Si Christum bene scis, satis est si caetera nescis;
Si Christum nescis, nihil est, si caetera discis."
Motto of Johann Bugenhagen.

[2] The word *chrisma*, not used in the Gospel, may be suggested by the word *antichristos*. All Christians are *christoi*, "anointed of God." Comp. Acts x. 38, "God anointed Him with the Holy Spirit."

[3] That is all things essential; all that we need.

[4] Is. lxi. 1. Kings and priests, Rev. i. 6; "a royal priesthood, a holy nation," 1 Pet. ii. 9; prophets, Joel ii. 28; Acts ii. 17, 18

[5] 1 Kings xix. 16 only.

listener, mark that holy and uncompromising severity of St. John's ideal, which resulted from his living in the atmosphere of contemplation, and regarding all things in their inmost nature and essence. Yet we should judge, from the affectionate title of "little children" by which they are introduced, and we know from the precious traditions of the Apostle's later days, that this stern theological inflexibility cannot be perverted, as it so often has been, into an excuse for theological hatred and party spirit, since it was combined with the tenderest charity towards erring souls.

But to save them from all this terrible defection, they had but to abide in the truth which they heard from the first, and to suffer it to abide in them. The exhortation resembles that of our Lord in the Gospel, "Abide in Me and I in you.[1] If ye abide in Me and My words abide in you, ye shall ask for yourselves whatever ye will and it shall be granted to you." Their active endeavours after constancy would be followed by a passive growth in grace. The abiding is secured by the constancy. The constancy is secured by the abiding. "It is a permanent and continuous reciprocation; the abiding of Christ in men furthers their abiding in Him; this again facilitates the former; and so it goes on."

This abiding is what He promised to us, and it is Eternal Life. For Eternal Life is fellowship with the Father and the Son. "This is Life Eternal, that they should learn to know Thee the Only the Very God, and Him whom Thou sendest, Jesus Christ."[2]

Then, in the last two verses (28, 29) comes the recapitulation and closing exhortation, before he passes to a new topic. "You have heard your danger. You are aware of that Unction which will secure you against it. I have told you what is the meaning of the Eternal Life, and of the fellowship on which I touched at the beginning of my letter. Abide in the Unction. It is a thing absolutely real, incommunicably dissevered from all that is false. Thus it is a source of all true teaching to you. That is the one command which is needful for you."

SECTION II.

THE CONFIDENCE OF SONSHIP.

Having thus shown at length that fellowship with God involves a walk in the Light, and a confession of sin, and that our fellowship with the brethren consists in general obedience to the commands of God, and special imitation of Christ in His love for all; and having shown that this common fellowship with God and with our brethren necessitates an absolute severance from the world in general, and from all antichristian teaching in particular, he enters on another topic—namely, on *the confidence inspired by Sonship as a sign of our possession of Eternal Life.*

[1] John xv. 4, 5, 7.   [2] John xvii. 2, 3.

THE MANIFESTATION OF CHRIST.   547

"And now little children abide in Him, that if He be manifested we may have confidence, and may not be shamed away from Him in His appearing.[1] If ye know that He is righteous, ye recognise that every one also who doeth righteousness has been born of Him.

"See what love the Father hath given to us[2] that we should be called children of God.[3] [And such we are.[4]] For this cause the world recogniseth not us, because it did not recognise Him. Beloved, now we are children of God, and not yet is it manifested what we shall be. We know that if He be manifested we shall be like Him, because we shall see Him even as He is. And every one who hath this hope in Him, purifieth himself even as He is pure"[5] (ii. 28—iii. 3).

The "and now," and the address, "little children," of ii. 28, together with the introduction of the four new thoughts—of Christ's "manifestation," of our having "confidence," of "doing righteousness," and of having been "born of God"—all indicate the beginning of a new section. And every one of these new thoughts is referred to and developed in the next great division of the Epistle.[6]

i. As regards the "*manifestation*" of Christ, that term, as expressive of His return to judgment, is peculiar to St. John, and marks his invariable point of view that all things in the Divine economy advance, not by sudden catastrophes, but by germinant developments in accordance with eternal laws. Christ is present now; His return will be but a manifestation of His Presence; and it is, perhaps, the consciousness that Christ is always present which has prevented St. John from elsewhere using the word *Parousia* for His second return, though that term is so common in the other sacred writers. Only by abiding in God can we meet that manifested Presence without shame, and answer with confidence at His judgment seat. Now, as St. John has already said that "every one who abideth in Him sinneth not," so now he expresses the same thought in a more developed form, by saying that the doing righteousness—as He is righteous—is the test of having been born of Him. He who does not sin has fellowship with God. He whose innocence is manifested in righteousness may know with confidence that he has been born of God. Here the Evangelist's point of view nearly resembles that of St. Paul, when he says that "the foundation of God standeth sure, having this seal,—'The Lord knoweth them that

---

[1] "Ne pudefiamus ab ejus praesentiâ" (Calvin). Matt. xxv. 41. πορεύεσθε ἀπ' ἐμοῦ.
[2] ἡμῖν, "indignis, inimicis, peccatoribus" (Corn. à Lapide).
[3] The missionary Ziegebalg tells an interesting story that in translating this passage with the aid of a Hindoo youth, the youth rendered it, "*that we should be allowed to kiss his feet*." When asked why he thus diverged from the text, he replied, "*A Child!* that is too much—too high!" (Braune, ad loc.).
[4] These words are found in א, A, B, C, Theophylact (γενέσθαι τε καὶ λογισθῆναι), Augustine, etc. They are omitted in K, L, and by Œcumenius. They may be genuine, but read like an awkward gloss. The Vulg. renders it wrongly "*et simus*."
[5] Comp. 2 Cor. vii. 1. The Apostles do not deem it necessary at every turn to introduce all the qualifications which would express the whole truth as to the Divine and human elements in the work of salvation; but of course the "purifieth himself" must be understood side by side with John xv. 5, "without Me ye can do nothing." "Castificas te, non de te, sed de illo qui venit ut inhabitet te" (Aug.). There seems to be no fundamental distinction between the uses of ἁγνίζω and καθαρίζω. The adjectives ἁγνός, καθαρός are used indifferently for טָהוֹר in the LXX. both of material (Num. viii. 21, etc.) and spiritual things (Ps. xi. 7, etc.).
[6] "Manifestation of Christ" (iii. 3—8); "Confidence" (iii. 21; iv. 17; v. 14); "Doing righteousness" (iii. 1—10); being "born of God" (iii. 24, seq.).

are His,' and 'Let every one that nameth the name of Christ depart from iniquity.'"[1]

The righteous man, then, is the son of God; and what love has the Father given us with this very object—that we may be called His children! St. John does not call us "sons" of God, as St. Paul does,[2] but "children," because he regards the sonship less as adoptive and more as natural. If the world does not recognise the sonship we are not to be surprised, since neither did it recognise the Sonship of Him from whom our sonship is derived. But there is another reason why St. John calls us "children" rather than "sons." It is because the word "childhood" involves in it the necessary idea of future growth, and this is true of our relation to God. Children we are, and something more than this we shall be hereafter, because we shall see God, and, therefore, become more and more like Him, though that new, and as yet unknown, relationship to Him will be but the full evolution of the old. And it is the constant aim of every one who really holds this hope to begin that ever-increasing resemblance, by even now purifying himself even as Christ is pure.

Our sonship of God is, therefore, *tested* at the Last Day by our lives; and to us it can only become a matter of present assurance by doing righteousness. He proceeds to illustrate this truth in four sentences, of which each consists of two clauses. First, he shows that sin is opposed to God and opposed to Christ (vs. 4, 5); then that to abide in Him is to be sinless, and that to be sinful is never to have seen Him (v. 6); nay more, he shows that to do righteousness is to be of God, and to do sin is to be of the devil (vs. 7, 8); then, in the last two verses of the clause (9, 10), he recapitulates the proof, and states the final result.

The section then is as follows:—

"Every one that committeth sin committeth also lawlessness, and sin is lawlessness. And ye know that He was manifested that He may take away sins,[3] and sin is not in Him" (iii. 4, 5).

"Every one who abideth in Him sinneth not. Every one who sinneth hath not seen Him nor even known Him"[4] (ver. 6).

[1] 2 Tim. ii. 19.
[2] "According to St. Paul we receive for Christ's sake the *rights* of children. According to St. John we receive through Christ the children's nature. According to St. Paul the old nature of man is transformed into a new. According to St. John an altogether new principle of nature takes the place of the former. It is most evident that the two views are substantially one, and true, but they depend on the respective general systems of the two Apostles" (Haupt, p. 156).
[3] "Tollit peccata et dimittendo quae facta sunt, et adjuvando ne fiant, et perducendo ad vitam ubi fieri omnino non possunt" (Bede).
[4] "In ipso peccati momento talis fit, ac si Eum nullo viderit modo" (Bengel). This verse, as Theophylact tells us, was regarded by Antinomian Gnostics as proving the indefectibility of grace, and so was turned into an excuse for lasciviousness. But that certain practical modifications must be admitted is clear, from previous passages in the Epistle itself. The older expositors generally adopted the method of toning down the Apostle's language. Modern expositors accept the language as meaning what it says, but regard it as only applying to the ideal. The two methods come to much the same thing in the end. Thus, in verse 9, some explain "he cannot sin," by—

    He cannot commit mortal sin (Romanists).
    He cannot sin deliberately and intentionally (Ebrard).

"Little children, let no one mislead you. He that doeth righteousness is righteous, as He is righteous. He that doeth sin is of the devil,[1] because the devil sinneth from the beginning.[2] For this purpose was the Son of God manifested that He may destroy the works of the devil" (ver. 7, 8).

"Every one that hath been born of God doth not commit sin, because his seed abideth in him; and He cannot sin, because He has been born of God" (ver. 9).

"In this are manifest the children of God and the children of the devil" (ver. 10a).

To careless and superficial readers many of these clauses might look like mere mysticism clothed in antithetic tautologies. To one who has tried to study the mind and manner of St. John, they are full of the deepest meaning. Take the very first clause. How deep and awful a conception of sin ought we to derive from the fact that all sin, however slight it may seem to us, is not a matter of indifference, but a transgression of the divine law! How does such a conception tend to silence our petty excuses, or our weak talk about pardonable human imperfections! How different will be our tone—how little shall we be inclined "to say before the angel 'It was an error'"—when once we have realised this "universal and exceptionless fact!" And still more when we remember that not only is every sin, in God's sight, the violation of the eternal law, but also a violation of the whole purpose of Christ's manifestation, which was expressly meant to take all sins away. And when St. John proceeds to say that he who sinneth hath never seen or known God, however much we may be inclined to introduce limitations into this language, both by the daily facts of Christian

---

He cannot sin in the way of hating his brother (Augustine, Bede).
It is alien from his nature to sin (Grotius).
His nature and habit resist sin (Paulus).
He does not wish to sin, or ought not to sin (various Commentators).
He cannot be a sinner (ἁμαρτάνειν) (Wordsworth, and so Didymus).
He does not sin, he only suffers sin (Besser; comp. Rom. vii. 17).
So far as he remains true to himself, he does not sin (Augustine).
So long as he is a child of God he cannot sin (others).

The only possible escape from some such modification, is by asserting the possibility of sinlessness in this life (which contradicts i. 8), or else by asserting that none of us have seen God, and none of us are children of God (which contradicts the whole Epistle). Hopkins says, "The interpretation which I judge to be most natural and unforced is this:—He that is born of God doth not commit sin—that is, he doth not sin in that malignant manner in which the children of the devil do; he doth not make a trade of sin, nor live in the constant and allowed practice of it. . . . There is a great difference between regenerate and unregenerate persons in the very sins that they commit. 'Their spot is not the spot of his children' (Deut. xxxii. 5). And as they differ in the committing of sin, so much more in the opposing of it." And if the Stoic was allowed to set before himself his ideal, why may not the Christian do the same? Seneca said that the wise man was not only able to do right, but even could not do otherwise. "Vir bonus non potest non facere quod facit; in omni actu par sibi, jam non consilio bonus, sed more eo perductus; ut non tantum recte facere possit, sed nisi recte facere non possit." And Velleius Paterculus said of the younger Cato, "Homo virtuti simillimus, et per omnia ingenio Diis quam hominibus propior, qui nunquam recte fecit ut facere videretur, sed quia aliter facere non poterat" (Hist. ii. 34); and he spoke of him as "exempt from all human vices." And Tacitus said that when Nero wished to kill Paetus Thrasea, it was as if he wished "to kill virtue herself." The Christian ideal is infinitely higher than the Stoic, and that is why the Christian knows that not even a saint can be absolutely sinless; yet he hates sin, and more and more wins the victory over it.

[1] He does not say, "born of the devil." "Neminem fecit diabolus, neminem genuit neminem creavit" (Aug.). His work is "corruptio non generatio" (Bengel).

[2] Not "ex quo diabolus est diabolus" (Bengel), but since sin began: "ab initio τοῦ peccare."

experience, and the recognition in this very Epistle that even the most advanced believer does not here attain to absolute sinlessness (i. 8—10), yet the awfulness of the stern, unbending language tends to convince us, more than anything else could, of the exceeding sinfulness of sin, seeing that every act of it is a proof, as far as it goes, of alienation from God; of affiliation, in some sense, to him from whom all sin began. It is a nullifying of all that Christ died to achieve. The summing up, then, of what he has said, is that in every one who has been born of God there is a principle of divine life which renders sin impossible. Sin, on the other hand, shows, by ethical likeness, its Satanic parentage. St. John divides all men simply into children of God and children of the devil, and recognises no intermediate classes. We do not see it to be so in the ordinary mixture and confusion of human life, but in the abstract and in the essence of things, so it is. To God, though not to men, it is possible to write the epitaph of each life in the brief words, "He did that which was good," or "he did that which was evil" in the sight of the Lord.

On the dread severity of this language, on the only possible explanation and alleviation of it, I have already dwelt.[1] The ideal truth must ever, so to speak, float above its actual realisation. But the warning force of St. John's high words lies in *this*:—We are children of God by birth and by gift, but unless we also approve ourselves as His children by act and life, we sink out of that sonship into Satanic depths. Every sin we commit is a proof that we are not yet children of light, children of God; but that darkness still has power over us. For each such defection we must find forgiveness, and against each such defection we must strive more and more. A child of God, as Luther says, may receive daily wounds in the conflict, but he never throws away his arms. If once we have fully and freely dedicated ourselves to God, sin may sometimes invade us, but it can never have dominion over us. Of the two seals on the one foundation—"God's knowledge of us as His own," and "Departure from iniquity"—where the one is found, the other will be never wanting.

The demonstration of sonship, then, in relation to God, is "to do righteousness"; and in relation to man this righteousness is manifested by loving our brethren, which he illustrates first negatively (10b—15) and then positively (16—18).

"Every one who doeth not righteousness is not from God, nor he who loveth not his brother. Because this is the message (ἀγγελία, A, B, etc.,) which ye heard from the beginning, in order that (ἵνα) we should love one another; not as Cain was from the wicked one,[2] and brutally slew his brother. And why did he brutally slay him? Because his deeds were evil, but those of his brother righteous. Wonder not, brethren, if the world hates you. We know that we have passed from death unto

---

[1] See *supra*, pp. 522—524.
[2] *I.e.*, "Let us not be of the wicked one as Cain was, who," etc. The construction is condensed, as in 1 Cor. x. 8. Some of the Rabbis said that "Cain was a son of Eve and the serpent" (Zohar).

life, because we love the brethren.[1] He who loveth not abideth in death. Every one who hateth his brother is a murderer,[2] and ye know that no murderer hath eternal life abiding in him" (iii. 10b—15).

Our duty to man follows as an immediate corollary from our duty to God, just as the second table of the Decalogue follows naturally as an inference from the first. No doubt in thus exhorting to brotherly love, St. John is thinking in the first place of the Churches which he is addressing, and therefore by "brother" he primarily means Christian. But to *confine* his meaning to Christian brethren would be to wrong the majesty of his teaching. It would also dwarf all that our Lord taught on the same subject—as, for instance, in the parable of the Good Samaritan; and the force of Christ's own example, who loved us and died for us while we were yet sinners. And to miss the truth that love is the very central command of Christianity—though that truth has been missed for centuries—though Church parties in their narrow and envenomed controversies daily prove how utterly they have missed it—though all kinds of glozing self-deceptions are practised to persuade the conscience that violations of it are *not* violations of it, but are "uncompromising faithfulness" and "burning zeal"—yet to miss that truth is inexcusable, for it was delivered from the first, and is repeated continually. It was, as the Apostle tells us, at once the matter ("this is the message") and the purpose ("in order that ye may love one another") of the Christian revelation.

In his usual manner of illustrating by opposites, St. John impresses the duty by showing the frightfulness of hatred, of which he selects Cain as an example, because it is the earliest and one of the worst. The word which he uses for the murder—(ἔσφαξεν "he butchered")—perhaps refers to some Jewish legend as to the manner in which the murder had been accomplished. The instance was peculiarly apposite, because the murder was but the ripened fruit of a secret envy caused by God's approval of good works in another. It was, therefore, well adapted to show the nature of the *world's* hatred to the Church, and to illustrate the fact that hatred belongs to the world—that is, to the realm of Satan and of darkness—and should therefore be utterly excluded from the Kingdom of Light and of Christ. Let not the Church be as Cain-like as the world. For hatred means death, and we have passed from death into life, as our love to the brethren shows.[3] On the other hand, if—though we call ourselves Christians—we still hate, we are still in death. For all hatred is potential murder; it is murder in the undeveloped germ; and it is impossible to conceive a murderer as having in him that divine, that spiritual life which alone corresponds to St. John's use of the word "eternal."

[1] "Bona opera non praecedunt justificandum sed sequuntur justificatum" (Aug.).
[2] Comp. Seneca's "Latro es antequam inquines manum."
[3] Here again we have the double fact of a warning accompanied by the assertion that (ideally) it is quite needless.

Passing from the negative to the positive illustration he continues:—

"Hereby we have learnt to know what love is—because He, on our behalf, pledged His life; and we ought to pledge our lives for the brethren. But whoever hath this world's sustenance, and contemplates (θεωρῇ) his brother suffering want, and locks up from him his pity,[1] how doth the love of God abide in him? Let us not love with word nor yet with tongue,[2] but in deed and in truth"[3] (iii. 16—18).

Cain has furnished the most awful warning against hatred. There can be but one example, which is the most emphatic exhortation to love—namely, He who loved even His enemies, and proved His love for them by His death. Cain slew his brother because he hated him for his goodness; Christ died for sinners because He loved them in their iniquity. The phrase rendered in the English version, "He *laid down* His life," is found in St. John only, but it is one of which he is specially fond.[4] He borrows it from the discourses of our Lord, and it is therefore coloured in all probability by Hebrew analogies. If the reference be to Isaiah liii. 10, it involves the conception of laying down life as a pledge, a stake, a compensation. We ought to do the same according to the measure of need. But how can any man do this who grudges, or coldly ignores, the simplest, most initial, most instinctive acts of kindness to his suffering brethren?—who, like the fastidious Priest and the icy-hearted Levite of the parable, can coldly stare at his brother's need, and bolt against him the treasure-house of natural pity? How can the man who thus shows that he has *no* love in him, love God who is *all* love? Thus we see that with St. John, as with St. Paul, the loftiest principles lead to the humblest duties, and even as it takes the whole law of gravitation to mould a tear no less than to shape a planet, so the element or obligation of kindness to the suffering is made to rest on the infinite basis that God is Love. The man who is capable of such unnatural hardness as St. John describes, is quite capable of the hypocrisy of profession. Like the vain talker in St. James (ii. 16), he will doubtless tell the sufferer how much he pities him; he will say to him, with a fervour of compassion, "Be warmed," "Be clothed," but he has ten thousand cogent and ready excuses to show why he cannot personally render him any assistance. For such lip-charity, such mere pleasantly-emotional pity, such eloquent babble of hard-heartedness, wearing the cloak of compassion, he warns them, substitute the activity and reality of love.

The recapitulation which follows is extremely difficult, and all the more so because the punctuation is uncertain, the construction unusual,

---

[1] σπλάγχνα *rachamîm*, Prov. xii. 10 (tender mercies).
[2] "Sermone otioso, lingua simulante" (Bengel).
[3] Μή μοι ἀνὴρ γλώσσῃ εἴη φίλος ἀλλὰ καὶ ἔργῳ Χερσίν τε συνίθοι χρήμασί τ' ἀμφότερα (Theognis); "Ye knot of mouth-friends" (Shaksp., *Timon of Athens*).
[4] John x. 11, 15, 17, 18; xiii. 37, 38; xv. 13.

the readings unsettled. I give the rendering which, on the whole, approves itself to my mind, but I am far from certain that it is correct. Other versions and other interpretations are almost equally tenable, and I incline to the view that there is either some corruption in the text, or that some confusion may have arisen in the dictation of the Epistle. The difficulty in interpreting the words of St. John is almost always the difficulty of fathoming the true depth of his phrases—the difficulty of understanding the full spiritual meaning of his words. His style is, for the most part, incomparable in its lucidity, and there must be *some* disturbing element which renders it impossible in the next two verses to be at all sure that we have ascertained what he meant, or even what he said.

"And hereby shall we recognise that we are of the truth, and we shall in His sight assure our hearts:[1] because if our heart condemn us, [because] God is greater than our heart, and recogniseth all things"[2] (iii. 19, 20).

"Beloved, if our heart condemn us not we have confidence towards God; and whatsoever we ask we receive from Him, because we are keeping His commandments, and are doing the things which are acceptable before Him. And this is His commandment, that we should believe in the name of His Son, Jesus Christ, and love one another even as He gave us commandment. And he who keepeth His commandments abideth in Him, and he in him" (iii. 21—24a).

Assuming that the *reading* which I have followed in the first two verses of this passage is correct, and the *grammatical construction* admissible, the meaning will be simple. It is that Brotherly Love is a proof that we belong to the kingdom of Eternal Reality, and that by this assurance we shall ever be able to still the misgivings of our hearts. For even if the individual heart of each one of us knoweth its own bitterness and condemns itself, still, since we are sincere, and have given proof of our sincerity by love to the brethren, we may fall back on the love and mercy of One who is greater, and therefore more tender, than our self-condemning hearts. He will "count the long Yes of life" against its one No, or its guilty moment. Because He recogniseth all things—because, knowing all things, He recognises that we do love

---

[1] πείσομεν seems to mean we shall still the questionings of our hearts; persuade them that the view which they take of our frailties is too despairing. Haupt's rendering, "we shall soothe," only lies in the context, not in the word (comp. Acts xii. 20, πείσαντες Βλάστον; E. V., "*having made Blastus their friend;*" (Gal. i. 10).

[2] I cannot at all accept the version of Haupt, or his explanation of this extremely difficult passage. He takes it to mean, "In this love rests our consciousness that we are of the truth, and by it may we soothe our hearts, *in all cases in which* (ὅτι ἐάν) our heart condemns us, for God is greater than our hearts and knoweth all things." The difficulty lies partly in the repeated ὅτι. If the first ὅτι means "because," the second must also mean "because," and this gives a very awkward clause, and makes no good sense. I therefore take the view of the old scholiast, who says "the second ὅτι is superfluous" (τὸ δεύτερον ὅτι παρέλκει). We find a similar instance of ὅτι repeated in Eph. ii. 11, 12, and in classic writers (Xen. *Anab.* v. 16, § 12, "They say that if not . . . that he will run a risk"). If it be thought an insuperable objection that in these instances ὅτι always means "that" and not "because," I can only suppose that the second ὅτι is really a confusion due to dictation. I take the consolatory, not the dark view of the passage. I think that St. John meant us to regard it as a subject of *hope*, not of *despair*, that God is greater than our hearts. This certainly is most in accordance with John xxi. 17—"Lord, Thou knowest all things: Thou knowest that I love Thee." It would be useless to repeat the tediously voluminous varieties of exposition which have been applied to the passage. [The Revised Version renders it, "and shall assure our heart before Him, whereinsoever our heart condemn us."]

Him[1]—because, where sin abounded there grace much more abounded[2]—because, as Luther said, the conscience is but a waterdrop, whereas God is a deep sea of compassion—therefore He will look upon us

> "With larger other eyes than ours,
> To make allowance for us all."

But if our heart condemn us not of wilful failure in general obedience or in brotherly love—if we can, by God's grace, say with St. Paul, "I am not conscious of any wrong-doing"—then, when faith has triumphed over a self-condemning despair—we have that confidence towards God of which St. John spoke at the beginning of this section (ii. 28), and are also sure that God will grant our prayers, both personal—that we may ever more and more do the thing that is right—and intercessory—that His love may be poured forth on our brethren also. And thus shall we fulfil the commandments to believe and to love. These two commandments form the summary of *all* God's commandments: for the one is the inward spirit of obedience, the other its outward form. He who thus keeps God's commandments, abides in God and God in him.

The thoughts of the writer in these verses are evidently filled with the last discourses of the Lord, which he has just recorded in the Gospel, and which he may assume to be fresh in the minds of his readers. In these verses he dwells on the same topics—faith, love, prayer, union with God, the Holy Spirit. In this clause he concludes the section, which has been devoted to the proof that doing Righteousness and Love of the brethren are the practical signs that we are sons of God. In the second clause of verse 24—which would better have been placed at the head of the next chapter—he passes to two new thoughts, which form the basis of his proof that the source of our sonship is the reception of the Holy Spirit of God, and therefore that our confidence towards God ($\pi\alpha\rho\rho\eta\sigma\iota\alpha$, ii. 28; iii. 21; iv. 17, 18) may be absolute, even to the end.

SECTION III.

THE SOURCE OF SONSHIP.

"And hereby we recognise that He abideth in us, from the Spirit which He gave us. Beloved, believe not every spirit, but test the spirits whether they are from God, because many false prophets have gone forth into the world. Hereby ye recognise the Spirit of God; every spirit which confesseth Jesus as Christ come in the flesh is from God, and every spirit which severeth Jesus is not from God, and this is the spirit of Antichrist of which ye have heard that it cometh, and now is it in the world already. Ye are from God, little children; and ye have overcome them because greater is He who is in you than he who is in the world. They are from the world; for this cause they speak from the world, and the world heareth them. We are from God; he who learns to know God heareth us; he who is not

---

[1] John xxi. 17, κύριε σὺ πάντα οἶδας, σὺ γιγνώσκεις ὅτι φιλῶ σε. [2] Rom. v. 20.

from God heareth not us.[1] From this we recognise the spirit of truth and the spirit of error" (iii. 24b—iv. 6).

The change of phrase from "abide in Him" (ii. 28) to "He abideth in us," and the introduction of the new thought involved in the mention of the Spirit, mark the beginning of a new clause. The subject of this clause is at once stated in the words "we recognise that He abideth in us." We are passing from the *tests* of sonship to the *source* of sonship. Following the same method of division which we have already found in the previous sections of the Epistle, the Apostle treats of this subject first in relation to God in Christ (iv. 1—6), and then in relation to our brother-man (7—12). He who rightly confesses God in Christ, and who proves the sincerity of that faith by love to the brethren, does so by the sole aid of the Holy Spirit of God, and it is thus proved that he is born of God.

This possession of the Holy Spirit, this abiding of God in us, is first illustrated by its opposite. The denial of Christ is a sign that we are under the sway of spirits which are not from God, even the spirits of false prophecy and of Antichrist. The characteristic of the men whom these spirits deceive is to deny the Lord that bought them,[2] and to apostatise from the worship of Christ to the worship of the Beast.[3] That such spirits were at work even thus early we have already seen in the warnings of St. Paul, St. Peter, and St. Jude. And the peril which they caused was enhanced by this; they were at work in the bosom of the Church itself. When St. John says that they have gone forth into the world, he does not mean that they are severed from the Church, for if this had been the case there would have been no need to test them, or to be on guard against them, since, as regards the Christian community, they would have stood self-condemned. But while still nominally belonging to the visible Church, the nature of their teaching stamped them as belonging really to the world. Every Christian, therefore, had need to "test the spirits;" he was required to exercise that grace of "the discernment of spirits" to which St. Paul had called the attention of his Corinthian converts.[4] In Corinth the terrible abuses of glossolaly had led to outbreaks which entirely ruined and degraded the order of worship. Amid the hubbub of fanatical utterances voices had even been heard to exclaim "Anathema is Jesus." Those hideous blasphemies, due to secret hatred and heresy, had sheltered themselves under the plea of uncontrollable spiritual impulse, and St. Paul had laid down as distinctly as St. John, and almost in the same terms, that the confession of Jesus as Lord could only come from the workings of the Holy Spirit of God, and that any one who spoke against Jesus, however proud his claims, *could* not be speaking by the Spirit of God. It is interesting to find the two Apostles so exactly

---

[1] "For this have I been born, and for this have I come into the world, that I should testify to the Truth. Every one who is of the Truth heareth my voice" (John xviii. 57).
[2] 2 Pet. ii. 2.   [3] Rev. xiii. 8.   [4] 1 Cor. xii. 10.

in accord with one another. It is even difficult to imagine that St. John could have written this passage without having in mind what St. Paul had said to the Corinthians.[1] But even if not, we have another proof how absurd is the theory which places the two Apostles in deadly antagonism, whereas again and again there is a close resemblance between them, not only in the expressions which they use, but also in the entire systems which they maintain.

Here, then, was to be the test which each Christian could apply. Every spirit was of God who confessed "*Jesus Christ come in the flesh*." There were even in those early days professing Christians who said that Jesus was indeed the Christ, but that the Christ had not come in the flesh. They maintained that during the public ministry of Jesus, the spirit of the Divine Christ had been with Him, but only till the crucifixion; so that the Incarnation of the Divine in the human nature was nothing but a semblance. These were the forerunners of the sect of Docetists. There were others, again, who regarded the life of Jesus as homogeneous throughout, but denied that he was the Christ in any other sense than that He was the Jewish Messiah; denied that He was Christ in the sense of being the Son of God. These were the early Ebionites. Against them both St. John had erected his eternal barrier of sacred testimony when he wrote "The Word became flesh," a testimony which he here repeats, and which he expresses no less plainly in verse 14, when he says, "We have seen and do testify that the Father has sent His Son as Saviour of the World." Every spirit was from God which, speaking in the mouths of Christian prophets, confessed that Jesus who was a man was also the Incarnate Son of God.

The next verse (3) begins in the Authorised Version, "And every spirit that confesseth not that Jesus Christ is come in the flesh is not of God." The first correction which must be made to bring back this verse to the true reading is to omit the words "*Christ is come in the flesh*." Not only are they omitted by the Sinaitic, Alexandrian, and Vatican MSS., and absent from the Vulgate, Coptic, and Æthiopic versions, but also it is more accordant with St. John's manner to vary the form of his antithetic clauses. The meaning, however, remains the same, for by "confessing Jesus" nothing can be meant but confessing that He is the Incarnate Son of God. But in my version I have ventured to follow the other reading, "Every spirit WHICH SEVERS JESUS (ὁ λύει). It is a reading of deep interest, and one which, if it be genuine, proves very decidedly the working of those Gnostic speculations—at least in their germs—which is also presupposed in the later Epistles of St. Paul. The authenticity of those Epistles has often been denied, on the ground that they are devoted to the refutation of heresies which, it is asserted, had no existence till at least the second

---

[1] 1 Cor. xii. 8.

century. I have already endeavoured to show that there is no weight in this argument;[1] but if the reading "which severs Jesus" be indeed the original one, it furnishes the clearest indication of the direction taken from the first by Gnostic error.[2] The Docetæ and Ebionites had already begun to "sever Jesus"—to say that He was a man to whom for a time only the Spirit of God had been united, or that He was a man only and not the Son of God at all.

It need, however, be hardly said that the interesting character of a reading furnishes no ground for accepting it. But we are under no temptation to introduce it on dogmatic grounds, seeing that even without it we have sufficient indication of the existence of these sects.

At first sight it might seem to be fatal to the reading that it is not found in any existing manuscript. This fact must perhaps suffice to exclude it from any accepted text of the Greek Testament, yet this seems to me to be exactly one of those cases in which the reading of the existing MSS. is outweighed by other authorities and other considerations.[3] In the first place, the reading is found in the Vulgate. Then, Socrates, the ecclesiastical historian, tells us that Nestorius "was ignorant that *in the ancient manuscripts* of the Catholic Epistle of John *it had been written* that, 'Every spirit WHICH SEVERS JESUS is not from God.'"[4] He adds, that those who wished to sever the Divinity of Jesus from His Humanity, "took away this sense (ταύτην τὴν διάνοιαν ἐκ τῶν παλαιῶν ἀντιγράφων περιεῖλον) from the ancient manuscripts." How Düsterdieck and others can here maintain that Socrates does not mean to assert that the reading "severs Jesus" *was actually found* in these old manuscripts is more than I can understand. There is no other reason for mentioning the manuscripts at all. Socrates clearly means to charge the Nestorians with the falsification of the text. Irenæus also, in denying all claims of Christian orthodoxy to those who, under pretence of *gnosis*, drew distinctions between Jesus and Christ, between the Only Begotten and the Saviour, refers to this passage and quotes it, "Et omnis spiritus QUI SOLVIT JESUM non est ex Deo."[5] Origen, again, on Matt. xxv. 14, quotes the verse in the same way, and adds, "we thus reserve for each substance its own proper attributes."[6] Again, Tertullian, in referring to the first, second, and third verses of this chapter, sums them up in the words "Joannes Apostolus . . . . antichristos dicit *processisse in mundum* (verse 1) . . . . negantes Christum *in carne venisse* (verse 2), et *solventes* Jesum" (verse 3).[7] Once more, St. Augustine has the expression, "He *severs Jesus*, and denies

---

[1] See my *Life of St. Paul*, ii. 620.   [2] See *supra*, p. 501.
[3] To express the same thing technically, the *diplomatic* is outweighed by the *paradiplomatic* evidence.
[4] ἠγνόησεν ὅτι ἐν τῇ καθολικῇ Ἰωάννου ἐγέγραπτο ἐν τοῖς παλαιοῖς ἀντιγράφοις ὅτι πᾶν πνεῦμα ὃ λύει τὸν Ἰησοῦν κ.τ.λ. (Socrates, H. E. vii. 32).
[5] Iren. c. Haer. iii. 8.
[6] "Haec autem dicentes non SOLVIMUS suscepti corporis hominem, cum sit scriptum apud Joannem, 'Omnis Spiritus qui SOLVIT Jesum non est ex Deo,' sed unicuique substantiae proprietatem servamus" (Origen, l.c.).
[7] Tert. *adv. Marc.* v. 16, and *adv. Psych.*, "quod Jesum Christum solvant."

that He has come in the flesh." Against these testimonies—unmistakable as they are—it is usual to urge the supposed silence of Polycarp, who in his letter to the Philippians, says, "but every one who does not confess that Jesus Christ is come in the flesh is Antichrist. Clearly, however, this may be a general reference to the second verse, and furnishes no proof that the reading "severs" may not have occurred in this third verse even in Polycarp's time. That he should not quote it is sufficiently accounted for by its difficulty. There is a compression in it which requires explanation. It involved a profound and prescient allusion to heresies which as yet were vague and undeveloped. It needed for its full understanding the light which was to be thrown upon it by subsequent history, when heresy after heresy was occupied in "*severing*" the One Person, or isolating one or other of the Two Natures. When we consider the proofs that the reading did really exist in early texts; that there was every temptation to add explanatory glosses to explain its difficulty; that it was easy for such an explanatory gloss as "*does not confess*" to creep in from the previous text; that the explanatory gloss "*Christ come in the flesh*" has actually so crept in; that the later addition is easily accounted for by the need of explaining the words "who does not confess Jesus," words which by themselves gave no adequate meaning; that, lastly, it is St. John's almost invariable manner—a manner founded on the laws of the Hebrew parallelism in which he had been trained—to introduce into the second clause of his antitheses some weighty additional element of thought;—when we remember, lastly, what force there is in this old reading—what a flash of insight it involves—then we may be reasonably confident that it represents what St. John really wrote. Nothing but its difficulty led to its early obliteration from the common texts. We have, then, this result :—that *the disintegration of the divine and the human in the nature of Jesus* was the distinguishing characteristic of the spirit of Antichrist. It is, he adds, the spirit which speaks out of worldly inspiration, and meets with worldly approval; but they who are of God have prevailed over the Antichrists by holding fast—unshaken, unseduced, unterrified—their good confession.

The power to make this good confession comes from the Spirit of God; and so also does the power to love our brethren.

"Beloved, let us love one another. For love is from God, and every one that loveth hath been born of God, and recogniseth God. He that loveth not never recognised God, because *God is Love*.[1] Herein was the love of God manifested in us, that God hath sent His Son, His only begotten, into the world, that we may live by Him. Herein is love, not that we loved God, but that He loved us, and sent His Son as a propitiation for our sins. Beloved, if thus God loved us, we also ought to love one another. God no one has ever seen. If we love one another God abideth in us, and His love has been perfected in us" (iv. 7—12).

---

[1] See Aug. *de Trinitate*, ix. 2. "God is Love," a sentence which is the summary and most simple expression of what the Scripture—the whole Scripture—teaches us throughout" (Hofmann).

In the deep language of St. John, the recognition of God—the learning to know Him (γιγνώσκειν)—is a much greater attainment than merely knowing *about* Him, and having *heard* of Him. "The knowledge of the Divine involves a spiritual likeness to the Divine, and rests upon a possession of the Divine." And this possession of the Divine emanates in love; love must of necessity radiate from its central light. The hatred which wells from a fountain of inward darkness proves at once that the knowledge and love of God does not exist in the heart of him who hates. His hatred is the more, not the less, guilty if it tries to hide itself under a cloak of religiousness. For GOD IS LOVE. If Light be His metaphysical essence, Love is His ethical nature. The unfathomable and inconceivable fulness of life which is named Light is, from eternity to eternity, existent only under the form of Love. If, then, God is Love, everything which He does must have love for its sole aim, and must, therefore, be a communication of Himself. Every one who knows Him is born of Him, for "Him truly to know is life eternal;" and every one who is born of Him is a child of Light, and reflects His Light in the form of love. For He has sent His Son into the world to give us life; and this life manifests itself in us as love, which is thus of its very nature Divine. The love we are enabled to show is not earthly, not human, not animal—it is Divine. It is an effluence of the Love of God poured into our hearts, and streaming forth from them upon others. St. John is not here speaking of the mere slightly expanded egotism of family affections, or personal likings; he is speaking of *Christian* love, of the love of man as man. That love is a flame from the Divine flame. Christ rendered it possible when He died as a propitiation *for* us; it becomes actual when He is Christ *in* us. When we possess the Light it will certainly shine before men. No one has ever *seen* God; our fellowship with Him is not *visible*. But it is much nearer, for it is spiritual. He is not only with us, He is *in* us; and, therefore, His Love, in all its perfection, dwells within us, proving its existence by continuous love to all our brethren, whether in the Church or in the world.

Then follows the summary of the last two sections :—

"Hereby we recognise that we abide in Him, and He in us, because He hath given to us of His Spirit. And we have beheld, and bear witness that the Father hath sent the Son as a Saviour of the world. He who has confessed that Jesus is the Son of God, God abideth in him, and he in God. And we have learnt to know and have believed the love which God hath in us. God is Love, and he who abideth in love abideth in God, and God in him" (iv. 13—16).

These verses state the conclusion to which the Apostle has led us— namely, that neither confession of Christ nor love to the brethren are possible without the aid of the Holy Spirit of God. If, then, we have so confessed Christ, and if we love the brethren, we have received the

Spirit of God, and, therefore, have fellowship with God and are His sons. We abide in Him, and He in us. It only remains to show that this gives us the confidence (παρρησία) of which he had spoken in ii. 28, at the very beginning of the entire section.

"By this" (i.e. by all that I have now urged[1]), "love hath been perfected with us,[2] in order that we may have confidence in the day of judgment, because as He (Christ) is, we also are in this world. There is no fear in love, but perfect love casteth out fear, because fear hath punishment, but he that feareth hath not been perfected in love"[3] (iv. 17, 18).

The best comment on the first of these verses will be found in the discourses of our Lord in John xvii. 14—26. If we have the fellowship with God of which he has spoken, then, though the Church is still in the world, we have become like Christ, and may answer with boldness on the Judgment Day. For, just as we are condemned already if, by not believing, we have rejected the Light for the darkness—so, if we have believed, we anticipate the sentence of acquittal. Fear is inseparable from the self-condemnation which results from being separated from God; it is an anticipated punishment; it cannot co-exist with love; where it exists, there the love is not real love, for it is still imperfect and impure.

Thus, then, St. John has completed one great part of his announced design. He has written in order that Christians may have fellowship with God, and fellowship with one another, and that so their joy may be full. It will and must be full if they have perfect confidence; if, being at one with God—they in Him, and He in them—they look forward with perfect confidence even to that hour when they shall stand at the judgment-seat of God. Here he might have closed this part of his subject; but in one last retrospect (iv. 19; v. 5) he shows that, though hitherto he has treated of our relation to God and our relation to our brethren in separate sections, the two relations are, in reality, indissolubly one. And for this purpose he gathers together all the leading conceptions on which he has been dwelling—namely, "believing on Christ" (v. 5) as the principle (positively) of "keeping God's commandments (v. 2), and (negatively) of "conquering the world" (v. 4, 5), and shows that they find their unity in "loving our brother." From love (iv. 19—21), and from faith (v. 1—5), spring alike our duty to God our Father, and our duty to our brother man.

---

[1] ἐν τούτῳ, as in ii. 6, refers to what precedes, as in John iv. 37, xvi. 30.
[2] "With us"—i.e., in the midst of the Church. "God magnified His mercy with her (μετ' αὐτῆς)" (Luke i. 58).
[3] "We received not the spirit of slavery again to fear, but ye received the spirit of adoption" (Rom. viii. 15). There is, of course, a *righteous* fear (Ps. xix.), but it has in it no alarm or terror. The highest state of all is to be without fear, and with love; the lowest to be "with fear, but without love;" or, without either fear or love (see Bengel, ad loc.). "Timor est custos et paedagogus legis, donec veniat caritas" (Aug.).

"Let us love, because He first loved us. If any one say I love God, and hate his brother, he is a liar; for any one who loveth not his brother whom he hath seen, in what way can he love God whom he hath not seen? And this command we have from Him, that he who loveth God love also his brother" (iv. 19—21).

"Every one who believeth that Jesus is the Christ,[1] has been born of God, and every one who loveth Him that begat loveth also Him who hath been begotten of Him. Hereby we recognise that we love the children of God, when we love God and do His commandments. For this is the love of God, that we keep His commandments. And His commandments are not heavy,[2] because everything that has been born of God conquers the world. And this is the victory which conquered the world—our faith.[3] Who is he who conquereth the world, except he who believeth that Jesus is the Son of God?" (v. 1—5).

In the first of these two sections he exhorts to universal love, and shows that, since God is Invisible, there are no possible means by which we can manifest our love to Him except by love to man, in whom God is made visible for us. If we neglect these means, our self-asserted love to God, since it fails to meet the test of action, can be nothing but a lie. For though God is Unseen, yet His Presence is represented to us by man; and again, though God is Unseen, He has revealed to us His will. And the will which He has revealed, the obedience which He requires, is, that we love one another. Not to do so is to violate His commandment, and to insult His image; and He who acts thus cannot love Him.[4]

In the second clause his summary consists in telling us that faith in Jesus as the Christ is a proof of our sonship, and therefore, can only issue in love to all God's other children. If we are loving God, and obeying Him, we cannot fail to recognise in this very love and obedience that they are being manifested by the spirit of Christian brotherhood. It is faith which won the victory over the world; and faith is manifested in love. Thus all the elements of thought are gathered into one. Sonship, Faith, Obedience, conquest of the world are all essentially blended into an organic unity; and Love is at once the result of their existence and the proof that they exist.

SECTION IV.

ASSURANCE.

At this point, then, the Apostle concludes that great main section of his Epistle, which consisted in setting forth the Word as the Word

---

[1] "In this part of his treatment," says Bengel, "the Apostle skilfully so arranges his mention of Love, that Faith may be observed at the close, as the prow and stern of the whole treatment."

[2] "My yoke is easy, and my burden light" (Matt. xi. 36). "Da quod jubes, et jube quod vis" (Aug.). "His commandments are not grievous, because love makes them light; they are not grievous because Christ gives strength to bear them. Wings are no weight to the bird which they lift up in the air until it is lost in the sky above us, and we see it no more, and hear only its note of thanks. God's commands are no weight to the soul, which, through His Spirit, He upbears to Himself; nay, rather the soul through them the more soars aloft, and loses itself in the Son of God" (Pusey).

[3] Because by faith in Christ we become one with Him, and share in His conquest over the world. "Be of good cheer, I have overcome the world" (John xvi. 23).

[4] John xiv. 15, "If ye love me, keep my commandments;" xiii. 34, "A new commandment I give you, that ye love one another."

of Life, in order that we may have fellowship with one another, and with the Father and the Son, and that our joy may be full. But this resulted from the historic revelation of which the Apostles were appointed witnesses. Life springs from the Word; but the Church could only be taught respecting that Word—the Logos who became flesh—by the testimony of the Apostles to His life on earth. Of that testimony in general his readers were well aware. It only remained to say something as to its cogency and its results. This he does in v. 6—9 and 10—12.

The witnesses are these :—

"This is He who came by means of water and blood, Jesus Christ;[1] not by the water only, but by the water and the blood. And the Spirit is that which witnesseth because the Spirit is the truth. Because there are three who bear witness, the Spirit, and the water, and the blood, and the three tend to the one thing (*viz.*, the possession of Eternal Life in Jesus Christ)"[2] (v. 6—8).

I have, of course, omitted the words "on earth" and the verse about the three heavenly witnesses.[3] The spuriousness of that verse is as absolutely demonstrable as any critical conclusion can be. It is omitted in all Greek manuscripts before the sixteenth century; it was unknown to any one of the Greek Fathers before the thirteenth century; it is not found (except by later interpolation) in a single ancient version; it does not occur in any one of some fifty lectionaries which contain the rest of the passage; in the East it was never once used in the Arian controversy. The only traces of it are in some of the Latin Fathers, and even then in a manner which seems to show that, though the verse may have been a marginal annotation, it did not occur in the actual text.[4] Had it ever been in the original, its disappearance is simply inconceivable, for it contains a clearer statement of the doctrine of the Trinity in Unity than any other in the whole Bible. This, perhaps, is the reason why it

---

[1] This (see *infra*, p. 565) can only refer primarily to historic facts in the life of Christ. "He came by Water—which is our laver (λουτρόν)—and by Blood—which is our ransom (λύτρον)."

[2] Comp. John xvii. 23. "I in them, and Thou in me," ἵνα ὦσι τετελειωμένοι εἰς ἕν (consummated into one); "brought to a final unity, in which they attain their completeness" (Westcott); see xi. 52. But the meaning *here* is not so certain. I have supposed the words εἰσὶν εἰς ἕν to mean, "are for"—*i.e.*, make for "one thing," viz., the truth in question, "*in unum consentiunt*." But the "one thing" may be "that Jesus is the Christ." Wordsworth renders it, "are joined into one substance," which suits John xvii. 23, but hardly this passage. Reuss's "*Ces trois sont d'accord*," is a mere untenable paraphrase.

[3] They were first translated in the Zürich Bible, 1529, and in Luther's edition of 1534. First they were printed in smaller type, or in brackets, but after 1596 without any distinction. In Greek they were first printed in the Complutensian edition of 1514, and the 3rd edition of Erasmus. In his editions of 1516 and 1518 he omitted them, but having pledged himself to introduce them if found in a single Greek manuscript, he did so, though believing the MS. to be corrupt—"Ne cui sit ansa calumniandi." On their appearance in a lectionary in 1549, Bergenhagen said, "Obsecro chalcographos et eruditos viros ut illam additionem omittant et restituant Graeca suae priori integritati et puritati propter veritatem."

[4] The first distinct quotation of the words is by Vigilius Thapsensis, at the end of the fifth century. "If the fourth century knew that text, let it come in, in God's name; but if that age did not know it, then Arianism in its height was beat down without the aid of that verse; and let the fact prove as it will, the *doctrine* is unshaken" (Bentley). It is not impossible that some transcribers may have taken them from St. Cyprian, and written them as a gloss on the margin of his MS. (Wordsworth refers to Valcknaer, *de Glossis in N. T.*)

has been so vigorously defended. But not to dwell on the gross immorality of defending a passage manifestly spurious because of its doctrinal usefulness, the passage is not in the least needed as a proof of the doctrine of the Trinity, which, even without it, is in this very paragraph distinctly indicated (vss. 6, 9). The demonstrable spuriousness of the verse renders it, then, unnecessary to show that it breaks and disfigures the reasoning of the passage, because it belongs to a totally different order of ideas. There can be little doubt that it will disappear, as it ought to disappear, from the text of any revised version of the English Bible.[1]

But, omitting the spurious words, what does the passage mean? It has a very deep and true meaning, for which, if Renan had sought more patiently and more reverently, he would not have called it an "Elchasaite fantasticality."[2]

He says that Jesus Christ came by means of water and blood, and that the water and the blood are, with the Spirit, three witnesses, which give one converging testimony. As to what they testify, he himself tells us—it is, that God gave us Eternal Life, and that this life is in His Son. And such being the high truth to which they bear witness, it is most important for us to understand in what way their testimony is valid—nay, in what sense it can be called a testimony at all. In what sense, then, did Jesus, as Christ—that is, Jesus as Son of God—come by water and blood? And how do this water and blood constitute two separate witnesses?

It would be simply impossible for any one to answer this question who had not the Gospel before him. The notion of "Witness" is one that plays a very prominent part in the writings of St. John. To him Christianity is emphatically "the Truth"—i.e., the eternal, all-comprehensive Reality, which must pervade alike the thoughts and the actions of men.[3] But the Truth, so far as it rests on outward facts, must be brought home to men's hearts by "witness." This, of course, was necessary from the first; but it was more than ever necessary in the days when but few could bear the testimony first-hand, and when many had begun to cavil and to doubt.

Now, in the Gospel, St. John has adduced and elaborated a sevenfold witness;[4] 1, that of the Father (v. 31—37; viii. 18); 2, that of Christ Himself (viii. 14; xviii. 37); 3, that of His works (v. 36; x. 25); 4, that of Scripture (i. 45; v. 39, 40, 45); 5, that of John the Baptist (i. 7; v. 33); 6, that of the Disciples (xv. 27; xix. 35; xxi. 24); and, 7, that of the Spirit (xv. 26; xvi. 14). These seven include every possible form of witness. The first two are inwards and Divine; the next two are outward and historical; the fifth and sixth are personal

---

[1] This anticipation was written before the Revised Version was published in June, 1881.
[2] In *Contemporary Review*, Sept. 1877.
[3] John i. 14, 17; viii. 32, 40; xiv. 17; xv. 26; xvi. 13; xvii. 11, 17; xviii. 37.
[4] See Westcott's *St. John*, pp. xlv.—xlvii.

and experiential, depending on the capacity and truthfulness of righteous men; the last is continuous and irrefragable.

Again, in this Epistle, though St. John alludes to the witness of God (v. 9), and of Christ (v. 6), and to the witness of the Apostles (i. 2; iv. 14), and to the witness of the Spirit (v. 6), he does not allude to the four other forms of witness, though he adds to them the witness of absolute inward assurance (v. 10) to which they give rise. And he lays special stress on the water and blood as the two separate and powerful testimonies of the Christ to His own Divinity. Now, in what way did He manifest Himself to be the Divine Saviour by water and by blood?

Clearly not by the Baptism of John, where the water played a most subordinate part, seeing that it was not by the water, but by the Spirit descending as a dove, that He was consecrated to His work.

Nor, again, by the Sacrament of Baptism, because in no conceivable sense of the words could it be said that "Christ *came*" by means of Christian baptism; nor is the institution of Baptism mentioned, though the symbolic significance of water—which, in that Sacrament, reaches its highest point—is indeed alluded to. Water, in the Gospel, is the symbol of new and saving life,[1] as it also is in Isa. xii. 3. More generally and simply, it is the symbol of purification. When our Lord speaks of "being born of water, and of the Spirit," the two things symbolised are seen in their unity—the water is the sacramental instrument of spiritual regeneration into a holy life.

Yet, since even thus the expression that Christ *came* "by the medium of water" would be strange, and by no means easy of interpretation, we must wait to see what light may be thrown upon it by the following expression, that Christ also came "by means of blood."

Here, again, it is obvious that the *primary* allusion cannot be to the Lord's Supper. The word "came" has, in St. John, a special and emphatic meaning. It implies the *manifestation of Christ as the Redeemer*. It cannot, then, be said, on any ordinary principle of interpretation, that Christ "came" by instituting the Lord's Supper. And that St. John, at least, would not have used a term so vague is clear, because there would be no explanation of it in the Gospel. There he has not so much as mentioned the institution of the Lord's Supper, though—in a manner which we have already seen to be characteristic of him—he has indicated its deepest meaning. Further than this, in all direct allusions to the Lord's Supper, the wine is never severed from the bread, the blood from the flesh. Indeed, for the interpretation of what St. John means by "blood," we need go no further than this Epistle,[2]

---

[1] John iii. 5; iv. 10; vii. 38.
[2] John vi. This discourse, interpreted by the known rules of Hebrew symbolism, is a most important protection against the superstitions with which literalism, and materialism, and ecclesiasticism, have surrounded the subject of the Lord's Supper. It shows, as plainly as language can show, that by "eating His flesh, and drinking His blood," our Lord meant the living appropriation of Himself by Faith.

where he mentions the blood of Christ as that which cleanses us from all sin.[1]

So far, then, we have seen that by "water" and "blood" St. John means the symbols respectively of purification and of redemption—of regeneration and of atonement;[2] and so far it may also be truly said that there may be an indirect and secondary allusion to the Sacraments, just as there is in the third and sixth chapters of the Gospel, because in the Sacraments the symbolism of the water and the blood finds its culminating application.

But even yet we have not seen how it can be said that "Christ *came by means of* water and blood," as the *means through which*, and "*in* the water and the blood" as the *element in which* He came. And it is no small corroboration of the suggestion that the Epistle was meant to accompany the Gospel as a kind of practical commentary upon it, that it would be impossible to find any simple or adequate explanation unless we had the Gospel in our hands. We find it there in a fact recorded by St. John alone, but placed by him in such marked prominence, and corroborated by such solemn testimony, that the allusion in this passage to the fact so emphasized cannot be mistaken. For *in these two passages alone, of all Scripture, are blood and water placed together*, and, as if to show yet farther the connexion between them, they are in both places prominently associated with the notion of witness. The *fact* is, that the soldier, coming to break the legs of the crucified, in order that their bodies might be removed before the sabbath, finding that Christ was dead, did not break His legs, "but one of the soldiers, with a lancehead, gashed His side, and FORTHWITH CAME THEREOUT BLOOD AND WATER."[3] Now if this were simply a physical fact, arising from the death of Jesus by rupture of the heart, and the natural separation of the blood into *placenta* and *serum*, both of which flowed forth when the pericardium was pierced,[4] even then (though in this case there can only have been, at most, a drop or two of water, visible, perhaps, to St. John[5] only, as he stood close by the cross), the symbols would not lose their divine significance. This circumstance in the death of Christ—which, if natural, is still to the last degree abnormal and unusual—would, even in that case, most powerfully suggest the symbolism which St. John attaches to it. It would have suggested to St. John the thought that Christ came—that is, manifested Himself as the Divine Redeemer—by virtue of the regenerating and atoning power of which the water and the blood were symbolic.[6] But it is doubtful whether the alleged fact ever naturally occurs; nor is it probable that St. John had enough scientific knowledge to be aware that *if* it occurs it must be a sign of death; nor

---

[1] i. 7. [2] ii. 2; iv. 10; [3] John xix. 34.
[4] See Dr. Stroud, *The Physical Cause of the Death of Christ*, and my *Life of Christ*, ii. 424. In my view of this passage I entirely follow Haupt.
[5] It is natural to suppose that, after conducting the Virgin to his home, St. John returned.
[6] "Why water? why blood? Water to cleanse, blood to redeem"—Ambr. (*De Sacr.* v. 1).

is it his object to show that the death was real, since at that early period—and, indeed, till long afterwards—the reality of the death was never for a moment questioned.[1] In the Gospel, as here, the fact is appealed to "that we may believe;" it is adduced as a witness that Jesus is the Son of God. Consequently, there as well as here, we must suppose that in St. John's view there was something supernatural in the circumstance; and that there was an obvious mystery—that is, the obvious revelation of a truth previously unknown—in that which it signified. The water and the blood are witnesses, because, in the culminating incident of Christ's redemptive work, their flowing from His side set the seal to His manifestation as a Saviour, and because they are the symbols of a living continuance of that work in the world. The Spirit, and the Water, and the Blood, are three witnesses; but it is more especially and emphatically the Spirit that beareth witness, because it is through the Spirit that the witness of the Water and the Blood—that is, of Christ's regenerative and atoning power—is brought home to the human heart. Thus "the trinity of witnesses furnish one testimony." Their threefold testimony is, as he proceeds to tell us, the testimony of God—

"If we accept the witness of men, the witness of God is greater: for this is the witness of God, because[2] He hath witnessed concerning His Son. He who believeth on the Son of God hath the witness in Himself: any one who believeth not on God hath made Him a liar, because he hath not believed in the witness which God had witnessed about His Son. And this is the witness that God gave to us Eternal Life, and this life is in His Son. He who hath the Son hath the life; any one who hath not the Son of God hath not the life" (vs. 9—12).

In these verses the witness is further analysed. It is not mere human witness. It is human in so far as the facts alluded to are established by Apostolic testimony; but it is infinitely more. It is divine testimony, and it is divine testimony echoed and confirmed by inward witness. If it be objected that the Purification, and the Redemption, and the quickening Spirit, are only in any case witnesses to the believer—that they are subjective, not objective, the answer is twofold. First, that St. John is writing to believers, and thinking of believers only; and, secondly, that both the perfected witness of God (μεμαρτύρηκε)—perfected in the death of Christ and the results which sprang therefrom; and the continuous witness of the Spirit—continuous in every conversion and every sacrament—are indeed primarily witnesses to believers, but, through believers, they are witnesses to all the world. Believers alone possessed Eternal Life, and it was their unanimous witness that they had received it solely through Jesus Christ

---

[1] It will be seen that subsequent study has a little modified the view which I took of this circumstance in the *Life of Christ*, ii. 424.

[2] ὅτι (A, B, Vulg., Copt., Armenian, etc.), not ἥν, is the true reading. The repeated ὅτι is no doubt harsh and slightly ambiguous, for the second ὅτι might mean "that." For these reasons, or perhaps by a mere slip, it was altered into the easier ἥν. But the meaning is, "we ought to believe (1) because this is God's witness; and (2) because He has borne witness concerning His Son."

the Son of God. The echo of the divine witnesses in the lives of Christians reverberated the divine testimony in thousand of echoes through all the world. The "*Nos soli innocentes*" of Tertullian,[1]—We alone, amid the deep and gross and universal corruption of a Pagan world, live innocent and holy lives—was the one argument which the heathen found it most impossible to resist or overthrow. It was the threefold witness of the Spirit, the Water, and the Blood, multiplied in the life of every Christian, and it became ultimately strong enough for the regeneration of the world. Thus was it that the Word manifested Himself to be that which St. John called Him—"the Word of Eternal Life."

SECTION V.
CONCLUSION.

The remaining verses of the Epistle have an interest more special. St. John has developed his main thesis; he has spoken of the witness by which the truths on which it rested were established. The rest is mainly recapitulatory. It touches again on faith in Christ, on Eternal Life, and on Confidence: and it applies that confidence to the special topic of trust in the efficacy of prayer (vs. 13—17). Then, with three repetitions of the words "we know," he once more alludes to Sonship and Innocence, and severance from the world, and union with God and with Christ, and Eternal Life. And he concludes with a most weighty and pregnant injunction. But so rich was the mind of the Evangelist that, as we shall see, he cannot even recapitulate without the introduction of new and most important thoughts.

"These things have I written to you that ye may know that ye have Eternal Life—to you who believe on the name of the Son of God.

"And this is the confidence which we have towards Him, that, if we ask anything according to His will, He heareth us. And if we know that He heareth us, whatsoever we ask, we know that we have the petitions which we have asked from Him. If any man see his brother sinning a sin which is not unto death, he shall ask and shall give him life [2]—to those who are sinning a sin not unto death. There is a sin unto death. For that I do not say that he should make request. All unrighteousness is sin, and there is a sin not unto death" (vs. 13—17).

The first verse of this passage sums up once more the aim of the Epistle—to give assurance to all true believers that they have eternal life. Such a belief makes us bold towards God in filial confidence,[3] and like beloved sons we can ask for what we need from our Heavenly Father. But if our minds are filled, if our lives are actuated by Brotherly love,—if our fellowship with God be of necessity fellowship

---

[1] Tert. Apol. 45.
[2] He, the petitioner, shall give life to his brother. St. James exactly in the same sense says that he who converts a brother, "shall save a soul from death" (James v. 20). Nor does this in the least contradict the truth that no man can save his brother, and make atonement unto God for him. Man is but the instrument of this deliverance; the real deliverer is God. (Comp. Jude 23, "And others save, pulling them out of the fire.")
[3] The παρρησία here does not refer to the Day of Judgment, as in iv. 17, but to trustful prayer, as in iii. 21, 22; and as in Eph. iii. 12; Heb. iv. 16.

with one another,—our prayers will constantly be occupied with our brethren; they will to a large extent be intercessory prayers:—

> "For what are men better than sheep or goats,
> That nourish a blind life within the brain,
> If, knowing God, they lift not hands of prayer
> Both for themselves and those that call them friend;
> For so the whole round world is every way
> Bound by gold chains about the feet of God."

The importance attached to such prayers by the early Christians, who, in passages like these, are not even thinking of personal prayers for any earthly blessing, may be shown by the fact that there is an allusion to exactly the same kind of intercessory prayer at the very close of the Epistle of St. James. Many a prayer for earthly blessings may be by no means in accordance with the will of God; and St. John finds it here necessary to touch on a prayer which is concerning spiritual things, and which yet he cannot bid a Christian offer. But as regards prayer in general, when a Christian prays he knows that God listens,[1] and he therefore has what he asks for. He has it even if the prayer be denied, for his prayer is not absolutely that something which is contingent may happen, but that God will give him the true and the best answer by making the will of the petitioner to be one with His.[2] Now St. John assumes that the Christian will pray for the salvation of his brethren, but he tells us that there is one instance in which such a prayer will be unavailing. It is when we see our brethren sinning a sin which is unto death. In *other* cases the Christian by prayer shall give his brother life; in the case of a sin which is unto death St. John cannot bid any Christian to offer up his filial, his familiar prayer.[3]

What, then, is this sin unto death? Is it a single act? is it a settled condition? Does it give any countenance to the distinction between mortal and venial sins? Is it the same thing as the blasphemy against the Holy Ghost? To enter fully into all these questions here would be to break the continuity of our endeavour to understand the general scope of the Epistle. I will therefore treat of them as briefly as possible.

1. St. John cannot be thinking of any one definite act of sin (as is indeed sufficiently proved by his use of the present and not the aorist participle), because it would be simply impossible for any man, apart from inspired supernatural eyesight, to declare that any particular sin was a sin unto death. Saul, under strong temptation, broke a ceremonial commandment of the Prophet Samuel; David committed adultery and

---

[1] ἀκούει (John ix. 31; xi. 41, 42).

[2] "We ignorant of ourselves,
Beg often our own harms, which the wise Powers
Deny us for our good. So gain we profit
By losing of our prayers."—(Shakspere).

[3] ἐρωτήσῃ. It is remarkable that this word should be used (see *infra*, p. 570).

murder under conditions which made those crimes peculiarly heinous. Who would not have said à priori that the sin of David was infinitely the more deadly of the two? Yet "the Spirit of the Lord departed from Saul," whereas David was still able to pray that God would give him a new heart and create a right spirit within him—and his prayer was heard. Again, the Pharisees attributed Christ's miracles to Beelzebub, and in so doing we are told that they came perilously near, if they did not actually commit, the sin against the Holy Ghost. The Sadducees and the Romans, on the other hand, crucified Him. Who would not have said that the Sadducees were the worse offenders? Yet Christ prayed unconditionally for His murderers, "Father, forgive them;" and if He gave the unconditional promise to His disciples that "whatsoever they asked in His name, believing, they should receive," must we not regard it as certain that His own prayer was heard? Clearly, then, a sin becomes a sin unto death not by its external characteristics, but by its interior quality, and that interior quality is for the most part undiscernible by the eye of man. The nature of the consummating act, the nature of the continuous state which constitutes the sin unto death, may be completely disguised, while the offender still walks among men in the odour of sanctity.

> "So spake the false dissembler unperceived;
> For neither man nor angel can discern
> Hypocrisy, the only evil that walks
> Invisible, except to God alone,
> By His permissive will, through Heaven and earth;
> And oft, though wisdom wakes, suspicion sleeps
> At wisdom's gate, and to simplicity
> Resigns her charge, while goodness thinks no ill
> Where no ill seems: which now for once beguiled
> Uriel, though regent of the sun, and held
> The sharpest sighted spirit of all in Heaven;
> Who, to the fraudulent impostor foul,
> In his uprightness, answer thus returned."
>
> *Paradise Lost*, iii. 681—694.

2. There is such a thing—as we have already seen in the Epistle to the Hebrews—as absolute and desperate apostasy, where a man cuts himself utterly loose from all the means of grace, and effectually closes their influence upon him. There is such a thing not only as wilful, but even as willing sin. There can be such a thing as a deliberate putting of evil for good and good for evil, of bitter for sweet and sweet for bitter; such a thing as a man selling himself to do evil, and trampling under foot the Spirit of God. This, in the view of the Apostles, is connected with Antichrist; the man who does it is a "man of sin"; it is a deliberate abandonment of Christ for Satan, of light for darkness, of life for death. When such a blaspheming apostasy occurred in the very bosom of the Church, he who was aware that it had occurred could

only feel that so far as mere human foresight or human prayers on his behalf could go, such a man would die in his sin.[1]

3. For such a man a Christian could hardly offer the prayer which is inspired with the divine conviction that it is heard; for it is impossible, humanly speaking, to renew such a man unto repentance.[2] St. John feels that he must refrain from exhorting Christians to offer the highest kind of prayer[3]—such prayers as Christ offered, and which are scarcely ever predicated of any other—for the most consummate form of sin.[4]

4. Yet it does not seem that he *forbids* even such prayers.[5] He *could* not do so, for he gives no criterion by which his readers could discern what was, and what was not, a sin unto death. He only says, "when you see your brother sinning a sin which you know may be forgiven"—and they would learn from the entire history of the Old Testament, as well as from the Gospels, that this might be any sin however apparently heinous, were it even such a sin as that which had stained the Church of Corinth, and against which the very heathen had exclaimed—"you may pray for it with the conviction that God will hear your prayer." But, he adds, "you must not expect that, in every possible case, every prayer you offer for the sin of a brother will be heard. For there is a sin unto death. Not respecting that sin am I saying that a sinner should make filial request." His prayers must in such cases take a humbler form (αἰτεῖν); they must inevitably be offered up with a less implicit confidence that they will be heard; they must rather consist of a committal of the sinner to God's mercy than an assured petition that that mercy will be extended in the form which we desire.

5. We may perhaps derive some insight into the meaning of the sin unto death from the language of the Old Testament, with the meanings which the Jews inferred from it, and from those passages in the New Testament which seem to offer the nearest parallel.

a. As regards the Old Testament, we find the phrase "a sin unto death" (LXX. *hamartia thanatephoros*) in Num. xviii. 22,[6] Lev. xxii. 9,[7] but this does not greatly help us, because there the reference merely is to sins which were punished with death, whereas St. John is, of course, referring to spiritual death, as in iii. 14.

---

[1] John viii. 21—24.
[2] Heb. vi. 4—6, and on that passage see Riehm, *Lehrbegr. d. Hebräerbriefs*, ii. 763, *fg.*
[3] ἐρωτήσῃ. The word αἰτῶ (peto), is used of the petition of an inferior; ἐρωτῶ (rogo), of the more familiar entreaties of a friend. Hence our Lord never uses αἰτῶ of His own prayers; and never uses ἐρωτῶ of the prayers of the disciples (John xiv. 16; xvi. 26; xvii. 9, 15, 20); which show that St. John felt and observed the distinction. We may humbly αἰτεῖν the forgiveness of sins not unto death; we may not even ἐρωτᾶν those of sins unto death.
[4] By a "sin unto death," St. John meant absolute and wilful apostasy from, and abnegation of, Christ, both theoretically and practically.
[5] "Ora, si velis, sed sub dubio impetrandi" (Calvin).
[6] "Sin with high hand," Num. xv. 30; Matt. xii. 31 (Schöttgen, *ad loc.*).
[7] למות חטא. The references are to the approach of non-Levitical persons to the sanctuary, and neglect of Levitical purifications. The Rabbis divided sins into חטאת למות and חטאת לא למות "a sin unto death," and "not unto death." In the Talmud we find "*Five* have no forgiveness of sins—(1) He who keeps on sinning and repenting alternately; (2) he who sins in a sinless age; (3) he who sins on purpose to repent; (4) he who causeth the name of God to be blasphemed." The fifth is left unexpressed (Avoth d' Rab. Nathan, 39).

ρ. Nor, again, is much light thrown on the passage by the crimes to which excision—"cutting off from the people" is assigned as a penalty under the Mosaic law. Whatever interpretation be attached to these words—whether death by divine interposition, as the Rabbis thought, or by the hand of the civil power, as others think, or exile, or excommunication[1]—it is quite clear that the sins upon which this excision (*careth*) is denounced are not unpardonable, not beyond the reach of repentance and forgiveness.

γ. Again, in no less than three places, Jeremiah is forbidden to pray for the Jews (Jer. vii. 16; xi. 14; xiv. 11); yet we certainly may not infer that the case of all these Jews was eternally hopeless, or that, though they were put beyond the range of the prayers of men, they were therefore for ever excluded from the tender mercies of God.

δ. In the New Testament we find St. Paul twice using the expression "delivering to Satan." The offenders to whom he applies it are the Corinthian sensualist (1 Cor. v. 5), and Hymenæus, and Alexander (1 Tim. i. 20). Again, for Alexander the Coppersmith, in 2 Tim. iv. 14, St. Paul offers no prayer but this, "May the Lord reward him according to his works." Now it is a reasonable inference that while a man was under the sentence of the Church's excommunication—while he was thus deliberately cut off by their act from the means of grace—he would not have been included in their prayers; not, at any rate, in such prayers as they were wont to offer up for one another. We see the character of the sins of these men. The sins of Hymenæus and Alexander consisted in deliberately rejecting (ἀπωσάμενοι "pushing away from themselves") faith and a good conscience, and, in consequence, making shipwreck of their faith. St. Paul delivered them to Satan. Why? In order that they might perish everlastingly? Far from it; but for a merciful and hopeful purpose—"that they may be trained not to blaspheme." A worse case cannot be imagined than that of the Corinthian offender. He was a Church-member, admitted into full fellowship, even supported by public sanction, and yet he was living in the open practice of a sin so shameful that, as St. Paul says, "it is not so much as named among the heathen." No conduct could be more infamous, not only in itself, but also because it caused the name of Christ to be blasphemed in that vile heathen world. With intense and burning indignation, St. Paul imagines himself present in spirit in the assembly of the Christian Church, and there solemnly, in the name of Christ he "hands over the offender to Satan." If any sin could be regarded as a sin unto death, must not this have been such a sin, seeing that it was shameless, continuous, against light and knowledge, the sin of a Christian which was not even tolerated by heathens? It was natural that the victorious prayer of triumphant confidence should be

---

[1] See Gesen. Thes. s. v. כרת p. 719.

suspended in the case of such a man. Yet what is St. Paul's object in handing him to Satan? Not by any means his everlasting damnation, but "the destruction of his carnal impulses, *in order that his spirit may be saved in the day of the Lord Jesus*."[1] The man *was* handed to Satan by the now-aroused conscience of the startled community. And what was the result? In his next letter, a few months afterwards, St. Paul is once more urging them to show mercy towards this very offender. The "handing to Satan" has done its work. The fleshly temptation has been annihilated. The man has repented. St. Paul is now afraid lest he should be injured by over-severity. He bids them restore and ratify their love towards the now penitent transgressor, "lest by any means he should be swallowed up by his superabundant sorrow."[2] Similarly, in the case of Alexander, St. Paul's *avoidance* of a prayer for him *is* practically a prayer for him. It is not equivalent, as is sometimes supposed, to a sort of curse, "May God do him evil as he has done to me;" for such a prayer—though a David or a Hebrew exile may have offered it in ignorance, in days before the new commandment had been uttered—in days when it had been said to them of old time, "Thou shalt hate thine enemy"—could not have been offered without sin by a Christian Apostle. St. Paul's ejaculation is only another way of saying "It is not for me to judge him; I leave him in the hands of God."

From this examination then we may infer that St. John's limitation belongs, like so many of his thoughts, to the region of the ideal, the theoretical, the absolute; that it is only introduced as a passing, but very solemn, reminder of the truth that there is a sin which is past the possibility of being benefited by the Christian's prayer—a sin which can be only left to God, because it is discernible by Him alone. Practically it is most unlikely that we shall ever become cognisant of any sin in a brother so heinous, so desperate, so darkly deliberate in the apostate condition of heart which it implies, so obviously beyond the possibility of repentance, that we dare not pray for it. On the analogy of the language used, both in the Old and New Testaments, we must infer that even though there be a sin unto death, it is not beyond the mercy of Him who died "that He might destroy him who hath the power of death, that is the devil." To God we may leave it, if we find that we are unable to offer up on its behalf the prayer of faith. How little we are ever likely to realise the existence of such a sin we may infer from this—that there are only two or three in all the long generations of Christian history about whose salvation the Church has ever ventured to express an open doubt.

We are told in the Talmud that Beruriah, the wife of the great Rabbi Meier, once heard him ardently praying to God against some ignorant people—*am haratsim*—who annoyed him. She came to him

---

[1] 1 Cor. v. 5. [2] 2 Cor. ii. 6–8.

and said, "Do you do this because it is written (in Ps. civ. 35) 'Let the sinners be consumed'? But there it is not written *chotaim*, 'sinners,' but *chittaim*, 'sins.' Besides, the Psalm adds, 'And let the wicked be no more,' that is to say, 'Let sins cease, and the wicked will cease too.' Pray, therefore, on their behalf, that they may be led to repentance, and these wicked will be no more." This he therefore did, and they repented, and ceased to vex him.[1]

The whole tenor of Scripture show that, as a rule, we must herein follow the example of the brilliant Rabbi. But the New Testament teaches the lesson far more fully than the Old. The Church herself teaches us to pray—

"That it may please Thee to have mercy upon ALL MEN,
We beseech Thee to hear us, Good Lord."

And accordingly St. John instantly leaves the subject of the sin unto death to which he has made this unique and passing allusion, and adds "All unrighteousness is sin, and there is a sin not unto death." Therefore you will ever have the amplest scope for your intercessory supplications. Practically, that scope is the whole range of unrighteousness, the whole range of human sin. If the sin for which we are interceding is a sin which God knows, and which we may *fear* to be unto death, St. John does not *forbid* such prayers; for he says, "I do not say that you should" (οὐ λέγω ἵνα), not "I say that you should not" (λέγω ἵνα μὴ). Clearly it can *never* be in our power to decide what sins are unto death. If we unwittingly pray for such a sin, the Apostle can give us no promise that the intercession is of any avail. But if there be any sin for which we feel the genuine impulse to pray, we may rest assured that that impulse is an inspiration, and therefore that the prayer may be offered, and will be heard.

Then the Epistle concludes with these words:—

"WE KNOW that every one who has been born of God sinneth not; but he who is born of God keepeth himself,[2] and the wicked one graspeth him not."[3]

"WE KNOW that we are of God, and the whole world lieth in the wicked one."

"But WE KNOW that the Son of God is come, and hath given us understanding that we recognise Him who is true, and we are in Him who is true, in His Son, Jesus Christ. This[4] is the true God, and Life Eternal.[5]

"Little children, keep yourselves from idols" (ver. 18—21).

---

[1] Avodah Zarah, f. 18, b.
[2] It is astonishing that Alford, following the Vulgate, should render this "but he that hath been born of God, if (i.e. his divine birth) keepeth him" ("sed generatio Dei conservat eum"). There is not the smallest theological difficulty involved in saying that "he keepeth himself" (see on iii. 3). It means that effort is always necessary even for the saint—οὐ φύσει εἰς ἀναμαρτησίαν τροβαίνει (Œcumen.).
[3] "The Evil one approaches him, as a fly approaches a lamp, but does not injure, does not even touch him" (Bengel). But ἅπτομαι with a genitive properly means "to lay hold of." Thus μή μου ἅπτου is not *Noli me tangere*, but "Cling not to me" (see my *Life of Christ*, ii. 431).
[4] Namely, the Father as seen in His Son (Jer. xi.).
[5] Thus the Epistle ends as it began, with Eternal Life (Bengel). Comp. John xvii. 3.

Here, as before, St. John is beholding all things in their idea. Here, and now, neither are we absolutely sinless, nor is the whole world absolutely absorbed in sin. But in idea, in the ultimate truth of things, it is so, and, in the final severance of things, it will be so. Our knowledge that it is and will be so rests deep among the bases of all Christian faith. We know it because Christ has come, and has given us discernment to recognise Him who is the only Reality. We are in Him, and in His Son; He, God the Father, is the Very God, and Eternal Life.[1] For St. John has already said in his Gospel (xvii. 3), "This is the Life Eternal, that they should learn to know Thee, the only true God, and Jesus Christ, whom Thou didst send."

The last verse is a most pregnant warning, introduced by the Apostle's most affectionate title of address—Little children!—"keep yourselves from idols." He is not, of course, thinking of the gods of the heathen. He is writing to Christians who had long abandoned these, who had not the smallest temptation to apostatise to their worship. He is speaking of "subjective idolism." He is putting them on their guard against seductive notions of false prophets subtle suggestions of Antichrists. He is warning them not against gross idols of gold and jewels, representing deities of lust and blood, but against false, fleeting, dangerous images—idols of the forum, of the theatre, of the cave; systematising inferences of scholastic theology; theories of self-vaunting orthodoxy; semblances under which we represent God which in no wise resemble Him; ever-widening deductions from Scripture grossly misinterpreted; earthly passions and earthly desires which we put in the place of Him; ideas of Him which loom upon us through the lurid mists of earthly fear and earthly hatred; notions of Him which we make for ourselves, which are not He; conceptions of Him which we have derived only from our party-organ or our personal conceit. It is the most pregnant of all warnings against every form of unfaithfulness to God—against violations whether of the First or of the Second Commandment; against devotion to anything which is not eternally and absolutely true; against perversions due to religionism quite as much as against open rejection of God; against the tyrannous shibboleths of aggressive systems no less than against the worship of Belial and of Mammon. These are the idols which in these days also are more perilous to faith and holiness than any which the heathen worshipped. They are dominant in sects and Churches and schools of thought. They are the work, not of men's hands, but of their imaginations. They have mouths, but do not utter words of truth; they have eyes, but not such as can gaze on the true light; they have hands, but they do not

---

[1] That the Father is referred to seems to be decided by John xvii. 3. There is nothing abnormal in the change of subject. The Father is the principal subject of the whole clause, though the Son is last named. For a similar change of subject see verse 16, and ii. 22, and 2 John 7.

the deeds of righteousness; feet have they, but only such as hurry them into error. "They that make them are like unto them; and so are all such as put their trust in them." Little children—all who love the Lord Jesus Christ in sincerity and truth—all who know that hatred is of the devil—all who have recognised that "Love is the fulfilling of the law"—little children, keep yourselves from idols!

CHAPTER XXXVI.

THE SECOND EPISTLE OF ST. JOHN.

"Amor non modo verus amor est, sed veritate evangelicâ nititur."—BENGEL.

APART from the truths inculcated in such private Epistles as the Second and Third of St. John and that of St. Paul to Philemon, it is a happy Providence which, in spite of their brevity, has preserved them for us during so many hundred years. They show us what grace and geniality reigned in Christian intercourse, and how much there was in this sweet communion of saints which compensated, even on earthly grounds, for the loss of the world's selfish friendships and seductive approbation. The love of the brethren more than counterbalanced the hatred of the enemies of Christ.

That these little letters are genuine there is good reason to believe. They may be treated together, because there can be no question that if either of them is genuine both of them are, since they may well be described as "twin-sisters."[1] Their close resemblance in style, phraseology, and tone of thought, shows that they were written about the same time, and by the same person. Further than this, they agree so closely with the First Epistle that if they were written by another the resemblance could only be accounted for by deliberate imitation. But what possible ground could there be for "forging" letters so slight as these,—letters which, though full of value, do not add a single essential thought to those which are already fully expressed and elaborated in the other writings of St. John? Their very unimportance for any doctrinal purpose, apart from the Gospel, the Apocalypse, and the First Epistle, is one of the proofs that no *falsarius* would have thought it worth his while to palm them off upon the Church. Containing no conception which is not found elsewhere, they have little independent dogmatic value; their chief interest lies in the glimpse which they give us of Christian epistolary intercourse in the earliest days.

The external evidence in their favour is even stronger than we could have expected in the case of compositions so short, so casual, and

---

[1] Jer. *Ep.* 85.

so unmarked by special features. There is but one passage (vss. 10, 11) in the Second Epistle which can be quoted as distinctive, and for that very reason it is the one to which most frequent reference is made; nor is there anything which specifically characterises the Third except the allusions to Diotrephes and Demetrius. There is scarcely a single expression in either of these letters with which previous writings have not already made us familiar. Indeed, no less than eight out of thirteen verses in the Second Epistle are also to be found in the First. It is not, therefore, surprising that they only became known gradually to the Church, and that they were regarded as comparatively unimportant, being written "out of feelings of private affection, though to the honour of the Catholic Church."[1] Yet the first of them is twice quoted by Irenæus,[2] and twice referred to by Clemens of Alexandria.[3] Cyprian mentions that the Epistle to the Elect Lady (of course the passage about "heretics"), was quoted by one of the bishops at the Council of Carthage. The testimony of the Muratorian Canon is ambiguous, owing to the corruption of the text, but it seems to tell in favour of the Epistles.[4] The Syrian Church, according to Cosmas Indicopleustes, did not acknowledge these Epistles, but, on the other hand, the Second Epistle is quoted by Ephraim the Syrian. Eusebius and Origen seem to have regarded the Epistles as genuine, though they rank them among the disputed books of the canon—the *antilegomena;* as also does Dionysius of Alexandria, the pseudo-Chrysostom, and Theodore of Mopsuestia.[5] St. Jerome says that there were many who assigned them to the authorship of "John the Presbyter;" but he seems himself to have accepted them.[6] The notion that they were written by "John the Presbyter" was revived by Erasmus and Grotius, and has since been maintained by some modern scholars.[7] But, as

---

[1] The Muratorian Canon says of the Epistle to Philemon and the two to Timothy, that they were written "*pro affectu* et dilectione in honorem tamen ecclesiae catholicae."
[2] Iren. *Haer.* iii. 16, 8; i. 16, 3.
[3] *Strom.* ii. 15, and *Fragm.* p. 1011, ed. Potter (but comp. Euseb. *H. E.* vi. 14); Tert. *De Praescr. Haer.* 33.
[4] See Wieseler, *Studien und Kritiken,* 1847, p. 846. The true reading and punctuation of the passage seems to be "Epistolae sane Judae et superscripti Johannes duae (or duas = δυάς, "a pair") in Catholica habentur." The words which follow, "ut Sapientia ab amicis Salomonis in honorem ipsius scripta," must then be referred to the Apocalypse, as though it was written by friends of John, as Wisdom by friends of Solomon.
[5] οὐ πάντες φασὶ γνησίας εἶναι ταύτας (Orig. ap. Euseb. *H. E.* vi. 25; *Dem. Evang.* iii. 5); εἴτε τοῦ Εὐαγγελιστοῦ τυγχάνουσαι, εἴτε καὶ ἑτέρου ὁμωνύμου ἐκείνῳ (Euseb. iii. 25); φερόμεναι Ἰωάννου (Dionys. Alex. ap. Euseb. vii. 25); ἀντιλέγονται δὲ αἱ λοιπαὶ δύο (Euseb. iii. 24). The pseudo-Chrysostom exaggerates when he says (*Hom.* in Matt. xxi. 23), "the Fathers reject the Second and Third Epistles from the Canon."
[6] "Opinio quam *a plerisque* retulimus traditam" (Jer. *De Virr. Illustr.* 9; but see *Ep.* 85). Cosmas Indicopleustes rejects *all* the Catholic Epistles, but his remarks about them (*De Mundo,* vii. p. 292) are so full of errors as to deserve no notice. Gregory of Nazianzus, in his Iambics, says—"Of the Catholic Epistles, some say that we ought to receive *seven,* and some only three—one of James, one of Peter, and one of John—but some say the three (of John)."
[7] Dodwell, Beck, Fritzsche, Ebrard, etc. The latter says (1) that all resemblances to the First Epistle vanish if 2 John 5—6, 7, and 3 John 11 are regarded as quotations; and

I have shown in the Excursus, there never was such a person as John the Presbyter in contradistinction from John the Apostle. The two were one.[1]

We see, then, that, taken in connexion with the internal evidence, there is sufficient ground for accepting these little Epistles. There is no difficulty in the fact that St. John should call himself "the Elder" and not "the Apostle." The dispute as to who was and who was not to be regarded as an Apostle had long since died away. St. Paul himself does not always care to use the title. He drops it, for instance, in addressing those who, like the Philippians and Philemon, had never disputed his apostolic authority. The other Apostles were all dead. The whole Church knew that St. John was the last survivor of the Twelve. He may have called himself "the Elder" out of humility; just as Peter, in addressing the elders, calls himself their "fellow-elder."[2] Or he may have used the designation because he belonged to that class of aged Christians to whom, at this time, the younger generation which was springing up around them often appealed under the name of "the Elders."[3] Or, again, he may have called himself "the Elder" because he desired to claim no higher authority than that which accrued to him from his great age and long experience.[4] And it must be observed that he calls himself "the Elder," not "an Elder." There were hundreds of elders, and, therefore, by calling himself "the Elder" in a pre-eminent and peculiar sense, he at once marks his age and authority. The phraseology, the style, the tone of thought, the method of treatment in every sentence, points directly to the authorship of the Apostle. The few trivial deviations from his ordinary expressions only show that we are not dealing with the work of an elaborate imitator.[5]

1. There has always been great doubt as to the destination of the Second Epistle of St. John. Even yet the question whether it was addressed to a lady or to a Church cannot be regarded as settled. It begins with the words, "The Elder unto the Elect Lady and her children, whom I love in the truth; and not only I, but also all who

---

(2) that it is inconceivable that the *authority* of an *Apostle* should have been disputed in such a way as is described in 3 John 9.
[1] See Excursus XIV., "John the Apostle and John the Presbyter."
[2] 1 Pet. v. 1, συμπρεσβύτερος ; Philem. 9, ὁ πρεσβύτης.
[3] Euseb. *H. E.* iii. 39. The word occurs in Irenæus and other Johannine writers in quotations from the Fathers of that earlier age.
[4] It is in exact accordance with his modest self-withdrawal. In the Gospel he entirely suppresses his own name, as in the First Epistle. In the Apocalypse he only calls himself "John." So far, therefore, the absence of any lofty title, such as a forger might have given him, is a mark of genuineness. There is nothing to support Ewald's notion that it was due to the dangers of the time.
[5] Such are εἴ τις for ἐάν τις (2 John 10), διδαχὴν φέρειν, περιπατεῖν κατά, κοινωνεῖν, μειζοτέραν, as pointed out by De Wette. To dwell on the occurrence of a few phrases which he had no occasion to use elsewhere (such as ὑγιαίνειν, φιλοπρωτεύων, φλυαρεῖν, προπέμπειν ἀξίως τοῦ Θεοῦ), is idle.

have learnt to know the truth."[1] Certainly the *primâ facie* impression created by the words would be that they refer to a lady. In that case the omission of the article seems to show that her name is not mentioned. For if either Electa or Kyria had been her name, then, just as we have "To Gaius, the beloved," in the address of the Third Epistle, we should naturally have expected here, "To Electa, the lady," or "To Kyria, the elect." Nor is this objection adequately answered by saying that if Kyria was the lady's name, the article might have been omitted by an unconscious analogy of the use of the word Kurios, "the Lord," without an article.

α. That her name was Electa[2] is asserted in the Latin translation of the fragments of Clemens of Alexandria, where he says, "The Second Epistle of John, which was written to virgins, is very simple; it was, however, written to a Babylonian lady, by name Electa." It may, however, be regarded as certain that this is a mistake. For although Electa may have been a proper name in the Christian Church, yet in that case the meaning of verse 13 must be, "The children of thy sister Electa greet thee;" and it is highly improbable that *both* sisters bore this very unusual name.

β. But may it be addressed to a lady named Kyria?[3] Kyria was a female name, for it is found in one of the inscriptions recorded in Gruter;[4] and from an expression of Athanasius, "he is writing to Kyria and her children," it has been inferred that this was his view. It is a possible view in itself; and since Kyria may be the Greek equivalent of the Hebrew name Martha, the lady may have been a Jewess. This view also gets over the difficulty of a *title* so lofty as Kyria, which, according to Bengel, was rarely used, even to Queens.[5] But the objection still remains that we should then have expected, not "To elect Kyria," but "To Kyria the elect;" just as in the next Epistle we do not find "To beloved Gaius," but "To Gaius, the beloved."

γ. But if we must render the words, "To an elect Lady," are we to understand by them a person or a Church?

In either case, the person or the Church is left unnamed. The modern view seems to incline in favour of a Church.[6] All sorts of

---

[1] 2 John 8; Ὁ πρεσβύτερος ἐκλεκτῇ κυρίᾳ καὶ τοῖς τέκνοις αὐτῆς, οὓς ἐγὼ ἀγαπῶ ἐν ἀληθείᾳ, κ.τ.λ. The possible renderings are (in order of their possibility)—
    1. To an elect lady.
    2. To the elect lady.
    3. To the elect Kyria.
    4. To the lady Electa.

[2] This is the view of Lyra, Grotius, Wetstein.
[3] This is the view of Bengel, Heumann, Lücke, De Wette, and Düsterdieck.
[4] Gruter, *Inscript.* p. 1127, "Phenippus and his wife Kyria."
[5] See, however, the following note.
[6] So Hofmann, Hilgenfeld, Huther, Ewald, Wordsworth. On the other hand, Bengel, Fritzsche, De Wette, Lange, Heumann, Alford, Düsterdieck, understand a person to be addressed. Epictetus says that "women from the age of fourteen are called 'ladies' (κύριαι) by men."

conjectures have been made as to the Church intended, and the most far-fetched and arbitrary reasons have been assigned for supposing that it was addressed to the Church of Corinth,[1] or of Philadelphia,[2] or of Jerusalem,[3] or of Patmos, or of Ephesus, or of Babylon.[4]

2. The latter is the view of Bishop Wordsworth. Starting from the ambiguous expression of 1 Pet. v. 13, "the co-elect (ἡ συνεκλεκτή) with you that is at Babylon saluteth you," and interpreting it to mean the Church in Babylon, he says that it is a greeting of the Babylonian Church sent through St. Peter to the Churches of Asia; and he supposes that the verse, "the children of thy sister, the elect one, greet thee," is a return salutation of the Churches of Asia, through St. John, to the Church of Babylon. He thinks that this is rendered more probable by the close relations between St. Peter and St. John; and he finds a confirmation of it in the remark of Clemens of Alexandria, that the letter is addressed "to a Babylonian lady," and in the curious incidental expression in the title of St. Augustine's tractate on the Epistle, "Tractatus in Epistolam Johannis *ad Parthos.*" At this time, he says, Babylon was under the rule of the Parthians, and, therefore, a letter to the Babylonian Church might have been called "a letter to the Parthians." Further, when Clemens says that the letter was written "to Virgins," he thinks that the Greek word "*parthenous*" was only a corruption of "*Parthous.*" Lastly, he adds that "there would be a peculiar interest and beauty in such an address as this from St. John to a Church at Babylon, which, in the days of her heathen pride, had been called 'the Lady of Kingdoms,' and had said, 'I shall be a Lady for ever.'"[5] Babylon had fallen; but St. Peter had preached to Parthians, among others, on the Day of Pentecost,[6] and so Babylon had arisen again in Christ, and become an elect Lady in Him, and could be addressed as such by the Apostolic brother of St. Peter, the beloved disciple St. John.

(i.) I must confess that to me the whole theory looks like an inverted pyramid of inference tottering about upon its extremely narrow apex. The phrase of St. Peter is of *most* uncertain interpretation. It is not certain that by "the Co-elect" he means a Church. It is still more uncertain that by Babylon he means Babylon and not Rome. We may say of the very basis on which the theory rests,—

"Nil agit exemplum quod litem lite resolvit."

(ii.) Then the theory seems to imply the supposition that St. John had at some time left Asia and travelled as far as Babylon—a journey

[1] Serrarius.   [2] Whiston.   [3] Whitby and Augusti.
[4] The notion of St. Jerome (*Ep.* xi. *ad Ageruchiam*) that it was addressed to the Church in general (though adopted by Hilgenfeld), may be at once dismissed. Quoting Cant. vi. 9 as referring to the Church, he adds, "to which John writes his Epistle, 'St. John to an Elect Lady.'" The opinion that the Lady is a Church is mentioned by Œcumenius, Theophylact, and Cassiodorus, as well as by an ancient scholion.
[5] Is. xlvii. 5, 7; גְּבֶרֶת *gevereth*, rendered Κυρία by the LXX., as in Gen. xvi. 4, etc.
[6] Acts ii. 9.

intrinsically improbable, and which has left no trace in any tradition of the Apostle. In ecclesiastical legends it is St. Thomas and not St. John who is said to have been the Apostle of the Parthians.

(iii.) Next, the vague tradition that the Epistle was addressed to the Parthians, is devoid of even the slightest value, for it is more than doubtful whether the words " *ad Parthos* " ever stood in the original edition of St. Augustine's *Tractates*; and when Bede says that it was the opinion of St. Athanasius that the *First* Epistle was addressed " to the Parthians,"[1] he is almost certainly mistaken. No such statement is found in any Greek Father. It is only found, according to Griesbach, in some late and unimportant Latin Fathers, and in the passage of St. Augustine.[2] Now nothing can be more improbable than that the First Epistle was addressed to the Parthians,[3] and we should require much stronger evidence than this isolated allusion of St. Augustine to establish the fact. We are driven to suppose that "ad Parthos" must be a misreading. Serrarius conjectures that it should be "*ad Pathmios*," to the people of Patmos, but these and many other conjectural emendations have nothing to support them.[4] On the other hand, the word *Parthos* may have arisen from some confusion with *Parthenous*,[5] and not, as Bishop Wordsworth supposes, the latter from the former. The sweet and lofty simplicity of the First Epistle may have led some one to suggest that it was written to Virgins—using the word in the sense in which it occurs in the Rev. xiv. 4—namely, to youthful and uncorrupted Christians. And this suggestion may have derived fresh force from the ancient belief that St. John himself was in this sense " a Virgin " (*parthenos*),[6] a title which is actually given to him in some superscriptions of the Apocalypse, and elsewhere.[7]

3. But if Bishop Wordsworth's suggestion comes to nothing, what are we to say of the theories of German critics? The remarks of Baur respecting this Epistle exhibit, almost in their culmination, the arbitrary

---

[1] Bede, *Prol. ad Ep. Cathol.* (Cave, *Hist. Litt.* i. 289).

[2] Aug. *Quaest. Evang.* ii. 39. "Secundum sententiam hanc etiam illud est quod dictum est a Joanne (1 John iii. 2) *in epistola ad Parthos.*" He is followed by the Spaniard, Idacius Clarus. Πρὸς Πάρθους is found in superscriptions of the Second Epistle in some late cursive manuscripts.

[3] Grotius, Hammond, and others accepted this view; and Paulus pressed it into his theories about the Epistle.

[4] Semler guesses "*adapertius;*" Paulus "*ad Pantas;*" and Wegscheider πρὸς τοὺς διεσπαρσμένους, *ad Sparsos!* (see Tholuck, *Introd.* p. 32, et seq.).

[5] So Whiston conjectures. For Clemens Alexandrinus, in his *Adumbrationes*, says (in a very confused passage) that the *Second* Epistle was written "to Virgins," which is manifestly erroneous. His words are—"Secunda Joannis epistola quae *ad Virgines* scripta est, simplicissima est;" then, after saying that it is written to a certain Babylonian lady named Electa, he adds, "it signifies, however, the election of the Holy Church."

[6] Gieseler, *Kirchengesch,* i. p. 139.

[7] Tert. *de Monogam.* c. 17; Ps.-Ignat. *ad Philad.* 4; Clem. Alex. *Orat. de Maria. Virg.* p. 380. In a cursive manuscript of the twelfth century (30) the superscription of the Apocalypse runs thus—"Of the holy, most glorious apostle and evangelist, the Virgin, the beloved, the bosom Apostle (ἐπιστήθιον) John the Theologian."

recklessness of conjecture which has defaced the usefulness and obliterated the existence of the school of Tübingen. His combinations are briefly these :—Electa is a Church ; she is called a Babylonian by St. Clemens to indicate the Church of Rome ; the Epistle expresses the views of the Montanists ; Diotrephes, the leader of the anti-Montanist section of the Church, had refused to hold communion with them ; by Diotrephes is meant, not " Victor," as Schwegler (by a demonstrable anachronism[1]) supposed, but perhaps Anicetus, Soter, or Eleutheros. The writer is so strong a partisan as to describe the faction of Diotrephes as "heathens"[2] (3 John 7) !

4. Not much more reasonable is the notion of Hilgenfeld that the Second Epistle was sent to a Church as a letter of excommunication against Gnostic teachers, and the Third as a letter of commendation (ἐπιστολὴ συστατική) to Gaius, issued to vindicate against Judaising Christians the right of St. John as well as of St. James to furnish such authorisations to travelling missionaries.

5. Nor less arbitrary is the suggestion of Ewald that both the Second and Third Epistles were addressed to one Church ; that it must have been an important Church, because three of its Elders—Diotrephes, Demetrius, and Gaius—are mentioned ; that the name of the Church is omitted because it would have been dangerous to mention it ; and that the Third Epistle was addressed to Gaius from a misgiving that Diotrephes might suppress the first letter, and prevent it from being publicly read in the Church.

Such theories are not worth refuting. They might be constructed in any numbers. They are mere ropes of sand, which fall to pieces at a touch. It can only be regarded as a misfortune that such multitudes of them should cumber, with their useless accumulations, the whole field of exegesis. They do but block up the way to any real advance in our knowledge of the history of the early Church. I would say of them what Baur says of certain theories of apologists : " It is not worth while to discuss vague hypotheses which have no support in history and no cohesion in themselves."[3]

While I do not deny that the Elect Lady addressed *may* have been a Church, it does not seem to me probable. To say that the Church is symbolised as a woman and a bride in the Apocalypse, is to adduce an argument which bears very little on the matter.[4] The question is not whether a Church *might* not be allegorically called "a Lady," which everyone admits, but whether it is natural that, in a short and simple letter, St. John should, from first to last, keep up, in this one particular, an elaborate allegory, and, unlike the other Apostles, address a Church

---

[1] For this Epistle is quoted long before Victor's day by Irenæus and Clemens of Alexandria. [2] Baur, *Montanismus.*
[3] Baur, *Ch. Hist.* i. 131.
[4] Rev. xii. 1—17 ; xxi. 9. To say that 'Ἐκλεκτὴ means "a Church" in Cant. vi. 8, τίς αὕτη ἰκλεκτὴ ὡς ὁ ἥλιος, is to pass off exegetical fancies as settled truths.

as if he were writing to a lady. If the letter were playful or mystic, such a supposition might be tolerable. As it is, unless there be some unknown factors in the history of the circumstances which called forth the letter, it would seem to savour of a euphuism unworthy of the great Apostle, and alien from Apostolic simplicity. So far as I am aware, there is not another instance in Christian literature, whether Greek or Latin, whether in apostolic or post-apostolic times, in which a Church is called Kyria, or addressed throughout as a lady.

6. I take the letter, then, in its natural sense, as having been addressed to a Christian lady and her children. Some of those children the Apostle seems to have met in one of his visits of supervision to the Churches of Asia. They may have been on a visit to some of their cousins in a neighbouring city, and St. John—always attracted by sympathy towards the young—finding that they were living as faithful Christian lives, writes news of them to their mother, whom he held in high esteem; and in writing seizes the opportunity to add some words of Christian teaching. That St. John should write to a Christian lady has in it nothing extraordinary. Women like Priscilla, Lydia, and Phœbe played no small part in the early spread of Christian truth. They represented that ennoblement of Christian womanhood which was one of the great results of Christian preaching; and they inspired the Apostles with a warm sentiment of affection and esteem.[1] That the lady should be left unnamed is in accordance with the feelings of the day. It was against the common feelings both of Jews and Greeks that virtuous matrons should be thrust into needless prominence. St. Paul indeed names them when occasion demands. In writing to the Philippians, among whom women occupied a more recognised position than among other Roman communities, he makes a personal appeal to the two ladies Euodias and Syntyche;[2] and he sends salutations to and from women among others. Yet he never wrote a letter, so far as we know, even to Lydia or to Priscilla, to whom he was so much indebted; and if he had written such a letter—intended (as this letter of St. John's may well have been) for perusal by all the members of the Church, and even meant to be read aloud to them in their congregation—it is probable that he would have left the name unmentioned. Much more would this have been the natural feeling of St. John, who had lived most of his life in Jerusalem. He would have been less inclined to infringe on the seclusion which was the ordinary position of Eastern womanhood, because his experiences had been less cosmopolitan than those of his brother Apostles. Who the Elect Lady was we do not know, and never shall know. To suggest, as some have done, that she may have been Martha the sister of Lazarus,[3] or the

---

[1] See Acts xvi. 14; xviii. 2, etc.; and St. Paul's salutation to nine Christian women, in Rom. xvi.
[2] Phil. iv. 2.
[3] Carpzov. Martha = Κυρία.

Mother of our Lord,¹ is to be guilty of the idle and reprehensible practice of suggesting theories which rest on the air, and are not even worth the trouble of a serious refutation.

Nor is there anything to indicate where these letters were written. They may have been sent from either Patmos or Ephesus. Eusebius says that they were written at Ephesus before a tour of pastoral visitation.²

The analysis of the letter is extremely simple. After a kindly greeting (1—3), he tells this Christian matron of his joy in finding that some of her children (whom he had chanced to encounter) were walking in the truth (4). He enforces on her the commandment of Christian love, which is both new and old (5—6); warns her against dangerous antichristian teachers (7—9), to whose errors she is not to lend the sanction of her hospitality or countenance (10—11), and concludes with the expression of a hope that he may soon visit her and her family, and with a greeting from the children of her Christian sister (12—13). The keynotes of the Epistle, as indicated by its most prominent words, are Truth and Love. Truth occurs five times and Love four times in these few verses.

"The Elder to the elect Lady³ and her children whom I love in Truth,⁴ and not I alone, but also all who have learnt to know the Truth,⁵ because of the Truth which abideth in us, and shall be with us for ever.⁶ Grace, mercy, peace,⁷ shall be with us⁸ from God our Father, and from Jesus Christ the Son of the Father, in Truth and Love.

"I rejoice⁹ greatly because I have found some of thy children¹⁰ walking in Truth, even as we received commandment from the Father.

"And now¹¹ I entreat thee, Lady, not as writing to thee a new commandment, but that which we had from the beginning,¹² that we love one another. And this is love, that we should walk according to His commandments.¹³ This is the commandment, even as ye heard from the beginning, that ye should walk in it. Because many deceivers went forth¹⁴ into the world, such as confess not Jesus Christ coming

---

¹ Knauer, *Stud. u. Krit.* 1833.   ² Euseb. *H. E.* iii. 23.
³ Comp. ἐκλεκτοῖς παρεπιδήμοις, 1 Pet. i. 1.
⁴ Truth is here used in the Johannine sense—the realm of eternal reality. "Whom I love in the truth of the Gospel."
⁵ It has been thought that this expression is too wide to apply to a single person, but it merely means that all Christians who know the character of the lady and her children love her.
⁶ Comp. John xiv. 16, 17.
⁷ "Votum cum affirmatione" (Bengel). A wish, with the assurance that it will be fulfilled.
⁸ For the full meaning of this triple greeting, see my *Life and Work of St. Paul*, ii. 516. "Grace" refers to man's sin; "mercy" to his misery; "peace" is the total result to both; and all three work in the region of truth and love. "Gratia tollit culpam *misericordia* miseriam, pas dicit permansionem in gratia ex misericordia" (Bengel).
⁹ Lit. "I rejoiced," but it is the epistolary aorist. "Avete, filii et filiae, in nomine Domini nostri Christi in pace; supra modum exhilaror beatis et praeclaris spiritibus vestris" (Ps.-Barnab. *Ep.* l.).
¹⁰ λίαν, 3 John 3. This does not of course *necessarily* imply that some were *not* so walking. Probably St. John had only met some of them.
¹¹ The words mark a transition, as in 1 John ii. 28, ἐρωτῶ. See on 1 John v. 16. "Blandior quaedam admonendi ratio" (Schlichting).
¹² See on 1 John ii. 7, 8; iii. 11.
¹³ The same identification of love with obedience which we have found in 1 John ii. 6—10, etc. *Praxis*, not *gnosis*, is the true test of faithful discipleship.
¹⁴ ἐξῆλθον, א, A, B, Syriac, Vulgate, Irenaeus. Not "came in," the reading adopted by our E. V. Comp. 1 John ii. 18, 22; iv. 1—3.

in the flesh.¹ This is the deceiver and the Antichrist. Take heed to yourselves that ye lose not what we have wrought,² but that ye receive a full reward. Every one who goeth forward³ and abideth not in the teaching of the Christ, hath not God. He who abideth in the teaching, he hath both the Father and the Son. If any one cometh to you,⁴ and bringeth not this doctrine, receive him not into your house, and bid him not 'good speed.' For he who biddeth him 'good speed' partakes in his evil deeds.⁵

"Having many things to write to you, I prefer⁶ not to do so by paper and ink,⁷ but I hope to come to you,⁸ and to speak mouth to mouth,⁹ that your joy may be fulfilled.¹⁰ The children of thy elect sister greet thee."¹¹

It will be seen, then, at a glance, that Truth and Love are keynotes of the Epistle, and that the conceptions which prevail throughout it are those with which we have been made familiar by the previous Epistle. And yet one passage of the Epistle has again and again been belauded, and is again and again adduced as a stronghold of intolerance, an excuse for pitiless hostility against all who differ from ourselves.¹² There is something distressing in the swift instinct with which an unchristian egotism has first assumed its own infallibility on subjects which are often no part of Christian faith, and then has spread as on vulture's wings to this passage as a consecration of the feelings with which the *odium theologicum* disgraces and ruins the Divinest interests of the cause of Christ. It must be said—though I say it with the deepest sorrow—that the cold exclusiveness of the Pharisee, the bitter ignorance of the self-styled theologian, the usurped infallibility of the half-educated religionist, have ever been the curse of Christianity. They

---

¹ The *present* participle is used to make the expression as general as possible. They denied the possibility of the Incarnation. See 1 John ii. 18, 22; iv. 2; v. 6. They seem to have been Docetic Gnostics.
² The readings vary greatly between the first and second persons. Matt. ix. 37; 2 Tim. ii. 15; John vi. 29. The *loss* which takes off from the full reward is explained, in the next verse, to be separation from God.
³ The true reading is not "who transgresseth" (παραβαίνων), but προάγων, א A, B. Vulg. Not, as some commentators here hint, as though all progress in Christian thought was a crime, and incapacity to advance beyond stereotyped prejudice a virtue, but referring either (1) to advance in *wrong directions*, or (2) to Christian teachers who go before their flocks (John x. 4; Mark x. 32).
⁴ The *indicative* following εἰ, implies that such *will* come. He is of course thinking of heathens, but of Christian false prophets.
⁵ See below. The meaning of course is that we are not to give to fundamental heresy an appearance of approval by pronouncing the deeper fraternal greeting. In some versions are here interpolated the words, "Ecce praedixi vobis ne in diem domini condemnemini."
⁶ Epistolary aorist.
⁷ If the letter was written at Patmos, these materials might not readily be procurable. The word χάρτης means Egyptian papyrus. For the manner in which it was prepared, see Pliny, *H. N.* xiii. 21. The ink was made of soot and water, mixed with gum.
⁸ γενέσθαι πρὸς ὑμᾶς. The same Greek construction as in John vi. 25.
⁹ A Hebraism, פֶּה אֶל פֶּה (Jer. xxxii. 4; 3 John 14).
¹⁰ 1 John i. 4.
¹¹ "Suavissima communitas! comitas Apostoli minorum verbis salutem nunciantis" (Bengel). It is impossible to say why the sister herself sends no greetings. We can hardly suppose that she was dead, because she is called "thy *elect* sister." But we may suggest a score of hypotheses which would suffice to explain the circumstance. Bengel says, "Hos liberos (ver. 4) in domo materternae eorum invenerat."
¹² Thus on the strength of this text John à Lasco having been expelled from England during the reign of Mary in 1553, was, with his congregation, refused admission into Denmark (Salig. *Hist. Conf. Aug.* ii. 1090; quoted by Braune *ad loc.* in Lange's *Bibelwerk*). Thus by the manipulation of a few phrases Hate is made to wear the guise of Love, and Fury to pose as Christian meekness.

have imposed "the senses of men upon the words of God, the special senses of men on the general words of God," and have tried to enforce them on all men's consciences with all kinds of burnings and anathemas, under equal threats of death and damnation.[1] And thus they have incurred the terrible responsibility of presenting religion to mankind in a false and repellent guise. Is theological hatred still to be a proverb for the world's just contempt? Is such hatred—hatred in its bitterest and most ruthless form—to be regarded as the legitimate and normal outcome of the religion of love? Is the spirit of peace never to be brought to bear on religious opinions? Are such questions always to excite the most intense animosities and the most terrible divisions? Is the Diotrephes of each little religious clique to be the ideal of a Christian character? Is it in religious discussions alone that impartiality is to be set down as weakness, and courtesy as treason? Is it among those only who pride themselves on being "orthodox" that there is to be the completest absence of humility and of justice? Is the world to be for ever confirmed in its opinion that theological partisans are less truthful, less candid, less high-minded, less honourable even than the partisans of political and social causes who make no profession as to the duty of love? Are the so-called "religious" champions to be for ever, as they now are, in many instances, the most unscrupulously bitter and the most conspicuously unfair? Alas! they might be so with far less danger to the cause of religion if they would forego the luxury of "quoting Scripture for their purpose." The harm which has thus been done is incredible:—

> "Crime was ne'er so black
> As ghostly cheer and pious thanks to lack.
> Satan is modest. At Heaven's door he lays
> His evil offspring, and in Scriptural phrase
> And saintly posture gives to God the praise
> And honour of his monstrous progeny."

If this passage of St. John had indeed authorised such errors and excesses—if it had indeed been a proof, as has been said, of "the deplorable growth of dogmatic intolerance"[2]—it would have been hard to separate it from the old spirit of rigorism and passion which led the Apostle, in his most undeveloped days, to incur his Lord's rebuke, by proclaiming his jealousy of those who worked on different lines from his own, and by wishing to call down fire to consume the rude villagers of Samaria. It would have required some ingenuity not to see in it the same sort of impatient and unworthy intolerance which once marked his impetuous outbursts, but which is (I trust falsely) attributed to him in the silly story of Cerinthus and the bath. In that case also the spirit of his advice would have been widely different from

---

[1] Chillingworth.
[2] So Renan, in his article on the Fourth Gospel in the *Contemp. Rev.* Sept. 1877.

the spirit which actuated the merciful tolerance of the Lord to Heathens, to Samaritans, to Sadducees, and even to Pharisees. It would have been in direct antagonism to our Lord's command to the Twelve to salute with their blessing every house to which they came, because if it were not worthy their peace would return to them again.[1] It would have been alien from many of the noblest lessons of the New Testament. It would practically have excluded from the bosom of Christianity, and of Christianity alone, the highest workings of the universal law of love. It would have been in glaring disaccord with the gentleness and moderation which is now shown, even towards absolute unbelievers, by the wisest, gentlest, and most Christlike of God's saints. If it really bore the sense which has been assigned to it, it would be a grave reason for sharing the ancient doubts respecting the genuineness of the little letter in which it occurs, and for coming to the conclusion that, while its general sentiments were borrowed from the authentic works of St. John, they had only been thrown together for the purpose of introducing, under the sanction of his name, a precept of unchristian harshness and religious intolerance.

But there is too much reason to fear that to the end of time the conceit of orthodoxism will claim inspired authority for its own conclusions, even when they are most antichristian, and will build up systems of exclusive hatred out of inferences purely unwarrantable. It is certain, too, that each sect is always tempted to be proudest of its most sectarian peculiarities; that each form of dissent, whether in or out of the body of the Established Churches, most idolises its own dissidence. The aim of religious opinionativeness always has been, and always will be, to regard its narrowest conclusions as matters of faith, and to exclude or excommunicate all those who reject or modify them. The sort of syllogisms used by these enemies of the love of Christ are much as follows—

"*My* opinions are founded on interpretations of Scripture. Scripture is infallible. *My* views of its meaning are infallible too. Your opinions and inferences differ from mine, therefore you *must* be in

---

[1] It is said that Polycarp was once accosted by Marcion, and asked by him, "Dost thou not know me?" "Yes," he answered, "I know thee, the firstborn of Satan" (Iren. *c. Haer.* iii. 3; Euseb. *H. E.* iv. 14). "So cautious," adds Irenæus, "were the Apostles and their followers to have no communication—no, not so much as in discourse —with those who adulterated the truth." The story, as might have been expected, is told by other ecclesiastical writers with intense gusto, down to modern days. But even if it be true, it by no means follows that the example was estimable. St. Polycarp was just as liable to sin and error as other saints have been. We have no right to treat any man with rude discourtesy. If to be a Christian is to act as Christ acted, then Polycarp's discourtesy was unchristian. Pharisees openly rejected our Lord, yet He even accepted their invitations, and told His Disciples to show them honour. Is a heretic so much worse than a heathen, that a Christian wife might live with a heathen husband (1 Cor. vii. 12, 13), while yet a Christian might not even speak without the grossest rudeness to a Gnostic teacher?

the wrong. All wrong opinions are capable of so many ramifications that any one who differs from me in minor points must be unsound in vital matters also. Therefore, all who differ from me and my clique are 'heretics.' All heresy is wicked. All heretics are necessarily wicked men. It is my religious duty to hate, calumniate, and abuse you."

Those who have gone thus far in elevating Hatred into a Christian virtue ought logically to go a little farther. They generally do so when they have the power. They do not openly say, "Let us venerate the examples of Arnold of Citeaux, and of Torquemada. Let us glorify the Crusaders at Beziers. Let us revive the racks and thumbscrews of the Inquisition. Let us, with the Pope, strike medals in honour of the massacre of St. Bartholomew. Let us re-establish the Star Chamber, and entrust those ecclesiastics who hold our opinions with powers of torture." But, since they are robbed of these means of securing unanimity—since they can no longer even imprison "dissenting tinkers" like Bunyan, and "regicide Arians" like Milton—they are too apt to indulge in the party spirit which can employ slander though it is robbed of the thumbscrew, and revel in depreciation though it may no longer avail itself of the fagot and the rack.

The tender mercies of contending religionists are exceptionally cruel. The men who, in the Corinthian party-sense, boast "I am of Christ," do not often, in these days, formulate the defence of their lack of charity so clearly as this. But they continually act and write in this spirit. Long experience has made mankind familiar with the base ingenuity which frames charges of constructive heresy out of the most innocent opinions; which insinuates that variations from the vulgar exegesis furnish a sufficient excuse for banding anathemas, under the plea that they are an implicit denial of Christ! Had there been in Scripture any sanction for this execrable spirit of heresy-hunting Pharisaism, Christian theology would only become another name for the collisions of wrangling sects, all cordially hating each other, and only kept together by common repulsion against external enmity. But, to me at least, it seems that the world has never developed a more unchristian and antichristian phenomenon than the conduct of those who encourage the bitterest excesses of hatred under the profession of Christian love.[1] I know nothing so profoundly irreligious as the narrow intolerance of an ignorant dogmatism. Had there been anything in this passage which sanctioned so odious a spirit, I could not have believed that it emanated from St. John. A good tree does not bring forth corrupt fruit. The sweet fountain of Christianity cannot send forth the salt and bitter water of fierceness and hate. The Apostle of love would have belied all that is best in his own teaching if he had consciously given an absolution,

[1] 1 John iii. 10, 11.

nay, an incentive, to furious intolerance. The last words of Christian revelation could never have meant what these words have been interpreted to mean—namely, "Hate, exclude, anathematise, persecute, treat as enemies and opponents to be crushed and insulted, those who differ from you in religious opinions." Those who have pretended a Scriptural sanction for such Cain-like religionism have generally put their theories into practice against men who have been infinitely more in the right, and transcendently nearer God, than those who, in killing or injuring them, ignorantly thought that they were doing God service.

Meanwhile this incidental expression of St. John's brief letter will not lend itself to these gross perversions. What St. John *really says*, and *really means*, is something wholly different. False teachers were rife, who, professing to be Christians, robbed the nature of Christ of all which gave its efficacy to the Atonement, and its significance to the Incarnation. These teachers, like other Christian missionaries, travelled from city to city, and, in the absence of public inns, were received into the houses of Christian converts. The Christian lady to whom St. John writes is warned that, if she offers her hospitality to these dangerous emissaries who were subverting the central truth of Christianity, she is expressing a public sanction of them ; and, by doing this and offering them her best wishes she is taking a direct share in the harm they do. This is common sense ; nor is there anything uncharitable in it. No one is bound to help forward the dissemination of teaching what he regards as erroneous respecting the most essential doctrines of his own faith. Still less would it have been right to do this in the days when Christian communities were so small and weak. But to interpret this as it has in all ages been practically interpreted—to pervert it into a sort of command to exaggerate the minor variations between religious opinions, and to persecute those whose views differ from our own—to make our own opinions the exclusive test of heresy, and to say, with Cornelius à Lapide, that this verse reprobates "all conversation, all intercourse, all dealings with heretics"—is to interpret Scripture by the glare of partisanship and spiritual self-satisfaction, not to read it under the light of holy love.

Alas! churchmen and theologians have found it a far more easy and agreeable matter to obey their distortion of this supposed command, and even to push its stringency to the very farthest limits, than to obey the command that we should love one another! From the Tree of delusive knowledge they pluck the poisonous and inflating fruits of pride and hatred, while they suffer the fruits of love and meekness to fall neglected from the Tree of Life. The popularity which these verses still enjoy, and the exaggerated misinterpretation still attached to them, are due to the fact that they are so acceptable to the arrogance and selfishness, the dishonesty and tyranny, the sloth and obstinacy, of that bitter spirit of religious discord which has been the disgrace of the Church and the scandal of the world.

CHAPTER XXXVII.

THE THIRD EPISTLE OF ST. JOHN.

"Ex operibus cognoscitur valetudo animae, et hanc prosequuntur vota Sanctorum."—BENGEL.

NOTHING can be ascertained respecting the Gaius to whom this letter is addressed, beyond what the letter itself implies—that he was a faithful and kind-hearted Christian. I have already explained that, from the circumstances of the time, hospitality to Christian teachers was a necessary duty, without which the preaching of Christianity could hardly have been carried on.[1] Gaius, like his namesake at Corinth,[2] and like Philemon,[3] distinguished himself by the cheerfulness with which he performed this duty. It could not always have been an easy or an agreeable duty, for some of the Christian emissaries, and especially those from Jerusalem, seem, according to the testimony of St. Paul, to have behaved with an insolence and rapacity truly outrageous.[4] But those to whom Gaius opened his hospitable house were not of this character. They were men who had followed the noble initiative of St. Paul, and who refused to receive anything from the Gentiles to whom they preached.

Some, from the identity of name and character, have assumed that the Gaius here addressed must have been the Gaius of Corinth. Such an inference is most precarious. Gaius was, perhaps, the commonest of all names current throughout the Roman Empire. So common was it that it was selected in the Roman law-books to serve the familiar purpose of John Doe and Richard Roe in our own legal formularies. It no more serves to identify the bearer of the name than if it had been addressed "To the well-beloved ——," for Gaius was colloquially used for "so-and-so."[5] There are at least three Gaiuses in the New Testament—Gaius of Macedonia (Acts xix. 29), Gaius of Corinth (Rom. xvi. 23), and Gaius of Derbe (Acts xx. 4). A Gaius is mentioned in the *Apostolic Constitutions* (vii. 40), as Bishop of Pergamum, and it is not impossible that this may be the person here addressed.

The main object of the letter was to encourage him in his course of Christian faithfulness and to contrast his conduct with that of the domineering Diotrephes. Diotrephes, in his ambition, his arbitrariness, his arrogance, his tendency to the idle babble of controversy, and his fondness for excommunicating his opponents, furnishes us with a

---

[1] Hence the importance attached to it (Rom. xii. 13; 1 Tim. iii. 2; Tit. i. 8; Heb. xiii. 2; 1 Pet. iv. 9).
[2] Rom. xvi. 23; 1 Cor. i. 14.
[3] Philem. 7.
[4] 2 Cor. xi. 20.
[5] Renan, in *Contemp. Rev.* Sept. 1877.

very ancient specimen of a character extremely familiar in the annals of ecclesiasticism.[1] There is something astonishing in the notion that the prominent Christian Presbyter of an Asiatic Church should not only repudiate the authority of St. John, and not only refuse to receive his travelling missionary, and to prevent others from doing so, but should even excommunicate or try to excommunicate those who did so! But we must leave the difficulty where it is, since we are unable to throw any light upon it. The condition of the Church of Corinth, as St. Paul described it, leave us prepared for the existence of almost any irregularities. The history of the Church of Christ, from the earliest down to the latest days, teems with subjects for perplexity and surprise.

"The Elder, to Gaius the beloved, whom I love in Truth.[2]

"Beloved, I pray that in all respects[3] thou mayest prosper,[4] and be in health,[5] even as thy soul prospereth. For I rejoice exceedingly at the arrival of brethren who bear witness to thy Truth, even as thou walkest in Truth. I have no greater[6] joy than this, that I hear of my children walking in the Truth.[7]

"Beloved, thou playest a faithful part in all thy work towards the brethren, and even to strangers,[8] who bear witness to thy love before the Church, whom by forwarding on their journey[9] worthily of God thou[10] wilt do well. For on the Name's behalf[11] they went forth, accepting nothing from the Gentiles.[12] We then ought to support such, that we may become fellow-workers with the Truth.[13]

"I wrote somewhat to the Church,[14] but their domineering Diotrephes receiveth us not.[15] On this account, if I come, I will bring to mind[16] his deeds which he doeth,

---

[1] Hymenaeus, Alexander (1 Tim. i. 20), Philetus (2 Tim. ii. 17), Hermogenes, and Phygellus (2 Tim. i. 18) are similarly mentioned as opponents of St. Paul.
[2] 1 John iii. 18; 2 John i. To love "in Truth," is the same as to love "in the Lord."
[3] Not "above all things," as in E. V. That meaning of περὶ πάντων is only found in classical poetry.
[4] εὐοδοῦσθαι (Rom. i, 10; 1 Cor. xii. 2); literally, to be "guided on a journey." Philo uses the word as here, both of body and soul, Quis Rer. Div. Haer. § 58.
[5] ὑγιαίνειν was not among Christians as it was among Stoics, a common form of address. Hence we must assume that Gaius suffered from ill-health.
[6] The doubled comparative μειζοτέραν may be intentionally emphatic, like ἐλαχιστότερος, in Eph. iii. 8, "Est ad intendendam significationem comparativus e comparativo factus" (Grotius).
[7] ἵνα. St. John's use of ἵνα is far wider than that of classical writers. It often loses its telic sense ("in order that"), and becomes simply ekbatic, or explanatory, as in Luke i. 43, John xv. 13.
[8] καὶ τοῦτο, א, A, B, C. The hospitality of Gaius was not only φιλαδελφία, but φιλοξενία.
[9] προπέμψας. Tit. iii. 13.
[10] ἀξίως τοῦ Θεοῦ. That is, giving them the maximum of help, as their sacred cause deserves (Comp. 1 Thess. ii. 12; Col. i. 10.)
[11] Acts v. 41; ix. 16, etc.; Phil. ii. 9. "I have been bound in the Name" (Ignat. ad Ephes. 3). "Some are wont with evil guile to carry about the Name, while they are doing deeds unworthy of God" (id. ib. 7). Similarly Christians, among themselves, spoke of Christianity as "the way" (Acts ix. 2; xix. 9).
[12] St. Paul's rule (1 Thess. ii. 9; 1 Cor. ix. 18; 2 Cor. xi. 7; xii. 16). Gentiles must of course mean, "Gentile converts." They could not expect the heathens to support them. This is perhaps implied by the adjective ἐθνικῶν, א, A, B, C.
[13] Comp. 1 Thess. iii. 2; Col. iv. 11.
[14] Evidently a brief letter, from the expression τι, א, A, B, C (Luke vii. 40; Acts xxviii. 17). It is now lost, like many other of these minor communications (1 Cor. v. 9). Diotrephes seems to have suppressed this letter, whatever it was. If he could behave so outrageously as he is said to do in the next clause, he would have thought but little of making away with a brief letter.
[15] That is, "rejects my authority." Perhaps it means that this turbulent intriguer refused to acknowledge St. John's "commendatory letter."
[16] John xiv. 26. St. John means that he will draw the attention of the Church to the proceedings of Diotrephes.

with wicked words battling against us;[1] and not content with that, he neither himself receives the brethren, and he hinders those who wish to do so, and expels them from the Church.[2]

"Beloved, do not imitate the evil but the good.[3] He that doeth good is from God: he that doeth evil hath not seen God.[4] Witness has been borne to Demetrius by all,[5] and by the Truth itself; aye, and we too[6] bear witness, and thou knowest that our witness is true.[7]

"I had many things to write to thee, but I do not wish by ink and reed[8] to write to thee, but I hope immediately to see thee, and we will speak mouth to mouth. Peace to thee.[9] The friends salute thee. Salute the friends by name."[10]

"*Salute the friends by name.*" Salute each of our Christian friends as warmly and as individually as though I had here written down their names. So fitly ends the last of the writings of St. John. The close of his messages to the Church of God is as calm and gentle as the close of his life. God cares for individuals, and therefore the Church of God cares for them also. They may be obscure, humble, faulty; but if they be true disciples they need fear nothing which the world can threaten, and desire nothing which it can offer, for "their names are written in the Book of Life." The aged Apostle speaks of them as "friends." The name, as applied to Christians, is peculiar to him, for Christians regarded each other as "brethren," and therefore as bound together by a tie even closer than that of friendship. But if he uses this word as well as "brethren" and "beloved," it doubtless is from the remembrance of what he alone among the Evangelists has recorded, that the Lord Jesus had called Lazarus "His friend," and that He had said, "Ye are my friends, if ye do the things which I command you. No longer do I call you servants, for the servant knoweth not what his Lord doeth; but I have called you friends, for all things that I have heard from my Father I have made known unto you."

He ends, therefore, fitly with this kind message to individual friends. And after this we know nothing more with certainty respecting him. He was not taken to Heaven in the fiery chariot of glory or of martyrdom,

---

[1] φλυαροί (1 Tim. v. 13); φλυαρεῖν, the French *déblatérer*. "Apposite, calumnias Diotrephis vocat *garritum*" (Corn. à Lapide).

[2] These proceedings seem so very high-handed, that we might take the words to mean merely that he excluded them from the congregation which possibly met at his house; or we might suppose the meanings of the presents to be "*tries* to hinder them, and *wants to* excommunicate them." Certainly the present often implies the unsuccessful *conatus rei perficiendae* (see my *Brief Greek Syntax*, § 136), but we know too little of Diotrephes, and of the Church in which he had so much influence, to be able to say that he might not have actually excommunicated (as unauthorised interlopers into *his* parish—schismatic intruders on *his own* authority) those who gave hospitality to Evangelists or who brought "letters of commendation" from St. John. If he was capable of prating against St. John, he might have been capable of this also.

[3] Heb. xiii. 7; 1 Pet. iii. 13. "τὸ κακὸν in Diotrephe; τὸ ἀγαθὸν in Demetrio" (Bengel).

[4] 1 John iii. 6—10; iv 8.

[5] "Demetrius was possibly the bearer of the letter" (Lücke).

[6] καὶ ἡμεῖς δέ (1 John iii. 6).

[7] John v. 32; xxi. 24.

[8] The κάλαμος is a split reed. St. John seems to have disliked the physical toil of writing, to which it is quite possible that he had not been accustomed. He probably dictated his longer and more important works.

[9] John xix. 28. "The inward peace of conscience, the fraternal peace of friendship, the heavenly peace of glory" (Lyra).

[10] The allusion is to personal private friends, not the brethren in general.

but in all probability he died at Ephesus, in a peaceful and honoured age, among many friends who deeply loved and greatly honoured him. And the last murmur of tradition which reaches us respecting him is that which tells us of his last exhortation. When he was no longer a "Son of Thunder," no longer even an "Eagle of Christ"—when he was a weak and worn old man, with scarcely anything left him but a feeble voice and trembling hands, he still uplifted those trembling hands to bless, and still strove to sum up all that he had taught, in words easy to utter, but of which, after so many centuries, we have yet so imperfectly learnt the meaning—

"Filioli, diligite alterutrum."
"Little children, love one another."

And this he did, as he himself explained, "because such was the Lord's command; and if this only be done, it is enough."

APPENDIX.

EXCURSUS I.

THE ASSERTED PRIMACY OF ST. PETER.

THAT St. Peter was a leading Apostle—in some respects *the* leading Apostle—none will dispute; but that he never exercised the supremacy which is assigned to him by Roman Catholic writers is demonstrable even from the New Testament. Anyone who will examine the list of twenty-eight Petrine prerogatives detailed by Baronius[1] will see in their extreme futility the best disproof of the claims of Roman primacy. St. Peter had, as Cave says, a primacy of order, but not a supremacy of power. Such a supremacy our Lord emphatically discountenanced.[2] In his Epistle St. Peter does not assume the title of Apostle, but only calls himself a fellow-presbyter, and rebukes all attempts "to play the lord over the heritage of God." The other Apostles send him to Samaria. The Church at Jerusalem indignantly calls him to account for the bold step which he had taken in the case of Cornelius. Paul, at Antioch, withstands him to the face, and claims to be no whit inferior to the very chiefest Apostle, assuming the Apostolate of the Uncircumcision—that is, of the whole Gentile world—as predominantly his own. St. Peter was not specially "the disciple whom Jesus loved;" and though he received from his Lord some of the highest eulogiums, he also incurred the severest rebukes. Even when we turn to the Fathers, we find St. Cyprian saying that "the rest of the Apostles were that which St. Peter was; endowed with equal participation both of honour and of power."[3] The Presbyter Hesychius calls, not St. Peter, but St. James, "the prince of priests, the leader of the Apostles, the crown among the heads, the brightest among the stars."[4] He calls St. Andrew "the Peter before Peter." St. Cyril says that Peter and John had equivalent honour. The Promise of the Keys was given to all the Apostles alike;[5] and in the Apocalypse no distinction is made

---

[1] *De Rom. Pontif.* i. 17, *seqq.*
[2] Matt. xx. 25—27; Luke xxii. 24—26.
[3] *De Unitat. Eccles.* p. 180.
[4] *Ap. Phot. Cod.* 275. Πέτρος δημηγορεῖ ἀλλ' Ἰάκωβος νομοθετεῖ.
[5] Matt. xviii. 17, 18; John xx. 21—23.

between Kephas and the rest of the Twelve.[1] Origen says that all who make Peter's confession with Peter's faithfulness shall have Peter's blessing.[2] He was eminent among the Apostles;—*supreme* he never was.[3]

EXCURSUS II.

PATRISTIC EVIDENCE ON ST. PETER'S VISIT TO ROME

St. Clemens of Rome († 101) says that "he bore witness," using the term which implies his martyrdom;[4] but he does not say that this took place at Rome. Ignatius († 114),[5] and Papias[6] (referred to by Eusebius († 340), use language which may be inferentially pressed into the implication that he had been at Rome. St. Clemens of Alexandria († 220), who tells the story about St. Peter's wife, does not mention Rome.[7] St. Dionysius of Corinth († 165) says that St. Peter and St. Paul both taught in Italy;[8] but the weight of even this slight allusion is neutralised by its being found in the same sentence with the erroneous suggestion that Peter had a share in the founding (φύτειαν) of the Church of Corinth. St. Irenæus († 202) makes the dubious statement that both Apostles took part in the appointment of Linus to be Bishop of Rome.[9] Gaius († 200), as quoted by Eusebius, says that the "trophies" of the Apostles were shown at Rome in his days.[10] Tertullian († 218) makes a similar remark in a passage where he also accepts the legend of St. John's escape from death when he was plunged into a caldron of boiling oil at the Latin gate.[11] Lastly, Origen († 254) is the first who says that Peter was "crucified head downwards;"[12] and St. Ambrose—or a pseudo-Ambrose—tells the story of the Vision on the Appian road. Later allusions to the Apostle's connexion with Rome, which grow more definite as time advances, are found in Arnobius,[13] in Lactantius,[14] in the *Apostolical Constitutions*,[15] and in the pseudo-Clementine *Homilies*.[16]

St. Peter's visit to Rome is of course testified by multitudes of later writers; but their assertions have no independent or evidential value.[17]

---

[1] Rev. xxi. 14.   [2] In Matt. xvi.
[3] See the question examined in Shepherd's *Hist. of the Ch. of Rome*, pp. 494, *f.*
[4] *Ep. ad Cor.* v.
[5] Ignat. *Ep. ad Rom.* iv.; οὐχ ὡς Πέτρος καὶ Παῦλος διατάσσομαι ὑμῖν.
[6] Papias, *ap.* Euseb. *H. E.* iii. *ad fin.* But the inference is of the remotest kind. It supposes that St. Peter needed Mark as his "interpreter" in Latin.
[7] Clem. Alex. *ap.* Euseb. *H. E.* vi.   [8] Dion. *ap.* Euseb. *H. E.* ii. 25.
[9] Iren. *c. Haer.* iii. 1 and 3, and *ap.* Euseb. *H. E.* v. 6.
[10] Gaius, *ap.* Euseb. *H. E.* ii. 25.
[11] Tert. *de Praesc. Haer.* 32, 36. See too *Scorpiace*, 15.
[12] Orig. *ap.* Euseb. *H. E.* iii. 1; ἀνεσκολοπίσθη κατὰ κεφαλῆς οὕτως αὐτὸς ἀξιώσας παθεῖν.
[13] Arnob. *c. Gent.* ii. 12.   [14] Lactant. *de Mort. Persec.* ii.
[15] *Const. Apost.* vii. 45.   [16] Ps.-Clem. Hom. *Ep. ad Jac.* 1.
[17] The denial, that St. Peter was ever at Rome, by the Waldenses, Marsilius of Padua

EXCURSUS III

USE OF THE NAME BABYLON FOR ROME IN 1 PET. V. 13.

It has been asserted that St. Peter could not be writing from the real Babylon, because that city was at this period ruined and deserted. Strabo and Pausanias say that it was a mere ruin; Pliny calls it a solitude.[1] But, although we learn from Josephus that the Jews in the city had terribly suffered, first by a persecution in the reign of Caligula, and then by a plague,[2] we have no reason to believe that many of them may not have returned during the twenty years which had subsequently elapsed. Again, it is not proved that St. Peter may not have used the word "Babylon" to describe the *country* or *district*, as is done by Philo,[3] so that he may have actually written from Seleucia or Ctesiphon, in which cities the Jews were numerous;[4] or even from Nehardea or Nisibis, in which they had taken refuge.[5] Parthians, Medes, Elamites, and dwellers in Mesopotamia, had been among his hearers on the day of Pentecost, and there is nothing *intrinsically* improbable in the notion of his having gone to visit these crowded communities of the Dispersion. They were so numerous and so important, that Josephus originally wrote his *History of the Jewish War* for their benefit, and wrote it in Aramaic, without any doubt that it would find countless readers.

It has been argued that the geographical order observable in the names "Pontus, Galatia, Cappadocia, Asia, and Bithynia"— the Churches to which his Epistle is addressed—is more natural to one writing from Babylon than to one who was writing from Rome; but this is an argument which will not stand a moment's consideration.

On the other hand, *against* the literal acceptance of the word

---

Salmasius, etc., was elaborately supported by Fr. Spannheim (*De ficta profectione*, etc., 1679). De Wette, Baur, Winer, Holtzmann, and Schwegler are led to a similar view by their belief in the virulent jealousies between Jewish and Gentile Christians, and Neander was shaken by the arguments of Baur. But the mass of learned Protestants, Scaliger, Casaubon, Grotius, Usher, Bramhall, Pearson, Cave, Schröckh, Gieseler, Bleek, Olshausen, Wieseler, Hilgenfeld, etc., to a greater or less degree, admit his martyrdom or residence at Rome. To enter into a discussion of the Papal claims is here wholly beyond my scope. If the reader has any doubt on the subject, he may read with advantage the articles on the "Petrine Claims," in the *Church Quarterly Review* for April, 1878, April, 1879, and January, 1880, and he will find some brief hints on the subject in Dr. Littledale's *Plain Reasons*. He will find all that can be urged on the other side in Mr. Allnatt's *Cathedra Petri* and Father Ryder's *Catholic Controversy*.

[1] See Is. xiii.; xiv. 4, 12; xlvi., etc. That the Babylon alluded to is the obscure Egyptian fort of that name (Strabo, xvii. 1, p. 807)—a place utterly unknown to Christian history and tradition—is a conjecture which may be set aside without further notice. No human being in the Asiatic Churches to which St. Peter was writing could ever have heard of such a place.

[2] Jos. *Antt.* xviii. 9, § 8.

[3] Philo, *Leg. ad Gaium*, 36.

[4] Jos. *Antt.* xv. 3, 1.

[5] Jos. *Antt.* xviii. 9, § 9.

"Babylon" there are four powerful arguments. (1). There is not the faintest tradition in those regions of any visit from St. Peter. (2). If St. Peter was in Babylon at the time when his Epistle was written, there is great difficulty in accounting for his familiarity with the Epistle to the Ephesians, which was not written till A.D. 63. (3). It becomes difficult to imagine circumstances which could have brought him from the far East into the very crisis of the Neronian persecution in the Babylon of the West. (4). If "Marcus" be the Evangelist, he was with St. Paul between A.D. 61—63,[1] and probably rejoined him just before his martyrdom in A.D. 68.[2] We should not, therefore, expect to find him so far away as Babylon in A.D. 67.

I strongly incline to the belief that by Babylon the Apostle intended to indicate Rome,[3] and we find this interpretation current in the Church in very early days.[4] The Apocalypse was written about the same time as—or not long after—the First Epistle of St. Peter; and in the Apocalypse[5] and in the Sibylline Verses[6] we see that a Western, and even an Asiatic, Christian, when he heard the name "Babylon" in a religious writing, would be likely at once to think of Rome. Throughout the Talmud we find the same practice of applying symbolic names. There Rome figures under the designations of Nineveh, Edom, and Babylon, and almost every allusion to Christ, even in the unexpurgated passages of the Amsterdam edition, is veiled under the names of "Absalom," "That Man," "So-and-so," and "The Hung." The reference to Rome as Babylon may have originated in a mystic application of the Old Testament prophecies, but it had its advantage afterwards as a secret symbol. It is therefore a mistake to suppose that the use of Babylon for Rome would be the sudden obtrusion of "allegory," into matter-of-fact, or that by using it the Apostle would be "going out of his way to make an enigma for all future readers." There is, in fact, a marked accordance between such an expression and the conception which St. Peter indicates throughout his letter, that all Christians are exiles scattered from the heavenly Jerusalem, living, some of them, in the earthly Babylon.[7] An early Christian would have seen nothing either allegorical or enigmatical in the matter. He would at once have understood the meaning, and have known the reasons, alike mystic and political, for avoiding the name of Rome.

---

[1] Col. iv. 10; Philem. 24. [2] 2 Tim. iv. 11.
[3] So the Fathers unanimously; and Grotius, Lardner, Cave, Semler, Hitzig, and the Tübingen school; as against De Wette and Wieseler. See too Lipsius, *Chron. der Röm. Bisch.* (1869); Hilgenfeld, *Petrus in Rom.* (*Zeitschr. f. wiss. Theol.* 1872); Zeller, *Petrusfrage* (ib. 1876).
[4] Papias, ap. Euseb. *H. E.* ii. 15, iii. 25; Iren. *c. Haer.* iii. 1, etc.
[5] Rev. xiv. 8; xvi. 19; xvii. 9, 18; xviii. 2, etc.   [6] *Sibyll.* v. 143, 159.
[7] 1 Pet. i. 1, παρεπιδήμοις; v. 13, ἐν Βαβυλῶνι. See Godet's *New Testament Studies*.

EXCURSUS IV.

THE BOOK OF ENOCH.

The quotation from the Book of Enoch by St. Jude, and the traces which it contains of the reciprocal influences of Jewish and Christian speculation, have always attracted the attention of the Church to that singular Apocalypse.

From the end of the 16th century till recent times nothing was known of it except by the quotations in the Fathers and the Greek fragments preserved in the *Chronographia* of Georgius Syncellus, and the *Testament of the Twelve Patriarchs*. In the 17th century it became known that the entire book existed in an Ethiopic translation. Three manuscripts of this translation were brought to England by Bruce, the Abyssinian explorer, in 1773. It was first translated into English by Archbishop Lawrence in 1821, and retranslated into German by Hofmann in 1833, and into Latin by A. F. Gfrörer in 1840.

It consists of an Introduction, i.—vi. 12, containing a Prophecy of Judgment.

vii.—x. Legends about the two hundred fallen angels who went astray with the daughters of men, and taught mankind the Arts, the Sciences, and many forms of luxury.

xi.—xvi. Enoch is sent on a mission to these fallen angels.

xvii.—xxxv. Visions, sometimes (as in the Apocalypse) in Heaven and sometimes on earth, in which Enoch is taught the origin of the elements and the general elements of Natural Science, and is shown the prison of the fallen angels, and the dwelling of the good, where the voice of the murdered Abel sounds.

xxxvii.—lxx.[1] A second "Vision of Wisdom," which (as in the Apocalypse) repeats—though with many variations—all the essential elements contained in i.—xxxv., which are treated as one vision. This section falls into three Parables or Maschals; these are xxxviii.—xliv., chiefly dwelling on the future abode and condition of sinners; xlv.—lv., on those who deny Heaven and God, and the Messianic Judgment which they incur; lvi.—lxx., chiefly on the blessings of the elect.

The section lxxi.—lxxxi. is entitled the Book of the Lights of Heaven. Enoch, orally and in writing, teaches his son Methuselah about the sun, moon, and stars.

The section lxxxii.—lxxxix. contains two dreams. In the first Enoch sees the vision of the Flood, and prays God not to destroy all mankind; in the second he sees an apocalyptic foreshadowing of future history down to the time of Herod the Great (?) with a picture of the days of the Messiah.

---

[1] Chapter xxxvi. is missing.

Chapters xc., xci. contain Enoch's words of consolation and exhortation to his children.

Chapter xcii. to verse 18 is a sketch of history in ten weeks or periods, of which the first is signalised by the birth of Enoch; the second by the Flood; the third by the life of Noah; the fourth by Moses; the fifth by the building of Solomon's Temple; the sixth by Ezra; the seventh by the encroachments of heathenism; the eighth by rewards, punishments, and the building of a new Temple; the ninth by the Messianic kingdom; the tenth by the judgment of men and angels, and the renovation of the world.

From xcii. 19—civ. the book is mainly didactic, being full of promises and threatenings. In the last chapter (cv.) Enoch relates the birth of Noah, and prophesies that he shall be the founder of a new race.

The Ethiopic text is undoubtedly translated from the Greek, of which we find fragments in St. Jude, in Justin Martyr, and other Fathers, and in the *Testament of the Twelve Patriarchs*.[1] Whether the Greek is itself a translation from an original Hebrew book is uncertain. Origen seems to imply that this was the case, for he says that the Books (libelli) were not regarded as authoritative "among the Hebrews." That the book in its present form is not by one author, and that the Noachian parts of it are by another hand, is clear. From internal evidence it appears that part at least of the book (chapters i.—xxxv., lxxi.—cv.) was written in the days of the Maccabees; and that chapters xxxvii.—lxx. are not earlier than the days of Herod the Great, and are full of still more recent interpolations. Volkmar has endeavoured to prove that, as a whole, it is not earlier than the reign of Hadrian, and that it expresses the views of R. Akiva.[2]

One reason for the slighting estimate of the book by the Jews may be that the writer shows no interest in the Ritual and Ceremonial Law, and makes no special mention either of circumcision or of the Sabbath.

EXCURSUS V.

RABBINIC ALLUSIONS IN ST. JUDE.

The direct citation of St. Jude (verses 14, 15) from the Book of Enoch is taken from the second chapter, but it is by no means the only trace of a similarity between the two writers.

i. Jude 6 dwells on the fall of the angels which "kept not their

---

[1] Orig. *Hom.* 28; *in Num.* xxxiv.
[2] For further information, see Abp. Lawrence's *Prelim. Dissert. and Translation* (1821); Hofmann, *Das Buch Henoch* (1833); and in Ersch and Grüber, *Encycl. s. v.*; Lücke, *Einleit. in d. Offenb.* i. 89—144; Gfrörer, *Jahrh. d. Heils*, i. 93 *fg.*; and especially A. Dillmann, *Das Buch Henoch* (1853).

own dominion," but "left their own habitation, and are reserved in everlasting bonds under darkness unto the judgment of the Great Day" (comp. 2 Pet. ii. 4, 5). This, as we have seen, is a topic which occupies a large part of the Book of Enoch. In vii. 2 we are told of two hundred angels who descended on Ardis, the top of Mount Armon. In xii. 5—7, we are told that they "have deserted the lofty sky and their holy everlasting habitation, . . . and have been greatly corrupted on the earth," and in xiv. 4, that they are "to be bound on earth *as long as the world endures*," and (xvi. 5) that they are "never to obtain peace." Their prison-house, where they are to be "kept for ever" (xxi. 6), is "a terrific place," and they are "confined in a network of iron and brass" (liv. 6), which nevertheless consists of "fetters of iron without weight." The last expression is an antiphrasis like the "clankless chains" of Shelley, and the "fetters, yet not of brass," of Æschylus. The author of the Second Epistle of Peter, with lyric boldness, speaks of these fetters as "chains of darkness," and the author of the Book of Wisdom (xvii. 2, 16, 17) evidently had a similar picture in his mind when he speaks of the Egyptians as "fettered with the bonds of a long night," "shut up in a prison without iron bars," and bound "with one chain of darkness." These fallen angels are shut up in a "burning valley," and yet its fires give no light, or only "teach light to counterfeit a gloom," for they are "covered with darkness," and they "see no light" (Enoch x. 1—9).

ii. Again, in v. 13 St. Jude compares the corrupted Antinomians whom he is denouncing as "wandering stars to whom is reserved the blackness of darkness for ever." We might have supposed that the metaphor was derived from meteors disappearing into the night, or comets rushing off into the illimitable void. But from the Book of Enoch (xviii. 14, 16), we are led to infer that, by the "wandering stars" are meant quite literally *planets* (ἀστέρες πλανῆται), not, as Bengel supposed, because they are opaque, but because they are regarded (with the sun and moon) as "seven stars . . . . . which transgressed the commandment of God . . . *for they came not in their proper season*." What was the exact conception in the writer's mind is impossible to say, but he may have identified the planets with evil spirits because they were objects of idolatrous worship, and were named after heathen deities.[1]

iii. Once more, in verse 7 St. Jude seems distinctly to imply that the sin of the Fallen Angels was analogous to that of the cities of the Plain, in that they, by unions with mortal women, went after strange flesh. This is exactly the view of the pseudo-Enoch. He makes Enoch reproach them (xv. 1—7), because being by nature spiritual, they "*have done as those who are flesh and blood do*," and have thereby transgressed the very law of their nature.

[1] For two remarkable parallels between the Book of Enoch and the Apocalypse, see the Notes on Rev. vi. 10, 11, and xiv. 20.

iv. Nor are these the only references to Rabbinic and other legends by St. Jude. In verse 5 it is said that "Jesus" led the people out of Egypt, and in the second instance destroyed them. The use of the name "Jesus" for "Christ" shows perhaps the somewhat late date of the Epistle. When St. Paul alludes to the legendary wanderings of the Rock in the desert (1 Cor. x. 4), he adds the allegory "and that Rock was Christ." In saying that "Jesus" saved the people out of the land of Egypt, St. Jude seems to be identifying Him with the Pillar of Fire, which is one of the many divine manifestations to which Philo compares the Logos.[1]

v. The strange reference to a dispute between Michael and Satan about the body of Moses has not yet been traced to any source whatever. Origen says that it was taken from an Apocryphal book called *The Assumption of Moses*; and Œcumenius says that Satan claimed the body of Moses because he had killed the Egyptian. The words "The Lord rebuke thee," are addressed to Satan by the Lord (who is perhaps meant to be the same as the Angel of the Lord in the previous verse), in Zech. iii. 2. The nearest approach to this legend is in the Targum of Jonathan on Deut. xxxiv 6, where we are told, with obvious reference to some similar story, that the grave of Moses was entrusted to the charge of Michael.

vi. Again, when it is said that these false and polluted Christians "went in the way of Cain," the reference cannot be to anything recorded in the book of Genesis. There the only crime laid to the charge of Cain is murder. The reference here seems to be mainly to presumption and blasphemy, and to that insolent atheism with which Cain is charged in the Jerusalem Targum on Gen. iv. 7, where he is made to deny that there is such a thing as a Judge or a judgment. The allusion cannot be to the blaspheming Gnostics who called themselves Cainites, for we do not hear of them till much later.[2] It is, however, remarkable that they chose Cain, the Sodomites, and Korah (who are all here mentioned), as their heroes, and as the representatives of the stronger and better spiritual powers, who were opposed to the Demiurge of the Mosaic Dispensation and the material world.

EXCURSUS VI.

SPECIMENS OF PHILONIAN ALLEGORY.

1. Commenting on Gen. xvii. 16, "*I will give thee a son from her,*" and explaining it of the joy of heart which God promises to the virtuous, Philo adds that some explain "*from* her" to mean "*apart*

---

[1] *Quis Rer. Div. Haer.*, and *De Vit. Mos.* 2.
[2] Iren. c. *Haer.* i. 31; Epiphan. *Haer.* 38.

from her," because Virtue does not spring from the soul, but from without, even from God. Others explain the Greek words as though they were a single word (*exautes*), meaning "*immediately*," because all divine gifts are speedy and spontaneous. Others, again, make "from her" mean "*from Virtue*," which is the mother of all good.[1] The simultaneous existence of three such strange devices of exegesis at least shows that Philo might take his premises for granted among the readers whom alone he wished to address.

2. On Gen. xv. 15 he says that in "*Thou shalt go to thy fathers*" some understood by "fathers," not "thy Chaldæan forefathers," but "the sun, moon, and stars;" others explained "father" to mean "archetypal ideas, and the things unseen;" others, the four elements and powers of which the universe is composed—earth, air, fire and water!"[2]

3. Each of the Patriarchs represents a condition of the soul. Abraham represents acquired virtue; Isaac, natural virtue; Jacob, virtue acquired by training; Joseph, political virtue. Sarah represents generic virtue, virtue in the abstract; Rebecca represents endurance; Leah is persecuted virtue; Pharaoh is the mind set against God; Moses is the prophetic word. Everything and every person stands for something else. Egypt represents the body; Canaan symbolises piety. A kingdom is an emblem of Divine wisdom; a pigeon, of human wisdom; a sheep, of the pure soul.

4. Writing on Gen. xviii. 6, he idealises the appearance of the three angels into the fact that the seeking soul recognises God, His love, and His might. The three measures of meal indicate that the soul must embrace and treasure up this threefold manifestation of God. The word for cakes (*enkruphias*) means that the Sacred word about God and His power must be concealed in the initiated soul.[3]

5. On Gen xxxii. 10, "*With my staff I passed over this Jordan*," he says it would be a poor thing (ταπεινὸν) to understand it literally. Jordan means all that is base, the staff means discipline: Jacob intended to imply that by discipline he had risen above baseness.

Only by such means could Philo get rid of the representation of God as having human parts and human passions. But with this method he can boldly set aside, as literally false and only allegorically true, whatever offends his philosophic convictions. Thus, on Gen. ii. 21, after saying that the letter of the narrative is mythical, he argues that otherwise it would be absurd. By "*ribs*" are meant merely the powers of life,[4] and the notion that Eve was formed out of a material rib seems to him degrading.

---

[1] *De nomin. mutat.* § xxv. (Mangey, i. 599).
[2] *Quis Rer. Div. Haer.* (Mang. i. 513). *De Migr. Abraham.*, *ad init.*
[3] ἐγκρυφίας means "cakes baked by being *hidden* in ashes" (*De Sacr. Abel et Cain*, Mang. i. 173).
[4] *Leg. alleg.* i. 18 (Mang. i. 70).

6. He often accepts the general fact, but allegorises all the details. The tree of Paradise, the serpent, and the expulsion, are merely symbols; and he confidently addresses his explanation of them to "the initiated." The heart of his system is seen in his comments on "*Let us make man in our image.*" The plural shows, he says, that the angels as well as God had a share in the making of man, and since man is of mixed nature, we must suppose that the good side of his nature came from God, the weak side from the angels. But he goes on to explain that the verse applies to the creation of man in the idea, not in the concrete.

EXCURSUS VII.

ADDITIONAL ILLUSTRATIONS OF PHILO'S VIEWS ABOUT THE LOGOS.

In God, no less than in man, Philo distinguishes between the speech and the reason. The Divine reason embraces the whole intelligible world, the world of ideas, what he sometimes calls "the idea of ideas." The Divine speech includes the whole world of active agents and Divine forces.

(i.) Hence it is that, in a phrase borrowed by Apollos (Heb. iv. 12), he calls the Word "the *cutter* of all things." The phrase is founded on an allegorical explanation of Gen. xv. 9. Philo says that in the sacrifice there described the she-goat symbolises the sense, the calf the soul, the dove Divine wisdom, the pigeon human wisdom. The wise man sees all these as gifts from above. The text says that "*he*" divided these sacrifices, and since the name of Abraham is not repeated, "*he*" must mean the Logos, and the truth indicated is that the Logos, "whetted to sharpest edge," divides all perceptible things to their inmost depths—the soul into the reasonable and the unreasonable; speech into true and false; the world of sense into distinct and indistinct phenomena. These divided parts are, by way of contrast, placed opposite to each other. The doves alone are not divided, because Divine wisdom is simple, and cannot be cleft into opposing contrarieties.[1] Thus God, whetting His Word, which cutteth all things, divides the formless and abstract essence of all things, and the four elements of the universe, and the animals and plants compounded from them. Hence the phrase, "the cutter Word," seems to be based on the distinction between the Logos as the primeval Idea, and the Logos as a creative Force.

(ii.) The world of Ideas, to which the existing world corresponds as a copy to its archetype, lies in the Divine Logos. Philo illustrates this by saying that, when God bade Moses to lift up a serpent in the

---

[1] *Quis rer. div. Haer.* § xlviii. (Mang. i. 491); see Gfrörer, *Philo*, i. 184—187.

wilderness, He did not say of what metal it was to be made, because the ideas of God are abstract and immaterial; Moses, in carrying out the concrete realisation, is obliged to use *some* substance, and therefore makes the serpent of brass.[1] Similarly he holds that GOD is not to be grasped by human knowledge, but that the WORD is. Hence, writing on Gen. xxii. 16, he says, "God is the God of wise and perfect beings, but the Logos is the God of us who are imperfect."

(iii.) Philo uses so many analogies to express his notion of the Logos that he falls into contradictions, and leaves his readers in confusion. The Logos, in various passages of his voluminous writings, is the creator of species, although He is Himself the Idea of Ideas; He is the seal of God; He is the Divine force which dwells in the universe; He is the chain or band which keeps the world together; He is the law and ordinance of all things; He is the giver of wisdom, the warden of virtue; He is the manna which nourishes the soul; He is the fatherland of wise souls, the pilot of the wise; He is their controlling conscience, their Paraclete; He is the Divine wisdom which is the daughter of God.[2]

EXCURSUS VIII.

PATRISTIC EVIDENCE AS TO THE AUTHORSHIP OF THE EPISTLE TO THE HEBREWS.

The canonicity of the Epistle to the Hebrews, its right to be accepted as a part of Holy Scripture, the perfect truthfulness of the contemporary character which it assumes, its greatness, importance, and authority, and the fact that it was written before the fall of Jerusalem, are not in question. These points have never been seriously disputed. Some have seen allusions to the Epistle in St. James and the Second of St. Peter.[3] Setting these aside as improbable, it was certainly known to St. Clemens of Rome, and largely used by him in his letter to the Corinthians;[4] and it is possible—though no more—that it was the source of some of the parallels adduced from the writings of Ignatius, Polycarp, Justin Martyr, and the Pseudo-Barnabas. But in the Western Church no single writer of the first, second, or even third

[1] *Leg. allegg.* ii. § 20 (Mang. i. 80).
[2] See various passages quoted in Gfrörer, *Philo*, i. 176 - 243.
[3] 2 Pet. iii. 15, 16; Ja. ii. 24, 25.
[4] Ἐν ᾗ ᾗ τῆι πρὸς Ἑβραίους πολλὰ νοήματα παραθεὶς ἤδη δὲ καὶ αὐτολέξει ῥητοῖς τισιν ἐξ αὐτῆς χρησάμενος σαφέστατα παρίστησιν ὅτι μὴ νέον ὑπάρχει τὸ σύγγραμμα (Euseb. *H. E.* iii. 38). " Omnino grandis in utráque similitudo est " (Jer. *De Virr. illust.*). " Der Hebräerbrief ist ganz und gar in sein Denken übergegangen " (Tholuck, *Einleit.* 2). Yet, strange to say, Clemens never *mentions* it by name. This alone seems almost fatal to the Pauline authorship.

century quoted it *as St. Paul's*. Not only did Basilides (*cir.* A.D. 125) exclude it, though he acknowledged the other Paulinic Epistles,[1] but we are expressly told that St. Hippolytus († 235 ?) denied that it was written by St. Paul. The authority for this fact is late and heretical,[2] yet there seems no reason to reject so positive a statement. And this remark of St. Hippolytus, together with the place assigned to the Epistle in the Peshito, indicates the opinion of the Syrian Church in the first half of the third century, if, as seems probable, the learned and eloquent Bishop of Portus came originally from Antioch.[3] We have the same assurance about St. Irenæus († A.D. 202). We find from Eusebius that in a work attributed to Irenæus (but which Eusebius had never seen)[4] he quoted from the Epistle to the Hebrews, and *from the Wisdom of Solomon*. But no such quotation was to be found in any of his best-known works, and in any case he did not assign the Epistle to St. Paul.[5] Indeed, the mention of the Epistle with the *Wisdom of Solomon* seems to imply that he regarded the two works as standing on the same footing. The Presbyter Gaius only recognised thirteen Epistles of St. Paul, and did not number this Epistle among them.[6] The Canon of Muratori (*cir.* A.D. 170) either does not allude to it, or only under the damaging description of a letter to the Alexandrians, current under the name of Paul, but forged in the interests of Marcion's heresy ("*ad haeresim Marcionis*").[7] It is remarkable that Marcion, in the middle of the second century, rejected it, though many passages might have been used to support his views. Novatian, useful as it would have been to him, and frequently as he quotes Scripture,

---

[1] Jer. *Proœm. in Ep. ad Tit.* Basilides was a Gnostic, but he seems to have adopted the ordinary Canon of his day; this, therefore, would seem to show that at that time the Alexandrians did not recognise the Epistle as St. Paul's.

[2] Steph. Gobar, *ap.* Phot. *Bibl. Cod.* iii. 291 (Migne); and also Photius himself (Wieseler, *Untersuch.* i. 12).

[3] Giesoler, i. § 341. On Hippolytus, see Kurtz, *K. G.* i. 106. Mommsen, *Abhandl. d. Sächs. Gesellsch.* i. 595.

[4] The Βιβλίον διαλέξεων διαφόρων.

[5] The fragment in which he is supposed to quote Heb. xiii. 14 (Stieren's *Irenæus*, i. 854, seq.; ii. 361, seq.) is of very doubtful genuineness, and even if genuine proves nothing.

[6] Gaius, *ap.* Euseb. *H. E.* vi. 20. As he makes this remark in immediate connexion with severe animadversions on the procipitance (προπετείαν) and audacity of those who admitted the authenticity of spurious writings, it would appear that he even regarded the Pauline hypothesis with some indignation; and as he was a λογιώτατος ἀνὴρ, his opinion is important. Nothing, however, is known of Gaius, and Bp. Lightfoot (*Journ. of Philology*, i. 98) has conjectured that he is none other than Hippolytus using his own prænomen as an interlocutor in the dialogue against Montanism.

[7] If "Gaius" was, as Muratori thought, the author of the celebrated Canon, the next remark, "fel enim cum melle misceri non congruit," would harmonise with the severe sentiments alluded to in the previous note, and there would be an additional sting in this if we accept the suggested allusion to Heb. xii. 15, and the reading, ἐν χολῇ for ἐνοχλῇ. The writer of the Canon says that St. Paul only wrote (like St. John) to seven Churches. Delitzsch and Lünemann say that the Epistle to the Hebrews cannot be meant by the "Epistle to the Alexandrians," because it is anonymous; but the writer of the Canon does not say that it was "inscribed" with the name of Paul. (See Wieseler, i. 27, and Hesse, *Das Murat. Frag.* p. 201 *f.*)

never even alludes to it. Tertullian († A.D. 240) ascribes it to
St. Barnabas,[1] and did not regard it as a work of St. Paul, for he
taunts Marcion with falsifying the number of St. Paul's Epistles
by omitting (only) the Pastoral Epistles. St. Cyprian († A.D. 258), in
his voluminous treatises, neither quotes nor mentions it. Victorinus
(† A.D. 303) ignores it. It is separated or omitted in some of the oldest
MSS. of the Vetus Itala.[2] The first writer of the Western Church
who ascribes it to St. Paul (and probably because he found it so
ascribed in Greek writers) is Hilary of Poictiers, who died A.D. 368.[3]
It was not till quite the close of the fourth century that in the
Western Church it began to be popularly accepted as St. Paul's. As
this popular acceptance at that late epoch does not possess any critical
importance, it is needless to enumerate the names of writers who
merely run in the ordinary groove. Among those writers who really
thought about the matter doubts as to the Pauline authorship were
expressed—as, for instance, by Isidore of Seville—as late as the
seventh century.[4] Now, even if this fact stood alone—that the
Western Church for nearly four centuries refused to admit the Pauline
authorship—we should regard it as fatal to that hypothesis. And for
this reason. If it had been written by St. Paul, it is inconceivable that
St. Clemens of Rome, his contemporary and friend, should not have
known that it was so. St. Paul was not thus in the habit of concealing
an identity which, on the contrary, he habitually placed in the foreground. But if St. Clemens had been aware that it was really a work
of St. Paul, nothing can be more certain than that he would have
mentioned so precious a truth to the Church of which he was bishop.
If he said anything at all about the authorship, it must have been that
whoever wrote it *Paul did not*. Thus, and thus only, can we account
for the conviction of the Roman Church for nearly four centuries that

---

[1] Tert. *c. Marc.* v. 20.

[2] No name is attached to it in the Peshito, and the fact that in that version it is placed *after* all the thirteen Epistles of St. Paul, in spite of its size and importance, seems to show decisively that the Syriac translators did not regard it as the work of the Apostle (Wieseler, *Eine Untersuchung über d. Hebräerbrief* (1861), i. 9). It is only in later Syriac versions that it is called "The *Epistle of St. Paul* to the Hebrews."

[3] In the fourth century neither Phœbadius, nor Zeno, nor Hilary the Deacon, nor Optatus once quote it, though they frequently quote St. Paul; nor, in the fifth century, Siricius, Caelestine I., Leo the Great, Orosius, Evagrius, or Sedulius. St. Ambrose († 397), a student of Greek writers, quotes it as St. Paul's, and so does his friend Philastrius; but the latter tells that it was not read to the people in church, or only "sometimes," and (in another passage) that it had been ordained by the Apostles and their successors that *only thirteen Epistles of St. Paul* (and therefore *not* the Epistle to the Hebrews) should be read in the Catholic Church. Latin writers misunderstood, and therefore found it difficult to accept, the phrase "To Him that made Him," τῷ ποιήσαντι αὐτόν ("quia et *factum Christum* dixit"), in iii. 2; and they looked with suspicion on the rhetorical style ("quia *rhetorice* scripsit sermone plausibili"), and disliked the use made by the Novatian schismatics of vi. 4—8, which St. Ambrose finds it hard to reconcile with St. Paul's conduct to the Corinthian offender (*De Poenitent.* ii. 2). The intrinsic greatness of the Epistle overcame these hesitations, and, when once accepted, it was accepted as St. Paul's on the supposed authority and undoubted custom of the Alexandrian writers.

[4] † A.D. 636.

the opinion about it in the Eastern Church was erroneous. To say that St. Clemens, "in his love for the author, would not do what the author himself has not done; he would not betray the secret, &c.," is to overlook plain facts in the desire to support current traditions. Any one may see for himself that the author, though he does not mention his own name, has no wish to conceal his identity from those to whom he wrote, and, indeed, assumes that they were perfectly aware who it was who was thus addressing them. The Apostolic letters, it must be remembered, were always conveyed to their destination by responsible and accredited messengers. No Apostolic Church would have paid attention to an unauthenticated epistle.

How very little weight can be attached to the quotation of the Epistle in a loose and popular way as St. Paul's may be seen in the case of two great men, St. Jerome († A.D. 420) and St. Augustine († A.D. 430). By their time—in the fifth century—the current of irresponsible opinion ran strongly in favour of the Pauline authorship, and to throw any doubt upon it was to brave the charge of being arrogant or unorthodox. It is not, therefore, surprising that both these remarkable men in an ordinary way speak of the Epistle as St. Paul's in passages where they merely wish to make an allusion without exciting a controversy. They were justified in doing this, because they saw that even though it could not have been written by St. Paul, yet it was Pauline in its main doctrines. In ordinary treatises it was not desirable to be constantly correcting the multitude. But when they are writing carefully and accurately they are too independent not to indicate their real opinion. St. Jerome over and over again quotes it as St. Paul's, yet often with the addition of some doubting or deprecatory phrase. When he deals directly with the question, he treats it as unimportant, but admits that the Epistle was accepted with some hesitancy,[1] and that many considered it to be the work of Barnabas or Clemens.[2] St. Augustine often quotes it as St. Paul's, and his authority had probably no small share in influencing the Synods which declared it to be authentic.[3] Yet in his later

---

[1] Even Rufinus, though he supposed it to be by St. Paul, adds, "Si quis tamen eam receperit." (*Invect. in Hieron.*)

[2] His opinion seems to have wavered more than once (see Bleek, *Introd.*), but he never felt at all sure that St. Paul wrote it. "*Quicunque est ille*, qui ad Hebraeos scripsit epistolam" (*Comm. in Amos*, 8). "*Si quis vult recipere* eam epistolam quae sub nomine Pauli ad Hebraeos scripta est" (*Comment. in Tit.*). "Relege ad Hebraeos epistolam Pauli, *sive cujuscunque alterius* eam esse putas, quia jam inter ecclesiasticas est recepta" (*id.*). "Et Paulus apostolus loquitur, *si quis tamen ad* Hebraeos epistolam suscipit" (*in Ezek.* xxviii.). "Omnes Graeci recipiunt et *nonnulli Latinorum*" (*Comm. in Matt.* c. 26). "Licet de eâ multi Latinorum dubitent" (*Catal.* 59). "Apud Romanos usque hodie quasi apostoli Pauli non habetur" (*in Is.* viii. 18). "Pauli quoque idcirco ad Hebraeos epistolae contradictur, quod ad Hebraeos scribens utatur testimoniis quae in Hebraeis voluminibus non habentur" (*in Is.* vi. 9). "Et nihil intersse cujus sit, cum ecclesiastici viri sit, et quotidie ecclesiarum lectione celebretur" (*Ep.* 129, *ad Dard.*), etc.

[3] Hippo, A.D. 393; Third Council of Carthage, A.D. 398; Fifth Council of Carthage, A.D. 419. But the two former Councils only say, "Thirteen Epistles of St. Paul, and one of his to the Hebrews."

writings he so constantly quotes it merely as "the Epistle to the Hebrews," that Lardner says, "One would think that he studiously declines to call it Paul's."[1] The "accommodation" to which these eminent writers condescended in popularly referring to it as being (in a sense) a work of the Apostle, led to the rigidity of the ordinary acceptance; yet even at the close of the sixth century "no Latin commentary on it was known to Cassiodorus."[2]

The opinion of the Eastern Church originated in Alexandria. To the Alexandrian School, though they did not discover the secret of the authorship, the Epistle was extremely precious, because it exactly expressed their own views, and was founded on premises with which they were familiar. It was, therefore, natural that they should desire to give it as high an authority as possible; and in the Epistle itself they found a general support for the notion that it was written by St. Paul.

(a.) But this assertion cannot be traced farther back than to the unsupported guess of the venerable Pantænus. "The blessed Presbyter," as Clemens of Alexandria († A.D. 220) calls him in a passage of his last work, the *Hypotyposes*,[3] assigned two reasons why St. Paul had not mentioned his own name in the salutation, as he does in every other Epistle. It was, he said, because the Lord Himself had been sent to the Hebrews as an Apostle of the Almighty,[4] so that St. Paul suppressed his own name out of modesty; and it also was because St. Paul was a herald and Apostle of the Gentiles, so that a letter from him to the Hebrews was, so to speak, a work of supererogation.[5] Both these attempts to explain a fact so damaging to the Pauline authorship of the letter are untenable. If St. Peter in writing to the Jews calls himself an Apostle, there was no reason why St. Paul should have scrupled to give himself the same title; nor was the division of

---

[1] The force of truth compels him to insert an occasional caution, such as "Quamquam nonnullis incerta sit;" "quoquo modo se habeat ista quaestio;" "quam plures apostoli Pauli esse dicunt, quidam vero negant," etc. See the many passages referred to in the exhaustive catalogue of Bleek, from whom all succeeding commentators have freely borrowed. Nothing can show more forcibly the manner in which writer after writer will snatch at the most futile explanation of something which tells against a current notion than that we find Augustine repeating the absurdity, which has lasted down to our own day, that St. Paul concealed his name in order not to offend the Jews! ("Principium salutatorium de industria dicitur omisisse, ne Judaei *nomine ejus offensi* vel inimico animo legerent, vel omnino non legerent," etc. (*Expos. Ep. ad Rom.* § 11).

[2] Davidson, ii. 227. That the old hesitation continued may be seen from the fact that it formed originally no part of D (Codex Claromontanus), is omitted in G (Cod. Boernerianus), and is only found in Latin in F (Cod. Augiensis). The two latter MSS. are of the *ninth* century. In the Vulgate it is placed after Philemon.

[3] Ap. Euseb. *H. E.* vi. 13. It is clear that if Eusebius had found any traces of an *earlier* tradition he would have mentioned them, for he brings together all the reasons he can in favour of the Pauline authorship. His statement, therefore, tends to prove that even in the Eastern Church the Epistle, in spite of its obvious phenomena, had not been assigned to St. Paul by any writer or by any tradition of importance in the first two centuries. (Wieseler, i. 15.)

[4] The expression was taken by Clemens from Heb. iii. 1.

[5] Διὰ μετριότητα . . . διά τε τὴν πρὸς τὸν Κύριον τιμὴν διά τε τὸ ἐκ περιουσίας καὶ τοῖς Ἑβραίοις ἐπιστέλλειν. (*Hypotyposes*; ap. Euseb. *H. E.* vi. 14.)

office between him and the other Apostles so rigid as to prevent his addressing Jews. The "Apostolic compact" did not prevent St. Peter from addressing Gentiles. If it was thus rigid, it tells against St. Paul's having written this Epistle at all, but not against his authenticating it with his name. He constantly addressed Jews and constantly maintained against them his independent right to the highest order of the Apostolate. In writing to them he would have been *least* inclined to waive the dignity which he had received directly from his Lord. No authority can therefore be allowed to the opinion of Pantænus. It was a conjecture derived from the references at the close of the letter, and possibly even from the false reading "*my chains*" (τοῖς δεσμοῖς μου) instead of "prisoners" (δεσμίοις) in x. 34.[1] The conjectural suggestions by which he tried to support his opinion are so weak that they actually tell against it, and show that the eminence of Pantænus by no means consisted in a power of critical discernment.

(*b.*) If the great St. Clemens of Alexandria accepted the Pauline authorship, he did so mainly in deference to the opinion of Pantænus, and only in a modified form. For although he often quotes the Epistle as St. Paul's, he was aware of the difficulties of such an opinion. He supposed that the letter was originally written in Hebrew, and was translated into Greek by St. Luke. This notion may have originated in the resemblance of style between it and the Acts. With this suggestion we shall deal later on. But meanwhile St. Clemens, not content with the explanation offered by Pantænus of the anonymity of the letter, relies on another, which is still more groundless. St. Paul suppressed his name, he says, because he did not wish to divert the attention of the Jews from his arguments, being well aware that they had taken a prejudice against him and looked on him with suspicion.[2] Thus even St. Clemens contents himself with a reason which will not stand a single moment's consideration. The tone of the letter throughout, as well as the closing salutations, prove that the writer is known to his readers;[3] and the supposition that he wanted to entrap their attention before revealing his identity is too singular for serious refutation.[4]

(*c.*) There is no ancient writer whose opinion on the subject would

---

[1] Euthalius (cir. 460) especially refers to τοῖς δεσμοῖς μου as one of the arguments for the Pauline authorship. (Migne, *Patr. Graec.* lxxxv. 776, ap. Bleek; Alford, iv. 1, p. 15.) Τοῖς δεσμίοις is the reading of A, D, the Vulg., Peshito, etc. But even if the received text be right (with א, E, H, K, etc.), there is no proof that the writer is St. Paul, but only that the writer had been in prison—a common case with Christians of the first century.

[2] Clem. Alex. *Hypotyp.*, ap. Euseb. *H. E.* vi. 14. *Adumbratt.* in 1 Petr., p. 1007. Clemens was, it must be admitted, somewhat credulous.

[3] xiii. 18, 23.

[4] See Bp. Wordsworth's surprising remarks on this subject. The unions of great learning with want of subtle discernment even in the Alexandrian School may be seen in their acceptance of the Epistle of Barnabas as authentic in spite of its extravagant allegorising and incipient Gnosticism.

carry more weight than that of ORIGEN, whose splendid originality was not crushed by his immense erudition. Now it is quite true that Origen frequently quotes the Epistle as St. Paul's,[1] but it is no less evident that he only does so in accordance with common custom, and that by such casual expressions he as little intends to prejudge the question of authorship as the authors of the Revised Version, who still retain the name of St. Paul in the title. A modern writer who should casually happen to quote the "Second Epistle of St. Peter," or popularly to refer to Ecclesiastes as a work of King Solomon, would have a right to feel himself aggrieved if such a general reference was interpreted as the deliverance of a final and critical opinion. Origen, like Jerome and Augustine, whenever he wishes to be accurate, introduces some phrase of caution which indicates his own opinion. We know what he thought on the subject, for he wrote Homilies on this Epistle, which are now unfortunately lost, but of which one or two fragments have been preserved by Eusebius. In these we have the deliberate conclusion of the greatest of the Fathers. "That the character of the style of the Epistle to the Hebrews," he says, "does not show the unlearnedness (τὸ ἰδιωτικὸν)[2] of the Apostle who confessed that he was unlearned in word (that is to say, in language), but that the Epistle is more Hellenic in the structure of its style, everyone would admit who is capable of judging the differences of language;[3] but, on the other hand, that the thoughts of the Epistle are wonderful, and not inferior to the acknowledged apostolic writings, *that* too is a truth which every one would acknowledge who attends to the reading of the apostolic works." He subsequently attributes the *thoughts* to the Apostle, and the composition to some one who made notes of what the Apostle said.[4] "If, then," he concludes, "any Church holds this Epistle to be the work of St. Paul, let it be congratulated (εὐδοκιμείτω) even for this, since it was not without some grounds that ancient authorities have handed it down as Paul's. But who actually wrote it God only knows. The historical tradition that has come down to us is divergent; for some say that Clemens, who became Bishop of the Romans, wrote the Epistle, and some that it was Luke, who also wrote the Gospel and the Acts."[5]

[1] Not unfrequently, however, he uses the phrase κατὰ τὸν ἀπόστολον. See the passages in Bleek's Introduction.
[2] On the exact import of this word, see my *Life and Work of St. Paul*, i. 106.
[3] Ὅτι . . . ἐστὶν ἡ Ἐπιστολὴ συνθέσει τῆς λέξεως Ἑλληνικωτέρα, πᾶς ὁ ἐπιστάμενος κρίνειν φράσεων διαφορὰς ὁμολογήσαι ἄν. (*Ap.* Euseb. *H. E.* vi. 25.)
[4] ἡ δὲ φράσις καὶ ἡ σύνθεσις ἀπομνημονεύσαντός τινος τὰ ἀποστολικὰ καὶ ὡσπερεὶ σχολιογραφήσαντος τὰ εἰρημένα ὑπὸ τοῦ διδασκάλου. (Ibid.)
[5] This limited and hesitating expression implies that the Churches generally rejected this opinion, and perhaps that it prevailed in the Alexandrian Church alone. Now the natural tendency would so absolutely be to ascribe the letter to St. Paul, and the grounds for doing so, if taken apart from the objections, are so reasonable (οὐκ εἰκῆ) that the fact that until this view became stereotyped there were many who rejected it, is of itself a proof how strong were the reasons which compelled them to run counter to the popular inference. The general ἱστορία was against the Pauline authorship: the local

The passage is expressed somewhat obscurely, because (as we are sorry to admit) Origen, with all his courage, accepted the expediency of concession, in certain cases, to popular ignorance and current prejudice. It is clear that he did not accept the Pauline authorship in the ordinary sense of the word. He was too good a scholar, too profound a student, too familiar with the niceties of Greek expression, and too unbiassed a critic, not to perceive that the "style" of the Epistle to the Hebrews is far more correct than that of St. Paul. He therefore held that Clemens of Rome may have written it, or that it might be attributed to St. Luke. But he also saw that it came from *the School* of Paul; that it expresses his sentiments, and is, so to speak, quite worthy of him. This is why he does not care to disturb the opinion of any Church which accepted it, and says that "the ancient authorities"—under which term he vaguely refers to Pantænus and Clemens'—had not been guided by arbitrary conjecture in handing down a tradition of its Pauline origin.

(*d.*) The opinion of EUSEBIUS OF CÆSAREA is no less hesitating and wavering. In common parlance he quotes the Epistle as St. Paul's, but he too was well aware that it did not belong to the *homologoumena*. He was induced by the style to conjecture that it was a translation by St. Clemens of Rome from a Hebrew original.[2] He does indeed say in one place that there were *fourteen* Epistles of St. Paul, and this Epistle to the Hebrews had its place as Pauline in the fifty manuscripts of the Canonical books of the New Testament which he caused to be written out for the Emperor Constantine, who wished to place them in the churches of his new capital. The example of Eusebius is therefore very instructive. Passage after passage might be adduced from his writings to show that he accepted the Epistle as genuine; and yet when he is writing definitely and accurately he says, "The *thirteen* Epistles of St. Paul are manifest and clear. It would not, however, be fair to ignore that some have regarded the Epistle to the Hebrews as spurious (ἠθετήκασι), saying that it is opposed (ἀντιλέγεσθαι) by the Church of Rome as not being by St. Paul." Popular reference is one thing, and accurate statement is another. In disputed questions a current allusion possesses no critical importance. And this statement of Eusebius is remarkable as showing that, in spite of the general truth of St. Jerome's remark that "all the Greeks accept," there were some even in the Greek Church who were in doubt about it.[3] Can any honest man read this review of the early patristic evidence without feeling that it is on the whole *unfavourable* to the theory of the Pauline authorship?

παράδοσις was for it; and even this was probably reducible to the loose opinion of Pantænus.

[1] Hug (*Einleit.* ii. 317), Delitzsch (*Hebr.* § xvii.), and Bleek all exaggerate the meaning of these expressions. (See Wieseler, i. 17.)

[2] Euseb. *H. E.* iii. 3, 38 ; vi. 13.

[3] We learn this also from the *Iambics* of Amphilochius, who says that τινὲς rejected it: τινὲς δέ φασι τὴν πρὸς 'Εβραίους νόθον οὐκ εὖ λέγοντες.

EXCURSUS IX.

MINOR RESEMBLANCES BETWEEN THE EPISTLE TO THE HEBREWS AND THE WORKS OF PHILO.

A few separate instances may here be thrown together of minor points of contact between the language of the Epistle to the Hebrews and that of Philo:—

(*a.*) In iii. 7—15 the writer lays great stress on the word "*to-day.*" Philo defines "to-day" as "the infinite and interminable æon," and says "Till to-day; that is for ever."[1]

(*b.*) In ii. 6 he quotes from a Psalm by saying that "*one, somewhere, testified*" (ποῦ τις). He was of course aware that the Psalm is assigned to David; but the same vague form of quotation is found frequently in Philo.

(*c.*) In iii. 2 we find the remark, "*He that builded the house hath more honour than the house.*" Philo uses the same argument.[2]

(*d.*) In iv. 15 he says that Christ shared in all our infirmities, "*except sin.*" Philo says that "the High Priest is not man, but the Divine Word, free from all share not only in willing but even in involuntary wrongdoing,"[3] and speaks also of the mercy and gentleness of His nature.[4]

(*e.*) The word μετριοπαθεῖν—literally, "*to suffer moderately*"—in v. 2 is found also in Philo, though it does not occur in the Septuagint or elsewhere in the New Testament.

(*f.*) In vi. 5 he speaks of "*tasting the utterance of God.*" Philo speaks of the utterance (*rhema*) as well as the Word (*Logos*) of God, and speaks of its nourishing the soul like manna.[5]

(*g.*) In vi. 13 we have the distinctions between God's *word* and His *oath*, and the impossibility of His swearing by any but Himself. We find in Philo the same thought and the same expressions.[6]

(*h.*) In vii. 17 the High Priest is said (without rigid accuracy) to offer sacrifices *daily*. Philo uses the same expression.[7]

(*i.*) In ix. 16, 17 he avails himself of the two senses of *diathēkē*, a "covenant" and a "will." Philo does the same.[8]

(*j.*) In x. 3 he speaks of sacrifices involving "*a remembrance* of sin." Philo says that the sacrifices of the godless do not work a re-

---

[1] *Leg. allegg.* iii. 8; *De profug.* § 11. (Mangey, i. 92, 554.)
[2] *De plant. Noe,* § 16; ὅσῳ ὁ κτησάμενος τοῦ κτήματος ἀμείνων καὶ τὸ πεποιηκὸς τοῦ γεγονότος.
[3] *De profug.* § 20. (Mang. i. 563.)
[4] *Id.* § 18. (Mang. i. 559, 561.)
[5] *De profug.* § 25; *Leg. allegg.* iii. 60. (Mang. i. 564, 120.)
[6] *Leg. allegg.* iii. 72; *De Abraham.* § 46. (Mang. i. 128; cf. 181, ii. 39.)
[7] *De spec. leg.* § 23. εὐχὰς καὶ θυσίας τελῶν καθ' ἑκάστην ἡμέραν. (Mang. i. 430.)
[8] *De nom. mutat.* § 6. (Mang. i. 586.) Cf. *De Sacr. Abel.* (Mang. i. 172.)

mission, but a remembrance of sin, and that they force us to recall our ignorances and transgressions.[1]

(*k.*) In xiii. 5 he uses the quotation, "*I will never leave thee nor forsake thee.*" In that form the words are not *exactly* found in Scripture, but Philo quotes from Scripture in the same words.

EXCURSUS X.

"SALEM" AND JERUSALEM.

One passage alone is adduced from Scripture in proof that Salem may be used as a shortened poetical form for Jerusalem, namely, Ps. lxxvi. 2, "In Salem also is his tabernacle and his dwelling-place in Zion." But not to dwell on the fact that this can only be a poetic licence, and that we should not expect to find an isolated recurrence of it in a plain historic narrative, the meaning of that verse cannot be regarded as indisputable. The Psalmist may be referring to the Salem of Melchizedek as a different place from Jerusalem. Again, the word may mean "peace;" and both the LXX. and the Vulgate render it, "His place has been made in peace."[3] Besides this, in the days of Abraham, and for centuries afterwards, Jerusalem was only known by the name Jebus.[4] But though the Targums render Salem by Jerusalem in this passage of Genesis,[5] it was an old tradition that the Salem intended is the city near Shechem which is mentioned in Gen. xxxiii. 18 and John iii. 23.[6] There was a town of this name near to Ænon, and its site has been traditionally preserved. The former passage is again doubtful. The verse is rendered by the Targums, by Josephus, and by many ancient scholars,[8] not "*Jacob came to Shalem, a city of Shechem,*" but "*Jacob came in safety to the city of Shechem.*" The Samaritans always maintained that it was at Gerizim that Melchizedek had met Abraham; and St. Jerome tells us that the most learned Jews of his day regarded *this* town as the Salem of Melchizedek, and the ruins of a large palace were shown there which was called the Palace

---

[1] *De plant. Noe*, § 25; *De vit. Mos.* iii. § 10. (Mang. i. 345, ii. 246.)
[2] *De conf. ling.* § 33. οὐ μή σε ἀνῶ οὐδ' οὐ μή σε ἐγκαταλίπω. (Mang. i. 430).
[3] LXX. ἐγενήθη ἐν εἰρήνῃ ὁ τόπος αὐτοῦ. Vulg., "Et factus est in pace locus ejus."
[4] Judg. xix. 10, 11, etc.; 2 Sam. v. 6.
[5] So, too, Jos. *Antt.* i. 10, § 2 x.
[6] It is mentioned also in Judith iv. 4.
[7] Jerome says, "Salem civitas Sicimorum quae est Sichem." It would be more accurate to say that it was *near* Shechem. He places it eight miles south of Bethshean (*Onom.* s. v. *Ep. ad Evang.* 1). The ruined well there is now called Sheikh Salm (Robinson, *Bibl. Res.* iii. 333).
[8] *E.g.*, Knobel, Tuch, Delitzsch, and Kalisch on Gen. xxxiii. 18.

of Melchizedek.[1] It is therefore doubtful whether Jerusalem is intended, especially since the writer touches so very slightly on the name. The word Salem[2] means rather "peaceful" than "peace;" and hence some again have supposed that "peaceful king" was a title of Melchizedek,[3] and one which marked him out still more specially as a type of the Messiah;[4] but this is a late and improbable conjecture. It may, however, be justly maintained that the typical character of Melchizedek would rather be impaired than enhanced by his being a king of Jerusalem. For Jerusalem was the holy town of the Aaronic priesthood, and it might seem more fit that the Royal Prince should have been connected with some other sanctuary as a type of Him in Whose day "neither in this mountain nor yet in Jerusalem should men worship the Father," but should worship Him in all places acceptably, if they worshipped in spirit and in truth.

EXCURSUS XI.

THE ALTAR OF INCENSE AND THE HOLIEST PLACE.

The altar of incense (like the altar of burnt-offering) was called Holy of Holies (Ex. xxx. 10), and in Ex. xxx. 6; xl. 5, it is expressly said to be placed "before the mercy-seat," and "before the ark of the testimony." From its very close connection with the ceremony of the Day of Atonement, on which it was (as well as the mercy-seat) sprinkled with the blood of the sin-offering (Lev. xvi. 18), it is called in 1 Kings vi. 22, "the altar that is by the oracle," or, rather, "which belongs to the oracle." It is clear, then, (1) that a peculiar sanctity appertained to the altar beyond the sanctity of the other things which were in the Holy Place;[5] and (2) that its position was close to the veil, and in immediate relation to the position of the Ark, of which it seems to have been regarded as an appurtenance. Even on these grounds the Holiest might be generally said "to have" or contain the incense-altar. But then (3) it must be borne in mind that the writer is thinking specially of the Day of Atonement, and on that day the inner veil was lifted by the high priest, so that the Holiest and the Holy Place might

---

[1] Jer. ad Evagr. See, too, the tradition preserved by Eupolemos (ap. Euseb. Praep. Evang. ix. 17), that Abraham was entertained at Gerizim (Ewald, Gesch. iii. 239; Stanley, Sin. and Pal., p. 237).
[2] שָׁלֵם.
[3] In Bereshith Rabba it is said that Melchi Salem means "perfect king," and that he was so called because he was circumcised—referring to Gen. xvii. 1 (vide Schöttgen, ad loc.). Philo calls him "king of peace (for that is the meaning of Salem)" (Leg. alleg. iii. 25). [4] Is. ix. 5; Col. i. 20, etc.
[5] Incense was supposed to have an atoning power (Yoma, f. 44, a; Num. xvi. 47).

(on that day) be regarded as a single sanctuary,[1] which would give still minuter accuracy to the term used. Nor is this a mere conjecture. In the vision of Isaiah (vi. 1—8) the prophet is supposed to be standing in the Holy Place, and he sees the Lord uplifted on His Throne above the six-winged Seraphim, just as the Shechinah was supposed to rest between the out-stretched wings of the Cherubim above the mercy-seat. Then one of the Seraphs flies from the throne with a live coal in his hand, which he had taken "*from off the altar.*" Similarly, in the vision of the Apocalypse (viii. 1—5) the seer sees an angel with a golden censer, to whom is given much incense, that he may offer it upon "*the golden altar which is before the throne.*" In these considerations, then, we may fairly see the solution of the difficulty. The writer is not speaking with pedantic minuteness, but his expression is justifiable, and even accurate if we place ourselves in his point of view, and imagine that we are looking at the Holy and the Holiest as they appeared on the greatest day of the Jewish year. But though he has made no mis-statement, he comes very near it, and it is clear that St. Paul would have written with more familiar accuracy about these ritual details.

EXCURSUS XII.

CEREMONIES OF THE DAY OF ATONEMENT.

At earliest dawn the High Priest chose a young bullock for a sin-offering and a lamb for a burnt-offering for himself and his house. After the ordinary[2] morning service, he bathed himself, and put on his holy linen garments of purest white and of great value.[3] Then he laid his hands on the head of the young bullock, and confessed the sins of himself and his house. He next took two kids for a sin-offering and a ram for a burnt-offering for the sins of Israel,[4] and cast lots upon them at the entrance of the Tabernacle. The lots were drawn from a golden urn called *calpi*, which stood in the Court of the Priests, but close to the worshippers. One lot was "for Jehovah," the other "for Azazel." The goat on which the lot for Jehovah fell was sacrificed for a sin-offering. He sacrificed the bullock as an atonement for himself and his house and the priesthood in general. The blood of the bullock was stirred by an attendant lest it should coagulate. Then

---

[1] See a Paper by Prof. Milligan, in the *Bible Educator*, iii. 230.
[2] All these bathings were done in a special golden laver in a little chamber called "Happarveh," above the room where they salted the hides of the victims (Middoth, v. 1; Surenhusius, *Mishnah*, v. 376 (quoted by McCaul, p. 155).
[3] On these see Yoma, iii. 7, and Edersheim, *The Temple*, p. 266.
[4] Altogether he offered fifteen animals, according to Maimonides (see Lev. xvi.; Num. xxix.).

came the most awful moment of all. Filling a censer with burning coals from the altar, and his hands with sweet incense beaten small, he slowly approached the sanctuary, and in his white robes entered into the presence of God through the veil of the Holiest Place. When he did so he was accompanied, the Rabbis say, by three acolytes, of whom one held him by each hand, and the other by the jewels of his robe. Entering the Holiest, he threw the incense on the burning coals of the censer, that the thick and fragrant smoke might rise in a cloud between him and the mercy-seat.[1] Through the smoke he sprinkled the blood of the bullock seven times against the front of the mercy-seat and in front of it.[2] Then, going out and sacrificing the goat for the sins of Israel, he sprinkled its blood in the same manner on the mercy-seat, thus making an atonement for the Holy Place because of the uncleanness of the children of Israel. Going forth with the blood of the bullock and the kid, he made a similar atonement for the great brazen altar of burnt-offering, the horns of which he sprinkled with the blood seven times. Altogether there were forty-three sprinklings of the blood, and the remainder was poured away at the base of the great altar. When the whole priesthood and sanctuary were thus cleansed he brought the live goat to the door of the Tabernacle, and, laying both his hands upon its head, confessed over it all the iniquities, transgressions, and sins of the people, and sent the goat to carry those sins away into the wilderness, into a land not inhabited, and thus to free the consciences of the worshippers from the sense of unforgiven guilt. Divesting himself of the holy linen garments, which he left in the Holy Place, and which were never to be worn again, he once more bathed, probably in the Court of the Tabernacle,[3] and putting on his glorious apparel of purple and gold and fine linen, with its bells and pomegranates and rich embroidery, he came forth and offered the burnt-offerings for himself and the people, and burnt the fat of the sin-offering.[4]

EXCURSUS XIII.

IMPRESSIONS LEFT ON THE MINDS OF THE JEWS BY THE CEREMONIES OF THE DAY OF ATONEMENT.

We can trace in Jewish literature how powerful was the impression which this day and its ritual had made upon the Jewish imagination. Thus, in the Book of Ecclesiasticus, after more briefly mentioning

---

[1] This somewhat mysterious proceeding arose from the dispute between the Sadducees and Pharisees, in which the former maintained that the incense should be kindled *before* the High-Priest actually entered the Holy Place, whereas the Halachah required that it should be done *after* he entered. [2] See Knobel on Lev. xvi. 14.
[3] Lev. xvi. 24, which should be rendered "in a" (not *the*) Holy Place, as in vi. 16.
[4] I have omitted some of the less certain minutiæ. These may be found in Dr. Edersheim's *Temple and its Services*, chap. xvi.

the other worthies and heroes of Jewish history, the writer lingers longest and most lovingly on the glorious figure of the High Priest Simon, the son of Onias, as he appeared on the great Day of Atonement.

"How was he honoured in the midst of the people in his coming out of the sanctuary! He was as the morning star in the midst of a cloud, and as the moon at the full; as the sun shining upon the Temple of the Most High, and as the rainbow giving light in the bright clouds. . . . As fire and incense in the censer, and as a vessel of beaten gold set with all manner of precious stones. . . When he put on the robe of honour, and was clothed with the perfection of glory, when he went up to the holy altar, he made the garment of holiness honourable. When he took the portions out of the priests' hands he himself stood by the hearth of the altar compassed with his brethren round about, as a young cedar in Lebanon, and as palm-trees compassed they him round about. So were all the sons of Aaron in their glory, and the oblations of the Lord in their hands, before all the congregations of Israel. And finishing the service at the altar, that he might adorn the offering of the Most High Almighty, he stretched out his hand to the cup, and poured of the blood of the grape, he poured out at the foot of the altar a sweet-smelling savour unto the Most High King of all. Then shouted the sons of Aaron, and sounded the silver trumpets, and made a great noise to be heard for a remembrance before the Most High."[1]

Five chapters earlier he has dwelt with similar enthusiasm on the person of Aaron—

"He exalted Aaron, a holy man like unto him (Moses), even his brother of the tribe of Levi. An everlasting covenant he made with him, and gave him the priesthood among the people; he beautified him with comely ornaments, and clothed him with a robe of glory. He put upon him perfect glory, and strengthened him with rich garments, with hosen, with a long robe, and the ephod. And he compassed him with pomegranates, and with many golden bells round about, that as he went there might be a sound, and a noise made that might be heard in the Temple, for a memorial to the children of his people; with a holy garment and gold, with blue silk and purple, the work of the embroiderer, with a breastplate of judgment, and with Urim and Thummim, with twisted scarlet, the work of the cunning workman, with precious stones graven like seals, and set in gold. . . . He set a crown of gold upon the mitre, wherein was engraved Holiness, an ornament of honour, a costly work, the desires of the eyes, goodly and beautiful. Before him there were none such, neither did any stranger put them on, but only his children, and his children's children perpetually. Their sacrifices shall be wholly consumed every day, twice continually. Moses consecrated him, and anointed him with holy oil: this was appointed unto him by an everlasting covenant, and to his seed so long as the heavens should remain. . . . He chose him out of all men living to offer sacrifices to the Lord, incense, and a sweet savour, for a memorial, to make reconciliation for his people. He gave unto him his commandments, and authority in the statutes of his judgments, that he should teach Jacob the testimonies, and inform Israel in his laws."[2]

Nor did these intense feelings of admiration grow less keen as time advanced. To the Jew of the days of our Lord, the High Priest—degraded as was his office by the vice and violence and unspiritual greed

[1] Ecclus. l. 5—16.   [2] Ecclus. xlv. 6—22.

of its Sadducean representatives[1]—was still the most memorable figure of all his nation; and even their princes—a Herod of Chalcis, and a Herod Agrippa—thought it no small enhancement of their dignities if they received from the Romans the special prerogative of keeping the "golden robes" of the great Day of Atonement. Nothing more nearly precipitated the civil war which ultimately ruined the fortunes of Judaism than the attempt of the Romans to hold the Jews under entire subjection by keeping these robes under their own control, and so having the power to hinder, if they chose, the one ceremony on which the national well-being was believed most immediately to depend.

Even long centuries after the observances of Judaism had become impossible, Maimonides, in his *Yad Hachazakah*, carefully preserves for us all the traditional precepts of the Day of Atonement—the fifteen sacrificial victims, the fumigation and cleaning of the lamps by the High Priests, the seven days' seclusion, the sprinkling of his person on the third and seventh day with the ashes of a heifer; the daily rehearsal of all the rites which he had to perform, the disputes between the Sadducees and the Pharisees about the minutiæ of the day; the five baths and ten washings of consecration on the day itself; the utterance ten times of the full name of God; the reason why the name was pronounced in an almost inaudible recitative: the sprinkling of the blood once above and seven times below the mercy-seat, which was traditionally developed into forty-three sprinklings; the watch-towers and signals by which it was indicated that the goat "for Azazel" had reached the wilderness; the reading and reciting by memory as he sat in the Court of the Women in his priestly robes; the tying of the scarlet cloth round the goat's horns;[2] the washing of hands and feet in golden bowls; and the multitude of the details to which the nation clung with fond devotion as representing the culminating splendour of the ritual with which they connected all their hopes of forgiveness.

It may be said that even now the impression of this high-priestly splendour on the great day (Yoma) is not exhausted. In the festival prayers still read for that day we read—

"Even as the expanded canopy of heaven was the countenance of the Priest."
"As the splendour which proceedeth from the effulgence of Angels was the countenance of the Priest."

He is compared to "the appearance of the bow in the midst of the

---

[1] The high-priestly duties were not only severe, but would be most trying, and even revolting, to any one who was not animated by deep religious feelings. When the tract *Pesachim* (f. 113, a) lays down the rule, "flay a carcase, and take thy fee, *but say not it is humiliating*, because I am a Priest, I am a great man;" this is doubtless a reminiscence of the days when families like the Boethusim were only anxious *to have had* the dignity, and so, like modern aldermen, to "pass the chair." The Rabbis long remembered with scorn and indignation the High-priest Issachar Kephar Barkai, who had *silk gloves* made for himself, that he should not soil his hands with the sacrifices! (Kerithoth, f. 28 b); and Elazar Ben Charsom, who wore a coat worth 20,000 minas, so thin that his brother priests forbade its use (Yoma, f. 35 b).   [2] Yoma, f. 66 b.

clouds;" to "a rose in the midst of a garden;" to "a garden of roses in the midst of thorns;" to "a star;" to "the golden bells in the skirts of the mantle;" to "the sunrise;" to "the congregation covered with blue and purple:" and to "the likeness of Orion and the Pleiades."[1]

EXCURSUS XIV.

THE IDENTITY OF "JOHN THE PRESBYTER" WITH "JOHN THE APOSTLE."

The majority of those who have questioned the authenticity of the Apocalypse have assigned it to a supposed younger contemporary of the Apostle, who, they say, was known in the early Church as "John the Presbyter." If it can be shown that the very existence of "John the Presbyter" is in the highest degree problematical, great additional force will be given to the already strong proofs that the Apocalypse, the Gospel, and the Epistles are indeed the work of the Evangelist St. John. In recent times the supposed existence of this "nebulous Presbyter" has been made an excuse for denying altogether the work and the residence of St. John in Asia.[2]

I have long doubted whether there ever was such a person as this "John the Presbyter," and I had arrived at this conclusion, and arranged my reasons for holding it, before I saw the paper of Prof. Milligan in the *Journal of Sacred Literature* for October, 1868.[3] The papers of Riggenbach (*Jahrb. für deutsche Theologie*, vol. xiii. p. 319), and of Zahn, in the *Studien und Kritiken* for 1866, I have not yet seen, nor Zahn's *Acta Johannis* (1880).[4] I have purposely abstained from consulting them in order that I might state my argument in my own way and as it occurred to myself. It will have been useful if it helps in ever so small a degree to get rid of "a shadow which has been mistaken for a reality," "a sort of Sosia of the Apostle, who troubles like a spectre the whole history of the Church of Ephesus."[5]

The question of the separate existence of a "John the Presbyter"

---

[1] See Hershon, *Treasures of the Talmud*, p. 200.
[2] Vogel, *Der Evang. Johannes*, 1800. Lützelberger, *Die kirchl. Tradition über d. Ap. Johannes*, 1840. Keim, *Gesch. Jesu von Nazara*, vol. i., p. 160, ff. Scholten, *Der Ap. Johan. in Klein-Azië*, 1871. Holtzmann, *Eph. und Kolosser-briefe*, 1872. On the other side see W. Grimm, *Johannes*, in Ersch and Grüber. Baur, *Gesch. d. christl. Kirche*, vol. i., pp. 82—147, etc. Krenkel, *Der Apost. Johannes*, pp. 133—178. Strauss, Schwegler, Zeller, Hilgenfeld, even Volkmar all reject the new theory. Renan (*L'Antéchrist*, pp. 557—589) only thinks that Scholten has succeeded in relegating the facts to a sort of penumbra.
[3] I differ from Prof. Milligan in his interpretation of the meaning of Papias.
[4] Subsequently to writing this paper I have read Zahn.
[5] Renan, *L'Antéchrist*, p. xxiii.

turns mainly upon the meaning of a passage of Papias, quoted by Eusebius, and upon the criticism of that passage by Eusebius himself.

Let us first see the passage of Papias.

In his *Exposition of Oracles of the Lord* (Λογίων Κυριακῶν ἐξήγησις) Papias had assigned to himself the task of preserving with his best diligence and accuracy, and of interweaving in his five books, the apostolic traditions which were still attainable.

"*I shall not scruple,*" he says, "*to place side by side with my interpretations all the things that I ever rightly learned from the Elders and rightly remembered, solemnly affirming their truthfulness.*" Then, after telling us that, unlike most men, he was indifferent to idle gossip and secondhand information, and sought for direct evidence as to the words of Christ, he adds: "*but if at any time any one came who had been acquainted with the Elders, I used to enquire about the discourses of the Elders—what Andrew or what Peter said* (εἶπεν), *or what Thomas or James, or what John or Matthew, or any one of the disciples of the Lord; and what Aristion and John the Elder, the disciples of the Lord, say* (λέγουσι). *For I thought that the information derived from books would not be so profitable to me, as that derived from a living and abiding utterance.*"[1]

The general meaning of this passage is clear. The good Bishop of Hierapolis tells us that he wished, in setting forth his "interpretations," to derive all the information he could from the fountain head. We learn from St. Luke himself that, before he wrote his Gospel, many had already attempted to perform a similar task, and the Evangelist evidently implies that he was dissatisfied with the majority of these efforts. It is a fair inference from the expressions which he uses that some of these narratives were founded on insufficient knowledge, and were lacking in carefulness. It is possible that these tentative sketches of the Gospel narrative—all of which have now perished—admitted apocryphal particulars or narrated true circumstances with erroneous details. Such documents would be sure to contain some contradictions, and would create much uncertainty in the minds of Christians. The Four Gospels were written in fulfilment of an imperative need. Now if imperfect or unauthorised works, such as the sketches to which St. Luke alludes, had come under the notice of Papias, he would naturally regard them with suspicion, and would feel that their uncertainties discredited their authority. He was indeed acquainted with the Gospels of St. Matthew and St. Mark, and perhaps, though I do not think that this can be

---

[1] As the question turns on the meaning of this passage, I append the Greek. οὐκ ὀκνήσω δέ σοι καὶ ὅσα ποτὲ παρὰ τῶν πρεσβυτέρων καλῶς ἔμαθον καὶ καλῶς ἐμνημόνευσα συγκατάξαι ταῖς ἑρμηνείαις διαβεβαιούμενος ὑπὲρ αὐτῶν ἀλήθειαν. Εἰ δέ που καὶ παρηκολουθηκώς τις τοῖς πρεσβυτέροις ἔλθοι τοὺς τῶν πρεσβυτέρων ἀνέκρινον λόγους· τί Ἀνδρέας ἢ τί Πέτρος εἶπεν ἢ τί Φίλιππος ἢ τί Ἰωάννης ἢ Ματθαῖος, ἢ τίς τῶν Κυρίου μαθητῶν, ἅ τε Ἀριστίων καὶ ὁ πρεσβύτερος Ἰωάννης οἱ τοῦ Κυρίου μαθηταὶ λέγουσιν. Οὐ γὰρ τὰ ἐκ τῶν βιβλίων τοσοῦτόν με ὠφελεῖν ὑπελάμβανον, ὅσον τὰ παρὰ ζώσης φωνῆς καὶ μενούσης.—Papias, ap. Euseb. H. E. iii. 39.

regarded as certain, with the Gospel of St. John.[1] But stories were floating about, such, for instance, as that respecting the death of Judas Iscariot, and that about "a woman accused before our Lord of many sins," which diverged more or less from the accounts in the Gospels. Papias felt that he would be rendering a service to the Church if he collected from eye-witnesses all the *authentic* information which could still be gathered as to facts. It was even more important to him and to the Church to learn the accurate truth about asserted *doctrines*. If "the books" to which he referred included, as Bishop Lightfoot has conjectured,[2] some of the mystic heresies and absurdities of the early Gnostics, they fully deserved the tone of depreciation in which he speaks of them. He was acting wisely in endeavouring to bring to a focus the last glimmerings of direct Apostolic tradition.

It seems then that he had long been in the habit—perhaps ever since his early youth—of gleaning from every available source the testimony of the Twelve Apostles. His book was probably written after the last Apostle was dead, and he considered that it owed much of its importance to the old traditions which he had gathered while it was yet possible to do so. In the passage which I have quoted he is not speaking of present times, but is referring to what he used to do in the days of his youth and early manhood.

Now certainly if Papias had been a careful modern writer, we should have inferred from this passage that the John mentioned in the first clause was a different person from the John mentioned in the second. In the first, he says, that it had been his habit to enquire from any who had known "the Elders"—of whom he especially mentions seven Apostles—what these "Elders" *said;* and also "what Aristion and John the Elder, disciples of the Lord, *say.*"

But although this would be the *natural* inference, it is by no means the *certain* inference. The antithesis may be between the past and present tense ("said" and "say") and not between two sources of original information. There is nothing to forbid the explanation that when Papias met any one who had known the immediate Apostles and disciples of the Lord—St. John among them—he made notes of what (according to his informant) these Elders said; but in writing this clause he remembers that, at the time when he was making his notes, two of the immediate disciples of the Lord were not dead but living: namely, Aristion—to whom, since he was not an Apostle, he does not give the direct title of "Elder"—and John, whom he identifies with those whom he has mentioned in the first clause by calling him, as he had called them, "the Elder."

---

[1] Eusebius does not quote any allusion of Papias to the Gospel of St. John, but in an argument prefixed to a Vatican MS. of the ninth century, we are told that he testified to its genuineness; and a quotation from "the Elders," in Irenæus, may be derived from Papias. Westcott, *On the Canon,* p. 77. It must be admitted that this evidence is somewhat shadowy.

[2] *Contemporary Review,* August, 1867, and August, 1875.

Certainly such a way of expressing himself would show that Papias was a man who wrote in a very simple and loose style; but this is exactly what we know to have been the case. It is true that, in one place, if the clause be genuine, Eusebius calls him "a man in all respects of the greatest erudition and well acquainted with Scripture."[1] But the genuineness of this eulogistic clause is very uncertain, since it is omitted in several manuscripts, as well as by Rufinus, and (which is important) in an ancient Syriac Version. Three chapters further on Eusebius tells us that Papias was "a man of exceedingly small intelligence, as one may infer from his own writings."[2] Such a man might easily write in a confused style. One at least of the passages which Eusebius quotes from the *Exposition* bears out his unfavourable opinion of the ancient bishop's ability. Nor are we left to form our judgment of his style solely on the opinion of Eusebius. Another of the passages which the historian quotes from Papias (and to which I have referred further on) is equally wanting in precision, and is therefore susceptible of more than one interpretation.

I. Now, first of all, no difficulty can arise as to the title given to St. John. Papias calls all the other Apostles "the Elders," and it is only natural to assume that he gives the same title to St. John in the same sense. The word "Elder," like the word "Apostle," had two different senses. In its ordinary sense it was applicable to many hundreds of persons, for it meant any Christian who was member of a Presbytery. But it had a *special* sense, in which it meant one who belonged to the earliest generation of Christians. In this sense it is constantly used by Irenæus, and is applied to Papias himself, though he was not a Presbyter, but a Bishop of Hierapolis, and though by the time of Irenæus the distinction between "Bishop" and "Presbyter," which is not found in the writings of the New Testament, had been gradually introduced. If the Second or Third Epistles of St. John be, as the Church has generally inferred, by the same author as the First, the case is strengthened for identifying "John the Elder" with "John the Apostle," for in both these Epistles St. John gives himself this very title. That it was in no sense inappropriate may be seen from the fact that St. Peter, in addressing Elders, calls himself their "fellow Elder."[3] Besides this, when used with the definite article, it would be a title of great significance, and yet would accord with the modesty and reticence which were habitual with St. John. There was no need for the last survivor of the Apostles to give himself the title of "Apostle," to which, in its loftiest sense, all men knew that he had an undisputed claim. He did not wish to assert his own immense authority. But in calling himself "the Elder" he used a term doubly impressive. He implies that he was an Elder in a peculiar sense, both

---

[1] ἀνὴρ τὰ πάντα ὅτι μάλιστα λογιώτατος. Euseb. *H. E.* iii. 36.
[2] σφόδρα σμικρὸς ὢν τὸν νοῦν ὡς ἂν ἐκ τῶν αὐτοῦ λόγων τεκμηράμενον εἰπεῖν. *Id.* iii. 39.
[3] 1 Pet. v. 1.

because he was entitled from his great age to respect and reverence, and also because he was raised above the rest of Elders by the dignity of his position as the last of the Twelve, and the last of those who could say "I have seen the Lord." So far, then, we see that, whether they were the same person or not, the John in the first clause and the John in the second are each characterised by two identical titles. Each is called an "Elder," and each is called "a disciple of the Lord." Surely if Papias had wished to describe two different persons he would have given some separate and distinctive title to the second and inferior John. It is a reasonable inference that Papias is only mentioning the same person twice over in an intelligible, though loose and inartistic, way, to distinguish between reports of his sayings which were brought to him when St. John was yet living and after he was dead.

But, besides this, I am far from sure that the sentence is not loosely constructed in another sense. By the figure of speech called zeugma, or rather, syllepsis, the same word, even in the most classical writers and in all languages, is often made to serve two purposes in the same sentence. A verb is often used with two clauses which is only appropriate to one of them, as in Pope's line—

"See Pan with flocks, with fruits Pomona crowned,"

where from the participle "crowned" we must understand the word "surrounded" to suit the first half of the line. In other instances we are compelled by the sense to borrow from one verb another which may be even opposite in meaning, as in St. Paul's—

κωλυόντων γαμεῖν, ἀπέχεσθαι βρωμάτων.[1]

"Forbidding to marry, [commanding] to abstain from meats," where from κωλυόντων (forbidding) we must understand κελευόντων (commanding) to suit the second clause.[2] It is then perfectly legitimate to understand Papias to mean that he *used to enquire* what Peter, John, etc., *said*, and when opportunity occurred *used to make personal notes* of what Aristion and John *say*.[3] What he derived from St. John would, if such were his meaning, have been of two descriptions, namely, (1) Reports of his conversations from others, and (2) Actual notes of his living testimony taken down in intercourse with the Apostle himself when Papias was young. And that Eusebius is not guilty of mere carelessness in interpreting him to mean that he actually heard "John the Elder" is, I think, shown by the words which follow, in which Papias, thinking mainly of his last clause, speaks of the importance of the "living and abiding voice." Indeed, he says in his opening sentence that some of his notes were derived from immediate intercourse with some of these

---

[1] 1 Tim. iv. 3, comp. γάλα ὑμᾶς ἐπότισα οὐ βρῶμα, 1 Cor. iii. 2.
[2] This is called *zeugma*; in *syllepsis* the same word is taken in *two different senses*.
[3] 'Ἀνακρίνω means "I examine," "sift," or "question."

"Elders" *as well as* (εἰ δὲ καὶ κ.τ.λ.) from trustworthy reports of what they had said to others.

There are, then, two strong arguments for construing the sentences of Papias as I have here proposed. They are all the stronger because they are both derived from Eusebius himself, though he may be called the original inventor of the theory about "John the Presbyter."[1]

(1.) One of these arguments is that Eusebius so construed the sentence. He indeed makes "John the Elder" of the first clause a different person from the "John the Elder" of the second clause; but he paraphrases the sentence thus: "Papias testifies that he had received the sayings of the Apostles from those who had been acquainted with them, but says *that he had been himself a hearer of Aristion and of John the Elder*." He has been accused of error and carelessness in thus understanding the sentence, but I think that I have shown his construction of it to be, so far, perfectly justifiable.

(2.) The other argument is that Eusebius, in an earlier book, the *Chronicon*, says without any hesitation, that *Papias was a hearer of St. John the Apostle*.[2] Now, that this was the truer and more unbiassed conclusion, seems clear on other grounds. I shall show later on that "the Elder" is quoted for statements which could hardly have come from any but an Apostle. And besides the ancient and frequent testimony that Papias had seen and conversed with St. John the Apostle, it would be inconceivable *à priori* that one who was searching for first hand and authentic testimony should never have taken the trouble to go from Hierapolis to Ephesus to consult an Apostle of the highest authority, who was then living at Ephesus as the acknowledged head of the Asiatic Church.

The argument, therefore, that Eusebius was more likely than we are to have known whether there was or was not a "John the Presbyter," and whether Papias was *his* hearer or the hearer of St. John the Apostle, because Eusebius possessed all the writings of Papias, and we do not, falls signally to the ground. Indeed, it tells the other way. In his *History* he *reasons himself into the belief* that Papias was only the pupil of "the Presbyter;" but he had all the writings of Papias in his hand when he wrote the *Chronicon*, and there he says, without any hesitation, that Papias was a pupil of the Apostle. "John the Presbyter" is the creature of Eusebius's later criticism. If he could have quoted from Papias a single other passage which in any way countenanced his existence, there would have been no need to base his existence upon a mere conjecture.

On the other hand, the belief that Papias really had seen and heard

---

[1] Dionysius of Alexandria had given a timid hint that there *might* have been such a person, but Eusebius, by a bold criticism, assumes that there was.
[2] So, too, Iren. c. *Haer.* v. 33. Ἰωάννου μὲν ἀκουστής, Πολυκάρπου δὲ ἑταῖρος γεγονώς. It is monstrous to suppose that Irenæus would use the simple word "John" if he only meant the Presbyter.

the Apostle St. John, rests not upon conjecture, but upon the distinct testimony of Irenæus, who says that Papias was "a hearer of John, and an associate (ἑταῖρος) of Polycarp."[1] Justin Martyr lays the scene of his dialogue with Trypho in Ephesus; and he quotes the Apocalypse as the work of the Apostle.[2] That the John intended is the Apostle—the only John of whom Irenæus knew anything—is sufficiently clear, because Irenæus, in his letters to Victor and to Florinus, distinctly says so.[3] Apollonius, Bishop of Ephesus, says that the Apostle lived at Ephesus, and wrote the Apocalypse.[4] Melito, Bishop of Sardis, must have held the same opinion, as is clear from the silence of Eusebius.[5] Apollinarius, who succeeded Papias as Bishop of Hierapolis, A.D. 170, and was therefore specially likely to be well informed, must have known that both Polycarp and Papias were hearers of the Apostle.[6] Jerome, in his *De Viris Illustribus*, says the same.[7] Till very recent times no one ever breathed a doubt that *Polycarp* had been a hearer of the Apostle, and had by him been appointed Bishop of Smyrna.[8] If, then, Polycarp was a hearer of the Apostle, there can be no difficulty in accepting the testimony that Papias, who was a friend and contemporary of Polycarp, had enjoyed the same peculiar privilege.

II. But now let us examine more closely the criticism of Eusebius[9] upon the passage of Papias. He says "that Papias mentions the name of John twice, and in the first clause places him with Peter and the rest of the Apostles, clearly indicating the Evangelist; but that in the second clause he ranks him with others who were not Apostles, placing Aristion before him, and he distinctly calls him 'an Elder;' so that even in this way he indicates the truth of the statements of those who have said that there were two who had the same name in Asia, and that there were two tombs in Ephesus, and that each is still called 'a tomb of John.' We ought to attend to these facts, for it is probable that it was the *second* John who saw the Apocalypse which passes under the name of John, *unless any one wishes to believe that it was the first.*"

It should be most carefully observed that Eusebius does not here profess to know anything whatever about this "John the Elder," and that he is not quite fair in saying that Papias calls him "*an* Elder." Papias did not call him "*an* Elder," but "*the* Elder," which may be a very different thing. Eusebius also fails to notice that the "John" of the second clause is described by exactly the same two designations as the John of the first clause, namely, as one of the "Elders," and as a

---

[1] Iren. *c. Haer.* v. 33. So too Œcumenius, on Acts ii.; Nicephorus, *H. E.* iii. 20; and Anastasius Sinaita (*Hexaem.* vii.), who calls him a pupil of the "bosom-disciple" (ὁ ἐπιστήθιος). See Routh, *Rel. Sacr.* i. 15.
[2] Just. M. *Dial.* 81.
[3] Iren. *c. Haer.* iii. 1, § 1, and *ap.* Euseb. *H. E.* v. 20—24.
[4] *Ap.* Euseb. *H. E.* v. 18.   [5] See Jer. *De Virr. Illustr.* 24.
[6] *Ap.* Euseb. *H. E.* iv. 27; v. 19. Jer. *De Virr. Illustr.* 26.
[7] Jer. *l. c. c.* xviii.
[8] Tert. *De Praescr. Haer.* v. 30.   [9] *H. E.* iii. 39.

"disciple of the Lord." Eusebius is only led to infer that there was a John who was not the Apostle, (1) by his criticisms of this single passage; (2) by the fact that "some" had said so; and (3) because these persons stated that there were still two tombs at Ephesus which were known by the name of John. And yet, after all, Eusebius is so little convinced by his own reasoning—he is so anxious "to steer between the Scylla and Charybdis of yes and no"—he sees that the evidence for the Apostolic authorship of the Apocalypse is so strong—that he is still obliged to leave the authorship of the book a matter of individual opinion. Whatever may be thought as to the ingenuity of his reasoning, Eusebius furnishes the most complete refutation of his own theory by the inability to produce a single grain of testimony or even of tradition in favour of the view that this separate "Presbyter" had ever existed.

Two questions then arise:—

α. Why was Eusebius so anxious to believe in the existence of this "John the Presbyter"?

β. Who were the "some" on whose testimony he relies?

α. The answers to both questions are very easy. Eusebius disliked the Apocalypse. He seldom quotes it. In one passage he refers to it as possibly (εἴ γε φανείη) spurious, and in another as possibly (εἴ γε φανείη) genuine, leaving the decision very much to the reader himself. He was extremely opposed to the fanatical and sensuous Chiliasm, which derived its sole support from this book; and on this very ground he was inclined to look down upon the old Bishop of Hierapolis, with his credulous stories and Judaic sympathies. If the millennial traditions which Papias had collected in his *Expositions* could be dissociated from the authority of the Apostle, and made to rest on that of an unknown and sub-apostolic personage, it would be more easy to set them aside.

β. As to the "some" to whom Eusebius alludes, they probably reduce themselves to Dionysius of Alexandria, just as the "some" to whom Dionysius himself alludes as disparaging the Apocalypse probably reduce themselves to the Alogi. At any rate, the only trace of any conjecture as to the existence of "John the Presbyter" previous to Eusebius, is in the famous criticism on the Apocalypse by Dionysius. In that criticism, preserved for us only by Eusebius,[1] the learned Patriarch of Alexandria says that it is clear from the testimony of the book itself that a "John" wrote the Apocalypse, but that instead of calling himself "the disciple beloved by the Lord" (as in the Gospel), or, "the brother of James," or "one who has actually seen and heard the Lord," which would have clearly indicated his individuality, he only calls himself "your brother and fellow in affliction," and "a witness of Jesus," and "blessed because he saw and heard these revelations." "Now I think," continues Dionysius, "that there have been many who

[1] *H. E.* vii. 25.

bore the same name as John the Apostle, who loved that designation out of their love and admiration and emulation for him, and because they wished to be loved of the Lord as he was; just as many children are named after Paul and Peter. Nay, there is even another John in the Acts of the Apostles, who bore the surname of Mark. I cannot say whether this be the John who wrote the Apocalypse, for it is not recorded that he went with them (Barnabas and Paul) into Asia; but I think that it was *some other John* of those who were in Asia, since some even say that there are two tombs in Ephesus, each of which is called 'the tomb of John.'"

If the "some" to whom Eusebius appeals include any one except Dionysius of Alexandria and those who had given him his information, we have at any rate no clue as to who they were. Had they been persons of special authority, or with special opportunities of knowing the facts, Eusebius would have told us something about them. And what does the evidence furnished by Dionysius amount to? *Not* (be it observed) to the statement that *there were two Johns*, but only that John was a common name, and that there were two tombs in Ephesus, each of which was pointed out by the local ciceroni as a tomb of John! He does not even pretend to imply that they were the tombs of *two* Johns. On the contrary, each was asserted to be the tomb of the Apostle.

III. Could any reader of modern German criticisms believe that beyond this we know absolutely nothing about John the Presbyter, as distinct from John the Apostle?[1] And how utterly baseless a foundation is this for such a superstructure! Dionysius wrote about the middle of the third century,[2] when John had been laid in his grave for at least a century and a half. There is no tradition worth the name as to the place and manner of the Apostle's death, and in the absence of authentic information it was believed or assumed that he died at Ephesus. Since this was the common belief, it was quite natural that the Christians who visited Ephesus should ask to be shown the grave of John.[3] Now the duplicate sites of many other "holy places" in Palestine and elsewhere show that if, in a case where there was no certainty, *one* supposed grave was pointed out, it was a very likely result that there would be *two*. The two graves were merely rival sites for a spot which, if either of them were genuine, would be full of interest. Yet, on grounds so slight as these, Dionysius—who, though he speaks reverently of the Apocalypse, could not persuade himself that it was the work of the Apostle—first infers that there were two Johns;

---

[1] No importance can be attached by any one to the guess or invention of the *Apostolical Constitutions* (vii. 46), that the Presbyter succeeded the Apostle as Bishop of Ephesus.

[2] He succeeded to the Presidency of the Catechetical School at Alexandria in A.D. 231.

[3] Similarly the "trophies" of Peter and Paul were pointed out at Rome as early as the days of the Presbyter Gaius (A.D. 213).

and, secondly, that one of them may have been sufficiently famous to be the author of the Revelation.

That Dionysius is merely clutching at a theory is proved by his half suggestion that the author may have been John Mark the Evangelist; a suggestion in which, so far as I am aware, he has had scarcely a single follower for 1,500 years.[1]

But, further than this, his suggestion proves a great deal more than he intended by it. This second John, if he existed at all, must have been an exile in Patmos, and a person of such immense and acknowledged influence as to be able to address the Seven Churches of Asia with almost more than Apostolic authority. But, as we can now prove, the Apocalypse was written about A.D. 68; and if John the Presbyter at that time exercised so powerful a sway over Asia, then there is little or no room left for the work of John the Apostle. Polycrates, Bishop of Ephesus (A.D. 196), spoke of John the Apostle and Philip[2] as the two great lights of Asia;[3] but if John the Presbyter is the exile of Patmos and the author of the second and third Epistles, he must have been, on the evidence of these writings, a "light of Asia" whose splendour was much more powerful than that of Philip, and so bright as to make the name even of the Apostle grow somewhat pale.

If the Presbyter wrote the Apocalypse, a large part of the evidence for the Asiatic residence of St. John falls to the ground. This is the actual result arrived at by Scholten, Lipsius, Keim, and other Dutch and German theologians, who fall back on an unauthorised and dubious quotation from Papias by Georgius Hamartolos, to the effect that John the Apostle was martyred by the Jews. Dionysius shows no trace of such wild conclusions, though they would naturally spring from his own conjecture; and, as for Georgius Hamartolos, we have the less scruple in setting aside his supposed quotation, because none of his predecessors for eight centuries know anything about it, and because in the very same sentence he has flagrantly mis-stated the known opinion of Origen.[4]

IV. Keim dwells much on the fact that little or no mention is made of the Asiatic work of St. John till the close of the second century. It is not mentioned, he says, in the Acts of the Apostles, nor in the Ignatian Epistles, nor in Polycarp's letter to the Philippians, nor in the letter of the Churches of Lyons and Vienne. The answer to this difficulty, if it be one, is twofold. It is that, in the first place, there was no special reason why it should have been mentioned in any

---

[1] The only exceptions are Beza and Hitzig. Beza, *Prolegom. in Apoc.* p. 744. "Quod si quid aliud liceret ex stylo conjicere, nemini certe potius quam Marco tribuerim, qui et ipse Joannes dictus est" (Lücke, *Einleit. in d. Offenbar.* p. 780). Hitzig, *Ueber. Joh. Markus*, 1843.

[2] The Apostle, not the Deacon (Euseb. *H. E.* iii. 39).

[3] Polycr. *ap.* Euseb. *H. E.* iii. 31; v. 24. See Routh, *Rel. Sacr.* p. 369.

[4] Georgius Hamartolos not only quotes Papias for the assertion that St. John had been martyred by the Jews, but says that Origen thought so to, which is the reverse of the fact (Orig. *in Matt.*).

one of these documents; and that, in the second place, the "argument from silence" is always a most untrustworthy way of attempting to throw doubts on facts for which there is positive evidence. Are we to doubt the existence of Milton or of Jeremy Taylor—of Bacon or of Shakspeare—because these contemporaries make no allusion to each other in their voluminous writings? Humboldt points out that in the archives of Barcelona there is no trace of an event so important as the triumphal entry of Columbus; in Marco Polo's travels no mention of the wall of China; in the archives of Portugal no allusion to the travels of Amerigo Vespucci.[1] Michelet, in his *History of France*, states that the two chief historians of the Sicilian Vespers make no mention whatever of Procida, though he was undoubtedly the chief mover in that terrible event.[2] The *argumentum ex silentio* may be set aside as wholly unimportant. Moreover, in this instance it is singularly inappropriate, since it tells with redoubled force against the very existence of any separate "John the Presbyter," who is passed over in still profounder silence by all sources of information alike.

It is quite certain that such an hypothesis as the denial of John's work in Asia would have appeared absurd to Dionysius. He was probably in possession of a stronger and more detailed tradition on the subject than we are. At any rate, he would not have listened for a moment to the supposition on which this recent theory depends. It requires us to believe that Irenæus (A.D. 180) *actually confounded John the Apostle with John the Presbyter!* Such a supposition is—I fear it must be said—utterly absurd. Irenæus repeatedly refers to "John," and "John the Lord's disciple," and fortunately it cannot be asserted that he is referring to this second John, because in one passage he expressly calls him "John the disciple of the Lord who leaned upon his breast, and himself published the Gospel while living in Ephesus of Asia."[3] There is in Irenæus no trace of any other John; nor was there any such trace in the writings of Polycrates, Bishop of Ephesus, or Apollinarius, Bishop of Hierapolis—two persons who were eminently likely to be well informed about the history of the Christian Church in those two cities. Irenæus tells us that Polycarp had been the disciple of St. John, and had always referred to him about disputed questions, and had felt for him an unbounded reverence. Now Irenæus too was of Asiatic origin, and knew the traditions of Ephesus. He had himself been a hearer of Polycarp, and has left a most graphic description of the manner in which the old man used to demean himself. And yet we are asked to believe that when he calls Polycarp "a hearer of John" he mistook John the Apostle for John the Presbyter, though of this John

---

[1] *Gesch. d. Geogr.*, vol. iv., p. 160.
[2] Varnhagen von Ense, *Tagebücher*, vol. i., p. 123. These two instances are quoted by Krenkel, *Der Ap. Johan.* p. 139.
[3] See Iren. *c. Haer.* ii. 22, § 5; iii. 1, § 1; iii. 3, § 4; v. 30, § 1; 33, §§ 3, 4; and ap. Euseb. *H. E.* v. 24.

the Presbyter there is not so much as a tradition, however faint, until we come to the middle of the third century; and no trace even then except a vague report that there were at Ephesus two graves known as graves of John! But St. Jerome furnishes us with conclusive evidence of the extremely valueless character of this grain of supposed fact in the ever-widening ocean of theory. He says (*De Viris Illustr.*) that " another tomb is shown at Ephesus as the tomb of John the Presbyter, ALTHOUGH SOME THINK THAT THEY ARE BOTH TOMBS OF JOHN THE EVANGELIST"! Had it not been for dogmatic reasons, it is probable that no one would have thought anything else.

There is overwhelming evidence that John the Apostle spent many of his last years in Asia. It is one of the most unanimous and best supported of Church traditions, and it can be traced in a continuous sequence of evidence from the days of those who were his contemporaries, and had enjoyed his personal intercourse. That there was any John the Presbyter *distinct* from the Apostle, there is no evidence whatever. For to say that a second-hand report about two graves in Ephesus is any evidence, is idle. We should never have heard a word about these two graves, or at any rate, *this* is not the inference which would have been drawn from them, if Dionysius had not disliked to attribute the Apocalypse to St. John, and if Eusebius, in common with many others, had not felt a scarcely concealed desire to get rid of the book altogether. But if this imaginary " Presbyter " wrote the Apocalypse he must, on the showing of the book itself, have been a very great man indeed, and one whose position enabled him to adopt a tone more authoritative than was adopted even by St. Paul. Is it conceivable that of such a man there would not be so much as a single other trace except the report of a dubious grave conjecturally assigned to him a century and a half after he was dead?

The ancient Fathers, both Greek and Latin, were not to be misled either by the specious suggestion of Dionysius, or by the bold assertion of Eusebius more than seventy years afterwards. Neither of these great writers found any one to follow them in their theoretic inferences from the loose clause of Papias. The Fathers had the works of Papias in their hands, and knew that he had nowhere disintegrated the individuality of the one and only "John," whom the Church would understand to be referred to when that name was mentioned. They also had in their hands the Acts of Leucius, which are probably the chief source of Johannine traditions; and it is clear from the silence of Eusebius and Dionysius that there the Presbyter had no existence. Accordingly, Apollinarius, Anastasius Sinaita, Maximus, and many others, go on repeating that Papias was a hearer of *John the Apostle*, without so much as noticing that there was anything doubtful in the passage out of which Eusebius has conjured his shadowy Presbyter.

V. But some will say, have we not two Epistles which profess to emanate from "John the Presbyter"? Undoubtedly we have, and this is one of the strongest evidences that "John the Presbyter" was no other than "John the Apostle," for as St. John nowhere claims his Apostolic authority, he would least of all be likely to do so in two private notes to otherwise unknown individuals; notes which do not contain a single item of importance except where they exactly coincide with the thoughts, and indeed the actual words, of the First Epistle; notes which no separate "John the Presbyter" could possibly have written unless his mind were an echo of the Apostle's as well as his name. The Apostle calls himself "the Presbyter" in these little private letters, because the title sufficiently indicated his personality as the aged Head of the Asiatic Churches, and as one who belonged to a past epoch.[1] No other designation would have been so simple, so dignified, and so suitable. And most certainly Papias was not influenced by this circumstance; for while he was acquainted with the *First* Epistle of St. John, he does not seem to have known of the existence of the Second or Third.

VI. But the use of this designation, "the Elder," is further illustrated by Papias himself. He prefaces one of his oral traditions with the words, "These things *the Elder* used to say." We have seen that he used the word "Elders" in its narrower sense as synonymous with "Apostles." He meant by the term those who were the oldest and most venerated sources of tradition. He certainly would not have given this specific title to any one who belonged only to the second generation, and who would therefore have been a contemporary of his own. By "the Elder" he has been always and rightly understood to mean John, who, as the last survivor of the Apostolic band, was "the Elder" κατ' ἐξοχήν. He does not give this title to Aristion, though he too was a living witness of facts connected with the life and ministry of Christ.

Again, the remarks ascribed to this intensely venerated "Elder" are such as we can hardly imagine that any one short of an Apostle, and such an Apostle as St. John, would have had authority to make. For instance, the Gospel of St. Mark is universally believed to have been written under the guidance of St. Peter. The numerous graphic and vivid touches in which it abounds, as well as many other circumstances, lend probability to this tradition. Now who is the original authority for this belief? None other than "the Elder" himself. He informs Papias that "Mark having become the interpreter of Peter, wrote accurately all that he (Peter) related."[2] But, such being the case, what ordinary disciple, even of the first generation, would have

---

[1] I do not refer to the parallel case of St. Paul calling himself "the aged" in Philemon 9, because the word πρεσβύτης may there mean "an ambassador."

[2] Euseb. *H. E.* iii. 39. Μάρκος μὲν ἑρμηνευτὴς Πέτρου γενόμενος ὅσα ἐμνημόνευσεν ἀκριβῶς ἔγραψεν. The words may mean, "Wrote accurately all that he (Mark) remembered;" or. "all that he (Peter) related" (Westcott, *On the Canon*, p. 74). Here, again, we notice the ambiguity of the style of Papias.

ventured to criticise *ex cathedra*—to criticise as though from the standpoint of wider and more intimate knowledge—a gospel which rested on the authority of the Chief of the Apostles? Surely there was no living man who would have ventured to do this, unless he were one whose opportunities of information were greater even than those of St. Peter? Yet "the Elder" does so. He informed Papias that though St. Mark wrote truthfully, to the best of his remembrance, he did *not* write the events of Christ's life and teaching in "chronological order" (οὐ μέντοι τάξει). Now this we should have thought, apart from the Fourth Gospel, is exactly what St. Paul does. But yet "the Elder" is right, because the Elder is none other than the Apostle and the Evangelist. He can speak even of St. Mark in a tone of superiority, as of one who "neither heard the Lord nor followed Him." He knew, as perhaps no other man knew, that the Synoptic Evangelists were but imperfectly informed as to the events and discourses of that ministry in *Judæa*, as apart from Galilee, which it was his own special privilege to make known to the world. Hence he can even venture to say of St. Peter himself, that "he used to frame his teachings with reference to the present needs of his hearers, and not as making a connected narrative of the Lord's discourses." What mere secondary Presbyter would have spoken in terms of such familiarity and even equality of "the Pilot of the Galilean Lake"? In such criticisms do we not hear unmistakably the accents of an Apostle?

VII. There is, so far as I can see, but one slight objection to the arguments which I have here stated. It is that, if our conclusion be correct, Papias mentions *Aristion* in the same breath with St. John the Apostle, and even puts Aristion's name first.

I fully admit that this mention of Aristion is perplexing. Of this Aristion we know absolutely nothing.[1] It is startling, and it is a little painful, to find Papias referring to him as an eminent contemporary witness to the truth of the Gospel narrative, when we can give no information whatever respecting him. He is a *nominis umbra* and nothing more.

So strongly has this been felt that some—and among them Renan—suppose, that instead of "the disciples of the Lord" in the second clause of the passage of Papias, we ought to read "*the disciples of disciples* (μαθηταὶ μαθητῶν) of the Lord," and that the word μαθητῶν—which would relegate Aristion and "John the Presbyter" to the second generation of disciples—has dropped out by the clerical error known as *homœoteleuton*. Another suggestion is, that the name of John in the *first* clause is simply interpolated. But since neither Eusebius nor any one else knew or dreamt of such readings, the conjectures merely rest on foregone conclusions. If we may thus tamper with ancient authors,

---

[1] There is no authority for the assertion of the *Apostolical Constitutions* (vii. 46), which speaks of his martyrdom, and connects him with the Church of Smyrna.

we may make them say anything that we please. Moreover, a person who belonged to the *second* generation of disciples would not have furnished the sort of authority which Papias required. To that second generation he himself may be said to have belonged, for he was a contemporary of the daughters of Philip, and (as we have seen reason to believe) had talked in his youth with John the Apostle. What he wanted for the purposes of his *Expositions* was oral testimony derived at first hand from the original sources.

I have sometimes thought, and still think, that Aristion is a name which conceals some well-known person.[1] The Jewish Apostles commonly bore two names; one among their own countrymen, and one for use among the Gentiles. There is nothing to forbid the supposition that the otherwise unknown designation may in reality refer to some Apostle or Apostolic man who, like St. John and St. Philip, had taken refuge in Asia from the storm of persecution and calamity which had burst over Judæa, and who was known at Hierapolis by the Greek name Aristion. If this very reasonable and moderate supposition be allowed, all difficulty vanishes. What Papias then means to say is, that long before he wrote his book it had been his habit to gather all he could about the statements of the Apostles, whom he calls "Elders" —and among them about the statements of John—from those who had seen them; and that he also took notes of the living "oracles" furnished to him *directly* by Aristion (who was evidently well-known to Papias's readers) and even—which is the reason why he keeps the name to the last as being the fact which he most wished to emphasize—by "John the Elder;"—the same John—ὁ ὤν—the only John of whom any one knew anything—who so long survived his brother Apostles, and to whose *indirect* testimony Papias has just referred.

VIII. We have then sifted to the bottom the whole of the so-called evidence for the existence of a "John the Presbyter" who was not John the Apostle.

It is—

1. A passage of Papias, capable of a quite different interpretation, and which seems to have received a quite different interpretation, not only for a full century after he was dead, but also (in spite of Eusebius) in subsequent times.

2. A hesitating and tentative guess of Dionysius, rising solely from his avowed inability to regard the Apostle as the author of the Apocalypse.

3. Some dubious gossip (φασὶν) about two tombs at Ephesus, which, if trustworthy at all, was believed by some to be due to an attempt to reconcile the inventions of rival guides.

---

[1] When I wrote this I was entirely unaware that Krenkel, in his *Der Apostel Johannes*, p. 117, had been led to make exactly the same conjecture. *Pereant qui ante nos nostra dixerunt!* Polycrates tells us that John and Philip were at this time the "two great lights of Asia." If "Philip" were not a Greek name, one might have suspected that Aristion was a local name borne by Philip.

4. Eagerness on the part of Eusebius to support this inverted pyramid of conjectures, out of positive dislike to the Apocalypse caused by the abuses of Millenarians.[1]

"Only this, and nothing more"! And these are the grounds on which we are now asked to set aside the direct or indirect testimony of Papias,[2] of Justin Martyr,[3] of Polycarp,[4] of Polycrates,[5] of Irenæus,[6] of Apollonius,[7] of Clemens of Alexandria, of Origen, of Melito,[8] of Andreas, of Arethas, and, in fact, of unbroken Church tradition, and to assign the works of the last and one of the greatest Apostles to an obscure and dubious Presbyter! It is on this evidence—so late and so tottering—evidence based on an awkwardly expressed but perfectly explicable passage of Papias, a simple writer who had no pretence to subtlety of intellect or grace of style—and on a professed quotation from Papias in the ninth century by Georgius Hamartolos, who, in the very same sentence, attributes to Origen an opinion which his own writings show to be false—that some critics have ventured to rewrite the history of the first century; to assert, in spite of overwhelming evidence, that the Apostle St. John never was in Asia at all; that Polycarp never saw him; that the John for whom Polycarp expressed so profound a reverence was only a "Presbyter" who, like himself, belonged to the second generation of Christians; that Irenæus was mistaken in supposing that Polycarp meant the Apostle when he only meant the Presbyter; that, if this be thought impossible, the letter of Irenæus to Florinus must be regarded as a forgery;[9] that this "Presbyter," whose very existence was only conjectured a century later, is quoted as an oracle by Papias; that Polycrates, himself Bishop of Ephesus less than a century after John's death, made the same preposterous mistake which is attributed to Irenæus;[10] and that nebulous as he is, unknown as he is to early writers, utterly as every fact about him has perished, the "Presbyter" was still the author either of the Gospel and Epistle, or of the Apocalypse, or of the Second and Third Epistles, or of all these writings alike. *Credat Judæus Apella—non ego!*

---

[1] Speaking of the "certain strange parables and teachings of the Saviour, and certain other somewhat mystical things," which Papias recorded, "from unwritten tradition," Eusebius specially mentions "some millennium of years after the resurrection from the dead, during which the kingdom of Christ shall be established bodily upon this earth.
[2] *Ap.* Anastas. Sinaita. *Hexaem.* i. (Routh, i. 15).   [3] *Dial. c. Tryph.* 81.
[4] *Ap.* Iren. etc., and Euseb. *Chrom. ad Olymp.* 220.
[5] See Jer. *de Virr. Illustr.* xlv.; Euseb. *H. E.* v. 26 (Routh, i. 372).
[6] *Ap.* Euseb. v. 20, etc.   [8] Euseb. *H. E.* iv. 26.
[7] Euseb. *H. E.* v. 18.
[9] This entirely baseless suggestion of Scholten does not at all help his cause, for, apart from the letter to Florinus, the testimony of Irenæus, in his great work, *Contra Haereses*, is quite distinct.
[10] Scholten sets aside the testimony of Polycrates, because he calls John "a priest wearing the *petalon*." But (1) It is by no means impossible that St. John, who, at one period, was so fond of symbols, may have adopted this symbol to express the truth which he so prominently states (Rev. i. 6; v. 10). (2) It is not clear that Polycrates, in this highly rhetorical passage, meant his words to be taken literally. (3) Even if he did, he may have been misled by giving a literal meaning to some metaphor of St. John.

But the impugners of St. John's Asiatic work raise one or two chronological difficulties. They say that if Irenæus knew Polycarp, who knew St. John, all three must have attained to extraordinary longevity. The longevity need not have been very unusual. Tradition has always supposed that St. John reached extreme old age. Supposing that he died as early as A.D. 90, and that Irenæus wrote about A.D. 180, then, as M. Renan remarks, the difference which separated the two would be the same as that which separates us from the last years of Voltaire. Yet, without any miracle of longevity, M. de Rémusat had often conversed about Voltaire with l'Abbé Morellet, who had actually known him. If the martyrdom of Polycarp took place, as Mr. Waddington seems to have proved, about A.D. 155,[1] Polycarp was then 86 years old. Consequently he must have been born in A.D. 69, and would have been at least 21 years old when St. John died, and there is no difficulty in the supposition that Irenæus, as a boy, had seen and known a man who had conversed with the Apostle who had laid his head on Jesus' breast.

A credulous spirit of innovation is welcome to believe and to proclaim that any or all of St. John's writings were written by "John the Presbyter." They were: but "John the Presbyter" is none other than John the Apostle.[2]

---

[1] *Mém. de l'Institut*, xxvi. 235.

[2] This argument has already been printed in the *Expositor*, because I wished to subject it to the test of criticism. Some of my arguments about the "Beast" and the "False Prophet" have, for the same reason, appeared in the same admirable journal. I am allowed, by the kindness of Messrs. Hodder and Stoughton, to use the same material here.

INDEX.

Aaron the first High Priest, as described by the son of Sirach, 616.

Abel—an example of faith, 253; subject of his dispute with Cain, 257; murdered by his brother, 550; referred to in the Book of Enoch, 597.

Aben Ezra respecting the identity of Melchizedek, 217.

Abgar, king of Edessa, 48.

Abarbanel and others respecting the tables in the Ark, 231.

Abraham—the test of his faith, 328 et seq.; known throughout the East as "The Friend of God," 336; his example as adduced by SS. Paul and James, ibid.; Talmudic legend as to his integrity, 357.

Absalom—a scurrilous epithet of the Talmud, 215.

Accsius (Bp.)—his views on mortal sin, 186.

Adam—a Kabbalistic inference drawn from the name, 197.

Adelphotheos, 270—278, 300, 324.

Advent, the Second, certain vagaries respecting, 432.

Aciperthenia defined and discussed, 274, 275.

Ælia Capitolina and the abrogation of Judaism, 297, 491.

Agapæ or Love-feasts, 111.

Agrapha dogmata, or sayings of Christ unrecorded in Holy Writ, 397.

Agrippa I.—his antipathy to the Christians, 299, 311; the patron of Ishmael ben Phabi, 344.

Agrippina—daughter of Germanicus, 14; born at Cologne, ibid.; married (1) to Cn. Dom. Ahenobarbus, by whom she became the mother of Nero, 15; banished to Pontia, ibid.; married (2) to Crispus Passienus, 16, and (3) afterwards to her uncle the Emperor Claudius, ibid.; she procures the Imperial adoption of Nero her son to the prejudice of Britannicus the heir-apparent, 17; she poisons her husband, 19, and claims the Imperial purple for Nero, 20, who dignifies her as "the best of mothers," ibid.; her life unsuccessfully attempted, 25; her eventual assassination, 27.

Akhiva—a noted Jewish Rabbi, his martyrdom by the Romans, 336, 352.

Alexander the Great—his patronage of the Jews, 139.

Alexandria—its geographical advantages, 139; its synagogue, the Diaplenston, ibid.; its Sanhedrin, 140; its artificers and the Temple at Jerusalem, ibid.; its epoch-making literature, 140, 141; the Septuagint 141—144; the writings of Aristobulus, 144 et seq.; the so-called "Wisdom of Solomon," 145; and Philonic literature, 146 et seq.; its part in paving the way for Christianity, 153; its Catechetical School, 154; its antidote to Gnostic mysteries, 155; its theosophy, 155 et seq.; its views on Inspiration, 158; its influence on the Pauline Epistles, 159, 160; other contributions to Christianity, 169; its indebtedness to Plato, 174; Barnabas regarded as the founder of the Church at, 184; Apollos a native of, 187; certain Jews of, burned alive, 253; Heb. xi. 37, a possible allusion thereto, ibid.

Alexandrianism, indications of, in the writings of SS. John and Paul, 51.

Aliturus, the court-jester of Nero, a proselyte to Judaism, 36, 477.

Allegory and its developments, 156 et seq.

Alphæus identified with St. James in the Church of England Scripture lessons, 270; but contra-distinguished by the Greek Church, ibid.

Altar of Incense and the Holiest Place, 613 et seq.

Amalthea's horn (the cornucopia) mentioned in the Septuagint, 143.

Amhaarets—its definition, application, &c., 365, 572.

Anagram of malediction upon the name Jesus, 215.

Andreas (Bp.)—his Comment on the Apocalypse, referred to, 468.

Andrew, St.—his missionary travels and martyrdom, 47.

Aneling—a practice of the early Church, provided for in the first Prayer Book of King Edward VI., 317.

Angel of Death—his inability to take the life of Moses, 129; his place in Rabbinic angelology, 199; his adventure with R. Simeon ben Chelpatha, 343; and with R. bar Nachman, 497.

Angels—the Fallen, Enoch's mission to them, 130; their sin as traditionally recorded, 133, 599; the Ministering, their service at Sinai, 257; the angelic heptarchy, 132.

Annas the younger, and his martyrdom of James, 302; himself massacred by his own co-religionists, 306; and his remains dishonoured, 306, 422.

Antar, an Arabic poem, quoted, 199.
Antichrist—the rise of, 10; identified with Nero, 11, 411; of Old Testament Apocalypse, 33, 411; a term peculiar to St. John, 514 *et seq.*
Antilegomena, or disputed books of Scripture, 122, 576. (See also *Homologoumena*.)
Antinomianism—a travesty of St. Paul's teaching, 50.
Antioch, and the origination of the term Christian, 82.
Antiochus Epiphanes the Antichrist of Daniel, 33, 411.
Apocalypse of St. John the Divine—not the *latest* book of the New Testament Scriptures, 405; dates next in order to the Synoptic Gospels, 407; its originating circumstances, 410; Nero depicted, 411; persecution of the Christians, 411, 412; outbreak of the Jewish war, 412 *et seq.*; siege of Jerusalem, 413; other historical surroundings, 414—428; its reception, 420 *et seq.*; the various schools of interpretation, 431 *et seq.*; their theories discussed in detail, 432—437; the letters to the seven Churches, 438—440; the Apostolic Twelve, 440; invectives against heretics, 441, 442; misapplied by the Rationalists, 443; the seals, *ibid.*; the first seal, 444; the second and third, 445; the fourth, 446; the fifth and sixth, 447; the sealing, 448, 449; the seventh seal, 449; the seven trumpets, 450; detailed with historic illustrations, 451—460; forecast of the doom of Jerusalem, *ibid.*; the wild beast from the sea, 461—467; identified with Nero, 467 *et seq.*; the mystic number χξϛ, 468—474; the False Prophet, &c., 474 *et seq.*; illustrations from Roman history, 479—483; the vials, 483 *et seq.*; fall of Jerusalem, 486—489; end of the old dispensation, 490; abrogation of Judaism 491 *et seq.*
Apocalyptic literature—Apocalypse of Baruch, 397, 428; of Esdras, 402, 428; of Peter, 100. (See also *s.v. Enoch*.)
Apocryphal gospels—the Protevangelion, 278; gospel to the Hebrews, 291; gospel of the Infancy, 278; gospel of Joseph, 278; gospel of Nicodemus, 458; gospel of Peter, 501; gospel of Thomas, 279. (See also *s.v. Epistles.*)
Apocryphal writings attributed to St. John, 491; Ascension of Isaiah, 456, 467, 480; Ascension of James, 297; Ascension of Moses, 129, 132; the Assumption of Moses, 600.
Apollonius, Bishop of Ephesus, 624.
Apollos—the probable author of Hebrews, 51; acquainted with Philonian philosophy, 154, 168; his method of interpretation, 169; compares favourably with that of Philo, 169—171; contrasted with that of Paul, 172—182; ten qualifications for writing such an Epistle, 183 *et seq.*; all exemplified in Apollos, 186; sketch of his character, *ibid.*; notices of him and his work in New Testament, 186 *et seq.*; his native place and early home, 187; no hint that he ever visited Rome, 190; last Scriptural mention of his name, 191. (See *s.v. Hebrews.*)
Apostasy as regarded by the compiler of the Mishnah, 238.

Apotheosis of Claudius Cæsar, 21; of Caligula and Nero, 466; of the Roman Emperors generally, 479.
Aquila and Priscilla, their departure from Rome, 12.
Aquila—his Greek version of the Old Testament, 119; accredited with the authorship of Hebrews, 184.
Aratus quoted by Paul, 134.
Archangels—Jude and John the only New Testament writers who mention them, 132; the SEVEN according to Apocryphal books and the Talmud, *ibid.* (note); the hierarchy according to IV. (II.) Esdras, 194.
Aretas, king of Arabia, his adventure with the High Priest Ishmael, 226.
Aristeas and the origin of the Septuagint, 141.
Aristion, as mentioned in the writings of Papias, 619 *et seq.*
Ark and tables of the Covenant, 229 *et seq.*
Arminian perversions of Scripture, 212.
Arthur and King John, a parallel from Roman history, 23.
Asinarii—a satirical term applied to the early Christians, 38, 82; the Jews similarly slandered, 38, 230.
Atonement, Day of—as regarded by Barnabas, 59; its paramount place in Judaism, 181; Rabbinic ceremonies, 614 *et seq.*; impressions on Jewish minds, 615 *et seq.*; its connexion with the overthrow of Judaism, 617; traditional reminiscences, *ibid.*
Augurs and auguries, their prevalence, 476.
Augustus—his part in the play of life, 10; import of his name, 464; his aversion to deification, 466; his edicts against sorcerers, 476.
Aulus Plautius and Christianity in Britain, 33.
Aureum Quinquennium of Rome, 22.
Autos da Fé and Te Deums, 338.
Avodath Hakkodesh—a Kabbalistic work, quoted, 220.
Azazel and the scapegoat of Jewry, 239, 614, 617.

B.

Babylon—covertly referred to by Jeremiah, 472; figuratively applied in 1st Epistle Peter, 595, 596.
Balaam—legend of, alluded to in the Septuagint and the Targum, 68; his apostasy, 102; compared with the impious and false, 110; with evildoers generally, 111; how slain by Phinehas, 143.
Bammidbar Rabba—a Rabbinic commentary on Numbers, 422.
Barcochba—a false Messiah of the Jews, his aversion to Christians, 36; shares in their persecution and massacre, 491.
Barnabas—his Epistle, its drift and tone, 53; publicly read in the church, 56; its marked inferiority to the canonical scriptures, 56; Alexandrian proclivities, 58 *et seq.*; its Kabbalistic vagaries and heretical tendencies, 59; quoted or referred to, 58, 59, 86, 186.
Bartholomew—his mission-work and martyrdom, 47.

Basilical Synagogue at Alexandria, 139; said to have been the grandest in the world, the glory of Israel, 140.
Bath Kol, or voice from heaven, 295.
Berenice, Queen—her intercession for the Jews, 48.
Bereshith Rabba—a Rabbinic commentary on Genesis, quoted or referred to, 142, 217, 218, 221, 489, 513, 613.
Beruriah—the wife of Rabbi Meier, her praiseworthy advice, 572, 573.
Blood—no remission without, parallel from the Talmud, 236.
Brethren of the Lord, 124 *et seq*.
Burning of Rome—possible reminiscences in Peter's Epistle, 37.
Burrus (Afranius)—a partisan of Agrippina, 18; by her made Prætorian Prefect and guardian of the youthful Nero, 20; his influence for good over his ward, 21; his reprehensible laxity in certain matters, 22; his compromise, 26; poisoned by order of the Emperor, 28.

C.

Cæsar. (See distinctive names.)
Cæsarian race—its premature mortality, 11, 13.
Cain—his parentage according to the Rabbis, 550.
Caligula, or Nero, covertly alluded to by Paul, 436.
Calvin's perversions of Holy Writ, 211, 212.
Camel and needle's eye explained, 213.
Carthage, Councils of, 100, 307.
Catacombs at Rome, 10, 59, 92.
Catholic—definition of the term, 51.
Catholic Epistles—Gregory of Nazianzus upon, 578.
Cato the Younger—his character described, 549.
Centre of the earth from a Rabbinic point of view, 230, 298.
Cerinthus—a Judæo-Christian heresiarch, 114; the immorality of his system, 135; taught in Asia, 391; accredited by Dionysius of Alexandria with the writing of the Apocalypse, *ibid.*; the earliest of the Christian Gnostics, 395; the story of his death at Ephesus, 396; his heretical views and legendary associations, 500–503.
Charlemagne and the pirate Norsemen, 116.
Chiliasts, or Millenarians, 50.
χξϛ, the mystic symbol for 666, 470.
Chrestos and Christos, an interesting paronomasia, 86.
Chrestus—a perverted form of Christus, 12; notion that Chrestus was a seditious Roman Jew, *ibid.*; Chrestian, a parody upon the term Christian, 95; possibly alluded to by Peter, *ibid.*
Christ—name ironically turned to Chrestus, 12; styled Christus by Tacitus, 34; his life and work objectively treated in the Synoptic Gospels, 49; but subjectively treated by John, *ibid.*; scarcely alluded to by James, 73; his example, sufferings, death, resurrection, and ascension dwelt upon by Peter *ibid.*; his mission to the spirits in prison, 77–80, 94, 95; the Desposyni descendants of the family at Nazareth, 123–125; the redemptive scheme, 178, 179; the atonement, 180; Christ superior to angels, 194–196; pre-eminent to Moses, 200; his high priesthood, 203, 204; above that of the Levites, 205; and of Melchizedek, 225; various points of supremacy, 240–242; his atoning blood, 243; his perfect obedience, 244, 244; recapitulation of the phases of superiority, 244 *et seq.*; the Second Advent, 480; end of the Mosaic dispensation, 490; abrogation of Judaism, 491; a denier of Jesus is Antichrist, 503; knowledge of Christ is life eternal, 511; doctrine of the Logos (the Divine Word) considered, 512. Disguised references to Christ in the Talmud and Rabbinic writings, 596.
Christendom and heathendom contrasted, 59, 60.
Christians not brought into collision with the Imperial government until Nero's time, 11; the Neronian persecution, 33 *et seq.*, brought on through jealousy, 36; Jewish malice its primary cause, 37; regarded by the world as a debased Jewish sect, 82; the name Christian originated at Antioch, *ibid.*; spoken against everywhere, *ibid.*; taunted as renegades and apostates, 192; took refuge at Pella in prospect of the fall of Jerusalem, 388, 412, 461; persecuted by the pseudo-messiah Barcochba, 491.
Christianity—a *religio illicita* at Rome, 67; how regarded by Pliny and Tacitus, 82; its relations to Judaism, 167; its superiority to Philonian philosophy, 169; more ancient than Judaism, 173; referred to Abraham by Paul, *ibid.*; and to Melchizedek by Apollos, *ibid.*; a reversion to Judaism the worst kind of apostasy, 174; in what its pre-eminence consists, 175–178; Judaic Christianity pre-disposed to Pharisaism, 303; the Sadducees its most pronounced opponents, *ibid.*
Christology of Paul, of Apollos, and of John, 178.
Chrysostom, his noble resolution in prospect of exile or martyrdom, 93.
Cities of the Plain—their overthrow, 129, 131.
Claudius—his edict for the expulsion of the Jews from Rome, 12.
Cleanthes, the Stoic philosopher, his death by suicide, 9.
Clemens of Alexandria—his account of Peter's family, 73; in favour of 1st Epistle Peter, 67; his literary labours referred to, 79, 93, 100, 121, 135, 154, 156; on the Pauline authorship of Hebrews, 180; unacquainted with the Epistle of James, 307; his story of John and the robber, 399–401; the martyrdom of the Apostles, 403.
Clemens of Rome—his epistle publicly read in the church, 56; syncretism of the writer, 57; his catholicity, theology, and mistaken notions, *ibid.*; the evidential value of his writings, 58; Bishop of Rome, 65; speaks more of Paul than of Peter, *ibid.*; though said to have been ordained by the latter, 66; his definition of Faith, 76; makes no reference to 2nd Epistle Peter, 99; his various writings mentioned, 118–121; the Book of Wisdom and Hebrews known to him, 178; accredited by some with the authorship of the latter, 185; made use of Epistle of James, 307; quota-

tion from his writings, 343; his record of Peter's martyrdom, 594.
Clementine Homilies and Recognitions—the product of Ebionites, 53; their disfavour of visions, 118; their polemic character, 322; their animus against Paul, 350; allusions to Peter's connections with Rome, 594.
Cleopas an abbreviation of Cleopater, 269.
Cleopatra, the wife of the Procurator Florus, a friend of the Empress Poppæa, 417.
Clopas, Chalpai or Alphæus, 269.
Coincidences (undesigned) between the narrative of Acts and the writings of James, 326.
Comforter—true meaning of word so rendered, 536; Talmudic adoption and use of the original Greek word, *ibid.*
Commandments, the Ten—Philo's idea of their utterance by God, and the rest of the Law by angels, 194; Talmudic notion that the first Commandment only was spoken by God, and that the others were uttered by angels, 198.
Compassion deprecated by the Romans, 9.
Confession in sickness a Jewish as well as a Christian ordinance, 347.
Cornelius à Lapide—his summary dealing with heretics, 588.
Cremation—the Empress Poppæa's objection to, 36.
Crispus Passienus, the father-in-law of Nero, 16.
Cromwell and the doctrine of final perseverance, 211.
Crurifragium—a Roman custom, described, 379.
Crusades, referred to, 372.
Cryptographs—Jewish and Christian, 46, 215, 408, 596.
Custom—its force in Rabbinic Judaism, 160.

D.

Daniel—Book of, known to Peter, 85; his prediction of the fate of Rome, how treated in Josephus, 487.
Days—the ten penitential days of modern Judaism, 238.
Debarim Rabba—a Rabbinic commentary on Deuteronomy, 343.
Deification of Poppæa, the murdered wife of Nero, 9.
Descent into Hades, 93—95.
Desposyni, The, or relations of the Holy Family, 123 *et seq.*, 278.
Diaspora—the Hellenistic designation of the dispersed Jews, 84, 325. (See also *Galootha*.)
Diatheke—classical sense of the word, its use in a twofold sense in the Hebrews, 234, 235; Rabbinic adoption and use of the word, 235.
Dikaiōma—in judicial and scriptural nomenclature, 177.
Dionysius of Alexandria, 625—627.
Divorce—the first on record in the annals of Rome, 5.
Domine, quo vadis? 63.
Domitia—aunt and guardian of Nero, 15; her neglect of her charge, *ibid.*; incurs the jealousy of Agrippina, 19; accused of sorcery and doomed to death, *ibid.*
Domitian—his adventure with the Desposyni, the grandsons of Jude, 123 *et seq.*; his banishment of John to Patmos, 407 *et seq.*
Domitius Ahenobarbus, father of Nero, his character, his ominous saying at the birth of his son, his impeachment, and the confiscation of his property, 15.

E.

Ebionites—an early heretical sect, 50; claimed the authority of James, 52; attempt to calumniate Paul, 64; their views and practices, 498 *et seq.*
Emperors of Rome—their autocratic position, 4; their moral characteristics, 11; premature death, 453; their deification, 466, 472.
Encaenia—the Feast of Dedication, 235.
Enoch, Book of—referred to by Peter and Jude, 111 *et seq.* (See also *Excursus IV.*, 597, 598; and Index of Quotations and References.)
Ephesian robber—a legend of the early Church, 399.
Ephesians, Epistle to—its style, 104; its influence upon 1st Peter, 105.
Epictetus, the Stoic philosopher, saying quoted, 247.
Epimenides, Aratus and Menander, Paul's quotation of, 134.
Epiphany at Sinai—how represented in the Septuagint, 144.
Epistles, the Catholic, 51. (See also under respective names.)
Epistles, Uncanonical—of Barnabas, 38, 39, 86, 198; of Clemens, 57, 58; of Ignatius, 216, 496, 531, 590; of Polycarp, 440, 529. (See also *s.v. Hermas.*)
Ethnic inspiration exemplified in Socrates, Plato, &c., 158 *et seq.*; in heathen literature generally, 174.
Euripides—Nero's significant comment upon a verse of, 30.
Eusebius' quotation of a non-extant passage of Josephus, 304.
Eutropius concerning the burning of Rome, 29.
Exodus—a term used for death in Josephus, the Book of Wisdom, and by Peter, 114.

F.

Faith—as defined by Peter, 75; by Clemens, 76; by Paul, *ibid.*; by the Author of Hebrews, 176; by Philo Judæus, 177; Patristic views of, 328; Abraham's faith as described in Rabbinic history, 357.
Famine at Rome, *temp.* Claudius, 445; another in time of Otho, *ibid.*; at Jerusalem during the final siege, *ibid.*
Fast—the consummate, of the Jewish Calendar, 237; the bi-weekly fast of New Testament times, *ibid.*
Felix—Roman Procurator of Judæa, 16.
Festus, the Procurator, befriends Paul, 12; his official character relatively considered, 302.
Filioli diligite alterutrum—favourite words of John, 403, 592.

Final perseverance, 211, 212, 248.
Forbidden books of Jewry, 284.
Foundation-stone of the world, 230.

G.

Gaius (Caligula)—his animosity to the Jews, 12.
Gaius of Corinth, and others of same name, discriminated, 589.
Galatians, Epistle to—its style relatively considered, 104; its date, 311.
Gallio, the Proconsul—his refusal to convict Paul, 12.
Galooths, The—the Aramaic designation of the dispersed Jews, 84.
Gamaliel I. counteracts the avarice of the priests, 314; interferes on behalf of the Apostles, 382.
Gamaliel II.—his characteristic compromise at the baths of Ptolemais, 396.
Ghetto or Jewry—of Ancient Rome, 12; of Alexandria, 139.
Gematria—the term explained, 468; various exemplifications, 58, 238, 468—472.
Gerizim—its place in the Samaritan cult, 183.
Germanicus, grandfather of Nero, 13; his tragic end, 14.
Gladiatorial shows at Rome, 6; of Nero's time with Christian victims, 39 et seq.
Gospels, the Synoptic—mainly present the historical aspect of Christ's life, 49; their fragmentary nature, ibid.; John's Gospel deals with subjective aspects mainly, ibid.; James never mentions the Gospel, 52; the Gospel preached to the dead, 77—79.
Gospels, the Uncanonical. (See Apocryphal Gospels.)
Gracchi, the mother of—referred to, 147.
Graffiti, or caricatures, at Pompeii, 89.
Greek proverb addressed from Heaven to Paul, 156.
Greek versions of the Old Testament. (See Aquila and Septuagint.)
Greek wisdom and the Palestinian rabbis, 141; how regarded by the Babylonian Jews, 142; its effect on Judaism generally, 174.
Gregory of Nazianzus alone among Christian writers after St. John worthily styled "The Divine," 437; his views as to the Catholic Epistles, 576.

H.

Habakkuk—his summary of the precepts, 248.
Hades—Christ's descent into, 93—95.
Hagadah and Halachah, their occurrence in the Septuagint, 143; both alike familiar to the writer of the Hebrews, 237; compiled by Rabbi Judah, forming the Mishnah, 281; how regarded by the rabbis, 295.
Hagadistic traces in Jude, 52, 129 et seq., 132—134, 263, 598—600; in Paul, 159; in Hebrews, 171 et seq.; not any to be found in James, 284.
Hapax legomena in 1 Peter, 73; in 2 Peter, 103 et seq.; in Jude, 131; in Hebrews, 193; in James, 319.

Heathendom, its salient features, 9; contrasted with Christianity, 59, 60.
Hebrew unknown to Philo Judæus, 146.
Hebrews, Epistle to—the work of Apollos, 51; an expression of Alexandrian Christianity, ibid.; a link binding us to the Church of the Jewish Fathers, 157; not written by Paul, 159—162; attributed to him in the superscription in the English Bible, ibid.; and twice so referred to in the Prayer Book, ibid.; its resemblance to Pauline writings considered, 163; its dissimilarity thereto, 164—166; its theological scope, 166, 167; its dealings with the relations of Christianity and Judaism, 167; its marked Alexandrianism, 168, 169; coincidences to Philonian literature, 169—171; topical detail, 172—182; account of the author, 187 et seq.; to whom addressed, 189, 190; where written, 191; outline, 191, 192; analysis, with literal version and commentary, 193—264; subjects embraced: Christ's supremacy, 194—197; man's position, 198; mission of Christ, 199; Christ above Moses, 200 et seq.; exhortation to prompt acceptance, 202; priesthood of Christ and Melchizedek compared and contrasted, 203—225; the Levitic priesthood and its service superseded, 226, 227; the new covenant, 228; the Tabernacle and its symbolic furniture, 229—232; Christ their antitype, 233, 234; the Day of Atonement, 237—240; Christ the true high priest, 240—242; summing up, 243—246; danger of apostasy, 247, 248; faith defined and exemplified, 248—253; final admonitions, 254—264.
Herculaneum and its relics, 2, 4.
Heresy defined, misconceptions considered, 494.
Hermas, a post-apostolic writer—his works, "The Pastor," &c., quoted or referred to, 96, 99, 327, 338, 342, 398, 454.
Herod Agrippa and the murder of James, 292, 383.
Hesiod—his story of the imprisoned Titans, 129.
Hexameter verse in the New Testament, 255, 328.
High Priests under the first and second Temples compared, 181 et seq.; degradation of the office, 206; mere nominees of the rulers, ibid. (See also Ishmael ben Phabi, Joshua ben Gamala, Simon son of Onias, &c.)
Hillel and Shammai, the accredited leaders of Jewish thought in the time of our Lord, 281, 282, 288.
Hippo, Ecclesiastical Council of, 100.
Holy of Holies—Caligula's attempt to profane, 12; Pompey's surprise thereat, 239; how often entered by the high priest on the Day of Atonement, 240.
Homologoumena, or admitted books of Holy Writ, 530.
Hymn, early Christian, quoted, 45.

I.

Icarus—his alleged attempt to fly, 40; dramatized on the Roman stage, ibid.; Balaam

640 INDEX.

and Simon Magus said to have perished in a similar manner, 63.
Idolatry—St. John's warning against the *latest* written words of the New Testament, 406.
I.H.T. in Judæo-Christian symbolism, 58, 469.
Incarnation, The, as restricted by Apollos, 167.
Infanticide—its prevalence in Imperial Rome, 7; contrary to contemporary Christian usages, 50.
Insulæ, or lodging-houses of ancient Rome, 3.
Irenæus—his strange assertion as to the age of our Lord, 398.
Isaac and his substitute—a Rabbinic legend, 132.
Isaiah—his martyrdom under Manasseh, 253.
Ishmael the High Priest—his decade of office, 314; stigmatised as taking after Phinehas (son of Eli) *ibid.*; raised to the pontificate by Agrippa, 344; his disqualifying adventure on the Day of Atonement, 226.
Isidore, Bishop of Seville, respecting the Epistle to Hebrews, 161; anecdote of the poisoned chalice, 388 *et seq.*; his statement as to the age of John the Divine, 403.
Isopsephia, or *equi-numeral* interpretation, 468. (See also *Gematria* and *Kabbalah*.)

J.

Jacob's blessing—circumstances of, strangely perverted in the Vulgate, 252.
Jaddua—the last historic personage of the Old Testament narrative, 1:39.
James—his relationship, 265—279; the home at Nazareth, 280 *et seq.*; his training, 281—283; his acquaintance with the Scriptures, 283; with uncanonical literature, 284; his religious status, 285, 286; his early opinions of Jesus and His mission, 287—289; his conversion to Christianity, 290; Bishop of Jerusalem, 292; presides at the Synod, 294 *et seq.*; his part in the Gentile controversy, 295; decision respecting proselytes, 296; his martyrdom, 302, 304; Rabbinic legends, 305 *et seq.*; and traditional details from Apocryphal Gospels, *ibid.*, note.
James, Epistle of—"the Gospel" never mentioned, 52; its indebtedness to Sermon on the Mount, 284, and to post-biblical literature, *ibid.*; authenticity of the Epistle, 307; date, 310, 311; historic surrounding, 312—314; genius, 315 *et seq.*; style, 319 *et seq.*; topical analysis, 320, 321; aim, 322 *et seq.*; character, 323; the valedictory expression of Hebrew prophecy, 323, 324; literal version with explanatory notes, 324—349; faith and works, 350, 355—357; Abraham's example, 358; comparison with other Apostolic writings, 360, 361.
Jeremiah—his death by stoning, referred to, 253.
Jerusalem—"the centre of the earth," a Rabbinic conceit, 230, 296; fall of the city, 487—490; Ælia Capitolina built upon its ruins, 491; its fall an epoch in history, 542.

Jerusalem, the New, 486; legendary detail, *ibid.*, note.
Jesus Christ. (See *Christ*).
Jesus son of Ananus—his warning cry and tragic fate, 306.
Jesus son of Gamala—same as Joshua ben Gamala (*q.v.*).
Jesus son of Pandera—a disguised reference to Jesus Christ in the Talmud, 305.
Jesus son of Sirach—author of "Ecclesiasticus," a work well-known to James, 284; prohibited by the Rabbis, *ibid.*
Jews detested by Gaius (Caligula), 12; Claudius orders their expulsion from Rome, *ibid.*; futility of the edict, 34; not involved in the Neronian persecutions and massacres, 35; sworn enemies of the Christians, 36; proselytes in the Imperial palace, *ibid.*; promise Nero the kingdom of Jerusalem, *ibid.*; their religion privileged at Rome, 37; their malice, the secret of the first Christian persecution, *ibid.*; patronized by Alexander the Great, 139; befriended by the Ptolemies, 140; certain of Alexandria burned alive, 253; revolt in Judæa, 415 *et seq.*, and its spread throughout Palestine, 418; epidemic of massacre, 419 *et seq.*; Josephus' opinion that the Jews were ripe for destruction, 426, 454; fall of Jerusalem, 486—490; Ælia Capitolina built upon its ruins, 491; Jews denied admission, *ibid.*; their religion abrogated, *ibid.*
Jochanan ben Napuchah—his temporising compromise, 142.
Jochanan ben Zaccai foretells the destruction of the Temple, 239.
John—one of the three Pillar-Apostles, 363; his religious majority synchronous with the insurrection in Galilee, 366; a key to his impetuous spirit, *ibid.*; and patriotic bias, 367; a disciple of John the Baptist, *ibid.*; his call by Jesus, 369; his characteristics, 370; ambitious request of his mother, 374, 375; his intimacy with Jesus, 376; at the cross, 378; entrusted with care of the mother of Jesus, *ibid.*; at the sepulchre, 379 *et seq.*; with "the eleven," 380; revisits Galilee, *ibid.*; in the Temple at Jerusalem, 381; before the Sanhedrin, 382; saved by the interference of Gamaliel I., *ibid.*; scourged, yet persisting in preaching "the Word," 383; once only mentioned in the Pauline Epistles, 384; his Judaic sympathies, 384, 385; absence of further mention in Scripture, till at Patmos, 386; his exile, *ibid.*; his work, 387, 391; the *Apocalypse* (*q.v.*) of prior date to his *Gospel* and *Epistles* (*q.v.*), 392; legendary anecdotes, 394—400; death of John, 592; his extreme old age, 634.
John, Epistles of — the last utterances of Divine Revelation, 53.
John, First Epistle of—its object and outline, 525; contents, 527, 528; structural peculiarities, 529; authenticity, 530; topical analysis, literal version, and comment, 531—574.
John, Second Epistle of — its authenticity discussed, 575 *et seq.*; Kyria to whom addressed, whether an appellative or a proper name, considered, 577—579, 581—583; topical analysis, literal version, and notes, 583—586.

John, Third Epistle of—Gaius to whom addressed, 589; object and aim, 589, 590; literal translation and notes, 590, 591; salutation, 591 et seq.
Josephus—inimical to the Christians, 36; a renegade Pharisee, 37; his eulogy of the abandoned Poppæa, ibid.; date of his writings, 103; verbal resemblances to Peter's second Epistle, 107; his use of Rabbinic *hagadoth* (anecdotes, &c.), ibid.; re-writes Jewish history for Roman readers, 145; his "Jewish War," originally in Aramaic, 189; the untrustworthiness of his writings, 306; his impeachment of the priesthood, 344; acts as Governor of Gamala, 420; his military services, 421; his character, 422; his treatment of Daniel's prophecy affecting Rome, 437.
Joshua ben Gamala acquires the High Priesthood by purchase, 303, 314; massacred by his co-religionists, 422, 459.
Judah the Holy, the compiler of the Mishnah, 281; biographical anecdotes from the Talmud, 2.5, 401 et seq.
Judaism a *religio licita* at Rome, 35; friends at court, 36; inimical to Christianity, 37; as understood by Philo Judæus, 168 et seq.; its spirit re-animated by secular inspiration, 176; its quasi-deification of the priesthood, 181 et seq.; abrogated, 491; its developments, 496.
Judas of Galilee, his insurrection, 366.
Jude, Epistle of — work of a non-apostolic writer, 51 (and 124); freely utilises Jewish *hagadoth* and Apocryphal literature, ibid.; compared with Peter's second Epistle, 110–112; its evident priority thereto, 113, 120; story of the Desposyni, his grandsons, 123; their adventure with Domitian, ibid.; family connexions of Jude, 124, 125; compared with Paul, 127 et seq.; literal version and commentary, 128–131; style considered, 131; structural peculiarity, 132; allusions to secular literature, 132–135 et seq.; its aim, 135 et seq.
Justin Martyr — his mistake about Simon Magus, 64, 499; charge against the Jews for tampering with the Septuagint, 142; his statement as to contemporary Jewish opinions, 352; his views respecting Antichrist, 443.

K.

Kabbalah—a species of Rabbinic exegesis, 155, 427, 500. (See also *Gematria* and *Isopsephia*.)
Kapparah, the substitutionary sacrifice of modern Jews, 240 et seq.
Kedar, tents of, and the scattered nation, 65.
Kenites, their part in the temple services, 296, 304.
Kephas-party at Corinth, 49. (See also s.v. *Peter*.)
Keren Happuk quaintly represented by Amalthea's Horn in the Septuagint, 143.
King, a provincial title of the Emperors of Rome, 90; disfavoured by the Romans generally, 431.
Kitzur Sh'lu, a Kabbalistic *epitome* of the

(Two Tables of the) Law, quoted 172, 200, 395.
Knowledge and Wisdom, compared and contrasted, 338.
Koheleth (Midrash) and the story of Moses' terror at Sinai, 256.
Korah — the *Way* of, 131; reproached by Moses, 206.
Kyria, in Second Epistle of John—whether an appellative or a proper name, considered, 577—579, 581—583.

L.

Laodicæa, Ecclesiastical Council of, 100, 405.
La Scala—the traditional retreat of John at Patmos, 393.
Last words, The (chronologically), of the New Testament, 406.
Latest historic name of the Old Testament narrative, 139.
Law of Moses—as regarded by Peter and by James, 52; its delivery on Sinai, 256; Rabbinic legends concerning, alluded to in the Acts and Hebrews, ib'd.; further detail from the Talmud, 257; its supersession, ibid.
Legendary traces in the Septuagint Version, 143.
Lex Papia Poppæa, and its connexion with Roman morals, 5.
Liturgy—Scriptural use of the word, 288; its classic meaning, ibid.
Locusta the poisoner, a paid agent of Nero, 14; her part in the murder of Claudius, 19.
Luther—on the authenticity of the Epistles, 55; as to the authorship of Hebrews, 161, 187; endorses the Jewish opinion concerning Melchizedek, 220; respecting James, 309; on justification by works, 355 et seq.; misquotes Romans (iii. 28), 361; on the Apocalypse, 430.
Lysias—his timely interference on behalf of Paul, 12.

M.

Maccabees, Books of, referred to in Hebrews, 342.
Maimonides—his "Moreh Nevochim," quoted, 294; the "Yad Hachazakah," quoted, 617.
Maranatha, 108, 429.
Marcion the Gnostic and Polycarp, 396, 586.
Marcionism, a perversion of Paul's teaching, 50.
Marcus, the first Gentile Bishop of Jerusalem, 297.
Marcus Aurelius—his view of Christianity, 89; his writings referred to, 315.
Maria del Popolo, The Church of, its superstitious connexion with Nero, 41.
Maries, The three, at the cross, 378.
Mark the Evangelist—referred to by Peter, 62; his indebtedness to Peter, 70; intimate with Paul, 73; interpreter to Peter at Rome, 318; accredited with authorship

of Apocalypse, 390; and with the founding of the school of Alexandria, 154.
Marriage—regarded with disfavour at Rome, 5; extreme views, 7; honoured and consecrated by Christianity, 60, 162; disparaged by the Essenes (a Jewish sect), 258; the Apostles not celibates, 363, 402.
Martineau's "Hours of Thought," quoted, 10.
Martyrdom, Era of, marked by the Apocalypse, 410.
Mary, the hostess of the Apostles at Jerusalem, 292.
Matthew—his mission and martyrdom, 47.
Melancthon, concerning Hebrews and Paul, 162.
Melchizedek—his priesthood, 205; historical account confined to two verses of Genesis, 217; traditional details from the Midrash, 218; as regarded by Philo Judæus, 219; of unknown parentage, ibid.; attempted identifications, 219 et seq.; his relative greatness, 223; his priesthood superior to that of the Levites, 225; but inferior to that of Christ, ibid.
Menander, the Greek poet, 134.
Messalina, wife of Claudius, 14; mother of Britannicus and Octavia, 16; her attempt upon Nero's life, and her wretched end, ibid.
Messiah greater than the patriarchs, &c., 192.
Messiahs, The false, 415, 491.
Metatron, a Rabbinic anticipation of Messiah, 219, 221, 303.
Michael the Archangel and the body of Moses, 111, 119, 120, 129, 132.
Midrash Koheleth, a Rabbinic commentary on Ecclesiastes, 256, 305.
Milton's "Paradise Lost," quoted, 569.
Minim, the appellative of Christians in the Talmud and Rabbinic writings, 305.
Ministering Angels—their office at Sinai, 256, 257.
Montanists and post-baptismal sins, 256.
Monotheism and Jewish thought, 336, 352.
Montanus, the nominal founder of an early Christian sect, 158.
"Moreh Nevochim" (Guide of the Perplexed), a work of Maimonides, 294.
Moses—legend of his death, 129 (see also 111, 119, 120, 132); the *Ascension of Moses*, an apocryphal work, quoted by Jude, 137; Moses the Good Shepherd, an anecdote from the Midrash Shemoth, 401.
Motto of the Alexandrian School, 155.

N.

Nazarenes, a Judæo-Christian sect, 407.
Nero—son of Agrippina and Ahenobarbus, 14; his parents banished, 15, and he consigned to the care of his aunt Domitia, ibid.; his bad training, ibid.; his life unsuccessfully attempted by the Empress Messalina, 16, who shortly afterwards is assassinated, ibid.; his mother then marries the Emperor, her uncle, ibid.; betrothed to the princess Octavia, 17; his mother's ambitious intrigues, 18; she poisons the Emperor, 20, and places Nero upon the throne, ibid., under the tutelage of Burrus and Seneca, ibid.; the early years of his reign are favourable, 21 et seq.; his liaison with Acte, a Grecian odalisque, 22; he quarrels with Agrippina, 23; poisons his brother-in-law, the rightful heir to the throne, 24; contracts a *mésalliance* with Poppæa Sabina, the wife of a boon companion, 25, who prompted his worst crimes, including the murder of his mother, 25, 27, and eventually meets her death from a kick by Nero, 28; suspected of the burning of Rome, 29, but he charges the incendiarism upon the Christians, 33, 34, and mercilessly persecutes them, 38, with cruel æstheticism making them act as the *tableaux vivants* of his realistic plays, 39, 40; justly regarded as the Antichrist, 41; saluted as THE SAVIOUR OF THE WORLD, ibid.; the Romans revolt, 42, 43; he ignominiously flees the city, 43, and commits suicide, 44.
Neropolis—its connexion with the rebuilding of Rome, 30.
New Year's Day and its solemnities, as observed by the Jews, 238.
Nicene Creed mis-read in the churches, 194.
Nicodemus, Gospel of, quoted or alluded to, 77, 458.
Nicolas the Deacon, 398.
Nicolaitans incur the indignation of John, 135; their origin and development, ibid.; the error of Irenæus as to their founder, 398, 441.
Nishmath Chayim quoted for a remarkable Messianic inference, 197.

O.

Octavia—daughter of Claudius, 16; married to Nero, 17; present when Nero poisoned her brother, 24; banished to Pandataria, 28; assassinated by order of her husband, ibid.
Onias' Temple at Leontopolis, thought by some to be "the Temple" referred to in Hebrews, 183, 225.
Origen—the greatest of the Christian Fathers, 155; his peculiar exegesis, 156; his opinion concerning Hebrews, 160; also respecting Ep. James, 307; his account of the banishment of John, 409, and Peter's crucifixion, 594.

P.

Paetus Thrasea a noble Stoic, 9; put to death by order of Nero, 28; his character sketched by Tacitus, 549.
Paganism—its decadence, 8.
Pantheon at Rome, 12.
Papyrus, the paper of John's Epistle, 584.
Paraclete—its adoption in Rabbinic writings, 325; its classic sense and patristic use, 535.
Paradise, its symbolic application by the Rabbis, 155.

Parashah and Haphtarah, as read in apostolic times, identified, 141.
Parousia, The, of early Christian anticipation, 108.
Pascal, noteworthy saying, quoted, 331.
Patmos, the exile home of John, 394 et seq.
Patristic views as to the authorship of Hebrews, 603, 610.
Paul—humanely treated by the politarchs of Thessalonica, 12; protected from the Jews at Corinth by Gallio, brother of Seneca, ibid.; delivered from the plots of the Sanhedrin at Jerusalem by Lysias and Festus, ibid.; his appeal to Cæsar, and his residence in Rome, ibid.; indications of Alexandrianism in his epistles, 51.
Pella—the refuge of the early Christians, 388; its geographical position, 412; massacre of Jews at, 419; present identification, 461.
Penates, or household gods, 17.
Peregrinus, Death of, a tract by Lucian illustrative of the Neronian persecutions, 238.
Peter—short sketch of his history, 60, 61; autobiographic touches in his Epistles, 62; his daughter Petronilla, ibid.; his wife's martyrdom, 63; further details from tradition, 64, 65; his connexion with Rome, 65 (and 594), his crucifixion, 66; his primacy considered, 593.
Peter, First Epistle of—approximate date, 67; characteristic features, 68; Gospel reminiscences, 69, 70; influence of Paul and James, 71—73; originality of the author, 73; subject-matter, 74—76; Gospel to the dead, 77—80; conciliatory tone of the Epistle, 80, 81; historical circumstances, 82; keynote of its teaching, 83; to whom addressed, 83, 84; acquaintance with Book of Daniel, 85; topical analysis, 86—95; acquaintance with Book of Proverbs, 95; closing admonitions, 96; salutation, 97.
Peter, Second Epistle of—its distinguishing peculiarities, 97; canonicity, 98; external evidence as to authenticity, 99; patristic testimony, 100, 101; outline of contents, 102; singularities of style and expression, 103—105; points of similarity to Josephus, 107 et seq.; contrasts, 108; coincidences to Jude, 110—113; authenticity discussed, 114; internal evidence, ibid.; date, 115; superiority to other contemporary writings, &c., ibid.; summing up of evidence, 116; new translation, with running comment, 117—122.
Petronilla, a daughter of Peter, 62.
Philemon, Probable date of Epistle to, 7.
Philo Judæus—the most celebrated of the Alexandrian writers, 145; his ignorance of the Hebrew scriptures, 146; his views and opinions, ibid.; his priestly origin, ibid.; and family connexions, 147; his wife and her noteworthy saying, ibid.; his visit to Jerusalem, and his political services, ibid.; not a Christian, as traditionally reported, ib d.; but helped to pave the way for Christianity by his literary labours, 148; his peculiar exegesis of Holy Writ, ibid.; his influence on Apostolic writings, 150 et seq.; his philosophy embodied in the Alexandrian School (see s.v. Alexan-

dria), 153; its part in the development of Revelation, 153, 154 et seq.; his influence on the writer of Hebrews, 170 et seq.; specimens of Philonian allegory, 6 0—602; Philo's views about the Logos, 602, 603; coincidences between the works of Philo and the Epistle to the Hebrews, 611 et seq.
Phinehas, "the seventh from Jacob," 130.
Phinehas, the son of Eli, referred to representatively, 314.
Phœnix—accredited by Tacitus, the Roman historian, 57; used illustratively by Clemens, ibid.
Phylacteries, their exalted sanction, 497.
Pilate—the story of his letter to Tiberius concerning the Crucifixion, 11.
Pilgrimage feasts of Judaism—Hillel's decision respecting, 282; taken occasion of for re-visiting Jerusalem, 293.
Pirke Rabbi Eliezer on the death of Isaac, 252.
Plato—a notable example of ethnic inspiration, 158; his influence on Philo Judæus, ibid.; and indirectly on Christianity, ibid.; his works quoted or alluded to, 104, 174, 349.
Plautus' "Epedicus," quoted, 335.
Pliny—his letter to Trajan, 67; his views as to Christianity, 85, 89.
Pompeii—its relics, 2; its sarcastic graffiti, 82.
Pompey's desecration of the Temple of Jerusalem, 229.
Pomponia Græcina—her possible connexion with Christianity, 33.
Poppæa Sabina—wife of Marcus Otho, transferred to Nero, 25; her baneful influence, 28; a proselyte to Judaism, 36; possibly connected with the persecutions of the Christians, 37; eulogised by Josephus, though Tacitus and Suetonius are unable to praise her, ibid.; premature death from a kick by Nero, 28.
Post-baptismal sins, 211.
Prayer, Efficacy of, 347.s
Prayer Book—its acknowledgment of Paul as the writer of Hebrews, 162, 163.
Primacy of Peter considered, 593.
Prodigality of Imperial Rome, 3, 4, 92.
Proselytes at the court of Nero, 36; inimical to Christianity, 37; injurious to Israel, 46.
Proverbs, Book of, familiar to Peter, 92, 95.
Ptolemy Philadelphus and the Septuagint, 140.
Pudens, a senator of Rome, 63.
Punishment, its disciplinary aim, 95.
Pythagorean Mysteries, 147, 150.

Q.

Quadratus and his reminiscences of John the Divine, 403.
Quartodecimans—observers of the 14th Nisan as Easter, 391.
Quirinus (Cyrenius) and the insurrection in Galilee, 360.
Quotations from Greek poets in the New Testament, 134; from Rabbinical writings, see s.v. Talmud, and respective names.

R.

Rabbinic account of the pattern of the Tabernacle, 175.
Rabbinism defined and estimated, 365.
Ruca, its interpretation and use, 336, 350.
Ransom—mistaken notion of the early Church, 180, 223.
Rechabites in the Temple service, 286, 304.
Redemption—the views of Peter and Paul compared, 73—75.
Renan—on the burning of Rome, 29; on the authenticity of First Epistle of Peter, 67; on the Second Epistle, 97.
Repentance, the primary lesson of the Gospel, 207; its importance, 349.
Resh Galutha, "Head of the Captivity," 312.
Rich and Poor providentially tested, 330.
Righteousness defined by Paul, 177; by Apollos, *ibid.*
Robespierre's housekeeper, a Neronian parallel to, 44.
Romans, Epistle to, its date, &c., 311.
Rome—its abnormal depravity, 1 *et seq.*; its wealth, prodigality, &c., *ibid.*; preponderance of its slave population, 2; its family life, 5; literature and art, 5, 6; public amusements, 6; its senate, &c., 7; its moribund religion, 7, 8; its contact with Christianity, 11, 12; its golden *quinquennium,* 21, 22; the burning of the city, 29—32; St. Peter's connexion with Rome, 65; forecasts of its downfall, 427; famine at, 445; pestilence, 446; Rabbinic legend of its founding, 463; burning of the Temple of Jupiter, 485; its overthrow, as regarded by Esdras, *ibid.*; Patristic evidence respecting St. Peter's visit, 594.
Rubellius Plautus, his assassination by Nero, 13.

S.

Sabbath of Sabbatism, 237.
Sakya Mouni (Buddha)—his mission, 158.
Salem and Jerusalem, 612, 613.
Salome—her ambitious request, 374.
Sammael, the Angel of Death, 199.
Sanhedrin of Jerusalem—its conspiracy against Paul, 12; its libel of the Christians, 36.
Satan—once regarded as the recipient of the world's ransom, 180, 223; Rabbinic conceit as to the aboyance of his adverse prerogative on Day of Atonement, 238.
Saturnalia of Rome, 23.
Sectarianism and its developments, 371.
Seneca—co-tutor with Burrus of the youthful Nero, 17; his benign influence over his pupil, 21; his untimely end, 29; his opinions quoted, 549.
Sepher-ha-Chayim—a Rabbinical treatise on eschatology, 347.
Septuagint version of Old Testament undertaken at instance of Ptolemy Philadelphus, 140; its bearing upon the Gentile world, *ibid.*; upon Jews and Judaism, 141; the anniversary of its publication kept as a *festival* by the Alexandrians, *ibid.*; and as a *fast* by the Palestinian Jews, 142; Justin Martyr's complaint respecting, *ibid.*; its mistranslations, 142 *et seq.*; its local bias, 144; regarded by some as an inspired translation, 398.
Sermon on the Mount compared with Epistle of James, 284, 317, 329.
Shabbath shabbathon—an appellation of the Day of Atonement, 237.
Shakespere—*Timon of Athens* (iii. 6) quoted, 552; *Antony and Cleopatra* (ii. 1), 568.
Shechinah—the sole prerogative of Israel, 200; a Jewish name for the Messiah, 534.
Shema Israel—its daily repetition, 336; the keynote of Judaism, 336, 352.
Shemoth Rabba — a Jewish commentary, quoted, 330, 401.
Sheshach—a scriptural pseudonym for Babel, 472.
Sibylline Oracles—their use at Rome, 35; their forecast of the downfall of Rome, 427 *et seq.*; their illustration of the Apocalypse, 456, 496.
Silanian law, 7.
Silas, or Silvanus, as a New Testament author, his claims, 184.
Simeon of Mispeh—one of the earliest writers in the Talmud, 238.
Simon Magus—the legend of his contest with Peter, 64.
Simon son of Giora—a renowned leader in the Jewish war, 418, 422, 424.
Simon son of Onias, the model high-priest, 616.
Simon Zelotes—his death by crucifixion, 48.
Simony of the priesthood, 314.
Sirach—the son of, his literary influence on the Epistle of James, 318.
Slavery—its prevalence at Rome, 2; Jews rarely enslaved, and why, 91.
Socrates, the Athenian philosopher, his inspiration, 158.
Socrates, the historian, and the Nestorian sect, 557.
Solfatara — its suggestive connexion with Hebrews, vi. 8, 215, 454.
Solomon, the Wisdom of, 145.
Stoicism—its prevalence in Apostolic times, 9; its premium on suicide, *ibid.*; its decadence, 10; compared with Christianity, *ibid.* (See also Cato, Cleanthes, &c.)
Stoning of Jeremiah, 253.
Suetonius—his idea of Christianity, 89, 416.
Suicide, the panacea of Stoicism, 9; its frequency, and its varied nomenclature, *ibid.*

T.

Tabernacle—its divine original, 175; reference thereto (and not to the Temple), by the author of Hebrews, 230.
Tableaux vivants of Roman plays, 40.
Tables of the Law, their traditional size and weight, 230.
Tacitus—his account of the Roman Senate, 7; of Nero, 28; his view of Christianity, 82, 89; his description of the Jews of his time, 416.
Talmud of Babylon—a compend of the traditions of the elders (Matt. xv. 2), its *matériel,* 281; its compiler, &c., *ibid.*
Tanchuma (Midrash), a Jewish comment, quoted, 302, 327, 489.

INDEX. 645

Targums, or Chaldee paraphrases of the Old Testament Scriptures, cited or alluded to, 63, 129, 144, 195, 196, 208, 209, 217, 220, 230, 247, 253, 256, 448, 449, 600, 612.
Tartarus, a classic term, made use of by Peter, 108, 119.
Te Deums strangely associated with autos da fè, 338.
Temple of Onias at Leontopolis, built in imitation of the Temple at Jerusalem, 183, 235.
Ten tribes of Israel never to be restored to Palestine, 325.
Tertullian—concerning Nero and the persecution of the Christians, 38, 67, 82; his mention of Jude the earliest on record, 122; accredits Barnabas with writing Hebrews, 184; his pronounced views on celibacy, 368, 402.
Testament of the Twelve Patriarchs, quoted or referred to, 178, 329, 342, 391, 497, 543, 597, 598.
Tetragrammaton, the ineffable name JEHOVAH, 240.
Theodore of Mopsuestia—his rejection of the Petrine Epistles, 67, 100; ignores the Apocalypse, 405; unfavourable to John's Epistles, 576.
Thomas, the Apostle of India, 48.
Tiberius Cæsar—his character sketched by Suetonius, 12; the tragic end of his family, 13.
Tiberius, Procurator of Palestine—his relation to Philo, 36; made Prefect of Alexandria, 419; his temporising character, *ibid.*
Tillin, Midrash, a Rabbinic commentary on Psalms, 197, 199.
Titus—his acquaintance with Nero, 24; the conqueror of Judæa, 479; his grant of land to Josephus the historian, 487; blockades Jerusalem, 488; anxious to preserve the Temple, *ibid.*; his purpose to destroy Christianity with Judaism, *ibid.*; the destruction of the city of Jerusalem, 489; eulogised by Josephus, but branded with infamy by the rabbis, *ibid.*, note.

U.

Unity of God—its pre-eminence in the creed of Judaism, 336, 352; unity not uniformity, 137.
Unpardonable sins from a Rabbinic point of view, 570.
Unstrung bow, a forceful metaphor, 401.
Uxoriousness of the Roman Emperors, 13.

V.

Vehmgericht, The (a mediæval *tribunal of punishment*), referred to, 415.

Veil of the Temple—its material, dimensions, &c., 228; its symbolic teaching, 246.
Vespasian—his miracles, 480; his history elucidative of revelation, 461, 482.
Victorinus of Pettau—his interpretation of the Apocalypse, 405, 450.
Virgin Mary—her tomb at Ephesus, 379.
Vine, The, an early ecclesiastical legend, 397.
Visitation of the Sick (Church Service), referred to, 162, 347.
Vulgate Version—one of its perversions, 252.

W.

Wills—unknown to the Jews, borrowed from Roman usage, 235.
Wisdom, Book of—its Alexandrian origin, 145; coincidences with the Pauline Epistles, 159. For various references, &c., see Index of Quotations.
World—condition of in Apostolic times, 1 *et seq.*; compared with the Church, 59; state of when Jerusalem was destroyed, 495.

X.

Xenophon, the physician of Claudius, 19.
Xenophon's Memorabilia, 328.

Y.

"Yad Hachazakah," a comprehensive digest of the Talmud, quoted, 617.
"Yalkut Chadash," a Rabbinic miscellany, quoted, 192, 341.
"Yalkut Shimoni," a Rabbinic miscellany, quoted, 192, 347, 485.

Z.

Zebdia, or Zebedee—his social status, 365; his death, 369.
Zachariah, the son of Baruch—his massacre, 422.
Zealots, a political faction, the *Home-Rulers* of Jewry, 340, 346, 415, 418, 446.
Zechariah, the son of Berachiah—the reference in Matthew probably an erroneous gloss, 422; his murder, 458.
Zeno, the Stoic philosopher, referred to, 9.
Zerubbabel, Temple of, 229.
"Zohar," a noted Kabbalistic work, referred to, 256, 368, 550.
Zuk, the destination of the scape-goat, 259.

Google

PASSAGES OF SCRIPTURE

QUOTED OR REFERRED TO.

GENESIS.

i.	1	p. 152
	2	250
	6	121
	14	328
ii.	17	207
	21	601
iii.	5	190
	18	214
iv.	4	143, 251
	7	600
	8—10	251
	10	251, 257, 343, 447
v.	24	251
vi.	2	119, 133
	3	342
	3—5	341
	6	144
	8	91
	9	251
vii.	11	121
	24	455
xiv.	18, 19	217
	22	218
xv.	2	249, 330, 357
	6	602
	9, 10	234
	15	601
xvi.	4	579
xvii.	1	613
	7	252
	16	600
xviii.	6	601
	12	92
xix.	3	328
	21	150
xxii.	12	357
	16	603
	17	209
xxiii.	4	252
xxv.	9	336
	23—30	258
xxvi.	24	252
xxvii.	35	255
	39	253
xxviii.	8	255
	13	252
xxxi.	42	207
xxxii.	10	252, 601
	24, &c.	152
xxxiii.	18	612
xxxiv.	49	333
xxxvii.	9	453
xl.	8	159

GENESIS (continued).

xli.	12	p. 119
	15, 16	119
xlvii.	9	81, 252
	31	252
xlviii.	2	252
	14, 17—20	252
xlix.	1	87
	10	143
	19	252
l.	24	89
	26	252

EXODUS.

ii.	1	p. 143
	14	253
iii.	1	144
	5	118, 531
	6	256
	14	333
iv.	6	143
	16	144
	22	256
	24	144
v.	2	151
vi.	12, 15	143
vii.	3	201
ix.	22	451
x.	21	256
xii.		243
	22	237
	36	87
xiii.	19	143
	19	252
xiv.	19	198
xvi.	16, 32	230
	31	230
	33, 34	230
xvii.	1—7	202
	16	144
xix.	1—6	256
	3	144
	4	462
	5, 6	71, 80
	6	88
	10	236
	10, 11	233
	16	256
	18	256, 257
xx.	5	89
	12	256
	21	235
xxi.	6	243
xxii.	22—24	329

EXODUS (continued).

xxiii.	7	p. 357
	20	198
	31	235
xxiv.	3—7	235
	5	236
	6—8	85
	7	237
	8	85, 262
	9—11	144
	10	144
xxv.	8	144
	16—21	230
	31—37	228
	40	227
xxvi.	6	243
	31—35	209, 229
	36, 37	228
xxviii.	1	206
	36	391
xxix.	4	233
	9	225
	16	236
	21	246
	36	193
	38—42	225
xxx.	6	613
	10	613
	20	246
xxxi.	8	231
xxxiii.	13	336
xxxiv.	7	232
xl.		230
	5	613
	9, 10	247
	20	230

LEVITICUS.

iv.	3	p. 246
	12	259
v.	3	329
	11—13	236
vi.	13—16, 20	225
	16	615
	19—22	622
	30	259
vii.	12	260, 261
viii.	6	246
	30	237, 246
ix.	7	206
x.	9	233
	10	225
xi.		233
xiv.	4, 5	417

PASSAGES OF SCRIPTURE

LEVITICUS (continued).

xiv.	4—6	p. 236
xv.	5	236
	8	233
	16, 17	112
xvi.		233, 614
	2, 13	240
	4	246, 296
	6, 11	232
	8—10	239
	12, 16	232
	14	85, 615
	17	240
	18	613
	19	85
	24	615
	26—28	236
	27	259
	30	238
	31	237
xvii.	5	233
	11	236
	11, 12	225
xxi.		246
	7, 13, 14	221
	10	225
	17	225
xxii.	2	225
	5	233
	6	236
	9	570
xxiii.	10	333
xxiv.	5, 9	226
xxvi.	29	343

NUMBERS.

v.	15	p. 243
vi.		233
	2	233
	3	233
	26	334
viii.	21	547
xi.	29	341
	38	371
xii.	7	201
	8	144
xiv.	14	144
	28—30	202
xv.	30	570
xvi.—xviii.		206
xvi.	22	255
	47	613
xvii.	10	230
	12	225
xviii.	7	232
	22	570
	22, 23, 20	222
xix.	6	237
	9	233
xx.	1—13	202
	13	130
xxix.		614
	12—36	240
xxxi.	6	63
	22—24	236
xxxii.	12	143

DEUTERONOMY.

i.	13	p. 336
iv.	6	339
	12	256
	24	257

DEUTERONOMY (continued).

v.	9	p. 341
vi.	4	336, 352
ix.	19	256
x.	2	230
	2, 5	230
	12	329
	16	201
xi.	14	344
xiv.	1	194
xv.	17	246
xvii.	2, 7	247
xviii.	15	201
xx.	5	235
	16	235
	22, 23	260
	23	91
xxiii.	14	143
	19	305
xxiv.	14, 15	343
xxv.	4	91
	26	233
xxvi.	2	333
	5	265
	17	327
	29	343
xxviii.	10	335
	25	325
	35	325
	36	230
xxix.	18	255
	23	215
xxxi.	6, 8	259
	21	227
xxxii.	5	548
	8	143, 196
	10, 11	341
	11	342, 462
	35	183, 190, 247
	40	247
	43	195
xxxiii.		448
	1—3	256
	2	196
	36	247
xxxiv.	6	600

JOSHUA.

i.	5	p. 259
	8	143
v.	15	118
x.	3	217
	20	214
xiii.	22	63, 143
	23	81
xxi.	45	253
xxiv.	30	143
	32	252

JUDGES.

v.	4	p. 257
	19	484
vi.	2	254
ix.	4	234
xiii.	8	211
xiv.	6	253
xviii.	6	335
xix.	10, 11	612

I. SAMUEL.

ii.	8	p. 344
xii.	6	201

I. SAMUEL (continued).

xv.	12	p. 143
	22	243, 339
xviii.	11	253
xix.	10, 12	253
xx.	30	143
xxviii.	6	193

II. SAMUEL.

v.	6	p. 612
vii.	14	194, 195
viii.	2	458
xi.	14	335
xii.	23	217
xvii.	34	253
xxiii.	20	253

I. KINGS.

iii.	11, 12	p. 327
vi.	22	232, 613
vii.	49	229
viii.	9	230
	63	235
xiii.	7	253
	29	458
xvii.	1	346
	22, 23	343
xviii.		347
	4, 13	254
	21	327
	42	348
xix.	8, 13	254
	10	253
	16	545
xx.	11	143
xxii.	26	253

II. KINGS.

i.	9—14	p. 373
	10	457
iii.	22	444
iv.	14	253
	35—37	253
v.	19	335
ix.	20	329
x.	15—23	296
xi.	7	77
xii.	2	211
xvi.	15	296
xvii.	14	201
xxi.	12, 13	458
xxiii.	29	484

I. CHRONICLES.

ii.	55	p. 296
iv.		448
xxi.	13	247
xxiii.	13	225
xxviii.	20	259
	22	448
xxix.	15	252
	23	195

II. CHRONICLES.

iv.	8, 19	p. 228
	17	214
v.	10	336
xxiv.	20, 22	253
xxvi.	16—21	206
	19	221
xxix.	22	236
xxxv.	3	230

QUOTED OR REFERRED TO.   649

Ezra.
ii. 61, 62   p. 221

Nehemiah.
iv. 5   p. 340
vii. 63, 64   221
x. 38   222
xi. 22   139

Esther.
ix. 19, 22   p. 458

Job.
i. 6   p. 194
iv. 19   226, 333
vii. 7   343
xiv. 2   327
xv. 30   327
xvi.   447
xix.   447
  26, 27   144
xxviii. 12   338
xxix. 18   343
  25   144
xxxi. 10   143
xxxv. 14   144
xxxviii. 23   328
  33   329
xlii. 14   143

Psalms.
ii.   p. 225
  7   194, 204, 209
vii. 12   444
viii. 6   195
x. 6   343
  27   313
xi. 7   p. 547
xii. 2   327
xv. 1—5   248
xvi. 10   225
xvii. 15   144
xix.   560
  8—11   329
xxi. 3   327
  6   197
  17   329
xxii.   198, 199
xxiv. 2   131
xxix. 1   194
xxxii. 1, 2   340
  6   350
xxxiii. 12—16   93
xxxiv. 8   88
  10   255
xxxviii. 7   209
xxxix. 12   352
  13   84
  14   81
xl. 6, 7   241, 343
  7   329
  12   243
xlii. 3   144
  4   120
xliv. 23   260
xlv.   195
  6   444
  6, 7   195
xlvi. 5   251
l. 5   254
  16—20   338

Psalms (continued).
lii. 2—5   p. 338
lvii. 5   203
lix. 15   346
lxviii. 17   196, 256
  28   238
lxix. 2   249
lxxi.   226
lxxii. 18   344
lxxiv. 19   447
lxxvi. 2   612
lxxviii. 2   156
lxxix. 5   247
lxxxiii. 5   224
lxxxv. 2   349
lxxxvii. 1   251
lxxxviii. 8   375
lxxxix. 50, 51   253
xc. 4   204
xcv. 6   201
  10   202
xcvi. 10   142
xcvii. 7   195
cii. 3   343
  15   327
  25   195
civ. 1   196
  4   195
  25   573
cx.   196, 218, 225, 244
  1   195, 218
  4   208, 209, 214
cxiv. 7   257
cxvi. 17   260
cxviii. 22   88
cxix.   282, 285, 308
  20   341
  5   84
cxx. 3, 4   338
cxxii. 3   485
cxxxvi. 6   121
  7   328
cxxxviii. 19   201
cxxxix. 11   328
  16   244
cxl. 13   338
cxlvi. 3   325

Proverbs.
iii. 5, 6   p. 318
  11   318
  11, 12   254
  21   196
  25   92
  34   318, 339
iv. 26   255
vii. 16—23   328
viii. 22   152
ix. 5   218
  31   96
x. 12   95, 318, 340
xii. 10   552
xiii. 3   326
xvi. 27   318
xvii. 9   95
  15   357
xix. 3   333
xxi. 10   341
xxiii. 27   143
  31   318
xxv. 14   120
xxvi. 11   120

Proverbs (continued).
  27   p. 338
xxvii. 21   95
xxviii. 21   255
xxx. 12   318
  15   323

Ecclesiastes.
v. 2   p. 318, 328
x. 8   299, 305
xii. 6   338

Canticles.
iv. 5   p. 108
vi. 8   581
  9   579
viii. 6   341

Isaiah.
i. 6   p. 347
  10   457
  10—17   236
  11—17   243
  18   239
  21   217, 425
  22   343
ii. 2   486
  5   553
  12   327
  12—19   447
iii. 4   130
  9   457
  10   304
  17   143
v. 1—30   323
  23   357
vi. 1—8   614
vii. 6   472
  9   155
viii.   198
  14   88
  18   109
  21   214
ix. 5   613
  6   144, 217
  8   118
x. 3   89
xii. 3   564
xiii.   595
  6   343
  9, 10, 17   453
  10   447
xiii., xxiii., xxiv. 485
xiv. 4—12   595
  12   452
  18   458
  31   343
xv. 3   343
xvii. 5   463
xxiv. 23   249
xxv. 7—9   236
xxvi. 11   247
  21   447
xxvii. 13   109
xxviii. 16   88
xxix. 13—21   260
xxx. 4   254
xxxi. 9   486
xxxii. 1   217
  15   121
xxxiii.   343
  15   246

ISAIAH (continued).

xxxiv.	3, 4	p. 447
	4	121
	11	458
xxxvii.	3	414
xxxviii.	11	144
xl.	6	331
	6, 7	327
xli.	8	336
	19	448
xliii.	20	89
xliv.	4	223
xlvi.		595
xlvii.	5–7	579
xlviii.	8	213
	9	89
	22	326
xlix.	2	448
l.	3	447
	5	243
lii.	5	91
liii.	7	343
	9	91
	10	552
	11	357
	11, 12	91
	12	91, 230
liv.	4	485
	5	339
	11	327
	12	485
lvi.	1	248
	7–lvii. 5	111
	10	129
lvii.	19	260
	20	130, 327
	21	326
lix.	16	225
lx.	1	223
	8	254
	21	352
lxi.	1	545
lxii.	4	227
lxiii.	1–6	458
	3	483
	4	447
	9	257
	11	202
	17	201
lxiv.	10	448
	10, 11	489
lxv.	25	121
lxvi.	7, 8	461

JEREMIAH.

ii.	12	p. 339
	17	331
iii.	3	344
	8	453
	14	227
iv.	3	214
	23	328, 453
	23–26	447
v.	14	457
	24	344
vi.	20	243
vii.	4	352
	16	571
	21–23	243
iii.	7–12	233
xi.	14	571
xiv.	9	335
	11	571

JEREMIAH (continued).

xv.	16	p. 456
xvi., xxv.		485
xvii.	26	260
xviii.	7–10 }	343
xxii.	13	
xxiii.	5	223
	14	457
	26	119
xxv.	29	96
xxvi.	23	253
xxxi.	22	227
	31–34	227, 234
	33, 34	242
xxxii.	4	584
	23	253
xxxv.		236
xxxviii.	33, 34	244
xl.		574
li.	1	472
	27	456
	41	472

LAMENTATIONS.

ii.	7, 8	p. 458
iv.	7	260, 296

EZEKIEL.

ii.	9 }	p. 456
iii.	3	
viii.	11	231
ix.	4, 6	448
xiv.	3	538
	21	446
xvi.	32	339
	48, 49	457
xvii.	6	223
	10	327
xviii.	23	121
xix.	1–9	463
	12	327
xxi.	26	181
xxii.	31	463
xxiii.	25	341
xxvi., xxvii.		485
xxxii.	7, 8	447, 453
xxxiii.	11	121
	21	260
xxxiv.	1	130
	1–10	343
	11	91
xxxvi.	5	247
	25	246
	25–27	227
	27	341, 342
xxxvii.		343
	10	458
xxxviii., xxxix.		485
xl.		457, 573
xliii.	2	448
xliv.	2	274
	17	286

DANIEL.

i.	1–3	p. 86
iii.		253
	25	196
	31	86
iv.	1	86
	14	77
vi.	23	253
	25	86

DANIEL (continued).

vii.	8–20	p. 466
	9	448
	10	256, 444
	13	448
	24	463
	25	457
viii.	10	318, 461
	13	457
	17	193
	26	457
ix.	24, 25	236
	27	425
x.	5	448
	6, 11, 12	448
	13	129, 449
	13, 20, 21	198
	20, 21	439
xi.	31	425
	36	460
xii.	1	129, 439, 456
	4–9 }	457
	7–11	
	11	425
	13	193
	31	357

HOSEA.

ii.	16	p. 227
	23	89
iv.	17	343
vi.	6	236, 243, 329
viii.	1	453
x.	7	44
	8	447
xii.	6	329
xiii.	14	414
	15	327
xiv.	3	200
	4	319

JOEL.

ii.	3	p. 451
	10–31	447
	23	344
	28	545
iii.	4, 15	447
iv.	2, 11, 14	463

AMOS.

ii.	6	p. 344
	7	243
	11, 12	301
iv.	1	131
	4	243
v.	12	283, 346
	21–24	243
vi.	5–7	485
vii.	6–9	458
ix.	1	144
	12	283, 335

JONAH.

iii.	10	p. 343
iv.	8	327

MICAH.

i.	4	p. 121
iv.	9	414
	13	463
v.	2	414

MICAH (continued).

vi. 6—8 p. 243
    6—9   329
    8   248
vii. 8   199

NAHUM.
i. 6 p. 447
iii. 5   143

HABAKKUK.
ii. 3 p. 121
   3, 4   248
   4   177, 178, 336
iii. 12   483

ZEPHANIAH.
iii. 8 p. 483

HAGGAI.
ii. 6, 7 p. 257
   7—9   229

ZECHARIAH.
iii. 1, 2 p. 120, 223
    1—3   130
    2   131, 600
    3, 4   334
iv.   457
   2   448
   3, 11   457
   4, 5   448
   10   449
   14   208
vi. 11—13   246
    12   206, 223
    13   214, 218
ix. 9   217
   11   263
xi. 1   240
xii. 10   483
    11   484
xiii. 1   233
    9   449
xiv. 11   486

MALACHI.
ii. 17 p. 120
iii. 1   257
    2   447
    5   343
    6   259, 331
iv. 2   217, 253

II. ESDRAS.
v. 3 p. 449
xi. 1   463
    1, 36   464
    30
    32, 35 } 479
    42—46   485
    45   285
xii. 42   105
xliii. 39—47   325
xv. 8   447

TOBIT.
i. 16, 17 p. 334
   17   458

TOBIT (continued).
viii. 3 p. 455
xii. 15   198, 449
xiii. 6   193

JUDITH.
iv. 4 p. 612
v. 18   84
ix. 20   333

WISDOM.
ii. 1—24 p. 318
   6—20   346
   8   318, 327
   12   327
   17   259
   24   199
iii. 2   114
   7   89
iv. 11   199
v. 8   318
  9—14   318, 343
  16   327
vi. 1—4   159
   12   86
   12, 23   341
vii. 17—19   329
    17—20   318
    25, 26   158, 178
    26   193, 329
ix. 15   145, 159
x. 5   318, 336
   7   129
xi. 6, 7   452
    15, 16   484
    17   145
xii. 10   256, 333
    16   318
xiii. 1   159, 251
xvi. 1, 9   484
xvii. 2   484
     2, 16, 17   599
     17   119
xviii. 15, 16   203
      22   178

ECCLESIASTICUS.
i. 1—11 p. 339
   28   318, 327
ii. 13   346
   18   247
iii. 3   200
    30   200
iv. 14   338, 341
v. 11   318, 326
   14   338
vii. 10   327
xii. 11   318, 343
    12   329
xiv. 19   343
    23   318, 329
xv. 9   338
   11   318
   11—17   332
xx. 7   318
   15   318, 327
   26   270
xxii. 24   338
xxviii. 10, 19   318
      15, 26   337
xxix. 15   224
xxxiv. 2   343

ECCLESIASTICUS (continued).
xxxiv. 19 p. 200
     22   343
xxxv. 2, 14   329
    22   121
xlii. 22   318, 327
xliv. 14, 15   404
xlv. 6—22   616
    11   225
xlviii. 1   457
    5—16   616

BARUCH.
iv. 35 p. 485

I. MACCABEES.
i. 21 p. 228
ii. 28, 29   254
   38   253
iii. 45, 51   457
    49   301
iv. 49   228
   60   457
ix. 26   253
xi. 12   253

II. MACCABEES.
i. 27 p. 84
ii. 7   227
iii. 39   118
iv. 48   129
v. 26   253
   27   254
vi. 11   253, 254
   18, 30
vii. 7—10 } 253
    9—36
    28   250
ix. 19   326
x. 6   254
xiii. 14   190

III. MACCABEES.
(Extra Apocryphal Book.)
ii. 5 p. 129

MATTHEW.
i. 5 p. 253, 351
   19   282
ii. 1—15   461
   12, 22   227
   23   342
iii. 8—12   207
    9   352, 358
iv. 1—11   342
   21   265
v. 3   318, 331, 334
   4   318
   9   339
   10—12   318
   10—14   259
   11   96
   12   86
   20   338
   22   318
   24   318
   25   70, 96
   33   310

PASSAGES OF SCRIPTURE

MATTHEW (continued).

v. 33—37	p.	318
33—36		347
44		282
48 }		318, 326
vi. 14 }		
15 }		318
19 }		
22		543
24		318, 327
25		251
26		156
30		331
vii. 1		335, 346
1—5 }		
7—12 }		318
16, 17		333
21, 23		318
viii. 29		334
ix. 34		198
37		584
x. 3		265, 269
23		489
xi. 19		330
36		560
xii. 28		233
31		570
31, 32		208
37		337, 357
39		339
43—45		204, 455
45		120
46		275
49, 50		289
50		124
55		273
xiii. 17		254
23		333
26		331
30, 40, 40		236
55		246
57		287
xiv. 10		254
31		190
xv. 1		263
1—9		260
16		370
22		454
xvi.		594
4		310
6—12		370
18, 23		69, 66
23		246, 489
xvii. 3		458
4		114
9—13		458
21		282
24—27		69
xviii. 6		541
6, 8, 9		441
17, 18		593
22		69
xix. 12		368
21		326
26		213
28		69, 326
xx. 2		445
12		327
23		375
24		376
25—27		593
28		233
xxi. 13		340

MATTHEW (continued).

xxi. 21	p.	120, 327, 334
22		327
xxii. 23		1,9
44		218
xxiii.		343
6		334
8—10		337
12		331
16—22, 25		261
25—37		253
35		251, 422
36		202
xxiv.		246
2		250
3		284
4, 7		444
5, 11		544
6, 8		446
7		445, 446
8		414
12		333
14		483
15		425
16		453
22		96, 259
28		434
29		121, 432, 453
29—34		448
31		440
34		202, 489
37		60
51		253
xxv. 5		119
14		557
21		86
35		259
35—46		335
xxvi. 64		204
69		265
xxvii. 32		259
46		199
51		246, 459
56		266
xxviii. 2		459
19		347
20		236

MARK.

15	p.	207
19		205
20		365
iii. 14		201
17		366
18		265
31		275
iv. 34		119
vi. 3		266, 273, 287
4		287
13		347
vii. 1—15		233
5—13		261
20—23		339
viii. 12		202
ix. 2		91
33, 38		336
43—47		441
x. 27		213
32		374, 584
42		376

MARK (continued).

xi. 21	p.	275
xiii. 7		318, 445
7, 8		446
8		414
9		318
14		425
29		318
32		318
xiv. 70		265
xv. 7		340
40		266
xvi. 18		207

LUKE.

i. 6	p.	222
11		251
36		273
43		590
50		275
52, 53		344
59		560
68		99
ii. 26		327
29		199
44		273
iii. 11		287
iv. 5, 6		253
24		287
25		347
35		71
v. 10		265
39		88, 265
vi. 15		366
16		124
20		334, 344
22		259
22, 23		336
32		91
35		86
36		346
vii. 40		590
42		118
50		335
viii. 19		275
24		327
31		454
48		335
ix. 26		347
31		259
35		118
46		370, 371
54		366
54, 55		573
x. 18		454, 463
20		256, 326
34		347
55		273
xi. 13		327
20		233
21		541
26		203
28		124, 275
31		329
40		339
xii. 25		97
35		71
54		283
55		327
58		70
xiv. 11		331

LUKE (continued).		JOHN (continued).		JOHN (continued).	
xiv. 12	p. 273	iv. 6	p. 493	xiii. 23	p. 369
xvi. 31	458	10	564	25	376
xvii.	246	14, 36 }	510	33	541
9, 10	357	22		34	560
xviii. 3	70	35—38	883	34, 35	538, 539
7, 8	447	37	560	37—38	552
13	282	44	287	xiv. 6	246, 403, 534
14	185, 331	v. 24	510	10	233
27	213	31—37	563	15	560
xix. 3	207, 266	32	591	16	523, 570
44	89	33	563	16, 17	583
xx. 17, 18	88	35	328	16—26	535
21	304	36	563	17	563
xxi. 9	327	39, 40, 45	563	26	590
19	247	vi.	564	xv. 4, 5, 7	546
20	388, 412	6, 61, 64	370	5	547
21	462	25	584	11	531
24	457	27	510	13	552, 500
25	449	29	584	26	535, 563
25, 26	484	40, 47, 54	510	27	563
26	257	45	365	xvi. 7	563
28	233	51—56	259	12	493
xxii. 20	236	vii. 1—10	276, 289	13 }	563
24	370	4	289	14 }	
24—26	523	5	271, 289	23	560
28	326	7	124, 329	26	570
31	70	33, 42	312	30	560
32	83	35	324	xvii. 2, 3	510, 546
43	207	38	564	3	531, 573, 574
xxiii. 34	304	viii. 12	533	5	334
36	448	14 }	563	9, 15, 20	570
46	91	18 }		11	128
xxiv. 12	71, 87, 329	21—24	570	11, 17	563
18	269	31	538	14—26	540
21	233	32	329	15	329
25	370	32—40	563	17	533
27	244	33	352	23	563
31	380	34	120	xviii. 4	370
39	531	44	199	14	422
41	207	51	493	15	377
51	91	56	252	26	273
		58	333	28	329
JOHN.		ix. 5	328	37	555, 563
i. 1	p. 531	31	568	xix. 11	90, 324, 443
2	510	x. 4	584	25	260, 269, 270
3	146	7—9	303, 316	26	275, 309
3—10	193	11, 15, }	552	27	307, 387, 510
4	531, 533	17, 18 }		28	370, 591
4—9	540	16	91	34	379, 505
5	533	22	235	35	379, 563
6	391	25	563	37	365
7	563	36	201	xx. 2	369
9	227, 531	xi. 9, 10	538	5—11	87, 329
11	510	33	370	6	380, 391
12	531	41, 42	568	12	493
13	331, 531	48—50	422	14	380
14	233, 493, 531	52	84, 563	21—23	583
14, 17	563	54	373	29	86
18	531	55	88	30	379
45	563	xii.—xvii.	516	31	525
ii. 2	565	xii. 16	370	xxi. 4	360
4	124, 275	25	510	5	541
13	493	30	118	6	206
17	391	31	462	7, 20	369
19	233	xiii. 1	539	8	380
iii. 3, 7, 31	328	1—6	69	15	581
5	564	1, 3, }	370	16	96, 381
16	542	11, 21 }		17	381, 553, 554
19	533	12, 15	539	17, 18	118
23	612	14	347	19	66
36	516	18	347, 365	21	381
		22	376	24	563, 591

Acts.

i.	8	p. 458
	13	124, 381
	14	276, 220
	16	88
	17	117
ii.	2	113, 118
	9	85, 579
	9—12	312
	15	114
	16—20	489
	17, 18	545
	17, 31	87
	20	109
	22	87
	27	225
	32	71
	32—36	71
	36	201
	38	347
	40	71, 489
	47	244
iii.	6	87
	12	109, 114, 117
	13	91, 262
	15	71, 185, 199, 254
	16	326, 347
	17	87
	18	71
	19—21	489
	19—26	71
	19, 31	90
	24	87
iv.	1	381
	1—6	335
	10	71, 347
	11	71
	13	365
	13, 19	404
	21	262
	24	114
v.	17	335, 494
	28—32	90
	30	71
	31	185, 199
	32	71
	40—42	90
	41	326, 590
vi.	1	189
	6	207
	9	263
vii.	2	268
	6, 29	84
	12	334
	16, 43	222
	20	252
	22	256
	38	203
	52	345
	53	198
viii.	1	499
	1	384
	11	477
	14	333
	17	207
	20	87
	38	203
ix.		500
	2, 16	590
	34	347
x.	2	71

Acts (continued).

x.	20	p. 131, 334
	22	227
	28	91
	34	87
	38	545
	39	
	40	
	41	71
	42	
	43	
xi.	19	64
	26	82
	30	294
xii.	2	266, 403
	14	207
	17	292
	20	553
	25	63, 294
xiii.	3	194
	15	262
	39	185, 358
	43	37
	44	236
xiv.	15	347
xv.	2	128, 295
	5	494
	7	65, 87
	9	88, 204
	10	233, 241, 329, 335
	11	52
	13	266, 296
	13—21	351
	14—21	324
	17	283
	19	296
	20	258, 262
	23	326
	24	64, 321
xvi.	14	37, 582
xvii.		517
	6	90
	12	334
	13	263
	29	117
	30	87
xviii.	2	582
	5	334
	18	184, 301
	24	187
	24—28	186, 187
	25	190
	26	186
xix.	1	186
	9	201, 596
	26	236
	29	599
	38	334
	41	262
xx.	4	589
	19	326
	20, 27	248
	28	80, 89
	29	130, 259
xxi.	8	266
	10	118
	17—25	351
	20	125, 293
	21	354
	24	88
	25	262
	27	263

Acts (continued).

xxi.	29, 30	p. 544
	38	340
xxii.	11	206
	12	302
xxiii.	1	262
	8	179
	12	340
	22	262
	26	326
xxiv.	5, 14	494
	16	77, 262
xxvi.	5	329, 494
	7	325
	10	345
	11	253
	19	201
	26	262
	28	82
xxvii.	14	97
xxviii.	17	500
	20	494
	28	82
	31	222

Romans.

i.	1	p. 324, 325
	4	194
	10	500
	16	328
	17	178, 248
	18	87
	20	159
	24	542
	28	105
ii.	4	105, 121
	6—10	360
	8	534
	13	357, 359
	17	327
	17—20	352
	18	207
	22	37
	24	335
	29	92
iii.	8	121, 127
	20	357
	21—24	56
	22	176
	24	249
	25	176, 179, 200, 536
	27	329
	28	350, 361
iv.	2	350
	3	359
	8, 9, 22	357
	4	308
	6	251
	11	92
	13	251
	17—19	252
	18	356
	20	327, 333
	25	76, 136
v.	1	350
	2	74
	16	328
	20	121, 534
vi.	1	
	1—15	75
	2	91

ROMANS (continued).

vi.	4	p. 75, 308
	6	72
	7	75
	13	542
	12—14	75
vii.	14	224
	17	540
	22	92
	23	72, 89
viii.	2	329
	3	75, 200
	4	103
	13	75
	15	76, 87, 333, 560
	18	72
	19, 20	548
	19—23	333
	21	120
	24	175
	24, 25	240
	34	72
ix.	2	121
	5	121
	15	180
	16	201
	19	332, 336
	25	89
	25—32	72
	29	343
	32	207
	32, 33	88
x.	7	261
	9	356
	32	207
xi.	22	92
	33	442
	36	163
xii.	1	88, 241
	1—21	190, 217
	2	72, 87
	5	356
	6	72
	8	327
	9 }	258
	10 }	
	13	258, 589
	18	163
	19	163, 183, 190, 247
xii.—xvi.		350
xiii.	1—4	72
	1—7	13, 33, 159, 443
	5	84
	10	335
	11, 12	489
	12	540
	13	260
xiv.		259
	7	190
	21	441
xv.	14	118
	25	208
	33	163, 190, 262
xvi.		562
	3	184, 186
	7	257
	11	83
	17	72
	20	263
	25	589

ROMANS (continued).

xvi.	25	p. 131
	27	131

I. CORINTHIANS.

i.	7	p. 489
	9	246, 534
	13—15	347
	14	589
	20	313, 314
	30	217
ii.	6	156
	10	442
	14	338
	14, 15	350
iii.	1	224
	1, 2	207, 210
	1, 10	88
	2	622
	4—6	186, 187
	10	121
	13	246, 360
	16	201
	19	346
	23	335
iv.	4	262
	9	247
	19	343
v.	1—11	126
	2	129
	5	571, 572
	9	590
	10	258, 395
vi.	1	189
	9	258
	9—18	128
	12—20	121
	17	356
	20	324
vii.	1	547
	5	92, 277
	12, 13	586
	19	360
	22	258
	23	324
viii.	13	441
ix.	1	162
	2	120
	5	65, 110, 126, 402
	13	259, 260
	18	590
x.	4	128, 134, 600
	7, 8	441
	8	120
	11	489
	13	259, 534
	20	465
	32	441
xi.	19	119, 404
	21	130
	23	162, 362
	25	234
	30	130
	31, 32	95
xii.	2	590
	3	129, 556
	8	327
	9	348
	10	118, 555
xiii.		339
	5, 6	95

I. CORINTHIANS (continued).

xiii.	9	p. 193
	12	242, 329
	13	240
xiv.	5	96
	26—34	337
	33	327
xv.		176
	1	74
	3	362
	7	208, 290
	21	489
	22	331, 542
	27	109
	32	247, 463
	35	336
	52	440
xvi.		350
	1	208
	13	187
	15	333
	22	489

II. CORINTHIANS.

i.	1	p. 189
	5	253
ii.	6—8	572
	7, 10	211
	9	339
	14	258
iii.		186
	1	301
	3	224
	6	224
iv.	2	28, 88, 163
	4	178, 211, 243
	16	92
v.	1	118, 159, 542
	7	240
	10	360
	14	75, 308
	21	179, 236
vi.	2	180
	16, 17	180
vii.	1	547
	10	2, 7, 256
	12	211
viii.	4	189
ix.		359
	4	240
	8	359
	13	260
xi.	2	330, 368
	7	500
	13, 14	439
	17	240
	20	128, 589
	22	189
	24	183
	20	441
xii.	12	183
	13	531
	16	590
	21	126

GALATIANS.

i.	1	p. 198, 362
	1—12	183
	1, 12	161
	5	262
	9	123

GALATIANS (continued).

i. 10	p. 553	
11–ii. 21	362	
11–15	162	
13	202	
18, 19	292	
19	206, 268, 385	
ii. 2	362	
4	128	
6	162, 304	
7, 9	65	
9	84, 266, 293	
	351, 362	
10	208	
12	128, 248	
14	259	
16	240	
19, 20	74	
20	176, 308	
iii. 1	223	
7	92	
11	218	
13	91, 179	
16	180	
19	173, 198	
19, 20	227	
26	249, 333	
iv. 3	207	
10, 24	335	
19	92	
24	52	
v. 1	320	
6	330, 363	
10	262	
12	128	
13	80, 120, 126	
13–26	121	
16	308	
20	119, 494	
24	75	
vi. 7	208	
12	128	
12, 13	259	
15	360	

EPHESIANS.

i.	p. 175	
3	72	
4–7	72	
7	533	
8	338	
13	333	
14	80	
15	176	
17	208	
20	72	
ii. 2	129	
3	87	
6	72	
8, 9	350, 355	
10	86, 200, 359	
11, 12	553	
15	190	
16	74, 203	
20	88	
iii. 2	162	
2, 3	183	
4–6	107	
8	590	
12	203, 246, 567	
16	92	
iv. 14	259, 327	

EPHESIANS (continued).

iv. 19	p. 7	
22	254	
25	533	
32	346	
v. 1, 2	538	
2	236	
3	126	
3, 5	258	
5	328	
7	395	
8	87	
8, 9, 11–14	533	
14	132, 342	
21 }	72	
22 }		
26	246	
v.–vi.	359	
vi. 5	72	
10	193	
12	129, 199, 409	
14	87	
23	128	

PHILIPPIANS.

i. 7	p. 247	
8	339	
21	356	
25	262	
27	87	
28–30	82	
ii. 2	531	
5–11	199	
6	200	
7	243	
8	190	
9	199, 590	
9, 11	79	
10	444	
13	262	
15	328	
24	262	
iii. 2	34, 517	
5	180	
7–11	356	
7–11	253	
12	337	
19	331, 338	
20	81, 489	
iv.	359	
2	582	
3	256	
5	489	
7	86	
8	107	
9	262	
22	33	

COLOSSIANS.

i.	p. 130	
4	176, 246	
5 !	193	
9	338	
10	118, 359, 590	
15	178	
17	193	
20	533, 613	
24	253, 326	
ii.	130	
3	327	
4	329	
9	233	

COLOSSIANS (continued).

ii. 10–15	p. 93	
14, 15	180	
16	333	
16–23	259	
17	242	
18	129, 329, 537	
18–23	277	
iii. 5	258	
9	254	
12	96, 178	
23	91	
iii.–iv.	359	
iv. 3	262	
10	274, 506	
11	580	
11–15	186	
18	247	

I. THESSALONIANS.

i. 3	p. 163, 206, 246	
4	85	
10	254	
14–16	517	
ii. 1	246	
9 }	590	
12 }		
14	326	
14–16	36	
15	82, 517	
18	262	
iii. 2	590	
4	82, 544	
iv. 3	244	
6	126, 258	
9	258	
13–17	489	
13–v. 11	121	
15	120, 543	
16	129, 236	
v. 1–16	489	
9	89	
20	118	
23	262	
24	246, 534	
25	262	
26	347	
28	326	

II. THESSALONIANS.

i. 4	p. 82	
7–10	489	
8	37, 236, 534	
ii. 3	41	
3–12	436	
10	120	
17	359	
iii. 2	82	

I. TIMOTHY.

i. 4	p. 118	
6	255	
17	193	
18	118	
20	439, 571, 590	
ii. 4	121	
5	227, 233, 533	
9	91	
10	359	
iii. 2	258, 539	
3	330	

I. TIMOTHY (continued).		HEBREWS (continued).		HEBREWS (continued).	
iii. 6	p. 326	ii. 1—4	p. 198	v. 11	p. 189, 328
15	201	1—5	200, 201	11—14	189, 204, 207
16	93	2	173	v. 11—vi. 20	245
iv. 1	193, 338, 489	3	161, 162, 173,	12	71
3	258		183, 190,	14	236
7	118		256	vi. 1	172, 176, 180,
16	213	3, 4	189		233, 540
v. 10	359	5	175	1—3	204
13	591	5—8	165	1—8	208
15	255	5—18	198—200	2	179, 186, 207,
17	344	6	180, 611		262
22	329	6—16	200, 201	4	162, 247
vi. 3	203	7	164	4, 5	175, 176
14	329	8	165	4—6	570
18	260, 359	9	179	4—8	170, 181, 185,
		9, 10	190		204, 248,
II. TIMOTHY.		10	163, 179, 185,		256
i. 7	p. 87		207, 225,	5	175, 196, 611
18	590		277	8	208
ii. 15	333, 584	11	177, 179, 244	9, 10	204
16	254	13	195	9—12	247
17	439, 590	16	87, 164, 167	9—20	208 et seq.
19	548	17	167, 179, 201,	10	163, 189, 258
24	343		203, 204,	11	208
iii. 1	489, 542		208	11—18	204
8	134	17, 18	200, 201	11, 18, 19	246
17	359	18	245	13	246, 611
iv. 4	255	iii.	203, 245, 607	14	164, 165
9	299	1—6	200, 201	15	254
9, 21	186	2	181, 605, 611	17	200
11	596	3	227, 251	19	176
14	571	6	186	19, 20	204
17	463	7	178, 180, 201	20	179, 180, 246
19	187	7—15	164, 611	vii. 1—3	204, 216
		7—19	200, 201, 202	1—17	168
TITUS.		9	173	1—28	245
i. 8	p. 258, 589	10	202	2—10	179
ii. 7—14	359	12	201, 208, 247	3, 10, 5	164
12	542	14	249	4, 10	204, 222 et
13	117	15	202		seq.
14	233	16	164	5, 6, 9	225
iii. 1	33	17	128	5, 11, 27	167
5	86, 246	iv. 1	173	6	216
8	259	1—10	168	6—8	228
9	254, 340	1—13	200, 201	11	228, 242
10	119	3, 4	164	11, 12	204
13	187, 590	4	202	11—19	224
		5	195	11—25	344
PHILEMON.		7	253	12	173, 224
ver. 7	p. 589	8	202	13, 14	204
9	577, 630	9	167, 227	14, 21	164
22	262	11	236	15—19	204
24	596	11—13	203	17	180, 611
		12	88, 173, 178,	18	227
HEBREWS.			250, 602	18—19	259, 260
i.	p. 179	12, 13	170, 178	19	165
1	165, 173	14	189, 233, 246	19, 22	174
1—4	178, 193	14—16	201, 203	20, 21	224
2	250, 489	15	179, 226, 611	20, 22	205
3	164, 165, 166,	16	245, 507	22	165, 227
	240, 262	v. 1—3	204, 206	22, 23	225
4	227	1—10	245	23, 24	165
5	195, 345	2	165, 247, 611	23, 25	205
5, 6	164	2, 3	232	25	203, 224
5—14	194, 195, 200,	3	164, 243	26	179, 236, 242
	201	4—10	204, 206 et	26—28	225
8, 9	164		seq.	27	161, 243, 244
13	244	5	164	29	165
ii	179	6	511	viii. 1	164, 166, 224,
1	208	8	165, 179		244
		9	180	1—6	235
		10	216	1—7	23: et seq.

HEBREWS (continued).
vi i. 1–ix. 28 p. 245
2	175, 233
3	201
5	175, 236, 242, 259
5—8	164
7, 8	165
7—13	205
8—12	242
8–13	227
9	199
10	167
10, 12	244, 458
ix. 1	175, 228
1—5	228 et seq.
1—10	168
1—14	205
3	246, 247
3, 4	161
4	225
5	208, 731
6—10	232, 333
7	253
7, 19	167
8	165, 253
8, 12	236, 246
9	175
10	207, 259
11	174, 242
11, 12	165
11—14	232
12	246
12—28	261
13	78, 85, 257
13, 14	179
14	174, 207, 227, 244, 246, 533
15	165, 179, 233, 234, 252, 254
15—17	224, 232
15—18	202
15—22	179, 205
16, 17	234, 611
17	234
18—28	85, 235 et seq.
20	234
22	179
23	174, 175
23—28	205
24	175, 227, 236
25	225
25—28	261
26	103, 236
28	91, 165, 237
x. 1—3	225
1—10	168, 205, 242, 244
1—18	245
1, 22	203
2	188
2, 22	179
3	611
5—7	164
9	253
10, 14	179
10, 14, 29	177
11	161
11, 12	226
11—14	242, 244

HEBREWS (continued).
x. 11–18 p. 205
12	166
14 } 15 }	180
15—18	242, 244
16	244
18	226
19	74, 189, 226
19—25	245, 246
19—31	247
20	180
21	175
22	227, 246, 247
22, 29	177
23	40
24	246
25	328
25, 37	489
26	162, 185, 211
26—29	170
26, 29	208
26—31	181, 208, 245, 256
27	37, 236
27, 28, 30	258
28	253
29	169, 174, 213, 250
29, 34 } 38, 39 }	165
30	163, 164, 167, 183, 190
32	190
32, 33	258
32, 39	247 et seq.
34	177, 183, 331, 608
35	186
35—39	177
37	121
37, 38	164
38	178
39	247
xi.	245
1	76, 176, 177
1—3	175
1, 2, 4	176
3	175, 193
4	250, 257
4, 5	177
5	251
6	203
7	177
8	87
9	165, 242
10	175, 177
11	246
13	81, 84, 253
14	175
16	315
17	253, 333
19	252
21	164
25	167
31	87
32, 33	326
33	177, 254, 463
33—40	253 et seq.
34	541
35	179, 233, 262
37, 38	342
39	253

HEBREWS (continued).
xi. 40	p. 177
xii. 1	165, 177, 244, 356
1, 2	165
1—7	254 et seq.
1–xiii. 19	245
2	179, 185, 190
6—11	180
9	164
13	162, 255
14	163, 328
14—17	255 et seq.
15	255, 604
15—17	259
15—28	259
16	258
16, 17	170, 181
17	162, 328
18	175, 256
18—21	173
18—22	203
18—24	164
18, 27	175
18—29	256 et seq.
19	173
22	175, 251
22, 28	177
24	85, 177, 223, 246
25	256
26	246
27	175, 185
28	175, 178, 207
29	247
xiii. 1—6	190
2	166, 589
3	247
4	257
5	164, 611
7	591
8	184, 256
8—16	259, 260
9	164, 190
10	91
11	226
12	167, 177
13	253, 255
14	165, 251, 253
14, 15	255
15	83, 253
18	163
18, 23	608
20	163, 176, 190
20—25	203
21	184, 188
24	190
26	255

JAMES.
i. 1	p. 315, 326
1—4	320, 321
2	326
2—4	72, 326, 330
2—15	321
2—18	320
3	321, 326, 329
3, 4 } 17, 25 }	326
3, 25	321
4	321, 326

JAMES (continued).		JAMES (continued).		I. PETER (continued).	
i. 5	p. 282,318,321, 326, 327, 330, 356	iii. 6	p. 317, 318	i. 3, 7, 13	p. 73
		8	327	3, 12	83
		13	308	3, 13	76
5—8	283, 320	13—17	283, 321	4, 12, 13	73
6	131,312,318, 328, 334, 359	13—18	320,339,350	5	69, 76, 86, 193
		15	320	6	73
		15—17	327	6, 7	72
6—8	327, 330	16	327	6, 8	73
8—12	318, 329	17	320	6—9	86
9	330	iv.	285	7	37, 76, 81, 88, 105, 328
9—11	320, 327	1	89		
10	72,318,331	1—6	339		
11	318, 331	1—10	320, 321	8	70, 71, 73, 83
12	318,321,327	1—12	320		
12—15	320, 332	2, 3, 8	282, 321	9	76, 103
13	318	4	308	10	71
13—15	322	4, 5	321	10, 11	254
14	105, 120	5	338	10—12	86, 87, 119
16—18	320,328,333	6	318, 338	11	86, 118
17	259,318,333	6, 7, 10	72	11—v. 14	83
18	76, 86	8	88, 327	12	71, 77, 329
19	317, 318	11, 12	319, 320	12, 25	74
19—21	320	13	312,317,319, 327	13	71, 118
19—25	328 et seq.			13—16	73
19—27	320	13—v. 11	320	13, 16, 22	73
20	318	13, 14	321	13, 17	83
21	318, 321	13, 17	320, 343	13—21	87
22	307,308,321	14	318	14	72
22—25	320	16	343	14, 18	81
22, 27	267	17	321	15	81, 309
23	318	24	318	15, 16	87
25	52, 87, 318, 321, 356	v. 1	309	15, 18	103
		1—6	267,313,318, 321, 343	16	81
26, 27	281,320,328			17	71, 76, 87
ii. 1	315,324,359	2	343	18	74, 233
1—4	193	3	193	18, 19	74
1—7	321	3—6	319	18—20	71
1—13	319,320,335	3, 8, 9	489	18—21	83
2	316	4	283, 321	19	73,103,105, 225, 233
5	296, 350	5	308		
5—13	317	6	315	20	87
6	313, 315	7	315, 321	21	86
6, 7	315	7, 8	310, 344	22	117, 256
7	34, 310	7, 11	321	22, 23	76
8	329	8	321	22—25	85, 88, 346
10	118	9—11	346	23	333
10, 26	321	10	321	23—25	81
12	52,356,360	11	321	24	72,327,331
14	350	12	316,317,320, 321, 329	ii. 1	88
14—18	313			1—10	84, 89
14—26	320, 321	13, 15	321	1, 2, 11, 12	73
15, 16, 19, 20	267	13, 18	282,320,321, 347		
				2	70, 71, 88
17	350	14	315, 316	3	103
17—26	360	15	327, 356	4—8	69
19	316, 320	16	321	5	80, 280
19, 26	338 et seq.	16—20	321	6	81
21	57. 91, 318, 350	17	457	6—10	72
		19, 20	320, 348	7	71, 489
21—26	310	20	72, 95, 318	8	69
22, 26	359			9	71, 80, 107, 117, 256, 545
23	357, 359	I. PETER.			
24	350,355,361	i. 1	p. 62, 72, 81, 325, 583, 506		
24, 25	603			9, 10	71, 81
25	57, 253			11	72, 84, 542
iii. 1—12	320, 338	1, 2	83	11, 12	84, 89
1—18	320, 321	1—ii.10		12, 15	82
2	118,321,326	2	71,177,246	13	33, 72
2, 3	329	3	72, 87, 311	13, 14—17	443
3	88	3, 4, 21	71		
4	312	3—5	86	13—16	69
5	318				

PASSAGES OF SCRIPTURE

I. Peter (continued).

ii. 13—17	p. 84, 91
13—25	73
13—iii. 7	84
14, 15, 20	76
16	80, 120, 126
17	105
18	71, 72
18—20	84
18—25	91
19	81
19, 22	71
20	70
21	75, 77
21—25	84
22	72
22—25	73
23	70, 82
24	70, 71, 74, 89
25	70, 83, 114
iii. 1	72, 112, 114
1—6	84
1—7	92
1, 9—12, 17, 18	73
2	103
6	80, 81
6, 11, 13, 16, 17	76
7	84, 117, 340
8	346
8—iv. 19	84
8—12	84
8—17	83
8—22	83
9	72, 82
9, 14, 17	82
10	81
11	255
13	93, 591
13—17	33
13, 18	84
13, 15, 21	73
15	76, 93, 117
16	82
18	74
19	76
19, 20	77
19—22	84
20	19, 93
21	70, 71, 76, 103, 233, 246
22	72, 73
iv. 1	72, 75, 103, 340
1—4	73, 75
1, 4, 6, 10, 11	73
1—6	84
2	542, 543
3	94, 103
3, 4	81
4	70, 94
5	71
5—7	86
6	69, 78, 79
6, 7	73
7—10	84
7—19	96
8	69, 72, 339
8, 9	228

I. Peter (continued).

iv. 8, 18	p. 105
9	589
10	72
11, 13	73
11—16	84
12	37, 81
12—17	96
12—19	33
13	75, 86
13, 14	73
14	34, 82
15	70, 73, 96, 337
15, 19	82
16	82
17	37, 87, 96, 447
17—19	84
18	81
19	76
v. 1	71, 72, 86, 114, 577, 621
1—4	84
1—11	96
2	70
4	69, 77, 86, 103
5	70, 72, 81, 339
5—7	84
5, 9	72
6	73
8	70
9	76, 81
9, 10	84
10, 11	73, 84
12	70, 73, 81, 84, 97, 118, 262
13	436, 579, 595, 596
13, 14	84
14	347

II. Peter.

i. 1	p. 103, 114, 128, 324, 325
1, 2	102
1—11	117 et seq.
2	86, 105
3	103
3—5	107
3—11	102
4	106, 107
5	103, 106, 259
9	103, 106
11	103
12	103, 107
12—15	102
12—21	118 et seq.
13	107
14	103
15	107
16	103, 106, 107
16—18	102
17	107
17, 21	114
19	106, 107, 223
19—21	102
20	107

II. Peter (continued).

ii.	p. 128
1	128, 404
1—3	106, 110
1—9	102
1—13	114
1—22	119 et seq.
2	555
3	103, 106
4	93
4, 5	134, 599
5, 7, 9	102
5, 8	108
6	106
7	103
10	103, 107
10—12	102
10, 12, 13, 15, 17	106
12	103, 112, 114, 116, 120
13	103, 117, 130
13, 14	102
14	87, 103, 105, 339
14, 15	110
14, 18	328
15—16	102
16	116
17	102, 103
18	110
18, 19	102
20	99, 213
20, 22	102
22	105, 117
iii. 1	103
1, 2	102, 130
1—13	108
1—18	120—122
2	106
3	106, 107, 110
3, 4	104
3, 16, 17	117
5	106
5—7	102, 121
7	103
8	103
8, 9	102
8—10	121
9	106
10	103, 109, 110
10—12	37
10, 16	102
11	103
12	110, 489
14	103
14, 15	110
15	105, 127, 266
15, 16	106, et seq.
16	116
17	103
17, 18	102

I. John.

i. 1	p. 531, 533
1, 2	531
1—4	526, 527, 531, 584
2	564
3	536
4	584

I. John (continued).

i. 5 p. 328,531,537
5—v. 5 526
5—v. 12 526
5—7 527,533,536
5—10 537
6 360,493,521, 537
6—ii. 2 527
7 71,537,565
8 537
8—10 522,527,534, 536
9 523
ii. 1 523, 541
1, 2 527,535,541
1, 28 541
2 508, 565
3 537, 538
3—5 536, 537
3—11 537
3—13 528
3, 14 536
4 504, 537
5 493,537,538
5, 18 524
6 560
6—8 537
6—10 583
6—11 528, 538
7, 8 583
8 521, 531
9—11 521. 537
10, 11 395
12 523
12—14 520,528,541
13, 14 524
15—17 521
15—19 528, 542 et seq.
16 342
18 193,201,489, 541
18, 22 508,542,583, 584
20 493,515,524
20, 26 518, 528
20—27 523, 545
20, 27 520
21 541
21, 22 567
22 544, 574
27 524, 528
28 554,555,583
28, 29 546
28—iii. 3 546 et seq.
28—v. 5 528
29 524
iii. 1 522,531,536
1—10 528, 547
2 569, 580
2—5 509
2, 14 424
3 71, 88, 573
3—8 547
4, 5 548
4—10 522
5, 15 524
6 548, 591
6—10 591
7, 8 548, 549
7, 10 128
8 462

I. John (continued).

iii. 9 p. 549
9, 10 548
10 549
10, 11 587
10—15 550
11 309, 583
11—18 528
12 251
14 515, 570
16 524, 542
16—18 550, 552
17 543
18 541, 590
19, 20 553
19—23 528
19, 24 524
21 547, 554
21, 22 567
21—24 553
24 547
24—iv. 6 555
iv. 1 524
1—3 583
1—6 518,528, 555
2 524,531,584
2, 3 503
3 542, 544
3, 15 503
4 541
6, 13 524
7—12 528,555,558
8 504
9 56, 560
10 523, 565
11 71
12 531
13—16 559
14 564
14—16 528
16 524, 538
17 507
17, 18 528,554,560
18 76, 87
19 560
19—21 528, 560
v. 1 531
1—3 528
1—5 560, 561
1, 10 503
2 524, 560
5 560
6 564, 584
6—8 562
6—9 528, 562
7 163
9 564
9—12 566
10 564
10—12 528, 562
13 520, 525
13, 14 510
13—17 528, 567
13—21 528
14 547
15 515
15, 18, } 524
19, 20 }
16 208,213,574, 583
18—20 528
18—21 574
20 406,508,531

I. John (continued).

v. 21 518, 541

II. John.

verse 1 p. 500
1, 2 541
1—3 } 583
4, }
5, 6 }
5, 6, 7 576
7 503,542,574
7—9 583
8 } 577
10 }
10, 11 32',30',576, 583
12, 13 583
13 577

III. John.

verse 2 p. 128
3 583
7 581
9 577
11 578
14 581

Jude.

p. 128—131, 324
verse 1 131, 263
2 86, 131
4 110
5 118, 600
5—7 137
6 93,134,598
7 103, 599
8 110, 131
8, 23 112
10 110, 112
11 110, 132
13 599
14 133, 342
14, 15 134, 598
16 132
16—18 110
17, 18 124
18 86
19 132, 338
20 } 132
22, 23 }
23 567
25 132

Revelation.

i. 1—8 p. 438
4 439, 471
5, 6 246
6 71, 89, 200, 545, 633
9 82
9—iii. 22 438
12—17 446
15 456
16 203
ii. 2 } 483
3 }
5, 16 432
6, 14, } 498
15 }

REVELATION (continued).

ii. 9	p.	344
9, 10, 13 }		82
10		327
13		82
14		457
20 }		120
24		28, 442
iii. 4		131
5		256
7		
8, 16 }		493
11		432
14		491
17		344
18		496
19		254
iv. 3		156
5		439
iv.—vii.		438
v. 10		633
13		444, 491
vi. 4		424
9		447
9, 10		82
10		120
10, 11		599
11		456
12		433
vii. 1		439, 448
5—8		326
9		38, 491
13		447
viii. 1—5		614
2		439
13		434, 453
viii.—xi.		438
ix. 1		434
4		448
11		471
18		449
27		457
x. 3		439

REVELATION (continued).

xi. 2	p.	466
3		456, 458
7		41
8		425
13		457
14		432
xii. 1—17		581
3		41, 439
5		449, 406
7		129
7—11		457
9		470
10		199
14		412, 435, 466
xii.—xiv.		438
xiii.		443
1, 6		41
3		44, 413
5		466
8		256, 555
9, 10		466
10		467
11—17		474
18		468
xiv. 4		333, 580
8		596
14		368
19, 20		423
20		431, 483, 599
xv. 1		439
xv., xvi.		438
xvi. 5		82
13		41, 454, 476
16		471
19		596
21		451
xvii.		443
xvii., xviii.		485
xvii.—xx.		438
6		447
8, 11		41
8, 10, 11		464
9		468

REVELATION (continued).

xvii. 9, 10	p.	439, 463
9, 18		596
10		433
10, 11		413
11		44
12		465
12, 13, 16, 17 }		481
14		491
15		463
18		465
xviii.		343
2		454, 596
4		395
8		37
9, 18		95
13		243
14		82, 463
xix. 1		444
1, 6		38
11		444, 493
13 } 16 }		491
20		475, 476
xx. 2		470
4		82, 409, 447
6		260
9		451
10		476
15		256
xx., xxi.		7, 438
xxi. 3, 4		254
5		486
9		581
10		251
14		594
16		486
xxii. 7, 9		493
8, 21		438
11		334
15		496
18, 19		121
20		432

TALMUDICAL PASSAGES QUOTED OR REFERRED TO.

BERACHOTH.

fol. 5, a	p.	352
6, a		497
7, a		200, 497
8, a		246
8, b		210
13, b		352
20, b		314
29, a		181
32, a		219
61, b		352
63, b		218

PEAH.

ch. ii. 6	p.	238

SHABBATH.

fol. 21, a	p.	181
32, a		347
55, b		200
56, b		463
57, a } 86, a }		352
88, b		256
89, a		172

P'SACHIM.

fol. 54, a	p.	172
57, a		223, 313, 314
113, a		617
113, b		277, 416

CHAGIGAM.

ch. ii. 4	p.	225

MOED KATON.

fol. 26, a	p.	489

Rosh Hashanah.

fol. 16, a p. 217
  16, b   238
  21, b   200
  23, a   416, 448

Yoma.

ch. iii. 7 p. 614
  iv. 4   231
      7   240
  v. 2   231, 212
  vii. 2   212
  viii. 9   243
fol. 2, a   225, 239
     5, b   238
     9, a   181, 313
     9, b   485
     14, b   238
     18, a, b 239
     19, a   181
     19, b   239
     20, a   238
     20, b   240
     23, a   353
     28, b   358
     29, b   240
     35, b   314, 617
     38, a   140
     44, a   225, 613
     52, b   230
     66, a   239
     66, b   617
     85, b }
     86, a } 238
     86, b }
     87, a } 349
Tosefoth, ch. 1. 303

Succah.

fol. 29, b p. 343
     51, b   140
     55, b   237, 238, 242

Taanith.

fol. 3, b p. 352
     5, a   485

Megillah.

fol. 6, a p. 417
     9, a   144
     14, b   358
     23, a   238

Yevamoth.

fol. 16, b p. 325
     49, b   200, 253
     62, 63   277
     63, b   284
     97, b   239

Kethuboth.

fol. 103, b p. 238
     104, a   230

Kiddushin.

fol. 29, b p. 277
     70, b   181, 314
     82, a   352, 358

Gittin.

fol. 7, a p. 181
     57, a   423

Nedarim.

fol. 31, b p. 352
     32, b   220
     38, a   230
     40, a   347
     64, b   277

Sotah.

fol. 47, b p. 353

Bava Kama.

fol. 113, b p. 416

Bava Metzia.

fol. 59, b p. 295
     85, b   215, 402
     86, a   407

Bava Bathra.

fol. 14, a p. 230
     25, a   485
     75, a   200
     75, b   486
     116, a   277
     121, a   238

Avodah Zarah.

fol. 3, a p. 172
     18, b   573
     27, b   279
     44, b   396

Sanhedrin.

fol. 37, a p. 340
     59, a   416
     64, a   534
     81, b   181, 239
     87, b   357

Sanhedrin (continued).

fol. 90, a p. 352
     99, a   203
     100, b   284
     103, b   253
     110, b   325

Shevuoth.

fol. 13, a p. 239

Maccoth.

fol. 23, b }
     24, a } p. 248

Avoth.

ch. i. 10 p. 337
      17   336
   iv. 15   335
    v. 21   280

Avoth d'Rab. Nathan.

ch. xxxix. p. 570

Sopherim.

ch. xv. p. 416

Gerim.

ch. i. p. 352

Zevachim.

fol. 88, b p. 181

Menachoth.

fol. 29, a p. 175
     99, b   142
Tosefta   313

Bechoroth.

fol. 4, a p. 222

Chulin.

fol. 90, b p. 239

Kerithoth.

fol. 7, a p. 238
     28, a   314
     28, b   617

Middoth.

ch. v. 2 p. 614

PASSAGES FROM THE BOOK OF ENOCH QUOTED OR REFERRED TO.

Enoch.	
	p. 129, 133, 449
i.—xxxv.	507, 508
i.—vi.	507
i. 6	121
8 } vi. 4 }	120
vii.—x	597
vii. 2 } x. 1—9 }	509
xi.—xvi.	501
xii.—xvi.	130
xii. 4	129
5—7	134, 509
xiv. 4	509

Enoch (continued).	
xiv. 5	p. 129
xv. 1—7	599
3	129
xvi. 5	509
xvii.—xxxv.	507
xviii. 13	454
14, 16	134, 509
xxi. 3	134, 454
6	509
10	120
xxxvii.—lxx.	597, 598
xxxviii.—xliv.	597
xl. 8 } xli. 1 }	129

Enoch (continued).	
xlv.—lv.	p. 507
liii. 6	134
liv. 6	599
lvi.—lxx.	597
lxxi.—cv.	508
lxxii.—lxxxi. } lxxxii.—lxxxix. }	597
xc., xci.	
xcii. 1—18 } xcii. 19—civ. }	598
xciii. 3	483
civ. 1—3	447
cv.	508

CASSELL AND COMPANY LIMITED, BELLE SAUVAGE WORKS, LONDON, E.C.